LENGTH

U. S. (customary)

Metric

TEMPERATURE

PSYCHOLOGY: THE EXPERIMENTAL APPROACH

PSYCHOLOGY: THE EXPERIMENTAL APPROACH

DOUGLAS K. CANDLAND

Professor of Psychology

Bucknell University

MᶜGRAW-HILL BOOK COMPANY

New York, St. Louis, San Francisco

Toronto, London, Sydney

PREFACE

This textbook was written, as the title implies, for courses in psychology in which the experimental approach is emphasized. Accordingly, I have emphasized the presentation of data of interest to contemporary psychology which can be examined in terms of experimental procedures. The text was written in the belief that a textbook should supplement, not supplant, lectures, discussions, and laboratory work. For this reason, I have attempted to provide the student with both a textbook and a source to which he may turn for information on some of the most important topics which constitute experimental psychology. A lecturer need not expect every student to understand fully every topic covered in a textbook: his emphasis may be made clear in the lecture. However, the student should be provided with a text which permits him to go beyond the level of the lecture in areas which are of interest to him, and it is to that aim that this work has been dedicated. Course integration is accomplished most efficiently by the lecturer, and I have attempted to avoid binding the unseen instructor with a textbook representing a special point of view. Thus the textbook is eclectic in design.

I have not discussed many issues concerned with the philosophy of science, including statistics, for I believe that competence in these issues is best acquired in the laboratory, where the examples have meaning which cannot be as effectively conveyed by the written word. I have considered experimental design superficially, compared to other topics, for the same reason. The variety of books concerned solely with these problems should permit the instructor to provide this information either in lecture, in the laboratory, or by assignments in these works (see the Sources for Chapter 1.).

Assessing the accuracy of the data or the competence of the investigator in the number of different fields covered in this book is a difficult task. Accordingly, I have tended to accept older data, if the procedures appear sound, so long as they have not been contradicted by more recent research. In doing so, I have assumed that older studies which have not been contradicted in the literature have probably survived tests in numerous laboratories: if they had not, we would expect revisions of the data to appear in the literature. At times, when the reason for discrepancies has not been clear to me, I have taken the liberty of showing alternate results in the hope that the discrepancies would contribute to independent laboratory work.

The ordering of topics is the one issue on which instructors disagree most often. This is an important concern, for the order of presentation of topics in a textbook often forces the lecturer, usually hesitantly, to keep pace. Although there is no perfect solution to this difficulty, I have attempted to prepare chapters which can be read individually with the aid of the cross references given in the text. This is not always reasonable, for, obviously, the understanding of the psychophysics of vision is retarded in a student who has not understood psychophysics. On the other hand, I would hope that individual lecturers could exclude sections of the book without penalty. I believe that this approach, while having created some obstinate writing problems, permits maximum adaptability of a book which can be used for introductory or advanced courses and for courses of different durations as well.

Douglas K. Candland

References are given in the text by the surname of the author and the year of publication. Initials are used in the case of two or more authors having the same surname. If in the same year an author has published a second work to which I refer, it is indicated as, for example, "(Smith, 1961a; 1961b)." Full references are provided in alphabetical order at the end of the text. The reference list is alphabetical by contributor. The names of coauthors too are listed alphabetically, with a cross reference to the surname of the first author.

In providing references for works originally published in a foreign language, I have attempted to provide the reference both to the original work and to an English translation in cases in which I was able to locate an English translation. The year of publication of both volumes is indicated in the text.

The abreviation n.s. in the reference list indicates that I was unable to consult the original source. The reference with n.s. is the secondary source which I used.

A discussion of sources follows each chapter. This section indicates books or articles from which the reader may acquire additional information concerning the topics discussed in the chapter. The references are keyed in the same manner as references in the text.

Words or phrases which appear in the text in italic type are important words or phrases. The italic type serves to remind the reader to be certain that he has understood the definition of the item before continuing to read. Italics are also used for emphasis in general, for foreign words, and for titles.

CONTENTS

Preface, v
Reader's Guide, vii

PREFACE: CHAPTERS 1–5   1

1: AIMS AND TECHNIQUES OF
EXPERIMENTAL PSYCHOLOGY   2

Introduction, 2

Kinds of experimental psychology, 3
  Applied research, 4
  Theory-oriented research, 4
  Theory-testing research, 4
Some approaches of experimental
psychology, 5
  Systematic change, 5
  The phylogenetic approach, 8
  Field or naturalistic observation, 9
The technique of systematic change, 9
  Independent and dependent variables, 10
  Presenting the stimulus, 12
  Measuring the response, 12
Procedures of investigation, 13
  The literature, 13
  The experimenter and the hypothesis, 13
  Definitions, 20
  Designing the experiment, 21
    One variable, 21
    Functional relations, 24
    Factorial designs, 26
  A moment of truth, 27
Problems of interpretation, 28
  The statistical language of psychology, 29
  Manipulation and correlation, 29
  Generalization of findings, 30
Can psychology be experimental? 33
Sources, 34

2: THE PHYSIOLOGICAL BASES
OF BEHAVIOR   36

Introduction, 36

Psychology and physiology, 36
A brief history, 39
The senses, 41

Neurons and nerves, 42
The neuron and behavior, 46
The synapse, 46
The central nervous system, 48
  The spinal cord, 48
  The brain, 50
  The cranial nerves, 53
  The spinal nerves, 53
The peripheral nervous system and
homeostasis, 55
Some important phenomena, 58
  Electroencephalography, 58
  Brain stimulation, 59
  Emotion, 60
  Level of arousal, 61
Afterword, 62
Sources, 62

**3: THE SENSES AND
THEIR STIMULI**   **64**

Importance of the senses, 64
  Preference, 64
  Psychophysics and thresholds, 65
Audition, 67
Vision, 70
Cutaneous sensitivity, 73
  Pressure, 74
  Pain, 75
  Temperature, 76
Olfaction, 77
Gustation, 79
Kinesthesis and the vestibular sense, 81
Afterword, 82

4: PSYCHOPHYSICS   **83**

Introduction, 83
Role of psychophysics in psychology, 84
Origins of psychophysics, 85
The classic methods, 90
  Method of limits, 90
  Method of average error, 94
  *Frequency methods: The method of
  constant stimuli, 95*
  Some additional sources of variation, 98
Reliability and validity, 100

The development of psychophysics, 101
  Fullerton-Cattell principle, 101
  *Thurstone's law of comparative
  judgment, 102*
  Helson's adaptation level, 103
  Stevens's power function, 104
  Decision theory, 105
Sources, 107

5: SCALING   **110**

Introduction, 110

The nature of numbers, 111
Methods based on ratio and interval
judgments, 115
  *Method of equal sense distances
  (bisection), 115*
  Method of equal-appearing intervals, 117
  Method of fractionation, 118
  Method of multiple stimuli, 122
  Development of ratio techniques, 122
Successive categories (rating), ranking, and
pair comparison, 124
  Method of successive categories (rating), 126
  Method of ranking, 129
  Method of pair comparison, 133
Some additional techniques, 136
  Method of first choices, 136
  Method of similar attributes, 137
  Method of balanced values, 137
  Multidimensional scaling, 137
  Factor analysis, 138
Reliability and validity of scaling
procedures, 140
Sources, 142

PREFACE: CHAPTERS 6–11   **145**

6: AUDITION   **146**

Introduction, 146

Anatomy of the ear, 146
  Muscles, 148
  Nerve transmission, 148
Physiology of the human ear, 149

Electrical activity of the cochlea, 151
Role of the central nervous system in
audition, 152
Evolution of the ear, 152
Thresholds and auditory phenomena, 154
　Frequency, 155
　Pitch and frequency, 160
　Amplitude, 160
　Loudness and amplitude, 161
　Other characteristics, 162
　Combination tones and beats, 165
　*Psychological attributes of complex
　tones*, 165
　Masking and adaptation, 166
　Aftereffects, 167
　Tonal pleasantness, 168
　Sound localization, 169
Pathology, 170
　Stimulation deafness, 171
　Tinnitus, 172
　Diplacusis, 172
　Presbyacusia, 173
　Otosclerosis, 174
　High-tone deafness, 174
　Recruitment, 174
The final question: the relationship
between the physical stimulus and the
psychological response, 174
Sources, 182

7 : LANGUAGE　　　　　　**1 8 4**

Introduction, 184

Production of speech and phonation, 184
Recording speech, 189
Information theory in speech, 191
Measuring meaning, 192
　Word association, 193
　Nonsense syllables, 194
　Some physiological procedures, 195
　Visual perception and meaning, 195
　Semantic differential, 196
　Type-token ratio, 198
　Content analysis, 198
Statistical analysis of language, 199
Articulation and intelligibility, 201

Development of language, 204
　The first word, 206
　Vocabulary development, 206
　Development of meaning, 208
Language among animals, 209
Pathology, 210
　Aphasia, 210
　Stuttering, 211
Sources, 211

**8 : VISION: PSYCHOPHYSICAL
AND RELATED MEASURES**　　**2 1 3**

Introduction, 213

Anatomy, 214
Physiology, 216
Defining the stimulus, 220
Duplicity of the photoreceptors, 220
Evolution of the eye, 223
Electrical evidence of visual activity, 225
Role of the central nervous system, 228
Thresholds, 228
　Wavelength and hue, 229
　*Illumination, brightness, and related
　measures*, 229
　Saturation, 233
Other measures, 234
　Perimetry, 234
　Flicker fusion, 236
　Adaptation, 239
　Aftereffects, 241
　Acuity, 243
Sources, 245

9 : VISION: PERCEPTION　　**2 4 8**

History of color vision, 248
　Identifying the stimulus for color vision, 249
　Color mixture, 252
　Development of color vision, 252
　Deficiencies in color vision, 254
　Theories, 258
　Land effect, -262
Some phenomena of visual perception, 263
　Figure and ground, 264
　Constancy, 266

Depth and space perception, 271
Perceptual organization, 274
The Ganzfeld, 282
Motion perception, 283
Visual causality, 284
Eye movements, 285
The role of experience, 287
Varying the amount of visual stimuli, 288
Sensory deprivation, 288
Innate preference, 289
Development of perception in children, 290
Perceptual defense and subliminal
perception, 291
Sources, 294

**10: CUTANEOUS, KINESTHETIC,
ORGANIC, AND
VESTIBULAR SYSTEMS   296**

Introduction, 296

Cutaneous receptors, 297
The problem: stimulus and receptor, 301
Role of the central nervous system, 302
Thermal sensitivity, 305
Heat and cold as separate systems, 305
Thresholds and adaptation, 308
*A brief history of theories of
thermal sensitivity,* 310
Touch and pressure sensibility, 311
The stimulus, 312
Thresholds, 313
Adaptation, 314
Patterning of pressure stimuli, 316
*Uses of pressure and vibratory
stimulation,* 316
Pain sensitivity, 318
The receptors for pain, 319
Thresholds, 320
Adaptation, 321
Pain and the central nervous system, 321
Some explanations, 322
Kinesthesis and the organic sensations, 324
Receptors, 325
Thresholds, 325
Adaptation, 326
Posture and the righting response, 327

Hunger and thirst, 327
Hunger, 328
Thirst, 331
The vestibular sense, 332
Sources, 335

**11: THE CHEMICAL SENSES:
SMELL AND TASTE   337**

Introduction, 337

Olfaction, 338
The stimuli, 338
Receptors and neural pathways, 338
Techniques for threshold measurement, 340
Thresholds, 342
*Adaptation, masking, and related
phenomena,* 344
Electrical activity, 345
Pathology, 347
Theories of sensitivity, 348
Gustation, 349
The stimuli, 349
Receptors and neural pathways, 351
Temperature, 353
Learning, 354
Electrical activity, 355
Thresholds, 358
Preference among animals, 360
Pathology, 360
Theories of sensitivity, 361
Sources, 361

PREFACE: CHAPTERS 12–16   363

**12: LEARNED BEHAVIOR:
AN INTRODUCTION   364**

Introduction, 364

Conditioning and training, 366
Discrimination learning, 366
Trial-and-error learning, 367
Motor and verbal learning, 369
Transfer of training, 369
Problem solving, 369
Critical problems for learning theory, 370
Strengthening a response, 371

Reinforcement, 372
Reward and punishment, 373
Extinction and spontaneous recovery, 375
Secondary reinforcement, 376
Measuring learning, 377
Chemistry and physiology of learning, 379
Sources, 383

**13: CLASSICAL
CONDITIONING**   **384**

Introduction, 384

Brief history of classical conditioning, 384
Types of classical conditioning, 386
The unconditioned response and the
conditioned response, 388
Temporal relationship between conditioned
stimulus and unconditioned stimulus, 389
Characteristics of conditioning, 389
Sensory preconditioning, 390
Sensitization and pseudoconditioning, 390
Summation, 390
Adaptation, 391
The inhibitions, 391
External inhibition, 391
Disinhibition (inhibition of inhibition), 391
Inhibition of delay, 391
Generalization, 392
Conditioning and the central nervous
system, 393
Extensions of classical conditioning, 395
Interoceptive conditioning, 395
Verbal behavior, 396
Orienting reflex, 397
Anxiety, 399
Experimental neurosis, 400
Sources, 401

**14: INSTRUMENTAL AND
OPERANT TRAINING**   **402**

Introduction, 402

Operant training, 403
Reinforcement, 404
Schedules of reinforcement, 405

Amount of reinforcement, 410
Number of reinforcements, 411
Changing the amount of reinforcement, 411
*Temporal relationship between response
and reinforcement,* 412
Secondary reinforcement, 413
Discrimination in operant training, 414
The effects of punishment, 419
Punishment as reinforcement, 422
Role of instructions in conditioning
and learning, 423
Comparison of classical conditioning and
instrumental learning, 424
Neurological correlates of learning
and conditioning, 427
Sources, 427

**15: HUMAN LEARNING
AND PERFORMANCE**   **429**

Introduction, 429

Measures primarily of acquisition, 430
Measures primarily of retention, 432
Savings method, 432
Relearning, 433
Recall, 433
Methods of recognition, 434
Methods of reconstruction, 436
Some factors influencing acquisition
and retention, 436
Whole-part learning, 436
Massed-distributed learning, 437
Reminiscence, 440
Qualities of materials, 442
Knowledge of results, 443
Overlearning, 444
Retention and forgetting, 445
*Immediate, short-term, and long-term
memory,* 445
Theories of forgetting, 448
Transfer, 452
Measuring transfer, 452
Some kinds of interference, 454
Experiment and theory, 455
Incidental learning, 456
Verbal "conditioning", 458
Samples of perceptual motor learning, 460

*Some common apparatuses and
techniques,* 460
Time-and-motion studies, 463
Common factors of different tests, 463
Feedback, 464
Problem solving, 466
Imitation, 473
Fatigue, 474
Sources, 475

**16: LEARNED AND
NONLEARNED BEHAVIOR   478**

Introduction, 478

The concept of nonlearned behavior, 479
Sensitive periods, 480
Imprinting, 480
Maturation of the ability to learn, 482
Sexual behavior, 484
*Nest building, egg laying, and
related activities,* 485
Mammals, 488
Hormones, 489
Role of the central nervous system, 491
Analyses of some instinctual behaviors, 492
Homing and migration, 492
The sucking reflex and licking behavior, 494
*Innate releasing mechanisms and fixed
action patterns,* 496
Instinctual consummatory behavior, 497
Physiological basis of instinct, 498
Sources, 500

PREFACE: CHAPTERS 17–19   503

**17: EMOTION AND
MOTIVATION   504**

Introduction, 504

Some methods of measuring emotion, 505
Physiological measures, 505
Projective testing, 506
Ablations and lesions, 506
Posture, 507
Development of activation theory, 508

*Emotion and the autonomic nervous
system,* 513
Emotion and psychosomatic states, 514
Stress and emotion, 515
*Biochemical and drug-produced changes
in emotion,* 515
An introduction to motivation, 516
Motivation and learning theory, 517
Motivation and reinforcement, 519
*Learned drives: the example of acquired
fear,* 521
Some views on human motivation, 523
The psychoanalytic approach, 523
Need achievement, 525
The ethological approach, 528
Sources, 530

**18: PSYCHOMETRICS:
TESTS AND MEASUREMENT   532**

Introduction, 532

A brief history of tests and measurement, 533
Developing a test, 535
Types of reliability, 536
Correlation, Spearman-Brown, and
Kuder-Richardson techniques, 537
Types of validity, 540
Construct validity, 540
Content validity, 541
Face validity, 542
Predictive validity, 542
Concurrent validity, 543
Types of questions asked, 543
Examples of tests, 544
A general-aptitude test, 544
Special-aptitude tests, 547
Achievement tests, 548
Projective tests, 548
Sources, 552

19: SOCIAL BEHAVIOR   554
by **Richard V. Wagner**

Introduction, 554

*The study of individual behavior in a
social context,* 555

*Social interaction and small-group
behavior*, 556
*General techniques for studying
small-group behavior*, 557
  Survey, 557
  Field study, 559
  Field experiment, 562
  Laboratory experiment, 563
Small-group behavior, 564
  Group composition, 569
    Abilities, skills, and experience, 569
    Attitudes, values, and interests, 572
    Demographic variables, 573
    Personality characteristics, 574
    Social needs, 575
  Group structure, 576
    Group size, 576
    Task structure, 578
    Power structure, 579
    Bases of social power, 579
    *Determinants of the distribution
of power*, 581
    Leadership, 582

    Limitations of power, 583
    Changes in power, 583
    Communication structure, 584
  Affect structure, 587
    Geographic and spatial proximity, 588
    Attractiveness, 589
    Similarity versus complementarity, 589
    Instrumentality, 591
    Effects of the affect structure, 592
      General group structure, 592
      Members' characteristics, 593
      Task performance, 594
  Group interaction, 595
    Task and social functions, 596
    Phases in group interaction, 597
    Measuring group interaction, 598
Sources, 601

**Acknowledgments, 603
References and author index, 605
Subject index, 689**

This book is divided into four general sections. The first section, consisting of five chapters, is concerned with the role of the central nervous system and the sensory systems in behavior. We shall be concerned also with the basic question "What is the relationship between the stimuli which are impinging upon our sensory systems and our judgment of the stimuli?" Or, asked another way, "What is the relationship between the physical world and our perception of those stimuli?"

In the second section (Chapters 6 to 11) each of the sensory systems is considered in detail. We shall study the anatomy and physiology and phenomenology of these senses.

In the third section (Chapters 12 to 16) we discuss the importance of learning and conditioning to an understanding of behavior. We shall find that the relation between the senses and the phenomena of learning is close. In these chapters we discuss operant training, classical conditioning, types of learning and performance, including verbal behavior, that are characteristic of human beings, and evidence regarding the complex relationship between "instinctual" behavior and learned behavior.

In the final section of the book (Chapters 17 to 19) three main areas are considered that have attracted experimentation and theory, namely, motivation and emotion, psychometrics, and the behavior of groups of persons. In these chapters, an attempt is made to apply the knowledge we have acquired from previous sections to such questions as "What factors determine how a person or persons behave together?" "How are tests constructed to discriminate persons on the basis of intelligence, personality, and other variables?" and "What do we know about the roles of motivation and emotion in altering behavior?"

Thus the content of this book varies from descriptions of the functions of specific receptors in the retina of the eye and of tiny receptors found in the skin to discussions of concepts such as emotion and group behavior. This variety demonstrates that in contemporary psychology data and information are gathered in a number of ways, each of which contributes toward an understanding of behavior.

CHAPTER ONE

AIMS AND TECHNIQUES OF EXPERIMENTAL PSYCHOLOGY

INTRODUCTION

Were we to try to imagine the thought processes of our ancestors of the remote and unrecorded past, we would probably conclude that men have always been curious about their own behavior as well as the behavior of others. That a science of psychology has come into being only recently only attests to the many complications involved in the development of such a science. Our predecessors had to acquire appreciable information about the external physical world and the internal anatomical and physiological world before they could approach the mysteries of behavior with the hope of finding solutions to them. This, perhaps, explains why so many methods have been used to describe and predict behavior. Contributions to psychology have come from the work of the novelist, the dramatist, the theologian, the philosopher, and others. Each has attempted in his own way, often awkwardly, to describe behavior. Some writers, in addition to describing behavior, have reached toward explanation and prediction. One critical difference between their goals and those of the experimental psychologist remains, however: the psychologist always wishes to predict behavior with precision, for accurate prediction is the absolute proof of the success of his formulations.

Prediction assumes control. If one has the information necessary to form laws so that he can predict behavior, it is reasonable to assume that he can also control behavior by altering events. Herein lies the basis for the power of psychology as well as the reason for fear. But behavior has always been controlled. The point is that only recently have we learned some of the principles concerning *how* it is controlled. Those who claim, often loudly and repeatedly, that behavior cannot be controlled are behaving like ostriches. Behavior is controlled every day by governments, advertisers, teachers, parents, and classmates. The fact that behavior can be controlled, at least partially, is neither good nor bad in itself; what is good or bad is the way control is applied and the end toward which it is used.

Although psychology is an infant among the sciences, man has, for centuries, employed the principles of the experimental method to study behavior. Pliny the Elder, of the first century AD, qualifies as an early animal psychologist. He reports training (that is, conditioning) his pet fish to surface for food upon hearing a particular noise (Pliny, trans. Melmoth, 1915). The well-known experiments of Ivan Pavlov at the turn of the twentieth century were also concerned with conditioning, and his experiments have contributed heavily to the ability of contemporary psychology to predict behavior. The same behavior was available for both Pliny and Pavlov to observe. However, it was Pavlov, who, nineteen hundred years after Pliny, realized the significance of the phenomenon of conditioning and *experimented* with it. Certainly, much of the advance in our knowledge of behavior is due to our learning to use the techniques of controlled observation and experimentation properly.

Let us mention an example of the way in which behavior has been manipulated and altered without the benefit of psychology. The dog—or the wolf—who learned that running to the call of a caveman resulted in food was exhibiting the process of operant training (see Chapters 12, 14). The principles of operant training are used today to control the behavior of primates used in space exploration and the behavior of pupils using teaching machines. The discovery that the number of responses an organism makes may be determined by selecting an appropriate *schedule of reinforcement,* that is, rewarding every response or only occasional ones, may be put to a good use—helping students to learn subject matter rapidly, thoroughly, and, perhaps, enjoyably—or to a dubious one—keeping people playing slot machines after they have lost next month's rent. The behavioral processes are identical. One purpose of contemporary experimental psychology is to find such processes. It is the purpose of other disciplines, such as politics, philosophy, and religion, to inquire into the application of the principles involved in the processes. But the people who select political officers, who organize their lives according to a philosophy, or

who deport themselves according to a religion, must have a knowledge of these principles in order to evaluate the way in which they are utilized by the politician, philosopher, and theologist.

Earlier methods of prediction—the dream, the position and movement of the stars and planets, or the location of lumps and bumps on the head—have been criticized by contemporary psychologists on the basis that the most accurate and efficient method presently available for investigating natural phenomena, including the behavior of living organisms, is the scientific method. The experimental method is one component of the scientific method. Experimental psychology has identified itself with the task of describing and predicting behavior through the use of the principles of experimentation.

Before we consider the data that have been derived from experimental procedures, we must know something about the ways in which data are collected and interpreted. Although this book is concerned primarily with the *content* resulting from psychological investigations, we must also understand the *methods* if we are to be intelligent readers. Accordingly, in this introductory chapter we shall discuss the kinds of experimental psychology and the advantages and disadvantages, procedures, and special problems of the experimental method when it is applied to behavior.

KINDS OF EXPERIMENTAL PSYCHOLOGY

If we examined the *Psychological Abstracts,* which, as the name suggests, provides abstracts of all papers concerned with psychological topics and classifies all journal articles and books concerned with psychology, we could, with little inconvenience and only a small bit of dishonesty, separate papers on experimental psychology into three basic kinds: The first category would include studies in which the experimental method was used for the purpose of answering a specific and practical question, such as "How much can a chewing-gum manufacturer shave from each piece of gum before the customer is able to notice the difference?" or "Do hallucinations occur if a man is kept in a totally dark room?" The second category would consist of research directed toward establishing a theory, or questions such as "How similar must distracting stimuli be to a controlled experimental stimulus before they interfere with the learning of the controlled stimulus?" The third category would include papers which attempted to test available theories. Some publications might fit into two categories, and a few, perhaps, into all three. However, when an experimenter begins work, he usually is motivated by one of three desires: to answer a specific question, to build a theory, or to test a theory (W. A. Scott & Wertheimer, 1962). In the following sections we shall discuss three types of research: applied research, theory-oriented research, and theory-testing research.

Applied Research: Applied research is most often concerned with the relationship between machines and the human beings who use them. Research of this type is common in industrial and military research units. For example, an automobile manufacturer might be concerned with designing easy-to-read dashboard dials. Different dial shapes—round, rectangular, and square—encourage different kinds of reading errors. Measurement of dial legibility is a common industrial application of psychological principles. Another question, "How can we distinguish secondary school students who will do well in college from those who will not?" is important to college admissions officers, as well as to students and parents. This problem is also of an applied nature, for it asks a specific, practical question. It is not concerned with explaining how the behavior of successful students came about but with predicting which students will be successful. If an investigator found that no successful students were redhaired and that all who failed were redhaired, he would have answered the question. It would be unnecessary to inquire further, because he would have shown how to predict successful students. An experimenter more concerned with theory or theory testing (if he were not completely dumbfounded by the astonishing results) would be interested in determining why red hair was such an important variable.

Theory-oriented Research: Much has been written on how theories are developed. Often, a theory comes from a hunch. The investigator muses whether A will affect B and, if so, what the relationship will be. We are all theorists to some degree, for we are constantly testing such hypotheses. "What will my roommate do if I squeeze the toothpaste from the middle instead of rolling it neatly from the end? What if I squeeze it near the end?" In research, investigators use this approach to develop experiments. A second source of theory construction comes from research in progress. Often an experimenter will find something unusual or unexpected in his results, and this finding will lead him to develop new theories.

The word *theory,* however, should not be used in place of *idea, notion,* or *opinion.* Even the most modest of theories is based on experimental findings or rigid observations. No theory exists outside some logical frame, and it is incorrect to refer to unfounded and unorganized speculations as theory. Most often, a theory provides a framework that, when the findings are compared with other data, permits one to interpret and unite the data. Once a theory is formulated, it must be properly tested. Thus, we are led to the third general category of experimental studies in psychology, theory-testing research.

Theory-testing Research: This type of research is the logical extension of theory construction, and in the realm of sound research procedures the two are commonly one. When a theory is constructed properly, it makes predictions. Some of these predictions are stated clearly in the theory, and others are discovered by alert readers. For example, if the relationship between A and B is linear (the more hungry the human infant, the more activity it generates) and if B has a linear relationship to C (the more active the human child, the louder it cries), then we should be able to predict the relationship between A and C. If our experiment or observation does not provide the expected results, a reexamination of either the theory or our logic is in order.

Often two theories disagree directly on a single point, thus permitting an investigator to perform an "ideal" experiment. Whatever the results, one theory is shown to be incorrect and the other correct on that particular point. Rarely, however, is a theory destroyed by one or even more failures to confirm a prediction. Usually a theory replaces another because it repeatedly predicts correctly while the other does not. Theories do not die overnight, nor do they stand or fall on the behavior of one group of subjects. The formulation of theory before enough facts are available to assure a reasonable chance of success is extremely risky, and in some areas of psychology the experimenter searches about for relations between factors long before he attempts to provide a theory or, sometimes, even a hypothesis. Such research is sometimes called *nontheoretical,* or *ahypothetical.*

Although some experimenters do only one kind of research and thus call themslves either applied psychologists or theoretical psychologists, other investigators vary their approaches, conducting research which cuts across these applied and theoretical lines. The major differences are not in technique or method so much as in the types of questions the investigator wishes to ask and answer.

In experimental psychology, we may approach an experiment in any of several different ways.

SOME APPROACHES OF EXPERIMENTAL PSYCHOLOGY

Many investigative procedures have been used in experimental psychology. Vogues come and go, and protagonists argue for one approach or another. As a science develops, it may be that one is more appropriate at a particular time than another. Students of experimental psychology should be familiar with the three

methods that have contributed most to the investigation of behavior: (1) the method of *systematic change,* which is employed most often in the controlled laboratory situation, (2) the *phylogenetic method,* which is also used in the laboratory but may be used in conjunction with (3) *field, or naturalistic, observations.* Let us consider these often overlapping methods in more detail.

Systematic Change: The majority of the studies which we shall discuss in this text were conducted in the laboratory. Under such controlled conditions, the experimenter is able to evaluate the systematic change on one variable produced by one or more other variables. Assume that our experimental question is whether or not distraction or noise interferes with learning. We have some commonsense information on this matter, for it is "well known" that one cannot study efficiently surrounded by blaring radios and talking friends. We do not, however, perform our experiment by going to the nearest dormitory and asking the inhabitants if noise distracts them from their studies. Such a procedure would introduce too many possible sources of error. For example:

1. We might pick subjects who are not a representative sample of students. We might select a group of students who have chosen to live close to one another because each wishes to study under conditions that are as quiet as possible. Alternatively, we might select a dormitory in which students chose to live together for just the opposite reason! In either case our sample would be biased, and it would be unscientific to generalize from the behavior of these students to the behavior of all students.

2. We would have no control over the kind of distracting noise, since we have not defined it. Some students might learn efficiently if classical music were played, while others might find it detrimental to their work.

3. We have failed to specify what we mean by "learning"—do we mean the kind of learning involved in studying for a final examination in a history course, the kind involved in memorizing

the vocabulary of a foreign language, or the kind employed in trying to understand a poem?

To avoid these sources of error, we design an experiment to be conducted under controlled conditions. We attempt to select an unbiased sample of students, we define clearly what we mean by noisy distraction, and we select some appropriate test of learning on which all subjects will be examined. Similarly, we insist that all our subjects be tested under the same conditions. Finally, we have the problem of *designing the experiment,* that is, specifying how subjects will be treated. One very simple design divides the subjects into two groups: one group, the *control group,* does not receive the distraction, while the second group, the *experimental group,* does. We may show the design of this experiment in the following notation:

Time

C ⟶ | — | B |
E ⟶ | A | B |

where

C = control group
E = experimental group
— = absence of the noise
A = presence of the noise
B = test of learning

The design, which reads from left to right, specifies in notation that the control group does not receive the noise distraction and is tested on the same measure of learning as the experimental group. An extension of this design is:

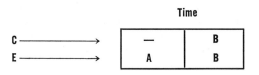

	Test	Condition		Retest
Subjects	Divide into	C ⟶	—	B
	E & C	E ⟶	A	B

In this design, both groups are tested to assure that they are of equal ability on the particular task and then divided into the control and experimental groups. The experimental group receives the distracting stimulus, while the control group does not. Finally, both groups are retested. Simply, if the final test shows the control group to be superior in learning, we may assume that the distraction did indeed inhibit learning.

The choice of design for an experiment is a very complicated affair. Often, the choice is dictated by mundane considerations, such as the number of subjects available and the kind of measure being taken. However, an experimenter always works to select the most efficient design, that is, the design which provides him with the greatest amount of useful information from the smallest number of subjects. The problem of design has been treated in detail in a number of excellent books (see Sources at the end of this chapter). Our purpose in demonstrating this simple design has been to show that the method of systematic change requires providing one set of conditions in contrast to a second set of conditions. In this example, the conditions are the presence or absence of the distracting noise. The technique of systematic change would include varying the levels of noise. The technique permits the experimenter to vary the parameters of the variables in any way he thinks fruitful.

Two points are noteworthy: the first concerns a matter of semantics, and the second, the reason that experiments such as these are performed in the laboratory.

First, we referred to "distracting noise." For the purpose of this object lesson, we equated the presence of music with distracting noise. However, the word *distraction* strongly implies an unwanted alteration in one's concentration. The word *noise* also denotes unpleasantness. Had we found that the experimental group performed better than the control group, we should have been in the interesting position of claiming that "distracting noise" is beneficial. If we made this statement to persons not acquainted with our definition of the phrase (in a newspaper report of the experiment, for example), we should not be surprised to find confusion, if not disbelief, among our readers. We would hardly want our findings to encourage students to study to the accompaniment of sound tracks, blaring bands, and collapsible chairs. Thus, the definition of terms is extremely important, especially in interpreting an experiment. More will be said about the whole matter of definitions later in this chapter.

Another comment on our experiment might be that we did not test our subjects under "real" conditions. Why should the experimental psychologist make subjects go to a laboratory, place them in soundproofed, light-controlled rooms, and force them to learn nonsense syllables while he intermittently disturbs them with loud noises? Few persons, if any, have any interest in whether one learns under these conditions. Classes are not taught in this way, and students, presumably, do not study under these conditions.

This objection can be answered by analogy. If one wishes to test whether or not a newly designed plane can withstand winds over 1,500 mph (miles per hour), one does not send the plane up, with the passengers, on its maiden run to find out. A model of the plane is tested in a wind tunnel in order to predict whether or not the plane will stand the stress. In a like manner one experiments with chemicals in a test tube before producing them in large quantities. The point is that the controlled experiment provides us with data under conditions which enhance our ability to predict. The laboratory experiment is, if you will, an abstraction. Although the laboratory investigation involving systematic change may bear little direct resemblance to the problem posed by the original question, it has two important advantages:

1. **The findings may be generalized to problems other than those posed by the original question.**
2. **It is less likely to produce erroneous or inexact results than an experiment conducted under nonlaboratory conditions.**

The laboratory permits us to control many more factors in the experiment than we otherwise could. There are exceptions, of course; some questions cannot be answered at all, or at least not easily, in the laboratory. Moreover, as in applied research, we are sometimes interested in a specific answer to a specific question under specific conditions. If we want to know whether workers in factory X (and only factory X) can perform a certain task (and only that task) more efficiently under certain conditions, then it is preferable to conduct the experiment under those conditions. However, the specificity of the design does not provide us with general rules of behavior which we can abstract and generalize to other situations.

The first statement is, perhaps, more difficult to tolerate than the second. Indeed, a person without experience in laboratory work might be unlikely to accept it at all. The point is this, however: although the controlled experiment is apparently artificial, its findings can be used for theory construction. The findings may seem limited in practical application because of the artificial methods. In the long run, the results may be applicable to a great number of problems.

One frequent objection to laboratory studies is that experimental psychology appears to be a psychology of white rats and college sophomores. Unfortunately, these two populations have been the favorites of investigators. Since most investigators, until recently, were in academic institutions, it is not surprising that they turned to the most easily available source of subjects. This, however, is not an appropriate objection to the experimental method of systematic change in the laboratory; rather, it is an appropriate criticism of the methods used in selecting subjects.

We have interpreted the experimental method to include both studies in which the experimenter manipulates the variables directly (an *experimenter-manipulated* experiment, such as the one in which the presentation of distracting noise was manipulated) and studies in which the experimenter investigates variables already present but does not manipulate them (the measurement of intelligence as a function of economic background or the measurement of adult anxiety as a function of childhood training). Some authorities regard the first type of study as the only proper sphere of experimental psychology. In this text, however, we adopt the broader view that any systematic collection of data requires the techniques of experimental psychology.

The Phylogenetic Approach: The phylogenetic approach involves the study of behavior in different species, the comparison of the behavior of species, and the search for ways in which behavior has developed in an evolutionary sense.

White rats and college students would appear to display quite divergent kinds of behaviors. There is no question that this is true. Rats do not drop bombs on one another, and they have never learned that the supermarket provides an easier method for obtaining food than foraging. By the same token, few college sophomores can burrow through wood with their front teeth or produce litters of twelve with regularity.

Infrahuman subjects are employed in psychological research for several reasons:

1. If we accept the premise upon which evolutionary theory is based—that behavior may be seen as a continuing line of development from the simplest to the most complex animals—infrahuman subjects provide us with information on how behavior has developed.

2. Whether or not the behavior of animals contributes to an understanding of human behavior is irrelevant to the purposes of the science. Psychology is concerned with the behavior of living organisms. Thus, any living organism is an acceptable subject for psychological research.

3. In some research, human beings are not appropriate subjects for experimentation. An obvious example is research on brain functions, where ablation or lesioning of the brain is necessary. Similarly, animals are often used when it is necessary to control genetic history and when the availability of organisms with shorter life spans than

human beings have permits the experimenter to observe many generations of organisms. In psychology, the study of animal behavior is commonly conducted in the laboratory. In zoology, animal behavior is most commonly studied in the field, or the natural habitat, of the animal. Although both approaches provide information on the behavior of animals, experimental psychologists are likely to use the experimental method of systematic change.

Often discoveries about the mental abilities of animals provide useful clues to what should be studied in human beings. For example, the development, but not the invention, of teaching machines and other devices for automatic teaching originated in experimental work on rats. Another example of a behavior that can be studied phylogenetically is *probability learning.* Suppose that you are facing an apparatus which has two lights and you may "guess" which light will be turned on by flicking a switch. Now, assume that the unseen experimenter has manipulated the lights so that light A will appear 80 percent of the time and light B the remaining 20 percent. Of course, the lights will be presented in a random fashion, so that you cannot know which light will appear. What will you do? Some animals *maximize* under these conditions; that is, they guess light A 100 percent of the time. Thus, they maximize the probability of their being right on any one trial. Other animals *match;* that is, they select light A 80 percent of the time, even though they are wrong on some occasions, and select light B 20 percent of the time, even though, of course, they are sometimes wrong.

As we go up the phylogenetic scale, a general shift from maximizing to matching occurs. Among human beings, we find more adults than children matching; we find more normally intelligent children than retarded children matching. If one suspected that matching or maximizing depended upon some elements of brain structure, the next step would be to compare the subject that matches with the development of its brain. Whether human beings match or maximize is probably of practical interest only to gamblers. However, it should be clear that variations in behavior follow phylogenetic lines, and this observation may provide us with information about the role of the structure and functions of the brain in determining behavior. We might also note that human beings, when told about the difference between matching and maximizing, assume that matching is the more intelligent behavior. A fish, however, might consider matching a waste of time, since maximizing provides success with little effort. The point to keep in mind is that the morphological phylogenetic scale might not correlate with the phylogenetic scale based on behavioral patterns.

Field, or Naturalistic, Observation: In the study of human and animal behavior, it is frequently impossible to bring either the subjects or the procedure into the laboratory. Social behavior under war conditions is not easily translatable into a correlative study, and if it were, the obvious artificiality would probably change the behavior of the subjects. Nor is it feasible to study the mating behavior of whales in the ordinary university laboratory. Studies conducted as the behavior occurs in the natural habitat are called *field studies,* and they employ the system of naturalistic observation. Rarely is any systematic change or manipulation of behavior attempted in such studies; rather, the experimenter watches and records the behavior and attempts to isolate and infer its causative factors through observations. Cause and effect are more likely to be confused in field studies than in the laboratory, for in the laboratory the investigator can always repeat the experiment or manipulate in different ways the variables that he has under control. Field studies, however, often provide valuable contributions to experimental psychology. Although they may provide data from which it is difficult to formulate laws of behavior, they often provide hypotheses and direct attention to phenomena which can be more clearly delineated in the laboratory. Moreover, many forms of behavior cannot be measured in the laboratory. For example, the sexual behavior of certain species is greatly inhibited by captivity, and the laboratory worker is likely to have no data to observe, much less to manipulate. Workers committed to field studies argue that the laboratory itself affects behavior. Laboratory workers contend that field studies lack rigor. Hopefully, the truth is somewhere between these two extremes, for both approaches have advantages and, certainly, both have disadvantages.

THE TECHNIQUE OF SYSTEMATIC CHANGE

Let us reiterate that there are many methods of investigating behavior. Each has its own special problems and each makes its own special contributions. No doubt, other methods will be invented, and improvements will be made on those currently in use, for the logic of the scientific method is not static. In the preceding section, we have only introduced some approaches which have provided useful data on behavior. Basic to experimental psychology, however, is the method of systematic change within the laboratory. The manner in which such experiments are designed and performed is therefore considered in greater detail in this section.

When we speak of technique, we really refer to two separate but complementary components: the apparatus and the design, or procedure, of the experiment. Some kind of physical apparatus is used in experiments to present the stimulus and to record the response. Clearly, measurement is only so accurate as the apparatus or measuring device. The apparatus may consist of highly specialized electronic equipment, or it may be paper and pencil used in scoring tests. An experimenter concerned with projecting light on a small portion of the retina is dependent upon the reliability and accuracy of the equipment which presents the stimulus, just as he is dependent upon the reliability and accuracy of the amplifier and recording instrument which record the effect of the light. The development of techniques employed in a field of study often parallels the history of advances in knowledge in that field; the development of new techniques (such as electrical recording from nerves or the ability to reach the other side of the moon) permits new discoveries. The refinement of techniques (such as the replacement of chronoscopes, mechanical devices for counting small fractions of time, by electric clocks) and the development of new techniques (most recently, electronic devices for measuring responses and programming experiments) herald changes in the emphasis of research and, eventually, advances in knowledge.

Technique also refers to the experimental design and the procedure of the experiment. The most accurate equipment is useless, even detrimental, if the experimental design is inappropriate. Although any experiment is limited by the sensitivity of the apparatus, the procedure and design are equally important. Indeed, attempting to assess whether apparatus or design is the more important attribute of an experiment is rather like deciding which right angle contributes most to a square.

We shall consider three important characteristics of design. The first concerns the terminology used to designate the variables; the second concerns some problems associated with measuring and presenting the stimulus; and the third involves the manner in which the response is measured.

Independent and Dependent Variables: When the experimental psychologist asks a question about behavior, he attempts to answer it by manipulating either the environment or the organism; he wants to discover the precise effect of such manipulation on behavior. That which is manipulated is called the *independent variable* of the experiment. The behavior which is measured and which is expected to change as a result of the presence, absence, or magnitude of the independent variable is called the *dependent variable.* In our attempt to discover the effect of distracting noise on learning, the noise was the independent variable, and the amount learned was the depen-

dent variable. An experimenter who designs an experiment to test the effect of a drug on reducing anxiety refers to the drug as the independent variable and the anxiety as the dependent variable. The independent variables are those elements of the experiment which the experimenter has under his control, and which he may vary as he chooses. However, he must always know which elements he has varied and how much he has varied them. Since the dependent variable is not under the control of the experimenter, it is assumed to be dependent upon the independent variable.

The nature of the independent variable must be analyzed precisely. In our experiment, "distracting noise" is too general a term. Among the many attributes of the major independent variable are:

1. **The intensity of the stimulus (the noise)**
2. **The pattern of the stimulus**
3. **The duration of the stimulus**

We could list a number of other independent variables in our experiment, for it is reasonable to assume that many factors would affect the dependent variable in some way. However, in any experiment only a few independent variables (or perhaps one) are of concern to the experimenter. Thus, these variables are manipulated and the remaining independent variables are *controlled;* that is, they are kept constant.

The universe is filled with independent variables. The problem of the experimenter is to decide which should be manipulated, which should be controlled, and which should be ignored. Indeed, the process of experimental investigation consists of determining which variables affect which behaviors. Some independent variables are known to be more effective in controlling specific behaviors than others; some are known to be irrelevant. Thus, a major concern of the experimental psychologist is to determine, both from his own experiments and from the literature, which independent variables are important.

Regarding dependent variables, it is obvious that any behavior consists of many discrete bits of behavior. A rat may be pressing a bar to obtain food, but he may also be twitching his whiskers, sitting on his haunches, and performing many other measurable behaviors. In selecting and defining the behavior that we wish to measure, we are selecting the dependent variable. Clearly, we might select a very effective independent variable but fail to notice its effect if the dependent variable were inappropriate. Once again, the experimenter selects the dependent variable as a function of several considerations. What bit of behavior is most accurately observed? Which provides the experimenter with the greatest magnitude of change? Which is most likely to be affected by the independent variable?

Over the years, a number of conventional dependent variables have been derived:

1. **The latency of the response**
2. **The amplitude of the response**
3. **The frequency of the response**
4. **The duration of the response**

In some situations the measures correlate very highly with one another; in others they may not correlate at all. Let us consider a selection of frequently used dependent variables.

Latency refers to the amount of time between the presentation of a stimulus and a response to that stimulus. One of the most common dependent variables which is measured by response latency is *reaction time*. In the standard reaction-time experiment (see Chapter 15), the subject is presented with a board containing lights and switches. He is instructed to turn off a light, when it appears, as promptly as possible by throwing the appropriate switch. In the early days of psychology, this technique was used in an attempt to measure the speed of transmission of the nervous system. Today, measures of reaction time are used for practical purposes, such as determining how rapidly a person can brake a car at a given signal. A second example of the use of latency as a dependent variable comes from studies of the behavior of animals in a maze.

Often an animal is placed in a starting box and calmed before a door is raised which permits him to enter the maze. The time between the opening of the door and the animal's leaving the starting box is referred to as *latency*. In this context, latency is sometimes regarded as a measure of motivation, on the assumption that the greater the motivation of the animal to reach the goal of the maze, the shorter the latency, or reaction time.

Amplitude is often used in studies of conditioning. When Pavlov measured the amount of salivation secreted by his dogs, he was using amplitude as the major dependent variable. He could have used another measure, such as the frequency of salivation; however, in this experimental design, amplitude would appear to be the more sensitive measure. Similarly, studies have been conducted that evaluate the force with which a rat presses a bar to obtain food. In such instances, one might expect amplitude to reflect the motivational state of the organism.

Rate of response is most commonly used in studies aimed at measuring relatively repetitive acts, such as bar pressing. Rate, of course, includes both the frequency and the duration of the response, although the two can be measured separately. Frequency is the dependent variable when the number of persons who behave in one fashion is compared with the number who behave in another. Measuring the probable outcome of a presidential election is one example of the use of frequency of response. Duration of response may be used if we wish to determine how long it takes for an organism to solve a particular problem.

It is wise to measure as many dependent variables as possible, unless one gives up precision by doing so. The strategy of using many dependent variables is especially appropriate when the effect of the independent variable is difficult to predict and when one wishes to explore the possible outcomes of manipulating a given independent variable.

The identification of independent variables and dependent variables provides us with a useful shorthand for describing research programs. An understanding of the terms also permits us to design an experiment intelligently. However, specification of these variables does not end the task of designing an experiment, for it is also necessary to stipulate the way in which measurements are to be made. Since the independent variable is usually a stimulus in one form or another and since the dependent variable is always a response of some kind, it is now necessary to examine the ways in which stimuli and responses are measured.

Presenting the Stimulus: Over the years, certain basic apparatuses have been developed for use in psychological laboratories. In advanced research, however, the experimenter must often construct equipment which suits his specific requirements. Both the availability of equipment and its accuracy and precision limit and determine the kinds of experiments which can be performed.

Stimulus-producing apparatus is of two kinds: one only presents the stimulus, while the second records or evaluates the stimulus or response. The oscilloscope, which is used to record the voltage generated by some other apparatus, such as a shock source, belongs to the latter group. It monitors the apparatus to make certain that it is producing voltage at the desired frequency and amplitude. In a similar way, illuminometers are used to measure a light source. These stimulus-recording instruments are most often used in physiological, sensory, and psychophysical research. However, the need to measure the output and to calibrate apparatus is a matter of consequence in any research.

Consider the obvious, but difficult, problem an experimenter has when he wishes to administer small amounts of electric current to an organism. Although it might seem a simple matter to apply current to the subject's feet, the amount of shock the organism receives will depend upon its electrical resistance. Since electrical resistance varies widely (in fact, such variations are used to measure changes in emotionality—see Chapter 17), the experi-

menter loses control over an important variable, namely, the amount of current the subject receives. The apparatus tells the experimenter that a certain amount of electric current is being administered, but it tells him nothing about the quantity which the organism receives. The experimenter's first step might be to monitor the amount of current on an oscilloscope. His next step might be to find a type of generator which would be uninfluenced by changes in resistance. Whatever his approach, it is clear that recognition of the problems of calibrating the apparatus and measuring its output are critical if an experiment is to be conducted successfully.

Since the selection of the design of an experiment depends upon the kinds of equipment in use and since appreciation of experimental results depends in part on one's ability to assess the apparatus which was used in determining the results, a list is presented in Table 1–A of some of the most commonly used apparatuses in psychological research with a brief description of the function of each. Most of the items are also discussed in the text at some point.

Measuring the Response: Many kinds of apparatuses both present the stimulus and record the response. Often, however, a different instrument is used for recording responses, and the experimenter may have to modify or invent recording devices to suit his needs. The comments made regarding the necessity of calibrating and using precise equipment to present the stimulus are equally valid when we consider devices to measure the response. Table 1–B presents some of the most common recording apparatuses and gives each item's function.

In many kinds of contemporary research, experimenters rely upon electronic switching devices to control the stimulus and upon intricate recording devices to record the responses. Switching devices are especially useful when the subject's response determines what events will occur next, as, for example, when a rodent is learning to delay or eliminate the presentation of electric current by a specific behavior, such as pressing a bar.

PROCEDURES OF INVESTIGATION

We have considered some of the kinds of investigations in which experimental psychologists engage and some of the techniques used. Let us now consider, in greater detail, what is involved in designing, conducting, and interpreting an experiment.

There are a number of ways to go about gathering information on behavior; some are correct and some are not. Although there is no single correct method, a model of how a research project is conceived, carried out, and concluded may nevertheless be valuable. For convenience in exposition, we shall talk about (1) using the literature of psychology, (2) developing the hypothesis, (3) designing the experiment, (4) conducting the experiment, and (5) problems of interpretation. The last item is extensive, and we devote the final portion of this chapter to it.

The Literature: The literature of psychology consists of all the material bearing on psychological topics that is published throughout the world. *Psychological Abstracts* provides summaries of publications. However, a summary rarely includes all the information about apparatus, procedures, and interpretation of results that is needed by the student or scientist who is contemplating a research project. Thus, it usually becomes necessary to consult the original source. Moreover, abstracts and summaries are not critical. That is, they do not assess errors in the design or interpretation of the work or point out praiseworthy characteristics. The burden of ascertaining how much value to place on the results of an experiment falls upon the reader.

When an investigator has selected a problem, a review of the appropriate literature is advisable for several reasons: (1) it may show that the problem has been solved, (2) it describes the procedures and apparatus that other investigators have used to solve similar problems, and (3) it tells how the findings of others have been interpreted.

With the expansion of experimental psychology to many countries, the probability of two or more experimenters inadvertently conducting identical experiments is increasing. It is rare, of course, that an experiment is repeated in every detail; the numerous procedures available tend to decrease such a possibility. In some instances, it may be worthwhile to repeat available experiments, but ordinarily, unless there is reason to doubt the validity of the results of a study, exact repetition is inefficient.

Use of the literature also generates new ideas and new hypotheses. If one reviews the literature thoroughly on any particular topic, he is very likely to devise several new hypotheses. Accordingly, a review of the literature may either precede the formulation of a hypothesis or follow it.

The Experimenter and the Hypothesis: Formulation of a hypothesis is a fundamental process and a factor which contributes heavily to the selection of design in research. An experimenter usually has an opinion or an expectation about the outcome of an experiment: he is human, and his behavior is subject to the same laws and principles as other men. He has hopes, beliefs, and prejudices. He may adhere to a theoretical position, or he may oppose a specific position. Realizing that beliefs may influence the outcome of an experiment, many experimenters automate their studies in order to minimize their role or, at least, to control it so that it does not affect the outcome. The use of prerecorded instructions to the subjects is one technique that keeps the experimenter's behavior constant during an experiment.

The following example illustrates the danger of "experimenter contamination." One investigator assigned his class a problem concerned with the running speed of rats in a maze. He told half the students that they were

TABLE 1-A: *Apparatus Commonly Used to Present the Stimulus in Psychological Studies and Apparatus Used to Study Learning.*

Apparatus	*Function*
Artificial pupil	Controls amount of light entering the eye.
Audiometer (audiooscillator)	Presents tones of variable frequency and intensity.
Autokinetic apparatus	Presents stationary point of light in dark room, giving illusion of movement.
Bárány chair	A rotating chair to create gross bodily motion.
Beat-frequency oscillator	Produces pure tones of variable frequency.
Blast injection bottle	Presents olfactory stimuli with controlled amount of air.
Camera inodorata	Removes background odors when olfactory stimuli are tested.
Color wheel	Mixes colors by rotating disks of several colors in varying proportions.
Dvorine plates	Tests for color blindness.
Episcotister	Rotating disk which cuts down amount of light reaching subject.
Esthesiometer	Finds minimum separation necessary for two points of contact with skin to feel like two points instead of one.
Flicker fusion apparatus	Presents light stimuli in controlled off-on cycle.
Flowmeter odorimeter	Presents olfactory stimuli by adding odor to air stream.
Fourier analyzer	Gives record of wavelength and intensity of frequency bands of visual and auditory stimuli.
Howard-Dolman apparatus	Three-needle apparatus for testing depth perception.
Humascope	Presents different stimuli (usually faces) to each eye to test visual rivalry and perceptual defense.
Illuminometer	Measures physical characteristics of light source.
Ishihara plates	Tests for color blindness.
Monochrometer	Light source which gives close regulation of wave frequency.
Novelty box	Tests curiosity drive in animal.
Obstruction box	Separates starting box and goal box by a grid.

Apparatus	Function
Olfactorium	Room for removing background odors when olfactory stimuli are tested.
Open field	Tests emotionality in animal.
Oscilloscope	Gives visual representation of electrical potential changes.
Perimeter	Presents visual stimuli to different locations on the retina; tests peripheral vision.
Phi-phenomenon apparatus	A series of light that gives an illusion of movement when illuminated sequentially.
Pseudophone	Reverses normal presentation of auditory stimuli (from left to right ear, for example).
Pseudoscope	Reverses normal presentation of visual stimuli leading to a reversal of depth effect.
Radiant-heat stimulator	Tests pain thresholds.
Reduction screen	Conceals surroundings and illumination conditions of visual stimuli.
Rod-and-frame device	Tests role of vision in orientation.
Sine- and square-wave generator	Generates tone, delivers electric current, and stimulates brain.
Stereoscope	Presents slightly different pictures of the same thing to the two eyes, giving depth effect.
Tachistoscope	Presents visual stimuli for very short periods of time.
Telereoscope	Increases depth effect.
Visual-test module	System for rapid presentation of simple stimulus patterns for discrimination learning.
von Frey hairs	Used in the study of tactile sensitivity.
White-noise generator	Produces wide-spectrum noise to mask sounds irrelevant to experimental conditions.
Zwaardemaker's olfactometer	Delivers olfactory stimuli.

Apparatus	Function
Activity cage and activity wheel	Records animal's activity.
Ataximeter	Measures body sway.
Automalograph	Measures motion.
Bitterman activity-count integrator	Translates small-animal and fish activity into a digital count.
Body plethysmograph	Records volume of air subject is breathing.
Chronoscope	Measures small periods of time mechanically.
Cohen Constant Weight Cage	Feeds rat automatically when his weight drops below a preset level, thus maintaining certain body weights.
Continuous-event recorder	Records changes in the intensity or frequency of some electrical event.
Cumulative recorder	Gives graphic record changes in rate of response.
Dermohmeter	Measures skin resistance.
Discrete-event recorder	Records onset and sometimes offset of events according to some threshold, i.e., above or below a certain voltage or current value.
Dynamometer	Measures strength of grip.
Electrocardiogram (ECG, EKG)	Records electrical changes in heart muscles.
Electroencephalogram (EEG)	Records electrical changes in brain patterns.
Electromyograph (EMG)	Amplifies and records electric potentials produced during muscular contraction.
Electroretinograph (ERG)	Records electrical change of retina.
Ergograph	Records effort involved in weight-pulling tasks.
Gasometer	Records breathing volume.
Hoffman analogue labs	The movement of a dial reproduces many changes in response strength typical of animals when certain environmental contingencies are imposed, such as reinforcement or extinction. Graphic means of demonstrating factors influencing response strength.
Keeler polygraph "lie detector"	Records breathing and blood-pressure changes and associative reaction time.

Apparatus	Function
Kymograph	Records small amounts of movements.
Lashley jumping stand	Animal must jump across a chasm to safety or food. Tests visual and auditory discrimination.

Mazes
  Finger maze
  Open maze
  T maze
  Runway maze
  Water maze
  Fly maze
  Continuous maze
  Multiple T maze
	Task in which blindfolded subject traces raised path to goal.
	All are variations on task requiring an organism to traverse some path or area to reach a goal area. They vary in difficulty and medium of travel, but critical measures are always amount of time required to begin travel, rate of motion, and number of errors.

Memory drum	Presents verbal material.
Miller-Mower box	Animal must shuttle back and forth between sides of box to avoid or escape shock through grid floor.
Mirror-drawing device	Allows subject to see only mirror image of hand movements as he draws a figure.
Ophthalmograph	Records eye movements on film.
Photokymograph	Records eye movements on film.
Plethysmograph	Records volumetric changes in the body.
Pneumograph	Records thoracic expansion with breathing.
Preference apparatus	Measures relative consumption of different foods and liquids.
Pursuit rotor	Tests motor learning.
Reaction-time apparatus	Measures latency of response from stimulus presentation.
Rotter level-of-aspiration board	Gives subject a task in which the experimenter has control of the score.
Skinner box	Apparatus in which the subject must perform operant response in order to receive reinforcement.
Sphygmograph	Records arterial pulse.
Sphygmomanometer	Records blood pressure.

TABLE 1-B (continued)

Apparatus	Function
Stereotaxic instrument	Fixes the heads of many vertebrate animals in a rigid position so that cranial electrodes can be coordinated to a precise position in the brain according to a brain atlas.
Switching circuitry	Electrical systems used to control experimental events and to record responses. Usually used when experimental conditions are too complicated to be controlled by hand. Switching devices include electromechanical relays, reed relays, and transistors.
Teaching machine	Presents material to be learned in such a way that the learner must make a response which confirms acquisition of the material before more items are presented.
Telemeters	Systems for remote recording of physiological processes by implanting or attaching a small transmitter and sensor to the organism.
Thermocouple	Measures temperature.
Transducer	Translates physical movement or pressure into electric potentials.
Voice key	A switch which is closed by speech sounds.
Wisconsin General Test Apparatus Purdue General Test Apparatus	Present stimuli for discrimination and problem-solving tasks.

working with a strain of rats which had been developed as quick learners and rapid maze runners; he told the other half that their rats had been bred to be slow maze runners. Actually, the rats were of the same strain. Curiously, the students found that the "speedy" rats ran much faster than the "slow" rats (cf. R. Rosenthal & Lawson, 1964; R. Rosenthal, 1966). In this illustration, we see how the outcome of an experiment may be influenced, often unintentionally, by the experimenter.

Before an experiment is designed, the experimenter has formulated some type of hypothesis. The hypothesis may be as simple as "*If* I deprive this animal of water for a period of time, *then* he will learn to press a bar to get water more rapidly than an animal who is not deprived," or it may be as complicated as "*If* a group of students in an introductory psychology course is divided into five subgroups equivalent in learning ability and if group I is taught the course by television, group II by lecture, group III by reading assignments and no lecture, group IV by the use of programmed materials and teaching machines, and group V by discussion groups, *then,* when tested for mastery of content four months later, the groups will differ significantly from one another in the order given, group I being superior on the examination." Often, the hypothesis is no better formulated than "I wonder what would happen if . . . ." This is not a true hypothesis, but it is a kind of questioning which generates many experiments.

Although the design and procedure which would be used to establish the validity of these hypotheses vary greatly, the hypotheses have much in common. Both hypotheses (we shall not include the third formulation) specify certain conditions and predict certain results. The specification of experimental conditions and the prediction of experimental results are the fundamental components of a hypothesis. The specification of conditions must be extremely clear and concise, so that there is no question about what they are to be. The specification "*If* this animal is deprived of water for a period of time" is not sufficient, for it fails to indicate the length of deprivation, the type of animal, the age and sex of the animal, and so on. Similarly, the predictive portion of the hypothesis must state clearly how the prediction is to be evaluated. The statement "*Then* he will learn to press a bar more rapidly than another animal" is not informative either, for "rapidly" may mean different things to different experimenters.

Many experimenters use the *null hypothesis* in designing and performing experiments. Both the preceding hypotheses make a specific prediction; that is, they state that one group or animal will be "superior" or more "rapid" than the other. The hypotheses are upheld if, *and only if,* one group or animal is superior. If the animals or groups had been equivalent or if the opposite animal or group were superior, the hypotheses would be rejected. A null hypothesis, however, predicts that *no* difference between the subjects will exist. An example, of a null hypothesis is "If I deprive this animal of water for a period of time, *then* he will learn to press a bar for water *no more rapidly* than an animal which is not deprived." The null hypothesis predicts "no difference." Accordingly, the hypothesis may be rejected if *either* animal behaves significantly differently from the other animal.

Although this distinction between a hypoth-

esis that predicts specifically which group will be better and one that predicts no difference may seem superfluous, it is of critical importance to the selection of the statistic appropriate for establishing any difference between the groups. Moreover, it emphasizes the point that the scientific method does not prove the presence of cause-and-effect relationships; it only disproves them. In short, once the hypothesis is formulated—long before the design and procedure are established—the type of statistic which may be used to evaluate the' data is stipulated. The wording of the original hypothesis is the beginning of a chain of interrelated plans which concludes with an experimental finding.

With careful nurture a hypothesis may grow up to be a law. The difference between hypotheses and laws, ultimately, is in the amount of supporting evidence which has accumulated. If a hypothesis is repeatedly rejected, it obviously cannot become a law. However, if it is not rejected (as in the case of a null hypothesis) or is accepted and if the results of other investigators continue to confirm the prediction, the hypothesis may become a law; for example, other things equal, the hungrier the animal, the more rapidly he will perform. At times, the original hypothesis is modified because of the results of experiments designed to test it. A single rejection does not mean that the hypothesis cannot become a law: rejection may only suggest the need for revision in the formulation of the hypothesis. Laws, in the beginning stages of their confirmation, are often named for (more often, by) their inventor or for some characteristic of their prediction.

The need for precision in defining terms within a hypothesis is obvious. One can prove anything if he defines the terms as he wishes. The problem of definition is bothersome in all scientific disciplines; however, it is unusually cumbersome in the field of psychology, because, unfortunately, words used in everyday language have another precise meaning within the field. The term *learning*, for example, means something specific to investigators of psychological phenomena, but it has many acceptable meanings within the English language. When it is stated, as a law, that "frustration leads to aggression," it is clearly important that *frustration* and *aggression* be defined precisely. Hypotheses, laws, and theories all require precision in definition. There are several acceptable ways to achieve precision, and the problem of which method to use in psychological investigation is of appreciable consequence in interpreting experiments.

Definitions: Dictionary definitions are sometimes called *conventional* definitions; that is, there is no a priori reason to attach a specific meaning to a specific word. Convention alone decrees the relationship. We use conventional definitions in almost all our written and spoken language. But they can be dangerous when applied to experimental science. If the conventional definition of *learning,* for example, is used to refer to precise experimental operations, misunderstanding will ensue.

One way of acquiring precision is to develop a new language or a set of symbols to replace conventional language. The symbolic logician does this, for he knows that he is likely to let the meanings of words interfere with his analysis of the logic of statements. He replaces words with symbols while solving the problem, and then when the solution is reached, he replaces the symbol with the conventional words, if that is necessary for explanation. Although psychologists have from time to time invented terms to stand for concepts, only a few of these remain in our scientific vocabulary. Thus, psychology is without its own language.

Experimental psychologists employ a system of definition originally expounded by the physicist Bridgman (1927). This approach to scientific definition is called *operationism,* or *operationalism,* for the system emphasizes the use of *operational definitions.* An operational definition defines words or concepts in terms of operations. Consider how we would operationally define a 3-inch piece of chalk so that no other piece of chalk could be confused with

it. Perhaps the most convenient way to begin is to formulate operations we might perform. Thus:

If we measure an item with a ruler and find that the item is 3 inches long, and

If we test the item and find that it is composed of calcium carbonate, and

If we perceive that the item is cylindrical in shape

At this point we have separated all cylindrical, 3-inch pieces of calcium carbonate from all the other items in the universe. In order to specify a particular piece of chalk (the one I hold in my hand), we must continue to provide specifications of measurement (texture, color, diameter, etc.). Thus, we arrive at an operational definition of a specific item. One objection to this procedure is that operational definitions require infinite regression. For example, what do we mean by 3 inches? What do we mean by cylindrical? To answer these questions, we must provide operational definitions for these terms too. This problem, however, should not prevent the use of operational definitions insofar as their use is reasonable. Some precision is better than none at all.

In psychology, operational definitions are applied primarily to concepts, such as intelligence, motivation, and learning, the meaning of which is most likely to provoke disagreement. Thus, when an experimenter claims to show that the intelligence of one group of subjects is different from that of another group and the critic asks: "But what do you mean by intelligence?" the experimenter replies: "I use the Stanford-Binet test as my measure of intelligence. Intelligence is what the Stanford-Binet test tests."

Because a reasonable amount of truth may be accompanied by a sleight-of-hand trick, such a reply should be evaluated thoroughly. What is a Stanford-Binet test? Operationally, we could define it by describing the operations that one uses in administering, scoring, and interpreting this particular test so that it would be impossible to confuse the Stanford-

Binet with any other test, or any other item in the universe for that matter. Whether or not the Stanford-Binet, once defined, is a test of intelligence is a different matter, for this question is concerned with whether the test validity distinguishes persons on the basis of intellectual ability. However, our respondent performs this feat simply by claiming that since intelligence is what the Stanford-Binet tests, he has defined both the Stanford-Binet and intelligence.

Our respondent may have been truthful, but he has misled us, perhaps, by defining one item by another. The same procedure would permit someone else to claim that the hypothetical *Short Test of Good Writers* (which consists of giving high grades to females and low grades to males) is a test of academic achievement, for, after all, the test certainly does differentiate students who get high grades from those who do not. You may reply that this test does nothing more than show that females will get high grades and males, low grades. You might continue to argue that a grade in one course is not an adequate test of a good student, and, especially if you were a male in the course, you would no doubt find many, many arguments against such arbitrary ways. You would be right, for this is a difference between the validity of a test and a useful operational definition.

When used properly, operational definitions have several advantages: (1) the experimenter is forced to know what *he* means when he uses a concept, and thus he can convey to everyone else what it means; (2) he may discover that he holds some unnecessary concepts which overlap other concepts and clog theory; and (3) he will be forced to consider the implications of his experimental design more thoroughly than he otherwise might.

We cannot, of course, always write books or take part in verbal discourse on the basis of operational definitions. Not only would the problem of infinite regression make such discourse unreasonable, but, worse, very little would be communicated if we could not resort to conventional definitions as a kind of short-hand. Nevertheless, when we wish to reason, when we wish to design experiments or talk about concepts, and when we wish to develop theories about concepts, the tenets of operationism provide experimental psychology with a very useful device for enforcing clarity of thought. In the discussion of the formulation of hypotheses, we converted the coarse hypothesis into a neat hypothesis by providing operational definitions of the terms. In designing the experiment on the effect of distracting noise upon learning, we took care to define the independent and dependent variables in operational terms.

Designing the Experiment: So far, we have acquired some of the principles regarding how a problem is developed and how a hypothesis is formed. Before getting into the problems of interpretation, we return to experimental design and consider some additional procedures.

ONE VARIABLE: In our inquiry into the effect of noise on learning, a specific level of noise was the only critical independent variable. Other independent variables were available, but they were controlled and not manipulated. In experiments involving just one independent variable, however, several design sequences are possible. Some of these designs are weak, in the sense that the validity of the results is difficult to evaluate. Nevertheless, all have been used at one time or another, and it is worthwhile to appreciate their disadvantages as well as their advantages.

In the first design sequence only one group of subjects is used, and all the subjects receive the application of the independent variable. For example, let us say that shortly before an election, a candidate makes an appearance in a small town. What is the effect of the candidate's appearance (the supposed independent variable) upon the votes cast by the people of the town (the dependent variable)? This is a naturalistic design in which the experimenter neither controls nor manipulates the independent variable: he merely isolates it from the other variables which are presumably active at the same time. This type of design requires the experimenter to have some way of measuring the behavior of the group prior to the application of the independent variable. That is, the observer must have some method of assessing how the people were going to vote before the candidate made his appearance. Any difference between the anticipated voting pattern before and after the appearance would indicate its effect. This type of design rarely leads to unequivocal results, because the experimenter has assumed the presence or manipulation of an independent variable *after* the dependent variable has been measured. Rarely does the experimenter have the independent variable completely isolated; that is, he cannot time the appearance of the speaker, determine how many persons shall be in the audience, and make certain that all other relevant variables are controlled.

When the investigator does have information on the condition of the group before the application of the independent variable, he can use a second type of design involving one independent variable. Consider a seventh-grade teacher who wants to know whether a movie on square roots teaches the principle of squaring numbers and taking square roots correctly. The teacher gives a test (pretest) on square roots to the class before the movie, presents the movie, and then gives a second test (posttest). Any change in test performance is assumed to be due to the movie.

Thus, in our experimental design shorthand, we have

where

T = pretest
I = movie on square roots (independent variable)
D = posttest (dependent variable)

The teacher has used only one group, an experimental group. This design does make one critical assumption, which, if untrue, can invalidate the results. The teacher has assumed that the two tests, the pretest and the posttest, are equivalent measures of the ability of the students. She cannot give identical tests for both the pretest and posttest, for then she could not determine whether the difference in performance, if any, was due to the movie or to the students' familiarity with the test.

Because of the difficulties involved in designs where only one experimental group is used, experimenters concerned with testing one independent variable commonly use two groups, an *experimental group* and a *control group*. The experiment on noise used a control group, which we may now define as that group which receives all elements of the experiment except the independent variable. The experimental group receives all elements, including the independent variable. The true independent variable must be correctly isolated in these experiments. For example, if an investigator is trying to determine whether a specific drug affects anxiety, he administers the drug to the experimental group. However, he also administers a dose of some ineffective substance to the control group so that they do not know which group they are in. Often knowledge of whether one is in the control or experimental group affects results. The wise experimenter also makes certain that *he* does not know which group received the drug and which did not, for he may influence the subjects' performance by some subtle gesture. Thus, he would probably have an assistant, who would never see the subjects, code the pills in such a way that the two groups could be identified only after the experiment was completed. The control group provides a base line of behavior. Thus, any change in the behavior of the control group in a pretest and posttest design represents the normal change in performance which occurs merely as a function of the passage of time.

In *two-group* experiments, the behavior of the experimental group is usually compared with that of the control group. If the two groups were equal on the basis of the dependent variable before the independent variable was applied, any difference between the groups must be due to the independent variable. The teacher who wants to assess the effect of a movie uses the results of the pretest in order to separate the class into two groups of students equal in test performance and, supposedly, equal in their ability to square numbers and to take square roots. For each student in the control group (group C) who received a score of x there would be a student in the experimental group (group E) who received the same score. The ideal situation is to have two groups whose scores are identical.

When two "equal" groups have been established, group E receives the independent variable (in this case, the movie); group C does not see the movie. Then both groups are retested. In this design the students' performance is not compared with pretest results but with the posttest performance of the other group. Thus, if group E is significantly superior to group C on the final test, it would appear that the movie was effective in improving ability to square numbers. This design answers the possible objections to the previous designs concerned with a single independent variable: the experimenter has information on the behavior of the group prior to the administration of the independent variable, and he is able to assume that the groups were equivalent in respect to the dependent variable before the independent variable was administered. Again, in our shorthand system, we have the design like that used for the effect of noise on learning

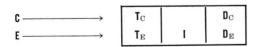

where

T = test to establish groups
I = presentation of movie (independent variable)
D = posttest (dependent variable)

Now, consider only the C group. The differ-

ence between T_C and D_C is the amount of change in performance to be expected as a function of time. There is no reason to suppose that it will be zero, for many activities are affected by maturation and previous experience with the stimuli, such as the pretest itself. However, considering the E group, $T_E - D_E$ does not tell us the effect of the independent variable, except in relation to the $T_C - D_C$. Thus, the difference between $T_E - D_E$ and $T_C - D_C$ represents the influence of the independent variable.

If we examine this design carefully, we can see that it is markedly superior to the two designs described earlier in this section. The first design (involving the election candidate) has no control group and no control at all over the independent variable, while the second (involving the one-group square-roots test) makes the often untenable assumptions that (1) no change in performance occurs between the pretest and the posttest and (2) the measures of performance used for the tests are equivalent. However, the two-group design, though superior, is not without limitations. The teacher who conducted the experiment may, quite appropriately, be interested in knowing whether the control group served its purpose. She may suspect that sending the students in the control group from the room during the movie changes their behavior. Perhaps being dismissed from class while the movie was shown had some effect. Accordingly, the teacher might want to know the effect of leaving the room.

In order to answer these questions, the experimenter must set up additional control groups. Experiments with a single experimental group (and a single independent variable) but with three or more control groups are not uncommon. For example, the teacher might include (1) a group that is shown the movie and told that a test will follow, (2) a group that is shown the movie and *not* told that a test will follow, (3) a group that is sent from the room and told to wait for a test, (4) a group that is sent from the room and *not* told that a test will follow. More groups, of course, could be delineated. In a real sense, such additional groups could pass easily as variations of the experimental group; however, the important characteristic of such designs for purposes of classification is that only one independent variable is present (in this case, the movie) and that it is only varied in one way (it is either present or absent).

Not all experiments which use two groups of subjects rely on a pretest to equate the groups. In many experiments subjects are assigned randomly to groups. The inherent danger in this procedure is, of course, that although it is possible to take elaborate steps to secure a random sample, it is impossible to guarantee such an achievement. We shall discuss some of the problems associated with selecting a random sample later in this chapter under the heading Generalization of Findings. Another method of equating the groups is to test subjects in both experimental and control conditions. We shall discuss this procedure in the next section.

FUNCTIONAL RELATIONS: A number of designs use more than one independent variable and attempt to determine *functional relationships*. In establishing a functional relationship, the experimenter varies the degree or amount of the independent variable and determines the effect of the variations on the dependent variable. For example, if he wished to assess the effect of caffeine on reaction time, the outcome might very well depend upon whether he used ½, 1, or 10 grams of caffeine. If the experimenter had to assess the effect of each of these quantities in a different experiment, he would find the task extremely time-consuming. He can, however, include the different magnitudes of the independent variable in the same experiment and establish a functional relationship. It may be, for example, that 1 and 3 grams of caffeine have the same effect as measured by the dependent variable; it may be that any amount under 5 grams is ineffective. Unless the experimenter is able to assess the relative effectiveness of these different amounts, he is likely to come to a false conclusion. Figure 1-1 shows the relationship

graphically and indicates how errors in interpretation may occur. The illustration should make it clear that supposedly functional relationships may be misleading, especially if the experimenter has not used enough different groups or different magnitudes of the independent variable to establish the trend appropriately. Figure 1–2, for example, shows some functions, all of which are consistent with the same two empirical data points. The problem of knowing when to stop adding empirical points is unanswerable, for there is always the chance that an additional point will alter the function. Although every experiment must stop somewhere; it is probably a greater sin to use too few points than too many.

Two basic experimental designs may be used to establish functional relations: (1) application of all the values of the independent variable to the same subjects and (2) application of different values of the independent variable to different groups of subjects. In the first design, each subject receives all the conditions of the independent variable. This type of design requires that the experimenter *counterbalance* in order to prevent practice effects from contaminating the results. For example, the investigator might use six different quantities of caffeine in order to assess the functional relationship of caffeine to reaction time. Table 1–C shows that each subject receives the dosages in a different order. Such a design cancels any cumulative effect of taking the caffeine. It does not remove the effect of practice or the effect of accumulative administrations of the independent variable, but it does balance presentations in such a way that the *results* are not affected by the order of presentation.

In the second design, an experimenter relies on random sampling rather than counterbalancing. He assigns to each experimental condition a reasonably large number of subjects and assumes that the subjects are "equal" in respect to the dependent variable before the experiment begins. If the investigator provides a pretest, he can divide the subjects into equivalent groups. If he cannot provide such a

FIGURE 1-1: *Possible results of an experiment involving the relationship between reaction time (the dependent variable is plotted on the ordinate) and amount of caffeine consumed (the independent variable is plotted along the abscissa). The top figure (A) shows data collected at only two points, 1 and 3 grams. From this figure, the experimenter might conclude that the amount of caffeine was immaterial. The bottom figure (B), showing a fictional study which includes more points, illustrates that the magnitude of the independent variable is important. The amount of caffeine is immaterial until approximately 5 grams has been consumed, but between 5 and 9 grams caffeine affects reaction time; more than 9 grams is also immaterial, in that no increase in reaction time is noted. Thus, the functional design shows that more than 5 but less than 9 grams is the maximal dose of caffeine which affects reaction time.*

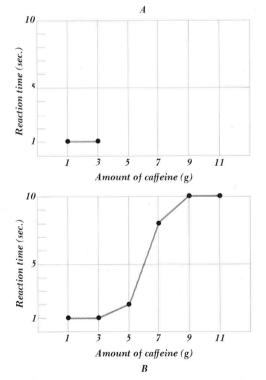

FIGURE 1-2: *The two points in each of the six functions are identical in regard to the ordinates and abscissas. Obviously, very different functions may be drawn using the same two points. This emphasizes the need to use a sufficient number of empirical points in constructing functional relations. (From W. A. Scott & Wertheimer, 1962, p. 40.)*

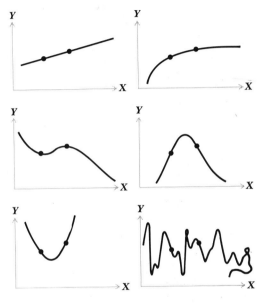

larger the number, the less the chance of a bias, or sampling error. We have previously confronted the problem of assuming that the subjects are randomly selected. Usually, an experimenter must counterbalance the presentation of the independent variable so that any practice effect is eliminated or assume that he has a random distribution of subjects in each of the groups.

Although matching the subjects beforehand by a pretest is an excellent method of equating the groups, this procedure usually requires a large number of subjects. With a small number, an accurate division into several groups is often difficult. Both designs yield functional relationships in which different magnitudes of the independent variable are used to predict

measure, the usual procedure is to increase the number of subjects, on the ground that the

TABLE 1-C : *A Counterbalanced Design to Test the Effect of Six Levels of Caffeine (1 through 6 Grams) on Reaction Time.*

Six different subjects (A through F) are listed in the left column. Six different sessions, twenty-four hours apart, were given, as listed in the right-hand side of the table. Thus, subject B received 2 grams on the first day, 4 grams on the second, and so on. Subject A received 1 gram on the first day, 2 grams on the second, and so on. Each column and each row contain all the dose levels.

	Session					
Subject	*1*	*2*	*3*	*4*	*5*	*6*
A	1	2	3	4	5	6
B	2	4	6	1	3	5
C	3	6	2	5	1	4
D	4	1	5	2	6	3
E	5	3	1	6	4	2
F	6	5	4	3	2	1

differences in the dependent variable. The selection of a design depends upon the type of problem, the number of subjects, and other variables which are of concern to the particular experiment.

FACTORIAL DESIGNS: When two or more independent variables are used and when each variable is itself varied in two or more ways, we have a factorial design. Consider an experimenter who wishes to determine what schedule of study is best for performance on a test. At least four different methods of study are possible, all of which are interrelated. In *massed* practice, the student continues to work on the material until he has learned it. In *distributed* practice, he distributes his time, or "takes time out." It is commonly assumed that distributed practice results in better retention than massed practice; at least this is the rationale behind coffee breaks.

We can also distinguish between *whole* and *part* learning. In whole learning the student rehearses the material in its totality. For example, if he were to memorize the Declaration

of Independence or a sonata, he would read the text or play the sonata from beginning to end, continuing to do this until the task was learned. In *part* learning, the subject rehearses parts of the material and then puts the parts together. A pianist might memorize one passage, then a second passage, and so on, until each passage was learned. Then he would put the memorized parts together and play the whole sonata. A student may study under the combinations of these procedures (see Chapter 15).

Depending upon the type of material to be learned and the way in which the material is to be recalled, one method is usually superior to the others. An investigator might wish to establish which combination of methods is superior for the learning of foreign-language vocabulary. A design which indicates possible relationships is shown in Figure 1–3. The subjects are divided into two equal groups on the basis of a pretest to determine initial ability in the foreign-language vocabulary. Two groups are formed: one learns the material under massed practice, and one learns under distributed practice. Within these categories, however, the subjects are further divided so that half the subjects in each group use the whole-practice method while the other half use the part-practice method.

In effect, the experimenter has formed four groups, although the groups are divided in such a way that the effect of the variables can be assessed independently. If groups MW and DW in Figure 1–3 were superior to groups MP and DP in learning or retention of the learned material, whole learning would seem to be superior regardless of whether massed or distributed practice was used. Similarly, if groups MP and DP were superior, the experimenter might assume that part learning was better regardless of whether massed or distributed practice was employed. On the other hand, if groups MW and MP were better than DW and DP, it would be assumed that massed practice was superior to distributed whether or not the whole or part method was used. The basic design may branch out indefinitely. If

FIGURE 1-3: *Schematic design of a factorial experiment in which the major independent variables are (1) massed versus distributed practice and (2) whole versus part practice. This combination yields a 2 × 2 factorial design. n indicates the number of subjects in each group. Note that each subgroup (e.g., massed-whole) contains half as many subjects as the parent group (e.g., massed). Additional variables, such as age and IQ, could be added by further dividing the subgroups.*

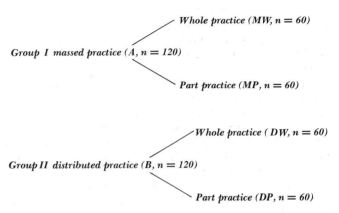

we wished to investigate the effect of the subject's age or sex on the learning of foreign-language vocabulary under various conditions of learning, we could subdivide in order to consider all these variables. This type of design is quite useful when the experimenter considers several independent variables and wishes to assess their relative effect upon one another. The design allows the experimenter to partial out superior and inferior combinations.

Interpreting the results of these designs is far more complicated than interpreting the results of the simple design involving only one independent and one dependent variable. On the other hand, most of the influences on behavior are not simple, and the ability to predict behavior accurately often depends upon findings which do not lend themselves well to generalization. For example, massed-whole practice may be superior for foreign-language vocabulary but quite inferior for other types of material.

A Moment of Truth: Now that we have rather courageously stated how research should be conducted, we should properly discuss some of the problems that plague an experimenter. It is one matter to write about the perfect experiment, another to perform the perfect experiment, and a matter of astonishment if one achieves perfect results.

In research, we have many "mini-max" problems, that is, problems where by maximizing efficiency in one direction we minimize efficiency in another direction. In such a situation, we attempt to find a compromise that provides the greatest relative efficiency. This situation arises when, in designing an experiment, we decide the degree of automation we wish to use. For instance, we can create an almost perfectly controlled experimental chamber in which the organism is presented with stimuli and responses are recorded. Temperature, humidity, sound, and light are controlled; no extraneous stimulus interevenes to interrupt behavior. Nevertheless, in attempting to achieve perfection we must not forfeit the observational nature of research. After all, the term *research* originally meant *to seek out*. When an animal is placed in an experimental chamber, he may press the bar with his paw or with his nose. Animals, like human beings, develop odd behaviors, and these are well worth investigation in themselves. The investigator who watches only the recorders that measure responses is blinding himself to the behavior; on the other hand, he should not become a part of the experiment and influence the behavior.

Our description of experimental designs illustrates the necessity of logical procedures in experimental science, but in practice few experiments are performed as they were designed. Commonly, unforeseen variables force alterations in the original design. For example, an experimenter who has planned to divide his subjects into two or more equal groups might find this impossible after examining the results of the pretest. In studies with human beings, subjects fail to appear for experimental sessions, or they appear with hangovers or with little sleep. In research with animals, subjects may be lost through illness or death, sometimes after the experiment has been in progress for weeks or months. Since the psychologist works with living organisms, he must contend with all the unplanned variations of which human beings and animals are capable. Unlike the chemist, the psychologist cannot put a test tube in the refrigerator for the weekend. The human being who is tested on Friday or the rat who has learned to press a bar for food on Saturday is not the same organism on Monday.

An axiom among experimental scientists goes thus: "If anything can go wrong with an experiment, it will." This pessimistic overstatement points up the difficulties that every scientist has had in attempting to control all the variables in an experiment. Curiously, it is often the "things that go wrong" that provide the most interesting information. An experimenter might be investigating the effects of ablation of a part of the brain on behavior.

He might find that one operated animal responds to the ablation differently from the other animals. Under these conditions, one experimenter might chalk up the unusual behavior as "just one of those things," or he might point out that random chance would produce such an abnormal effect every once in a while. A wiser experimenter would be sufficiently curious about the unusual behavior to pursue it further. He might perform an autopsy, for example, to ascertain exactly where and how much ablation was done, or he might investigate the experiences of the animal up to the time of the operation in an attempt to find some independent variable which would account for the unusual behavior.

Many discoveries have been made by experimenters who were careful observers and who attended to unusual data. Sometimes the eventual outcome has little or nothing to do with the original problem. A good investigator is something like a gambler: he decides which data might turn out to be most important, and he "bets" his energy accordingly. Mme. Curie's observation that her photographic slates had developed spots led her to inquire further into the cause of the spots. A lesser, or perhaps unluckier, investigator might have thrown out the plates and accused an assistant of incompetence.

It is sometimes pointed out that many great discoveries in science have been "accidental"; the implication is that the investigator found something quite irrelevant to the original objectives. Such accidents are real phenomena, and they occur every day both inside and outside the laboratory. The difference is that with some "accidents" a watchful investigator perceives the phenomenon and attempts to isolate it.

PROBLEMS OF INTERPRETATION

We have now discussed some of the major designs used in psychological research. From a simple design using only one independent variable, we have progressed through designs involving more than one independent variable, to a design which includes several independent variables and varies these. Now we must consider the interpretation of the results.

The Statistical Language of Psychology: The ultimate aim of an experimental science is generalization from the experiment to prediction of events. The test of the competence of a physicist or engineer who plans a rocket or space missile is whether the collection of drawings and calculations are generalized to a real rocket or a missile that does fly. Similarly, the psychologist who watches a rat scurry down a runway or measures the activity of an organism hopes that his findings may be generalized to other species. He also hopes that his results will permit some generalizations about human behavior. But before his findings may be generalized, the results on which they are based must be established as *reliable;* that is, repetition of the experiment or recollection of the data must produce the same results again and again.

One method of ascertaining the reliability of data is the use of statistical devices. Statistics are generally divided into two types, descriptive and inferential. *Descriptive statistics* involve a kind of shorthand; a mean or median which describes a population of subjects is a useful example. When the Census Bureau reports that the average male in the United States is 25.9 years of age, it is using descriptive shorthand. Some precision is lost, of course, for we do not know the range of ages or whether they are normally distributed or skewed. *Inferential statistics* are used to predict the reliability of data. They may use means or medians in computations, but their purpose is not usually descriptive. Most commonly, inferential statistics predict how often a given result is likely to occur again.

Consider the teacher mentioned earlier who was interested in establishing the effect of a movie on learning. Had she executed the experiment, she would have measured a dependent variable expressed in terms of the number of correct answers each student in each group, experimental or control, received on the test. Could she be confident that under apparently identical conditions she would get the same results, or is the difference she found between the groups a chance difference—one that would not be likely to occur again? She needs to know how likely it is that she would get the same results again and again before she attempts to form a generalized statement about the meaning of her results. To answer such questions, the experimenter uses an appropriate statistical device.

A number of such devices are available, each serving different kinds of experimental designs and different types of data. For example, a *t test* can be used to test the difference between two populations. We would use this test to evaluate the study on learning in which both a control and an experimental group were available. For the functional relation design, we would use the *F test,* which permits us to analyze interactions between various factors present in an experimental design. These and other statistical devices are considered in texts listed under Sources at the end of this chapter.

Statistics are tools—they neither change data nor make them more meaningful. They are only as useful as the experimental design is sound, and only as capable of interpretation as the researcher is capable of applying them properly. Detailed advice on selecting and interpreting statistical devices is far outside the scope of this book, but the student of psychology needs to understand statistics so that he can understand his own work and evaluate the meaningfulness and the "generalizability" of the work of others.

Manipulation and Correlation: Although the idea of causality has prompted numerous philosophical treatises, the experimentalist commonly accepts, at least tacitly, the tenet that every effect must have a cause. When an outcome in the laboratory is not as predicted, the scientist does not ascribe the negative result to a whim of the gods. He assumes a cause-and-effect relationship, although he may not be able to isolate the cause of the unexpected reaction. The manipulation of an independent variable does not guarantee the discovery of a causal relationship. However, when the same independent variable produces the same result time after time, our faith in the cause-and-effect relationship increases. Some experiments are designed solely to determine the *correlation* between two variables. For example, the experimenter who injects a drug into psychotic subjects to determine whether or not the drug is effective in ameliorating psychotic conditions is concerned with establishing a relationship between the drug and the mental condition of his subjects. Either the drug has an effect on the recovery of the subjects, or it does not, in the same way that a chemical reaction either does or does not occur as predicted. The statistical devices used to evaluate the effect of the supposed cause (the independent variable) on the supposed effect (the dependent variable) are based on probability theory, and, generally, they predict the probability that the independent variable would continue to have the same effect on the dependent variable in future repetitions of the experiment.

Correlation, on the other hand, is most often concerned with establishing the relationship between two dependent variables. For example, a college admissions officer may use test scores, such as College Boards, to predict which students will do well in college and which will not. In order to make this prediction, he must know the relation between the test and success in college. Success may be measured by grades or, more simply, by whether or not a student is permitted to continue. Accordingly, the *correlation* between the test and success is the result desired, not whatever causal relationship may exist between the test scores and success in college. Most likely, College Board scores and college grades are both *effects*, the cause being some unknown factor or combination of factors such as intelligence and motivation. The use of correlation does not imply the absence of a causal factor. It is only that correlation can-

not demonstrate causality because of the nature of the questions it asks concerning the data. In this example, both measures are dependent variables (test scores and freshman grades, let us say) and the investigator is solely concerned with how well he can predict the second variable by knowing only the value of the first.

Although correlation is used most frequently in predicting behavior from test scores, it is also used, sometimes unknowingly, in designs which purport to establish cause and effect. An experimenter who compares the amount of a chemical with the incidence of cancer is also concerned with a problem in correlation. The finding that those who have most contact with the chemical are also those who most commonly develop cancer does not *necessarily* indicate a cause-and-effect relationship, since no independent variable has been investigated. On the other hand, the finding of high correlations often suggests where to look for the "cause." Thus, correlational studies have two fundamental functions: (1) they permit prediction of one kind of behavior from knowledge of a second kind, as when one predicts college grades from a test score, and (2) they suggest possible cause-and-effect relationships.

Generalization of Findings: A basic issue in science is the extent to which one may generalize from an experiment. Generalization is a part of daily life. From our first meeting with a person, we form opinions about his behavior and his basic nature—whether he is pleasant or unpleasant, intelligent or unintelligent, kindly or malicious. From a sample of his behavior we generalize and, perhaps, tacitly make predictions regarding his future behavior. Similarly, when we design an experiment to study a certain behavior, such as foreign-language learning and how it is affected by caffeine, we assume that we can generalize from the findings to a sample larger than the experimental one. Experimental control gives the scientific technique an advantage over casual observation. Clearly, however, the most perfectly designed experiment will yield useless results if those results cannot be generalized accurately to a large population. The purpose of an experiment is to provide an accurate model of the behavior under consideration.

Let us refer to any deviation between the model (the experimental results) and the accurate prediction of behavior as *error*. The greater the error, the greater the probability that generalizations will be incorrect. There are no simple statements to tell us how to maximize the probability of successful generalization. There are, however, ample examples of how one may increase the amount of error.

The first major source of error is the apparatus used for presenting the stimulus and recording the response. Although this is an obvious source, the experimenter is often so concerned with possible errors of other kinds that he overlooks it. Measurement is a matter of degree. The less accurate the apparatus, the greater the error. Obviously, some amount of error from this source is always expected and must be tolerated. With technological advances, new equipment can be produced which will reduce this kind of error.

A second source of error is the experimental design. Here error may occur in three basic ways:

1. The design may not include enough control groups to draw proper conclusions from the data. This can be corrected if the experimenter pays attention to what he can justifiably conclude from his results when the experiment is completed. Not a few experimenters have had the experience of finishing an experiment only to find that results which appear to be clear are actually equivocal because they can be interpreted in several ways. The use of appropriate control groups can often reduce the number of possible interpretations.

2. The design may be such that no appropriate inductive statistic is available. The statistic, as we have noted, is a vital part of the experimental design. Investigators sometimes design apparently faultless experiments only to find that the data are uninterpretable.

3. Error may occur in the selection of subjects.

There are basic techniques for selecting subjects which reduce the probable error. Some of the procedures become complicated and time-consuming. However, the more effort expended in selecting subjects appropriately, the less error from sampling.

Sampling is the technique used for selecting subjects, and *sampling errors* are those which arise from the method used to select subjects. Two kinds of sampling will be discussed: (1) random and systematic sampling and (2) stratified sampling.

When *random sampling* is used, all members of the population under consideration have an equal chance of being chosen. Random sampling may be either without replacement or with replacement. In random sampling *without replacement,* a subject cannot be chosen twice. This form of random sampling is used most often in psychological experiments, for once a subject has been used, it makes no sense to use him again. However, in this sampling method, the probability of a particular person's being selected varies with the number of persons already selected. If the experimenter starts with 40 subjects and selects 1, the chance of any of the remaining persons being chosen is now 1 in 39. In random sampling *with replacement,* once a subject has been chosen, he is replaced by himself. In either case, the probability of a particular person's being chosen on the first draw does not change: it is 1 in 40.

A random sample of the population of a country would be met if the country had a population of 1 million and the chance of any given person's being selected was 1 in 1 million. Similarly, if an investigator wishes to test a random sample of a college population, each student must have an equal opportunity of being chosen. Thus, the experimenter cannot stand in front of the library and ask people who pass by to be subjects unless all students in the college pass by the library equally often. If they do not, he will acquire a biased sample, loaded in favor of those persons who pass by the library. Several procedures are used for selecting a random sample. One involves the use of a table of random numbers to select names from the telephone directory or a list of students. Note, however, that using a telephone directory biases the sample in favor of persons who have telephones.

Systematic sampling is a variation of random sampling. Consider a college with 400 sophomores. An investigator wishes to use 20 percent of the available population of sophomores, or 80 subjects, for his study. Using a table of random numbers and starting at an arbitrary point, he picks the first number he finds between 1 and 80. If the number is 3, then the third person on the list is chosen. Now, the sampling interval is determined by

$$\frac{N}{n} = k$$

where

N = total number of population
n = number to be selected
k = sampling interval

In this case, $k = 5$. Thus, 5 is added to 3 to determine the next subject. Accordingly, $x + k = 8$, and subject number 8 is chosen. The next subject selected is $x + 2k$ (or 13), and so on, until all subjects have been selected. Note that, following the first selection, other selections are not independent. All selections are totally dependent upon the first selection. Assuming that the subjects were listed randomly, the group might be treated in the same way as a random population. However, a list of subjects may be biased in certain subtle ways. One might think that an alphabetical listing would be appropriate, but it is possible that the factor of national origin would be reflected, since some letters are used more often in one language than in another.

Stratified sampling represents an attempt to make certain that the subjects are a truly representative and random sample of the population under consideration. A stratified sample uses several random samples, representing some characteristic within the total sample. Suppose that an investigator wishes to form a stratified sample of a college population. He knows that two characteristics within the total sample are sex and class standing. Class standing, however, is not distributed evenly, for class size tends to diminish each year, with the senior class the smallest. Similarly, the college may or may not have as many males as females. If an investigator wishes to find a stratified sample of the total population of a country, he would want to consider age, sex, occupation, marital status, economic status, and so on. The stratified sample is formed by selecting the subsamples that are regarded as relevant. It would not be necessary, for example, to consider both age and class standing in our college population, for these two variables probably correlate very positively. Once the subsample categories have been selected, a *proportionate stratified sample* is selected by choosing subjects in such a way that every category is selected in accordance with its true proportion within the total population. Sometimes a *disproportionate* sample occurs when certain categories are difficult to use. We shall note, in Chapter 18, the effect that the use of disproportionate samples has had on determining intelligence scores.

Stratified sampling is the type most commonly used in public-opinion or voting polls. If selected carefully, a small number of subjects may permit generalization to the total population. Since a small number is used, errors or biases in the procedure of questioning the subjects become greatly magnified. Accordingly considerable attention is given to reducing error by using unbiased questionnaires. The stratified sample also guards against the biasing that occurs normally under random sampling. Given a college with 1,000 males and 1,000 females, it is possible that the first 1,000 subjects chosen could all be males. The use of random procedures certainly does not guarantee a true random sample. A major difficulty with the use of stratified samples is that the investigator needs to know a good deal about the characteristics of the sample before he can arrange subsample categories and select subjects. Thus, stratified samples are expensive to select.

Assuming that the experiment is correctly designed, that the statistical treatment is both appropriate and revealing, and that the subjects are properly selected, the experimenter must still determine how far he can generalize from his findings. Is it possible to use one's findings on rats to make assumptions about the behavior of monkeys, human beings, or planaria? From a study of the child-rearing practices of 1,000 mothers, is it safe to generalize to the behavior of an individual? There is no "yes" or "no" answer to these questions, unless one actually does discover whether the behavior of the rat and the monkey is the same or whether the behavior of one mother can be predicted. But science must work by generalizations, just as any experiment must be limited to a finite number of subjects and restricted by the design and apparatus employed. The more often generalizations are validated, the more confidence one has in the method employed.

CAN PSYCHOLOGY BE EXPERIMENTAL?

In its most restricted sense, an experimental science requires the manipulation of a physical or psychological stimulus by the experimenter and the observation of the effect of the stimulus on the matter or on the organism's responses. However, if this definition of *experimental* were strictly followed in scientific inquiry, then theoretical physics, astronomy, and parts of biology would be classified as nonexperimental sciences, for no physicist manipulates cosmic rays or natural irradiation and no astronomer manipulates the orbit of the planet Mars in his laboratory.

Many problems do not readily submit to the experimental approach. First, a question may be too loosely phrased to admit of a direct answer—for example, "Why do people engage in wars?" Although an explanation may be found for an individual's aggressive behavior, it would be imprecise to generalize from one individual or a few to all humanity. Second, some questions may be unanswerable at the present time because techniques are not available for their investigation—for example, "Do dogs dream about cats?" Only through speech can we know the content of dreams today, but it is possible that in future years we shall find techniques (such as electrical recording from the brain) that will allow us to answer the question. The first type of question will remain unanswerable because it is poorly phrased. Questions of the second type may become answerable, however, as new techniques are invented. One hundred years ago the question "What is on the other side of the moon?" would have been unanswerable; today it is a meaningful question and the object of research.

Third, some questions are unanswerable because they imply some kind of teleology, and teleology is not a suitable paradigm for experimental investigation—for example, "Why do dogs dream?" Questions of this type are common, and many are regarded as the most important questions in life, such as "Is there an afterlife?" and "If so, how do I obtain it?" Although not admitting to experimental verification, they are clearly questions which motivate human behavior, and their effect on behavior is measurable.

The quest for knowledge is in some ways analogous to the way in which a cancerous patient is bombarded with X rays; separate rays with different origins are aimed at the same point. No *single* ray is strong enough to destroy tissue, and within limits any one of the rays can be excluded without altering the result. But when all the rays terminate at the same part of the body, their strength combines to destroy diseased tissue. Similarly, many areas of inquiry, ranging from folk philosophy through common sense to physics, are concerned with behavior. Each area has its own special characteristics, language, and methods. Within limits, any one can be eliminated without greatly altering the advancement of knowledge. Together, they complement one another. Experimental psychology is not the only science which can explain behavior, but it is an approach which has contributed greatly to knowledge of behavior.

The different branches of science differ basically in the data they consider and the natural phenomena they analyze. If one were to ask a group of scientists to describe an ashtray, the physicist might analyze the object in regard to its gravitational pull or its weight. He might also define the ashtray in terms of its effect on other bodies or its heat conductance, while the chemist would be more likely to analyze it in terms of its chemical components, its hardness, its solubility, and so forth. The biologist, on the other hand, is not likely to define a static object of this kind. Consider the various descriptions that would result, however, if these scentists were describing a human being as he would the ashtray—in terms of physical characteristics. The chemist might point out the chemical constituency of the human body. The biologist might analyze the human being in terms of his anatomy and physiology and of how organs regulate one another. The experimental psychologist would discuss him in terms of behavior. He might refer to the physical specification, chemical constituency, and physiology of the organism, but his major concern would be to define the organism in terms of behavior. Each of these scientists defines the human being within the framework of his own language.

The nineteenth-century philosopher Auguste Comte (1927) saw psychology (or "moral philosophy," as he called it) as the *propaedeutic* science, the science on which all other sciences depended. We have assumed that man must first understand the workings of nature before he can hope to understand himself; that is, only by understanding the physical, chemical, and biological aspects of the organism will we be able to understand the behavior of the organism. In contrast, Comte argued that the practice of science was merely a type of human behavior and that in order to understand physics, one must first understand the physicist, for his findings and theories are dependent upon his behavior. For this reason, if for no other, experimental psychology provides a useful method for organizing natural phenomena.

SOURCES

General: A sound introduction to the general relation between psychology and science is Andreas (1960). Chapter 1 is particularly useful. On a less theoretical level, the excellent discussion by Bugelski (1951, chaps. 1–6) contains comments on this subject as well as some very sound advice for the beginning investigator. Hyman (1964) has written a thorough introduction to psychological methodology. Lastrucci (1963) provides a superb discussion of scientific methodology.

Students who wish to consider the relation between experimental design and statistical valuations of data will find Edwards (1960) a useful text and a handy reference work as well. McGuigan (1960) is largely concerned with the practical problems of research in psychology, as is Zimney (1961). In McGuigan, the discussion of randomization and factorial designs is particularly useful.

A book which devotes considerable attention to the more mundane, but important, problems of psychological research, such as where to acquire research funds and the types of journals available to psychologists, is W. A. Scott and Wertheimer (1962). This book also considers sampling and associated problems in detail and is very thoughtfully written. It covers areas of research and suggests solutions to many research problems. Sidman (1960) provides an interesting and valuable consideration of certain methodological problems which occur in procuring and interpreting data.

An excellent handbook by Townsend summarizes a good many methods and is a very useful text (1953, also paperback). Sections A and B are of particular interest, since they are concerned with some of the basic problems of causality, hypothesis formulation, inference, and apparatus.

Techniques: Andreas (1960) devotes his second chapter to the design and execution of experiments. Frank (1961) presents some good papers concerned with validation on a theoretical level. The presentations are of interest to students concerned with the more philosophical aspects of experimental design and procedure. A philosophical position underlies every design, whether the experimenter recognizes the fact or not; thus, the study of design in these terms is very valuable. Hammond and Householder (1962) is a very good source book on the relation between technique and statistics. The book is written for students less experienced than those who might use Edwards (1960), and the first chapter presents a thoughtful essay on generalization and variability in science from the point of view of the statistician. Townsend (1953) presents discussions and diagrams of apparatus; although this book was written more than a decade ago, the information on apparatus remains very useful, particularly to the beginning experimenter. Lyons (1965) has provided a far-ranging book which discusses many aspects of experimental psychology. His examples of experimental problems are noteworthy. Bakan (1966) discusses the role of tests of statistical significance for the advanced reader.

Other Viewpoints: For those who prefer to supplement study with historical precedents, Boring (1950) has written the more or less standard work in the field. An understanding of the history of experimental psychology is requisite to an understanding of the contemporary field. Skinner (1953) provides one of the most influential statements regarding the relation between psychology and science, drawing upon considerable evidence to support his position. The book is important to students not acquainted with the Skinnerian position, and, like Boring (1950), it is a must for serious students. Underwood (1957a) considers many of the actual problems that occur in design and provides references to sources which either have corrected the problems or have failed to do so. The book is written primarily for students who have had experience with designing and performing their own experiments and is more meaningful for such students. Nevertheless, it is a wealth of reasoned thought about psychological problems. Like Boring (1950) and Skinner (1953), Underwood is essential for every student, whether he plans to perform research or to use and interpret the findings of others. The chapter on operational definitions is excellent. Mandler and Kessen (1959) also discuss the problem of language in psychology.

Dictionaries: The beginning student and the scholar often come across terms they do not understand. This is a natural difficulty in a field in which data have been culled from other sources and disciplines. English (1958) provides a dictionary of both psychological and psychoanalytic terms. Harriman provides a comprehensive dictionary (1959a; 1965) as well as a handbook (1959b) of terms used in psychology. Verplank (1957) has compiled a dictionary of terms used primarily in experimental psychology.

CHAPTER TWO

THE PHYSIOLOGICAL
BASES OF BEHAVIOR

INTRODUCTION

The review in Chapter 1 of some of the methods and procedures used in experimental psychology emphasized the attention which the experimenter, the reviewer, and the interpreter must give to problems of design and interpretation. Interpretation, however, depends upon the kinds of explanatory principles which are used. Should psychology limit itself to explanatory principles which deal solely with observable behavior, or should it extend these principles in order to deal with unobservable or unconscious behavior? May psychology advance more rapidly by extending its observations to the fields of anatomy, physiology, neuroanatomy, and neurophysiology? Can the study of the relations between these fields and observable behavior lead to useful discoveries for the field of psychology? Or is the study of such relations premature, and would it, in the long run, lead us in wrong directions? In short, once observations have been made, how shall we use them to the best advantage?

PSYCHOLOGY AND PHYSIOLOGY

The proper relationship between psychology and physiology remains a matter of debate among psychologists, as well as among physiologists. Those who perceive psychology as a biological science point out that behavior, however measured, does not occur without the occurrence, as well, of some physiological process. Accordingly, they argue that physiological changes are epistemologically prior to behavioral changes. Before one can fully understand why a rat presses a bar at a certain rate or why a child learns to speak, he must understand the nature of the physiological changes which accompany these behaviors. The most engaging argument is made, perhaps, in the applied areas of psychology, such as clinical or school psychology. Consider a child who is referred to a school psychologist as a behavior problem. Teachers complain that the child interrupts, does not pay attention in class, and seems to be always thinking of something else. Although these symptoms are described in psychological terms, the cause of the behaviors may be a hearing disorder. The child is inattentive because he does not hear what is said; he interrupts because he is unaware that other people are speaking. Often a hearing loss progresses so slowly that the child adjusts to each slight change and never notices the gradual deterioration. The behavior problem, however, can be accounted for (and cured, hopefully) if the physiological process involved is understood. Similarly, an adult who complains of hallucinations, blacking out, or forgetfulness may suffer from brain damage or a brain tumor rather than from a personality defect.

Those who contend that behavior can be studied without reference to physiology point out that psychology is a descriptive science which does not need to refer its findings back to assumed physiological change. Indeed, they argue, to do so is to confound cause-and-effect relationships; the study of behavior, they say, can even be retarded if the psychologist looks in the wrong place for the keys to behavior.

In effect, the argument between those who wish to base behavior upon physiological concomitants and those who wish to exclude physiological considerations is an argument over "how much" is necessary for explanation. One is reminded of the scientist who wanted to do research on seed growth. To understand how seeds grew, however, he needed to know the effect of the chemicals in the earth on seeds; but to understand how the chemicals interact he needed to know the effect of temperature on the chemicals; but to understand the effect of temperature, he had to understand how climatic conditions affect temperature; but to understand climatic conditions, he had to understand the earth's stratosphere; but to understand the stratosphere, he had to understand the movement of the planets; but to understand the movement of the planets, he had to understand their relation to the universe. From a "simple" research project con-cerned with seed growth, the scientist found that he had to explain the universe. Although the example is exaggerated, each scientist must make his own value judgment about how far explanation must be pushed before findings are meaningful. B. F. Skinner (1953, pp. 27–29), probably one of the most frequently quoted contemporary spokesmen of the dangers involved in using physiological *concepts*, points out:[1]

The layman uses the nervous system as a ready explanation of behavior. The English language contains hundreds of expressions which imply such a causal relationship. At the end of a long trial we read that the jury shows signs of brain fatigue, that the nerves of the accused are on edge, that the wife of the accused is on the verge of a nervous breakdown, and that his lawyer is generally thought to have lacked the brains needed to stand up to the prosecution. Obviously, no direct observations have been made of the nervous systems of any of these people. Their "brains" and "nerves" have been invented on the spur of the moment to lend substance to what might otherwise seem a superficial account of their behavior.

The sciences of neurology and physiology have not divested themselves entirely of a similar practice. Since techniques for observing the electrical and chemical processes in nervous tissue had not yet been developed, early information about the nervous system was limited to its gross anatomy. Neural processes could be only inferred from the behavior which was said to result from them. Such inferences were legitimate enough as scientific theories, but they could not justifiably be used to explain the very behavior upon which they were based. The hypotheses of the early physiologist may have been sounder than those of the layman, but until independent evidence could be obtained, they were no more satisfactory as explanations of behavior.

[1] Reprinted with permission of The Macmillan Company from *Science and Human Behavior*, by B. F. Skinner. Copyright 1953 by The Macmillan Company.

Direct information about many of the chemical and electrical processes in the nervous system is now available. Statements about the nervous system are no longer necessarily inferential or fictional. But there is still a measure of circularity in much physiological explanation, even in the writings of specialists. In World War I a familiar disorder was called *shell shock*. Disturbances in behavior were explained by arguing that violent explosions had damaged the structure of the nervous system, though no direct evidence of such damage was available. In World War II the same disorder was classified as *neuropsychiatric*. The prefix seems to show a continuing unwillingness to abandon explanations in terms of hypothetical neural damage.

Eventually a science of the nervous system based upon direct observation rather than inference will describe the neural states and events which immediately precede instances of behavior. We shall know the precise neurological conditions which immediately precede, say, the response "No, thank you." These events in turn will be found to be preceded by other neurological events, and these in turn by others still. This series will lead us back to events outside the nervous system and, eventually, outside the organism. However, we may note here that we do not have and may never have this sort of neurological information at the moment it is needed in order to predict a specific instance of behavior. It is even more unlikely that we shall be able to alter the nervous system directly in order to set up the antecedent conditions of a particular instance. The causes to be sought in the nervous system are, therefore, of limited usefulness in the prediction and control of specific behavior.

On the other hand, the relationship between physiology and psychology is conceived differently by Wenger, F. N. Jones, and M. H. Jones (1956, pp. 2–3), who point out:

With the development of specialization among the sciences, there has grown up a rough division of the study of the activities of the living animal into several disciplines, among which are physiology and psychology. It should be emphasized at once that this is not a natural division, but rather a division of convenience. In general, those investigators who are identified as physiologists have chosen to study activities localized within the organism, and to deal with internal systems and changes; thus, physiology is sometimes defined as the study of organ and tissue functions. Typical physiological investigations are concerned with such problems as the processes of digestion, the chemistry and circulation of blood, and the characteristics of muscular contraction. Psychologists on the other hand, are more concerned with activities which involve the total organism. Typical investigations of a psychological nature are studies of learning, of the development of personality, or of the effect of motivation. There is, however, no hard and fast line between these two fields. Psychologists have sometimes studied part activities, such as the neuromuscular activity in a single finger, the functions of parts of the eye, or the activity of a few segments of the spinal cord; and physiologists have studied such total organismic activities as homing in birds and orientation in the bat.

It is well to keep in mind that the general division of labor between the physiologist and the psychologist is partly a methodological one. We may expect the physiologist to be competent in techniques for the electrical recording of activity in a nerve, the biochemical assay of the by-products of nervous activity, or the changes induced in starches by the action of digestive enzymes. The psychologist, on the other hand, has at his command techniques for measuring learning, for assaying ability or efficiency, or for studying other organismic behavior familiar to the student who has had a beginning course in psychology. But the physiologist sometimes finds it necessary to pay attention to psychological controls when dealing, for example, with the effects of low oxygen intake on the human subject or with effects of various drugs, and the psychologist must often be concerned with sensory end organs or the physiological changes occurring in such behavior as drug addiction.

Skinner is not arguing that all of physiology is inapplicable to psychology, any more than Wenger et al. are arguing that physiology should supplant psychology. The former warns against unwarranted generalization between physiological principles and observations of behavior. The latter turn our attention to the usefulness of physiology in explaining and understanding many events of interest to psychologists. These writers are not so much protagonists as they are elucidators of the problems of generalization and explanation.

Nevertheless, physiological findings have had considerable influence on the science of behavior and have resulted in reorganization of psychological theories. If a psychological theory assumes that the brain operates in a certain way and if it is discovered that the brain does not operate in that fashion, the physiological discovery about the brain is important to psychology. In the past few centuries, many important physiological discoveries have influenced the development of psychology.

A BRIEF HISTORY

It is not easy to trace the origins of psychology, but two sources are apparent: One is the physiological approach to behavior begun by German scientists of the nineteenth century. Men trained as physiologists began to study psychology when they became interested in the problems of behavior. Wundt (1832–1920), although not trained as a physiologist, is often credited with founding the first laboratory of experimental psychology in 1869. A second approach might be the British schools of the philosophy of empiricism and associationism. Contemporary psychology appears to be a marriage between the two approaches, although in its early years, the marriage was anything but placid.

In the first half of the nineteenth century, the major discoveries about behavior were essentially physiological discoveries. Sir Charles Bell (1774–1842; see Sources) and François Magendie (1783–1855; see Sources) independently discovered the relationship between the spinal cord and the motor and sensory nerves. This discovery demonstrated that the nervous system, like behavior, has two components: a sensory component and a motor, or behavioral, component. This discovery, along with others, reinitiated an interest in the problems of how the senses operate. By this time, however, it was clear that there were more than the five senses suggested by Aristotle. As investigators dissected the sensory systems, it became clear that these systems operated in a very complex way. Slowly, the relations among the sensory receptors (the eye, for example), the nerves which served them (the optic nerves), and the eventual sensations (vision) became both more clear and more mystifying.

Applying his name to a doctrine announced in part by Bell and many other investigators, Johannes Müller (1801–1858; see Sources) gave his authority to the doctrine of specific nerve energies. The use of the term "energies" is somewhat misleading according to today's usage, for the doctrine gave reference to the qualities of sensation, rather than to the actual electric energy of nerves. Müller's doctrine, stated simply, was that one is not aware directly of external objects. One is aware only of their effects upon the nervous system. It is our nervous system that describes the external world.

Müller's doctrine prompted the development of several theories which we shall discuss later. Over the years, some experimental findings and a large number of theories, especially theories about the functioning of the skin and the sensory systems of taste and smell, suggested refinement of the doctrine. These theories suggest that the nerve is able to code incoming information in such a way that the pattern of frequency of firing of the nerve is instrumental in setting a pattern to be uncoded by the brain.

In England, at the beginning of the nineteenth century, Franz Joseph Gall (1758–1828; see Sources) had begun his work on physiognomy, or *phrenology,* as it came to be called. The concept that behavior could be predicted from physiognomy fell into disrepute, particularly among writers who saw the concept as a glorious example of the evils of nonscientific psychology. Yet the idea that behavior was related to various areas of the brain and that excesses in particular areas of behavior would result in enlargement of the particular area of the brain corresponding to that behavior was a useful concept. As the lay person interpreted this idea, one only had to investigate the skull and determine which areas were enlarged in order to understand an individual's personality. Phrenologists' "busts" enjoyed a brisk sale, as employers, prospective mates, and even college presidents used the technique of head holding to predict personality characteristics. Figure 2–1 indicates the proposed regions of the skull which correspond to various behaviors.

Gall was only one of a series of investigators who had perceived the brain as the center of physiological and behavioral functioning. Discoveries about the nature of electricity by Alessandro Volta (1745–1827; 1800; 1816), Luigi Galvani (1737–1798; 1791), and Georg Simon Ohm (1787–1854) in the first part of the nineteenth century were eventually applied to physiology and behavior. Emil du Bois-Reymond (1818–1896; 1848; 1849; 1860–1884) used a galvanometer on animals and discovered the presence of an electric discharge in the nerve. This was the beginning of a series of important discoveries concerning the electrical and chemical nature of nerve transmission. Moreover, as we shall learn later in this chapter, electric stimulation is now used to stimulate various areas of the brain.

A second type of discovery came from the work of Luigi Rolando (1770–1831; 1809) and Pierre Flourens (1794–1867; 1824). The former suggested that specific components of the brain controlled sleep and another controlled mood. Gall, of course, used this assumption in his theory of phrenology, but the work of Rolando and Flourens was appropriately grounded in experimental investigation. Flourens developed the methodology of extirpating a section of the brain in order to determine the function of that section. This technique marked the beginning of an experimental approach to brain physiology. The same approach is used today by physiologists and physiological psychologists who remove small sections of the brain to determine their function and to determine the relations among the various parts.

The work of Fritsch and Hitzig (1870), which indicated that electric stimulation of the various areas of the cerebral cortex results in movement of different parts of the body, was a major advance in identifying the relationship between parts of the brain and behavior. Indeed, perhaps the most important work in physiological psychology within the last few decades has been concerned with electric stimulation of the brain and behavior. W. R. Hess (1954a; 1954b) perfected the first useful technique for implanting electrodes in the brain. Contemporary work in brain physiology, which has indicated centers in the brain for eating, sleeping, and so forth, bears a superficial resemblance to the technique used by Gall. The discovery that there are eating centers in the hypothalamus (reviewed by Teitelbaum and A. N. Epstein, 1962) and the finding that organisms will learn a bar-press response in order to stimulate their own brain through implanted electrodes (Olds & Milner, 1954; Sheer, 1961) are examples of more recent discoveries that have emanated from the approach of artificially stimulating the brain.

Although the distinction between voluntary and involuntary movements has its basis in the philosophic distinction between free will and determinism, the discovery of reflexive reactions in the nineteenth century laid the groundwork for the research of Ivan Pavlov (1849–1936; 1927; 1928a; 1928b) on conditioning and for the emphasis on learned behavior which has concerned psychologists in the twentieth century.

FIGURE 2-1: *The phrenologist's head, showing the areas assumed to correspond to various traits, or "faculties," as they were called by phrenologists. Such "busts" were in surprisingly wide use during the last part of the nineteenth century. (From J. D. Davies, 1955, p. 6.)*

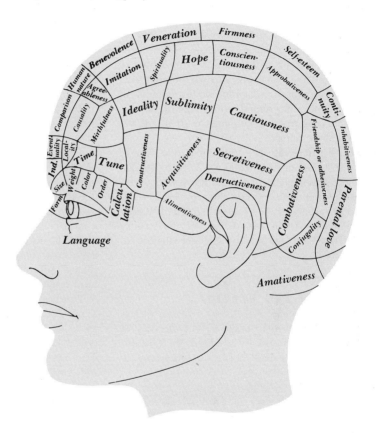

THE SENSES

The dictum that "nothing enters the mind save by means of the senses" provides the rationale of physiological psychology. Since the beginnings of psychology in the laboratories of the European scientists, such as Hermann von Helmholtz (1821–1894) in the middle of the last century, physiological psychologists have believed that the first step in understanding behavior is to understand how the external world comes to be part of the "mind." They have argued that a human being can learn only by what he perceives and that he perceives only by means of his sensory apparatus; that is, all knowledge and all behavior come about because of what is perceived of the external world by vision, audition, taste, smell, kinesthesis, and the cutaneous receptors.

The human organism is like a house with several windows, each window (or sense) giving a different view of the external world. What a person inside the house learns is limited by what the windows allow him to perceive. A student who is nearsighted will not be a good outfielder, and a person who cannot distinguish small differences in taste will not become a gourmet. Sometimes the windows yield contradictory information, as when our eyes tell us one thing and our ears another. Perception is the stuff of which behavior is made; thus, one of the traditional areas of experimental psychology is the study of the sensory systems—a concern with how well or how much an organism perceives.

As dependent as we are upon our senses, it is curious that we know so little about them. Such basic questions as how we hear the many tones which the human ear is capable of discriminating or how we perceive all the different colors that the normal human eye is capable of perceiving have remained unanswered, resisting the onslaught of physicists, biologists, and psychologists alike. Like the scientist who merely wanted to explain the growth of a seed, we must begin at the beginning. The first step we must take in the analysis of the sensory systems is to find out how the nervous system operates.

NEURONS AND NERVES

The discovery that tissue is a collection of cells, which is usually credited to Theodor Schwann (1801–1882), was as important to physiological psychologists as the isolation of the atom was to chemists. By showing that the basic "building blocks" of animal tissue were similar, cellular theory emphasized the similarities between species and indicated that progress in understanding the human nervous system could be made through comparative and phylogenetic studies. The history of medical research indicates that until human dissection became a general practice (in the eighteenth century), most of man's knowledge about the anatomy and physiology of his own body came by generalizing from dissection of animals. Today, the comparative approach is employed when research on human beings is impossible. However, this is neither the only reason nor the main reason that animals are used in medical and psychological research.

The study of animal behavior, comparative psychology, and comparative anatomy and physiology is valuable in itself for the information it provides about the world we inhabit; there is no need to have to justify it by generalizations to human anatomy or behavior. On the other hand, the phylogenetic scale indicates close relationships among various organisms. Although it may be difficult to generalize from one species to another, discoveries about a lower animal may suggest research possibilities for higher animals.

Research has shown that among vertebrate species, the three major types of excitable cells are *neurons,* or nerve cells, *muscle cells,* and *gland cells.* The primary structure of the nervous system is the neuron. The most important attribute of the neuron is that it is differentiated in such a manner that it may cover large areas, thus allowing transmission of a message throughout the body. Although neurons are tiny in diameter, there is tremendous variability in their length: some may be less than a millimeter long, while others may extend several feet.

The basic structure of a neuron is shown in Figure 2–2. The dendrites connect with the axons, cell bodies, or dendrites of other nerves and form a chain of interconnecting links. The connection of two neurons is known as the *synapse.*

Neurons in the *central nervous system* (CNS), which includes the brain and the spinal cord, are somewhat different from those in the rest of the body. Neurons which are not in the CNS (peripheral neurons) are generally found in trunks. These trunks of neurons are called *nerves,* a word not to be confused with such unscientific terms as being "nervous" or "having nerves." Properly, a physiological nerve is a collection of neurons outside the CNS. A bundle of fibers inside the CNS is called a *tract.* At birth man has all the neurons he will ever have, for they do not reproduce. If the cell body of a neuron is destroyed through damage to the tissue or disease, the cell is dead. If the dendrite or axon is damaged and the cell is left intact, in the periphery few, if any, nerve fibers will regenerate (Windle, 1955). Neuronal processes in the CNS, however, do not regenerate. This is one of the reasons that damage to the brain, such as that which occurs from a lack of oxygen (as in certain birth defects), is irreparable in most cases.

All excitable cells have the ability to react to a change in stimulation. This change is reflected physiologically by a change in the ionic permeability of the membrane and is transient; that is, after stimulation the membrane returns to its original state. In the excitable cells found in the nerves and muscle tissue the change caused by the stimulus is not only local but, indeed, continues to nearby tissue, spreading in a wavelike manner over the entire membrane. Clearly, the conductivity of these cells permits considerable variety in the system, for it allows messages to be passed throughout the body. If the stimulation had a purely local effect, such transfer would not occur, for each cell would have to be stimulated separately.

The change in potential which accompanies the stimulation of cells is known as the *impulse*. The impulse is the result of ionic movement which produces an electric discharge, the *action potential* (or electric potential), which is measurable. The action potential is measured by the use of two electrodes: one rests on the outside of the tissue, while the other is inserted "inside" the tissue. Figure 2–3 shows, schematically, how the electrodes measure the electrical changes of the nerve.

Commonly, only a single electrode is used, while the second electrode is grounded on some inactive part of the tissue. This technique is used for simplicity, rather than for any theoretical reason. Figure 2–4 shows, schematically, how a monophasic (single-electrode) recording is made and indicates the typical reading reported from this technique. It should be remembered that taking an electrical recording from a nerve is rather like measuring the depth of an ocean with a long rod. The rod is stationary, but at one minute the depth might read 1.3 miles and the next minute, 1.45 miles. When plotted, depth appears to vary as

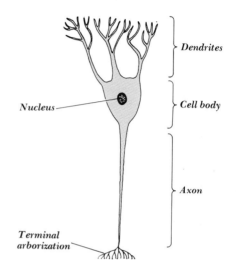

FIGURE 2–2: *Greatly enlarged schematic diagram of the "typical" neuron. (From* Physiological Psychology, *by M. A. Wenger, F. N. Jones, and M. H. Jones, copyright 1956 by Holt, Rinehart and Winston, Inc.)*

Dendrites

Nucleus

Cell body

Axon

Terminal arborization

a function of time. In recording from a nerve, the electrode is stationary and records the impulse as it passes at a stationary point. Figure 2–5 shows an example of what the electrode might record.

The *spike potential* represents the period of most rapid ionic exchange, or passage of the impulse. It also represents the *threshold* of the nerve, for it indicates the point at which the stimulus is sufficiently strong to elicit firing of the nerve. If the stimulus is so weak that the nerve does not fire (just as a tone may be too quiet for a person to hear), the stimulus is referred to as *subthreshold*. If it is sufficiently strong that the nerve fires, it is called *suprathreshold*. So far as the nerve is concerned, either the stimulus is strong enough to fire the nerve, or it is not: if it is not strong enough, the nerve does not fire; if it is strong enough (and it does not matter how much stronger), the nerve does fire.

Indeed, the action of a nerve is similar to the action of a gun. If one pulls the trigger

FIGURE 2–3: *Representation of an excitable fiber. The membrane presumably separates the negatively charged ions from the positively charged ions. A schematic diagram of a galvanometer, which records changes in electric potential, is shown on top of the membrane. The galvanometer on the left records no change in potential, since the electrodes are on the outside of the membrane. However, if one electrode is inserted in the tissue (as is recorded by the right galvanometer) and the other is placed on the surface, a change in electric potential is recorded by the galvanometer. If two electrodes were placed inside the membrane, there would be no difference in potential. (From D. P. C. Lloyd in Fulton, 1955, p. 8.)*

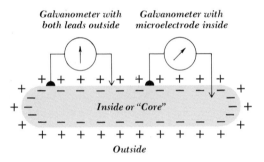

Galvanometer with   *Galvanometer with*
both leads outside   *microelectrode inside*

past the firing point, the gun fires with full force; it does not matter how far past the firing point the trigger is pulled, for the gun always fires with the same intensity once the threshold has been passed. The general statement that a nerve, like a gun, either fires with full intensity or does not fire at all is known as the *all-or-none law*. Precisely, the law states that once threshold is passed, the neuron will discharge completely with the energy that it has at that moment. The law implies that a fiber does not give small spikes for weak stimuli and stronger spikes for more intense stimuli; however, on some occasions a suprathreshold stimulus can fire the spike before it has recovered freely from the effect of the previous stimulus. In this case, the spike is smaller than would be the case normally. Apparently, the

law applies to the axon, but not to the dendrite. Dendrites yield graded responses. This suggests that conduction along axons follows the all-or-none law but that dendrites function with graded responses.

Although the spike potential records the passage of the message along the nerve, the full recording of the firing of most nerves includes two potentials which follow the spike potential and which also indicate the changing position of charged ions. These are known as the *negative afterpotential* and the *positive afterpotential,* the adjective referring to the state of ionization. Although their presence is correlated with composition of the nerve and other measures, at the present time their basic importance is their correlation with the excitability cycle, for it is this cycle which determines whether the nerve will fire at all. This cycle is shown in the bottom part of Figure 2–5. This cycle shows that following the refractory period the spike potential may undershoot the resting level resulting in a *supernormal* period or overshoot resulting in a *subnormal* period. If a supernormal period occurs, the neuron shows an increase in sensitivity. A subnormal period is a decrease in sensitivity.

During the period of *latent addition,* the application of a threshold stimulus will add to the effects of the initial stimulus. In effect, a series of subthreshold stimuli may *summate* to reach threshold and produce firing of the nerve. Clearly, *threshold* is a term which is relative to the state of the nerve. It may be higher or lower, depending upon the position in the excitability cycle. The first portion of the refractory period is known as the *absolute refractory period,* for during this period no stimulus, no matter how intense, may fire the nerve. So far as conduction is concerned, the nerve is dead, figuratively speaking. However, during the *relative refractory period* only suprathreshold stimuli can elicit the firing of the nerve; that is, a stimulus as intense as the original stimulus which caused the spike potential will not fire the nerve during the refractory period, but a stronger stimulus may. The all-or-none law still holds during this period, but the intensity of the stimulus must be increased to produce a response from the nerve. Superficially, this corresponds to the phenomenon known as stimulus *adaptation:* we cease to perceive an odor after repeated contact with it; the sound of a passing train or the ticking of a clock ceases to disturb our sleep after the first few nights. Although it is certainly not clear that *adaptation* (the change in threshold of a stimulus due to repeated presentation of the stimulus) is caused by the physiological phenomena of afterpotentials, the phenomena are basically similar in their behavioral consequences.

The doctrine of the specific energy of nerves set forth by Bell, Müller, and others emphasized that the mind was limited, not by the number or kind of external objects, but by the nerves and receptors. Just as the Copernican revolution removed man from his place in the center of the universe, this doctrine corrected the fallacious idea that man's senses recorded external events perfectly. Today, we accept the fact that we perceive only a portion of the external world—that we perceive color only within a limited range, that our hearing range is inferior to that of many animals (notably, cats and dogs), and that we have very poor taste and smell sensitivity. Indeed, man is limited by his receptors and nerves. His genius is in his ability to develop apparatus to extend his sensory powers—telescopes, radar, and radio.

In spite of the limitations of our sensory systems, our nerves transmit a wide variety of sensations. How can a single nerve transmit gradations in hue or pitch or intensity? If the all-or-none law is true, a single nerve has no way of reporting the intensity of a stimulus, but many animals, as well as human beings, are capable of fine discriminations in intensity. Consider how one might explain this. Most stimuli are sufficiently strong to fire many nerves; perhaps intensity merely reflects the number of different nerves that are fired.

FIGURE 2–4: *Diagram indicating action potential and action current. The dial at the top of each illustration is a galvanometer which reflects differences in electric potential. In illustration 1, the galvanometer reads zero. In the illustration the potential (depicted in dark gray) has not yet reached the left-hand electrode, and the galvanometer reads zero. In illustration 2, the potential has reached the left-hand electrode, changing it to a discharge, as shown by the galvanometer which deflects to the left. In illustration 3, the potential is between the electrodes, and no difference in potential is reported. (From Tuttle and Schottelius,* Textbook of Physiology, *15th ed., The C. V. Mosby Company, St. Louis, 1965.)*

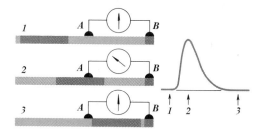

As we shall see in our discussion of cutaneous sensitivity, this theory is not universally true, but it appears to be a reasonable explanation of intensity in some sensory systems. A second technique is that an increase in amplitude increases the rate of firing of cells by forcing them to fire earlier in the relative refractory period. Thus, intensity would be conveyed by frequency of nerve firing.

A third method by which the nerves could transmit intensity is *local action*. The concept of local action refers to the phenomenon that the firing of a nerve may fire another nerve, without separate stimulation of the second. Theoretically, nerve 1 could fire nerve 2, nerve 2 could fire nerve 3, and nerve 3 could fire nerve 1, continuing the circuit again. This type of conduction is known as a *reverberating circuit*. Conceivably, intensity could be trans-

FIGURE 2–5: *The action potential of a mammalian fiber, with magnitude of the discharge along the ordinate and time along the abscissa. Note the positions of the spike, the negative afterpotential, and the positive afterpotential. The bottom portion shows the excitability cycle. (From C. T. Morgan, 1965, p. 65.)*

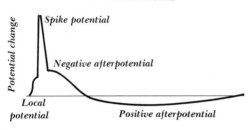

ACTION POTENTIAL

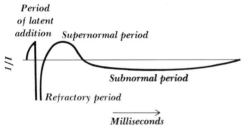

EXCITABILITY CYCLE

mitted by the number and type of such circuits or by the degree of local action.

A further possible explanation of intensity is that not all nerve fibers are alike. Nerves differ both in regard to their size and in regard to the presence or absence of *myelination*. Generally, nerves are divided into *A-*, *B-*, or *C-type fibers*. Both A- and B-type fibers are myelinated; that is, they are coated with a whitish substance called *myelin*. Myelination is most noticeable in the whitish nerves of the CNS. Unmyelinated cell bodies and nerves do not have this coating, and they are grayish; these are C-type fibers. Table 2–A shows some characteristics of different types of nerve fibers. In the table, C-type fibers are divided into two subgroups, s.C and d.r.C. The former are found in certain axons; the latter, in peripheral nerves (as well as elsewhere).

THE NEURON AND BEHAVIOR

Although the last sections have been concerned with the neuron, the nerve, and conduction, the process of conduction is only a portion of the total process by which an impulse is translated into behavior. Figure 2–6 shows a schematic example of the translation of an impulse into behavior. The stimulus is applied at the point labeled *A;* in this case the simulus is of a type to which the cutaneous sense would react—it might be heat, cold, touch, or perhaps an injury causing tissue damage. Stimulated, the impulse is passed along the path designated *B* to the spinal cord by way of the *dorsal* route. The nerve under discussion is known as an *afferent* nerve (sensory). Afferent nerves are those which travel away from the stimulation and toward the CNS. At points *C* the afferent nerve meets a nerve cell in the CNS called an *interneuron*. The impulse is passed to a second interneuron *C'*, one which is an *efferent* neuron. The impulse is then passed along *B'*, which is an *efferent nerve* (motor). It is a motor nerve because it is going to a muscle, and it is efferent because it conducts away from the CNS. The efferent impulse *B'* passes through the ventral portion of the spinal cord. The end of the process need not be a muscle as shown here; it may be a gland or an organ, such as the heart.

THE SYNAPSE

Although the properties of the nerve must determine the quality and quantity of the sensation, impulses must be transmitted across neurons. In this way the impulse may be routed throughout the organism. The junction between nerve cells is known as a *synapse*. It was long thought that nerve cells grew together physically at the synapse, but there is some experimental evidence that this may not be so. The findings indicate that the transmission of an impulse may be discontinuous—at times it must jump across neurons. This discontinuity in conduction means that the

TABLE 2-A: *Some Basic Properties of a Mammalian Nerve Fiber.*
A and B fibers are myelinated. C fibers are unmyelinated. s.C fibers are generally a part of the sympathetic nervous system, and d.r.C fibers are found in the peripheral system. Note that the fibers differ in such basic properties as size, conduction rate, and amplitude of the discharge. B fibers are most susceptible to oxygen lack, followed by A-type fibers. (From Ruch, Patton, Woodbury, & Towe, 1961, p. 81.)

	A	*B*	*s.C*	*d.r.C*
Fiber diameter, μ	1–22	< 3	0.3–1.3	0.4–1.2
Conduction speed, msec	5–120	3–15	0.7–2.3	0.6–2.0
Spike duration, msec	0.4–0.5	1.2	2.0	2.0
Absolute refractory period, msec	0.4–1.0	1.2	2.0	2.0
Negative afterpotential amplitude,				
percent of spike	3–5	None	3–5	None
Duration, msec	12–20		50–80	
Positive afterpotential amplitude,				
percent of spike	0.2	1.5–4.0	1.5	
Duration, msec	40–60	100–300	300–1000	
Order of susceptibility to asphyxia	2	1	3	3

nervous system has several properties which would not be characteristic of a continuous, pipelike system. For one thing, there is a delay in time of transmission. There has been a tendency among theorists to speculate on the relation between learning and the synapse. To date, there is no clear evidence that learning correlates with changes in the nervous system, although some theories are based on the supposition that such correlations can be found.

An important functional property of the synapse is that it allows impulses to pass in only one direction. Accordingly, the analogy of the nervous system as a telephone system in which impulses and information are relayed back and forth fails. A more suitable analogy is that of a town which has made *all* its streets one-way: a driver may have to make many devious turns to get headed in the right direction, and if one road is blocked, no traffic can get through, since the driver cannot turn around. The synapse, then, determines the direction the impulse can take.

How it is that the synapse is able to reproduce the impulse is as mysterious as the way in which the neuron itself is able to conduct various gradations of sensations. One general

theory emphasizes the electrical nature of the impulse. It states that the electrical field set up by the impulse would be broad enough to affect (or cross over) the synapse. This theory is useful, for it also explains how one nerve may fire another and how *summation* may occur. A second general theory is that a chemical change is responsible both for the transmission of the impulse and for the crossing of a synapse. Some support for this position

FIGURE 2-6: *Schematic diagram of sensory-motor integration.*

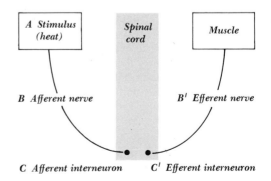

A Stimulus (heat)   *Spinal cord*   *Muscle*

B Afferent nerve   *B' Efferent nerve*

C Afferent interneuron   *C' Efferent interneuron*

comes from the finding that, at least with some neurons, a chemical called *acetylcholine* is secreted. The impulse is transmitted as the chemical is secreted. Acetylcholine is supposedly chemically degraded rapidly by the enzyme *cholinesterase*.

THE CENTRAL NERVOUS SYSTEM

The CNS includes both the spinal cord and the numerous structures of the brain. The neurons and nerves of the CNS are different in several respects from peripheral nerves, most notably in size and the presence of myelination in fibers forming tracts. Although the process of conduction is basically the same for both peripheral and central nerves, transmission in the CNS has received more experimental attention, because almost all bodily or behavioral activity affects the CNS. In the CNS the neurons are grouped into structures. Just as the various geographic areas of the world received their names in a haphazard fashion depending upon the date of naming and the language used by the discoverer, so the structures of the brain have been named: sometimes the name signifies a function of the area; sometimes it represents the name of the discoverer. In order to discuss the functions of the CNS efficiently, it is necessary to be able to identify its main structures. However, just as it is easier to remember the names of streets or towns once you have been in them, so it is easier to learn the names of the parts of the brain during dissection. In describing the areas of the body, and particularly the components of the CNS, we have adopted terms which define the positions of areas in relation to other structures. Most directional definitions are determined in relation to the spinal cord, *dorsal* (from *dorsum,* the Latin for *back*) referring to the side at the back and *ventral* (from the Latin *venter,* meaning *belly*) referring to the inside, or the side nearest the abdominal cavity. It does not matter whether the animal walks upright or not: dorsal and ventral are relative to the position of the spinal cord.

The terms *anterior* and *posterior* are most commonly used only in reference to the brain, since they denote the front (anterior) and the back (posterior) of the head. One might speak of the ears as being posterior to the eyes. The terms *rostral* and *caudal* refer to the upward or downward direction of the spinal cord, respectively. When one pets a dog, one usually does so in a *cephalocaudal* direction, meaning the strokes are from the head toward the tail.

Other terms commonly used to define areas of the CNS are *medial,* which refers to the midline of the body, and *lateral,* which refers to locations away from the midline. A medial cut is one in which the body is divided in equal halves. The terms *proximal* and *distal* indicate whether a given area is near (proximal) or far (distal) from a second area. Since the CNS is three-dimensional, a combination of two or more terms is often necessary to specify a location with precision.

The Spinal Cord: Because the spinal cord is often associated with the conduction of nervous impulses and the brain is often associated with higher mental processes, we sometimes think of the spinal cord and brain as vastly different structures. Although they are different functionally, the same processes of nervous transmission and synaptic transmission which are found in the spinal cord are found in the remainder of the CNS. In the same way, although the anatomy of the spinal cord and of the brain indicates some different relationships, similarities are far more noteworthy than differences.

The basic anatomy of the spine is the same no matter where it is sectioned: unlike the brain, it is a very homogeneous structure. Figure 2–7 shows a transverse section of the spinal cord.

The cord shows two distinct components: (1) the white matter and (2) the gray matter, which forms the shape of a butterfly. Surrounding the cord are three layers of tissue which constitute the *meninges.* These are known as the *pia mater, arachnoid layer,* and *dura mater.* We shall discuss meninges again

FIGURE 2–7: *Transverse section through the fourth cervical vertebra, showing the coverings of the cord. (Copenhaver & D. D. Johnson, 1958, p. 209.)*

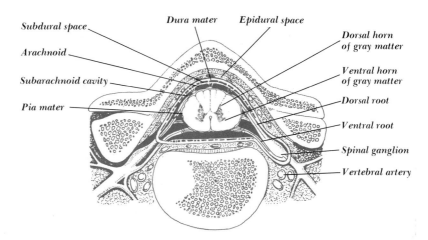

when we consider the brain, since they also surround it and have several critical functions.

The white matter is composed of columns of myelinated nerve tracts which allow nervous transmission up and down the spinal cord. Generally speaking, the columns to the dorsal side are *afferent;* that is, they conduct impulses of a sensory nature toward the brain. Columns to the ventral side are generally *efferent,* for they carry impulses from the brain to connections with the motor system. In discussing the various senses later in this volume we note the importance of being able to locate and follow a given tract of nerves in both its sensory and motor components. For example, the question whether there is an identifiable tract which conducts impulses from the temperature receptors in the skin to the CNS or a tract which conducts only sensations of pain to the CNS is clearly of importance.

Tracts are generally divided into two types on the basis of length: long tracts appear to run between the brain and the spinal cord without interruption; short tracts—*intersegmental tracts*—appear to connect different portions of the cord. Tracts which have been identified are usually named by their apparent be-

ginning and their apparent end (e.g., the spinothalamic tract).

When the tracts reach the brain, the respective positions of the white and gray matter are reversed, so that the gray matter lies outside the white matter. This relationship is known as a *cortex.*

The basic functions of the spinal cord appear to be twofold: first, the conduction of afferent and efferent messages, and, second, the ability to short-circuit messages to and from the brain by means of a *reflex arc.* Certain afferent impulses, such as intense pain and intense temperature, do not need to go all the way to the brain before synapsing with an efferent fiber which leads to a motor response, such as withdrawing the hand. The synapse occurs in the spinal cord itself. Thus the time lapse between the sensory stimulus and the motor response is greatly lessened. This "protective" feature of the spinal cord, the basis of the principle that certain stimuli are followed by predictable responses (such as removing the hand from a hot stove), gave credence, if not incubation, to the idea of the conditioned response, which became an essential component of behavioral theory.

The Brain: Figure 2–8 shows a medial aspect of the brain. Grossly, the major areas of the brain, moving anteriorly, are the *medulla, cerebellum,* and *cerebrum.* The medulla, both anatomically and functionally, is an extension of the spinal cord and is a transitional structure between the brain and spinal cord. The medulla transmits fibers from the spinal

FIGURE 2–8: *The medial aspect of the brain. Note particularly the location of the structures described in the text. (From the Ciba Collection of Medical Illustrations by Frank H. Netter, M.D., copyright Ciba.)*

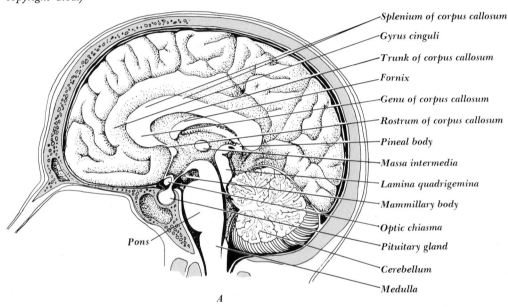

Splenium of corpus callosum
Gyrus cinguli
Trunk of corpus callosum
Fornix
Genu of corpus callosum
Rostrum of corpus callosum
Pineal body
Massa intermedia
Lamina quadrigemina
Mammillary body
Optic chiasma
Pituitary gland
Cerebellum
Medulla

Pons

A

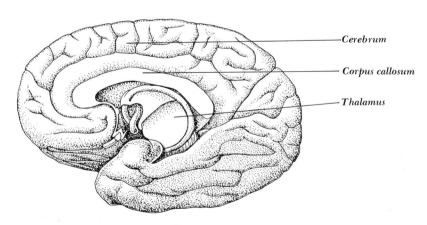

Cerebrum
Corpus callosum
Thalamus

B

cord to the brain and from the brain to the spinal cord. It also controls certain reflex actions, such as breathing. Recent evidence indicates that portions of the medulla may be associated with "alertness." The enlargement near the top of the medulla is known as the *pons.* One of the more important anatomical aspects of the pons is that fibers from the cerebellum cross over to the ventral side and return to the cerebellum on the opposite side. The pons is important for the sensory and motor components of the mouth and face, since the cranial nerves which serve these sensory and motor functions have their nucleus in the pons.

The cerebellum is perceived immediately as different from surrounding structures because of its rough texture and darker coloring. In Figure 2–8 it is seen as a bulb at the back of the brain, with branchlike areas running through it. In the cerebellum, the relation between gray and white matter is the opposite of what it is in the spinal cord. The gray matter, on the outside, forms a surface, or cortex. The cerebellum is associated with motor movement, coordination, balance, and so on.

The largest portion of the CNS is the cerebrum; it is composed of many specialized areas which differ from one another both anatomically and functionally. The medial portion in Figure 2–8 shows the cerebrum in silhouette, as if the brain had been sliced in half.

Among the more important structures for the study of behavior are:

Corpus callosum: In Figure 2–8 this markedly white area joins the two cerebral hemispheres (one of which has been cut away in the figure) and is a "roof" over the important structures beneath it, such as the thalamus and hypothalamus. The corpus callosum is composed of fibers transversing the two hemispheres of the cerebrum, and, as such, it serves as a center for the transmission of information in either direction.

Fornix: The fornix is directly beneath the corpus callosum. It too is comparatively white in appearance.

Frontal lobes: The large area in front of the corpus callosum is one of the two frontal lobes. These lobes are apparently of importance to higher mental functions such as ability to think about the future. In performing frontal lobotomies and lobectomies, the clinical psychiatrist severs the connecting fibers between this area and the rest of the brain in order to reduce severe anxiety.

Thalamus: Although the thalami cannot be seen in Figure 2–8, their location is identifiable. The area marked massa intermedia represents the tissue that connects the two thalami. In the figure, one thalamus has been severed, while the other is behind the massa intermedia. A portion of the thalamus may be seen more clearly in the lower portion of the figure (*B*) in the area marked thalamus.

Hypothalamus (not shown in the figure): The hypothalamus has received considerable attention recently as the seat of the "eating center." The hypothalamus lies directly below the thalami.

Pituitary: The pituitary gland is a major part of the endocrine system, and accordingly it is important in emotionality, sex behavior, and growth.

Optic chiasma: The optic chiasma is the place at which the two visual nerves cross and bisect themselves in such a way that a portion of the fibers from each nerve joins a portion of the fibers from the other. This crossing of fibers influences some critical aspects of the visual system (Chapters 8 and 9).

Amygdala: The amygdala is located on the lower surface of the lateral hemisphere of the cerebellum. It functions in emotional and sexual behavior.

Among the other landmarks of the brain which are thought or known to be important for the study of behavior are the gyrus cinguli, the mammillary bodies, and the lamina quadrigemina.

The cerebrum also has a cortex (the cerebral cortex) which is composed of gray matter, white fiber tracts running from the cortex to the subcortical structures, and the corpus callosum, which is composed of fibers running between the two hemispheres.

The presence of a cortex is one of the major distinctions between mammals and other forms of life. The general relation of the cortex to other structures may be seen in Figure 2–9.

Certain areas of the brain are referred to as *lobes.* We have already noted the area of

FIGURE 2–9: *The upper drawing (A) shows the surface of the left hemisphere of the brain. Note the* Central sulcus *and* Fissure of sylvius, *which serve as landmarks. The major lobes are labeled. The lower drawing (B) shows the medial aspect. Note the* Corpus callosum, *through which fibers pass from one hemisphere to the other.* (*From* Physiological Psychology, *by M. A. Wenger, F. N. Jones, and M. H. Jones, copyright 1956 by Holt, Rinehart and Winston, Inc.)*

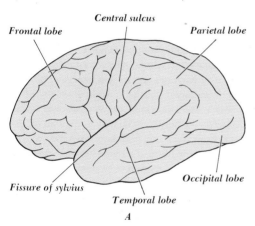

Central sulcus
Frontal lobe
Parietal lobe
Fissure of sylvius
Occipital lobe
Temporal lobe
A

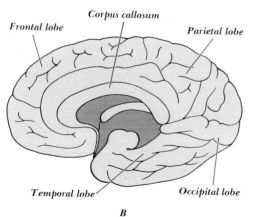

Corpus callosum
Frontal lobe
Parietal lobe
Temporal lobe
Occipital lobe
B

the frontal lobes. Posterior to the frontal lobes and to the *central sulcus* is the *parietal* lobe, which appears to be concerned primarily with incoming sensory messages. The parietal lobe includes the *somesthetic cortex,* where the senses of touch, pain, and temperature are projected. Posterior to the parietal lobe is the *occipital* lobe, which appears to be the area where impulses traveling from the eyes through the optic nerves terminate. This lobe is commonly called the *projection area,* even though it is not delineated by any sulcus or fissure. Ventral to the *fissure of Sylvius* is the *temporal lobe.*

The cortex in higher mammals is commonly folded, or convoluted. The folding over of tissue, of course, allows more cells per unit of space. The ridges of the cortex are known as *gyri,* while the valleys are known as *sulci.* The *central sulcus,* which divides the frontal from the parietal lobes, is a deeply indented area.

In discussing the spinal cord, the presence of the *meninges* was noted. These are the three layers of tissue surrounding the CNS. One function of the meninges is to separate the brain tissue from the skull.

The ventricular system has a superficial resemblance to a canal system. In some places it is very wide and in others, quite narrow. The places where the ventricular system widens are designated by roman numerals, beginning with the posterior portion of the brain. Of considerable importance are the third ventricle, between the thalamus and hypothalamus, and the fourth ventricle, which appears at the separation between the cerebrum and cerebellum. One of the meninges (or subarachnoid spaces) comes close to the fourth ventricle, and, through a permeable membrane, fluid from the ventricular system comes in contact with fluid from the subarachnoid spaces. The resultant cerebrospinal fluid superficially resembles blood but has different components. It does not, for example, carry red or white corpuscles. Although comparatively little is understood about the function of cerebrospinal fluid, one of its contributions is to supply the brain with the chemicals necessary for nervous transmission and to protect the brain. A blow to the head has its pressure absorbed and equalized over the entire brain surface by the presence of the cushion provided by the fluid. Malfunctioning of the systems which provide cerebrospinal fluid results in pathological conditions, such as hydrocephalus, in which the head sometimes grows so large, owing to an accumulation of cerebrospinal fluid, that it cannot be held upright.

Although the chemical components necessary for transmission in the brain are not fully identified, the need for oxygen is well annotated. The newer structures of the brain appear to be most rapidly affected by the lack of oxygen, for the cerebral cortex will cease firing after 10 seconds of oxygen elimination (and will be irreparably damaged in a few minutes) although the medulla can tolerate longer periods of oxygen lack. When a circulatory deficiency occurs, as in a heart "attack" or in infantile strangulation from being wrapped in the umbilical cord, reflexes may remain normal, but there may be permanent damage to the brain.

The Cranial Nerves: In some portions of the organism, thousands of neurons merge to form a nerve trunk, just as thousands of separate telephone lines eventually merge and are conducted by a single cable. Some nerves have a single function, such as the optic nerve, which transmits impulses from the retina of the eye to the projection areas for vision at the back of the brain, or the olfactory nerve, which appears to be solely concerned with the transmission of impulses from the olfactory system. Other nerves, however, have more than one function. For example, the auditory nerve, which conducts impulses from the ear, also serves as a pathway for sensations of balance which come from the nonauditory labyrinth also located in the ear.

Figure 2–10 and the accompanying text indicate the origin, course, termination, and function of the various cranial nerves. Psychologists are most interested in the nerves that service the sensory systems of vision, audition,

olfaction, gustation, and balance, and these will be considered in detail in later chapters. Note, however, that a sensory system may be serviced by several nerves. Although the major nerve for vision is the optic nerve, the motor functions of visual perception (accommodation, movement of the iris) are cared for by the IIId cranial nerve (oculomotor). The fact that this nerve also services parts of the internal organism is one of the reasons that visual perception is related to certain types of internal illnesses, most notably motion sickness. Similarly, the receptors on the tongue which report taste sensations are serviced by several different nerves. The VIIth cranial nerve (facial) handles the anterior portion of the tongue, while both the IXth (glossopharyngeal) and the XIIth (hypoglossal) handle the other areas.

The Spinal Nerves: The human being has 31 *pairs* of spinal nerves placed at regular intervals along the spinal cord. The nerves are named according to their location, as shown in Table 2–B. Perhaps the most important aspect of the spinal nerves in their relation to behavior is the separation which they make between sensory and motor impulses. As the spinal nerves enter the spinal cord, they separate. Each of the connections formed by the separation is called a *root,* and the relationship between each connection and its function to the nervous system is known as the *law of*

TABLE 2–B: *The Name, Number, and Position of the Spinal Nerves in Man.*
The location of some of the nerves may be seen in Figures 2–11 and 2–12. (From C. T. Morgan, 1965, p. 28).

Name	Number	Position
Cervical	8	Neck
Thoracic	12	Chest
Lumbar	5	Loin
Sacral	5	End of spinal column
Coccygeal	1	End of spinal column

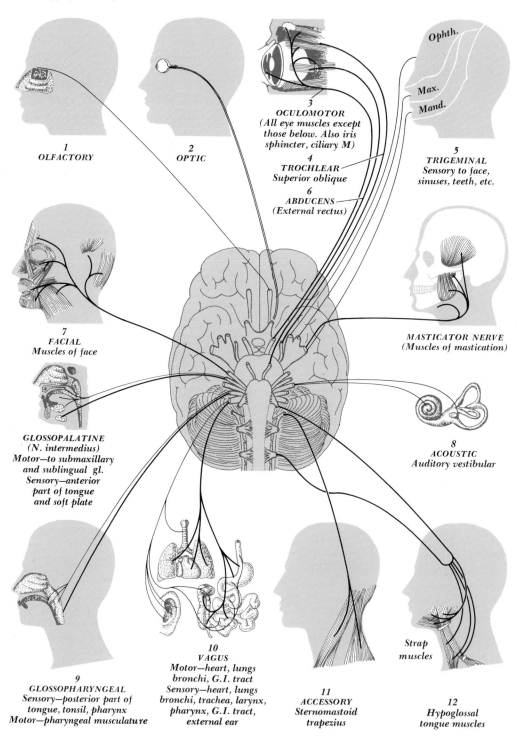

FIGURE 2–10: *Location and basic function of the cranial nerves. (From the Ciba Collection of Medical Illustrations, by Frank H. Netter, M.D., copyright Ciba.)*

Ophth.

Max.

Mand.

3
OCULOMOTOR
(All eye muscles except those below. Also iris sphincter, ciliary M)

4
TROCHLEAR
Superior oblique

6
ABDUCENS
(External rectus)

1
OLFACTORY

2
OPTIC

5
TRIGEMINAL
Sensory to face, sinuses, teeth, etc.

7
FACIAL
Muscles of face

MASTICATOR NERVE
(Muscles of mastication)

GLOSSOPALATINE
(N. intermedius)
Motor—to submaxillary and sublingual gl. Sensory—anterior part of tongue and soft plate

8
ACOUSTIC
Auditory vestibular

Strap muscles

9
GLOSSOPHARYNGEAL
Sensory—posterior part of tongue, tonsil, pharynx Motor—pharyngeal musculature

10
VAGUS
Motor—heart, lungs bronchi, G.I. tract Sensory—heart, lungs bronchi, trachea, larynx, pharynx, G.I. tract, external ear

11
ACCESSORY
Sternomastoid trapezius

12
Hypoglossal tongue muscles

roots. Generally the *dorsal root* has a sensory function (for example, it mediates pain or temperature sensation and reports sensations from joints and perhaps from visceral structures), while the *ventral root* has a motor function (it mediates movement of the structures).

The dorsal root contains a "swelling" which is the *dorsal spinal ganglion.* The swelling contains cell bodies of the sensory fibers which emanate from the sensory receptor and which are on their way to the spinal cord. The cell bodies of the motor fibers, however, are within the spinal cord itself; they form a swelling of gray matter and are known as *ventral horn cells.* Since the relationship between the spinal nerves and their motor and sensory components is responsible for mediating the relationship between perception and behavior, any theory of behavior should consider existing knowledge regarding the abilities and limitations of the nervous system. At the same time, evidence from the nervous system in regard to its normal or pathological functioning contributes heavily to psychological theory by indirectly indicating the relationship between the stimulus and the response.

THE PERIPHERAL NERVOUS SYSTEM AND HOMEOSTASIS

The peripheral nervous system is composed of two subsystems, the *sympathetic* and the *parasympathetic.* Together, these two components make up the *autonomic nervous system* (ANS). The sympathetic and parasympathetic component (see Figures 2–11 and 2–12) is concerned with the rate of functioning of the heart, kidneys, and other visceral organs. A comparison of the two figures shows that the two subsystems perform antagonistic functions on certain organs. For example, the sympathetic system increases heart rate, and the parasympathetic system decreases heart rate. When it is said that the two divisions of the ANS are antagonistic, it is pointed out that one "slows down" and the other "speeds up" functioning, or that one conserves energy while the other mobilizes energy. These descriptions are adequate to

differentiate the functions of the systems, and, except for some specific relationships in which the systems are not antagonistic, the description is a reasonable evaluation of the different functions. In general, the sympathetic system has the function of the expenditure of energy, while the parasympathetic system has the function of the conservation of energy.

During stressful situations the sympathetic system usually is dominant: increases are noted in blood pressure, respiration, and the like, while the functions of the parasympathetic system, such as digestive actions, are retarded. Thus, the ANS is extremely important in the physiological attributes of emotional behavior.

The course which the fibers from the two systems follow is one way in which they can be differentiated. In the sympathetic system, the course is from cell bodies in the spinal cord through the ventral root, where synapse occurs with ganglia. In the parasympathetic system the course is from the brainstem (e.g., medulla) or spinal cord to the appropriate organ (e.g., heart) and then to the synapse with ganglia near the organ.

The antagonistic functioning of the two subsystems of the ANS suggests a concept important to psychology—*homeostasis.* Although the concept may be traced to Greek philosophy, it has been given a contemporary behavioral meaning by the physiologist Walter B. Cannon (1871–1945; 1932). Homeostasis refers to the process by which the body is able to regulate itself by maintaining a relatively constant state. On a simple behavioral level, this means that when I am thirsty, I drink. Thirst is assumed to represent a disruption of the normal state of the internal system; the mouth becomes parched, and so on. Departure from homeostasis creates a *drive.* In thirst, the drive is for water. When water has been taken, the organism returns to its normal state, and the drive becomes latent. This concept has been used in many theories of behavior, especially those concerned with factors motivating or driving the organism.

The translation of the concept of homeostasis from physiology to a motivational state of the organism may be a bad analogy, at

FIGURE 2–11: *The sympathetic division of the autonomic nervous system. The left-hand column shows the brain and spinal cord. Note the spinal nerves. The broken lines indicate the organ innervated by the several nerve and ganglionic connections. The right-hand column shows the action to the organ which is under the control of the sympathetic system. (From Rothe, 1963, p. 144.)*

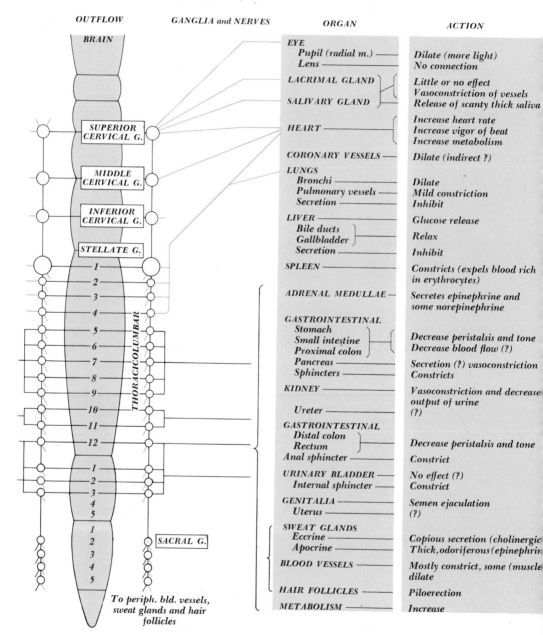

OUTFLOW	GANGLIA and NERVES	ORGAN	ACTION
BRAIN		EYE	
		Pupil (radial m.)	Dilate (more light)
		Lens	No connection
		LACRIMAL GLAND	Little or no effect
			Vasoconstriction of vessels
SUPERIOR CERVICAL G.		SALIVARY GLAND	Release of scanty thick saliva
		HEART	Increase heart rate
			Increase vigor of beat
			Increase metabolism
MIDDLE CERVICAL G.		CORONARY VESSELS	Dilate (indirect ?)
		LUNGS	
		Bronchi	Dilate
INFERIOR CERVICAL G.		Pulmonary vessels	Mild constriction
		Secretion	Inhibit
STELLATE G.		LIVER	Glucose release
		Bile ducts	
1		Gallbladder	Relax
2		Secretion	Inhibit
3		SPLEEN	Constricts (expels blood rich in erythrocytes)
4		ADRENAL MEDULLAE	Secretes epinephrine and some norepinephrine
5	THORACICOLUMBAR	GASTROINTESTINAL	
6		Stomach	Decrease peristalsis and tone
7		Small intestine	Decrease blood flow (?)
8		Proximal colon	
9		Pancreas	Secretion (?) vasoconstriction
10		Sphincters	Constricts
11		KIDNEY	Vasoconstriction and decrease output of urine
12		Ureter	(?)
1		GASTROINTESTINAL	
2		Distal colon	
3		Rectum	Decrease peristalsis and tone
4		Anal sphincter	Constrict
5		URINARY BLADDER	No effect (?)
		Internal sphincter	Constrict
1		GENITALIA	Semen ejaculation
2	SACRAL G.	Uterus	(?)
3		SWEAT GLANDS	
4		Eccrine	Copious secretion (cholinergic)
5		Apocrine	Thick, odoriferous (epinephrin)
		BLOOD VESSELS	Mostly constrict, some (muscle) dilate
To periph. bld. vessels, sweat glands and hair follicles		HAIR FOLLICLES	Piloerection
		METABOLISM	Increase

FIGURE 2-12: *The parasympathetic division of the autonomic nervous system. The brain and spinal cord are shown in the left-hand column. Note the position of the cranial nerves at the top of the spinal cord and the sacral nerves at the base. The organ affected by the parasympathetic system and its parasympathetic function is shown in the center and right-hand columns. (From Rothe, 1963, p. 145.)*

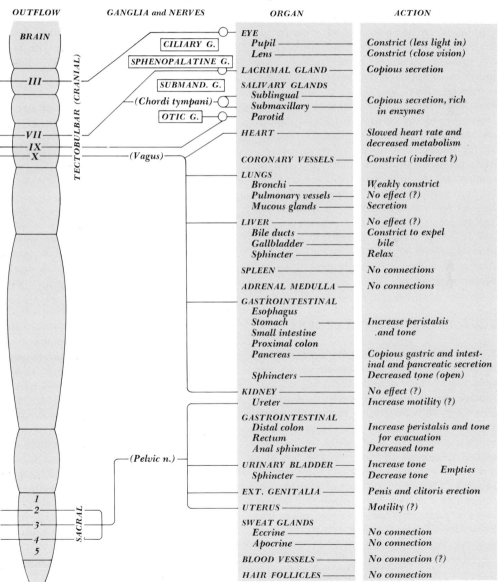

PARASYMPATHETIC DIVISION OF THE AUTONOMIC NERVOUS SYSTEM
(*All nerve fibers are cholinergic*)

worst, or a great simplification, at best. Biologically, the homeostatic mechanism does more than create motives or drives. It may restrict the behavior of the organism. For example, the bear hibernates and the frog lives at at the bottom of the pond during the winter, since neither has a homeostatic mechanism to handle temperature changes. Primates do have such a mechanism as do many other animals. The use of temperature as an example of the working of the homeostatic mechanism is apt, for in many ways the mechanism is similar in concept to a feedback system such as that found in thermostats: the temperature of the thermostat affects the "behavior" and, eventually, the temperature of the furnace, and the "behavior" of the furnace, in turn, regulates the "behavior" of the thermostat. The systems are not independent: they regulate each other. Although the concept of homeostasis and its complement, the concept of feedback, are useful, care should be taken in applying them to theories of behavior. When we consider the problem of explaining how organisms acquire new repsonses, how they adapt, and how they learn (Chapters 12 to 16), we shall find the concept of homeostasis widely used as an explanatory principle.

SOME IMPORTANT PHENOMENA

For several reasons, an understanding of some of the basic physiological functions of the nervous system must precede the study of psychology. First, such knowledge permits the grounding of psychological theory. One cannot, or at least should not, devise theories which contradict the workings of the nervous system. Second, an understanding of how the sensory systems work permits us to analyze behavior. (Chapters 6 to 11 are concerned with this subject.) Further our physiological system forms a limit to which we may apply our knowledge of how learning occurs. When a new response is acquired or an old response forgotten, it is reasonable to assume that some processes are going on in the nervous system.

We shall now discuss (1) the recording of electric potential from the CNS by the technique of electroencephalography, (2) brain stimulation, in which small amounts of electric current or certain chemicals are applied to the brain, (3) the relation between centers within the CNS and emotional responses, and (4) the role of the brain in determining alertness, sleep, and other factors associated with the level of arousal. Some of the physiological phenomena involved here are so basic that we refer to them throughout the book. Others are discussed in considerable detail in Chapters 12 to 16.

Electroencephalography: Since 1929 (H. Berger) and perhaps as early as 1875 (Brazier, 1961), it has been known that the cortex and possibly other areas of the CNS yield small amounts of electric current which can be amplified and measured. It is also known that the frequency and amplitude of the current vary as a function of the behavior of the organism. For example, a sleeping organism yields a record quite different from a wakeful, attentive organism. The apparatus used to amplify and record electric potentials is called an *electroencephalograph*, the record itself is called an *electroencephalogram* (EEG), and the study of these records is *electroencephalography*. When electrodes are placed on the scalp and the electric potential is amplified and recorded, several distinct rhythms are noted. *Alpha rhythms*, or alpha waves (8 to 12 Hz[2]), are recorded from adult individuals who are awake but relaxed; *beta rhythms* (14 to 30 Hz) are characteristically associated with the motor areas of the brain; and *delta rhythms* (0.5 to 5 Hz) are recorded from individuals in deep sleep. The different rhythms appear throughout the structures of the CNS, indicating that the EEG is reporting gross changes in brain function as opposed to precise alterations. When a person is beginning to sleep, higher frequencies are noted, along with occasional

2 The expression Hz (for *Hertz*) is currently being used to replace cps (cycles per second).

alpha waves. In deep sleep, the slow delta waves appear. During sleep, sudden shifts in the waveform are noted, and these may correlate with dreaming. The EEG pattern is also sensitive to changes in the blood supply, oxygen supply, and many drugs. The EEG is in widespread clinical use, for it often shows abnormalities of the CNS caused by tumors or pathological states, such as epilepsy.

Of interest to behavior theory is the evidence provided by Hearst, Beer, Sheatz, and Galambos (1960) that both the frequency and the amplitude of the EEG may be changed in response to a negative stimulus, such as shock or a positive stimulus, such as food. As we shall note in detail in Chapter 13, there is evidence that the EEG pattern can be controlled through conditioning procedures. In our search to correlate behavioral measures with changes in the nervous system, the EEG provides one of the most useful tools, for it permits recording of the electrical activity of the nervous system without interfering with the system through surgery.

Brain Stimulation: The study of brain stimulation by electric current may be said to have begun when Alessandro Volta passed current through his own CNS while experimenting with electricity. Happily, he survived to continue his work. In 1870 Fritsch and Hitzig systematically used electric stimulation, applying it to the cortex and noting that it resulted in movement of the appendages. Technique refinements have made it possible to apply electric stimulation to discrete areas of the brain in several different ways. The most common method is that of permanently implanting an electrode holder (a *chronic* implant) in the skull of the animal, a minor operation. Once the holder is in place, the experimenter can stimulate a specific area of the brain at different frequencies and amplitudes by inserting a conductive lead into the implant. A similar procedure may be used to make a lesion in specific areas by applying a current of sufficient intensity and duration. A *stereotaxic* instrument is used to determine the placement of the electrode. The instrument has three coordinates, corresponding to each spatial plane. Stereotaxic atlases of the brain, showing the settings of the coordinates, are available for a number of different species (Snider & Niemer, 1961; Snider & Lee, 1961; Gergen & MacLean, 1962). Figure 2–13 shows the placement of a chronic electrode.

Electric stimulation of the brain has produced information on such behaviors as sleep and wakefulness, food and water intake, sexual behavior, and the fundamental properties of learning. Although we shall mention the specific findings of experiments at the appropriate location in the book, we may here give one example of the type of discovery made possible by the development of the technique of brain stimulation. In 1954, Olds and Milner implanted an electrode in the forebrain of a rat. The animal was placed in an open arena, and a small electric current was passed into the CNS through the implant. It was noted that the animal spent more time in the section of the arena where stimulation first occurred. When the rat was placed in a maze in which stimulation was given if the animal went to one side of the maze but not if it went to the opposite side, the animal more and more often went to the side which produced electric current. In further experiments, rats learned to press a bar in order to receive stimulation. Indeed, animals so trained would produce many hundreds of responses when electric current followed each response but would cease to respond when the current was eliminated. It is noteworthy that none of the usual reinforcers such as food or water was used. Apparently the sensation associated with the current was sufficient to motivate the animal to learn a new response.

This phenomenon has been replicated in various animals, including rodents, pigeons, goldfish, dolphins, and human beings (Sem-Jacobsen & Torkildsen, 1960). The number of responses emitted in the experiment varies as a function of the placement of the electrode, the intensity and duration of the current, and the kind of animal. The importance of this

FIGURE 2–13: *A chronic electrode placement in a rat. Two placements have been made in this animal. Each contains a two-prong female plug into which the connecting cable is inserted. (From U.S. Army Photo, courtesy of Dr. Bernard Beer.)*

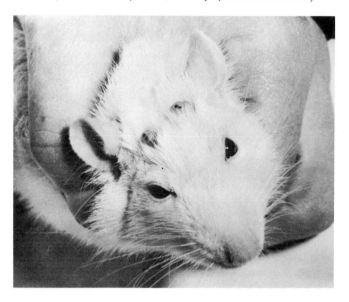

finding to psychology is that the organism learns a new response without apparent reward. Moreover, it would appear that certain areas of the CNS are more responsive to this form of stimulation than other areas, insofar as learning is concerned. Brain stimulation has come to be an important technique in the investigation of the physiological sources of emotion and motivation, of the effects of certain drugs on the CNS, and of the way new responses are acquired (Chapters 13 and 16).

Emotion: Emotional states, especially among infrahuman beings, are necessary for survival. The emotion which accompanies flight from an enemy or aggression in a predator is related to how well and how quickly the organism can respond. Thus, emotion is a necessary part of behavior. Part of Chapter 17 is devoted to the problems of measuring and evaluating emotion; however, we may note at this point the importance of the CNS to emotional states.

All mammals have a set of structures in the brain called the *limbic* system, or, sometimes, the *visceral brain.* Figure 2–14 shows the general area of the limbic system in the rabbit, cat, monkey, and human being. Two points are salient: First, moving up the phylogenetic scale, the limbic system occupies proportionately less of the brain, or, put another way, the cortical areas consume proportionately more of the available space. Second, the limbic system includes structures of the "old" brain—structures necessary for survival, such as the hypothalamus, rather than structures concerned with higher mental functioning, such as the cortex. The general area of the limbic system consists of the thalami, hypothalamus, hippocampus, mammillary bodies, fornix, amygdala, and septal area, among others. Each of these areas appears to have different functions. For example, ablation of the amygdala results in hypersexual animals, and a lesion in the hypothalamus results in changes in food and water intake. Stimulation of the hypothalamus may result in animals who eat continuously and become obese or in animals who refuse to eat at all. Stimulation of the hippocampus and certain nearby areas results in penile erection in males. Stimulation of other areas will produce a rage reaction in dogs and cats. It is apparent that the limbic system is directly involved in the production of emotional behavior. Systematic exploration of the CNS continues to yield information on the role of these areas in the important psychological processes of emotion and motivation (see Chapter 17).

Level of Arousal: Emotion is often related directly to the level of physiological arousal of the organism. In an angry human being, the posture and visceral mechanisms show heightened arousal. Indeed, many theorists have concluded that emotion is best understood in terms of the degree to which the organism is activated: how much adrenalin is pumped into the system, what happens to heart rate, blood pressure, and so on. Sleep and arousal, or wakefulness, would appear to be anchors on a continuum of arousal level. With the improved technology that permits brain stimulation, the accurate location of lesions and ablations, and the use of the EEG, information has become available on the processes of sleep and wakefulness. Why organisms sleep (or why they remain awake) is an unanswered question. Kleitman (1963) has shown that human beings are able to tolerate only a few days without sleep before gross physical and mental aberrations appear.

As we have noted, during deep sleep delta waves are prominent. Aserinsky and Kleitman (1953) and Dement and Wolpert (1958) have reported the presence of *rapid eye movements* (REMs) during sleep. This has sometimes been called *paradoxical sleep,* because the EEG is similar to that during light drowsiness. It appears that dreaming is correlated with REM activity (Dement & Kleitman, 1957). If REMs during sleep do represent dreaming, we dream every eighty to ninety minutes and have five

FIGURE 2-14: *The limbic system. (A) In the rabbit, (B) in the cat, (C) in the monkey, and (D) in man. Note that as position on the phylogenetic scale approaches man, the limbic system takes up proportionately less of the brain. (From Russell in Sheer, 1961, modified from MacLean, 1954.)*

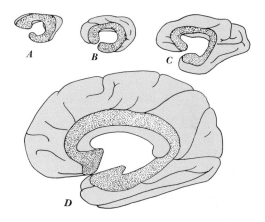

or six dreams per night. Kleitman (1960) reports that when external stimuli, such as a light or a water spray, are applied to sleeping subjects, the dreams contain elements of the external stimuli. Similarly Jouvet (1960) reports a correlation between EEG pattern and muscle tonus for the cat. It has been suggested that the pons is responsible for this patterning, since stimulation of this area produces the pattern.

An arousal system, located primarily in the pons and medulla, and spreading to the thalami, is called the *reticular activating system* (RAS). Because of the importance of these areas to emotional states, we shall discuss the subject in detail in Chapter 17. However, it may be noted that this system, when stimulated electrically, produces waveforms similar to those obtained from a person who is awake (Moruzzi & Magoun, 1949). Other evidence suggests that tumors in this area produce somnolent animals (Lindsley, Bowden, & Magoun, 1949).

Another area which appears to be concerned

with sleep and wakefulness is centered around the hypothalamus, which is a prominent member of the limbic system. It has been known since the early part of the century that tumor growth in the forward part of the hypothalamus affects sleep. However, it appears that both sleep-producing and wakefulness-producing centers are located in this area (Hernandez-Peón & Ibarra, 1963). This is analogous to the presence of structures affecting both eating and noneating in the same region.

It appears likely that the origins of sleep and wakefulness within the CNS are both complex and vast. Indeed, several different systems, such as the reticular activating system, the structures associated with the hypothalamus, and the pons, all contribute a share. Level of arousal is clearly related to such psychological functions as motivation and speed of learning; the relationship between level of arousal and the functioning of the CNS makes it apparent that the structures of the CNS are important in determining the quality of behavior.

AFTERWORD

The discussion of some of the physiological bases of behavior in this chapter prepares us to consider other aspects of experimental psychology in appropriate detail. Although, for convenience, we often speak of stimuli and responses, we should note that a stimulus must act upon a receptor (one of the sensory systems), which then transfers the stimulus to the CNS, which controls the response made to the stimulus. If we are to understand how an organism learns to make new responses, it is first necessary to understand how external stimuli reach the CNS. Human beings are limited by the kind and quality of the stimuli to which their bodies are attuned. The sensory systems are complex, and we shall devote a chapter, and sometimes more, to each of the systems. First, however, we shall consider the nature of the stimuli to which human beings respond.

SOURCES

Any discussion of the history of physiological psychology (as well as any discussion of the history of psychology) is a footnote to Boring (1950). This is the authoritative source, and the copious notes at the conclusion of each chapter furnish an excellent start for the scholar of the history of psychology. A second valuable source is Postman (1962), in which chapters written by specialists review the history of selected concepts in the history of psychology. In another work Boring (1942) restricts himself to sensation and perception. It is also an authoritative work, and, again, the annotations are very useful to both scholar and student.

Relationship between Physiology and Psychology: Almost everyone who has published a paper or written a book in the field of psychology has adopted a position on the relationship between physiology and psychology. Although Skinner (1953) is the most commonly cited contemporary spokesman against the use of physiological concepts in psychology, his position, as indicated in his writings, is not quite so strongly antiphysiology as some followers have suggested. From the quotation on page 37 it is clear that Skinner perceives that a true finding should fit both psychological and physiological concepts but that explanation in terms of physiology is not necessary for the advance of psychology. Pavlov (1932) provides the argument against "psychologizing" on the principles of physiology.

One of the soundest of commentaries on this topic is found in Geldard (1953). In chap. 1 of this excellent text, Geldard relates the study of the senses to the history of experimental psychology and, in a more contemporary setting, to the problems of engineering and industrial psychology. Hebb (1955) has provided a very thoughtful essay on this topic which deserves attention.

Brief History: Bell's original paper appeared

in 1811 and was reprinted in 1869 and 1948. See also Carmichael (1926). Magendie's contribution is represented by papers appearing in 1822 and 1839. See also Boring (1950). J. Müller's papers bearing on the doctrine of specific nerve energies appeared in 1826 and 1838. See also Rand (1912). For Gall's work on phrenology, see Gall (1810–1819). See also Spurzheim (1825; 1826; 1832), Cuvier (1808), and Boring (1950).

Neurons and Nerves: Standard sources in this area differ both in the level of knowledge assumed on the part of the reader and in the recency of the publication. However, for the general reader, advances in this area are not so rapid that a well-written text that is ten years old is useless. Among the sources found valuable in the preparation of this section were Boring (1950), Fulton (1955), C. T. Morgan and Stellar (1950), C. T. Morgan (1965), and Ochs (1965). Netter (1957) includes a supplement on the hypothalamus. Although the book consists mostly of medical illustrations of very high quality, the accompanying text is useful in orienting the reader. Wenger, F. N. Jones, and M. H. Jones (1956) and Ranson

and S. L. Clark (1959) are standard sources and texts. In Ruch, Patton, Woodbury, and Towe (1961), a very useful reprint for psychologists includes the sections from Howell's *Textbook of Physiology* which relate to cells, nerves, and the sensory and motor functions. J. A. Deutsch and D. Deutsch (1966) have written a fine text on physiological psychology as has R. F. Thompson (1967). An advanced handbook is S. P. Grossman (1967).

The Central Nervous System and the Cranial Nerves: The sources named above discuss the CNS and cranial nerves at different levels. Netter (1957) is a very useful reference work. While the Ciba drawings in this book are instructive, they are most useful during the process of dissection. A dissection of the rat brain will point up the basic structures mentioned in this text.

Phenomena: This section of the chapter is intended as a general introduction to these phenomena. Since each is to be discussed in detail in later chapters, sources will be found following the more detailed discussions in Chapter 17.

CHAPTER THREE

THE SENSES AND
THEIR STIMULI

IMPORTANCE OF THE SENSES

We are so accustomed to using our sensory systems that we do not always recognize the ways in which they limit our behavior. We may become aware of our own limitations by noting, for example, that other people have an easier time hearing the phone ring, that they are quicker in hearing money dropped on the sidewalk or deer moving in the bushes, that they are more sensitive to the smell of perfume or leaking gas, that they find a food filled with unusual flavors whereas we find the same food bland, that they find a light touch on the back of the neck sensuous which we hardly notice. Some of these experiences indicate a difference in preference, on the one hand, or a difference in sensitivity, on the other.

Preference: Preference is used in the psychological sense to indicate a subject's selection of one item from among several possible alternatives. The rat who is allowed to choose among drinking tubes, one of which contains a small percentage of alcohol, one water, and one sucrose solution, is expressing a preference if, over a given period, he selects 0.25 ml (milliliters) of the alcohol solution, 0.20 ml of water, and 0.15 ml of sucrose. We would say that he had a preference for alcohol over pure water but a preference for water over sucrose. When the psychologist studies preference behavior—such as preference for music, paintings, a politician, or a kind of food—he is usually concerned with both innate and learned behavior. The preference between a Brueghel and a van Gogh may depend upon such innate capacities as the ability to distinguish the colors used by the artists or upon what we have learned to prefer through experience with the preferences of other people. Accordingly, the study of many kinds of behavior is reducible to the study of how preference comes about and an evaluation of the individual's capacities of perception. If we wish to understand why a person prefers one painting to another, one beverage to another, or one girl to another, the first step is to measure the innate perceptual abilities of the individual.

Psychophysics and Thresholds: The study of the relation between physical stimuli, such as sound, light, or touch, and the accompanying sensation (usually identified by some response to the stimulus) is known as *psychophysics.* In psychophysics, an equation is obtained between a physical stimulus and the behavioral response to that stimulus. Specifically, we are concerned with the determination of *thresholds*—the detection of changes in the stimulus which elicit different responses. Two kinds of thresholds are recognized, *absolute* and *differential.* Within the class of absolute thresholds (AL)[1] we may note two kinds: The first, the *stimulus* (or *lower*) *threshold* (RL), refers to the point at which a stimulus is of such a magnitude that it is just as likely to be perceived as not perceived. For example, an individual may be able to hear a pitch of 48 Hz but may never report hearing a pitch of 46 Hz. Accordingly, the stimulus threshold lies somewhere between 46 and 48 Hz. Table 3–A shows some approximate threshold values for several senses.

The term *limen* means *threshold* or *doorway* in Latin. Many of the abbreviations of psycho-

[1] The abbreviation AL is used in experimental psychology for both *absolute threshold* and *adaptation level.* To avoid confusion, in this text the term *adaptation level* will always be spelled out, and AL will always mean *absolute threshold.*

physical phenomenon use L for limen, but the terms *limen* and *threshold* are interchangeable. In addition, because psychophysics began in Germany and most of the early articles on the topic were published in German, the German word for stimulus (*Reiz*) is used. Thus, a stimulus threshold is sometimes abbreviated RL (for *Reiz* limen). The RL for sound then, indicates the threshold, or doorway, which separates nonperception from perception. Although this historical development of nomenclature has resulted in an odd collection of Latin and German, most psychologists retain the traditional terms.

The second kind of AL is the *upper* or *terminal threshold,* or *terminal limen* (TL). It applies to some sensory systems, such as audition, but not to all. The TL is the statistical point at which the stimulus is too high in frequency to be perceived more than 50 percent of the time. Thus, perception passes into nonperception. For example, a person may be able to hear a tone of 17,000 Hz 100 percent of the time, be unable to hear a tone of 17,500 Hz at any time, and be able to hear a tone of 17,250 Hz 50 percent of the time. The third figure represents the TL, for it is the point at which a stimulus which has been perceivable is no longer perceived. Accordingly, sound maintains two ALs for frequency (or pitch), one at the low end of the frequencies and one at the upper end of the frequencies. A human being may therefore have an RL of 48 Hz and a TL of 17,250 Hz. Figure 3–1 applies these terms

TABLE 3–A: *Some Approximate Threshold Values.*
(From *New Directions in Psychology,* by Roger Brown, Eugene Galanter, Eckhard H. Hess, and George Mandler, copyright 1962 by Holt, Rinehart and Winston, Inc.)

Sense modality	Stimulus, or lower threshold
Light	A candle flame seen at 30 miles on a dark clear night (ca. 10 quanta)
Sound	The tick of a watch under quiet conditions at 20 ft (ca. 0.0002 dyne per cm²)
Taste	One teaspoonful of sugar in 2 gal water
Smell	One drop of perfume diffused into the entire volume of a 3-room apartment
Touch	The wing of a bee falling on your cheek from a distance of 1 cm

FIGURE 3-1: *Schematic representation of the location of key psychological terms. The abscissa shows sound waves from 48 to 17,250 Hz. The arrows indicate the location of the absolute thresholds.*

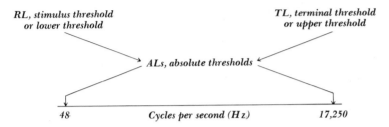

and abbreviations to our example of auditory ALs.

Vision is another sense which has both RLs and TLs. The human eye perceives wavelengths from approximately 400 mμ (millimicrons), which is in the deep-blue and violet range of perception, up to around 710 mμ, which is perceived as red. Although this range is perceived under ordinary conditions, there is evidence that the thresholds may be from 312.5 mμ (Goodeve, 1934) to 1,050 mμ (Griffin, Hubbard, & Wald, 1947). All senses have RLs. Individual differences, inherited or learned, are quite common, and the members of a single species may differ widely in sensitivity, as measured by ALs.

Although ALs indicate the limits of perception, insofar as they establish where perception begins and ends for a given sense, they do not say anything about the precision of perception within the limits. Within the perceivable range stipulated by the determination of ALs, there exists a second kind of threshold determination known as the *difference threshold* (DL). The DL represents the least amount of change in a physical stimulus which is necessary for an organism to report (50 percent of the time) that a change has occurred. For example, when in the shower, how much do I have to change the "hot" spigot before I am able to detect a difference? When someone asks me to turn down the radio or TV, how much do I have to decrease the volume before the person perceives that it has

been lowered? When dividing a cake in half, how much can I deviate from a fifty-fifty split (so I can get a larger piece) without the other person's discerning that the "halves" are not equal? In preparing a product for marketing, how small can I make the can (thus saving costs in producing the package) without having the housewife think she is getting less of the product than she would get from the larger package of a competitor? All these are practical examples of the calculation of the DL. The DL is not a constant. It varies not only as a function of the individual and of the technique used to measure it but primarily as a function of the level of stimulation.

The determination of sensory thresholds is an exacting process of considerable importance to experimental psychology. Many industrial and engineering psychology problems are concerned with the determination of thresholds. Determination of the appropriate location for panel mountings often requires measuring the perceptual ability of those who will be working with the equipment. A gum maker can cut production costs by shaving an amount off each stick of chewing gum which is "below" threshold, so the consumer does not perceive the difference.

Since the determination of sensory thresholds requires determining the response of the subject as well as measuring the original stimulus, a knowledge of the way in which physical stimuli are measured is basic to an understanding of psychophysics. A physical stimulus does not always correspond to the psychological perception of that stimulus. For example, a 5,000-Hz tone is played at 20 db (decibels, a measure of loudness). If this tone is now changed by increasing the loudness to 40 db, a person will tell you not only that the tone is louder but that it has been increased in frequency, or pitch, as well, even though no alteration in frequency has been made. Because of these disagreements between the physical stimulus and the psychological response, this chapter begins our discussion of psychophysics by considering how stimuli are measured. Chapter 4 describes the methods by which thresholds are determined. We shall now consider the nature of the stimuli to which human beings and other animals are responsive.

AUDITION

For human beings, hearing is certainly one of the two most used senses. Our ability to perceive sounds is well developed, even though we are far from being the most able animals in this regard. However, such everyday activities as speaking with people, responding to the honk of a car or the whistle of a train, turning our heads toward the source of a sound, or discriminating the slight inflections in voice which determine whether someone is pleased or irritated—all rely upon the sense of audition. Perhaps one of the main reasons why audition is so useful is that it is a so-called distance sense. Like vision, it enables us to perceive stimuli that are not directly in contact with us. If, like the human infant and some lower animals, we had to rely on "direct senses," we would spend most of our day running to objects in order to hear, smell, or see them. As a matter of fact, the human infant relies upon such direct senses as touch and taste until he learns to interpret the complicated messages which come through his eyes and ears. The baby crawls to an object to feel and taste it, for these are among the only senses which are well enough developed for identification. The older child and adult do

not have to waste such motions, for they may identify many stimuli by one of the distance senses.

The sense of audition is used primarily in communicating with other human beings, and an understanding of how normal hearing (as well as normal speech) comes about is important for evaluating pathological states. It is no surprise that many of the advances in understanding the processes of audition have come from the telephone laboratories, where communication is a major concern. A communications company may devise elaborate systems for the reproduction of sound, but in the long run, the product is only as good as the ear which receives the stimulation.

Audition has also received wide attention for aesthetic reasons. Music has been a part of human existence since earliest historical times, and even animals, if one is to believe anecdotal evidence, are not beyond a response to music. An orchestra creates physical stimuli by its instruments into a pattern of frequencies and amplitudes which are perceived by the listener. With little imagination one can imagine a similar "civilized" use of the other senses—a cutaneous concert, where the various modalities of the skin—hot, cold, pressure, pain, touch, tickle—are intermingled in a symphonic pattern, or a kinesthetic concert, where the body would be stretched, pulled, and pushed, activating the internal receptors of balance and position into a light sonata.

Sound may be generated through any medium. The transmission of sound bears some resemblance to the process of nerve conduction: not only must there be a source of the sound, a place where the vibration begins, but there must be some method for the vibration to continue and be transmitted. Although human beings and other mammals rely primarily on sound generated through the air, other forms of life rely primarily on sound waves generated through other mediums; the snake, for example, receives stimuli through the ground. Solids, such as walls and doors, do not usually eliminate sounds transmitted through the air, but the sounds they themselves transmit are of a different quality. Underwater sounds strike us as "eerie," just as the sounds transmitted through the air must sound strange to a fish.

The fact that sound is qualitatively different when transmitted by different mediums is evidence that the perception of sound depends on the physical stimulus (and what has happened to it during transmission) as well as on the ear. Sound is generated by a vibrating body in an elastic medium. Since the air particles in the medium of transmission are separated by space, the particles bounce back and forth creating a wave effect. It is believed that the particles do not move along the course of conduction but rather that the individual particle strikes the next in line and then bounces back to its original position while the second particle repeats the process with the third, and so on. As the particles bounce back and forth, they produce a compression and rarefaction, or a wave. Figure 3–2 shows a sample sound wave as it might be recorded.

The wave shown in Figure 3–2 is the simplest of sound waves: it is characterized by steady compression and rarefaction: there is no distortion evident from the recording. Sound waves of this type (which are virtually unknown in nature, where some distortion almost always occurs) are known as *sine waves*. In the figure, note that when the wave has

reached point *A*, it has made a complete circle: this is known as a *cycle*. When we spoke earlier in this chapter of a 5,000-Hz *tone*, we meant that 5,000 of these cycles would be completed every second. The fact that the wave completes a circle is the reason that the wave is called *sine,* for strictly speaking, a sine wave is one which covers all the angles, from 0 to 360°, of a full circle. Point *A* in Figure 3–2 indicates the point of 360°, while the point marked *B* is half a sine wave or 180°. As a tone passes through the cycles, it may be interrupted at any time. For example, it may cease at point *C*, where it has almost, but not quite, reached 360°, or a full cycle. Sometimes we want to refer to a particular point in the cycle, equivalent, for example, to 102°. This point is known as the *phase*, and it is very important for the study of audition. Two tones may be exactly alike in every way except phase—one may have started its cycle just before the other—and differences in phase are audible to the ear.

Sine waves or tones may also differ from one another in frequency and in amplitude. Frequency is the number of cycles completed each second. A tone of 500 Hz is perceived as much lower than a tone of 15,000 Hz. Thus, frequency is a major feature in describing differences in sound waves and, eventually, differences in perception. Although frequency is used in specifying the physical attribute of the sine wave, *pitch* is commonly used in describing the psychological counterpart of frequency. It is improper to say that we perceive frequency—we perceive pitch. We are able to say that one tone sounds higher than another or that two tones sound equally high or equally low, but as we noted, if the loudness of some tones is changed, the human ear perceives a change in pitch, even though no change was made in frequency.

The peaks of the sine wave (at 90 and 270°) may be slight or deep. *Amplitude* refers to the amount of deflection from the line point along the ordinate. Two tones each oscillating at 500 Hz may differ in their amplitude, and this difference will be perceived as a difference in

FIGURE 3–2: *A sine wave resulting from the electronic transformation of a series of sound waves. At point A it has completed its 360° cycle of compression and rarefaction. At point B it has completed half its cycle (180°), or the compression phase. Point C indicates a phase in the wave.*

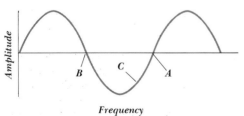

loudness. The tone with the largest deflection will sound louder (or have greater amplitude) than the one with the lesser deflection. *Amplitude* is the physical term for the intensity, or power, of the wave, while *loudness* is the psychological term. Different terms are needed because the physical and psychological aspects of the wave are different. As with variations in frequency and pitch, amplitude may vary without a corresponding perceptible difference in loudness; or if frequency is varied, we note a difference in loudness when there has been no alteration in amplitude.

Amplitude is described in terms of decibels. The decibel scale is the log of the ratio between two physical energies times a constant. One of the physical energies is the reference point. The usual reference point in acoustics is 0.0002 dyne per cm² (dynes per square centimeter). This reference point arises from the observation that it is very near to the human absolute threshold for a 1,000-Hz tone. The reference level of 0.0002 dyne per cm² is taken as *sound pressure level,* or SPL. The term *bel* is used to refer to 10 db. Figure 3–3 shows some common threshold measurements.

In summary, while sound may be described in terms of its physical characteristics, it may also be described in terms of the sensation perceived by the listener. At times, the physical characteristics of sound are important, but at other times, especially when apparatus is constructed for human use, the psychological specification is more useful. Sometimes the physical and psychological descriptions are equivalent. Table 3–B summarizes the physical and psychological terms used to describe sound.

The sounds which interest us in everyday life are rarely, if ever, pure. Indeed, a perfect

FIGURE 3–3: *The intensity levels (in decibels) of some familiar sounds. (From Chapanis, Garner, & Morgan, 1949, p. 194.)*

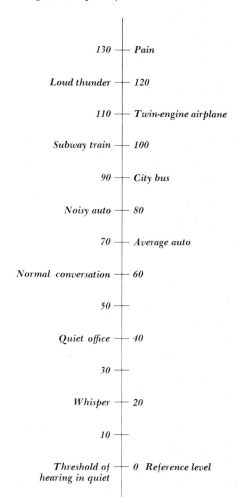

TABLE 3–B: *Physical and Psychological Equivalent Descriptions of Sound.*

Physical	Described in	Psychological	Described as
Frequency	Hz (cps)	Pitch	Higher, lower, or the same
Amplitude	db	Loudness	Louder, softer, or the same
Harmonic content	Contribution of waveforms	Quality, or timbre	Full, tinny, and so on

sine wave (that is, a tone without measurable distortion) is difficult to produce even with the most expensive equipment. Accordingly, our attention should be given to the characteristics of impure or distorted sine waves.

In general, there are two types of impure waves: The first type consists of a wave which may be broken down into sine waves; that is, it is composed of various sine waves in different phases, different frequencies, and different amplitudes. These different components may be analyzed electrically, and the ear itself is able to differentiate them to some degree. In this *complex wave,* the components must repeat themselves so that a pattern is formed. When they do not, that is, when the tone is composed of different tones varying in frequency, amplitude, and phase in a random order, the tone is referred to as *noise. White noise,* the second type of impure wave, contains so many different tones that the component sounds cannot be analyzed. It is commonly used in research when the experimenter wants to mask the presence of any other tone. For example, an experimenter who is training an animal to press a bar for food may want to make certain that the animal is being conditioned to the bar and not to the click the bar makes when it is depressed. If the experimenter cannot eliminate the click, he may use white noise to mask its presence.

Figure 3–4 shows the analysis of the complex tone produced when the note C is played on a piano. The lower part of the figure shows the contribution to the whole note by each of the components. The way a note is played will affect the composition, and the nature of the source of the sound, whether it be the human vocal cords or a musical instrument, will determine some of the components and, hence, affect the quality of the tone. With a violin, for example, the string vibrates in such a manner that it produces not only the sine wave corresponding to the frequency of the vibration but separate vibrations as well. If the tone is 256 Hz (the *fundamental* frequency), the string also vibrates at one-half the fundamental (the first *partial*), as well as at one-third,

FIGURE 3–4: *The waveform produced by a piano when C is played (128 Hz). The upper figure shows the waveform; the lower figure shows component tones and their relative contribution to the sound form. (From Fletcher, 1929, p. 92.)*

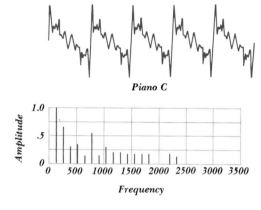

one-fourth, and so on. A piano and a violin may both be played to yield a fundamental tone of 256 Hz, but the fact that a piano sounds different from a violin is due to the different overtones and partials they produce. Figure 3–5 shows a spectrographic analysis of the waveforms produced by several different instruments.

The absolute thresholds for human beings range from approximately 50 Hz to 15,000 to 20,000 Hz. Moreover, the amplitude affects the absolute thresholds.

VISION

Few would challenge the statement that man receives more information about the external world through vision than through any other sense. Although deafness presents problems in adjustment, blindness is far more debilitating. As with audition, man must *learn* to use his sense of vision. Only slowly does he learn how to judge visual distance, how to tell which objects are closer than others, or how to determine which objects are moving and which are stationary. Indeed, it is possible that we rely too much on our sense of vision, for at times we prefer to believe what we see rather than what we reason logically to be true. Perceptual illusions are discussed more fully in Chapter 9. We shall discover, however, that it is possible that certain kinds of visual perception depend less on learning than has been believed.

Although most of the stimuli perceived by the eye are produced by light, light is not the only stimulus to which the eye responds. This fact may be demonstrated by pressing the eyeball: the resultant patches of color, in accordance with Bell's and Müller's comment (see Chapter 2), furnish evidence that a visual sensation occurs whether the method of stimulation is light or pressure. A person who stares at a bright light or a spot of color for a few seconds may close his eyes and remove most of the light, but he still perceives color, or *after images,* after his eyes are closed.

In spite of this, when we think of the stimulus which is perceived by the visual apparatus, we often think of light. Physicists are not in agreement on the properties of light. The difficulty is that it appears to behave in two quite different ways, and two theories have been developed to account for its two "personalities." One theory suggests that light, like sound, travels in waves (the *wave,* or *undulatory,* theory), while a second theory contends that light is essentially masses of particles (the *quantum theory*). Each theory is able to account for specific facts, and each has difficulty with other facts. When two or more theories are needed to account for observations, physics, like other fields, follows a pragmatic approach: the theory that predicts most accurately for a given set of circumstances is used. Although allowing two contradictory theories to exist side by side strikes some observers as unscientific and hypocritical, the most common defense is merely that one must use the best tool one has.

Light is measured in terms of wavelengths, generally in millimicrons. Waves of different forms of physical energy vary from infinitesimal length to well over 40 feet. However, only a small portion of the electromagnetic spec-

FIGURE 3-5: *Different instruments produce different waveforms: (A) A saxophone playing in the middle register, (B) a trumpet sounding F_4, (C) a clarinet playing G_3 on the left and D_4 on the right, and (D) an English horn sounding A at 200 Hz on the left and A at 440 Hz on the right. The height of the waveform indicates the amplitude, and the number of cycles per second represents the frequency. (Culver, 1951, pp. 204, 207, 211, and 220.)*

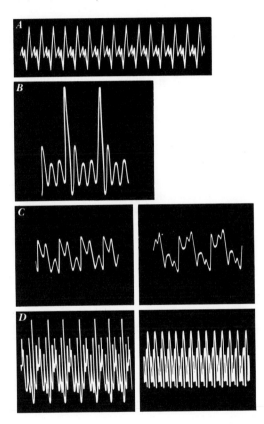

trum is visible to the human and to most animal eyes. (Only wavelengths within the 380- to 720-mμ range are perceived by human beings.) This small portion of the spectrum is delineated by ultraviolet wavelengths at the lower range and infrared wavelengths at the upper range. The thresholds for vision are, then, in the infrared–ultraviolet portion of the spectrum. Figure 3–6 shows the electromagnetic spectrum.

In visual perception, the wavelength determines the *hue* to the normal eye. But wavelengths may be identical and still be perceived differently, depending upon two other factors: the *homogeneity* of the light and the *illumination,* or amount of light (radiant energy). The three physical components of light (wavelength, homogeneity, and amount of radiant energy) have psychological components. The wavelength is basic to *hue;* the homogeneity—how many different wavelengths are included and how diverse they are—is known as *saturation,* or *purity,* of hue; and the amount of radiant energy is known as illumination, or *brilliance.*

The statement that white and black are not colors, while probably true technically, often leads to misunderstandings about what color is. When we speak of color, we speak of a combination of hue, saturation, and brightness. Any color may appear black, depending upon the saturation and illumination. In this sense, black has no specific wavelength associated with it, as do green, red, and other hues. A green coat in a dark room appears black because of the illumination. Things may be perceived as white because of strong illumination or, more commonly, the combination

of a number of different wavelengths so that no single one dominates. *White light* is a conglomeration of all the wavelengths to which the eye is sensitive. It is, thus, analogous to white noise. Psychologically, not all wavelengths need to be present for the perception of white. So long as any single hue is obscured, white is perceived. Thus, red, green, and blue may combine to yield the perception white.

The psychological descriptions of light may be varied independently of one another and independently of the physical descriptions. This variability was true of audition, as well. One may vary the illumination of a hue in such a way that an observer perceives the hue as changing when actually only the illumination changed. This phenomenon is similar to the changing of the perception of two sound frequencies by changing the intensity. The perception of "color" may present critical problems in industry. The operation of many safety devices is contingent upon instant recognition of color, and certainly in such areas as art, aesthetics, interior decorating, and the design of clothing and material, the physical and psychological attributes of vision are as important to the artist or designer as are the properties of sound to the musician.

Since the human eye can discriminate a large number of DLs in saturation, purity, and

TABLE 3–C: *Physical and Psychological Equivalents of Visual Stimuli.*

Physical	*Described in*	*Psychological*	*Described as*
Wavelength	mμ	Hue	Color—green, red, etc.
Homogeneity of wavelength	Identification of component wavelengths	Saturation	Purity of color—a pure green vs. a muddy red
Amount of radiant energy	Foot-candles (ft-c), (foot-lamberts (ft-L), candlepower (cp), etc., depending upon specific type of measurement	Illumination	Brightness

FIGURE 3-6: *The electromagnetic spectrum, showing the area visible to human beings. The energy waves are the same, although they differ in length. The human eye is sensitive to particular lengths, notably those between 380 and 720 mμ. The thresholds are inexact, for different persons have different reactions to the threshold between ultraviolet light and visible light and between infrared light and visible light. Moreover, for various reasons discussed in the text, people differ in their perception of color. (From Chapanis, Garner, & C. T. Morgan, 1949, p. 68.)*

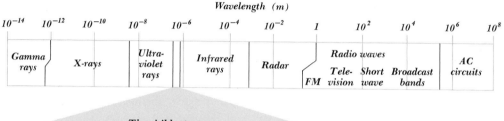

CUTANEOUS SENSIBILITY

Cutaneous sensibility may well be called the "forgotten sense," for although man is everywhere concerned with deficiencies in audition and vision, he seldom notices cutaneous reception, whether deficient or not. However, we use our cutaneous senses whenever we note that the day is warm or cool or that the humidity is high, when we perceive that sandpaper is rough and a cat's fur soft, and when we cut ourselves and receive the sensation of pain. Clearly, the cutaneous senses provide us with a great deal of information about the

illumination, man is able to discriminate just over one million "colors," each representing a different combination of the three components of light.

world. Unlike the stimuli for auditory and visual perception, however, the stimulus for cutaneous sensitivity generally comes in contact with the receptor (the skin). Cutaneous sensitivity is not a distance sense, and perhaps for that reason, we fail to realize how much vital information about our surroundings it provides.

In a very real way, the human skin is a large data-processing machine. For example, it continually transmits information to the brain about the relative temperatures of the external and internal environments, and, accordingly, the brain uses this information to make internal adjustments, such as changes in perspiration rate and in blood distribution. At the same time, our skin provides the brain with information about the texture and shape of objects, pain, and the amount of pressure that objects exert upon the skin.

The fact that the skin is replete with thousands of receptors which may be classified into four or five different types has led to the theory that each type of receptor is responsible for a particular kind of cutaneous sensation. In this theory, one type of receptor is responsible for receiving the sensation of pain and reporting it to the CNS; a second type of receptor is responsible for sending impulses of warmth; a third type, for impulses of cold; a fourth type, for sensations of pressure. This approach is reinforced by the finding that receptors of one type may be plentiful in one part of the body but rare in another section and that some parts of the body are more sensitive to warmth and some to cold and some to pain. In general, many investigators have found rough correlations between the type of receptor and the type of sensation which is recorded in particular parts of the body. However, there is sufficient negative evidence to suggest that cutaneous sensibility is more than only the stimulation of specific receptors.

The theory that each sensation has its own corresponding receptor has been popular for the last century, largely because no other theory handled the data and phenomena quite so well. On the other hand, the assumption of correspondence between the cutaneous receptor and the sensation has never quite accounted for *all* the phenomena that have been noted, and accordingly, several alternative theories have been propounded. Although these issues are discussed more thoroughly in Chapter 10, we should be aware that the basic process which underlies cutaneous sensitivity is not well understood and that the theory that separate receptors in the skin record separate sensations is useful but not necessarily a fact.

Classically, cutaneous sensations have been divided into *pain, pressure, cold,* and *warmth*. Introspectively, at least, these appear to be the major categories people use when attempting to describe their cutaneous experiences. The fact that a receptor may report changes in temperature, without reporting a corresponding change in pressure, has also led theorists to regard these categories of sensation as separate. They are not entirely separate, however.

For example, a light tap on the forearm with a pencil yields a sensation of touch; if the pencil is pressed more firmly, so that the skin is displaced from its usual position, a subject may report the sensation of pressure; if the pencil is pushed still farther so that the skin is grossly displaced, the subject is likely to report a sensation of pain. That is, one way in which pain is perceived is an intense increase in pressure.

On the other hand, there is surgical evidence that the four categories do represent reliably different processes. For example, when a local anesthetic is applied to a portion of the skin, sensitivity to the four categories is lessened at different rates. The sensation of temperature may disappear first, followed by loss of the sensation of pressure. Similarly, operations on the spinal cord have indicated that a person may lose his sense of pain (through severance of certain nerves in the spinal cord) and retain his other cutaneous senses. There are a number of cases in which one cutaneous sense was lost through disease, although the others remained intact. Finally there are cases of congenital absence of a certain cutaneous sense. For example, some individuals have been born with a condition which renders them insensitive to pain (*hypoalgesia*). Although we may think of such persons as fortunate, actually they are in constant danger and rarely survive childhood without the use of extreme precautions. A person who does not sense pain is untroubled when he places his hand in a flame, and only the odor of burning flesh may warn him that he is injured.

Pressure: Introspectively, there are many kinds of pressure. Some sensations of pressure may be described as dull, others as sharp; some are steady, and others appear to vibrate or tickle. In some ways, the category of "pressure" is used to designate sensations which do not easily fall into other categories.

The stimulus for pressure appears to be deformation of the skin or deformation of certain receptors within the skin. Apparently, bending the hairs which grow out of the skin gives a sensation of pressure, because, as we shall see more fully in Chapter 10, the appropriate receptor is nearby.

The absolute amount of pressure exerted upon the skin does not appear to be correlated with the amount of pressure felt; that is, the amount of pressure is not reported accurately by the receptors. Rather, the *change* in pressure as a function of both time and the area of contact appears to be the sensation which is reported. This fact is easily proved by demonstrations in which vastly different pressures are given to two contiguous areas. Placing a finger in mercury, or even in water, indicates that only at the place where the finger is under *uneven* pressure is the sensation of pressure reported. That is, the portion of the finger under water pressure does not report the sensation of pressure. Only where the pressure is unequal—at the water-air interface —does one report the sensation. Thus the sensation of pressure appears to be a result of the *gradient of deformation*. Whenever the gradient is sufficiently large, or the difference between the pressures on two areas sufficiently great, the sensation of pressure is reported.

Pain: Although pain may appear to be a separate category because it can be eliminated with surgical techniques, it is not a simple sensation. We have noted already that pain may be perceived when pressure becomes intense, which explains why some theorists have considered pain as nothing more than overstimulation of the receptor. Although this view has the advantage of agreeing with common sense (everyone "knows" that too much pressure, too much heat, or too much cold produces pain of one kind or another), it does not have the advantage of agreeing with anatomical observation. Since present knowledge makes it unproductive to argue whether pain is or is not a separate sense, we might just as well consider some of the phenomena associated with pain stimulation in the expectation that specific knowledge may be more useful than general theory, at least so far as pain sensitivity is concerned.

A large number of stimuli may elicit the sensation of pain, but we do not know precisely what factor is responsible for the sensation. Among the more common stimuli associated with pain sensation are puncture or cutting of the skin, intense heat, electric current, certain chemicals (such as alcohol or Merthiolate applied to an open wound), or mechanical stimulation, such as intense pressure. Perhaps we have become so accustomed to finding a single, major stimulus for each of the various senses (light for vision, sound waves for audition, change in pressure for pressure sensation) that we feel uncomfortable when we find a supposed sense that does not have a simple stimulus. The theory that the appropriate stimulus for pain is tissue damage does not stand up when it is noted that electric stimulation causes no apparent tissue damage and yet is clearly painful. Nor does the *amount* of tissue damage appear to bear any relation to the amount of pain perceived. Nor is "sharp" cutaneous pain the same as the "dull" pain which is felt internally, as when we have a stomachache. Although internal sensations of pain will be discussed more fully in Chapter 10, it is important to note at this point that cutaneous pain is different in quality from other pain sensations.

Some investigators have attempted to isolate the various sensations of cutaneous pain, in the hope that categorization would lead to a better understanding of the processes underlying pain perception. Weddell (1941a; 1947) assumes two different qualities of pain—pricking and burning—and has found some anatomical correlations between the type of pain sensation and the receptors involved. According to Weddell, the sensation of "pricking" pain is short in duration and usually brings about an immediate withdrawal response by the subject. Further, the subject cannot define the stimulus; that is, without further sensory information he cannot specify whether the stimulus was mechanical, chemical, or electric. The "burning" pain is longer in duration and characteristically has a "deeper" sensation.

As has been pointed out, no single factor

has been suggested which accounts for all the stimuli—chemical, electric, and mechanical—which are capable of eliciting a pain response.

Temperature: Although it is convenient to think that the perception of temperature involves a single sense which reports the temperature in much the same way as a thermometer, it may be incorrect to do so. The evidence is by no means clear, but there is reason to believe that there are two relatively separate senses, one concerned with the perception and reporting of warmth (temperatures above 31°C) and a second concerned with the perception and reporting of cold (temperatures below 31°C). One theory holds that our skin reports not absolute temperatures but changes in temperature, just as it reports relative changes in pressure.

On the other hand, Hensel and Zotterman (1951c) suggest that absolute temperature of the receptor determines thermal sensitivity. The procedure employed by Hensel and Zotterman involves measuring the temperature of the receptor *in situ;* the results indicate that the number of impulses per second emitted by the receptor corresponds generally to the perception of absolute temperature, not relative change. The theory is growing, at least in number of supporters (Kenshalo & Nafe, 1962), that the receptor is capable of responding to absolute temperature and that a thermal gradient, similar to the pressure gradient believed to be necessary for the sensation of pressure, is not necessary.

In addition to the theory outlined in the preceding paragraph, a second theory has competed actively. Although this theory assumes that the thermal gradient is important, it suggests that the stimulus for thermal sensitivity is found in the constriction and dilation of the blood vessels. This approach is called the *vascular theory.* A major problem with the theory is that if warmth and cold are perceived as a result of the receptors in the arterial walls, the theory should be able to identify the nature of the receptor system which precedes or activates such vasodilation or vasoconstriction.

The basic argument for two separate thermal sensory systems rests on evidence that the skin appears to have "hot" and "cold" spots and that, anatomically, some receptors appear to yield a sensation of cold and others a sensation of warmth, no matter what the temperature of the stimulus. The hot and cold spots and areas of the human skin have been plotted by a number of investigators, and no doubt by a large number of students, in physiological and psychological laboratories. Table 3–D shows some data on the number of warm and cold spots found in various parts of the body. It should be noted in interpreting this figure that the number of "spots" does not necessarily reflect the number of appropriate receptors in the areas designated. Factors such as the sensitivity of the skin and the area stimulated also affect the perception of temperature.

A demonstration which does not necessarily reject the view that receptors are able to react to absolute temperature comes from phenomenological evidence. The "three bowl" experiment of Ernst Heinrich Weber (1795–1878; 1846) is often used to demonstrate the argument. One bowl contains water of 20°C, a second contains water of 30°C, and a third, water at 40°C. The subject places one hand in the coldest water and the other hand in the warmest water. After a few moments he places both hands in the 30°C water. Usually, the hand that was previously in the cold water is perceived as hot, while the hand that was in the hot water is perceived as cold, even though both hands are immersed in water of the same temperature. Although this demonstration is striking, it probably indicates the effect of *adaptation* to temperature, rather than the perception of temperature itself.

Clearly, identification of the appropriate stimulus for thermal sensitivity is dependent upon the type of theory chosen, or perhaps, more correctly, the type of theory determines what is to be called the stimulus for thermal sensitivity. In summary, although the adequate

TABLE 3-D: *A Comparison of Cold- and Warm-spot Concentrations in Various Parts of the Body.* (From Geldard, 1953, p. 212, after Rein, 1925, and Strughold and Porz, 1931.)

Part of body	Cold "spots" per cm²	Warm "spots" per cm²
Forehead	8.0	0.6
Nose	8.0 (side)	1.0
	13.0 (tip)	
Upper lip	19.0	
Chin	9.0	
Chest	9.0	0.3
Upper arm, volar side	5.7	0.3
Upper arm, dorsal side	5.0	0.2
Bend of elbow	6.5	0.7
Forearm, volar	6.0	0.4
Forearm, dorsal side	7.5	0.3
Back of hand	7.0	0.5
Palm	4.0	0.5
Fingers	2.0–9.0	1.6–2.0
Thigh	5.0	0.4
Lower leg	4.0–6.0	
Sole of foot	3.0	

stimulus for thermal sensitivity may be any of a number of stimuli, it is not clear how the stimuli transmit the sensations of warmth and cold or if there is a single thermal sense or two.

OLFACTION

Olfaction is the process of perceiving stimuli with the olfactory receptors usually by means of odors transported by air through the nose cavity. Olfaction is intimately involved with gustation (the process of perceiving stimuli in solution with water or saliva through receptors in the tongue or mouth). Most foods are both smelled and tasted. When we speak of the taste of an object, we are usually commenting on its smell as well. The importance of smell to taste may be demonstrated by asking a subject to identify a variety of spices by taste alone, that is, without being allowed to smell them. Although the taste of a substance, as

well as its texture and composition, gives clues to its identity, the number of errors in identification is surprisingly high and sometimes amusing. Some subjects will call cinnamon "sugar," some will call it "salt," and some, "nutmeg." Similarly, a thin slice of potato and a thin slice of apple, which are left at room temperature for a few hours so the smell will dissipate, commonly taste similar. Since smell, temperature, texture, and vision all contribute to taste, one can imagine the difficulties faced by research workers attempting to understand the mechanisms that govern these senses.

Although the human sense of smell is not nearly so accurate, either in terms of absolute thresholds or difference thresholds, as that of many animals, it is still a useful sense. For example, it may be used as a safety device. Natural gas, which is piped into homes and factories, is odorless to human beings, but an added chemical with an odor that can be detected serves to warn the user of any dangerous leakage.

Animals, especially domestic pets, such as cats and dogs, and members of the Rodentia, use their sense of smell far more than do human beings and other primates. When we take a dog for a walk, we learn about our surroundings largely by vision and audition, although our sense of smell may give us some information, such as whether it is fall (the smell of burning leaves) or spring (the smell of flowers) or whether we are passing a bakery or a stockyard. The dog, on the other hand, shows little evidence of using the cues to the environment provided by sight and sound. He pokes his nose into cracks and corners, sniffs, and appears to enjoy the mass of odors which are perceivable by him. Animals appear to use their sense of smell in order to find their way home, to greet their master, to distinguish friends of the family from strangers, to find food, or to find a mate, and accordingly the sense of smell is to many animals what the senses of vision and audition are to man.

Olfaction is limited to the perception of substances in a gaseous state. Neither solids nor liquids are perceived by the human olfactory apparatus. However, substances commonly found in a liquid state, such as perfume, may be smelled if vaporization occurs. If perfume were somehow retained in a liquid state with no evaporation, no odor would be perceived. Other substances, such as sulfur, generally found in nature in a solid state, change to a gaseous state with changes in temperature. In its solid state at room temperature sulfur is odorless, but the application of heat results in a definite odor, as any student of chemistry is well aware.

The physical or chemical properties which permit human beings to differentiate odorous stimuli are unknown. This is not to say that clues are lacking but rather to point out that although one theory may adequately explain the relation between the stimulus and the perception for a majority of odors, no theory is able to explain the relationship for all odors. For example, we have evidence that there is a relationship between odor and its vapor pressure—the more odorous a liquid, the higher its vapor pressure as a gas. However, the overpowering odor of musk, which has a low vapor pressure, and the slight odor of water, which has a high vapor pressure, argue against the inclusiveness of this theory.

As we noted in our discussion of the stimuli for cutaneous perception, when a physical stimulus is not well defined and its relation to perception is not well understood, there is a strong tendency to resort to psychological dimensions as descriptions of physical stimuli. The establishment of psychological dimensions of perception is useful, but the psychological definitions lose a great deal of their usefulness when they cannot be compared with the physical dimensions. It is as if, in audition, we knew how to measure loudness, pitch, and timbre without knowing anything about frequency, amplitude, and phase. On the other hand, pragmatically, half a definition is more useful than no definition at all. Accordingly, there have been a variety of attempts to define the stimuli for olfaction by defining the psychological qualities characteristic of the perception of the olfactory receptors.

Before Carolus Linnaeus (1707–1778) designed his system for the classification of plants, botany faced a confusion in nomenclature similar to that which presently engulfs the study of olfaction. Linnaeus' contribution lay in suggesting a nomenclature for plants which was acceptable to most scientists throughout the world. The problem in the study of olfaction is that when one person reports that an odor smells "burnt" or "fruity" or "foul," there is no assurance that another person will use the same adjective. There is no agreed-upon way of describing the perception. The problem arises because the process of olfaction is not separated clearly from the reports of other sensory systems and because we do not know how to compare the perception of olfactory stimuli with the physical properties of the stimuli. Linnaeus himself suggested one of the first systems of odor classification when he developed a system of olfactory descriptions as part of his system of plant classification. He distinguished seven categories of odors. Hendrik Zwaardemaker (1857–1940) reconstructed this system and arrived at nine olfactory categories: ethereal, aromatic, fragrant, ambrosiac, alliaceous, empyreumatic, hircine, foul, and nauseous. As Geldard (1953, p. 283) comments, "There are some obvious difficulties with this grouping of odors. Among the thousands of specific smells that have to be accommodated by the nine categories there are doubtless many hundreds that could not reasonably be pressed into so simple a scheme. Moreover, it is quite possible to find odors in two different categories of Zwaardemaker's listing that have more resemblance to each other than they do to their fellows in the same odor class."

Hans K. F. Henning (1916) developed a system of olfactory descriptions which employed six "primary" odors placed in such a relation to one another that a prism resulted. Figure 3–7 shows a common representation of the "smell prism." Supposedly, all odors could be located in a physical space on the prism. The position that an odor occupied would depend upon its similarity to the primary odors delineated by the corners of the prism. The approach bears a superficial resemblance to the color wheel and to the use of primary colors in describing hue.

The technique of identifying odors by using other odors as reference points has been continued by E. C. Crocker and L. F. Henderson, who have developed a system of odor classification employing four basic odors: fragrant, acid, burn, and caprylic (goaty). An odor is rated on a scale of 0 to 8 for each of the dimensions represented by the basic odors. Accordingly, 7122 represents vanillin; it is rated as highly fragrant (7) but rated low in the other categories. In the same way, 7213 represents cinnamic acid, which is rated equal in fragrance to vanillin but slightly different in the other categories. The standard Crocker-Henderson kit[2] consists of 32 vials of odors,

2 The Crocker-Henderson Odor Classification Set, Cargille Scientific, Inc., 33 Village Park Road, Cedar Grove, N.J.

FIGURE 3–7: *The smell prism suggested by Henning. The six primary odors are set at the corners of the prism. The surfaces contain odors which resemble the coordinates. Thyme would, theoretically, resemble both spicy and flowery, and it would occupy a position on the continuum anchored by those two primaries. (From Geldard, 1953, p. 283.)*

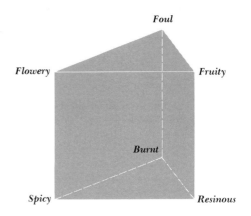

representing examples of each degree of each dimension (four dimensions times eight degrees). A substance to be rated is compared with the standard examples to determine which standard it is most similar to. Although using standard solutions for comparative purposes is no doubt more reliable than depending on the judgment of a subject to evaluate a substance, the Crocker-Henderson system is still at the mercy of all the variability to which the human organism admits.

As has been pointed out, there is no standard method for evaluating or naming olfactory qualities. Perhaps this lack accounts for the ambiguities encountered in the study of olfaction at the present time.

GUSTATION

Each of the sensory systems contains mysteries which plague the investigator, but gustation and olfaction have retained their secrets particularly well. One reason that we know so little about gustation is that, with the exception of persons involved in the production and marketing of food, the phenomena associated with taste are of little concern to human beings. Although taste is of importance to tea-tasters, winesippers, and gourmets, this sense does not supply the adult with anywhere nearly the quality and quantity of information about the external world provided by vision, audition, and the cutaneous senses.

No doubt the lack of research interest in how our gustatory receptors operate has contributed to this lack of knowledge, but it is also true that gustation is a most complicated sensory system. We have noted before (Chapter 2) that, unlike any other receptors, three different cranial nerves serve to report the sensation of taste to the brain.

All receptors change with age. The shape of the eye changes, causing nearsightedness or farsightedness among other difficulties; sometimes the small bones of the ear fuse, creating a loss in hearing acuity, and changes in the gustatory receptors alter our food preference as well as our appetites. A nearsighted person may resort to glasses, and a person with a hearing loss may wear a hearing aid, but the person whose sense of taste has become deficient does nothing about it, even though the changes which have taken place in the receptors are quite sufficient to alter his selection of food. A text in physiological psychology (Wenger, F. N. Jones, & M. H. Jones, 1956, p. 134) reports the following example:

One advertising campaign for a new beverage was directed at young people. It failed miserably, and the company was wise enough to attempt to discover why instead of simply hiring a new advertising agency. The facts of the matter were that the beverage had a slightly bitter taste, which young people, on the average, do not like but middle-aged people find pleasant. It was then a simple matter to direct the advertising to the middle-aged group.

The stimuli which activate the gustatory receptors are somewhat better understood than those which activate olfactory receptors. But gustation and olfaction present the investigator with similar problems in identifying the stimuli and understanding how the receptor is able to transmit information about them.

The stimulus for gustation may be liquid, solid, or gaseous, provided that it is capable of going into solution upon contact with water or saliva. The way the solution acts upon the receptor to yield perceptions of taste is not well understood. That is, there is no consistent method for predicting the perception which will result from a given substance. The perception of the stimulus depends on many factors, such as the chemical composition of the stimulus, its concentration, and its temperature.

Although theorists concerned with olfaction have predicted a varied number of primary odors, theorists concerned with gustation have been surprisingly consistent in claiming only four primary tastes—*sweet, sour, salt,* and *bitter*—based on both psychological and physiological information. The human being appears to be quite able to discriminate taste on the basis of one of the four qualities. Physiologically, different areas of the tongue are differentially sensitive to the four qualities. Although we shall discuss this type of threshold data more thoroughly in Chapter 11, it is important to note at this point that the detection of the appropriate stimulus for gustation depends at least partially on the area of the tongue which is stimulated. There is ample evidence that in human beings the location of maximal and minimal sensitivity may vary as a function of age. There is also ample evidence that animal forms have vastly different requirements for a stimulus for taste. The postulation of the four qualities of taste may be applicable only to man or other primates.

The receptors for gustation may be stimulated electrically; that is, electric current applied to the receptors in the tongue yields sensations of taste. The quality of the sensation brought about by electric stimulation appears to vary as a function of both the type of current (alternating or direct current) and the frequency and amplitude of the current. For example, low-frequency ac current provides the sensation of sour, but if the frequency is increased to 1,000 Hz, a bitter perception is reported. Similarly, with the use of dc current perceptions vary, depending upon whether the anode or cathode is applied to the tongue.

There is some evidence that chemicals carried in the blood may provide an adequate stimulus both for taste and for smell. Subjects given an injection of an arseniclike compound report olfactory and gustatory perception shortly after injection (Bednár & Langfelder, 1930). Although the phenomenon of taste and smell by blood chemistry appears to be very real, its significance for understanding these two sensory systems has been limited.

KINESTHESIS AND THE VESTIBULAR SENSE

Kinesthesis, derived from the Greek root for *movement,* is concerned with the way in which we sense our own bodily movement. It is a broad term which refers to the receptors in the muscles, tendons, and joints that transmit information regarding the position of the various parts of the body; that is, these receptors transmit information about whether the fist is taut or loose, the arm outstretched or relaxed, the stomach muscles tight or slack, and the foot arched or flat. Clearly, the absence of kinesthetic receptors or interference with the transmission of the reports of kinesthetic sensation would seriously curtail the ability of an individual to "know where he is going and where he is." Indirectly, kinesthesis also provides information regarding position; that is, one cue to whether our arm is flexed or our head bent comes from the perception of the stretching and relaxing of the muscles and joints involved. We "know what it feels like" to have our head bent, because we have learned through experience which kinesthetic sensations appear when our head is in that position.

The bodies of higher animals contain a re-

ceptive system which reports sensations of position. The kitten is well known for its ability to land upright, and this *righting reflex,* as it is commonly called, is the result of the sensation of position interacting with various motor connections. The sense which reports position of the head is known as the *vestibular sense* in man. The primary receptor for determining position is located in the *nonauditory labyrinth,* a part of the ear located near the cochlea, the organ of hearing.

By dividing the senses into two types, *exteroceptive* and *interoceptive,* Sherrington (1906) pointed out the distinction between stimuli which emanate from the external world (exteroceptors, external to our body) and those which emanate from the internal world (interoceptors, from within our own bodies). Such senses as vision, audition, olfaction, gustation, and to a large degree the cutaneous senses are concerned with interpreting stimuli external to the body; as such, their perception can be validated insofar as more than one person can perceive the stimulus. If I look up at the sky and ask, "Is that a plane or a bird?" I am attempting to validate my perception by the experience of another person. Other senses are concerned only with "private stimuli" perceived within the body solely by the individual. External verification of interoceptive phenomena is difficult, if not impossible. While we may all agree that there are such sensations as headaches, stomachaches, and back pains, we cannot perceive the sensations of another person, and we have no convenient way to describe the sensations. I may maintain that my headache is more painful than your headache, but we cannot establish which is actually more painful. Although there appears to be a gross correspondence between various descriptions of the sensations reported by the kinesthetic and the vestibular senses, there is no guarantee that the sensations of two people are similar either in quality or quantity.

Sherrington used the term *proprioceptive* to refer to senses which were neither fully exteroceptive nor fully interoceptive. The vestibular sense is one example of a proprioceptive sense, for while it is concerned with reporting sensations of position, it is also acted upon by external forces—such as a blow to the head and the placing of the head under water. Some forms of kinesthesis would also be proprioceptive, since movement of the arms, legs, head, and muscles and joints of other parts of the body results in sensations of what is stimulated internally as well as what is stimulated externally.

The sufficient stimulus for the kinesthetic receptors appears to be any movement, change in position, or alteration of muscle tonus which is perceivable by the receptors within the muscles, joints and tendons.

The vestibular system reports position through the nonauditory labyrinth. Thus, the appropriate stimulus for vestibular sensation is the position of the head. Since the nonauditory labyrinth is both functionally and anatomically associated with the ear and the eye, the perception of head movement usually has some bearing on either hearing or vision. This complication makes precise determinations of the nature of the stimulus difficult and at the same time it means that phenomena associated with the nonauditory labyrinth often concern other senses as well.

AFTERWORD

In this chapter, we have been concerned with the importance of physiological and sensory psychology, and with the stimuli which are appropriate to the various senses. We have noted that an organism is able to perceive, and thus to process, only a portion of the available stimuli in the external and internal world. Accordingly, the first step in understanding behavior which comes about as a result of the perception of stimuli is to ascertain how the stimuli are perceived. The next chapter is concerned with measuring the stimuli which are perceived.

CHAPTER FOUR

PSYCHOPHYSICS

INTRODUCTION

Although we have emphasized that psychology is concerned with the relationship between stimuli and responses, until this point we have been purposely cavalier about defining either term. A *stimulus* is some occurrence in the external environment which is sensed by the organism, and the *response* is a measurable change in the organism. When a pilot is alerted that he has reached the appropriate height to lower his landing gear, he does so. It is a simple matter to describe this behavior in terms of the stimulus (the alerting) and the response (lowering the landing gear). Similarly, when a student learns to say "casa" when the instructor says "house," we may describe this situation in terms of the stimulus-response connection present.

We define a response only if we can identify some stimulus which accompanied it, and, conversely, we identify a stimulus only if a response has accompanied it.

When we attempt to answer a question such as "Why did fifteen-year-old Johnnie steal a car?" we often violate the concept of stimulus-response by confusing it with cause and effect. An appropriate answer to the question might be that the identification of a single stimulus-response relationship would be impossible. On the other hand, we might be tempted to give a simple answer and to say that the response, car theft, was the result of some "stimulus"— homelife, economic status, and so on—which, upon examination, does not turn out to be a stimulus at all. This violation of the concept of stimulus-response by artificially equating stimulus with cause is a source of confusion in contemporary psychology.

In Chapter 3, we considered one side of psychology: the measurement of stimuli. Here, we shall begin our study of psychophysics in psychology. Psychophysics is concerned with establishing the relationship between physical stimuli and our psychological responses to such stimuli. Since behavior is measured by responses, an understanding of how our perceptions occur and how they are related to our environment—the physical stimuli—is fundamental to an understanding of behavior.

ROLE OF PSYCHOPHYSICS IN PSYCHOLOGY

Experimental psychology may be said to have been born when investigators began to direct their attention to evaluating the stimuli which affect the senses. Historically, the problems associated with identifying the type and properties of stimuli which organisms perceive and to which they react have occupied a large part of psychological thought, but in recent years the growth of military and industrial psychology, which are concerned with identification and detection of stimuli (instrument panels, radarscopes, and so on), has awakened renewed interest in measurement. Although the so-called psychophysical methods evolved during the early stages of experimental psychology (ca. 1860) to measure the effects of stimuli upon an organism are still in use today, the last twenty years have witnessed the invention of new methods. To some degree early psychophysicists saw psychophysics as a method for finding a true threshold, or series of thresholds, within the organism. Generally, when they noted that sensory thresholds varied from time to time, they blamed the variations on their apparatus and technique and not upon the organism. Studies in recent years, however, have emphasized the role that learned behavior plays in perception. Indeed, certain procedures used in making psychophysical determinations may alter the reported sensation in a predictable way. For example, consider a man who devotes his time to watching a radarscope for the blips of unknown aircraft. If blips appear rarely or never, his threshold for detecting a blip when it does appear is likely to be quite different from that of a man who watches a scope on which blips come and go at irregular but frequent intervals. The psychophysical behavior of the two men in regard to the probability of detecting a sensory stimulus when it *is* present is more the result of

the manner in which the stimuli are presented than of any innate difference in the perceptual abilities of the men.

Human beings make psychophysical judgments constantly. While showering we adjust the hot and cold water in an effort to keep a constant temperature. In doing so, we are responding in such a way as to assure no noticeable difference in the temperature of the water. We are attempting to keep the change in water temperature smaller than the difference threshold. When cake is passed for dessert or drinks are poured, we try to make certain that all the portions are the same size. These are psychophysical problems, for they are concerned with judging whether two stimuli are different or equivalent.

The methods of psychophysics have an important application to subhuman behavior. Comparative anatomy and physiology indicate that the human being represents modifications, and in some respects enhancements, of lower organisms. Accordingly, discovery of how the sensory systems of other animals operate is useful in pointing the direction which human development has taken. The human eye, for example, is very similar to the eye of other primates, while the eye of the crab *Limulus* operates on an entirely different neurological principle. On the other hand, the eye of some birds contains a structure not even found in the human eye (the *pecten*). The ear of the human being is similar to the ear of other primates but almost totally different from the hearing organ of a snake, turtle, or bird.

How are we able to apply psychophysical methods to the measurement of perceptual thresholds in animal subjects? How can we estimate thresholds such as the upper range of hearing for a rat, guinea pig, macaque, or pigeon? In the absence of verbal behavior from these animals such as "I hear it" or "I don't hear anything," it would appear impossible. Fortunately, such is not the case. By combining the techniques of psychophysical measurements and operant training or classical conditioning (Chapters 13 and 14) we can determine the various thresholds of animal forms. Rather than responding verbally to the presence, absence, or change of a stimulus, an animal can be trained to jump a barrier when he hears a tone. If the tone is presented and the animal jumps, food or some other preferred object is available. If the animal jumps the barrier when there is no tone, he receives no food or perhaps is given a mild punishment as a "reminder" of his error. Eventually the animal learns to jump (respond) only when a tone is perceived and to remain behind the barrier when a tone is not perceived. By slowly varying the frequency or amplitude of the tone over many trials, an experimenter is able to apply the same techniques of psychophysical measurement which he would use with human beings. The difference is that the animal jumps or responds in some behavioral way, whereas the human being speaks. But speaking, after all, is a behavioral response much as is jumping: it involves the movement of appropriate muscles to a specific cue.

The behavioral fact that a seventeen-year-old human male is able to perceive a tone of 20,000 Hz at 10 db and that a collie dog is able to respond to the same tone does not mean that both are perceiving the identical physical stimulation as equal psychologically. On the contrary, all that one may say is that both are able to respond to the same stimulation. As Ehrenfreund (1948) pointed out in regard to earlier experiments by Lashley (1942), although rats are able to discriminate between a square and a triangle, they do not respond to the entire figure but only to the bottom portion of it. Thus, although behavioral evidence indicates that both rats and human beings are able to discriminate squares from triangles, it is an error to assume that they necessarily distinguish the same characteristics of the stimulus.

ORIGINS OF PSYCHOPHYSICS

By the middle of the nineteenth century, German science and German philosophy had produced the proper milieu for investigating the relationship between the external world and the organism. It is one of those ironies of the history of science that the man who made the major contribution to work on this relationship and who derived the classic psychophysical methods was concerned with aesthetics and had no interest in the young science of experimental psychology. Gustav Theodor Fechner (1801–1887) had many interests and wrote about all of them (physics, which was his original vocation, philosophy, and religion); between 1850 and 1860 he was particularly involved in the mind-body problem.

He was concerned, as have been so many thinkers both before and after his time, with the relationship between the physiological aspects of the organism and its spirit, or soul. With his background in physics, it is not surprising that Fechner should have perceived that the solution to the problem lay in relating "physical energy" to "mental energy"; that is, if you want to measure the mind, one way would be to measure how it changes in respect to changes in physical energy. Does an increase in physical energy (such as change in illumination or saturation of colors) correspond with a "mental" increase? If I am in a darkened room which contains one lighted candle and if a second candle is added, do I now perceive the room as "twice" as bright? From the physical aspect, the room has twice as many candles, but from the mental aspect it is unlikely that I should perceive the room as twice as bright. Moreover, if, instead of one candle, the room contained 1,000 candles and if one more candle were added, it is unlikely that I should even notice the difference. Yet the physical change is exactly the same as the change in the first example—only one candle has been added. Fechner suspected that it was possible to work out arithmetic or geometric relationships between the amount of physical energy and the amount of mental energy.

Fechner was not the first to concern himself with this relationship. The idea that perception was not equivalent to the physical stimulus but that it followed its own laws of measurement appears to have lain just below threshold for many writers for some time. Ernst Heinrich Weber (1795–1878) had expressed the same point in 1846, but he had not developed it. Fechner worked on the problems of what came to be known as psychophysics for ten years, and in 1860, after publishing two short papers on the topic he published the classic *Elemente der Psychophysik,* which contained, among other items, the three psychophysical methods which Fechner had refined for the assessment of thresholds. These three methods have various names, but for purposes of simplicity, rather than out of reverence for origin or purity of nomenclature, we shall call them the *method of limits,* the *method of average error,* and the *method of constant stimuli.* Each of these methods provides statistical estimates of sensory thresholds. Fechner developed them so that he could evaluate the change in mental energy (or perception) which accompanied a change in physical energy (the stimulus). Fechner was concerned primarily with psychophysics as a means of measuring the perceptions of the mind, but the psychophysical methods have been used most commonly in the determination of sensory thresholds.

After the publication of *Elemente,* Fechner's interests vacillated between aesthetics and psychophysics. In 1882 he published a text in which he considered the criticisms of psychophysics as well as what E. G. Boring (1950, p. 283) calls the "unexpected demands of experimental psychology" upon the science of psychophysics. This rarely read but important treatise was his last, for Fechner died five years later. He had lived to see the onset of experimental psychology in the German universities (Wilhelm Wundt [1832–1920] had founded a separate laboratory for the study of experimental psychology at Leipzig in 1879) and had, unknowingly and perhaps disinterestedly, begun the separation of psychology from philosophy and physics by providing convincing evidence that the real world of physical energy does not necessarily correspond to the world of mental energy but that mental energy was as lawful as physical energy.

The proposed relationship between the physical and the mental stimuli is shown schematically in Figure 4–1. The relationship is represented by two continua, the physical continuum, labeled *S,* and the psychological continuum, labeled *R.* Note first that the *R* continuum is nonexistent at either extreme. You may recall from Chapter 3 that sound stimuli may be placed on a continuum but a tone may be of too low a frequency to be perceived or it may be too high. This is indicated in the figure by RL (the stimulus threshold) and by TL (the upper threshold, or terminal threshold). At these points the subject reports sensation of the physical stimulus 50 percent of the time when they occur.

Differential thresholds are indicated by the three pairs of vertical lines which connect the physical and psychological continua. The DL is concerned with establishing the point at which two stimuli appear to be different. The fact that psychophysical methods have been used most commonly for the determination of sensory thresholds may have obscured the fact that psychophysics is concerned with determining the perceived equality of stimuli as well as the perceived difference. When the acuity of our eyes is being examined, the examiner sometimes presents two lines which he slowly moves together and asks us to state when the lines appear to merge into one. On other occasions, the examiner may show a single line from which another is separated slowly, and we are asked to state when the single line becomes two lines. This latter determination is similar to the concept of the DL, for the subject's task is to state when two stimuli are different. The former example, in which the subject is asked to judge equality, is of equal importance.

If I give a subject a 30-gram weight to hold in one hand, using it as a standard, and I give him a series of assorted *comparison* weights (such as 28, 29, 30, 31, and 32 grams) in the other hand and I ask in each case which is the heavier weight, the results can be plotted as shown in Figure 4–2. The percentage of presentations of the two stimuli on which the sub-

FIGURE 4–1: *Schematic representation of the relation between the stimulus continuum S and the response continuum R. The text describes the DL relationships. In this diagram the RL and TL are represented on the R continuum for ease of understanding. (From Guilford, 1954, p. 21.)*

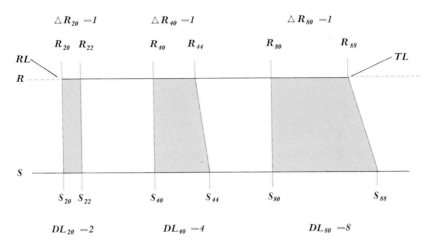

ject judged the comparison weight to be heavier is plotted along the ordinate, and the physical weight of the *stimulus* weights are plotted along the abscissa. When the subject is asked to discriminate between a 28- and a 30-gram weight (the latter being the standard), he correctly judges the 30-gram weight to be the heavier 90 percent of the time. Or, conversely, he judges the 28-gram weight to be heavier 10 percent of the time. As the weights approach the weight of the standard, the decision becomes more difficult. This is represented in the figure by the fact that weights of 29 and 31 grams are judged heavier approximately 50 percent of the time. If we ask the question "What weight is judged to be equal to the standard half the time?" we draw a line from the 50 percent mark on the ordinate until we reach our data point. By interpolation, the answer to our question is 29.4. This point is called the *point of subjective equality* (PSE). We shall have much more to say about the development of the concept of the PSE as we continue our historical review.

Returning to Figure 4.1, consider the stimulus marked S_{20}. The DL for this point will be that point on the continuum which will be judged greater than S_{20} half the time. In the figure, this point on the continuum is S_{22}. The DL, then, equals 2 units for S_{20} which must be increased by 2 units before the difference between S_{20} and S_{22} is noted half the time. This DL for S_{20} is represented as ΔR_{20} on the R continuum, and it is equal to 1 *response* unit. The figure also calculates the DL for two greater values of the stimulus, S_{40} and S_{80}. In the former, the DL equals 4 units along the *stimulus* dimension and in the latter, 8. Nevertheless, ΔR_{40} and ΔR_{80} still equal 1 unit along the *response* continuum. Thus, at any point along the R continuum, ΔRs are equal, although the DL changes along the physical continuum as a function of the stimulus.

The point is that although the DL may vary along the stimulus dimension (as it does in Figure 4–1), the DL is a constant along the R dimension. This is true by definition, since in terms of the response dimension a DL equals

FIGURE 4-2: *The abscissa shows the comparative stimulus weights; the ordinate shows the percentage of times the comparative stimulus is judged heavier. The standard is a 30-gram weight. By drawing a horizontal line from the 50 percent mark on the ordinate, we define the PSE, by interpolation, at 29.4 grams.*

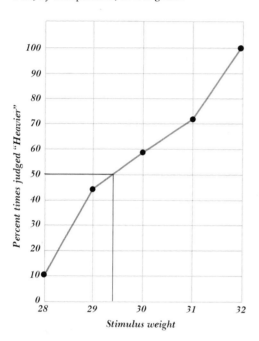

the amount of change necessary for a difference to be perceived. The R units, then, are all equal, even though the number of S units which they represent depends upon the location of the particular stimulus along the S continuum. Most commonly, the formula is given in the form

$$\frac{\Delta S}{S} = K$$

where

ΔS = **increment in the physical continuum corresponding to an increase in the R continuum**

S = **point on physical continuum**

K = **a constant which is a function of the observer**

Let us now plot this function, using the data from Figure 4-1. If we plot $\Delta S/S$ on the ordinate and plot the stimulus along the abscissa, we have the result shown in Figure 4-3. The result is a straight line.

The constant K is the *Weber ratio*, and one of its obvious applications is the assessment of the sensitivity of organisms to various types of stimulation. For example, Weber (and others) has determined the ratio for weight lifting to be around 1:30; that is, given a 100-gram weight, one would have to increase the weight by one-thirtieth of its original weight for the difference to be noted 50 percent of the time. Thus, a second weight of 103.33 grams would be equally likely to be judged heavier than the original weight, but a weight of 101 grams would not be so judged. These ratios are generally particular to the observer, and individual differences among persons are noted. A Weber ratio may be calculated for each dimension (intensity, frequency, etc.) of each sensory modality. The smaller the ratio, the more sensitive the modality.

As various critics have pointed out, Weber's ratio is not a true psychophysical law: since it is concerned with the relation between ΔS and S, it is concerned solely with the physical continuum. The R continuum is used merely to furnish an anchor of equal units, but the measurements made are made only on the S continuum. Indeed, if the units on the R continuum are not, in fact, constant, the law says nothing about psychological sensation at all.

Weber's ratio has some weaknesses. The most critical is that most measurements of the relationship between ΔS and S do not show the function to be linear, as Weber's ratio suggests. We shall note in our study of the individual senses (See Chapters 6 to 11) that although Weber's ratio is often an accurate description of large parts of the $\Delta S/S$ function, it rarely describes the whole function.

Now, it may be that there is no law which can express the relationship between the stimulus and response continua for all sensory modalities. The search for this perfect psychophysical law may be ill-advised, for it may be that no such universal law exists. Nevertheless, students of psychophysics have continued to investigate the relationship between sensory and mental events with the result that although we may be little closer to finding *the* psychophysical law, we know a great deal about the relationship between sensory and mental events. Accordingly, we turn now to discuss the contribution which Fechner made.

Fechner referred to Weber's ratio as the "fundamental formula" and succinctly described its usefulness by saying: "The fundamental formula does not presuppose the measurement of sensation, nor does it establish any; it simply expresses the relation holding between small relative stimulus increments and sensation increments" (Fechner, 1860, trans. Langfeld in Rand, 1912). However, starting from the fundamental formula, Fechner suggested that the relationship between the increments in the formula is logarithmic. Just as sensation begins with some value above zero (the threshold), so logarithms begin with a finite number. Thus, the relationship between sensation and stimulus is a relationship between logarithm and number. With this logic —that sensation depends both upon the threshold and the stimulus value—the sensation, then, is dependent upon the logarithm of the magnitude or intensity of the stimulus. This reasoning leads to Fechner's law:

$$R = K \log S$$

where

R = response (the sensation)
K = a constant
S = stimulus dimensions measured in distance from the threshold

The plot of Fechner's formula may be seen in Figure 4–4, in which *equal* units of R are plotted against *ratio* units of S. This is the important characteristic of Fechner's formulation: as R increases in *equal* steps, S increases in *ratio* steps.

Since Fechner suggests that we plot equal *proportions* (the S continuum) against equal units (the R dimension), the function becomes

FIGURE 4–3: *A diagram showing Weber's ratio for the data in Figure 4–1.*

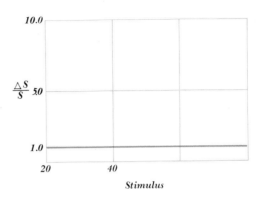

FIGURE 4–4: *According to Fechner's law, the ordinate shows the response continuum (note that the units are equal), while the abscissa shows the stimulus dimension (note that the units are unequal but proportional). (Guilford, 1954.)*

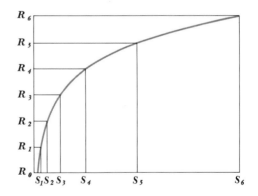

logarithmic. Fechner's proposal makes two assumptions: The first assumption is that the DL is a function of all DLs which have come before it. Thus determining any given DL requires knowledge of how many DLs have preceded it and the location of the RL. Second, the proposal assumes that all DLs are subjectively equal. We shall see later that these assumptions have been attacked; however, they form the basis of the psychophysical methods which Fechner proposed.

In the hundred years since Fechner's time,

other formulations have been suggested as the psychophysical law. However, to appreciate classic psychophysics as defined and described by Fechner and to understand why changes have become necessary in psychophysical formulations, we must consider the basic methods Fechner proposed. Although both Weber's ratio and Fechner's law have been used to describe many kinds of data, the techniques which were used to validate them—the psychophysical methods—have been retained and put into use not only in the study of thresholds and sensory psychology but in many other fields of experimental psychology, as well. Contemporary psychology has found vastly different methods for studying the relationship between the stimulus and the response, but it is to the credit of Fechner that he contributed the original, and hence classic, methods for measuring this relationship.

THE CLASSIC METHODS

If someone were to ask you to invent methods for determining thresholds, you would probably derive the same methods that Fechner evolved in his work. For, after some consideration, you would probably see that there are several options involved in deciding how to measure a sensory threshold:

1. **Either the experimenter presents the stimulus (limits, constant stimuli), or the subject manipulates the stimulus (average error).**
2. **The subject is asked to determine whether the standard and the stimulus are *equal* (average error) or whether they are *different* (limits, constant stimuli).**
3. **In successive trials, the stimulus is presented in such a way that it approaches and recedes from the standard (limits, average error), or it is presented in a random fashion (constant stimuli).**

Given these three options, the operations of psychophysical methods become clearer. The three methods we shall describe are most commonly used and represent the methods from

which others have been derived to handle different types of data. An understanding of the operations and basic postulations of the classic methods and a knowledge of the assumptions underlying the mathematical calculations of the data aid one in assessing the assumptions and accuracy of derived methods.

Method of Limits: Originally called the "method of minimal change," the *method of limits* operates in a fashion described by its names. The subject compares one stimulus (the *comparison stimulus*) with a second stimulus (the standard stimulus) through a series of trials in which the magnitude of the comparison stimulus is changed. Trials in which the comparison stimulus starts above the standard are *descending* trials; the reverse are *ascending*. The technique is most commonly used in the assessment of stimulus and terminal thresholds, and it is for this reason that the contemporary name for the method is *limits*. It may be used in determining the DL, although in general other methods are more efficient for that purpose.

Assume that we wish to test the terminal frequency threshold of a subject for a tone at a specified intensity. Equipment would be an audiooscillator, such as that described in Table 1–A. When coupled with an amplifier and speaker, the audiooscillator enables the experimenter to present tones of known frequencies and to hold intensity constant. For purity, we would probably ask the subject to use earphones, so that unwanted sounds from the surroundings would be masked. For research purposes, tones are often presented in rooms especially prepared with acoustic forms to prevent reverberation of the sound.

The determinations are shown in Table 4–A. In the sample the experimenter has presented 14 trials. In each trial, the frequency has either increased or decreased in units of 10 Hz. The initial range in the example (22,000 to 21,820 Hz) may be determined in several ways, but the most common technique for isolating the range of frequencies to be presented is by exploratory trials in which the

TABLE 4–A: *Sample Determination of Terminal Threshold for Sound Frequency by the Method of Limits.*

Hz	D	A	D	A	D	A	D	A	D	A	D	A	D	A	D
22,000					N										
21,990	N		N		N						N		N		N
21,980	N		N		N						N		N		N
21,970	N		N		N		N				N		N		N
21,960	N		N		N		N		N		N		N		N
21,950	N		N		N		N		N		N		N		N
21,940	N	N	N		N		N		N		N		N		N
21,930	N	Y	N	N	N		N	N	N		N		N		N
21,920	N	Y	Y	Y	N	N	N	Y	N	N	N	N	N		N
21,910	Y	Y		Y	Y	Y	N	Y	Y	Y	Y	Y	Y	N	Y
21,900		Y		Y		Y	Y	Y		Y		Y		Y	
21,890		Y		Y		Y		Y		Y		Y		Y	
21,880		Y		Y		Y		Y		Y		Y		Y	
21,870		Y		Y		Y		Y		Y		Y		Y	
21,860		Y		Y		Y		Y		Y		Y		Y	
21,850				Y		Y		Y		Y		Y		Y	
21,840								Y						Y	
21,830														Y	
21,820														Y	
X̄ =	21,915	21,935	21,925	21,925	21,915	21,915	21,905	21,925	21,915	21,915	21,915	21,915	21,915	21,905	21,915

$$*\overline{X}_A = 21{,}919.28$$
$$\overline{X}_D = 21{,}915.00$$

$$\frac{\overline{X}_A + \overline{X}_D}{2} = TL = 21{,}917.14$$

where

$\overline{X}$ = average
A = ascending trial
D = descending trial
Y = yes
N = no

subject reports whether or not he hears the frequency. A few such trials are usually sufficient.

On descending trials, the experimenter begins with a stimulus believed to be sufficiently above threshold that the subject will respond "No" when asked if he hears the tone. On ascending trials, the experimenter begins with a stimulus thought to be sufficiently below threshold that the subject will respond "Yes." On succeeding trials, the origin of the series will vary so that the subject is unable to predict the proximity of the stimulus to the standard from the number of presentations within the trial.

The data shown in Table 4–A are of a nature most fortunate for the experimenter, for the subject's discriminations are excellent. In the real world of data collection, subjects are rarely so consistent. Various techniques are available for calculating thresholds when the subject responses are equivocal. It is for this reason that the determination of the threshold is considered a statistical approximation.

The TL value may be determined in one of three ways: (1) The individual values of the series threshold (T) may be added and divided by the number of determinations. An equal number of ascending and descending trials must be given, for the threshold will differ depending on whether the trial was ascending or descending. (2) The experimenter may compute the T for one ascending and one descending trial. The average of these pairs of ascending and descending trials is calculated. (3) All ascending trials may be averaged, as are all descending trials. The TL is the average of all ascending and all descending averages. This figure will equal the average found under both the preceding methods, but this technique will indicate differences in the threshold which are a function of whether an ascending or a descending trial was used. As mentioned above, the T for ascending trials is usually not identical to the T for descending trials. This fact is usually explained by reference to a *persistence effect*. These persistence effects include *errors of habituation* or *errors of anticipation*. In the former (perhaps

correctly) a subject has made the same response a number of times, and he continues with the response, even when it is erroneous. For example, a person is given a stack of red and black cards and is asked to state the color of each card as he turns it over. He may find a string of red cards and become so habituated to saying "Red" that when a black card appears, he says "Red" again. Errors of anticipation represent the opposite effect—the subject expects or anticipates a change and therefore changes his response before it is applicable.

The method of limits may also be used for the determination of DLs. Usually, the experimenter presents the standard and then the comparative stimulus. The subject is required to state whether the comparative stimulus has "more" or "less" of the appropriate attribute than the standard. For some determinations, a judgment of "equal to" is permitted. The allowance of the "equal to" response (which, of course, may be used in the determination of absolute thresholds [ALs] also) requires slightly different calculations, for the mutual exclusiveness of two choices is lost.

Table 4–B shows a sample calculation of the difference in DL by the method of limits. The experimenter is interested in determining the DL for a tone frequency of 1,000 Hz at 20 db. The experimenter starts the tone at a point clearly greater or clearly less than the standard (depending on whether it is a descending or ascending trial) and extends the series until the subject has reported all three responses— "more," "equal to," and "less." It is important to appropriate calculation that this be done, or critical data will be lost. This procedure yields the *interval of uncertainty* (IU), which appears in measurements of the DL and which refers to the area where neither "yes" nor "no," neither "plus" nor "minus," and neither "more" nor "less" judgments are in the majority. If one uses only two responses, as in Table 4–A, there is no IU, since either one response or the other must be in the majority, or they will both be equal. When three responses are allowed, however, an area appears where no single judgment occurs a majority

*TABLE 4-B: *Sample Determination of Differential Threshold for Sound Frequency by the Method of Limits.*

Comparative stimulus	A	D	A	D	A	D	A	D
1,010	..	M	..	..	..	..	..	..
1,008	..	M	..	..	..	..	..	..
1,006	M	M	..	M	M	..	M	..
1,004	M	M	M	M	M	M	M	M
1,002	=	M	=	M	=	M	M	M
St = 1,000	=	=	=	M	=	=	=	M
998	L	=	L	=	=	L	=	=
996	L	L	L	L	L	L	=	L
994	L	L	..	L	L	L	L	L
992	..	L	..	..	L	..	L	..
990	..	..	..	..	L	..	..	..
T+	1,003	1,001	1,003	999	1,003	1,001	1,001	999
T−	999	997	999	997	997	999	995	997

*Standard (St) = 1,000 Hz; A = ascending trial; D = descending trial; M = more; L = less; "equals" sign = response of "equal to" or "not certain"; T+ = change between M and equal; T− = change between L and equal.

$\bar{X}T+ = 1,001.25$
$\bar{X}T- = 997.50$
$\quad$ IU $= (\bar{X}T+) - (\bar{X}T-) = 3.75$
$\quad$ DL $= 0.5$ (IU) $= 1.875$
$\quad$ PSE $= \dfrac{(\bar{X}T+) + (\bar{X}T-)}{2} = 999.375$
$\quad$ CE $=$ PSE $-$ St $= -0.625$

where

$\quad$ T $=$ series threshold
$\quad \bar{X}$T $=$ average threshold
$\quad$ IU $=$ interval of uncertainty
$\quad$ DL $=$ difference threshold
PSE $=$ point of subjective equality
$\quad$ CE $=$ constant error
$\quad$ St $=$ standard

of the time, and this area is the IU. The IU (see Table 4–B) is calculated by subtracting the average of the T+ values from the average of the T− values.

When the IU is determined, calculation of the DL is simple. The DL is merely one-half the IU, since by definition the DL represents the point at which discrimination is successful half the time. It should be noted that this is merely a method of approximating the DL.

At times, an experimenter is more interested in determining the PSE than the DL. The PSE may be found by adding the mean for the T+ and for the T− values and dividing by 2. This yields an average of the place where T+ and T− change to equality. Presumably, perfect discrimination would yield a PSE equal to the standard. The difference between the PSE and the standard is considered the *constant error* (CE). Since the PSE may extend on either side of the standard, the CE may be either positive or negative. If the CE is positive, it may be said that the subject overestimates the quality of the comparative stimulus relative to the standard; if negative, the subject underestimates.

The method of limits, then, may be used to measure both ALs and DLs. When the DL is calculated, subsidiary calculations, such as PSE, IU, and CE provide additional information about the relationship between the standard stimulus and the comparative stimulus. The method may be adapted for other problems, but the calculations reported in Tables 4–A and 4–B are the standard techniques for expressing the data.

Method of Average Error: This method has also been called the *method of adjustment* and the *method of equation.* As the names suggest, a major characteristic of the method is that the subject decides when the comparative stimulus is equal to the standard stimulus. It may be recalled that with the method of limits the subject's task is to determine when the stimuli were different. The method of average error is concerned primarily with matching two stimuli and calculating the "error" resulting from the match.

In the method of average error the subject is usually allowed to adjust the comparative stimulus until he considers it equal to the standard. Using the method of average error, an experimenter might want to determine the extent of the illusion for the Müller-Lyer illusion shown in Figure 4–5. In this well-known illusion, the line indicated by *B* appears longer than the line indicated by *A*, although the

FIGURE 4–5: *The Müller-Lyer illusion. The horizontal lines marked A and B are of equivalent length, although human beings and apparently other mammalian subjects perceive B to be of greater length. The slant and size of the arrows contribute to the illusion. The illusion is used in the text to indicate how the method of average error may be applied to measuring the extent of the illusion.*

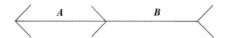

lines are of the same length. An apparatus may be constructed which allows the subject to adjust the *A* and *B* segments until he perceives the lines to be equal. A scale on the reverse side of the apparatus is marked from the point at which the lines are equal in physical length, so that the experimenter may determine how close the subject comes to matching the lines. Either of two sets of directions can be given to the subject:

1. **"I am going to set this apparatus so that one line is obviously longer than the other. I want you to push the longer segment of the apparatus in slowly until you believe the two lines to be equal in length. When you believe they are equal, remove your hand from the apparatus. You may not *pull* the segment at any time, you must always push it, so be certain you do not overshoot the place where you think the lines to be equal."**

2. **"I am going to push this segment of the apparatus slowly in. I want you to tell me when you believe the two lines are equal."**

Under either set of directions, the experimenter sets the comparative-stimulus segment so that it is pushed in on some trials (descending trial) and on other trials pushed out (ascending trial). Assume that the length of the standard line is 25 centimeters. Table 4–C shows the data from four descending and four ascending determinations.

From the table, it may be noted that the investigator gave four descending trials (i.e., the original setting is such that the comparative segment is obviously longer than the standard) and four ascending (i.e., the original setting is such that the comparative segment is obviously shorter than the standard). As when ascending and descending trials are used in the method of limits, different results occur depending on the direction from which the subject's manipulation approaches the standard.

In the example, the average descending trials and average ascending trials have been calculated separately, although since an equal number of trials was given with each tech-

TABLE 4-C: Finding the Point of Subjective Equality of the Müller-Lyer Illusion by the Method of Average Error.

Trial	Descending-trial, cm	Ascending-trial, cm
1	26.5	....
2	....	26.0
3	....	25.5
4	25.5	....
5	....	25.0
6	27.0	....
7	25.5	....
8	....	27.0

*Standard = 25 cm.

$$\overline{X}_D = \frac{104.5}{4} = 26.125$$

$$\overline{X}_A = \frac{103.5}{4} = 25.875$$

$$PSE = \frac{\overline{X}_D + \overline{X}_A}{2} = \frac{26.125 + 25.875}{2} = 26.00$$

Since CE = PSE − St
CE = 26 − 25 = 1.0

where

$\overline{X}_D$ = average of descending trials
$\overline{X}_A$ = average of ascending trials
PSE = point of subjective equality
CE = constant error

nique, the average for all eight trials would yield the same result. The resulting average is the PSE. It should be noted that the method of average error does not lead directly to a measurement of the DL but to a measurement of the PSE—the point where the stimuli are considered equal. The CE may be calculated as in the method of limits by subtracting the standard from the PSE.

The method of average error is convenient, because it tends to maintain the interest of the subject since he responds actively to the stimuli and it allows rapid and uncomplicated calculation of the PSE. There are disadvantages to the method, however, which may dis-

qualify it for particular problems. First, it does not allow direct estimation of the DL. An indirect estimate may be made from assumptions about the PSE, but this technique is probably not so reliable as the method of limits. Second, the method is not useful in cases where it is impossible or impractical for the subject to manipulate the comparative stimulus.

The method is theoretically applicable to the determination of absolute thresholds but is unwieldy. Consider the example used for the method of limits (Table 4–A), in which the experimenter wished to ascertain the TL for a sound frequency at a given amplitude. In order to make a similar determination with the method of average error, the standard would be varied from trial to trial. For example, if the subject's TL was thought to be around 21,000 Hz, the first trial might use a standard of 21,100 Hz, and the subject would attempt to adjust the comparative stimulus to the standard. Since the standard is believed to be above threshold and therefore not perceptible to the subject, he would have considerable difficulty in matching the two stimuli, and the "average error" would be great. However, if the standard was below threshold—clearly within the perceptual range of the subject—his adjustment would be finer, and the error would be less. Accordingly, through a series of determinations it would be possible to approximate the RL or the TL by using the average error associated with each standard as a threshold approximation.

Frequency Methods: The Method of Constant Stimuli:
This technique has also been called the *method of right and wrong cases* and the *method of constant-stimulus differences.* As the names imply, a major characteristic of the method is the computation of the threshold by determination of the frequency with which the subject was "right" or "wrong" in his judgments. In this method, comparative stimuli are presented repeatedly in random order in comparison with the standard. When it is used to measure the RL or TL, the general procedure consists of warning the subject that

the stimulus may or may not appear and recording whether he perceives the presence of the stimulus. For example, assume that an investigator is interested in discovering the TL for a sound frequency at a given intensity. Through pilot work, he assumes that the TL is around 20,000 Hz. His apparatus is designed in such a way that it can emit frequencies of 19,940 to 20,080 Hz in discrete steps of 10 Hz.

The experimenter who is concerned with determining the TL in this case conducts the study as shown in Table 4–D. The various stimuli are each presented four times in random order, and the subject is asked whether he perceives them or not. The frequency of "yes" answers is then computed. (Since "yes" and "no" are mutually exclusive, it is equally reasonable to compute the number of "no" responses.) A computation of the frequency of responses for the data reported in Table 4–D is shown in Table 4–E.

The frequency data may be plotted as in Figure 4–6, which shows the percentage of "yes" responses along the ordinate and the value of the physical stimulus along the abscissa. Since the threshold, by definition, is that physical unit perceived half the time, a line drawn from the 50 percent mark on the ordinate will bisect the threshold value. In this example, the TL lies at 19,990 Hz. Further presentations of the stimulus in and around the area isolated by this preliminary calculation would indicate the veracity of the interpolation. There are various techniques for interpolating data from experiments which use the method of constant stimuli in order to assess absolute threshold (AL), and each technique makes different assumptions about the nature of the data and about the manner in which the data were collected (Woodworth & Schlosberg, 1954; Underwood, 1949, 1966; and, especially, Guilford, 1954). Most of these interpolations and transformations are based on the assumption that since the judgments are varied randomly around the threshold, the proportion of "yes" responses should be normally distributed.

Although the method of constant stimuli is quite suitable for the measurement of ALs, it is more commonly used in the measurement of DLs. When applied to DL determinations, the technique requires the presentation of a standard stimulus, against which the comparative stimuli are judged. The statistical manipulations employed when the DL is measured are the same as those employed when the AL is measured; the frequency or proportion of one class of response is plotted, and the threshold is considered to be the stimulus which is perceived as different from the standard half the time. Table 4–F shows data arising from the

*TABLE 4–D: *Using the Method of Constant Stimuli to Determine the Stimulus Threshold for a TL.*

Comparative stimulus, Hz	Judgment	Comparative stimulus, Hz	Judgment
19,950	Y	19,990	Y
20,000	Y	19,970	N
19,970	Y	20,050	N
20,040	N	19,980	Y
20,050	N	20,040	N
19,980	Y	19,950	Y
19,950	Y	19,960	Y
19,960	Y	20,000	N
20,010	N	20,040	N
20,020	N	20,010	N
20,000	N	19,990	N
20,040	N	20,000	N
20,030	N	20,010	N
19,990	Y	19,950	Y
20,050	N	19,960	Y
19,960	Y	20,020	N
20,010	N	20,030	N
19,990	N	20,050	N
20,030	N	20,030	N
19,970	Y	20,020	N
19,980	Y	19,980	N
20,020	N	19,970	Y

*N = no; Y = yes.

determination of the DL by the method of constant stimuli for weight. The apparatus consists of 21 cylinders which are weighted by shot, so that the cylinders range between 90 and 110 grams in units of 1 gram. Although the cylinders have different weights, each appears the same outwardly. The 100-gram weight is the standard. On each trial, the experimenter places two of the weights before the subject. One of the weights is always the standard weight of 100 grams. The experimenter asks the subject to lift each weight simultaneously, one in each hand, and to tell him which is heavier or lighter. Ten trials are given with each comparative weight: on five trials the comparative stimulus is on the left, and on the other five it is on the right. The placements are random, however, insofar as the experimenter follows a preset "random" pattern.

The data from Table 4–F are plotted in Figure 4–7, in which the ordinate shows the percentage of "heavier" responses and the abscissa shows the weight of the comparative stimuli. When the comparative stimulus is 90 grams, the subject never claims that it is heavier than the standard of 100 grams, but as the weight of the comparative stimulus approaches the weight of the standard, the subject is less certain. At least, he is more variable in deciding whether the comparative stimulus is heavier or lighter than the standard. The PSE may be determined by the same technique that was used when the method of constant stimuli was applied to ALs; i.e., the 50 percent point is taken as the PSE. In our example, PSE = 98. The DL is the difference between 25 and 75 percent $(102.5 - 92.5 = 10)$. The CE is St − PSE, or $100 - 98 = 2$.

It should be clear that in classic psychophysics upon each presentation of the stimulus, four possible conditions may prevail: two of these are determined by the experimenter and constitute the independent variable of the experimenter and of the determination, while two are determined by the subject and constitute the dependent variable. Figure 4–8 indicates the contingencies. Note that the ex-

TABLE 4–E: *Frequency of "Yes" Responses.* Data are based on those reported in Table 4–D.

Stimulus	No. of "yes" responses	Proportion, percent
19,950	4	100
19,960	4	100
19,970	3	75
19,980	3	75
19,990	2	50
20,000	1	25
20,010	0	0
20,020	0	0
20,030	0	0
20,040	0	0
20,050	0	0

TABLE 4–F: *Determining the DL for Weight by Using the Method of Constant Stimuli.*

Comparative-stimulus weight, grams	No. heavier responses	Percent of total
90	0	0
91	0	0
92	1	10
93	3	30
94	2	20
95	3	30
96	4	40
97	4	40
98	5	50
99	6	60
100 = St	6	60
101	6	60
102	6	60
103	8	80
104	7	70
105	9	90
106	10	100
107	9	90
108	10	100
109	10	100
110	10	100

FIGURE 4-6: *A plot of the frequency data shown in Tables 4-D and 4-E. The proportion of "yes" responses is presented along the ordinate, while the stimulus frequencies are reported along the abscissa.*

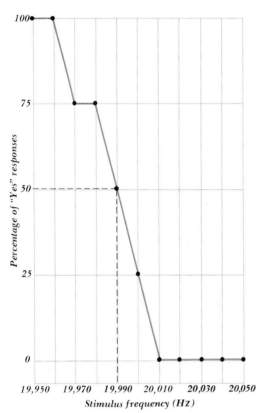

order to be certain that the subject does not come to believe that the stimulus is always present. In recent years, investigators have noted that the responses which occur when the stimulus is not presented form an interesting class of behavioral responses, for as we shall see later in this chapter, the occurrence of such responses may be manipulated experimentally.

Some Additional Sources of Variation: Perhaps one of the reasons that psychophysical methods have remained an active area of research interest, in addition to their usefulness in determining thresholds, is that small changes in procedure often produce vastly different results. We noted that with the method of limits the threshold would vary depending on whether ascending or descending trials were used. Such a variation also occurs with the method of average error and calls for balancing the comparative and standard stimuli. This counterbalancing provides opportunity for an error in the opposite direction, but it does not eliminate the variation. Research on the source of error when the comparative stimulus ascends or descends or when the standard stimulus is placed on the left or on the right has provided experimenters with information, not only about the accuracy of the psychophysical methods, but also about the behavior of the individual making the determinations.

The example of the methods of constant stimuli and of limits which have been shown in this chapter have used simultaneous presentation of the comparative stimulus and the standard. However, the results of the threshold determination may differ markedly if the stimuli are presented successively, rather than simultaneously. This effect is known as the *time error*. A simple case of time error occurs when the standard is presented followed by the comparative stimulus. When the comparative is judged greater than the standard, it is called a *negative* time error. The reverse is known as a *positive* time error. If the order of presentation of the stimuli is random, the time errors balance out.

perimenter may present the stimulus or he may *not* present it. Similarly, the subject may perceive the stimulus when it is present, or he may not see it. When the stimulus does not appear, the subject may perceive it as present, or he may perceive it as absent.

In traditional psychophysics, the "absent" category is not used. The experimenter presents the stimulus and records whether the subject did or did not perceive it. As a check experimenters often include a few trials on which the stimulus really does not appear, in

A source of error which was accounted for in the example was the *space error*. This occurs when the subject prefers the stimulus on one side over the stimulus on the other side. Most mammals show a preference for one side or one hand. A child learning to hold a pencil or a rat running a T maze usually shows a preference for either the right or the left alternative. This space error would appear in assessing the DL for weight with the method of constant stimuli if the standard were always on the left of the comparative stimulus or if it were always on the right. The space error has also been noted in determining the PSE for the Müller-Lyer illusion with the method of average error. This source of error could be balanced by turning the Müller-Lyer illusion apparatus upside down on half the trials in random order.

A corollary of the space error is the *error of movement,* which refers to the difference in judgment that a subject may make depending upon whether he is pushing the apparatus in or pulling it out. This error is counterbalanced in the method of average error by using an equal number of trials on which the comparative stimulus both approaches and recedes from the standard.

Experimenters sometimes talk about *practice effects* and *fatigue effects* in accounting for the results of studies in which the subject has been required to make several determina-

FIGURE 4-7: *A plot of the DL for weight with the method of constant stimuli. The ordinate shows the percentage of responses in which the subject reported the comparative stimulus as heavier than the standard, and the abscissa shows the weights of the stimuli in grams.*

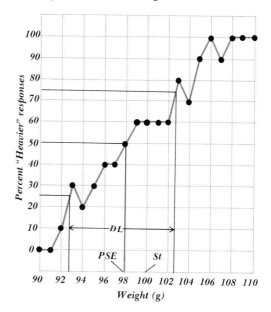

tions. A practice effect is an increase in efficiency or performance with continued trials. Although some subjects performing under cer-

FIGURE 4-8: *Possible contingencies in the determination of thresholds.*

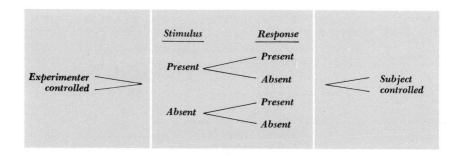

tain experimental conditions perform better as the number of trials increases, the explanation of why this should occur is difficult. A fatigue effect is a decrement in efficiency or performance with increasing trials; this is explained by the assumption that the subject tires and becomes less accurate.

Although the process of *assimilation* is not an error in the usual sense, it is nevertheless of concern in certain types of psychophysical experiments. The term refers to a situation in which a third stimulus is interpolated between the standard and the comparative stimuli. For example, consider an experiment in which the investigator is determining the DL for weight by the method of constant stimuli. Assume that the subject is required to pick up the standard stimulus, then to pick up an irrelevant stimulus (in the sense that the subject is not being asked to compare it with anything), and then to pick up the specified comparative stimulus. Under these conditions, the subject tends to "assimilate" the interpolated stimulus by using it as the standard, rather than the original standard stimulus. The interpolation of a stimulus (or a response) between the comparative and standard stimuli has some interesting effects on human and animal learning, as will be noted in Chapter 13. Some experimenters have varied the nature of the stimuli in studies of assimilation with curious results. Lauenstein (1932), for example, worked with auditory stimuli and noted that if the interpolated stimulus was loud in tone, the subject tended to consider the standard louder than it had been. Although assimilation may have the same causes as time errors, the two are not operationally similar, since assimilation involves the interpolation of a third stimulus (which must, of course, occur in time) whereas the time error does not.

RELIABILITY AND VALIDITY

The concepts of *reliability* and *validity* are concerned with evaluating the usefulness of data. Reliability is concerned with whether the

same results would appear if the experiment were repeated. In psychophysics, the reliability of a measurement can be expressed in two ways: (1) *intertest,* or *intersession, reliability*—whether an experimenter continues to find the same thresholds on repeated testings as he did on the first test—or (2) *intratest reliability* —whether the subject responds in the same way to identical stimuli during a single trial. In psychological testing, the concept of reliability is extremely important. If a subject scores high on a test on one day and low the next day, and if the performance of many subjects varies with repeated administrations, the test has low reliability, and the scores are useless for predictive purposes. Reliability, then, is one of the problems confronted in preparing a test. Some of the techniques used in evaluating and constructing tests are discussed in Chapter 18.

Blackwell (1953, p. 1) has expressed the relationship between psychophysics and reliability succinctly: "Reliability within a session is directly proportional to the goodness of fit of threshold measurements to a theoretical curve. Reliability from session to session is inversely proportional to the extent of the variance obtained with repetitions of measurements with a given procedure."

Validity is concerned with whether the data measure what they were expected to measure. For example, if a test that purports to be an IQ test does not really distinguish students on the basis of their intelligence, the test is not valid; that is, it is not really a measure of intelligence. Similarly, if the method of average error does not really evaluate the PSE, it is not a valid test for the PSE. A test may be highly reliable without being valid. An "IQ test," for example, may continually separate students in the same way but not on the basis of intelligence. Such a test would be very dangerous if interpreted by someone not acquainted with how to measure validity and reliability, for the person might take the high reliability as evidence that the test was "good" or successful, when actually the test was not valid. If a test or measure is reliable, it is likely that the absence of validity indicates that the wrong measure of validity is being used. After all, in evaluating validity, one should always ask, valid according to what standard? An IQ test may be valid when the measure of validity is success in school as evaluated by grades but become invalid when the measure of validity is earning power ten years after school. The evaluation of validity always requires some *external criterion* (for example, amount earned, grades, or on-the-job performance), and the criterion used obviously affects the assessment of validity. Although it is possible that a test or measure could be valid without being reliable, lack of reliability would make the test useless for continual use. In psychophysics, the most meaningful external criterion by which validity may be judged is the threshold itself. Besides electrical recording of nerve functioning and similar indirect evidence, there are few other sources for the external criterion.

THE DEVELOPMENT OF PSYCHOPHYSICS

Psychophysics is not a sterile area of research. As Fechner prophesied, "The tower of Babel was never finished because the workers could not reach an understanding of how they should build it; my psychophysical edifice will stand because the workers will never agree on how to tear it down" (Fechner, 1877, trans. Stevens, 1957, p. 153). Although the contribution of psychophysics to an understanding of the "mind" and its dimensions has not been so great as Fechner and other pioneer psychophysicists predicted, psychophysics has contributed a wealth of information regarding the sensory systems. The contribution of psychophysics during the past one hundred years has been in the practical application of measuring sensory thresholds.

It would be incorrect, however, to believe that psychophysics is merely a discipline of applied or sensory psychology or that the idea that psychophysics may measure the "mental energy" has been dispelled. On the contrary,

the work of twentieth-century investigators indicates clearly that both the measurement of thresholds and the search for the universal psychophysical law remain open questions. Although some of this work is discussed in Chapter 5, it should be clear that attempts to measure the mind or to show that techniques can be derived which uncover psychophysical relationships not only continue but account for a reasonable percentage of ongoing psychological research.

Of the many refinements in technique and measurement that have been made on the classic Fechner type of psychophysics, we may note four landmarks along the way which have greatly advanced psychophysical methodology and which will undoubtedly contribute to the final task of finding the psychophysical function, should that ever be accomplished. Two of these landmarks are (1) the *Fullerton-Cattell principle* and (2) *Thurstone's law of comparative judgment.* Both of these are concerned with the way in which psychophysical measurements are distributed. Both provide refined statistical techniques for measurement. The other two landmarks are (3) the contributions of Helson and his colleagues on interpreting psychophysical measurement in terms of *adaptation-level (AL)*[1] *theory* and (4) the development of psychophysical scales by Stevens and his associates, which has suggested a different form for the psychophysical law. Let us consider these wayposts along the unending path of psychophysics.

Fullerton-Cattell Principle: This says that *"equally often noticed differences are equal, unless always or never noticed"* (Fullerton & Cattell, 1892). The principle assumes and originally gave some data as evidence that the dispersions are unequal if the stimuli are of such a nature that subjects either never perceive a difference or always perceive a difference. In short, the principle is intended to apply only if the relationships between the

---

1 Since AL is also the abbreviation for *absolute threshold*, the term *adaptation level* will always be spelled out in this text.

stimuli are not consistently perceived in the same way. Fechner assumed his law to be related to Weber's ratio, but, as both Thurstone (1927) and Guilford (1954) have argued, this is true only if the dispersions along the stimulus continuum are equal.

In their investigations of dispersion in psychophysics, Fullerton and Cattell asked subjects to reproduce a stimulus a number of times; they then computed the probable error of the reproductions. If both Weber's ratio and the Fullerton-Cattell principle are true, the dispersion should be constant; i.e., the ratio of the probable error to the mean should be constant. They noted, however, that the mean error of the reproductions increased in direct proportion to the square root of the stimulus. Hence, the Fullerton-Cattell principle suggests that

$$\Delta S = C \ \sqrt{S}$$

where C = constant, the probable or mean error.

Guilford (1932), noting that most empirical data were somewhere between Weber's ratio and the Fullerton-Cattell principle, suggested what has come to be called the *nth power law*. Guilford pointed out that since the Fullerton-Cattell principle could be written $\Delta S = CS^{.5}$ and since in Weber's ratio the power is 1.0, data which fit between the two functions could be evaluated by allowing the power to vary as a function of the data. Accordingly, the Guilford function may be written $\Delta S = kS^n$ where n is derived from the data, and is probably, but not necessarily, between 0.5 (Fullerton-Cattell) and 1.0 (Weber).

Thurstone's Law of Comparative Judgment: Consider a psychophysical experiment in which the subject is presented with two stimuli. He is asked to judge whether they differ in some quality. If the subject perceives them as at all different in respect to that quality, two responses are possible: either stimulus α has "more" of the quality or stimulus β has

more of it. If the two stimuli are sufficiently different in respect to the quality, the subject will always respond in the same manner; i.e., he will always contend that stimulus α is greater, or, perhaps, that stimulus β is greater. If the subject never perceives them as different, the effect is the same, for in both cases the subject is consistent and never alters his judgment. It is for that reason that the Fullerton-Cattell principle was modified by the statement "unless the differences are always or never noticed," for under these conditions there is no dispersion, or variability, in the response.

However, stimulus α and stimulus β may be so similar that the subject does not always give the same response. In this case, the dispersions of the two stimuli overlap. Figure 4–9 shows how an overlapping dispersion results.

The problem of dispersion is to evaluate the actual size of the distance between the two stimuli. Indeed, this may be determined by evaluating the proportion of time that stimulus α is judged to be greater than stimulus β and the proportion of time that both α and β are judged to be different from other stimuli. Clearly, this determination bears on both Weber's ratio and the Fullerton-Cattell principle, for it is an indirect evaluation of the variability associated with the measure of central tendency of each judgment. This is the problem with which the law of comparative judgment is concerned. The law is

$$\bar{X}_1 - \bar{X}_2 = Z_{ab} \ \sqrt{\sigma^2_a + \sigma^2_b - 2r_{ab}\sigma_a\sigma_b}$$

where Z_{ab} = normal deviate and σ_a and σ_b = standard deviations (SD) associated with dispersion around $\bar{X}_1$ and $\bar{X}_2$, and r_{ab} = correlation between $\bar{X}_1$ and $\bar{X}_2$ (i.e., between the dispersions). $\bar{X}_1$ and $\bar{X}_2$ may also represent the scaled values of the stimuli.

The equation contains three unknowns, σ_a, σ_b, and r_{ab}. Z_{ab} may be calculated from the data. If it is assumed that the correlations are zero (i.e., that there is no correlation between the dispersions for α and β or between their standard deviations), the third unknown is zero and is eliminated from calculation of the equation. The equation then may be solved for a series of possible numbers of substitution, since only the observable variable Z_{ab} remains. (Thurstone, 1927b)

Thurstone's law is valuable not only for the contribution it makes to an understanding of the problems of traditional psychophysics but also because of its usefulness in several scaling techniques. The problems of variability and dispersion are not the sole property of the psychophysical method, for any technique which requires judgment of the differences between two stimuli involves evaluation of the dispersion.

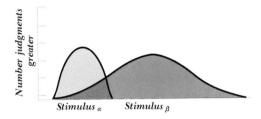

FIGURE 4–9: *Representation of dispersion from two stimuli, stimulus α and stimulus β. The dark gray area indicates the area of overlap. The ordinate shows the number of judgments of "greater."*

Helson's Adaptation Level:

Helson's Adaptation Level: Adaptation-level theory, which was originated and developed by Helson (1938; 1964), was intended to handle many disparate and seemingly contradictory phenomena which result from psychophysical investigations. This approach to psychophysics has been so successful that it has been applied to other complex sensory and behavioral processes. Theory and research on adaptation level have led to a reformulation of Fechner's law and to the application of the principle of adaptation level to the processes of learning and conditioning. The principle is complex, however, and is most easily understood by reference to its origins and development.

Consider first the obvious fact that every subject in a psychophysical experiment has been making psychophysical judgments of one kind or another throughout his life. The classic psychophysical methods take great care to remove various sources of error from their determinations. In so doing they manage to remove from the experiment any investigation of how judgment differs or changes as a function of previous experience. Such experience may result from a subject's previous judgments or from the way the psychophysical procedure is designed.

Helson (1938) designed an experiment to examine the relative influence of four attributes of color: constancy, contrast, conversion, and adaptation. (These terms are discussed

fully in Chapters 8 and 9: their precise meaning need not detain us from understanding the point of the experiment.) In classic psychophysics, each of the aspects were investigated separately; that is, functions were derived for constancy, for contrast, and so on, with little or no attention given to the ways in which the functions might be interrelated. Moreover, the literature on these aspects of color indicated a surprising lack of agreement in findings, which is probably attributable to apparently minor differences in experimental design.

Helson varied the four attributes under three conditions: the color of the object, the background, and the amount of illumination present. Under this experimental approach, the interrelations between these factors and the subjects' judgments of them became apparent. Judgment of the color of the object depended upon the other variables introduced into the experiment. This finding suggested that the level to which the subject had adapted in respect to illumination, for example, determined in part his eventual judgment of color. Thus, judgment depends upon the *level of adaptation* to other stimuli. The adaptation level presents the theorist and the investigator with two problems: first, it must be defined in an operational manner; second, data must be collected to show the way in which adaptation level varies as a function of specific stimulus dimensions.

It is assumed that adaptation level is "... a pooled effect of all stimuli impinging upon the organism both from without and within and includes residuals from past experience..." (Helson, 1964, p. 127). Further, it is assumed that adaptation level is a weighted mean of all these stimuli. Thus each of the judgments previously acquired is weighted in some fashion to predict the eventual judgment.

The fact that the function representing subjects' judgments differs as a function of the procedure used can be seen from Figure 4–10, which shows three judgment scales of weight. The scales were derived under three experimental conditions depending upon where the scale was *anchored*. Anchoring refers to providing the subject with a stimulus on which other judgments are based. It is clear that experience with different anchor points affects the shape of the judgment function.

The results of many studies conducted by Helson and others have led to several impor-

FIGURE 4–10: *Three functions showing judgments of weight. The functions differ in the type of anchor used. The use of an anchor apparently provides the subject with experiences which alter his judgments. (From* Adaptation-level Theory, *by Harry Helson, Harper & Row Publishers, Incorporated, 1964, p. 193.)*

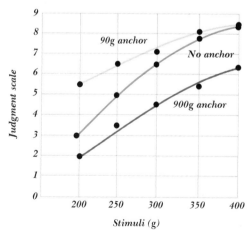

tant changes in approach to psychophysical measurement. One of these, recommended by Michels and Helson (1949), is a reformulation of Fechner's law. In part, it suggests that a subject's response on trial *x* is determined by his judgment on the immediately preceding trial and all other prior trials, each contributing different values to the final prediction.

Since the concept of adaptation level may be generalized to many other areas of behavior, including abstract thinking, emotion, and cognition, and conformity and deviation, its uses have become widespread, although it was intended originally to solve certain discrepancies in studies of psychophysical judgments. The fact that an attack on psychophysical problems leads to new and, perhaps, better methods for examining other complex behavior, suggests the tempting conclusion that psychophysics is, after all, the place from which understanding of behavior originates.

Stevens's Power Function: Some laws of science are useful, often repeated, generally taken for granted, and probably wrong. In the one hundred years since the formulation of Fechner's law, textbook writers have cited it as the example of the relationship between the physical and the psychological worlds, and experimenters have sometimes strained to make their data fit the expected function. In this chapter, we chose to introduce the development of Fechner's law and the methods employed in the classic psychophysical techniques so that we could understand why Fechner's formulation requires improvement. It may be recalled that Fechner's basic assumption was that equal stimulus ratios correspond to equal sensation differences. However, what if this basic assumption, which appears to be both logical and validated, is incorrect? If it is incorrect, it may be incorrect for only a few subsidiary assumptions, whereas other basic postulates of the law, such as using the threshold in the formulation, may be appropriate.

Stevens has suggested that this is the case. Following the results of several experiments to be examined later, Stevens suggested that the physical stimulus related to the psychological sensation is

$$\psi = K \, (\gamma - \gamma_0)^n$$

where

K = a constant, determined by choice of units
n = an exponent, which varies with sensory system
ψ = psychological magnitude of stimulus
γ = physiological stimulus
γ_0 = effective threshold: point on physical scale from which measurement of effective stimulus begins

Notice that Stevens's function includes characteristics of both Weber's ratio and Fechner's law. An important point of correspondence with Fechner's law is the inclusion of a measure of the threshold value at which the psychological determination is made. The formula contains an important element of Weber's ratio in the use of the exponent n, which varies with the sensory modality under consideration. Through experimentation, Stevens and his colleagues have found that n varies with the sensory modality. Brightness is rated 0.33, and electric shock, 3.5. (Pain was a sensory modality ignored by Fechner except for his unfortunate habit of staring at the sun at great length in order to study certain visual processes.)

The power function, when plotted on a log-log plot (that is, where both the abscissa and ordinate are in logs, unlike the typical Fechner plot, where only the abscissa is in logs), yields a straight line. If the plot of the same data were linear-linear, curvilinear relations would result. Figure 4–11 shows the log-log plot for three sensory modalities: electric shock, length, and brightness. We have already indicated the values of electric shock and brightness; length assumes the exponential function of 1.1.

The question remains whether the power function describes the same data that Fechner attempted to accommodate in his law. The answer is probably not. The classic psychophysical methods have some special characteristics in regard to measuring sensation. In some methods, the subject is asked to judge whether two stimuli are equal, and in other methods he is asked to judge whether they are different. Moreover, the classic methods ignore a rather interesting characteristic of psychophysical judgments. This may best be explained by example. Assume that a subject is asked to relate one physical dimension to another. For example, an electric current applied to the subject's finger produces the sensation of vibration. The subject is then asked to adjust an apparatus which provides tones of differing loudness until the loudness is perceived to be of the same magnitude as the vibration. At first, this procedure appears bizarre. Yet if the power function is an apt description of sensation, the subject's judgments result in an "equal sensation" function which is also a power function (Stevens, 1959). Figure 4–12 shows the plot which results from this. Several other experiments, using different sensory modalities, have verified the general statement that cross-modality comparisons result in power functions.

An important outcome of these findings is that the resulting function will depend upon the method used. Classic psychophysical methods are more likely to yield one kind of function than contemporary techniques, for the simple reason that the determinations requested of the subjects are different today. The experiments reported by Stevens and his colleagues demonstrate this fact. In contemporary procedures, the subject is asked to judge the stimuli in relation to one another: When is a tone as loud as a shock? When is tone α twice as loud as tone β? These procedures are regarded as *scaling* techniques, and an understanding of their important details must await an understanding of the theory of numbers (see Chapter 5).

Decision Theory: Hopefully, the point has been made clear, both explicitly and by example, that the sensory threshold is a statisti-

FIGURE 4–11: *Three sensory modalities, electric shock, length, and brightness, plotted on a log-log plot as described in the text. The resulting plot is a straight line. The exponent, which is a function of the sensory modality under investigation, determines the slope. (Stevens, 1962, p. 30.)*

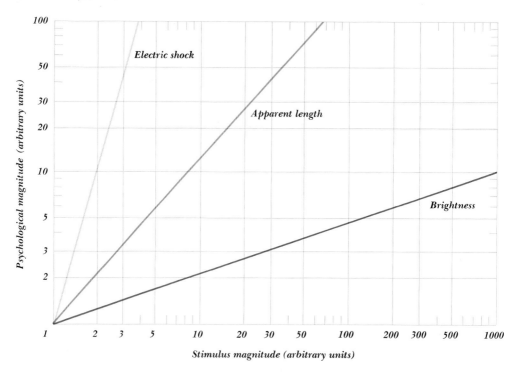

cal approximation. It changes rapidly sometimes; however, we are never quite certain whether the threshold itself has changed or whether the technique for measurement, such as one of the psychophysical methods, is in error. For many years, the threshold has been referred to as a statistical device, but it is quite possible that the threshold is something less than that.

Decision theory is a general term for studies which are based on the assumption that psychophysical measures may be considered a measure of *detection* and *recognition* thresholds. Detection refers to the point at which one is able to say that a stimulus is present, while recognition refers to the point at which

one is able to say that the stimulus is of a certain character. For example, you may ask me to watch a screen until a red light appears. When I can detect the stimulus, my detection threshold has been reached. However, it is quite likely that I am unable, at this point, to determine the color of the light. When I am able to recognize the color, my recognition threshold has been reached. This area of sensory investigation is often referred to as *decision theory,* for it emphasizes the need for the subject to make decisions regarding stimuli.

Classic psychophysics permits one of two decisions: yes or no. That is, the techniques are so structured that the subject's only decision is to state whether or not he perceives the stimulus, whether or not he perceives a change in the stimulus, and whether one stimulus differs from another. These techniques lead to the concept that a threshold is a real point. By definition, it is the place at which detection occurs 50 percent of the time. Thus, some writers prefer to refer to this point as the *detection threshold,* rather than the absolute or stimulus threshold. The stimulus threshold, then, becomes the point at which the number of "yes" responses equals the number of "no" responses. One may go further and say that a threshold is merely a statistical convenience, not only because thresholds are nothing more than statistical approximations but because they vary continuously, owing to physiological changes within the sensory system and to what we have learned about the probability that the stimulus will appear.

This last point represents one of the major contributions that detection theory has made to psychology. Assume that we design an experiment in which the probability that the stimulus will appear is varied. The experimenter instructs the subject to tell him whether or not he perceives the stimulus. The experimenter warns him when he may expect the stimulus (a trial), but the probability that the stimulus will appear is varied from 10 to 90 percent. This technique has the effect of altering the probability that the subject will report perceiving the stimulus. The resulting function is known as an *isosensitivity contour,* or a *response operating characteristic.* Figure 4–13 shows such a function. The ordinate represents the probability of the subject's saying, "Yes, I perceive it" when the stimulus (signal) does appear, and the abscissa shows the probability of his saying "Yes" when the stimulus does not appear. The solid line shows a strong stimulus, while the broken line shows the function for an undetectable stimulus. The important point is that even when the stimulus is presented, the subject is not likely to report perceiving it if it has rarely appeared.

Is there a sensory threshold? Or is the threshold little more than a combination of the strength of the stimulus and the subject's

FIGURE 4–12: *A cross-modality comparison between vibration and loudness. Circles represent the loudness adjusted to match the amount of stimulation, and squares show stimulation adjusted to match loudness. Each produces a slightly different slope, although both slopes are a power function whose exponent is equal to the ratio between the exponents for the two stimuli, loudness and vibration. (Stevens, 1962, p. 33.)*

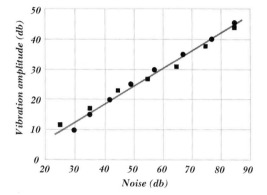

experiences and expectations regarding the stimulus? Even if there is no true sensory threshold, it is a useful approximation of the limits and ranges of the sensory systems. It is, after all, a remarkably useful concept, as may be seen from the fact that it has been with us for many years. However, in our quest for the psychophysical law—even though we have expressed doubts about whether there is such a law—we turn in the next chapter to a consideration of another approach to the problem, that of scaling.

SOURCES

History: The most thorough, if not the only, introduction to the history of psychophysical theory is in Boring (1942; 1950). It is curious that no text devoted solely to psychophysics and its development is available; the rich history of the subject begs for attention, and not even an elementary text in psychology is com-

FIGURE 4-13: *An isosensitivity curve. The probability of a "yes" response when the stimulus does appear is shown on the ordinate, and the probability of a "yes" response when there is no stimulus is shown on the abscissa. The dark line is the curve for a strong stimulus. The broken line is the curve for an undetectable stimulus.* (From New Directions in Psychology, *by Roger Brown, Eugene Galanter, Eckhard H. Hess, and George Mandler, copyright 1962 by Holt, Rinehart and Winston, Inc.)*

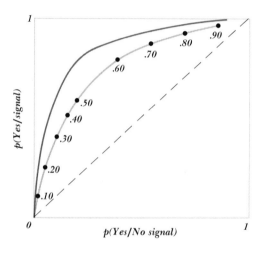

plete without some discussion of it. It appears that within the last decade psychophysics has become an object of idolatry to which textbook writers feel the need to pay homage without necessarily showing respect.

Methods: Psychophysical methodology is discussed, at least to some extent, in every text in experimental psychology. For readers who desire more advanced treatment of the subject, the following works are suggested: The text by Edwards (1957) covers many psychophysical problems, but not the classic methods of limits, average error, and constant stimuli. Edwards is most concerned with scaling methods.

Guilford's text (1954) is superb. It is difficult, but thorough. The discussions of the psychophysical methods are on a fairly complex level and are most palatable to students interested in the mathematical assumptions of proofs underlying much of psychophysical theory. In addition, Guilford is concerned with many intriguing attributes of psychophysics which have been eliminated from the present text.

Woodworth and Schlosberg (1954) have excellent chapters on the psychophysical methods. An advantage of this work is that the writers show, by example, how the various threshold measures may be calculated. Alternative techniques are given which are not included in the present book, particularly for the method of constant stimuli.

Underwood (1949; 1966) is another excellent source. The sections on psychophysical methods (or "discriminal processes," as Underwood calls them) are thorough. In a step-by-step analysis, Underwood shows the controls and procedures necessary for accuracy in each method. In addition, he cites appropriate literature both on the methods and on the type of data which result from the techniques.

Stevens (1951) discusses psychophysical theory in a chapter that is valuable to anyone interested in this aspect of scaling and psychophysics.

Bugelski (1951) is especially useful for the reader who prefers to begin the study of psychophysics with a less detailed discussion than that presented here in Chapter 4. This text is both lucid and accurate.

Reliability and Validity: One of the few major discussions of reliability and validity in regard to psychophysics is found in Blackwell (1953). The report includes experimental data.

Development of Psychophysics: Among useful contemporary sources, in addition to those listed above under other categories, is Galanter's chapter in R. Brown et al. (1962). The chapter discusses some of the applied problems of psychophysics and indicates the directions in which research has moved. Swets (1961) presents an interesting discussion of the basic problem of psychophysics: Is there a sensory threshold?

Adaptation Level: The complexity of adaptation-level theory is due, no doubt, to the fact that the concept is often talked about but rarely discussed thoroughly. The best source is Helson (1964), who reviews the enormous number of studies bearing on adaptation-level theory. This is a difficult book, but it is mandatory if one wishes to follow the development of the theory and understand the derivations which adaptation level suggests for many basic psychological problems.

Stevens's Power Function: Stevens's formulations have appeared over a number of years. His writings contain a complete statement of the development of the power function theory and provide an excellent casebook of the scientific method. Four sources especially summarize the contributions Stevens has made to psychophysics: 1960, 1961, 1962 and 1965. The 1962 paper is, perhaps, the most clear to the beginning student. The 1965 paper applies scaling to the "social consensus."

Decision Theory: Galanter (1962) presents a most interesting and vivid account of this approach to psychophysics. A book of readings, all of which consider decision theory in detail, has been compiled by Swets (1964). His article "Is There a Sensory Threshold?" is, perhaps, most germane to the problem discussed here in Chapter 4.

CHAPTER FIVE

SCALING

INTRODUCTION

A scale results from the assignment of numbers to objects, events, or mental phenomena. A thermometer, for example, is a temperature scale, for it is a dimension on which certain events have been located, e.g., freezing and boiling of water. A ruler and a calendar are also scales, for both consist of a series of intervals on which objects or events may be placed.

We may reinterpret psychophysics, then, as a *scaling technique*. Fechner's intention was to assign numbers to mental events, and the history of the development of psychophysical methods and psychophysical laws shows a concern for scaling mental phenomena in such a way that the resulting scale correlates in some way with a physical-stimulus scale. The determination of Fechner's law for brightness, for example, is concerned with constructing a scale of the mental impression of differences which corresponds to a scale of the physical amount of brightness.

Many judgments we make, such as evaluating which of several candidates is most beautiful or deciding whether we shall select brand X over brand Y, are of a psychophysical nature. The candidates in the beauty contest could be described in terms of a physical continuum. Indeed, they often are. However, many physical attributes may constitute a single stimulus. Thus, the traditional psychophysical measures are not particularly efficient when we wish to judge stimuli more complex than the attributes of weight, brightness, or other dimensions.

Theoretically, all our behavior can be placed upon one scale or another. When one says that he prefers to date X rather than Y, he is providing us with two values on a scale which we might call "preference for dates." We might pursue the matter by inquiring how much he prefers X to Y? Would a presentation of cash, on the condition that Y were dated, make a difference in preference? If so, how much money would be necessary? We then have a scale which we might call "amount of money necessary to change preference." There is an infinite number of possible scales, and each type of scale has specific mathematical properties. These properties dictate the kinds of conclusions which we can draw from our data. For example, I might ask, "What is 3 plus 2?" Your answer would be 5. Then, I might change the question slightly by asking, "What is 2 oranges plus 3 apples?" You would reply, I hope, that it is a meaningless question. Both questions ask for a computation of the sum of two numbers. But when properties are applied to the numbers, the second question becomes meaningless. Numbers are numbers, and as such they stand resolute. Nevertheless, the stimuli to which the numbers refer govern the usefulness of the scale. There is a stimulus consisting of 2 oranges, and there is another stimulus of 3 apples. The question is whether some mathematical operation can be applied to both sets of stimuli.

As Stevens points out (1951, p. 23), "Scales are possible in the first place only because there exists an isomorphism between the properties of the numeral series and the empirical operations that we can perform with the aspects of the objects." That is, the properties of the numbers assigned to the scale correspond, at least partially, to the properties of the objects themselves.

The expression "2 degrees Fahrenheit" is meaningful only because a command, such as "Increase the room temperature 2 degrees," can result in some operation by which the temperature increases by the stipulated amount. Similarly, if you have a piece of wood 12 inches long and I ask you for 4 pieces, each 3 inches long, the request is meaningful only because operations may be performed on the object (the wood) that will fulfill the request (a 12-inch piece, divided into 3-inch lengths, yields 4 pieces). If the operation cannot be performed as required by the scale (in this case, if the wood could not be cut into the units required), the usefulness of the scale is greatly decreased.

THE NATURE OF NUMBERS

Why are some scales able to correspond more accurately to the objects which they purport to measure than other scales? At least two reasons present themselves: First, the nature of the object being scaled contributes to the amount of correspondence. For example the very nature of the concept "intelligence" makes it more difficult to scale accurately than length. The lack of agreement as to what constitutes intelligence, compared with universal agreement as to what constitutes length, is an example of one cause of this problem. Second, the actual operations used in constructing the scale affect the accuracy of the scale. There is always the possibility that the correspondence of a scale may be enhanced by improving techniques or statistical procedures. The fact that the possibility exists of improving procedures means that the investigation of scaling techniques is by no means sterile, for experimenters interested in scaling may be concerned not only with the interpretation of the data they collect but also with the improvement of the procedures by which the data are collected and of the techniques with which the data are evaluated.

The nature, or property, of the objects being scaled is related to the techniques which may be used to establish the scale. Consider the numbers 7, 34, 18, and 21. If you were asked to scale these numbers, you would most likely find a ruler, plot points equally distant from one another, and mark the seventh line as 7, the thirty-fourth line as 34, and so on, as shown in Figure 5.1. But in so doing you would be imposing upon the numbers an order which does not necessarily exist. For example, when you finished your drawing, I might say, "That is all very good, but the numbers I gave you happen to refer to the numbers on the uniforms of four baseball players. Now, what does your plot have to do with baseball players?"

Depending upon whether your reaction was one of indignation or one of chagrin, you might reply that your plot had nothing to do with baseball players, that I should have told you what the numbers represented, and that you would not have gone to the trouble of scaling the numbers. Your point would be well taken, for if the numbers represent ballplayers, it is

FIGURE 5-1: *A probable plot of the numbers 7, 18, 21, and 34 when no further instructions are given regarding the meaning of the numbers. Because of our experience, we would be likely to plot the numbers on an equal-interval scale, although, as the text describes, the numbers may have different interpretations.*

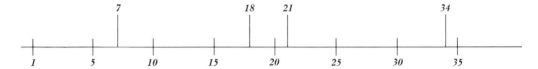

obvious that 21 is not 3 times 7. It is meaningless to say that the player numbered 21 is 3 times more of *anything* than the player numbered 7, for the reason that the numbers do not represent any quality or characteristic of the object. The numbers are used merely to *distinguish* one player from another, and player 7 could as easily be player 21, or player 756386957482. The purpose of the numbers is to "name" the objects and to show that they are somehow distinct. We could have given each player a different color, a different uniform, or any other distinct quality. The essential point is that the numbers represent only *difference* and tell us nothing about the magnitude of the difference. Such a scale is called a *nominal scale*.

Stevens (1951), following von Neumann and Morgenstern (1947), includes a nominal scale in his analysis of kinds of scales. More recently, Torgerson (1958), in his analysis of kinds of scales, omits the nominal category on the ground that since the use of numbers is not a necessary utensil for the development of a nominal scale, it is not properly a scale. After pointing out that there are two subclasses of nominal scales, depending upon whether one is distinguishing objects from other objects or groups of objects from other groups of objects, Torgerson says: "Here, the numerals serve to identify classes of objects. . . . It should be noted that the use of numerals here is unnecessary. Other sets of distinguishable marks would serve as well. As a matter of fact, words are ordinarily used for that pur-

pose" (Torgerson, 1958, p. 17). That is, we might just as well (and probably would) refer to the ballplayers as Smith and Jones.

Assume, however, that, rather than ballplayers' numbers, I had been referring to scores which had been given on a test; i.e., one student received a score of 7, another a score of 18, a third a score of 21, and the last a score of 34. The raw score does not matter, for I have converted these test scores into letters grades of A, B, C, and D. The student with the score of 7 received an A, and the student with a score of 34 received a D. Now, if these letter grades are transposed for the numbers shown in Figure 5-1, we have a scale with considerably more meaning than before. Not only does an A *differ* from B, but it is also possible to note that an A has more, or less, of the quality being scaled than does B. From this scale, it may be assumed that B has more of the attribute or quality than C and D, but not more than A; similarly, C has more of the quality than D, but not more than A and B. Thus, the numbers indicate not only that the objects are different but also the direction in which the difference occurs. With this scale, it is possible to say that one number is greater or less than another number but it is not possible to state the magnitude of the difference. It is not possible to say that the student with a score of 21 is 3 times worse than the student with the score of 7, nor even that 21 is 14 more than 7. This kind of scale is called an *ordinal scale*. Ordinal numbers are numbers such as first, second, and third. They are ranked in order; however, the order tells us nothing regarding the distance between the ranks.

Now, it might be claimed that not only were the two students with scores of 18 and 21 second and third on the test but in addition that they differed by 3. The question is 3 of what? If the numbers represent scores from an examination, in which the units appear at equal intervals (as inches appear at equal intervals on a ruler), it may be said that they differ by 3 correct answers on the examination. In this case, it is meaningful to say that the students scoring 18 and 21 were 3 units apart. The criterion is whether the scale has equal-appearing units. This type of scale is an *interval scale,* for the intervals between the units are measurable. An interval scale has all the characteristics of both nominal and ordinal scales, but it has one additional characteristic, namely, that the magnitude may be specified in terms other than greater or less. Thermometers and calendars are examples of interval scales. The difference between March 1 and March 15 is the same as the difference between December 1 and December 15 in terms of number of days. Similarly, the difference in degrees between 10 and 20°F is the same as the difference between 80 and 90°F.

Regarding scores on the examination, note that as soon as the scores are converted to letter grades (e.g., A, B, C, D), the equality of the units is lost, and we have reverted to an ordinal scale. It is not meaningful to say that an A is twice a B, or three times a C. Thus, ordinal scales are not quantitative in a real sense. This is a property of the scale that is commonly overlooked by computing grade-point averages which are treated as interval data from letter grades which are actually ordinal data. A note on zero is in order: Not all apparent zeros, of course, are true zero points. Some zero points are largely a matter of convention. For example, 0°F is not the absence of temperature. That point on the scale could be called 100 or 165 without affecting the qualities of the scale.

The area between ordinal and interval scales is, to some extent a quagmire. Many scales which appear to be interval scales (such as IQ scales) do not meet completely the requirements of interval scaling, yet they are commonly treated as if they represented interval numbering. For example, it is not uncommon to hear teachers or parents treat the difference between an IQ score of 110 and an IQ of 120 as if the 10-point difference represented 10 units of *something.* Or they may assume that the difference in intelligence between a person with IQ 125 and a person with IQ 135 is the same as the difference between IQ 75 and 85. Similarly, teachers commonly assume that the grades with which they evaluate students are at least of an interval-scale nature, when, in reality, the absence of a zero point and of equivalent units indicates that the scale has many of the characteristics of an ordinal scale but only a few characteristics of an interval scale. Many tests produce scales which may be described as "ordinal scales striving to become interval scales." Some of these scales are very useful in ascribing behavior to categories. On the other hand, there is a tendency to ignore the meaning of the numbers and to assume that the scales are more accurate or more meaningful than they are. It is inconceivable that someone would suggest playing a football game by multiplying the numbers of each player and determining the team with the most points in that way. Yet sometimes the uses of IQ and other test scores make assumptions about the resulting scores which are hardly more tenable.

The highest form of scale is the *ratio scale.* It is "highest" in that it contains the other scales. It has all the qualities of the nominal, ordinal, and interval scales, as well as one additional characteristic, namely, that with the ratio scale one can perform operations on the data in such a way that the equality of ratios is maintained. An absolute zero is implied. The usual technique for constructing a ratio scale is to begin with the zero point and plot equal units. These units must be equal in the sense that multiplying each value by a constant yields equal ratios. Because of this characteristic, all mathematical tools may be applied to data applicable to ratio scaling, since the ratios are not distorted. Consider two boards, one 12 inches long and one 3 inches long. Given the numbers 12 and 3, I may perform any mathematical operation on both numbers, and the ratio between the numbers is not altered; Table 5–A shows the basic operations of the scales of measurement as cited by Stevens.

Just as the importance of a number will vary depending upon the kind and characteristics of the scale on which it is placed, so we may expect to find differences in judgment as a function of the scale. Consider an experimenter who presents a light of four different intensities to a subject. He may ask the subject to rank the lights in order of brightness (an ordinal scale), or he might ask the subject to assign each light a number from 1 to 100, with 100 as bright as possible (an interval and perhaps a ratio scale, depending upon the instructions). It should be clear that the design of an experiment and the kinds of judgments the subjects are asked to make result in differences which are a function of the scale imposed by the experiment. That is the important point of this chapter. Just as in the pre-

TABLE 5–A: *Characteristics of the Four Types of Scales Discussed in the Text.*
(From Stevens, in Rosenblith, 1961, p. 4.)

Scale	Basic empirical operations	Permissible statistics (invariantive)	Typical examples
Nominal	Determination of equality	Number of cases Mode "Information" measures Contingency correlation	"Numbering" of football players Assignment of type or model numbers to classes
Ordinal	Determination of greater or less	Median Percentiles Order correlation (type O: interpreted as a test of order)	Hardness of minerals Grades of leather, lumber, wool, etc. Intelligence-test raw scores
Interval	Determination of the equality of intervals or of differences	Mean Standard deviation Order correlation (type I: interpreted as r) Product moment (r)	Temperature (Fahrenheit and Celsius) Position on a line Calendar time Potential energy Intelligence-test "standard scores" (?)
Ratio	Determination of the equality of ratios	Geometric mean Harmonic mean Percent variation	Length, density, numerosity, time intervals, work, etc. Temperature (Kelvin) Loudness (sones) Brightness (brils)

ceding chapter we studied the classic psychophysical methods in order to understand the kinds of data used to formulate psychophysical laws, in this chapter we shall consider several scaling techniques, so that we may understand the ways in which the techniques contribute to the evaluation of data.

We shall discuss, first, three scaling methods which are based upon ratio and interval scaling. Then we shall discuss three more classic methods, *rating, ranking,* and *pair comparison,* which are widely used, particularly in industry, to evaluate preference or judgment of stimuli. Next we shall consider briefly some additional techniques which are used to solve problems somewhat different from those with which the above techniques are concerned. Finally, we shall consider, as was done with psychophysics, the reliability and validity of scaling procedures.

METHODS BASED ON RATIO AND INTERVAL JUDGMENTS

Guilford (1954) distinguishes between *interval judgments* and *ratio judgments.* This distinction, however, is not intended to imply that one group of techniques uses interval numbers while the other uses ratio numbers. Rather, the distinction refers to the type of task required of the subject.

Method of Equal Sense Distances (Bisection): This method is characterized by the stipulation that the subject judge the point at which some psychological continuum is *bisected.* For example, the experimenter may present a tone at 15,000 Hz and a tone at 5,000 Hz and ask the subject to select a tone halfway between the two standards. Or the experimenter may give the subject two substances to taste and ask him to select a substance midway in sourness or sweetness between the two standards. The fact that the subject is always required to "bisect" the two standards accounts for the fact that the technique is also called the *method of bisection.* It should be noted that

the actual task required of the subject is that of equating intervals, for through further bisection trials the subject establishes intervals which are psychologically equated in the specific continuum.

Consider an experiment in which the experimenter wishes to evaluate degrees of brightness. The apparatus consists of three lights, the brightness of which may be altered independently from 0.20 to 0.42 ft-L (footlamberts). The light in the middle serves as the comparative stimulus, and the lights on either side as the standard stimuli. One standard is set at 0.42 ft-L, and the other is set at 0.20. In emulation of both the method of limits and the method of constant stimuli, the experimenter decreases or increases the brightness of the comparative stimulus. The subject's task is to estimate the brightness which is halfway between the two standard stimuli by indicating whether the comparative stimulus is brighter than, equal in brightness to, or less bright than the estimated halfway point. In addition, the experimenter varies the standard stimulus of the brightest magnitude from left to right in a random order, so that any possible position preference is counterbalanced. Table 5–B shows the results of the experiment.

Since the process of bisection allows three responses (more, less, or same), the PSE is a useful measure of discrimination. It is found, theoretically, by taking the midway point of responses of "same." Obviously, the other measures commonly taken by the method of limits or constant stimuli are applicable (see Chapter 4; also, Woodworth & Schlosberg, 1954, pp. 196–199). An approximation of average error can also be used in which the subject adjusts the comparison until he believes it to be half the standard.

Having determined the bisection of the original standard stimuli, we can now perform further bisections. For example, the PSE found in the data shown in Table 5–B could form a new standard stimulus, and bisections could be made between the PSE and the lower standard stimulus and between the PSE and the higher standard stimulus. A series of such bi-

*TABLE 5-B: *Data on Brightness Derived by the Method of Equal Sense Distances.*
Two standard stimuli, one at 0.20 ft-L and one at 0.42 ft-L, are used. The comparative stimulus is varied, and the subject is asked to estimate the brightness that is halfway between the two standards.

Comparative stimulus, ft-L	S_l A	S_r D	S_l D	S_r A	S_l A	S_r D	S_r A	S_l D	S_r A	S_r D	S_l D	S_l A
0.42	..	..	..	..	..	M	..	..	..	..	M	..
0.40	..	M	..	..	..	M	..	M	..	..	M	M
0.38	M	M	..	..	M	M	M	M	..	M	M	M
0.36	M	M	M	M	M	M	M	M	..	M	M	M
0.34	M	M	M	S	M	M	S	M	M	M	M	S
0.32	S	M	S	S	S	S	S	M	M	S	M	S
0.30	S	S	S	S	S	S	S	S	M	L	S	L
0.28	S	L	L	S	L	S	L	L	S	L	L	L
0.26	L	L	L	L	L	S	L	L	L	..	L	L
0.24	L	L	..	L	..	L	L	L	L	..	L	L
0.22	L	L	..	..	..	L	L	..	L	..	..	L
0.20	..	..	..	..	..	L	..	..	..	..	..	L
PSE	0.30	0.30	0.31	0.31	0.31	0.29	0.32	0.30	0.28	0.32	0.30	0.33

*S_l = the standard of 0.20 is on the left; S_r = the standard of 0.20 is on the right; A = ascending trial; D = descending trial; M = response of "more than half"; L = response of "less than half"; S = response of "same" or "half"; PSE = point of subjective equality.

sections each time using a derived PSE as a new standard stimulus, results in a plot of *equal sense distances.* Figure 5–2 shows the application of this technique to the psychological quality of auditory loudness. Some writers have pointed out that there is a danger in using a *series* of bisections, because any error in the first determination is reflected and possibly magnified in succeeding determinations.

In the example shown in Table 5–B, the method of limits was employed in determining the point of bisection. Other basic psychophysical techniques may also be used, however, depending upon the nature of the task and the available apparatus. For example, the method of average error could be employed; thus, the subject would manipulate the comparative stimulus until he judged it equal to the midway point of the standard stimuli. In this case, the measurement of the PSE is appropriate for the same reason that it is appro-

priate in the pure method of average error: the subject is asked to find the point where the stimuli are the same, rather than the point where they are different. Similarly, the method of constant stimuli could be employed.

In the method of equal sense distances, the subject may be instructed to divide the standard stimuli, not into two equal parts, commonly called *fractionation,* but into three, four, or as many equal parts as the experimenter selects. This avoids using the first bisection as the new standard stimulus. In essence, it requires the subject to make the same series of determinations but without the presence of a new standard stimulus on each trial. The technique has been used by Stevens and Volkmann (1940) in relating pitch perception to frequency. In this study, the subjects were given three overlapping sets of standards (one from 40 to 1,000 Hz, a second from 200 to 6,500 Hz, and a third from 3,000 to 12,000 Hz) and asked to separate *each* into four equal parts. Figure 5–3 shows the results. Although we shall discuss these data again in the next chapter, it should be pointed out that this scale yields data that are somewhat different from what common sense would suggest. It may be noted that frequency and pitch are not related in a linear fashion. Is this a function of some characteristic of the method used to determine the function? Is it merely a function of the organism, that is, does the human ear not perceive a linear relation between these two variables? We shall see.

Method of Equal-appearing Intervals: This method is distinguished by the requirement that the subject is given all the stimuli that he is to evaluate at one time. He is asked to sort the stimuli into *x* number of categories. Clearly, the method is most easily employed when the stimuli can be manipulated by the subject. It is, for example, not an especially appropriate method if tones are the stimuli, for the presentation of all stimuli and the task of sorting one from the other would result in bedlam. On the other hand, the technique has some of the advantages of the method of average error in that the subject is likely to remain interested in a task in which he can manipulate the stimuli. The term *equal-appearing intervals* refers to the fact that the subject's sorting of the stimuli into categories results in groupings which are, to the subject at least, equivalent in regard to the continuum stipulated.

Consider the technique applied to the following problem: The experimenter is interested in determining a subject's perception of length. The experimenter uses 33 sticks identical to one another except in length. The sticks range from 1 to 2 inches in length, differing from one another by $\frac{1}{32}$ of an inch. The subject may be told to arrange the sticks in *x* number of categories (usually an odd number is selected so that there is a theoretical midpoint), or he may be instructed to arrange the sticks in as many categories as he deems appropriate. It is worthwhile for the

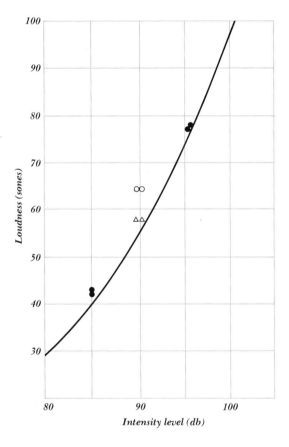

FIGURE 5–2: *Using the method of equal sense distances (bisection) to determine a scale for loudness. The ordinate indicates loudness in sones (a sone is an arbitrary unit of loudness and is discussed in Chapter 6). The abscissa indicates intensity in decibels at 1,000 Hz. Each point represents the bisection of the interval between two standard stimuli. Thus the perception of loudness is related to the physical intensity. (From Newman, Volkmann, & Stevens, 1937, p. 136.)*

experimenter to include several stimuli in each category (in this case, of identical length) in order to be able to measure variability, for the frequency with which each stimulus is placed in each category could provide the scaled values of the categories. Alternatively, the experimenter might ask the subject to perform

FIGURE 5–3: *The curve shows how pitch, scaled in subjective units called* mels *(ordinate), varies with frequency. The circles, squares, and triangles represent data obtained in the experiment. The filled figures mark the ends of three frequency ranges, and the hollow figures show the points arrived at when the experimenters divided the ranges into equal intervals of pitch. (Stevens & Volkmann, 1940, p. 336.)*

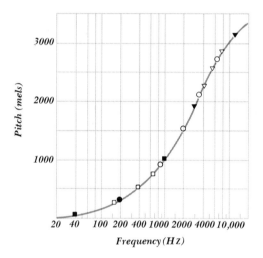

Frequency (H z)

the complete operation of placing the stimuli into categories several times. Either way, the data may be presented in terms of the frequency with which each length falls into each category. The technique has many characteristics in common with the method of constant stimuli and other frequency methods. For example, assuming that the subject has arranged the stimuli in categories equally distant from one another, the assumptions of interval numbers are met.

Table 5–C shows the results of a study of length and the manner in which the data are treated. Means, medians, and standard deviations have been computed in order to give information regarding the skewness of the scores. When the mean and the median differ appreciably, it may be assumed that the scores

are skewed. If the scores are not skewed, the standard deviation may be taken as an estimate of the dispersion. The data from Table 5–C are plotted in Figure 5–4.

As we shall note later in this chapter, many of the scaling techniques become cumbersome when many stimuli are to be scaled. Often, in this case, the method of equal-appearing intervals is used in a preliminary way to determine the categories from which a smaller number of stimuli may be chosen which will be characteristic of the total sample. Similarly, the method is often used (sometimes unknowingly) in rating term papers or tests. When a large number of examinations or papers are to be graded, the instructor sometimes places the papers in 9 or 10 groups, each group composed of papers very similar in quality. The instructor then scales each group separately, checking to be certain that the paper of lowest quality in one category is not lower in quality than the highest paper in the next lower category. By concentrating on a small sample of stimuli, the instructor is better able to distinguish one paper from another in the categories. By putting the categories in order, the instructor has arranged the papers on a scale of quality.

Method of Fractionation: The method of fractionation is distinguished by the fact that the subject is required to select a comparative stimulus which is one-half (or some other fraction) of the standard stimulus. In its pure form, the method has several disadvantages: the stimulus dimension must be of such a nature that standard stimuli may be presented and evaluated conveniently by the subject; the number of stimuli to be evaluated must be small enough that the subject can compare them effectively, yet a sufficient number of comparative stimuli must be available to permit the subject to make accurate discriminations.

As an example, consider an experiment in which the experimenter wishes to determine the relationship between the subject's sensation of "sweetness" and the physical dimension of sweetness as measured by percentage

TABLE 5-C: *Use of the Method of Equal-appearing Intervals.*
The frequency is shown with which sticks of varying lengths were placed in each of several categories in an experiment in which the investigator was concerned with establishing a scale for length.

Stimulus, in.	Categories 1	2	3	4	5	6	7	Mean	Median	Standard deviation
1	5	1	..	..	..	..	..	1.16	1.10	0.40
1 1/32	4	1	1	..	..	..	..	1.5	1.25	0.76
1 2/32	4	2	..	..	..	..	..	1.33	1.25	0.48
1 3/32	3	2	1	..	..	..	..	1.66	1.5	0.76
1 4/32	3	1	1	1	..	..	..	2.0	1.5	1.15
1 5/32	2	3	1	..	..	..	..	1.83	1.83	0.69
1 6/32	1	4	1	..	..	..	..	2.0	2.0	0.57
1 7/32	..	3	3	..	..	..	..	2.5	2.5	0.50
1 8/32	..	5	1	..	..	..	..	2.16	2.10	0.41
1 9/32	..	4	1	1	..	..	..	2.5	2.25	0.76
1 10/32	..	2	2	2	..	..	..	3.0	3.0	0.82
1 11/32	..	3	1	1	1	..	..	3.0	2.5	1.15
1 12/32	..	2	1	2	1	..	..	3.33	3.5	1.11
1 13/32	..	1	2	2	1	..	..	3.5	3.5	0.96
1 14/32	..	..	..	1	4	1	..	5.0	5.0	0.57
1 15/32	..	..	..	2	2	2	..	5.0	5.0	0.82
1 16/32	..	..	..	4	1	1	..	4.5	4.25	0.76
1 17/32	..	..	..	5	1	..	..	4.16	4.10	0.45
1 18/32	..	..	..	4	1	1	..	4.50	4.25	0.76
1 19/32	..	..	..	2	2	1	1	5.16	5.0	1.10
1 20/32	..	..	..	1	3	2	..	5.16	5.16	0.73
1 21/32	..	..	..	..	5	1	..	5.16	5.10	0.32
1 22/32	..	..	..	..	5	1	..	5.16	5.10	0.32
1 23/32	..	..	..	..	4	1	1	5.50	5.25	0.76
1 24/32	..	..	..	..	3	1	2	5.83	5.5	0.92
1 25/32	..	..	..	..	2	2	2	6.0	6.0	0.82
1 26/32	..	..	..	..	2	1	3	6.16	6.5	0.95
1 27/32	..	..	..	..	3	2	1	5.66	5.5	0.79
1 28/32	..	..	..	..	1	2	3	6.33	6.5	0.77
1 29/32	..	..	..	..	1	1	4	6.50	6.75	0.76
1 30/32	..	..	..	..	..	1	5	6.83	6.90	0.42
1 31/32	..	..	..	..	..	2	4	6.66	6.75	0.55
2	..	..	..	..	..	..	6	7.0	7.0	0.00

FIGURE 5-4: *A plot of the data shown in Table 5–C. The ordinate shows the categories, and the abscissa shows the stimulus length in inches. Both means and medians are plotted.*

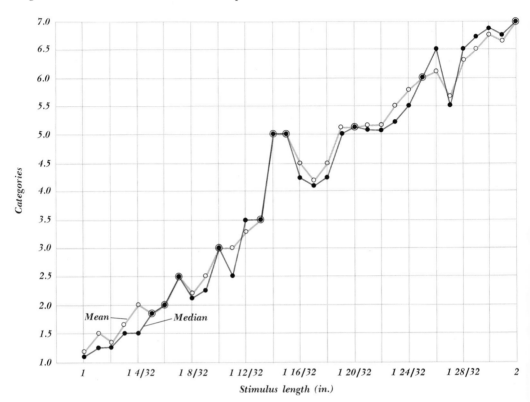

concentration of sucrose. Such a determination would have practical implications for soft-drink or candy industries, for example, in which the DL for the taste of sweetness is an important consideration. Table 5–D shows the standard stimuli (sucrose concentrations from 0.01 to 0.20), the comparative stimuli employed (from 0.05 to 0.20), as well as the results in terms of the median and mean concentrations of the standard judged one-half as sweet as the comparative stimulus.

The experimenter presents the subject with the stimuli and allows him to examine them so that he is familiar with them. The experimenter then may present the subject with the concentrations and ask him to select the stim-

ulus which is closest to one-half the standard stimulus. The subject is permitted to smell, taste, lift, or manipulate the standard stimuli in order to make the determination. After the determination has been made, the experimenter presents the subject with another stimulus, and the sequence of presentations and determinations is continued until each stimulus has been evaluated. In practice, the experimenter usually presents each stimulus several times, in random order, so as to assess the reliability of the determinations and to account for practice effects. In Table 5–D it is assumed that each stimulus was presented several times. Very slight variations in procedure can alter results appreciably. For this reason, execution of the

TABLE 5–D: *The Method of Fractionation Applied to the Judgment of the Relationship between Sucrose Concentrations and the Sensation of Sweetness.*

Concentrations of sucrose available	Stimuli	Median concentration judged "half as sweet"	Mean concentration judged "half as sweet"
0.01			
0.02			
0.03			
0.04			
0.05	0.05	0.02	0.035
0.06	0.06	0.03	0.0375
0.07	0.07	0.03	0.04
0.08	0.08	0.04	0.0425
0.09	0.09	0.05	0.045
0.10	0.10	0.04	0.0525
0.11	0.11	0.06	0.0525
0.12	0.12	0.06	0.0575
0.13	0.13	0.08	0.06
0.14	0.14	0.07	0.065
0.15	0.15	0.08	0.075
0.16	0.16	0.09	0.075
0.17	0.17	0.08	0.09
0.18	0.18	0.09	0.09
0.19	0.19	0.10	0.09
0.20	0.20	0.11	0.095

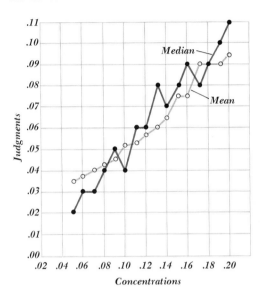

FIGURE 5–5: *A plot of the data shown in Table 5–D. The ordinate shows judgments of sweetness, and the abscissa shows sucrose concentrations. Both mean and median judgments are noted.*

technique requires that considerable attention be given the problems of counterbalanced presentations so as to minimize the effects of adaptation, fatigue of the subject, and possible practice effects.

Figure 5–5 shows the data from Table 5–D plotted with standard concentrations along the abscissa and the median and mean judgments of "half as sweet" along the ordinate. The plot for both medians and means is roughly linear.

The advantage of plotting such data is that for any given point on one axis we are able to interpolate a corresponding point on the other. For example, although the experimenter did not use a standard concentration of 0.13575 in the experiment, it is possible to predict what concentration would be judged "half as sweet" by drawing a straight line from the ordinate at 0.13575 to the function and a line from that point on the function to the abscissa. The point on the ordinate which corresponds to 0.13575 on the abscissa is approximately 0.075 if one uses the median and 0.058 if one uses the mean. Similarly, the plot permits the reverse determination; i.e., given a concentration judged half as sweet, what concentration appears to be twice as sweet? By following the procedure of drawing straight lines between the abscissa and function and between the function and the ordinate, we can make this determination.

To avoid such uncomfortable terms as "half as sweet," and "half as heavy," various experimenters have invented terms to correspond to units which result from fractionation methods. The *sone* is a psychological unit of loudness, the *veg* refers to perceived weight, the *gust* is an arbitrary unit of taste, *bril* is used for brightness, and *mel* for pitch. We shall discuss the use of these measures in the chapters on the sensory systems, but it may be noted at this point that fractionation methods have produced units of measurement which, since they are arbitrary, avoid some of the theoretical problems inherent in the definition of DL.

Some of the disadvantages of the basic method of fractionation may be overcome by alternative experimental procedures. If a large number of comparative stimuli or many standard stimuli are required, it is possible to separate the stimuli into two or more groups. For example, if one wished to use weights varying by 1 gram from 100 to 300 grams, it would be possible to use three different groups of stimuli (the first from 100 to 200 grams, the second from 150 to 250 grams, and the third from 200 to 300 grams). This procedure reduces the number of comparisons which any one subject must make. Since each range can employ a different group of subjects, the fact that the comparative stimuli overlap in weight allows the experimenter to check the consistency of the measurements by determining whether the 150-gram comparative stimulus (for example) receives the same judgment in the first series as it does in the second.

Method of Multiple Stimuli: The distinguishing characteristic of this method is that the subject is required to select a stimulus which is a multiple of the standard, i.e., twice as much or five times as much. It is an extension, or an inversion, of the method of fractionation, for while fractionation requires the subject to "fractionate" the standard, the method of multiple stimuli asks the subject to compare the standard to multiples of the standard. For this reason, the two methods may be used as checks upon one another, for a

stimulus which is judged to be four times the standard in the method of multiple stimuli should be judged one-fourth of the comparative stimulus in the method of fractionation.

Table 5–E shows data from an experiment in which the strength of the odor of hydrosulfuric acid was judged. The data are presented both in terms of means and medians and in terms of judgments of "twice as strong" and "four times as strong." In this study, the experimenter would follow the procedure in a random order, and each stimulus would be presented several times in order to assess variability. Figure 5–6 shows the data plotted, with the concentrations along the abscissa and the judgments along the ordinate. The data reported here form a linear relationship across concentrations. However, as concentration decreases, the two functions—one for four times as strong and one for twice as strong—come closer together. Thus, as concentration is increased, the difference between twice as much and four times as much also increases.

A variety of modifications of both procedure and calculation are available in ratio scaling techniques. Quite often the inapplicability of a standard method, owing to the physical limitations of a problem, leads to the development of alternative techniques. In all methods, however, the subject is required to make a judgment regarding the ratio of the stimuli to one another.

Development of Ratio Techniques: The scaling techniques discussed above are the bases of several additional techniques. As is true of the classic psychophysical methods, different scaling techniques have appeared in order to solve special problems and to show the results of requiring the subject to make different kinds of discriminations. Stevens and his colleagues (1957) have developed three methods which attempt to force the subject to make *ratio* judgments directly. These are the methods of *ratio estimation, ratio production,* and *magnitude estimation.*

In ratio estimation, the subject is presented with two stimuli (as in a frequency method)

TABLE 5–E: *The Method of Multiple Stimuli Used to Measure Judgments of the Odor of Hydrosulfuric Acid.*
The subject is instructed to select a concentration which is four times as strong as the stimulus and to select a concentration which is twice as strong. Both means and medians are shown.

Concentrations of hydro-sulfuric acid available	Stimuli presented	Median judgments "four times as strong"	Mean judgments "four times as strong"	Median judgment "twice as strong"	Mean judgment "twice as strong"
0.02	0.02	0.06	0.075	0.04	0.035
0.04	0.04	0.18	0.15	0.10	0.075
0.06	0.06	0.28	0.265	0.14	0.125
0.08	0.08	0.36	0.375	0.18	0.175
0.10					
0.12					
0.14					
0.16					
0.18					
0.20					
0.22					
0.24					
0.26					
0.28					
0.30					
0.32					
0.34					
0.36					
0.38					
0.40					

and asked to estimate the ratio between them. For example, two lights of differing brightness are presented, and the subject is asked to state that, say, light A is equal to 10 and light B is equal to 50. Notice that he is not asked to say that one light is five times as bright as the other, for that is a different question. In effect, the subject taking part in an experiment using ratio estimation and the subject in a classic psychophysical experiment are asked to perform in opposite fashions. In the latter, the ratios are given, and the subject is evaluated on his ability to recognize ratios properly. In ratio estimation, the subject is given the stimuli and asked to make the ratio judgment himself. The procedure has the advantage of using ratio scales, rather than scales lower on the mathematical hierarchy.

In ratio production, which we have met before under a different name, the subject is asked to produce a fraction of the original stimulus. Thus, the technique is that of fractionation or bisection, or, perhaps, of multiple stimuli. Again, the apparent advantage is the approximation of a ratio scale. Note, however, that the experimenter specifies the desired fraction. Thus, it is the subject's "error" which is measured, rather than his direct sensory experience as in ratio estimation.

In magnitude estimation, the experimenter provides the subject with a continuum or dimension of the physical stimulus. Various

FIGURE 5-6: *Plot of the data shown in Table 5–E. The ordinate shows judgments, and the abscissa shows concentrations of the stimulus. Means and medians are shown for judgments of "four times as strong" and "twice as strong."*

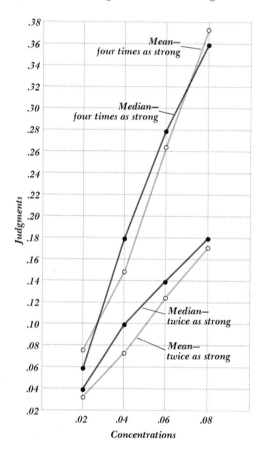

presented with the standard, whether it is demonstrated only once, or whether it is presented, as a reminder, every third trial. It is advisable to select a standard which is easily multiplied or divided, such as 10 or 100. The experimenter may, of course, use more than one standard if he wishes to plot a function across a variety of stimuli, but only one standard should be used in each session. These techniques are based on the assumption that subjects are able to generate ratio scales themselves. Note, however, that the tasks set for the subjects are different from those used in the classic psychophysical methods.

SUCCESSIVE CATEGORIES (RATING), RANKING, AND PAIR COMPARISON

Probably the most commonly used scaling techniques are *successive categories* (also called *rating*), *ranking*, and *pair comparison*. The popularity of these methods is no doubt due to the ease with which they may be applied to a variety of scaling problems, the ease of computation and interpretation, and the simplicity of the task required of the subject. Each technique produces either ordinal or interval data, depending upon the procedure.

The method of successive categories is a general term for a variety of similar techniques. The one most commonly used for scaling problems is the method of rating. The critical factor in rating is that the subject is asked to arrange the stimuli into groups, ranks or categories. When an instructor decides which students will receive grades of A and which will receive C, he is sorting the stimuli (in this case, the students' performance) into ranks or successive categories. Sometimes a series of determinations is made, as when the instructor gives several grades during the semester and then evaluates this series of ranks at the end of the term in order to decide the final rating. A second application of this method could be with the *semantic differential* shown in Figure 5–7. The semantic differential is a technique which permits scaling of the

values of the physical stimulus are then presented randomly, and the subject is required to assess each in terms of the continuum. Often, some standard is provided at the onset of the investigation; e.g., the instructions may be "This light is worth 10 in brightness. Now tell me what these other lights are worth in brightness." Apparently, the subject is providing ratios insofar as he measures each stimulus against the standard. Clearly, the results may vary as a function of how often the subject is

meaning of words. As you will note from the figure, the subject has been asked to evaluate the word "mother" on two continua, each with defined end points and anchors. The subject locates the placement of the term in regard to the end, or anchor, points. He may decide that the concept "mother" is 60 percent hard and 40 percent soft.

The method of rating has certain statistical similarities to the method of ranking. However, a basic characteristic of ranking is that the subject must place each stimulus in only one category. For example, a track steward whose job requires him to rate racehorses at the finish decides which horse is first, which is second, and so on, until one horse has been assigned to each category. Essentially, the steward is ranking the horses on the quality of speed. We encounter similar scaling problems where rank is required—that is, where each stimulus is placed in only one category and where ties are not permitted—in evaluating beauty contestants and selecting clothing. In some uses of this procedure tie ranks are permitted. The terms used in the semantic differential could be used with the method of ranking by presenting, say, 10 categories. The first would be defined as "completely hard"; and so on. The subject would be required to place each of the descriptive titles (hard, soft, warm, cold, etc.) in rank order, beginning with the characteristic that is most descriptive of the term "mother" and ending with the characteristic that is least descriptive.

If repeated scaling tests are given, the method of ranking and the method of rating may produce ties, although in ranking the presence of a tie might imply that the subject was contradictory in his judgment; in rating the implication is that the stimuli were judged to be equal. Figure 5–8 shows the results of an experiment in which the terms used in the semantic differential shown in Figure 5–7 were both ranked and rated by the same subjects. Note that rating generates interval data. "Soft" and "warm," for example, are close together, as compared with "hard" and "cold." This distinction does not appear in the method of

FIGURE 5–7: *A semantic differential scale of the word "mother." The subject has been provided with two continua and asked to scale the word on the continua. This is an example of a rating scale.*

FIGURE 5–8: *Use of both the method of ranking and the method of rating to evaluate the word "mother." The left-hand column shows the ranking of four terms in decreasing order of applicability. The right-hand column shows the ratings of the four categories. Note that rating, as shown in the right-hand column, permits the collection of interval data, while ranking permits only ordinal data.*

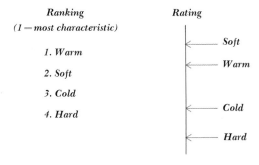

ranking, since only one stimulus may be placed in each category. Although ranking appears to restrict the subject, we shall note that both techniques have disadvantages and advantages.

In the method of pair comparison, the subject is presented with pairs of stimuli. He then selects the member of the pair which has more, or less, of the quality under measurement. For example, a judge in a beauty contest in which 10 girls were entered might find that gazing at all 10 at once (as is done in the method of ranking) would result in his being unable to keep his "mind" on the job and his rankings would be contradictory. That is, the rankings might not prove reliable. Rating each girl independently might lead to the same result. The method of pair comparison, however, not only permits more occasions for examining the stimuli but also reduces the magnitude of the decision to be made to a choice between two stimuli. The pairs of stimuli are presented several times in random order, and the presentation of the stimuli is counterbalanced in order to eliminate position effects. However, as the number of stimuli increases, the number of comparisons to be made increases dramatically, according to the formula

$$\frac{n\,(n-1)}{2}$$

where n = number of stimuli. If 10 stimuli are used, 45 pairs must be presented. If 20 stimuli are used, 190 comparisons must be made, and if 100 stimuli are used, 4,950 comparisons are needed. Clearly, the technique becomes unwieldy with large numbers. On the other hand, it appears to have the advantage of maintaining the subject's alertness and of—perhaps, but not necessarily—providing a more reliable determination than other methods.

Method of Successive Categories (Rating): Variations of this general method are useful for scaling a number of different kinds of stimuli. Although the technique can be applied to analyses of physical stimuli, it has most often been used for scaling continua in which the dimensions are less clearly defined. For example, "best fraternity" and "most beautiful sophomore" are less clearly defined (less agreement is reached on them) than degrees of brightness or loudness. In some ways scaling techniques, such as the method of successive categories, force the subject to define what he means by the stimulus and the categories; for this reason, they may be perceived as techniques which result in the subject's providing definitions for the stimulus and the categories without his being informed that his task is one of definition.

In this regard, one of the basic problems of psychology has been the stipulation of definitions of so-called emotional reactions. Facial expressions have been used as examples of emotional reactions such as fear, fright, love, and hate (see Schlosberg, 1941, 1952). The method of successive categories can be used to scale the subject's categorization of facial expressions. Note the facial expressions shown in Figure 5–9. Assume that an experimenter presents you with the following categories:

A. Completely pleasant
B. Mostly, but not completely, pleasant
C. Slightly pleasant
D. Neither pleasant nor unpleasant
E. Slightly unpleasant
F. Mostly, but not completely, unpleasant
G. Completely unpleasant

Then the experimenter presents you with each of the pictures and asks you to assign each to one of the preceding categories. Assume that 19 other persons are also presented with the same task. The experimenter would have completed the gathering of data when he had the ratings supplied by each subject. It may be noted at this point that scaling techniques admit to the same problems of random sampling and generalization as any other measurement. Whether the 20 subjects represent a random sample of any population is a matter of considerable consequence if the findings are to be generalized to groups beyond those used in the experimental population.

Table 5–F shows the raw data which resulted from the ratings of the 20 subjects. Table 5–G shows the same data in terms of cumulative proportions. The proportions are derived by multiplying each number by 5 (since $n = 20$, then $n \times 5 = 100$) and dividing by 100 to convert to decimals with 1.00 equaling unity. The proportions are added from left to right.

Figure 5–10 shows the cumulative proportions from Table 5–G plotted with categories along the abscissa and cumulative proportions

TABLE 5–F: *Data from an Experiment Using the Method of Successive Categories (Rating).* The subjects were asked to rate the facial expressions shown in Figure 5–9 as representative of one of seven categories ranging from "completely pleasant" to "completely unpleasant." The numbers in the table represent the number of subjects rating the designated expression in the designated category.

	Category						
Expression	A	B	C	D	E	F	G
1	4	5	4	3	2	2	0
2	8	4	3	3	1	1	0
3	2	8	6	0	0	2	2
4	0	12	6	0	1	1	0
5	0	7	7	6	0	0	0
6	3	3	2	3	3	3	3
7	1	0	0	9	3	5	2
8	1	0	1	1	7	8	2
9	0	0	0	6	8	3	3
10	0	0	1	0	9	5	5

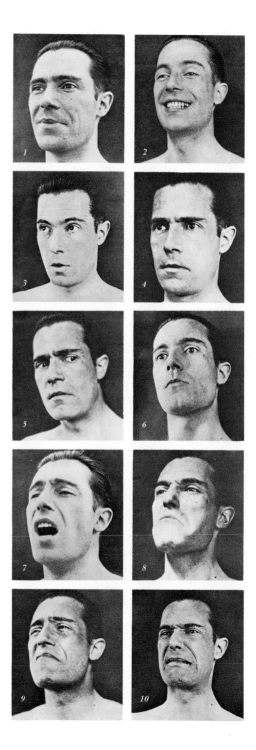

along the ordinate. The slope of the function for each expression is indicative of the variation in category placement of an expression. If there were no variation, the expression would reach a cumulative proportion of 1.0 at a single category. If, however, maximum discrepancy in evaluation existed, the function would be linear and would reach 1.0 at the last category. Expression 6 is nearest to linearity, implying maximal dispersion at that evaluation.

Perhaps one reason this method is used so frequently is that the interpretation of the results seems fairly simple. It appears appropriate, for example, to say that expression 2 could be characterized as the expression most similar to "completely pleasant" while expres-

FIGURE 5–9: *A display of pictures from the Frois-Wittman series. The pictures are to be ranked as described in the text. (From Schlosberg, 1952, p. 235.)*

TABLE 5–G: *Cumulative Proportions for Values Shown in Table 5–F.*

Expression	Category						
	A	B	C	D	E	F	G
1	0.20	0.45	0.65	0.80	0.90	1.00	1.00
2	0.40	0.60	0.75	0.90	0.95	1.00	1.00
3	0.10	0.50	0.80	0.80	0.80	0.90	1.00
4	0	0.60	0.90	0.90	0.95	1.00	1.00
5	0	0.35	0.70	1.00	1.00	1.00	1.00
6	0.15	0.30	0.40	0.55	0.70	0.85	1.00
7	0.05	0.05	0.05	0.50	0.65	0.90	1.00
8	0.05	0.05	0.10	0.15	0.50	0.90	1.00
9	0	0	0	0.30	0.70	0.85	1.00
10	0	0	0.05	0.05	0.50	0.75	1.00

FIGURE 5–10: *The cumulative proportions of Table 5–G plotted. The plot provides information on the amount of variation or dispersion associated with each expression.*

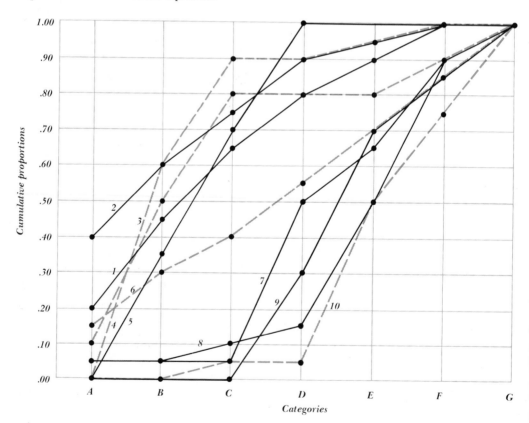

sion 4 is "mostly, but not completely, unpleasant." Within reason, such interpretations are useful. They overlook a wealth of information, however. In many applied problems, it is not merely the most common, or even the average, rating which is important, but the *variation*. For this reason, calculations of standard deviations and regression equations are sometimes more useful. Descriptions of additional refinements are cited in the Sources at the end of the chapter.

For simplicity, we can arrange the mean (or median) category values along a continuum, as shown in Figure 5–11. You will note that such a plot assumes interval scaling, since the scale is composed of equal units.

Although the preliminary technique for assigning category values to stimuli is relatively simple, both in regard to the task required of the subject and the ease of calculation by the experimenter, the eventual transformation to intervallike data is tedious and fairly complicated. The danger is that preliminary calculations, such as those shown in Tables 5–F and 5–G and Figures 5–10 and 5–11, will be interpreted as if they represent interval data when they do not. If interval data are required, they may be found by additional assumptions and statistical treatment of the data.

Rating scales are very popular in employee and student selection. To a degree, the "letter of recommendation" has been replaced by rating scales in which the recommender is required only to select an appropriate location on a scale corresponding to some quality of the person being rated. Refinements of such techniques include asking the recommender to determine the percentile into which the intelligence of the person being rated might fall. The general advantages of such techniques are that recommendations from a variety of persons may be compared on a similar continuum, the designer of the recommendation form may be certain of gaining information that is of particular interest to him, and the task of the recommender is simplified. The disadvantages are that the recommender may not offer information not requested by the designer of the form and, furthermore, that the mere fact that the same scale is used by several recommenders does not assure the designer that the judgments are equivalent.

Method of Ranking: The basic characteristic of the method of ranking is that the subject is required to place one, and only one, of the stimuli available in each rank. Moreover, the category continuum or series of ranks is defined in some term, such as "best," or "brightest," or "most beautiful," in such a manner that the subject may be instructed that he is to select the "most beautiful" stimulus for the first category, the "second most beautiful" for the second category, and so on, until the "least beautiful" stimulus is placed in the last category.

In ranking, as in the method of successive categories, the subject is required to place each stimulus in a category, but in ranking, only *one* stimulus may be placed in each category. Resemblances between the two methods are thus superficial, for the use of defined categories or a defined continuum is a resemblance only in operation. Actually, in terms of technique, the method of ranking is similar to the method of pair comparison, since in both these

FIGURE 5–11: *Mean or median ratings of 10 expressions plotted along a continuum ranging from pleasant to unpleasant.*

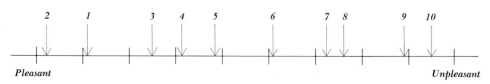

Pleasant   Unpleasant

methods the subject is supposedly comparing each stimulus with each other stimulus. The difference is merely that in ranking all the stimuli are presented simultaneously, while in pair comparison they are presented two at a time.

It should be noted, however, that ranking, unlike either successive categories or pair comparison, forces the subject to be consistent. He may not assign the same value to more than one stimulus. In some experimental designs, it may be desirable for the subject to be forced to make a choice when two stimuli appear equal in respect to the dimension under consideration. In most designs, however, the method of ranking results in a loss in the precision of measurement, since the subject is asked to perform operations characteristic of ordinal scaling. That is, his task is to indicate whether one stimulus has more or less of the quality being scaled; he is not asked to indicate the quantity of the difference. This does not imply that interval data may not be ranked, but if interval or ratio data are subjected to ranking, some of their original precision is lost, since the rank order is no respecter of the content of the original data. For example, assume that five animals run down a runway with the following speeds: 2.5, 2.6, 14.6, 16.1, and 17.1 seconds. By ranking these running speeds in order from 1 to 5 we lose the amount of difference in speed in *seconds*. Animal 2 (2.6 seconds) is merely 1 rank higher than animal 3 (14.6 seconds), even though the difference in running speed between these animals is much greater than the difference between ranks 1 and 2 and ranks 3 and 4.

Assume that the facial expressions shown in Figure 5–9 (and later subjected to the method of successive categories in Tables 5–F and 5–G and Figures 5–10 and 5–11) are to be ranked rather than rated. The subject is presented with the series of stimuli and asked to rank them in order, with the "most pleasant" expression first and the "least pleasant" expression last. Note that we have used "pleasant" for the entire continuum, calling the lowest rank on the scale "least pleasant," rather than

"unpleasant." When both "pleasant" and "unpleasant" are used as extremes (as was done in successive categories), it may be assumed that there is some neutral point, presented by a category which is "neither pleasant nor unpleasant." However, when a single continuum is used (as with ranking), it may be assumed that the subject is evaluating the quantity of a single continuum (the amount of "pleasantness") and that even the lowest rank has some of the quality. Needless to say, either technique can be used for either method, but it is useful to notice that slightly different tasks are being required of the subject depending upon the type of continuum or categories established.

If only one subject is used, there is no technique by which the experimenter can be certain that equal "attention" is given to all the stimuli. Indeed, with stimuli such as facial expressions it is apparent that the subject must see one of the stimuli first, and it is possible that the nature of the stimulus could affect judgment of the others. The problem may be counterbalanced by using as many subjects as there are stimuli; thus, the experimenter may present each subject with the stimuli in a different order with the restriction that each stimulus will have appeared in each position when all the subjects have been tested. A counterbalanced design similar to that shown in Table 1–C could be used.

Table 5–H shows the frequencies with which each of 10 facial expressions were ranked by 20 subjects. As is true of all scaling methods, there are several ways in which the data may be analyzed, depending upon the needs of the experimenter. One can, for example, compute the mean or median ranks. This technique makes certain assumptions about the nature of the data, for with the method of ranking deviation is artificially lowered by permitting only one stimulus to be placed in each rank. However, if the experimenter is willing to assume that this restriction is ineffective—that each category represents the mean of judgments which would have been dispersed around that category had such measurements been per-

TABLE 5–H: *Frequencies with Which Each of 10 Facial Expressions Shown in Figure 5–9 Were Ranked by 20 Subjects.*

Rank 1 is defined as the expression showing the most pleasantness.

Subjects	Expression									
	1	*2*	*3*	*4*	*5*	*6*	*7*	*8*	*9*	*10*
1	6	2	7	4	1	3	5	9	8	10
2	4	1	3	8	5	2	10	6	9	7
3	1	8	9	2	4	3	5	6	7	10
4	9	1	8	7	3	4	5	2	6	10
5	4	9	2	3	1	8	7	5	10	6
6	5	1	3	2	4	6	9	7	10	8
7	2	3	6	4	1	5	7	8	10	9
8	1	7	2	3	4	8	6	9	5	10
9	2	3	6	8	4	7	5	1	10	9
10	5	1	7	4	3	8	9	6	2	10
11	8	3	4	6	2	9	7	1	10	5
12	2	1	3	5	6	9	8	10	7	4
13	1	4	2	3	8	7	10	9	6	5
14	4	9	8	6	2	3	1	7	5	10
15	6	1	7	10	4	2	9	5	8	3
16	6	5	4	7	2	1	8	3	9	10
17	1	5	2	4	3	9	6	8	7	10
18	3	5	4	7	2	1	5	9	6	10
19	1	2	6	8	3	5	4	7	10	9
20	1	8	4	3	2	5	9	6	10	7
$\overline{X}$	3.60	3.95	4.85	5.20	3.20	5.25	6.75	6.20	7.75	8.10

mitted—then computation of means or medians may be useful. This would be true if the experimenter were interested only in which stimulus received the most judgments of first, that is, if the method were used to determine the first-prize winner in some event and the placement of the remaining contestants was not an issue.

It is true that if only one subject ranks the stimuli (and only one stimulus is placed in each rank), each stimulus appears to be equidistant from the next, but if more than one subject takes part in the rankings, the equidistant relationship disappears. As may be noted from Table 5–H, the use of more than one subject can result in occasional ties in ratings as a function of disagreement among the subjects.

When one subject places each stimulus in a distinct category, the frequency distribution is rectangular; there is a frequency of one stimulus for each category. Most stimuli being scaled, however, do not exhibit a rectangular distribution. Ordinarily the stimuli are normally distributed, since this type of frequency function is common when living things subject to the laws of random distribution are evaluated.

Table 5–I shows the data from an experiment in which one subject was asked to rank the same stimuli several times. Although it is tempting to claim that the subject is "reliable" because he tends to give the same rank to the stimuli upon retesting, it should be remembered that he may permit his judgment on previous tests to influence succeeding ones. Subjects probably prefer to appear to be reliable judges; accordingly, successive rankings by the same subject are probably not independent of previous rankings. However, a series of determinations, as shown in Table 5–I, does permit the experimenter to scale the rankings in a manner characteristic of interval scaling, since a stimulus *may* appear in more than a single category. Similarly, the use of more than one subject permits the same type of scaling for the same reason. The concept of *dispersion* (see Chapter 4) is applicable here, for it may be assumed that judges will make determinations around the mean in such a way that the determinations are normally distributed.

Many times it is useful to be able to convert raw scores to some common scale. One technique, which indicates the amount of devia-

tion from the mean of the sample, is to convert to z scores. The advantage of using z scores is that data from different psychophysical or scaling procedures may be compared more easily and meaningfully than if only raw scores, or "choice scores," were used. In order to determine the z score, the mean and standard deviation (SD) of the sample must be known. The z score for any raw score is determined by the following formula:

$$z = \frac{\text{Raw score} - \text{mean}}{\text{SD}}$$

Hence, if the raw score is 40, the mean 35, and the standard deviation 10,

$$z = (40 - 35)/10$$
$$z = 5/10$$
$$z = 0.5$$

Note that the z may be a minus number if the raw score is less than the mean. Hence, a z score of −0.5 would indicate the same deviation from the mean as 0.5, but on the other side of the mean. z scores are generally distributed between +2.96 and −2.96.

In both psychophysics and scaling, z values are often computed from the proportion (p)

TABLE 5–I: *Ranking of 10 Facial Expressions by One Subject on 10 Different Occasions.* The apparent reliability between successive rankings is probably exaggerated, since the subject is able to remember his prior rankings and is influenced by them.

	Trial										
Expression	*1*	*2*	*3*	*4*	*5*	*6*	*7*	*8*	*9*	*10*	*Mean*
1	3	2	3	3	3	2	4	3	3	3	2.9
2	1	1	1	1	2	1	1	1	1	1	1.1
3	2	3	2	2	1	3	3	2	2	2	2.2
4	4	5	4	4	5	4	2	4	5	4	4.1
5	6	6	7	6	6	6	7	6	7	7	6.4
6	7	7	6	7	7	7	6	7	6	6	6.6
7	5	4	5	5	4	5	5	5	4	5	4.7
8	10	8	10	9	10	10	10	10	10	10	9.7
9	9	10	8	10	9	9	8	9	9	9	9.0
10	8	9	9	8	8	8	9	8	8	8	8.3

of responses. For example, in the method of constant stimuli or in the method of pair comparison, the p of responses in a given category is computed, and the p value may, in turn, be translated into z scores. Table 5–J shows this conversion. Note that if $p = 50$ (if the stimulus is selected half the time), $z = 0$, since the mean proportion of choices is 50 percent if two alternatives are available. An example of the use of z scores, computed from choice scores, is shown in Table 5–M.

In addition, data from experiments in which ranking scales have been used may be translated into *pair comparison* techniques. For example, if stimulus$_1$ is judged greater than stimulus$_2$, and if stimulus$_2$ is judged greater than stimulus$_3$, it may be assumed that *three* pair comparison evaluations have been made, since stimulus$_1$ should be judged greater than stimulus$_3$. This technique assumes that the subject does not contradict his choices. The data are now in the same form as most pair comparison data, in which a series of "greater than" or "less than" determinations are made between pairs of stimuli. This technique also permits eventual translation onto a common scale, such as z scores.

Method of Pair Comparison: The basic characteristic of the method of pair comparison is

TABLE 5–J: *Table for Converting p Values to z Scores.*

p	01	02	03	04	05	06	07	08	09	10
z	−2.33	−2.05	−1.88	−1.75	−1.64	−1.55	−1.48	−1.41	−1.34	−1.28
p	11	12	13	14	15	16	17	18	19	20
z	−1.23	−1.18	−1.13	−1.08	−1.04	−0.99	−0.95	−0.92	−0.88	−0.84
p	21	22	23	24	25	26	27	28	29	30
z	−0.81	−0.77	−0.74	−0.71	−0.67	−0.64	−0.61	−0.58	−0.55	−0.52
p	31	32	33	34	35	36	37	38	39	40
z	−0.50	−0.47	−0.44	−0.41	−0.39	−0.36	−0.33	−0.31	−0.28	−0.25
p	41	42	43	44	45	46	47	48	49	50
z	−0.23	−0.20	−0.18	−0.15	−0.13	−0.10	−0.08	−0.05	−0.03	0.00
p	51	52	53	54	55	56	57	58	59	60
z	+0.03	+0.05	+0.08	+0.10	+0.13	+0.15	+0.18	+0.20	+0.23	+0.25
p	61	62	63	64	65	66	67	68	69	70
z	+0.28	+0.31	+0.33	+0.36	+0.39	+0.41	+0.44	+0.47	+0.50	+0.52
p	71	72	73	74	75	76	77	78	79	80
z	+0.55	+0.58	+0.61	+0.64	+0.67	+0.71	+0.74	+0.77	+0.81	+0.84
p	81	82	83	84	85	86	87	88	89	90
z	+0.88	+0.92	+0.95	+0.99	+1.04	+1.08	+1.13	+1.18	+1.23	+1.28
p	91	92	93	94	95	96	97	98	99	99.5
z	+1.34	+1.41	+1.48	+1.55	+1.64	+1.75	+1.88	+2.05	+2.33	+2.58

that the subject is presented with the pairs of stimuli and is required to select which member of the pair contains more, or less, of the quality being scaled. As with the other methods, a single subject may judge a given pain on several occasions, or several subjects may judge the same stimuli, thus providing a measure of dispersion. Either technique permits more than a single assessment of each pair and permits variation to appear in the final evaluation. The amount of variation for a given stimulus provides additional information regarding the attributes of that stimulus.

Some determinations (such as lifting weights or making fine physical discriminations) should include some trials in which each stimulus is presented with itself (unknown to the subject, of course), to permit evaluation of the amount and location of discriminal dispersion. In showing preference for names of perfumes or similar scales, such comparisons are not meaningful, because the identity of the stimuli is readily apparent to the subject.

The advantages of the method are that it contains some built-in controls not possessed by other methods. Since the stimuli are presented in pairs, the techniques of counterbalancing permit elimination of time and space errors as relevant variables affecting the data. Similarly, the fact that each stimulus is presented with each other stimulus on at least one occasion leads to an a priori assumption that the technique permits the subject to make more reliable judgments than are possible when a large number of stimuli are presented at once. The basic disadvantage of the method is that it becomes unwieldy with a large number of stimuli. Although there are various techniques for reducing the number of comparisons that need to be made when a large number of stimuli is used, even with a small number the technique is time-consuming and possibly tedious.

Assume that a perfume manufacturer is interested in determining the appropriate name for a new perfume compound. The manufacturer believes, probably correctly, that the name of the perfume will affect sales and that

it is worthwhile to use scaling devices to determine the name most attractive to potential buyers. Eight names are recommended: Abattoir, Southside, Caprylic, Butterfly, Beeoh, Formalin, Tiger Milk, and Getim. A sample of women is selected, as described in Chapter 1. Each subject is tested individually. The stimuli (the names) are arranged in pairs in such a way that no single stimulus appears in succession and that each stimulus appears equally often on the left and the right. Table 5–K shows a sample of the order in which the pairs might be presented. Since eight stimuli are to be evaluated, 28 pairs are to be presented to each subject.

It may be noted at this point that the method of pair comparison is similar to the psychophysical method of constant stimuli in that the subject is required to determine whether one stimulus is greater or less than a second stimulus. The results for a single subject are shown in Table 5–L, and the proportion of times each stimulus was chosen over each other stimulus is shown in Table 5–M. These proportions may be plotted in the same way as data from experiments using the psychophysical method of constant stimuli. A useful method of evaluation in many cases is shown in Figure 5–12, where the stimuli have been rearranged in order of choice. Although Butterfly appears to be the preferred name for the new perfume, Abattoir is so close that the manufacturer might choose either one, depending upon other considerations. For example, if the stimulus had been the color of the packages, if red had been preferred only slightly over blue, and if red packages were significantly more expensive than blue ones, the manufacturer might decide to use blue.

Although the strict procedure of pair comparison uses stimuli in pairs, nothing prevents the use of three stimuli in each sample, or even more. When three stimuli are used, the technique is sometimes called the *method of triads*. The subject may be asked to select only one of the items, or he may be asked to select the stimulus which has "most" of the attribute as well as the stimulus which has "least" of the

TABLE 5-K: *A Sample Order of the Presentation of Pairs in the Method of Pair Comparison.*
Each name is paired with each other name, and no name is permitted to succeed itself on the list.

1. Butterfly—Abattoir	15. Beeoh—Formalin
2. Tiger Milk—Getim	16. Southside—Getim
3. Caprylic—Butterfly	17. Formalin—Tiger Milk
4. Getim—Beeoh	18. Getim—Caprylic
5. Formalin—Abattoir	19. Beeoh—Tiger Milk
6. Butterfly—Beeoh	20. Abattoir—Getim
7. Caprylic—Tiger Milk	21. Caprylic—Butterfly
8. Getim—Beeoh	22. Tiger Milk—Abbatoir
9. Formalin—Butterfly	23. Formalin—Caprylic
10. Southside—Beeoh	24. Butterfly—Southside
11. Butterfly—Getim	25. Tiger Milk—Getim
12. Southside—Caprylic	26. Abattoir—Beeoh
13. Tiger Milk—Butterfly	27. Southside—Formalin
14. Abattoir—Southside	28. Beeoh—Caprylic

TABLE 5-L: *Results from a Single Subject on Scaling Eight Perfume Names by the Method of Pair Comparison.*
The "number of choices" is determined by counting the number of times that the stimulus is selected. For example, when Abattoir and Southside are compared, Southside loses and receives a 0 in its horizontal row, while Abattoir receives a 1 in its horizontal row.

	Abattoir	South-side	Caprylic	Butter-fly	Beeoh	Formalin	Tiger Milk	Getim	Choice
Abattoir	x	1	1	0	1	1	1	1	6
Southside	0	x	0	0	0	0	0	0	0
Caprylic	0	1	x	0	1	1	1	1	5
Butterfly	1	1	1	x	1	1	1	1	7
Beeoh	0	1	0	0	x	1	1	1	4
Formalin	0	1	0	0	0	x	1	1	3
Tiger Milk	0	1	0	0	0	0	x	0	1
Getim	0	1	0	0	0	0	1	x	2

attribute, the remaining stimulus being considered neutral or between the other two. The number of comparisons necessary in this method is given by the formula

$$\frac{(n-2)(n-1)n}{6}$$

where n = number of stimuli. Accordingly, if 10 stimuli are to be evaluated by the method of triads, 120 comparisons must be made. Clearly, comparatively more determinations must be made by the subject with the method of triads than with pair comparison; on the other hand, some additional useful information may be given by the method for special problems.

TABLE 5-M: *Eight Perfume Names Arranged in Order of Highest to Lowest Scale Value by One Subject (Table 5-L).*

The scale is determined by conversion to p scores, where $p =$ number of times chosen / $(n-1)$, and z is computed from p as indicated in Table 5-J.

Stimulus	*p*	*z*
Butterfly	1.0	More than +2.58
Abattoir	0.857	+1.08
Caprylic	0.714	+0.58
Beeoh	0.571	+0.18
Formalin	0.428	−0.18
Getim	0.285	−0.58
Tiger Milk	0.142	−1.08
Southside	0	Less than −2.33

SOME ADDITIONAL TECHNIQUES

As is true of the basic psychophysical methods, the basic methods of scaling admit to apparently endless variations. Some variations in scaling techniques have the essential characteristics of one of the parent methods, and others are crosses between several parent methods. Although the development of new scaling techniques sometimes appears to be based on the desire merely to invent a previously unused concoction, most often it is the physical or technical problems presented by the stimuli to be scaled which leads to the invention of novel

FIGURE 5–12: *A plot of the p values of perfume names used in the experiment with the method of pair comparison.*

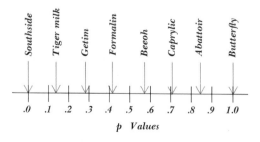

p *Values*

scaling techniques. Among the general techniques are *multidimensional scaling* and *factor analysis.* The first technique involves the use of more than one continuum and the second technique involves the assessment of the intercorrelations among continua. Both techniques attempt to handle more complicated data than those which are considered by the scaling techniques we have discussed in which only a single continuum is used.

There are, however, several older techniques which bear clear resemblances to the standard techniques of ranking, rating, and pair comparison and which are useful in particular situations. Those to be discussed are the *method of first choices,* the *method of similar attributes,* and the *method of balanced values.* All these methods are concerned with scaling along a single continuum, and all have weaknesses which make them useful only for restricted types of data.

Method of First Choices: The method of first choices was named by Fechner, who called it *der Wahlmethode.* The technique is not applicable to one subject, for it consists solely of calculating the stimulus which was judged "first" or "best" by the subjects. The frequency with which each stimulus is judged first represents the rank of that stimulus. If the eight perfume names used in the pair comparison experiment were evaluated by the method of first choices, the experimenter would merely ask each subject which name she preferred and would tabulate the number of times each name was selected. If Abattoir received 13 first-place votes, Butterfly, 8, Beeoh, 2, and Getim, 2, Abattoir would receive a rank of 1, Butterfly a rank of 2, and so on. Needless to say, if a large number of stimuli are used or if the difference between the stimuli is great, an unusual number of tied ranks may be expected among stimuli which receive few or no first-place votes. Also, a relatively large number of judges is required to prevent tied ranks.

The advantages of the method are that the subjects may be tested very quickly and that a larger sample of subjects may be tested than is possible with other methods, such as pair comparison, in which the testing of each subject is lengthy. The major disadvantage is that few useful data are accumulated on stimuli ranked less than 1. On the other hand, the technique is useful where an efficient determination of the first rank is needed, as in elections. Indeed, the method of first choices is used whenever we vote, since the matter of who received the second, third, and nth place in the election is a matter of comparatively little interest.

Method of Similar Attributes: The method of similar attributes was developed by Thurstone and Chave (1929) to handle the scaling of attitudes of human judges. The method is based upon the realization that although the experimenter may present the subject with a continuum specifying the quality on which he wishes the subject to base his judgments, there is no guarantee that the subject will make his judgment with reference only to that continuum. As we have noted, this is the basic problem to which multidimensional scaling and factor analysis of scaled values is directed. In order to appreciate the problem to which the method of similar attributes is addressed, as well as to understand the assumptions it makes regarding scales, consider a study by D. Katz and Braly (1933) in which college students were presented with a list of attributes supposedly characteristic of races (such as humorless, musically inclined, and thrifty) and asked to indicate the statements which were characteristic of certain racial groups.

Now, if two statements of attitudes receive the same scale value, that is, if they are rated as being characteristic of a particular group an equal number of times, they are interchangeable. If they are interchangeable, if the attitudinal statements were presented singly, subjects who accept one as a characteristic of a particular race should also accept the other as characteristic. If the two statements are not interchangeable—if, when presented with the attitudinal statements individually, a subject accepts one as characteristic of a race, but not the other—it would appear that the two statements were actually being rated on different continua but that they happened to receive the same scale value on whatever continuum the experimenter selected.

If it appears that equal locations on the scale do indicate consistency (in the sense that one statement can be substituted for another at the same location), then the difference in location between two stimuli represents the "nearness" of the attitudes to each other. If two statements are far apart in location, it is quite likely that subjects accepting one statement as characteristic would not accept the other. The nearer statements are to each other, the more likely it is that they represent "similar attributes" to the subjects. This technique is used often in research in social psychology (see Chapter 19).

Method of Balanced Values: Certain continua, such as those used in rating, assume a zero point by identifying such a point on the continuum. For example, the supposedly neutral term "neither pleasant nor unpleasant" was used in an earlier example in this chapter. It is possible, however, that subjects find that the very presence of the word "unpleasant" in the definition slants the concept toward the negative side. One technique for avoiding this problem is to reverse the process, i.e., to require the subject to locate the zero or neutral point on the scale. Horst (1932) has described such a technique. Its operations are similar to those of pair comparison, except that the subject is not asked merely to select one stimulus from a pair. Rather, he is required to select from a number of stimuli the one he would choose if he could *not* select one stimulus. By arranging the stimuli, the experimenter can determine the stimulus the subject would least accept, and, by a series of determinations, he can find the zero, or neutral, point of indifference—where the subject does not care which stimulus is chosen.

Multidimensional Scaling: In discussing the method of similar attributes, we noted that it attempted to investigate a phenomenon basic to problems of scaling, namely, that any object has many properties and that separate scales can be devised for each property. Even though scaling procedures commonly specify the type of scale on which the subject is to make his judgments, it is unlikely that any subject is sufficiently "objective" to remove all properties of an object, save those specified, from consideration. Indeed, the very act of scaling implies that the subject has acquired, or possesses, through his sensory abilities, beliefs about the nature of the object being scaled which are not necessarily consistent with the beliefs of other subjects.

Unidimensional judgments, such as those made when the subject is instructed to judge which stimulus is "heavier," "brighter," "tastier," or even "more beautiful," may be represented along a continuum which consists of a straight line. The distance between any two points on the line may represent the difference in "heaviness" or some other singular quality. Multidimensional judgments, on the other hand, are represented by several dimensions or continua, and they are represented in space, rather than as points on a straight line. When an object is scaled by multidimensional methods, the scale value is some point in space which is identified by the axes or coordinates of the space.

It should be noted that some attributes of objects are purely unidimensional. Length is a clear example of a unidimensional attribute. Color is an example of a multidimensional attribute, since it is composed of two unidimensional attributes, saturation and hue. When color is used in unidimensional scaling (as when colors are scaled in order of preference), the subject is really being asked to evaluate several dimensions of the stimuli in making his judgments. The data may be analyzed in terms of the distance between each scaled point and the dimensions of the continua. Figure 5–13 shows two dimensions, D_1 and D_2. They might be dimensions of saturation and hue. The figure shows four scaled values. Note that if only D_1 were under consideration and if the quality of D_1 increased from right to left, the rank order of the stimuli would be

4, 2, 3, and 1. If D_2 were under consideration, with the quantity increasing upward, the order would be 3, 4, 1, and 2. The rankings are not the same, because the dimensions represent different attributes. If the rankings were identical, it would appear that the dimensions were not different, and this, it may be recalled, was the basic procedure used by Thurstone in the method of similar attributes. In addition, techniques may be used to discover the relative "weighting" the subject gives each dimension in the determination of the scale value of each object. This procedure has some obvious industrial and practical uses in situations in which it is necessary to evaluate the importance or value the subject gives to various dimensions.

Figure 5–14 shows a sample of an object scaled when three dimensions are employed. Each scaled value is related to three planes, and the distance between each plane and the scaled value may be computed. There is nothing to prevent the use of any number of A dimensions, since any number may be conceptualized. Various techniques and procedures have been used in determining interstimulus distances. Both the method of equal-appearing intervals and the method of successive categories have been adapted to the needs of multidimensional analysis.

Multidimensional scaling is a relatively new technique in the development of scaling procedures, even though the basic problem to which it is addressed has long been known. Thurstone's technique of similar attributes was developed from a concern that unidimensional scaling was overlooking useful data. The technique has been applied to various problems. Analysis of colors has been particularly prominent (e.g., Richardson, 1938; Torgerson, 1951), probably because the dimensions which compose color are established and a considerable quantity of material is available on unidimensional scaling of color. The procedure has also been used for scaling "friendliness of foreign powers" (Klineberg, 1941).

Factor Analysis: Although the process of factor analysis was not developed specifically for problems in scaling, it has proved useful in determining the source of common elements and individual differences in scaled values. Factor analysis has its origin in the assessment of mental abilities. Assume that an investigator wishes to find a series, or a battery, of tests which, taken together, predicts mental ability accurately. Assuming that the investigator knows how to measure mental ability accurately, it is reasonable to assume that it is wasteful to use every test devised, since there is likely to be some overlap between tests. The problem of the investigator is to find the least number of tests, or parts of tests, which can predict mental ability accurately. The process of factor analysis is a mathematical technique which permits discovery of which tests have these common elements and which measure different attributes.

The basic procedure of factor analysis is the evaluation of the correlations between tests, subtests, or other groups of data. If we are concerned with a series of multidimensional judgments, represented as scale values, we have the same format as if we had a series of test scores purporting to measure mental ability. Accordingly, the application of factor analysis to a series of judgments permits the investigator to determine the variables which are common (i.e., correlate highly) and to determine each subject's variance from these common loadings on correlations. Although multidimensional scaling is concerned with the same problem, it may be noted that here the data are represented in terms of the distance of each scaled value from the established dimensions. In factor analysis, however, the mathematical variance from the common factors is taken as the dependent variable. One final difference is worth noting: with multidimensional techniques, the dimensions are established at the onset of the collection of data. With factor analysis, the relation between the established dimensions may be determined by the analysis, thus indicating how similar or different they are in terms of the origin of the communality of the scale values.

In factor analysis, variance is composed of

FIGURE 5–13: *Four stimuli (1 to 4) are evaluated along two dimensions, D_1 and D_2. The hatched lines indicate the distance between the scaled values and the continua.*

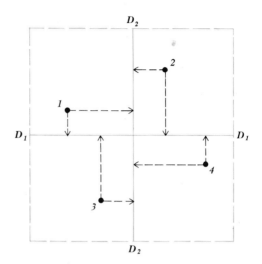

three subforms: The first, *common-factor variance,* is that variance accounted for by agreement between two or more subjects. Objectivity is defined by factor analysis as an increase in the number of judgments of a given type. The greater agreement there is among judges, the greater the contribution to common-factor variance and, by definition, the less contribution to the other two subforms, *specific* and *error variance.* The judgments of a subject may be influenced by a determinant which operates only on his judgments; that is, it does not affect the judgments of other subjects. This is known as *specific variance,* since the variance resulting from the determinant is specific and to an individual subject. Some specific variance is found in almost all subjects. *Error variance* merely implies that there is some identifiable variance which is not due to either common-factor or specific variance. Error variance may occur merely because the subject gives contradictory judgments on different occasions.

The use of factor analysis in such areas as aesthetics has been shown by Guilford and

FIGURE 5-14: *Multidimensional scaling on three dimensions, D_1, D_2, and D_3. The analysis is performed the same way as in Figure 5–13; however the third dimension is added. Thus, the scale value lies in space on three dimensions.*

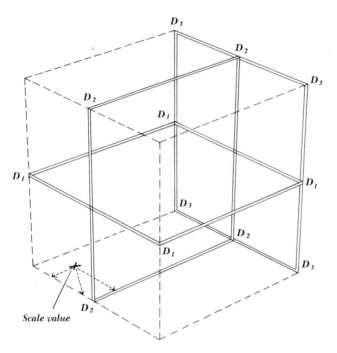

Holley (1949), who had subjects judge the artistic merit of a series of pictures. Four different types of instructions (which directed the attention of the subjects to a particular characteristic, such as color) were used. The experiment was repeated to permit assessment of reliability, and the sex of the subjects was evaluated in the factor analysis. It is clear that factor analysis yields a great amount of useful information when applied to problems such as those of aesthetics. In addition to being able to locate the source of agreement or disagreement among subjects on judgments, the experimenter may also evaluate one aspect of scaling commonly overlooked by other methods by determining the sources of the variance, namely, the analysis of the source of individual differences.

RELIABILITY AND VALIDITY OF SCALING PROCEDURES

It is useful to distinguish between intramethod and intermethod reliability and validity. The reliability of a given method is most easily evaluated by retesting. This reliability may be expressed as the correlation between different administrations of the procedure. Other tests of intramethod reliability are available (Chapter 18).

Reliability between different methods is a somewhat more complicated task, since it is often difficult to determine whether the absence of agreement is due to error contributed by the subjects or to differences in procedures in the methods. Very small procedural differences can cause large differences in measurement, since procedural differences probably affect *all* subjects tested under one method while affecting *none* of the subjects tested by a second method. Fortunately, experimental designs which concentrate on ·discovering which procedures produce differences in results between methods may be constructed to answer this question. One way of measuring intermethod reliability is to use two or more procedures on the same task. Table 5–N shows

T A B L E 5 – N : *Some Comparative Studies of Scaling Techniques.*

Techniques	Author	Task	Result
Pair comparison and equal-appearing intervals	Thorndike (1910)		Did not agree
Pair comparison and equal-appearing intervals	Guilford (1938)	Spots pattern	Pair comparison shows greater units among higher intervals
Multiple stimuli and fractionation	Geiger & Firestone (1933)	Sound intensity	Greatest discrepancy in ratios between ½ and 2
Multiple stimuli and fractionation	Ham & Parkinson (1932)	Sound intensity	Good agreement
Multiple stimuli and fractionation	Hanes (1949)	Time patterns and hues	Agreement best in central portion
Pair comparison and ranking	J. Bernard (1934)	Human questionnaire	Ranking was quicker and as reliable as pair comparison
Pair comparison and rank order	Eng & French (1948)	Human questionnaire	Near-perfect correlation between mean ranks and pair comparison
Pair comparison and ranking	Wilkins (1950)	Incentives	Dissimilar results
Pair comparison and rank order	R. T. Ross (1955)	Preferences	Linear relationship between choices from pair comparison method and rank-order method
Magnetic-board rating technique versus pair comparisons, equal-appearing intervals, ranking, Likert, and graphic ranking	C. J. Bartlett, Hermann, and Rettig (1960)	Human ratings	Pair comparison and ranking were superior

some of the intertest reliability checks which have been made. It should be noted that different investigators may have used slightly different procedures or variations in technique, which could account for some of the discrepancies. In addition, it is likely that the task itself will result in disagreement, since some tasks are better adapted to certain methods than are others. Table 5–N is not an exhaustive survey of intermethod reliability; however, it does indicate the need for further comparisons.

To question the validity of scaling methods is, in some ways, meaningless. One might argue that to talk about the validity of the ruler as a technique of measurement is meaningless because of the absence of any external criteria and the fact that the measure itself is often the only criterion available. The concept of validity faces the same problems when applied to scaling as when applied to psychophysics. The only meaningful "external" criterion is whether the threshold or scaled value is consistent and whether it varies predictably with the application of known independent variables. Although the possibility of electrical recording from nervous tissue means that an external criterion may be available for some physical threshold determination, a similar external criterion is not readily available for the "mental" phenomena usually investigated through scaling techniques.

SOURCES

Nature of Numbers: A general discussion of the relation between the nature of numbers and psychological phenomena is found in Stevens (1951). The chapter is broad in scope and includes some remarks on the mathematical development of psychophysics. For a slightly different viewpoint, see Chapter 2 in Torgerson (1958), which relates the qualities of the different number systems to scaling problems and hence is germane to our discussion here. In addition, Torgerson's chapter provides an excellent introduction to the problems and techniques of scaling. For the advanced reader or the reader interested in derivations rather than in a cookbook approach to scaling, the Torgerson work is probably the most useful. Guilford (1954) includes a general discussion of the problems of measurement in his first chapter. This excellent section of an excellent book is useful to the reader who has a general knowledge of statistical techniques.

Methods Based on Interval and Ratio Judgments: The most compact source of information on this topic is Guilford (1954). Guilford's text is considerably more detailed and imaginative than the present volume and indicates refinements of analysis not discussed in this chapter. In addition, the methods discussed are based on assumptions of considerable importance to the entire field of scaling, and a knowledge of the methods based on internal and ratio judgments; it is a very useful book for work in the more common methods, such as successive categories. Woodworth and Schlosberg (1954) have two chapters on psychophysics and scaling, in which they give examples of these methods. Both the fractionation methods and the method of equal sense distances receive thorough treatment.

Successive Categories (Rating), Ranking, and Pair Comparison: These techniques are so commonly used that all experimental psychology texts and many introductory books contain discussions and examples of them. However, many texts fail to indicate the underlying assumptions, both psychological and mathematical. Because it is simple to collect data from these techniques, the uninitiated worker is led to make analyses and interpretations which are incomplete and perhaps misleading. If the worker does not understand the assumptions and does not know what mathematical or statistical analyses of the data are permissible, the techniques become useless, if not dangerous. In this chapter, I have attempted to show a variety of techniques of analysis, so that an investigator can determine which method is most appropriate for a particular problem and what the various disadvantages and advantages, both operational and theoretical, are for each technique. However, for adequate experimental work, a reader would need to consult a more advanced source. I recommend especially (in order of increasing difficulty) Woodworth and Schlosberg (1954), Guilford (1954), and Torgerson (1958).

In addition, Edwards (1957) offers a detailed account of pair comparison, equal-appearing intervals, and successive categories, citing data from questionnaires and social psychology and thus indicating a wider use of scaling techniques than does the present chapter. Edwards also covers scaling techniques appropriate for the type of scaling most often required in opinion polling and similar work, such as scalogram analysis.

Some Additional Techniques: The techniques discussed under this topic are covered (more thoroughly) by Guilford (1954) and Torgerson (1958). Other than these sources, the reader will need to consult the literature cited in the text.

Validity and Reliability: Textbooks say remarkably little about these characteristics of scaling methods. While experimental psychologists express concern over the reliability and validity of mental or projective tests, they seem uninterested in similar measures of psychophysics and scaling.

The first five chapters of this book have emphasized the importance of the central nervous system and the sensory systems to the study of psychology. Our first task was to acquire some techniques and procedures for the measurement of stimuli and for the measurement of responses to the stimuli. This task considered the search for a psychophysical law which would relate stimulus dimensions to psychological judgment. We now must consider the nature of the sensory systems themselves.

It is, perhaps, in the study of sensory psychology that the distinction between research for applied purposes and research of a basic nature is most clear. Any basic discovery concerning how a sensory system operates has implications for persons with such diverse interests as consumer behavior, industrial psychology, training practices, and problems of military psychology. However, many times the implications of basic discoveries for applied endeavors are not readily apparent.

George Santayana (1934) once remarked that "those who cannot remember the past are condemned to repeat it." Similarly, the applied psychologist who is not aware of basic data and theory is compelled to rediscover them when a practical need appears. Rediscovery, as opposed to confirmation, of research findings is an obvious waste of research talent. Accordingly, although the presentation of the "facts" of sensory physiology may not make for as lively reading as the applications of this information, it should be remembered, analogously, that any person who learns to write has to begin by learning the alphabet. Since we must begin with the basic units of behavior, we turn now to the anatomy, physiology, and phenomenology associated with the sensory systems, for it is from these elementary letters that the words of behavior are formed.

CHAPTER SIX

AUDITION

INTRODUCTION

The stimulus for audition, which for the human being is usually alterations in the form of waves transmitted through the air to the ear through an elastic medium, is described in terms of its frequency (cycles per second of the wave) and its amplitude (decibel rating). The psychological counterparts of these terms are pitch and loudness. The need for two sets of definitions, one based on the physical stimulus and the other on the psychological response to the physical stimulus, indicates again that there is a difference between physical units and sensation. This difference, to which Fechner, Stevens, and others have added quantification, is the basis of both psychophysics and scaling.

ANATOMY OF THE EAR

The human ear is a delicate but precise instrument which has the capacity to convert the original physical sound wave into mechanical energy and then, probably, into electrical energy, before the stimulation is transmitted via a branch of the VIIIth cranial nerve to the brain. Although the ear is a clearly defined receptor (unlike, for example, the receptors for touch or pain which are diffused throughout the skin), it shares its nerve with another sensory system, the *nonauditory labyrinth* (see Chapter 10). This system is concerned with reporting the position of the head, and it is a major contributor to the sense of balance. The fact that both head balance and audition share the same cranial nerve (VIIIth) explains the basic phenomenon that in man hearing and balance derangements appear together in many normal as well as many pathological states. Dizziness, which involves the labyrinth, is often accompanied by difficulties in auditory perception, such as a "ringing" in the ears.

Figure 6–1 shows the major structures of the human ear. The term *meatus* refers, anatomically, to any canal or opening in the body. The meatus shown in the figure is called the *external auditory meatus,* to distinguish it from other meatuses. The external portion of the ear—the flap that we commonly call the "ear"—is the *pinna.* Since the pinna blocks and scatters sound waves, it helps us to locate sounds. For example, a sound coming from the left will enter the meatus of the left ear first and the meatus of the right ear afterward. The temporal difference between stimulation of the two ears gives us an important clue to the location of the sound.

For convenience in describing the ear, we shall divide it into three sections: The *outer ear* is composed of the pinna and meatus, defined above. The *middle ear* is composed of structures which are mobilized by stimulation into mechanical energy. The basic structures of the middle ear are the *tympanum,* or *tympanic membrane* (eardrum), the three small bones which operate together—the *malleus, incus,* and the *stapes*—and the oval window (not shown in Figure 6–1) on which the stapes rests. Sometimes called by their anglicized names the *hammer, anvil,* and *stirrup,* the three bones are known collectively as the *ossicles.* The *inner ear* is composed of the *round window* (not shown in Figure 6–1), the *cochlea,* which is a snail-shaped structure containing membranes and hair cells, and the *nonauditory labyrinth* (semicircular canals). As we have noted, the nonauditory labyrinth is concerned with balance rather than with audition, although its location and its sharing of the VIIIth cranial nerve are responsible for certain interactions among the two senses. In addition, the middle ear has contact with the throat through the *eustachian tube.* This tube affects the amount of pressure on the tympanic membrane and on the oval window. You may feel its effect by merely swallowing hard and noting the resulting pressure change perceived in the middle ear.

The *cochlea* is coiled 2½ times in human beings. If uncoiled, it is approximately 30 mm (millimeters) long (for comparison, the following line is 30 mm: _____). The *basilar membrane* runs along the cochlea from the base toward the apex and divides the

FIGURE 6–1: *Schematic diagram of the outer, inner, and middle ear as well as the nonauditory labyrinth (noted as semicircular canals in the drawing). (From Schaeffer, 1953, p. 1263.)*

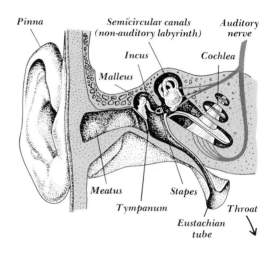

cochlea into an *upper gallery* and a *lower gallery.* The basilar membrane ceases before reaching the apex of the cochlea, thus permitting contact between the two galleries. The area at the apex where contact is made between the two galleries is called the *helicotrema.* Figure 6–2 shows a section of the cochlea and indicates the relationship between the two galleries. Figure 6–3 is a simplified diagram of the unfolded cochlea; it shows the relationship between the galleries, the membrane, and the helicotrema. Note that the lower gallery begins at the round window, while the upper gallery terminates at the oval window. This anatomical relationship is important; since the stapes (stirrup) pounds against the oval window, sound energy may affect the cochlea in that pressure may bend the basilar membrane.

The basilar membrane has many parallel fibers which run transversely, implying that the membrane is stronger in the transverse direction than in its longitudinal direction. There is some evidence that the fibers increase in length as they approach the apex (even

FIGURE 6-2: *A highly schematic cross-sectional view of the cochlea showing the relationship betwen the galleries. (Modified from Poirier & Charpy, 1907, p. 1353.)*

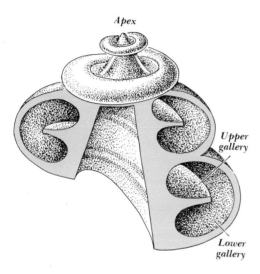

FIGURE 6-3: *A simplified schematic diagram of the cochlea uncoiled. Note the location of the stapes (stirrup) in relation to the oval window, and the basilar membrane in relation to the helicotrema and the round window. (From Beatty, 1932, p. 12.)*

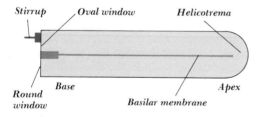

though the cochlea itself is decreasing in width). The obvious parallel to the manner in which sound is produced by a piano or harp has led to several theories of hearing based on the principle that long fibers, like long strings, would produce low frequencies and short fibers would produce high frequencies.

The basilar membrane is not the only struc-

ture of note in the cochlea, as Figure 6–4 shows. Other important structures are *Reissner's membrane,* the *tectorial membrane,* the *organ of Corti,* and the *hair cells* on the basilar membrane. Reissner's membrane is thin compared with the basilar membrane. The organ of Corti rests upon the upper surface of the basilar membrane and is composed of nerve endings. When the stapes forces a change in liquid pressure in the cochlea, the basilar membrane is moved, and the arched hair cells of Corti rock back and forth, moving the tectorial membrane with them. Effectively, the organ of Corti has the role of a lever in magnifying the motion of the hair cells. The hair cells are more or less evenly spaced throughout the basilar membrane. They are arranged in three groups (or columns), and it is estimated that there are 3,500 inner cells and 20,000 outer cells. Reissner's membrane is relatively more receptive to changes in liquid pressure than the basilar membrane. It separates endolymphatic fluid, which bathes the organ of Corti, from the perilymph, which bathes the remainder of the cochlea.

Muscles: The ossicles are attached to two small muscles, commonly called the *tensor tympani* (hammer muscle) and the *stapedius* (stirrup muscle). The stirrup muscle is considered the smallest muscle in the human body. When the two muscles operate together, they aid smooth mechanical transmission among the ossicles. Although they can facilitate transmission through the middle ear at some frequencies, the amount of facilitation is slight. These muscles are apparently primarily protective.

Nerve Transmission: The organ of Corti and its hair cells appear to be a critical link in the transmission of sound pressure. Although each inner hair cell is connected to one nerve fiber (or sometimes several hair cells use the same fiber), the outer cells take part in *multiple innervation,* in which a single fiber is connected with hair cells located throughout a large area. In places, a single fiber may carry impulses from hair cells as far apart as half of

FIGURE 6-4: *A cross-sectional view of the cochlea. Using the basilar membrane as a reference point, note especially Reissner's membrane and the tectorial membrane. (From Rasmussen, 1943, p. 45.)*

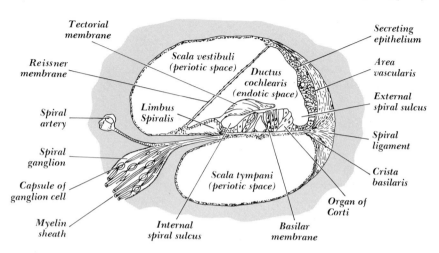

one turn of the cochlea. The cell bodies of the auditory nerve fibers are imbedded in the walls of the cochlea. The axons come together and leave the base of the cochlea, where they become part of the VIIIth cranial nerve. The auditory nerve enters the medulla (the two structures are only 5 mm apart in man). Here the fibers cross on their way to the thalamus. From the thalamus (actually, the *medial geniculate body*), the fibers radiate into the temporal lobe of the cerebrum.

One technique that has been used to explore the projection area for audition in the temporal lobe involves stimulating the nerve cells in the cochlear wall and recording the resultant electrical discharge from the cortex. Later in the chapter, we shall consider the role of the CNS in hearing.

PHYSIOLOGY OF THE HUMAN EAR

In order to understand the conversion of the original sound wave into the perception of auditory phenomena, we shall trace the path of a sound source through the various parts of

the ear, pointing out the function of each part. Our goal is to answer the question "How does one hear?" This apparently simple question turns out to require extremely complex answers. When we understand the workings of the ear, we should be able to understand the various pathological conditions, the facts regarding correspondence and lack of correspondence between physical stimuli and the psychological sensation, and the contributions made by each part of the ear.

In many animals, including dogs and cats, the pinna may be lifted voluntarily. It is not clear how useful this ability is in permitting the animal to alter the amount of sound energy entering the ear, but ear lifting is often associated with emotional behavior. The bat folds his pinna downward as a protective reflex in order to eliminate intense stimuli. It is likely, however, that some animals are able to direct auditory attention by appropriate movement of the pinna muscles. In man, most of these muscles are dormant. Although individuals who have retained voluntary control over the pinna muscles are not uncommon, the ability to wiggle one's ears has little relation to auditory perception. The horse, on the other hand, has 17 active muscles which permit him to alter auditory attention without changing the position of his head. There is some evolutionary evidence that man's ancestors were able to fold the ear lobe over the external meatus. There are obvious practical advantages to the possession of a pinna which folds, most of which are concerned with the elimination of unwanted sounds.

The external meatus is both cartilaginous and bony and lies within the temporal bone of the skull. Both waxy secretions and hair serve to protect the meatus from foreign objects. The membrane, which forms the termination of the meatus and the beginning of the middle ear, is a tightly stretched, diaphragmlike structure called the *eardrum*. Of importance to auditory perception is the fact that the eardrum reproduces the forces which act upon it by vibrating, much as the top of a drum vibrates to a single blow. The eardrum is approximately 0.01 mm thick, and it has the advantage of regeneration; i.e., if it is torn or damaged, the wound will often heal. On the other hand, lesions of the membrane are among the most painful to the human body.

The malleus is attached to the tympanic membrane, and it vibrates in unison with the membrane. Békésy and Rosenblith (1951) have shown that with sounds up to 2,400 Hz the drum vibrates as a rigid system; with frequencies above that point, different segments of the membrane perform in different ways. The three ossicles (the malleus, incus, and stapes) form a lever arrangement, resulting in the action of the stapes on the oval window. Although some force is lost in transmission from the tympanic membrane to the stapes, the relative size of the stapes to the tympanic membrane indicates that the system does produce a mechanical advantage by the time the stapes hits against the oval window. It is suggested that "per unit of area, the pressure on the oval window from the stapes is from 25 to 30 times as great as the original force upon the membrane" (Geldard, 1953, p. 106).

The eustachian tube is responsible for main-taining balance between the middle ear and the surrounding environment. Normally, the tube is closed at the throat end, but it may be opened by the voluntary act of swallowing. When the system is in good working order, the air pressure in the tube matches the middle ear pressure, so that there is no differential pressure upon the tympanic membrane. This equilibrium may be altered by a variety of factors, however. A head cold, which may block the tube, is the most common source of disturbance in this balance. When the membrane is subjected to changes in pressure, as when we are flying or skin-diving, the unequal pressure causes pain. Swallowing or movement of the jaw permits the eustachian tube to alter the pressure applied to the middle ear and to match the external pressure on the tympanic membrane, thus eliminating the pain. On occasion the tube may fail to close, with the result that we are able to hear our own speech loudly. This perception is echolike, as we would expect if the ear were to hear sounds made inside the mouth before they were emitted through the lips.

The final bone of the ossicles—the stapes—continues the process of translating sound energy into sensation by driving the oval window. The driving of the oval window alters the fluid in the cochlea and stimulates the basilar membrane and the hair cells. This in turn stimulates the VIIIth cranial nerve, which transfers the impulse to auditory projection areas. The manner in which the cochlea and its components are able to translate information from the stapes and oval window to the cranial nerve is, as we shall see, a primary question in auditory theory. An immense number of stimuli, varying as a function of pitch, loudness, and other sensory characteristics, are perceivable, and several theories have been proposed to explain how the cochlea is able to translate them. Some more or less obvious answers might be based on the guess that the transverse fibers of the basilar membrane respond much as a piano responds, or on the assumption that the motion of the basilar membrane in response to waves of pressure changes set up by alterations in the oval window by the stapes results in the sensation of hearing, or on the compromise solution that audition is a function of both these processes.

Theory, however, must be consistent with the anatomical and physiological facts concerning the receptor, as well as account for the phenomena associated with the receptor. In addition, a good theory must be able to handle reception in both normal and pathological receptors. Accordingly, before examining the theories which attempt to explain how audition occurs, we must consider further discoveries about the process of hearing. These include (1) evidence regarding electrical activity of the cochlea, (2) evidence regarding the function of higher-order elements of the nervous system, (3) the evolution of the ear, (4) evidence regarding auditory thresholds, (5) pathological conditions, and (6) the way in which the ear is able to localize tones.

ELECTRICAL ACTIVITY OF THE COCHLEA

In the late 1920s two psychologists, Ernest Glen Wever and Charles Bray, placed an electrode on the auditory nerve of an anesthetized cat, amplified the signal, and sent it through a telephone receiver (Wever and Bray, 1930b). One investigator remained in the room with the cat, while the other had the receiver in a second room. The rooms were shielded from each other in order to prevent the system from picking up unwanted signals. The cat's ear was stimulated with various frequencies, and the experimenter in the adjoining room was able to hear the frequencies through the receiver so long as the frequencies were below 5,000 Hz. In addition, when one investigator spoke, so that his voice stimulated the cat's ear, the other was able to report accurately what had been said. The initial report on this discovery was published in 1930 (1930a), and the phenomenon became known as the *Wever-Bray effect.*

When a number of checks on controls indicated that the phenomenon was real and not an artifact of the amplification or receiving equipment that was used, Wever and Bray reached the initial conclusion that the auditory nerve was able to reproduce both amplitude and frequency faithfully (Wever and Bray, 1930b). The actual nature of the electrical response in the ear was not in the nerve, however, but was an electrical discharge from the cochlea, perhaps from the organ of Corti. The phenomenon has been called the *cochlear microphonic* by some investigators (H. Davis and Saul, 1931); however, the term *cochlear potential* is appropriate.

When the impulses from nerve action potential are removed from the recording of the cochlear potential (since the electric discharge is usually composed of both the cochlear potential and nearby nerve discharge), the potential is remarkably similar in form to the original stimulus sent to the ear. Figure 6–5 shows the similarity between the potential and the original stimulus. A different pattern of cochlear potential will occur for the same frequency depending upon the function of the location of the electrode on the cochlea. If cochlear potentials represent an indication of the area of the cochlea which is being stimulated by different frequencies, considerable information regarding how the ear distinguishes

FIGURE 6–5: *Figures A and B show the form of the stimulus, while figures C and D show the cochlear potential associated with the waveform. These examples demonstrate the agreement between the form of stimulus and that of the cochlear potential. (From Wever, 1949, p. 137.)*

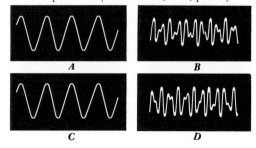

various frequencies and amplitudes can be gained by recording at different locations in the cochlea. This has been done, with the general result that low frequencies appear to stimulate more of the basilar membrane (or hair cells) than high frequencies, for as may be noted from Figure 6–6, which shows recordings taken at various places in the cochlea from the base to the apex, low frequencies result in a potential from all areas of the cochlea. As the frequency becomes higher, maximal response is found at the base. With a tone of 10,000 Hz, only a small potential is found at either the apex or the second turn of the cochlea.

For auditory theory, the important question regarding cochlear potentials is "What do they represent?" One point is certain, however: the cochlear potentials are not the same as nerve discharge, for none of the classic phenomena associated with nerve transmission, such as the all-or-none law or the presence of refractory periods, is characteristic of the cochlear potential. Evidence that the location of the potential is from the organ of Corti is based, in part, on studies that show that the potential is not recorded from certain albino animals which do not have hair cells in the cochlea (Howe, 1935; Stevens & H. Davis, 1938). In addition, animals whose hearing at some frequencies has been destroyed through excessive stimulation show, upon autopsy, destruction in the organ of Corti.

One of the most curious features of the cochlear potential, and possibly the most significant, is that its range of reportable frequencies is more extensive than the auditory range. When tested with conditioned response techniques (see Chapters 12 and 14), cats and dogs will respond to frequencies of well over 20,000 Hz. Similarly, cochlear potentials have been reported in the guinea pig to frequencies as low as 5 Hz (Wever, Bray, & Willey, 1937). Wever's research on a variety of species indicates that auditory thresholds are considerably narrower than the band of frequencies which elicits a cochlear potential.

ROLE OF THE CENTRAL NERVOUS SYSTEM IN AUDITION

We have traced the source of hearing to the cochlea and commented on certain special properties of that organ, for it is certain that the cochlea is responsible for translating the impulse through the cranial nerve to the centers of the brain. The hair cells in the cochlea are connected to the VIIIth cranial nerve through nerve fibers which collect at the base of the cochlea and become the auditory section of the cranial nerve. The fibers from the nonauditory labyrinth also meet and form a section of the VIIIth nerve. These two branches join outside the cochlea. The neurons of the cochlea are known as the first-order neurons; those in the medulla, as the second-order. The areas within the medulla are called the *cochlear nuclei;* one is ventral and the other dorsal. Some neurons terminate at this point. Others continue to the *inferior colliculi* via the *lateral lemniscus.* This is known as the *lemniscal pathway.* Although other neurons form other pathways, the lemniscal pathway appears to be the most important. The cortical projection area for audition is not clearly delineated. Work on the cat suggests that the projection area is diffused and is in the temporal lobe cortex.

It is clear that the role of the CNS in audition is extensive. It is not merely a recorder onto which impulses from the cochlea are directly recorded. Indeed, structures beyond the cochlea are responsible for the final attributes of audition. We shall return to these considerations after we have discussed the evolution of the ear (see Ades, 1959).

EVOLUTION OF THE EAR

Although the study of the evolution of the structure of a sensory system may give clues to how human beings hear, the process of evolution does not provide absolute proof for the validity of any theory. Analysis of hearing ability in subhuman forms through conditioned response techniques and through destruction of parts of the ear in order to determine the relationship between location and function contributes to information regarding the comparative anatomy, comparative psychology, and physiology of the ear.

Many fish have a circular system similar to the human nonauditory labyrinth. Since each ring is filled with a liquid or gelatinous substance, movements of the body of the animal are apparently reflected in changes in the location of the substance. If receptors are available to register the change in location of the substance, the animal may learn to determine the position of his body through these organs. Some fish have only a single ring (which limits greatly the amount of information provided), although the lamprey, one of the more primitive forms of fish, has two. Most fish have the three-ring arrangement, as do human beings. The suspicion that these organs are also used in hearing comes from the observation, through conditioned response techniques, that most fish are able to discriminate sounds passed through water. One of the difficulties with data derived from conditioned response techniques is that the subject may be responding to some change in the environment other than the stimulus which the experimenter is presenting. However, the number of reports of successful conditioning of various forms of fish life to sound stimulation appear convincing. The possibility that the fish responds to sound pressure because of its vibration against his body cannot be ignored. The skin, which gives human beings cutaneous sensations, may provide the receptors for auditory stimulation in fish. It would appear that the labyrinth organs of the fish are useful in discriminating sound waves passed through water, even though the labyrinth does not have this function in human beings.

It is in Amphibia that the first ear is found, if by *ear* we mean a separate organ concerned solely with hearing. The important attribute of the amphibian ear is that it is formed with

FIGURE 6-6: *Relation between location on the basilar membrane from which recording is made (base, second turn, or apex) and the resulting cochlear potential. A 200-Hz tone results in similar potentials at each point on the membrane. At higher frequencies the base provides relatively more output than other locations along the membrane. (From Tasaki, H. Davis, & Legouix, 1952, p. 509.)*

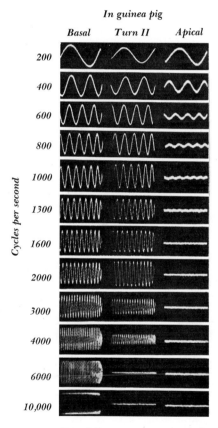

Intensity adjusted for constant response in basal turn paired electrodes, scalae vestibuli and tympani, in each turn

a membrane interrupting the hard skull. The implications of the possession of a membrane are immense, since the possibilities for acute hearing are obviously considerably greater with an ear that has a thin membrane, thus permitting more rapid transmission of stimuli impinging against it, rather than a hard bone. In amphibious animals, a *columella auris* is found, which is usually attached to the membrane. The columella is capable of moving in response to stimulation of the membrane, and it appears to perform as a matching transformer similar to the ossicles of the human ear.

In some amphibia a rudimentary cochlea is found. Figure 6–7 shows schematic drawings of the development of the cochlea from fish to mammal. Although amphibia do not have a

FIGURE 6–7: *Development of the cochlea. (A) Fish: the three-ringed labyrinth is noted but no true cochlea exists; (B) frog: the small swelling on the right shows the beginnings of a rudimentary cochlea; (C) bird: a curved cochlea is noted; (D) mammal: a spiral cochlea is noted. In human beings the cochlea has 2½ turns. Some mammals have fewer turns, and some have more. (From Beatty, 1932, p. 27, adapted from Hesse.)*

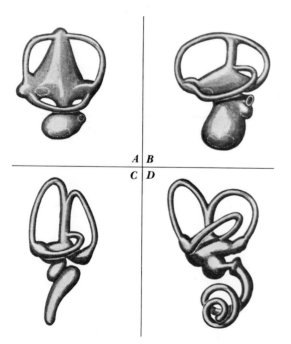

A | B
C | D

coiled cochlea, the ear contains the equivalent of a basilar membrane and hair cells. Some reptiles, notably snakes, have a columella which is attached to the skull. Such animals are adept at hearing by *bone conduction*. The snake is relatively insensitive to airborne sounds but is sensitive to sound passed through the ground. The advice to "stand still" when in the presence of a harmful snake is based as much upon preventing the animal from hearing your location as it is upon not exciting his visual apparatus. Other reptiles, such as the crocodile, have an external meatus, along with a covering flap and a tympanic membrane. Many birds have a columella as well as a cochlea, and, in general, the development of their ears is similar to that of the reptiles.

In mammals, the cochlea is coiled. Variation appears in the number of coils; in duck-billed platypuses, which are sometimes regarded as both reptile and mammal, the cochlea has a ¼ turn compared to the 2½ turns of the human cochlea. Cats have three complete turns and pigs four. This suggests that the number of turns does not correlate well with either acuity or phylogenetic level. The number of hair cells on the basilar membrane also varies dramatically. Estimates of the number of hair cells in the human cochlea range from 24,000 to 30,000 compared with 16,000 in the cat and around 3,000 in some birds. In mammals, the ossicles take the place of the columella arrangement common in birds and reptiles.

THRESHOLDS AND AUDITORY PHENOMENA

Auditory thresholds are of importance to psychologists for at least two reasons: The first is the puzzle of how perception occurs. Clearly, the psychological facts regarding how an organism responds to stimuli must correspond to the physical and chemicals facts about how the sensory organ responds. For example, a reasonable theory of audition must explain (1) why thresholds exist and why they are located as they are, (2) why, among human beings, the upper threshold diminishes with the age of the organism, (3) why different organisms have different thresholds, and (4) what the relationship is between the abnormal or pathological ear and anatomical and physiological impairment. For example, if a theory of audition assumes that frequency is perceived as a function of the length of the transverse fibers on the basilar membrane, then an ear which fails to perceive high tones should show impairment in the shorter transverse fibers. Since much of the evidence by which we are able to evaluate theories of hearing is based on threshold measurements, a study of the techniques of threshold determination, as well as the data from threshold measurements, is primary to formulating a theory of auditory functioning.

The second major reason for determining auditory thresholds is practical. In many areas of applied psychology, it is important to know thresholds under given circumstances. Cognizance of auditory and visual pathology is an important function of the school psychologist. Although he is not necessarily trained in *audiometry* (the procedures for measuring thresholds) or in evaluating the significance of a loss in sensitivity at different frequencies or amplitudes, a school psychologist does need to recognize the basic symptoms of an auditory threshold pathological condition. A child who is suffering from hearing loss should not be punished for inattention. Unless one is aware of the limitations of the normal human ear, one is not likely to notice deviations. Similarly, many military and industrial problems, such as determining the amplitude of machinery noise which might damage the ears of workers and determining the appropriate frequency and amplitude for warning buzzers, are concerned with auditory thresholds.

The process of determining thresholds is complicated by the relationship of one attribute of the stimulus to other attributes. For example, pitch and loudness are related in such a way that an increase in amplitude may be reported as an increase or decrease in pitch.

Accordingly, unless one wishes to study this particular relationship, threshold determinations of pitch require that other aspects of the stimulus, such as loudness, be controlled. It may be recalled that the major physical aspects of sound are frequency and amplitude, while the major psychological aspects are pitch and loudness. Other psychological characteristics have also been investigated, including *volume* and *density*. Many phenomena which are known to affect thresholds, such as fatigue and the presence of masking tones, have been investigated. In addition to the usual psychophysical methods (see Chapter 4), a variety of other procedures have been employed in measuring auditory thresholds. Some of these procedures, such as scaling techniques (see Chapter 5), have yielded data of considerable theoretical interest.

Let us consider data on thresholds for sound stimulation, as well as certain other important phenomena, remembering that our goal is to learn how the physical stimulus becomes the psychological sensation. That is, we return to the hoary psychophysical question, this time applied to the specialized sense of audition: what is the relationship between the physical event and the psychological result?

Frequency: For the human ear, the thresholds for frequency are *approximately* 25 Hz and 20,000 Hz. The precise threshold depends upon the individual ear as well as the amplitude of the stimulus. The RL is difficult to assess, since, as we shall note, we may distinguish between a threshold for tone, for noise, or even for pressure sensations at low frequencies. Figure 6–8 shows hearing loss, especially in the higher frequencies, as a function of age.

The threshold for frequency is often affected by *tonal gaps* and *tonal islands*. A tonal gap is an area in which there is a loss of sensitivity. Usually, this means that the *amplitude* must be raised beyond normal in the area of the tonal gap for perception to occur. A tonal island is an area of normal sensitivity surrounded by areas of a loss of sensitivity. In

FIGURE 6–8: *Changes in the TL for audition as a function of age.*
The ordinate shows hearing loss in converted sensation units, and
the abscissa shows different frequencies. As one grows older, hearing
loss is clearly greatest in the high frequencies (above 2,000 Hz),
although little loss is noted in the lower frequencies. The problem of
why aging should affect high but not low frequencies is critical in
formulating a theory of audition. (From Bunch, 1929, p. 634.)

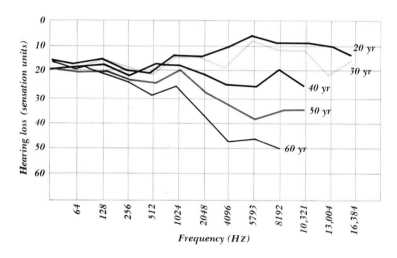

primates, including human beings, it is not unusual to find a tonal gap around 4,096 Hz. The RL provides some curious phenomena, for the perception of tonal frequency does not appear suddenly. Rather, subjects report "chugging, piston-like slaps, and high frequency bursts" (Wever & Bray, 1937). There is some difficulty in distinguishing tone from these sensations, a fact which probably accounts for some discrepant findings in regard to the RL for tone. For this reason, a distinction is often made between *feeling thresholds* and *auditory thresholds*. The former refer to sensations which arise from presenting stimuli to the ear but which are not clearly identified as "hearing." The sensations of "chugging and piston-like slaps" are examples of feeling thresholds. Needless to say, the point at which "feeling" becomes sensation of tone is not well defined, although it is a point of considerable theoretical interest.

Figure 6–9 shows the results of several studies, plotted along the same ordinate and abscissa, which have measured the feeling threshold and the auditory threshold. Although different procedures were followed in measuring these thresholds, there is considerable agreement among the studies as to the slope of the function. Sensitivity is at its finest in the 1,000- to 4,000-Hz range. This fact is of considerable industrial importance, for it permits telephone companies and others concerned with communication to eliminate most high frequencies (thus saving the expense of developing high-fidelity apparatus) without greatly altering the perception of the stimulus.

Determination of absolute thresholds (ALs) in human beings almost always employs a psychophysical technique in which the subject indicates his perception of the tone by verbal report. Conditioned response techniques (Chapters 12–14) have not been generally used with human subjects, no doubt because verbal reports are thought to be adequate for most

FIGURE 6-9: *Measurement of feeling thresholds and auditory thresholds. Curves 1 to 6 are attempts to measure the AL. MAP (minimal audible pressure) represents measures made at the eardrum, while MAF (minimal audible field) represents measures in a free field. Curves 7 to 12 are attempts to measure the point at which sounds become too intense for comfort or at which the sensation of hearing is replaced by some other sensation, such as tickle or discomfort. (From Licklider, 1951, p. 995; data for 1, 2—Sivian & White, 1933; 3—Békésy, 1936a, 1936b; 4—Waetzmann & Keibs, 1936a, 1936b; 5, solid line—Steinberg, Montgomery, & Gardner, 1940; 5, dashed line—Montgomery, 1932; 5, dotted line—Beasley, 1938; 7, 8—Silverman, Harrison, & H. S. Lane, 1946; 9—Wegel, 1932; 10–12—Békésy, 1936b.)*

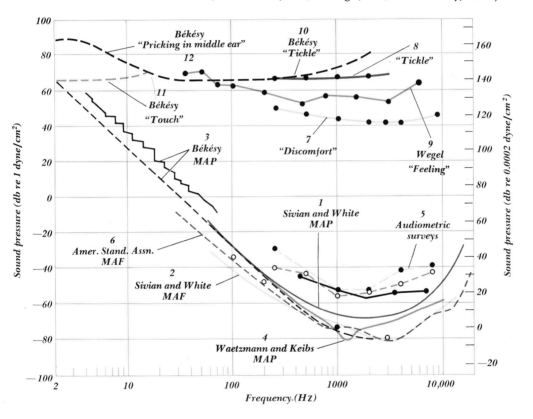

purposes. On the other hand, comparisons of thresholds derived from conditioned response techniques and from psychophysical techniques might yield useful data.

Research on the ALs for animals has employed both the conditioned response technique and the recording of cochlear potentials.

For dogs the TL for frequency is reported to be 26,000 Hz (Anrep, 1920), and in cats cochlear potentials in response to tones as high as 30,000 Hz have been reported (Wever, 1930). It is probably inappropriate to equate cochlear potentials with thresholds, since it is likely that potentials may result without the organism's showing any behavioral signs of hearing. The TL for rats is less than that for primates, although it is not clear whether it is closer to 12,000 or to 8,000 Hz. The TL for reptiles does not appear to be above 7,000 Hz —considerably lower than for primates. The absence of perception of high tones is interesting when it is remembered that most reptiles have a columella, rather than ossicles. It would seem reasonable that a columella could not vibrate so rapidly as is necessary for the perception of high tones.

Among fish, minnows have been conditioned to distinguish DLs of 2 to 3 Hz; catfish appear to have a TL of around 13,000 Hz. Insects vary widely in regard to auditory thresholds. Although little work has been done on bees, it is reported that they show no evidence of auditory perception (von Frisch, 1950). For purposes of audition theory, the most important aspect of studies on animal hearing is the establishment of the relationship between function and structure. An example of this is observed clearly in the TLs for animals which have a columella as opposed to the thresholds for animals which have ossicles and a cochlea.

Since the DL varies as a function of the frequency selected to serve as the standard, it is necessary to define the DL in terms of the standard. For example, one might speak of a DL for a frequency of 10,000 Hz at 4.5 db, or of a DL of 15,000 Hz at 11.3 db. However, one may begin at the RL and measure successive DLs by ascending and descending frequencies. This permits evaluation of the size of successive DLs as well as the general discriminative ability of the ear by Weber's fraction:

$$\frac{\Delta f}{f} = K$$

where

$\Delta f =$ **increment necessary in frequency (f) for a difference to be observed**

$f \ \ =$ **frequency**

$K \ =$ **the constant, Weber's fraction**

Probably because of the many variables which affect determinations of the DL and what appear to be inappropriate sampling techniques in the selection of subjects in many experiments, estimates of the number of DLs for human beings vary considerably. Luft (1888) calculated 11,000 DLs, but later experimenters have persistently found that number high. In a well-controlled study (but with only five subjects), Shower and Biddulph (1931) estimated 1,500 DLs. Figure 6–10 shows composite data from four experiments. The ordinate represents the ratio $\Delta f/f$, and the abscissa indicates the frequencies employed. Although the data are in agreement beyond 500 Hz, the Shower and Biddulph (1931) study indicates a much higher fraction at low frequencies when sinusoidal, rather than abrupt presentation of the stimulus, is employed. This difference, which results from a simple change in the manner of presentation, is characteristic of the sensitivity of DL and AL measurement to a number of factors. In this case, if the stimulus is abrupt, there is the problem of transient tones which accompany the onset of the stimulus. If the stimuli are not presented abruptly and if a gradual transition is used as the frequencies are decreased, the subject is less likely to note a difference, since the DL for gradually changing stimuli is higher than that for stimuli which are presented and concluded abruptly.

The data reported in Figure 6–10 indicate that the optimal area for frequency perception is between 1,000 and 2,000 Hz, for it is in this range that the smallest variation produces a perception of change. We can see, however, that the Weber ratio is not a constant. Although Western music plots octaves in ratios of 2:1, with each octave twice the frequency of the preceding octave, it is apparent from the threshold data that the human ear does not perceive this ratio; that is, the discrimination of pitch does not correspond to the measurement of frequency. In addition, Western music is characteristically written in semitones (the distance between a white and black key on the piano, for example). The DL for a 400-Hz tone is around $\frac{1}{10}$, so Western music is writ-

FIGURE 6-10: *Summary of three experiments which evaluated DLs for human audition. The ordinate shows the Weber fraction Δf/f, and the abscissa shows frequency in cycles per second. The difference in the two curves provided by Shower and Biddulph (1931) is created by whether or not the stimulus was presented abruptly or sinusoidally. Note that this difference in procedure is effective at the lower frequencies. (From J. D. Harris, 1952, p. 755; data from Shower & Biddulph, 1931; J. D. Harris, 1948; Koester, 1945.)*

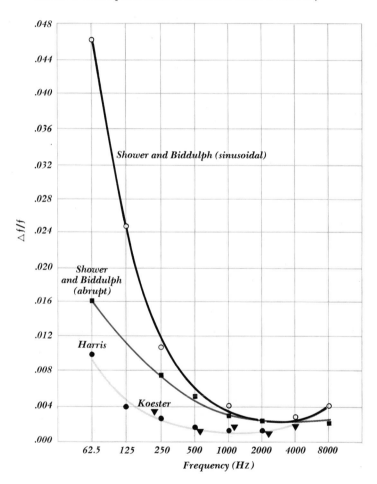

ten well within the discriminatory ability of the listener. The fact that the human ear is able to make much finer discriminations than are called for in most musical compositions has permitted the contemporary emphasis on mus-

ical compositions based on scales of smaller units.

The ability of some people to distinguish small changes in tone is related to the belief that some human beings are able to emulate tones exactly. Such persons are said to have *absolute pitch*. It is often implied that absolute pitch is the result of genetic makeup, rather than training. If one considers that DLs for pitch are probably randomly distributed throughout the population, it would be expected that some persons would be able to reproduce pitch without large error. Choral conductors contend that such persons are in the majority. As Licklider points out, it does not seem necessary to postulate a separate ability for absolute pitch. "We do not, for example, postulate a special kind of vision to account for unusual accuracy in color naming" (Licklider, 1951, p. 1004).

Pitch and Frequency: One of the greatest uses of scaling procedures has been the evaluation of the psychological characteristics of sensory quality. In 1937, Stevens, Volkmann, and Newman used the method of fractionation in an attempt to establish a scale of pitch. With intensity constant, subjects were required to fractionate 10 standard frequencies by selecting the tone that was half as high as the standard. A frequency of 1,000 Hz was arbitrarily given a scale value of 1,000. Accordingly, the tone selected as half as high in pitch as a 1,000-Hz standard was given a value of 500. Figure 6–11 shows the results from such a study. The ordinate presents pitch in mels. The term *mel* was selected by Stevens et al. to be the standard unit of *pitch*. Taken from the word "melody," mels are defined on the following basis: a tone of 1,000 Hz is arbitrarily given a scale value of 1,000 mels. Accordingly, the pitch which is perceived as half as high as the 1,000-Hz standard is given the value of 500 mels. Note that 500 mels is not equal to 500 Hz. As Figure 6–11 shows, 500 mels equals 400 Hz, although 2,000 mels equals approximately 3,000 Hz. These data indicate that the relationship between pitch and frequency is not 1:1. Up to approximately 1,000 Hz, pitch and frequency are in reasonable agreement. Over 1,000 Hz the deviation becomes increasingly greater.

Amplitude: Just as frequency may be interpreted only if the amplitude is known, so the reverse is true—it is meaningless to discuss amplitude without specifying the frequency. For example, one speaks of a 32-db hearing loss at 8,000 Hz. The statement means that, starting with an amplitude sufficient to place the frequency at threshold for the normal ear, the amplitude has to be increased 32 db for the subject to report the sensation of the tone. Since most information on thresholds, particularly intensity thresholds, comes from audiometric measurements, it is necessary to review physical conditions under which audiometric determinations are made. Two practices are common: In the first, an earphone is placed against the external auditory meatus. A variant of this technique includes placing a tube against the tympanic membrane itself. The results are expressed in terms of the *minimal audible pressure* (MAP). A second common technique is to place the subject in a specially designed area where reflection is nearly eliminated. This technique is commonly called the *minimal audible field* (MAF) technique, since it attempts to reduce the surrounding sounds to zero. The subject usually faces the source of the sound (termed 0° azimuth), and the stimulus may be presented either *monaurally* (to one ear) or *binaurally* (to both ears). The differences in results between these two techniques may be noted from Figure 6–9.

The intricate relationship between amplitude and frequency makes separation of one from the other difficult. The relationship between amplitude and frequency is complicated by the fact that one does not exist without the other. There is no amplitude above or below the stimulus thresholds for frequency, and unless a frequency has some amplitude, it is not heard. In addition, absolute silence does not exist for the ear. The sounds of pulse, respiration, and other physiological functions make certain that the ear is continually perceiving stimuli and that threshold measurements are always partially masked by these stimuli.

Figure 6–12 indicates data showing the percentage of subjects who were able to perceive a given tone at the indicated frequencies and amplitudes. Perhaps the most revealing aspect of these data is the effectiveness of different amplitudes upon the percentage of persons able to perceive the frequency. Again, the area of maximum sensitivity is somewhere between 1,000 and 4,000 Hz.

The determination of DLs for amplitude is, if possible, an even more difficult process. One experimenter (Riesz, 1928) employed a steady tone to which a second tone, differing from the steady tone by 3 Hz, was added. Sometimes the second tone was introduced so that it augmented the standard and sometimes so that it was masked. The result was heard as a continuous variation in amplitude three times per second. The subjects described the sensation as one of "beats." The results indicate that for the average subject, given a 1,000-Hz tone at 30 db, the intensity must be raised 1 db for the subject to report the sensation of change in amplitude.

One method for showing the relationship between frequency and loudness is to plot equal-loudness contours as shown in Figure 6-13. In the diagram, the lowest line represents the RL. That is, to the average observer, the RL for a 40-Hz tone is 70 db. Consider the ordinate, which indicates loudness in decibels. Any point on any contour will be perceived as equally as loud as any other point on the contour. For example, all tones on contour 50 sound equal (in loudness) to a tone of 50 db at 1,000 Hz. Thus, a tone of 200 Hz at 65 db will sound as *loud* as a 1,000-Hz tone at 58 db. Equal-loudness contours are of considerable value for industry and for the amateur acoustical engineer who builds home music reproduction assemblies. It is clear that alteration in amplitude will occur at the extremes. That is, high and low notes will sound appreciably softer than notes in the middle ranges, even though the amplitude is identical.

Loudness and Amplitude: Just as pitch does not maintain a 1:1 relationship to frequency, so loudness does not maintain a 1:1 relationship to amplitude. Various scaling techniques have been used to establish the relationship, including fractionation and bisection. An ad-

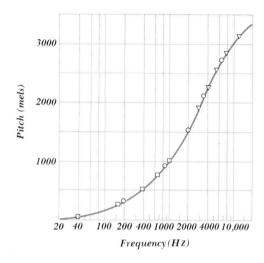

FIGURE 6-11: *The relationship between frequency and the perception of pitch as determined by the method of fractionation. The subjects adjust the frequency of one tone (as expressed on the abscissa) until it appears to be half as high in pitch (ordinate). (From Stevens & Volkmann, 1940, p. 336.)*

ditional technique, more or less restricted to the auditory apparatus, since two organs are available, is sometimes called the *monaural-binaural equation*. The "equation" is concerned with the increase in amplitude or loudness which is perceived when the tone is introduced into both ears as opposed to the sensation resulting from the introduction of a tone into a single ear. Some writers have reported a reasonable approximation of a 2:1 ratio (Stevens & H. Davis, 1938), although others report that the ratio varies with the frequency of the stimulus (Hirsh, 1948).

Using the method of fractionation, Churcher (1935) evaluated the relationship between loudness and amplitude. He established a tone of 1,000 Hz at 40 db to be equal to 1 *sone*. A sone is a standard of loudness, just as a mel represents a unit of pitch. In this case, a tone which was perceived as twice as loud as 1,000 Hz at 40 db would be equivalent to 2 sones, while a tone which was perceived as half as loud would equal 0.5 sones. Figure

FIGURE 6-12: *Percentage of subjects showing absolute auditory thresholds at different frequencies and amplitudes. (From Fletcher, 1940, p. 48.)*

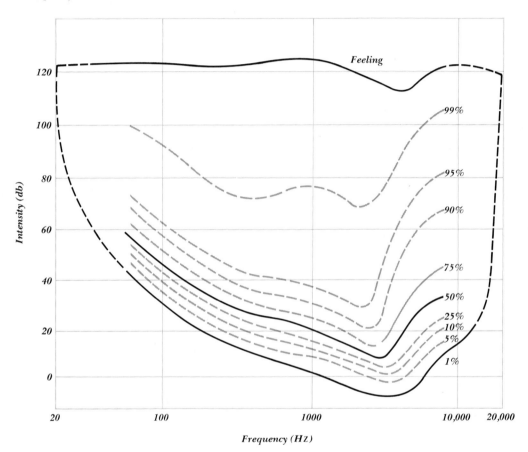

6-14 indicates the relationship, in sones, between loudness and the decibel rating. Variation in the ratio between loudness and amplitude is small for tones of 1,000 Hz. As the extremes of frequency are approached, loudness "grows" more rapidly. This is particularly true of low-frequency tones, where, as may be noted from the figure, the curves for 10, 25, and 50 Hz bend sharply at the upper levels of amplitude. When the scaling method of magnitude estimation is used to relate loudness to physical amplitude, we find a power function, as shown in Figure 6–15. In this study, each subject selected his own standard, which was then converted to yield the ordinate. The lower the frequency, the more rapidly loudness grows as a function of frequency.

Other Characteristics: Various experimenters have suggested that there are qualities of audition besides pitch and loudness. In music, these are grouped under *timbre*, which is assumed to represent such aspects of sound as brilliance, volume, density, and tonality. The

FIGURE 6-13: *Equal-loudness contours as a function of intensity. The contour marked zero is the function for MAP. The function at the top (from Wegel, 1932) represents the feeling threshold (see Figure 6-9). The numbers along the contours refer to the level of loudness. (From Stevens & H. Davis, 1938, p. 124.)*

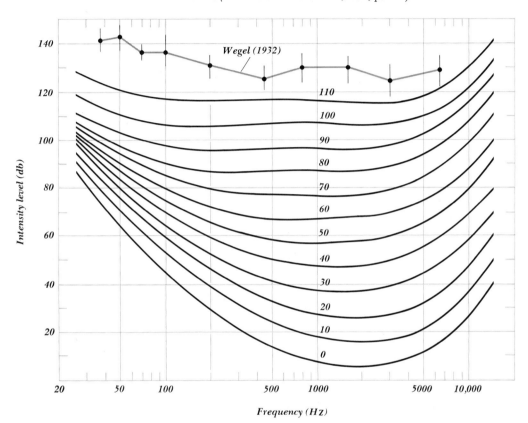

evidence for the presence of another dimension to auditory sensation is that a violin and a piano may both play a note of the same frequency and amplitude but that the two tonal sensations are different. Part of the discrepancy is due to the phenomena of *overtones, beats,* and *masking.* However, there seems to be adequate evidence that certain sensations may be discriminated by the human ear which are not accounted for by frequency and amplitude and their interactions.

The term *volume* is sometimes used in auditory research to mean the *expansiveness* of a tone. It should not be used as a term equated with "loudness," as when we speak of turning down a "volume control" to decrease "loudness." If we play a series of tones and ask a number of subjects to indicate whether the individual tones are "small or large," considerable agreement in the ratings will result. Generally, tones of high frequencies are considered "small," while those of low frequencies are considered "large." Indeed, agreement among subjects is sufficiently high that equal-volume contours may be constructed which are similar to equal-loudness contours (Thomas, 1949).

FIGURE 6–14: *The relationship between physical intensity and frequency (numbers on the functions) of the stimulus and perceived loudness expressed in sones. (From Stevens & H. Davis, 1938, p. 118.)*

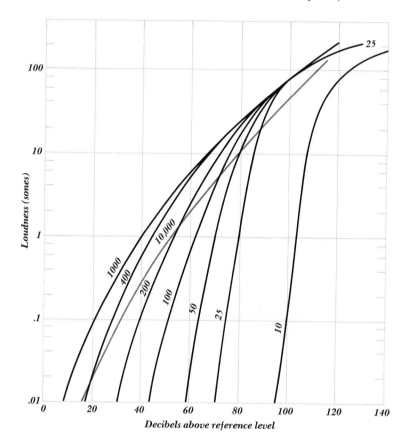

Not all experimenters have been able to find agreement among subjects, however. Characteristically, experimenters who find agreement have used techniques which required subjects to report *equality,* while those who do not find agreement have required subjects to report sensations of *difference.* Such are the intricacies of scaling.

The term *density* is used to refer to the *hardness* or *softness* of tones. Low tones are sometimes perceived as softer and less compact than high tones, which are perceived as full and hard. *Equal-density contours* have been developed (Stevens, 1934) which indicate that both density and volume are separate characteristics of perceived tone. *Brightness,* which was once thought to be a separate attribute of auditory sensation, appears to follow the same form as density, and it has been suggested that the concepts are operationally identical (Boring & Stevens, 1936). One might suspect that pitch and brightness would bear a high positive correlation, since low tones are commonly thought to be lusterless compared with high ones. At least, thresholds for pitch and brightness are not demonstrably different (Rich, 1919). Accordingly, the useful distinctions of the sensation of tone are loudness, pitch, volume, and density. Figure 6–16 indicates contours for these four characteristics, based on data derived by Stevens (1934). The ordinate plots amplitude, and the abscissa indicates frequency. The contours of tonal sensation are equated by locating the point at which the characteristics are equal. For example, a tone of 450 Hz at 58 db has the volume of a tone of 500 Hz at 60 db and a tone of 550 Hz at 62 db. Note that the curves for pitch and loudness do not vary greatly compared to frequency and amplitude.

Combination Tones and Beats: We have noted before that very few of the tones perceived by the human ear are pure tones. When two tones of different frequencies are presented, one of two sensations may result: First, the frequencies may be sufficiently far apart that an interaction occurs which results in the sensation of frequencies in addition to the original frequencies. These tones are known as *combination tones*. Second, the frequencies may be sufficiently similar that the resulting sensation is one of a single tone varying in amplitude. This phenomenon is known as *beats*.

Combination tones are divisible into *difference tones* and *summation tones*. As the names imply, difference tones represent the difference between the two original frequencies, while summation tones represent a summation of the two original frequencies.

These phenomena present several puzzles for any theory of acoustics. Clearly, the ear does not reproduce faithfully what is put into it, and an adequate theory of hearing should explain how the ear produces combination tones and beats.

Psychological Attributes of Complex Tones: Our discussion of loudness, pitch, and other psychological attributes has been based on experimental findings in which the attribute was regarded as a function of a pure tone. Although the procedure of using pure tones in experimental investigations furnishes basic data for both theoretical and practical refer-

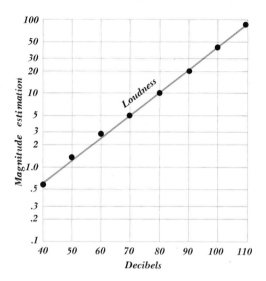

FIGURE 6–15: *The relationship between physical intensity and perceived loudness as a function of the method of magnitude estimation. (From Stevens, 1961, p. 19.)*

ence, it is quite possible that these psychological attributes follow different functions when they are evaluated as a function of complex tones, such as those we hear every day. There is evidence, for example, that if the components of a complex tone are sufficiently separated in frequency, the loudness is rated as equal to the sum of the loudness of the frequencies presented separately (Licklider, 1951). However, if the frequencies are close together, the perceived loudness of the complex tone is greater than the loudness of the components presented separately. When we deal with pure tones, pitch is not a direct function of frequency, but the effect is not so pronounced when we use complex tones (Fletcher, 1935). This phenomenon is of considerable importance to auditory theory. Does the ear respond to the frequency of the fundamental regardless of the amplitude? How does it "decide" which of several frequencies is to be considered "strongest" in the sensation of the tone? Or does the phenomenon indicate that the ear

FIGURE 6-16: *Equal contours for loudness, volume, density, and pitch. (From Stevens, 1934, p. 458.)*

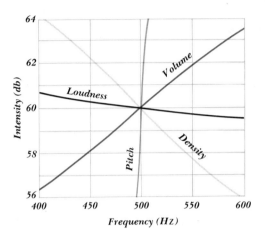

responds to fundamental tones primarily, and, if so, how does the structure of the ear permit it to isolate fundamental tones from other tones?

Masking and Adaptation: *Masking* refers to the combining of stimuli in any sensory system. In audition, this procedure alters the basic sensation in predictable ways. *Adaptation* refers to changes in sensation as a function of repeated stimulation. In vision, for example, we say that our eyes "adapt" to the darkness of the theater. Masking (which may be particular to audition), fatigue, and adaptation all have received considerable experimental attention because of the importance of findings to theoretical formulations and because of the practical applications in industrial psychology.

Wegel and C. E. Lane (1924) worked with only a single subject, but the data derived from their investigations on the effect of masking in audition have remained classic in the literature. Figure 6–17 shows the relationships determined by these investigators. To determine the effect of masking, the secondary tone is used to mask the primary tone: the primary

tone is measured twice, once in the presence of the secondary tone and once without it. In this study, the primary tone was 1,200 Hz at 80 db. Several generalizations regarding masking may be made: first, high tones are affected more than low tones; second, when the primary and secondary tones are presented to separate ears, masking still occurs, but it is not nearly so severe as when the tones are presented binaurally; third, low tones are more effective in masking high tones than high tones are in masking low tones.

From Figure 6–17 we note that the relationship between the primary and secondary tones is straightforward until they approach each other in frequency. Here, some overtones interfere, and when the two frequencies are sufficiently close, beats are perceived. As the frequency of the secondary tone surpasses the frequency of the primary tone, difference tones interfere, and when the overtones are reached, beats are perceived again. The mixture of overtones, difference tones, and beats continues as the frequency is increased, thus providing, in general, greater effects of masking.

Experiments on fatigue and adaptation in audition have usually been conducted for applied purposes. Both terms refer, in general, to the effects of continued stimulation. With repeated stimulation, receptors become less sensitive to stimulation. A ring placed on the finger soon ceases to stimulate the cutaneous receptors: at least, one ceases to be aware of its presence. When one enters a room he may be aware of an unusual odor, but in time he ceases to notice it. The effects of adaptation are easily apparent in vision, cutaneous sensitivity, olfaction, and gustation. The fact that the effects of adaptation on hearing are less readily apparent has led to the supposition that the ear does not adapt. As we shall see, a simple experiment indicates that the supposition is fallacious. On the other hand, recovery from adaptation—usually measured as the amount of time necessary for the receptor to return to its normal sensitivity—is remarkably rapid for hearing in comparison with recovery rates of other sensory systems. Let us

FIGURE 6-17: *Masking, as demonstrated by sensations produced by two-component tones. The primary tone is 1,200 Hz at 80 db. When the secondary tone falls below the heavy line, it is masked. When it falls above, a variety of sensations may result. For example, beats appear in the range on either side of the primary tone. Depending upon the relation between the two tones, a mixture of difference tones may be perceived. (From Wegel & C. E. Lane, 1924, p. 272.)*

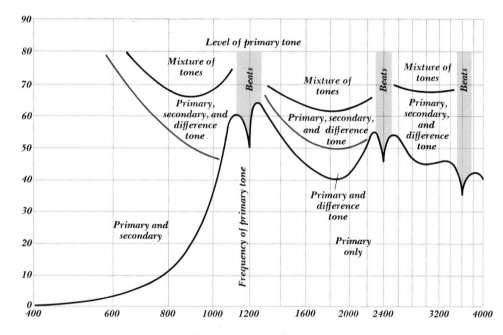

present a subject with a 1,000-Hz tone at 50 db for ten minutes binaurally. Now, we remove the tone and substitute a tone of a different frequency. Using common psychophysical techniques, we can determine the amount which the second tone must be changed to be perceived as equal to the first. This amount indicates the effects of adaptation.

Data from such a study are shown in Figure 6–18, in which a 1,000-Hz tone was used as the standard. Adaptation is most rapid in the first few seconds and reaches asymptote at around sixty seconds. The shape of this curve is typical of adaptation in all senses. Recovery

from auditory adaptation is shown in Figure 6–19, in which it may be noted that the amplitude of the tone determines the rapidity of recovery from adaptation. One difficulty with assessing auditory adaptation as a function of both frequency and amplitude is that the tone may be sufficiently intense to cause damage to the cochlea or other parts of the ear.

Aftereffects: Aftereffects occur with most, and perhaps all, sensory systems. They are most obvious in vision. If a subject stares fixidly at a colored surface for at least ten seconds and then turns his gaze to another uniform surface

FIGURE 6-18: *Auditory fatigue. A tone of 1,000 Hz is presented. Then the percentage of the original intensity which is required to produce a sound as loud on the unstimulated ear is plotted. (Wood, 1930, n.s., from Geldard, 1953, p. 135.)*

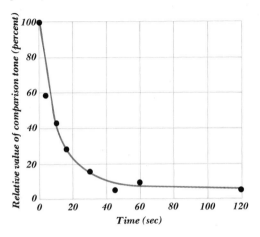

FIGURE 6-19: *Recovery from auditory fatigue from a 3,000-Hz tone. The amount of time required for recovery is a function of the original level of stimulation. (From Rawnsley & Harris, 1952, p. 140.)*

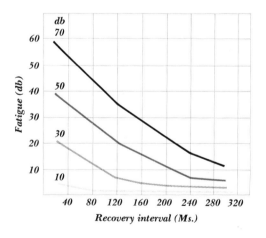

of a different color, he notes a fleeting sensation of the color of the original surface. This sensation is called the *positive afterimage:* the term *positive* indicates that the perceived color of the aftereffect is the same as the color of the initial surface. However, the positive afterimage disappears rapidly and is followed by a sensation of the color which is the complement of the color of the original surface. This is known as the *negative afterimage.* A similar aftereffect occurs in kinesthesis. If one leans against a wall, pushing his weight against his arm held downward, and if, after twenty seconds or so, he moves from the wall and stands upright, he notes a very strong tendency for the arm to raise. In audition, just as it is sometimes said that there is no adaptation effect, it is also argued that there is no aftereffect. It is certainly true that it has not been positively established that an aftereffect occurs in audition. Rosenblith, G. A. Miller, Egan, Hirsh, and Thomas (1947), however, have noted that the quality of a tone is sometimes transferred to other tones after the original tone is removed. But since this does not occur in the absence of stimulation, it is not properly an aftereffect in the same sense that afterimages are aftereffects of the visual system. On the other hand, the finding does indicate an interesting ability of the auditory mechanism.

Tonal Pleasantness: Although part of our judgment of whether tones are pleasant or unpleasant is undoubtedly learned, it appears that we innately judge some combinations of tones to be more pleasant than others. If this is true, the implication is strong that the ear and the brain must be so constructed as to report sensations in such a way that these distinctions are made. The octave, which involves a frequency ratio of 1:2, is generally regarded as pleasing. Certain combinations or chords are also selected as pleasant more commonly than other combinations, and all these are direct ratios; e.g., the major fifth chord is a 3:2 frequency ratio, and the major seventh is a 15:8 ratio. One possible explanation is based on the assumption that octaves are pleasant because the partials produced by the two tones coincide and are not dissonant. In any case, organized music presents a very real problem for theories of hearing, for it represents an additional set of phenomena for which a theory must account.

Sound Localization: In addition to the perception of tones, the auditory system has another function which is very useful; namely, it may be used to *localize* sounds. Adult human beings are so accustomed to localizing sounds as coming from the left or the right that localization may seem to be an innate capacity. However, one has only to watch a young child attempt to determine the location of sounds to discover that localization is an ability which requires considerable practice. At first thought, sound localization seems to be a simple matter. If a tone emanates from the right, it strikes the right ear before it strikes the left ear. This temporal difference in stimulation may be the cue that the tone is from the right. Similarly, if a tone emanates from directly in front of me or directly behind me, I am unable to distinguish its location, perhaps because the tone stimulates both ears at the same time. When a tone *is* presented directly in front (or directly behind), I characteristically tilt my head slightly, thus making certain that the tone strikes one ear more quickly than the other, permitting me to judge its location.

Sound localization is, of course, an important attribute of the ability of the blind to perceive obstacles. Although it is sometimes said that the loss of one sense (such as vision) results in a sharpening of other senses, it is far more likely that persons without vision merely learn to rely to a greater degree on cues available from another sense. For example, so long as a person has his sense of vision, he does not need to use much of the information provided by cutaneous sensations. Without the sense of vision, however, he comes to make finer discriminations regarding cutaneous stimuli. This is probably true of sound localization as well. The classic studies of Karl Dallenbach (Cotzin & Dallenbach, 1950; Supa, Cotzin, & Dallenbach, 1944) indicate that the blind rely upon echo location and sound localization in order to avoid obstacles.

If the ears did not come in pairs, the ability to locate sounds would be greatly diminished, if not absent. On the other hand, the manner in which sound localization occurs is not nearly so simple as the theory of temporal difference in receiving sounds would indicate. The technical problems associated with studying sound localization are immense. For example, if one presents a sound in a closed space of any kind, reverberations occur which provide an artifact in measuring the temporal lag between one ear's perceiving the original tone and the other ear's perception.

In classic studies which attempted to overcome this difficulty, Stevens and Newman (1934; 1936a; 1936b) placed their subjects on a pole on top of a building. The sound was presented from a speaker on a rotating boom. At each selected location, the tone was presented, and the subject was asked to locate the source of the sound. Figure 6–20 shows the average error in degrees of localization for two subjects as a function of frequency. The amount of error increases to around 3,000 Hz and then declines. Why should sound localization be worse at 3,000 Hz than at other frequencies? Apparently, localization is not a simple matter of which ear receives the stimulus first. Rather, since localization depends on frequency, phase, and intensity differences, it seems likely that the hearing apparatus itself is somehow concerned with localization, because only the hearing apparatus can differentiate frequencies. Figure 6–21 shows the percentage of "reversals" made by the subjects, that is, the percentage of times the subjects confused the front and rear in locating the sounds. This too appears to be a function of frequency, for the number of reversals drops sharply in the 2,000- to 3,000-Hz range.

Since frequency affects localization, the next question is obviously whether amplitude and phase have similar effects. A sound emanating from the right will be louder to the right ear than to the left, so that amplitude is an additional cue to the source of the tone. However, differences in amplitude appear to be far more useful in localization with high-frequency

FIGURE 6–20: *Error of localization as a function of frequency. The different points represent data collected at different times. The heavy line represents an approximation of the curve from the data. (From Stevens & Newman, 1936a, p. 302.)*

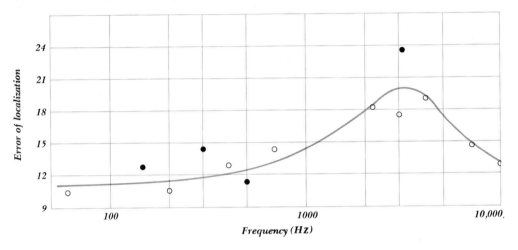

tones than with low-frequency tones. However, differences in phase are apparently useful only in localization with low-frequency tones.

Improvements in the techniques of electrophysiology and ablation of parts of the CNS, coupled with military and industrial interest in the problems of sound localization, have added considerably to our information in this area. As Rosenzweig points out (1961, p. 387), it is "shown that the cortex is required for binaural localization, although neural interaction first occurs low in the brain stem. Some evidence suggests that the cortex of a single hemisphere may be sufficient to permit localization." If so, it seems that the concept of localization as merely a function of the location of the ears is too simple.

PATHOLOGY

The psychologist studies pathological conditions of the sensory systems for two reasons: First, for practical purposes, psychologists must be able to distinguish learned or culturally derived behavior disorders from those which have a physiological origin. Second, the study of pathology is of considerable importance to theory, since a theory of hearing must be able to explain the function of the abnormal as well as the normal ear. Indeed, pathology furnishes one of the most useful checks on the validity of theories of hearing. For example, if high tones are presumed to be perceived by the short transverse fibers along the basilar membrane, then persons with a hearing loss of high tones should show some abnormality in these fibers. If a subject reports a constant "ringing in the ears," examination should reveal that a pathological condition exists in certain fibers. The location and the type of the pathological conditions are very useful in indicating the relationships between structure and function in the sensory apparatus.

Pathological conditions of the ear are of two types: *conduction deafness* and *nerve deafness*. Conduction deafness refers to abnormalities in the structure or functioning of the parts of the ear (the ossicles and the cochlea). Nerve deafness refers to an abnormality in the cranial nerve or in the conductive aspects of the cochlea which prohibits the sensation of complete hearing.

Stimulation Deafness: Stimulation deafness is caused by excessive stimulation. Since it results in destruction of the cochlea, it may represent either conduction or nerve deafness. Most research on stimulation deafness has been done on the guinea pig, since his cochlea is similar to that of man. Figure 6–22 shows the effect of an intense tone on different areas of the basilar membrane as a function of frequency. The white areas indicate the location and extent of damage to the membrane and hair cells. The zero along the abscissa indicates the base of the membrane. It is noteworthy that low tones (300 and 1,000 Hz) produce extensive damage near the apex. As the frequency is increased, the location of the destruction is nearer the base of the membrane, and the amount of destruction decreases. The

implication is that the sensation of low tones requires a great many hair cells or fibers, although the sensation of high tones uses very few. In addition, there is a correlation between place on the membrane and frequency, with the base of the basilar membrane concerned with high frequencies and the apex concerned with low frequencies. Evidence from cochlear potential recordings indicates a similar pattern.

One important phenomenon associated with studies of stimulation deafness is that an unusual amount of destruction in the 1,000- to 2,000-Hz area is noted, regardless of the frequency of the original tone. The effect of the duration of the exposure is shown in Figure 6–23, in which a 1,000-Hz tone at 130 db was presented for 1, 2, 4, and 8 minutes. The stimulation is far more effective on frequencies above 1,000 Hz. Both 4 and 8 minutes' exposure result in severe loss at the high frequencies.

FIGURE 6–21: *Percentage reversals in sound localization as a function of frequency. The points represent data collected at different intervals. The critical region appears to be around 3,000 Hz, as was true of the data shown in Figure 6–20. (From Stevens & Newman, 1936a, p. 302.)*

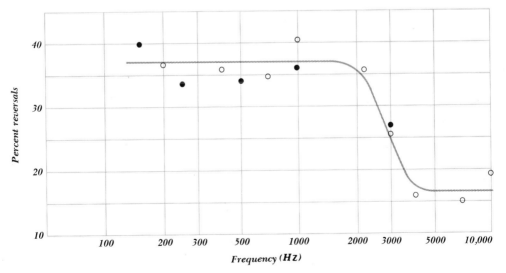

FIGURE 6-22: *The effects of intense stimulation on the cochlea. For each of four frequencies, 300, 1,000, 5,000, and 10,000 Hz destruction is shown at two areas, the organ of Corti and the tympanic lamella. The unfilled areas show the regions where damage occurs, as measured in millimeters from the base of the cochlea. The abscissa shows the number of millimeters from the base. Note that low tones produce more extensive damage than high tones and that low tones damage the membrane nearer the apex of the membrane. Higher tones produce limited destruction nearer the base. (From Wever, 1949, p. 213; K. R. Smith, 1947; and K. R. Smith & Wever, 1949.)*

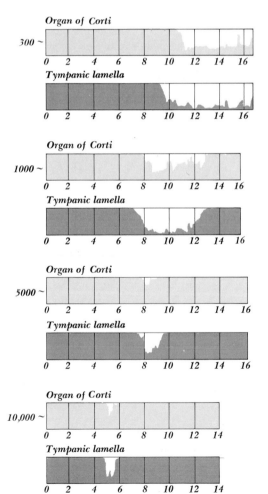

Tinnitus: Tinnitus is a very common disorder of the ear; it appears in almost all auditory disorders. In its mildest form, tinnitus is perceived as a "ringing in the ear" of short duration. The pitch is usually high. Many persons who have never suspected tinnitus in themselves become aware of it if they are placed in soundproofed rooms. Tinnitus occurs quite commonly after extreme stimulation of the ear, and it is often experienced after a blow to the ear. Wever (1949, p. 354) points out that some tinnitus may be vascular (in that an artery is partially blocked) and that another type may be the result of muscle spasms, perhaps of the tympanic muscles. He notes that in some cases a second observer has been able to hear the tone, thus indicating that it is not always cochlear in origin. Of importance to auditory theory, however, is the observation that tinnitus often accompanies progressive losses in high-tone perception and that the frequency of the tone heard corresponds with an area where pitch perception is impaired.

Tinnitus is present in *Ménière's disease.* The syndrome is typified by sudden attacks of nausea, vertigo, and tinnitus. The disease is sometimes attributed to an intestinal disorder, rather than to its origin in the auditory and labyrinth system. Tinnitus also occurs often with *otosclerosis,* which is a bone growth that immobilizes the stapes in the oval window. When this occurs, they cannot reproduce the energy impinging upon the tympanic membrane, and conduction is impaired.

Of significance to theory is the observation that the pitch of the tinnitus is usually accompanied by a selective hearing loss in nearby pitches and that the offending tone is almost always above 2,000 Hz. This latter observation corroborates findings which indicate that the perception of high tones involves smaller areas on the basilar membrane than does the perception of low tones. Low-tone tinnitus is not unknown, however; cases of tinnitus over wide areas of pitch have been reported.

Diplacusis: This disorder is commonly called

FIGURE 6–23: *The amount of hearing loss produced by a 1,000-Hz tone at 130 db for 1, 2, 4, and 8 minutes. Maximal loss occurs in the 1,000- to 2,000-Hz range. The longer the duration of the exposure, the greater the hearing loss. (From H. Davis, C. T. Morgan, Hawkins, Galambos, & F. W. Smith, 1950, p. 13.)*

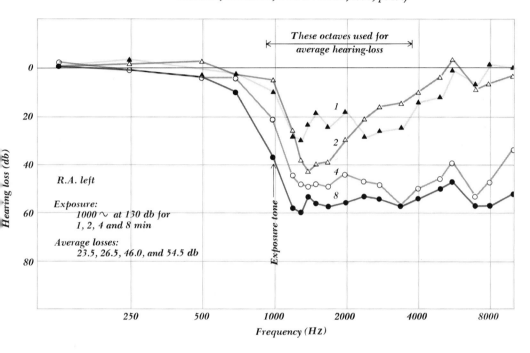

double hearing. Ordinarily, the subject reports that an identical tone yields the sensation of different pitches in different ears. Rather than imply that diplacusis is an abnormality, one might just as easily wonder at the fact that our ears are so finely tuned that both normally perceive the same frequency as being of the same pitch. Transient diplacusis occurs in many unrelated pathological states, including high fever or infection of a single ear. Where the difference in perception between the ears is large, the subject reports echolike sensations. Sometimes diplacusis is noted only under higher amplitudes, such as a public address system. Cases are reported of monaural diplacusis, in which the subject perceives the echo in a single ear. The basic difficulty encountered by theories of audition in regard to diplacusis is that of explaining why it occurs

at all and, especially, how it can occur in only one ear.

Presbyacusia: That there is a decrease in the TL for pitch with age is well known. As one ages, the ring of the telephone becomes softer, and high-fidelity sets become unnecessary. Figure 6–8 showed the effect of age upon the TL for frequency. It is clear that the loss is at the high-tone frequencies and not especially at the low-tone. The implications of this for industrial design are immense. The implications for theories of audition are more questionable, since presbyacusia is probably the result either of increasing immobility of the ossicles with age or of a combination of minor diseases and infections throughout life. On the other hand, it is significant that, once again, it is the high tones which are affected.

Otosclerosis: This malfunction involves the stapes immobilizing the oval window. Surgical procedures are required for correction of otosclerosis. The older technique was merely to rattle the stapes in the hope that it would be freed from the window. Sometimes, of course, the stapes became detached from everything else in the process. In recent years, some successes have been reported with the replacement of the original stapes by a plastic stapes.

High-tone Deafness: Distinct from presbyacusia (in which age is the determining factor), some individuals show a considerable and often debilitating loss of high-tone perception. In some cases, the impairment is graduated; i.e., it increases as the frequency is increased. In others, it is abrupt, for perception is normal to a certain point and then is impaired for all higher frequencies. Once again, it is impressive that the deficiency is in perception of high tones, not low tones.

Recruitment: One of the curious phenomena associated with the various forms of high-tone deafness is that, given a subject with high-tone loss, if the pitch is now raised in amplitude in slow steps, the subject reports that the sensation of the tone begins abruptly. That is, he does *not* report the tone as becoming louder and louder; rather, when it reaches a specific amplitude, it is "suddenly" heard. Such persons may ask you to "turn up" the TV and then complain it is too loud. The problem of how amplitude is perceived is a problem for a theory of audition. Recruitment, however, indicates again that pitch and loudness are intertwined.

THE FINAL QUESTION: THE RELATIONSHIP BETWEEN THE PHYSICAL STIMULUS AND THE PSYCHOLOGICAL RESPONSE

When we compare verbal reports regarding auditory sensations with qualities of the physical stimulus, it becomes clear that auditory sensations are not directly predictable from our measurement of the physical stimulus. This is hardly surprising, for it was this problem—the lack of correspondence between the physical and psychological worlds—that led to Fechner's development of psychophysics. Many theorists have attempted to solve this relationship for audition, and it is worth our time to review the elements of some of the basic theories chronologically, so that we can understand more clearly how we have arrived at the present concept of how hearing occurs. Naturally, the history of theory is filled with wrong guesses—certainly, many more wrong guesses than right guesses, assuming that we know what is a right guess even now. Nevertheless, there is much to be learned about how theory is formed, developed, modified, and perhaps rejected.

Hermann von Helmholtz, who was born in 1821, was truly a Renaissance scientist. His interests were catholic, and he made important contributions to the study of both audition and vision. In school, he was influenced by the work in physiology and physics of Johannes Müller, whose name we associate with the law of specific nerve energies and the law of spinal roots. He was also associated with du Bois–Reymond (p. 40). At the age of twenty-six, Helmholtz delivered a paper before the Physical Society of Berlin on the conservation of energy. He had worked on the paper during his tour of duty with the army. Publication of this paper procured sufficient prestige that Helmholtz was called to Königsberg as a professor of physiology. There he met, and admired, William Thomson, who was to become Lord Kelvin. Lord Kelvin was already famous at this time.

When Helmholtz was thirty-four, he moved to the University of Bonn, where he began work on the origin of combination tones. He uncovered the relationship between summation tones and the fundamental and published a paper on harmony. In 1856, the first volume of his work on optics (*Handbuch der physiologischen Optik*) appeared. The second volume was published in 1860, and the third in

1866 (see Helmholtz, 1867; 1962). In 1858 he transferred to Heidelberg where he was to remain for thirteen years. In 1859 he published a paper on vowels and air vibrations. In 1863 he published the results of his thinking and research on acoustics in *Der Tonempfindungen* (see also Helmholtz, 1930).

In 1871 Helmholtz moved to Berlin and into the professorship in physics. During the next few years he served in various administrative capacities and continued his research. In 1893, at the age of seventy-two, Helmholtz finally visited the United States to attend the electrical congress in Chicago and, incidentally, to attend the Columbian Exposition which was presented in Chicago at the same time. The next year, Helmholtz died. With his death, science lost perhaps the last and certainly the greatest all-around scientist (see Koenigsberger, 1902–1903; Riggs, 1967).

Helmholtz made a number of significant contributions to sensory physiology and sensory psychology and postulated an ingenious theory of how the auditory apparatus works. Although 1863 is commonly cited as the date of the theory, since that date marked the publication of his classic work on audition, Helmholtz altered his ideas from time to time. Some of Helmholtz's suppositions may appear naïve in retrospect, but it is unsophisticated to overlook the fact that his argument cleverly integrated most of the phenomena associated with audition at the time. In regard to the process of audition, Helmholtz suggested that the cochlea in general and the organ of Corti, in particular were the locus of hearing. It should be recalled that the *zeitgeist* of nerve physiology during Helmholtz's time was a belief in the specific energies of nerves, in one form or another. It is not a far step from the idea of specific nerve energies to the supposition that each pitch has a separate receptor in the cochlea. How else can one conveniently account for the vast number of distinguishable pitches available to the human ear? At first, the hair cells on the organ of Corti seemed an obvious choice. Later, Helmholtz shifted to a belief that the transverse fibers on the basilar membrane were the locus of pitch discrimination.

When Helmholtz first suggested the organ of Corti as the locus of the receptors for pitch, the anatomy of the basilar membrane was not well known. The observation that the ear had a series of fibers which varied in length implied that the ear perceived pitch much as a piano or a harp vibrates strings of different lengths to produce tones of different frequencies. As often happens in theory, the analogy was too appealing to be avoided by any but the most dogmatic theorist, and Helmholtz was quick to see the significance of the analogy and to alter the postulations accordingly. To Helmholtz, the sensation of pitch depended upon the length of the fiber vibrated.

It is sometimes said that Helmholtz had a theory of pitch, rather than a theory of hearing, for he was somewhat reticent to comment on how loudness and other complexities were perceived. How *force* (Helmholtz's term for amplitude) was perceived did not appear to have occurred to Helmholtz as a difficult problem, since he did not know that limitations of the nervous system made it unlikely to assume that a nerve could carry separate impulses, such as pitch and loudness. Obviously, if there were a separate fiber for each pitch, the amount of force on that fiber would determine the loudness.

Although one must admire the ingenuity with which Helmholtz applied the available data on audition to the observations of the anatomy and physiology of the ear, it has been clear for at least fifty years that the theory is not tenable considering the abilities and limitations of the nervous system. For reasons which we shall note below, the "piano string" theory of hearing does not hold up under discoveries made after Helmholtz postulated his theory. The simplicity of the theory, however, has led to its widespread repetition, although even Helmholtz's contemporaries objected to the postulation of 20,000 different fibers for hearing, particularly when it was noted that the anatomical relationship in length between the longest and shortest fibers along the basilar membrane is 12:1—just enough for three octaves, and far less than the capacity of the human ear. Moreover, was it not hard to believe that 1 fiber out of 20,000 could operate independently of all the rest? Would it not be likely that the vibration of a single fiber would activate surrounding fibers? Anatomically, the fibers are connected within the tissue of the basilar membrane, and to expect a single tone to affect a single fiber was as reasonable as trying to find a needle in a haystack without moving any of the hay. The postulation of the all-or-none law (see Chapter 2) in the early part of this century was a telling blow, for if it was true that a nerve either fired completely or not at all, how could the supposed 20,000 fibers report loudness and pitch together?

With the all-or-none law, Helmholtz's postulation was in trouble, but not for long. The *Forbes-Gregg hypothesis* of 1915 suggested an alternative as an explanation of how a single fiber can report two dimensions and still follow the all-or-none postulation. The Forbes-Gregg hypothesis suggested that the relative refractory period permitted a single nerve to report intensity as well as frequency. It may be recalled (Chapter 2, p. 000) that during the relative refractory period, a nerve may be fired again if the stimulus is more intense than the stimulus originally required to fire the nerve. In other terms, during the relative refractory period a suprathreshold stimulus could fire the nerve, whereas a normal stimulus could not. In this way, a single nerve fiber could report frequency (the original threshold stimulus) as well as intensity (whether the nerve continued to respond after its initial firing and before returning to its resting state). The more intense the stimulus, the more rapidly the nerve would be able to fire, and the rapidity of firing would be responsible for the sensation of loudness (Forbes & Gregg, 1915). The hypothesis was a clever prediction. Not only did it make Helmholtz's theory tenable again, but the concept of the firing of a single nerve under different levels of intensity during the relative refractory period turned out to be accurate.

Although some research findings argued against Helmholtz's postulation, others corroborated his speculations. A critical test of the pitch portion of the theory is whether or not different parts of the membrane do respond to different frequencies. Data from cochlear potentials and from stimulation deafness indicate that this relationship is generally accurate in that low tones appear to stimulate the apex of the basilar membrane while high tones stimulate the base. These findings do indicate that there is not a single fiber for every pitch and that, accordingly, Helmholtz would need even more fibers than 20,000 to account for the number of different pitches perceived by the human ear. Pathological states too tend to support the concept that it is the place or location on the cochlea which determines the pitch; although evidence from the human being is difficult to secure, many persons with high-tone deafness do show abnormal nerve function at the base turn of the cochlea.

Experimenters who attempt to destroy a theory by designing a "critical experiment" which is expected to leave the theory in ruins have always found that theories are remarkably resistant to destruction from a single shot. As we have noted, although the all-or-none law appeared to limit Helmholtz's theory, the total effect was to drive other experimenters to postulate new methods for explaining the so-called critical finding. It is for this reason that theories are never murdered with one neat swipe; rather, they die slow deaths, fading away, as newer theories manage to account for more and more facts.

Among the theories which have opposed Helmholtz's emphasis upon the organ of Corti as the location of auditory perception are several which consider the basilar membrane the important organ of hearing. These so-called telephone and frequency theories suggest that the basilar membrane behaves very much like the diaphragm in a telephone receiver. Vibrations are created by the action of the stapes on the oval window and by the fluid which, in turn, pushes against the membrane. The vibration of the membrane stimulates the hair cells. Rutherford (1886) is credited with the first telephone theory, which was later modified by Wrightson and Keith (1918). Meyer (1907) proposed a theory which assumed that the basilar membrane was solid and that its parts did not vibrate separately but that the entire membrane was lifted and dropped by the action of the stapes on the oval window. Troland (1929b) suggested that both the Helmholtz and the telephone theories were correct but that certain frequencies followed one whereas other frequencies followed the other. Compromise is not so suspect in theory construction as it is in moral endeavors, for compromise usually implies that the theorist has taken the best from available theories and formulated a better theory.

Curiously, the telephone and frequency theories handled loudness well (for the amount of displacement of the basilar membrane would indicate the intensity of the stimulus by stimulating more receptors) but had trouble with determining the location of pitch perception. The solution was to relegate this function to the brain. The assumption that the brain was somehow capable of performing the fine pitch discriminations had the virtue of not being readily testable at the time and the disadvantage of requiring as much credulity as Helmholtz's 20,000 fibers for pitch alone. Moreover, it does not seem possible that the cranial nerve could conduct as many pulses so rapidly as would be required by telephone and frequency theories.

Clearly, both *place theories* (Helmholtz type) and *frequency theories* (Rutherford type) had something to offer: one handled pitch, and the other handled loudness. The need for compromise between these two positions became clear. Wever and Bray (1930a; 1930b; 1937) and Wever (1949) have made the compromise and have produced some additional evidence in what is known as the *volley theory*. This theory suggests that perception of certain frequencies is dependent upon the location in the cochlea but that the perception of other frequencies depends upon the volleying of fibers.

The volley theory takes advantage of the Forbes-Gregg hypothesis regarding the relative refractory period as well as the finding that frequencies may be shown to volley (when measured by the auditory nerve) up to around 4,000 Hz and perhaps beyond. Figure 6–24 indicates, systematically, the way in which the volley theory predicts the perception of pitch and loudness. The diagram shows two frequencies, 800 and 3,000 Hz, and two intensities. Intensity 1 is less intense than intensity 2. The lines *a, b, c, d,* and *e* are nerve fibers. Now, when the frequency is 800 Hz and the intensity is low (upper left), three nerves fire, all at the same time. When the amplitude is increased but the frequency is unchanged (upper right), *more* fibers are fired, either because fibers *b* and *d* have a higher intensity threshold than *a, c,* and *e* or because the increased amplitude fires nerves in their relative refractory period.

Now, consider a higher tone—one of 3,000 Hz—at both low and high amplitude. Note that although all five fibers *(a, b, c, d, e)* are fired, they fire at different times. The firings are staggered, since each nerve must await the completion of its absolute and, perhaps, its relative refractory period before firing again. If the intensity is increased, however, as shown in the lower left portion of the figure, each nerve fiber is able to fire more frequently, since the stimulus is sufficiently intense to fire the nerve during its relative refractory period. It should be noted that there is no reason to suppose that all nerves have relative or absolute refractory periods of the same duration. The differential time lapse between different nerves is also useful in predicting the variations in individual fiber threshold expected by volley theory. Low tones, then, result from volleying. Higher tones depend on stimulation of the appropriate receptor.

Among the virtues of the volley theory are that it does not require unusual assumptions about the physiological nature of the ear and that it is capable of explaining pathological conditions which feature partial loss of hearing. Atrophy of a single fiber would not destroy perception of a given pitch, for other fibers would still be volleying to the appropri-

FIGURE 6-24: *The volley principle. The figure shows two frequencies (800 and 3,000 Hz) at two intensities (1 and 2). At 800 Hz fibers a, c, and e fire. When the intensity is increased, fibers b and d are brought into play. Under the higher-frequency, 3,000-Hz tone, the fibers fire at different times. (From* Method and Theory in Experimental Psychology, *by Charles E. Osgood, copyright 1953 by Oxford University Press, Inc. Reprinted by permission.)*

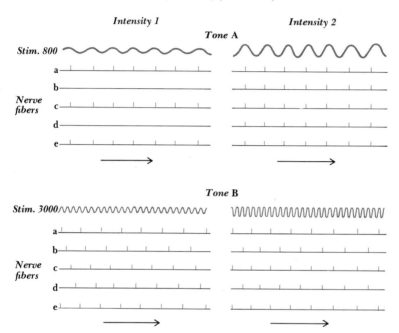

ate frequency. On the other hand, loudness would be impaired by such atrophy, since the frequency of the volley would be reduced. This is exactly what happens in cases of partial loss, for the subject shows a reduction in loudness threshold, rather than a minute, selective loss of pitch perception. Although the fact that frequencies above 4,000 Hz do not appear to volley is offered as a criticism of the volley principle, it appears that the criticism is directed to the generality of the volley theory, rather than to the principle of the volleying of fibers. One of the most serious questions is that if the volley principle holds, how is it possible to hear two low tones near to each other in frequency? It would seem likely that one tone would be severely masked by the other, yet human beings are able to hear two low tones simultaneously.

The volley theory, like Helmholtz's theory, has withheld attack longer than most theories. With improvement in techniques and equipment, contemporary research on theories of hearing has concentrated on understanding the functioning of the cochlea and, especially, the functioning of the basilar membrane. A series of brilliantly conceived experiments by Georg von Békésy and his colleagues has resulted in a theory of hearing often called the *traveling wave* theory, since it emphasizes the motion of the basilar membrane. The basic assumption of this approach, which is supported by observational evidence, is that the basilar membrane responds mechanically to stimulation against the oval window and that the location of maximum displacement varies as a function of the frequency of the stimulus. The location of maximal mechanical displacement is near the stapes for high tones (which has been established as the source of high-tone perception since Helmholtz's time) and farther from the stapes for low tones. Thus, it is assumed that the basilar membrane is a frequency analyzer and that the movement (or traveling wave) of the basilar membrane stimulates the hair cells. Pitch, then, is determined by the form of the traveling wave set up by the stimulus. Loudness, on the other hand, is supposedly mediated by the number of hair cells stimulated.

It is suggested that more fibers will be excited by high intensities than by low intensities, because an intense tone will be suprathreshold for more fibers than a soft tone. Since the mechanical analysis performed by the basilar membrane in this theory cannot be expected to produce the fine discriminations available to human and other ears, it is suggested that the CNS is able to integrate and differentiate in such a way as to make fine discriminations of the nerve impulses. Let us now examine this approach in greater detail.

A theory of audition is concerned primarily with answering three questions: (1) How does the ear, especially the cochlea, discriminate frequencies and loudnesses as well as the many other phenomena of auditory sensitivity? (2) How is this information coded and sent to the brain? (3) Once this has occurred, what role do the brain structures play in auditory discrimination? The earlier theories which we have reviewed were chiefly concerned with the first question, because it is the primary question and also because little was known about the auditory functions of the brain at the time.

Let us begin by reviewing what is presumed to occur when a sound enters the ear. The three important components, the tympanic membrane, the ossicles, and the cochlea, each have limitations in the transportation of the sound pattern. The external canal has a resonant frequency of around 4,000 Hz. When combined with the resonant frequency of the middle ear, the range is approximately 800 to 6,000 Hz (H. Davis, 1959). This range matches the estimates of thresholds shown in Figure 6–25. The transmission of this pattern by the stapes (via the oval window) to the cochlea produces a *traveling wave* within the cochlea. The wave increases in amplitude as it moves toward the apex and is at its maximum when the resonant frequency of the basilar membrane matches the frequency of the traveling wave. As the frequency of the wave is increased, the location of maximal amplitude moves toward the oval window. If it is decreased, movement is toward the apex.

This relationship is seen in Figure 6–25, which shows the effect of a 200-Hz tone in terms of the traveling wave established along the membrane. Since the basilar membrane varies in stiffness (the base is stiffer than the apex), the wave creates only a small movement when it enters. However, as it travels along the membrane and the membrane becomes less stiff, the magnitude of the wave increases until it reaches a maximum at some point along the membrane. Following the point of maximal magnitude, the wave declines and dies out. Now, a low-frequency wave will travel farther

FIGURE 6–25: *The traveling wave to a 200-Hz tone. The abscissa shows the distance from the stapes. The two lines show the pattern at two instants of time separated by a phase angle of 90°. (From Békésy, 1947, p. 455.)*

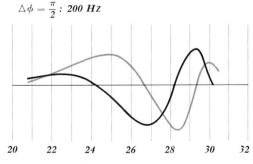

$\triangle \phi = \frac{\pi}{2} : \textbf{200 Hz}$

| 20 | 22 | 24 | 26 | 28 | 30 | 32 |

Distance from stapes (mm)

than a high-frequency wave. The latter travels only a short distance before reaching its maximum. The data suggest that the cochlea is able to analyze and report the frequency of the stimulus in terms of the location on the membrane whose resonant frequency matches that of the wave. In human beings, a tone of 100 Hz reaches its maximum magnitude near the helicotrema. The basal end of the membrane, however, resonates to all frequencies. In compiling these data, Békésy (1963) examined the cochlea microscopically under stroboscopic illumination.

Research on the second question—how the cochlea transmits its information to the brain and the role of the brain in auditory perception—has profited from remarkable advances in neurological techniques and from a shift in emphasis. For several reasons earlier investigators had concentrated their research on two characteristics of sound—frequency and amplitude. Surely, these are easier to present and quantify than mixed tones. Moreover, earlier theories of hearing emphasized the ear as an analyzer of pure tones (e.g., Helmholtz). More recently investigators have used clicks or other reasonably complex stimuli. As we shall see, the CNS apparently handles pure tones somewhat differently from complex tones. Let us trace, so far as we can, what occurs to the auditory stimulation as it leaves the cochlea.

The afferent neurons at the point where the auditory nerve leaves the cochlea are bipolar cells. There are perhaps 28,000 in each ear (H. Davis, 1959). As we have noted, all these fibers arrive at the cochlear nucleus in the medulla. If we measure the output of the VIIIth cranial nerve in response to a single click, a volley of action potentials results. This volley is known as N_1. If we increase the intensity of the click, a second potential N_2 appears shortly after N_1; an even more intense click is likely to produce an N_3 response (Tasaki, 1954). The time lapse between the action potentials is approximately 1 msec (millisecond); thus, we assume that the nerve cannot reproduce, by the rate of firing, frequencies above 1,000 Hz. This implies that some mech-

anism other than simple response rate is responsible for high frequencies reaching the brain. An important finding is that fibers have different latencies and that the same fiber does not fire with the same latency on successive recordings. From 1,000 to around 4,000 Hz the action potential volleys appear to follow the stimulus frequency reasonably well, although the amplitude of the volley is reduced. This would appear to be the result of cells skipping and responding only on every nth presentation. We have seen this principle before as the volley theory (H. Davis, 1959). For example, the response of a single auditory nerve fiber is shown in Figure 6–26. The curved line inscribes the response area of the nerve fiber. Clearly, the nerve fiber has its special area to which it will respond in terms of intensity and frequency. Fibers differ greatly in thresholds and in whether or not they repeat the response upon continued stimulation. Thus, we may conceive of a nerve which contains fibers responsive to a variety of frequencies and amplitudes, although each fiber appears to have its area of specialization.

Earlier in this chapter, we stated that the auditory system continues from the cochlea through the brainstem to the thalamus and, eventually, to the cortex. We noted previously the importance of the lemniscal tracts. It is obvious, however, that many other areas of the brain are concerned with interpreting auditory sensations, even though the number of areas and their functions are not fully understood. First of all, when the VIIIth nerve reaches the cochlear nuclei, each fiber appears to terminate on approximately one hundred cells. Each cell within the nucleus appears to receive impulses from more than one fiber. We may identify at least three different pathways from the cochlear nuclei (Barnes, Magoun, & Ranson, 1943). The complexity of the auditory system, once it leaves the ear, if not before, may be noted from the large number of third-, fourth-, and fifth-order synapses which occur before the thalamus is reached (Ades, 1959). In some sensory systems, second-order synapses are the rule. The large number of fibers, in addition to the unusual amount of synapsing, provides the system with the possibility of sending messages to many areas of the brain. W. D. Neff and his colleagues (1956), for example, offer strong evidence that the cortex is necessary for the discrimination of tonal patterning. On the other hand, it appears that some areas of the brain exercise an inhibitory effect on auditory sensation. Stimulation of an area in the medulla either destroys or lessens the N_1 and N_2 responses. Further, areas up to the cortex may be inhibited by such a stimulation (Galambos, 1956; Ruben & Sekula, 1960).

We have noted on several occasions that the cochlea is organized according to frequency. When such an organization occurs, it is said to be *tonotopic*. Thus, the organization along the cochlea should be repeated elsewhere in the system. Such organization does indeed occur in several locations along the auditory pathways, including the separation into dorsal and ventral sides of the cochlear nuclei and in the auditory cortex. Two areas of the cortex, known as AI and AII, also represent the cochlear formation.

The most common experimental procedure for investigating the role of the cortex, or any other structure, in auditory perception is to train an organism, usually a cat, to discriminate two or more tones and then to remove a specific area of the cortex. If the animal retains the discrimination, evidence is provided that the area removed is not necessary for that particular perception. If the animal does not retain the discrimination, the results favor the finding that the area is necessary for the perception. Goldberg and W. D. Neff (1961) have shown that large areas of the auditory cortex can be removed without damaging the ability to learn frequency discriminations. The originally learned discriminations may be lost following the operation, but the animals are able to relearn them. However, if we require the organism to make a pattern discrimination, in which, for example, one pattern consists of a low tone followed by a high tone and concluding with another low tone while a second

FIGURE 6-26: *The response area of a single auditory (VIIIth cranial) nerve fiber. The response is to tone pips of different amplitudes and frequencies. (From H. Davis, 1959, p. 580, after Tasaki, 1954.)*

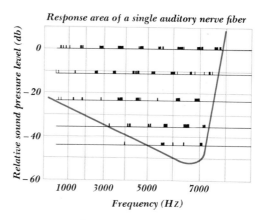

Response area of a single auditory nerve fiber

Relative sound pressure level (db)

Frequency (Hz)

discrimination is high-low-high, any of several combinations of removal of areas of the auditory cortex results in loss of the discriminative ability (Diamond & W. D. Neff, 1957).

Similar findings relate to the perception of intensity (W. D. Neff, 1961a). With removal of the auditory cortex, cats retain the ability to discriminate intensities. Thus, the source of the perception of loudness appears to be within structures lower in the brain. However, the cortex is very important in the ability to localize sounds. If sections of the cortex are removed (W. D. Neff, 1961a), cats do not retain a learned discrimination of sound localization, but they are able to acquire the ability again with retraining. However, if all the major areas of the auditory cortex are removed, the animal is unable to localize sounds. At the present, it appears that the cortex is necessary for such complex acoustical phenomena as sound localization and temporal patterning but not for the more simple recognition of frequency and amplitude.

It should be evident from our review of auditory theory that the fate of many reasonable theories has been gradual and piecemeal invalidation. The characteristics of a theory which hold up over years of investigation are given rebirth by being incorporated into new theories, while other attributes are dropped. Thus, there is still much of Helmholtz's thinking in contemporary theory. Certainly, the basic idea of a place theory holding for some tones remains. Nevertheless, new techniques and developments, especially those concerned with recording from single fibers, have transferred attention from the cochlea to the brain.

It is hard to say how far we are from a comprehensive theory of audition. However, it is quite evident that much has been learned since the days of Helmholtz's formulations. We shall see, when we study vision, that some old theories have remarkable powers of rejuvenation.

SOURCES

Experimental reports on audition make up a substantial proportion of the literature of psychology. In one recent review of the literature (covering a three-year period) 297 articles on audition were considered of sufficient value to be noted. On the other hand, there are few books on the topic. Among the more prominent are Stevens and H. Davis (1938); Wever (1949), which includes an excellent review of auditory theory and data as well as the presentation of the volley theory, as it stood in 1949; and Hirsh (1952). Hirsh deals with the practical attributes of hearing—those which are of value to a hearing therapist or a school psychologist—and is a superb sourcebook for data on the process of hearing.

Anatomy and Physiology: Students who have gone on to do research on the ear have often pointed out that until they actually saw an ear *in situ,* they believed it to be much larger than it is. This impression probably comes from diagrams and anatomical drawings, which enlarge the ear in relation to the head in order

to show its parts clearly. The ear is imbedded in bone and tissue, and its parts are difficult to locate, even for the reader who is quite familiar with anatomical drawings. Perhaps the finest medical illustrations of the ear are by Max Brödel (1946). These drawings are of the ear *in situ* and are difficult for the reader who has not formed a good idea of the anatomy of the ear. Netter (vol. I, 1957) has a good illustration (schematic) of the relationship between the cochlea and the VIIIth cranial nerve and its passage to the temporal lobe, although the drawings representing the cochlea and the temporal lobes are overly imaginative. *The Atlas of Normal Anatomy* (medical student edition) presents a useful drawing of the ear, showing the relationship between the cochlea and the nonauditory labyrinth.

Thresholds and Audiometry: There is a dangerous aspect to the presentation of data in textbooks. Quite often neat threshold measurements which appear in the technical literature are repeated in texts, and a student can easily form the impression that data are valid only because they have been repeated so often in print. Although the thresholds reported here have some validity, if for no other reason than that they have been published time and time again without criticism or rebuttal, this type of validity is not nearly so convincing as that which arises from a threshold measurement's being repeated and corroborated in the literature. Unfortunately, technical journals are rarely interested in publishing pure repetitions of data, and the textbook writer, as well as the professional, is never certain that the data he presents are accurate. This is a difficulty common to all sciences, and the student should consider the difficulty as the explanation for the need to remeasure and to establish procedures of validification on even the most common data.

Of use to the student interested in the problems of auditory thresholds is Licklider (1951). Although the data reported in Licklider's chapter are over ten years old, his considered opinions on the problems of measuring auditory thresholds are valuable. The chapter by Békésy and Rosenblith (1951) is also very useful. Hirsh (1952) discusses thresholds and the procedures of audiometry in detail. Geldard (1953) offers a careful opinion of the usefulness of many of the common data regarding thresholds. Osgood (1953) also offers a thorough description of auditory thresholds. The chapters by H. Davis (1959) and Ades (1959) in Field, Magoun, and Hall are technical; however, the student interested in detailed information should use these sources. C. T. Morgan (1965) is somewhat easier to understand, although not nearly so complete.

Pathology: The Hirsh (1952) volume is especially good on recruitment. Wever (1949) considers the nature of the basic pathological states and their relation to auditory theory.

Sound Localization: Rosenzweig (1961) offers a detailed review of the literature on sound localization. In addition to its historical interest, the paper offers comments on contemporary theory of localization.

Theory: Helmholtz's formulations were translated into English in 1930. A presentation of the volley theory is presented in the work by Wever (1949). Wever has translated and edited collected papers of Békésy (1960). Wever and Lawrence (1954) present basic data on the ear and on techniques of investigation. Several chapters in Rosenblith (1961) indicate the trends in auditory theory: Cherry's "Two Ears —but One World" (1961b), H. Davis's "Peripheral Coding of Auditory Information" (1961), Woolsey's "Organization of Cortical Auditory System" (1961), and W. D. Neff's "Neural Mechanisms of Auditory Discrimination" (1961b).

CHAPTER SEVEN

LANGUAGE

INTRODUCTION

One of the most useful functions of the ear is that it enables us to perceive speech. Many of the sensory stimuli impinging upon us are the speech sounds of other human beings. Lower animals also use speech. For example, various types of dog speech can be discriminated by a dog owner: the whine of pain, the sharp bark noting an intruder, the "begging" sounds connected with the desire for food or handling or to be let out of the house to search for a lady friend. Comparatively little is known about the use animals make of auditory perception in their speech, but it is likely that we underrate its importance.

Auditory perception of speech requires two components: the production of sound by the speaker and the reception and transmission of the sound stimuli by the auditory apparatus. It is clear that auditory perception is not innate to the organism, for both the speaker and the listener must learn to distinguish sounds. Accordingly, an understanding of how speech develops requires knowledge of the principles of conditioning and learning (discussed in Chapters 12 to 15) as well as an understanding of the principles of audition discussed in the last chapter. Speech is both a motor function and a sensory process. It differs from some senses, such as vision, in certain obvious ways, yet it is similar to other processes, such as cutaneous sensitivity, in that one can talk to oneself just as one can touch oneself. The capacity to speak is indebted to what is learned, and this is true of any of our senses. Thus, although we shall not discuss the fine points of the process of learning until later in this volume, it appears appropriate to review some of the fundamental findings regarding speech now that we have discussed the auditory apparatus.

PRODUCTION OF SPEECH AND PHONATION

Speech is intertwined with the process of breathing. It occurs "on top of" respiration, and for this reason, the measurement of speech sounds always involves, to some degree, measurement of respiration. The most common method for providing an index of respiration is known as the *I fraction,* in which

$$I \text{ fraction} = \frac{I}{D}$$

where

I = duration of inhalation
D = duration of whole breathing cycle (inhalation and exhalation)

For example, if a person inhales for 5 seconds during a total cycle of 12 seconds, the *I* fraction is

$$5/12 = 0.416$$

When a person is quiet and breathing at a normal rate, the *I* fraction is reported to be between 0.40 and 0.45. When a person is speaking, the *I* fraction decreases to around 0.16 (Fossler, 1930).

The production of sound begins in the lungs. Under normal conditions, the speaker inhales prior to speaking and slowly exhales during the process of speech. During inhalation, the chest cavity expands while the lungs fill with air. Thus, the volume of air available for use in speech is increased. Although shortness of breath in athletics or in singing is sometimes ascribed to small lung capacity, it appears that training is far more important than innate capacity in this respect (G. A. Miller, 1951a, p. 12).

Speech depends upon the coordination of several organs, including the mouth area—the lips, tongue, teeth, and palate, which may be moved to alter the type of sound produced—and the respiratory system. In human beings, speech is vastly more complex than the simple production of sounds, just as writing is considerably more intricate and requires far more coordination than the scribblings of a child. Areas of the CNS are also important in, and

have appreciable control over, speech production. Parts of the fish's respiratory mechanism resemble a rudimentary mechanism for speech found in the frog and other amphibians. This mechanism appears to have been commandeered when the supposed transition from sea to land rendered the gill slits useless.

Mammals, as well as birds and reptiles, have a device for closing off the lungs. This device may be as simple as a group of muscle fibers, or it may be as elaborate as the cartilaginous bones which form the *larynx* in man and the other primates. Since this apparatus serves to contain the air in the lungs, its manipulation can permit the organism to let air escape in controllable quantities, an ability which is essential to the production of precise speech sounds. The larynx of man and the primates is more elaborate than that of other mammals, including the ruminants, rodents, and domestic animals. The location of the larynx is easily observed externally in man, for it may be seen on the throat as the "Adam's apple." When swallowing, one can feel the movement of the larynx and nearby structures.

The structure of the larynx is shown in Figure 7–1. Note that the Adam's apple, vocal folds, and cartilage rest on top of the windpipe. Muscles are attached to the cartilages, and these muscles can contract or relax to control the position of the *vocal folds.* When the muscles are relaxed, as when one is resting and breathing lightly, the folds form a V shape known as the *glottis.* The glottis permits air to pass into, and out of, the windpipe. When the glottis is closed by the folds' coming together, pressure from air in the windpipe can be applied to the folds, forcing them apart and producing noise or speech. The air "pops" and forces the folds to open suddenly. This popping is so rapid that the number of openings and closings per second may be between 100 and 200. The patterning and extent of the pops form the beginning of speech. There is evidence, however, that sounds may be independent of air passage, for Laget (1953) has induced vocal chord vibration in a dog merely by stimulating the laryngeal nerve.

FIGURE 7–1: *Sketch of the larynx, as seen from the left side. Note the position of the glottis, epiglottis, and vocal folds. (From G. A. Miller, 1951a, p. 13.)*

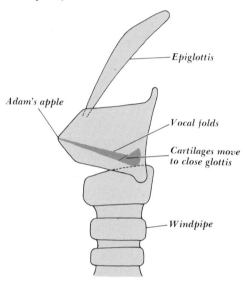

mouth which modifies the pitch and intensity of the air, a change in the shape of the throat so that different sounds are produced (much as organ pipes are of different lengths and diameters in order to produce different tones), and alteration of the pattern of frequencies and intensities associated with the original pop from the folds. The folds are not limited to a single vibration; they are capable of producing several vibrations of different frequencies at the same time. This too permits the production of different complexities.

The range of frequencies and amplitudes is remarkable. Licklider and G. A. Miller (1951) cite data which indicate that the difference in amplitude between a whisper and a shout is around 60 db. A whisper may generate only 0.001 microwatt, while a yell may approach 1,000. It is possible to record the amplitude of different syllables or different sounds (Sacia & C. J. Beck, 1926). If the amplitude is recorded from several persons under conditions of normal conversation, clear differences appear. For example, the vowel *u* has an average power of 13 microwatts, while *l* has a value of 0.33.

The complexity of speech produced by variation in the size and shape of the throat, mouth, or nose is called *resonance*. Any pop will contain a fundamental tone (usually around 125 Hz, or 125 pops) as well as overtones and other harmonics. What happens to the fundamental tone and the overtones before they pass out of the mouth, into the air, and into the ear of the listener may be analogous to what happens to a note played in an auditorium. A note played in an auditorium with a vaulted ceiling and an identical note played in a square room with a low ceiling will sound different because of the size and shape of each room. In a similar manner the pop in the larynx differs as a function of the size and shape of the throat and mouth. Indeed, in speaking, all of us alter the shape of the throat and mouth in order to produce different sounds. The process through which different sounds are produced by varying the physical characteristics of the organs connected with speech is known as *articulation*.

Accordingly, speech may differ in regard to the frequency of pops, the intensity of pops, and the complexity of the vibrations, just as auditory stimuli differ in frequency, amplitude, and complexity. As the number of vibrations is increased, the pitch of the sounds is increased. In English and in many other languages pitch is not an especially important attribute of speech. Changes in pitch may denote accent, but they are rarely used to communicate; e.g., the word *dog*, spoken at different pitches, it still understood as *dog*. In some languages, however, a sound may have three different meanings at three different pitches. Of course, some consonant sounds, such as *t* and *k*, are of high frequencies themselves. Intensity, which is determined by the size of the pops and the amount of air pressure placed on the folds, is employed in English to form different speech sounds.

Complexity is also important in communication. It is produced by several different techniques, including a change in the shape of the

In general, five broad categories of movement, or *types of articulation,* may be identified. These categories are *vowels, plosives, aspirants* (or fricatives), *laterals,* and *trills.* The differences between these movements are most easily learned by pronouncing word examples and noting the position which the organs assume in order to produce the tone.

Vowels. When we make the sound of *a, e, i, o,* or *u* (and of other letters which have some characteristics of vowels), the entire passageway is, more or less, left open. The vowel is determined by the position of the folds, rather than by changes in the structure of the mouth or lips. If you say *a, e, i, o, u* rapidly, you may feel the folds change position.

Plosives. In sounds such as the *p* in *please* or *pop,* the air stream is stopped. The *g* in *gosh* is an example of a plosive.

Aspirants. In sounds such as *th* and *sh* the entire mouth and lip region is narrowed.

Laterals. Sounds which are formed by closing the center of the mouth and allowing air to pass around the outsides (the lateral sides) are called *laterals.* The *l* in *limit* is an example.

Trills. Trills are not common in English but are widely used in Latin languages. For example, the English pronunciation of *burro* does not include a trilling of the *r*; however, in the Spanish pronunciation of the word the *r* is trilled by placing the tongue farther back in the mouth than in the English pronunciation and letting the air play against the tongue. The tongue is moved back as the trill is made, as in *bur-r-r-r-r-o.*

Nasals. Although not a category, nasalization may be added to any of the basic categories. Nasal sounds occur when air is released through the nose, as in the last part of the word *rung.*

Some of the organs of the throat and mouth, such as the tongue and lips, are mobile. They are known as *mobile articulators. Fixed articulators* are immobile. There are five mobile and six fixed articulators. The mobile are (1) lower lip and jaw, (2) tip of tongue, (3) front of tongue, (4) back of tongue, and (5) vocal folds. The fixed are (1) upper lip, (2) upper teeth,

(3) gum ridge, (4) hard palate, (5) soft palate, or velum, and (6) glottis. Clearly, not every mobile articulator can combine with every fixed articulator. The lip does not move back to articulate with the glottis; this is physically impossible. But we can close or open the lips and raise or twist the tongue. These changes affect the quality of sound. Actually, only eight *positions of articulation* are possible. These are articulation between the upper and lower lip *(bilabial),* the upper teeth and lower lip *(labiodental),* the tongue tip and upper teeth ridge *(dental),* the tongue tip and the gum ridge *(alveolar),* the tongue tip and the hard palate *(cacuminal),* the front of the tongue and the soft palate *(palatal),* the back of the tongue and the soft palate *(velar),* and the folds and the glottis *(glottal).* These combinations refer to positions assumed in producing the sounds made in speaking the English language. Other languages include additional positions.

Both vowels and consonants are classified phonetically by the positions the articulators assume to produce the sound. Each position and its accompanying sound has a name composed of its type of articulation and its position of articulation. In addition, a symbol is used to denote the type and position. For example, the *p* in the word *pie* is a plosive (type) and a bilabial (position); the symbol ʃ, representing an aspirant and a palatal sound, occurs in the *sh* of the word *she.* Table 7–A shows the classification of *consonants* used in English.

Three articulators affect vowels: the tongue (either the tip, center, or back may be used, yielding three different tongue positions); the extent of the tongue's movement (how high it is raised—seven heights are distinguished); and the position assumed by the lips (either rounded or unrounded). The combination of three tongue positions, seven tongue heights, and two lip positions yields 42 possible vowel sounds. Figure 7–2 shows the English *vowels* as a function of their articulators.

These classifications of sounds, along with some variations, constitute the *phonetic* system. In this system, each articulation has its own name and symbol, and spoken sounds in

TABLE 7-A: *Classification of Consonants Used in English by the Type and Position of Articulation.*
(From G. A. Miller, 1951a, p. 25.)

Type of articulation	Position of articulation							
	Bilabial	Labio-dental	Dental	Alveolar	Cacuminal	Palatal	Velar	Glottal
Plosives	p (*p*ie) b (*b*y)			t (*t*o) d (*d*o)			k (*k*ey) g (*g*o)	?
Nasals	m (*m*e)			n (*n*o)			ŋ (si*ng*)	None
Fricatives	w (*w*e)	f (*f*ine) v (*v*ine)	θ (*th*in) ð (*th*en)	s (*s*ip) z (*z*ip) r (*r*ip)		ʃ (*sh*e) ʒ (a*z*ure) j (*y*es)		h (*h*e)
Laterals				l (*l*ip)				None
Trills						None		None

any language may be recorded with the same basic symbols. Thus, phonetic classification is a universal shorthand, permitting sounds to be coded and duplicated.

Speech and language, however, differ in many attributes, such as pitch and amplitude. For example, the phrase "I am here" may mean "*I* am here," "I *am* here," or "I am *here*," depending upon the intonation and accentuation of the words. Regardless of the intonation, the phrase would have the same phonetic classification. Characteristics of speech, such as pitch and amplitude, are called *prosodic features.* They are clearly important in communicating meaning, but they do not distinguish phonetic classifications.

Not all phonetic distinctions appear in every language, or if they do appear, not all are necessary to understand the language. A unit which appears often enough in a language to be useful in describing the sounds of the language is called a *phoneme.* For example, English is thought to have between 7 and 15 vowel phonemes: the person listening to English speech needs to discriminate only this many different vowel sounds to distinguish almost all the vowel sounds he will hear. Languages differ in the number and type of phonemes they use. When phonemes are combined, *dipthongs* are produced, such as the *oi*

FIGURE 7-2: *Classification of vowels in English. The chart is arranged according to the part of the tongue (front, center, back) and the height of the tongue. Regional differences in pronunciation may be noted, as, for example, in the different sounds given /a/ in American Eastern and American Southern speech.*
(G. A. Miller, 1951, p. 24.)

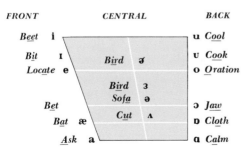

in *boil*. In the symbolic system, sounds which are expressed phonetically are placed in brackets [ ], and those expressed phonemically are placed between slanted lines / /.

Phonemes do not occur randomly in a language, as crossword-puzzle solvers know: long strings of either vowels or consonants are rare. Generally, there is an alternation of consonant and vowel sounds. No word begins with the phonemes *rt*, for this combination is unpronounceable. The fact that phonemes occur under different probabilities—the probability that *q* will be followed by *u* is almost 1—is useful in uncoding messages and in understanding communications.

The fact that combinations of vowels and consonants follow one another with a predictable frequency leads to *redundancy* in language. Some redundancy is useful, for it permits the listener to miss some parts of speech without losing the meaning of what is said. However, redundancy clearly makes the language more verbose and cumbersome than is necessary under some circumstances. In normal communication, extra words or letters are worthwhile, for they enhance correct communication. If we are hurried or have a limited amount of space in which to communicate, redundancy can become a problem. Telegram writing is a behavioral example of this observation. I might want to communicate the fact that I shall be arriving on a certain plane, at a certain airport, on a certain date, but when putting this message into telegraphic form (where verbosity is expensive) I remove as much redundancy as possible. The telegram is written, rather than spoken, so the recipient will take time to read it and be certain of the message; were I to speak the same message, there would be greater opportunity for misunderstanding. Determining how much redundancy may be removed without altering successful communication is a practical problem which has received attention in both military and industrial settings. W. Epstein (1961) has provided data to show that the syntactical structure of messages contributes to the ease of verbal learning, as do meaningfulness and familiarity. Just as the statistical probability of the occurrence of words or letters provides information to the listener, so it appears that the statistical probability of grammatical structure provides information.

RECORDING SPEECH

Two general methods are used for recording speech sounds: the *graphic* technique involves analysis of the waveform of the speech frequencies and amplitudes through Fourier analysis; the *electrical recording* technique is used more commonly. Figure 7–3 shows the way in which filters are used to record speech sounds. The subject is at the microphone. Appropriate measurements are made in order to relate the microphone to the intensity and distance of the speaker's voice. A series of analyzing filters, each tuned to a different frequency, is used. For example, one filter may cover frequencies between 50 and 100 Hz, while another covers those between 100 and 150 Hz. Usually, the filters control the intensity of a light placed at the output of the filters. In this way, changes in the intensity of the light reflect those frequencies and intensities which the filter has permitted to pass. A photograph is then made of the lights, as shown in the figure, so that a permanent record of changes in intensity and frequency is available. Since the photographic film moves at a constant speed, time or duration can be read from the base, or abscissa, of the film. If the filters have been arranged from low to high frequencies, then the photographic record repeats this order; i.e., a recording at the top of the record indicates high-frequency stimuli. Similarly, the intensity of the stimulus is represented by the brightness of the lights and, accordingly, by the amount of darkening on the record (since the film is light-sensitive). The resulting record is known as a *spectrogram*. An example of a spectrogram is shown in Figure 7–4, in which the sentence "Speech we may see" is recorded.

Graphic analysis is appreciably more difficult than electrical analysis. Figure 7–5, for

FIGURE 7-3: *The spectrograph. Sounds passed through the microphone are filtered by wave-band filters, each of which records selected frequencies of the original sound. These are recorded on the moving belt. The amplitude of the sound is reflected by the amount of light produced. Thus, the density of the pattern indicates amplitude, and the location of the recording shows the frequencies represented. The image may then be read, with time along the abscissa and frequency along the ordinate. (From Potter, Kopp, & H. C. Green, 1947, p. 17.)*

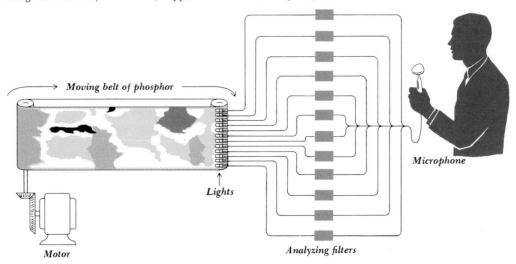

FIGURE 7-4: *A spectrogram, made from apparatus similar to that shown in Figure 7.3, of the spoken words "Speech we may see." The abscissa indicates both time and the speech. The ordinate shows frequency, and the light patterns indicate amplitude. (From Potter, Kopp, & H. C. Green, 1947, p. 12.)*

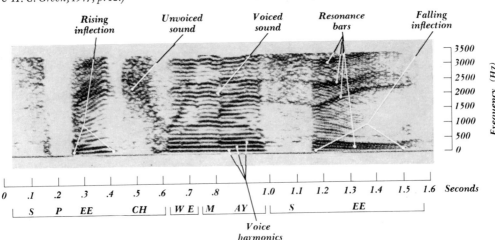

example, shows a graphic analysis of the diphthong in the word *out.* Amplitude is plotted on the ordinate and frequency on the abscissa. The numbers 1 through 12 along the right side of the figure indicate successive stages of the fundamental. The height of the lines indicates the intensity of the vibrations at the frequencies indicated. It is clear that the fundamental frequency changes with successive periods and that amplitude shows a similar shift.

We have noted that sounds may be classified regarding the positions of the vocal apparatus used in producing them. Similarly, recordings of the frequencies of sounds provides a technique for classification. If the speech sounds of sustained vowels are recorded and plotted, it can be seen that the frequencies used by the vowels take up a limited area of the spectrum.

INFORMATION THEORY IN SPEECH

Although the function of speech is to communicate information, not all speech provides the same amount of information. The term *information* refers to the precision with which a sound may be identified. The amount of information conveyed depends upon the number of alternatives. For example, one word selected from the thousands of possible words in a language differs in the amount of information it carries from the appearance of a single dot or dash in Morse code in which only two alternatives are available. Note that the amount of information does not depend only upon the single occurrence of the stimulus: in order to evaluate the amount of information carried by a stimulus, one must know the number of alternative stimuli which might have occurred. If you are playing the party game twenty questions and the respondent answers "Yes" to *all* questions regardless of veracity, you receive little information from his responses. If he answers either "Yes" or "No," more communication is obtained, since as questioner you know not only what is right but what is wrong. If the respondent increases the number of alternatives by saying "Maybe," you acquire

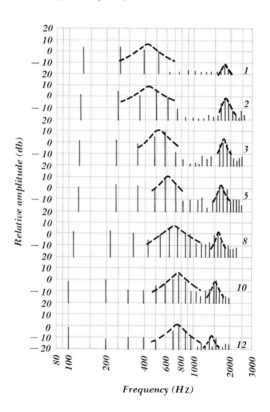

FIGURE 7–5: *A graphic analysis of the diphthong in the word* out. *The numbers 1 through 12 indicate successive stages of the fundamental. Amplitude is plotted along the ordinate and frequency along the abscissa. (From Steinberg, 1934, p. 22.)*

even more information, for if the answer "Maybe" is given to a question, you know that neither "Yes" nor "No" is a correct answer. As the number of alternatives increases (in this example, the number of answers which the respondent may give), more information is gained from any single answer.

Since information is dependent upon the number of alternatives, the amount of information conveyed by an occurrence may be defined as the natural logarithm of the number of alternatives (Shannon, 1948). Figure 7–6 shows this relationship. From the figure it may be noted that the occurrence of 1 out of 10

FIGURE 7-6: *The amount of information gained as a function of the number of alternatives.*

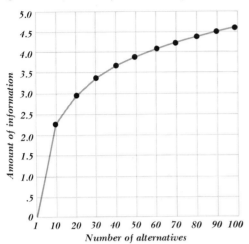

Amount of information

Number of alternatives

sible alternatives assumes that the alternatives are equally probable. That is, it is assumed that each alternative has as great a chance of occurring as every other alternative. With phonemes, it is obvious that this is not so, for some combinations do not exist in the language. Indeed, the fact that the probabilities of occurrence are not equal is very useful in decoding material. As we noted, the probability of *u* following *q* is almost 1. What is the probability of any given letter following *s?* The consonants *t, n,* and *p* have a higher probability of occurring than *b, d,* or *f.* If the probability of occurrence of all alternatives is equal, the logarithmic function will be adequate. If the probabilities are not equal, as occurs in languages, the function may be determined by taking the *average* probability of the logarithms of the alternatives. This formulation yields the *average* amount of information conveyed and provides an estimate of the amount of information.

H. L. Lane (1962) has developed procedures for psychophysical measurements of speech perception. This work (along with that of H. L. Lane, Catania, & Stevens, 1961) has shown a difference between the speaker's own perception of his speech and the perception of listeners. The speaker's assessment of the loudness of vowel sounds in his own speech increases as a power function of the actual sound pressure being produced, although the function for pitch is logarithmic. Changes in amplitude and frequency appear to be greater to the speaker than to listeners. These data suggest, as we have noted in other sensory systems, a lack of perfect correspondence between the physical world and the sensations of physical stimuli.

alternatives carries only half the information carried by the occurrence of 1 out of 100 alternatives, and so on.

The basic idea that the amount of information increases logarithmically as a function of the number of alternatives may be expanded in order to estimate the amount of information conveyed in a unit of speech. If we take a speech wave as a basic unit, the amount of information contained in the wave will be a function of (1) the duration of speech, (2) the range of the frequencies of the speech, and (3) the intensity. In other terms, an increase in the amount of information may occur through (1) extending the length of speech, (2) providing greater range of frequencies within the speech, or (3) varying the amplitude so that more distinctions can be made.

In order to evaluate the amount of information carried in a message, it is not always necessary or useful to analyze appropriate sound waves. One may also evaluate the phonemes of the language. Since a finite number of total phonemes exist (probably between 30 and 50 in English), the number of alternatives to any occurrence may be calculated. The definition of information in terms of a number of pos-

MEASURING MEANING

It is not simple to define *meaning*. Obviously, sounds have different connotations and denotations to different individuals. The word *dog* may arouse feelings of distaste in one person but feelings of tenderness in another. It is probable that the feelings, associations, and emotions that we assign to words are acquired, although there is extensive variability among individuals. The manner in which words acquire meaning presents psychology with one of its most useful avenues of investigation, for many experiments and psychological measurements use verbal behavior as a dependent variable. Accordingly, the way in which language is learned and developed becomes critical for the interpretation of data. Moreover, it is no exaggeration to point out that many misunderstandings and misconceptions appear because of individual differences in the meanings assigned to words. Those who know more than one language know that each language has words or expressions which convey meanings not found in English. This suggests that one's thoughts and, ultimately, one's rationality are governed by the meanings available in the language used. This point is made clear in the difficulties confronted in translating from one language to another. The importance that personal word meanings have in determining behavior cannot be overstated.

In the assessment of personality, individual differences in the meaning ascribed are believed to provide clues to an individual's patterns of thought. If it is assumed that thoughts are restricted to the meanings provided by one's language, then it is reasonable to assume that an analysis of the meanings attached to language provides information on individual patterns of thought. For these reasons, among others, several techniques have been developed to analyze meaning. We shall discuss these in detail in Chapter 15.

Word Association: Originally developed by Francis Galton (1822–1911; 1879) and extended by Carl Jung (1875–1961; 1919) to personality assessment, word association tests are based on the supposition that a sequence of words is not a purely random event. One word prompts the occurrence of the next word, because the meanings of the two are related. For example, consider the following lists of words given in response to the original word "dog."

Subject₁	*Subject₂*
cat	bite
mouse	pain
fur	hit
cheese	injure
trap	fear
hurt	run

It is obvious that the types of associations differ. $Subject_1$ continues to associate the *stimulus word* "dog" with other animals, and eventually with mice and the injury afforded by mousetraps. $Subject_2$ associates quite different meanings with "dog." His associations are concerned with injury and fear. If you were asked which subject would probably be afraid of dogs, your answer would, no doubt, be $subject_2$.

The testing of word association was examined in Wundt's laboratory in Leipzig in 1883 (Trautscholdt, 1883). The important addition made by Wundt and his workers was the use of *reaction time*. This measurement records the time lapse between the presentation of the stimulus word and the reply by the subject, that is, the time lapse between stimulus and response. Reaction time became a useful measure of meaning, for it led to the development of several laws which predict the type of response that will be given. For example, *Marbe's law* states that frequently used words have a more rapid reaction time than words used less frequently (Thumb & Marbe, 1901). Karwoski and Schachter (1948) classified reaction time as a function of the type of response, i.e., whether the response was an opposite word, a word in the same category as the stimulus, or some other category. They found reaction time to be shortest for response words which were direct opposites of the stimulus.

Several types of word association tests have been used. In *free association,* the subject is instructed to respond with any word he wishes. In *controlled association,* the response is limited in some way. For example, the subject may be instructed to reply with the names of animals, or with the word most clearly the opposite of the stimulus word. In *discrete association,* the subject is instructed to reply with the first word that occurs to him. He is limited to the response of a single word. After the response has been made, the experimenter usually provides another stimulus word. In *continuous association,* the subject is instructed to provide as many words as he can. In the pure case of association, the subject's own response becomes the next stimulus word. Often combinations of these types are used, such as *free-discrete, free-continuous, controlled-discrete,* and *controlled-continuous.*

Measures of association include reaction time, the frequency of the response word in terms of its occurrence as a response word among the general population, and the number of words mentioned (in continuous association). To evaluate the rarity of a response, one must compare the response words selected by the subject with the responses provided by other subjects who are representative of the general population or of the population to which the subject belongs. For example, certain response words found among college students are not representative of words used by the general population. Frequency tables, showing the percentage of subjects who respond with given words to specified stimulus words, have been calculated from time to time (Kent & Rosanoff, 1910; Schellenberg, 1930; J. J. Jenkins & Palermo, 1964). Unfortunately for the stability of frequency tables, changes in language, such as idioms and colloquialisms, come and go at a rapid rate. Moreover, it is not a simple matter to prepare a frequency table based on data from subjects who constitute a true sample of the whole population (see Chapter 1). Nevertheless, word association tests remain a useful measure of meaning.

Nonsense Syllables: Although nonsense syllables are not commonly used as a measure of meaning as such, they are used in many studies of verbal learning. If words are used on tests of ability to memorize and retain learning, there is a clear experimental danger that some subjects may form associations with test words which permit them to learn and remember them. In order to overcome this difficulty, nonsense syllables with as little meaning as possible are used as test items. The most common nonsense syllables are composed of two consonants separated by a vowel—for example, ZOK, GEK, and MIP. Few nonsense syllables are totally devoid of meaning. Some syllables, such as JUG, CAT, and GOD, form words, while others, such as DUZ and GOP, are names or abbreviations. For this reason, nonsense syllables are evaluated in regard to their meaningfulness by asking subjects to associate to them.

In an early study on the meaningfulness, or *association value,* of nonsense syllables, Glaze (1928; see Hilgard, 1951) asked 15 subjects to note the syllables to which they were able to associate. The syllables were then evaluated on the basis of the percentage of subjects who formed an association. HAZ, for example was reported as having an association value of 100 percent, since all subjects reported an association to the syllable. DAX, however, is reported to have an association value of 0 percent. As is true of words, nonsense syllables change value over time, and some of the syllables used by Glaze and reported to have low association values probably have higher values now because of their use as trade names or abbreviations of government agencies (Hull, 1933a).

The amount of association value affects the ease with which words and nonsense syllables may be learned. McGeoch (1930) prepared lists of nonsense syllables and asked subjects to study them for two minutes. The subjects were then asked to recall as many of the syllables as possible. Meaningful three-letter words were most often recalled, followed in order by nonsense syllables of 100, 53, and 0 percent association value. This finding was duplicated when the syllables were to be spelled (as opposed to pronouncing them). Lindley (1960) has reported that familiar syllables are easier to learn than unfamiliar syllables, even when the association values of the syllables are identical. In addition to the classic three-letter nonsense syllables, four-letter syllables such as MEEV, NOWK, and THOG have been used (Woodworth & Schlosberg, 1954, p. 703) as well as *paralogs*. Paralogs contain five letters; the second and fourth are vowels. GOKEM and TARUP are examples. Some experimenters have used sets of numbers, and these have been scaled for meaningfulness (Battig & Spera, 1962), although groups of numbers are more difficult to learn than combinations of letters.

Nonsense syllables were first used by the German psychologist Hermann Ebbinghaus (1850–1909; 1885). Since he used but a single subject in his studies of memory (himself), Ebbinghaus took the precaution of finding material which he had not learned previously. He developed over two thousand nonsense syllables in German. In contemporary psychology, meaningfulness is established by scaling procedures, such as those described in Chapter 5.

Some Physiological Procedures: Several techniques exist for the measurement of meaning by recording physiological changes associated with the presentation of words. The most popular technique is the recording of *galvanic skin resistance,* which is the basis of the "lie detector." The electrical resistance of the skin in human beings and animals is variable, and investigators have noted that changes in resistance occur in response to "emotion-provoking" stimuli (Chapter 16). It is probable that emotion is mediated by meaning and that the galvanic skin response (GSR) indirectly records meaning. Indeed, the use of the lie detector (which records a variety of physiological responses, such as blood pressure and respiration) is based on the assumption that the subject will respond to those words or questions which have an emotional and, hence, a meaningful value. The GSR as a measure of meaning has several difficulties: first, GSR recordings are not notably reliable; second, skin resistance can shift quickly, even when apparently unemotional stimuli are used; third, the subject must be wired into the apparatus,

which makes the situation highly artificial for the subject. Few experiments have been reported which use the GSR as a measure of meaning (see Bingham, 1943; M. Mason, 1941).

The principles of classical conditioning (Chapter 13) have also been used to measure meaning. Razran (1935; 1936) used an adhesive coil containing a substance which changed color when it came into contact with saliva. Using himself as the subject, Razran examined the extent of his salivary responses to the word "saliva" expressed in different languages. The amount of salivation was greatest in the writer's childhood language (Russian), next greatest in the language in which he was most proficient (English), and lowest in languages in which he was not so proficient.

The idea that thought is subvocal speech has appeared in the literature from time to time. Max (1934; 1935a; 1937) and E. Jacobson (1932) made recordings of muscle movements of subjects when the subjects were asked to think about actions, such as hammering a nail or solving mathematical problems. In general, the form of the muscle potentials approximate those which would have appeared had the subject actually performed the task. Max also studied dumb persons who had learned sign language. When they were asked to think of a word, small muscle potentials were recorded from their hands similar to those obtained when they made the sign for the word overtly. These experiments have been interpreted as supplying evidence that thought is subthreshold speech. Possibly some evidence regarding the meaning of words could be derived from this procedure. For example, it is possible that different subjects would attach different meanings to different commands or instructions and that there would be corresponding differences in the location of muscles which react.

Visual Perception and Meaning: As we shall note in the next two chapters, the sense of vision has often been used to provide information on meaning. It is well established that one's motives (whether hungry or satiated, elated or depressed) can affect visual perception and that measurement of individual differences in visual perception can provide information on the meaning which individuals attach to visual stimuli.

Semantic Differential: In Chapter 5, the semantic differential was used as an example of a scaling technique, for it requires the subject to evaluate the relationship between stimuli. Since the subject is usually asked to rate words or concepts in terms of his concept of the meaning of the words, the differential technique provides a direct measure of meaning. Figure 7–7 shows the semantic differential ratings provided by two subjects in response to the stimulus word "father." An examination of the placements of the checks by the two subjects suggests that the meanings attached to "father" are different. Subject₁ rates "large," "soft," "valuable," and "bass" at the extremes followed by "happy," "loving," and "brave." Subject₂ considers the concepts "delicate," "old," and "loving" to be most extreme.

It has been pointed out (Osgood, Suci, & Tannenbaum, 1957) that the semantic differ-

ential is a combination of a scaling method and of controlled association. The subject's possible responses are controlled by the choice of words which anchor the scales at either end. Although the use of established anchor words does restrict the rating and consequently the number and type of meanings which a subject may ascribe to a concept, it is necessary to use controlled association with the semantic differential if comparisons between subjects are to be made. The choice of the stimulus words is critical.

It has been noted that some words *cluster* together; i.e., if the subject rates one high, he will rate other words in the cluster high. One cluster, noted by Stagner and Osgood (1946), is "fair-unfair," "high-low," "kind-cruel," "valuable-worthless," "Christian–anti-Christian," and "honest-dishonest." Since all these pairs are evaluated similarly, it is not necessary to use all of them in a semantic differential test. If the subject rates "valuable" high along the "valuable-worthless" line, the probability is high that he will rate "fair," "high," "kind," "Christian," and "honest" high. Moreover, these clusters provide useful information on the concepts held by various groups or indi-

FIGURE 7–7: *The responses of two subjects to a semantic differential test. The check marks indicate the subjects' assessment of the place of the stimulus word "father" on the continua.*

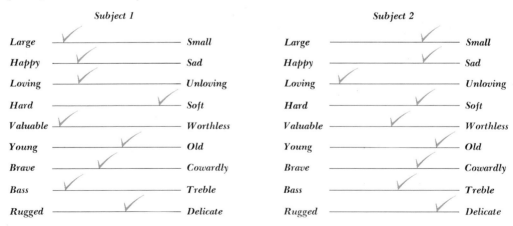

viduals. Although natives of Christian countries might associate "fair," "high," and so on with Christianity, the same cluster would not be likely to appear from the evaluations of natives of countries with different religions. By using the techniques of factor analysis (Chapter 5), one can "factor out" clusters of word pairs which correlate highly with one another. The "factors" which emerge are labeled *evaluative, activity,* and *potency.*

The semantic differential may be used in research on changes in personality. Subjects may be asked to make differential ratings under different stressful conditions or at differ-

ent times in their lives. These ratings are placed in a *D-matrix* (D = distance) in which the distance between the concepts is plotted in order to indicate changes in the subject's conceptual thinking. Figure 7–8 shows D-matrices for a patient before, during, and after therapy. Note the change that occurs in the evaluation of "mother," "father," and "me." It is obvious that certain concepts have changed, presumably in meaning, while others remain essentially unchanged. Probably because of the importance of the measurement of meaning to theories of behavior, semantic differentials have been used to measure a number of re-

FIGURE 7 – 8 : *D-matrices, using the semantic differential, for a female subject. Assessment was made before, during, and after therapy. Note the changes that occur in the nearness of the terms she was asked to evaluate. (From Osgood, Suci, & Tannenbaum, 1957, p. 244.)*

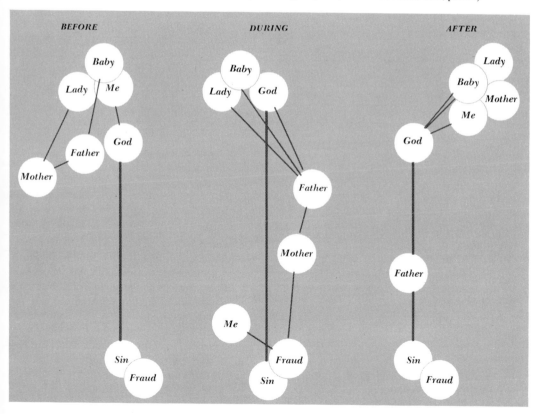

sponses, including responses to color (Karwoski & Odbert, 1938) and to music (Odbert, Karwoski, & Eckerson, 1942).

Type-Token Ratio: This ratio, the TTR, is a commonly used statistical device which measures the *variability* of language. Each different word is known as a *type,* while the total number of words is known as the *token.* The type-token ratio is defined as

$$TTR = \frac{type}{token}$$

Hence, if a sample of 10,000 words is selected and if 5,000 *different* words appear in the sample,

$$TTR = \frac{5,000}{10,000} = 0.5$$

Note that the TTR is concerned only with the variability of language. The formula does not distinguish between a token of the Sunday supplement and a scientific treatise.

The TTR has been shown to differ as a function of several variables. For example, Fairbanks (1944) analyzed spoken samples of language from schizophrenics and from college freshmen. The TTR for the schizophrenics was significantly lower than that for college students, showing that college students use more different words than schizophrenics. Chotlos (1944) analyzed the writing of 108 subjects varying in intelligence, age, sex, and environmental background. He analyzed TTRs for different parts of speech used by his subjects, e.g., verbs, adjectives, and nouns, on the assumption that individuals or groups may differ in this regard. The frequency of both nouns and adjectives increased with age and IQ.

A similar but simpler method for determining variability in speech has been developed by Carroll (1938). This method assumes that the greater the variability, the greater the number of words that will intervene between two usages of any given word. For example, if the word *the* is selected as the standard, the more words which intervene between occurrences of *the,* the more variable the speech. Since only words are counted in this method, assessment is rapid. In general, the number of intervening words between the instances of *the* is between 10 and 15 words, a relatively small number.

Sentence length has also been used as a measure of variability. W. S. Gray and Leary (1935) evaluated the sentence length found in various popular magazines. The compilation of sentence length is also a method for distinguishing authors from one another. This procedure has been used in providing evidence regarding the author of disputed works. If it is assumed that an author's writing style does not vary greatly from one work to another, one may compare the TTR or sentence length of Shakespeare's works with those of the known works of authors who may have been responsible for Shakespeare's writings. Similarly, an analysis of the use of punctuation marks provides descriptions of the techniques of authors. Today, with the use of computers, such analyses and comparisons may be compiled rapidly. For example, Mosteller and Wallace (1964) analyzed the language of James Madison and Alexander Hamilton in an effort to establish the authorship of the 12 Federalist Papers whose authorship is disputed. By analyzing sentence length, incidence of words such as *enough, while,* and *whilst,* and the percentage of nouns and adjectives, it appeared that Madison wrote 10 of the papers.

Content Analysis: The aim of content analysis is to distinguish the *type* of meaning conveyed in language. Two examples of speech or writing may have the same TTR but vary considerably in content: one example may be a political speech, while the other may be a report of scientific research. The technique used to analyze content depends upon the nature of the material and the purpose of the analysis. In some cases, classification of sentence type may be sufficient. No doubt, speakers may be distinguished on the basis of the number of rhetorical questions, exclamatory sentences, and so on, which they use. Whatever technique of analysis is used, it is critical for the reliability of the analysis that the rules specifying categories be clearly formulated. Indeed, the rules should be formulated so that a person unaware of the purpose of the analysis could classify the content. For example, say that one wishes to perform content analysis on the speech of a person undergoing psychotherapy in order to assess changes in verbal behavior as a function of the therapeutic process. One might establish categories which distinguish whether the subject is talking about himself, his parents, or his relations with the therapist.

STATISTICAL ANALYSIS OF LANGUAGE

Words and people have some characteristics in common. If we were to measure the characteristics of all the people in the world, we would find that some are tall, some short; some have light skin, some dark; some have curly hair, some straight hair, and some no hair at all. We describe these characteristics by descriptive statistics (see Chapter 1). For example, our measurements may show that the mean height of people is 5 feet, 7 inches. This figure describes the population but tells us nothing about a particular individual. If we know the height of the individual, however, it does tell us something about the relationship between him and the rest of the population. Similarly, words may be long or short, may start or end with any of a number of sounds, and may be used often or rarely. Accordingly, words provide data for descriptive statistics.

In two major publications, Zipf (1935; 1949) analyzed the use of words and provided some statistical laws of language. After comparing three languages (Chinese, Latin, and English) Zipf noted a negative correlation between the length of a word and its frequency of use; i.e., more frequently used words are shorter. Indeed, there is some evidence that a word be-

comes shorter as its frequency of use increases. The word *automobile* was used years ago when automobiles were rare. Now that they are common and references to them are made more often, the word *car* is used. Similarly, *television* has become *TV, moving pictures* has become *movies* or *flicks,* and so on.

Zipf (1945) compared the frequency of occurrence of the 20,000 most commonly used words (Thorndike & Lorge, 1944) with the number of meanings ascribed to these words in a standard dictionary and found a positive correlation. For example, words such as *get, come,* and *can* occur frequently and have more different meanings than words such as *horoscope, multiplicity,* and *investigation.*

If you took a sample of the words in this book—say, 10,000 consecutive words—and counted the number of different words that appeared only *once* in the sample, then the number of different words that appeared only *twice,* continuing in this manner until you could plot the rank order of frequency of occurrence against the frequency, you would probably derive a plot similar to that shown in Figure 7–9. In the figure, this comparison has

FIGURE 7-9: *Plots of Joyce's* Ulysses *(A) and samples from newspapers (B). A double log plot is used. The ordinate shows the frequency with which words of different ranks (abscissa) appear. Note that both functions are approximately linear. (From Zipf, 1949, p. 25, modified.)*

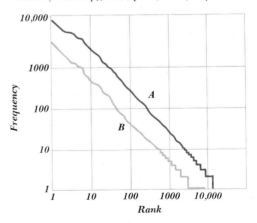

been made between a work known to contain a variety of words (James Joyce's *Ulysses*) and a work which probably contains relatively few different words (a newspaper). Both functions are almost linear, and both indicate that the lower the rank order in frequency, the more different words appear at that rank. For example, from the sample of 10,000, it is probable that many words would occur only once, fewer would occur only twice, and even fewer would occur only three times. The number of different words which would appear 400 or 500 times in the sample would be small, for probably the only candidates would be words such as *a* and *the*.

A group of laws of langauge, based on statistical analysis of the components of speech, has been determined by Zipf. From these laws he has developed a theory of the development of language (1945; 1949). The theory is based on the *principle of least effort*. Zipf suggests the analogy of a workman who has tools (words) of many sizes on his tool bench. As he works along doing different tasks and requiring different tools, he will order the tools in such a way that those most frequently used are placed in the most easily accessible positions. A housewife eventually arranges her kitchen so that the items used most—the plates, glasses, and silverware—are the easiest to reach. Items used only occasionally—the pressure cooker or large roast plate—are generally relegated to the less accessible shelves. This analogy is applied to the development of language, for it is reasonable to suppose that we make the words we use most often convenient—by shortening them.

We have noted that the frequencies with which any letter or word follows any other letter or word are not equal. The rules which govern the statistical frequency of the occurrence of words or letters in a language may be uncovered by constructing a new language. If, following Shannon (1948), we take the 26 letters of the English alphabet, plus one space, and if we select the letters and spaces at *random,* so that each letter has an equal chance of appearing, we find a *zero-order approxima-*

tion of a language. An example of a sequence of letters with zero-order approximation is the following:

bqudjksg halukegwn jnpshcalddhrvj

However, a *first-order approximation* uses information on the relative frequency of each letter (and each space) in language. If, for example, the letter *e* appears 4,300 times in a sample of 100,000 letters, the same proportion of *e*'s should appear in the sample. An example of a first-order approximation would be the following:

ghemnopse dwpoil utfeac

A *second-order approximation* occurs when the letters are chosen with respect to the frequency of *pairings* of letters in the language. For example, the pairing *zy* is rare compared with the pairing *ie*. If letters are selected on the basis of statistical information on the frequency of *pairs* of letters, we might find a message such as

ouph gomyclie cisetrylo

Since the selection is made upon the basis of frequency of pairs, the second-order approximation provides the opportunity for the words to approach pronounceableness. Successive orders of approximation (third, fourth, fifth, and so on) are derived from approximating the statistical appearance of groups of three, four, or five letters in the language. In third-order approximations, short words such as *bit, can,* or *lie* may result.

The same procedure may be applied to words. In zero-order approximation of words, each word in the dictionary would have an equal chance of selection. In a first-order approximation the frequency of occurrence of each word would be considered; in a second-order approximation the frequency of pairs of words would be evaluated; in a third-order approximation the frequency of three-word groups would be evaluated; and so on.

The importance of frequency of occurrence in language analysis is clear when it is considered that many words are repeated in speaking or writing; repetition of any word may occur within 10 or 15 words (G. A. Miller, 1951a, p. 89). The preceding sentence, for example, contains 35 words; however, only 28 different words are used. Words such as *of, the, a,* and *or* occur very frequently, even in technical writing. G. A. Miller (1951a, p. 89) estimates that 50 words form about 60 percent of spoken tokens and 45 percent of written tokens.

ARTICULATION AND INTELLIGIBILITY

A spoken message may be understandable and may carry information; however, if it is not intelligible to a listener, both the meaning and the information may be lost. The question of the *intelligibility* of speech is important both in establishing the thresholds of speech perception and in providing data regarding the most appropriate communication systems to use under specific conditions. A loss or decrement in intelligibility may come from the speaker, from the listener, or from interference between the two, such as masking (see Chapter 6). The speaker may speak indistinctly. On the other hand, the speaker may speak clearly, but difficulties in the ear of the listener may reduce the intelligibility of the material.

The simplest and most common measure of intelligibility is the *articulation* test. The listener is presented with a sample of speech and asked to write what he hears. If he reports every word correctly, he has an articulation score of 100 percent. If he reports only 50 out of 200 words correctly, he has an articulation score of 25 percent. The articulation score will depend on the ability of the listener, on physical variables, such as the amplitude of the spoken material, and on the type of material used. The articulation score of a biochemist listening to a paper in his own field will be higher than the score of someone unfamiliar

with the field, even though their articulation scores for material with which they are equally familiar may be identical. The term *articulation test* seems to suggest that the test provides a measure of the speaker's clarity; in reality it is a measure of the listener's speech perception.

The practical questions associated with speech perception are numerous. What frequencies can be eliminated from telephone transmission without reducing speech perception? What portions of speech are most commonly misperceived? Can speakers avoid certain combinations which are generally misperceived? Are some words more intelligible than others? What is the effect of background noise, such as that from a machine, on intelligibility? The effect of the intensity of speech upon intelligibility is shown in Figure 7–10. Under quiet conditions maximal intelligibility is not achieved until the intensity of speech is increased to between 40 and 60 db. Even at 60 db, however, it is not at all intelligible with a 120-db background noise. These findings suggest that when background noise is present, the range of intensity of speech which can be made intelligible is shortened. Under both conditions there is a decrement in intelligibility if the speech in-

FIGURE 7–10: *The effect of intensity of intelligibility under two conditions, quiet and a 120-db noise. (After Egan & Wiener, 1946; from Chapanis, Garner, & C. T. Morgan, 1949, p. 221.)*

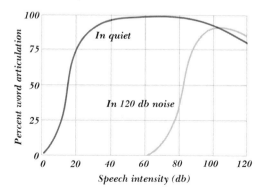

tensity becomes too great, for even under quiet conditions, a loss of intelligibility is noted if the speech approaches 100 db.

Since some background noise is almost always present and since its effect depends not only upon its intensity but upon the intensity of the speech as well, it is common to express the relationship between speech and noise in the *speech-to-noise ratio:*

$$\frac{\text{Speech db}}{\text{Noise db}} = \text{speech-to-noise ratio}$$

Assume that you are listening to a radio in which the static (background noise) is so intense that you cannot understand the speech. The principle of the speech-to-noise ratio offers several alternatives that may help to increase intelligibility. You may decrease the noise, thus increasing the ratio. Ordinarily, this is accomplished by changing the tuning. If, however, the static is coming from some source other than the radio (for example, high-voltage equipment in use near the receiver), you may increase the speech intensity by turning up the volume of the radio. This will increase the numerator of the ratio without altering the denominator and will increase intelligibility. If the static comes from within the radio and if you cannot tune more finely, it is useless to increase intensity, since the speech and noise will be increased together. Savin (1963) has suggested that a difference in intelligibility between common and uncommon words will occur as a function of the speech-to-noise ratio; that is, common words will probably be perceived under less favorable speech-to-noise ratios than will uncommon words.

The presence of noise as a background has a different effect on intelligibility from the presence of tone. Both phenomena are cases of masking (Chapter 6). Figure 7–11 shows the amount of masking of speech which occurs when noise, a 300-Hz tone, and a 1,000-Hz tone are used. Even at high amplitudes, pure tones do not mask speech so well as noise. The difference in masking between a low tone (300

Hz) and a relatively high tone (1,000 Hz) follows the general rule that low tones are more effective in masking high tones than are high tones in masking low tones. The effect of noise may be traced to the fact that noise contains a variety of frequencies, so the probability is high that speech frequencies will be masked. If one is interested in jamming radio communication, noise is clearly the most effective masking agent. The relationship between speech-to-noise ratio and the articulation score, as a function of the type of material used in the articulation tests, has been investigated; digits, words in sentences, and nonsense syllables were used (G. A. Miller, Heise, & Lichten, 1951). Figure 7–12 shows the results. Comparisons may be made by noting the speech-to-noise ratio when a given articulation score, say, 50 percent, is reached. According to this measure, nonsense syllables require 17 db more than digits to reach the 50 percent articulation rate.

The removal of particular amplitudes and frequencies from sound is called *clipping*. Most commonly, clipping involves high, rather than low, amplitudes. Communication devices such as the telephone regularly clip both amplitudes and frequencies. Clipping detracts from the quality of the message, as the common remark "I didn't know your voice over the telephone" suggests. Figure 7–13 shows the effect of both peak (high) and center clipping on articulation scores. With peak clipping, articulation scores are above 70 percent through a clip of 36 db. Center clipping, however, renders speech unintelligible even with small amounts of decibel clipping. The effect of peak, center, and no clipping on frequency and duration is shown in Figure 7–14. This figure represents amplitude by the height of the "mountains," and frequency is recorded by its location on the depth of the "plain." The top figure (*A*) shows the speaking of the words *shoe bench* without clipping. The highest amplitudes occur in the *oe* of the *shoe* and the *ben* of *bench*. With peak clipping these characteristics remain, but the amplitude of other parts of the phrase is lost. With center clipping, there is an overall reduction in amplitude. Two low ranges of mountains appear for the *oe* and the *ben*. This makes the sound reasonably undistinguishable and leads to unintelligibility.

A type of clipping occurs in written language when letters are eliminated from a message. As experienced manuscript typists know only too well, book manuscripts often provide the typist with ample opportunity for practice at decoding. For example, the first sentence of this paragraph in the original draft was typed:

A t pe of crippin occurs in wrotten kanguage....

The ability to make this sentence intelligible depends on several factors, including experience with the subject matter of the message and the amount of the material deleted or mistyped. Indeed, Howarth and K. Ellis (1961) have shown that subjects recognized their own names more rapidly than any other word.

In order to study the problem of reconstructing written language, Chapanis (1954) selected 13 prose selections. Some represented technical material taken from scientific textbooks, and other passages came from magazines. In either random or in regular order, 10, 20, 25, 33.3, 50, or 66.7 percent of the letters and spaces of each text were eliminated. The bowdlerized texts were then given to 91 subjects with instructions to repair the text, i.e., to write in the missing marks. Figure 7–15 shows the percentage of deleted items which were restored correctly. When 10 percent of the units were deleted, 90 percent of the items were restored correctly; however, when the deletion rate was increased to 30 to 40 percent, the number of correct restorations dropped to 50 percent. If the number of correct insertions was examined in terms of whether the material had been deleted randomly or in a regular order, slight, but indicative, differences appeared in performance. Figure 7–16 shows these results. Correct insertion was slightly higher for regular deletions until approximately 30 to 40 percent of the subject matter had been deleted. As the percentage of de-

FIGURE 7–11: *The effect of background noise on intelligibility of speech. This experiment used tones of 300 and 1,000 Hz and a masking noise composed of many frequencies. The amount of masking (in decibels) is shown along the ordinate, and the intensity of the masking sound is shown along the abscissa. (From G. A. Miller, 1947, p. 108.)*

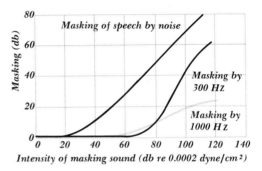

leted items was increased beyond 40 percent, random deletions were slightly easier to replace correctly. Oléron (1960) has obtained similar findings among French children using

FIGURE 7–12: *Articulation scores as a function of the speech-to-noise ratio. The curves are for three types of items: digits, words used in sentences, and nonsense syllables. (From G. A. Miller, Heise, & Lichten, 1951, p. 330.)*

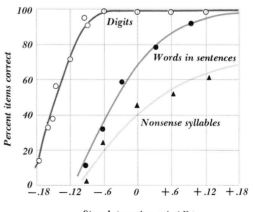

FIGURE 7-13: *The effect of peak and center clipping on articulation scores. Articulation is plotted against clipping in decibels. Peak clipping affects articulation scores less, although as intensity increases, the articulation scores decrease slightly. On the other hand, center clipping has drastic effects on intelligibility as measured by articulation scores. (From Licklider & G. A. Miller, 1951, p. 1058.)*

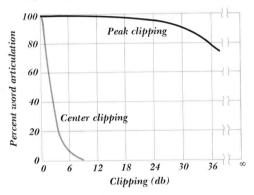

French prose. He notes that reconstruction is easier for pronouns and articles than for nouns, verbs, and adjectives.

DEVELOPMENT OF LANGUAGE

How long does it take to learn a language? College faculties often suppose that two years of study are sufficient for a reasonable understanding of a second language. However, it may take fifteen years to learn our native language well, and evidence is abundant that some people never become proficient in their own language. Does it matter when a language is learned? Can the mature student learn a language more rapidly than a young child? These questions are answerable experimentally, and they provide us with basic knowledge concerning the development of language.

The importance of speech to overall physical and mental development may be noted in the derivation of the word *infancy*. Schultze

(1880) suggests that the word comes from the Latin *in* (without) and *fari* (to speak). Although the definition of infancy as the "period without speech" is not used today, the derivation points out the importance of the acquisition of speech to the maturation of the child.

The first speech emitted by the child and heard by others is the birth cry. Although some commentators have interpreted the birth cry as having emotional significance, it would appear that its main importance is that it is the first speech the individual produces—at least, it is the first perceived by others. A child's crying is only indirectly related to speech. The vocal patterns of crying do not become refined into speech; rather, speech develops independently as the child gains control over the vocal apparatus. Osgood (1953, p. 684) recorded the speech of an infant throughout the first year of life. Recordings averaged ten minutes per week. Analysis indicated that all the speech sounds that the vocal system is capable of producing were present in this first year. These data suggest that the development of speech reflects changing the frequency of appearance of sounds rather than learning to make new sounds, as some investigators have suggested. Osgood also suggests that the type of speech sound produced depends on the state of the child: during feeding time soft vowels appear, but during a period of hunger harsher sounds are evident.

If the infant possesses a full repertoire of sounds, how does he come to speak English, German, or Zulu? As any student of language knows, the major difficulty in learning to pronounce a foreign language is that it contains sounds which the student has not used since infancy, if then. The gutteral sounds of German and the vowel sounds of French may have been in the student's repertoire of sounds during infancy, but they have not been used for many years. There is no simple answer to the question of how one language develops to the exclusion of other possible languages. The statement that the child will learn to speak only what he hears spoken is so obviously true that it misses the point: the real question is how the child learns to reproduce sounds at all. Does he learn by imitation or under the principles of operant training (see Chapter 14), in which new responses are acquired if they are followed by reward? A review of the data available on changes in the frequency of use of speech sounds will help us to uncover the principles of speech development. We should not be surprised at the apparently contradictory findings: the difficulties in selecting a sample recording, judging the sounds, and assessing the reliability of findings are substantial.

There is considerable agreement that vowels predominate among the sounds made by the infant. Those vowels which are produced from the front of the mouth are heard first and those formed in the back of the mouth, later. Consonants, however, appear to develop in the opposite direction, with those produced by the back of the mouth appearing before those produced from the front (Irwin, 1947). Although there is disagreement over this general principle (see works reviewed by D. McCarthy, 1954), there is agreement that *b, m,* and *p* are the first consonants to be recognized by investigators. One difficulty with these data is that the experimenters recorded those phonemes which they *heard.* Clearly, one is far more likely to perceive phonemes in one's native language than to recognize sounds which are heard rarely.

Osgood's data (1953) suggest that all vowels and consonants occur in the speech of the child, although not necessarily with the same frequency. Profiles of the frequency of occurrence of vowel sounds as a function of age have been published by Irwin (1948). Figure 7–17 shows these results. The upper right graph represents data from adults. In adult speech, all vowels appear, and the differences in frequency of occurrence are considerably less than the differences found among children. These data suggest that the "leveling" of frequencies occurs around twenty-three to twenty-four months of age. It is noteworthy, however, that sounds which are not heard, or

FIGURE 7–14: *The effect of no clipping, peak clipping, and center clipping on the words* shoe bench. *Frequency and intensity are the parameters. Intensity is shown by the height of the "mountains," and frequency is indicated by the depth of the figures. (From Licklider, Bindra, & Pollack, 1948, p. 18.)*

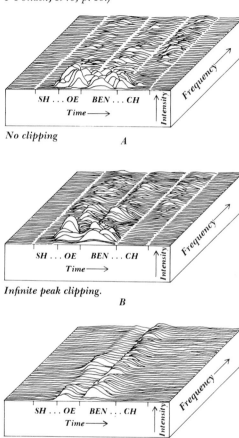

are heard rarely in English, also appear in the infant's speech.

The change in the relative frequency of occurrence of vowels and consonants has been studied by Irwin and Chen (1946). See Figure 7–18 for the results. In a child one month old, the ratio is approximately four vowels to one

FIGURE 7-15: *The percentages of deleted items which were correctly restored as a function of the number of items deleted in median percentages. (From Chapanis, 1954, p. 501, modified.)*

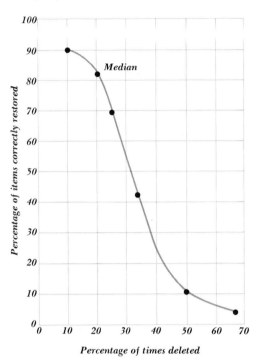

Percentage of times deleted

consonant (a consonant-vowel ratio of 0.25). By the age of thirty months, the child uses an equal number of vowels and consonants. Adult speech, as measured by telephone conversations, used 1.4 consonants for each vowel (G. A. Miller, 1951a).

The First Word: It is difficult to discriminate the child's first word from his parents' projection of a babblelike sound as a word. Moreover, it is clearly impossible to say when the first "word" is a word. Is "de-de" close enough to "da-da" to count? Or do we wish the first word to have reference to the environment? If the child says "da-da," it may be true that a sound similar to a word used in English has

been made. But if he says it while looking at his mother, it is not certain that the referent to the word is understood. Observationally, the so-called first word is usually a repeated monosyllable, such as "bye-bye" or "ma-ma," and some appear to be onomatopoeic (sounding similar to their meaning), such as "tick-tock." It should be remembered that a word is only a word if it is understood by a listener. It would perhaps be more accurate to replace the phrase "baby's first word" with the more descriptive "parents' first understanding." The few data available on the age at which the first word appears indicate that the median is around eleven months (C. Buhler, 1931; Terman, 1925).

Vocabulary Development: The major difficulty in obtaining estimates of vocabulary growth in children is that very young children do not write. Among literate adults, vocabulary tests may be given in which the subject responds by writing the meaning of words presented to him. Or he may be questioned orally. Children, however, acquire a large vocabulary before they are able to write. The only sure method for ascertaining the vocabulary of a child is to follow him with a tape recorder throughout the day (and night) and tabulate the words he uses. Anyone who has attempted to follow a child for even a few minutes dismisses this technique immediately.

The procedures which have been used for measuring the vocabulary of children have (1) measured samples of speech and projected the number of words in the sample to the total number of words which the child would use in a larger sample of speech (clearly, this technique is liable to sampling errors); (2) presented the child with a picture and either (*a*) asked the child to provide a word describing the picture or (*b*) used the word in a sentence and determined whether the word was understandable in context to the child; (3) used free association and requested the child to say as many words as possible. Although each of these methods has advantages, it is not surprising that we should note discrepancies among the results of the studies. There is some agreement, however, that vocabulary first increases slowly, then increases rapidly before four or five years of age, and expands slowly again through secondary school age. There is evidence that the acquisition of new words slows down at the time the child is learning to walk (Shirley, 1933a; 1933b). New environments and experiences lead to an observable increase in vocabulary. For example, a trip to a farm provides a city child with new objects to be named and assimilated into the vocabulary.

Some studies of vocabulary size have failed to distingush between *basic* words and *derived* words. Basic words are the *root* words found in a dictionary, while derived words are those formed by altering the endings of basic words. *Recognize* is a basic word, while *recognition, recognized,* and *recognizes* are derivatives. The child is not noted for using derivatives, for their use generally requires knowledge of the fine points of grammar and syntax. Accordingly, it is important in vocabulary measurement to distinguish basic from derivative words.

M. K. Smith (1941) measured the vocabulary size of children of school age, separating basic from derivative words. The results are shown in Figure 7–19. The plot of total words represents the combination of both basic and derived words, and the number of derived words represents the difference between basic and total words. Two points deserve attention: first, the number of derived words increases as a function of age; second, the total number of words in the vocabulary of the first-grade child (age six) is estimated at around 25,000. Should this figure seem unlikely, it may be noted that other studies have reported vocabulary sizes between 5,000 and 200,000 words for these six-year-old children. If Smith's figure of 25,000 is correct, it would suggest that the child learns an average of about 4,000 words per year.

Changes in the types of words used (nouns, adjectives, etc.), in the kinds of sentences used (simple, compound), and in the egocentricity

FIGURE 7–16: *The percentage of items correctly restored as a function of the percentage of items deleted and as a function of whether a random pattern of deletions or a regular pattern was used. (From Chapanis, 1954, p. 502.)*

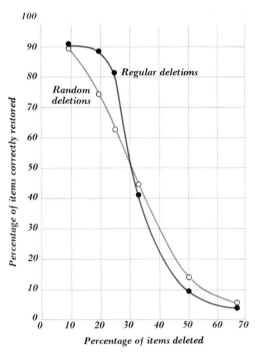

of speech (*I* opposed to *it*) have also been reported. Most investigators have found the percentage of nouns to be high in the speech of the child, although it is worth noting that a child may say "choo-choo" without necessarily using the word as a noun; in childen's speech a noun often represents an entire sentence, such as "See the choo-choo go by." Zyve (1927) recorded story telling from third-graders and calculated the percentage for each part of speech, as well as the percentage for the number of different words. Pronouns composed 17.2 percent of the total words used but only 1.5 percent of the number of different words. The implication is that although pronouns occur commonly in speech, only a few different pronouns are used, no doubt because few

FIGURE 7-17: *The proportionate number of vowels produced at certain levels of maturation. The graph at the upper right is based on data from adults. The other graphs show the percentage of vowels produced at birth and through thirty months of age. Note the changes in percentage of the vowel sounds with maturation and training. (From Irwin, 1948, p. 32.)*

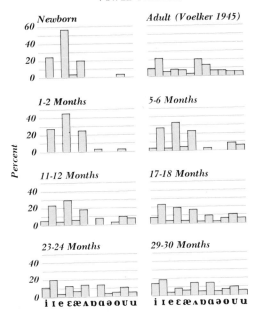

VOWEL PROFILES

total sentences) and more compound and complex sentences (F. K. Heider & G. M. Heider, 1940).

Piaget (1924) suggested that a distinction be made between *egocentric* speech (in which the presence or reaction of an audience is immaterial to the speaker) and *socialized* speech (in which the speech is directed toward others). If these definitions are employed, a surprisingly small percentage of the child's speech may be classified as egocentric. D. McCarthy (1930) reports less than 10 percent of the sentences as egocentric. However, if the definition of egocentric speech is altered to include sentences about the child ("I want . . ."), the percentage increases to between 30 and 40 percent. It appears that egocentric speech is not the prerogative of children, for adults show the same percentage (Henle & Hubbell, 1938).

Development of Meaning: A dictionary does not "define" words: it only suggests other words which have similar meanings. This emphasizes the idea that the meaning of words is derived from their context. One technique which has been used to study the development of meaning through context uses sentences which contain an invented word (Werner & Kaplan, 1950). For example, try to give the meaning of the word *bojum* in each of these statements:

1. **A bojum is used to write on.**
2. **Some people keep papers and pencils in a bojum.**
3. **Bojums usually have four legs.**

This type of study provides information on the way in which the subject arrives at the concept. To a degree, the problem is one of reducing alternatives and is similar to the game twenty questions. Although statistical analysis of the results from this technique is difficult, the procedure does provide an indication of the development of the ability to identify words by context.

In addition, the frequency of occurrence (and probably the meaning) of words may be

exist. The three articles *a, an,* and *the* appear so commonly in speech that they compose 7 percent of the total words but only 0.1 percent of the number of different words.

Data on the length of sentences as a function of age show as much variability as measures of vocabulary. D. McCarthy (1954) has summarized various studies in tabular form. The average length of sentences follows the child's age through age 5; i.e., the child of 2.5 years speaks sentences with an average of 2.5 words. Then the length of sentences remains at around six words until the child reaches 9.5 years of age. From age 8 to 14, children use fewer simple sentences (as a percentage of

altered by the reaction of the hearer. Using 21 three-month-old infants, Rheingold, Gewirtz, and H. W. Ross (1959), without accompanying speech or special facial expression, recorded the social responses of the infants. These records provided a base line of the infants' speech patterns. Then certain sounds were selected to receive attention from the experimenters: the experimenters responded to the appropriate sounds by smiling, chuckling, or patting the infants' abdomens. During the final phase of the study, no social responses were given. The results indicated that an increase in speech was noted during the second phase. This procedure, sometimes called *verbal conditioning,* is discussed in detail in Chapters 14 and 15.

LANGUAGE AMONG ANIMALS

If by "language" we mean sounds produced through the vocal apparatus, primarily only the higher mammals are capable of communicating through language. However, animals communicate in other ways. It appears likely that many species communicate through movement. Von Frisch (1950) has investigated the patterns (or "dancing") which the honey bee uses to convey information regarding the location of food. The finding that a recording of a particular vocal signal given by a starling causes other starlings to depart from the area (Frings & Jumber, 1954) indicates the likelihood of verbal communication among these birds as well as a possible technique for eliminating starlings from areas where they are a nuisance.

There is strong evidence that among some birds the typical song or warble must be learned, most commonly from the parent (Thorpe, 1956). The speech of the mynah bird has received considerable attention (Mowrer, 1947a; Grosslight & Lively, 1963), because its vocalizations closely approximate human speech. Parrots have learned as many as 100 words; however, their ability to associate the sounds with symbols is probably lacking. The

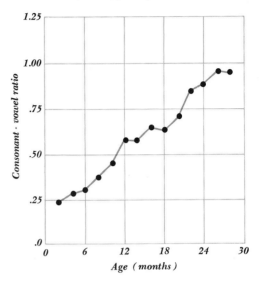

FIGURE 7–18: *Changes in the relationship between vowels and consonants as a function of age in months. (After Irwin & Chen, 1946; from G. A. Miller, 1951a, p. 143.)*

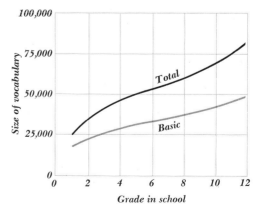

FIGURE 7–19: *The number of total and basic words as a function of grade in school. The total vocabulary includes both basic and derived words. (After M. K. Smith, 1941, p. 338–339; curves fitted by G. A. Miller, 1951a, p. 150.)*

mockingbird takes its name from its ability to reproduce the sounds of other birds. Bird sounds can be very complicated: the blue wood thrush can sing up to four notes simultaneously, sustaining some while changing others, like an organist.

K. J. Hayes and C. Hayes (1951) report that a chimpanzee, which they raised in their home as a member of the family, learned only three English words, although considerable time was spent trying to train the chimp to reproduce human sounds. Investigators report that monkeys emit sounds which have compound meanings such as *let's go* and *run*. Lilly (1961) has suggested that the sounds of dolphins may serve to communicate messages between them.

It is vital to discriminate the ability of an animal to reproduce humanlike sounds from the ability of the animal to respond to human sounds. Well-trained dogs are able to respond to a variety of verbal commands, although they do not reproduce these sounds. Similarly, a dog is able to convey information to his human keepers by the use of vocalizations. Most persons who have trained animals have had the experience of discovering that an animal trained to a verbal command will respond appropriately to other *similar* sounds. It is quite possible to train domestic animals to respond to a command given by a particular person but not to respond to the same command given by anyone else. This process of discrimination which occurs in animal learning suggests that similar processes may be responsible for the development of human speech (Chapters 13 and 14).

PATHOLOGY

Since the production of the precise sounds required for human communication involves the cooperation of several structures, organs, and muscles, it is not surprising that individual structural differences may result in failure to produce certain sounds. Such difficulties may arise from any of the areas concerned with speech: a misshaped mouth roof renders the production of many sounds impossible, as does an irregular shape of the lip. However, other difficulties in the production of precise speech appear to be central in origin; i.e., the CNS fails to make the necessary connections for speech to be perceived or reproduced. The child born deaf (from malfunctioning auditory apparatus) is slow to speak, for the sufficient reason that, not having heard sounds, he has no model to imitate. Stuttering is a common speech disorder, and it may be due to a number of causes.

Aphasia: Paul Broca (1824–1880; 1861) is credited with having discovered an area of the brain, located in the frontal lobe, which is the motor area responsible for speech. The corresponding sensory area is *Wernicke's area,* located in the parietal lobe. Patients with a lesion in *Broca's area* are aphasic. *Aphasia* is the general term to describe the inability to understand speech. It may be noted, however, that it is one thing to discover an area which is *necessary* for verbal communication and quite another thing to show that this is *the* area responsible for speech. Since attempts to correlate particular speech defects with particular parts of Broca's area have been inconclusive, analysis of the various forms of speech disorders remains in the descriptive stage. Among the forms of aphasia which have been noted are the following:

Central, or auditory, asphasia: **The subject has difficulty in understanding the meaning of spoken words and in selecting the appropriate word or structure when composing sentences. At times the subject uses words which he coins or invents. It is important to note that the subject experiences difficulty both in understanding and in reproducing words and sentences.**

Nominal, or amnesic, aphasia: **The subject has difficulty in noting the symbolic reference of words. This, in itself, is not uncommon in verbal behavior, for persons with normal speech patterns sometimes fail to *recall* words or names momen-**

tarily. In nominal aphasia, however, the subject is unable to select the proper name for objects. When shown a variety of foodstuffs and asked which is "bread," he may hesitate and point to the incorrect object. Even though corrected, he may continue to mislabel.

Verbal, or Broca's aphasia: The subject is apparently able to understand the meaning of words but is unable to speak them. In severe cases, the subject is unable to speak at all. In less severe cases, he may use only a few words, while indicating by motions that he understands that he is using the wrong word.

Word dumbness: Although similar to verbal aphasia, this condition is distinguished by the subject's ability to indicate an appreciation of the sound of the word. He may, for example, be able to tap out the number of syllables contained in a spoken word, although he is unable to reproduce the word.

Various combinations of these and other forms of aphasia occur. Pure cases are the exception, rather than the rule. It may be noted that these examples fall into three general classes: (1) those in which talking is more impaired than speech perception *(expressive)*, (2) those in which the perception of speech is more impaired than the speech *(receptive)*, and (3) those in which the names of objects cannot be recalled *(amnesic)* (see Laffal, 1964; Brain, 1961; Goldstein, 1948).

Stuttering: Stuttering is not uncommon among children and adolescents. If it continues into adulthood, the disorder may be sufficiently mild that only difficulties in articulation are noted, or it may be so severe that little articulation occurs. Many theories regarding the causes of stuttering have been suggested, and although each can find cases supportive to its contention, no theory is completely acceptable. Some investigators have traced stuttering to handedness and to the forcing of handedness common in the educational techniques of an earlier day (Orton, 1937). Some theories have regarded the "domi-

nance" of the cerebral hemispheres as significant. The psychoanalytic literature generally interprets stuttering as having an emotional cause (Laffal, 1964).

SOURCES

A frequency plot of the number of research articles published on speech, language, and related topics would probably show two distinct peaks: The first would represent the period from approximately 1925 to 1935. During this period "normative" studies were in vogue, and this fact is evident in the section on Development of Language, in which the primary data are vintage. The second period is that following World War II through the present.

Much of the impetus for work on speech and language has come through the development of computers and information theory. A survey of books and texts written on the topic of language follows the same general trend. Happily, the area has profited from some excellent works. G. A. Miller (1951a) presents a lively and meaningful text on language and communication, written with a basic interest in psychological problems. Cherry (1957, 1961a) has produced a literate and informative work on communication. The section on information theory is excellent. His chapter in Rosenblith (1961b) is also excellent, but more advanced. Discussions of the role of communication in engineering and other disciplines give the reader an idea of the importance of communication to many areas of inquiry. Broadbent (1958), in a book of wider scope, unites apparently divergent data into a discussion of the role of perception and communication. His reviews of the literature are informative and carefully prepared.

Discussions of speech and language are not commonly found in textbooks in psychology, but there is a trend toward including such topics in books devoted primarily to child psychology. D. McCarthy's review (1954) of language development in children is competent and serves to evaluate the rather extensive portion of the literature where agreement is lacking. Chapanis, Garner, and C. T. Morgan (1949) have a good chapter on the role of speech in industrial problems. Osgood (1953) presents an enlightening section on language behavior. He includes information on the origins of language, the development of language, and theories of language.

Some excellent but older books are available. Eisenson (1938) provides chapters on the relationship between language and personality and between speech and thought. Pillsbury and Meader (1928) contains a general survey, with special attention to mental processes. Fletcher (1929) presents a classic review of speech and hearing. It is noteworthy that much of the basic material found in this work is still useful. A summary of the physiological aspects of speech is provided by Curry (1940) and by Zangwill (1960). A. W. Staats and C. K. Staats (1963) interpret the development of speech and language according to the principles of reinforcement theory, and this is probably the best-developed single source for this viewpoint.

The chapters in Stevens by G. A. Miller (1951b) and by Licklider and G. A. Miller (1951) are excellent, although difficult, summaries of the literature on speech. J. S. Gray (1954) offers a comprehensive chapter on speech correction which covers a variety of disorders and considers the theoretical significance of such disorders for an understanding of speech. Brain (1961) discusses speech disorders in a brief but compact volume. Hirsh (1952) includes a chapter on speech intelligibility in his book *The Measurement of Hearing*. See also Luchsinger and Arnold (1965).

A chapter on the use of information theory in behavioral science is offered by Frick (1959). Although not concerned with speech as such, the chapter may satisfy the desire of those who wish to pursue the concepts supplied by information theory. Luria (1961) has written an informative book on speech and the regulation of behavior.

Church (1961) presents a very useful chapter on the development of speech. It analyzes many studies in the field and is probably the best single reference for students. Attneave (1959) has provided an excellent, although difficult, work on the applications of information theory to psychology.

R. Brown (1958) has published an interesting book on language which considers at great length many of the topics discussed in this chapter. The book provides a fine starting point for the student interested in studying language.

CHAPTER EIGHT

VISION: PSYCHOPHYSICAL
AND RELATED MEASURES

INTRODUCTION

Fechner's contribution—that measurements of the physical world do not necessarily correspond to sensations of the psychological world—is nowhere more demonstrably true than among phenomena associated with the sense of vision. The large number of visual illusions attests to the fact that the visual sense often reports psychological sensations which differ from the physical stimulus, for an illusion is nothing more than a notable discrepancy between the physical and the psychological worlds. Consider the common experience of noting that straight roads appear to come to a point in the distance. Most of us choose to believe that the point is an illusion, for if we travel to it we find that the road has not changed and that another point has appeared farther ahead. Accordingly, the experience does not worry us at all as we drive on. Moreover, as distinct from a hallucination, this illusion is common to everyone. This is only one of a large number of illusions in everyday life that we have learned to ignore or, sometimes, to use.

Consider Figure 8–1, which shows two objects. If you were asked what you saw in the figure, you would reply "chalk." Yet it is obvious that the objects are of two very different natures. Indeed, if you considered only what was actually perceived, you would point out that what you "really saw" was a cylindrical object and an oblong object. The ability of the central nervous system to translate these dissimilar images into the sensation of "chalk" is remarkable, and it is, no doubt, one of the capacities which contributes to intelligence. We are so accustomed to recognizing objects from various directions and views that we often ignore the power of the central nervous system to form concepts and to permit generalization from perceptions. These are, however, some of the critical aspects of visual perception which provide one of the most fruitful topics for research in perception.

Visual perception has played an important role in the development of philosophical

FIGURE 8-1: *Although the two shapes have vastly different images on the retina, the adult interpreter has little trouble in describing both as "chalk." How does the eye come to accept two vastly different shapes as members of the same class? This is one of the key problems in understanding our visual process.*

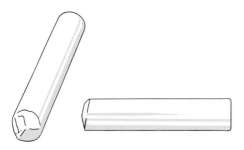

thought. One need only recall the contributions of Berkeley, Hume, Mill, and Kant, among others, to acknowledge this fact. The reasons the philosophers found visual perception important are very similar to those which attract psychologists to the study of vision, for they are concerned with similar questions. Consider, for example, the following problems:

Is the mind of the newborn organism a *tabula rasa* (a blank slate), or are some neural patterns already available at birth which allow us to separate an object from its background?

Are spatial and temporal concepts innate, or are they learned through interaction with the environment?

If sensations are learned by experience, *how* are they learned?

If perceptual organization is innate, can differences in perceptual organization among persons be accounted for by any way other than inheritance?

Solutions to these problems are basic to our study of the causes of behavior. The visual process provides psychology with one of its most useful sources of information regarding the elements of behavior. It is probably the sense most often used by human beings. Like audition, it is a distance receptor that permits us to interpret stimuli with which we are not in direct contact. The visual system, including the central nervous system, is able to learn; that is, perception of objects and events apparently change as a function of the previous experience of the organism. It is probably fair to say that, for the human being, most of the information received about the external world comes by way of the eye. Since the eye is known for the lack of correspondence between what is presented to it by the physical world and the sensation it reports, the human being's behavior is limited by the restrictions imposed by the visual process. This is not meant to imply that the visual process is misleading or to deny that the eye is a remarkably able and useful organ, but only to point out that our most useful and most sensitive sensory organ is also one of the most adaptable.

For vision to be possible, protoplasm must be available which contains substances altered by radiant energy of specific wavelengths. The irritability of protoplasm to light waves is probably a function of all organisms—even the lowly ameba is light-sensitive in this sense. However, it is only among the more advanced animals that we find specialized receptors for radiant energy.

Although a major part of vision is the chemical reaction which occurs in response to radiant energy, the visual system of higher animals is arranged in such a way that this energy is transfigured by the time it reaches the point at which the chemical conversion occurs. In order to understand the role of the structures involved, let us consider the anatomy and physiology of the human eye.

ANATOMY

The eyeball of human beings is roughly spherical. Stimuli impinge upon specialized nerve cells, called *photoreceptors*, after having passed through several refracting structures, including the cornea and the lens. The photoreceptors convert the energy (image) into nervous impulses which terminate in the *occipital lobe* by way of the *geniculate bodies.* Although the eye is primarily sensitive to electromagnetic energies of approximately 380 to 720 mμ, it is also sensitive to pressure, as was mentioned in Chapter 3.

The antero-posterior length of the human eye is approximately 24 mm; each of the other axes is between 21 and 22 mm. Unlike the ear, the eye has the ability to alter its structure as a function of the stimulus: muscles contract depending upon the distance or brightness of the stimulus. This ability is not possessed by all organisms, and it is one of the features that makes the eye of higher mammals very useful.

The adaptability of the human eye also enables it to provide information about the exact location of the objects. If the muscles contract to permit viewing of stimuli close at hand, the physical contraction of the muscles supplies kinesthetic cues as to whether the object is near or far. In addition, the fixation point may be shifted very quickly to permit the rapid gathering of information regarding a large number of stimuli. Although the eye is well arranged to permit these special functions, it is not so obviously well arranged for the transmission of radiant energy to the photoreceptors. Light must pass through two solutions (the *aqueous humor* and the *vitreous humor*) as well as the lens, cornea, and some tissue on the retina, before the photoreceptors are stimulated. The photoreceptors are densely packed, with some on top of others; thus the functioning of some receptors is always impaired. The receptors are inverted; that is they face away from the source of light coming through the lens.

Figure 8–2 shows a cross section of the eye in a schematic diagram. The *cornea* is the relatively clear, tough coat without blood vessels; it is an extension of the *sclerotic coat.* The cornea is easily observed as the transparent coating over the eye (J. L. Brown, 1965a). Next to the sclerotic coat, but not extending to the cornea, is the *choroid coat,*

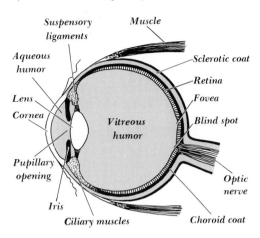

FIGURE 8–2: *Cross section of the human eye. (From Munn, 1961, p. 519.)*

which is darkly pigmented, as the figure indicates. The *retina* lies next to the choroid coat; it contains the photoreceptors. Pushing against the cornea is the aqueous humor, or liquid, which separates the *lens* from the *iris,* just as the vitreous humor separates the lens from the retina. The ciliary muscles affect the shape of the lens by contracting and elongating it; in this way the refraction of light striking the retina is altered, depending upon the shape of the lens.

The photoreceptors are found at the portion of the retina near the choroid coat. Between the receptors and the vitreous humor are layers of nerve fibers, ganglion cells, and other tissue. The retina contains 10 distinguishable layers (Polyak, 1941). The most important are labeled in Figure 8–3, which shows a cross section of the retina. At the *fovea* (Figure 8–2) the retina is invaginated, permitting many more photoreceptors to be located in a single place than is possible elsewhere in the retina. Near the fovea is the path of the optic nerve. Since the nerve interrupts the retina, there are no photoreceptors at the origin of the nerve, and for this reason it is known as the *optic disk.* The photoreceptors are called *rods* and *cones.* These terms are de-

FIGURE 8-3: *A cross section of the retina, showing its relation to the choroid coat. (Modified from Polyak, 1941, p. 36.)*

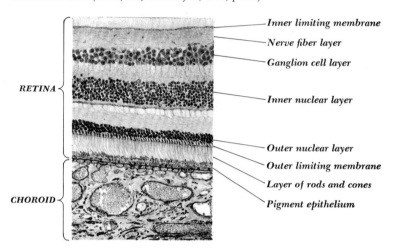

RETINA
- Inner limiting membrane
- Nerve fiber layer
- Ganglion cell layer
- Inner nuclear layer
- Outer nuclear layer
- Outer limiting membrane

CHOROID
- Layer of rods and cones
- Pigment epithelium

scriptive of their approximate shape, for rods are generally cylindrical and longer than the cones, which are, as the name implies, conical. In lower vertebrates the distinction becomes vague, for the photoreceptors are often not easily separable into rods or cones. Intermingled with the rods and cones in the retinochoroid area are *bipolar cells.* These act as mediators for the nervous impulse from the photoreceptor by channeling the impulse through the ganglion cell layer (Figure 8–3), into the optic nerve (IId cranial nerve), to the lateral geniculate body, and eventually to the occipital lobe. It is important to note that a single bipolar cell may mediate both rods and cones.

Figure 8–4 shows the anatomy of the optic nerve. Although the auditory (VIIIth cranial) nerves do not meet until reaching the appropriate projection area of the central nervous system, the optic nerves not only meet on their way to the projection areas, but they decussate.

As may be noted from Figure 8–4, the nerves divide; the location of the cross is known as the *optic chiasma,* or the *optic cross.* Consider the left eye and the left nerve. At the chiasma, fibers from the right half of the left eye cross to the right geniculate body. They are joined by fibers from the right half of the right eye. Fibers from the left side of the left eye are joined by fibers from the left half of the right eye and continue to the left geniculate body. Posterior to the geniculate bodies, some fibers continue to the occipital lobe, which is considered the projection area for vision. Figure 8–5 shows a ventral aspect of the brain and the position of the eyeballs and the optic nerves.

PHYSIOLOGY

Let us follow the course of radiant energy from its striking the eye at the cornea. Since the cornea is curved, some refraction of the light occurs at this point. The cornea is transparent, even though the sclerotic coat, from which it derives, is opaque. The cornea is of particular interest in cutaneous sensitivity, since it appears to lack certain cutaneous receptors found elsewhere in the skin. The threshold for pain is low in the cornea (see Chapter 10).

After striking the cornea, the refracted energy passes through the aqueous humor, through the lens, and through the vitreous humor, before striking the retina. Just as the sclerotic coat becomes differentiated to form the cornea, so the choroid coat is differentiated to form the *iris*. The iris is under the control of two muscles which are antagonistic and which permit the center of the iris, the *pupil*, to expand and contract. Since these muscles are responsive to a variety of changes within the body, the dilation or constriction of the pupil is often symptomatic. Many narcotics inhibit the muscles, and the pupil fails to respond to changes in light. This is the *Argyll-Robertson effect*. Other pathological states influence the behavior of the pupil, so that responsiveness to light stimulation may be indicative of physiological states quite unrelated to vision. Under normal conditions, the iris constricts, thus reducing the size of the pupillary opening.

The lens also has the capacity to change its shape. Through the action of the ciliary muscles, which are under the control of the autonomic nervous system, the lens may become elongated or shortened. Since light must pass through the lens to reach the photoreceptors, the shape of the lens influences the refraction of light. The lens is useful in the process of *accommodation*, in which the shape, and hence the refraction index, of the lens is changed according to the distance of the stimuli. If the lens did not accommodate, one useful means of determining the distance of objects would be lost. The lens hardens with age; thus, as a human being grows older, his ability to accommodate quickly and efficiently declines. Figure 8–6 shows the characteristic

FIGURE 8–4: *A diagram of the central visual pathways passing to the left hemisphere. The shaded areas in the inserts indicate the visual defects to be expected from lesions at points indicated by the corresponding letter. For example, A shows complete loss of vision in the left eye, no loss in the right eye. This would occur by severing completely the nerve coming from the left eye. However, a lesion at D, past the chiasma, results in a loss of vision in the nasal side of the left eye and in the temporal side of the right eye. (From John Homans,* A Textbook of Surgery, *6th ed., 1945. Courtesy of Charles C Thomas, Publisher, Springfield, Ill.)*

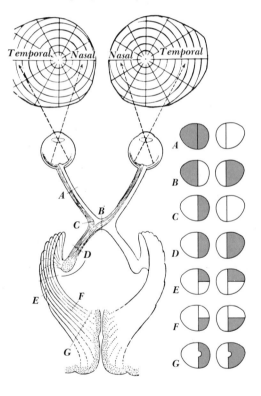

changes in the lens as a function of the distance of the stimulus.

The aqueous humor, as its name implies, is watery, although it is similar to blood plasma in composition. Its source is primarily the blood supply to the ciliary muscles. The fluid

FIGURE 8–5: *A ventral aspect of the human brain showing the parts of the visual system. Note the two eyeballs and optic nerves which bisect at the chiasma. The left geniculate body appears in the left hemisphere of the picture, as does the optic thalamus and the medial geniculate body. The right hemisphere is intact; the left hemisphere has been partially removed to show the mamillary bodies. (From Polyak, 1957, p. 291.)*

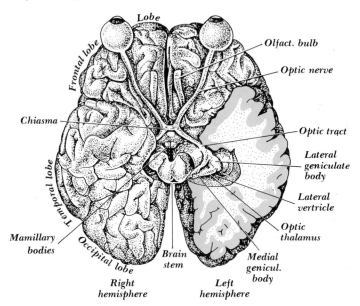

FIGURE 8–6: *A diagram of accommodation of the lens. With distant objects (figure A), the lens flattens. With near objects (figure B), the lens becomes more circular. (From C. T. Morgan, 1961, p. 339.)*

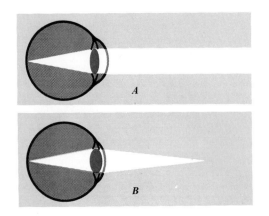

is drained so that it is changed completely in an hour (J. L. Brown, 1965a). The vitreous humor has a yellowish-white pigment and is more viscous. It helps maintain the spherical shape of the eyeball by its force upon the retina.

Following refraction by these structures, the light now strikes the retina, in which the photoreceptive structures are found. Curiously, the light-sensitive portions of the rods and cones do not face the light (the external surface of the retina); they are inverted, with their light-sensitive area facing the choroid coat. Accordingly, the light must pass through additional barriers, the collection of cells on the outer surface of the retina (see Figure 8–3), before reaching the sensitive parts of the receptor. This feature is one characteristic of the vertebrate retina. Through the appropriate bipolar cell, each cone is connected with its nerve fiber in the optic nerve. Although this is not always true in the periphery of the retina (the areas of the retina closest to the lens), the relation holds for the cones in the fovea. A single bipolar cell may serve several rods, and in some cases a bipolar cell may serve both rods and cones. Cones are concerned primarily with color vision; rods are concerned with color vision only to a small degree, if at all. As one moves from the fovea through the periphery toward the lens, relatively fewer cones and more rods are found. Although cones are distinguishable from rods, many photoreceptors are similar anatomically to both rods and cones, an observation which serves to confound research on the relation of the photoreceptors to color vision.

The fovea lies within the center of an area known as the *macula lutea,* or *yellow spot.* Figure 8–7, made through an ophthalmoscope (which shines light on the retina, permitting the examiner to evaluate the condition of the retina), shows the macula lutea of a young woman. The spot on the right is the macula lutea. The fovea, of a darker color, may be seen within the macula lutea. To the left is the origin of the optic nerve, or optic disk, and the arteries and veins. Rods are not found within the macula lutea, although they begin to appear at its edges. Curiously, severe damage to the occipital lobe may destroy all vision except that impinging upon the macula lutea. This suggests that receptors in this area use a projection area different from that used by other receptors.

Figure 8–8 shows one count of the number of rods and cones in the retina of the right eye. The *nasal retina* refers to that area nearest the nose, and the *temporal retina,* to the area farthest from the nose. The optic disk lies around 17° from the fovea, which is taken as 0°. The number of cones at the fovea per degree is around 17,000 by this count. On either side of the fovea, the number of cones is relatively constant, although the number of rods decreases. As the periphery is approached, there are fewer photoreceptors, largely because of the decrease in the number of rods, al-

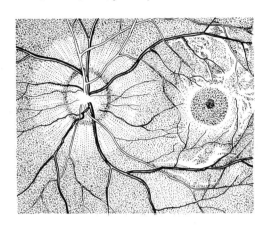

FIGURE 8–7: *The macula lutea from the left eye of a twenty-year-old woman. Note the optic nerve fibers extending beyond the disk. (From G. L. Johnson, 1901, plate 1.)*

though rods predominate in total number. It is estimated that there are approximately 6.5 million cones and perhaps 100 million rods in the human retina, with an average of 140,000 to 160,000 photoreceptors for each square millimeter (Geldard, 1953, p. 26).

It has been shown that the substance *rhodopsin,* or *visual purple,* is associated with the rods but not with the cones. Since rhodopsin may be extracted, its chemical characteristics have been compared with the physiological characteristics of the rods. It is sensitive to all observable frequencies, except red under low illumination. This particular characteristic has been of considerable use to the military. In order to avoid *night blindness* (nyctalopia), pilots have worn red goggles, which permit the rods to maintain normal functioning and, at the same time, permit the wearer to function normally in a lighted room. Rhodopsin appears to bleach at about the same rate that the rods are known to alter their adaptation, and it seems reasonable to conclude that rhodopsin is the major substance responsible for the responsiveness of rods to illumination.

Wald (1936) has named what appears to be a similar chemical substance in the cones,— *iodopsin,* although the substance has not yet been isolated chemically. Clearly, the source

FIGURE 8–8: *Distribution of rods and cones throughout the retina. The ordinate shows the number of photoreceptors per unit area, and the abscissa shows the location along the retina, from the periphery of the nasal side of the retina, through the fovea, and through the temporal retina. (See Chapanis, 1949, p. 7.)*

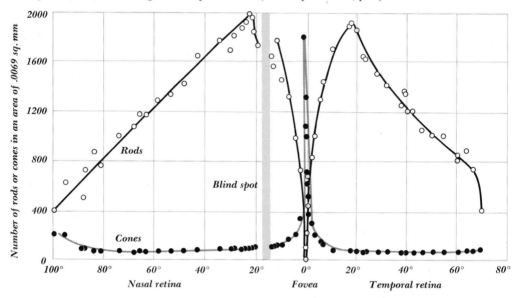

Distance from the fovea

of the answers for many questions regarding vision lies in the characteristics of the chemical reaction in the retina. Four chemicals, all carotenoid proteins, are either known or strongly suggested: in addition to rhodopsin, the rods contain *porphyropsin;* in addition to iodopsin, the cones contain *cyanopsin* (Wald, 1959).

DEFINING THE STIMULUS

As we noted in Chapter 3, the visual stimulus is generally broken down into wavelength (corresponding roughly to hue), the amount of radiant energy (brilliance or luminosity), and the homogeneity of the wavelength (saturation of the hue). Other measures are in common use, however, and the differences between systems of nomenclature are often con-

fusing. Table 8–A indicates the major measurements of various characteristics of the visual stimulus. Some are rarely used today, but all will be found in textbooks and other sources.

DUPLICITY OF THE PHOTORECEPTORS

The overwhelming weight of evidence now suggests that we should think of the primate eye as composed of two receptor systems rather than one. This evidence is based upon the demonstration that rods and cones function in different ways and that the same light source will be perceived differently depending upon whether it strikes rods or cones. Rods are primarily sensitive to stimuli under low illumination, and they are rarely sensitive to

TABLE 8-A: *Common Measures of the Visual Stimulus.*

Flux:	Rate of flow of light energy.
Lumen	Luminous flux from standard candle; 1 lumen = light falling on 1 m² at distance of 1 m from standard candle.
Wavelength:	
Millimicrons (mμ)	1/1,000 of 1 μ; 1 μ = 1/1,000,000 m.
Angstrom (Å)	10 Å = 1 mμ; hence, 5,600 Å = 560 mμ.
Intensity:	
Candlepower (cp)	Intensity of one standard candle. This has been replaced by the international candle, which is defined in terms of the electrical consumption of a standardized source.
Foot-candle (ft-c)	Level of illumination on surface 1 ft from one candle.
Meter-candle (lux)	Level of illumination on surface 1 m from one candle.
Brightness:	Reflectance.
Foot-lambert (ft-L)	Reflectance from a perfectly reflecting surface 1 ft from standard candle, i.e., with 1 ft-c of illumination on it.
Apparent foot-candle	Same as foot-lambert.
Millilambert (mL)	1 mL = 1.076 ft-L.
Troland (formerly called *photon*)	Luminance of one standard candle per square meter passing through a pupil of 1 mm².

wavelength. Cones, on the other hand, are primarily receptive to wavelength and are less sensitive under low illumination. For this reason, visual perception which involves the cones (color perception under medium or high illumination) is known as *photopic* vision. Perception which involves the rods (discrimination of illumination at low intensities) is known as *scotopic vision*. This distinction is still known as the *duplicity theory* (or *duplexity* by some authorities), even though it has been a proved relationship since the beginning of this century. The theory states that cones are for color and daytime vision, and that rods are for nighttime vision. Figure 8–9 shows strong evidence for this relationship by indicating the absolute threshold values for different wavelengths, with the curves for rods and cones compared. These are called *visibility curves*. For cone vision, the lowest threshold, and hence the point of maximum sensitivity, is at 550 mμ (greenish yellow). For rod vision, on the other hand, maximum sensitivity is at 510 mμ (green). Note that rod vision reaches its limit around 670 mμ; this indicates that the oranges and reds stimulate primarily the cones.

Figure 8–10 (following p. 242) shows the spectrum as a function of both photopic and scotopic vision. The green wavelengths for scotopic vision appear brightest, because this is the area of maximal sensitivity of the rods. Perception under medium or high illumination is most acute in the fovea, as we would expect, since the fovea is composed entirely of cones. Perception under low illumination, at nighttime, is most sensitive at an area around 20° from the fovea, for this area is the one in which the rods are packed most densely. In addition, the macula lutea is "night-blind"; it has no rods, so it is insensitive to stimulation of low illumination. This is experienced when one is driving at night and attempts to fixate upon a light in the distance. One must "look

FIGURE 8-9: *Cone and rod (photopic and scotopic) vision visibility. The ordinate shows the threshold, and the abscissa shows the wavelength. (From Chapanis, 1949, p. 10; data on cones from K. S. Gibson & Tyndall, 1923; data on rods from Hecht & R. E. Williams, 1922, p. 13.)*

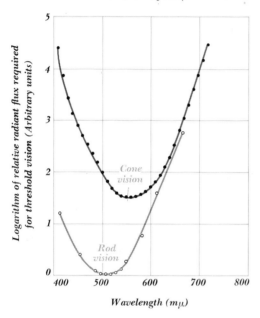

Wavelength (mμ)

ment for duplicity is that the Purkinje phenomenon has not been shown to occur in the macula lutea, which has only one type of receptor. In addition, individuals whose rods do not function (night blindness) do not report the Purkinje phenomenon.

The concept of duplicity of the photoreceptors handles data regarding illumination well, but it says nothing about how the cones translate the stimulus into different hues and colors. As we shall see, how the stimulus is perceived as color has been a matter of considerable concern to theories of vision at least since Newton. Men such as Goethe, Berkeley, and da Vinci attempted to solve the problem of how color is perceived, with results considerably less than successful.

The major difficulty in theories of color vision is presented by pathological cases of color blindness; although many credible theories of color vision have been developed, few are able to explain color blindness adequately. Every theory of color vision has postulated more than one kind of cone: some have suggested two, some three, some four, and one theory, at least, has postulated complementary pairs of cones. Unfortunately, although duplicity may be a useful concept to account for the difference between daylight and nighttime vision, it does not serve to explain color vision, since it has not been demonstrated that the cones differ anatomically from one another in such a way that discrete types may be identified. A growing body of data suggest that different types of cones exist, but most of these data come from electrical recordings of the retina in response to different hues, rather than from evidence of anatomical differentiation.

In addition, although the concept of duplicity is useful in explaining the different reactions of the photoreceptors of the human eye, it is not so successful in accounting for data from other vertebrate eyes. There is no question that the human eye has two fairly discrete photoreceptor systems; however, the finding may not be generalized to other organisms

away" from the stimulus in order to perceive it; that is, the head or eye must be turned so that the stimulus impinges upon receptors in the retina other than those in the macula lutea.

The level of illumination affects rods and cones differently. As illumination is decreased, colors at the upper end of the visible spectrum (reds and oranges) become dark or black very quickly, although colors at the low end of the visible spectrum (blues and greens) grow darker at a much slower rate. This effect may be seen easily at sunset, for the blues and greens of the landscape remain identifiable far longer than do the reds and oranges. This phenomenon, which would be expected from the duplicity of function of the photoreceptors, is known as the *Purkinje phenomenon,* or *Purkinje shift.* Perhaps the cinching argu-

with similar success. Since information regarding the evolution of the eye forms a basis of speculation regarding its functioning, we shall now consider this evidence.

EVOLUTION OF THE EYE

A specialized organ sensitive to light is found in many animals, but the diversity of types of organs is large. Eyes differ in regard to the presence of cones or rods, the blood supply and circulation, the presence of ciliary muscles (which permit accommodation), the development of the choroid coat (in terms of thickness or thinness), and the presence in birds, including some fowls, of the structure called the *pecten,* which penetrates from the retina at the optic disk. The pecten, shown in Figure 8–11, is composed of retinal blood vessels and pigment. It is found in a rudimentary form in other animals and is most highly developed in those fowls and other birds which use daylight vision rather than night vision.

Although all primates have cones and hence presumably have color perception, color perception is not common throughout animal life. The color vision of some birds and fish is excellent. Some psychophysical measurements have shown the color vision of some fowls to be superior to that of human beings. It should be remembered, however, that color vision, like beauty, is in the eye of the beholder and is not a characteristic of the external world. The external world produces only wavelengths, their homogeneity, and illumination. The color which is assigned to these combinations is a product of the photoreceptors of the particular eye being stimulated. A flower may be called "red" by you or me, but a bee, which may be able to perceive the ultraviolet wavelengths below the threshold of the human beings, will perceive the flower differently. The dog would probably describe the flower as having a greenish tinge. Although it is comforting for human beings to think of the

world as having green grass and a blue sky, this judgment is a product merely of the primate cones.

Many organisms which do not have a specialized light receptor have photoreceptors scattered throughout the body, much as we have pain receptors scattered throughout our skin. Such organisms are sensitive to the light from the sun but are probably incapable of perceiving reflected light unless the illumination is high. *Amphioxus,* for example, has light-sensitive cells scattered along the length of the central nervous system, although it has no specific cranial optic organ. When it is recognized that almost all the stimuli perceived by the primate eye are reflected light, the importance of the distinction between the possession of a specific eye with its specialized structures and the possession of photoreceptors is clear. A specialized eye has the advantage of permitting such activities as accommodation, judgment of the distance of the stimulus (particularly for animals which have two eyes, rather than only one), and fixation (the ability to follow a moving stimulus as its reflected

FIGURE 8–11: *The pecten in birds. Note the fovea and the three coats (sclerotic, choroid, and retinal) and the artery serving the pecten. (From J. H. Prince,* Comparative Anatomy of the Eye, *1956. Courtesy of Charles C Thomas, Publisher, Springfield, Ill.)*

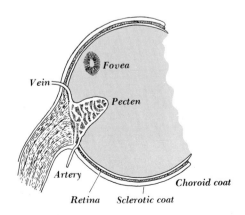

light moves across the retina). Although we have noted previously that a number of structures interfere with light entering the eye before it reaches the photoreceptors, causing inaccurate perception, it appears that the advantages provided by each of these structures far outweigh the loss of perceptual acuity.

Many organisms which perform unusual feats (such as the apparent communication system of the bee and the logistic ability of many ants) appear to use visual cues. Many animals appear to use light as a cue for orientation, just as man uses the sun and the stars to determine direction. An artificial change in the direction of light on ants sends them into

mass confusion for a brief period, but they promptly orient to the new light source. Sensitivity appears to vary widely, even among animals anatomically similar. Figure 8–12 shows the results of a study in which the receptivity of various butterflies to different wavelengths was measured by a preference technique (see Chapter 4). The differences in receptivity are immediately obvious.

Relatively little, or in some cases nothing, is known about the psychophysical functioning of many animals, even though the anatomy of the particular eye or photoreceptor is well documented. This is especially unfortunate for the student of animal behavior, be-

FIGURE 8–12: *The color preference of different butterflies. The ordinate shows preference in terms of percentage of flights, and the abscissa shows hue. Note the bimodal distribution, with one kind of butterfly selecting yellow stimuli most often and other kinds selecting blue and violet most often. (From Buddenbrock, 1958, p. 76, after Ilse, date unreported, n.s.)*

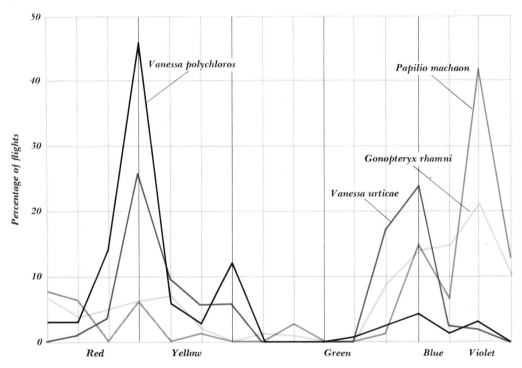

cause much behavior, especially in experimental investigations, requires the animal to use visual perception. Unless something is known about the thresholds associated with visual perception, experiments which require visual functioning are suspect unless it can be shown that the required task was within the animal's visual ability. Many reports of color vision in animals have failed to consider the multiple properties of light. For example, great care must be taken to be certain that the animal is discriminating wavelength and not intensity.

ELECTRICAL EVIDENCE OF VISUAL ACTIVITY

It has been known since the turn of the century that various parts of the visual system yield electrical discharges which may be recorded. Until quite recently the complexity of the problems associated with electrical recording and the need for precise electronic apparatus, however, have hampered the development of a reasonably systematic body of knowledge regarding electrical activity. A considerable portion of the work concerned with electrical recording of the sensory systems has been on the retina, both because of the importance of understanding the functioning of the visual sense and because the retina is located propitiously for recording purposes. The fact that recordings may also be made from the optic nerve and the occipital lobe means that separate recordings of the transmission of visual impulses may be made, and this possibility permits analysis of the functions of the components of the system. The development of techniques for electrical recordings from receptors and nerves *in situ* is an obvious example of the way in which improvements in the techniques of apparatus construction parallel advances in knowledge. The first reports of success with electrical recording techniques appeared in the early 1920s. Adrian, writing in 1953 (Granit, 1955, p. 2), recalled the attitude of workers at the time:

No one in those days who was interested in electrophysiology could have failed to realize what it might mean to his own work when the initial difficulties were overcome, and then came the papers of Forbes and Gasser and Newcomer to show that the difficulties were already yielding. The technique they were using was clearly not to be undertaken lightly: it involved all sorts of unfamiliar components, high tension batteries, condensers and resistors—electrical gear which now overflows our cupboards but then had all to be made by hand in the laboratory.... [The technique] promised direct information about events which formerly we had only been able to study by inference.

A recording made from the electrical activity of the retina is known as an *electroretinogram* (ERG). Figure 8–13 shows a sample ERG recording. The lower line indicates the passage of time, with each peak representing the passage of 0.2 seconds. The middle line, which breaks abruptly and then returns to its original level, indicates the presence of the stimulus. The onset of the stimulus is the first

FIGURE 8–13: *An electroretinogram from the octopod,* Eledone moschata. *The base line shows time: each blip is 0.2 second. The middle line shows the onset and termination of the stimulus. The top line shows the electroretinogram. (From Fröhlich, 1921, vol. I.)*

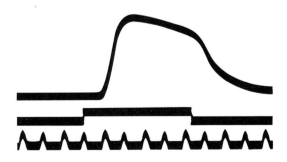

break, and the offset, or termination, is the second break. The upper line indicates the electrical recording. In the figure, it may be noted that the electrical response begins shortly after the onset of the stimulus, shows a variation in wave pattern at its peak, decreases in amplitude slowly as the stimulus remains on, and decreases more rapidly as the stimulus is terminated. Note that the potential is still above the original state even after termination of the stimulus. Figure 8–14*A* shows the simultaneous recording of the electric response to a flashing light (indicated by peaks along the bottom line) from both the retina and the optic nerve in the rabbit. The recording from the optic nerve contains far more "noise" than does the recording from the retina, even though both areas discharge at the same time. The bottom portion of the figure (*B*) indicates the same measures in response to different wavelengths. Again, noticeable differences occur depending upon whether the discharge is from the retina or the cortex.

The variety of eyes among animals, particularly in regard to the kind of photoreceptor, has permitted the gathering of useful comparative data on the electrical functioning of various forms of receptors. In one type of clam, two distinct layers of photoreceptors are found. One yields an electric potential at the onset of a stimulus, and the other yields a potential at the termination. Granit (1955) calls this the *on-off system,* since it implies that receptors may fire both at the onset of a stimulus and when the stimulus is removed. Some organisms do not show the on-off effect, and others, such as the human being, appear to show it only after the impulse has appeared beyond the retina.

The ERG is sensitive to changes in wavelength, as well as to changes in intensity. It may be recalled that a persistent problem in understanding audition is that it is difficult to account for the way in which *intensity* is sensed. For example, Figure 8–15 indicates the response of a small portion of the retina of the guinea pig to the same wavelength at different intensities. As the intensity is increased, there are more points of discharge.

Of considerable relevance to a theory of visual functioning is the fact that separate components of the electric potential may be identified. Figure 8–16 indicates a typical discharge analyzed into its components. Note that the filled line is similar to that shown in Figure 8–13: the onset of the stimulus produces a rapid change in potential, called the *b* wave, the potential increases slowly, but at the offset the discharge decreases slowly and continues to discharge after termination of the stimulus. Granit (1933; 1947; 1955; 1962) has suggested that the resulting function may be analyzed into three components, *PI, PII,* and *PIII,* for it is known that the administration of various drugs selectively removes one or more of the components from the recording.

FIGURE 8–14: *Figure A shows the response of the rabbit eye and the nerve to repeated flashes of white light. The base line shows time, and the left-hand legend shows the amplitude of 1 mv (millivolt). Note that the waveform is more complex from the nerve. Figure B shows the response of the monkey eye and the cortex to different wavelengths. The longer the wavelength, the greater the cortical response. (From Adrian, 1946, pp. 32, 35.)*

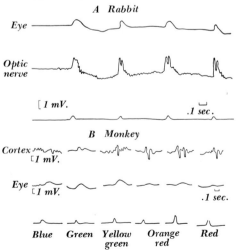

For example, under anesthesia, *PI* is eliminated first, then *PII*, and last, *PIII*. If *PII* is
eliminated, there is no discharge in the optic
nerve. *PII* is very susceptible to a lack of
oxygen (asphyxia). Similarly, there is evidence
that *PIII* originates and thus represents the
action of the photoreceptors.

Although the basic setups for ERG recordings differ, recordings are usually made of
electrical changes resulting from stimulation
of a tissue by amplifying the signal which is
received from electrodes in contact with the
tissue. With human beings, recordings are
often made from a contact lens arrangement
(Riggs, 1941; 1956; 1965b). Among vertebrates,
the cornea is positive in respect to the macula
lutea; however, this arrangement is reversed
in invertebrates (Riggs, 1965b). The exact
source of ERG impulses is not definite. It appears that the retina is involved (Riggs, 1954)
but that other structures also contribute to the
final ERG.

Of major interest is the reflection in the
ERG of such basic physical properties of light
as intensity and wavelength, for eventually
we shall be concerned—as we were in our
study of auditory phenomena—with how visual
perception occurs. The ERG reports the intensity of the stimulus. If the course of dark
adaptation is followed by ERG recording, a
wave may be identified which is correlated
with scotopic vision (E. P. Johnson and Riggs,
1951). Although difficult to observe, characteristic responses on the ERG have been identified for specific wavelengths. In general, the
intensity of the stimulus is independent of the
wavelength: thus, as is true of amplitude and
frequency of sound waves, the two appear to
be separate aspects of the light source. There
appears to be a specific component of the
ERG which may be identified, with the wavelengths generally perceived as red (Adrian,
1945; Boynton & Riggs, 1951; Armington,
1952); Adrian (1945) has reported separate
components for orange-red and blue. As we
shall see, information from electrical recordings from the eye become very useful in our
attempt to uncover the relationship between

FIGURE 8–15: *Effect of increasing the
intensity of the stimulus on the response of an
isolated retinal element of the guinea pig. Relative
energy values of the stimuli (from above
downward): 1 (threshold), 1.3, 1.48, 2.22, 3.91, 9.31.
Wavelength of stimulus: 530 mμ. Time markings:
1/50 second. (From Granit, 1942, p. 323.)*

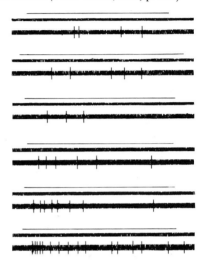

the physical stimulus and the response to that
stimulus. Before considering these problems,
we shall discuss what is known regarding
visual thresholds.

FIGURE 8–16: *The on-off responses of the
ERG and the massed activity of the retina.
Granit's (1933) analysis is indicated by the dashed
lines PI, PII, and PIII. The main waves of
response are indicated by A, B, C, and D.
(Bartley, 1939, p. 347.)*

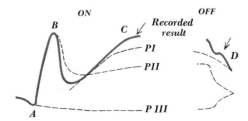

ROLE OF THE CENTRAL NERVOUS SYSTEM

The units of the central nervous system which are of greatest importance to the process of vision are the optic nerve, the optic chiasma, the lateral geniculate nucleus, and the visual cortex. We have noted previously the role of the chiasma. The optic nerve has been investigated most commonly by recording electric potentials. The electrode is placed on the nerve, and recordings are made of changes in the electric potential which accompany various kinds of visual stimulation, such as a flickering light.

The optic nerve reports on-off effects, just as do electrical measurements emanating from the retina. The effects seem to vary as a function of intensity. Under weak intensities, a single "on" response appears. If the light is more intense, the termination of the stimulus is followed by an "off" response. As intensity is increased, what seem to be additional "on" responses appear. These, it is believed, have different latencies for firing. They may represent more than one kind of receptor in the optic nerve, differing perhaps in size and thus in conductance rate, and they may represent more than one kind of receptor.

Impulses from the optic nerve terminate at several locations within the brain. For example, one group travels to the lateral geniculate body, which is the group of visual nuclei in the thalamus, and then is relayed to the cortex. After leaving the geniculate body, most fibers go to the striate cortex (see below). Some travel down the brainstem, where they eventually serve to integrate vision with the organs of balance. It appears that the lateral geniculate body is topographically organized in relation to an area of the cortex. That is, each area of the retina is served by a point in the lateral geniculate body and in an area of the cortex. In human beings and primates, the lateral geniculate body has six layers. Alternately, three layers represent one eye, and three represent the other eye.

We may note several characteristics of the lateral geniculate body which have been identified through studies measuring electrical changes. First, some cells appear to fire spontaneously when the eye is in darkness (Erulkar & Fillenz, 1960). It is possible that these are the "off" units, for we have noticed that an "off" response occurs at the termination of a light stimulus. Second, although in some cases a single fiber from the optic nerve is sufficient to fire a cell in the lateral geniculate body, most often a single fiber is not sufficient to yield a measure of the well-known spike potential. Rather, several fibers must pulse a cell for the spike to appear. Third, according to the wavelength which impinges upon the retina, the lateral geniculate body may respond with either an "off" response or an "on" response (De Valois, 1960). This suggests that the geniculate body fires differently, depending upon the wavelength of the stimulus. Fourth, on-off responses appear in the geniculate body just as they do from the retina (Bartley & Nelson, 1963). We shall reconsider the role of these bits of knowledge in the determination of color vision and other perceptual processes in the next chapter.

The visual cortex is the projection area for the lateral geniculate bodies. It is also known as the *striate cortex,* since it has a striped appearance. When light stimulates the eye, recordings may be made of changes in electric potential in this area of the cortex. The area is related topographically to the retina. It may be recalled that within the lateral geniculate body alternate layers represent each eye. In the cortex there is no such simple pattern. Most cells may be pulsed by stimuli from either eye. These factors lend support to the idea that the fusion which appears in vision between the two eyes is cortical. This fusion is extremely important, especially in the eyes of higher mammals, for, as we shall see, much of visual perception depends upon the eyes' fusing the images each receives (Hubel, 1963).

THRESHOLDS

Threshold measures are possible for wavelength, illumination, homogeneity, saturation, hue, illumination and brightness, saturation and homogeneity, and other less common specifications as well (N. R. Bartlett, 1965). Since proper threshold determination requires holding all specifications constant save the ones under investigation, a large number of measures are available. Many threshold determinations are useful for very specific needs only. Our discussion is limited to determinations of the major specifications of the visual stimulus.

Wavelength and Hue: The absolute thresholds (ALs) for human beings are estimated at 380 mμ for the RL (blue) and 720 mμ for the TL (red). These are estimates only, for in addition to individual differences in ALs, wavelengths which are normally subthreshold may combine with those which are suprathreshold to produce the perception of hue. Similarly, there is some evidence that ERG recordings report nerve responses for wavelengths well above the TL estimate of 720 mμ, even though perception is not reported by the subject verbally. The thresholds will vary, of course, as a function of illumination and saturation, so that specification of a precise threshold for wavelength requires information regarding the accompanying specifications of the other aspects of wavelength.

The ALs for other primates appear to be similar to those for human beings. There is evidence that the TL is extended in the rat and perhaps in other rodents, permitting perception of reds beyond those wavelengths perceivable by primates. Similarly, the RL wavelength in the bee is less than 380 mμ, permitting perception of wavelengths which are ultraviolet and imperceptible to the human eye.

Figure 8–17 shows the detection threshold for various wavelengths of the human being. The lowest thresholds are for wavelengths which correspond to yellow and yellow-green hues. The higher thresholds are at the extremes.

The DL for wavelength varies as a function of the spectral wavelength, so that the DL, measured in mμ, is smaller in the middle

ranges of the visible spectrum and larger nearer the AL points. When DLs are plotted across all wavelengths, one common procedure is to use one AL as the first standard, to mark off the DL from that standard, and to use the DL plus the standard as the second standard. For example, if the first standard were 370 mμ, and the DL were 6 mμ, 376 mμ would serve as the next standard. This procedure reveals the progression of DLs throughout the visible spectrum but does not indicate the DL for any particular point other than the standards employed on the spectrum. Figure 8–18 shows a plot derived from this procedure. The DL is largest as the RL and TL are approached, but the pattern of sensitivity is neither the linear nor the curvilinear relationship that we have come to expect in the sensory systems. Maximal sensitivity is at approximately 490 mμ (greenish blue) and 580 mμ (yellow), while a sharp loss of sensitivity appears at approximately 540 mμ (greenish yellow). This procedure accumulates 128 DLs between the RL and TL, most of which are between 1 and 3 mμ in length. Experimenters report wide individual differences among human beings. The form of the function, however, including the inversion at 540 mμ and the two locations of maximal sensitivity, is commonly found in studies which have used the step procedure.

The relationship between wavelength and hue is complex. The perception of hue is dependent on such factors as illumination, level of adaptation of the eye, and sensitivity of the individual eye, although the wavelength itself is the most important single contributor to perception. Wavelength and illumination are intertwined intimately, for a wavelength within the visible spectrum is not perceivable unless its illumination is sufficiently intense.

Illumination, Brightness, and Related Measures: The psychophysics of illumination and brightness must consider the amount of radiant energy, as well as such matters as the location and size of the area of the retina under stimulation and the adaptation level of the retina at the time of measuring. The relationship of these factors may be appreciated by

FIGURE 8–17: *Spectral sensitivity in the fovea following a thirty-minute dark-adaptation period. A modified method of limits was used. The threshold is lowest in the middle ranges and highest at the extremes; however, if the subject is asked to name the color he perceives, blue and red (the extremes) are reported most frequently at the threshold level and yellow is reported less frequently. That is, although wavelengths within the yellow area have the lowest threshold, they are not so easily identified by color as those at the extremes. (From Hurvich & Jameson, 1953, p. 489.)*

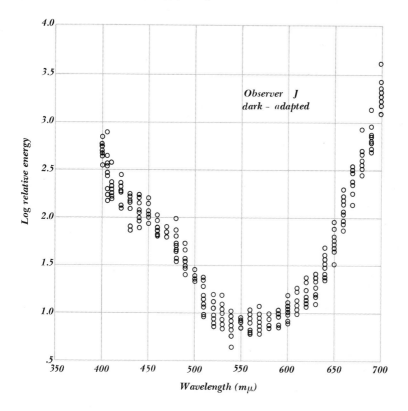

analogy to photography: depending upon the amount of illumination, a camera must be adjusted to account for the intensity of the scene by altering the duration (exposure time) of the stimulus. If the light is strong, the exposure time is small; if the light is weak, the exposure time is lengthened accordingly. This relationship is called the *Bunsen-Roscoe law,* and it takes the form of the equation

$$I \times T = C$$

where

I = intensity
T = time, or duration
C = constant representing threshold value

Thus a light which lasts 1/100 second appears as bright as a light which is ten times as intense but which lasts for 1/1000 second. There is evidence that the relationship holds only for relatively short durations but that the general applicability of the formula applies to events as diverse as the growth of oat seedlings (Hecht, 1934) and the bleaching of rhodopsin. Figure 8–19 shows one determination of the relationship between intensity and the duration of the stimulus. This determination deviates from the Bunsen-Roscoe law beyond 0.1 second and indicates that short durations require greater intensities of the stimulus. Thus, the Bunsen-Roscoe law has severe restrictions.

The general validity of the Bunsen-Roscoe law is also dependent upon the size of the location stimulated. The relationship between the area stimulated and the intensity of the stimulus is known as *Ricco's law,* and its equation is

$$I \times A = C$$

where

I = intensity
A = area stimulated
C = constant representing threshold value

In general, the law states that a constant threshold value may be maintained by increasing the area stimulated while decreasing intensity. Figure 8–20 shows acuity at different levels of brightness, with 0° representing the fovea. The graph indicates that the fovea is most acute at high brightness, although under low brightness, around 5 and 7 $\mu\mu$L (micro-microlamberts), the area about 4° from the fovea is most acute. Various investigators have proposed alterations of Ricco's law, since it appears to fit only within relatively small areas of the intensity function. There is no question that intensity and area interact reciprocally, but the exact relationship which might apply for all intensities and all areas is unknown. The principle by which perception varies as a function of the area stimulated implies that the number of rods and cones stimulated is a

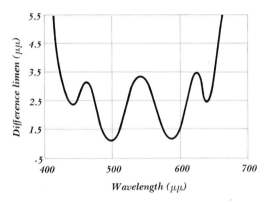

FIGURE 8–18: *The perception of hue as a function of wavelength. The function shows two areas of minimal hue sensitivity, at approximately 490 mμ and 580 mμ. The threshold is highest at the extremes. (Data from Nutting, 1908, as plotted by L. A. Jones, 1917, p. 65.)*

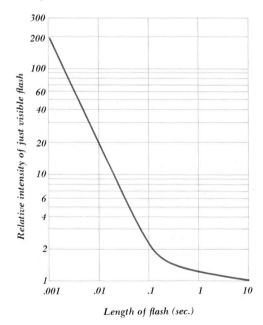

FIGURE 8–19: *Relationship between the duration of a flash of light and its relative intensity. Note the break in the function at 0.1 flash per second. (From Chapanis, Garner, & C. T. Morgan, 1949, p. 87, after Blondel & Rey, 1911.)*

FIGURE 8–20: *Visual acuity in different areas of the retina at different brightness levels. At high brightness, the fovea of the eye (0°) is most acute. At very low brightness, between log 5 and log 6μμL (micromicrolamberts), the eye is most acute about 4° from the fovea. (From Chapanis, Garner, & C. T. Morgan, 1949, p. 99, after Mandelbaum & Sloan, 1947.)*

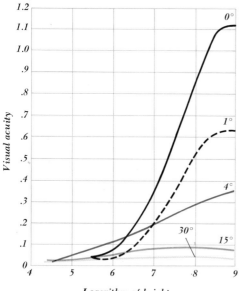

Logarithm of brightness
(micromicrolamberts [μμ L])

by pointing out that the amount of energy from a single pea's falling 1 inch would be sufficient to yield a suprathreshold sensation to every person who has ever lived (Pirenne, 1948, p. 78). Indeed, the deductions of Hecht (1944) indicate that one quantum of energy is sufficient to fire one rod. The fact that the smallest unit of light and the single rod are matched has been a fact of considerable and continuing interest to many fields of inquiry, for as Hecht points out, in an evolutionary sense, when one quantum excites one rod, the limit of sensitivity of the photoreceptor has been reached.

Since the DL varies as a function of the stimulus selected as the standard, in any sensory aspect there will be as many DLs as there are discriminable standards. For most purposes, however, it is useful to plot DL functions by the technique used to plot hue discrimination. In this technique, each standard, plus its corresponding DL, is summed in order to derive a new standard. The result is a series of sensitivity steps. Similar measures of brightness discrimination present smoother curves than are found with successive DLs of hue, but they do not fit the Weber fraction. Rather, it appears that the fraction decreases as the intensity is increased. Figure 8–21 gives one function indicating the relationship between brightness DLs and the standard. In the figure, the abscissa is represented in log Trolands, at 535 mμ. A *Troland,* it may be recalled from Table 8–A, is what was formerly called a *photon,* and it represents illumination when intensity and area of the pupil are held constant. The data indicate a cleavage at 0 Trolands, and this cleavage probably represents the different contributions to the perception of illumination of the cones and the rods. According to the data shown in Figure 8–21, there are over five hundred discriminable steps in the DL function for brightness.

As is true of the AL for intensity or brightness, the factors of intensity, duration of the stimulus, and the area of the retina which is stimulated determine the DL. In general, the relationships between these characteristics of

critical factor in perception and carries the names *areal summation* and *spatial summation.* Areal summation itself varies in its effect as a function of the area of the retina; summation is more pronounced in the periphery than in the foveal region. Spatial summation refers to the amount of the retina stimulated.

From these established interactions of area, intensity, and duration, it follows that all three aspects are critical in the determination of intensity thresholds. Accordingly, it is the *quantity* of the stimulation *(A × I × T)* which is the determining factor in intensity stimulation. The quantity of light energy required to reach threshold is small. Pirenne describes this

the physical stimulus which were noted in regard to the AL also hold for the DL, although, as usual, they appear to hold only within limits.

The application of scaling techniques to determining the function of "brilliance" has been unusually successful. Hanes (1949), using the method of fractionation, varied light from 0.00001 to 500 mL (millilamberts) and derived the scale shown in Figure 8–22. Hanes used the term *bril* as the scaled equivalent of "brilliancy," defining 100 brils as equal to 1 mL. In Figure 8–22, the ordinate represents brils, and the abscissa represents Trolands. The close correspondence between brils and DLs is indicated by the fact that they may be readily converted to each other by the application of a constant. For example, the bril may be multiplied by a constant of 1.6 in order to convert to DLs.

Saturation: We have defined saturation as homogeneity of wavelength. However, human subjects are able to discriminate not only differences in the amount of white light added to a dominant wavelength but differences between wavelengths matched for purity, as well. That is, if presented with a yellow and a blue of the same luminance, most human subjects will judge the blue to be more saturated than the yellow. Thus, differences exist in apparent saturation as a result of the nature of the dominant wavelength. This fact, as we shall see later, is of some practical consideration in such matters as the design of lighting systems.

Generally, two light fields are used in experiments concerned with measuring saturation thresholds. Both fields are made equal in luminance, although one is constructed so that the amount of white light or the amount of spectral light may be altered. Thus, if we wish to assess the difference in purity for a given wavelength that is necessary for the difference to be noticed, we may use standard psychophysical procedures by varying the amount of white light or spectral light in one field and requiring the subject to judge when the two fields are different or the same in saturation.

FIGURE 8–21: *Brightness discrimination, with log ΔI/I on the ordinate and log intensity along the abscissa at 535 mμ. (From Hecht, Peskin, & Patt, 1938, p. 15.)*

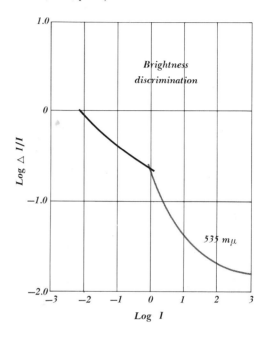

FIGURE 8–22: *A subjective scale of brightness which plots brilliance against illumination. (From Hanes, 1949, p. 450.)*

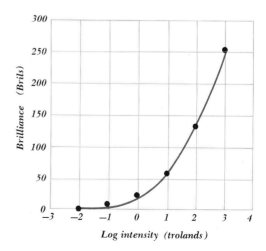

It is important, of course, that luminance be kept constant to assure that the subject judges on the basis of saturation and not on the basis of luminance. Figure 8–23 shows the results of one experiment which measured saturation as a function of wavelength. The threshold increases with an increase in wavelength through 570 mμ in the yellow region and then declines through the reds. L. A. Jones and Lowry (1926) determined the number of DLs for eight different spectral wavelengths. They found 16 DLs in the yellow region and 23 in the red and blue regions.

OTHER MEASURES

Perimetry: Indirect evidence for duplicity of the photoreceptors comes from studies which have plotted the threshold for different hues as a function of the area of the retina to which the hue is presented. If you hold an object in

FIGURE 8–23: *The perception of saturation as a function of wavelength. Data are shown for two observers. To one side of a field of a specific brightness of white light, the investigators added homogeneous spectral light and took out as much white as necessary to keep the two sides of equal brightness. They then determined the minimal amount of color that had to be added to make the half of the field appear colored. Appreciably more yellow, orange, and yellow-green are required, compared with red, blue, or violet. (From Hecht, 1934, p. 801; data from Priest & Brickwedde, 1926.)*

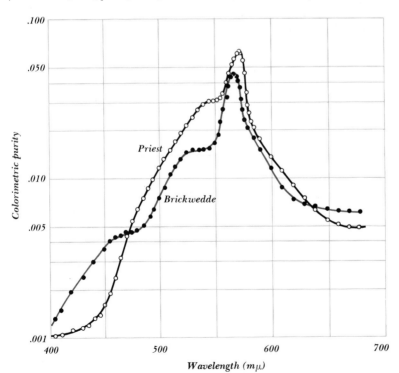

your outstretched hand, so that the image of the object is focused upon the temporal periphery of the retina, you will be unable to describe its color: it appears gray. As you move the object in front of you, the image on the retina is moved nearer to the fovea, and the color of the object becomes identifiable. This demonstration indicates that the periphery of the retina is relatively color-blind but that color perception improves as the image nears the foveal area. The plotting of areas of the retina which are sensitive to color is known as *perimetry,* and the apparatus which is commonly used for such assessments is called a *perimeter,* or, in the older literature, the *campimeter.*

Figure 8–24 shows a perimeter. The arm marked by an arrow holds a small colored patch which may be moved along the rim on which it rests. The subject's focus is held constant by the use of a chin rest. Patches of different colors are moved from the extreme periphery toward the foveal area either at a slow rate or in steps until the subject is able to identify the color of the patch. A modified method of limits is commonly used in determinations, but it should be noted that trials may be conducted in only one direction, i.e., from the periphery toward the fovea. It is useless to counterbalance by having the stimulus move from the fovea, where it is easily discriminable, to the periphery, since the subject is then aware of the color of the stimulus at the outset of the trial. If the experimenter wishes to determine when a color becomes gray, it would be appropriate to move the stimulus from the fovea to the periphery. Figure 8–25 shows a sample perimetric result for the right eye.

The results from perimetric studies provide fuel for the theoretical fire. First, some colors are perceived more quickly than others. Blue and yellow objects are identified before red or green. Although the subjects may be responding to intensity rather than to hue, it seems probable that even when intensity and saturation are controlled, the peripheral retina is more sensitive to blue and yellow hues than to

FIGURE 8–24: *A perimeter. A small colored object may be moved around the semicircular apparatus in order to locate the place at which colors become identifiable.*

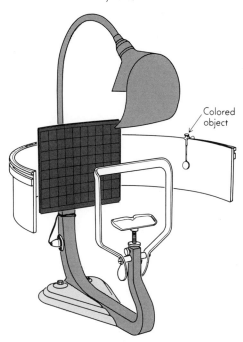

Colored object

others. A second finding from perimetric studies is that an object of a given color will appear to *change* hue as it approaches the fovea. Subjects do not always perceive the hue of an object correctly when they first detect it. Four hues, however, are usually identified correctly when they are detected. Red, yellow, green, and blue are perceived to change from gray to the appropriate color without being first perceived as a different hue. Intermediate hues, such as orange and yellow-green, are commonly misidentified at first.

Perimetric investigations have also been used to measure the effect on vision of damage to parts of the central nervous system. Destruction of parts of the visual cortex result in a loss of pattern vision (Teuber, Battersby, & Bender, 1960). When visual acuity is measured by perimetric techniques, the areas in

FIGURE 8–25: *A perimetric plot of the eye. The color patterns indicate the overlapping areas in which the color is perceived.*

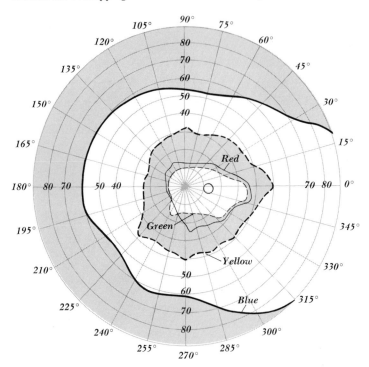

which vision is lost are called *scotoma*. Sometimes this may be a large area of the perimetric plot, or it may be a large donut-shaped area in which the center of the scotoma may retain vision while the surrounding area does not.

Flicker Fusion: If a light is made to turn on and off 10 times a second, the human eye is able to distinguish when the light is on and when it is off. The photoreceptors and the optic nervous system are able, under these conditions, to distinguish the presence of light from its absence. If the frequency is changed, with the light going on and off at such a speed that individual receptors, or groups of receptors, are unable to fire so rapidly as the onset and termination of the stimulus demand, the sensation is that the light is constantly on. Standard ac lights, for example, alternate at

60 Hz, so that in any second the light goes on 60 times and goes off 60 times. This on-off relationship is so rapid that the light is perceived as constantly on. It follows that thresholds may be determined for the rate of firing necessary to produce the sensation of constancy or, alternatively, the sensation that the light is "blinking." These thresholds will vary as a function of illumination, wavelength, and the other characteristics of radiant energy which are known to affect thresholds. The phenomenon is called *flicker fusion,* and the point at which a light appears constant, as opposed to its appearing to be flicker, is known as the point of *critical flicker fusion* (CFF).

Flicker fusion has been of considerable interest to psychologists for many reasons. The CFF varies as a function of certain physiological changes, such as oxygen deficiency, and it has been reported that it is affected in some psychopathological states, such as schizophrenia. In addition, the CFF threshold, or *flicker fusion threshold* (FFT) has been shown to be a predictor of "stress," as measured by patients' reactions to the prospect of surgery (R. A. Buhler, 1961). Workers concerned with the physiology of the retina and the problems of color vision are required to interpret the data associated with CFF, for it presents another well-developed area of research in which a unifying theoretical framework is needed. Flicker fusion is of practical importance to motion pictures.

Determinations of FFT are usually made with the method of limits. Uniformity of psychophysical measures has not, however, removed contradictory findings from the literature on flicker fusion. CFF is similar to other visual measures in that the kinds of controls used for intensity and other variables mean that there will be wide differences in the specification of individual studies. The most important single component determining CFF is the rate of flickering, which is usually expressed in terms of the number of cycles (composed of one onset and one termination) of the light per second. However, since the cycle may be altered so that the light is on longer than it is off or the reverse, a concomitant aspect of the flicker is the light-dark ratio (LDR). Most studies of CFF have employed a 50 percent LDR in which the stimulus is present half the time.

Figure 8–26 shows the relationship between intensity and cycles per second with a 50 percent LDR. The function appears to have two components, one for low intensities and one for high intensities. As the figure indicates, when intensity is increased, the number of flashes must be increased also. This means that the more intense the stimulus, the higher the cycles per second must be for the threshold to be reached.

When the CFF is above threshold, the apparent brightness of the stimulus may be evaluated by *Talbot's law.* From the formula, if

FIGURE 8–26: *Critical flicker fusion with an LDR of 0.50. The abscissa shows intensity, and the ordinate shows number of flashes per second. Note that two curves are found: one probably represents the functioning of the rods and the other the functioning of the cones. (Modified from Crozier & E. Wolf, 1941, p. 639.)*

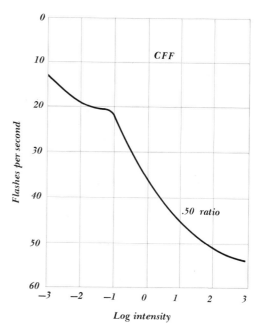

the LDR is known, the intensity needed for a standard source to be matched to the CFF source may be determined. Talbot's law applies only when the CFF is above threshold, for it underestimates the apparent brightness of the "on" phase for subthreshold CFF. This differential effect of subthreshold CFF is known as *brightness enhancement* (Bartley, 1941; 1951; 1958), and the maximal values for brightness under these conditions have been computed. The phenomenon is also called the *Bezold-Brücke effect.* Figure 8–27 shows the effect of brightness enhancement. The horizontal line represents the effect of a steady light. When the CFF is near threshold (Talbot level), the apparent brightness is less than that of a constant source. However, if the flicker is

FIGURE 8-27: *Talbot's law of brightness enhancement. The horizontal line shows the brightness of steady illumination. The three curves show three different LDRs. The abscissa shows the number of flashes per second. The curves show the shift in apparent brightness. (From Bartley, 1939, p. 344, modified by courtesy of Professor Bartley.)*

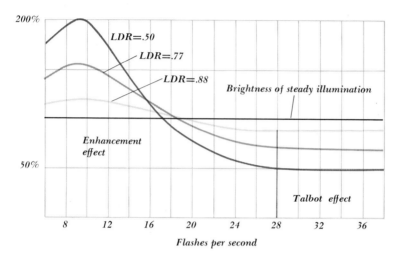

increased sufficiently, its apparent brightness is greater than that of the standard up to the point at which the flicker is around 10 Hz. As the cycles per second are decreased from 10, the relative brightness of the CFF compared with a constant source decreases.

Flicker fusion varies as a function of other attributes of the visual system. The area of the retina stimulated appears to be a critical variable, for it appears that the periphery maintains a lower threshold than the foveal area. On the other hand, Granit and Harper (1930) have shown that if the area stimulated is small, flicker fusion is comparatively higher in the foveal area. Similarly, it has been reported (Hecht, 1938) that under high intensities the foveal area has a higher CFF than the periphery. Lindsley (1958) has been successful in making electrical records of flicker fusion from the retina and the cortex. The electric discharge faithfully follows the frequency of the "on" phases to a point; however, the cortex is the first part of the visual system to cease following the "on" phases when they become too rapid.

Flicker fusion is one example of the general area of *temporal patterning*. As the name suggests, research in this area is concerned with the effects of the duration of stimuli, rather than with location, or spatial, effects. Many studies of temporal patterning use a variable-speed motor which permits cardboard or plastic disks to be joined and rotated at different speeds. To study CFF, for example, one could place a black disk in such a way that it covered half a white risk. CFF could be measured using psychophysical methods by calculating the point at which the black and white sectors become indistinguishable. As we shall note in the next chapter, this procedure may be used with disks, or sectors, of different colors. Under these conditions, laws of color mixing, as well as other phenomena, may be investigated. One of the more curious products of disk rotation is the sensation which results from a disk such as that shown in Figure 8–28, in which half the disk is black and the other half consists of four sets of three curved lines. This arrangement is called *Benham's top*. When rotated at the appropriate speed, colored rings appear to surround the center. Those nearest the center appear yellow, red, or orange, and those on the outside appear blue. Reversing the direction of the rotation reverses the location of the hues. Although it is likely that the phenomenon is a product of afterimages, it is clear that speed of rotation, or CFF, is an important variable in producing the effect. Of importance to theorists, of course, is the problem of how color may be seen from the mere rotation of black and white. The magical trick of producing color out of the absence of color remains one of the mysteries of the visual system.

Adaptation: The term *adaptation* was originally applied to the adjustment of the pupil and the photoreceptors to light intensity. When one enters a darkened room, it is almost as if one were blind. After a little while, shapes can be distinguished. This process is known as *dark adaptation,* and it is accompanied by improvement in acuity as time passes. *Light adaptation* is the reverse effect, in which one enters a bright room from a darkened one and discovers that for a time the eye is blinded by the light intensity. Applied to vision, *adaptation* connotes an improvement in performance due to changes in the pupil size and the reactivity of the photoreceptors where, because of the bleaching of rhodopsin in the rods, there is a time lag between the initial stimulation of the rods and their maximum responsiveness. The term has been expanded, however, to describe related phenomena in other senses (Harriman, 1959a). In some respects, this usage is unfortunate, for adaptation in other senses is commonly associated with a decrement, rather than an increment, in sensitivity. For example, when we enter a room which has an identifiable odor, the olfactory receptors soon cease to respond to the stimulus.

Visual adaptation is a function of such variables as the wavelength and intensity of the preadaptation and adaptation stimuli and the length of time that the eye has been stimulated. Light adaptation, in which the cones become sensitive to light and the rods become

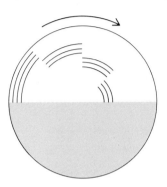

FIGURE 8-28: *Benham's top. The disk is half black and half white. The white half contains sequences of three curved lines. When the top is rotated at an appropriate speed, colors are observed. (From Helmholtz, 1962, vol. II, p. 449.)*

insensitive, is far more rapid than dark adaptation. Under most conditions, complete light adaptation occurs within a few minutes (Wald & A. Clark, 1937). These data do not fit common experience, for when a person leaves a darkened theater and enters a brightly lighted street, he is often not fully comfortable in the bright light for some time. Most measures of dark adaptation indicate that around 30 minutes is required for the eye to reach its maximum sensitivity.

Figure 8–29 shows a typical function of dark adaptation, with intensity plotted along the ordinate. Each point represents the RL for white light as a function of time. Two functions are shown: one represents the administration of white light to the entire eye, and the other represents the administration of red light to the fovea. The similarity between these two functions during the first 7 minutes of adaptation indicates that the initial stage of dark adaptation is a function of the cones. After 10 minutes, the cones have adapted, and no improvement is noted, but the rods continue to adapt until maximum sensitivity is reached after approximately 30 minutes. The break in the function appears to be a result of the need of rhodopsin to reach a critical point in the bleaching process before the rods are able to respond at all.

FIGURE 8-29: *Two sets of data showing adaptation. The open circles show the effect of the presentation of white light to the entire eye. Two stages of adaptation are apparent: the first may be noted as a gradually decelerating curve to approximately seven minutes of time in the dark, and the second, which shows a similar form, lasts from seven minutes until the longest test sessions used. The filled circles show data from the presentation of a nearly monochromatic light of between 660 and 700 mμ which illuminated a portion of the retina assumed to have no rods. Thus, this adaptation rate is for cones. These data show that both rods and cones adapt. (From Hecht, 1934, p. 727.)*

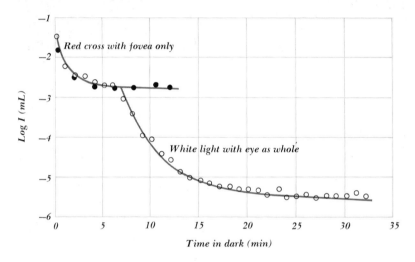

The relationship between the intensity of the stimulus during the preadaptation period and the adaptation function is shown in Figure 8–30. Five different 2-minute preadaptation intensities were used, ranging from 263 to 400,000 Trolands. Thresholds during the adaptation session were measured by violet light. The break noted in Figure 8–30 appears in all the functions, but it occurs later in the adaptation period following the more intense preadaptation stimulus.

Although the wavelength of the preadaptation session is important, its effect is most easily observed when red wavelengths are employed, since, as we know from the discussion of duplicity theory, the rods are fairly insensitive to those wavelengths. Figure 8–31 shows the relation between adaptation to white light and adaptation to red light. The data indicate that for adaptation to red light to be as rapid as adaptation to white light, thirty times as much red light would be needed. The practical implications of this finding are commonly applied to military and industrial situations where the problems of dark adaptation are a consideration. In addition, as we shall note in Chapter 9, dark-adaptation functions for color-blind persons produce characteristic differences which provide useful information for color theorists. The dark-adaptation function may change dramatically in persons who have a vitamin A deficiency, since this vitamin is known to be important in the regeneration process of rhodopsin. Such persons will show a dark-adaptation curve only in cone adaptation, and not in rod adaptation. Such people

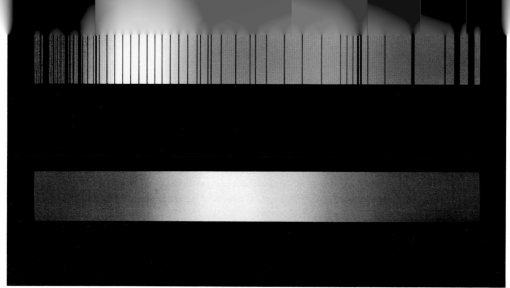

FIGURE 8–10

FIGURE 8–32

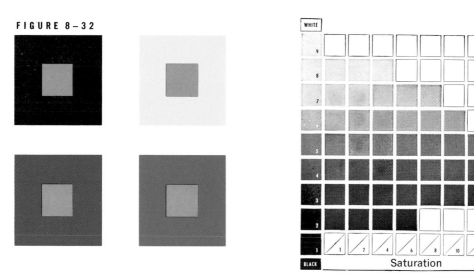

FIGURE 9–3

FIGURE 8–10: *The spectrum as seen by photopic and scoptopic vision. Note the areas of maximal sensitivity for the two sets of receptors. (From Helmholtz, 1962, vol. II, plate II.)*

FIGURE 8–32: *Examples of simultaneous contrast. Does the gray in the center of each pattern appear equally light in all the patterns? Actually, the gray squares are all of the same saturation: they appear different because of the presence of the surrounding color—red, yellow, blue, or green.*

FIGURE 9–3: *An example of the Munsell system of identifying colors. Colors are identified in terms of hue, chroma (saturation), and value (brightness). The brightness continuum is along the vertical axis, and saturation is along the abscissa. Each hue is represented on a separate page. (From Munsell, 1929.)*

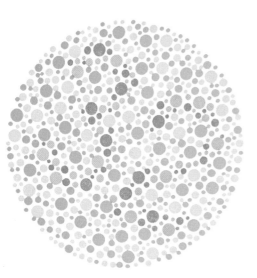

FIGURE 9-6

FIGURE 9-10

FIGURE 9-6: *An example of a commonly used test of color deficiency. The eye with normal color vision sees the number 32. (This plate has been reproduced with permission of the author of the Dvorine Pseudo-Isochromatic Plates, published by the Scientific Publishing Co., Baltimore, Md.)*

FIGURE 9-10: *Colored objects in the top picture were photographed with the special dual camera which appears at left. Here the two ground-glass screens of the camera are left uncovered to show that one image is photographed through a green filter and the other through a red filter. The images are photographed on ordinary black-and-white film; then black-and-white positive transparencies are made from the negatives. In the bottom photograph the "red" transparency is projected through a red filter and the "green" without a filter. When the two images are superimposed on the screen at the right, they reproduce the objects in a full range of colors. (E. H. Land, 1959, pp. 85, 87. Photographs courtesy William Vandivert.)*

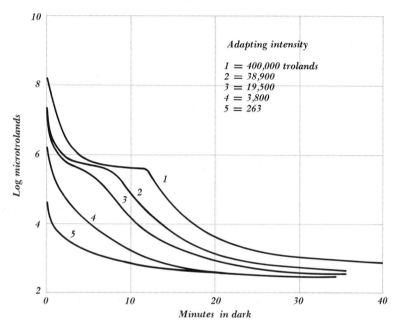

FIGURE 8–30: *The effect of light adaptation on the course of dark adaptation. Following different amounts of preadaptation stimulation, dark-adaptation thresholds were taken under violet light. (Modified from Hecht, Haig, & Chase, 1937, p. 837.)*

are "night-blind," for even with a lengthy adaptation period, their visual acuity at night or under low illumination is severely impaired.

Hues are apparently inhibited with continuing stimulation. If a hue is presented and maintained, the observer eventually reports that the light has become more gray, or desaturated. Hues which are naturally desaturated, such as yellow, are more prone to inhibition than other hues. White light does not show inhibition, however, and this fact is useful in industrial situations where workmen or buyers should be prevented from perceiving changes in hues.

Aftereffects: Aftereffects of the visual system are such a large part of common experience that many kinds of literature are replete with

FIGURE 8–31: *The difference between adaptation to red light and adaptation to white light. (Hecht & Hsia, 1945, p. 265.)*

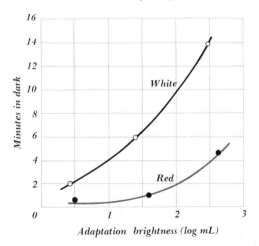

comments about them. Both Ptolemy and Aristotle mentioned them. We noted in Chapter 6 that a simple demonstration of visual aftereffects may be performed merely by having the subject fixate upon a color patch and then look away. Similarly, a glance at the sun or other bright light is sufficient to yield the sensation of a myriad of colors. Such sensations have been employed often in a manner suggesting the occult (Boring, 1942).

Aftereffects are conveniently, if not precisely, divided into two kinds: those based on the principles of *simultaneous contrast* and those based on the principles of *successive contrast*. The latter refers to aftereffects in which there is a temporal lag between the original stimulus and the sensation of the aftereffect. Fixating upon a color patch and looking away is one procedure for producing successive contrast. Simultaneous contrast refers to situations in which the subject perceives the aftereffect while still observing the original stimulus. Figure 8–32 (following p. 242) indicates two attributes of simultaneous contrast. Although all the gray squares are of the same reflectance, the color of the surrounding square influences perception so that the grays appear to vary in brightness.

Brightness is not the only aspect of vision which may be altered by simultaneous contrast. If you look at the center of each square, you will begin to note that the gray appears to be tinged with the color which is the complement of the surrounding square. For example, a greenish tinge may be seen at the line separating the red from the gray square. The laws of chromatic simultaneous contrast and brightness simultaneous contrast are important to the theorist; they are also of practical concern in decorating and fabric design. If you look at a green dress with gray prints, you will receive the sensation that the prints are surrounded by red. The laws are also useful in industrial situations where clear perception is important and maximum contrast is desirable. Studies have indicated that yellow on black produces the least contrast and hence the greatest acuity; such findings are reflected in the contemporary use of these colors in road signs.

There is some evidence that contrast is not necessarily a retinal process. Largely, this evidence is based upon the demonstration that perceptual organization, whether learned or innate, determines the sensations of contrast phenomena. If so, it would appear that contrast is a product of the higher centers of the brain, rather than of the retina alone.

Although many aftereffects are temporal, a spatial aftereffect may be demonstrated when a light is moved so that different areas of the retina are stimulated. Bidwell (1898) reported that the effect of moving a light across the retina was the sensation of pale blue semicircles which appear to float; hence, the term *Bidwell's ghosts* for this phenomenon. When the process is examined closely, it may be seen that the sensations are similar to those reported in successive contrast: the first sensation is of a color similar to the original, and the succeeding sensation is one of either the complement of the original color or, more commonly, a bluish hue.

The *figural aftereffect* has received a considerable amount of attention. J. J. Gibson made the first extensive reports of work on this phenomenon in 1933, but it appears that the name was applied by Köhler (Köhler & Dinnerstein, 1947; Köhler & Emery, 1947). If a subject views a curved line for a period of time and then shifts his attention to a straight line, the straight line appears to curve in the *opposite* direction from the original curved line. Thus, the figural aftereffect is a phenomenon of space perception, although it appears to fit the definition of an aftereffect. In general practice, the term refers to aftereffects which alter the size, shape, or location of an object, and such phenomena have been noted in sensory systems other than vision. Figure 8–33 shows a commonly used figural aftereffect design by Köhler and Wallach (1944). The legend describes the procedure for achieving the effect. Köhler and Wallach explain figural aftereffects as a function of the brain. Their work in support of their "electrical field theory" (which postulates a relationship between the brain and its *satiation* from the perception of an object) provided considerable information on the mechanisms of the effect. Osgood and Heyer (1952) interpreted similar data in terms of neurophysiology.

Acuity: Acuity is the analogue of CFF, for while the latter is concerned with the temporal problem of when two stimuli appear different or the same, acuity is concerned with the spatial problem of when two stimuli appear as one or as separate. Since assessments of visual acuity are important for many kinds of activities and for the selection of personnel for various tasks, a large number of theoretical and practical data have been accumulated on the topic. As is true of CFF, acuity is influenced by such variables as wavelength, intensity, and the area of the retina under stimulation.

No single technique appears to provide complete data regarding acuity (Rabideau, 1955), and for this reason, an oculist or psychophysicist interested in assessing acuity will use several measures. Possibly the most commonly used measure is the *Snellen chart.* A reduced example of such a chart is shown in Figure 8–34. It consists of letters of varying sizes which the subject is required to name. Since the subject's head is held still, so that the letters subtend a known visual angle of the retina, his performance may be compared with the average performance of other individuals. If a person is able to perceive an object which subtends 1 minute of the visual angle from a given distance, he is said to have 20/20 vision. If the same object cannot be seen unless it subtends 2 minutes of the visual angle, he is said to have 20/40 vision.

The letters on the Snellen chart are correlated in height with the distance from which they may be perceived by the average eye. Thus, the largest letter can just be discriminated by the average eye at 200 feet; the next row of letters is half as high and can be discriminated at 100 feet; and so on. If you can stand 20 feet from the chart and see the row

FIGURE 8–33: *A test for figural aftereffects. Using one eye, stare at the x in the inspection figure at the left for about one minute while holding the page about 20 inches from the eye. (Cover the test figure while looking at the inspection figure.) Then transfer the fixation to the x in the text figure at the right. The two T rectangles to the left of the x in the test group will appear to be farther apart than they are, while the two rectangles to the right will appear closer together. (Woodworth & Schlosberg, 1954, p. 424, after Köhler & Wallach, 1944.)*

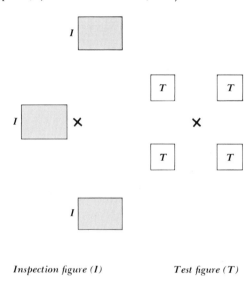

Inspection figure (I)   *Test figure (T)*

of letters which can be perceived by the average person at 20 feet, you have 20/20 vision. If you have to stand 10 feet from the chart to see the same letters, you have 10/20 vision, which indicates a decrement from the perceptual acuity of the average or normal eye. In practice, numbers below 20 are not used. Hence, if visual acuity is 10/20, it is multiplied to 20/40, and if it is 20/10, it becomes 40/20. Although this system has the advantage of simplicity, it does not yield information about the norm which was used, unless all measurements are made with the same standard.

One difficulty with the use of letters as a

FIGURE 8-34: *A Snellen chart (reduced in size) which is used to test visual acuity. (From Chapanis, Garner, & C. T. Morgan, 1949, p. 94.)*

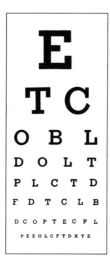

test of acuity is that their shapes provide information which aids discrimination. Two classes of tests of visual acuity exist. *Minimum visible* tasks are those in which the subject is required to indicate when an object is visible or identifiable. Other tests are called *minimum separable,* since they require the subject to indicate when two objects are separated. For example, two lines, circles, stars, or other common objects may be used. Acuity is measured in terms of the separation required before the two figures are perceived in different locations. *Grating,* which consists of a series of parallel and alternating black and white lines, is also used. When the lines are viewed from a distance, the sensation is one of uniform gray, but at the appropriate distance the difference between the lines is identifiable. *Vernier* acuity tests use two continuous juxtaposed lines which may be horizontal or vertical. The subject is asked to state whether the two lines are continuous or offset. Acuity is measured by the amount of change necessary for the two lines to be perceived as offset. *Landolt rings,* which consist of an unclosed circle similar to the letter C, may be used as a minimal separable task, for the subject is required to indicate when the circle is closed and when it is not. In addition, the subject may be asked to indicate the part of the circle on which the gap appears.

Although the various measures of acuity do not always produce results which correlate perfectly with one another, the similarity in results is sufficient that measures of acuity as a function of wavelength, retinal locus, and other factors do not differ appreciably as a function of the test used. The relation between two measures of acuity may be noted in Figure 8-35, in which both C rings and grating were used under different intensities of illumination. The functions are similar in shape, even though they cross one another. Figure 8-36 shows the relationship between intensity of illumination and acuity (measured in terms of the visual angle). Once again, the function appears to have two factors, one representing the acuity of the cones and the other representing the acuity of the rods. The break between the functions disappears if red light is used, as we would expect from our knowledge of the functioning of the rods.

In regard to visual acuity, the relationship between duration and the area of the retina stimulated is similar to that found in other visual measures of the RL; i.e., there is a reciprocal relationship between intensity and duration and between intensity and the area stimulated. As Osgood points out, the fact that illumination affects acuity is a curious paradox (1953, p. 164). Since the photoreceptors are fixed within the retina and since in studies of acuity the stimulus is held constant as it impinges upon the retina, how can differences in intensity be reported?

The immense amount of research on visual psychophysics and related phenomena has provided us with a good many questions regarding how the visual system operates. However, a second body of knowledge, regarding the processes of color vision and perceptual organization, also exists, and an understanding of the visual system with respect to behavior requires that both areas be considered. Accordingly we shall now consider these other aspects of visual sensation.

SOURCES

Two excellent discussions of the role of perception in philosophy are by Boring (1942) and Hochberg (in Postman, 1962). Chapter 3 in Boring discusses the development of the study of visual phenomena and indicates the nature of the contributions of Newton, Young, Goethe, and Helmholtz, among others. The section on Nativism and Empiricism, which appears in chap. 7, is germane to the problem of whether perception is learned, innate, or both. Hochberg covers much of the same ground, but includes a section on more recent evidence bearing on the nativism-empiricism controversy. See also Flieandt (1966).

Anatomy, Physiology, and the Stimulus: A large number of works is devoted, in whole or in part, to this topic. Polyak's (1957) monumental study of the vertebrate visual system is a definitive work, although the general reader will find it difficult. The student who wishes to pursue a particular topic will do well to start with Polyak's comments and make use of the superior bibliography he provides. Somewhere in the 1,390 pages of this work the student will find seasoned reports on the status of every aspect of the vertebrate eye. The illustrations are magnificent and are useful even without the accompanying text.

Walls (1942) has also published a tome on the vertebrate eye, and although it is not so detailed as Polyak, it serves the general reader very well. Much has happened in the field of vision since 1942, however, and the reader would, no doubt, want to consult recent sources in addition. Davson (1962) presents detailed information on particular aspects of the eye, such as vegetative physiology, intraocular pressure, the vitreous body, the lens, the cornea, and the sclera, and comparative anatomy. Pirenne's (1948) short but concise work

FIGURE 8–35: *The relationship between two measures of visual acuity, grating and C rings. Log acuity is plotted against log Trolands. The two functions are similar, although the C yields estimates of better acuity at higher intensities and grating yields estimates of better acuity at lower intensities. Modified from Shlaer, 1937, p. 183.)*

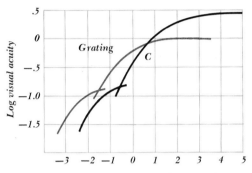

Retinal illumination (log trolands)

FIGURE 8–36: *Relationship between background intensity and the visual angle subtended by the thickness of a wire when it is revolved against the background. The different functions for rod and for cone vision may be noted. (Modified from Hecht & Mintz, 1939, p. 597.)*

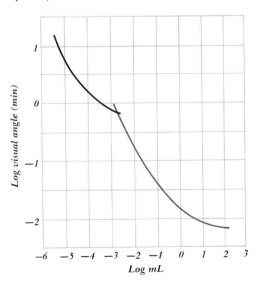

is an appropriate source for the student whose understanding of vision is at the level of the present text. It is written clearly and has the advantage of providing interesting and often curious aspects of vision, for the writer has the talent of making even the most difficult concepts lucid.

Students interested in rhodopsin and the general study of the pigments of the photoreceptors will find Dartnall (1957) very useful. Judd's chapter in Stevens (1951) reviews the problems of identifying and correlating the stimuli for vision. A general source is edited by Graham (1965a). Especially relevant to the subject we are concerned with here are the chapters on light as a stimulus (Riggs, 1965a), anatomy and physiology (J. L. Brown, 1965a), basic terms and methods (Graham, 1965b), electrophysiology (Riggs, 1965b), photochemistry (Hsia, 1965), thresholds (N. R. Bartlett, 1965), acuity (Riggs, 1965c), and afterimages (J. L. Brown, 1965b).

Evolution of the Eye: The sources listed above are useful, although Polyak's account (1957) is the most thorough. Buddenbrock (1953; 1958), in a factual and entertaining work and provides some useful information, but the lack of detailed references is a barrier to the student, regardless of the student's level of sophistication.

Electrical Evidence of Visual Activity: This is a remarkably difficult area, and few sources useful to the general reader are available. Granit's work (1955) is a classic and is "must" reading for anyone interested in pursuing this area. Much has been published since 1955, but it is found mostly in widely scattered journals. Some sections of Rosenblith (1961) are also helpful. Probably the most useful information is found in the chapters on perception, color vision, and vision which are reported yearly in the *Annual Review of Psychology* and in Riggs (1965b).

Thresholds: The variety of possible threshold measurements requires that the student in-

terested in information on a particular type of threshold consult *Psychological Abstracts* for appropriate references. The continuing development of apparatus useful for threshold determinations means that new results are reported at a rapid pace. However, most texts which review visual threshold have used older measurements, largely because a group of apparently accurate measures are available for the major threshold determinations. Bartley (1951) and N. R. Bartlett (1965) cover the area well. Although Bartley is less concerned with thresholds than with other phenomena, he provides information regarding some useful determinations not reported in the present text.

Threshold determinations which are of concern to industrial and military problems are reviewed in Chapanis, Garner, and C. T. Morgan (1949); this work may be recommended highly to persons interested in the application of thresholds to practical problems. Dember (1960) discusses thresholds in terms of "detection" and "recognition" and summarizes the contributions of visual psychophysics to this important area. Luce (1963) and Luce and Galanter (1963) also discuss this use of psychophysics on a more detailed level. Geldard (1953) presents threshold data with his usual clarity.

The student interested in the development of visual thresholds is well advised to consult Helmholtz (1910; 1962) if for no other advantage than the respect he will gain for the precise measurements made in older psychophysics. In addition, Helmholtz's speculations about the underlying causes of the determinations provide fruitful ideas for research.

The review by Mueller (1961) indicates the variety of contemporary threshold problems under consideration. Osgood (1953) presents a more detailed account of thresholds than that of the present text, and his ability to integrate material from various sources renders the text most useful to the student. Postman and Egan (1949) is a useful reference. Troland's (1929a) classic work on psychophysics makes useful reading, not only because of its historical interest, but because of the writer's speculations on the nature of visual processes as reflected in thresholds at an intermediate level. Woodworth and Schlosberg (1954) provide their usual competent account and include an enormous amount of information on other aspects of vision, such as eye movements and depth perception, not readily available in other literature. Mueller's (1965) short text on vision also reviews threshold determinations.

Other Phenomena: For information on perimetry, both Wenger, F. N. Jones, and M. H. Jones (1956) and Geldard (1953) are very satisfactory. The student interested in the development of perimetry will want to read Titchener (1901a; 1901b; 1905a; 1905b), a classic source. Indeed, the student of experimental psychology would do well to read all of Titchener, if only to show that Boring may no longer say that "probably no one has ever read either of the Instructor's Manuals through" (Boring, 1950, p. 413). Flicker fusion is usually treated as a threshold measure, and the references cited above under Thresholds are appropriate. The topic has been subjected

to a variety of reviews in the literature, and the student should consult *Psychological Abstracts* to locate the review appropriate to his interests.

Similarly, adaptation is often treated as a threshold measure, and the sources cited above are useful. Dartnall (1957), in a work concerned with the nature of the visual pigments, includes information on adaptation as it concerns changes in pigmentation, although his work is difficult for the general reader.

Aftereffects have been treated by all the writers mentioned under Thresholds. Boring (1942) gives a brief summary of the historical development of the study of afterimages. As is true of illusions, the data regarding aftereffects are best located by reference to journal articles, and the *Psychological Abstracts* serves as the best source for locating appropriate articles.

Acuity is also a threshold measure. Chapanis, Garner, and C. T. Morgan (1949) provide information on industrial interest in acuity. Riggs (1965c) reviews the techniques and findings of studies of visual acuity.

CHAPTER NINE

VISION: PERCEPTION

Few scientific problems have persisted with such tenacity as that of explaining how some organisms are able to perceive color. The number of different approaches to the problem testifies to the confusion that surrounds attempts to understand it. The first reasonable theory of color vision developed from Newton's work, which showed that color is dependent upon the refrangibleness of light. Newton's assumption that there are but seven basic colors upon which all other hues are dependent is incomplete. It is a curious, but understandable, observation that when the nature of the stimulus is not well understood, as is the case now in both taste and smell and as it was with light in Newton's time, theorists attempt to specify a limited number of primary stimuli. However, when the nature of the stimulus becomes understood more completely, theories which attempted to reduce the stimuli to a small number of basic types are usually found to be inappropriate. What Newton failed to note was that infinite degrees of refraction are available. By the early nineteenth century, color theorists (e.g., T. Young, 1807) were aware of the infinite number of stimuli.

This realization led to an outbreak of theoretical speculations throughout the remainder of the century. Probably the most influential of these theories was Helmholtz's, based on Young's earlier work, that the presence of three discrete types of nerve endings in the retina—one for each of the supposedly three primary colors—could produce most of the phenomena associated with color vision. When the structure of retinal structures became known through the work of von Kries in 1894, theorists designated the cones as the color receptors.

The postulation of three types of cones was able to account for some important phenomena, such as afterimages. Although three primary colors are sufficient in certain cases, the primaries do not correspond with the "psychological" primaries. Since there appear to be four invariant psychological primaries (Chapter 8), at least from results of perimeter studies, it was not long before a theorist suggested six "primaries" (actually, three pairs of complementary primaries) to correspond with the psychological perception of color (Hering, 1874; 1920).

Neither Helmholtz's nor Hering's formulations explained the various forms of color blindness, and this was a critical failure. If there are two, or three, or four basic types of cones which correspond to the primary perceptions, then deficiencies in color vision should be predictable from the basic types. For reasons which we shall discuss, they are not predictable. This state of affairs produced another theory (Ladd-Franklin, 1893), which adopted an evolutionary approach to color vision. Although it handled some forms of color blindness better than previous theories, it failed to account reasonably for some of the phenomena that the previous theories had explained. Accordingly, at the turn of the twentieth century, several theories of color vision flourished side by side, each showing success in interpreting some areas but failure in interpreting others. This situation is not unusual, for in contemporary work we have two major theories of the transmission of light and at least two theories of geometry; each is successful with some phenomena, but not with others.

It was not until the last part of the nineteenth century that Fechner's approach to psychophysics led to the determination of visual thresholds. Once applied, however, the basic formulations regarding the various DLs for the qualities of visual stimuli were found rapidly, thus presenting theories with a large number of useful data not available previously. The determinations of the DLs made the assumption of three or four primaries appear untenable. The fact that one could have 128 DLs for hue and still have three or four primary colors was interpreted as contradictory, for it led to the question whether a nonprimary color, such as orange, was also a primary color or was composed of other primaries. At the turn of the century, many of

the best minds in psychology devoted their attention to this apparent problem. As Boring puts it (1942, p. 130), "Is an orange from homogeneous light a psychological mixture of red and yellow, or is it psychologically as elementary as red and yellow?" The great psychologists lined up on one side or the other, and as often occurs in divided houses, the problem merely disappeared from view without settlement. To contemporary psychology, the problem smacks of intrepid philosophy, but to the generation just beginning to find the complexity of color vision, it provided a choice battleground, although any victory would have been Pyrrhic.

Identifying the Stimulus for Color Vision: In their attempts to identify stimuli, such as color, which are composed of several distinct aspects, such as wavelength, homogeneity, and saturation, investigators sometimes resort to geometric patterns which show the dimensionality of the relationships between the aspects. One such attempt is the color spindle in Figure 9–1. Brightness is represented along the vertical axis, with white at the top and black at the base. Saturation is represented horizontally; the most saturated hues are placed on the circumference, with hues decreasing in saturation toward the center. The center is gray. The *spindle* appears to assume that each hue is in some sense primary, because each has its private location on the horizontal axis. Opponents of the spindle system contend that although orange is similar to red and yellow (and is between them on the spindle), yellow does not resemble green and orange or green and red, even though it is between them on the spindle. This problem permeates many aspects of color theory, for continuities along physical dimensions of light do not correspond with continuities along dimensions of color perception.

Nickerson and Newhall (1943) have proposed a *color solid* which reflects the number of DLs for hue, saturation, and brightness. This approach does not result in a simple geometric form, as may be noted from Figure

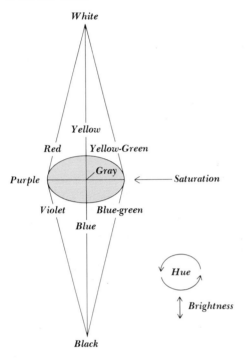

dardize color, since standardization has obvious practical use in industrial situations. With standardization, a homeowner could order the exact color of paint he desired without having to specify the stimulus in terms of its wavelength, homogeneity, and saturation. The problem is made more acute by the fact that people do not agree on the naming of colors: what is "aqua" to one person is merely "blue-green" to another. Manufacturers do not help the situation when they invent new names for old colors for advertising value. The Inter-Society Color Council recommends the use of nine basic hues (e.g., brown, pink, olive, red) coupled with 11 descriptions of intensity (weak, deep) among other descriptive aspects. This results in 312 distinct colors. Although the number is far from the 7,500,00 calculated by Nickerson and Newhall (1943), it is sufficient for most uses.

The generally accepted method for describing color involves the use of a *chromaticity diagram.* If one selects colors of three wavelengths, one short, one long, and one in the middle range, all other colors may be produced from appropriate mixing of these primaries. Since violet or blue, green, and red are of the appropriate wavelengths, these primaries may be used (W. D. Wright, 1928–1929; 1946). The red which we see looks yellowish, for a true red is beyond the human spectrum. If we add blue to the nonspectral red, it appears red to the human eye. There is some contemporary evidence that colors of only two wavelengths, one long and one short, may also produce all other colors under given conditions, but it is not certain that this phenomenon is a product of color mixing (E. H. Land, 1959). The amount of each of the three primary wavelengths needed to produce all colors is shown in Figure 9–4. The results are similar to those proposed by Helmholtz in discussing Young's three-color theory, for each primary contributes most around its own wavelength. Violet, at 460 mμ, is the major component until colors of around 530 mμ are produced: at this point, green (at 530 mμ) becomes the dominant contributor to the mixture. As the

9–2. From this approach, these writers conclude that the number of distinguishable colors is around 7,500,000.

Another technique in common use is the Munsell system, which is based on matching. Colors are specified in terms of their *hue, chroma* (saturation), and *value* (brightness). Patches are arranged as shown in Figure 9–3 (following p. 242), with the black-white brightness continuum along the vertical axis and saturation along the horizontal axis. Each hue is represented on a separate page. The chart permits one to specify, for example, a red with a value of 6 and a chroma of 8. Independent observers may then match the specified color from the description.

Various attempts have been made to stan-

oranges and reds are approached, red (650 mμ) becomes the major contributor.

These data permit the specification of any color in terms of the relative contribution of each of the primaries. For example, we may specify a hue as

$$0.04R + 0.32G + 0.64B$$

where

$R = $ **red**
$G = $ **green**
$B = $ **blue**

When mixed in the specified proportions, this would yield a bluish green. In 1931, the International Commission on Illumination (ICI) established a chromaticity diagram which standardized the proportions by utilizing data based on color matching of a number of subjects. The results collected from these subjects provided a makeup of what the ICI termed the *standard observer,* and these data were compiled to produce the ICI chromaticity diagram shown in Figure 9–5. The ordinate is the amount of the green coefficient, while the abscissa is the amount of the red component. Since the addition of the coefficients of the three primaries must equal unity, it is necessary to stipulate only two of them; the third (in this case, the violet component) is determined if the other two are known. The light line, forming a cone, indicates the resulting hues at complete saturation, with violet (400 mμ) at the base of the cone and red (700 mμ) to its right.

The C at the center of the plot represents a standard illumination. The distance between C and the hue curve indicates saturation. Consider the sample color marked by A in the diagram. Its saturation is around 33 percent, since it is one-third of the way between C and the hue curve. Its dominant wavelength is around 550 mμ, since a straight line drawn through A from C to the hue curve ends at that point. It may be noted that the diagram yields information about two of the basic com-

FIGURE 9–2: *The Nickerson-Newhall color solid. The models are arranged to show each change in hue, saturation, and brightness. Unlike the color spindle, the color solid reflects the irregularity of these measures. (From Nickerson & Newhall, 1943, p. 420.)*

ponents of color—wavelength and saturation—while holding illumination constant. If the location of C is altered, plots for different illuminations may be developed. The diagram permits investigators to specify colors accurately. Accordingly, it has many uses in the study of color perception.

Although these systems are useful in permitting the specification of colors, they tell us

FIGURE 9-4: *The three (trichromatic) coordinates for two subjects, using frequencies of 460, 530, and 650 mμ. (From W. D. Wright, 1928–1929, p. 148.)*

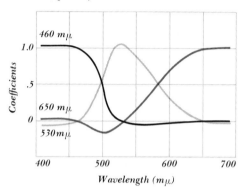

little, if anything, of how color is perceived. Specifying the stimulus is, however, fundamental to understanding the visual system. Data from perimeter studies, reports on afterimages, data from color mixing, and results of color mixture and electrophysiology all raise questions and contribute information about the process of color vision.

Color Mixture: In everyday color perception, a pure hue is rarely observed. Although we might agree that a wall was green, spectrometric evaluation would indicate that a variety of wavelengths was present. Accordingly, the way in which colors mix is an important aspect of the data on color vision. Color mixture is of two kinds: In *subtractive color mixing,* the resulting color is what remains after some wavelengths have been absorbed. For example, colored filters absorb wavelengths in given areas, and the resultant color is the remainder (hence the term *subtractive*). Subtractive mixing is used in the mixing of paints. In *additive color mixing,* the original wavelengths are added to produce a different color. When colors are projected upon a screen without the use of filters, the resultant color is a product of the original colors. The laws which predict the resultant color are quite different, depending upon whether an additive or a subtractive process is used. The artist, who uses pigments in his work, follows a different set of color-mixing laws from the individual who mixes colors by projecting them on a screen. The artist mixes all colors together, and black results. In additive color mixing, however, the mixture of all colors produces white. Indeed, the artist's conception of primary colors is based on the priciples of subtractive color mixing, and therefore his primaries are different from those which are noted in the psychological study of color perception. The artist does not consider green a primary color, since it may be mixed from yellow and blue. Yellow is considered a primary color. The reverse is true of the study of color perception, where green is regarded as a primary and yellow is not, since it is the additive mixture of red and green.

Development of Color Vision: Research on color perception in animals is packed with technical difficulties, and many of the data reported are unacceptable. The conditioned response technique (Chapters 4 and 13) is used often to measure whether an organism is capable of discriminating one wavelength from another. If such experiments are to be interpretable, both saturation and brightness must be held constant to be certain that the animal is not judging on the basis of characteristics of the stimulus other than wavelength. This is a difficult technical feat in itself, for it requires elaborate measuring equipment. A second problem is that a given animal may be sensitive to a few hues, but not to all those perceived by human beings. Some animals are sensitive to hues which are not perceivable by human beings.

In addition to the use of the conditioned response as a measure of hue discrimination, a second technique for measuring color perception in animals is based on the observation that if various hues are projected over an area inhabited by many animals, the animals tend to congregate in regions associated with particular colors. This suggests that certain wavelengths are aversive. The technique is useful

FIGURE 9-5: *The ICI chromaticity diagram. The diagram permits investigators to specify colors. (Modified from Judd, 1951, p. 843.)*

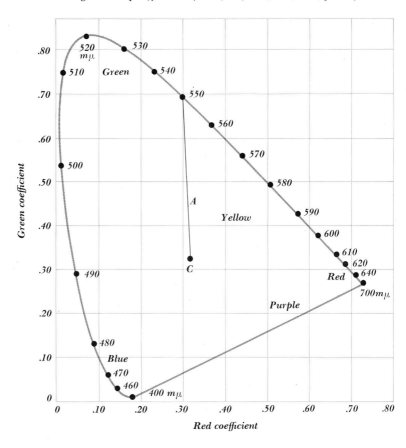

for studies of aquatic animals, where different hues may be projected into different areas of the aquarium and a count may be made of the number of animals selecting each region. Both AL and DL measures may be made with this technique, for appropriate statistical techniques indicate the probability of animals' congregating as a function of changes in the stimulus.

Acceptable contemporary evidence indicates that color vision may be demonstrated in several forms of fish and insects. It is quite common among birds, including fowls, although some birds that are primarily nocturnal in be-

havior do not show evidence of color vision. As was true of the development of audition, it appears that we are indebted primarily to fish for the initial development of a visual system.

Among the mammals, color vision is noted only in primates, although there is scattered evidence that some mammals may be sensitive to wavelengths within a small range. Among subhuman primates, color vision appears to vary as a function of the nocturnal or diurnal habits of the species. The higher subhuman primates, such as the chimpanzee and squirrel monkey, appear to have color vision almost identical to that of human beings. Color vision is also widespread among insects, and as Pickford has noted (1951, p. 30), with the exception of man and the subhuman primates, animals who have color vision have a skin or fur that is generally highly colored with a variety of hues, but animals which are color-blind are of nondescriptive hues, such as black and white.

Several theories have used a phylogenetic approach, assuming that the human system of color vision arose from several distinct evolutions of color perception. There is, for example, ample evidence that color defectiveness is a racial characteristic. The incidence of color deficiency among whites in Great Britain ranges between 5.3 and 9.4 percent (P. E. Vernon & Strakar, 1943), although American Indians show an incidence of less than 2 percent (Clements, 1930). Some workers have reported that the incidence of color defects is lower in children than in adults and have suggested that color deficiency may develop as a function of age. It seems more likely, however, that these results arise from the difficulties involved in testing for color discrimination in children. Since the tests cannot require verbal reports from very young children, the same problems of measurement arise which occur with the testing of animals. One may measure choices and get an approximation of psychophysical measurements by presenting a child with blocks of different hues. Staples (1932) reports that by this method the primary colors (including yellow) can be differentiated by children of fifteen months. Studies in which all attributes of the physical stimulus have been controlled are notably few. However, even with accurate measurement it is difficult to be certain whether the results show color perception or indicate only the maturation of motor responses, such as the physical ability to point to stimuli.

Deficiencies in Color Vision: Human beings with deficiencies in color vision have been a source of useful data in the understanding of color vision. More appropriately, deficiencies in color vision have provided the theorist with one of his most troublesome sources of information. A theory of color vision makes assumptions about the workings of the photoreceptor and other parts of the visual system. Often, these assumptions appear reasonable in terms of many of the known phenomena of color vision but become untenable with the additional observations of color deficiency. The various types of color deficiency make it difficult, but not impossible, to assume the presence of three or four discrete types of photoreceptors.

Color deficiency, or color blindness, as it is erroneously called, is of considerable concern in many practical situations. School children are sometimes inappropriately remonstrated for inattention or error in tasks which involve color vision, for sometimes the child is unable to make the desired discrimination of color. Similarly, color deficiency is undesirable in many industrial positions. Since persons with minor deficiencies may learn to discriminate colors as a function of brightness or saturation, it is not at all uncommon for a deficiency to escape notice until a test of color deficiency is administered. Indeed, it is difficult to know where the normal variation in hue sensitivity ends and where variation becomes pathological. There are, no doubt, reasonably wide variations in so-called normal color vision.

The first general test of color deficiency was reported by Baron John W. S. Rayleigh in 1881. He prepared an apparatus for projecting and mixing red and green, and asked persons to match the mixture to a yellow provided separately. The process of mixing red and green in order to produce yellow is known as the *Rayleigh equation*. Rayleigh asked several persons to perform the matching experiment, and he noted, fortuitously, since so few subjects were used and many were members of his family, that five persons far exceeded the others in their need to add green to the red-green mixture in order to match the yellow. Devices which measure color deficiency by requiring the subject to match spectral lights are called *anomaloscopes*. Various other devices have been developed for testing color deficiency. Most techniques are based on the principle that a color-deficient person will be unable to match hues. This matching procedure is used in Holmgren's wool test, in which the subject is provided with a set of wool skeins which he is required to match to a standard skein. The procedure is similar to Rayleigh's in that a matching process is required of the subject. Less commonly used tests based on the same principle are the Edridge-Green bead test (1891; 1920) and Nagel's card test. The reliability between these methods, and between tests which used matching and other tests, is not so high as to make the tests interchangeable (E. Murray, 1943).

Another series of tests requires the subject to distinguish hues rather than to match them. Ordinarily, the subject is shown a page of small colored spots, similar to that shown in Figure 9–6 (following p. 242). The spots are so arranged that a subject with normal vision is able to distinguish a letter or number. A person with a deficiency sees either no number or a different number. On other plates, the normal eye does not distinguish the figure, but the color-deficient eye does. Brightness is controlled by mixing the brightness of the spots randomly. Probably the most commonly used tests of this type are the *Ishihara pseudoisochromatic plates* (Ishihara, 1920) and the *Dvorine pseudoisochromatic plates* (Dvorine, 1953).

Pickford (1951) has devised a test based upon the principles of psychophysics and the Rayleigh equation. Known as the *four-corner test*, it uses red, green, yellow, and blue filters. The subject is able to alter the projectors so that he may change the intensity and amount of filtering. The procedure consists of presenting the subject with two distinct spots, such as red and green. The subject is asked to adjust the spots until they appear to be of equal brightness. When he perceives the spots to be of equal brightness, he is asked if there is a difference in the colors. If a difference is perceived, the spots are made nearer in hue, following standard psychophysical techniques, until the subject cannot report a difference. This basic procedure is repeated with yellow and blue. Some advantages of the test are that it permits some control of brightness and more precise measurements than other methods.

Several kinds of color vision are distinguishable: *monochromatism* (total color deficiency), *dichromatism, normal trichromatism* (three-color perception, or normal vision) and *anomalous trichromatism* (almost normal vision, although the anomalous trichromat requires different amounts of the primaries to match than the normal trichromat does). The terms refer to the number of colors which an observer needs to mix in order to match all the hues that he sees. The trichromat can match the full spectrum with only three sources: red, green, and blue. Table 9–A shows the basic forms of color vision, including the normal hue distinctions made, the luminosity peak in the visibility spectrum, the neutral points, and the name for the condition. The neutral point is the wavelength selected to match white. This is an impossible task for the normal or anomalous trichromat. The dichromat, however, is able to match the white. Under trichromatism are listed the normal eye, as well as eyes which are red-weak *(protanomaly)*, green-weak *(deuteranomaly)*, and yellow-blue–weak *(tritanomaly)*. In protanopes, the upper wavelengths are not visible, and greens appear gray. In deuteranopes, the visible spectrum is the same as for the normal, but red and/or green is confused with gray. Most color deficiencies are of these types. Dichromats show normal vision of illumination (light-dark), since the rods do not affect color blindness. The protanopes and deuteranopes lack red-green perception, although the yellow-blue combination is intact. Tritanopes and *tetartanopes* have red-green perception, but lack yellow-blue. The latter two types are rare.

Monochromats have no color perception at all. They depend entirely upon differences in intensity to make discriminations. Two types exist: those without functioning rods and

TABLE 9-A: *The Basic Forms of Color Vision.*
The three main types of color deficiency are given,
with the discriminations made in each category,
the wavelength of the maximum luminosity function, and the wavelength of the neutral point.
(Adapted from Judd, 1943, p. 297.)

Designation of type according to number of components	Discriminations possible by the type	Wavelength of the maximum of luminosity function, $m\mu$	Wavelength of neutral points in spectrum, $m\mu$
Trichromatism (normal)	Light-dark Yellow-blue Red-green	555	None
Anomalous trichromatism	Light-dark Yellow-blue Red-green (weak)	540	None
	Light-dark Yellow-blue Red-green (weak)	560	None
	Light-dark Red-green Yellow-blue (weak)	560	None
Dichromatism	Light-dark Yellow-blue	540	493
	Light-dark Yellow-blue	560	497
	Light-dark Red-green	560	572
	Light-dark Red-green	560	470 580
Monochromatism	Light-dark	510	All
	Light-dark	560	All
	Light-dark	540	All

those without functioning cones. The former
see all wavelengths as gray, and the latter see
all colors as one hue. Although monochromats
are very rare, Geldard (1933) has reported extensive work with a monochromat. The subject read and worked under low illumination,
since normal illumination was painful. The
visibility curve of the monochromat corre-

sponded almost exactly with the normal rod visibility curve. The implication is that the cones were either absent or totally nonfunctioning, since the monochromat appeared to function with only rod vision. Table 9–B shows the frequency of the various types of color deficiency (Judd, 1943). It should be noted, however, that the analysis of frequency depends to some extent on the type of test which is used. Pickford (1951) summarizes results of studies of the frequency of color deficiency in various ethnic groups.

Although it is difficult to know what a person with color deficiency "sees," introspective judgments from such persons are useful. Both protanopes and deuteranopes confuse red and green: either hue is perceived as a yellowish gray. In addition to differences in the TL, the brightest hue for the protanope is shifted around 15 mμ from the brightest hue for the normal eye. The protanope will perceive a maroon sock as black and a red-brick building as brownish yellow. Most color-deficient individuals are quite adept at identifying colors properly by their name, even though it is clear that they do not see the same hue as the normal eye. The few cases in which an individual is color-blind in one eye but not in the other provide some of the most useful information on the perception of color by the color-deficient (e.g., Sloan & Wollach, 1948; Graham, Hsia, & E. Berger, 1955; Graham & Hsia, 1954). It is clear, however, that the various types of color deficiency argue against a tristimulus theory of color vision. In order to identify color deficiency, at least four colors are needed —the three usual primaries plus yellow—and this corresponds neatly with the fact that yellow is regarded as a psychological primary.

The genetic determinants of color deficiency are reasonably well understood, at least in regard to red-green blindness. Red-green blindness is a sex-linked characteristic, like baldness, hemophilia, and other traits. Since the trait is sex-linked, the mother is the usual carrier, and she passes the trait to her male children but

TABLE 9–B: *The Frequency of Various Types of Color Deficiencies.*
(From Judd, 1943, p. 300.)

Designation by number of components	Nontheoretical designation (Kries)	Percentage of population that have these visual systems	
		Male	**Female**
Anomalous trichromatism	Protanomaly	1.0	0.02
	Deuteranomaly	4.9	0.38
	Tritanomaly	0.0001	0.0000
		5.90	0.40
Dichromatism	Protanopia	1.0	0.02
	Deuteranopia	1.1	0.01
	Tritanopia	0.0001	0.0000
	Tetartanopia	0.0001	0.0000
		2.10	0.03
Monochromatism	Total color blindness	0.003	0.002
Abnormal systems		8.0	0.43
Normal systems		92.0	99.57

not to the female children. Figure 9–7 shows hypothetical patterns of protanopia and deuteranopia.

Theories: It is difficult to determine whether theories of color vision have contributed to the literature by indicating appropriate lines of experimental attack or whether they have hampered the eventual understanding of color vision by providing a myriad of conflicting

FIGURE 9–7: *Hypothetical patterns of sex-linked protanopia and deuteranopia. X and Y indicate genes; a dot under X or Y indicates a recessive defective gene; filled circles represent color-blind persons; hatched circles represent carriers; open circles represent persons with normal vision. For example, at the top of the figure, the combination of a color-blind male with a recessive gene and a female without the recessive gene would produce three male children who were not color-blind and did not carry the gene and one male who was color-blind and carried the gene. Among the females, both are carriers of the recessive gene. (From Hsia & Graham, 1965, p. 507.)*

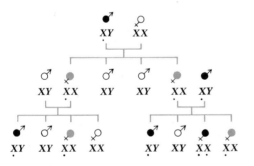

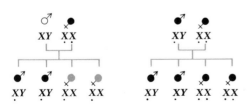

viewpoints. The task of a theory of color vision is to suggest how the visual system is able to function in such a way that all the phenomena associated with color vision are predictable. Accordingly, speculation has centered on the role of the photoreceptors in the retina. The result is that, superficially, color theories differ primarily in regard to the number of functions postulated for the photoreceptors. The issue, however, is not so much whether one or more types of receptors are involved but whether we can deduce from the data on color vision what the characteristics of the photoreceptors must be.

Basically, theories of color vision have adopted a tristimulus approach similar to that of Young and Helmholtz in which three primary colors are presumed to interact in order to produce intermediate hues, or they have emphasized an anabolic-catabolic reaction in which the opposing process of the receptors is responsible for intermediate mixtures (Hering, 1874; 1878; 1920). There are ample variations on these themes. Table 9–C indicates some of the characteristics of some major interpretations of color vision. The second column indicates the anatomical location of the major source of color vision according to the theory. The third column indicates the fundamental, or primary, colors assumed by each theory. When two colors are hyphenated (e.g., red-green), it is implied that a single type of photoreceptor is antagonistic, so that both hues are produced from the same source. The final column indicates the area in which each theory has experienced most difficulty. It may be noted readily that most theories experience some difficulty in interpreting certain types of color deficiency and that every theorist finds it necessary to postulate the presence of more than one kind of photoreceptor.

The Young-Helmholtz postulations were based originally on data from color-mixing experiments which indicated that all colors could be produced from a small number of fundamental or primary colors. For tristimulus theories, color is a function of the contribution of each of the three primaries. Bright-

TABLE 9-C: *Description of Some Major Theories of Color Vision.*
The second column indicates the location of the major source of color vision according to each theory, the third column shows the fundamental colors assumed by each theory, and the last column lists the major limitation of each theory. (Adapted from Graham, 1959, pp. 220–221.)

Name	Anatomical location	Fundamental colors	Chief limitation
Young, three components	Cone pigments	Red Green Violet	Fails to explain dichromatic vision as intended
Helmholtz, three components	Cone response	Red Green Violet	Fails to explain color perception of protanopes and deuteranopes
Dominator-modulator, late König	Cone response	Red Green Violet	Fails to explain color perception of protanopes and deuteranopes
Ladd-Franklin, three components, early König	Cone response	Red Green Blue	Implies that the blue function has a negative luminosity for normal subjects and deuteranopes, positive for protanopes
Hering, opponent colors	Optic nerve	Red-green White-black Yellow-blue	Fails to give an account of protanopia and tritanopia

ness too is dependent upon the mixture of the brightness of each of the primary components. There is no a priori reason, however, to forbid spectral wavelengths other than red, green, and blue from serving as the primaries. Indeed, some color phenomena suggest the choice of primaries other than red, green, and blue.

Theorists have also postulated some types of anabolic-catabolic reaction of the photoreceptors. The classic theory of color vision based on the assumption that the postulation of antagonistic photoreceptors could explain color perception is that of Karl Ewald Hering (1834–1918). The original data which prompted the theory were more psychological in nature than the Young-Helmholtz data. Hering believed four psychological primaries were needed, and he postulated three pairs of antagonistic receptors, red-green, blue-yellow, and black-white. It was assumed that each of these pairs could be "dissimilated" or "assimilated" by some physiological or chemical process. White, red, and yellow were dissimilative, in that they were produced through a decrease in the efficiency of the receptor; the remaining members of each pair were assimilative. Figure 9–8 shows this relationship schematically. If the red-green component were fully assimilated, green would be perceived. In this way, each of the primaries could be produced, while intermediate hues resulted from the dissimilation process in more than a single receptor. For example, if red were dissimilated and blue were assimilated, violet would result. Similarly, the schematic diagram indicates why we do not perceive "yellow-blues" or "red-greens." Given these assumptions, the data

FIGURE 9-8: *Schematic representation of Hering's three-component theory. (From Hurvich & Jameson, 1957, p. 385.)*

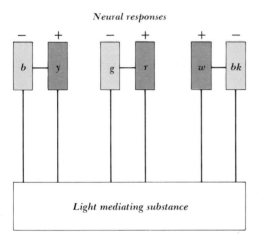

Neural responses

Light mediating substance

from color-mixing experiments could be explained, and one could predict the perception which would result from simultaneous contrast and changes in hue as a function of brightness by assuming that the addition of white (under strong stimulation) produced the sensation of an increase in the intensity of the stimulus.

The fact that the various kinds of color deficiency require more than a simple tristimulus theory has prompted separate theories for color deficiency. These theories, which often account for color deficiency, but do not always explain normal color functions satisfactorily, are of two general types: In the first, color deficiency is interpreted as a loss in the efficiency of one of the fundamentals. This idea, postulated by T. Young (1807), is an extension of tristimulus theory. Unfortunately, a loss in efficiency of each of the fundamentals is not sufficient to predict the various forms of color deficiency. The second type of theory has suggested that deficiency in producing dichromatic vision is a result of the amalgamation of two fundamentals, such as red and green. This idea was apparently suggested by Helmholtz

(see Ladd-Franklin, 1893), even though he did not pursue the possibility.

One theory which attempted to account for varieties of color deficiency was formulated by König (1886), who postulated from color-mixing data that the fundamentals formed a *Grundempfindungen* (perceptual foundation). König assumed that protanopes lacked the red fundamental and deuteranopes lacked the green fundamental. A second theory was proposed formally by Leber (1869) and Fick (1879). It assumed that, probably through evolutionary development, the red and green receptors failed to become differentiated. Deuteranopia will result if in addition to some receptors that are sensitive to red there are some which are similar to both the red and green receptors but in which the red is more sensitive. If the green component of the red-green receptor dominates, then red will be perceived as green, and protanopia results. This approach accounts for the discrepancy in the extent of the RL for hue among protanopes and deuteranopes, and the difference in threshold for the two deficiencies is taken as evidence in favor of the *Leber-Fick–type fundamentals*. The Leber-Fick suggestion also accounts more readily for differences in brightness perception in the color deficiency.

Additional data on the luminosity curve for dichromats have been collected by Graham and Hsia (1954; 1958). These data indicate a luminosity loss for the protanopes in the red region and for the deuteranopes in the green and blue regions. One of the more intriguing questions raised by the work of Graham and his collaborators (Graham, Sperling, Hsia, & Coulson, 1961) comes from work with a unilateral color-blind person; i.e., she was color-blind in one eye but not in the other. By projected hues, it was determined that she perceived only two hues in the color-blind eye. She matched wavelengths longer than her neutral point by a yellow (as perceived by the normal eye) and the wavelengths shorter than the neutral point by a blue. As Graham points out (1959, p. 228), this type of data raises a neat problem for tristimulus theory: how can the deuteranope see yellow, since a sensitivity to green is lost?

Quantification of Hering's system has been undertaken with considerable success by Hurvich and Jameson (see particularly 1955, 1957; Jameson & Hurvich, 1955; and Graham's review of their work, 1959). Their purpose has been to measure the components and functions of the three proposed pairs of receptors. In general, they have met with success in providing measurements which are consistent with the Hering approach and which handle information from color mixing, brightness, saturation, hue, and the Bezold-Brücke effect. Graham (1959, p. 264) suggests that some modification of the theory is necessary to account for some phenomena of color deficiency.

In recent years many of the problems posed by earlier theories have been solved. Two major findings are (1) evidence that the eye does use three types of cone pigments in its ability to produce the spectrum of colors and (2) the discovery of ways in which certain cells in the visual system operate in response to stimulation. It appears that the Young-Helmholtz theory of three receptors is essentially correct but that Young was incorrect in postulating three separate pathways to the brain, one for each of the colors. Moreover, it appears that the brain plays an important role in the perception of color.

The discovery that the eye uses three cone pigments is based on advances in technology as well as clever experimentation. By 1938, the individual optic nerve fibers in the retina of the frog had been isolated by H. K. Hartline. A year later, several investigators discovered the technique of recording directly from a cell by using microelectrodes. In 1957, Svaetichin, working with the retina of fish, found several distinct kinds of electrical activity. The activity was recorded in response to brief light flashes and was characterized by an uncommonly slow change in potential. These are called *S-potentials,* and they are of two kinds: The first kind is a large, negative resting potential which occurs in the presence of light. A second kind appears as a negative potential that becomes more strongly negative when the light used as a stimulus is in the blue range of the spectrum. When longer wavelengths are used as stimuli, the extent of the electric response diminishes until a point is reached at which stimulation produces a positive potential. The availability of the "on" response and the "off" response in responses to flashes of light has been shown to appear in the retina of a number of animals. We may note that this finding is not antithetical to the suggestion by Hering, discussed earlier, of complementary pairs of color receptors.

MacNichol (1958; 1964) has succeeded in the complex task of analyzing the absorption spectrum of the visual pigment in cones. This is a difficult procedure, because both the size of the cone and the amount of pigment within a cone is small. Investigators in several laboratories were able to record the absorption spectrum in higher mammals, including primates and man. All investigators report three distinct curves, although data differ in regard to the points at which the curves peak. Figure 9–9, for example, shows spectral sensitivity curves developed by MacNichol (1964). The peak sensitivities are blue-violet (447 mμ), green (540 mμ), and yellow (577 mμ). This last curve, the yellow system, actually projects far enough into the red portion of the spectrum to provide for the sensation of red. It should be noted that this procedure provides data on the pigment of the individual cone studied and not necessarily of all similar pigments. These three curves are similar, of course, to those found in psychophysical studies. Thus, it is likely that there are three kinds of cones, differing in regard to the nature of the pigmentation of each.

The combination of the work of Svaetichin, MacNichol, Wald, and Hurvich and Jameson has led to the *stage theory* of color vision. In essence, this approach suggests that color vision is more than a single process. It is consistent with the formulations of Young and Helmholtz in regard to the presence of three types of receptors in the retina and with the suggestions of Hering regarding complemen-

FIGURE 9–9: *Color vision in primates is mediated by three cone pigments responsible for sensing light in the blue, green, and red portions of the spectrum. Their spectral-sensitivity curves are shown here: 447 mμ (blue-violet), 540 (green), and 577 (yellow). Although the "red" receptor peaks in the yellow, it extends far enough into the red to sense red well. Symbols accompanying curves trace shapes of hypothetical pigments with peaks at each wavelength. (From Three-pigment Color Vision, by E. F. MacNichol, Jr. Reprinted with permission. Copyright 1964 by Scientific American, Inc. All rights reserved.)*

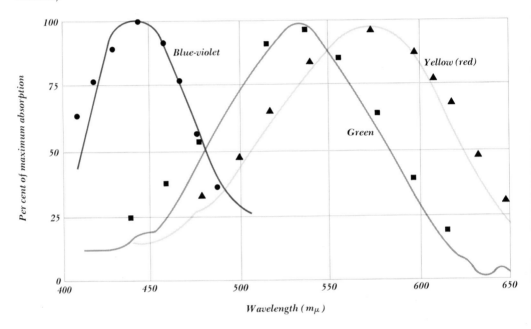

tary opposites at the optic nerve and the remainder of the brain. Thus, the photochemical pigments of the cones operate on the trichromatic system suggested 150 years ago by Young and reintroduced by Helmholtz, but the visual nervous system operates on the complementary pair system, as first suggested by Hering. The availability of different potentials for different wavelengths, as noted by Svaetichin (1957) links the two processes.

There is much to be learned about the process of color vision. Nevertheless, it is apparent that the speculations and psychophysical measurements made in the last century and the present one has reached fruition through the ingenuity of experimenters and the development of equipment, such as electron microscopes, which makes the verification of theory possible at the physiological level.

Land Effect: The Land effect is one of the most controversial discoveries to appear in color vision theory in recent years. At first glance, the effect appears to be damaging to tristimulus theories, but the influence of the effect on theories of color vision is indeterminate. By mixing *two* bands of wavelengths, one long and one short, E. H. Land (1959) produced accurate full-color images on a screen. Two identical photographs of the same scene are taken through two filters, commonly a red and a green filter (a "long" and a "short" wavelength, respectively). This results in two black-and-white photographs which differ in shading. By superimposing the photographs on a screen through the long (red) and short (green or nothing) filters, the original full-colored images are produced. Effectively, it appears that two bands of wavelengths can act as primary colors which produce nearly all the other colors in a scene. However, the blue in these photographs is very weak and often absent.

Figure 9–10 (following p. 242) shows how the Land effect is demonstrated. Any two wavelengths, not necessarily complementary, can act as "primary" colors. The only requirement is that the long-wavelength photograph be illuminated by the longer-band filter and the short-wavelength by the short-band filter. One wavelength band may be the entire spectrum; e.g., white light (from the projector) may be used as a short record or a long record, depending on the wavelength of the other stimulus. There must be a minimum difference between the long and short wavelengths; however, this minimum difference usually is very small. The so-called Land color effect is quite predictable in determining what minimum difference is necessary between wavelengths and what colors will be available from their combination. Figure 9–11 shows the limits on color obtainable with different pairs of wavelengths. Note that in the larger area all colors except purple are obtainable. The shaded area along the diagonal indicates the region in which wavelengths are too similar to produce any kind of color.

Land is careful not to suggest a theory for the phenomenon, since there is no available physiological evidence that can readily account for it. He suggests that the colors arise from an interplay of longer and shorter wavelengths over the entire scene and speculates that the eye somehow establishes a balance point and divides the wavelengths into short and long. Conventional theories of color vision and color mixing do not have difficulty explaining the extra colors which appear in the projected image. Walls (1960) accounts for the extra colors in terms of simultaneous contrast; i.e., the hue induced at a certain spot on the screen is complementary to whatever light in the surround is doing the inducing. If this explanation is correct, then it would appear to account for the blues which sometimes appear in the images and which could not be predicted by the laws of color mixing. The phenomenon still remains unclear, but Land's demonstrations have provided the stimulus for determining both the nature and the location of the phenomenon (Geschwind & Segal, 1960).

One interesting implication of the effect is that our visible spectrum need not be so large as it is for the production of color. It is possible that if the visible spectrum were reduced from its present range of approximately 300 $m\mu$ to between 50 and 100 $m\mu$, most of the colors would still be perceivable provided the range were in the middle portion of the spectrum.

SOME PHENOMENA OF VISUAL PERCEPTION

In many ways the eye is a miniature organism: what it senses is a function of its physiological limitations but also a function of such variables as learning (for it may be shown that what we perceive is to some extent determined by past experiences), motivation (for the eye sometimes sees what it "wants" to see), attention (for one can measure eye movements as well as electric discharges from both the retina and the cortex), and other factors as well. Further, whatever may be discovered about the functioning of the eye has immense practical and theoretical significance.

The composition of an accurate definition of *perception* which subsumes the variety of topics associated with the concept is exceedingly difficult. Bartley (1958, pp. 8–12) reviews many definitions and concludes that most writers have merely assumed that the concept

FIGURE 9–11: *The limits of color obtainable with different pairs of wavelengths. Long and short wavelengths are shown along the axes. Within the light gray area, the wavelengths are too close for color to appear. (From E. H. Land, 1959, p. 89. Reprinted with permission. Copyright 1959 by Scientific American, Inc. All rights reserved.)*

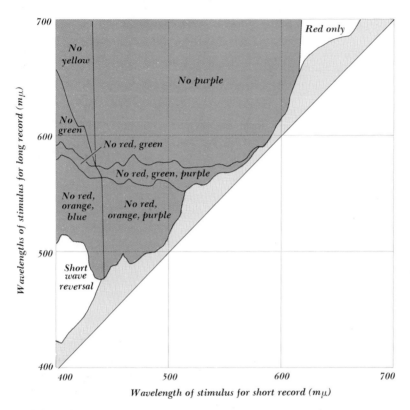

is so general as to defy formal definition. Generally, however, perception refers to the content of sensory experience. The distinction between perception and *sensation* is commonly made (Boring, 1942) on the assumption that sensation refers to the action by a receptor when it is stimulated and perception refers to the meaning given the sensation. Sensation is the mosaic of stimulated receptors within the retina. Perception is the cognition or supposition added to the mosaic; e.g., "I see a man swimming."

The laws and phenomena of visual percep-

tion may be grouped around several fairly independent areas of research interest, although there is some overlap. First, we shall consider some general laws which each of the groups has produced, and in the next sections we shall consider the effects of learning, motivation, and attention, among other variables, upon visual perception.

Figure and Ground: One of the fundamental observations regarding visual perception is that human beings, and probably many animals, perceive *objects* distinctly from their *surround*. Indeed, this ability is so fundamental that our speech reflects the *figure-ground* relationship of our perception. We speak of words being *on* a page, of tractors *in* the field, and of a group of men *beside* a crowd. The objects—the words, the tractors, and the group—are the *figure*, and the remainder of the perception is the *ground*. There is some evidence that these relationships are learned through experience, but there is probably more evidence that they are an innate characteristic of the nervous system. A blob of ink on a white paper is perceived as different from the surrounding whiteness, even though we have never experienced the particular shape of the ink blob before. That we have not previously experienced it means that it has less content or meaning than familiar objects, even though we are easily able to distinguish it from its surround. This fact is one assumption underlying *projective tests* of personality, such as the Rorschach inkblot test, in which the subject is presented with ambiguous blobs and required to describe his perception of them. In order to ascribe content, such as "a bear" or "a policeman," to the blob, the subject must supply his own meaning to the perception of the figure. Since perceptions are a function of what he has experienced, among other variables, the choice of content indicates something about the perceptual selection which the individual uses.

Several demonstrations of the figure-ground relationship are shown in Figure 9–12. Part *A* shows a reversible figure-ground. If the white area is seen as the figure, an object similar to a vase, or urn, is noted. If the black is seen as the figure, two heads, facing each other, are perceived. Once you have seen both figures, you have little trouble shifting your attention from one perception to the other. Part *B* shows the wife–mother-in-law figure-ground. Either you may see an old woman with her chin embedded in her coat, or you may see a young woman with her face in profile. The nose of the old woman is the cheek and jaw of the young woman. Part *C* shows the rat-psychologist. The ears of the rat form the eye-

FIGURE 9–12: *Four examples of the figure-ground phenomenon. (A) The reversible figure-ground. The picture may be seen either as a vase or as two profiles, but not as both at once. (C. T. Morgan, 1961, p. 312.) (B) An ambiguous figure, in which one may see either the "wife" or the "mother-in-law." Put less dogmatically, one may see a young woman with her face turned away and to the left or an old woman with her chin embedded in a heavy coat. From Boring, 1930, p. 444.) (C) A rat-psychologist. One may see a white rat with its tail wrapped around itself, or one may see a "psychologist" with either large eyes or glasses which are also the ears of the rat. (From* An Introduction to the Principles of Psychology, *by B. R. Bugelski, copyright 1960 by Holt, Rinehart and Winston, Inc.) (D) A royalist print from the French Revolution. Imbedded in the scene are the heads of Louis XVI, Marie Antoinette, the dauphin, and a fourth profile of an unknown person. (From Gombrich, 1961, p. 64; copyright, 1961, The Curtis Publishing Company.)*

Fig. 9-12A

Fig. 9-12B

Fig. 9-12C

glasses of the "psychologist." The fact that you may shift your attention from one perception to the other is not easily explicable, and it is one of several phenomena which are not incorporated easily into contemporary psychological theory. The figure-ground relationship is not new; it was used by eighteenth-century French royalists to circulate profiles of Louis XVI, Marie Antoinette, the dauphin, and one

other hapless but nameless figure of the revolution. Part *D* shows the print which was circulated among royalist supporters. Although the figure is ostensibly a vase, the careful observer will note four profiles hidden at the base of the vase and within the twigs.

Constancy: If I am watching a football game and I turn my head to the side (or even if I stand on my head), the figures of the players are still identifiable as people, even though the image on the retina may be "upside down." I have no difficulty in recognizing familiar objects even when their position on the retina is changed drastically. This is one example of a second observation regarding visual phenomena—that objects maintain perceptual stability through transformations of varying types. Indeed, the constancy of the object, even though the retinal image has changed, is an important characteristic of the intelligent behavior of human beings and animals. A dog who could recognize bones only when they were horizontal and viewed from the side would miss many pleasures, and if I only recognized coins when they were perceived as perfectly circular, I would have considerable difficulty dealing with the necessities of everyday life.

The principle of constancy, like that of the figure-ground relationship, is a part of our language, and for that reason we are rarely aware of the lies that we tell about the world. What is the shape of a window? Most likely, you will say that it is rectangular. But so far as the retinal image is concerned, it is rectangular only if you are looking at it directly. Actually, if you are at all off center, the image on the retina is that of a trapezoid. Clearly, language would become cumbersome if we spoke honestly of the actual size and shape of objects as projected on the retina, rather than about their "real" size and shape.

Size constancy refers to the fact that in spite of the difference between the actual size of the retinal image of a tree 200 feet away and a similar tree only 10 feet away, we still are aware that both objects are trees and that they are of the same height. The different size of the image on the retina does not lead us to say that the trees are of different heights, but it does give us information about the distance of the trees. If cues to distance and to size are eliminated and if the subject matter of the image is one with which we are not familiar, the actual size of the image on the retina tells us nothing. Figure 9–13 shows an unfamiliar scene. Is it a small sand hill, or is it a crater on the moon? Without additional cues we cannot tell. It is for that reason that geologists and other persons who photograph unfamiliar scenes usually include in the photograph an object of known size, such as a person or a pencil.

Our inferences regarding size constancy can be demonstrated by reversing the expected relationship artificially. Figure 9–14A shows a demonstration using three sets of cards. Most observers agree that the card on the left in the left and center sets is closest. In addition, the king appears to be much larger than the plain card, although the six appears to be closer. The second portion of the figure (B) shows how this demonstration is arranged. In the second and third sets, portions of the cards have been cut out. The cards are actually of the same size in the third set. The lower left-hand corner of the king has been cut away so that the plain card appears to cover it. The result is that the six appears to be the nearest card but much smaller than the king, even though the king and six are the same size and the king is the nearest card.

This demonstration includes two additional indications of constancy: first, the unequal brightness of the cards (note the second set particularly) gives some cues to depth; second, the artificial interposition of the cards confuses our estimate of depth. We assume that faraway objects are blocked by near objects. Accordingly, we see the six as nearer than the plain card, since the plain card is partially blocked by the six. This is a false assumption in this demonstration. Since the assumed distance of an object influences our perception of its size *(size constancy)*, our perception is

Fig. 9-12 D

that the six must be small. Certainly, our perceptual process is logical, but, as with any other logical system, if the major premise is wrong, the remaining deductions may appear logical, but they are in error.

The texture of the image is also an important cue to both size and distance perception. Just as fabrics have different textures detectable by our cutaneous sense, so visually perceived scenes have different textures. J. J. Gibson (1950) has emphasized the role of texture in distance and in other kinds of perception. For example, examine Figure 9–15A. Which of the rectangles is nearer? Now examine Figure 9.15B. It becomes clear that the texture of the bricklike cloth has given us an uncalled-for belief in depth, and rather than discard our well-learned inferences regarding depth, we have made an untenable assumption about the distance of the blocks.

Brightness and color perception are two additional areas in which constancy is important. If I take a white shirt and decrease the brightness, the shirt still appears white. A black shirt under high illumination still appears black, even though the amount of brightness may be more than that on the white shirt. There is,

FIGURE 9-13: *The usefulness of size constancy. Is this a small hill or a crater on the moon? Without additional cues, we cannot tell. (From J. J. Gibson, 1950, p. 97.)*

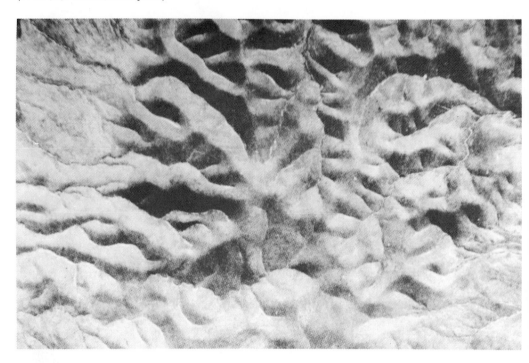

however, a sound physical reason for brightness constancy, A white shirt reflects almost all the light impinging upon it, while a black shirt reflects very little. The percentage of the total light which is reflected is known as *albedo*. Albedo does not change as a function of illumination, for if the albedo of a white shirt is 80 percent in sunlight, it is still 80 percent indoors even under low illumination. Accordingly, although the absolute amount of brightness may be altered, the albedo function remains constant. Brightness constancy is a function of the albedo function, and it is independent of absolute brightness, or luminance, which will vary in proportion to the amount of illumination.

Hue constancy is often confused with brightness constancy, for shifts in illumination will alter the apparent hue of a stimulus.

However, if a common scene, such as a row of houses, is projected on a yellow screen, white houses are still perceived as white, even though the white hues have been mixed with yellow (Cramer, 1923). It is interesting to note that if the projection is out of focus so that cues to depth, size, and so on, are reduced, the house is seen as yellowish. If a blue light is projected on a yellow screen, the perception of gray results. However, if the blue is identified with a common object, such as a dress, it is identified as blue. These demonstrations argue strongly for the presence of hue constancy as another characteristic of the constancy effect.

Constancy effects have been studied in a variety of animals and in children. Much of this research is prompted by the question whether constancy is learned through the prior

FIGURE 9–14: *The role of interposition. Figure A shows the demonstration as it appears to the viewer. Figure B shows the actual arrangement of the cards. (From Your Eyes Do Deceive You, Life, Jan. 16, 1950, p. 61.)*

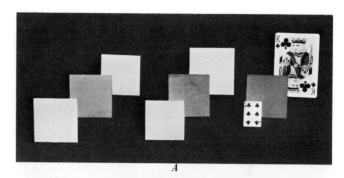

A

B

FIGURE 9–15: *A demonstration of the effect of the dependence of distance on the nature of the background. In figure A, which of the rectangles is nearer? Now consider figure B, which shows the arrangement from a different perspective. (From J. J. Gibson, 1950, p. 179.)*

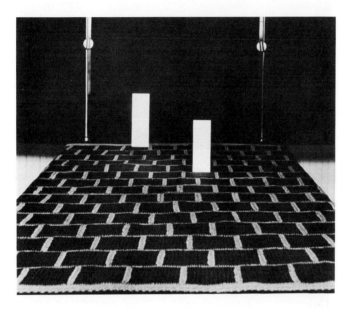

A

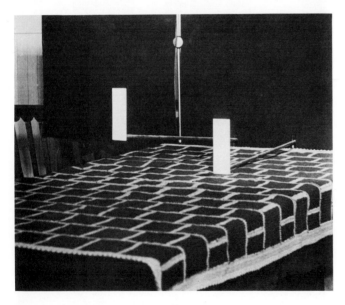

B

experiences of the organism or whether there is some type of innate neurological pattern. It is reasonable to assume that such cues as interposition in depth perception are learned, even though it is difficult to show the development of interposition as a function of age. If it is learned, children would show progressively more reliance upon interposition as a cue as they become older. Experimental attempts to examine the development of various cues to vision are equivocal because of the inherent difficulties in requiring children to make motor responses to visual stimuli. It is never clear whether it is the motor response which is learned or the perception.

Examinations of brightness constancy in a variety of animals, including monkeys, chickens, and fish, indicate that these animals operate according to the constancy principle as much as, or more than, human beings. Investigations of constancy phenomena in animals, however, have the same problems as investigations of other visual phenomena, since an immense amount of control over the various aspects of the visual stimulus is necessary to produce unequivocal results.

Depth and Space Perception: When the reflected light of objects and scenes falls upon the retina, the image is two-dimensional. In contradiction, the perceptual world in which we live is three-dimensional. The scenes which we observe are not flat, two-dimensional scenes such as those in a newspaper photograph: they have depth. How does an image which is two-dimensional on the retina become translated into the perception of three-dimensional space?

The fact that a large number of fairly obvious principles are known to contribute to depth perception has obscured the fact that no single theory of depth perception exists which adequately handles all the phenomena that occur. The principles which "explain" depth perception are commonly called *cues,* since it is assumed that the organism is provided with a cue (but not the complete story) for distance and depth. By describing these effects as cues, we verbally sidestep the problem of whether depth perception is learned or innate. However, the question is similar in nature to those concerning the innateness of hue discrimination, the constancy effects, and other perceptual characteristics.

The most commonly cited cue to depth perception is related to the fact that many organisms have two eyes. Since the two retinas are located at different points in space, the sensation on each is slightly different from that on the other. According to this principle, when the two perceptions are compounded to form the perception of the scene, the difference in overlap between the two images provides us with the sensation of depth. This principle is known as *retinal disparity,* and it is similar to the principle which assumes that sound localization occurs because each ear occupies a different position in space.

The eye provides several cues to depth perception in addition to retinal disparity. The accommodation and convergence processes of the lens yield kinesthetic cues of distance if the objects are sufficiently close. The philosopher George Berkeley (1685–1753; 1709) initially pointed out this use in his studies of perception.

The concept of *parallax* is important for understanding the visual scene observed by the organism, and it has special relevance to depth perception. In general, parallax refers to changes in the scene as a result of the observer's movement. For example, the fact that the two retinas are located in different places permits me to see "around" objects by moving my head. This accounts for retinal disparity, which is an example of *binocular parallax,* for both eyes are utilized. *Monocular parallax* refers to only one eye: if I close one eye and move my head, I am able to perceive slightly different views of the scene; these different views give me some indications of depth. If I am in motion, *motion parallax* occurs: if I am riding on a train and looking out of the window, all the objects in the scene move across my visual field, but the nearer an object is to me, the more rapidly it passes; if a line of poles follows the course of the train and if there is a forest half a mile in the distance, the poles appear to move more rapidly than the trees, even though they may be spaced equally far apart.

Interposition is one common cue for depth perception. We noted, when discussing the constancy effects, that objects which are interposed between other objects are judged to be nearer. This cue is very valuable for the determination of the relative distance between objects, even though, as we noted in Figure 9–14, it may be misleading. The *shading* of stimuli also furnishes cues for depth perception. A practical application of this cue is notable in art, where shading is used to give the illusion of depth on a two-dimensional canvas. Since shadow patterns produce a relief effect, they influence the *texture* of a scene, and, as we have noted, overall texture appears to be an important component of depth perception.

J. J. Gibson (1950) has discussed the role of texture gradient in depth perception. If a scene includes a notable pattern (for example, if one is looking upward at a brick building or if one is looking at acres of fallow ground), the texture becomes finer with increased distance. In the scene of the brick building, the bricks at the top of the building appear more tightly packed and hence more dense than those at eye level. The density, or the texture, gradient gives information about depth.

The observation that straight lines appear to join in the distance is another cue to depth perception *(linear perspective)*. In addition, the presence of an object of known size in the scene aids the sensation of depth. If I am standing next to a person who is 6 feet tall and if he moves to a position 200 feet from me, not only am I able to recognize him (even though his apparent size has changed), but also I am able to judge how distant he is. This effect, *apparent size,* is used in driving, in which we estimate the distance of an approaching car by its size. If the car is actually of an unusually small size, we often err in predicting its distance. Many drivers have noted difficulties in parallel parking when a small car or motorcycle is at the curb, since

the previous estimates of depth were made with larger cars and perspective must be re-learned for use with smaller cars.

All these cues to distance are useful for the perception of depth. Although there is some overlap in their roles, each has a slightly different function. Some cues tell us the relative depth relation between two objects but do not help us to estimate the actual distance. It is quite difficult to study one cue without the interfering presence of other cues. The difficulty in the isolation of a single cue is no doubt largely responsible for the fact that the cues have not been brought together to form a unified theory of depth perception. Put another way, the influence of each cue is not well documented, even though there can be no question that each contributes something to the possibility of depth perception under some circumstances.

As is true of the constancy effects, the cues to depth perception may be artificially varied in order to provide some striking demonstrations. One of the most convincing is the Ames distorted-room demonstration. Although the demonstration employs cues other than those associated with depth perception, the major effect is created by inferences made regarding depth. The Ames room is badly distorted in construction: three of the walls are actually trapezoidal. However, because of the use of shading, size constancy, and interpositon, the room appears to be rectangular to the observer, particularly if he views it monocularly. Once the room is accepted as a rectangle, several distortions appear to the observer. Faces or hands placed in the window appear to be badly distorted, and a ball appears to roll uphill. These effects occur because the subject assumes the room to be normal in shape. Figure 9–16 shows the viewer's perception of the room and the outside of the structure. As Ames (1955, p. 53) explains the effect:

You make this particular assumption because your past experiences of acting to satisfy your needs and effect your purposes compounded and recorded horizontal rectangular surfaces, i.e.,

FIGURE 9–16: *The Ames room from two viewpoints. Photograph A shows the distorted room from the outside. Note the shapes of the walls and windows. Photograph B shows the inside of the room from the subject's viewpoint. (From Ittelson, 1952, p. 44.)*

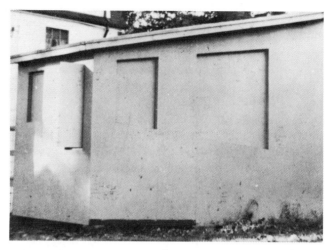

A

B

floors, with binocular stimulus patterns having specifically characterized disparity patterns related to those successful actions. When, on a later occasion, objective events give rise to similar disparity patterns, you assume you are looking at a horizontal rectangular surface instead of one of the innumerable other surfaces that could give rise to the same binocular disparity patterns.

Like many other aspects of perception, the question of how much learning and innate patterning contribute to depth perception is unanswered. Consider Figure 9–17, which shows three patterns. Most observes agree that *A* is two-dimensional: it does not yield the perception of depth. Both *B* and *C* do give the impression of depth, however, even though it seems unlikely that either comes about from previously learned experiences regarding this form. (It may be argued that form *B* uses interposition and that we all have experience with block shapes, but this argument does not appear to hold for the form shown in *C*.) The solution to this problem will lie with discovering how much *generalization* may occur in perceptual activities. For example, I do not have to have actual experience with a given cube to be able to label it a "cube" and to make judgments regarding its shape and depth that I would make about other cubes. Unfortunately, few data exist on the development of generalization in perception.

Since depth perception is of practical con-

cern to many persons, including flyers and people who drive automobiles, acuity of depth perception has received a good deal of study. The most commonly used apparatus for determining acuity is probably the *Howard-Dohlman apparatus,* which consists of two rods that run on horizontal tracks parallel to the line of sight. Using standard psychophysical techniques, we may place the standard rod at a given point on the track and require the subject to adjust the comparison rod until it appears equal in depth to the standard rod. The average error in adjustment may be computed. Depth perception, as determined by the Howard-Dohlman or other procedures (Woodworth & Schlosberg, 1954, p. 469–474), is sensitive to changes in illumination (Mueller & V. V. Lloyd, 1948), amount of parallax permitted, and other familiar cues.

Perceptual Organization: The study of perceptual organization is concerned with how we perceive the figure-ground relationship, how we organize visual patterns into scenes which include depth, and similar questions. In a very real sense, the problem of understanding how these abilities are developed and modified is the same problem as that which pervades most phenomena of visual perception, for if we agree that human beings and many animals perceive figure-ground groupings, then two basic questions appear:

1. **What laws describe which part of the scene will be perceived as figure and which will be perceived as ground? Similarly, why are stimuli perceived as patterns and not as isolated stimuli?**
2. **Even if laws are formulated which predict these relationships, how does the organism come to function in accordance with the laws? Is our sensation of perceptual organization a basic, innate attribute of the system, or do we acquire perceptual organization through experience?**

The most dedicated attempt to solve the first problem has been made by *gestalt psychologists.* The term *gestalt* means *form, figure,* or *whole* in German, and investigations

FIGURE 9–17: *Dimensionality of figures. Most observers agree that* A *does not have depth. It is easy to perceive depth in* B, *and many viewers see depth in* C. *(From Osgood, 1953, p. 255.)*

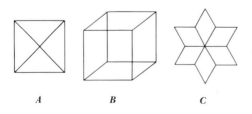

A   *B*   *C*

of perceptual organization by gestaltists have emphasized the role of innate patterning in visual perception. The basic problem which has catalyzed gestalt thinking is this: although it is possible to analyze stimuli in terms of units (a DL, a response to a stimulus, or similar molecular units of both the stimulus and the response), such analyses are not satisfactory when one wishes to explain behavior such as problem solving, thinking, ideation, and sensations. In short, the question is whether discrete measurements can lead to an understanding of complex behavior.

As such, the gestalt viewpoint takes issue with the type of psychology which assumes that the molecular level is the most efficient approach for arriving at an understanding of behavior. This latter form of psychology is one brand of *behaviorism,* and it assumes, by analogy to chemistry, that once the atoms are defined and measured, the resulting compounds become predictable. It emphasizes the measurement of the psychological equivalent of atoms—the single stimulus and its accompanying response. But if complex behavior (the compounds in the analogy) may not be predicted from its parts, e.g., if perception is not predictable from a knowledge of the past responses of an individual, then psychology may not assume this atomistic-molecular approach to behavior without failing to explain many kinds of behavior.

The basic premise of the gestaltist is that identification of the atoms of behavior cannot be sufficient to explain all behavior and that one must begin the study of behavior by studying the complex phenomena and by developing laws which predict them. The distinction between these approaches is between emphasis on units and emphasis on complexity, between examining behavior on a molecular level or on a molar level, and between emphasizing the discrete components which supposedly make up complex behavior and emphasizing the unity of perceptions and complex behaviors. The argument, if we can call it that, is over the best way to arrive at explanations of complex phenomena. Both the gestaltist and

the behaviorist want to understand perception and other complex behavior; however, they disagree on the most efficient method for arriving at an answer. The gestalt approach, particularly in methodology, is contrary to the behavioristic approach, which has strongly influenced American psychology. The debate between the warring factions has been acrimonious and, at times, unfair. The arguments have tended to overlook the similarity of positions—that both are seeking laws of behavior and physiological mechanisms—and to emphasize the weak points in the other's approaches. Fortunately, the subject matter of psychology has been the victor in this battle, for both schools of thought have contributed useful data to the study of visual perception.

Visual perception is an ideal battleground for these conflicting approaches. It contains both psychophysical units (Chapter 8) and complex phenomena (described in this chapter). It was natural then, perhaps, that the major work of the gestalt approach should be concerned with perception, and that the gestaltist should develop an approach to visual perception different from that of the behaviorists. The behavioristic tradition has emphasized examining perception in terms of defining the relation between the physical stimulus and the response and in terms of the learning process involved in constancy, depth perception cues, and other effects. The gestalt approach has emphasized investigations of configurations, and gestalt-oriented literature has produced a number of laws concerned with configuration. In many respects, such laws are similar to the behavioristic emphasis placed on cues: on the other hand, it appears that the gestalt approach has been more successful in organizing its laws into a unified theory, even though the validity of the theory may be questioned. Helson (1933) has isolated 114 laws formulated by gestaltists regarding the principles of configuration.

The development of the gestalt viewpoint on configuration and perceptual organization may be traced to Max Wertheimer (1912; 1923; 1958), who begins his discussion of perceptual organization with the following: "I stand at the window and see a house, trees, sky. Now on theoretical grounds I could try to count and say: There are ... 327 brightnesses and hues. Do I *have* 327? No, I see sky, house, trees; and no one can really have 327 as such" (Max Wertheimer, 1923, trans. Michael Wertheimer, in Beardslee & Michael Wertheimer, 1958, p. 115).

What are the principles that account for perceptual organization? One of the most important is the principle of *nearness* or *proximity*. The principle states that, other effects being equal, those objects near to one another will seem to be part of a group. For example, consider the next line:

. . . .

Now consider this line:

.. ..

If you were asked the nature of the first line, you would reply, "A row of dots." But if you were asked about the second line, you would be more likely to reply, "Groups of dots." Again, consider these dots:

. . . .
. . . .
                    .

And these:

.   .   .   .
   .   .   .   .

The first set is perceived as groups of dots, slanting from left to right, but the second set is perceived as less well organized than the first. Max Wertheimer (1923; 1958) points out that the principle of nearness is not only a visual phenomenon. Auditory stimuli follow much the same pattern, as may be noted by tapping your finger in the rhythm of the dots in the first example.

A second important principle is *similarity*, which states that objects which are similar to

one another in some dimension (color, brightness, etc.) will be grouped perceptually. Max Wertheimer (1923; 1958) provides a neat demonstration of this in Figure 9–18. Note that all the stimuli are circles: Some are filled and some are not. In figure *A*, the "similar" objects run vertically, and our perception is that of a vertical pattern. In figure *B*, our perception is of a horizontal pattern. This principle also occurs in audition. For example, tap your finger in the following pattern, where (.) is a soft tap and (!) is a loud tap:

. . ! ! . . . ! ! ! . . ! ! !

The last three elements of each set are perceived as grouped together, as are the first two elements. We group them because of the similarity in loudness in this case, although pitch groupings are also possible.

In any perceived scene, of course, the elements are not so neatly distributed as they are in these examples. In some scenes, for example, the principle of similarity could run into contradiction with the principle of nearness. Then what determines the perceptual organization? Several second-order principles have been developed. Among the most important are *closure, good continuation, good whole, experience, common fate,* and *set.*

Closure may be demonstrated by reference to Figure 9–19. If you supply a name for each of the figures, most likely you will call *A* a circle, even though it is not completely closed. The principle of closure says that you will complete, or close, the figure. Form *B* may be called a circle by some viewers and a C by others. Form *C* is seen as a C or a semicircle. Here, the circle is so incomplete that closure does not occur.

Good continuation is demonstrated in Figure 9–20. Which circle *A, B, C,* or *D,* should be filled to complete the scene? It would be *C,* of course, because it *continues* the form. However, if *C* were omitted as a choice, it is likely that *D* would be selected, even though both *A* and *B* are nearer the end of the figure and thus could be selected on the basis of nearness.

Max Wertheimer (1958, p. 129) refers to these figures as having an "inner belongingness, resulting in a *good whole* or *good configuration* which exhibits its own definite inner requirements."

Although good continuation refers to patterns which appear to move in a smooth manner, the principle of *common fate* is used for stimuli which are actually in motion. A neon sign in front of a restaurant is in the shape of an arrow. If the firing of the lights is arranged properly, the arrow seems to move downward and into the restaurant. The lights are all moving toward the same "fate," or termination. Dember (1960, p. 166) suggests that animals who appear camouflaged and then move are examples of the perception of common fate. While the animal is moving, all the elements are moving toward the same termination. When the animal stops, there is no further common fate of the elements, and the animal no longer stands out distinctly from the foliage.

In general, the foregoing principles of perception are considered relatively inherent and invariable. Among the principles, however, are several which emphasize the prior experiences of the individual. One of these principles is called *Einstellung*, or *set*. The term *Einstellung* implies an attitude or a tendency to respond in a given way. Set is not necessarily a product of past experiences. For example, if a row of dots is presented and if the space is increased slowly after every second dot until this pattern is attained:

•• •• •• •• •• ••

the observer will fail to see the grouping until the dots are further apart than would be necessary if the demonstration had begun with the uneven pattern. This is similar to the error of habituation in psychophysical measurement (Chapter 4), where the subject continues to make a response longer than is appropriate.

A second principle which is concerned with the experience of the organism is called *habit*,

FIGURE 9–18: *The principle of similarity. In figure A, one sees the direction of the surface as vertical. In figure B, the direction is seen as horizontal. (From Max Wertheimer, 1958, p. 118.)*

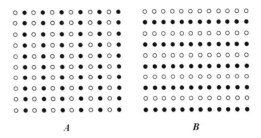

A   *B*

FIGURE 9–19: *A demonstration of closure. The text describes the differences in perception which the diagrams elicit.*

A   *B*   *C*

FIGURE 9–20: *The principle of good continuation. Which circle should be filled in to complete the pattern, A, B, C, or D? (From Psychology of Perception, by W. M. Dember, copyright 1960 by Holt, Rinehart and Winston, Inc.)*

or *experience*, by Max Wertheimer. His example of the effect of past experience is shown in Figure 9–21. Wertheimer points out that the original components of the written word "jump" were purely arbitrary and, as such, there were no perceptual laws involved. The organization "jump" comes about through "external, extrinsic, arbitrary habit or drill" (Max Wertheimer, 1958, p. 132). If the organization is broken, as in the right portion of the figure, the perception is lost, because the only rules which have determined its organization are arbitrary. This effect of past experience is one of the few crumbs which the gestaltist drops to the behaviorist. Max Wertheimer (1958, p. 133) comments:

Arbitrary materials can be organized in arbitrary ways through a sufficient amount of drill. . . . Some scientists, with very strong theoretical orientations, will be inclined to view [all the principles] as simply due to a factor of "past experience" and think they have solved all of the problems by the glib use of this magic word. . . .

One might say, for instance: Are not organizations to which we have become accustomed the ones that are favored? Are not the straight line, the right angle . . . all familiar from past experience? . . . Does not past experience drill into us to see equal colored areas as belonging together?

But it by no means solves the problems. It is the duty of the doctrine of past experience to demonstrate concretely for each of these cases and for each of the factors the actual past experiences and times of drill that are involved.

All the principles of organization contribute to the basic tenet of visual perception in the gestalt approach, the *law of Pragnanz*. This law states that perceptions will be as simple, whole, and good as possible. The implication is that we always reduce any scene to the simplest perception which accounts for all the elements. For example, consider Figure 9-22. Form *A* is embodied in both forms *B* and *C*. It is simple to perceive form *A* in form *C* but fairly difficult to perceive it in form *B*.

The basic question remains, however, whether organizations are innate or acquired. Two general methodological approaches have been used to solve this problem. The first procedure has been to examine the development of perceptual organization in organisms deprived of vision until adulthood. For example, a chimpanzee may be raised in the dark or with special opaque lenses which prohibit the perception of configurations until the glasses are removed. Similar data are provided from human beings who are congenitally blind but who gain sight in adulthood. The second general procedure has been to alter the perceptual environment of the adult human being in such a way that motor responses to visual stimuli must be relearned. For example, lenses have been developed which reverse the image on the retina. Individuals who wear such glasses must relearn their spatial orientation, and examination of the development of the new responses yields information on the way in which the original perceptual learning developed.

Probably the most comprehensive account of the reactions of persons who gain sight after congenital blindness is that of von Senden (1932). Von Senden's data were based on 66 human subjects who received sight suddenly either in late childhood or adulthood after congenital blindness. Since the majority of these reports were culled from other sources, there was no possibility of examining the persons by means of standard tests when sight was gained. Accordingly, the general finding that persons required months and often years to gain normal vision and that learning is an essential component of adult visual perception is suggestive at best, for one may only speculate from case studies of abnormal individuals as to the processes involved in the development of normal visual perception.

It is not clear from von Senden's data how much of the lack of normal perception was due to the lack of practice in making appropriate motor responses to visual stimuli and how much was due to perceptual learning. Dennis (1934) has reported on 32 cases of individuals whose sight was restored after partial blindness. He reports that they showed difficulty in discriminating both colors and shapes and that accurate distance perception took some time to appear (see also Miner, 1905; Latta, 1904). Riesen (1947; 1950) has reported that a chimpanzee raised in the dark for the first sixteen months of life showed retinal and optic nerve degeneration. This animal showed difficulty in fixation and in the avoidance of obstacles for as long as fifty hours following the restoration of sight. An animal who received diffuse light, but not total darkness, took less time to gain normal vision than the subject raised in total darkness.

Mowrer (1936) sealed the eyelids of pigeons for six weeks after birth and found that the pigeons had difficulty in avoiding obstacles when the lids were opened. Siegel (1953a; 1953b) reports that ring doves who were permitted only diffuse light had difficulty in discriminating objects (circles from triangles). Apparently, both spatial coordination and form discrimination are hampered by visual deprivation in pigeons and ring doves. Breder and Rasquin (1947) found that fish taken from dark caves into light were unable to avoid objects and failed to find food. Fish reared in lightproof tanks for over two years had similar problems when light was permitted. Both Lashley and J. T. Russell (1934) and Hebb (1937a; 1937b) had reported that rats reared in darkness had initial difficulties in discriminating form.

The question whether depth perception is innate or learned has been examined by E. J. Gibson and her associates. These experimenters arranged a test situation which used what they have termed the *visual cliff*. Their apparatus may be understood by reference to Figure 9–23. Square patterns are used to provide subjects with cues to depth. One portion of the test area is solid and "safe," while the other is apparently deep. Glass over the deep side prevents the subject from falling and hurting himself. The child or infant of another species is placed on the runway between the safe side and the cliff. E. J. Gibson and

FIGURE 9–22: *The simple form shown as* **A** *is included in both* **B** *and* **C**. *It is difficult to locate the form in* **B** *but easy to see it in* **C**. *(A and B from Gottschaldt, 1926, p. 296; C from Osgood, 1953, p. 217.)*

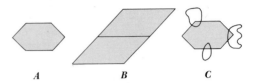

A   *B*   *C*

Walk (1960)[1] report that of the 27 human infants who moved from the runway, all went to the safe side at least once, and three subjects moved to the glass over the deep side. The children's mothers took part in the experiment by calling to the infants, sometimes in such a way that the infant would have had to cross the deep side in order to reach the mother. Even the mother's calling was not sufficient to encourage most infants to cross the "deep" side of the cliff. Through several experiments based on the principle of the visual cliff, Gibson and Walk concluded that the "perception of depth had matured more rapidly than had locomotor abilities" (E. J. Gibson & Walk, 1960, p. 64).

Similar observations were made on chickens, turtles, rats, lambs, kids, pigs, kittens, and dogs. Although turtles showed the poorest depth perception, other animals generally preferred the shallow side after only one day of life or as soon as they were able to stand and walk. Cats, dogs, and lambs froze when placed on the glass but showed no fear of the shallow side. Chicks less than twenty-four hours old always selected the shallow side. Although the data do not indicate that depth perception is innate, they argue strongly for the viewpoint that if depth perception is not innate, it is certainly learned in a very brief period of time.

The question that occurs when the retinal

[1] Reprints available at 20 cents of offprint no. 402 from W. H. Freeman and Company, 660 Market Street, San Francisco, Calif.

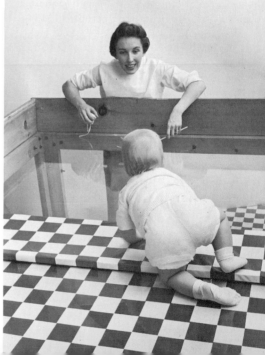

images are distorted or reversed has intrigued experimenters for many years. Leonardo da Vinci worked on the problem (see Argentieri, 1956), and Helmholtz and von Kries adopted the position that space perception was largely learned from experience with the perceptual world. Both were aware of evidence that children born with cataracts showed a deficiency in spatial orientation when sight was restored. Largely because of the disagreement about the origin of space perception between Kantian philosophers and the assumptions of physiological psychologists, the early years of this century witnessed considerable experimental attention to what happens when retinal images are inverted. Stratton (1897a; 1897b; 1899) used double convex lenses on himself for a period of several days. (Since this procedure strained the eyes considerably, Stratton eventually used one lens for one eye and blindfolded the other eye.) At first, he found it difficult to make appropriate motor responses to the altered visual stimuli. By the fifth day, he experienced little difficulty in coordinating his movements with the visual stimul: he no longer hit against objects as he had during the first days of the experiment. By the eighth day, his reactions to the reversed visual environment were normal. Indeed, he had learned to respond so well to the new environment that when the glasses were removed, he experienced difficulties similar to those which had appeared when he first wore the glasses. From

FIGURE 9–23: *The visual cliff. The checkered pattern is directly below the glass on one side but several feet below it on the other side. One subject, in this case a child, is placed in the center (figure A). The child crawls to his mother across the "shallow" side (figure B). Called from the "deep" side, he pats the glass (figure C), but despite this tactual information that the "cliff" is a solid surface the child refuses to cross to the mother over the deep side (figure D). (From E. J. Gibson & Walk, 1960, p. 65. Reprinted with permission. Copyright 1960 by Scientific American, Inc. All rights reserved.)*

these experiences, Stratton postulated that spatial vision was learned and not innate. Stratton had certainly demonstrated that one could relearn motor responses to altered visual stimuli, but his work did not exclude the possibility that spatial vision was an innate ability of the organism.

Wooster (1923) measured her subjects' accuracy in localizing objects and sounds. She had 72 subjects wear prisms which distorted the visual field less than the lenses used by Stratton. The subjects showed the difficulties in localization that Stratton had experienced. However, adjustment to the change in the visual field, as measured by localization, did not occur unless the subjects were permitted to reach for the objects. That is, merely wearing the prisms was not sufficient for learning localization: motor responses were necessary. This finding reinforces the viewpoint that space perception and localization are primarily a matter of learning to make appropriate motor responses and that mere visual adjustment to a new visual field does not provide the subject with sufficient cues to permit motor coordination with objects in the field.

G. G. Brown (1928) has reported that when the lenses are distorted with greater displacement than used by either Stratton or Wooster, depth perception did not appear to improve even with practice. Ewert (1930; 1936; 1937) repeated Stratton's work, using standardized tests of visual ability. His results indicate that normal functioning among the other sensory systems, such as audition and kinesthesis, was impaired by the change in the visual field. J. Peterson and J. K. Peterson (1938), Kohler (1951a; 1951b; 1955), F. W. Snyder and Pronko (1952), and F. W. Snyder and C. W. Snyder (1957) indicate that within the time limits of their studies (around thirty to thirty-seven days) subjects never reach their normal level of performance while the lens distorts. As K. U. Smith and W. M. Smith (1962) point out, the use of such lenses alters so many characteristics of the normally operating visual system that it is difficult to assess the cause of many noted effects. For example, lenses and similar devices which alter the visual field also interrupt processes such as convergence and accommodation.

Fractional information exists on the effects of altered visual environments of animals. Foley (1938) reports that a rhesus monkey equipped with a binocular lens which forced right-left, up-down, and depth reversal made backward movements and then refused to move at all. By the eighth day the animal showed appropriate localization movements, and upon removal of the lenses the rhesus showed little difficulty in readjustment. E. H. Hess (1956) has raised chickens with goggles and studied their pecking at food. Chickens mispecked in accordance with the amount of displacement of the lenses and had not learned to locate food at the termination of the experiment. The animals showed no sign of learning to correct for the discrepancy created by the lenses. This study indicates that spatial localization is not a process of learning in the chicken and that localization is an innate, and perhaps unchangeable, characteristic in this form of life. Other evidence on the innate perception organization of the chicken gives the same indication (Fantz, 1957; Rheingold & E. H. Hess, 1957; E. H. Hess & Gogel, 1954).

Some useful information on the effects of alterations in the visible field come from the work of Sperry (1943; 1944; 1945; 1956; 1961) and L. S. Stone (1944), who have developed techniques for grafting afferent and efferent circuits. One technique involved rotating the eye of a frog and grafting it to the opposite side of the head. Under these conditions, the frog showed errors in striking at objects equivalent to the amount of displacement. Practice did not appear to correct the error. L. S. Stone (1944) has shown that the grafting of neurological components of amphibian embryos resulted in a permanent disruption of visual functioning. These results indicate that it is the neurological connections which control orientation and that artificial alterations do not permit adaptation.

The Ganzfeld: The answer to the problem "How do the perceptions of configurations

occur?" lies in understanding how such perceptions develop. Since data from developmental studies of configuration are difficult to assess because of the problems of interpreting the verbal responses of infants and children, there have been several attempts to arrange an environment in which the responses of adult human beings are studied. Various techniques have been developed for presenting the subject with an artificial visual field in which the light is homogeneous and in which there are no figures. This perceptual environment is called the *Ganzfeld* (German for *whole field*). Anyone can arrange a Ganzfeld for himself merely by placing half a ping-pong ball over each eye (Hochberg, Triebel, & Seaman, 1951, originally developed by R. S. Harper).

Although studies employing the Ganzfeld technique have not been notably successful in solving the problem of how the perception of configuration develops, they have provided some useful information on color vision. W. Cohen (1958a) noted that subjects who were provided with a Ganzfeld of homogeneous red light perceived the light as red immediately upon presentation, but as time passed (approximately three minutes), the color faded and eventually produced the perception of a homogeneous gray field. Although the same effect occurs with homogeneous green light, blue light yields the immediate perception of grayness. These data suggest that color perception is dependent, at least partially, upon the presence of configuration within the perceptual field.

One method of introducing heterogeneity into the perceptual environment is to use different Ganzfelds for each eye. When a gray circle is used with a red background, an enhancement in saturation occurs, and the circle is seen as a saturated blue-green. Saturation, it would appear, is not dependent totally upon homogeneity of wavelength, for it is also a result of the presence of configurations in the perceptual environment. On the other hand, when the difference between the fields is in intensity (e.g., when a light red and a darker red are used), the perception is of gray, just as if only a single homogeneous red source were used. The implications of this finding are that a difference in hue is needed to produce color under the conditions of the Ganzfeld and that differences in intensity of the same wavelength are not sufficient to produce stable color perception. The fact that color perception disappears under the conditions of the Ganzfeld unless a configuration is present suggests not only that heterogeneity of the stimuli provides cues for depth perception and other phenomena but that heterogeneity is necessary for accurate color perception as well.

Motion Perception: One of the most useful characteristics of the human eye, as well as of many other animal eyes, is that it is able to perceive motion. This ability provides us with basic information regarding the location and speed of oncoming cars and people, permits us to watch motion pictures and television, and, in general, allows us to assess the location and path of moving objects. As is true of many other characteristics of vision, we are so accustomed to judging the rates and directions of objects and correlating our motor responses with these judgments that we overlook the complexity of motion perception. At first thought, motion perception appears to be a simple matter: as objects move across the retina, the retina reports a different sensation depending upon the location of the stimulus. The first indication that motion perception was not so simple came from demonstrations which indicated that objects may be perceived as in motion even though they are stationary. One of the more common demonstrations of this effect is the waterfall illusion. If you watch a waterfall, or any other set of stimuli moving continually in one direction, and then look at a stationary object, the stationary object appears to move in an *opposite* direction from the direction of the waterfall. These afterimages which yield the perception of movement in the opposite direction from that of the original stimulus conditions are indications that motion perception provides as many problems in the search for satisfactory explanatory principles as other aspects of vision.

Two major sources of movement are commonly identified: *Real movement* consists of the perception of objects being displaced. Said more directly, but less accurately, it is perception of the real movement of physical objects. However, under appropriate conditions, stationary objects appear to move. These examples, known collectively as *apparent movement,* provide the psychologist with some of the more interesting visual phenomena. Apparent motion is of appreciable practical importance, for motion pictures, certain electric signs, and other commercial products rely upon the human being's perception of apparent motion.

Part of the interest in real movement has been generated by the practical need to determine the perceptual thresholds for real movement. Objects may move too rapidly or too slowly for movement to be detected. Particularly in industrial situations, it is often critical that detection apparatus be constructed so that the observer may evaluate the relevant aspects of the object in motion. Obviously, the blips on a radarscope must be within the threshold limits of the individual for detection to be possible. The kinesthetic perceptions from eye movements are an important aspect of the perception of real movement. In watching a scene in motion, such as a parade or patterns on an oscilloscope, or if I am in motion and watching a scene, as in looking out of a car window, the eyes characteristically follow one moving point in the scene until it passes to the periphery of the retina, and then they are turned to fixate upon another moving object which appears in the opposite periphery, and that object is followed until it passes across the retina. This *saccadic* movement is a combination of both eye pursuit and alternating kinesthetic movements similar to those which occur in reading a book. The eye follows the line to its end, and then returns to pursue a new line.

Apparent movement provides us with an entirely different set of principles and phenomena. Indirectly, the study of apparent movement led to the founding of gestalt psychology through Max Wertheimer's (1912) classic paper on stroboscopic movement, in which he pointed out that two lights flashing on and off at appropriate intervals will provide the perception of movement. Although a variety of such demonstrations exist (each prefaced with a Greek letter, e.g., beta phenomenon), the phi phenomenon has received most attention. Laws predicting the perception which results following experimental manipulation of the phi phenomenon have been postulated by Max Wertheimer (1912) and by Korte (1915). *Korte's laws* indicate that the perception is determined by such variables as the intensity of the illumination, location of the lights, and latency between the onset and termination of the lights. By employing the apparatus shown in Figure 9–24, the experimenter may vary each of these characteristics: For example, if three lights are of the same intensity and the fourth light is dim, the motion appears to hesitate at the dim light before continuing. One of the more curious findings is that if lights of different hues are

FIGURE 9–24: *A phi phenomenon demonstration apparatus. The four lights may be varied in intensity and duration to produce different effects of the phi phenomenon.*

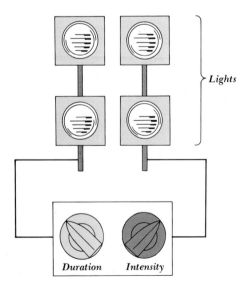

used, the line of apparent motion appears to change hue.

It has been reported (Boring, 1942) that if an object is placed in the line of the apparent motion, the apparent motion curves around the protusion. This finding suggests that some form of inference may be employed by the subject in the perception of apparent movement. In addition, both practice and set have been shown to influence the perception (Zeitz & Werner, 1927; W. S. Neff, 1936; Neuhaus, 1930). Three-dimensional apparent motion may be produced. One of the simplest procedures is, first, to expose lights in the form of an inverted V and then promptly to expose lights in the form of a V placed slightly lower than the first. Various examples of depth in apparent motion have been presented (Fernberger, 1934).

Another type of apparent motion, which has been used quite successfully in experimental investigations of attitude and leadership qualities (Chapter 19), is the *autokinetic effect*. A single light in a darkened room appears to waver if one fixates upon it. The light appears to move in spatial patterns under these conditions. Apparently the critical variable which encourages the autokinetic effect is the presence of a homogeneous background, for the effect does not occur if configurations are present in the surround. W. Cohen (1958b) reports that subjects perceive the effect when a Ganzfeld, which assures homogeneous background is used. Illumination also influences the perception of the autokinetic effect, since with an increase in illumination the surround becomes perceivable and the autokinetic effect is lessened.

Visual Causality: Albert Michotte (1946; 1963) has investigated the perception of causality. Michotte has shown that perceptual inferences are made regarding the *cause* of motion. For example, if billiard ball *A* moves and comes into contact with ball *B* and if ball *A* now stops and *B* moves, we assume that *A* caused the motion of *B*. Woodworth and Schlosberg (1954, p. 517) call this effect *appar-*

ent *visual kinetics.* Figure 9–25 shows apparatus for the demonstration of causality. When the disks are rotated as described in the legend, line *A* appears to strike line *B* and to place it in motion. Michotte has varied the stimulus conditions and derived several laws concerning the necessary circumstances for the perception of causality. A single object is not sufficient to yield the effect, even if it starts and stops unevenly. Two distinct objects are necessary. When *A* appears to strike *B,* the fixation must be foveal. If it is not, the perception is that two distinct objects are moving but not that they strike. Other factors, such as apparent speed, location, and direction of the movement, are critical in producing the effect of causality.

Eye Movements: We have noted that the action of the various muscles surrounding the eye are important for such processes as accommodation and convergence. In addition, their combined efforts permit the *fixation* which occurs when the light falls directly on the fovea, the source of clearest vision under illumination. When we observe the environment, these muscles, along with other muscles in the neck and face, sometimes contract rapidly and sometimes slowly in order to alter the fixation point. The kinesthetic sensations of the speed and force of these muscles' reactions provide us with important cues regarding distance and other characteristics of the visual scene. The eyes of human beings and many animals are capable of rapid movement.

Over the past eighty years, several techniques have been used to measure eye movements. For example, Figure 9–26 shows a recording of the eye movement of a subject asked to inspect the painting shown in figure *B.* The recording in figure *A* was taken when the subject was told, without further instructions, to look at the picture for ten minutes. The recording in figure *C* was taken when the subject was told to think "what the family was doing when the visitor arrived," and the recording in figure *D* was taken when the subject was told to estimate the ages of the mem-

FIGURE 9–25: *The Michotte disk. Assume that the disk rotates behind an aperture outlined by the dotted rectangle. As the disk is turned clockwise, line A appears to move, to strike B, and to place B in motion. Various other effects associated with apparent motion and causality may be investigated with this technique. (From Michotte, 1963, p. 30.)*

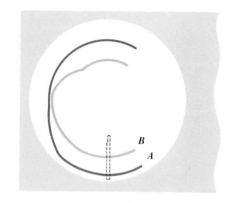

bers of the family. The eye movements under these three conditions are obviously different, but it is not easy to quantify the differences.

Most techniques for the measurement of eye movements have used either motion pictures or electrical recordings. Although motion pictures have some obvious advantages, the experimenter is still faced with the problem of converting the pictures into some form of quantifiable data. It is possible to plot each frame separately, but this procedure is tedious. Nevertheless, motion-picture recordings are often useful in such applied problems as discovering the parts of an advertisement or a newspaper which receive the most attention. In Figure 9–26, it is clear that when the subject is asked to estimate the ages of the persons, his eye movements are largely confined to the area occupied by the individuals in the picture.

If electrodes are attached to appropriate areas of the eye and if the response is greatly amplified, electrical recordings—*electrooculograms* (EOGs)—of the eye movements appear.

The electric discharge is not a product of changes in muscle tonus. Rather, it appears to be the result of metabolic differences between the cornea and the retina. Deflection of the light by movement of the cornea may be recorded. Among other techniques, W. M. Smith and Warter (1960) have designed a photo-electric circuit which appears to permit fine measures, and Johansson and Backlund (1960) have described a technique in which an infra-red or blue light is directed to the cornea.

The process of reading is one of the more important human functions involving eye movements. Tinker (1936; 1958) has reviewed

FIGURE 9–26: *Eye movements in response to the picture shown in figure B. Eye movements in figure A were taken from a subject who was given no instructions but to look at the picture. Figure C is the recording when the subject was told to think what the family was doing when the visitor arrived. Figure D is taken when the subject was asked to estimate the ages of the persons in the picture. (From Razran, 1961, p. 113.)*

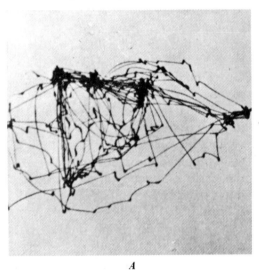

A

B

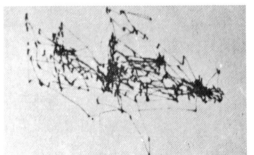

C

D

studies concerned with the relationship between eye movements and reading. As noted previously, reading consists of saccadic movements alternating with periods of fixation, during which the actual reading occurs, since clear vision is not present during saccadic movement. Rapid reading, then, is a function of both the period of fixation and the speed of the saccadic movements. Regressive movements often occur in reading when previously fixated material is reexamined. These movements detract from reading speed, even though they appear among very rapid readers. Perhaps the most objective evaluation of a textbook would be a quantification of the number of regressive movements required by students to understand the text. It is an error to assume that reading speed in itself is a testament to the ability of the reader. Schlosberg (1954c, p. 505) reports finding, in an informal study, that legal judges showed more fixations per line than the average third-grade student. It is reasonable to assume, however, that judges and other persons whose work is concerned with understanding each word of a sentence would learn to read material in a way appropriate to their needs.

With an increase in age (as measured by school grade), students show a decrease in the number of fixations per line of print and a decrease in the mean duration of the fixations and in the number of movements per line (Buswell, 1922). Following Tinker (1936), the percentage of the total reading time devoted to fixation is sometimes taken to be a measure of reading efficiency. L. C. Gilbert (1959) attempted to measure the influence of both eye movements and saccadic movements in college students by presenting two sets of reading tasks: in one set, the material was presented so it could be read without eye movements; in the second set, the material was arranged in such a way that movements were necessary. His results indicated that although all readers showed a decrement in ability when eye movements were necessary, the effect was most detrimental to previously slow readers who apparently require longer fixations than do rapid readers.

Quite often the first implications of deficiencies in visual acuity are noted in grade school when the child is learning to read. Some children exhibit a tendency to read words or syllables in reverse (*saw* for *was, god* for *dog*). This condition, known as *strephosymbolia,* is commonly attributed to a lack of dominance of one cerebral hemisphere over the other, although the cause is, no doubt, far more complicated. Improper functioning of the muscles of the eye, which limits fixation, is generally classified as *strabismus*. In *internal* strabismus, the eyes converge toward the nasal sides. This cross-eyedness, which is common in infants, can be debilitating both intellectually and socially if the muscles do not gain strength and the condition is not corrected. In *external* strabismus, the eyes diverge toward the temporal sides, and the person appears to be looking in two directions. On occasion, one fixation point is above the other. Accordingly, one eye sees the top portion of a work, and the second eye sees the bottom portion. Squinting, which may result from poor correlation of the muscles, may make one eye weaker than the other.

THE ROLE OF EXPERIENCE

One approach to the question as to whether perceptual phenomena are innate or learned (or a combination of both explanatory principles) involves depriving organisms of sight and studying their reactions to visual stimuli when vision is restored. Investigators have examined the effects of different amounts or kinds of visual stimulation on the development of intelligence, docility, and so on. In some studies, the amount of visual stimulation has been used as an independent variable. In others, the number and quality of objects in the visual environment have been manipulated. Although these studies contribute more to an understanding of the effect of the environment in shaping behavior than an understanding of visual phenomena, they do indicate that variation in the perceptual environment can have dramatic effects on such factors as intelligence, docility, and learning.

Basically, three kinds of studies have contributed indirectly to our knowledge of perceptual processes: In the first, animals are raised in "visually rich" or "visually poor" environments in order to determine the effects of the quality of the visual environment on behavior. In the second type, the subject, usually a human being, is placed in an environment with all sensory stimulation reduced to a minimum. These studies of *sensory deprivation* have provided information on perceptual processes and on the organism's response to isolation from stimuli. Studies of the third type, which investigate the perceptual preferences of subjects, are less common.

Varying the Amount of Visual Stimuli: As a general finding, animals which are exposed to stimulus-rich environments (varied visual stimuli, physical contact with human beings or other animals, visual patterns, an unrestricted environment) are superior in learning tasks to animals in "normal" or restrictive environments. It should be recalled, however, that interspecies comparisons are only suggestive, since the visual system varies widely from species to species. The rat, for example, uses olfaction more than vision, and conditions which constitute visual enhancement or deprivation for one species may have little effect on another.

The relationship between exposure to specific visual stimuli and learning which involves discrimination of the same stimuli has been investigated in the rat. Unfortunately, this relationship has not been investigated systematically in animals with a visual system more similar to that of human beings. Forgus (1954) raised three groups of rats in combinations of complex visual and proprioceptive environments from twenty-four to forty-eight days of age. The subjects were tested on a problem which required them to differentiate shapes.

When sufficient learning had occurred that the subjects selected the appropriate shape 90 percent of the time, the shapes were rotated 90 degrees, and the discrimination tests were continued in order to examine the subjects' ability to generalize to the rotated visual stimulus. Animals raised in a restricted environment with a minimum of visual and proprioceptive stimuli were notably inferior to subjects raised in richer environments.

Forgus (1956) has also reported that the age at which the visual environment is modified is a significant independent variable in the generalization of shape discrimination. Similarly, the type of visual environment provided affects the ability to learn a simple maze (Forgus, 1955). E. J. Gibson and Walk (1956) raised one group of rats in cages which had triangles and circles applied to the walls. A second group was raised without the presence of the forms. After ninety days in these environments, both groups were trained to discriminate triangles from circles; the group which had visual experience with the forms was superior. It was also superior in avoiding the forms (E. J. Gibson, Walk, Pick, & Tighe, 1958). The ability of the subjects to generalize to forms similar but not identical to those placed in the cages was also tested. The original stimuli were equilateral triangles and circles, and the stimuli used during the discrimination test were isosceles triangles and ellipses. Again, the subjects raised with the forms were superior.

Many studies indicate that visual experiences applied during infancy are more efficient in producing behavioral changes than similar experiences applied during adulthood. The reason for this is not clear. It may be that the infant of the species has fewer past experiences which interfere with his learning, or it may be that the infant's rapid growth renders his early experiences more efficacious.

Sensory Deprivation: What happens when an individual is deprived of as much stimulation as possible? Research on this question has yielded few solid conclusions but many areas for conjecture. Prior to the 1950s, many of the data came from the anecdotal experiences of groups or individuals trapped in isolation, such as the experiences of Shakleton's men isolated for several months on an ice flow in the Antarctic or stories concerning wolf-children who were isolated from mankind and grew up in forests with wild animals (Lilly, 1956). In the first controlled studies which attempted to assess the effects of sensory isolation, Bexton (1953) and Bexton, Heron, and T. H. Scott (1954) confined volunteer college students in an isolation chamber. An air conditioner provided a masking tone which decreased auditory stimulation, goggles prevented form discrimination, and gloves prevented tactual cues. A variety of tasks concerned with learning and visual and motor coordination were administered after release from confinement. Heron, Doane, and T. H. Scott (1956) reported that subjects experienced visual hallucinations during confinement. In another series of studies, J. A. Vernon, McGill, Gulick, and Candland (1959; 1961) confined subjects under more severe conditions for 24, 48, and 72 hours and administered a battery of perceptual and motor tasks. They reported a significant decrease in color perception in subjects confined for 48 hours or longer.

It is likely that all forms of visual acuity are hampered by deprivation. Freedman, Grunebaum, and Greenblatt (1961) report significant changes in such diverse perceptual measures as figure-ground stability and perceptual distortion with less severe deprivation procedures than those used in the above studies. In some cases, sensory deprivation (or *restricted motility,* as these writers describe their procedure) appears to improve some kind of perceptual performance. There is evidence that visual hallucinations occur during confinement only if some visual stimulation is present (J. A. Vernon, McGill, & Schiffman, 1958) but that few, if any, hallucinations occur when there is no visual stimulation (J. A. Vernon et al., 1959; Ruff & E. Z. Levy, 1959). The procedural difference among studies of human sensory deprivation, as well as differences in the severity of the confinement, make the generalization of findings tenuous. However, they do indicate that the process of visual hallucination apparently requires external stimulation and that color vision is affected by long-term confinement.

Innate Preference: In exploring the question of what an organism perceives at birth, an investigator is dependent on the verbal descriptions and motor coordination of his subjects. Since the chicken is able to peck for food at birth and has well-developed perceptual abilities, it has been used to study color, form, and stimulus preferences. Fantz (1957) arranged a simple, but effective, apparatus in which objects of different shapes (sphere, ellipsoid, pyramid, and star) were connected to microswitches. If a chicken pecked at a form, the microswitch for that form was activated. In this way, the experimenter was able to measure the number of responses made to each form. The subjects were permitted 20 test periods of fifteen minutes' duration. Both the sphere and the ellipsoid received 25,000 pecks from the 100 subjects used in the study, and the pyramid and star each received just over 2,000; this indicated a preference for rounded objects. In a second study, chicks were hatched and retained in darkness, so the possibility of their acquiring information about forms from visual experiences was limited. When they were placed in the light, these animals showed an immediate preference for circular forms, and Fantz thus concluded that immediate preference for visual forms exists in the chick.

E. H. Hess and Gogel (1954) have shown innate color preferences in the chick. Rheingold and E. H. Hess (1957) examined the chick's response to water, since chicks are able also to locate and drink water immediately after birth. In order to isolate the aspects of water to which chicks respond the investigators presented newly hatched chicks with the option of selecting from a variety of cups. One cup contained ordinary tap water, a second contained water with a blue dye, a third contained water with a red dye, a fourth cup contained polished aluminum but no water, a fifth cup contained plastic which looked like water to the human being but not necessarily to the chicken, and a sixth cup contained mercury. The chicks were deprived of water from birth (chicks do not normally eat for the first days following hatching). On the third and again on the seventh day of life, the chicks were placed in the test situation for three minutes and permitted to select a substance. In general, the cups containing mercury, the plastic substance, and the blue dye were selected by both experimental (food- and water-deprived) and control groups (permitted food and water). The evidence indicates that the attraction of the newly hatched chick to water is a result of an apparently innate preference for bright, reflecting surfaces.

Fantz (1958) has recorded the length of time that human infants fixated upon different patterns. From these observations, it was concluded that the infant discriminated different patterns during the first six months of life, because different patterns received different fixation times. If the patterns were not discriminated, it would be reasonable to assume that the fixation time would have been equal for all patterns. Fantz noted that a change in preference occurred around two months of age in many infants and that this shift did not appear to be related to the amount of testing or other readily identifiable variables. Fantz suggests that "consistent visual preferences were present as early as the first two months, thus arguing against an extreme empiricistic view of the development of visual organization and pattern discrimination" (1958, p. 47).

These studies support the view that innate pattern perception is evident in infant chickens and human beings. How much this innate perception is changed by learning and maturation is an open question. However, the use of measures of preference eliminates some of the difficulties inherent in studying the development of perception, although supportive data using eye movements and other measures of perception are lacking.

Development of Perception in Children: A large body of knowledge concerning the development of perception in children exists, but results must be treated with caution; not only are there inherent difficulties in the use of such data, but, as well, an unusual number of design problems render the results difficult to interpret. Some of the most suggestive work, although not necessarily the most experimentally defensible, is that of Jean Piaget and his collaborators (1926; 1929; 1930; 1954; see Kessen & Kuhlman, 1962). Piaget has investigated a number of attributes of the mental and perceptual development of children; some of his most suggestive work, however, deals with the development of the perception of geometric illusions.

Data from a variety of studies show that children and adults perceive visual illusions differently (Wohlwill, 1960). For example, most studies show that error in adjusting the lines of the Müller-Lyer illusion (Chapter 4) decreases as the age of the subject increases. Other types of visual perceptions also change with age. Some form of space perception indicate that experience leads to more efficient utilization of perceptual cues and more "realistic" perception, although other visual tasks involving space perception do not appear to change with age (Witkin, H. B. Lewis, Hertzman, Machover, Meissner, & Wapner, 1954). Several investigators have found the perception of brightness constancy to improve with age (Brunswik, 1928, 1956; W. Walker, 1927; Burzlaff, 1931; Akishige, 1937), but differences in experimental procedure lead to different results, and there is considerable disagreement on the validity of the findings. Space constancy also appears to improve with age (Akishige, 1937; Klimpfinger, 1933). Depth perception, which appears to be efficient quite early in life under the conditions of the visual cliff, has been shown to be well developed in tasks, such as the Howard-Dohlman apparatus, that require the estimation of which of two or more rods is most distant. Similarly, Gatenbein (1952) has shown that the perception of many kinds of apparent motion decreases as the age of the subject increases. That is, children are more apt to perceive apparent motion than adults.

The implication is strong that although many visual phenomena are present at birth, these innate patterns are greatly altered by learning and visual experiences. There is ample evidence that visual perception is innate, and there is perhaps more evidence that it is learned. Accordingly, it seems most likely that the argument as to whether perception is learned or innate is moot: it is both.

PERCEPTUAL DEFENSE AND SUBLIMINAL PERCEPTION

Since much of an organism's sensory input is visual and since perception varies as a function of learning, motivation, set, and other factors, it is not surprising that perceptual responses are used as a dependent variable in studies which attempt to uncover information regarding the nature of learning and motivation. We noted earlier in this chapter that visual perception is often used as a measure of personality in projective tests and that the wise use of such tests must indicate, at the least, that individual perceptions differ sufficiently from one another to permit the discrimination of one individual from another.

Broadly interpreted, studies of perceptual defense have attempted to show that perception is influenced by learned experiences. For example, some words which are not commonly used in speech and rarely in writing, often called *taboo words,* may go unnoticed in reading, not because we lack experience with them, but because we have learned, often by the soap-in-the-mouth technique of punishment, that the words should not be used. Similarly, if I *say* the word *stake* (steak), your perception of the meaning of the word is likely to depend upon whether you are hungry or whether you are a gardener. When I show you a visually ambiguous figure, if you are tired and hungry,

your description of the form is more likely to be in terms of forms commonly associated with food and bed than would be true if you were neither hungry nor tired.

Bruner and Goodman (1947) demonstrated this point neatly by projecting the form of a circle on a screen and asking "poor" children, "rich" children, and a control group consisting of children of unspecified economic backgrounds to manipulate the circle until it was equal in size to pennies, nickels, dimes, quarters, and half dollars. When a child had made the required determinations, he was shown the appropriate coins and again asked to make the circle equal in size. When the actual size of the coin was compared with the size selected by the child, some suggestive results were obtained. All children overestimated the size of the coins, but the greater the value of the coins, the greater the overestimation. Now, in the United States monetary system, the size of the coin is not always proportional to its value. Even though dimes and pennies are almost the same size, the children overestimated the size of the dime more than they overestimated the size of the penny.

A second important finding was that the poor children overestimated the size of the coins more than rich children. Some writers have assumed that the results imply that poor children have a greater "need" for money and thus overestimate the size of the coins. Although this is a temptingly simple deduction, its validity is questionable. It is possible that poor children have less contact with money and that their lack of familiarity with coins results in different estimations. Moreover, one might argue that rich children have a greater need for money, since they presumably have more to spend and are aware of its use.

The idea that visual thresholds may vary as a function of the personality of the individual has been an attractive hypothesis to many experimenters. Similarly, there have been occasional suggestions that visual stimuli near threshold may be undetected by an individual but may still have an effect on behavior. This possibility, known as *subliminal perception,* or sometimes as *subception,* has also attracted considerable attention among advertisers, for it suggests that motivation may be controlled without the subject's awareness. We have no dependable evidence that the presentation of subliminal stimuli is effective in *motivating* behavior; there is, however, evidence that stimuli presented below threshold are "perceived," even though the subject does not verbally report having perceived them.

McGinnies (1949) used a *tachistoscope* (Table 1–A) and projected a series of words on a screen for different durations. Some durations were below threshold, one dependent variable in the study being the determination of the perceptual threshold in terms of the duration of the exposure of the words. Some of the words were "neutral," such as *dance, glass,* and *broom.* Others were selected as taboo words: *raped, bitch, penis,* etc. The threshold for recognition among undergraduates averaged around 0.07 second for the neutral words and around 0.12 second for most of the taboo words. The implication is clear that taboo words are not recognized so quickly as neutral words, although the reason for this is not clear. Howes and Solomon (1950) pointed out that the results might reflect frequency of usage or familiarity of the words and supplied evidence that recognition is a function of frequency of usage. The interpretation that the results indicate some type of perceptual defensive mechanism on the part of the subjects has been suggested (see McGinnies, 1949; Bitterman & Kniffin, 1953; Postman, Bronson, & Gropper, 1953; Postman, 1953; Eriksen, 1954; Murdock, 1954; Lazarus, 1954; J. T. Freeman, 1954; Andrieux, 1954; G. S. Blum, 1955; Wiener, 1955).

Although the mechanisms underlying perceptual defense are not well understood, there is no question that visual thresholds may vary as a function of the experiences of the individual and that these variations may be manipulated experimentally. It is important to remember, however, that the term *threshold* usually means only that the stimulus is ob-

served half the time. Further, most psychophysical procedures employ a verbal response, such as "I see it" or "I don't see it." When we speak of a threshold for visual perception, we make the assumption that the verbal response is equivalent to the visual perception. In all likelihood, the correspondence is not 1:1, for it is reasonable to assume that a visual perception may occur which is above the threshold for perception but below the threshold for verbal response. Hence, it is helpful to recognize at the onset that the presence of subliminal perception may reflect nothing more than the lack of perfect agreement between perception and verbal response. As Goldiamond says: "The response 'I see' is not accepted as an indicator of vision when made by a blind man, nor for that matter, by many experimenters when the subject has vision worse than 20/20. Thus, the danger of using the . . . [verbal response] for subjective inferences is that such use tends to lead the experimenter to classify responses on a semantic basis, rather than in methodological terms" (Goldiamond, 1958, p. 403).

On the other hand, a variety of experimental conditions have shown *behavior without awareness* (J. K. Adams, 1957). Although this phrase is not easily definable without reference to specific experimental conditions, the phenomena which the concept describes are, in general, those in which the subject makes a response predicted by the experiments and by the experimental conditions but in which the subject is unable to state or recognize the conditions which prompted the change in behavior. J. K. Adams (1957) notes several types of experiments which have produced behavior without awareness. Although not all have employed purely perceptual tasks, the expectation is strong that all occur when perceptual tasks are employed in the experimental design.

In the first type of study the subject is not aware of the behavior itself. For example, J. G. Miller (1939) presented five geometric figures at illuminations determined to be below threshold. Under four illumination conditions, the percentage of figures recognized correctly was above that which would be expected statistically. A number of experiments of this type have been performed (see J. K. Adams, 1957). Most have shown that the recognition level is above that which would be expected statistically. In addition to methodological difficulties in these studies, however, it is also possible that the fact that the threshold is a statistical approximation rather than a definite point may account for this kind of "awareness."

In a second type of study the subject is unaware that he is responding, even though subsidiary measures, other than verbal responses, indicate a reaction. Lazarus and McCleary (1951) presented 10 syllables to subjects. A light shock was administered with the presentation of 5 of the syllables. Later, the threshold for all the syllables was determined while recordings of the *galvanic skin response* (GSR), a commonly used measure of emotion, were taken. Even though the subjects were unable to identify verbally anything special about the syllables, the GSR record indicated an increase in emotion when the five previously shocked syllables were presented. These results indicate that the subjects had learned to respond differently to some syllables, even though they could not state the difference between shock and nonshocked syllables. The interpretation of these findings in terms similar to the interpretations of studies of perceptual defense has promoted disagreement (C. W. Eriksen & Kuethe, 1956; Howes & Solomon, 1950; Lazarus, 1956; McGinnies, 1950).

In a third type of study which has occasionally supported the behavior-without-awareness principle, the subject is told that some information is being given which is expected to influence behavior, but he is not told anything more than the general nature of the cue. The subject might be presented with a group of blocks of different shapes and colors and be asked to arrange them in appropriate groups. The solution might be that red or green circles belonged in one group and blue and yellow squares in another, or it might be that red and blue squares belonged in one

group and yellow and green squares in the other. The subjects readily identify the major dimensions of the problem, e.g., that the clue lies in associating colors with shapes. It is probable that learning under these conditions comes about through nonverbal thinking and is not a true case of behavior without awareness. I might solve the problem without speaking, but it is likely that I "talk to myself" about possible solutions.

In a fourth and similar type of study, the subject has no information about the nature of the solution or the cue. For example, the subject may be asked to say all the words that come to him, and the experimenter might say "Right" or "Wrong" according to a previously arranged pattern which is dependent on the subject's choice of words (Postman & Jarrett, 1952; Philbrick & Postman, 1955). As we shall note, the format for this type of study is also used often in studies of verbal "conditioning" (Chapter 14).

There is no question that behavior without awareness occurs, but the real question is "Awareness of what?" A subject may show a change in motor behavior without being able to describe the change verbally, and, conversely, he may change his verbal behavior without changing other responses. Subliminal perception may occur under these circumstances; i.e., a subject may indicate that he is responding to a stimulus when one measure of response, such as verbal behavior, is used and fail to show a response to another measure. Reviewers have been notably reluctant to find conclusive proof of the presence of subliminal perception as a phenomenon in its own right (see particularly Coover, 1917, for the older literature; J. G. Miller, 1942; Lazarus & McCleary, 1951; J. K. Adams, 1957; Goldiamond, 1958).

The field of visual perception pervades many aspects of contemporary psychology. This reflects the fact that the influence of visual stimuli is greater than that of other sensory systems for the human being. In addition, the visual apparatus appears to be influenced by learning, motivation, and other psychological principles more than other sensory systems. Accordingly, visual perception is a convenient independent variable for many studies which are concerned with understanding the development of behavior.

SOURCES

In Chapters 8 and 9 I have attempted to touch upon many topics which compose visual perception at the expense of treating selected topics more thoroughly. On the other hand, I have attempted to provide references to recent reviews, so that the student may seek out more detailed information. The following sources are suggested in addition to the reviews cited in the text.

Color Vision: The development of theories of color vision is reviewed by Boring (1942) in a straightforward historical account. In a book of readings, Teevan and Birney (1961) present some of the original papers since Newton. Of particular interest is the work of many theorists whose original publications are not easily obtainable. Graham's review of the history and current status of color theory (1959) is excellent. In the same volume, Pirenne and Marriott (1959) review the relation between quantum theory and visual psychophysics.

In textbooks, the tradition has been to present various theories of color vision in chronological order, with indications of the agreements and disagreements between various theories. In this text, however, I chose to show that most theories have been of two polar types. Accordingly, some of the classic work of Ladd-Franklin, Fick, Mary Collins, Green, and others has been omitted or has received only scattered attention. The student interested in the development of these theories may consult the standard sources, such as Geldard (1953), Osgood (1953), Pirenne and Marriott (1959), Woodworth and Schlosberg (1954). The only reviews which fully consider contemporary work are by Graham (1959; 1965c). He also considers the development of statistical theory

of color vision, a topic not often mentioned elsewhere. Brindley (1960) includes a chapter in his physiology book, as does Weale (1960). In Reuck and Knight (1965) see chapters by Crawford and G. Svaetichin, K. Negishi, and R. Fatehchand.

Identifying the Stimulus and Color Mixture: Consultation of the original sources reported in the text is the most efficient way of gaining further information in these areas. Judd's chapter (1951) is a competent, although difficult, source. Geldard (1953) discusses these matters in depth. W. D. Wright (1958) presents a thorough book on measurement. Another source is Burnham, Hanes, and Bartleson (1963).

Development of Color Vision: Wohlwill's review (1960) of the development of visual perception includes some studies concerned with color vision. Other useful sources include E. J. Gibson and Olum (1960), Riesen (1961), and Pickford (1951). Waters, Rethlingshafer, and Caldwell (1960) contains some information on color vision in animals. Munn's book (1955) includes a valuable section concerned with technical problems in measuring color discrimination, as does a chapter by K. U. Smith (1951) and L. J. Milne and M. Milne (1959).

Deficiencies in Color Vision: The standard texts by Geldard (1953), Woodworth and Schlosberg (1954), and Wenger, F. N. Jones, and M. H. Jones (1956) provide summaries similar to that presented in this text. Pickford's book (1951) contains a detailed discussion of color vision, although the reader should remember that the purpose of the review is closely associated with the writer's theoretical position. Pieron's text (1952) is also useful. Hsia and Graham (1965) have provided an excellent chapter on deficiencies. The topic is reviewed periodically in the *Annual Review of Psychology*. In Reuck and Knight (1965) see the chapter by Pickford.

Phenomena of Visual Perception: The literature in this area is so vast that one could write several tomes which did nothing except review the relevant literature. Reviews of selected portions (space perception, constancy, etc.) appear often, particularly in the *Psychological Bulletin.* For example, see Zuckerman and Rock (1957), who present some cogent arguments regarding past experience and innate visual perception; Sagara and Oyama (1957), who discuss some important work on figural aftereffects; and Wohlwill (1960), who reviews the development of perception. Perception is often used as a dependent variable in studies of leadership, defensiveness, brain damage, and personality disorders. The present chapter has, for the most part, left discussion of these topics to later chapters.

For further information on the special topics treated in this section, Woodworth and Schlosberg (1954) provide the most thorough account. This source is especially useful, since the writers discuss problems of procedure, technique, and interpretation of results of great value to anyone anticipating a project in the areas. One trend in research in visual perception has been unnecessary duplication: the vastness of the topic and the number of approaches make it difficult for even the most faithful to be aware of all the literature. Accordingly, the fact that Woodworth and Schlosberg do not omit the older literature is of inestimable value to the reader. Dember's book (1960) includes more recent references, although he does not attempt the detail of Woodworth and Schlosberg. Hochberg (1964) has written a concise book on this topic with many illustrations and demonstrations. On figural afterimages, see the review by Ganz (1966).

In addition to the original works of gestalt-oriented writers, both Ellis's sourcebook (1938) of gestalt psychology and Henle's (1961) collection of important papers concerned with the gestalt approach furnish the student with greater depth in the gestalt view of perception than is afforded in the present chapter. The book of readings by Beardslee and Michael Wertheimer (1958) contains some important gestalt articles, some of which are not available elsewhere in English (see also Köhler, 1959).

Blake and Ramsey (1951) present a useful book of readings consisting of papers concerned with the relationship between perception and personality. A similar book by Ittelson and Kutash (1961) presents papers on perception and psychopathology, although the papers are largely concerned with the transactional approach to perception, which is discussed only indirectly in the present volume. Another useful source for information regarding the transactional approach is Kilpatrick's (1961) collection of papers. In addition, see chapters by Ogle (1959) on stereoscopic vision, Blank (1959) on binocular space perception, Prentice (1959) on the work of Wolfgang Köhler, J. J. Gibson (1959) writing about his own contributions, Postman and Tolman (1959) on Brunswick's "probabilistic" approach to perception, and Helson (1958) on adaptation-level theory. Also, see Postman (1963) on perception and learning, Schoenfield and Cumming (1963) on behavior and perception, and Guttman (1963) on the laws of behavior and facts of perception.

Mussen's (1960) *Handbook of Research Methods in Child Development* contains some relevant sources, particularly in regard to perception in children. Similarly, Jaensch's (1930) classic work on eidetic imagery presents an old but still living set of data on this phenomenon.

CHAPTER TEN

CUTANEOUS, KINESTHETIC, ORGANIC, AND VESTIBULAR SYSTEMS

INTRODUCTION

We refer to the sensations produced through the stimulation of the skin as *cutaneous sensibility*. The skin contains many structures, including several different kinds of receptor bodies, which may be classified into major groups. In places the skin is extended by underlying vessels and veins; in places it is smooth or rough; in other places it is withered and wrinkled. It is taut in certain locations, such as the heel, and flabby in others, such as the earlobe. The skin may be regarded as a large, irregular, and nonspecialized receptor for cutaneous sensibility. It is not an isolated, separate, or specialized receptor, for it maintains several sources of contact with the remainder of the body through nerves and blood vessels. Unlike either the eye or the ear, the skin is sensitive to many kinds of stimulation (e.g., mechanical, thermal, chemical), and it produces a variety of sensations (e.g., hot, cold, itch, pain, pressure). The cutaneous receptors are stimulated from outside the body. In this way, the cutaneous sense is like vision and hearing but unlike kinesthesis and the vestibular sense.

In *kinesthesis* stimulation comes from sources within the body. Receptors, sometimes similar to those found in the cutaneous system, are located in the deeper body tissue—the muscles, tendons, joints, and linings of the viscera. The receptors are stimulated by the motion of the various components of the body. The kinesthetic receptors provide information necessary for motor coordination, and they report the condition of internal portions of the body, conditions such as stomachache, intestinal discomfort, or whether a muscle is taut or stretched. Because these receptors are internal, it is difficult to get reliable data on their functioning *in situ*.

In *vestibular sensitivity* the receptor system responds to changes in the movement of the head. As we know from Chapter 6, the receptor, called the *nonauditory labyrinth*, is related anatomically to the ear. The receptor is posterior to the cochlea, and the vestibular system shares the vestibulocochlear nerve, more commonly known as the auditory nerve or the acoustic nerve (the VIIIth cranial nerve), with the ear. It is for this reason that many pathological conditions of hearing are associated with pathological conditions of balance. The vestibular receptor does not report an easily identifiable sensation, such as heat or pain, yet it does provide information regarding the position of the head.

In this chapter, we shall analyze these sensory systems and discuss the organic sensations of hunger and thirst, which are important drives in the behavior of all animals, including man. Since hunger and thirst have kines-

thetic associations, we shall include them in our discussion of kinesthetic sensibility.

Cutaneous Receptors: The skin may be conveniently, if not completely accurately, described in terms of several layers of tissue. The external surface, the *epidermis,* may be divided into five separate segments, as shown in Figure 10–1; in reality, the distinction between these segments is not so clear as it is in the diagram. The outer layer is the *stratum corneum.* It is composed largely of epithelial cells which have become hardened. The cells nearest the surface are the hardest, probably because they are stimulated and damaged most

FIGURE 10–1: *Layers of the epidermis, greatly magnified. (From Andrews, 1963, p. 3.)*

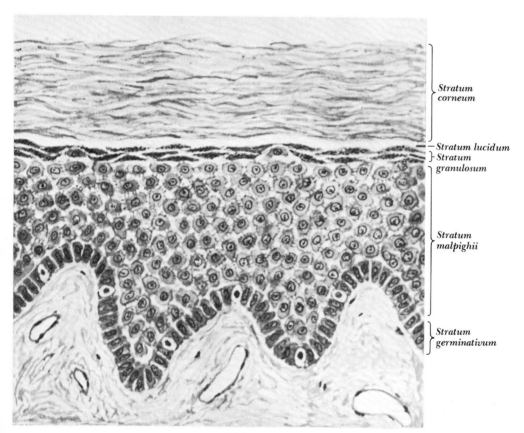

Stratum corneum

Stratum lucidum
Stratum granulosum

Stratum malpighii

Stratum germinativum

often and because they are farther from the nutrients furnished by the blood supply. The depth of this layer varies. It is thick on the palm of the hands and the soles of the feet and relatively thin in such places as the eyelids, cheeks, and prepuce. The primary function of this segment appears to be protective. The *stratum lucidum* is thin, translucent, and usually colorless. The *stratum granulosum* is thicker than the stratum lucidum. It is thickest on the palms and soles. The malpighian layer *(stratum Malpighii)* contains a series of cells built upon one another in a mosaic pattern. These cells contain living nuclei. The last segment, the *stratum germinativum,* is usually only a single cell in depth. The cells in this stratum are undergoing mitosis; as a cell is produced, it moves slowly upward through the succeeding layers. Thus a new cell grows, dies, and becomes hardened as it passes through the layers of the epidermis from the stratum germinativum to the stratum corneum.

Under the epidermis lies the *corium*, which contains the supportive tissue, glands, blood system, and hair follicles that may be the major receptors for cutaneous sensations. The corium is generally believed to have two segments, the *papillary* layer and the *reticular* layer. The papillary layer lies next to the epidermis. It contains a rich blood supply and nerve endings, which appear to be sensitive to different types of stimulation. These receptors often protrude into the epidermal layers. The reticular layer is dense and lies next to the *subcutaneous tissue*. This tissue supports the vessels and nerves passing through it and contains some deep hair follicles, specialized receptors which are assumed to be sensitive to specific types of stimulation. Figure 10–2 shows the general structure of these layers.

In human skin, a variety of cellular endings is present. These endings are presumed to be the receptors for the sensations associated with cutaneous sensitivity. There are several problems in assuming that specific receptors are associated with specific sensations. However, there is certainly a correlation between the type of receptor stimulated and resulting sensation. Before we consider the problems asso-

ciated with connecting a specific receptor to a specific sensation, we shall consider the major receptors found in the skin.

Free nerve endings abound in every layer of the skin. In the epidermis, they extend as far as the stratum granulosum. Usually a number of free nerve endings are supported by a single nerve. This means that stimulation of one of a number of endings will produce the sensation of stimulation of a single nerve. Therefore the ability of the organism to localize the stimulus is less than it would be if each receptor were served by a single nerve. Some free nerve endings are covered with a myelinated sheath, known as a *medullary substance*. Others are *nonmedullated*. These are commonly found near the root of hair follicles. Some medullated free nerve endings are looped; i.e., they pass into the papillary layer and then return to the reticular layer or subcutaneous tissue. These endings are abundant; they overlap in intricate patterns and are extremely delicate. The free nerve ending appears to be the prototype of more finely differentiated medullated structures which appear in various segments of the skin. It is convenient, although conceivably erroneous, to think of the free nerve endings as the basic structure from which other receptors have developed. Among the other major receptors are *Pacinian corpuscles, Merkel disks, Krause end bulbs, Meissner corpuscles, Ruffini cylinders, Golgi-Mazzoni corpuscles,* and *basket endings.*[1]

Pacinian corpuscles are elongated and contain an outer surface composed of a series of concentric sheaths, much like an onion. They are the largest of the specialized receptors, averaging around 2 mm in length, though some approach 5 mm. Each corpuscle has a blood supply, and capillaries may be found between the sheaths. The nerve carries into the center of the corpuscle, gradually losing

[1] Other names are often used for these structures: for Pacinian corpuscles, corpuscles of Vater; for Merkel disks, touch cells; for Krause end bulbs, bulb corpuscles, *kolbendorperchen;* for Meissner corpuscles, corpuscles of Wagner, tactile corpuscles; for Ruffini cylinders, terminal cylinders, arboriform terminations.

its medullation as it does so. Compared with other receptors, Pacinian corpuscles are found in deep tissue, generally in the subcutaneous tissue, and occasionally in the corium.

They are also found deep inside the body and near the joints, an observation which suggests that they may be used in kinesthetic sensations as well as pressure. Figure 10–3

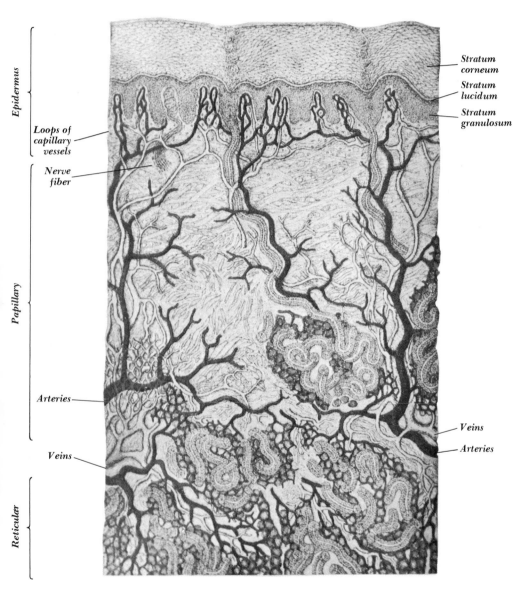

FIGURE 1 0 – 2 : *A section of the palm of the hand magnified 150 diameters, emphasizing the segments of the corium. Certain components described in the text are labeled in the figure. (From Ormsby, 1927, p. 19.)*

shows a schematic diagram of a Pacinian corpuscle taken from a duck's bill.

Merkel disks, which are oval-shaped receptors with a nucleus, are found in the corium and in the epidermis. They are flatter and smaller than Pacinian corpuscles and are most commonly noted in the mouth, lips, and fingertips, as well as in the skin surrounding the abdomen.

Krause end bulbs are more rounded than either Pacinian corpuscles or Merkel disks. The center is nonnucleated, and the external surface is formed of connective tissue. They are commonly found in the tongue, lips, glans penis, clitoris, and around the eye and the cornea of the eye. They are located throughout the corium.

Meissner corpuscles are elongated, like Pacinian corpuscles, but are smaller. A Meissner corpuscle may be formed from several capsules. As in the Pacinian corpuscles, the attending nerve is medullated. The nerve not only penetrates the corpuscle but also separates in such a way that portions of it encircle the receptor itself. Meissner corpuscles are generally found in the papillary layer of the corium and in hairless regions of the skin. Quite often they are packed densely.

Ruffini cylinders (Figure 10–4) are unusual in shape, compared with other receptors. They are greatly elongated, and the nerve enters from the side. One nerve may serve several cylinders. They are usually found in the subcutaneous layers, and they have been reported in deep tissue.

Golgi-Mazzoni corpuscles are found throughout the body but are most widely distributed in the corium, in subcutaneous layers, and in the muscles and joints. Accordingly, they may have a kinesthetic as well as a cutaneous function.

Basket endings are found near the locus of hair follicles, either in the corium or in subcutaneous tissue. In appearance, they form a "basket" for the hair root from a series of nerves.

It is commonly speculated that the free nerve endings provide the rudimentary method of nerve communication for the receptors. The observation that some structures have developed specialized endings composed of additional tissue implies that each structure is sensitive to slightly different forms of stimulation. For example, the presence of a specialized ending means that the nerve may not be stimulated directly; the surrounding tissue must be bent or manipulated in some manner to stimulate the nerve. In addition, the fact that more than one receptor may be served by the same nerve in some cases means that accurate localization of stimulation is difficult. Since stimulation is transmitted by the nerve and since stimulation of any of several receptors may activate the same nerve, it is difficult to determine the particular receptor which has been stimulated.

Nor can the receptors be easily differentiated from one another. None except Pacinian corpuscles can be observed under the microscope without staining, and not all are sensitive to the same stain. One of the major advances in the identification of the cutaneous receptors has been the development of refined staining techniques. In addition, an isolated receptor may be difficult to classify, for it may have characteristics which confuse it with another kind.

Figure 10–5 shows a purely schematic dia-

FIGURE 10–3: *Diagram of a Pacinian corpuscle from a duck's bill. (From Ormsby, 1927, p. 30, after Renault, n.s.)*

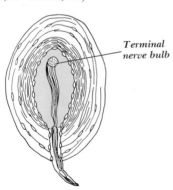

Terminal nerve bulb

gram of the location of certain receptors and other aspects of the cutaneous system. The representations are greatly stylized, and the receptors have been located in the area which they occupy within the cutaneous layers.

The Problem: Stimulus and Receptor: In the 1880s, Blix (Swedish), Goldscheider (German), and Donaldson (American) each reported separately that the skin is differentially sensitive to several types of stimulation. They reported that if a section of the skin was marked in a grid pattern and if the areas within the grid were stimulated systematically with cold, hot, pressure, and painful stimuli, particular areas within the grid appeared to be sensitive to one kind of stimulus but not to others. Figure 10–6 shows a plot of a section sensitive to hot and to cold within an area of 1 square centimeter on the forearm. Even though some of the *sensitive spots,* as they are often called, changed position during the four-day interval, they remained in the same general location.

The discovery of differential sensitivity of the skin led, quite naturally, to a search for specialized receptors. As we know from the previous section, such receptors exist. After both differential stimulation and separate receptors had been found, the next step was to correlate the stimulus with the receptor in order to discover which type of receptor was sensitive to which type of stimulation. This was done by mapping a section of the skin and examining the underlying structures histologically. If there is a correlation between the receptor and the sensation, then the cold spots should always be found in locations where a specific receptor is available, and warm spots should be found at the location of another type of receptor. It has been established that some sensations correlate with the presence of particular receptors but not always. In some parts of the body, only one kind of receptor is present, and only one type of sensation is reported; yet elsewhere the same kind of receptor fails to produce the expected sensation. Certain kinds of pain, most types of pressure, and certain temperature

FIGURE 10–4: *A Ruffini cylinder. The connective tissue sheath covers the terminations of the axis cylinders. The nerve fibers leave the organ in a bundle. (From Lickley, 1912, p. 117, after Ruffini, 1894.)*

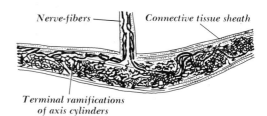

Nerve-fibers — Connective tissue sheath

Terminal ramifications of axis cylinders

FIGURE 10–5: *Some possible relationships between organs and the accompanying sensations. Note the relative depths of the receptors. Cutaneous innervation: (A) groups of Meissner corpuscles subserving the sensation of touch; (B) beaded nerve nets subserving pain; (C) Merkel disks subserving touch; (D) beaded nerve fibers derived from nerve nets subserving the relative pain and associated with blood vessels (probably slow pain); (E) nerve terminals around the sheath of a hair subserving touch; (F) a Pacinian corpuscle subserving touch; (G) a group of Ruffini endings subserving warmth; (H) and (I) groups of Krause end bulbs subserving cold (these lie at somewhat variable depths beneath the skin surface). The organized endings are accompanied in every instance by fine-beaded nerve fibers subserving pain. (Weddell, 1945.)*

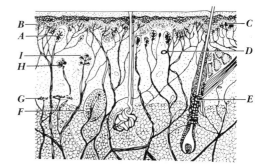

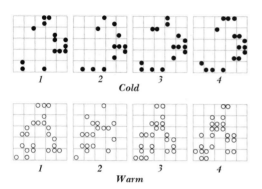

Cold

Warm

sensations appear without the presence of any particular set of underlying receptors. In short, the search has been fruitful in providing information about the receptors and the nature of the skin but unsuccessful in establishing correspondence between stimulus, receptor, and sensation.

Whereas the stimuli for audition and vision are known, many types of stimuli can trigger cutaneous sensations. For example, the sensation of pressure can result from a change in temperature; changes in temperature can be produced by chemical changes; the amount of pain that is sensed can result from a change in the pH value of a chemical; and sensations of pain, pressure, and temperature can be produced by electric stimulation. Apparently, the receptors are not differentiated in terms of the kind of stimulus required for stimulation, for a variety of stimuli may provide similar sensations. Little wonder that the skin poses a difficult problem.

Role of the Central Nervous System: Several receptors are commonly served by different fibers from the same nerve. Similarly, several nerves combine into larger bundles which transmit the impulse up the spinal cord and into the brain. Consider a simple free nerve ending, which is itself a neuron. It differs from endings such as the Pacinian corpuscle in that its dendritic process has no capsule. The proximal process of the free nerve ending is through an axon. It joins fibers from other endings, and eventually nerve fibers from other receptors are included. If the nerve is severed at this point, sensation is lost for all the modalities.

With one exception, each of the pairs of spinal cord roots receives cutaneous impulses from the periphery. Impulses from the single free nerve ending have now joined other cutaneous impulses and have reached one of the roots of the spinal cord. Once impulses reach the spinal nerves, a reorganization occurs, so that the sensations of each of the modalities join and proceed toward the brain together. For example, sensations of touch join and approach the brain via the *ventral spinothalamic tract*. The sensations of pain and temperature are transmitted by way of the *lateral spinothalamic tract* (see Chapter 2). If a tract is severed, the corresponding sensation is lost throughout the body below the cut. For example, if the lateral spinothalamic tract is cut in the spinal cord at, say, the fifth lumbar segment, only the legs would be affected. The upper regions would continue to be sensitive. Accordingly, peripheral fibers cannot be separated from one another in terms of the type of sensation they convey at any point peripheral to the spinal cord, for this may be done only when the fibers have reached the spinal cord and have grouped themselves into spinal tracts. There is, of course, a surgical advantage to the presence of separate tracts within the spinal cord, for the tract carrying pain sensations may be severed without interfering with the sensations of touch. Temperature sensitivity is likely to be lost, however, since it shares the tract with the fibers for pain. Both tracts continue to the brain centers by way of the medulla and the thalamus and eventually reach the cortex of the parietal lobes, where the impulses project upon the postcentral gyrus.

An area of skin in which all afferent fibers connect to a single nerve root is called a *dermatome*. Figure 10–7 shows the dermatomes of the human being. The plots were determined by sectioning the peripheral spinal nerves to destroy sensations connected to a single nerve root. This procedure is known as the technique of *remaining sensibility*. It may be noted that the technique of severing a nerve does not tell us the function of that nerve or dermatome; rather, it tells us the effect of severing one nerve on the function of the nerves and dermatomes which remain intact. As might be expected, the dermatomes overlap far more than is indicated in the figure. It is likely that any given point on the skin is handled by more than a single nerve root. Also, the size and location of the dermatome will vary as a function of type of stimulation; "pain" dermatomes, for example, are smaller in area than "temperature" or "touch" dermatomes.

In addition to dermatomes, which are determined by a single nerve root in the spinal cord, areas known as *peripheral nerve fields* have been noted. These areas are supplied by a single cutaneous nerve fiber. They are, of course, quite small. However, several zones of sensibility may be identified within a peripheral nerve field. The *autonomous zone* is served only by the nerve. Severance of the nerve results in loss of the sensation in the zone. The *intermediate zone* is formed by the overlap of peripheral nerve fields. Even following severance of the single nerve, there is some sensation from the area which it serves, since the nerve from a second peripheral nerve field may carry the impulse. If the nerve is severed, the sensations arising from the intermediate zone are qualitatively different from those reported prior to the severance. Head (1920) showed that when the nerve is severed, the threshold for pain increases, so that a stronger stimulus is required to produce the sensation. Further, if the threshold is exceeded, the quality of the pain is different, for it is reported as both intense and burning. Similarly, changes in the sensation of temperature

FIGURE 10–7: *Location of the dermatomes as viewed from the front of the body. Note the relative size of the dermatome areas in the legs as compared with those on the trunk. Similar dermatomes appear if one looks at the back of the body, rather than the front. The letters C, T, L, and S are used for general identification. (T. Lewis, 1942, p. 20, as plotted from Foerster, 1933.)*

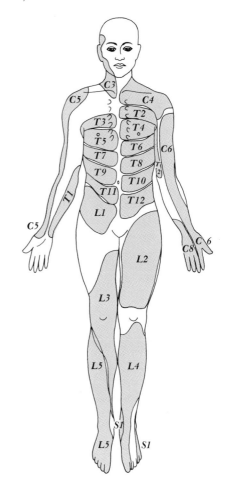

are reported. This finding led Head to provide a theory of the evolution of pain sensitivity which we shall consider later in this chapter. Four cranial nerves are also involved in the transmission of cutaneous sensations: the trigeminal (Vth), facial (VIIth), glossopharyngeal (IXth), and vagus (Xth). Of these, the trigeminal appears to be the most influential.

Figure 10–8 shows a schematic diagram of the relationship between the original receptor (in this case, the free nerve ending) and other nerve fibers.

Pathways between the tracts within the spinal cord and the nuclei are well established. They are, however, complex. Some fibers synapse with motor units forming the physiological basis for reflexive behavior. Sensory roots are divided into two bundles, the *medial bundle* and the *lateral bundle*. The former has large myelinated fibers and serves the pressure receptors. Small unmyelinated fibers make up the lateral bundle which serves the pain and temperature receptors. Accordingly, we have two systems, one for conducting pressure impulses and one for conducting pain and temperature sensations.

The medial bundle enters the dorsal aspect

FIGURE 10–8: *A schematic diagram showing the relationship between the receptor and nerve fibers. Within the dermatome, the autonomous and intermediate zones are shown. The diagram shows the probable effect of severing nerve fibers at points along the pathway.*

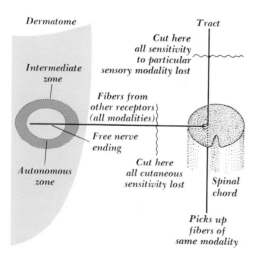

of the cord and eventually crosses to the ventral side. The cord has two dorsal columns: *fasciculus gracilis* and *fasciculus cuneatus*. In the medulla these pathways end at the *gracile nucleus* and the *cuneate nucleus*. Fibers from the lateral bundle cross the cord to the gray matter of the dorsal horn and approach the brain through the lateral spinothalamic tract (see Chapter 2). The medial bundle, on the other hand, ascends through the ventral spinothalamic tract.

The lateral spinothalamic tract appears to contain two tracts, one for temperature and one for pain. The former continues directly to the thalamus, where it synapses. The pain tract sends fibers throughout the gray matter. However, the tract synapses in the thalamus with fibers that continue to the projection area.

Within the brain, the pathways for sensation from the head, the trunk, and the limbs join at the medulla. Here the cranial nerves associated with the head meet the pathways from the rest of the body which ascend to the brain via the spinal cord (trigeminal, facial, glossopharyngeal, and vagus nerves.) Thus in the area of the medulla, different sensations are separated by the tract their fibers use. Cutaneous pressure is in the ventral spinothalamic tract; pain and temperature, in the lateral. Kinesthetic sensations are served by a separate set of tracts, comprising the lateral spinocerebellar tract. In some way, information about the nature of the sensation is coded at the thalamic level and uncoded at the level of a projection area. The projection area is the *postcentral gyrus* (Chapter 2), and it is topographic. Two characteristics of the topographic arrangement are important: first, the location of the representation from toes to head is ordered, the top of the projection area representing the legs, followed by an area for the trunk, arms, and face; second, the amount of space devoted to each area appears to be a function of the complexity of the area. Thus, among human beings, the face consumes more space on the projective area than, say, the legs or toes, but less than the hands. The face region is an exception, for it is bilaterally represented.

If we measure the location of electric potentials on the cortex, we find areas, in addition to the locations described above, which are responsive to cutaneous and kinesthetic stimulation. *Somatic area I* corresponds with the postcentral gyrus. From this area, we may record potentials in response to stimulation of the skin or muscle. It has been noted, however, that when kinesthetic sensations are provided, potentials come from the *precentral cortex* (which lies anterior to the postcentral cortex) as well as from the postcentral gyrus. Thus, cutaneous sensations are limited to the postcentral cortex, although kinesthetic sensations appear in both the precentral and postcentral cortex as well as the cerebellum. The precentral cortex is known as the *motor cortex,* for it is from this area that motor impulses begin their descent through the spinal cord to the muscles. Moreover, the recordings provide us with a more complete understanding of the topographical arrangement of the cortex (Rose & Mountcastle, 1959). *Somatic area II* lies near the temporal lobe and the area of the auditory cortex. Apparently, impulses to area II come from both sides of the body. In area I, the side of the body from which the sensations originate is also represented on the cortex; i.e., area I is *contralateral*—the left side of the body is reproduced on the right side of the cortex, and the right side of the body is reproduced on the left side of the cortex except for the face (Rose & Mountcastle, 1959).

THERMAL SENSITIVITY

Heat and Cold as Separate Systems: There is compelling evidence that human beings and other animals possess two distinct sensory systems for temperature, one for cold sensations and one for hot sensations. Using a warm stimulus (40 to 50 degrees Centigrade), one may find certain spots on the skin which yield the sensation of cold. This is paradoxical, since a stimulus of this temperature is clearly perceived as warm in most cutaneous locations. The fact that a warm stimulus may produce the sensation of cold is known as *paradoxical cold.* The opposite, *paradoxical warmth,* has been reported in the literature (Woodworth & Schlosberg, 1954, p. 283), although this phenomenon does not appear to be so clearly established or so easily obtainable as paradoxical cold.

A second source of data which supports the idea of two separate sensory systems is that a map of the skin based on response to hot and cold stimuli indicates the presence of "warm spots" and "cold spots." In general, cold spots are more numerous; they are especially prevalent in the upper lip, nose, chin, chest, elbow bend, forearm, and back of the hand, with over 6.5 spots per cm² reported in these areas. The greatest accumulation of warm spots appears in the fingers and nose (see Table 3–D). The presence of a large number of cold spots does not exclude the possibility of a large number of warm spots in the same area. The number of spots for heat and the number for cold vary independently of each other. Thus, temperature sensitivity itself is variable throughout the skin. Moreover, the estimates of the number of cold and warm spots are based on stimuli of one intensity protruding into the skin at a uniform depth. Changes in the intensity, depth, and duration of the stimulus would yield differences in the number of spots reported.

A third source of data informs us that the skin responds differently to warming and cooling. Bazett and his colleagues (Bazett & McGlone, 1932; Bazett, McGlone, & Brocklehurst, 1930; Bazett, McGlone, R. G. Williams, & Lufkin, 1932) developed the technique of implanting tiny thermocouples into the skin. A thermocouple, when used with a bridge circuit, may serve as a small thermometer capable of measuring the temperature inside tissue. These experimenters located cold and warm spots by the mapping process and then placed the thermocouple at various depths under the spots while applying an appropriate stimulus to the surface of the skin. A series of explorations with both warm and cold stimuli produced two general findings: (1) The temperature of the physical stimulus is not accurately reflected even on the surface of the skin directly below the stimulus. With moderate and nonpainful stimuli, the difference between the physical stimulus and the external surface of the skin is often 10°C. (2) Rather large changes in the temperature of the stimulus, up to 15°C, produce only slight changes in the temperature of the underlying tissue. The speed with which the stimulus penetrates the underlying tissue is not constant but appears to vary as a function of the state of dilation of the blood vessels. Heat stimulation travels more slowly through tissue which contains dilated blood vessels. This finding has formed the basis of a major theory of temperature reception (Nafe & Wagoner, 1936; Kenshalo & Nafe, 1962), which suggests that the primary receptor for temperature is the tissue surrounding the blood vessels.

A fourth source of data indicating the presence of separate sensory systems for warmth and cold comes from studies which show that the nerve itself is responsive to thermal changes. A single nerve yields different electric potentials, depending on whether it is being warmed or cooled (Granit & Skoglund, 1945). Bernhard and Granit (1946) surrounded a nerve bundle with a thermode cuff. The cuff emitted specified temperatures and was used to warm or cool the nerve. Using standard procedures for recording the electric potential of the nerve bundle, the investigators measured the change in potential as a function of the warming or cooling of the nerve. A difference was noted between the nonstimulated portion and the stimulated area. This difference was called the *generator potential;* it indicated the electric potential generated by the change in temperature in one portion of the nerve compared with the potential generated in other parts. Some of the data is shown in Figure 10–9, which graphs the generator potential produced by warming or cooling the nerve bundle. The more the nerve is warmed *or* cooled, the greater the change in the generator potential. Within the limits of the temperature used in this study, it appears that the gradient of the generator potential for warming is greater than that for cooling.

Figure 10–10 shows the same determinations but with the number of impulses per second from the nerve fiber presented as the dependent variable. One curve represents the number of impulses when the nerve is cooled, and the other represents the number when it is warmed. Clearly, the frequency changes with the change in temperature. The point is clear that nerves (and not necessarily only those responsible for temperature, if they exist as separate receptors) are able to respond to changes in temperature independently of any receptor.

Bazett and his colleagues have reported measurements taken with a thermocouple placed within the various layers and segments of the skin. Because of the expected importance of the blood supply to temperature sensitivity, the skin segment used in this determination was flushed with blood. Figure 10–11 indicates the suspected areas of cold and warm receptors and projects the expected vascular network. The solid line indicates changes in temperature recorded when the skin was flushed so that the capillaries were extended. The dotted line indicates measurements taken when the skin was nonflushed, or in a normal state. The presence of filled capillaries clearly exaggerates the temperature change when compared with the function that results when normal skin is employed. Moreover, there appear to be two locations where the temperature change is maximal: one is between the corium and the epidermis, and the other is in the subcutaneous tissue.

Zotterman and his colleagues (Dodt & Zotterman, 1952; Hensel & Zotterman, 1951b; Zotterman, 1953, 1959) have isolated and investigated specific fibers which are responsive either to cold or to warmth. These fibers fail to respond to mechanical or painful stimuli, but they do respond to warming or cooling. Accordingly, they are called *thermal fibers.* These fibers show the characteristic spike when stimulated.

Data from several sources indicate that there

is not a single thermal sense. At the very least, two systems exist—one for heat and one for cold. Superficially, there is some correlation between the type of receptor and the sensation. For example, cold receptors are nearer the surface of the skin, as are Krause end bulbs. Thus, it is tempting to assume that Krause end bulbs are the receptors for cold. However, it is known that certain nerve fibers, namely, thermal fibers, respond either to heat or to cold, but not to both and not to other cutaneous stimuli, such as pain or mechanical stimulators. It is possible that the single cell may serve as a thermal receptor. Wall (1961) has isolated two groups of cells. One group is found in the dorsal horn of the spinal cord (lumbar region), and the second is found in the gracile nucleus. The cells are the way station for fibers, and each cell is responsive to fibers from more than a single afferent fiber. The cells in the dorsal horn are responsive to all the peripheral fibers from the skin which converge upon them; those in the gracile nucleus are apparently responsive only to large fibers. The combination of (1) the type of afferent fibers converging upon a single cell and (2) the relationships among the cells determines the type of sensation which results from stimulation.

Wall isolated a single dorsal horn cell and applied both heat and pressure to the surface of the skin. The reaction of the single cell to the stimulus was then recorded. Figure 10–12 shows an example of the results. Parts *A, B,* and *C* indicate reactions to pressure. The ordinate, in milliseconds, indicates the interval between the recorded stimulus and the stimulus which preceded it. It may be noted that the weaker the stimulus, the more rapid the adaptation. In parts *D* and *E,* heat was applied to the skin surface area for fifteen seconds at the point marked by the arrow on the abscissa. The pattern of firing following the presentation of the warm stimulus is clearly different from the pattern prior to application.

In the study of thermal sensitivity, research emphasis has shifted from the receptors in the external surface of the skin to the nerve fibers and individual cells which aid in the trans-

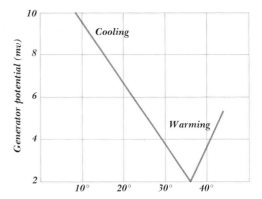

Temperature of thermode around nerve

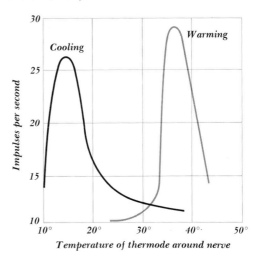

Temperature of thermode around nerve

mission of impulses. This shift parallels technical advances. It is clear, however, that the operation of cutaneous sensation (and, as we shall note in Chapter 11, that of olfaction and gustation) is different from the relatively

FIGURE 10–11: *Thermal gradients of the skin. The solid line represents measurements taken when the skin was flushed with blood, and the broken line represents measurements taken when the skin was normal. The temperatures are the difference between the temperature at the surface of the skin and the temperature at the various depths indicated along the abscissa. The probable areas of cold and warm receptors are indicated by shading. (From C. T. Morgan & Stellar, 1950, p. 240, after Bazett, 1941.)*

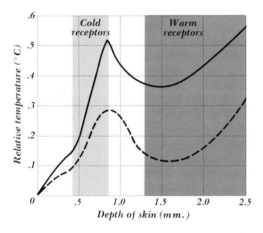

"simple" operation of vision and audition. It seems likely that the nerve, and perhaps the individual cells, "code" information which is later decoded in the nervous system.

Thresholds and Adaptation: Computing thresholds for temperature sensitivity is difficult because (1) the precise location selected on the skin is extremely important in determining the sensation, (2) the threshold varies as a function of the previous thermal state of the organism, and (3) the process of adaptation is not specific to warm or cold: adaptation to one system often affects the threshold of the other system. That is, when a spot is stimulated with a warm stimulus, a change may be noted in the threshold of succeeding cold stimuli. This finding supports the view that the temperature system is a single system.

On the other hand, at any location on the skin there is a temperature, usually around

32°C, which may be considered the transition temperature between warm and cold; i.e., any temperature above this transition temperature is perceived as warm, and any temperature lower is regarded as cold.

Under most circumstances, stimuli above 32°C result in the sensation of warmth, and stimuli cooler than 32°C result in the sensation of cold. For this reason, this point of thermal insensibility is known as *physiological zero*. However, once a stimulus of an appropriate temperature is applied, the "zero" point shifts to a new level. If the skin is cooled to 26°C until adaptation is complete, this point becomes insensitive and assumes the properties of physiological zero. Some evidence (E. A. Culler, 1926) indicates that the physical area in the state of physiological zero grows wider as the temperature is *either* increased or decreased from between 28 to 32°C. Accordingly, the zone gets progressively larger as the level of adaptation is increased or decreased.

The process of sensory adaptation is extremely important in temperature sensitivity. The receptors (and thus the skin) are able to adapt quickly to changes in temperature. Individual spots appear to have different RLs, and the adaptation rate appears to be correlated with the basic RL. The lower the RL, the longer the time required for complete adaptation. There is also evidence that the effects of stimulation are cumulative; the more a spot is stimulated without reaching complete adaptation, the longer it takes to reach complete adaptation.

A technique developed by Hardy and his associates (J. D. Hardy & Oppel, 1937; J. D. Hardy, Wolff, & Goodell, 1940) for the study of cutaneous pain has produced results with implications for the study of thermal thresholds. This technique uses *radiant heat* as the stimulus. Radiation is projected through both a condensing lens and a shutter, which permits accurate measurement of the stimulus in terms of energy, duration, and location. This procedure, in which the stimulus is projected onto the skin, produces sensations of temperature unlike those produced when the stimulus is actually placed in contact with the skin, as has been done in most studies of thermal thresholds. The disadvantage of the latter type of study is that the application of the stimulus directly may excite receptors sensitive to pressure and pain, as well as those sensitive to temperature. J. D. Hardy and Oppel (1937) report that when small areas of skin are stimulated by radiant heat, warmth is not per-

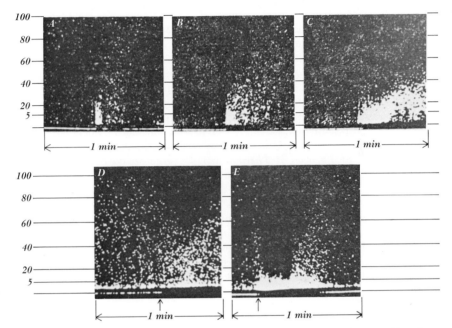

FIGURE 10-12: (A, B, C) *Reaction of a dorsal horn cell to three pressure stimuli of increasing intensity. The recordings are made by a microelectrode placement within a single cell. Stimuli: (A) 2 grams suspended from hairs in the middle of the cell's receptive field; (B) 20 grams suspended from a hair; (C) pinch applied directly to the skin. On the left of each picture, the cell is firing spontaneously without disturbance of the skin; in the middle, the stimulus was applied and remained on for the rest of the recording. Each dot represents a nerve impulse; the height above the base line represents the interval, shown in milliseconds on the scale, between the recorded impulse and the preceding one. Dots on the bottom line represent impulses that occurred at intervals greater than 100 msec after the preceding one. The pictures show the rapid adaptation to the small stimulus and the decreasing adaptation as the stimulus intensity is increased. (D, E) Reaction of a dorsal horn cell that is sensitive to skin pressure and to changes in skin temperature. The method of recording is the same as that shown in A through C. Heat was applied to the cell's receptive field by a radiant lamp for fifteen seconds after the arrow on the abscissa. In D, the skin temperature rose a maximum of $4°C$, and in E, $12°C$. The activity of the cell is shown before, during (arrow), and after the application of heat. (Wall, 1961, p. 484.)*

ceived. Under this condition, if the stimulus is sufficiently strong to elicit a response, the response is one of pain rather than warmth. A *thermal-summation* effect occurs with radiant heat, but not with direct contact. If two separate skin areas in the same part of the body, such as the forehead, are stimulated simultaneously, the threshold is lower than when the areas are stimulated separately. These findings add intriguing data to the mystery of thermal sensitivity, for the implication that the system may react differently to stimuli applied directly and those applied radiantly presents some interesting possibilities for theories of thermal sensitivity.

A Brief History of Theories of Thermal Sensitivity: We should not be astonished to find that theories of thermal sensitivity differ chiefly in the type of receptor which is considered responsible for the sensitivity. This reflects the fact that a theory is dependent upon the anatomical, physiological, and psychological knowledge of its day. For convenience, we may distinguish three major types of theories: The first assumes that specific receptors exist for all cutaneous sensitivity and that receptors for warmth and cold may be identified separately from other receptors. The second type suggests that it is the concentration of the receptors which is responsible for sensations of temperature. The third type of theory suggests that the blood vessels and vascular system are primarily responsible for thermal sensations.

Typical of the specific-receptor theory is the suggestion by Max von Frey (1852–1932; 1896) that Krause end bulbs mediate cold sensations and Ruffini cylinders mediate warm sensations. Two sets of experimental data supported this early hypothesis: First, the latency between application of the stimulus and the sensation varies, the warm stimuli having the longer latency. Accordingly, it is reasonable to assume that the specific receptors for warmth are deeper in the skin than the receptors for cold. In addition, there is a rough correlation between sensitivity and the skin areas known to

be most sensitive to temperature. The lower the threshold for thermal sensitivity, the more Krause end bulbs and Ruffini cylinders. Second, certain areas of the skin are sensitive primarily to cold alone. Histological examination indicates the presence of Krause end bulbs in these areas (Strughold & Karbe, 1925; Bazett, McGlone, R. G. Williams, & Lukin, 1932; for criticism see Dallenbach, 1927; W. L. Jenkins, 1940, 1941, 1951; Kenshalo & Nafe, 1962). Although it is possible that Krause end bulbs and Ruffini cylinders are especially sensitive to temperature stimulation, it seems unlikely that they are the only receptors responsible. There is too much evidence that temperature sensations appear in areas of the skin where these receptors do not appear in sufficient quantity to permit unequivocal acceptance of the theory of special receptors.

Jenkins (1939a; 1939b; 1939c; 1939d) has argued against the specific-receptor theory and has suggested that thermal sensitivity is a result of the concentration of receptors. The *concentration theory* assumes that many structures, including free nerve endings, may report thermal sensitivity. Since it is assumed that these receptors have different thresholds, the intensity of the thermal sensation depends upon the threshold and the number of receptors stimulated. So-called warm and cold spots are interpreted as areas where the receptors are most densely concentrated. Jenkins has suggested that the receptors (whether they be actual receptors or nerve fibers) take part in a chemical reaction similar to that proposed by Hering to account for the function of the cones in color vision. It is suggested that a change in temperature is sufficient to cause the chemical change, probably through the breakdown of an unspecified compound, and that this breakdown stimulates the nerve fiber. Separate reactions are proposed for warmth and for cold.

Although the suggestion of chemical breakdown fits the facts of adaptation and of different latencies of response to warm and to cold stimuli, the chemical content of the proposed compound is only speculative. However, this general type of theory is supported by the work of Hensel and Zotterman (1951a) who, as we have noted, examined the properties of nerve fibers. They noted that axons which respond to thermal changes are relatively insensitive to mechanical stimulation and axons which are responsive to mechanical stimulation are not so sensitive to thermal changes. Smaller axons are more receptive to thermal changes than larger ones. This finding has led Zotterman (1959) to suggest a chemical process similar to that proposed by Jenkins. In addition, Zotterman assumes that the chemical reactions are of two kinds: one for cold sensitivity and one for warm. This viewpoint is supported by the observation (Hensel & Zotterman, 1951a) that some fibers appear to respond only to an increase in temperature and others only to a decrease. This approach emphasizes the presence of a separate system for the two thermal sensations.

Nafe has suggested that temperature sensibility is mediated by the neurovascular system. It is proposed that warmth and cold result from the constriction and dilation of the blood vessels and smooth muscle tissue. This hypothesis suggests that thermal sensitivity is similar to kinesthesis in origin. Perhaps the most appealing virtue of this theory is that it postulates a single mechanism for thermal sensitivity. Physiological zero represents the point at which the vascular system and the smooth muscle walls of the blood vessels are neither dilated nor constricted. As temperature is increased, the system dilates, producing the sensation of warmth. When heat becomes sufficiently intense, the muscles and tissue contract spastically, yielding pain. Similarly, when the temperature is decreased from physiological zero, the system contracts, producing the sensation of cold. When it is sufficiently contracted, the accompanying spastic contractions result in pain.

The fact that the neurovascular theory accounts for the pain from intense thermal stimulation is advantageous, for other theories must depend upon a separate receptor system to explain it. In addition, the fact that, apparently, smooth muscles contract and dilate in response to temperature stimulation (T. Lewis, 1927; C. L. Evans, 1956) gives credence to the hypothesis. The theory is said to account for paradoxical cold because of the observation (C. L. Evans, 1956) that even when a muscle is relaxed at warm temperatures, portions of it are constricted. In addition, Evan's work supports the idea that at extreme temperatures spasticity results. When smooth muscle is warmed to around 45 degrees Celsius, the muscle dilates, but some parts of the tissue constrict.

Although the neurovascular theory is parsimonious, some major problems exist for it. Perhaps the most critical objection is that it fails to account for the observation that warm and cold spots may be located. If both warmth and cold have their origin in kinesthetic sensations of smooth muscle dilation and contraction, why should the sensation of warmth appear in some location but not in others? In addition, the observation that cold spots are more numerous than warm spots is not readily explained by the theory.

The neurovascular theory also has a great deal to say about the way pressure is perceived. As a theory of thermal sensitivity, it has some clear advantages and probably no more disadvantages than any other theory. However, the fact that all these basic theories of thermal sensitivity have persisted so long is a clear indication that insufficient relevant data exist to destroy any of them. One commonly cited virtue of a good thory is that it should encourage research, and it seems likely that the neurovascular theory has excited as much research as any other theory of cutaneous sensitivity (Nafe, 1929, 1934, 1938; Nafe & Wagoner, 1936; Kenshalo & Nafe, 1962).

TOUCH AND PRESSURE SENSIBILITY

Phenomenologically, at least, our sense of tactile stimulation may be placed on a continuum ranging from light touch through pressure to pain. However, this placement might encourage us to believe that all three sensations originate in the same sensory system. As we shall see, there is evidence favoring the theory that there are separate receptors for touch and pressure. There is also evidence that specific fibers are sensitive to mechanical stimulation. Pain, of course, is experienced whenever a sensory system is stimulated excessively. Loud noise hurts the ears, bright light hurts the eyes, and extreme pressure to the skin is painful. However, we must not assume that pain is nothing more than the result of overstimulation. It is possible that pain is a separate, identifiable sensory system. For this reason, a section of this chapter is devoted to a discussion of pain, even though the sensation must be mentioned in connection with other systems.

The most evident problems associated with mechanical sensibility are (1) What is the effective receptor? Is there a specialized receptor—a Pacinian corpuscle, for example—or do nerve fibers respond to the stimulus directly? (2) What are the effective stimuli that create tactile sensibility? What do electrical energy, light hairs, or certain chemicals have in common which renders them able to create the sensation of tactile stimulation? (3) What does our knowledge of thresholds tell us about the working of the system? Can pain and tactile sensitivity be isolated from each other? For example, do they adapt at different rates? What is tickle? Is it a separate sensory system, or is it a part of mechanical reception? When we have provided some answers to these questions and, as one might expect, turned up new ones, we shall consider some techniques for using the skin as a means of communication.

The Stimulus: It is generally agreed that the stimulus for pressure sensitivity is *deformation* of the skin. Von Frey demonstrated this point neatly by showing that one can produce sensations of cutaneous pressure by lifting the skin. If a wire is glued to the skin, so that the skin may be lifted, one perceives pressure, even though the actual pressure upon the skin

is *decreased*. Both the amount of deformation and the rate of deformation must be sufficient for pressure to be perceived. It is likely that the intensity of pressure sensations is the result of the sharpness of the gradient of deformation. The more rapid and the greater the deformation, the more intense is the resulting sensation. Accordingly, the adequate stimulus for pressure sensitivity is often called the *gradient of deformation.* Geldard has pointed out: "...If a finger is dipped into a jar of mercury only the 'ring' at the surface of the liquid is felt. Considerable pressure is being exerted on the immersed part of the finger, but the pressure is evenly distributed, and one local area of tissue is not deformed with respect to its neighbor except at the region of transition from mercury to air" (1953, p. 178).

Although the concept of the gradient of deformation is a second general principle which explains many of the phenomena associated with pressure sensitivity, there is ample evidence that much remains to be learned about the manner in which the gradient operates. Von Frey (1919; von Frey & Kiesow, 1899) attached small hairs to a handle in such a way that the hairs could be applied to small areas of the skin. By using hairs of different sizes and weights, he was able to make rough threshold determinations of the size and weight required to produce sensations of pressure throughout the skin. This technique made use of the fact that the extent of the bending of the hair indicates the pressure which has been exerted upon the skin. With this procedure, touch spots may be identified throughout the skin, suggesting the presence of a specialized receptor which mediates pressure sensibility. Touch spots are commonly found on the windward side of external hairs but not ordinarily on the leeward side (Geldard, 1953), a finding that correlates with the fact that certain types of receptors (basket endings) are usually found near hair follicles.

The gradient theory would predict that the rim, rather than the size or area, of an object would be responsible for sensation, since the gradient would occur only at the point where a difference in pressure occurred. Holway and Crozier (1937a; 1937b) tested this deduction by using glass tubes of different perimeters, but equal surface areas, filled with water. With these stimuli, subjects could not discriminate differences in pressure sensitivity. According to these writers, it is the pressure per unit area of skin which reports pressure sensations, rather than the size or shape of the perimeter.

The specialized receptors, if any, which mediate sensations of pressure are not well identified. Pacinian corpuscles, which are found in subcutaneous tissue, are known to respond to pressure (J. A. B. Gray & Malcolm, 1950), but apparently other receptors are responsible for pressure elsewhere in the skin. It is known that the receptor, and not the fiber alone, adapts to mechanical stimulation (J. A. B. Gray & P. B. C. Matthews, 1951). Moreover, mechanical stimulation of the pacinian corpuscles yields a potential which comes from the receptor and not from the nerve (J. A. B. Gray & Sato, 1953). Basket endings, which surround the roots of hairs, appear to respond to pressure, and there have been reports that Merkel disks, Meissner corpuscles, and free nerve endings may report pressure also. Indeed, the postulation that many receptors mediate pressure is probably necessary if the gradient hypothesis is to be accepted: for the skin to be sensitive to slight changes in deformation, a large number of receptors throughout the skin is required. However, the sensations of touch are apparently mediated by a different pathway in the central nervous system from those of similar qualities, such as pain, itch, and tickle. Severance of the anterolateral tract in the spinal cord does not diminish touch sensation, although sensation of the other qualities is lost (Bickford, 1938).

Thresholds: Both RLs and DLs vary considerably as a function of the locus of the skin selected for measurement. Table 10–A shows the RLs derived by von Frey (1894) using the technique of applying small hairs to various areas of the skin. The table indicates that greatest sensitivity (in terms of the lowest RL)

TABLE 10–A: *Thresholds Derived by von Frey (1894) by Using Small, Stiff Hairs as Stimuli.*
(From *Experimental Psychology*, by R. S. Woodworth and H. Schlosberg, copyright 1954 by Holt, Rinehart and Winston, Inc.)

Part of body	Grams per mm²
Tip of tongue	2
Tip of finger	3
Back of finger	5
Front of forearm	8
Back of hand	12
Calf of leg	16
Abdomen	26
Back of forearm	33
Loin	48
Thick parts of sole	250

is found on the tongue and fingers. There is a relationship between threshold and the "toughness" of the area. The sole of the foot, which has a high RL compared with other areas of the body, is heavily padded in the human adult. The relationship suggests that pressure thresholds are a function of the number of receptors available and of the density of the tissue. In most areas of the body, the TL for pressure represents the RL for pain. However, as we shall note in our discussion of pain, some areas do not report sensations of pressure but do report sensations of pain. This is among the most convincing arguments for regarding pain as a separate sense with its own specialized receptor.

Since relatively small amounts of energy are sufficient to provide the sensation of pressure, we often overlook the fact that the skin is remarkably insensitive to external stimulation. Geldard (1953, p. 182) estimates that the skin requires from 100 million to 10 billion times as much energy to reach threshold as the eye or the ear.

The DL for various areas of the skin varies widely. Moreover, there is a positive correlation between the RL for a given area and the DL. If the RL is low, the DL is also small, and vice versa. Such variables as the size of the skin area tested, the amount of time between tests, and the physiological state of the subject affect sensitivity.

Gatti and R. Dodge (1929) computed the Weber ratio for pressure. Figure 10–13 shows the results. The ordinate is plotted in $\Delta I/I$, the Weber fraction. The ratio is at its minimum between 3 and 6 grams per mm skin area.

Two additional measures have been investigated thoroughly: The first seeks to determine the accuracy with which a person can localize an area that has been stimulated. If pressure is applied to a small area on my back and then removed, how accurately can I point out the place that was stimulated? L. A. Cohen (1958) asked subjects to localize an area in the following manner: they were instructed to touch a reference point on their outstretched arm; then they were asked to close their eyes, drop the arm to the side, and then locate the reference point. The error for 90 adult subjects varied from 1.75 to 5.75 cm, with a mean of 3.25 cm. The second measure is concerned with determining when two stimuli are so close together that they are perceived as one. It is called the *two-point threshold* and has been investigated by many writers. Consider

the apparatus shown in Figure 10–14. If the two points are near one another when applied to the skin, the stimulus is most likely perceived as a single point. As the distance between the two points is increased, the likelihood of perceiving two different points increases. The two-point threshold is defined in terms of the distance between the two points when they are perceived as different. It is lowest in areas of the skin which have been found to be sensitive by other threshold measurements. A two-point threshold of 1 mm is reported for the tip of the tongue, but 70 mm is reported for the calves, the back, and the upper arm. Figure 10–15 shows measurements of the two-point threshold as a function of skin locus.

Adaptation: Without the ability to adapt to pressure, organisms would be bombarded constantly with pressure sensations. Through adaptation, we cease to perceive the presence of a ring on the finger, cloth covering the skin, or the constant pressure applied by students and scholars to the gluteus maximus. Among the variables which affect the rate of pressure adaptation are the intensity of the stimulus, the size of the area stimulated, and the locus of the area. In general, the more intense the stimulus and the larger the area stimulated, the longer the time to adapt. For example, von Frey and Goldman (1914) measured adaptation under constant pressure stimulation on the forearm. A negatively accelerating decay function resulted, similar to that found for adaptation in other sensory modalities. Zigler (1932) examined adaptation as a function of intensity on several areas of the body, including the hand, forearm, forehead, and cheek. The forearm appeared to adapt most rapidly (within 3 seconds with a 50-gram intensity and within 8 seconds with a 2,000-gram intensity) and the cheek most slowly.

Two sources of variation in assessing pressure are the variety of sensations subsumed under the rubric *pressure* and the wide individual differences in verbal reports of these

FIGURE 10–13: *Weber ratio for pressure. (From Boring, 1942, p. 496, after Gatti & R. Dodge, 1929.)*

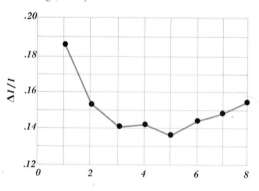

Tension (I): g/mm

sensations. Nafe and Wagoner (1941) arranged a series of finely graded weights which could be dropped into the skin at varying rates of speed. When a weight of, say, 9 grams was slowly lowered onto the skin and permitted to sink into the skin without a gradient's being established, the subject reported sensations of pressure. However, when the weight ceased

FIGURE 10–14: *An aesthesiometer being used to measure the two-point threshold. (Photograph courtesy Lafayette Instrument Company, Lafayette, Ind.)*

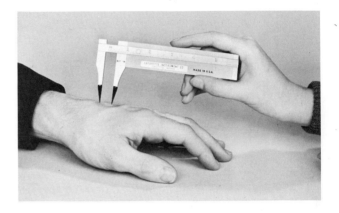

FIGURE 10–15: *Variation in the two-point threshold as a function of location on the body at which the threshold is measured. The length of the vertical lines is approximately equal to the magnitude of the two-point threshold. (Data from Weber, cited by Sherrington in Schäfer, 1900; from Ruch, Patton, Woodbury, & Towe, 1965, p. 316.)*

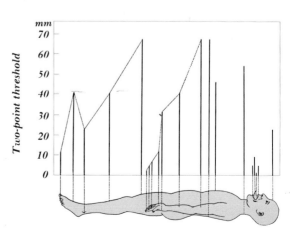

moving, so that it was in tension with the surrounding tissue, the subject reported no sensations of pressure. When the weight was raised from the skin, the sensation of pressure was again reported. Accordingly, it is clear that the sensations of pressure and of pressure adaptation are not merely a matter of the depth to which the skin is deformed but of the rate of deformation.

These data suggest that pressure adaptation is of two kinds: receptor adaptation (for there is evidence that some receptors cease firing promptly after the application of a stimulus) and stimulus adaptation (for the stimulus, as noted in the Nafe and Wagoner study, can move so slowly that it is below the deformation threshold). Either kind of adaptation results in a cessation of pressure sensation, even though the reasons for the cessation are quite different.

Patterning of Pressure Stimuli: The temporal or spatial patterning of stimuli produces a variety of phenomena in the visual system, such as the phi phenomenon, figural aftereffects, and apparent movement. Similarly, the pattern of pressure stimuli produce phenomena differing in quality from those commonly associated with pressure sensitivity. Foremost among the cutaneous sensations which result from the pattern of the stimuli are *tickle* and *vibration.* Both phenomena provide some useful clues to the functioning of the cutaneous system in pressure reception.

Tickle appears to be the result of alternating pressure stimulation within a relatively small area. It usually involves pressure of mild intensity, and it may occur through a light brushing of hairless parts of the skin, such as the lips, or through the bending of hairs to and fro. This concept of tickle is different from that employed when we tickle the ribs or the soles of the feet, for stimulation of this type produces more intense reactions which appear to vary in threshold as a function of age. The sensation of tickle has been rarely studied, and little, if any information exists on thresholds or adaptation.

Geldard and his associates have devoted a considerable amount of attention to the phenomena of vibratory sensitivity. The sensation of cutaneous vibration may be experienced by striking a tuning fork and then holding the vibrating fork lightly against the skin. This sensation is distinct from other cutaneous sensations. With large or intense stimuli, of course, the pattern of vibration travels far from the original source, just as a sound wave continues far past its origin.

Geldard presented the stimulus by using a small needle or hair which could be made to vibrate rapidly. He reports (Geldard, 1940a, 1940b, 1940c, 1940d; see also Weitz, 1939) that vibratory sensitivity is distributed throughout the skin in much the same way as other cutaneous modalities: some areas have low thresholds and others have relatively high thresholds. In short, vibratory "spots" which are sensitive to different frequencies of alteration may be located, but the intensity (in terms of the amount of depression of the skin necessary to arouse vibratory sensations) is fairly stable. Regardless of its frequency, the stimulus must be implanted around 0.025 mm into the skin for the sensation to result. Spots which appear to be insensitive to vibration do not report the sensation of vibration up to 1,024 Hz. However, spots which show any sensitivity at all do so at all frequencies. This indicates that the difference between sensitive spots and nonsensitive areas is not only a matter of their possessing different thresholds for frequency. On the contrary, a type of all-or-none law exists which stipulates that if a spot is sensitive to vibration, it will respond at all frequencies; if it is not sensitive, an increase in frequency has no effect. For areas on the fingertips, the frequency eliciting maximal sensitivity appears to be around 128 to 512 Hz (Knudsen, 1928; Hugony, 1935; Setzpfand, 1935; Gilmer, 1942; Geldard, 1940a). The curve is similar to that found for loudness thresholds for auditory stimuli.

Uses of Pressure and Vibratory Stimulation: Geldard and his colleagues (1957; 1960; 1961) have demonstrated that the skin may serve as a useful system for communication. As Geldard comments: "In all this debate about eyes and ears there has been scarcely a voice raised about other possibilities. Yet the human integument, housing several modalities, rivaling the ear as a temporal discriminator and greatly excelling the eye in this respect, sharing with the retina the property of somewhat orderly spatial extension, has many of the message-transmitting features commonly extolled in the eye and the ear" (Geldard, 1960, p. 1583).

For many military and industrial purposes it would be an advantage to be able to "hear" or "see" through some modality other than audition and vision. For example, a pilot often must use his eyes and ears to watch the instrument panel and listen for instructions. A third sensory modality could provide additional information as well as serve the useful function of permitting communication should one of the other systems fail. Geldard has pointed out that the cutaneous system has many advantages as a communication system: (1) a variety of locations are available for stimulation because of the large area covered by the skin; (2) the skin is rarely used as a sensory modality, and therefore few stimuli interfere; (3) compared with other senses, excluding audition and vision, the skin is highly sensitive to stimulation.

Consider the potential of cutaneous communication. A test pilot would have small stimulators placed on various parts of his body. Stimulation of one location might indicate a letter of the alphabet or a simple word. The number of possible alternatives could be expanded by varying the frequency, intensity, and duration of the stimulus. Depending upon the combination of these factors, messages could be spelled out, in a kind of "cutaneous Morse code" which the pilot would decipher. This is the basic design behind the invention of *vibratese,* or the language of the skin (Gault, 1927; Geldard, 1961). In the coding procedure commonly employed in vibratese, five locations on the rib cage, three intensities, and three durations are used. This permits 45 possible combinations. Although it would be possible to use more locations and a greater

variety of intensities and duration, the decision to use 5 by 3 by 3 combinations was made in order to permit maximum sensitivity and minimal confusion between the dimensions. The code suggested by Howell (1956) is shown in Figure 10–16. Some possible combinations are blank, pending further assignments. Each combination conveys a particular letter or a common preposition or conjunction. With well-trained subjects, the transmission rate is 67 words per minute, a figure well in excess of the transmission rate for Morse code. Frequency is not used in the combinations for various reasons, including the fact that intensity and frequency become confused (as they do in audition).

The attempt to determine the appropriate types of stimulation to use in vibratese has provided some useful information on the psychophysics of vibration and electric stimulation. Thus, research on a practical problem—communication through the skin—has provided us with basic information regarding cutaneous sensitivity. Hawkes (1960) determined that two levels of intensity provided the most ac-

FIGURE 10–16: *The code used in vibratese. Intensity is represented along the ordinate and duration of the signal along the abscissa. (From Howell, 1956, n.s.; Geldard, 1961, p. 80.)*

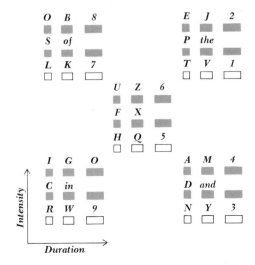

curate transmission; three levels provided more information but also led to some errors. Accordingly if accuracy is essential, only two intensity levels can be used; however, if speed of transmission is the goal and if some error can be tolerated, three channels are most efficient (see also Hawkes, 1961a, 1961b).

Touch and pressure are among our most useful sensory systems, but many of the basic questions regarding their operation remain unanswered. Perhaps this state of affairs is due to the eminence which is given audition and vision, or perhaps it is due to the complexity of our cutaneous senses. Certainly the volume of research on cutaneous sensitivity is appreciably less than that on the "major" senses. Moreover, whether cutaneous receptors are specialized endings, distinct nerves or fibers, or some combination of both, the fact that the receptor and the adequate stimuli are so difficult to identify renders our knowledge of cutaneous sensibility elementary.

We have noted that pain may be regarded as a sensation resulting from excessive stimulation, but there is ample evidence that this interpretation falls far short of explaining many observations regarding pain. Pain is one of the most important sensations for human beings and, no doubt, for animals. A good part of our education and training, especially during infancy and childhood, is motivated by attempts to avoid or escape the pain of punishment. As we shall see, especially in Chapters 12 to 15, the role of punishment and pain in human and animal behavior has been thoroughly, but far from definitively, investigated. However, the functioning of the sense of pain is easily as substantial a mystery as the operation of other cutaneous senses.

PAIN SENSITIVITY

Unlike many other senses for which a specific physical stimulus activates the receptor, pain may be triggered by many stimuli. Pressure, cold, warmth, and deformation of the skin— all are able to evoke sensations of pain if the stimulus is sufficiently intense. The observation indicates one reason why it is unclear whether pain should be regarded as one sense or two. Superficially, pain occurs when receptors are stimulated excessively; e.g., a stimulus may be so hot that it causes sensations of pain, rather than of warmth. Similarly, extreme deformation of the skin may evoke the sensation of pain, rather than of pressure. On the other hand, certain areas of the skin yield only pain sensations, thus suggesting the presence of a specialized receptor for pain.

Sensations of pain are not limited to cutaneous sensitivity. All sensory systems, including the ear and the eye, will yield sensations of pain if they are stimulated sufficiently, but not all these systems include specialized receptors, such as those found in the skin, which could mediate pain. For example, a light may be so intense that the retina is damaged and intense pain occurs, but where are the supposed specialized receptors which could produce this sensation? Thus, it is speculated that pain may be produced in two ways: by the stimulation of specialized pain receptors or by intense stimulation of *any* receptor.

Even though the appropriate stimulus for pain may be included among several general types, such as electric current, deformation, chemical application, intense temperature (either warm or cold), or cutting, the sensations are reasonably similar—sufficiently similar, at least, that we have little disagreement about when a sensation is painful and when it is not. However, we differentiate a sharp pain (as when the finger is cut) from dull pain (when we have a stomachache). Cutaneous pain is usually sharp, and internal pain is usually dull. Cutaneous pain, however, is not always sharp. Often, after a cut on the finger, for example, the pain is sharp and intense at first, but within a few moments it becomes dull and throbbing. The area immediately surrounding the stimulated area becomes *analgesic,* that is, insensitive to pain. A few hours later, the area becomes *hypersensitive,* or *hyperalgesic;* that is, the threshold for pain decreases, and the area is more sensitive than usual. If threshold is reached during this period, the resulting pain sensation is not sharp, as it was originally, but has a slow, burning quality. This finding has led to a major theory of pain sensibility which suggests that, owing to evolutionary development, there is more than one kind of pain. We shall consider this theory later in the chapter. It is worth noting, however, that the qualities of pain sensation vary over time. Whether this is merely a matter of the adaptation of specialized receptors or whether some other factor accounts for changes in threshold as a function of time is unclear.

The Receptors for Pain: A good deal of evidence has accrued on the problem of identifying the receptor or receptors for pain. Von Frey (1896) and others have suggested that the receptors are the free nerve endings. The fact that they are the only receptors located in almost every area of the skin provides credibility for this speculation. In addition, there are so many free nerve endings that one or more may be found near each specialized receptor. This fact might account for the observation that intense stimulation of any receptor produces pain. This appeared to be strong, suggestive evidence of the projected relationship between free nerve endings and pain in the cornea of the eye (which has only free nerve endings and is extremely sensitive to pain) until Nafe and Wagoner (1937) performed the classic experiment of lowering weights slowly onto the cornea. When the weights were lowered sufficiently slowly, the subjects reported the sensation of pressure and sometimes of sharp pressure, but rarely of pain. Accordingly, it seems likely that the cornea is able to report pressure as well as pain (Lele & Weddell, 1956). It should be noted, however, that these results do not rule out the idea that free nerve endings mediate pain: they indicate only that free nerve endings may mediate pressure as well as pain. Sjöqvist (1938) carried this problem a step further when he surgically severed the trigeminal (Vth cranial) nerve in the human being.

The purpose of this operation was to eliminate all pain in the patient's face, and it was successful. However, some remnant of pressure sensitivity remained after the operation, even in the cornea. This indicates that although free nerve endings may serve as receptors for pain, data based on the cornea alone do not provide convincing evidence for this belief.

Several theorists have looked to the nerves themselves as the receptor for pain. T. Lewis (1942; see also T. Lewis & W. Hess, 1933) suggested that the hyperalgesic state which follows injury could have two components, *primary* and *secondary hyperalgesia*. For example, the area of hypersensitivity extends into undamaged skin beyond the boundaries of the original cut. This finding implies that some type of neural network is involved which transcends the location of the original source of pain. Moreover, although primary hyperalgesia usually dissipates within two days, secondary hyperalgesia may continue much longer. T. Lewis has suggested (1942) that the nervous pathways short-circuit; impulses thus return to the area of their source, and this return movement releases a chemical which is responsible for secondary hyperalgesia. These supposed neurological pathways have not been isolated, although histamine has been suggested as the chemical (Habgood, 1950; Rosenthal, 1950). J. D. Hardy and his coworkers (J. D. Hardy, 1950) have suggested that the cause of secondary hyperalgesia is cortical, not peripheral. They noted that repeated stimulation of the areas of secondary hyperalgesia resulted in a reduction of its size, although the area expanded when stimulation was withdrawn. On the basis of these data, they suggested that the impulses from an injured area made contact with other afferent paths of adjoining areas.

Whatever principle may account for the presence of primary and secondary hyperalgesia, it is clear that the phenomena exist and that an adequate theory of pain must account for them. It should be remembered, however, that an injury to the skin does more than only stimulate pain receptors, if they exist. Injury also causes changes in the blood, the vascular network, and the surrounding tissues. The presence of these other effects may very well mask the origins of the simple pain produced by tissue injury. Both A- and C-type fibers (Table 2–A) are presumed to report sensations of pain (Maruhashi, Mizuguchi, & Tasaki, 1952; Zotterman, 1939; Sweet, 1959). It is possible that different sensations of pain are carried by different types of fibers. A related phenomenon is *referred pain*. This phenomenon is well known in pain experienced internally where, at times, pain in one area of the body may be perceived as coming from an entirely different area. This is common in angina conditions, where the person reports pain in the arms even though the heart is undergoing damage.

In addition to referred pain, *causalgia* has received attention in the study of pain because of its relevance to understanding the functioning of the nervous pathways. Causalgia, which is the result of injury to peripheral nerves themselves, is experienced as a continuous pain. It is usually a burning pain, and the affected area is hypersensitive to any form of stimulation. It has been suggested that causalgia is the result of a *reverberating circuit,* i.e., a neural circuit which has the ability to restimulate itself. Neuron A fires neuron B, B fires C, and C *re*fires A. The condition may be corrected by the severance of appropriate nerves; however, the phenomenon itself suggests again the complexity of the neural networks concerned with pain.

Clearly, the sensation of pain is not simple. It is doubtful that only a single receptor is responsible, and it seems clear that even if the receptors were identified, further understanding of the functioning of the nervous system is required, particularly of those nerve pathways responsible for the transmission of pain.

Thresholds: Perhaps the major difficulty in determining thresholds for pain sensitivity is the selection of the stimulus to be employed to produce pain. If the stimulus is electric, mechanical, or thermal, stimulation spreads over a larger area of the skin than the point of presentation of the stimulus itself, and this interferes with the determination of the threshold. Moreover, these stimuli may cause damage to the tissue. Bishop (1943) used an electric spark gap in which the stimulus was placed 0.5 mm from the skin and a spark crossed to the skin, providing a discrete electric stimulus. As is true of other cutaneous modalities, "spots" may be located. Von Frey (see Strughold, 1924) plotted the number of pain spots for various areas of the skin. Needless to say, the determination of the number of spots per area is not exact, for individual variations are noted and difficulties in the experimental procedure are many. However, there appear to be clear differences in pain spots in various areas of the skin. For example, both the back of the knee and the neck show around 200 pain spots per square centimeter; the sole of the foot and the tip of the nose show only around 45. The absolute number of pain spots found in each area is not so significant as the relative number.

Both the cornea of the eye and the tympanic membrane of the ear are extremely sensitive to pain. Pain stimulation in the latter is a common experience for persons who have inadvertently poked the membrane while cleaning the ear cavity. A few skin areas, such as the interior lining of the cheeks and the back part of the tongue, appear to be highly insensitive to pain. This fact has been used in various displays in which a person sticks a sharp object through the cheek without apparent pain. It is not, however, suggested as a laboratory exercise. Internal organs also appear to be insensitive to pain, at least on their exterior surface.

One method of measuring pain DLs has used scaling techniques. J. D. Hardy, Wolff, and Goodell (1947), using the radiant heat device discussed previously in relation to thermal sensitivity, have scaled pain differential in terms of millicalories per second per square centimeter. According to their data, the Weber fraction holds from 240 to around 300 mcal per second per cm² with a fraction of 0.03; with greater intensities the fraction is larger. These writers suggest *dol* as a name for the scaled unit of pain intensity. A dol is considered equal to two successive DLs. RLs have also been determined by the radiant heat procedure. Using a 3-second exposure, investigators have found that the RL is approximately 0.220 g-cal (gram-calorie) per second per cm², although above 480 mcal burns are produced. Indirect evidence of the success of this method of determining pain thresholds comes from similar measurements taken when the skin is made insensitive artificially by the use of such drugs as morphine and codeine. These drugs and certain others render the skin insensitive to pain but leave other cutaneous systems intact. H. G. Wolff and S. Wolf (1958) have reviewed the techniques for measuring pain sensitivity.

It has been noted, at least in the study of thermal sensitivity, that radiant heat and warm or cold stimuli applied directly to the skin produce different results. Several writers have measured pain thresholds by applying stimuli directly to the skin. Bishop (1949) used small solder balls of various sizes cemented to needle tips and found that the size of the stimulus was not the determiner of the pain; all sizes produced pain sensations at the same level of depression of the skin. This evidence suggests that the appropriate stimulus for pain is the stretching of the skin, and it is supported by the observation that injury to the skin is painful only if the skin is stretched or depressed. If a cut is made into skin which is held immobile, there are often no pain sensations.

Adaptation: The question "Are pain sensations capable of adaptation?" has been subject to strenuous argument, possibly because an answer forces one to take a stand on whether pain is overstimulation of receptors or whether it is a separate sense. Those who consider pain nothing more than excessive stimulation must also assume that adaptation does not occur, at least in the usual meaning of the word. If pain is simply overstimulation, adaptation should provide a sensation identical to that of the receptor before it was overstimulated. That is, if overstimulation of pressure receptors causes pain, then adaptation should be perceived as a return to the original sensation of pressure.

Relatively few data on pain adaptation exist. Dallenbach has provided classic studies in the field (1939) by stimulating the skin with a variety of stimuli, including needles for pressure, radiant heat for warmth, and dry ice for cold. In all cases, pain gradually subsided and eventually became the sensation of the original stimulus, i.e., pressure, warmth, or cold. The fact that the pain subsided and that the sensation returned to the original sensation only after the *pain itself had decreased* suggests that pain is a separate sense modality, for it shows adaptation. Accordingly, it seems clear that although pain may accompany other sensory systems (for it is certain that excessive stimulation causes pain regardless of the receptor system), it does not rely upon the same receptors as other sensory systems. It has an independent existence and will adapt with time, similar to other sensory systems, yet it is also clearly intertwined with the other sense modalities.

Pain and the Central Nervous System: The relationship between the sensation of pain and the central nervous system has been examined by the usual techniques of lesions and ablation. The general concern is to locate those areas of the brain which are involved in the sensation of pain. J. M. R. Delgado (1955) has implanted small electrodes into sections of the thalamus of the monkey brain, with the result that he can stimulate these areas electrically from outside the animal. At specific points, stimulation results in the animal's making the same general response that he makes to such stimulation as having his tail pinched. Of course, the monkey is not able to report the sensation of pain verbally, and investigators must rely upon analogous behavior as evidence of sensation. Several experimenters have reported similar observations from conscious man. For example, Talairach, Hecaen, David, Monnier, and Ajuriaguerra (1949) and Hecaen, Talairach, David, and Dell (1949) stimulated the thalamus and found that human subjects failed to respond with pain sensations, even though they reported varying degrees of loss of pressure and vibratory sensitivity. A number of studies show that if areas of the cortex and subcortical white matter are destroyed, hyperalgesia results. Curiously, few experimenters have found analgesia to occur.

Some Explanations: Theorists have given a great deal of attention to primary and secondary hyperalgesia. No doubt, one reason for this concentration of interest is that this phenomenon displays most of the major questions which must be explained by a useful theory of pain sensitivity. Among these questions are (1) What is the adequate stimulus for pain? (2) Is pain one sense or two? (3) Does pain adapt? (4) Why is the skin differentially sensitive to pain? Few theories of pain sensitivity attempt to answer all these questions. More commonly, each question has presented so many problems that theories have been developed to account for particular facets of pain, with little attempt to generalize the minor theories to other related problems. In noting the characteristics of pain, we have mentioned some of these "suggestive theories."

One of the more noteworthy theories of cutaneous pain was developed by Head (1920). With an obvious appreciation for the observational side of science rare in contemporary laboratories, Head severed nerves in his forearm and observed the process of regeneration. In addition, he studied the changes in pain sensitivity which accompanied regeneration. Upon severance of the nerves, Head noted a total absence of pain sensitivity within a given region. Surrounding this anesthetized area was an "intermediate zone" which was sensitive to pain only if stimulated by a stimulus considerably more intense than the stimulus originally necessary for eliciting pain sensation;

i.e., the intermediate zone had a higher threshold for pain than it had shown before the severance of the nerves. Moreover, once pain was produced in this area, the sensation was of a different quality from that commonly perceived. The sensation was of an unpleasant, burning type.

On the basis of these observations, Head suggested that two pain systems, one evolutionarily older than the other, were present. The older system was called *protopathic;* it was assumed to be more primitive than the newer system, which was called *epicritic.* The epicritic system had the function of inhibiting protopathic pain. In addition, the epicritic sense was assumed to be responsible for pressure and fine discriminations of tactual stimuli and moderate thermal stimuli. Head interpreted the observations made on his own forearm by assuming that he had disassociated the protopathic and epicritic systems. The change in threshold in the intermediate zone was assumed to represent the presence of the protopathic system without the inhibition of the epicritic system. Later theorists have suggested that the epicritic system is mediated by the cortex and the protopathic system by the thalamus.

In a better-controlled study, Lanier (1934) anesthetized two nerves in three persons, including himself. The cutaneous area was mapped prior to the anesthetization for reference during the regenerative process. Threshold measurements of pain, pressure, warmth, and cold were taken during recovery. Lanier reports that the four senses recovered continuously for two years following the anesthetization. Of these stimuli, warmth was the slowest to recover its function. Lanier also reported finding the intermediate zone with its accompanying qualitatively unusual pain sensations. He did not, however, find it necessary to assume the presence of two separate pain systems to account for the results.

Several investigators have correlated pain sensitivity with histological examination (Bishop, 1944; Weddell, 1941b), finding that free nerve endings are solely responsible for pain sensations, since they are found throughout the skin. Although it is commonly accepted that free nerve endings are the receptors for pain, theorists, such as Hebb (1949), make a good case for regarding pain as the result of intense stimulation.

Weddell and his colleagues have devoted attention to the histology of regenerating nerves. They noted (1948) that when an area undergoing regeneration had isolated nerves, rather than intertwined "nets" of nerves, the sensation of pain was similar to that ascribed by Head to the intermediate zone; however, when nerve nets were found, the resulting sensation was that of the normal sharp pain. Thus, the problems associated with primary and secondary hyperalgesia and of protopathic and epicritic pain may be traced to the concentration of nerve endings. Feindel, Weddell, and Sinclair (1948) have examined deep internal tissue and found it to be composed of relatively isolated nerves. This finding fits neatly with the observation that internal pain is more unpleasant and dull than cutaneous pain. Accordingly, the presence of pain spots, as well as the availability of at least two kinds of pain sensations, may be due to the concentration of nerve nets.

It seems likely that the action of the higher centers of the brain holds the clue to how pain is perceived. Although the peripheral pathways for pain are well understood and traceable to the thalamus, evidence regarding what happens after the thalamus is both meager and contradictory (W. Edwards, 1950). It may be recalled that Hardy, Lewis, and other theorists mentioned in this section made assumptions regarding the functioning of the central nervous system in pain. One of the most thoroughly presented speculations of this type is that of Hebb (1949), who discusses the possible source of pain sensation and presents a more general theory of brain functioning. Hebb suggests that pain may be the result of an imbalance in the number of fibers firing into the central nervous system. If too few impulses are received or if too many arrive, massive firing occurs in the thalamus, and this firing is

perceived as pain. A moderate number of firings, however, is perceived merely as pressure or perhaps as some other cutaneous modality.

The idea that pain is the product of the massing of nerves firing into the central nervous system has been developed by Melzack and Wall (1965). These theorists stress two phenomena of pain sensitivity which appear to be unusual: first, persons suffering severe injury often deny sensing pain, even though there has been extensive tissue damage; second, when a peripheral nerve has been injured, as in a cut finger, the tissue becomes highly sensitive, and the sensation of pain often persists long after the injurious stimulus has been removed. It is suggested that the central nervous system receives spatial and temporal patterns from the periphery, which codes painful stimulation, and thus the central nervous system is actively involved in decoding and transferring messages to the appropriate area of the brain.

To show how perception of pain may occur under this theory, the writers suggest that an area in the spinal cord is composed of two columns which run the length of the cord and which serve as "gates." These columns, the *substantiae gelatinosae,* are joined by two kinds of afferent nerve fibers from the dorsal roots: large fibers, along which impulses travel rapidly, and small fibers. These fibers make connection with specific neurons, called *T cells;* the T cells, in turn, connect with the brain. It is suggested that the large fibers close the gates and the small fibers open it. Thus, when an impulse traveling from the brain reaches a gate, it closes. The brain, however, receives impulses from nerve fibers which have branched before entering the gate. Thus, the brain may (1) close down the gate system, thus cutting off pain sensations, or (2) select impulses from certain fibers but not from others. Thus one might feel no pain following an immense trauma resulting in extensive brain damage but would feel pain at the insertion of a hypodermic needle. The gate system accounts for a variety of pathological pain states and the difference in painful sensations between the peripheral and the central nervous system. Moreover, it emphasizes the coding system of the nerves, which appears to be a necessary assumption in explaining how pain is perceived.

Theories of pain sensibility are far less sophisticated than theories of vision and audition. Data on pain are extensive, but, curiously, they are often more confusing than helpful in the formulation of theory. Probably no other area of sensory psychology is so susceptible to experimental error. One difficulty is that experimenters must usually rely upon the subject's verbal report that he perceives pain—although some have used conditioning techniques, such as finger withdrawal to painful stimuli, as a dependent variable. A further difficulty is that there is no generally accepted definition of pain; therefore investigators are usually at the mercy of subjects who have different perceptions of what is painful and what is not.

It may be noted that much of the evidence about pain is based on the peripheral mechanisms and the search for the receptor. We may recall that until the central mechanisms underlying vision and audition became available for study, theory in those areas was as uncertain as it now is in pain sensitivity. As techniques for investigating central process become more useful and more reliable, it is possible that theory of pain sensibility will also develop rapidly. Few areas of psychological interest have greater practical application.

KINESTHESIS AND THE ORGANIC SENSATIONS

Kinesthesis, the sense of muscle movement, is one of several internal sensations. We are apt to lead full lives without ever realizing our dependence upon kinesthetic sensations, although pathological conditions of kinesthesis do occur. In general the basic receptors for the kinesthetic system are specialized endings found in the muscles, joints, and tendons. They report the movement of these structures

and provide us with basic sensory cues about what the structures are doing. It is hard to imagine how it would feel to raise one's arm and not sense the changes in the muscles and tendons. We have learned to interpret these movements so well that we are able to make very fine kinesthetic discriminations, such as those involved in throwing a football, without "thinking" about it. The viscera are sensitive not only to kinesthetic stimulation but also to pain and temperature: we feel stomachaches, food that is too hot, and pain from distension of the viscera because of gas. The system that provides for sensations concerning the functioning of the viscera is one kind of *organic sensibility*.

Closely related to organic sensibility are two sensations of considerable concern to experimental psychology—hunger and thirst. At first thought, hunger and thirst may seem to be such basic psychological drives that there is little to be said about them. They are, however, responsible for motivating a significant portion of behavior. Nor are hunger and thirst so easily explained as one might suppose. To claim that one becomes thirsty because of a lack of water or hungry because of a lack of food is to oversimplify. Thirst and hunger are complex, involving at least two, if not more, processes. Foremost among the difficulties inherent in investigating these sensations is the difficulty in getting to the receptors. Although several techniques for reaching the receptors are available, each involves contact with other receptors and other sensory systems.

One procedure, useful for investigating deep receptors below those associated with cutaneous sensibility, is to anesthetize the cutaneous receptors. This procedure is similar in principle to the technique used by Head (1920) when he severed nerves in the forearm. Indeed, some investigators have inquired whether the peculiar pain observed by Head was merely the result of stimulation of subcutaneous receptors.

A second technique is to remove the receptors, place them in preparation, and investigate their function by electrophysiological means. This presents difficulties, for the receptors are isolated from other structures which may be involved in the sensory process and the electrophysiological recordings are not likely to provide complete information.

A third technique, which is more accidental than intentional, is the observation of internal organs that are bared during surgery. Such observation has provided at least one interesting fact: the structures of the viscera, such as the bladder, may be touched and cut without their showing any sensations of pain. Let us begin by examining what is known about the receptors for kinesthesis and other internal sensations.

Receptors: Kinesthesis is apparently mediated by four different types of specialized receptors. Two of these, *annulospiral endings* and *flower-spray endings,* are associated with muscle spindles. The former is mediated by a large fiber, the *primary afferent fiber,* from the muscle spindle. The flower-spray endings are mediated by a smaller fiber, the *secondary afferent fiber,* from the muscle spindle. Both receptors show an electric discharge when the muscle is at rest. If the muscle is stretched, the rate of the discharge increases. If the muscle is contracted, the rate decreases or the discharge ceases altogether. Because of these reactions, it is often said that the appropriate stimulus for movement of the muscles is stretching of the muscle. For simplicity, flower-spray endings are sometimes called A_1 and annulospiral endings are called A_2. A_1 receptors fire with slow stretching of the muscle. If the muscle contracts rapidly, they cease to fire. A_2 receptors respond to slow stretching, but, unlike A_1 receptors, A_2 receptors continue to fire during intense contraction.

The tendons contain Golgi organs, or receptors. Unlike A_1 and A_2 receptors, B receptors appear to be stimulated by a change in tension of the tendons. Type C receptors, which may be pacinian corpuscles, are found in the sheath of muscles. They respond to stimulation in a fashion similar to B receptors. Pa-

cinian corpuscles are found elsewhere throughout the body, where they are presumed to be responsive to deformation. Thus, they may be responsible for internal sensations of pressure.

Receptors for pain are no more evident in the internal structures of the body than they are in the cutaneous structures. It is apparent that a variety of internal pain sensations exists: some are dull and some are sharp. Internal structures are reasonably well equipped with free nerve endings but not with other receptors.

Thresholds: Threshold determinations for kinesthesis present many problems, most of which are concerned with the internal position of the receptors. It is reported, however, that Golgi organs maintain a threshold approximately 100 times greater than that of annulospiral endings (Wenger, F. N. Jones, & M. H. Jones, 1956). Accordingly, it is reasonable to assume that the muscles are more sensitive to movement than the tendons. At the turn of the century Goldscheider, whose work on cutaneous sensitivity we have discussed, measured DLs for kinesthesis in a thorough series of determinations. He used two dependent variables: the minimum angular displacement that could be detected, with movement held constant, and the minimum velocity that could be discriminated. Of the nine joints he tested, Goldscheider found the shoulder to be the most sensitive; the wrist was second; and the ankle was last. Other results indicate that the main joint of the big toe and the hip are perhaps as sensitive as the shoulder (Laidlaw & Hamilton, 1937).

Kinesthetic discriminations using the fingers are common, and identification of the Weber fractions is often useful in industry. Dietze (1961) asked subjects to judge the lengths of rods held between the thumb and forefinger. The method of constant stimuli was used, with standards of 10, 30, and 50 mm. Weber fractions of 1/50 for the 30- and 50-mm standards and of 1/20 for the 20-mm standard were obtained, indicating fine discrimination in kinesthetic finger-span determination. In addition,

Stevens and G. Stone (1959) scaled the apparent thickness of stimuli held between the thumb and middle finger using magnitude estimation. The results in terms of the Weber fraction and Δs are shown in Figure 10–17. Apparently, Δs increases in subjective size with an increase in the width of the stimulus.

Another technique which has been used to assess the DL for kinesthesis is that of lifting light weights. The apparatus usually is a series of graded weights, all of the same size and shape. The subject's task is to judge the weights by lifting them with the same finger and, supposedly, with the same motion. It is assumed that whatever differences exist in judgment are due to kinesthetic sensitivity. Oberlin (1936) found the Weber fraction to be between ⅙ and ⅛ with standards varying from 3 to 600 grams. In addition, he found the shoulder to be most sensitive, while the wrist was the least sensitive part of the arm.

Adaptation: It is sometimes said that kinesthetic receptors do not adapt. This statement is based on the belief that these receptors, like those for pain, merely report what is going on (whether the muscle is stretched or not, whether tissue is cut or not) and have no

reason to adapt in the same sense that a cone in the retina adapts. Apparently, however, kinesthetic receptors *do* adapt, but they do so very slowly. Our world would be very different if they adapted as rapidly as receptors for other sensory systems. Figure 10–18 shows adaptation to continuous stimulation in several sensory systems. The rate is quite rapid in the single nerve fiber, but adaptation to pressure and in the muscle spindle is very slow.

When weights are used as the stimuli, kinesthetic adaptation shows the typical function, although the time to complete adaptation is long compared with other sensory systems. The length of time required for complete recovery after stimulation varies both as a function of the intensity of the original stimulus and the length of time the stimulus is in place. The heavier the weight or the longer it remains in place, the less sensitive the organism is, in terms of DL, to kinesthetic weight.

These data fit those acquired from electrical recording from the muscle spindle (Lippold, Nicholls, & Redfearn, 1960). Figural aftereffects, which provide an unusual phenomenon in the study of visual perception (Chapter 8), have also been noted in kinesthesis. Generally, the kinesthetic phenomenon refers to the overestimation or underestimation of length or width when the stimuli are held between the fingers. Subjects may be satiated in such a way that they overestimate the standard (just as subjects may see a straight line curve in the opposite direction from a previously curved line in the visual figural aftereffect), or they may be satiated in such a way that they underestimate the standard (R. W. Gardner, 1961; Costello, 1961).

R. L. Reid (1954) has reported a kinesthetic illusion similar to the visual horizontal-vertical illusion. In vision, if two lines are at right angles and of equal length, the horizontal line is generally perceived as longer. This experimenter required blindfolded subjects to manipulate a stylus in one direction and then asked them to make the same movement at right angles. Reid reports that horizontal movements are underestimated and vertical

FIGURE 10–17: *Differential sensitivity for finger span. (From Stevens & G. Stone, 1959, p. 93.)*

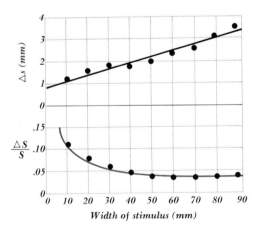

movements are generally overestimated. Although we do not commonly associate "after-images" with kinesthesis, they do exist. If a subject presses his arm against a door or wall and then steps away from the structure, the arm rises without volition on the part of the subject. This demonstration is commonly cited as a kinesthetic aftereffect, but it is surely different from the visual aftereffect in which complementary colors may appear following stimulation.

Posture and the Righting Response: Although the muscles are responsive to internal stimulation, they also give us information about the external world. For example, the ciliary muscles (Chapter 8) provide us with important cues regarding the accommodation of the lens of the eye, giving useful information on depth perception. Similarly, adjustments to depth and other visual situations are made by motor response, and motor responses always require kinesthetic involvement. Kinesthesis is also important in the study of reflexes. As we shall note in Chapters 12 and 13, an entire area of learning phenomena, called *classical conditioning,* is concerned with the action of the various reflexes of the body. Many of these reflexes are well known, such as the *patellar reflex* (knee jerk).

Pathological conditions of kinesthesis are so rare that they are seldom brought to our attention. Most often, if a disease is sufficiently disruptive to kinesthesis, paralysis or some other serious disorder masks the kinesthetic deficiency. In *tabes dorsalis,* however, the neurons in the spinal cord concerned with synapsing kinesthetic sensations are destroyed. A person with this disease, usually caused by syphilis, is able to walk only if he looks at his feet; that is, without kinesthetic cues, he can determine the location of his feet only by looking at them. This condition indicates an important characteristic of kinesthesis: not only does the sensory system tell us when movement is occurring, but it provides useful cues on the location of the organs being moved. As such, kinesthetic sensitivity is concerned with bal-

FIGURE 10–18: *Adaptation rate to a continuously presented stimulus in several sensory systems. The muscle spindle shows the slowest adaptation. The nerve fiber (without receptor) shows a single, brief response. (From Adrian, 1964, p. 79.)*

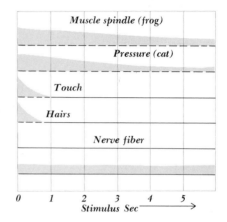

ance, posture, and precision as well as with motion.

Many animals exhibit a *righting response* when they fall. It is perhaps most obvious in cats, where the observation that "a cat always lands on his feet" is well documented but not always accurate. When a cat is dropped with his feet in the air, he rights himself by making the half turn necessary to land with the feet downward. This response has been studied because it is a complex function involving kinesthetic as well as vestibular receptors and because in some animals it appears to be an innate response; i.e., they are able to execute the maneuver shortly after birth and without apparent training.

HUNGER AND THIRST

The viscera are not insensitive, even though many of the internal organs may be manipulated without notable pain. We have all swallowed a liquid so hot that the viscera burned, and we have all experienced pains caused by the distension of the viscera. Indeed, the viscera are able to supply kinesthetic and cutaneous sensations as well as information about two very basic sensations, hunger and thirst. Hunger and thirst are, of course, neither sensory systems nor receptors, yet there is ample evidence that they result from kinesthetic and cutaneous sensations. If you were asked to describe thirst, you would most likely select dryness of the mouth as the most obvious sensation. Similarly, if you were asked to describe the sensation associated with hunger, you would most likely name hunger "pangs" in the stomach.

Consider the sensory events that follow eating. For example, recall the sensation of placing a small piece of freshly broiled steak in the mouth. The mouth cavity permits cutaneous sensations, for the lining of the mouth is skin containing cutaneous receptors. You taste the steak as warm and chewy. The sensation of warmth, of course, comes from cutaneous thermal receptors. The sensation of chewyness comes about because of the muscle action involved in chewing the steak; hence kinesthesis is also part of the sensation. Note that neither of these sensations involves *taste*, yet both are important aspects of the pleasure derived from eating.

Now the piece of steak is swallowed. As the food drops down the esophagus, thermal sensations are lost. Yet the esophagus and the stomach lining are thermally sensitive. Under careful observation, it may be shown that there are thermal receptors in the esophagus and that the stomach cavity is responsive to changes in the temperature of its contents. Drink ice water, and the stomach reports the sensation of cooling. Measurements indicate that the temperature of the stomach has been reduced under these conditions, even though skin temperature itself does not appear to be affected. The problem of which receptors are responsible for mediating thermal sensitivity in the stomach cavity is unsolved. It seems unlikely, however, that they could be the same receptors that are found in external skin. Clearly, hunger and thirst are intertwined with both kinesthetic and cutaneous sensitivity.

Hunger: Peripherally, hunger appears to be related directly to contraction of the stomach walls, but this observation fails to provide the complete explanation of why and how hunger occurs. Cannon and Washburn (1912) examined the hypothesis that hunger correlates directly with contractions by inserting a balloon into the stomach of Washburn. Once he had become accustomed to the technique of swallowing a balloon, the sphere was enlarged so that it filled the stomach cavity. A tube inside the balloon was connected to a recording apparatus, and Washburn was instructed to press a key whenever he felt hunger pangs. These observers noted that stomach contractions correlated with the sensation of hunger pangs as measured by key presses. Their data also indicated that unless food was placed in the stomach, the hunger pangs became more and more violent.

These basic data have been repeated in other laboratories with some success, but they do not go very far toward answering the many questions about hunger. The fact that a person experiences hunger at the same time that the stomach walls are contracting does not necessarily indicate that contraction is the source of hunger. Indeed, some change in the chemistry of the blood may be responsible for both the contraction and the sensations of hunger. Moreover, hunger pangs may be eliminated with a very small amount of food. When one starts to eat a meal, the first few mouthfuls are usually sufficient to calm the hunger pangs, even though the eating continues for some time. Indeed, one may satisfy the contractions with substances other than food. A cigarette, for example, is often capable of calming both the contractions and the hunger pangs, and this is one reason why one's food intake usually increases dramatically when one stops smoking. Because the process of hunger does not account for the amount which is eaten, the term *appetite* is commonly applied to eating behavior which does not satisfy particular physiological needs. We finish a meal because of appetite, not because of hunger. If we were satisfied to stop eating when the physiological need was resolved, few of us would eat beyond the soup course.

Ivan Pavlov, who is remembered as the investigator of classical conditioning (Chapter 13), performed a study shortly before the turn of the century in which he surgically partitioned about 10 percent of the stomach of a dog. This pouch had the same nerve and blood supply as the remainder of the stomach cavity and was arranged so that it could be observed by means of a fistula. Some animals were operated on in such a way that food could be sent directly to the stomach by means of another fistula. Pavlov studied the secretions of gastric juice in these animals. Figure 10–19 shows the results. The function labeled *A* indicates the gastric secretions in a normal stomach. Part *B* indicates the secretion when the food is induced directly into the stomach, the mouth and esophagus not coming into contact with the food. Although the curve shows the same general pattern as *A,* it is clearly of considerably less magnitude. Part *C* represents the secretion from animals which were sham-fed; i.e., the food passed down the esophagus but never reached the stomach. Part *D* is the sum of secretions reported in *B* and *C;* it is very similar in function to the results for normal animals shown in *A.* Apparently, hunger is determined not merely by what occurs in the stomach, for stimulation of the mouth

FIGURE 10–19: *Pavlov's data on gastric secretions.* (A) *Secretion under normal conditions; the ordinate shows the amount of gastric secretion, and the abscissa shows time.* (B) *The result when food is introduced directly into the stomach.* (C) *Results after sham feeding, in which the food is introduced into the mouth but never reaches the stomach;* (D) *A composite of* B *and* C, *showing the combined effect of feeding directly into the stomach and sham feeding. Note the similarity between* A *and* D. *(From G. A. Kimble, 1961, p. 244; data from Pavlov, 1910, n.s.)*

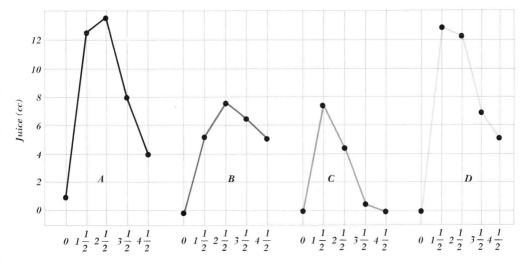

Time (hr)

and esophagus, without food's reaching the stomach, results in an increase in gastric secretion.

The problem of when hunger is satisfied and when it is not or of whether hunger or appetite is present is a matter of considerable concern to theories which attempt to account for learned behavior. Some theories assume that a reduction in drive (such as a reduction in hunger, thirst, or some other deficit which moves the organism to action) is necessary if learning is to occur. The *drive-reduction* concept, of course, requires information on what a drive is and what it is not, on when a drive is being reduced and when it is not. Is a drive being reduced when a person takes a second dessert? Hunger itself is no longer being reduced, since it is believed that the stomach contractions associated with hunger cease fairly rapidly after a small amount of food enters the stomach. Needless to say, it is not a simple matter to determine what is a drive and what is not, although the importance of this concept to theories of how learning occurs has led to a variety of studies concerned with isolating hunger and appetite. The presence of stomach contractions does not account for the amount which is eaten or for food preferences. Indeed, rats whose nervous pathways from the stomach to the brain have been severed show eating behavior similar to unoperated rats (Bash, 1939a; 1939b).

A number of experiments have pointed to the possibility that chemical changes, perhaps in the blood, are responsible for hunger or appetite. When blood from a hungry dog is injected into a satiated dog, the satiated dog becomes hungry. Similarly, when blood from a satiated dog is injected into a hungry dog, his stomach contractions decrease (Luckhardt & Carlson, 1915). Among human beings, there is evidence that the blood-sugar level is lower prior to eating than after (Carlson, 1916), although there are also normal variations that do not necessarily correlate with hunger.

Some investigators have suggested that one or more "hunger hormones" exist which mediate the sensation of hunger, but the hormones have not been identified. Some drugs, however, such as *d*-amphetamine, depress the appetite, even though the rate or intensity of gastric contractions is not affected. The suspicion that the pituitary and hypothalamus were involved in regulating food intake was prevalent by the end of the last century, for several cases had been reported in which uncontrollable obesity followed the growth of tumors in these areas of the central nervous system. It remained for Hetherington and Ranson (1940) to show that it was the hypothalamus, not the pituitary, which was responsible. Overeating (*hyperphagia*) also occurs following a lesion in the ventromedial nuclei of the hypothalamus. A lesion of the lateral areas was found to result in the behavioral opposite of hyperphagia, *hypophagia,* or *aphagia.* In this condition, the organism refuses to eat voluntarily. Some rats, if not force-fed, will starve to death following such lesions. The eating will reappear, however, if the animal is maintained on an appropriate diet, force-fed through a stomach fistula (Teitelbaum & Stellar, 1954).

In addition, the hypothalamus appears to be responsible for water intake. A lesion causing aphagia also produce *adipsia,* a condition in which the organism does not drink. Apparently, hunger and thirst are interwoven. Following lesioning, the rat appears to find both food and water aversive: he neither eats nor drinks. When he reaches a point of semistarvation, he will accept wet food. Teitelbaum and A. N. Epstein (1962) report that the animal then shows a sudden acceptance of both dry and wet food. Finally, he drinks water but only when food is also available. Thus, it appears that the normal pattern of drinking does not reappear, although the animal consumes sufficient water to survive. Apparently there is some separation between the two drives, for eating behavior reappears more rapidly and more completely.

It is convenient to think that the ventromedial nuclei serve as a center of satiation. Thus, destruction of the nuclei results in a loss of the inhibitory center of feeding and leads to overeating. If cats are administered the drug amphetamine, which is known to decrease food intake, recorded electrical activity from the medial hypothalamus increases (Brobeck, Larsson, & Reyes, 1956). It appears that the area does not activate eating so much as it removes the inhibitory center for eating. This suggestion is supported by the observation of N. E. Miller, Bailey, and Stevenson (1950) that hyperphagic animals do not seek out food. Moreover, they do not tend to learn a new response, such as bar pressing, in order to acquire food. These data suggest, again, that destruction of the medial hypothalamus deprives the animal of the inhibitory check that, in effect, informs him when it is time to stop eating. Other reports suggest that there are centers, other than the satiety center, which serve to increase appetite. Morgane (1961) made a lesion in the mid- and far lateral hypothalamus and found that although hyperphagia appeared, only animals with lesions in the far lateral area were willing to cross an electrified grid to get food. These results suggest that the satiety center for food and water intake and the mechanism which controls motivation for intake are located in the hypothalamus.

One complication in the study of hunger is that the sensation of hunger is not general: many times there is hunger for a specific kind of food. *Specific hunger* refers to such hungers as the need of the adrenalectomized organism for salt, the occasional craving for particular foods that most persons experience, and the peculiar desires of pregnant women for bizarre foodstuffs. When a specific deficit in the organism occurs, such as a deficit in salt or some other substance necessary for survival, the person commonly develops a hunger for that substance. This is not hunger in its full sense, for specific hungers may develop even when the person is satiated.

It has been reported that animals will select a diet that is appropriate for their needs. Richter (1942–1943) has shown that if rats are presented with a variety of foodstuffs, they will select an appropriate amount of each.

Human beings might not do so well at such a task, for much of our preference for foodstuffs is apparently learned. Some writers have suggested that specific hungers appear because the development of a particular need in the organism decreases the organism's threshold for that substance. The result would be that the organism would find it easier to identify the appropriate substance. Other experiments have emphasized the learned nature of specific hungers: it is unlikely that many of us would "like" caviar unless social reasons dictated that it should be appreciated. Similarly, there is evidence (Chapter 11) that taste sensitivity changes as a function of age, and thus differences in thresholds may account for some examples of what appear to be specific hungers.

Thirst: Mammals eliminate water in a variety of ways, such as perspiration, evaporation, and evacuation, and water must enter the system in sufficient quantity. Whatever mechanism is responsible for the maintenance of this balance, it is fairly precise. Slight decrements in body weight due to giving off water are reflected in immediate increase in water intake. However, the basic sensation of thirst for human beings is dryness of the throat. This sensation may occur because of an imbalance in water within the body, because one has eaten salty food or delivered a long speech, or for a variety of other reasons not directly related to thirst.

Experiments using fistulas, in which either the stomach cavity or the mouth and esophagus may be bypassed, have been performed in order to determine the influence of these areas, much as Pavlov attempted to find the relationships for hunger. In sham drinking, in which the water passes through the esophagus but out of a fistula, so that it does not reach the stomach, dogs drink as they would normally; i.e., they drink what would be enough to overcome the deficit, even though the water fails to get to the stomach. In addition, if water is placed directly in the stomach, so that the throat, mouth, and esophagus are bypassed, dogs do not stop drinking unless the water has been in the stomach for some time, generally around half an hour. Apparently, the reporting of sensations of thirst is slow. Neither the presence of water in the stomach nor the bathing of the dry throat appears to satisfy thirst. Indeed, removal of the salivary glands does not affect water intake. Structures in the brain are known to affect water intake. Portions of the pituitary and the hypothalamus appear to control water intake, for if these areas are destroyed in human beings, excessive thirst and constant urination result.

Various theories of thirst have been presented. Some emphasize the possible presence of a "thirst hormone," similar to the projected "hunger hormone." Others have concentrated on dehydration of the cells. No doubt these influences affect water intake and thirst, but conclusive evidence on the underlying cause of thirst is no more available than similar evidence on the cause of hunger.

It is difficult to compare hunger and thirst experimentally, for in many species the hungry animal does not drink, nor does the thirsty animal eat. Thirst and hunger are compound drives, and it is difficult to treat them as totally different sensations. Rats which are deprived of food or water or both food and water for varying periods of time show shifts in their preference for one substance or the other as a function of their age and the length of the deprivation. For example, young rats who are deprived of both food and water select water after 1 hour of deprivation but shift to a preference for food after 12 hours. By 72 hours the preference is again for water. Older rats, under the same conditions, prefer food regardless of the period of deprivation (Candland & Culbertson, 1963).

THE VESTIBULAR SENSE

The vestibular system has characteristics of both audition and kinesthesis. The sense organ, which is housed in the nonauditory labyrinth, is part of the ear. Hearing and balance share the same nerve, and as we shall note, events within the cochlea can affect the vestibular sense. Other receptors, however, also provide information on balance. The eyes give information on spatial patterns and the various components of the kinesthetic system inform us about tonus, position, and balance.

The structure of the vestibular system is shown in Figure 10–20. The figure shows the cochlea, as well as the facial (VIIth cranial nerve) and the cochlear and vestibular nerves, which combine to form the auditory (VIIIth cranial) nerve. The nonauditory labyrinth has two principal components, the *semicircular canals* and the utricles. The *utricle* and *saccule* are membranous sacs filled with a fluid, the *endolymph*. Each contains a static receptor called the *macula*. The macula may be compared to a platform on top of which are small calcium stones, called *otoliths*, which, when pulled by gravity, serve to deform the hair cells. The three semicircular canals are in three planes in man at approximate right angles to one another. The canals are known as *lateral, superior,* or *posterior,* depending upon their location and plane. Since there are two sets of labyrinths, one on each side of the head, six canals are present in man. The canals are between 15 and 25 mm long, or about this long: ——————. Each is approximately 0.8 mm in diameter, or about this wide: ˍ. Each has a common cavity in the utricle, although it is also true that each functions independently of the other. Within the canals lie membranous semicircular canals. The space between the membrane and the bone is filled with a fluid called *perilymph.* The perilymph has free access to the other canals. Within the membranous canals is a fluid, *endolymph,* which does not circulate into other canals: its only exit is into the utricle.

The end of each canal forms a swelling at the junction with the utricle; this is known as the *ampulla.* Within the ampulla lies the *crista,* which contains hair cells, similar to those found in the cochlea. The hair cells synapse with other nerve fibers; the movement of the hair cells was considered by earlier theorists to be the receptor for vestibular sensitivity (Mach, 1875). On top of the hair cells and the crista is a gelatinous body, known as the *cupula*, which extends to the roof of the ampulla. It has been described as a swinging door, for it covers the entire ampulla, yet it can be pushed aside under pressure. Figure 10–21 is a photograph of the ampulla of a fish. The cupula is the white area; the crista and its nerve cells lie underneath the cupula, making contact with the nerve.

The perilymph apparently acts as a lubricant in preventing the membrane from rubbing against the bony external surface of the canal. The endolymph, however, moves back and forth, pushing against the crista and cupula. It is believed that the endolymph is responsible for stimulating the hair cells. The vestibular section of the auditory (VIIIth cranial) nerve consists of large fibers, although some small fibers are present. Since the large fibers provide for rapid transmission, it appears that vestibular sensitivity is reported rapidly.

Vestibular sensations result from two kinds of stimulation: The first is a change in position of the head. The macula is apparently the receptor responsible for this stimulus. The vestibular organ is also responsive to changes in the rate of movement of the head. Apparently, the crista registers such changes. In addition, the vestibular apparatus is sensitive to mechanical, thermal, and electric stimulation but it is not presented with these stimuli under normal conditions.

In the early nineteenth century Marie J. P. Flourens (1794–1867; 1830a, 1830b) laid bare the nerves and vestibular apparatus of several birds and mammals and noted that destruction of the canals resulted in changes in other senses, particularly in vision and audition. Flourens also noted that the adequate stimulus for the vestibular sensation was not merely movement but a change in the rate of movement; that is, like pressure sensitivity, the vestibular sense does not respond to absolute stimulation so much as it responds to changes

FIGURE 10–20: *Detail of the nonauditory labyrinth, showing the cochlea, attending nerves, the utricle and saccule, and the position of the semicircular canals. (From M. Hardy,* Anatom. Rec., *1934, 59:112, fig. 7.)*

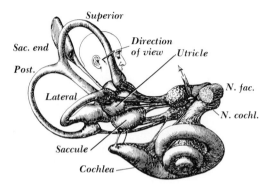

in stimulation. If a human being is turned around in a chair, the speed of which may be controlled, he does not report vestibular sensations unless the speed of rotation is altered; if the speed is held constant, no vestibular sensation is reported.

Steinhausen (1931) and Dohlman (1935; 1944; 1960) devised a technique which permitted observation of the ampulla in fish. A drop of oil was placed in the endolymph, so that the investigator could observe its path through the canals during acceleration of movement. The evidence indicated that when the endolymph flows into the ampulla, the cupula is bent toward the utricle; when acceleration is completed, the cupula returns to its usual station. The evidence for this conclusion is shown in Figure 10–22, which presents photographs taken by Dohlman (1935). Point *B* represents the drop of oil (photograph). Point *C* represents the drop of oil during acceleration. Points *a* and *b* represent the cupula before acceleration. Dohlman has noted that the time it takes for the cupula to return to its neutral position is equivalent to the time it takes for nystagmus to cease.

Bárány, whose name is given to the chair (the Bárány chair) used to whirl subjects at

FIGURE 10-21: *The ampulla of a living fish (pike). The cupula is the vertical white area. Note the ampullar nerve and the ampulla. (From Dohlman, 1935, p. 1371.)*

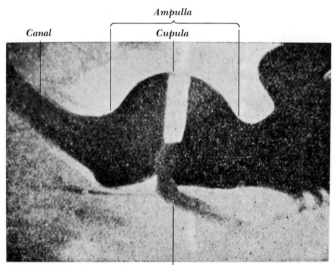

Ampulla

Canal   Cupula

Ampullar nerve

different accelerations during tests of the vestibular apparatus, noted in 1908 that nystagmus could be produced by filling the external meatus with cold water. Dohlman has suggested that when the vestibular system is under such thermal stimulation, the endolymph is cooled and this cooling sets the liquid in motion. Thermal reactions of this type are used extensively in clinical tests of the performance of the vestibular system.

The utricle is found where the three semicircular canals meet. Within it is the macula. In mammals, the utricle contains endolymphatic fluid which has a specific gravity very nearly that of water. The macula itself, because of its composition of sensory cells and a gelatinous substance, has a greater specific gravity than the endolymphatic fluid. When one stands erect, the macula is in a nearly horizontal position. Changes in one's posture are reflected by changes in electrical recordings from the macula and adjacent areas. Ledoux (1960), for example, recording from the am-

pulla, has noted several characteristics which determine the intensity of the vestibular response. Among these characteristics are the extent of the acceleration and the difference between the temperature of the ear and the temperature of water placed in the external meatus. Trincker (1962) has recorded inside the macula of the guinea pig and found that neural responses appeared only with specific movements of the hair cells. Stimuli applied at right angles to the macula do not appear to produce electric discharges. The saccule may be destroyed, at least in animals, without producing notable effects on balance or posture. Indeed, in some cases in which congenital brain damage renders the human being deaf and speechless, the nonauditory labyrinth is completely destroyed. So long as vision is present, however, appropriate postural responses may be learned without difficulty, and the individual does not show an obvious lack of balance or posture.

Because of the importance of the vestibular

system to aviation and other military endeavors, the past years have seen an increase in attention to vestibular sensitivity. Many studies (see Walsh, 1960; Meek, Graybiel, Beischer, & Riopelle, 1961; B. Clark & Graybiel, 1960) have focused on the practical problem of determining how much rotation or acceleration a person can take without nystagmus or other debilitating symptoms. Individual differences in thresholds are wide, however, and consistent threshold data are not plentiful. Adaptation may or may not be a characteristic of the vestibular system; although it appears that individuals may learn to accommodate to increasingly severe acceleration, it is doubtful that this represents adaptation of the receptor so much as it indicates the ability of the organism to adjust kinestheically to acceleration.

The vestibular apparatus is directly concerned with motion sickness of all kinds. Motion sickness usually involves a number of responses. Occasionally ear difficulties are noted, such as tinnitus. There is evidence that proneness to motion sickness varies as a function of age. In addition, there is evidence that vertical motion, e.g., the sudden drop of an airplane or a boat, is most likely to produce motion sickness. Several drugs are available that inhibit the symptoms of motion sickness.

SOURCES

The student of the sensory systems discussed in this chapter will find a perusal of classic textbooks instructive. Titchener's classic student manual (1902) presents details of experiments on locating the "spots," and most of the questions it poses about cutaneous sensitivity are still alive. Both Ladd's text (1911) and the various editions of Woodworth (1918, 1938; Woodworth & Schlosberg, 1954) present a ready method for studying the history of cutaneous sensitivity. The study of kinesthesis and the vestibular sense has received considerable impetus from military and industrial programs, such as the space program.

FIGURE 10–22: *The path of a drop of oil during acceleration. Photograph 1 (top) shows the drop of oil (B). During acceleration, the drop moves toward the ampulla. The cupula, originally almost vertical, bends toward the utricle as a result of the flow of the endolymph into the ampulla. C shows the drop of oil during acceleration. Point a shows the original position of the ampulla in both the top and bottom pictures. Point b is the top of the cupula before acceleration. Point c shows the top of the cupula during acceleration. (From Dohlman, 1935, p. 1373.)*

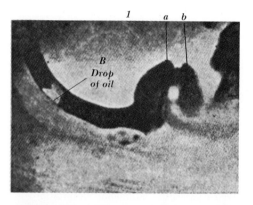

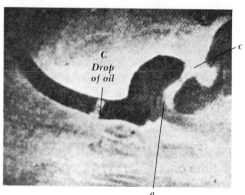

Textbooks vary widely on their interpretation of the structures within the skin which serve as receptors. Certainly, uncritical acceptance of von Frey's speculation that each cutaneous sense has its own receptor is a disservice to the student, even though complete acceptance appears in many physiology texts which choose not to discuss the subject at length. More reasonable discussions of this problem are presented by Geldard (1953), Osgood (1953), and Wenger, F. N. Jones, and M. H. Jones (1956). C. T. Morgan and Stellar (1950) and C. T. Morgan (1965) also provide useful summaries. See also Rose and Mountcastle (1959) on touch and kinesthesis, Zotterman (1959) on thermal sensations, Sweet (1959) on pain, and Gernandt (1959) on vestibular mechanisms. Mountcastle (1961) presents a difficult and fascinating discussion of the relationship between certain cutaneous systems and the central nervous system. In addition, a chapter by Wall (1961) provides an excellent summary of the contributions of this writer to certain aspects of skin sensations. The chapter presents a useful theory of conduction as well as data which may alter some old views about cutaneous perception. Rosner (1961) discusses some experiments concerned with cutaneous responses to "successive stimuli." This chapter is concerned with how discrimination occurs between successive cutaneous stimulations.

Zotterman's review (in the *Annual Review of Physiology*, 1953) summarizes work on cutaneous sensitivity during the preceding few years. More recent reviews have appeared in Field, Magoun, and V. E. Hall (1959), in Rothman (1954), and in the review by Nafe and Kenshalo of the somesthetic senses (1962).

For information on advances in the study of thermal sensitivity, Hensel's review (1959) and Zotterman's review (1959) are very useful. Several other reviews exist (see Kenshalo & Nafe, 1962), but many are technical reports from the armed services, and they are not readily obtainable. Pain is reviewed in a book by J. C. White and Sweet (1955). Iggo (1959) presents a useful discussion of the cutaneous receptors involved in itch and pain.

Reviews of the relationship between the hypothalamus and eating and drinking have been provided by Anand (1961), Hightower (1962), and Teitelbaum (1961). Theories of hunger are rampant. Mayer's glucosity theory is based on the idea that the hypothalamus is sensitive to changes in the glucose level of the blood (see J. Mayer, 1952; 1955). Brobeck (1957; 1960) has suggested that food intake is regulated thermally. This idea suggests that the hypothalamus has thermal receptors (not of the kind found cutaneously) which regulate the hypothalamus and, in turn, the intake directed by it.

CHAPTER ELEVEN

THE CHEMICAL SENSES: SMELL AND TASTE

In this chapter we discuss the last of our major sensory systems, the "chemical senses." The chemical senses are said to be *olfaction* (smell), *gustation* (taste), and the common *chemical sense*. An example of a reaction from the common chemical sense is that which occurs when a speck of pepper comes into contact with the lining of the esophagus and evokes a sensation of pain. Several receptors, generally the cutaneous ones, respond to chemical stimulation. We have stated previously that cutaneous receptors are sensitive to various kinds of stimulation, including chemical and mechanical stimuli. For this reason, the common chemical sense might be classed as a special case of cutaneous sensation rather than a separate sensory system. The term "chemical senses" is a misnomer for at least two reasons: first, most sensory systems may be stimulated by chemicals, although chemical substances are not the most common type of stimulation; second, although certain sensory systems, such as taste and smell, appear to be primarily receptive to odors and foodstuffs, which are described most efficiently by their chemical composition, we are not sure that the chemical composition alone is the aspect of the stimulus that is responsible for the sensation.

It is often stated that less is known about taste and smell than about other sensory systems. Nonetheless, there is no lack of data concerning taste and smell. The difficulty is that these data do not form a completely acceptable theory concerning how we smell and taste. Part of the difficulty originates from the fact that both the gustatory and olfactory receptors are minute and difficult to examine. Also, there are problems in controlling the stimulus. It is much easier to measure and reproduce light waves or sound waves than to manipulate and measure gustatory and olfactory stimuli accurately. Further, both taste and smell are intimately involved with other sensory systems. For example, odors affect taste; the composition of foodstuffs, whether they are hot or cold, chewy or liquid, affects taste.

These associations interfere with experimental control.

The chemical senses are sometimes called "minor senses," since they are, supposedly, less important to human behavior than others. They are of minor importance only in that they are usually ignored by human beings: deficiencies in hearing or vision are corrected, but deficiencies in smell or taste are rarely noticed. Removal of noxious odors and the presentation of palatable food are of concern to many industries, however, and a major portion of the research on smell and taste has been instigated by the practical needs of industry.

OLFACTION

The Stimuli: As we learned in Chapter 3, the adequate stimulus for olfaction is certain chemicals in a gaseous state. Among the elements, only fluorine, chlorine, bromine, iodine, phosphorus, arsenic, and oxygen (ozone) are odorous in their natural state. Many organic compounds, however, are odorous. One of the characteristics of the olfactory system is that the individual can alter the amount of the stimulus he receives. If I present a bottle to you and say, "Smell this," you will probably sniff. By taking deeper breaths, you enhance the possibility of perceiving the stimulus. Accordingly, whenever we breathe, we are in the process of smelling, although we are not often aware of the accompanying sensations. Only if an odor is unusual in quality or intensity are we apt to note its presence.

Breathing and sniffing through the nose are the most common ways in which odors are perceived, but the fact that the receptor for olfaction is anatomically associated with respiration means that other methods for perceiving odorous materials exist. One can smell, for example, by holding the nose and taking in air through the mouth. Further, since the olfactory stimulus can remain in contact with the receptor long after the stimulus has been inhaled, the sensation may continue for some time after the physical stimulus has been removed, although generally olfaction occurs during inhalation, since the greatest volume of the stimulus reaches the receptor in this manner.

There is evidence, however, that the stimulus must move from the nasal cavity to the receptor before sensation can occur. Take a bottle containing ammonia and hold it under the nostrils while holding the breath. Olfaction does not occur, although there may be some stinging sensations from the membranes (the common chemical sense). If you then move away from the location of the test (so that ammonia remaining in the air will not be perceived) and then inhale, the ammonia will be perceived. The point of this demonstration is that the odorous chemical must be transported to the receptor if there is to be a sensation. It is likely, then, that smell is not a distance sense, such as audition and vision, but that the stimulus must make physical contact with the receptor. As we shall discover in the next section, although the receptor system is identified easily, the manner in which the sensation is transmitted is unclear.

Receptors and Neural Pathways: Figure 11-1 shows the general location of the structures associated with olfaction. The openings provided by the nostrils (*nares*) meet at the nasopharynx (10) at the top of the throat. Within this area are three bones and membranes, known collectively as the *turbinates*. In the figure, these are identified as 3, 4, and 5 (the *inferior, middle,* and *superior turbinates*). These structures are of primary use in the process of breathing, for they filter, warm, and hydrate the air. The major receptor for olfaction is the *olfactory cleft,* 6 in the diagram. There are two olfactory clefts (approximately 2.5 square centimeters in area), one associated with each nostril, but separated by the nasal septum (not shown). Although the nasal cavities are reddish, the olfactory cleft is yellow because of the presence of a pigment. It would seem reasonable to assume that the special pigment found in the olfactory cleft is associated with the process of olfaction.

Two kinds of cells are found in the epithelium: (1) sustentacular cells, which are large and wide, and (2) olfactory cells, which are pigmented, long, and thin. Figure 11–2 shows, schematically, the sensory organ and the central pathway of the olfactory nerve. The olfactory cells in the epithelium may be observed.

Figure 11–3 shows an electron micrograph of the surface of a human olfactory cell. The cells connect to the cranial nerve through the *cribiform plate* (Figure 11–2). Each olfactory cell maintains between 5 and 10 hair cells, similar to those found in the cochlea on the basilar membrane. The hair cells are thought to be the actual receptor for odorous substances; it is believed that chemicals reaching the hair cells make contact with, or become imbedded in, the mass of these cells. This region is kept moist by the mucus from surrounding tissue (the *mucosa*). Overproduction of mucus, as during a cold, results in congestion of the hair cells, which limits olfactory reception. Olfaction is one of the oldest sensory systems, and it follows that the receptor is an extension of cell matter. The fact that the receptors are morphologically simple, however, does not mean that it is also simple to uncover the way they code and uncode the olfactory messages.

Two large olfactory nerves carry the impulses arriving from the receptor to the brain. Each is associated with a nostril and with its corresponding olfactory cleft. Each olfactory nerve is composed of 20 or more bundles of fibers; each bundle contains many fibers. Curiously, in man the olfactory nerves are not medullated, although medullated fibers and nerves are common in the central nervous system (see Chapter 2). The place at which the receptors meet the nerve is known as the *olfactory lobe*. This represents the first synapse of the receptor system. This lobe is especially large in some animals, primarily those which

FIGURE 11–1: *Diagram of the structures concerned with olfaction. (1) Vestibule, (2) antrum, (3) inferior turbinate, (4) middle turbinate, (5) superior turbinate, (6) olfactory cleft, (7) sinuses, (8) hard palate, (9) soft palate, (10) nasopharynx, (11) posterior nares, (12) pharynx. (From Moncrieff, 1951, p. 34.)*

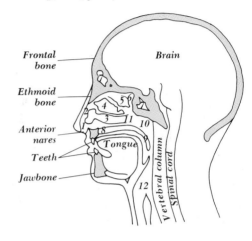

FIGURE 11–2: *A schematic representation of the olfactory system. (From The Ciba Collection of Medical Illustrations, by Frank H. Netter, M.D., copyright Ciba, 1957, p. 62.)*

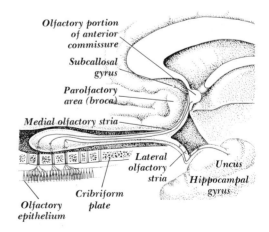

FIGURE 11–3: *Electron micrograph of the surface of a human olfactory cell, showing a great number of fingerlike processes 1.5 to 2.0 mμ long. Magnification × 23,430. (From Bloom & Engström, 1952, p. 700.)*

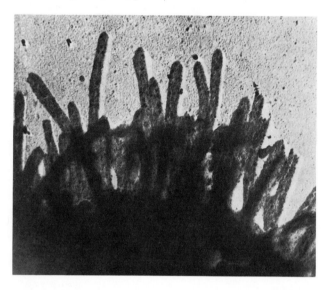

depend heavily upon the sense of smell for food and safety.

The olfactory nerves use various and devious pathways in their travels to the brain. Indeed, as may be noted from Figure 11–2, the pathways are elaborate, compared with those of other senses. The history of the study of olfaction indicates that a variety of central structures have been suggested as the projection area. The nerve fibers are known to reach the *uncus* (Figure 11–2), and there is evidence that some fibers continue to the *amygdala* (Chapter 2). Although there is a suggestion that other fibers reach the *subcallosal gyrus* (Figure 11–2), the presence of this pathway is not certain. It has been suggested that the *pyriform area* is involved, for electrical recordings from this area correlate with the presentation of olfactory stimuli. Unlike other cranial nerves, the olfactory nerves do not pass through the thalamus, although pathways to the hypothalamus are available.

As we consider, in the next sections, data on thresholds, adaptation, electrical activity, and pathology, it is instructive to keep in mind the two critical questions that plague theories of olfaction: (1) How do the hair cells translate the chemical stimulus into sensations? (2) Where in the brain does the sensation of olfaction occur?

Techniques for Threshold Measurement: A major difficulty in the determination of olfactory thresholds is control over the stimulus. Although one may prepare a solution with specified components, one cannot be sure that this precise concentration actually reaches the receptor. Certainly such factors as breathing rate, amount of mucus on the epithelium, and individual differences in the morphological features of the receptor encourage variation in the reception of the stimulus when it acts upon the receptor. For these reasons, a variety of techniques and apparatuses exist for the determination of thresholds. Since the results of threshold measurements vary as a function of the technique employed, it is necessary to review some of the more common techniques.

ZWAARDEMAKER'S OLFACTOMETER: Invented in the nineteenth century by Hendrik Zwaardemaker (1857–1930), this device has been among the most widely used apparatuses for olfactory thresholds. Figure 11–4 shows the device. The glass tube, usually 0.08 cm in diameter, is inserted into the nostril. A *double olfactometer,* which contains two tubes, one for each nostril, is also used—both to increase the amount of the stimulus administered and to investigate the effects of presenting different odors or different concentrations of the same odor through different nostrils. The rubber cylinder contains the stimulus, and, like a syringe, it has appropriate markings so that the amount of the stimulus administered may be determined. The calibration is in centimeters; 1 centimeter of the stimulus is sometimes called an *olfactie,* or *olfacty.* Hence, the threshold may be described in terms of the number of olfacties presented before the subject reports a sensation. More precisely, the term *olfactie* represents the number of molecules detectable per cubic centimeter. Thus, 1 olfactie for a given stimulus represents the RL. One difficulty with the olfactometer is that the rate of inhalation by the subject is uncontrolled. In the older literature the subjects were instructed to make "standard sniffs." More recently, a continuous-flow pump has been used to ensure standard speeds of inhalation.

BLAST INJECTION: The blast injection technique, developed by Elsberg and I. Levy (1935), improved the Zwaardemaker technique. A bottle is used which serves as a receptacle both for a syringe and for tubes placed in the nostril. Figure 11–5 shows the device. A determined volume of air may be pumped into the bottle by the syringe. When the cock is removed, the air and the odors from the bottle are blasted into the nostrils. This technique assumes that all air and its odorous substances have equal pressure, for otherwise the force of the blast would vary.

OLFACTORIUM: Dallenbach has designed an

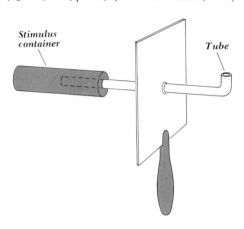

FIGURE 11–4: *A diagram of Zwaardemaker's olfactometer, used for presenting olfactory stimuli in the measurement of olfactory thresholds. (From Pfaffman, 1948, p. 284, after Zwaardemaker, 1920.)*

olfactorium which takes the precaution of employing the whole subject, rather than his nostrils alone. The olfactorium consists of two rooms, one inside the other. The air in the inner chamber is controlled by a variety of devices that attempt to establish purity of the air. The subject bathes and is encased in a plastic suit before entering the inner, experimental chamber. When he is in the chamber, different odors are presented, and he communicates his sensations. Clearly, this procedure is time-consuming, for once a stimulus of given intensity has been presented and noted, the subject should be removed and rewashed and the chamber air purified before the next session.

CAMERA INODORATA: Invented by Zwaardemaker and later improved by several investigators, the *camera inodorata* is a box large enough to hold the head. Unwanted odors are removed by a mercury vapor lamp. The subject places his head in the device, and the olfactometer is employed. This technique represents a small version of Dallenbach's olfactorium and has the advantage of attempting to control unwanted odors during the measurement of thresholds. An improvement of this

FIGURE 11-5: *Apparatus used in the blast injection technique. When the cock is released, a substance of known concentration is blasted through the tube into the nostril. (From Elsberg & Levy, 1935, p. 11.)*

technique has been used in the determination of thresholds by Wenzel (1954).

CONSTANT FLOW: Le Magnen (1942–1943; 1944–1945) has developed an apparatus employing an air whistle that sounds as the subject inhales. The subject is required to maintain a constant pitch, thus supposedly ensuring constant intake of the odorous substance.

MEASURING SUBHUMAN THRESHOLDS: A considerable portion of the work on thresholds has used animal subjects. One reason for this concentration is the relative ease of employing animals in the long sessions required for threshold determinations. Another reason, however, is that the evolution of the olfactory system is of scientific interest, since lower organisms that rely heavily on olfaction and have larger and sometimes better-developed systems provide data useful for understanding human sensory behavior. One classic technique for determining thresholds in animals is to require the subject to learn a maze for a reward of food or some other suitable substance. The alleys or goals are differentiated by the types of odors associated with them. If the subject learns to select one odor over another, it is assumed that he has discriminated the odors (Gerebtzoff & Phillipot, 1957; Munn, 1950). Pfaffman and his collaborators (Pfaffman, Goff, & Bare, 1958) have used an apparatus in which a rat, or another suitable animal, learns that odorized air is the signal to cease bar pressing. As we shall note in Chapter 14, rats and other animals learn this response rapidly. Odors are blasted into a chamber. If the rat perceives the odor, he does not press; if he does not perceive the odor, he presses the bar. In this way, the threshold for the odorous substance may be determined.

Thresholds: Since a large number of stimuli are capable of producing olfactory sensations, each stimulus maintains its own characteristic DLs and RLs, which may be expected to vary as a function of such factors as temperature and concentration. Accordingly, statements regarding thresholds for olfactory stimuli depend upon the precise stimulus used. Clearly, there are large individual threshold differences among compounds. A small dab of paint in a room is obvious immediately, as is the presence of rotten eggs or perfume. Other odors, however, appear to have very high thresholds, including, unfortunately, some lethal gases. Moreover, the quality of the sensation may vary as a function of the intensity. One chemical, for example, is perceived as having a mild violet odor in low concentration but as having a powerful and somewhat repugnant cedar odor when the concentration is increased.

Table 11–A indicates the threshold in terms of milligrams per liter for some common substances. Note that some odors, such as musk, are perceived when the concentration is extremely low. Other, such as wintergreen, require higher concentrations. When one considers that 0.000000075 mg per liter of trinitro-

TABLE 11-A: *Some Representative Thresholds of Odiforous Substances.*
The left column gives the chemical or name, the center column gives the common name of the odor, and the right column shows the thresholds in milligrams per liter. (Adapted from Wenger, F. N. Jones, and M. H. Jones, 1956, p. 148. Data from studies by V. C. Allison and S. H. Katz, 1919; Baldus, 1937; J. Jung, 1936; S. H. Katz and Talbert, 1930; Ohma, 1922; and Schley, 1934.)

Substance	Odor	Threshold, mg per liter
Carbon tetrachloride	Sweet	4.533
Methyl salicylate	Wintergreen	0.100
Amyl acetate	Banana oil	0.039
N-butyric acid	Perspiration	0.009
Benzene	Kerosine	0.0088
Safrol	Sassafras	0.005
Ethyl acetate	Fruit	0.0036
Pyridine	Burned	0.00074
Hydrogen sulfide	Rotten eggs	0.00018
N-butyl sulfide	Foul, sulfurous	0.00009
Coumarin	New-mown hay	0.00002
Citral	Lemon	0.000003
Ethyl mercaptan	Decayed cabbage	0.00000066
Trinitro-tertiary-butyl xylene	Musk	0.000000075

tertiary-butyl xylene is at threshold, olfactory sensitivity appears to be acute. Even this small amount may require billions of molecules, however. Accordingly, olfactory sensitivity seems to be remarkably adept when it is remembered that in vision between 1 and 2 quanta is sufficient to stimulate a rod. Among the chemical senses, though, olfaction is the most acute by far. Moncrieff (1951) estimates that olfaction is 10,000 times as sensitive as taste.

In general, threshold studies report a Weber ratio of approximately 0.2 in the middle ranges. The fraction is no more a constant for smell than it is for other senses, for as intensity is increased, the fraction is lowered. Geldard (1953) has pointed out that if the RL is high, the DL is low. Accordingly, there appears to be a relationship between the RL and the precision of discriminations within the intensity range.

The intensity of olfactory stimuli has been scaled by F. N. Jones (1958). His results indicate that the discrimination of intensities follows Stevens's power function (see Chapter 5). In this study, the Weber fraction for intensity was 0.38. This finding indicates that although the RL for olfaction is thought to be considerably lower than that for taste, the DL is considerably larger. That is, although it is easier to detect odor than taste, it is difficult to detect changes in intensity.

A further problem in threshold measurement is that a threshold may be determined without the subject's being able to identify the stimulus. Engen and Pfaffman (1960) found that human subjects are able to discriminate and label approximately sixteen different olfactory qualities. This number is considerably smaller than the number of chemically different substances which can be smelled. Untrained human subjects are able to discriminate approximately three levels of intensity, although persons given practice are able to identify four levels. Clearly, the human being discriminates only a small number of the available stimuli and intensities.

Thresholds of animals are remarkably different from those of human beings. The most common technique for investigating thresholds in animals is to train the animal to make a given response when the odor is present and to make no response, or another response, when the odor is not present. Adequate control of the stimulus is of importance in research on animals, and failure to control for relevant problems may explain some of the divergence of reported results. Data have been collected on animal thresholds by electrical recording techniques. Recordings are taken from the olfactory bulb and related areas. Although these data provide useful information on the differences in nerve discharge as a function of the type and intensity of the stimulus, they are not well suited to the determination of thresholds. Adrian's studies (1951) indicate that animals live in a vastly different olfactory world from human beings, a fact well known to dog and cat owners. Many animals show heightened electric response to dead or decaying material; some, such as rabbits, are apparently more sensitive to fruit odors. Many animals, including cats, appear insensitive to the aroma of flowers, although this odor is ordinarily pleasant to the human being.

Olfactory thresholds among human beings vary, just the thresholds of other senses do. Since perfect control over the olfactory stimulus is often doubtful, there is a tendency to consider deviations the result of the experimental method. Data exist, however, which suggest that the deviations have other causes. For example, Elsberg, Brewer, and I. Levy (1935) have found that a lowering of the threshold (i.e., more acute olfactory perception) occurs both before and after the men-

strual period in women. The data of Hansen and Glass (1936) indicate that although there is no increase in the threshold during pregnancy, an aversion to some odors may develop. Olfactory acuity also varies as a function of the time of day. Goetzl and F. Stone (1947) report that acuity increases from awakening until lunchtime, after which it decreases.

Adaptation, Masking, and Related Phenomena: Adaptation occurs in olfaction just as in the other senses we have studied. We noted in Chapter 3 that adaptation to smell often occurs rapidly: we appear to adapt very quickly to the strange odors of a house, animals, flowers, and cooking. Researchers working with animals commonly report an inability to smell the subjects, although a novice in the laboratory has no difficulty in perceiving the odor. Most of the problems faced in controlling the stimulus also appear in measuring adaptation. The odors of some chemicals seem to change the longer we are in contact with them. Moreover, a second odor may mask the original odor or change its threshold.

Relatively little information exists concerning adaptation rate. Zwaardemaker (1925) furnished an experiment in which the adaptation rate of benzoin and rubber was measured under two different concentrations. Figure 11–6 shows the results. Intensity is indicated by the number of olfacties. It is clear that benzoin adapts more rapidly than rubber. Furthermore, the more intense the original stimulus, the more rapid the adaptation. It should be noted, however, that these functions are almost linear. In other sensory systems, adaptation usually results in a decelerating function as the rate of change approaches zero. It is possible, of course, that this is not a characteristic of olfactory adaptation and that the threshold merely becomes infinitely high. Data compiled by Woodrow and Karpman (1917) suggest that adaptation is a function of vapor pressure and thus of the number of molecules impinging upon the receptor. Stuvier (1958) reports that the relationship is indeed linear when relatively high intensities of the stimulus are used. When the intensity is lower, however, rapid adaptation followed by slower recovery occurs.

Electrical Activity: The advances in knowledge emanating from the recording of electrical activity associated with olfaction have not been so dramatic as advances from similar studies in vision and audition. One difficulty is that the central nervous pathways for olfaction are apparently more complicated. However, the recent technical advantages provided by single-cell recording have provided valuable data on the olfactory process. Gesteland, Lettvin, Pitts, and Rojas (1963) recorded from individual receptors in the frog mucosa. Separate receptors respond differentially; i.e., one may respond strongly to some stimuli and not at all to others. These data suggest that receptors may be grouped into stimuli to which each group is sensitive. For example, one group is sensitive to musk, which has a heavy putrid odor, but not to several odors which smell like bitter almonds. Moreover, the divergence of structures in the olfactory system among animals is so great that it is difficult to generalize findings from one species to another.

A further problem in obtaining electrical recordings from the olfactory system is that it is difficult to reach the minute and densely packed receptors. Nevertheless, some valuable and intriguing clues are to be found in data from electrical recordings. Commonly, recordings are made from second-order neurons or from the olfactory bulb where refinement in electrode placement is possible. Some animals possess a large olfactory bulb or stalk. For this reason many studies have used fish, such as the carp and catfish, whose receptors are more conducive to the implanting of tiny electrodes. As we noted, however, there is ample evidence that the olfactory thresholds and olfactory pleasures of subhuman animals are different from those of human beings.

Adrian has recorded from several areas of the olfactory bulb while forcing odors into the receptor. In general, the several areas produce different potentials to different stimuli. Several experimenters have recorded from the mucosa of various animals. Takagi and Shibuya (1959)

FIGURE 11–6: *Adaptation to two intensities of benzoin and two intensities of rubber expressed in olfacties. Adaptation is more rapid for benzoin than for rubber; with both substances, the more intense the stimulus, the more rapid the adaptation. (Form Pfaffman, 1951, p. 1165, after Zwaardemaker, 1925.)*

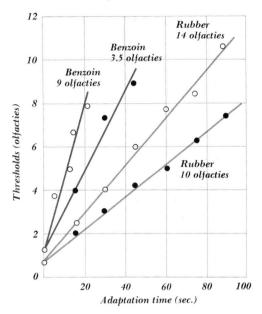

report the presence of on, on-off, and off responses similar to those found in vision. On the other hand, Loed (1959) found potentials which decline exponentially under repeated stimulation. Ottoson (1956; 1959) reports only slow potentials. In a study of the human olfactory bulb, electric current from 25 to 39 Hz was employed and differences both in frequency and in amplitude appeared between the two bulbs (Sem-Jacobsen, Petersen, H. W. Dodge, Jacks, & Lazarte, 1956). Recording from the mitral cells, Adrian (1956a; 1956b) reports that different areas of cells respond to different intensities of a stimulus; i.e., a given odor may produce electric discharge in one area at one intensity but in another area when the intensity is changed.

It is possible, of course, that these differences represent nothing more than the fact that an increase in intensity will produce a spreading of the stimulus over a wider area of the epithelium. It is also possible, however, that the mitral cells are differentially sensitive, so that the manner in which they code and decode information depends upon the combination of areas stimulated. This is similar to the postulates of the volley theory of hearing. Although the differences in results may be attributed to the technical difficulties in acquiring electric potentials, it appears that there is not total agreement upon the characteristic potential that accompanies olfaction. It is also possible that olfaction is affected by other sensory systems. For example, in one study (Lavín, Alcocer-Cuarón, & Hernandez-Peón, 1959), the investigators implanted electrodes in the olfactory bulb of the cat and noted that the electric discharge increased when visual, auditory, or gustatory stimuli were applied to the appropriate receptor.

Adrian's work (Adrian & Ludwig, 1938) on the catfish indicated variations in the frequency of the impulse as a function of the type of olfactory stimulus. Such a recording is shown schematically in Figure 11–7. A "defi-

nite" discharge was recorded from such succulent stimuli as extracts of fresh earthworms, fresh blood, decayed earthworms, frog muscles, decayed liver, and decayed alligator head. Neither oil of cloves nor oil of cedar gave a recordable discharge. The investigators did not report their own reactions to the stimuli.

Using small electrodes, investigators have recorded olfactory discharges from the mucosa of the frog (Gesteland, 1961; Gesteland, Lettvin, Pitts, & Rojas, 1963). The electrode is an irritant to the organism, however, and may block olfactory sensitivity around the area in which it is inserted. Data on adaptation are shown in Figure 11–8, which presents the recordings from two successive administrations of an acid. Although the spikes are apparently equal in amplitude, the frequencies are different. The application of the stimulus a second time results in a decrease in the number of potentials. When the concentration of the stimulus is varied, differences in frequency of discharge also occur. Figure 11–9 shows the application of the same acid in three different concentrations. The lowest concentration is represented by recording *A* and the highest concentration by recording *C*. Again, the amplitudes of the spikes are relatively equal, although an increase in concentration produces an increase in the number of spikes.

Using the rabbit, Moulton (1963) has recorded from both the olfactory bulbs and the mucosa. He reports "marked disconformities" between the recordings. These results emphasize the discontinuity between electrical activity around the receptor and activity within the nerve or olfactory bulb. The implication is clear that some transition occurs in or around the receptor. Schneider (1963) has reported work on olfactory sensitivity in insects, and Dethier, Larsen, and J. R. Adams (1963) have reported on the blowfly. They found that temperature affected a large fiber of the tarsus, which in turn affected the nature of the substance the blowfly would accept. The fly extends its proboscis in response to sucrose but withdraws it in the presence of such unacceptable compounds as hydrochloric acid.

FIGURE 11–7: *Schematic diagrams of nerve discharge to different solutions. Curve* A *shows the response to extract of decayed earthworms, and curve* B *shows the discharge to a diluted concoction of the same substance. Apparently the intensity of the stimulus is reflected in the intensity of the discharge. (From Adrian & Ludwig, 1938, p. 450.)*

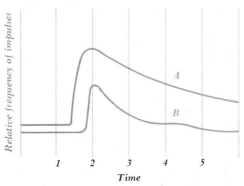

Relative frequency of impulses

A

B

1   2   3   4   5

Time

Pathology: It is sometimes difficult to separate pathological conditions of the receptor from the olfactory sensations that are sometimes reported under atypical conditions, such as olfaction during sleep and that which results from the rubbing and striking of certain stones. Aronsohn (1884; see Moncrieff, 1951, p. 94) filled the nasal cavity with salt solution and stimulated the solution with electric current. Ambiguous olfactory sensations reportedly followed this procedure. Also, it has been reported that certain chemicals injected directly into the blood produce immediate sensations of an olfactory nature, even though the olfactory receptor has not been stimulated directly (Maybee, 1939). Unfortunately, a survey of the literature does not indicate that these phenomena have been examined closely or that replications have been reported. Although not technically a pathological condition, several investigators have noted that the striking of two stones together produces an olfactory sensation (Piccard & Piccard, 1908; Schwarz, 1913; see Moncrieff, 1951, p. 95). Schwarz took the precaution of warming the stones as a control for the possibility that the odor was produced by the decomposition of some impurities in the composition of the stones, but he reported that warming alone was not sufficient to create an odor.

Pathological states may result in an enhancement or lowering of acuity. Accordingly, pathology refers to an abnormal functioning of olfaction by either an increase or a decrease in threshold. We have noted that acuity for various stimuli is increased under specific conditions such as pregnancy or menstruation. In addition, some drugs, including cocaine, enhance olfactory acuity briefly. Individuals or species that possess acute olfactory perception are said to be *macrosmatic;* those whose perception is relatively less acute are *microsmatic.* Human beings are generally microsmatic, although some individuals have acute perception. The term *anosmia* refers to cases in which olfactory perception is either lacking or greatly reduced. Anosmia may be permanent (as in brain damage or congenital deficiency)

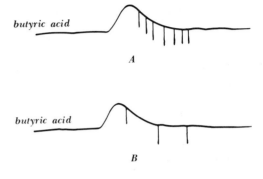

FIGURE 11–8: *Electric response to two puffs of butyric acid. Diagram* B *represents the response one minute after the response recorded in diagram* A. *The entire time of the discharge is ten seconds. (From Gesteland, Lettvin, Pitts, & Rojas, 1963, p. 24.)*

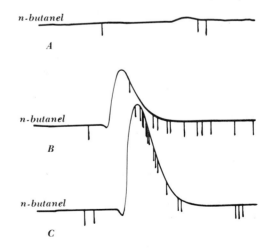

FIGURE 11–9: *How the electric discharge is influenced by increasing the strength of the stimulus. Part* A *of the diagram shows the smallest intensity of n-butanel, and part* C *shows the response to the greatest intensity. The length of the recording is ten seconds. (From Gesteland, Lettvin, Pitts, & Rojas, 1963, p. 24.)*

or temporary (as when one has a cold). One of the common sources of temporary and partial anosmia is tobacco, for it dulls olfactory, as well as gustatory, sensitivity. Temporary anosmia may be produced by olfactory fatigue. Anosmia of any kind is rarely debilitating, for human beings can survive quite well without olfactory sensations. Data on anosmia in animals, especially those which rely upon olfactory cues for food, mating, and survival, are lacking. Such data would be useful in understanding the evolution of olfaction as well as in the study of survival among animals.

Theories of Sensitivity: Most theories of olfaction are concerned with how the receptor reacts to the stimulus, a problem which appears to be reasonably settled in the other sensory systems we have discussed. For example, although there are several theories of audition (see Chapter 6), there is agreement concerning the nature of auditory stimuli and the action of the receptor. In the area of color vision (Chapter 9), however, we find that conflicting theories arise, because the physiology of the receptor is not completely understood. A similar situation exists among olfaction theories, where different assumptions are made regarding how the receptor operates. Until the nature of the receptor and the characteristics of the stimulus are better understood, it is not likely that a comprehensive theory of olfaction will be suggested. Nevertheless, or perhaps for these reasons, theories of olfaction are abundant. Moncrieff (1951), Geldard (1953), Adey (1959), and C. T. Morgan (1965) have reviewed them. Consider the following postulates that have been suggested. They are placed in nearly chronological orders, so that one may notice the development of olfaction theory.

1. The molecules of the stimulus vibrate as a function of the ultraviolet wavelength absorbed. Thus, the stimulus does not have to come in contact with the receptor. The different frequencies of vibration determine the quality of the odor (Heyninx, 1917).

2. The molecular structure of the substance determines the quality of the olfactory sensation. For example, if the compound forms a ring, the odor is resinous; if it is forked, the odor is fruity; if the compound is fragmented, the odor is foul (Henning, 1916). For each corner of Henning's smell prism (Figure 3–7), a different structure is predicted.

3. The molecules must make contact with the receptor, where they are dissolved or altered, probably by the mucus. Accordingly, a stimulus must be soluble to be sensed. The quality and quantity of the sensation are determined by the degree of solubility of the stimulus; the more soluble stimuli have lower RLs (Backman, 1917).

4. The intensity of the odor is a function of several factors, including (*a*) volatility and diffusibility and (*b*) rate of absorption (Zwaardemaker, 1922). Nine groups of substances are projected. The common element of some groupings is suggestive, but that of other groupings is unknown. For example it is suggested that nauseating stimuli have a common pyrrole nucleus, whereas ethereal odors contain an ether linkage.

5. The "dipole" theory is based on the assumption that the critical determiner of the sensation is a function of the electric charge of the molecule. If the positive charges do not correspond to the negative charges, the compound has an electric potential as well as "poles." The discrepancy between the poles is considered the critical aspect of the stimulus. Compounds without poles are said to have the same general odor. Those with poles are thought to stimulate the receptor differently, depending upon the difference in polarity (A. Müller, 1936).

6. Several theories are based on the principle of the *Raman shift.* If monochromatic light is scattered, the resultant light is not homogeneous but is a combination of both longer and shorter wavelengths. The difference in wavelength is known as the Raman shift. Dyson (1937; 1938) has suggested that only those substances which show a Raman shift between 140 and 350 mμ have odors. Dyson has also suggested that substances must have sufficient vapor pressure and sufficient solubility for sensation to occur. It is suggested that the quality of the odor corresponds with the amount of the Raman shift. For example, the various forms of mercaptan have similar qualities

of olfactory sensation, and all show a Raman shift of 256 to 258 mμ. This theory, then, considers the frequency of shift to have a function similar to frequency of wavelength for vision. Just as we may discriminate colors as a function of their frequency, so olfactory stimuli may be discriminated in quality by the extent of the Raman shift.

7. The receptor is a source of infrared radiation, and receptors radiate differentially. When the stimulus has an appropriate absorption band, it absorbs the radiation and stimulates certain receptors (L. H. Beck & Miles, 1947).

8. There may be primary receptors, just as the presence of three distinct types of cones are postulated to account for color vision. The difference in receptors could arise from the amount of protein covering them, so that the rate of solubility of the stimulus would differ from receptor to receptor. Or the shape of the molecule may be critical, for a given molecule will correspond only with the appropriate structure of a particular receptor (Moncrieff, 1946; 1951).

9. Enzymes present in the olfactory epithelium catalyze reactions with certain stimuli and thus lead to a sensation. An odor may inhibit the action of certain enzymes, thus signaling a change in stimulation to the olfactory nerve (Kistiakowsky, 1950).

10. The size and shape of the impinging molecule is critical in determining how much of the olfactory epithelium is displaced. An area of 64 Å^2 (square Angstroms) must be altered for sensation to occur. Because of their size and shape, some molecules may stimulate a single area, and other stimuli must stimulate larger areas. Strong odors supposedly stimulate only a small portion of the epithelium (J. T. Davies & F. H. Taylor, 1957; 1959).

11. The pigment of the epithelium is stimulated by a metabolic process produced by the impingement of chemical stimuli. When the stimulus is absorbed by the pigment, the membrane potential is altered, and this change in potential is translated into the sensation (R. H. Wright, C. Reid, & H. G. Evans, 1956).

Amoore, Johnston, and Rubin (1964) have developed the suggestion by Moncrieff (1951) that the different sizes and shapes of different molecules "fit" into receptor sites on the membranes. Amoore et al. have suggested seven receptor sites that correspond to seven primary odors: camphoraceous, musky, floral, peppermint, ethereal, pungent, and putrid. Further, it is suggested that the charge of the molecule affects the nature of the odor. Mixed odors occur because a molecule may fit into several different receptor sites. Amoore et al. have shown that it is possible to predict the odor of a compound when it is altered.

GUSTATION

Taste, like olfaction, is often relegated to sensory limbo, for it is considered a less useful sense than vision and audition. When we consider the number of people who are concerned with processing, packaging, and selling food, however, as well as those who eat, it is apparent that everyone has some practical interest in gustatory sensitivity. Two types of taste can be differentiated: (1) the sensations that result from stimulation of the taste receptors on the tongue and (2) the sensations that result from other factors which affect one's reaction to food, such as the odor, texture, temperature, and stimulation of the common chemical sense. Not surprisingly, investigators concerned with the practical uses of taste have concentrated on the second type. Relatively few have been concerned with how "pure" taste occurs. Nevertheless, data concerning the relationship between the gustatory stimuli and the receptor appear to be more logical than comparable data on olfaction. One reason for this is that relatively more is known about the receptor for taste; the tongue is much easier to investigate than the corresponding olfactory receptor.

The Stimuli: There is unusual agreement on the statement that four basic tastes exist: acid (sour), sweet, bitter, and salt. Salt and acid are sometimes thought to be more basic than the other two. One theorist (Moncrieff, 1951, p. 131) suggests that this is due to the evolutionary development of taste, which supposedly begins in fish. It is proposed that fish require sensitivity to both salt and acid for survival; the former serves as a primitive system of sensitivity to the environment, and the latter serves as a warning of foul waters. In man, taste is confined to the region of the mouth, although it is possible that in other animals, such as fish, the common chemical receptors located throughout the body report the equivalent of taste sensations. Moreover, in man, the location of the receptors varies as a function of age. Allara (1939) has suggested that full development of the taste receptors is reached at puberty in human beings and that a decrement in sensitivity begins at approximately age forty-five. It has also been suggested that children have active taste receptors along the lining of the mouth which become inactive as they grow older.

Sour tastes are thought to be the result of acid compounds. Sour tastes are often, but not necessarily, repulsive. For example, they occur in fruits (citric acid) as well as in other common food substances. The intensity of the sour taste appears to depend upon the concentration of hydrogen ions. For this reason hydrochloric acid, which has a relatively high concentration of hydrogen ions, tastes more sour than citric acid, which has a lower concentration. Similarly, the intensity of the sour taste depends upon the intensity of the solution and the nature of the particular compound. The presence of other chemicals besides the acid may alter the taste. For example, even though some fruits taste sour, they also excite a sweet taste, because they contain other chemicals. Most foodstuffs are combinations of basic tastes and hence evoke a sensation different from the components.

In general, salt compounds produce a salty taste. Some, however, such as potassium bromide, taste both salty and bitter; others, such as potassium iodine, have a bitter taste primarily. A reasonable explanation is that the taste depends upon the molecular weight of the components: salts of low molecular weight taste salty, and those of high molecular weight taste bitter. In addition, the presence of other compounds may alter the taste. If sugar is

added to sodium chloride, the salty taste is reduced, but if acid is added to sodium chloride, the salty taste is increased (Fabian & H. B. Blum, 1943).

It is noteworthy that both sour and salt, which are regarded as evolutionarily primary to the other basic tastes, are also the most easily correlated with characteristics of compounds. Sweet tastes, for example, may result from a variety of compounds which possess no common characteristics other than the fact that they are not usually ionized. Saccharin, which is commonly regarded as a sweet substance, actually tastes bitter under high concentrations. Moreover, some substances yield different tastes depending upon the location of the receptor. Bittersweet tastes sweet when placed on the tip of the tongue but bitter when placed at the back. Epsom salts has a similar characteristic, for it is bitter at the back of the tongue but salty at the tip. Since the prediction of which compounds will taste sweet is complicated, it is understandable that predicting the intensity that a compound will convey is also difficult. In complexity at least, bitter is similar to sweet. We have noted that some salts taste bitter. Similarly, some compounds taste sweet at low concentrations and bitter at higher concentrations. Probably the most commonly used bitter substance is quinine, but such chemicals as strychnine also have a strong bitter taste, unfortunately for poisoners. Although it is difficult to construct general laws which account for the relationship between the basic sensations that are perceived and the chemical composition of the stimulus, it is notable that few tastes exist which cannot be identified with one or more of the basic tastes. One exception may be the reports that some chemicals have a metallic taste.

In addition to the normal means of gustatory stimulation via the tongue, other techniques may produce taste sensations. The injection of some chemicals into the blood results in the sensation of taste (Bednár & Langfelder, 1930). One arsenic compound is reported to be both smelled and tasted approximately eight seconds after an injection. Systematic investigation of this phenomenon is lacking. Tellurium gives "garlic breath" when eaten, and injected sodium pentothal gives the immediate sensation of a garlic taste.

Electrical taste has received greater attention. In the nineteenth century it was reported that the application of current through the tongue resulted in a sour taste. This effect is not due entirely to the electrolysis that would occur in such a procedure, and it appears that all receptors, not only those commonly identified with acid sensitivity, react to electric stimulation. There is additional evidence that the sensation depends upon the frequency and intensity of the current (Bujas & Chweitzer, 1937). Alternating current and direct current appear to produce different sensations. The frequency appears to determine whether the taste is sour, sweet, or another sensation. Thorough development of this phenomenon could lead to the inexpensive simulation of caloriless meals.

Receptors and Neural Pathways: The basic receptor for taste is the *taste bud.* It is estimated that man has at least nine thousand separate taste buds, and some authorities suggest that there are many more. The taste bud resembles certain cutaneous receptors, as may be noted from the schematic diagram shown in Figure 11–10. The bud is roughly circular, with its tips extending into a pit in the tongue or skin tissue. Sustentacular cells are found in the taste bud, but their function is uncertain (de Lorenzo, 1958; Engström & Rytzner, 1956). The bud is composed of a number of gustatory receptors which form the larger receptor diagramed in the figure. It has been suggested that the taste bud contains a hair cell which serves as the primary receptor, but this observation has not been confirmed by electron microscope techniques (Beidler, 1961). The number of individual receptors within the bud may vary from two to two dozen. There is evidence that the sustentacular cells develop into gustatory receptors, so that new receptors are developed over time (Beidler, 1961).

The taste buds are often found in bunches which are observable on the surface of the

FIGURE 11–10: *Schematic diagram of a taste bud. The surface of the tongue is represented horizontally at the top of the drawing. The pit in the tongue contains the tips of the specialized cell. (From* Psychology, *by Robert S. Woodworth, copyright 1940 by Holt, Rinehart and Winston, Inc.)*

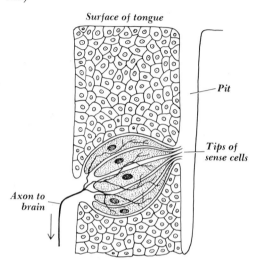

tongue. These structures are commonly called *papillae,* and different types have been noted. Figure 11–11 indicates the relative location of the different types. *Fungiform (FU)* papillae have the general shape of a mushroom. *Foliate (F)* papillae are seen as a series of groves. The *circumvallate (C)* variety form a chevron at the rear of the tongue. *Filiform* papillae are distributed over the surface.

Figure 11–12 shows the areas of the tongue where each basic taste is most acutely perceived. The tip is maximally sensitive to sweet substances, and the back to bitter. The nerves enter the taste buds and form a clublike ending. Accordingly, one nerve ending may serve several different taste cells (de Lorenzo, 1958). The enzyme cholinesterase (see Chapter 3) is found in the taste bud, as well as in the nerve fibers. This implies that the taste cells somehow alter the stimulus before the nerve reacts. De Lorenzo (1963) has reported that the "turnover" of taste buds occurs mostly among

FIGURE 11–11: *Upper surface of the human tongue. F represents foliate papillae, C are circumvallate papillae, and FU are fungiform papillae. Filiform papillae are scattered throughout the surface. (From Moncrieff, 1951, p. 42.)*

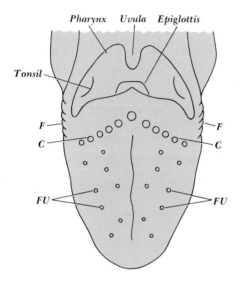

Pharynx   Uvula   Epiglottis

Tonsil

F   F

C   C

FU   FU

FIGURE 11–12: *The areas where the four basic tastes are perceived most easily. Taste buds are numerous in these areas. All the basic tastes are sensed in each area, but the threshold appears to be lower for the specific substances designated for each area. (From Moncrieff, 1951, p. 43.)*

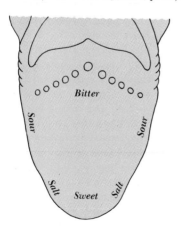

Bitter

Sour   Sour

Salt   Sweet   Salt

foliate papillae and is usually centered in the margins of the bud rather than the center. It is estimated that the turnover is from one cell every thirty hours (de Lorenzo, 1963) to one cell every ten hours (Beidler; see de Lorenzo, 1963). This evidence suggests that the life of a taste cell is very short. It is not surprising, then, to find difficulty in establishing the reliability of threshold measurement, for the receptor is continually changing.

The central pathways for gustation are relatively complicated. Four different cranial nerves transmit gustatory messages. A branch of the facial (VIIth cranial) and the glossopharyngeal (IXth cranial) nerves have the definite function of transmitting taste sensations. The vagus (Xth cranial) nerve probably services the taste buds not on the tongue, namely, those in the pharynx and larynx. The trigeminal (Vth cranial) nerve possesses a curious history. At one time it was thought to handle both taste and smell. Later it was considered responsible for taste alone, and now there is some doubt that it handles taste at all. Apparently, the trigeminal nerve does report *cutaneous* sensations from the mouth, so its primary responsibility appears to be to the common chemical sense. This nerve reports chemical sensations which contribute to the total sensation of taste, such as temperature. One may sever the trigeminal nerve without producing a loss in gustatory sensation.

The cranial nerves have vastly different pathways through the brain. The facial nerve services the anterior two-thirds of the tongue by means of its trunk, the *chorda tympani*. As may be suspected from the word *tympani*, the nerve passes near the tympanic membrane of the ear before reaching the medulla. Investigations which record the electric discharge emanating from gustatory stimuli have used this nerve. The posterior third of the tongue is served by the glossopharyngeal nerve. Fibers from both nerves pass through the thalamus before reaching their cortical projection areas. The cortical projection area for taste lies near those for chewing and hearing. The taste and chewing areas overlap, thus furnishing further evidence of the relationship between taste and cutaneous sensitivity. Potentials have been recorded from the cortex of the cat following stimulation of the tongue (M. J. Cohen, Landgren, Ström, & Zotterman, 1957; Landgren, 1957). Some areas respond to cutaneous as well as gustatory stimulation; this finding reinforces the view that these senses are related. In addition, a center in the thalamus is reported to be responsive primarily to gustatory stimuli (Emmers, Benjamin, & Ables, 1960). It is probable that these centers, or projection areas, vary in location depending upon the species.

A clear evolutionary line of development of the gustatory receptors is not evident. Species vary drastically in the number, type, and location of taste buds. Also, there is compelling evidence from recordings of electric discharges that species differ in the substances to which they are sensitive. One method of determining the sensitivity of different animals is the preference technique (see Chapter 3). For example, a rat may be presented with the option of drinking from two containers, one containing distilled water and the other containing an additional gustatory stimulus, such as sugar or salt. If the animal drinks from the containers in equal amounts, we can assume that he does not sense a difference between the stimuli or that, if he does, he has no preference for either. By increasing or decreasing the intensity or type of substance, we can determine thresholds. Neural activity, in the form of electric discharges, has been recorded from a variety of animals and has provided information concerning species differences.

Unfortunately, it is not possible to correlate the discharge with the subject's perception of gustatory sensations. An animal may show a large discharge to a certain substance, but such a finding does not necessarily indicate that this is the subject's preference or threshold unless it is correlated with some behavioral measure, such as preference. The crab *Limulus,* for example, does not respond strongly to the four basic tastes found in man. There is a strong discharge, however, to extract of marine bivalves (Barber, 1956). Monkeys respond to the same four basic tastes as man; in addition, they respond to water. Zotterman and Diamant (1959) have reported that recordings from the chorda typmani of man (during ear surgery) show responses to the four basic substances, but not to water. The chicken responds to quinine, but not to sugar or salt (Kare, Black, & E. G. Allison, 1957). The reverse is characteristic of the pigeon, which responds to salt, acid, and sugar, but not to quinine (Kitchell, Ström, & Zotterman, 1959). In a series of experiments, Dethier and his colleagues (cf. Dethier & Arab, 1958) have examined the gustatory sensitivity of the blowfly.

Temperature: In our discussion of olfaction we noted that some odors change in quality as a function of temperature. This phenomenon occurs also in gustation, where the temperature of a substance is a critical factor in determining the sensation. Cooks are well aware (or should be) that temperature affects taste and is an important aspect of flavor. Flavor, however, by which we mean the pleasurable or unfavorable characteristics of foodstuffs, is probably influenced more by odor than by taste.

It is commonly believed that taste is most acute when the temperature of the stimulus is at the temperature of the body (Weber, 1847; Moncrieff, 1951). Hahn (1936) has reported that sensitivity to sugar increased between 17 and 42°C, with optimal sensitivity at 37°C. The taste of acid appears to be unaffected by temperature; sensitivity to both quinine and salt decreases between 17 and 42°C. Electrophysiological studies that have used temperature as a variable report either little or no alteration in the electric discharge as a function of temperature (see Abbot, 1953; Beidler, 1954; Fishman, 1957). Recording from the chorda tympani, Sato (1963) has reported decided differences in discharge as a function of temperature. Figure 11–13 shows characteristic results for different concentrations of sodium chloride under three different temperatures. It is apparent that the thresholds for

FIGURE 11–13: *Responses of the chorda tympani to stimulation of the tongue with Ringer's solution, water, and sodium chloride solutions of different temperatures. The figures at the top show the temperature of the solution; the bottom record shows changes in the surface temperature of the tongue. (From Sato, 1963, p. 153; Nagaki, Yamashita, & Sato, 1964.)*

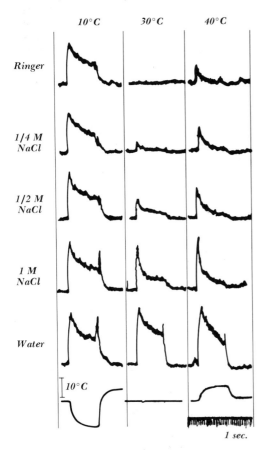

salt and Ringer's solution vary as a function of temperature. The data also show that the magnitude of the electric response varies as a function of both concentration and temperature (Nagaki, Yamashita, & Sato, 1964). The relationship between temperature of the taste solutions and sensitivity in human beings is shown in Figure 11–14. These results are not entirely consistent with those provided by Hahn (1936).

Learning: Learning plays an important role in visual perception, and it may be important in audition for sound localization. The determination of whether taste preference is learned or is innate in the particular sensory system of the species is complicated by the fact that taste preference changes as a function of age. Does this change indicate learning? Or does it mean merely that, in man at least, the number and quality of taste buds change with age? Warren and Pfaffman (1959) fed infant guinea pigs a substance that is usually regarded as unpleasantly bitter by human beings. The baby guinea pigs' preference for the substance and for water was measured. The animals were then permitted to mature for three months on a normal diet. Then they were given another preference test, with both water and the experimental solution available. Initially, there was no difference in preference, but as the animals aged, an aversion to the substance developed. Control guinea pigs, who had never received the substance, refused to take it when the choice was presented. It appears that the guinea pigs' preference was altered by their early "training."

Brush and Amitin (1960) injected quinine hydrochloride into rats which were suckling their young, so that the rat pups would receive the substance through the mother's milk. A number of pups refused the milk under these conditions. Those which did take the milk showed a marked change in quinine preference when older, although the change was temporary. Apparently, infantile experience with substances may alter preference, but only briefly.

Osepian (1958; 1959) has conditioned both children and dogs to respond to taste. The eye-blink response (Chapter 13) was conditioned in infants through eighteen months of age. It is reported that infants are able to differentiate solutions by the third month of life. Using the same technique, investigators have reported that dogs can differentiate taste stimuli by thirty-five to forty days of age. Conflicting results appear from studies that have attempted to examine taste sensitivity in the aged or merely as a function of age (Byrd & Gertman, 1959; T. Cohen & Gitman, 1959; Bouliere, Cendron, & Rapaport, 1958).

Electrical Activity: Through surgical procedures, an individual nerve fiber can be isolated from the remainder of the nerve. The electric discharge of this fiber in response to substances placed on the tongue may be recorded and measured. As we might expect, the size of the discharge is fairly uniform. Figure 11–15 shows electric discharges from the rat in response to sodium chloride solutions and to water. Note that the spikes are of the same height. As the concentration is increased from 0.001 to 0.3 *M* (molar concentration), the number of impulses increases. Hence, it appears that the degree of concentration is reflected by the frequency of discharge. When water is applied to the tongue (lower right part of figure), a response is also recorded.

Pfaffman (1941) has reported that three types of fibers may be found in the cat. One type responds primarily to sodium chloride and acid, a second to quinine and acid, and a third only to acid. This evidence suggests that all taste nerves respond to acid, and some respond to other substances as well. In later work, Pfaffman (1959) suggested that a fiber may translate information regarding different qualities of the sensations, depending upon the activity of nearby fibers. That is, it is inappropriate to conceive of a system in which each basic taste has its own receptor and accompanying nerve. Rather, some receptors and nerves may be primarily sensitive to some chemicals but be capable of transmitting information regarding other chemicals as well. For example, Pfaffman suggests (1959, p. 228) that if one nerve conveys acid-salt and a second nerve transmits acid, stimulation of both nerves will lead to the sensation of sour. Moreover, this is not merely a matter of direct stimulation, for a receptor or nerve may in-

FIGURE 11–14: *The relationship between taste sensitivity of 27 human subjects and the temperature of the taste solutions. (From Shimizu, Yanase, & Higashira, 1959, n.s.; see Sato, 1963, p. 163.)*

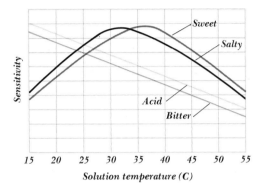

FIGURE 11–15: *Response of a single element from a rat to sodium chloride and water. (From Pfaffman, 1955, p. 432.)*

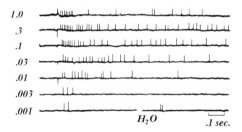

hibit sensation, too. Accordingly, if a single nerve ceases to discharge, one of two events has occurred: (1) the stimulus has been removed, or (2) a new stimulus which inhibits the action of that nerve has been presented.

Further, the relative difference between discharges of two fibers may correlate with the sensation. Consider the data shown in Figure 11–16. Each part of the figure represents a separate nerve fiber; both fibers are responsive to salt and sugar, but the left fiber is primarily salt-sensitive, and the right is primarily sugar-sensitive. Note the changes in frequency of discharge as a function of concentration. Since frequency changes with con-

FIGURE 11-16: *The relationship between frequency of discharge and concentration in two fibers, both of which are sensitive to sugar and salt. (From Pfaffman, 1955, p. 430.)*

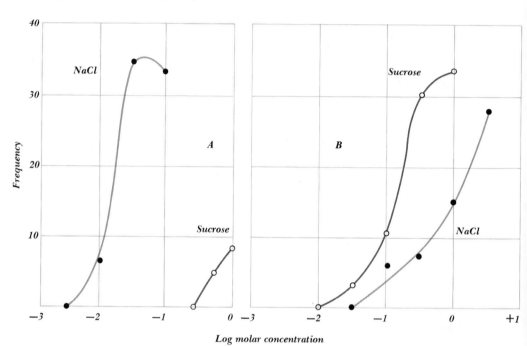

Log molar concentration

centration, the frequency can be related to the sensation. For example, if the concentration of salt is low, only the left-hand fiber will fire. If the concentration is increased, both fibers will fire, but the left-hand fiber will provide greater activity. It is the relationship between these fibers that determines the sensation. If activity is greater in the left-hand fiber, the sensation will be one of salt; if the right-hand fiber contributes most activity, the sensation will be of sweetness.

Accordingly, we find again that the physical stimulus does not always correlate with the psychological sensation. Just as it is impossible to discuss "red" only in terms of its wavelength, so it is improper to discuss "salt" as if it were a single stimulus that always evoked the same sensation. The sense of taste does not translate the stimulus into the sensation without some alteration any more than the eye

translates light energy into sensation without refracting and changing the original stimulus.

The question as to whether the receptor responds to several stimuli or to one specific stimulus remains, however. In an attempt to answer this question, Kimura and Beidler (1956) inserted a tiny electrode into a taste bud of the rat and measured electrical changes when different substances were placed on the tongue. They were unable to find evidence that the receptor was stimulated by a single substance, for no clear pattern appeared.

Many problems appear in measuring electric discharge. One of the more serious is the usual difficulty in presenting the stimulus. Some stimulation is always present, even though it may be adapted or may be below threshold. Accordingly, the tongue of an organism being tested is usually rinsed with water or Ringer's solution. As we have noted, some animals are sensitive to water alone; at least electric discharges appear. In addition, some chemicals, notably the acids and quinines, inhibit the receptors. This may have two important effects: (1) no potential may be evoked to these substances, even though they are present in sufficient quantity to reach threshold under normal conditions, and (2) the inhibiting effect may mask the response of other substances. These effects may be noted in Figure 11–17, which shows recordings taken from a chicken under different conditions. Note the effect of adding distilled water. Merely touching the receptor may produce a potential. Figure 11–18 shows the response of the cat's glossopharyngeal nerve to a touch on the papilla before, during, and after the application of 0.02 *M* quinine hydrochloride. It is clear that the discharge is a function of both the movement of the receptor and the application of the gustatory stimulus.

Records have been reported from the chorda tympani of man (Zotterman & Diamant, 1959; Zotterman, 1961; Diamant, Funakoshi, Ström, & Zotterman, 1963). During an operation on the stapes, electrodes were inserted into the chorda tympani while various substances were placed on the tongue. Figure 11–19 shows the results. Note the discharge associated with touch. In addition, it is noteworthy that distilled water does not produce a discharge. Although some animals, including monkeys, do respond to water alone, man apparently does not. Electric reactions have also been recorded to sweet stimuli (Diamant, Funakoshi, Ström, & Zotterman, 1963).

It is possible to make recordings from the various brain centers concerned with taste. The records may be correlated with responses from the nerves and with the type of stimulus. As we noted, the central pathways for taste are treacherous indeed. Recording from the thalamus of the rat, Frommer (1961) found records for sodium chloride very similar to those reported in Figure 11–15 from the lingual nerve. Unfortunately, recording from the thalamus and recording from the nerves present different problems. Background noise (dis-

FIGURE 11–17: *Records from the lingual nerve of the chicken during application of different solutions to the tongue. In each pattern, the upper line represents the stimulus: the deflection in the line indicates the presentation. The lower line in each section represents the integrated response. Note the response to distilled water. (From Kitchell, Ström, & Zotterman, 1959, p. 145.)*

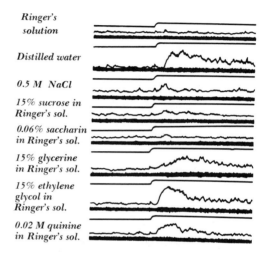

Ringer's solution

Distilled water

0.5 M NaCl

15% sucrose in Ringer's sol.

0.06% saccharin in Ringer's sol.

15% glycerine in Ringer's sol.

15% ethylene glycol in Ringer's sol.

0.02 M quinine in Ringer's sol.

FIGURE 11–18: *Recordings from the glossopharyngeal nerve of the cat to touch on the circumvallate papilla before, during, and after the application of 0.02 M quinine hydrochloride solution to the tongue. (From Appelberg, 1958, p. 134.)*

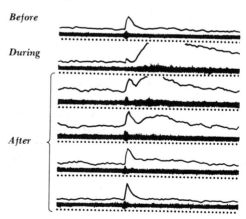

Before

During

After

FIGURE 11-19: *Responses of the chorda tympani of a human being to various solutions passed over the tongue. (From Zotterman, 1961, p. 214.)*

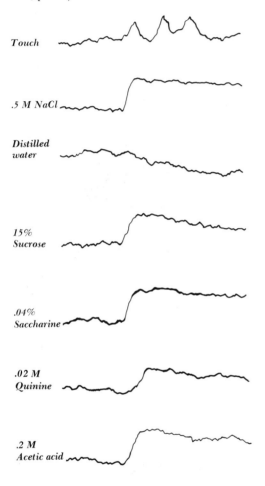

Touch

.5 M NaCl

Distilled water

15% Sucrose

.04% Saccharine

.02 M Quinine

.2 M Acetic acid

response to salt when concentration is increased.

Landgren (1961) has investigated thalamic and cortical responses to taste and tactile stimulation. Responses to electric stimulation of the tongue were recorded in the thalamus 3 to 6 msec after stimulation. Responses were recorded from the cortex 4 to 8 msec after stimulation. Similarly, when the tongue is warmed or cooled, changes may be recorded from the thalamus. When the tongue is cooled, the thalamic area shows an increase in electrical activity (M. J. Cohen, Landgren, Ström, & Zotterman, 1957). Warming the tongue results in a decrease in frequency (Landgren, 1959).

Recordings may also be taken from the medulla (Pfaffman, Erickson, Frommer, & Halpern, 1961). In general, they are similar to those taken from the thalamus. In addition, data from the medulla indicate that the area responds differentially, as does the nerve; i.e., there may be a discharge to salt and acid but not to bitter or sweet. Figure 11–21 shows a sample of this effect in which there is sensitivity to sodium chloride and hydrochloric acid but not to quinine or sweet solutions. It was noted previously that the correlation between the stimulus and the character of the nerve discharge was not perfect. Neither does the relationship between the stimulus and the response in the central nervous system represent a perfect correlation. It is clear that because of the characteristics of the receptor, nerve, or synapse, a transition takes place between the receptor and the nerve.

Thresholds: Taste thresholds depend upon many variables, including the site of stimulation on the tongue and the difficulties inherent in controlling the stimulus. The RL for taste is, moreover, different from the point at which the subject is able to *name* the stimulus correctly. In addition, the fact that the tongue is constantly bathed in fluids implies that stimuli are diluted when presented on the tongue. The four basic tastes reach RL at the

charges from other areas near the thalamus) probably masks all but the strongest discharges. Halpern (1959) has reported that with sweet (sucrose), the deeper the implantation, the greater the response. He has also recorded responses from both the thalamus and the chorda tympani to the four basic substances. See Figure 11–20. Recordings from both areas show a decelerating curve for magnitude of

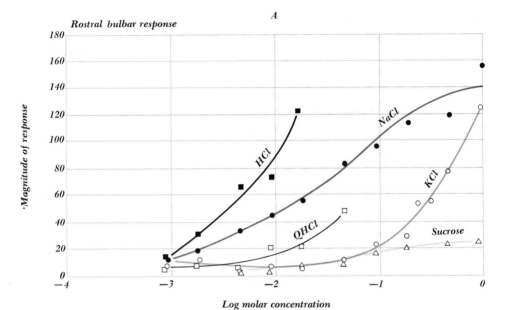

FIGURE 11–20: *Responses following stimulation of the anterior tongue of the cat. Figure A shows responses from the rostral bulbar area; figure B, from the chorda tympani. Responses to different solutions are shown as a function of concentration. (From Kare & Halpern, 1961, p. 56, after Halpern, 1959.)*

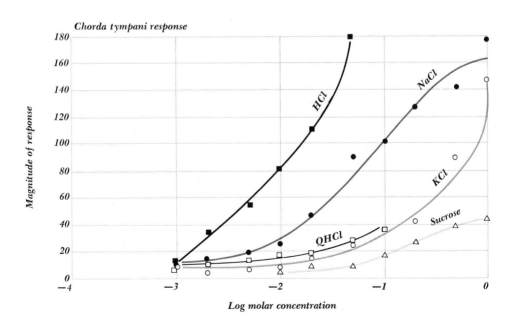

FIGURE 11–21: *Response of a unit to various substances. The unit is responsive to sodium chloride and hydrochloric acid but not to quinine hydrochloride or sucrose. (From Pfaffman, Erickson, Frommer, & Halpern, 1961, p. 462.)*

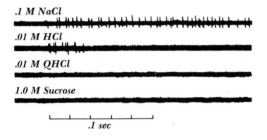

.1 M NaCl

.01 M HCl

.01 M QHCl

1.0 M Sucrose

.1 sec

following concentrations: bitter (quinine sulfate), 0.0000004 M; acid (hydrochloric), 0.002 M; salt (sodium chloride), 0.35 M; and sweet (sucrose), 0.2 M (Pfaffman, 1951).

DLs, in terms of the Weber fraction, are reported as follows: bitter, 0.3; sour, 0.125; salt, 0.15; sweet, 0.17 (Schutz & Pilgrim, 1957). For bitter, the fraction is fairly constant over a range of intensities. The relationship with intensity is not linear for salt, sour, or sweet, all of which vary near the RL. Salt also varies in intensity near the TL. Beebe-Center and his coworkers (Beebe-Center, M. S. Rogers, & O'Connell, 1955; Beebe-Center, M. S. Rogers, & W. H. Atkinson, 1955) have applied the principles of information theory (Chapter 7) to taste thresholds and report that sensitivity, in terms of the amount of information conveyed, is near that reported for auditory discrimination. Sex differences in thresholds have been found by Tilgner and Barylko-Pikielna (1959), who report that women are more sensitive than men to sweet and salt and less sensitive to sour; they are equally sensitive to bitter.

The major factors that determine the adaptation rate are the location of the stimulus on the tongue and the quantity and quality of the stimulus. The general finding is that bitter and sour adapt most rapidly and that sweet and salt take longer (Abrahams, Krakauer, & Dallenbach, 1937; Krakauer & Dallenbach, 1937). Adaptation as a function of concentration follows a predictable course: the greater the concentration, the longer the time to adapt.

D. R. Lewis (1948) used the method of fractionation to determine the scaled relationships of taste stimuli. This procedure resulted in fairly consistent fractionations and indicated that reliable data could be obtained from subjects who were asked to "cross" the stimuli; e.g., a subject was asked to select a salty substance which was half a sweet substance. The basic unit of scaled gustatory stimuli is called the *gust*. The gust is arbitrarily equal to the intensity of a 1 percent sucrose solution (Beebe-Center & Waddell, 1948). Figure 11–22 shows the relationship of gusts to intensity for the four basic tastes. It may be noted that the relationships are approximately linear.

Preference among Animals: One method for determining the threshold of taste sensitivity in animals is to examine preference. If a rat is presented with two calibrated tubes, one containing water and the other containing a salt solution, an experimenter may measure the amounts consumed by the animal. By altering the concentration of the salt solution, the experimenter may find a concentration that the subject finds pleasurable (e.g., he accepts it in preference to the water) or which the subject rejects (i.e., he drinks only water and ignores the solution). In addition, the experimenter can determine the concentration and thresholds for different substances that the subject regards as equally pleasurable. When two compounds are equally pleasurable (or equally rejected), they are said to be *isohedonic,* and isohedonic contours, similar in assumption to equal-loudness contours, may be developed (P. T. Young, 1960; Christensen, 1960).

Pathology: Because of the extreme variations

in thresholds, it is uncertain whether true pathological gustatory conditions exist. Obviously, taste will be lost if any of the nerves serving the various areas of the tongue are severed or destroyed; however, there is no evidence that a loss of taste for given qualities (*ageusia*) occurs.

The synthetic compound phenylthiocarbamide (PTC) is tasted by some persons but not by others. Approximately 70 percent of the population is able to taste this bitter substance. Whether a person is a taster or a nontaster appears to be determined by the Mendelian laws of inheritance, and for this reason PTC has been studied by geneticists. It is unlikely, however, that nontasters are totally unable to perceive PTC. Rather, it appears that their thresholds for the substance are so high that large concentrations are required for taste to occur. Accordingly, PTC does not actually distinguish between tasters and nontasters but between differences in the RL for the substance (J. Cohen & Ogden, 1949). PTC has a curious effect on rats; Richter and Clisby (1941) report that the hair of rats which are fed the substance turns gray within three months but that withdrawal of the substance results in the hair's reverting to its original color.

Theories of Sensitivity: A variety of theories of taste sensitivity have been put forward, but considerably fewer than the number proposed for olfaction. The advances in electrophysiological knowledge of the functioning of the receptors and the nerves have provided many new data, but as yet no theory covers all the mysteries of taste.

From time to time, the presence of enzymes has been suggested and reported (El-Baradi & Bourne, 1951; also see Beidler, 1961). Dethier (1956) has reviewed theories of gustation and has concluded that biophysical explanations are probably more reasonable than biochemical theories. Moncrieff (1951) has suggested that his theory of olfaction, in which the receptor is assumed to "match" the molecular

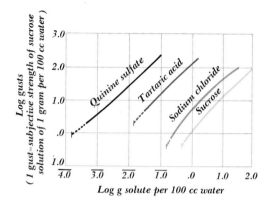

FIGURE 11–22: *The relationship between concentration (abscissa) and gusts for aqueous solutions of sucrose, quinine sulfate, tartaric acid, and sodium chloride. A gust equals the strength of a 1 percent sucrose solution. (From Beebe-Center & Waddell, 1948, p. 522.)*

organization of the stimulus, may also be applied to taste. Beidler (1957), following the same line, has suggested that each taste cell contains units which can absorb only certain stimuli.

SOURCES

Relatively few texts devote attention to the problems of the chemical senses, and most of the books published in the area are symposia containing technical reports from investigators in the field. One general source is Moncrieff (1951). Zotterman (1963) contains many excellent papers on the electrophysiology of taste and smell. Although the papers are rewarding, they are difficult. In addition, several important papers, comprising summaries of research, appear in Rosenblith (1961). A number of papers on gustation has also been collected by Kare and Halpern (1961). Moncrieff has extended his 1951 book on taste (1966).

Pfaffman's chapter in Stevens (1951) is written at a moderately complicated level, although it precedes many of the advances in electrophysiological recordings. See also Pfaffman (1959) on taste and Adey (1959) on smell. Michaels, D. S. Phillips, R. H. Wright, and Pustek (1962) have published on unannotated bibliography on olfaction. Fortunately, the bibliography is divided into subgroups; this source is vital to anyone contemplating research in the area. Beidler's review (1961) of

literature is helpful, although a stronger background than that supplied in the present chapter is necessary for its comprehension. Also see C. P. McCord and Witherage (1949) and R. W. Miner (1954) on olfaction.

The vast literature resulting from industrial or applied experiments in taste and smell has not been covered in this chapter. These studies are of limited interest to the general field, for they are concerned with particular problems. For further basic information on the topics covered in this chapter, the student is advised to consult the sources given in the text.

With an understanding of the physiological bases of behavior, we may now turn to the general topics to which the experimental psychologist devotes his attention. The major contribution of psychology to universal knowledge is that it has provided a systematic approach to the study of how learning occurs. Chapter 12 examines several kinds of experiments on learning and considers a number of problems that have prompted research and have traditionally impeded construction of adequate theories of learning. Chapters 13 and 14 review classical conditioning and operant training—two topics introduced in Chapter 12—in considerable detail. Chapter 15 considers studies of human learning and performance. Verbal behavior, as we noted in Chapter 7, is probably the most important single capacity of the human being, and we should not be surprised that investigators have devoted elaborate attention to uncovering the facts about, and establishing theories of, human verbal behavior. Chapter 16 discusses learned and nonlearned behavior. Years ago, when it was fashionable to divide behavior into its innate components and its learned components, this chapter would not have appeared. As Chapter 16 shows, however, we are no longer so certain that such a division exists, and we are sure that the division is harmful to inquiry. Animals maintain many behavior patterns that have elements of both innate and learned behavior, and our treatment of the role of learning in behavior is concluded on this note.

CHAPTER TWELVE

LEARNED BEHAVIOR: AN INTRODUCTION

INTRODUCTION

Our discussion of the sensory systems has been concerned implicitly with *change*. For example, when we talked about the adaptation function for the rods, we plotted time along the abscissa and units of magnitude along the ordinate. In effect, we were showing the change in the receptor's performance as a function of time or some other variable. The more general concept of change is basic to psychology, for the use of an experimental design assumes the presence of some dependent variable, and a dependent variable is always measured in terms of change from some base rate.

At this point, we may distinguish two types of change that are important to psychological theory. The first includes changes that take place in the sensory receptors. Taste preferences change; detection or recognition thresholds may be permanently altered by experience and experimental manipulations; perception of visual figures may depend upon one's experiences. Some of these changes, such as those we have discussed under Pathology are permanent. Others, such as those shown by adaptation curves, are only temporary, for they depend upon some characteristic of the stimulus, e.g., its duration or intensity. After a period of rest, the adapted receptor turns to a different state. Given sufficient time with an oxygen deficiency, however, parts of the central nervous system never return to their normal state. A second kind of change proceeds more or less independently of changes in the sensory processes, even though it is dependent upon them—this is the change that we call "learning."

Although learning is probably the most important single topic of concern to psychology, the concept becomes elusive when one attempts to define it. The student claims to have "learned" the material for a test; the rat is said to have "learned" if he presses a bar more and more rapidly and gets more food; the inveterate gambler is said to have "learned" *not* to respond when he ceases to play slot machines. A rat is placed in a maze that contains no food or preferred substance. After he has meandered through the maze, food is introduced. He now runs through the maze with few errors. He is said to have "learned." Each occurrence is thought to be an example of the occurrence of learning, and all the organisms are believed to be engaged in learning. Although psychologists agree on the importance of "learned behavior," they agree only superficially on a definition of the term. Shown below are some representative definitions of "learning." It is clear that those theorists and writers who have had the courage to provide a definition consistently talk about the same kind of phenomena, but they differ on details. Notice the emphasis on change and on the relationship between the stimulus and the response.

Keeping the above restrictions in mind, we may say that *learning is the acquisition of new responses or the enhanced execution of old ones* **(Underwood, 1949, p. 341).**

. . . There has always been general agreement among authorities on the subject that *learning refers to a more or less permanent change in behavior which occurs as a result of practice* **(G. A. Kimble, 1961, p. 2).**

Learning is no more than transient modification of behavior which presumably results from past experience and not from known organic change (Wenger, F. N. Jones, & M. H. Jones, 1956, p. 456).

Learning: a broad term referring to modifications of behavior as a result of experience. The theories most mentioned are the following (q.v.): association, trial and error, conditioning, and insight (Harriman, 1947, p. 199).

Two basic problems render a definition of learning difficult to achieve. First, learning is an *inferred* process; one never observes it directly. The student who finishes studying for an examination *says* that he has learned; however, the evidence that he has learned comes from his *performance* on the examination. Similarly, the rat that presses the bar

more and more often is said to be learning, but the only measure of his learning is his *performance* with the bar. Accordingly, one really measures performance and judges a change in performance to indicate the occurrence of learning. In studies of learning, performance is the dependent variable, and learning is an unobserved construct used to account for the change in performance.

Less rigidly, "learning" is often used to describe behavior that the organism acquires. For example, when I say that I have learned to drive a car, I mean simply that I once did not drive and that now I do. In this example, the learning is the performance of the specified behavior. This use of the term is complicated, however, by the second problem: the influence of such factors as maturation. For this reason learned behavior must be distinguished from unlearned behavior. For example, as the child grows older, he is able to throw a baseball faster. Is this change in performance due to learning, or is it due to maturation and the increased strength of the child? We might answer this question by raising two children, one who is never permitted to throw a baseball and another who is permitted to practice throwing and thus is given the opportunity to learn. We might measure the speed of baseball throwing of each child at a given age. If the child with practice throws faster, it is tempting to say that he has learned. If the two children throw equally fast, we might conclude that no learning occurred and that the change in speed as the children grew older was due merely to maturation. This type of experiment really begs the question of the relationship between learning and maturation. Although it succeeds in measuring differences in performance, it fails to indicate any difference between learning and maturation. Thus, it is important to distinguish the different processes implied by learning, performance, practice, and maturation.

A description of the distinction between learned and unlearned behavior is often unclear. If we were able to define the inferred construct "learning" with precision, the behaviors not covered by the definition would be, by exclusion, regarded as "unlearned." We shall present data on the relationship between unlearned and learned behavior in Chapter 16. Happily, these problems have not prevented research on "learning," no matter how it may be defined. Indeed, it is possible that the absence of agreement has prompted studies that have contributed to our overall understanding of the phenomena associated with learning.

The range of behaviors investigated under the name of learning includes studies of such diverse subjects as the ameba turning away from a light source and the complex actions involved in learning differential equations or in learning how to play a musical instrument. Naturally, this diversity leads to the creation of subtypes of learning and different techniques for the study of learning, such as animal learning, motor learning, and verbal learning. Moreover, it is undetermined whether all kinds of learning follow one general set of laws or whether different sets of laws are required to account for different kinds of learning. For example, can the principles used to explain classical conditioning be used to explain problem solving or human verbal learning? This chapter considers the kinds of learning that have received the most detailed attention and certain critical problems, such as whether different sets of principles are required to explain different kinds of learning. First we shall consider several major types of learning.

Conditioning and Training: Conditioning studies involve observation of a simple form of behavior. In *classical conditioning,* the dependent variable may be the amount of saliva deposited by a dog in response to the presentation of various stimuli. Typically, the experimenter controls the temporal relationship between the stimuli and studies the effects on the dependent variable, saliva. The response selected is from among the several involuntary responses (e.g., knee jerk, eye blink) characteristic of the organism. In *instrumental*

training, a response is selected (e.g., pressing a bar, pecking at a circle), and the experimenter manipulates the giving of a reward (e.g., food or water) contingent upon the prior occurrence of the correct response. The way in which the response is acquired and the way the response is lost *(extinguished)* are studied as a function of many factors, such as the temporal relationship between the response and the reward.

Classical conditioning and instrumental training differ both in the procedures involved in establishing the response and in the ways in which performance changes. Conditioning studies occupy an especially large portion of the psychological literature. Some theorists contend that conditioning and instrumental training are the basic processes of all learning and that other forms of learning are variations. Although precision in defining a response is useful in the design of experiments, the responses selected are rarely among the more important responses available, especially in classical conditioning. The amount of saliva secreted by a human being in the hour before lunch is not generally considered of monumental significance. On the other hand, the choice of a simple response that can be controlled and studied thoroughly permits a more thorough analysis of the laws that underlie learning. Therefore, conditioning studies commonly use such responses as eye blink, patellar reflex (knee jerk), or salivation. It should be noted that the concern is not specifically with the response itself but with the development of laws governing how learning occurs in relatively simple situations. We teach a child to count cars, cows, and books, not because we are concerned that he be able to count cars, cows, and books specifically, but because we want him to learn to count items in general. Similarly, the psychologist studies small units of behavior because he wants to understand the general principles that underlie learning.

Discrimination Learning: In one form or another, discrimination occurs in all types of learning. Obviously, an organism must be able to discriminate stimuli if it is to learn to respond to some and not to others. Some learning studies emphasize the role of discrimination. For example, a rat learns to choose the goal that is lighted and to avoid a goal that is darkened. Human beings learn to step on the accelerator when the light is green and to brake when the light is red. In either case, the organism has learned to discriminate stimuli.

Two general procedures are used in discrimination studies: *successive stimuli* and *simultaneous stimuli*. In the method of successive discrimination, the subject is confronted with one stimulus on each trial. A human subject might be placed in front of an apparatus containing a screen, a switch, and a coin box. He is told that he will be shown a series of figures on the screen and that if he pushes the switch following the presentation of the "correct" figure, he will receive a dime in the coin box. In order to make certain that he discriminates the correct figure, that he does not merely press the switch after each figure in order to enhance the opportunity for reward, he is also warned that if he presses the switch following incorrect figures, he will receive a slight shock. A series of figures is then presented on the screen, one at a time, and the investigator records the number of trials required for the subject to make the appropriate response to the correct figure. Note that on those trials in which incorrect figures are shown, the subject's most efficient response is to do nothing at all. Since only one stimulus is presented on each trial, the subject must remember characteristics of the stimulus from trial to trial. Moreover, he may be said to be learning to make two responses: (1) a response to the correct stimulus and (2) restrain from making a response to incorrect stimuli. As any child knows only too well, much of the learning in life is concerned with learning *not* to make a response.

When the technique of *simultaneous discrimination* is used, both stimuli are presented at the same time. The subject selects the appropriate stimulus and makes the correct response to it. If he were presented with a set of figures and told to select the "correct" figure from among them, he would be discriminating under the principle of simultaneous, rather than successive, discrimination. A rat running through a simple T maze must choose between turning left and turning right at the choice point. Assuming that the two paths are discriminably different, the rat is involved in an experiment on simultaneous discrimination, since the two response alternatives appear simultaneously. Under simultaneous discrimination, the subject does not learn *not to respond* to the incorrect stimuli, as he does in successive discrimination. Rather, he learns to respond to one stimulus and to ignore the others.

Trial-and-Error Learning: Although trial-and-error learning is a special case of instrumental training, the attention that it has received requires that it be discussed as a major method of learning. We may understand trial and error by reviewing the studies of learning that used a puzzle box (Thorndike, 1898). Figure 12–1 shows the apparatus used by Edward L. Thorndike (1874–1949) in his classic studies. The subject, often a cat, was placed inside the box. The door was closed and could be opened only if the animal performed a desired response, such as pulling a loop of string, pushing a pole in the center, or performing another complicated set of movements. Food was placed outside the apparatus, as shown in the diagram. Note that this arrangement is very similar to contemporary experiments in instrumental training in which the subject is required to make an appropriate response, such as pressing a bar, in order to acquire food. Thorndike measured the progress of the subject's learning to escape from the box under a variety of conditions. He noted that the subject performed in a characteristic manner: (1) When placed in the box, the subject attempted to escape by finding an opening or by clawing the bars. The subject did not appear to be concerned with the food but was engaged only in random movements which might permit escape. (2) Accidentally,

FIGURE 12–1: *Diagram of a puzzle box similar to that used by Thorndike. By pushing the pole, the animal can open the door and find food. The animal must turn away from the door, which is near the food, in order to make the correct response.*

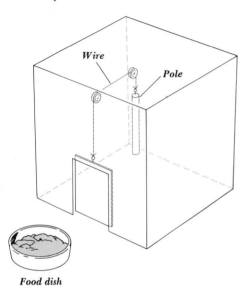

Food dish

the subject made the response that led to the opening of the door and the finding of food. After a number of trials, the subject isolated the distinct response that opened the door. Random movements became fewer as trials continued, and eventually the animal learned to make the appropriate response with as little effort as possible.

These observations correspond with those made of subjects learning a more restricted response, such as bar pressing, and there is no reason to suppose that trial-and-error learning, as described by Thorndike, differs from other forms of instrumental training. Thorndike's work, however, made two contributions to the study of learning. First, his data showed that the cat did not *suddenly* learn to make the correct response. The subject did not show "insight" by abruptly noting the pole and thinking, "Aha! The pole opens the door."

Had insight been present, the amount of time taken to escape would have shown a sudden drop between trials. With few exceptions, the course of performance was not abrupt; the subject showed slight improvement on each trial. Second, Thorndike's approach emphasized breaking down complex behavior into its components, thus establishing the pattern of subsequent experiments in learning.

The application of the term *trial and error* to this procedure pointed up the supposed mental activity of the organism. In certain ways *trial and error* is an unfortunate label, for it suggests that the organism consciously tries one motion after another until it finds the correct response. In short, the term assumes a purposiveness on the part of the subject. This interpretation of the term *trial and error* is not that made by Thorndike, however, for he emphasized the presence of random behavior.

As a simple description of what occurs when an organism is attempting to solve a problem, the term *trial and error* describes the process of random attempts very well. If a subject has no cues to the solution, he resorts to apparently random movements. When a vending machine fails to produce after money has been inserted, the typical human being resorts to trial-and-error performance. He bangs the machine on the side and then on the top. If these movements fail, he administers a sharp kick. Although these movements are purposive in the sense that the subject has one goal (either the appearance of the object or the return of the money), they are random in the sense that the subject has no idea which movement will produce the result.

Trial-and-error performance is common in the problem-solving behavior of human beings. If you were to learn to type on a typewriter with blank keys, your initial movements would be of a trial-and-error nature. At first you would select keys randomly. Once you had learned to identify the result of each press, you would still have to practice until you could strike the correct keys efficiently, just as Thorndike's cats required extensive trials in order to make the appropriate response efficiently. Trial-and-error learning occupies a prominent position in the history of learning. The concept, if not regarded as implying more than a pure description of behavior, retains its importance to animal and human instrumental learning.

Motor and Verbal Learning: In studies of motor learning, the subject is required to perform some activity requiring motor coordination, and his performance is measured. In studies of verbal learning, the subject's performance is measured by his verbal behavior. In motor learning, a variety of independent variables have been employed, many of which are of practical importance in industry and education. Among these variables are investigations of fatigue, motivation, and the most efficient method of practice (massed, distributed, whole, part) (see Chapter 1). Studies of verbal learning have also emphasized these variables as well as those concerned with assessing the amount of material that can be recalled. Clearly, a variety of both independent and dependent variables may be used in the study of verbal learning. The importance of verbal behavior in human activity is reflected by the large number of studies that have been made. These are discussed in detail in Chapter 15.

Transfer of Training: Transfer is concerned with the effect of previously learned behavior on more recently acquired behavior. When presented with a task to learn or a problem to solve, the organism does not begin his process of learning in a vacuum; he is able to call upon previously learned material that may be beneficial in learning the new behavior. For example, other things being equal, the person who knows seven languages has less trouble learning a new language than the person who knows only one. Similarly, a person who plays many instruments has less difficulty learning to play a new one than a person who has never learned to play any instrument. Some of the principles already acquired may

be generalized, or transferred, to tasks. When the learning of previous tasks is instrumental in reducing the amount of time or the number of errors involved in learning a new task, we have *positive transfer*. If the reverse occurs— if the learning of the new task is hampered by previously learned material—we have *negative transfer*. A further transfer phenomenon is called *learning to learn*. If a subject is given 10 different lists of nonsense syllables to learn every day, a notable improvement in the speed of learning will occur. That is, practice is not specific for the items learned, for the similarity in the process of learning nonsense syllables leads to the subject's "learning how to learn the material." As such, learning to learn is a case of positive transfer.

In motor learning, studies of *bilateral transfer* are common. Bilateral transfer refers to learning in which a skill acquired by one hand (or leg) is transferred to the contralateral side. For example, I may write with my left hand. If you ask me to write with my right hand, I can form letters and sentences—I do not need to learn to write all over again with the right hand. Some information acquired by the left hand is transferred to the right hand.

Problem Solving: Problem solving includes those behaviors commonly called "thinking," "reasoning," or "creating." As such, it is concerned with the supposed higher mental processes that permit monkeys to unravel knots and men to build computers. Problem solving is sometimes set apart from the other categories of learning on the grounds that it involves tasks far more difficult than pressing a bar or running a maze and that the course of learning complex tasks is rarely so observable or so measurable as the learning of simpler tasks. Research in problem solving has two distinctive characteristics: first, there is, initially, a low probability that the correct response will occur; second, research emphasizes the "discovery" process which is assumed to occur in problem solving. In problem solving, human subjects may confront the problem, stare out of a window for a few minutes, and then supply the correct answer. Clearly, it is difficult to measure the learning process that occurred while the subject was gazing; the amount of observable, quantifiable behavior was indeed small. Although there is some tendency to attribute somewhat mystical qualities to the events involved in problem solving, it would be unfortunate if this important attribute of behavior were eliminated from experimental investigation merely because of its complexity. After all, the course of learning to escape from Thorndike's puzzle box appeared mysterious, too, until Thorndike took the trouble to analyze the components of the learning process.

Animals have been used in many problem-solving experiments. In the *delayed-reaction* type of experiment, a test is made of the animal's memory capacity. The *direct* delayed-reaction experiment requires that the appropriate response be of a kind well practiced by the subject. As an illustration, a chimpanzee is placed in a room with two containers. The experimenter places food in one container. The chimp is permitted to watch this procedure, but is not permitted to approach the container. Later, the chimp is allowed to move, and his ability to select the appropriate container is measured (Tinklepaugh, 1932). The direct method requires that the subject have previous experience with food getting, or with whatever response is used. The *indirect* delayed-reaction experiment differs only in that the appropriate response must be learned. Hunter (1913) first trained rats to select the one doorway of three which was lighted. After the task was learned, the light was turned off as the rat left the detention area: that is, the rat had to remember which door had been lighted, for in that passageway he would find food. This procedure can be used on a variety of species as well as on human beings.

Two other learning situations in common use required the organism to remember the correct response. These are the *double-alternation* problem and the *multiple-choice problem*. In the former, the organism must learn to make sequential movements. Figure 12–2 shows a double-alternation maze. Note that whenever the organism completes a sequence, he returns to the starting point. He may, for example, receive food only after he has made three left turns followed by three right turns. This test of memory differentiates the learning (or remembering) ability of animals. Rats are notable failures at double-alternation problems, but cats are able to learn the sequence.

In multiple-choice problems, the organism is presented with several alternatives. An animal, for example, may be placed in a chamber with four doors, one of which leads to a reward. The correct door is varied randomly. Given the problem, the human being tries one door, then another, and so on, until he finds the right door. He does not tend to try a door that he has already tried. Some animals, including the rat, return to try an incorrect door; that is, they do not appear to remember the doors they have already tried.

The examples we have discussed have ranged from types of learning (classical conditioning or instrumental training) to techniques used to study learning (delayed reaction, etc.). We have certainly not exhausted the subject. Nevertheless, our discussion should provide us with a general sensitivity to the types of questions that are asked in studies of learning and with an appreciation of the dependence of studies on apparatus. More complete discussions are cited in the Sources at the end of the chapter.

No matter what our approach to learned behaviors, certain basic theoretical and practical questions are evident. We shall consider seven of the most important questions and, in this way, develop a framework on which to hang the results of studies to be taken up in later chapters.

CRITICAL PROBLEMS FOR LEARNING THEORY

The purpose of learning theory is to formulate laws which permit accurate prediction of the course of learning, performance, and forgetting. Of the theories that have been proposed (see Hilgard, 1956; Hilgard & Bower, 1966), it is noteworthy that most have dealt with the same critical problems. Although these problems have been subjected to experimental attack through the years, no definitive answers to the questions they pose are available. The questions are so important to learning theory, however, that any theory must provide an answer to them if it is to be sufficiently comprehensive to permit predictions of the course of learning under a variety of learning conditions. The problems we shall now discuss are among the most critical.

Strengthening a Response: *How does the probability of a response's occurring increase or decrease?* Characteristically, a negatively accelerated curve occurs during the learning, or *acquisition,* of a response. For example, if a subject is requested to learn a list of nonsense syllables, a typical learning curve, shown in Figure 12–3, results. Note that the greatest improvement in performance occurs during the first few trials. As the process of acquisition continues from trial to trial, the rate of improvement decreases. This curve is typical of the performance of human subjects learning nonsense syllables, of rats learning to bar-press more frequently, of human beings learning a motor task, and of a variety of other learning tasks.

The curve suggests that learning is *incremental* and that the response becomes more probable as the trials continue. In labeling learning as incremental, we mean that when examined in the fashion described, learning appears to occur in steps, or increments. As we shall see later, this observation may be in error. We say that the response becomes stronger in the sense that the rat presses the bar at a faster rate and in the sense that the human being remembers more and more nonsense syllables. More specifically, the probability of the occurrence of the specific response under identical or similar conditions is increased. The increments observed in the typical learning curve suggest that repetition is necessary for the "strengthening" of a re-

FIGURE 12–2: *A double alternation maze. The double-alternation problem requires the animal to run twice in one direction and then twice in the other direction for reward. The left side of the maze requires the animal to make right turns, and the right side requires him to make left turns. (From Deese, 1958, p. 282.)*

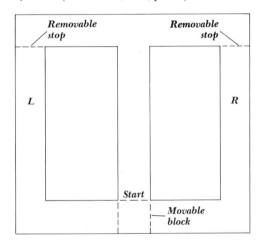

FIGURE 12–3: *A typical learning curve, with number of trials plotted along the abscissa and number of syllables correct along the ordinate. The curve is negatively accelerated, the greatest increase in performance occurring in the first few trials.*

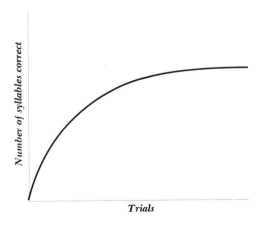

sponse. This suggestion fits the commonsense notion that "practice makes perfect." The tacit supposition in these statements is that the effect of practice is to strengthen the response. This supposition may be incorrect. It is possible, for example, that the effect of practice or repetition is only the elimination of wrong responses, rather than the strengthening of right responses. Some theorists suggest that the response is learned completely the first time the stimulus and response occur together, and that repetition serves only to eliminate inappropriate or competing response patterns (Guthrie, 1952; Estes, 1950).

The difference between these viewpoints is the basis of the distinction between two broad classes of theories of learning, the difference between *continuity* and *noncontinuity* theories. The position that learning is an incremental and gradual process, as suggested by the learning curve shown in Figure 12–3, underlies continuity theories of learning. On the other hand, noncontinuity theories assume that not all kinds of learning are continuous. The belief that problem solving is accomplished through insight or other forms of sudden learning is an example of the noncontinuity approach to learning. Noncontinuity theorists suggest that learning typically represents the acceptance and rejection by the organism of various hypotheses regarding the nature of the proper response. As the learning-how-to-learn type of experiment demonstrates, it is possible to show that at least some forms of apparently noncontinuous learning are actually continuous.

Reinforcement: What is the role of reinforcement? We speak of rewarding or reinforcing the behavior of a rat by giving it a pellet of food for each bar press and of rewarding a student by giving him an A for a well-written examination. Other times, we speak of providing *negative reinforcement* to the child who misbehaves by applying an appropriate stimulus to the child's posterior or of providing negative reinforcement to an animal by electric shock following some responses. In other cases, providing a student with knowledge of how well he is doing or what the correct answers are is called *reinforcement*. Since reinforcement is such a critical concept in learning theory, let us consider some of the applications and misapplications of the word.

We may distinguish two main uses of the term *reinforcement*. The first usage is biological. When an organism is deprived of any substance necessary for survival so that a homeostatic imbalance occurs (Chapter 2), the organism, in some fashion, searches for the substance that will restore homeostasis. That is, the dog who has not been fed searches for food: the human being who is deprived of water for a week is willing to learn complicated tasks, if he is strong enough, in order to obtain water. The nature of the reinforcement will depend upon the state of the organism. If the dog is hungry, food is reinforcement; if he is not hungry, food is not likely to be reinforcing. The man arising from the dinner table will not consider food as reinforcing as the man who has not eaten all day. Reinforcement, then, is identified as whatever leads to a return of homeostasis, and the strength of the reinforcer is assumed to depend upon the extent and type of deprivation to which the organism is subjected.

A second use of the term *reinforcement* is operational: any stimulus that leads to an increase in the rate or quality of the response is called a reinforcer. This usage does not restrict the concept of reinforcement to the satisfaction of biological needs, and it has the advantage of defining reinforcement in terms of its effect on the behavior of the organism rather than in terms of a supposed internal process. As examples, if a child, learning to spell, spells a word correctly, he is given permission to move on and attempt to spell the next word. Another child may be given words of praise for his performance. In either case, the child's spelling improves. Accordingly, both the permission to proceed and the praise are said to be reinforcers, even though they have not satisfied a biological drive. This approach to reinforcement assumes that organisms *learn* to ascribe reinforcing properties to some stimuli and that the reinforcing power of stimuli is not necessarily biologically determined. Money may be highly reinforcing for some individuals in some cultures, but for other individuals and cultures a different stimulus may be equally or more reinforcing.

An important subtype of the operational use of *reinforcement* is *knowledge of results*. It is obvious that in a learning task, performance is most efficient when the learner is informed immediately of the outcome of his attempts. In some types of learning, especially motor learning, knowledge of results is inherent in the task: a boy learning to pitch a baseball knows fairly quickly after each pitch whether or not the pitch was successful. The umpire provides knowledge of results by indicating "ball" or "strike," and the batter may provide even more effective information by hitting the ball over the fence. In other types of learning, such as writing themes, knowledge of results is not inherent in the task. The teacher may collect the papers, return them in due course, and provide knowledge of results by attaching a grade and comments to the work. Acquisition is often assumed to proceed more rapidly when immediate knowledge of results is given. For this reason, knowledge of results satisfies the operational definition of reinforcement, since it leads to an increase in the quality of the response.

G. A. Kimble (1961, p. 137) makes a useful distinction between the factual and the theoretical definitions of reinforcement. He interprets the factual definition to mean "any of a wide variety of conditions which may be introduced into the learning situation to increase the probability that a given response will appear in the same situation."[1] On the other hand, the theoretical definitions of reinforcement vary widely among theorists. One theorist may adopt a theory of reinforcement using homeostasis as the model; others may

1 From Hilgard and Marquis's *Conditioning and Learning*, revised by Gregory A. Kimble, 2d ed., copyright 1961 by Appleton-Century-Crofts, Inc. Reprinted by permission of Appleton-Century-Crofts, Inc.

regard reinforcement as nothing more than a change in the stimuli impinging upon an organism.

Reward and Punishment: Thorndike expressed an elementary view of the nature of reinforcement in his statement of the *law of effect* (1925, vol. II, p. 4):

The Law of Effect is: When a modifiable connection between a situation and a response is made and is accompanied or followed by a satisfying state of affairs, that connection's strength is increased: When made and accompanied or followed by an annoying state of affairs, its strength is decreased. The strengthening effect of satisfyingness (or the weakening effect of annoyingness) upon a bond varies with the closeness of the connection between it and the bond. This closeness or intimacy of association of the satisfying (or annoying) state of affairs with the bond in question may be the result of nearness in time or of attentiveness to the situation, response and satisfying event in question.

Although Thorndike later modified his views on the role of the law of effect, the law remains a classic statement of a hedonistic position regarding the nature of reinforcement. The difficulty with tautologies such as the law of effect is that, at once, it explains everything and explains nothing. Assume that a laboratory rat has been placed in an apparatus with two compartments. One compartment contains a grid floor through which current may be administered. The other compartment has a smooth floor with neither grids nor current. When placed in the "shock" compartment, the animal soon learns to run to the safe compartment. Now the question is "What is the nature of the reinforcement in this learning situation?" Does the animal run from the shock side because it is unpleasant, or does he run to the safe side because it is pleasant? If we assume that shock is unpleasant and, hence, a negative reinforcer, does it then follow that the safe compartment provides a positive reinforcement? Not necessarily. The most serious difficulty with the law of effect is that it is a *post hoc* law: you do not know whether a stimulus is a reinforcer or not (or unpleasant or not) until after the subject has responded to it. Prediction by hindsight is bad science, for the reason that it encourages serious mistakes regarding the connections between events. Nevertheless, by varying experimental operations, one may generalize to statements regarding what reinforcing conditions are.

Although the term *negative reinforcer* is commonly used to denote those stimuli which an animal will avoid, we may identify from behavior several kinds of negative reinforcement or punishment.

On many occasions, reinforcement is used to decrease or extinguish an unwanted response. The child receives this training early in life when he is taught to keep his hands out of electric sockets, for his hands are slapped when he makes the response. Later he will be punished similarly for putting his hands in the cookie jar, and eventually he may be punished by being sent to jail for having his hands in someone else's pocket. Note that the reinforcement here is used with the intention of destroying a response already within the organism's repertoire of available responses; it is not used to establish a specific new response. Several variants of punishment may be identified.

In *omission training,* reinforcement is given if the response is *not* made. The parent who says, "Don't bite your brother all day, and I'll give you dessert at dinner," is using omission training, for he is reinforcing the failure to respond. It may be noted that omission training does not provide negative reinforcement, for the organism does not learn to avoid the reinforcer. Omission training eliminates a particular behavior by the use of a positive reinforcer.

In *punishment training,* the negative reinforcer is applied whenever the organism makes the specified response. Whenever the child puts his hand in the electric socket, negative reinforcement appears, in this case in the form of electric shock. From this example, it may be noted that the reinforcement does not appear *unless* the response is made. Omission training and punishment differ in regard to whether reinforcement follows the response or occurs when the response is not made.

Another kind of punishment involves the *withdrawal of reinforcement.* Consider this example: A monkey has been trained to press a bar in order to get banana-flavored pellets. Now the food reward is eliminated. No matter how often he presses, no pellets appear. Another example: A child receives an allowance of $2 per week on the condition that he behave. Suddenly the money is no longer forthcoming, regardless of his behavior. Eventually the monkey ceases to press the bar, and, conceivably, the child ceases to be good. In both examples, an acquired response—pressing the bar or behaving in a particular fashion—has been extinguished by *eliminating* the reinforcement. By extinction we mean the antithesis of the acquisition of a response, namely, the decrease in the rate of the response. Extinction will occur also if, rather than withdrawing reinforcement, we punish the organism for the response. For example, we might attach current to the bar, so that the monkey would not only fail to receive food but would also receive a slight shock for pressing. Both procedures lead to extinction, or elimination, of the response, but there is ample evidence that the course of extinction will differ depending upon the procedure used (Chapters 13 and 14).

Two important training techniques are *avoidance training* and *escape training.* In avoidance training, negative reinforcement is employed if the expected response fails to occur. The apparatus used may be the two-compartment chamber, one side of which administers current and one side of which does not. Assume that the apparatus has been designed so that a bar, when depressed, opens a door between the two chambers. If a tone or other discriminable stimulus is presented and followed by current a few seconds later, the subject soon learns to respond to the tone by pressing the bar that opens the door and permits him to leave the compartment and avoid the shock. If the subject fails to press the bar or leave the compartment, he receives the current. Note that the negative reinforcement occurs only if he fails to respond in a certain way. If he responds to the tone properly, he will not experience shock. The observer may well believe that the subject considers the tone the negative reinforcement, for whenever the tone sounds, the subject presses the bar and moves to the safe compartment. Sidman (1953a; 1953b) has shown that an external stimulus is not a necessary component of avoidance learning. Using rats and the bar-press response, he presented current every twenty seconds unless the rat had pressed the bar during the interval. If he did press the bar, the shock was postponed for a specific duration. Under the design, rats learned to press the bar at a rapid rate. Note that no external stimulus is employed: the organism must use his ability to "tell time" if he is to avoid the shock.

In *escape learning,* the subject cannot avoid the stimulation. If electric current is the stimulus, then it is turned on without a warning cue. The animal usually runs from the area to a safe compartment. Thus, he always receives the stimulus (i.e., he cannot avoid it), and some behavior (such as running) is necessary to terminate the negative reinforcement.

In avoidance training, which is the opposite of punishment training, the reinforcer appears only if there is a failure to make a response and thus appears before the response. In punishment training, the reinforcer appears only if the response is made and thus follows the response. In the next chapter we discuss how these two training procedures lead to different kinds of behavior.

Extinction and Spontaneous Recovery: When reinforcement, either positive or negative, is terminated, the response decreases in rate and in quality. If an organism trained to bar-press

for food finds that food no longer follows the response, the rate of bar pressing decreases. Similarly, if a human being discovers that a particular vending machine neither furnishes the product nor returns the money, he ceases to put coins in the machine. The term *extinction* refers to those situations in which a decrement in the performance of the response follows the withdrawal of the reinforcer. Extinction of a response, however, does not necessarily mean that the response has been unlearned, as the phenomenon of *spontaneous recovery* (an increase in responding after being returned to the acquisition-extinction environment) demonstrates. Extinction means only that the performance of the response ceases.

It is sometimes tempting to equate the word *forgetting* with extinction; however, a caution about this usage is necessary. The only method by which we can determine that a subject remembers or forgets is to measure his ability to perform the response. Although it is possible to show that the response has *not* been forgotten, it is impossible to show that it has been forgotten. The basic problem that extinction presents to learning theory is the need to explain why an organism continues to respond, often for some time, after the reinforcement has been withdrawn. The apparent simplicity of the question is deceptive. Human beings "know" from their own experiences that we often continue to respond long after a reward has been withdrawn. We try and try again. Accordingly, it does not strike us as strange that specific patterns of behavior continue to occur without reinforcement. The problem of the learning theorist is to uncover the principles or functions that lead to the organism's responding during extinction. There is ample evidence that many variables affect the extinction rate, including the effects of massed and distributed practice and the number of reinforced trials prior to extinction —the *schedule of reinforcement,* by which we mean whether reinforcement is given for each response, for every *n*th response, or perhaps, for a response only after *n* minutes have passed. Extinction and acquisition are closely related: indeed, the rate of extinction is often believed to represent the strength of original conditioning.

A phenomenon associated with extinction is spontaneous recovery. If a specific response has been extinguished and the subject is removed from the environment in which the response was acquired, he will usually exhibit an increase in the response rate when he is returned to the environment. For instance, a rat in which the bar-press response has been extinguished will often show a burst of responding when he is placed in the conditioning box, even though no reward is given. The response was apparently extinguished, but the occurrence of spontaneous recovery reminds us that learning and performance are very difference concepts. Moreover, the fact that the response rate increases in spontaneous recovery, even though no reward is involved, provides a neat puzzle to drive-reduction theories.

Extinction and spontaneous recovery following a response acquired under positive reinforcement show a predictable typical pattern. The rate of extinction can be predicted from knowledge of the variables employed during acquisition of the response. Prediction of the course of extinction of tasks which involve painful stimuli, however, such as avoidance training, is less accurate. There is evidence that under some conditions rodents retain an avoidance response over long periods (Mowrer & Lamoreaux, 1942). There is also evidence that under other conditions an avoidance response may be extinguished within very few trials (Moyer, 1958). A probable reason for the difference in behavior during extinction between positively and negatively reinforced responses is that under negative reinforcement a variety of responses in addition to avoidance are being learned. An animal which is bar-pressing for food has to contend with few competing responses: the required response is simple. When shock is applied, however, the animal reacts with many responses, such as crouching, freezing, and defecating. Presum-

ably, these responses are also being conditioned: the simultaneous conditioning of the responses may mask or interfere with acquisition of the avoidance response. Nevertheless, the fact that extinction following negative reinforcement is variable is of considerable importance to the development of learning theory and to the practical problems that arise in attempts to alter behavior patterns.

Secondary Reinforcement: The concept of secondary reinforcement is used to explain how relatively simple responses develop into complex responses and how responses may occur without the presence of the originally reinforcing conditions. Consider a dog who salivates at the presentation of food. This response is well established in dogs: they do not need to be trained to salivate. A tone or other discriminable stimulus is presented at the same time as the food. With repeated pairings of the food and the tone, the food may be omitted, and the animal will respond to the tone alone. The tone is now the *conditioned stimulus* (CS). Under some conditions it is possible to pair the tone with another stimulus, such as a light. After pairing the two stimuli—tone and light—for several trials, the tone may now be omitted, and the animal will respond to the light. If this procedure can be continued, it is clear that any stimulus may become a reinforcer, as long as it has been paired with the stimulus used originally during conditioning.

In operant learning, a rodent learns to bar-press for food. Each time the bar is depressed, the animal receives food, and a light blinks near the bar. A second animal acquires the same response, although there is no light. Now the food is eliminated, but each bar press turns on the light. The rodent who received the light will make more bar presses during extinction than the animal who did not receive the light. To some degree, the light has assumed the properties of the original reinforcer: it is a *secondary reinforcer*. Both examples, the one from classical conditioning and the other from operant training, show

how a stimulus may become a reinforcer. The traditional description of secondary reinforcement is operational: whenever a neutral stimulus is paired with a reinforcer and the neutral stimulus eventually assumes the power of eliciting the original response, the previously neutral stimulus has become a secondary reinforcer.

The critical test of whether a stimulus has become a secondary reinforcer is to determine whether the stimulus can be used to reinforce the acquisition of a new response. As an illustration, an animal is placed in the two-compartment chamber that we have used previously for examples in this chapter. He learns to avoid electric shock in one compartment by responding to a tone that always precedes the shock. When he hears the tone, he runs to the other compartment. Now, let us place a doorway between the two compartments which can be opened only if the animal presses a lever near the door. If he learns to press the lever when the tone alone occurs, we can say the tone is a true secondary reinforcer, for it has assumed the power of serving as a reinforcer for the acquisition of a new response, namely, the pressing of the lever. Note that electric shock was not present. Rather, a chain of pairings was used. Originally, the tone signaled shock, but then the shock was omitted, and the tone served as the reinforcement in the animal's learning to press a lever.

The concept of secondary reinforcement explains how stimuli which have no primary value in satisfying a drive may come to serve as reinforcers. Returning to our discussion of the role of reinforcement in which the biological definition of reinforcement was distinguished from the operational definition, we may note that secondary reinforcement may account for the observation that many stimuli appear to assume reinforcing properties through learning. Indeed, the distinction between stimuli that are innate reinforcers to the organism and stimuli that are reinforcers acquired through learning is embodied in the use of the term *primary reinforcement* to refer to reinforcers which satisfy biological needs and the term *secondary reinforcement* for those which have assumed the function of primary reinforcements through learning.

It is difficult to imagine that all nonprimary reinforcers—that is, every stimulus that has the potential to increase response rate or the quality of the response—are members of a long chain of associations originating with a primary reinforcer. This viewpoint suggests that a quest for money or blondes is only one of a long chain of associations. Nevertheless, stranger concepts have been shown to be true when subjected to experimental attack, and for the moment there is a practical advantage to assuming that many, if not all, higher-order behaviors are the product of secondary reinforcement. Because of the suspected relationship between primary and secondary reinforcement and complex learned behaviors, secondary reinforcement assumes an important position as a critical concept in learning theory. We shall study it in greater detail in Chapter 14.

Measuring Learning: There are many ways of measuring performance of responses. Some methods are determined by the type of apparatus employed and others by the way in which data is analyzed. The ingenuity of experimenters has provided many new procedures for presenting data, and there is no reason to suppose that the number is decreasing. The way in which data is analyzed and presented, however, often reflects the theoretical position of the experimenter. This is to be expected, since the experimenter wants to emphasize the aspects of the data he considers important.

The major problem in interpreting data from learning studies is variability. On a series of trials, a subject may show unexplained decreases and increases in performance. Rarely is an individual learning curve so smooth as is suggested by the theoretical functions (Figure 12–3). The most common procedure for making the results of a series explicable is to combine trials. Figure 12–4 shows hypothetical data from subjects and the change in the

FIGURE 12–4: *Part A of the figure shows the mean number of times (in 12 trials) that the subjects were able to avoid punishment in an avoidance chamber. Drawing B shows these means averaged over 3 trials.*

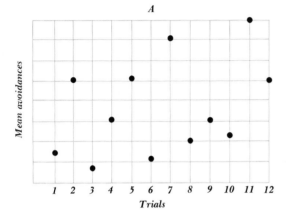

A

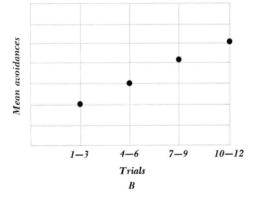

B

function that results when trials are combined. Although the combining of trials permits the reader to perceive the general function easily, it also masks the variability of the data. Most investigators search for the "happy medium" in which the data show the function clearly without masking variability. Variability may be indicated, of course, by plotting ranges or standard deviations. When this is done, vertical lines are commonly used to show either the range or the standard deviations. Figure 12–5 shows hypothetical data in which the means, standard deviations, and ranges are indicated.

Some investigators prefer to emphasize control over possible extraneous variables at the expense of using large numbers of subjects. Other things being equal, the larger the number of subjects, the greater the chance that a random population has been selected. If the population were perfectly random, we would expect the variability of one subject to be canceled by variability in the opposite direction from another subject. Other investigators prefer to work with a small number of subjects and to attempt to reduce variability by controlling for the effect of all variables. Often, the nature of the experiment determines which approach is used. The choice of approaches is not merely a value judgment; in most cases an experimenter chooses one technique over the other for reasons of expediency. Rarely is a perfectly random sample available; in investigations concerned with specific types of subjects, such as psychotics or retardates, it is often difficult or impossible to select a random sample. Sometimes absolute control over all variables is impossible, and appropriate statistical techniques and experimental designs, such as counterbalancing (Chapter 1), are used to circumvent the problem.

Studies of operant learning do not, characteristically, use large numbers of subjects. The emphasis is on absolute control over a few organisms. Ordinarily the data are presented in their entirety, without combining trials. For example, Figure 12–6 shows a schematic drawing of a *cumulative record* of a rat's acquisition and extinction of the bar-press response. Accordingly, the slope of the function indicates the rate of learning: the steeper the slope, the more rapid the acquisition. The inset is included to indicate the relationship between time and the number of responses. These data are recorded automatically. The paper on which the data are recorded moves at a constant speed, and each bar press moves the pen an equal amount up the ordinate. A hash mark is used to indicate responses that are reinforced.

One of the most common procedures when measuring learning in both human and animal studies is to use a *criterion*. Criteria are used because there is no simple procedure for determining when a person has learned: generally some arbitrary point in performance is chosen to represent learning. This point is called the criterion. We may set the criterion as the correct recall of 8 out of 10 syllables, the running of the maze in less than thirty seconds, or the making of 100 bar presses in less than an hour. Similarly, it is necessary to set a criterion for extinction, such as no bar presses within thirty minutes or simply three hours in the conditioning chamber without reinforcement. The difficulty is that subjects reach criterion at different levels. If one subject reaches criterion on the ninth trial and a second reaches criterion on the fifteenth trial, the problem of averaging performance on trials 10 through 15 appears. Is it fair to say that the first subject would have continued to perform at the level of the criterion for these trials? How can one construct a learning curve that shows the rate of learning without distorting the fact that the subjects reach criterion at different times?

One technique is to use the Vincent curve (Woodworth & Schlosberg, 1954, pp. 536–537). This procedure uses a "rubber" abscissa. The individual subject's percentage of total gain in performance is plotted for successive intervals. Unfortunately, this procedure masks the slopes of the learning function, but it does solve the problem of how to report the data of subjects who reach criterion on different trials. Criteria are used when we wish to match two or more groups on the basis of acquisition. If we wish to study the effects on retention of different periods of delay between acquisition and retention, it is vital that the groups perform at the same level when acquisition is terminated, for otherwise we cannot determine whether the differences in retention are a function of the independent vari-

FIGURE 12-5: *An example of a method for showing the mean, ranges, and standard deviations of data.*

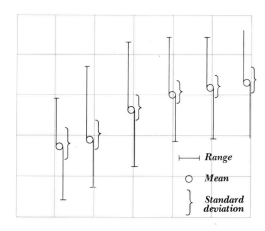

able (delay) or of the speed of acquisition. On the basis of the criterion used for acquisition, the subjects are divided into "equal" groups (Chapter 1).

Chemistry and Physiology of Learning: We infer that learning occurs in the organism, presumably, somewhere and somehow within the central nervous system. Some authorities argue that a proper theory of learning cannot be developed until the functions of the central nervous system are understood. Others argue that until more is known about the nervous system, it is misleading to form hypotheses about supposed relations between learning and changes in the nervous system. It is likely, however, that both analysis of the nervous system and experimentation on the factors that alter performance will contribute to an understanding of the principles of learning. Indeed, some rather striking findings have appeared which suggest that learning and forgetting are correlated with certain changes in the central nervous system.

The neurophysiology of learning has been approached in at least two major ways: First, there have been attempts to show the physiological changes that accompany particular

FIGURE 12–6: *A schematic drawing of a cumulative record. Time is shown along the abscissa and cumulative number of responses along the ordinate. Since the responses are plotted cumulatively, observation of the rate of responding and of changes in the rate describes the course of acquisition and extinction. The inset shows the relationship between slope and number of responses per unit of time. The vertical line shows the pen resetting.*

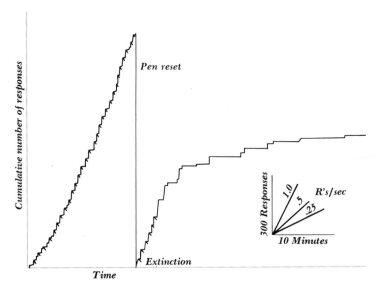

types of learning, such as classical conditioning. One question, for example, is whether a cerebral cortex is necessary for an organism to acquire a conditioned response. Answers to this question and others of a similar nature contribute to our understanding of the locations in the brain that are involved in special kinds of learning. Second, there have been more global attempts to unite all learning under some theoretical physiological mode. The first approach will be considered in Chapters 13 and 14, which discuss conditioning and instrumental training. Several theoretical models are available, however, which attempt to provide a unified framework for the physiological or neurological processes responsible for learning. Hebb (1949) has suggested that the synapses provide an obvious location for chemical changes in the nervous system which occur with learning. Since nervous system activity requires some chemical changes (Chapter 2), it is possible that these changes alter the shape of the axons or the size of the synapse. If a "learning chemical" exists (and there are some guesses about its constitution), perhaps the more often a particular neural network is used, the more secure the connection becomes. Thus, the probability of occurrence of the response connected with that neural network is increased.

Hebb has used this concept to explain a variety of psychological problems, including the effects of brain damage on intelligence and certain problems concerned with configuration in perception. Hebb's detailed analysis of the relation between supposed activity in the central nervous system and both learned and perceptual factors has provided a major attempt to unify these two areas.

Although the suggestion that learning is

paralleled by chemical changes in the neurons of the central nervous system dates from the last century, the idea remained undeveloped until the later 1950s because of the technical problems involved in studying such chemical changes. In Chapter 2 we noted the relationship between acetylcholine (ACh) and cholinesterase (ChE) and the possibility that these chemicals are responsible for nerve conduction. Rosenzweig, Krech, and Bennett (1960) have summarized a series of studies that they conducted in an attempt to relate these chemicals to the instrumental activity of maze running. They suggest that (1) learning ability correlates with the amount of available ACh at the synapses and (2) although ACh and ChE are related, ChE is not a consistent predictor of amount of ACh, since there are genetic differences, at least among rats, in regard to the relationship between ChE and learning ability.

The chemical basis of memory—the changes that occur at the molecular level in the nervous system—has received considerable experimental attention. The impetus for this research has come from work on the mechanisms involved in the storage, replication, and transfer of molecular information in biological systems. These mechanisms involve the nucleic acids, *deoxyribonucleic acid* (DNA) and *ribonucleic acid* (RNA). Figure 12–7 illustrates the structure of the DNA molecule as suggested by J. D. Watson and Crick (1953). It is generally believed that the sequence of the various bases along the molecular chain is the foundation of the genetic code (J. D. Watson & Crick, 1953). The DNA molecules function as templates for the formation of RNA molecules, which carry in their own sequence of bases the "message" which was coded on the DNA. These RNA copies of the DNA message then direct the synthesis of proteins in the cytoplasm. The capacity of DNA and RNA to retain molecular information, which led to their implication in the genetic mechanism, has prompted investigators to look to them for an explanation of memory.

Before scientists realized the relationship that existed between nucleic acids and protein

FIGURE 12–7: *Formula of a single chain of deoxyribonucleic acid (DNA). (From J. D. Watson & Crick, 1953, p. 965.)*

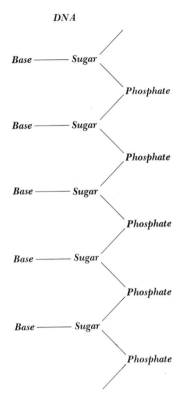

synthesis, suggestions had been made that alternations in neural proteins served as the basis of the memory process (J. J. Katz & Halstead, 1950; McCulloch, 1950). Some evidence along these lines came from work with the flatworm *Dugesia*. After apparently demonstrating that worms could acquire a conditioned response, experimenters cut trained flatworms in half and let them regenerate. The old-head–new-tail specimens retained the learned response, as might be expected, but a surprising result was that the old-tail–new-head specimens did the same. The memory of the response seemed to have been transmitted from the tail tissue to the new head (R. Thompson & McConnell, 1955; McConnell, A. J. Jacobson, & D. P. Kimble, 1959).

To ensure that actual transmission of the memory had occurred and that the trained tail was not simply reacting for the head, a double-regeneration experiment was performed. The trained *Dugesia* were cut in half and allowed to regenerate the missing half; then a second cut separated the newly regenerated tissue from the old tissue, and this new tissue also displayed the learned response (McConnell, R. Jacobson, & Maynard, 1959). Evidence for the direct involvement of RNA in this phenomenon was produced by Corning and John (1961), when they observed that if trained tails were allowed to regenerate in a medium containing ribonuclease (an enzyme which destroys RNA), the learned response was lost. Even more dramatic evidence for the role of RNA in memory appeared when trained worms were subjected to a chemical treatment which extracted their RNA. When this "trained RNA" was injected into untrained worms, these animals were conditioned more easily than uninjected subjects (Zelman, Kabat, R. Jacobson, & McConnell, 1963).

That RNA is involved in the learning process of higher animals has been suggested by a number of experiments. Hydén and his collaborators (Hydén & Egyhazi, 1962; 1963) found that rats which had been trained to climb a string to a food platform showed an increase in the amount of RNA in the vestibular nuclei but not in other parts of the brain. Furthermore, changes in the base ratio of the RNA in this area were detected, possibly reflecting the coding of the learned event on this molecule. That the base-ratio change was not simply a result of the increased neuronal activity was shown by giving a group of rats vestibular stimulation in a centrifuge. These animals showed an increase in RNA in the area but did not have an altered base ratio. Other experiments have shown that learning ability is improved in rats (L. Cook, Davidson, D. J. Davis, H. Green, & Fellows, 1963) and in human beings (Cameron, Solyom, & Beach, 1961; Cameron & Solyom, 1961) after they are supplied with large quantities of yeast RNA. Finally, memory has been found to be disrupted by chemicals that interfere with the normal activity of RNA (Chamberlain, Rothschild, & Gerard, 1963; Dingman & Sporn, 1961; J. B. Flexner, L. B. Flexner, & Stellar, 1963).

Although some evidence supports the notion that RNA is somehow implicated in the learning process, the precise mechanism of the events is unknown. Since RNA is involved in protein synthesis and since the proteins are the basis of all structural properties of the cell, the variety of possible mechanisms is virtually unlimited. Several suggestions, however, have been made. Gaito (1961) postulates that electrochemical changes, which occur as a result of nervous conduction, cause dislocations in the DNA or RNA molecules of the cell, thus transforming the genetic code directly into the memory code. Another suggestion is that memory involves the induction of enzymes that facilitate the release of transmitter substances at the synapse (M. H. Briggs & Kitto, 1962; C. E. Smith, 1962). Hydén has inferred from his work that sensory stimulation produces a modulated frequency in the neuron which changes the sequence of bases in one of the cell's RNA molecules. This changed RNA is then able to produce a new protein, which Hydén suggests has the property of dissociating rapidly when stimulated by the same frequency that produced its parent RNA. The result of this dissociation is the production of molecular fragments in the cell that cause the explosive release of the transmitter substance at the synapse (Hydén, 1959; 1961). Landauer (1964) speculates that the basic event of conditioning or learning is the transfer of RNA molecules from the glial cells into the conducting neurons, with the subsequent modification of the neuron's synthesizing mechanism. This new synthetic ability is supposed to result in changes in the protein composition of the neuron's membrane, making it more sensitive to some characteristic of the spreading electrical activity generated during the learning situation.

It is clear that information on learning and memory is being gathered in many ways by specialists trained in different disciplines. Any meaningful theory of the chemistry and physiology of learning or memory must interpret the data available on the psychology of learning, and any new theory of learning, if it is to be fruitful, must pay attention to the possibilities and restrictions imposed by the nervous system and its chemical action. For the moment, research on learning is proceeding in two directions: first, ·investigators look to the chemistry of the brain to reveal the nature of learned behavior; second, investigators attempt to identify the factors that alter performance. The two most important kinds of performance are those resulting from classical conditioning and instrumental training. We shall now begin a more thorough discussion of learning by examining these topics. We should, however, keep the critical problems in mind, so that we can apply them to our review of classical conditioning and instrumental training.

SOURCES

This chapter introduces the student to the field of learning. Writers vary considerably in the emphasis they place on various attributes of learning; most textbooks attempt a broad survey before presenting a more thorough discussion of important concepts and techniques.

Both Mednick (1964) and Hill (1963) have written short but useful paperbacks on learning. The former reviews methodology and data primarily, and the latter emphasizes theory. Hill's book is written at an appropriate level for students; it succeeds admirably in placing the bits and pieces of data on learning into theoretical frameworks.

For further analysis of critical problems in learning, Osgood (1953) provides an excellent section that reviews the problems mentioned in the present chapter, as well as other issues. Osgood's comments deserve careful study, for his dissection and interpretation of studies is very valuable. G. A. Kimble (1961), in his revision of the Hilgard and Marquis' work (1940), provides a thorough and updated review of several important areas of learning. The introductory chapter considers the problem of defining learning. Woodworth and Schlosberg (1954) have a chapter that introduces the subject area of learning; their analysis of how data may be presented is both useful and thorough. On a less difficult level, Deese has written (1958) a sound text which includes an introductory chapter on the types of learning. J. A. McGeoch and Irion (1952) review studies of human learning; the reader may find perusal of the vast number of topics in this area instructive. See also Deese and Hulse (1967).

Hilgard's chapter in Stevens (1951) on "Methods and Procedures in the Study of Learning" discusses basic problems in learning and provides useful information on methodology. The chapter also discusses learning curves, their analysis and construction. Underwood (1957a), in his excellent discussion of problems in psychological research, emphasizes the design of experiments concerned with learned behavior. The serious investigator will profit greatly from study of this book. Bugelski (1956) devotes the first two chapters of his text to the problem of defining learning and to an overview of experiments.

Magoun's (1963) informative book, *The Waking Brain,* includes chapters on the electrophysiology of learning and on how the brain processes and stores material. Further information on chemical approaches to learning is found in Hydén (1960) and in Schmitt (1962). Hydén's chapter discusses the properties of the neuron and introduces that writer's work on memory storage. It is highly recommended. Schmitt's collection includes chapters by workers who are concerned with how memory is stored; a wide variety of interests is represented (such as chemical engineering and psychology).

CHAPTER THIRTEEN

CLASSICAL CONDITIONING

INTRODUCTION

Classical conditioning is sometimes called *Pavlovian conditioning* in honor of one of its most able investigators. Some authorities also refer to it as *type I learning* in order to distinguish it from operant training *(type II)*. The paradigms and procedures describing the necessary conditions for each of these two principal types of learning are well understood, but as we shall learn in this chapter and the next, some elements of classical conditioning are found in operant-training situations, and possibly the reverse is true as well. The two may not be so distinct after all.

BRIEF HISTORY OF CLASSICAL CONDITIONING

The process of conditioning is not new, nor is it a discovery of psychology. Living organisms and perhaps plants have been conditioned since time began. Experimental concern with the process, however, did not appear until the latter part of the nineteenth century, and the implications of conditioning for behavior were not appreciated until the twentieth century.

The Russian physiologist, Ivan Pavlov (1849–1936), is properly called the "father of conditioning," although he did not "discover" the process. Experiments on what we now call conditioning had been conducted, primarily in Russia, for some years before Pavlov began his systematic investigations of the phenomenon. The association of Pavlov's name with conditioning has masked the contributions of other Russian workers. Vladimir Bekhterev (1857–1927) was far more concerned with behavior than Pavlov. His views on psychology and his work on the "association reflex" were reported in a book called *Objective Psychology,* which appeared serially in Russian from 1907 to 1912, in French and German in 1913, and in English in 1928. The association reflex was the original concept which developed into the idea of the *conditioned response* (CR). Bekhterev's work gave American psychology its fundamental tenets. The American psychologist, John B. Watson (1878–1958; 1916), expounded these tenets in the philosophy of behaviorism, beginning in 1916.

G. A. Kimble points out (1961, p. 22) Bekhterev's contributions to psychology: (1) the idea that thinking is subvocal speech (see Chapter 7 of the present volume), (2) the fact that conditioning can be used to determine the sensory thresholds of animals and of nonvocal subjects (see Chapter 4), and (3) the idea, later used by Watson as the tenet of behaviorism, that introspection is not an appropriate tool for psychology. In spite of the seminal quality of Bekhterev's works and beliefs, Pavlov's terminology has been retained in the literature of psychology and physiology. It is noteworthy that Bekhterev had studied with Wundt, who had founded the first laboratory for psychological research in 1879 at Leipzig.

The concept of stimulus-response connections as the prevailing explanatory device in learning theory may be traced to another Russian, Ivan Sechenov (1829–1905; 1935). Sechenov had studied under J. Müller, who is remembered for the formulation of the law of specific nerve energies (Chapter 2), Du Bois-Reymond, who was among the first to note the electric potential of nerve conduction, Helmholtz (Chapter 6), and Claude Bernard, whom we remember for the concept of homeostasis (Chapter 2). Since Sechenov's work preceded that of Pavlov and Bekhterev, it may be surmised that his view of behavior as the relationship among sensory events, the ongoing processes of the central nervous system, and the resultant motor response influenced their thought. Sechenov suggested the concept of the reflex arc to describe the relationship, and he spoke of the effect of the excitation and inhibition of the central nervous system upon behavior. These concepts were adopted by Pavlov, and they are still in use today by neurophysiological theorists (cf. Hebb, 1949; Melzack & Wall, 1965).

Pavlov began to study for the priesthood, but he eventually undertook studies at St. Petersburg and gave up his seminary training.

By 1888 he had taken his degree in medicine and had made two important contributions to this field: (1) the discovery of the secretory nerves of the pancreas and (2) the discovery that sham feeding of an animal (Chapter 10) produced secretions, just as if food had actually entered the stomach. In 1904, he was awarded the Nobel prize for his work on the digestive glands.

When Pavlov turned his attention to conditioned reflexes, his work received strange criticism. Some critics argued that he was reporting nothing that dog trainers did not already know. It should be noted, however, that Pavlov's work on the digestive system led rather directly to his work on the association reflex. The important clue that he followed was his discovery that the digestive secretions were not simple physical responses. They could be produced by presenting stimuli other than the original stimulus. Thus, the mere sight or odor of food was sufficient to cause the response. Once Pavlov realized this, he had the germ of the idea that responses could be learned through the appropriate pairing of an *unconditioned stimulus* (US) with a novel stimulus. He selected the salivary response as his unit of measurement of conditioning, for the simple reason that saliva is easier to measure accurately than digestive secretions.

He had perceived the relationship between stimulus events outside the organism and internal changes; it was to this basic problem that he devoted the remainder of his career, and for this his reputation is firmly established. Parenthetically, it may be noted that at the same time in Vienna Sigmund Freud (1856–1939) was similarly beginning a new stage in his lifework. Having already established a reputation in physiological research, Freud turned to the work of dream interpretation and eventually developed basic postulates concerned with the development of behavior. His work too received an uncommon amount of abuse.

After 1910, American psychologists became concerned with conditioning. But for the most part the interest was minimal, and no one attempted the kind of systematic investigation that Pavlov had initiated. It is a curious historical oddity that the American psychologist Twitmyer (1873–1943) discovered the classically conditioned response by accident in 1902 (Dallenbach, 1959). While training human subjects to respond to a stimulus by lifting the knee, he noted that if he withheld the stimulus, the knee-jerk response persisted. He reported his findings in 1904 (see Twitmyer, 1905) at a meeting of the American Psychological Association; however, the chairman of the session, William James[1] (1842–1910), ignored the importance of the finding and cut short the discussion of the report, so that the members might not miss lunch, for which they were already late. Florence Mateer (1887–1961) also did work in this area. Her doctoral dissertation (1916) and a book (1918) review her studies of classical conditioning in children. She placed a bandage over the eyes of children shortly before presenting food; eventually the placing of the bandage was sufficient to cause "consummatory responses" such as swallowing.

By 1916, J. B. Watson had adopted the objective point of view proposed by Bekhterev. At first, this approach was a negative reaction to the introspective techniques employed by E. B. Titchener and others. By 1925, however, Watson's book *Behaviorism* spelled out how objective psychology, or behaviorism, could use conditioning as its major explanatory tool. This text prompted studies of human classical conditioning throughout the next decade.

In 1930, B. F. Skinner began a series of experiments on the bar-pressing behavior of the rat, which culminated in the book *The Behavior of Organisms* (1938). Skinner distinguished between classical conditioning, such as that investigated by Pavlov in which the original response (the unconditioned response) is already within the behavior patterns of the organism, and instrumental training, such as

bar pressing, in which the response, although within the ability of the organism, is not innate for a specific stimulus.

TYPES OF CLASSICAL CONDITIONING

Before discussing the various kinds of temporal arrangements between stimuli used in classical conditioning, we must distinguish certain basic features found in classical conditioning from those found in instrumental training. For the moment, it is sufficient to note that the two differ in respect to (1) the kind of response with which we begin and (2) the use of reinforcement.

In classical conditioning, the response to be conditioned, the eye blink, for example, is effectively the response with which we begin the experimental manipulations. Conditioning serves to train that response to occur following a stimulus other than the stimulus that originally evoked it. In instrumental training, however, the response is often very far removed in quality from the response with which training was begun. A bar press, which is not a common response for a rat, must be shaped by the investigator. The rat must be reinforced for going to the area of the bar, then for touching the bar in some manner, and eventually for pressing the bar. Thus the original response, which must be shaped, is quite different from the eventual response.

Classical conditioning does not rely upon reinforcement. Although there may be some reinforcing power in the sensations of salivating, it is difficult to find a reinforcer for eye blinking or knee jerking. In instrumental learning, reinforcement is used to train or shape the desired response. It is possible that the conditioned response can be the same under both procedures. For example, we might classically condition the eye blink to a tone, or we might instrumentally train the eye-blink response. In the one paradigm, however, we would take advantage of an available response and pair a stimulus, such as a puff of air, with

[1] James had already contributed his *Principles of Psychology* (1890) and was to be elected president of the association twice—an honor accorded to only one other person, G. Stanley Hall (1846–1924), who founded the association in 1892.

a tone until the tone itself brought about the eye-blink response. In instrumental training, we would offer some form of reinforcement after each eye blink in order to obtain an increase in the rate of eye blinking.

Consider the example of the human eye blink being conditioned to a tone. Let us assume that the stimulus which originally evoked the blink was a bright light. The light is called the *unconditioned stimulus* (US), for it is able to evoke the response without previous conditioning. The eye blink, given in response to the US, is called the *unconditioned response* (UR), for it occurs without previous conditioning. Thus, the original relationship between the stimulus and response is

$$\text{US} \xrightarrow{\hspace{3cm}} \text{UR}$$
$$\text{(light)} \qquad\qquad \text{(eye blink)}$$

The tone, which is paired temporally with the US, is called the *conditioned stimulus* (CS), and, diagrammatically, we have the following situation:

(light)
US

⟶ UR
(eye blink)

CS
(tone)

When the US is eliminated and only the CS appears, the UR becomes a CR (conditioned response) and

$$\text{CS} \xrightarrow{\hspace{3cm}} \text{CR}$$

Note that, behaviorally, the UR and CR are theoretically identical; a UR becomes a CR when the CS takes over the function of the US. Actually, the UR and CR only appear to be similar. If various characteristics of the CR, such as amplitude or frequency, are measured against those of the UR, one finds that the resemblance between the two is incomplete. The term *conditioned* in the nomenclature of classical conditioning is perhaps unfortunate.

Pavlov's original term, *conditional,* emphasizes the probability of the occurrence of the response, rather than the *shaping* of the response which is implied by *conditioned.* However, *conditioned* is the term that has acquired acceptance in the speech and writings of psychologists.

A variety of stimuli have been used as the US, including light, shock, acid, food, drugs, and air puffs. URs include such responses as salivation, skin resistance, intestinal secretions, nausea, knee jerk, eye blink, and eye movements. In addition, classical conditioning procedures have been used on organisms of diverse kinds. In human studies the eye blink is probably the most commonly used response, although the patellar and salivary reflexes have been used extensively. There is some evidence that the human fetus can be conditioned (Sontag & Wallace, 1935). E. L. Hunt (1949) has reported conditioning of chicken embryos. It is noteworthy that some chicks retained the CR after hatching. Conditioning studies with dogs have most often used either the salivary response or the eye blink. R. Thompson and McConnell (1955) and other investigators report successfully conditioning the flatworm *Planaria.* It is unlikely that pure classical conditioning occurs phylogenetically below the flatworm, but other kinds of learning may take place.

Pavlov's original studies were duplicated on children (Krasnogorski, 1909; 1913) with success, although it was noted that conditioning became more unstable as age increased. Studies of adults have generally upheld the basic laws and reproduced the phenomena that Pavlov found with dogs. Since classical conditioning deals with such fundamental and simple physiological responses, it probably accounts for few behaviors in the life of the human being and other advanced mammals. Instrumental training appears to account for many more responses and types of behavior. Nevertheless, classical conditioning procedures have been used with some success in psychotherapy (Bandura, 1961; Feldman, 1966).

Several factors contribute to the speed of

conditioning and to the quality and quantity of the CR. Foremost among these is the temporal relationship between the US and CS. This relationship is usually expressed in a diagram by a horizontal line to represent time:

20 seconds

and a block to indicate the onset and termination of either the US or the CS. The following, for example, indicates that the CS came on after 10 seconds, remained on for 5 seconds, and was then terminated.

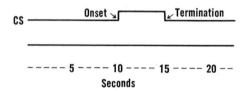

The next paradigm shows a case of simultaneous conditioning, for the US and CS are presented at the same time:

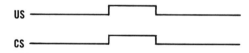

Delayed conditioning occurs when the CS is presented *prior* to the US and remains until the appearance of the US. The CS and US may overlap and may take several forms, as shown in the following four paradigms:

1. The CS may terminate at the onset of the US.

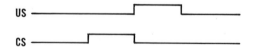

2. The CS may terminate with the termination of the US.

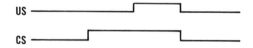

3. The CS may terminate after the termination of the US.

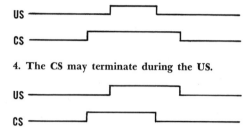

4. The CS may terminate during the US.

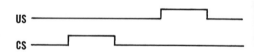

Note that in delayed conditioning, the US and CS are always in some kind of temporal contiguity. There is always some point at which the two appear together.

If the CS and US are not in temporal contiguity, as in the following paradigm, the conditioning is called *trace conditioning* (presumably because a memory "trace" is required for the organism to associate the two events).

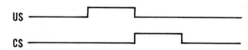

In trace conditioning, the CS precedes the US, but the two have no temporal overlap. When the US precedes the CS, as in the following example,

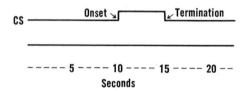

the schedule is known as *backward conditioning*. There is considerable doubt that true backward conditioning occurs.

THE UNCONDITIONED RESPONSE AND THE CONDITIONED RESPONSE

Although investigators once believed the UR and the CR to be identical, accurate measuring devices indicate clearly that they are not. Classical conditioning is not only the substitution of one stimulus for another; it also represents a change in the quality of the CR when compared with the UR. As an example, the amount of saliva deposited after conditioning is not so great as that deposited originally to the US. Similarly, the number of conditioned eye blinks to the CS may be less than the number evoked by the US. These findings suggest that the CR may be considered a *portion* or *fraction* of the UR. Yet it is clear that the CR is more than merely a fraction of the UR, for the CR often includes behaviors that were not part of the UR. In short, the CR is both something more than the UR and something less. It is a different response, but it has elements of the UR. We must keep in mind that the CR is artificial, because the experimenter chooses to observe only a fraction of behavior. When measuring salivation, one might measure heart-rate changes, blood-pressure changes, gastric changes, and pupillary size, too. These are all responses of the organism to the conditioning procedure. Classical conditioning may profitably be regarded as a set of manipulations determined by the experimenter and, ultimately, by the experimental procedures. We know that if a procedure is followed, certain changes in behavior occur, such as a change in salivation rate. We must remember that (1) salivation is only one response which is being changed by the experimental manipulations, and (2) the quantity of the response after the manipulation is not likely to be the same as that of the response before.

When measuring a CR one typically ignores all behavior except that being measured, e.g., the amount of saliva deposited. Obviously, the organism is behaving in other ways: he may swallow, chew, gnash his teeth, twitch his tail, or tap his fingers. Some of these behaviors, such as chewing and swallowing, are related to salivation. Others appear to be unrelated to the conditioning, but if we measure them, we will find that they too are undergoing modification. If the UR is the amount of salivation, it is possible that the CS produces less salivation but more swallowing. Which is the true CR—salivation or swallowing? Obviously, there is no single CR, for the CR is selected by the conditions of the experiment. Although it is vital to consider discrete responses in conducting experiments on conditioning, these responses do not provide the full picture of all that is undergoing conditioning.

TEMPORAL RELATIONSHIP BETWEEN THE CONDITIONED STIMULUS AND THE UNCONDITIONED STIMULUS

What is the most efficient temporal relationship between the CS and the US? The answer depends upon the nature of the CR. If hand withdrawal to shock is the conditioning situation, we shall find that the most efficient relationship is that in which the CS precedes the US by approximately 0.5 second. If heart rate is the measure, we shall expect a different relationship to be maximal. Using finger withdrawal to shock, H. M. Wolfle (1932) obtained the data shown in Figure 13.1. The zero point on the abscissa indicates the point of simultaneous presentation of the CS and US. Points to the left of the zero point represent intervals in which the US precedes the CS (backward conditioning), and points to the right represent delayed conditioning. When the CS precedes the US, the percentage of conditioning increases to approximately 0.5 second and then decreases rapidly, at least for the eye-blink response. Conditioning does not occur in this situation with lags over 1 second. Some evidence for backward conditioning appears from the data, for the "percentage conditioning" hovers around 10 percent when the US precedes the CS for 1 second or less. It is doubtful that this is conditioning. We shall note a possible explanation for this finding in the next section.

CHARACTERISTICS OF CONDITIONING

Over the years a number of characteristics of conditioning have been discovered and examined. All of these enable us to understand conditioning better.

FIGURE 13-1: *The results of an experiment that measured the temporal relationship between the CS and US. The ordinate shows the amount of conditioning, and the abscissa shows the temporal relationships. To the left of the zero point the US precedes the CS; to the right of the zero point the CS precedes the US. Thus, the area to the left of the zero shows backward conditioning. Note that little, if any, conditioning occurs under this arrangement. The temporal relationship that yields the greatest conditioning is around 0.5 second; however, this duration holds only for shock and finger withdrawal. Other responses show different relationships to be maximally effective. (Modified from H. M. Wolfle, 1932, p. 90.)*

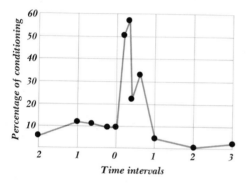

CS is "transferable"; i.e., one stimulus may assume the power of another stimulus through association and without conditioning (see Seidel, 1959).

Sensitization and Pseudoconditioning: During conditioning, the US sensitizes the reflex, or UR. Sensitization results in the animal's making the response, not only to the CS and US, but also to any extraneous stimuli he might perceive. This phenomenon may account for those cases of backward conditioning which have been reported. In backward conditioning, the US sensitizes the organism's response so that when the CS is presented, the response occurs. If a subject is being trained to withdraw his hand on being given a shock, the hand response is sensitized: the subject is ready to move his hand. At this point any sudden stimulation, such as the sound of a door slamming or a sudden movement by the experimenter, will lead to the hand-withdrawal response.

Pseudoconditioning, a special type of sensitization, occurs when the US is so strong that it will sensitize the UR to such an extent that almost any stimulus will bring about the response. In this situation, the first presentation of the CS after the pairing of the US and UR will bring about the CR. Although pseudoconditioning has not received extensive experimental attention, it is clear that one must know what it is and the circumstances under which it may occur if one is to talk with confidence about conditioning.

Sensory Preconditioning: If two stimuli, such as a light and a tone, are presented together on several trials and if the light is then selected as the CS in a conditioning study and is presented until conditioning occurs, the tone, which has not been used as a CS, may still evoke the CR. For example, a light and a tone are presented to a dog for a number of trials without the US. The dog is then conditioned to the light, and the tone is ignored. When conditioning has occurred, the investigator may substitute the tone as the CS, and the CR may be noted, even though the tone has never been used as the CS. Apparently the temporal contiguity of the two stimuli prior to conditioning is sufficient to permit the organism to generalize at the later time. This procedure reemphasizes the fact that the

Summation: If the same response is conditioned to two stimuli separately and if the two stimuli are now presented simultaneously, summation of the CSs occurs. Summation results in an increase in the strength or quality of the CR, but it is not a simple additive function. If stimulus₁ normally produced 10 percent CRs and stimulus₂ produced 20 percent CRs, the summation of the stimuli would not necessarily produce 30 percent CSs. The percentage of CRs refers to the number of conditioned responses which occur in proportion to the number of presentation of the stimulus. Generally, the effect of summation is to produce something less than the sum of the two stimuli.

Adaptation: Adaptation may occur, particularly when the US is unpleasant if the US is presented in a series of trials before conditioning is begun. When an animal that received "adaptation" trials is compared with one that did not, the number of CRs is greater for the latter animal (MacDonald, 1946; G. A. Kimble & Dufort, 1956). The parameters affecting adaptation have received little attention. For example, the relationship between number of adaptation trials and conditioning is relatively unexplored: USs of a nonnoxious nature have received little attention, and adaptation of the CS, as opposed to the US, has not been thoroughly considered, although McAllister (1953) reports adaptation of the CS in eye-blink conditioning.

In sensory preconditioning, pseudoconditioning, and sensitization, an unexpected response occurs often to an unexpected stimulus. Pseudoconditioning and sensitization are scientifically awkward in that investigators may mistakenly report conditioning when they are really reporting pseudoconditioning or sensitization. Controls have been developed to eliminate or measure these artifacts (G. A. Kimble, 1961). In adaptation there is a decrease in the appearance of a CR. Thus these four aspects of conditioning are concerned with (1) a CR appearing when it should not and (2) a CR not appearing when it should. The occurrence or disappearance of a CR leads us to the theoretical construct of inhibition.

THE INHIBITIONS

Pavlov's theory included two constructs, *inhibition* and *excitation*, which described the functionings of the central nervous system during conditioning. The constructs of inhibition and excitation are so useful that they, or their equivalent, appear in the work of later learning theorists, especially those who attempt to point out the possible neurological correlates of learning.

External Inhibition: The period of acquisition of a conditioned response can be trying for both the experimenter and the subject unless external stimuli are well controlled. Observationally, the subject is hyperattentive to stimuli, and irrelevant noises or other stimuli noticeably affect performance. Pavlov noted that during acquisition any stimulus that occurred with the US created a deficit in the CR. He referred to this deficit as *external inhibition* and to the inappropriate stimulus as the *external inhibitor*. Experiments with operant training, where the phenomenon also appears, suggest that the greater the strength of learning at the time of inhibition, the less the effect of the external inhibitor (Winnick & J. McV. Hunt, 1951).

Disinhibition (Inhibition of Inhibition): Although external inhibition refers to a decrement in the quantity of the response during acquisition, disinhibition refers to an improvement in the quantity of the response during extinction. For example, Pavlov (1927) extinguished the conditioned salivary response by presenting the CS without the US. Then he presented meat with a novel stimulus, such as a tone or a touching of the skin. This procedure increased the amount of saliva deposited. The effect was to *disinhibit* the extinction of the response. That is, during the extinction process, the response was inhibited; when a new stimulus was supplied, however, the inhibited response was disinhibited, and the response reappeared. The important point is that an extinguished CR can be rejuvenated in several ways that do not involve pairings of the CS and US. This finding suggests that responses are not truly extinguished but that they are merely inhibited until an appropriate disinhibitor appears.

Inhibition of Delay: Pavlov also reported that when the CS was present for a relatively long period (say, three minutes), as the time for the presentation of the US approached, the animal "anticipated" the US by salivating before its presentation. When the CS first appeared, no saliva was deposited; however, as the time for the US approached, more and more saliva was secreted. We shall note that a similar effect occurs in operant training under certain schedules of reinforcement. In classical conditioning this effect only occurs when the response has been well conditioned; i.e., the animal must have had sufficient presentations of the stimuli to anticipate that the US bears the same temporal relationship to the CS on each trial. If the temporal relationship between the CS and US is varied from trial to trial, the effect does not occur. Pavlov also stated that the effect could be disinhibited by the presentation of a novel stimulus.

GENERALIZATION

An organism does not respond *only* to the specific stimulus used in conditioning. If the CS is a 510-Hz tone, a stimulus of 505 Hz will evoke the response. As the second stimulus becomes more unlike the original CS, however, a diminution in response strength is noted. The ability of an organism to respond to stimuli different from, but in the same dimension (e.g., cycles per second, mμ) as the original CS, is called *stimulus generalization*.

Figure 13–2 shows a gradient which might occur in classical conditioning when a dog is trained to salivate to a 5,000-Hz tone and tested on stimuli of other frequencies. The resulting function is called the *stimulus-generalization gradient*. Thus, organisms respond to stimuli other than the precise stimulus used during conditioning. It would be a simple and clocklike world, indeed, if organisms did not generalize.

Response generalization is said to occur when the response changes but the stimulus remains the same. The classic example of response generalization is supplied by Bekhterev (1928), who conditioned a dog to respond by lifting one foot. That foot was then immo-

bilized and the stimulus presented; the animal lifted the other foot. Thus, the stimulus did not change, but the response was generalized from one foot to the other. Both stimulus and response generalization assume a "spreading" effect, i.e., the extent of the stimuli to which the organism responds or the extent of the responses made by the organism increases.

Generalization may also occur during extinction. Bass and Hull (1934) used four parts of the skin as the location for conditioning, with weight as the CS. When all four areas were conditioned equally, one area was extinguished. Following the extinction of this area, the other areas showed a decrement in response strength, even though they had not been extinguished specifically. Pavlov referred to this effect as *irradiation of inhibition*, for he assumed that the inhibition (extinction) "radiated" within the nervous system.

The concept of irradiation as an explanatory principle for the process of generalization, as well as for other conditioning processes, is no longer in vogue, largely because of a series of papers by Hovland (1937a; 1937b). Hovland selected auditory perception as the dependent variable, for there is evidence that loudness does not depend, neurologically, on a spatial phenomenon. Since the concept of irradiation assumes a spatial, rather than a temporal, relationship, a generalization gradient for loudness would, according to some theorists, indicate that irradiation is not the complete explanation for generalization. Hovland conditioned one tone, measured the GSR, and then tested for generalization to other stimuli by measuring GSR changes. The results are shown in Figure 13–3.

An important contribution of Hovland's studies was the use of psychophysical measurements for the selection of the generalization test points. Hovland used points which were 25, 50, and 75 just noticeable differences (jnd's) in frequency from the CS. Individual differences in auditory thresholds may account for the variation between subjects. Slivinske and J. F. Hall (1960) have found that the stimuli used by Hovland were not always discriminable, and Prokasy and J. F. Hall (1963) suggest the possibility that the subjects in studies of this type respond to the "whole" tone, rather than to its particular loudness or pitch.

CONDITIONING AND THE CENTRAL NERVOUS SYSTEM

One of the first problems that Pavlov and his colleagues investigated was the source of the classically conditioned response. Did it occur through some connection in the spinal cord or in the brain? Was the cortex necessary for conditioning to occur? The answer was sought by training animals and removing the cortex *(decortication)*. The first attempts failed (Zeliony, 1929; see C. T. Morgan, 1964), leading Pavlov and others to believe that the cortex was necessary. Later work, however, both in Russia and in the United States, shows that an animal could acquire a classically conditioned response without a cortex (Poltyrew & Zeliony, 1930; Bromiley, 1948; see also Chapter 14). Further evidence comes from the observation that classical conditioning occurs in invertebrates, which do not have a cortex. It has been argued that studies which have used decorticate preparation (see, for example, Ten Cate, 1934; Bromiley, 1948) are open to some question, because the investigators cannot prove that the decortication was complete. In spite of this argument, the weight of experimental evidence suggests that the cortex is not an essential structure in conditioning.

Studies that attempt to correlate the anatomical or physiological state of an organism with learning ability are hampered by two kinds of methodological difficulties: those associated with the learning process and those associated with operative and surgical techniques. Preferably, although it is not always possible, the performance should be measured prior to the operation and after the operation, and the number of trials necessary to relearn the task should be measured. A control group should be used to provide the same measures, although the operation would be omitted. Some investigators prefer to include a third group

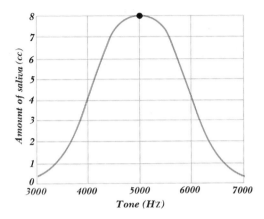

FIGURE 13–2: *A dog is trained to salivate to a 5,000-Hz tone. Then the other tones noted along the abscissa are presented in a random sequence, and the salivation rate is recorded. The data shown represent a possible curve, not obtained data.*

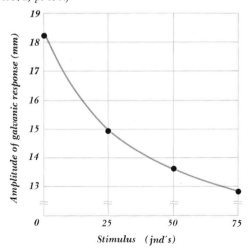

FIGURE 13–3: *An example of generalization. The abscissa shows the original tone used for conditioning marked as zero. The other stimuli are 25, 50, and 75 jnd's removed in frequency from the original tone. The exact curve which results is not germane, since the response dimension is not scaled. The curve clearly shows a decrease in the GSR amplitude, however, as the tone became less similar to the original one. (From Hovland, 1937a, p. 136.)*

which receives a *sham operation,* i.e., one in which all surgical procedures are followed except the ablation or lesion of neural tissue. In some cases, the lesion or ablation is performed on apparently unimportant areas and, depending on the design of the experiment, rather different interpretations may be made. Osgood (1953, p. 475) lists the inferences that may be made regarding the importance of the ablated or lesioned structure:

The influence of localization: Localization refers to the specific area that is thought to be essential for the response or performance. For example, the visual cortex is essential for vision in the human being, but so are the retina, optic nerves, and other structures. Localization does not mean that this specific area is the *only* area concerned with the performance but that the response or performance desired cannot occur unless the specific area is available.

The influence of replication of function: Replication occurs when two areas are found to have the same function. In the human being, for example, where there are two hemispheres in the cerebrum, ablation of the right hemisphere may not disrupt performance, for the left hemisphere which has an identical function may take over. When both areas are ablated, however, the performance will be lost.

The influence of equipotentiality and mass action: These terms refer to the amount of loss in performance as a function of the amount of destruction done to a particular area of the brain. If a section of a large area is removed and if the specific *location* of the area chosen for destruction has no effect on the response being studied, the area is said to be equipotential. If removing a given amount from the front, back, right, or left has the same effect on performance, the area is equipotential. Equipotentiality, then, is concerned with the effect of the location of the destruction. An area is described as possessing mass action if the *amount* of tissue removed is related to the loss in performance. Mass action implies the presence of equipotentiality, but equipotentiality does not necessarily imply the presence of mass action.

The fact that the cortex is apparently not

necessary for classical conditioning does not indicate that it is *unimportant* for conditioning. Some studies provide evidence that decorticated animals do not develop the precise motor response required for eliminating shock in an avoidance-learning situation so well as normal animals (Girden, Mettler, Finch, & E. Culler, ¬1936), although Bromiley (1948) did not find this difference. A major difficulty in these and similar studies is that the procedures do not permit replacing the cortex after the experiment.

Many investigators have searched for methods to render the cortex nonfunctional, so that the effects of decortication could be studied without actually removing the cortex. In one study dogs were trained to avoid shock by pressing a panel whenever a stimulus light went out (Solomon & Turner, 1962). After they had learned this task, their muscles were paralyzed by an administration of curare. While the dogs were immobile from the drug, a neutral stimulus was paired with current. Another neutral stimulus was presented, but never with the current. Following recovery from curarization, the dogs were returned to the original training problem, and all three stimuli—the light used originally plus the two neutral stimuli—were presented. The animals' responses (pressing the panel) were recorded. The responses indicated that learning occurred during the curarization, for the animals pressed more often to the stimulus that had been paired with shock than to the stimulus that had not been. The writers conclude "that certain types of transfer of training or problem solving can occur without the benefit of mediation by peripheral skeletal responses or their associated feedback mechanisms" (Solomon & Turner, 1962, p. 218).

Determination of the level of the central nervous system involved in conditioning has been an unresolved but noisy issue since Shurrager and E. Culler published data which indicated that dogs could be conditioned at the level of the spinal cord (1940; 1941). These investigators dissected out muscles to the hind legs at the third lumbar root. Shock was applied to the hind paw, and the reaction of the muscle fiber was observed. Twitches of the muscle (CR) were found to follow the established laws of conditioning; e.g., the acquisition rate followed the usual pattern, and the twitches could be extinguished by eliminating the US. This finding was challenged by other investigators on the general principle that the twitch represented a sensitization process, rather than true conditioning. The unfortunate fact that these investigators varied parts of the experimental procedures, such as current intensity and the interval between the US and CS, renders it difficult to ascribe the lack of agreement to any single source (see Deese & W. N. Kellogg, 1949).

The technique of using EEG recordings to follow changes in learning within the central nervous system has also received attention. EEG recordings show characteristic potentials during certain types of activity. For example, *alpha* rhythms appear when the subject is awake, but relaxed, and *delta* rhythms are recorded when the subject is asleep. EEG rhythms are themselves capable of classical conditioning. The alpha rhythm, for example, may be suppressed by conditioning procedures. Moreover, Galambos (1960) has provided data which indicate that both frequency and amplitude of the EEG may be changed in response to either shock or a positive reinforcer, such as food. These changes appear throughout the structures of the central nervous system and imply that the EEG is reporting gross changes rather than precise ones.

Other studies of the role of the central nervous system in classical conditioning have developed conditioning techniques which require description. Confusion is sometimes expressed over the type of learning that takes place in the avoidance situation. Avoidance training involves the presentation of a warning stimulus followed by electric shock which the animal can avoid by responding in some particular way (See Chapter 12). Such training is thus instrumental training rather than classical conditioning. Some classical conditioning is involved, however, in the learning of the response—mainly that part of the response which is associated with physiological reactions to fear. If the animal is placed in a somewhat similar situation in which a tone is followed by electric current but he cannot escape the current, then we have a case of classical conditioning. The twitching or other attempted movement that follows the tone upon repeated pairings of the tone and shock qualifies as a conditioned response.

The finding that an animal placed in this situation also exhibits generalized fear responses led to the development of an important technique, the conditioned emotional response (CER). The typical paradigm for this technique is to present a click or other stimulus which is followed by the administration of electric current. Within a few trials, the animal shows the CER to the tone. The CER is manifested by increased defecation and urination, decreased activity (called *freezing*), whining, or other responses commonly associated with fear.

EXTENSIONS OF CLASSICAL CONDITIONING

Because classical conditioning concentrates on supposedly small aspects of behavior and possibly because Pavlov's grand reputation discouraged investigators, this type of learning has received less attention than it deserves among theorists or experimenters. Once Pavlovian findings were recognized and validated, classical conditioning seemed to slip into the background. Instrumental training came to the front because of its apparent relevance to a variety of complex behaviors. We may, however, identify five major areas in which studies of classical conditioning have revealed implications for some important forms of behavior. These areas are (1) conditioning of the interoceptive system, (2) conditioning of verbal behavior, (3) conditioning of the orienting reflex, (4) conditioning in relation to anxiety and, (5) experimental neurosis. The Russian contributions to the first three areas have been reviewed by Razran (1961).

Interoceptive Conditioning: Although there is no doubt that interoceptive processes are involved in conditioning, the methodological difficulties confronted in examining their role prohibited the collection of accurate data on the topic for many years. Pavlov himself attempted interoceptive conditioning early in his research career but discarded it in favor of work on the salivary response, which he found easier to measure and observe. Two methods have been employed in interoceptive conditioning: (1) fistulas, which permit direct stimulation of the viscera from the exterior of the animal and (2) balloons, which are swallowed and then inflated to provide a stimulus to the interoceptive system. These techniques have been used, especially in Russian laboratories, on both animals and human beings.

Using fistulas in different intestinal locations on dogs, Moiseyeva (1952) trained the animals to differentiate between stimuli applied to the ileal and cecal sections of the small intestine. Using salivation and paw withdrawal as the CRs, she was able to train dogs to respond when one area was distended but not when the other was. Vasilevskaya (1948; 1950) conditioned paw withdrawal in response to distension of the duodenum. The distension was paired with shock. After 129 trials, the shock was replaced by, not paired with, a buzzer. This is known as *second-order conditioning.* After a few trials, the buzzer produced paw withdrawal even though it was never paired simultaneously with the shock.

It has been suggested that interoceptive conditioning may explain the observation that persons sometimes report kinesthetic and cutaneous sensations from an amputated limb. Ayrapetyants (1952) has written of a patient with a colostomy who continued to report the urge to defecate even after the surgical removal of the rectum. Razran (1961) considers this phenomenon a result of "natural" interoceptive conditioning, by which he means that the normal physiological responses have been conditioned to external stimuli. It is important to remember that such conditioning is occurring continuously and that conditioning is not merely an artificial, isolated phenomenon obtained in the laboratory.

Verbal Behavior: The great majority of work on conditioning verbal behavior has used the principles of instrumental training (Chapters 7 and 15), but classical conditioning has been used successfully to alter verbal responses. Razran (1939) conditioned salivary responses in three human subjects to the words "style," "urn," "freeze," and "surf," and noted that the magnitude of the response was greater to "fashion," "vase," "chill," and "wave" than to "stile," "earn," "frieze," and "serf." The data suggest that the subjects generalized along the dimension of meaning, rather than along the dimension of sound, for the homonyms (surf-serf) showed less generalization than synonyms (surf-wave). Using salivation as the CR, Volkova (1953) conditioned a boy to respond to the Russian word for "18," and to differentiate between "18" and "14." He then presented the subject with mathematical problems, such as $9 + 9 = ?$ and $9 + 5 = ?$ In general, those problems which had 18 as the answer produced more saliva than those which had 14 as the answer.

Lacey, R. L. Smith, and A. Green (1955) presented a list of words to human subjects and asked them to say any word in response to the original stimulus words. For some of the subjects, the word "cow" was a critical word; after providing the response to "cow," the subjects received a small electric shock. For another group of subjects, the word "paper" was critical, for electric shock followed the response. Among the list were some words that would be commonly associated with farms, such as "tractor" and "haystack." GSR, heart rate, and blood flow were measured as the subjects responded to the words. The farm words were used, of course, to provide a measure of generalization to the critical word "cow." The investigators also included two important variables in their design: (1) a measure of the extinction rate of the CR (this was measured on the assumption that one test of the strength of acquisition is the amount of time required for extinction to occur) and (2) a measure of the effect of awareness of the difference between the critical word and other test words.

In order to examine the effect of awareness, the experimenter informed some subjects but not others that they would be shocked on the critical words. When the changes in heart rate were examined, the informed subjects showed a much higher rate (presumably indicating a higher level of anxiety) than uninformed subjects, although the heightened response adapted as the trials were continued. One result of informing the subjects was that the emotional reaction was heightened before conditioning was begun. Figure 13–4 shows the amount of generalization of the CR to other farm words as a function of whether the subjects were aware or not. Note that there is little difference between the aware and unaware groups in terms of amount of generalization. Note, too, that the extinction procedure shows a decrease in the amount of generalization.

A serious experimental problem arises, however; note that on trial 1 the two groups were unequal in performance. If we set the performance on the first trial as equivalent for each group, the functions shown in Figure 13–5 appear. Treated in this fashion, both groups continue to show generalization, as well as extinction of generalization, but the difference between the aware and unaware subjects appears greater. It may be argued that the fact that the subjects differed on trial 1 is ample evidence that they were not from the same population and that adjusting the scores so the groups start at an equal point does not remove the objection that they were different in response rates before additional trials were conducted. Nevertheless, the results indicate the probability of both conditioning and generalization of classically conditioned verbal behavior.

Orienting Reflex: One of the tacit assumptions of classical conditioning is that the US and UR are stable. In a somewhat mechanistic fashion, it has been assumed often that a specific US always evokes a specific UR. Observation indicates, however, that this is not necessarily true. Anyone who has attempted

FIGURE 13–4: *The effect of awareness on the generalized heart-rate response. A positive response indicates greater heart-rate response to the farm words, excluding the conditioned word "cow," than to nonfarm words. The first block of trials compares reactions to the second, third, and fourth farm words with reaction to the second, third, and fourth nonfarm words. This procedure for presenting the results appears as "moving blocks of three," which are plotted along the abscissa. The ordinate shows the response difference between farm and nonfarm words in heart-rate units. (From Lacey, R. L. Smith, & A. Green, 1955, p. 212.)*

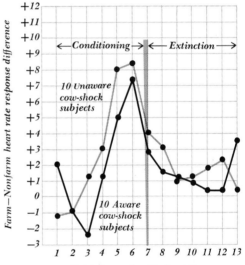

Trials in moving blocks of three

to train a dog to "sit" or "beg" by reinforcing the animal with food for the appropriate response knows that the attention of the animal varies from trial to trial. On some occasions he is alert with ears upright, and on other occasions he is placid with ears drooping. Animal trainers are aware that a dog must be slightly excited if rapid conditioning is to occur; conditioning is difficult if the animal is either placid or too excited. The reaction that accompanies the simple presentation of sen-

FIGURE 13–5: *A replot of Figure 13–4, showing the functions when the initial-response differences of the two groups are equated and set equal to zero. (From Lacey, R. L. Smith, & A. Green, 1955, p. 212.)*

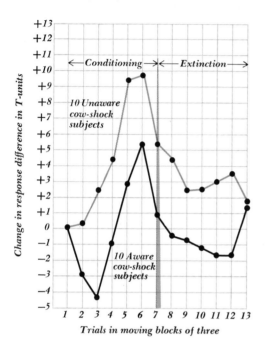

previous presentations of the stimulus but merely that the stimulus possesses the **OR** evoking novelty for only a limited number of presentations—the exact number depending upon a variety of parameters... after which the stimulus either evokes no reaction at all or a reaction that is different from an **OR**.

One of the changes in experimental procedures which has made the study of the OR useful has been the reliance, particularly among Russian investigators, on taking a variety of measurements during conditioning, such as GSR, vasoconstriction of vessels, kinesthetic reactions, and respiratory changes. The emphasis on measures other than a single CR has indicated that many disparate responses are both acquired and extinguished during conditioning.

Phylogenetic differences in the kind as well as in the strength of CRs have been noted. Although the dog shows an OR to "rustling sounds" similar to those which may be produced by the presence of another animal, the OR extinguishes rapidly. Hares show a strong OR to rustling sounds (Klimova, 1958). After 240 presentations of the stimulus of rustling sounds, the hare's respiratory responses to the sound failed to extinguish. Among other strong ORs cited by Razran (1961, p. 115) are "the sight of a cat for owls, the odor of rosemary and hunters' decoy sounds for ducks, the displacement of objects in the field of vision and sucking sounds for hares, the sound of wood splintering for beavers, and the sound of waves splashing for fish."

sory stimuli is known as the orienting reflex (OR). One of the reasons the OR has failed to receive the experimental attention it deserves is that experimenters have been concerned more with the parameters of conditioning than with the parameters of preconditioning. Pavlov recognized the existence and importance of the OR, but he considered it too subjective to admit to experimentation. Advances in recording techniques and in physiological measurements have led to a revitalization of interest in the OR, especially among Russian psychologists and physiologists.

Razran (1961, p. 111) defines the OR as:

...the organism's normal first reaction to any adequate normal stimulus or, in terms of the stimulus, it is the organism's normal reaction to a normal *novel* stimulus. Novelty does not mean no

There is some evidence that the OR may be used to differentiate "normal" from schizophrenic persons. Figure 13–6 shows the number of schizophrenic, normal, and brain-injured subjects who responded with an OR to an auditory stimulus. Differences of this kind are also found between retarded and normally intelligent children (Dolin, Zborovskaya, & Zamakhover, 1958). Biryukov (1958) has reported that ORs appeared strongly in fox cubs who were presented with the sounds of squeaking mice. Eventually, the OR extinguished. When the cubs were permitted to dine on one of the mice, however, the OR became strong again and was, within the limits of the experiment, unextinguishable. Thus the OR can be reinstated, at least in some situations, by the re-presentation of the extinguished stimulus.

The importance of the study of the OR is that it represents an attempt to understand the nature of unconditioned stimuli and responses which have long been neglected in favor of the conditioned stimuli and responses. Available data suggest that the UR is not so stable as has been supposed and that it too may be "conditioned"; the finding that the UR can be extinguished provides the opportunity for a variety of URs to be used for classical conditioning.

Anxiety: Anxiety is of great importance to several theories of personality development, probably because it appears to accompany many neurotic conditions. There is, however, lack of agreement on which behaviors indicate anxiety. Changes in the GSR, in respiration, or in blood pressure are used as physiological indicators of anxiety; defecation and urination are commonly used to measure anxiety in animals; and certain types of tests are designed to evaluate the level of anxiety in human beings.

The concept of anxiety appears to have two general interpretations: First, it is sometimes assumed to be a normal component of organisms. Its strength or level is believed to vary, depending upon the kind of stimulation. Second, anxiety is sometimes assumed to be a response to unpleasant and noxious stimuli; it is assumed to be a drive, for organisms will learn responses that reduce or eliminate anxiety. This interpretation is used to explain why responses that have been conditioned by the use of negative reinforcers are often difficult to extinguish. Most commonly, the experimental literature uses the second interpretation of anxiety, perhaps because the concept of anxiety as a drive is a useful explanatory device in the study of learning.

The role of anxiety in learning and performance is complicated. Although it is true,

FIGURE 13-6: *The proportion of schizophrenic, normal, and brain-injured subjects giving either an OR, a defensive reaction, or no reaction at all to a stimulus yielding equal auditory stimulation. The numbers within the areas indicate the number of subjects giving the response within that group. (Modified from Gamburg 1958, pp. 273, 278, n.s.; see Razran, 1961, p. 115.)*

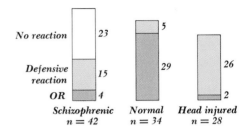

in general, that a little anxiety is efficacious for conditioning, too much anxiety renders conditioning difficult, if not impossible. If anxiety is a drive, however, it should also motivate behavior; e.g., the anxious student should be more highly motivated and should perform better than the student who is not anxious. Nevertheless, the student who is very anxious about an examination often finds himself making unnecessary mistakes and attributing his errors to excessive anxiety.

Studies concerned with the relationship between anxiety and performance have most often used the *Taylor Manifest Anxiety Scale* (MAS) (J. A. Taylor, 1953) to assess the anxiety level of human subjects. This kind of assessment uses the first interpretation of anxiety, i.e., that individuals have different basal "amounts" of anxiety. The scale, which was taken from the *Minnesota Multiphasic Personality Inventory* (MMPI), asks the subject to determine whether a number of statements are descriptive of his behavior. The items are largely concerned with physical symptoms, such as "I sweat a great deal." The validity of the MAS, as measured by the correlation between test scores and independent judgments of clinical psychologists, is not entirely satisfactory. J. A. Taylor (1951) selected a "high-anxiety" group and a "low-anxiety" group on the basis of scores on the MMPI and then conditioned the eye-blink response. The anxiety levels of the two groups were experimentally manipulated through the use of instruction. One-half of each group (designated plus) was told that the intensity of the US (an air puff) would be increased; the other half of each group (designated minus) was told that the intensity would be decreased. In all cases, however, the intensity of the US remained constant throughout testing.

Figure 13–7 shows the results in terms of the percentage of CRs given by the four subgroups as a function of the number of trials. First, high-anxiety subjects are apparently easier to condition than low-anxiety subjects. This finding supports the general idea that anxiety is useful in increasing the probability of conditioning. It does not, however, indicate whether too much anxiety limits conditioning. Second, for both low- and high-anxiety subjects, the percentage of conditioned re-

sponses evoked increases as a function of the number of trials. Studies that have used a simple conditioning technique, such as the eye blink, have consistently noted this difference, but results of studies using more complex tasks, such as learning a maze, have often been equivocal. Such findings suggest that the complexity of the task may determine the role of anxiety in learning (see G. A. Kimble, 1961, p. 448, for a review of these studies). Third, Figure 13–7 shows that the use of different instructions for the various subgroups did not increase or lower anxiety enough to affect conditioning.

Experimental Neurosis: Around 1914, Pavlov reported the following experiment: A dog was conditioned to salivate when a circle was presented as the CS. This was accomplished by feeding the animal whenever the circle was shown. Then the dog was taught to differentiate between the circle and an ellipse with a ratio between the semiaxes of 2:1, by providing punishment when one stimulus was shown and food when the other stimulus appeared. In Pavlov's words (1927, p. 291):

A complete and constant differentiation was obtained comparatively quickly. The shape of the ellipse was now approximated by stages to that of the circle (ratios of the semi-axes of 3:2, 4:3, and so on) and the development of differentiation continued through the successive ellipses. The differentiation proceeded with some fluctuations, progressing at first more and more quickly, and then again slower, until an ellipse with ratio of semi-axes 9:8 was reached. In this case, although a considerable degree of discrimination did develop, it was far from being complete. After three weeks of work upon this differentiation not only did the discrimination fail to improve, but it became considerably worse, and finally disappeared altogether. At the same time the whole behavior of the animal underwent an abrupt change. The hitherto quiet dog began to squeal in its stand, kept wriggling about, tore off with its teeth the apparatus for mechanical stimulation of the skin, and bit through the tubes connecting the animal's

FIGURE 13–7: *The percentage of conditioned responses plotted against trials in an experiment designed to determine whether performance, in terms of the learning curve, is superior in anxious or nonanxious subjects. (From J. A. Taylor, 1951, p. 86.)*

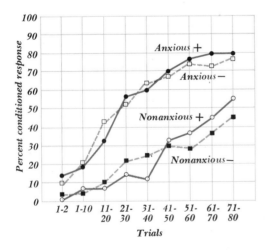

room with the observer, a behavior which never happened before.

Pavlov also reported (1927, p. 293) that neurotic behavior could be produced by extending the delay between the CS and US. Although conditioning was simultaneous at the onset of training, the delay was extended by five seconds each day. One dog, selected for his mild temperament, learned to tolerate increasing delays without undue difficulty. Another, selected for his excitable temperament, showed "neurotic" behavior when the delay surpassed three minutes. According to Pavlov, "the animal became quite crazy, unceasingly and violently moving all parts of its body, howling, barking and squealing intolerably" (1927, p. 294).

Classical conditioning procedures have been used to produce experimental neurosis in sheep (Liddell, 1938), rats (S. W. Cook, 1939), and cats (Masserman, 1943). They have also been used to extinguish "neurotic" or inappropriate behavior. Max (1935b) reports the use of electric shock on a subject who showed homosexual behavior following the presentation of a certain stimulus. By pairing the shock with the stimulus, Max claims to have extinguished the homosexual reaction.

A form of interoceptive conditioning has been suggested by O. H. Mowrer and W. M. Mowrer (1938), who developed a procedure for eliminating enuresis. The subject's bed is wired in such a way that a buzzer is sounded as soon as the bed becomes wet. The buzzer serves to awaken the subject, and the kinesthetic reactions associated with a full bladder also serve as cues to awaken him. In their original study these investigators reported success with all thirty of their subjects. B. Martin and Kubly (1955) report that of 118 parents who used the method on their children, 74 percent reported success.

Both classical conditioning and instrumental learning are being applied to a variety of maladaptive behaviors. The assumption is that since most, if not all, such behaviors are learned, the way to eliminate them is to discover how they are acquired and how they may be extinguished. Most approaches use instrumental training.

SOURCES

Discussion of classical conditioning can be found in the major sources that discuss principles of learning, such as Bugelski (1956) and Deese (1958). G. A. Kimble (1961) has revised the Hilgard and Marquis' book (1940) to provide the most comprehensive discussion of classical conditioning available. Prokasy (1965) has edited a volume on various aspects of classical conditioning. The advanced reader will find many of the papers in this book stimulating and useful. Deese and Hulse (1967) also consider this material.

Two collections of Pavlov's works are available in English (Pavlov, 1927; 1928a; 1928b). The latter has been published in paperback (1960). In his classic textbook, Woodworth (1938) discusses the relevance of classical conditioning, as it was understood at the time of writing, to human behavior. C. T. Morgan (1965), in a text on physiological psychology, has a chapter on conditioning which includes some information on the role of the central nervous system.

CHAPTER FOURTEEN

INSTRUMENTAL AND OPERANT TRAINING

INTRODUCTION

One important characteristic of the classically conditioned response is that reinforcement, if it occurs at all, is not involved in the conditioning process. Depending upon one's definition of *reinforcement* (Chapter 12) it is possible to consider the US as a reinforcement in classical conditioning. Nevertheless, there is little that is gratifying in salivation, jerking the knee, of blinking the eye. It is reasonable, although not entirely accurate, to think of classical conditioning as a type of stimulus association, for the experimental manipulations involve the substitution of one stimulus for another by pairing. In the manipulations used to achieve instrumental learning, however, reinforcement is an essential component of the procedure, for the response determines whether or not there will be reinforcement.

This important distinction in procedure explains why the term *instrumental* is used, for the response is instrumental in the acquisition of the reinforcement. Thorndike's experiments with cats (Chapter 12) demonstrate an example of instrumental learning; the act of escaping from the cage is instrumental in the acquisition of food. Moreover, in several critical attributes, the procedures used in Thorndike's studies clearly differ from those used in classical conditioning: (1) Thorndike did not select a reflex as the response. The response (escape from the cage) is an action of which the animal is capable, but it is not a reaction already attached to a given stimulus. (2) The animal acquired a *new* response. The precise movements required in manipulating the puzzle box were not within the animal's repertoire of responses before the procedure began. Rather, the investigator selected the appropriate response and reinforced the animal when it occurred. (3) Reinforcement was given only if the animal completed the specified response. Effectively, the investigator waits until the animal makes the appropriate response. In classical conditioning, on the contrary, the stimuli are presented at predetermined intervals.

Skinner (1938) points out that classical conditioning might be called *respondent learning,* for the response is evoked by a given stimulus. Instrumental learning is separate, for the correct response appears, more or less spontaneously from among the responses available to the organism. Some authorities (e.g., Mowrer, 1947b) have suggested that the term *conditioning* be applied only to classical conditioning situations, for there is reason to suppose that instrumental behaviors are not conditioned so much as they are trained. Since the number of possible operant behaviors is limited only by the number of responses that an organism can make, instrumental learning may include trial-and-error learning, such as that investigated by Thorndike, problem solving, and many other kinds of learned behaviors that are not necessarily "conditioned." These fine distinctions are somewhat more than mere quiblings over terminology, for the different usages and the intensity with which one argues for his own particular definition indicate that the differences between classical conditioning and instrumental learning are complex. As we shall note, classical conditioning involves some operant responding, and instrumental learning usually involves some classical conditioning.

OPERANT TRAINING

A baby in his crib makes many movements which, to an observer, appear to be random. His legs and arms move, his eyes dart, he responds to sudden sounds by lying still or by turning his head, he gurgles or cries. The number of possible responses is infinite, determined only by the precision with which the observer cares to define them. The baby cries, and suddenly he is given a bottle of warm milk. The movements cease for the most part, and the responses are relegated to movements in and around the mouth as the baby drinks. Soon the bottle is empty, and the random movements begin again, or he falls asleep.

To be anthropomorphic, we might say that the baby does not know which of his random movements led to the appearance of the bottle, but he soon learns that there is some connection, particularly between his vocal responses and the bottle. Soon he learns that not all vocal responses have the same affect: gurgling and cooing fail to produce the milk, but crying is effective in producing it. Now the physiological changes that accompany hunger become associated with crying, and the hunger pangs bring out the response of crying. So long as the parent is willing to provide milk whenever the baby cries, the baby has learned that a particular response brings about a particular end.

This example suggests two important characteristics of operantly controlled behavior: (1) The connection between response and reinforcement is not learned suddenly. The organism learns to discriminate these responses which lead to reinforcement from those which do not. (2) Any response can serve; if movement of the left leg resulted in the appearance of the bottle on every occasion, the response of moving the left leg would be acquired. Any of a number of discrete responses can be used as the appropriate response in studies of operant behavior. Finally, it is interesting to inquire *who* has been conditioned: the child who cries or the parent who provides milk each time he hears crying.

In studies of operant behavior, learning is assumed to exist if the frequency of the response is increased. If the frequency declines, it is assumed that the response is undergoing extinction. From the example of the baby, Figure 14–1 shows the frequency of occurrence of a variety of behaviors: left and right leg movement, left and right arm movement, respiration rate, gurgling, and crying. From the onset, reinforcement (in the form of milk) is given only when the child cries for more than ten seconds. It is evident that the frequency of crying for ten seconds or longer is increasing, although the frequency of other operant behaviors is decreasing. The figure indicates that operant learning may be thought of as a specific response, the reinforcement of that response alone, and the eventual increase in fre-

FIGURE 14-1: *Records of a baby's behavior. The rectangles indicate the presence and duration of a response. For example, four discrete movements are recorded from the right leg early in the record. Respiration is recorded in waves rather than in discrete units. The baby is given a bottle only if he cries long enough, in this example over ten seconds. Note that the first two cries are unreinforced, for they are not of sufficient duration. When the baby cries for longer than ten seconds, reinforcement in the form of a bottle of milk is given, and the response rate of the other responses declines.*

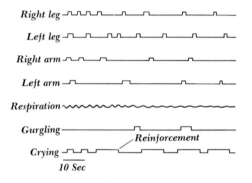

quency of the response selected. Note that the first reinforcement occurs not only when crying has persisted but also at the time of left-arm and right-leg movement and gurgling. Since these responses will not always occur simultaneously, and since only crying is reinforced, the child will learn that it is the crying, not the other responses, that produces reinforcement.

Just as the chemist analyzes complex compounds by breaking them into their molecular parts, so the psychologist interested in operant behavior reduces complex behavior into smaller segments in order to permit accurate measurement. Accordingly, the kinds of responses selected for experimental attention *appear* trite, such as pecking responses of chickens and pigeons, bar-pressing responses among rats or primates, including human beings, and other precisely defined movements

in many types of organisms. Theoretically, no matter what response is selected, so long as it is sufficiently discrete to permit accurate measurement, acquisition and extinction functions are very similar. In addition, the characteristic phenomena of operant learning, which we shall discuss later in this chapter, occur regardless of the nature of the response selected. The choice of a response, then, is often determined by the equipment available or by other experimental considerations. Investigators concerned with operant behavior are not interested in the chicken's pecking responses as such: they merely use this response for experimental convenience, assuming that their findings will be representative of other operantly controlled behavior.

REINFORCEMENT

The role of reinforcement is the major distinguishing feature between classical conditioning and instrumental learning. We noted in Chapter 12 that the term *reinforcement* has several meanings. When it is used in reference to operant behavior, however, it is used operationally; that is, whatever stimulus serves to increase the frequency of responding is called a *reinforcer*.

Although we have no completely satisfactory definition of *reinforcement*, the quality and quantity of the reinforcer have definite effects upon performance. The distinction between *learning* and *performance* renders it impossible to note the effects of reinforcement upon learning, but there are ample data to show that performance varies as a function of the reinforcer. The quantity of reinforcement refers to the physical specification of the reinforcer: it may be 5 grams of food or 1 ml of water. The quality of reinforcement refers to the organism's preference for the reinforcer. Monkeys generally prefer bananas to steaks, and a 10-gram steak does not have the same reinforcing value for them as a 10-gram banana. Similarly, a hungry human being will find

20 grams of food preferable to 20 grams of water. The quality of the reinforcer is determined by (1) the innate physiological and sensory preferences of the organism, (2) the learned preferences, particularly among human beings, and (3) the physiological state of the organism, e.g., whether he is hungry or thirsty.

Among the parameters of reinforcement are (1) the schedule of reinforcement, (2) the amount of reinforcement, (3) the number of reinforcements, (4) a change in the amount of reinforcement, (5) the temporal relationship between response and reinforcement, and (6) the secondary reinforcement. We shall consider these parameters in some detail.

Schedules of Reinforcement: It is advantageous, in considering the descriptions of the major schedules of reinforcement, to keep in mind a particular experimental situation. We may wish to think of a rat pressing a bar, with food or water as the reinforcement, of a chicken pecking at a disk in order to acquire grain, or of a child pulling a lever to acquire candy. Perhaps most usefully, we may think of how we ourselves would behave under the different schedules. The apparatus shown in Figure 14–2 is commonly used in studies of operant training. In the laboratory, the apparatus is connected to a group of electronic panels which automatically record responses, reinforcements, or any of several other features of the experimental situation which the experimenter wishes to control or measure.

We may distinguish two classes of schedules: the first is known as *continuous reinforcement;* the second class, in which not every appropriate response is reinforced, is known as *intermittent,* or *partial, reinforcement* (D. J. Lewis, 1960). Generally, organisms are trained under *continuous reinforcement* (crf) in order to encourage rapid learning. In real life, of course, very few responses are reinforced under a crf schedule.

The basic schedules are determined by two variables: (1) whether the number of responses or length of time is critical and (2) whether the number of responses or length of time is fixed or variable.

The four basic intermittent schedules of reinforcement are the following:

1. *Fixed ratio* (FR): **A fixed number of responses must be emitted before reinforcement. For example, if five responses are required, we have an FR5 schedule. In this schedule the rat must press the bar five times: on the fifth response, reinforcement occurs. He must then press five more times to acquire another pellet of food. Note that crf is identical to FR1.**

2. *Variable ratio* (VR): **The same ratio rule holds, i.e., that reinforcement depends upon the number of previous responses; however, the number of required responses is variable. For example, the rat may have to make 5 responses for reinforcement, then 2, 1, 7, 6, 9, and so on. For descriptive purposes, the VR designation is followed by the mean number of responses required for reinforcement. In the example, 5, 2, 1, 7, 6, and 9 responses were required, so the schedule is a VR5.**

Both these schedules are concerned with the number of responses required of the organism. For that reason they are both called *ratio schedules,* although the ratio may be either fixed or variable. One may also develop schedules based upon time. These are known as *interval schedules.* There are two classes, fixed and variable, of interval schedules too.

3. *Fixed interval* (FI): **In an FI schedule, the first appropriate response *after a given length of time* is reinforced. For example, the subject must wait five minutes—any responses made before that will not be reinforced. The first response after the termination of the five-minute period will be reinforced. After reinforcement, the five-minute period begins again. Note that a response is required: it does not matter how much more than five minutes elapses before the response is made, so long as the five-minute period is completed. In this textbook, the required interval of time is noted in minutes; e.g., FI5 means that a five-minute delay is required, and FI.5 means that an interval of half a minute is required.**

FIGURE 14-2: *An operant-training chamber, commonly called the* Skinner box. *The bar, or whatever feature of the chamber is manipulated by the organism, is called the* manipulandum. *In experiments where the animal must be able to discriminate one feature of the chamber from another, such as the color of the light shown in the chamber, these characteristics are called* discriminanda. *(Courtesy of Ralph Gerbrands Co.)*

4. *Variable interval* (VI): The length of the delays required in a VI schedule is variable. The required time may be 5 minutes, then 10 minutes, no minutes, and so on. As with VR, the mean of the intervals is usually shown, as VI5, VI7, etc.

It is possible, of course, to combine these four basic schedules in a variety of ways. Seven combinations are common:

1. *Alternate* (alt): Reinforcement is provided under either a ratio or an interval schedule, whichever the organism satisfies first. For example, consider an *alt FR20 FI5*. Reinforcement will occur in either of two ways: (*a*) after 20 responses have been made (assuming that the five minutes have not elapsed) or (*b*) upon the first response after five minutes (assuming that less than 20 responses have been made).

2. *Conjunctive* (conj): On a conjunctive schedule, reinforcement appears only after *both* schedules have been satisfied. Either may be satisfied

first, or both may be satisfied simultaneously. For example, using a *conj FR20 FI5*, reinforcement would appear after one of three ways of reaching the criteria had been reached: (*a*) the organism could respond 20 times, then wait five minutes, after which his next response would bring reinforcement; (*b*) the organism could wait five minutes, then respond 20 times, after which reinforcement would occur; (*c*) the organism could respond 20 times in a five-minute period to receive reinforcement. In all three modes of responding, *both* schedules have been satisfied. It is important to note the distinction between this type of schedule and a tandem schedule (discussed later) in which only one method of responding will produce reinforcement.

3. *Interlocking* (interlock): In this schedule, reinforcement is determined by the number of responses made, but the number required changes as a function of the intervals between reinforcement. The change in the requirement is usually linear. For example, 200 responses are required for the first reinforcement, 150 for the next, and so on. In this case, each reinforced response changes the schedule by x − 50. The more responses the organism makes, the quicker he passes into the next category, and the fewer responses are required to reach the next category.

4. *Tandem* (tand): The completion of one schedule starts another schedule. When the second schedule is completed, reinforcement occurs. For example, in a *tand FI20 FR10*, the organism must wait twenty minutes (no responses during this interval are reinforced) and then make 10 responses. The 10 responses must occur after the twenty-minute interval has elapsed.

5. *Chained* (chain): Chained schedules are identical to tandem schedules with one important exception: a stimulus is used to indicate the end of the first schedule. Under a *chain FI20 FR10*, a light, tone, or other stimulus appears when the FI portion of the schedule is completed. In tandem schedules, no stimulus is used.

6. *Multiple* (mult): Two or more schedules are used, and the schedules appear randomly. Moreover, a stimulus is used to indicate which schedule is in effect. Under a *mult FI20 FR10*, a 5,000-Hz tone may be used to indicate that the FI

schedule is effective and a 2,000-Hz tone to indicate that the FR schedule is effective.

7. *Mixed* (mix): A mixed schedule is identical to a multiple schedule, except that cues are not used. That is, the schedule in effect is determined by some random process, and no stimulus signals which schedule is effective. In a *mix FI20 FR10*, either part of the schedule may be effective: the reinforcement for the first response may occur after twenty minutes, or it may appear after 10 responses.

Any intermittent schedule involves extinction during the acquisition sessions. Since one example of extinction is the occurrence of a response which does not result in reinforcement, only a crf schedule involves acquisition alone, for when some responses are unreinforced, as they are in intermittent schedules, extinction is present. The fact that different amounts of extinction occur during different schedules of reinforcement may account for the differences that occur in acquisition when different schedules are used.

Figure 14–3 shows an acquisition curve for an organism trained under crf but switched

FIGURE 14-3: *A cumulative record showing an animal on an FR25 schedule. The earlier section of the record, in which he was trained on crf, is shown for comparison. The downward hash marks indicate the occurrence of reinforcement.*

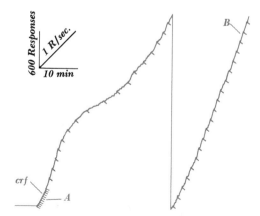

to FR25. The hash marks indicate the presentation of reinforcement on this cumulative record (Figure 12–6). The slopes in the box indicate the number of responses per minute in order to permit determination of the number of responses involved in any section of the record. Note that after the organism was trained on the FR25 schedule, the slope of the curve (point *b*) became very similar to that obtained when the organism was under a crf schedule (point *a*). When the pen reaches its upper limit, it resets rapidly to the starting position. Thus the vertical lines indicate the resetting of the pen.

Figure 14–4 shows a well-trained animal's record under an FR75 schedule. A well-trained organism on the FR schedule shows even responding. The *time intervals* between reinforcements are approximately equal, indicating that the responses are given at an even rate. After each reinforcement, there is a pause in responding (the pen moves horizontally) while the organism consumes the reinforcement. The FR schedule is clearly useful

FIGURE 14–4: *A well-trained organism operating under an FR75 schedule. The hash marks indicate points of reinforcement. The vertical lines represent the resetting of the cumulative recorders pen.*

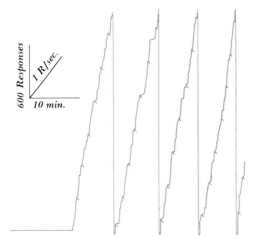

if one wishes to obtain a large number of responses by offering few reinforcers.

Figure 14–5 shows the extinction of the response acquired under an FR75 schedule. The extinction function is not smooth: the animal commonly shows a burst of responses and then has long periods without responses. In general, the slope of the functions decreases as the extinction test continues.

Under a VR schedule, the subject typically responds at a rapid and consistent rate. Like a slot-machine player, he never knows whether or not the next response will produce reinforcement. If the ratio is too high, extinction will occur. Figure 14–6 shows an organism operating under VR300. In order to achieve high VR rates, investigators usually train the organism progressively on higher and higher ratios. The animal, whose performance is shown in the figure, was trained on crf, followed by VR10, 30, 100, 240, and 300. The data indicate that between 2.5 and 3.5 responses are emitted per second under this schedule, although reinforced responses are few.

Extinction following training on VR schedules usually results in a high rate of responding. Since the organism is accustomed to variable periods of extinction during the acquisition of the VR schedule, the actual extinction session is very similar to acquisition. For this reason, a VR schedule is comparatively difficult to extinguish. The form of the extinction function will depend upon several factors, such as whether the ratios used during acquisition were relatively low or high, whether the ratios were changed upward or downward during acquisition, and the number of reinforcements that the organism received during acquisition. Compared with a typical FR schedule, VR schedules produce more responses with fewer reinforcements and are more difficult to extinguish.

The critical component of FI schedules is that a specified period of time must elapse before the appropriate response will be reinforced. Organisms trained under crf and shifted to FI schedules show a characteristic response pattern to the schedule. The organism learns not to make responses during the critical interval and to make responses near the end of the time period. Typically, the animal gives a burst of responses at the end of the period. Figure 14–7 shows the responses of an organism trained on crf but shifted to FI1. As the session continues, the animal ceases to respond immediately after reinforcement. Eventually he responds only as the time for reinforcement approaches. Thus, the FI schedule typically yields a scalloped cumulative record. We have noted a similar effect in classical conditioning, where the animal begins to salivate shortly before the presentation of the stimulus. An animal who has been on an FI schedule for some time yields few responses compared with an animal on a ratio schedule. Extinction following acquisition of an FI schedule generally results in a loss of the scalloping effect. The organism begins to respond during the intervals.

The VI schedule resembles the VR schedule in that there is no way for the organism to discriminate the pattern of reinforcement. Under both FI and FR the organism can learn to discriminate either how many responses are required or how much time must elapse. Under the variable schedules, the possibility of such discrimination does not exist. Figure 14–8 shows acquisition of a VI2. This schedule produces a rapid response rate, like the VR schedule. Apparently, since a variable pattern is in use, the organism has no way of determining whether he is being reinforced for responding or for permitting time to elapse.

There is no question that the schedule of reinforcement used in operant learning affects the rate of responding during both acquisition and extinction. Moreover, training on one schedule of reinforcement clearly affects the acquisition of responses on another schedule. There is an obvious difference in behavior between an organism trained on crf and shifted to FR20 and one trained on the FR schedule without the benefit of the crf training. Two questions regarding the importance of schedules of reinforcement may be noted: First,

FIGURE 14–5: *Extinction following training on an FR75 schedule. The bottom portion of the figure is a continuation of the top portion. Responding continues at a rapid rate through two resettings of the pen and then begins to be spotty. Finally (lower part) the animal fails to respond at all. For some species and certain schedules, responses during extinction can number in the ten thousands.*

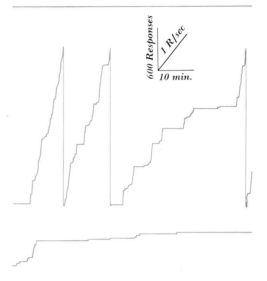

how stable are the effects of schedules within species? Do all animals of a given species respond to the schedules in the same way, or are there individual differences which lead to different response rates? Second, can one generalize from the behavior of the rat or chicken to the behavior of human beings? That is, are the effects of scheduling specific to the species tested? Both questions are available for experimental attack.

In regard to genetic differences, Skinner has argued that the effect of establishing functions by taking the average response rate of a group of subjects may mask true individual differences. This argument contains a blade that cuts two ways: first, if individual differences are presumed to be the result of conditioning and learning, then thorough investigation of the behavior of one organism should be under-

FIGURE 14-6: *An organism working under a VR300 schedule. The arrows point to the hash marks which show where reinforcement occurred. Since the ratio of responses to reinforcements is variable, the organism responds at a rapid and consistent rate.*

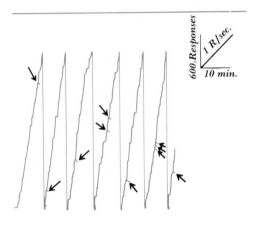

FIGURE 14-7: *Responding under an FI1 schedule. Reinforcement occurs following the first response after a time lapse of one minute. Note the scalloping that occurs when the animal begins to press just before the end of the period.*

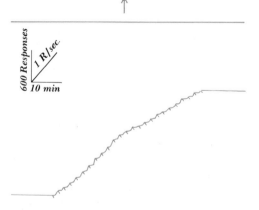

taken in preference to assessing the average behavior of a number of animals; second, if we are concerned with establishing general functions, the behavior of a single animal may be misleading; i.e., we cannot assume that the functions produced by one animal will necessarily be found in other animals.

Heron (1940) reports that response rates in the Skinner box differ between "maze-bright" and "maze-dull" rats. Rats were bred over many generations to produce one strain that learned mazes easily and one that did not. Heron found that maze-bright animals produced more responses than maze-dull animals under operant training. He also found that animals differed in the amount of activity they emitted. Figure 14–9 shows the cumulative records for an inactive and an active strain of rats (Heron, 1940). The records show a clear difference between the strains. There is an established relationship between hunger and activity, and it is probable that one source of the differences that appear in studies of operant conditioning is attributable to different levels of deprivation. Unfortunately, it is difficult to equate "degree of hunger" among animals. The strength of deprivation depends not only upon how long the animal has been without food but upon such factors as age, weight, sex, and previous deprivation history.

In regard to the problem of cross-species generalization, the major attributes of the schedules are similar for a variety of species. The FI schedule produces a scalloped record of responses, and the VR produces a relatively higher rate of responding. The species differences that do appear are probably attributable to the basic problems of establishing identical conditions for two or more species. For example, it is not a simple matter to make a human being as hungry as a rat, and since reinforcement value depends upon degree of deprivation, the degree of deprivation of the subject becomes a critical factor in response rate.

Amount of Reinforcement: As a general law, the amount of reinforcement is positively correlated with the strength of performance, in terms of the quality or quantity of the response. It should be mentioned, however, that the amount of reinforcement and the quality of the reinforcer are related: the greater the amount of reinforcement given, the less "quality" the reinforcement is likely to have. If a hungry rat is given a 1,000-gram pellet of food for responding, it is not likely that he will respond again, either because he will no longer be hungry after consuming this large pellet or because the food will no longer have the qualities of a reinforcer for him. Accordingly, the number of responses will be affected by the amount of reinforcement, even though within reasonable limits the greater the amount of reinforcement, the greater the performance (e.g., Hull, 1943; Zeaman, 1949; Guttman, 1954). Studies of the effect of the amount of reinforcement have commonly used a positive reinforcer, such as food, but data on the effect of a punishment, such as electric shock, suggest that the same general law holds (e.g., Boren, Sidman, & Herrnstein, 1959; G. A. Kimble, 1955).

Number of Reinforcements: The relationship between the strength of acquisition and extinction as a function of the number of reinforcements varies with many factors. For example, in a VI schedule we have many responses for very few reinforcers, and extinction is slow compared with a crf schedule in which each response is reinforced. Among partial schedules, there is a rough correlation between number of reinforcements and extinction, in that the greater the proportion of reinforced responses to unreinforced responses, the more difficult it is to reach extinction. The relationship between number of reinforcements and strength of learning is specific for the experimental situation, and no general law holds for all occasions.

Changing the Amount of Reinforcement: Changing the quantity of reinforcement will affect performance but will not necessarily alter learning. In a classic study, Crespi (1942) trained rats to run down a straight runway for food. Of the several groups used in this study, three are of special significance: one group trained on a large reward, one on a medium reward, and a third on a small reward. Dur-

FIGURE 14–8: *The responses of an organism on a VI2 schedule. Reinforcement occurs after the lapse of an average of two minutes.*

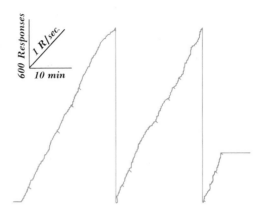

FIGURE 14–9: *Cumulative records for an active and an inactive strain of rats. (From Heron, 1940, p. 28.)*

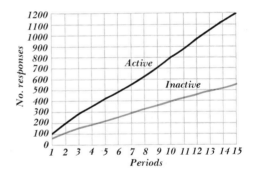

ing the period of acquisition, the running speeds of the animals were recorded as they ran down the alley to the food. The group that received the large reward ran fastest, and the group that received the smallest reward ran slowest. Then all three groups were placed on the medium reward. The large-reward group, upon being shifted to the medium reward, showed a *depression effect.* The small-reward grup showed an *elation effect.*

Figure 14–10 shows a schematic graph of these effects. It represents a reversal of rein-

FIGURE 14-10: *A stylized drawing of the Crespi effect. Curve A is for organisms trained under high reinforcement and curve B for those under low reinforcement. At point E the amount of reinforcement is shifted, resulting in the functions labeled C and D. (From J. A. McGeoch & Irion, 1952, p. 247.)*

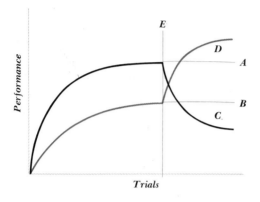

reinforcement affected performance during acquisition; second, the relationship between the amount of reinforcement before and after the shift was effective in decreasing or increasing the running speed.

The Crespi effect has been shown to occur mostly in higher organisms; some investigators, however, have been unable to obtain the effect. It appears that an important variable is whether or not the subjects have reached an asymptotic level of performance (i.e., a level over which performance will not usually increase) when the change in reinforcement is introduced (Spence, 1956; Heber, 1959; O'Connor & Claridge, 1958; J. B. Wolfe & Kaplon, 1941).

Temporal Relationship between Response and Reinforcement: In classical conditioning, the temporal relationship between the US and CS is a critical variable in determining the speed and quality of conditioning. In instrumental learning, the reinforcement may appear prior to, simultaneous with, or after the response. The exact relationship between the response and the reinforcement depends upon the type of response required. Pressing a bar for food is a reasonably discrete response: certainly it is more discrete than the complex pattern of movements involved in running down a runway.

Using the Skinner-box technique, Perin (1943) altered the period of delay of reinforcement—the time between the response and the reinforcement—from zero (simultaneous) to 20 seconds in intervals of 5 seconds. The speed of responding was found to be inversely related to the length of delay. The response speeds were highest when the reinforcement was simultaneous with the response and decreased as the interval was lengthened. There was almost no responding under the 20-second delay condition. Grice (1948), using a runway, found that the gradient was steeper. Zero delay produced the greatest performance; however, the function dropped off very quickly. The response strength at 0.5-second delay was only one-fourth of the strength at zero delay. Simi-

forcement levels for the large- and small-reward groups, rather than a shift to medium reward. Curve *A* shows the performance level of a group working under continuous high reinforcement. Curve *B* represents performance under low reinforcement. The shift in reinforcement levels occurs at point *E*. Curve *C* represents the performance of the group originally working under high reinforcement after the shift to low reinforcement. Note that the level of performance falls *below* that expected for a group working under continuous low reinforcement. This decrease in performance below curve *B* is representative of the depression effect. Curve *D* shows the performance of the low-reinforcement group after shift to the high level of reinforcement. Here the performance rises *above* curve *A,* representing the elation effect.

Presumably, the animals in all groups had learned to run equally rapidly (for they were able to do so when the reinforcement was shifted), but the actual running speed—the performance—depended upon the reinforcement in two ways: first, the actual amount of

lar results are obtained when aversive instrumental training is used: learning (or performance) is maximally efficient when the CS is terminated immediately by the response (Kamin, 1957a; 1957b). Accordingly, the general statement regarding the temporal relationship between the response and the reinforcement is that the more contiguous the two events, the greater the strength of performance.

Secondary Reinforcement: We noted in Chapter 12 the important role of secondary reinforcement in learning. Its chief characteristic is its ability to acquire the motivating properties of a reinforcer. Whenever a previously neutral stimulus becomes associated with a reinforcer, it may come to have the power of the original reinforcer in eliciting a response. In this case, the neutral stimulus is called a *secondary reinforcer*. In one study Mowrer and Aiken (1954) used punishment in order to examine the role of the secondary reinforcer. They first taught rats to bar-press. Then, a flickering light (CS) was paired with a shock (US) under the temporal arrangements shown in Figure 14–11. Note the differences in these arrangements. Group I received the light *before* the shock; the termination of the light—the secondary reinforcer—signaled the onset of shock. Group II did not receive a warning, for the light and shock appeared simultaneously. Group III was signaled that the shock would be terminated, for the light came on after the onset of the shock but they terminated together. Group IV was given the light at the termination of the shock, and group V, a control group, received only the shock, although the light was presented two minutes later. This design produces what has been called the "hope and fear" study, since, for some groups, the light signals the termination of shock (hope) and for other groups it signals that shock is on the way (fear).

Later, when the rats were bar-pressing for food, the CS—the light—appeared. Figure 14–12 shows the effects of the punishing secondary reinforcement—the light—on response

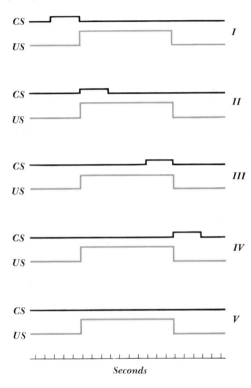

FIGURE 14–11: *Diagram of the five groups used in the "hope and fear" study. The diagrams show the relationship between the CS and the US in each of the groups. (Mowrer & Aiken, 1954, p. 28.)*

Seconds

rate. The light appeared after five minutes, and the data for the first five minutes represent control data accumulated without the introduction of the secondary reinforcer. Clearly, the presence of the secondary reinforcer depresses the rate of responding. The extent of the depression is in the order in which the groups were described. The greatest interference is for those groups in which the secondary reinforcer functioned as "fear," and the next greatest is for the groups in which the light functioned as "hope." Apparently, stimuli associated with the termination of punishment may also acquire the properties of a secondary reinforcer.

FIGURE 14–12: *Results of the "hope and fear" study. The first five minutes show free responding in which animals may bar-press. Then the light, which has been paired with shock, appears. Note the depression in the number of bar presses. Compare the degree of depression with the schedule each group received (as shown in Figure 14–11). (From Mowrer & Aiken, 1954, p. 29.)*

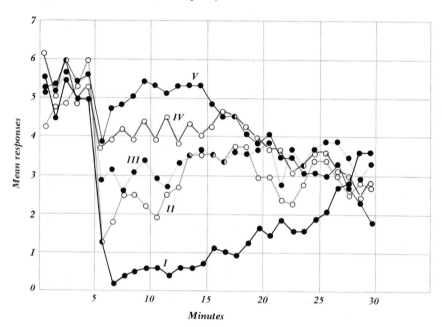

As is true of reinforcement in general, secondary reinforcement is affected by such variables as number of pairings with the original reinforcer, the interstimulus interval, and the amount of reinforcement. Although this issue is complicated by methodological differences, there is reason to suppose that drive level—in terms of the extent of deprivation—does not affect the development of a secondary reinforcer (see J. L. Myers, 1958).

DISCRIMINATION IN OPERANT TRAINING

Generalization occurs when the subject makes the appropriate response to stimuli similar but not identical to the stimulus used in prior conditioning or training situations. In classical conditioning, a dog may respond to the original CS of a 1,000-Hz tone as well as to a 1,005-Hz tone. Generalization occurs in operant learning as well as in classical conditioning, and there do not appear to be any major differences between the generalization gradients produced by the two. S. H. White (1958), among others, has shown that generalization gradients similar to those which occur in classical conditioning appear among children trained to press a lever when a visual stimulus appears (see Mednick & J. L. Freedman, 1960).

In operant training, reinforcement is used to set up the discrimination process. Generally, the organism learns to discriminate stimuli because a response to one is reinforced and responses to the others are not. We soon learn that driving through red lights brings a different kind of reinforcement from driving through green lights. Similarly, we learn to make some verbal responses in the presence of certain people (stimuli) but not in the presence of others.

In the terms of operant learning, the stimulus that results in reinforcement is known as the S^D (pronounced *ess dee*), and the stimulus that does not result in reforcement is called the S^Δ (pronounced *ess delta*). For example, the child who is learning the response necessary to obtain milk when he is hungry soon finds that crying serves as a stimulus to his parents which results in feeding. Gurgling and moving the right leg do not lead to feeding. The crying, therefore, is the S^D, and the gurgling and right leg movement are S^Δs. This type of operant learning may be investigated with subhuman forms. The organism may be trained to press a bar or peck at a key whenever the S^D appears but not to perform when the S^Δ appears. Indeed, an FI schedule of reinforcement requires the organism to determine the S^D (the time when the interval has elapsed) from the S^Δ (the lapse of time). The determination of appropriate S^Ds and S^Δs depends upon ascertaining the differential threshold of the organism for the stimuli.

One problem in learning to speak is the confusion of a minor category with a major category. One may point out to a child the presence of a "red car" in response to a child's question. The child may then refer to *all* cars as red until corrected. How is he to know that "car" and not "red" is the discriminative stimulus? Viewed in this way, the development of speech may be considered a process of discrimination. In part, literacy is determined by the precision with which one makes verbal discriminations. The person who distinguishes "she doesn't" from "she don't," "envy" from "jealousy," or many other refinements in a language is considered more literate than the person who does not. Moreover, the process of discrimination is closely related to what is commonly called "abstract" thinking. The

shape "circle" does not, for example, usually appear alone—it appears in conjunction with some other discrimination, such as a white circle or a large circle. Colors too do not exist without shape or size.

These "abstractions" are not simple stimuli which may be distinguished from other stimuli. Rather, they are components of many stimuli; they do not maintain an independent existence. We are not taught to discriminate "goodness" from other stimuli, for "goodness" is an abstraction that we learn by being told some of the characteristics of a "good" person. In the absence of perfect agreement on such characteristics, different people will make different discriminations regarding the concept. Similarly "Democrat" and "Republican" are stimuli which are discriminated because they are associated with other stimuli. There is no a priori difference between the terms, nor would we find anything approaching agreement on what the terms stand for. The abstractions that ultimately result in calling some persons "Democrats" and other persons "Republicans" may be created through many processes of discrimination.

Some authorities (cf. Keller & Schoenfeld, 1950) have suggested that an S^D, since it is associated with reinforcement, assumes reinforcing properties itself. If one has learned that Republicans are good, kind, generous, and warm, if this discrimination has become an S^D that has been reinforced, and if the S^Δ, consisting of alleged characteristics of the Democrats, has not been reinforced, the mere identification of an individual as a Republican could be sufficient to bring about reinforcing properties to the appendage "Republican."

The tendency to assume that higher-order behaviors are operantly learned, on the basis that they could not be learned through the principles of classical conditioning, may reflect an error in logic. On the other hand, the assumption may prove to be true. One difficulty is that it fails to account for achievement through maturation; e.g., it fails to account for our doubt that a one-month-old infant would learn to write legibly, no matter how much operant training was administered. Operant learning requires that the desired response or its components be among the responses already possessed by the subject; if the desired response is one that is quite frequently used by the subject prior to training, the training process will be easier.

It is possible to gain valuable knowledge about the development of behavior by observing the way a simple operant response is acquired and extinguished. Acquisition and extinction involve continuing processes of generalization and discrimination. Similarly the behavior of organisms represents an ongoing process of generalization and discrimination in which new responses are acquired and other responses are extinguished. Consider that we are training a rat to press a bar or a child to hold his head high. The rat is placed in a rather uninspiring chamber which contains a food cup and a bar; the child may have a more illustrious environment. Electric photocells are placed throughout the child's environment so that whenever the beam is broken by the presence of an object—hopefully, the child's head—an electric response is reported which can be used to trigger the presentation of some form of reinforcement. Similarly, the rat's bar press sets off an electric impulse which may be used for the same purpose.

Now, we wait for the correct response to occur. Eventually it will, provided it is within the organism's repertoire; however, the general lack of patience notable among both experimenters and parents suggests the need for aiding the process of acquiring the response. The technique that is used—whether by the knowing experimenter or the exasperated parents—is that of *successive approximations*. In this procedure, not greatly different from the childhood game of "You're getting hot, you're getting cold," we lead the subject to make the appropriate response by reinforcing the responses that are nearer and nearer in quality to the one we desire. That is, we do not wait for the child to lift his head the desired height. Rather, we reinforce the first response

that shows any raising of the head; next, we give reinforcement when he lifts his head a little higher. As to the rat, we reinforce him for approaching the general area of the food cup, then for standing on his hind legs, and finally, for touching the bar. When one level of achievement has been reached, it is unwise to continue to reinforce the same response; each time the organism should be required to approach the final goal a little more before reinforcement is given. Otherwise, a form of inertia will occur in which the organism learns to discriminate which movements "pay off" and which do not, just as a slot-machine player will learn which machines offer the greatest opportunity for reinforcement.

A knowledge of the development of operant learnings is essential for anyone charged with the control of the behavior of others. Consider the lesson to be learned from the child who throws temper tantrums (let us ignore the somewhat embarrassing question of how tantrums come to be a part of the behavioral repertoire in the first place). When parents decide that temper tantrums have gone too far, i.e., that they have become an embarrassment, the parents withdraw all recognition of the tantrums. The child screams louder. Still recognition or reinforcement is withheld: the parents wait for the tantrums to subside. No doubt, if all attention and reinforcement were actually withheld, the behavior would extinguish; however, we should not expect parents to be any less trained by operant techniques than their children. If occasional attention is given to the tantrums, the child is thus placed on a partial schedule of reinforcement. Accordingly, we would expect the behavior to be more difficult to extinguish, for partial reinforcement typically results in greater resistance to extinction than does continuous reinforcement. Following the procedures of the method of successive approximation, the parents might reinforce the lessening strength of each tantrum. Each tantrum that was notably less severe than the former would be reinforced, until, finally, the severity of the tantrums would be reduced to a minimum.

This procedure has a second advantage: we do not want to extinguish most responses totally. We want to permit them to appear under appropriate circumstances. During peacetime, aggression is not considered appropriate, during wartime, it is rewarded with medals. Generally, we do not want an overly aggressive child to lose all aggression, any more than we normally want a person with unusual sex desires to lose all sexuality. Usually, we want to establish an S^D and an S^Δ so that aggression and sexual behavior appear under appropriate circumstances.

In addition, generalization may be expected to occur. The reinforcement of aggression under one condition may generalize to produce aggression under other circumstances. In order to discriminate appropriate responses successfully, we must learn to discriminate the *response class*—those responses of the same nature (aggression, for example) which are produced by different stimuli. Operant learning is a constant process of generalization and discrimination; as one response is strengthened, another is weakened.

One of the more bitter debates in psychology raged over the problems of the processes underlying the generalization of stimuli that have been discriminated successfully. Consider the two stimuli shown in Figure 14–13. Assume that you have been trained to select the circle marked *B*. Now, consider the stimuli shown in Figure 14–14. Which do you choose?

If circle *C* is selected, you have responded to the actual, or absolute, size of the circle, since this circle is of the same size as *B*. If, however, you chose circle *D*, you have responded to the relationship between the size of the circles, for circle *B* is smaller than circle *A* and circle *D* is smaller than circle *C*.

There are ample data to support both the *absolute* theory (choosing *C*) of the generalization of discriminated stimuli and the *relational* theory (choosing *D*). Whether transposition is relational or absolute appears to depend upon the precise method used in training and the nature of the transposition test as well as upon the type of stimuli used. An

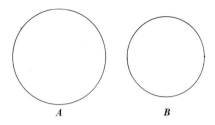

FIGURE 14–13: *Two stimuli used in a demonstration described in the text. Assume that you have been trained to respond to circle* B *but not to circle* A.

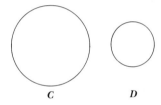

FIGURE 14–14: *Remembering that you have been trained to respond to circle* B *in Figure 14–13, to which circle in this figure do you respond?*

apparently neat test of the relative veracity of the two interpretations is offered by the technical difference between simultaneous and successive discrimination learning (Chapter 12). Under successive discrimination learning, the organism must retain some memory of the stimuli; under simultaneous learning, the stimuli are presented at the same time, and thus direct comparison is possible. Relational theory predicts that successive discrimination will be more difficult, and absolute theory suggests that the two techniques will not produce different results. The long series of conflicting results from studies based on this deceptively simple problem suggests only that rats and/or experimenters differ appreciably from laboratory to laboratory. In short, it is possible to get either result, depending upon the conditions used and the degree of similarity of the stimuli employed (see, for example, Spence,

1952; Bitterman & Wodinsky, 1953; MacCaslin, 1954). For Spence's theory of transposition learning see Spence (1936; 1937), and for experimental evidence see, especially, T. S. Kendler (1950), Ehrenfreund (1952), and D. H. Lawrence and DeRivera (1954).

Learning sets (Chapter 12) provide evidence regarding another form of generalization. Harlow (1949) presented monkeys with 312 discrimination problems (each set was presented six times) and measured the number of correct responses. Figure 14–15 shows the course of improvement. The four lower curves in the figure indicate progress during the first 32 trials, broken down into segments of 8 trials, and the top four curves show the percentage of correct responses during blocks of 100 successive trials. If one were to observe only the last few trials, one might conclude that in-

sightful learning had occurred (just as observation of Thorndike's cats would have suggested the same inference if one had watched them escape from the puzzle box). It is clear, however, that learning to learn is a measurable process which proceeds in an orderly fashion. Learning sets have been shown to occur in a variety of species from man (retarded and unretarded) to rats (see Harlow, 1949).

Reversal learning is often used in experiments as a rudimentary measure of learning to learn. The organism is trained to reverse his responses, e.g., to turn left on one trial and right on the next or to turn left one day and right the next day. If an organism is given 10 trials in which the right turn is the correct response and the rules are changed so that a left turn is the correct response, negative

FIGURE 14–15: *Discrimination-learning curves on successive blocks of problems in the learning-to-learn experiment. (From Harlow, 1949, p. 53.)*

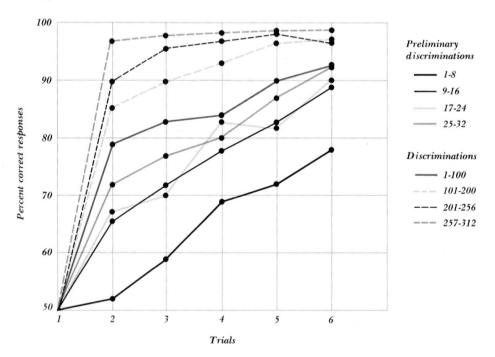

transfer occurs in that the organism will continue to make some right-turn responses before reversing himself. The less difficult the transfer (i.e., the fewer incorrect responses at the start of each session of trials), the better the organism has learned to reverse his responses.

THE EFFECTS OF PUNISHMENT

Punishment is one of the most common methods used by human beings to control behavior. But does punishment effectively alter behavior? An accurate answer requires precise stipulation of the type of punishment that is used and the conditions under which it is administered. Punishment does not always eliminate behavior. It may have very little effect, or in some cases it may increase the response.

Thorndike's influential law of effect (Chapter 12) stated in its initial form that punishment had an equal but opposite effect on performance compared to positive reinforcement. For example, if a child were praised for a given response, the strength of that response would increase at a certain rate. If, however, the child were given a comparable negative reinforcement for the response, the strength of the response would decrease at a comparable rate. Because of a series of experiments performed between 1913 and 1932, Thorndike altered his view of the efficiency of punishment (1932a). His data suggested that punishment did not necessarily render a response weaker. In a representative study, Thorndike (1932b) selected human subjects who were unfamiliar with the Spanish language. He gave them English words and asked them to guess the equivalent in Spanish. If the subject made the correct response, the experimenter said "Right"; if he made the wrong response, the experimenter said "Wrong." Note that the words "Right" and "Wrong" were presumed to have secondary reinforcing properties. The final test consisted of reexamining the subjects to determine the frequency with which they identified those words which had resulted in a "Right" reinforcement and those which had

resulted in a "Wrong" reinforcement. The results suggested that although "Right" increased the frequency of accurate responses, the reinforcement "Wrong" had little or no effect.

This study was criticized by several sources (see Stephens, 1934). One major criticism was that the response "Right" clearly identified the correct response while the response "Wrong" only signified that one of the alternatives was not correct but failed to indicate which was correct. Nevertheless, the weight of Thorndike's studies indicated that punishment and positive reinforcement were not merely opposite sides of a coin. Thorndike suggested that punishment lessens the strength of a response only indirectly; that is, when a response produces positive reinforcement, it is evident that repetition of that particular response will also produce positive reinforcement. When punishment follows a response, however, there is no obvious way for the organism to determine which of the alternative responses will produce positive reinforcement. Thus, punishment may be expected to produce more variability in behavior than positive reinforcement.

There is evidence that some forms of punishment can improve learning when applied to the correct response. Tolman, C. S. Hall, and Bretnall (1932) shocked human subjects when they made the correct turn in a maze and found that they learned the maze rapidly. Muenzinger (1934) found the same result using rats. These studies indicate the difficulty in defining *punishment*. If punishment is defined as an event that leads to a weakening of the strength of the response, these studies are not concerned with punishment at all, for the response was strengthened. The studies do indicate that if a normally noxious stimulus is used at appropriate intensities, it may serve as a cue for discriminating the correct response. There is additional evidence (Lohr, 1959) that shock may become a secondary reinforcer for rats. Moreover, it may be argued (Holland & Skinner, 1961; Mowrer, 1960a) that the withdrawal of positive reinforcement—during extinction, for example—is also punishment.

Negative reinforcement may be used in several different ways. In escape learning (Chapter 12), for example, the punishment is presented, and the organism must perform a specified response in order to escape it. In this kind of learning, a response is learned in order to terminate the punishment. In some avoidance situations, punishment is not present at all, but the organism learns to perform a response in order to avoid punishment. In this type of learning, the organism is not punished unless he fails to make the appropriate response. In another type of training, the organism's response produces the punishment. Clearly, these procedures differ greatly in regard to the relationship between punishment and response. Parents generally rely upon the last two procedures in training children. Typically, the child is told, "Either eat your dinner or you'll be punished," or "For putting your brother's hand in the waffle iron you shall receive a spanking." These are two very different types of training; in the first, punishment is administered if the appropriate response (eating) is not made, and in the other punishment occurs because a response was made. The first type of training attempts to generate behavior, and the second type attempts to suppress it.

The suppression of behavior has received considerable experimental attention, perhaps because suppression is the usual goal when punishment is administered. B. F. Skinner (1938) trained four rats to bar-press for food. Two rats were slapped each time they made the appropriate response, and two were not slapped. Figure 14–16 shows the results of this study in terms of the number of responses during two-hour sessions on two successive days. The animals that were punished emitted fewer responses during the first day of extinction than the control group. As the extinction was continued, the response rates of the two groups approached one another, and eventually the number of responses was identical for both groups. Skinner (1938) suggested that the results indicate that punishment is not really effective in altering the number of responses: it merely changes the rate of responding. If this conclusion is correct, the effect of punish-

FIGURE 14–16: *The effect of punishment on extinction. During the first ten minutes of extinction (indicated by the blackened area), all responses are slapped. Note that, although the rate of the slapped group is depressed for a time, it eventually returns to the rate of the group that was not punished. (Reproduced from The Behavior of Organisms: An Experimental Approach, by B. F. Skinner, copyright, 1938, by Appleton-Century-Crofts, Div. of Meredith Publishing Company.)*

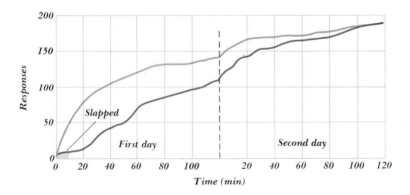

ing a child for a particular response will not lead to a weakening of the response; it will merely decrease the rate of responding for a time.

Estes (1944) continued the investigation of punishment in a thorough series of studies. He supplied current to the bar, so that the rat could receive either food or shock for the bar-press response. Estes too noted that shock suppressed the rate of responding but did not lower the total number of responses. He did note that if the shock was especially severe, the total number of responses tended to be suppressed slightly. In addition, Estes varied the schedules of punishment by supplying punishment on partial schedules. The effects of the partial schedules were similar to those noted when partial positive reinforcement was given: the decrement in response rate was not so severe as with continuous reinforcement, but extinction was more difficult.

The general finding that punishment is not successful in eliminating behavior has led some writers to emphasize the advantage of using positive reinforcement for training. Although punishment may not affect the total number of response, it does affect the probability of a response's occurring after punishment has been administered. There are certain responses, such as walking in front of moving vehicles, which, if not suppressed, do not permit the organism the opportunity of making additional responses. Although punishment may have a particular effect on the response that is punished, few data show the relationship of punishment to other similar responses: does punishment for the bar-press response generalize to similar responses?

The studies of Estes and B. F. Skinner show that punishment may result in what R. M. Church (1963) describes as *temporary* and *partial suppression*. In temporary suppression, complete recovery is indicated by the observation that the punished organism eventually produces as many responses as the nonpunished. In partial suppression, complete recovery never results. Total suppression, in which the response ceases altogether, has not been demonstrated, but it has been tacitly sug-

gested by the psychoanalytic theories of personality which assume that a single traumatic experience is sufficient to cause widespread changes in behavior.

Electric shock has been used as the punishing agent in the majority of studies concerned with punishment. The reason for the selection is that shock permits, superficially, control over the stimulus. The appealing fact that current may be defined in terms of its amperage and voltage, however, ignores two important considerations: First, electric shock is not a common punishing agent in the lives of animals, including human beings. More often punishment is administered to human beings by verbal comments or by bodily punishment. Second, although it is easy to specify the amount of current delivered, it is considerably more difficult to specify the amount the animal receives, because organisms provide resistance in electric circuits. Indeed, differences in electrical resistance are the major variable in the use of the GSR. The problem may be circumvented by measuring the resistance that the organism provides, but since resistance varies in short periods of time, continual adjustment of the input is necessary if the amount of shock is to be kept constant. Moreover, different kinds of electric currents produced different effects upon organisms (Campbell & Teghtsoonian, 1958).

Estes found that a slight decrement in total responses occurred when punishment was severe in either the intensity or the duration of the shock. This finding has been further considered by several investigators who have measured the effects of intensity of punishment on behavior. Azrin 1959, 1960; Azrin & Holz, 1961) trained pigeons to peck at a key under several schedules of reinforcement. Following the training, the subjects received currents of different intensities administered through small implanted electrodes. This procedure for administering shock is necessary with fowls, because the resistance furnished by their tough feet all but precludes the possibility of their receiving measurable amounts of current through the feet. Each animal served as his own control, for through a variety of sessions the subjects received each of the different intensities of shock available. The data indicate that low intensities fail to alter the response rate, moderate intensities depress the response rate, and severe intensities, such as 130 volts, suppress responses completely.

These results, along with those of other experimenters (see Appel, 1963; G. C. Walters, & J. V. Rogers, 1963; Karsh, 1962; Dinsmoor, 1952) indicate that the effect of punishment depends upon its intensity and duration. The finding that punishment merely reduces the rate of responding without altering the total number of responses is apparently true only when the punishment is relatively mild.

PUNISHMENT AS REINFORCEMENT

As Muenzinger (1934) and others have reported, punishment may lead to more rapid learning. Muenzinger's data were based on the performance of rats on a maze problem. Studies that have shown punishment to be ineffective have used a discrete response, such as bar pressing or pecking. Accordingly, investigators have suggested that the effects of punishment may depend upon the particular task, in addition to other features, such as the intensity or duration of the punishment. Holz and Azrin (1962) trained pigeons on an FI schedule with various intensities of current administered during the "time-out" interval. They found that the resultant pattern of responses was similar to that obtained from subjects trained without shock but with a green light used as a cue during the intervals. High intensities of current produced suppression of the response. Apparently, shock may serve as a discriminative stimulus, as may a neutral stimulus such as a light.

Muenzinger's (1934) study, which showed that punishment of the correct responses leads to an increase in the rapidity of learning, triggered a series of experiments that served to define further the relationship between punishment and learning. In the first study (1934)

rats shocked for the correct response did not differ in learning from those shocked for the wrong response. This finding emphasized that punishment did not have a specific effect on behavior. Muenzinger suggested that shock might slow the animal down at the choice point and force him to take more time to select the turn he would take. Muenzinger and A. Wood (1935) shocked one group of rats just before they made the choice and shocked another group just as they made the choice. The group shocked after making the choice learned more rapidly, indicating that the advantage of punishment was to slow down the organism.

In these studies, the *correction* method of learning was used. In correction, when the organism has erred in a choice, he is permitted to choose again until he makes the correct response. In *noncorrection* learning, the organism is not given the opportunity to try again. Wischner (1947) used the noncorrection method in a simple discrimination task. Animals punished for the wrong response learned more rapidly than those that did not receive punishment. A group that received punishment for correct responses did not differ from the group given no punishment at all in regard to number of errors. Wischner emphasized not only the likely effects of using different procedures in the learning problem but the possibility that the measures of learning used may have affected the results. For example, differences may appear between groups if the total number of trials to criterion is taken as the measure but not if the number of errors made during training is used. Muenzinger, W. O. Brown, Crow, and Powloski (1952) have shown that pretraining trials in which shock is presented to the subject will also affect the role of punishment in learning. Although it is clear that punishment is effective in producing rapid learning, the conditions under which this occurs are not understood in detail.

The question of why the effect of punishment on behavior would be different from the effect of positive reinforcers has intrigued many theorists. The fact that punishment typically results in behavior which may be called "emotional" has led theorists to the repeated suggestion that the anxiety produced by punishment is at the core of the answer. Theorists have suggested that one effect of punishment is to establish an emotional-response syndrome and that the punishment becomes a CS for the emotional response. The behavior of the organism following punishment is, then, a *conditioned emotional response* (H. F. Hunt & Brady, 1951). It is was noted that evidence is equivocal on whether or not classical avoidance conditioning produces long-term avoidance of the stimulus. Several investigators have shown that long-term inhibition of feeding is developed in organisms punished for eating (Lichtenstein, 1950, with dogs; Masserman, 1943, with cats). Solomon and Wynne (1954) found that the conditioned emotional response established with punishment is so resistant to extinction that it may be unextinguishable.

One technique for comparing punishment and positive reinforcement is to compute *approach-avoidance gradients*. This technique, developed by N. E. Miller (1944; 1959), assumes that an organism's preference for stimuli provides a useful measure of the reinforcing properties of the stimulus. J. S. Brown (1948) fitted rats with a harness and trained them to run down a straight alley for food. The harness was attached to a spring arrangement which permitted the experimenter to measure the amount of pull exercised by the animals as they ran down the alley. The pull was measured both near the goal and near the starting box. Figure 14–17 shows the data for this approach gradient. Note that the mean pull (in grams) increases slightly as the animal gets closer to the goal.

Now, an *avoidance gradient* may be determined by administering shock in the goal box and measuring the pull the animals produce in order to get away from the stimulus. Figure 14–18 shows two avoidance gradients—one with weak current and one with strong current —and Figure 14–19 shows the two avoidance gradients and the approach gradient noted in

FIGURE 14–17: *The approach gradient as represented by the mean force exerted by rats under forty-six hours of food deprivation when restrained at two points in the alley, 30 and 170 cm. Although the two points are connected in a linear fashion, it is not assumed that the relationship is actually linear. (From J. S. Brown, 1948, p. 457.)*

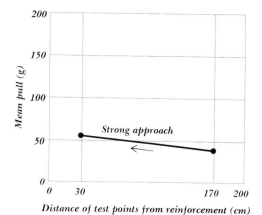

Distance of test points from reinforcement (cm)

Figure 14–17. Like the approach gradient, the avoidance gradients show greater pull the nearer the animal is to the goal box. Note that the strong avoidance gradient crosses the approach gradient. At this point, one might argue that the severity of the electric current was identical in its motivating properties to the severity of food deprivation. This experimental design permits the scaling of the reinforcing or motivating properties of various kinds of stimuli.

ROLE OF INSTRUCTIONS IN CONDITIONING AND LEARNING

In contrast to subhuman subjects, human subjects in learning experiments are generally instructed verbally. This procedure is somewhat unfortunate, for it has added to the legend that "conditioning," especially of the classical type, is involuntary and hence suitable primarily for subhuman animals. The type of instructions given a subject is as much a part

FIGURE 14-18: *The avoidance gradient represented by the mean force of rats attempting to get away from the stimulus. Two negative reinforcements, strong and weak electric current, were used. (J. S. Brown, 1948, p. 459.)*

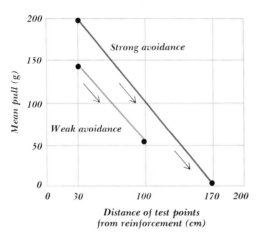

FIGURE 14-19: *A composite of Figures 14–17 and 14–18. Note the difference in slope between the approach and avoidance gradients. Note also that the approach gradient crosses the gradient for strong avoidance. At this point, the gradients are equally strong. (J. S. Brown, 1948, p. 457 and 459.)*

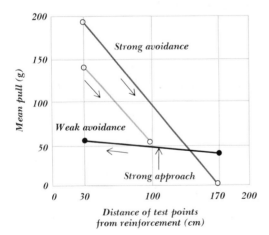

of the experimental procedure, however, as is the humidity or the tightness of straps on an animal subject. In both classical conditioning and operant learning there is evidence that instructions can alter the acquisition rate of the response. Figure 14–20 shows the results of an experiment by Norris and Grant (1948). The figure gives the acquisition rate of human subjects being conditioned to give an eye-blink response under two different types of instructions. There is a clear difference in acquisition rate. Hilgard and Humphreys (1938) used several groups of subjects which differed in the "restraint" implied by the instructions. The instructions varied from one group which was told not to respond to the stimulus, through a group given no instructions, to a group told to respond. In general, strongest conditioning (in terms) of the percentage of CRs, amplitude of the response, and its latency) decreased from those told to respond through those told not to respond.

In studies of human verbal conditioning in which the experimenter provides a verbal reinforcement (such as "Mm-hm" or "Good") for a correct response, the subjects are often asked if they are aware of the purpose of the experiment, i.e., if they are able to identify the response that produced the reinforcement or if they even noted the reinforcement. Although some experimenters automatically eliminate subjects who show "awareness," others do not find that the response rates differ between aware and unaware subjects.

COMPARISON OF CLASSICAL CONDITIONING AND INSTRUMENTAL LEARNING

As was noted previously in this chapter, it is not easy to separate completely classical conditioning from operant learning. Consider the basic experiment in classical conditioning in which a dog is being conditioned to salivate to a tone. The dog eventually anticipates the reinforcement by discharging saliva. This is the appropriate CR; however, it alters the

FIGURE 14-20: *An example of the effects of instructions on learning. The two groups are given different instructions by the experimenters. Note the difference in the development of the conditioned responses. (From Hilgard and Marquis' Conditioning and Learning, revised by Gregory Kimble, 2nd ed., copyright, 1961, by Appleton-Century-Crofts, Div. of Meredith Publishing Company, after Norris & Grant, 1948.)*

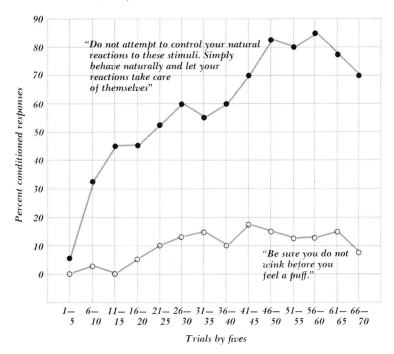

effect of the US, the presentation of the meat, for the salivation has assumed the properties of a secondary reinforcer. Thus an operant or instrumental behavior is present during a supposedly clear example of classical conditioning. Similarly, the rat who performs the common operant and instrumental response of bar pressing for food is not free of classical conditioning, for the presence of a variety of stimuli during reinforcement parallels the typical classical conditioning paradigm.

Although these influences may appear to be of minor interest, they become significant when one attempts to determine whether there is but a single kind of learning (classical conditioning and operant learning being only different procedures) or whether there is more than one kind of learning. A review of the similarities and differences between classical conditioning and instrumental behavior have led theorists to write different assumptions regarding the nature of learning. Depending upon whether one emphasizes the importance of the differences or of the similarities between the two forms of learning, one may believe that the two are so different that they should be treated as different forms of learning, or one may believe that they differ only in the technique used to produce learning but that the learning is essentially identical.

Further, it may appear to be a simple matter to design experiments that separate the two kinds of learning or, at least, offer the possibility of comparing them. Such is not the case. The fact that each kind of learning includes some attributes of the other is only one of the problems. The classic study that attempted to compare the two kinds of learning was reported by Brogden, Lipman, and E. Culler (1938). The experimenters placed guinea pigs in a running wheel. This apparatus, commonly used to measure activity in rodents, is turned by the animals' feet, which move it in the fashion of a treadmill. A shock and a tone were used as stimuli. The purpose of the shock (in the classical conditioning segment of the experiment) was to evoke running in the wheel. Animals in one group (classical) received the shock whether they moved or not. Those in a second group (instrumental) did not receive the shock if they ran.

The results are shown in Figure 14–21. During the first four days of training, acquisition is equal for the groups; however, after that time, the animals that could avoid the shock (the instrumental group) show a decided increase in the frequency of the running response. Sheffield (1948) pointed out that one difficulty with the experiment was that the

subjects in the classical group might receive a shock while they were running, thus establishing the paradoxical situation in which the subject was being punished for the response that he was expected to learn. Repeating the earlier study, but noting what the subject was doing when the shock was applied, Sheffield (1948) found essentially the same results as Brogden et al., although he pointed out that his suspicion was verified by the observation that subjects that received a shock while running sometimes ran and sometimes stopped running with the onset of the shock stimulus. This observation indicated that two different responses—running and not running—were being learned. Similar studies, using different responses, such as the eye blink, have shown classical conditioning to lead to more rapid learning than instrumental learning (G. A. Kimble, Mann, & Dufort, 1955). As we have come to expect in our discussion of various learning problems, the answer to a seemingly simple question will depend on the precise techniques employed and the exact response measured.

The differences in acquisition during classical or instrumental learning suggest that the two differ, at the least because of the methodology employed to produce learning, but the similarities between the two are impressive. Although different names are often employed for phenomena, depending upon whether one is talking about classical conditioning or instrumental learning, many phenomena appear to be very similar, such as extinction, spontaneous recovery, the various forms of disinhibition and inhibition, stimulus and response generalization, and discrimination.

Whether these two types of learning turn out to be fundamentally identical or whether they are clearly separated remains a matter of considerable concern, particularly to those who attempt comprehensive theories of learning. The interest reflects the considerable importance placed by psychology on learning and conditioning as fundamental concepts in the understanding of behavior. Indeed, the interest, particularly among American psycholo-

FIGURE 14–21: *A comparison of learning under classical conditioning and instrumental training. (From Brogden, Lipman, & E. Culler, 1938, p. 110.)*

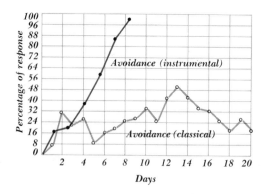

gists, in learning theory and conditioning has had the negative effect at times of deemphasizing the importance of behaviors that may be regarded as innate, instinctual, or unlearned (Chapter 16).

NEUROLOGICAL CORRELATES OF LEARNING AND CONDITIONING

More attention has been given to the neurological correlates of instrumental learning than to those of classical conditioning. Attention has been devoted to higher-order instrumental tasks, such as discrimination learning. Much of the data suggests the importance of vicarious functioning of the cortex in discrimination tasks. The studies of Lashley (1920; 1922; 1929; 1933; 1935a; 1935b) first directed attention to the possibility of investigating the importance of brain functions, particularly of the cortex, in the study of learning and contributed the concepts of equipotentiality and mass action to the literature (Chapter 13). Lashley's work emphasized the importance of vicarious functioning in discrimination tasks. In some studies, he noted that the ability to learn a light-dark discrimination was actually enhanced in rats deprived of a portion of the cortex. This finding reemphasized the fact that while one commonly thinks of the intact organism as most efficient, areas of the brain may serve to inhibit or to support one another. There is no reason to suppose that partial decortication enhances the general ability of an organism to learn, but it may well have the effect of removing conflicting stimuli and of making it easier for the organism to acquire certain specific habits. Several investigators have attempted to discover whether bar-pressing behavior in the Skinner box is related to particular brain centers. Although some observers report relatively mild changes (such as a change in the length of time that the animal holds the bar down), lesions do not appear to have gross effects on bar-pressing behavior in the rat (O'Kelley; see G. J. Thomas, 1962).

Discrimination-learning studies indicate that two factors are important: (1) the type of animal used and (2) the type of discrimination problem employed. As we have noted, a light-dark discrimination problem can be learned by the rat with most of the visual cortex removed. This does not appear to be true of primates. Moreover, different areas of the central nervous system are necessary for discrimination; the exact area depends upon whether the discrimination involves color patterns, brightness, or other variables.

In general, it would appear that simple conditioning procedures show replication of function, but more complicated discrimination learning shows vicarious functioning.

SOURCES

Further study of instrumental learning should begin in two places: in Thorndike's original work (1898) and in B. F. Skinner's monumental book (1938), which inspired interest in operant training. Interest in operant training has represented the most dramatic change in psychology in the decades since 1940. It is noteworthy that Woodworth in his comprehensive text on experimental psychology (1938) did not discuss operant training. The "Skinnerian viewpoint" is also expressed in a book which goes into considerable detail on the effects of schedules of reinforcement (Ferster & B. F. Skinner, 1957). B. F. Skinner's more general work (1953) is an excellent starting point for students interested in the application of operant learning to many higher-order processes of human behavior. In addition, Skinner cogently presents his arguments regarding appropriate procedures for the investigation of psychological problems. Holland and B. F. Skinner (1961) have presented a programmed book on the same general topic.

Keller (1954) has contributed a short, but effective, book on the role of reinforcement in learning. Further information on conditioning and learning in animals is available in Waters, Rethlingshafer, and Caldwell (1960) and in

Thorpe (1956; 1962). More difficult, but certainly rewarding, books have been published by Mowrer (1960a; 1960b) and Spence (1956). The student will note a difference in the way these writers approach the solution to problems of learning. A. W. Staats and C. K. Staats (1963) contribute several important chapters which relate operant learning to higher-order behaviors, such as language development. The review of stimulus generalization by Prokasy and J. F. Hall (1963) will provide the reader with a detailed analysis of this area. J. Hirsch (1962) has reviewed some studies concerned with the genetics of operant learning. As Solomon (1964) has noted, few textbooks are concerned with the effects of punishment on behavior. Both R. M. Church (1963) and Solomon (1964) have contributed reviews and analyses of studies of punishment, and both are highly recommended.

The *Annual Review of Psychology* publishes reviews of this area from time to time, although they tend to be highly technical. Two works edited by Delafresnaye (1954; 1961) contain contribution to the general area of neurological correlates. In addition, some of Lashley's contributions have been reprinted with commentary (Beach, Hebb, C. T. Morgan, & Nissen, 1960). The Solomon and Turner (1962) paper on curarization of dogs presents an excellent review of the literature. Osgood (1953) presents a chapter on neurophysiology and learning which neatly summarizes research in the area.

CHAPTER FIFTEEN

HUMAN LEARNING
AND PERFORMANCE

INTRODUCTION

There is no reason to suppose that the laws which govern learning and performance in human beings and in subhuman animals are different, but the study of human learning presents some problems not found in the study of animals. The human being is capable of a greater variety of learned responses than the rat or monkey. Determination of the variables that affect learning in subhuman animals may explain some behavior at the human level or demonstrate learning in its more rudimentary and basic forms. It is not likely, however, that a thorough knowledge of rat behavior would lead to an explanation of human behavior, any more than a complete knowledge of the laws of human behavior would necessarily explain the behavior of rats.

Although most animals emit sounds and appear to respond to sounds made by other animals, the most important difference between man and other animals is the ability to speak and to attach meaning to the sounds spoken by others (Chapter 7). Animals do not listen to lectures, use telephones, or read books. Probably a large percentage of all that is learned by human beings involves some form of speech and speech perception. For this reason, studies of human learning commonly use speech as the dependent variable: the subject is asked what items he remembers from among those previously learned, or he is asked to memorize according to various techniques. From these studies, knowledge regarding how human beings learn has been accumulated.

In addition to speaking, human beings make motor responses, just as do other animals. The rat pressing a Skinner-box bar is making a motor response, just as is the worker drilling holes in each specimen on the assembly line. Much of human existence involves motor skills, both simple and complex: we learn to print, to write, and perhaps to type. These are nonverbal behaviors, but, like speech, they are learned. Knowledge of how they are learned has many practical applications. In industry, one must design equipment that is within the capacities of the human motor system, and in many endeavors it is useful to isolate the most efficient method for acquiring motor skills.

In studying human learning, one should remember the scientific rule that the phenomena under investigation should be explained in the simplest way possible; one should invent new constructs to explain observations only when a simpler explanation is not sufficient, only if one cannot explain human learning by the laws that apply to other animals. For example, before regarding verbal behavior as a complex phenomenon that requires special explanatory devices, one should first ask whether established principles, such as the laws of operant training, account for the behavior. We shall ask such questions later in this chapter.

The study of human learning, particularly verbal learning, provides valuable lessons; it is here that the importance of methodology is most obvious. The problem of differentiating learning and performance is accented in the study of human learning, for in order to measure acquisition we must measure *retention*. We have noted before that it is one thing for a student to say that he has learned material and often quite another for us to measure how much he has learned by examining his retention of the subject matter. Our evaluation will vary considerably depending upon the technique of measurement we select—whether we give an oral examination, a multiple-choice test, or an essay examination. We can hardly assume that these measures reflect a difference in his original learning; rather, they tell us that different measuring techniques measure different attributes of the original learning.

MEASURES PRIMARILY OF ACQUISITION

Until the last part of the nineteenth century, discussions of memory were concerned primarily with the question of *association*. Investigators who were interested in how information is gained and retained generally assumed that memory was a fundamental property of organisms and that learning occurred through the association of stimuli with responses already acquired. By the turn of the century, two events had provided impetus to the study of memory. The first was Pavlov's work on conditioning, for a fundamental characteristic of classical conditioning is that the paradigm includes association. That is, through repetition the conditioned stimulus is paired with the unconditioned stimulus and eventually replaces it.

The second event was the work of one man, Hermann Ebbinghaus. In 1885 Ebbinghaus published the results of his studies on memory (1885; 1913). Like Thorndike, in his study of instrumental learning, Ebbinghaus chose to measure the detailed way in which memory operates. From the study of small discrete responses, he obtained data which produced general laws governing the development of human memory and learning. Ebbinghaus, like Fechner and Thorndike, was inventive: in order to conduct experiments that permitted him to isolate the process of learning, he invented nonsense syllables (Chapter 7) and developed several methods for the study of memory. Indeed, Ebbinghaus's approach to the study of memory was the result of his accidentally discovering a copy of Fechner's *Elemente der Psychophysik* (1860). The procedures described by Fechner for measuring mental energy prompted Ebbinghaus to apply the principles of human memory. Since he was greatly limited in his choice of subjects (his experiments were conducted on himself), he was forced to develop methods of control, such as nonsense syllables, that would eliminate contamination of the results. That these controls and methods are in wide use today attests to his ingenuity.

Although we distinguish the methods used to measure acquisition from those used to measure retention, the two methods are intertwined. In some cases, a retention measure is the only measure of learning, as when a student is told to memorize a poem and his performance on this task is measured later. In other cases, the process of learning is measured during acquisition, as when a person is asked to repeat a list of names over and over again until he has mastered them; here the number of errors on each trial yields a measure of acquisition as well as a measure of retention.

Among a variety of methods of stimulus presentation that have been used, two have received the most attention: *paired-associate learning* and *serial learning*.

In paired-associate learning, the subject is presented with pairs of words or items (such as "house"-"casa"; "I"-"je"). His task is to learn which two words or items go together. In the purest application of paired-associate learning, the order of the pairs is unimportant, for the subject is required only to associate one of the pair with the other. Sometimes, however, the subject is required to remember the order of the pairs: this procedure has elements of both paired-associate and serial learning. In practice, paired-associate learning is used when we memorize telephone numbers (Jones–717-523-0352), learn equivalent foreign and English words, or pair names with faces.

In serial learning, the subject is presented with a series of items, each item presented individually. The subject is instructed to remember the order of the stimuli. A common example of serial learning is memorizing a poem or musical composition. A child in the process of learning the sequence 1, 2, 3, 4, 5, 6, . . . 10 is learning in serial fashion. Note that in its methodology, serial learning has elements of paired-associate learning, for it may be that the subject is learning to pair 1 with 2, 2 with 3, 3 with 4, and so on. The essential difference between the methods is whether the items are presented individually or in pairs.

Other methods of presentation have been used in the study of human verbal learning. Some of these methods were employed in order to isolate a particular phenomenon of learning. For example, the relationship between retention and length of material is as-sessed by the *method of immediate memory span*. The subject is presented with a set of stimuli of increasing lengths, such as the numbers 157; 1938642; 1497362157823. After each presentation, he is asked to repeat the stimuli in order. Although numbers are ordinarily used in studies of immediate memory span, other items may be used. Immediate memory span is of considerable concern to telephone companies, for the user is often required to retain a series of numbers long enough to dial correctly. In less complex times, telephone subscribers needed to remember only 4 numbers; then they were required to remember 7 (although the first 2 were usually disguised with an exchange name, e.g., JA 30352); eventually 10 numbers, including the area code were required. These changes have been accompanied by tests of immediate memory span of the population in order to select the length that can be recalled.

The *method of retained numbers*, or, as it is now commonly called, of *free recall*, is used in a variety of commonplace situations, although its nonspecificity has resulted in minimal use in human learning studies, until recently. In its simplest form, the subject is asked to remember a series of stimuli usually in excess of his expected ability. For example, a poem or composition may be given to the subject. He is then asked to recall as many of the words as possible. His score is the number of correct items recalled. This procedure, of course, is used in educational tests. Woodworth and Schlosberg (1954, p. 697) note a subtle attribute of the technique: it gives a measure of the *amount recalled*, not necessarily of the *amount retained*. Although this distinction is like the one between performance and learning, it should be noted that when the technique is used in education tests, it is a measure of recall rather than of retention. This fact becomes clear if the subject is tested for retention more than once. He sometimes recalls items on the second test but not on the first; this suggests that these items had been retained but not recalled on the first test. Thus, the method should be described as a method of *recalled* members, rather than *retained* members.

The *learning-time* method is applicable to material that cannot be divided easily into discrete stimuli, such as musical composition. A criterion is set, say, one perfect performance or a performance with no more than two errors. The time taken to reach the criterion is measured. Under some circumstances, the number of trials to criterion may also be used as the measure. There are very real difficulties with this method, as anyone knows who has taken music lessons and prepared a piece to the satisfaction of the instructor. The pessimist may practice far beyond the limits set by the criterion and thus yield an overevaluation of his speed of learning. The optimist may assume that he has reached criterion before he actually has and be asked to continue his labors. Moreover, the use of a criterion may bias results from individuals who consistently make one specific error; such an individual may have progressed at a more rapid rate than one who reached criterion more quickly, but he may be held back by the single error. This is always a problem to be considered when criteria are used; the experimenter has no information on the rate with which the criterion is approached unless he tests the subject in discrete trials.

In order to overcome some of these difficulties, experimenters have added *prompting* to the experimental task. The subject is corrected or prompted whenever he makes an error: the criterion usually established is one complete trial without prompting. Either the number of trials or the number of prompts to criterion may be measured. The advantage of prompting is that the experimenter is able to record the course of learning.

MEASURES PRIMARILY OF RETENTION

Savings Method: Ebbinghaus suggested the *savings method,* which, essentially, consists of requiring the subject to *relearn* material. For example, the subject learns a list of items to a given criterion. The experimenter may wait forty-eight hours and then ask the subject to relearn the list. Presumably, the subject should relearn the material to the same criterion in less time (or with fewer errors) if he remembers anything from the first learning. Thus, the amount *saved* in relearning the stimuli is represented as a *savings score*. Note that the savings method can be used in any situation in which the subject relearns. If a subject took 20 trials to learn a list of nonsense syllables and 10 trials to relearn it, his score would be

$$\frac{\text{First learning} - \text{relearning}}{\text{Number of trials to learning}} \times 100$$

or

$$\frac{20-10}{20} \times 100$$

or

$$0.5 \times 100 = 50$$

Thus the subject saved 50 percent. The multiplier is used to convert the score into a percentage.

A difficulty arises with the savings method if a criterion, such as one correct trial, is used. The difficulty is that, by definition, the subject must take at least one retention trial to reach criterion; thus, he cannot score 100 percent savings. This difficulty is corrected by the following formula (Hilgard, 1934):

$$\frac{100\,[(OL{-}C) - (RL{-}C)]}{(OL{-}C)}$$

where

$OL =$ **trials required for original learning**
$C\ \ =$ **trials required to meet criterion**
$RL =$ **trials required for relearning**

Thus, a subject who took 10 trials to reach criterion at acquisition but who took only 1 trial to reach criterion during the retention test would have a savings score of

$$\frac{100\,(10-1) - (1-1)}{10-1}$$

or

$$\frac{100\,(9-0)}{9}$$

or

$$\frac{900}{9}$$

or

$$100$$

The savings method may be used on any memory task, for it does not require that the materials be learned in any particular way; it merely measures the relationship between original learning and relearning of the material. The experimenter must, however, design the experiment to control such effects as learning to learn and other factors that can contaminate the validity of the results. Some authorities believe that the measure should not be used on identical material when an independent variable is placed between the two sessions. For example, assume that we wish to study the effect of the tranquilized chlor-promazine on memory. The subject learns a list of stimuli, receives the drug, and then is asked to relearn the list, It is argued that the proper measure is the determination of how long it takes to learn an equivalent, but not identical, list of items, rather than how long it takes to relearn the same items. The subject should be asked to learn two sets of stimuli during the posttest: not only the set learned originally, but a set equal in difficulty. The savings method then may be used to determine how much time is saved in learning as a function of having learned a previous test.

Relearning: *Relearning* is obviously a measure of retention. In this technique, the subject relearns the original material, usually, but not necessarily, under the same conditions as the original learning. When relearning is used to measure retention, the experimenter should be aware that he is actually presenting another acquisition trial. For example, if the subject is given a series of 10 words and asked to repeat them in order until he can say the entire sequence correctly, each new trial is both a relearning trial and a measure of retention from the previous trial. If the independent variable is time between original learning and relearning, care must be taken to design the experiment in such a way that supposed retention trials do not represent relearning trials as well. If we wish to measure retention after one, two, and three days, the same subject should not serve under all three conditions, for the first test of retention serves as a learning trial for the second day.

Recall: *Recall* is another commonly used measure of retention. The subject is asked by the experimenter to say all that he remembers from the learning task. If the task was the learning of 15 nonsense syllables, the subject is asked during retention to name all the syllables he can remember.

Robinson (1927), in a statement which has come to be called the *Skaggs-Robinson hypothesis,* suggested that the degree of similarity between the two tasks determines the efficiency of recall. Figure 15–1 shows the relationship involved. Recall is most efficient when the two tasks are so similar as to be identical (maximal), less efficient when there is some similarity (minimal), and least efficient in between at the point between the two tasks. Several experiments (Kennelly, 1941; Robinson, 1927) suggest that the hypothesis is reasonably accurate, although the *C* point—that representing neutrality—has not received as much verification as has the distinction between points *A* and *B*. J. A. McGeoch (1942) has summarized several of his earlier experiments which indicated that when meaningful words

FIGURE 15-1: *The Skaggs-Robinson hypothesis. Along the abscissa the points of maximal similarity and minimal similarity or neutrality are represented. B is the low point in the curve for efficiency of recall. (From Osgood, 1949, p. 136.)*

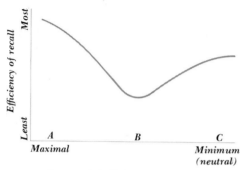

Degree of similarity— Descending scale

are used, interference increases as similarity increases. Osgood (1946), however, has reported the reverse.

Studies using this technique have pointed out the distinction between *errors of omission* and *errors of inclusion*. The former refer to the subject's inability to report an item learned originally. The latter refer to the substitution, during the retention test, of an item or response not included in the original list. For example, consider the following:

Original learning	*Recall (first trial)*
horse	horse
woman	—
desk	book
car	—
bank	tank

The subject commits two errors of omission ("woman," "car") and two errors of inclusion ("book," "tank"). It may be "recalled" that successive recall tests may show that the subject is able to report previously omitted words, such as "woman" and "car," thus suggesting that recall and retention are different characteristics of the learning situation.

Methods of Recognition: Under *methods of recognition* the subject is presented with one or more stimuli and asked whether each was or was not a member of the originally learned stimuli. The subject may have learned a list of 10 names. The experimenter then asks, "Was Smith one of the names?" "Was Jones one of the names?" Typically, some of the names included in the questioning were not in the original list. The subject may be given 20 cards, 10 containing the names originally learned and 10 containing names not included in the original learning. The subject is asked to separate the cards into two categories —names learned and irrelevant names. There is no reason to tell the subject how many cards belong in each category. The simplest technique for scoring the results is to calculate the number of correct recognitions; however, this fails to account for the number of incorrect recognitions a subject may make. Assume that subject 1 places 8 cards in one pile and 12 in the other. All 8 in the first pile are correct; however, he has omitted 2 correct cards. Subject 2 places 18 cards in one stack and 2 in the other; of the cards in the 18-card stack, 8 are correct. Thus, both subjects receive the same score, for both correctly identified 8 of the names learned originally, yet subject 2 had more incorrect responses. To avoid this problem, we can subtract the wrong responses from the right responses, using the following formula:

$$\frac{|C|-|I|}{N} \times 100$$

where

$C =$ **number of correct identifications**
$I =$ **number of incorrect identifications**
$N =$ **total number of items**

Thus, subject 1 receives a score of

$$\frac{|18|-|2|}{20} \times 100$$

or 80. Subject 2 receives a score of

$$\frac{|8|-|12|}{20} \times 100$$

or 20.

A score of 0 would indicate pure chance, and a score of 100 would indicate perfect retention. The problems involved in evaluating true recall by the methods of recognition are similar to those noted in giving examinations. When the subject is asked to place the cards in either of two piles, he is, effectively, taking part in a "true-false" examination. He must decide whether the card is true (e.g., learned originally). As any student knows, one would expect a subject to be correct 50 percent of the time by chance, provided the number of irrelevant cards is equal to the number of learning items. In order to minimize the effects of guessing, multiple-choice examinations are given in which only one item out of four or more is correct. Indeed, generations of students have gained and suffered from Ebbinghaus's invention of the multiple-choice method of measuring retention. With the multiple-choice technique, the probability of being correct by chance is reduced 25 percent or more. Similarly, some investigators have used the multiple-choice technique in studying the method of recognition by inserting one correct card in a set of four or more alternatives. One procedure for distinguishing answers derived by guessing or by chance from those derived from knowledge is as follows:

Guilford (1936) has suggested that the usual method of correcting for chance be applied to items as well as test scores. This method involves two assumptions:

1. That the persons can be divided into groups, (*a*) those who know the answer and (*b*) those who guess the answer

2. That those who guess are equally likely to select any one of the alternatives given

Let f designate the number of different answers given for an item: then $1/f$ of those who

"guessed" would guess correctly, and $(f-1)/f$ would guess incorrectly. Since this latter group includes all who answer incorrectly (by assumption 1 above, there is no misinformation leading to the incorrect answer), $1/(f-1)$ of those who answer incorrectly is equal to the number of lucky guessers; hence, subtracting the number wrong divided by $(f-1)$ from the number right will give the number who got the right answer, not by guessing, but by knowledge. The percentage who know the answer (designated p') may be written

$$p' = \frac{R_i - \dfrac{W_i}{f-1}}{T}$$

where

R_i = number of correct answers to the item
W_i = number of incorrect answers to the item
f = number of possible answers given for each item
T = total number who tried the item (T may be considered equal to rights plus wrongs [$R_i + W_i$] or may also include those who skipped the item)
p' = estimate of the percentage knowing the answer to that item

It should be noted that one implication of this method is that the same number of persons will select each of the incorrect alternatives and that some number greater than this will select the correct alternative. Investigation of any multiple-choice test will show that rarely, if ever, are all the distractors (incorrect answers) equally attractive (Gulliksen, 1950, p. 371).

The selection of the irrelevant items used in the methods of recognition affects the recall score, for in effect the subject is taking part in a psychophysical experiment in which he is asked to judge when stimuli are identical and when they are different. The more similar the irrelevant stimuli are to the original stimuli, the more difficult the task for the subject and the greater the number of errors. Moreover, the correction for guessing assumes that the alternatives will be selected equally often. Unfortunately, although this is a condition that can be met by the careful selection and testing of alternatives or irrelevant items, it is rarely a part of the experimental procedure.

Methods of Reconstruction: The *methods of reconstruction* are most efficiently employed on physical stimuli. The subject is asked to remember the location of a set of stimuli; then the stimuli are rearranged, and the subject is asked to reconstruct them in their original sequence. The measure may be as simple as the number of stimuli placed correctly, although under some conditions one may wish to measure the degree of error by noting how far the subject places a stimulus from its original position. In a variation of this procedure, each attempt by the subject to reconstruct the stimuli may be treated as a trial, and the subject may be asked to continue his reconstructions until he correctly places the stimuli. Thus the rate of learning may be measured by noting the number of correct reconstructions on each trial.

Other variations of these procedures are available. One may read the items, project them visually, or introduce them by recording. One may develop techniques that are offshoots of basic methods, just as many psychophysical measures are derived from the basic methods. Characteristically, learning and performance are affected by slight changes in procedure. Similarly, performance may vary appreciably as a function of the method used to measure retention.

SOME FACTORS INFLUENCING ACQUISITION AND RETENTION

A number of factors and experimental conditions affect the rate of learning and the degree of retention. Among these factors are the meaningfulness of the material (Chapter 7), whether the subject is corrected when errors occur, the lapse of time between the original learning and the retention measure, whether the subject is expected to rehearse all the material until some criterion is reached (*whole* learning) or whether he is expected to learn segments of the material and then put the segments together (*part* learning), and whether trials are conducted in succession (*massed* learning) or with a noticeable time lapse between (*distributed* learning). It is impossible to examine the role of one factor without examining other factors. For example, we may wish to examine meaningfulness, but the influence of meaningfulness will vary as a function of other factors, such as whole or part learning and time lapse between acquisition and testing of retention. Accordingly, as we review the influence of certain factors, it should be remembered that indirect information on the effect of other factors is also being reported.

Whole-Part Learning: Although the question "Which is more efficient, whole or part learning?" appears to have prompted many studies in the early 1900s, the simple question is beyond answer. Under some circumstances whole learning is superior, and under others part learning is more efficient. Moreover, efficiency depends upon the type of material, its length, whether acquisition or retention is measured, and upon a variety of other factors. Yet the question recurs, somewhat naggingly: if all conditions were kept constant, would it not be possible to show that either part or whole learning was superior?

Learning by the whole method assumes that the subject continues performing until some criterion is reached. If the material is a list of 20 names to be remembered in order, the subject repeats the entire list over and over again until his performance is adequate. In part learning, the material is divided into sections, and the subject learns each section to criterion before continuing to the next section. There are three basic ways in which material may be learned by the part method:

In the *pure part method,* the material is

divided into *x* parts, and each part is treated as if it were a whole. The subject learns each part, and then puts the parts together until criterion is reached. For example, if the criterion is one perfect trial, the 20 names can be divided into four sets of 5 names each. The subject practices the first set, then the second set, then the third, etc., until each set has been learned. He then repeats the five sets in order until the criterion is reached.

In the *progressive part method,* the first set is learned, then the second, and then the two sets are combined. When the criterion has been reached for the combined sets, the third set is learned. Then the subject is tested on all three parts. The characteristic of this method is that a new set is learned and added to the sets already learned before the subject is permitted to continue to the next set.

In the *repetitive part method,* the first set is learned, then the second set is added to the first set, and the first two are learned together. The third set is then added to the first two sets, and all three are practiced together. This method is distinctive in that it forces the subject to repeat information already learned, and the parts (composed of the combined sets) get larger as learning continues.

Some general conclusions regarding the effects of whole and part learning are possible:

1. **The more intelligent the subject or the older the subject, the more advantageous the whole method becomes (G. O. McGeoch, 1931a; Rubin-Rabson, 1940).**

2. **As the length of the material increases, the part method becomes more advantageous (Orbison, 1944).**

3. **Practice with the whole method appears to increase its efficiency; practice with the part method does not. That is, the more one uses the whole method, the more efficient it becomes (Lakenan, 1913; Wylie, 1928).**

4. **The type of material (e.g., poetry, serial lists) does not appear to favor one type of learning over the other, although the degree to which the parts must be organized into a whole makes a difference in the efficiency of learning. It would appear that** "logically" placed material, such as a poem, would favor the whole method, but experiments have not shown this (Crafts, 1929, 1930, 1932; Seagoe, 1936a, 1936b; Hoskins, 1936; Jonckheere, 1939).

5. **In part learning, putting the parts together after they have been learned separately consumes 50 percent or more of the total learning time (Perkins, 1927). For human beings, most of the errors (studies suggest 60 to 80 percent) occur during the reconstruction of the sets learned by parts.**

6. **Because the human being possesses bilateral symmetry, we should ask whether practicing with both hands separately and then using the hands together (part method) has different results from using both hands together at the onset (whole method). The question has practical implications, particularly for musicians, who differ on the most efficient method to learn to play an instrument. Some piano teachers recommend that a composition be learned by the part method, whereas others prefer the whole method. In piano playing, the hands-together or each-hand-alone distinction appears to be immaterial in the early stages of training, although some studies suggest that the part method is more efficient for difficult assignments (R. W. Brown, 1933; O'Brien, 1943).**

Most human learning is done by a combined whole-part method, but few data are available on the effect of various combinations. When learning by the whole method, one may select segments of the material for special attention and rehearse them separately: this yields a combination of the part and whole methods.

Massed-Distributed Learning: Our discussion of whole and part learning assumed that the subject learned all the material in one session. The differences in procedure were dependent upon the way the material was organized. For many activities, we do not complete the learning in one session; rather, we return to the task later to practice it. Indeed, with complex skills, such as playing the piano, many sessions are required for performance to reach an adequate level. When time elapses between practice sessions, we use the term *distributed,* or spaced, learning. When all learning takes place during one session, we speak of *massed* learning. Distributed learning permits forgetting to become a factor in efficiency. If we study French only every fifth year, we can expect to forget a considerable portion of the material in the interim. Thus, the temporal scheduling of distributed learning—whether trials are conducted every 5 minutes, 12 hours, or 1,000 days—permits different amounts of forgetting and different rates of learning. If there is no rest period, however, the repetition of trial after trial is accompanied by fatigue and boredom, thus reducing the efficiency of learning.

Because these assumed factors—forgetting and inattention from boredom—affect learning, it is suggested that some optimum time level exists at which the two factors are minimally effective. The optimum will vary, however, as a function of the type of material, the methods used for learning and for measuring retention, the length of the material, etc. Moreover, problems in experimental design of studies concerned with the effects of distributed practice suggest that many studies are not comparable. For example, if the experimenter keeps the number of trials during the practice session constant but varies the length

of the rest period, the experimental and control groups will complete the task in different times; if the experimenter keeps the length of the "rest periods"—the time between learning trials—constant, the groups will receive different numbers of trials during the learning session; if the experimenter keeps the rest periods constant and varies the time between the items within a series given during the practice session, again groups will finish at different times.

Table 15–A shows these paradigms. In design I, trials are constant, but the rest period varies; in design II the rest period is constant, but the trials vary; in design III, both the trials and the rest periods are constant, but the time between presentation of items during each trial is varied. All three methods test the effects of distributed practice; however, it may be more precise to say that although all the designs are concerned with the effect of presentation rate, designs II and III deal with distributed trials, and design I deals with distributed rest periods.

Most studies have found distributed practice to lead to greater retention and more rapid learning than massed practice. Since learning may be expressed in either (1) number of trials to criterion or (2) amount of time to criterion, the expression *rapid learning* re-

TABLE 15–A: *Three Experimental Designs Discussed in the Text*

Group	Practice	Rest, hr	Practice	Rest, hr
Design I:				
A	Trial 1	None	Trial 2	None
B	Trial 1	1	Trial 2	1
C	Trial 1	2	Trial 2	2
Design II:				
A	Trials 1, 2	1	Trials 3, 4	1
B	Trials 1–6	1	Trials 7–12	1
C	Trials 1–9	1	Trials 10–18	1
Design III:				
A	Trial 1 (10 sec between items)	1	Trial 2 (10 sec)	1
B	Trial 1 (20 sec between items)	1	Trial 2 (20 sec)	1
C	Trial 1 (30 sec between items)	1	Trial 3 (30 sec)	1

quires qualification. Although distributed practice may require fewer trials, it may still take more time. Figure 15–2 shows two graphs representing acquisition under massed practice and under distributed practice. The graph on the right *(B)* would suggest distributed practice to be far more efficient than massed practice. When the data are plotted in terms of time, rather than in number of trials, however, it is clear that massed practice consumes less time. In speaking of "efficient learning," one must distinguish the absolute amount of time consumed from the amount of time actually spent in learning the material.

Distribution of practice is far too vast an area of experimental attention to yield a simple statement on the effects of practice. Nevertheless, some general conclusions may be outlined:

1. For many tasks, distributed practice—even with just a brief rest period—is more efficient than massed practice.

2. Distributed practice is more efficient for motor than for verbal tasks, but a few tasks are more easily learned under massed practice. Underwood (1961, p. 230) suggests that if efficiency is the goal, distributed practice is not useful in verbal learning, since it is slower (in terms of total learning time). This comment is based upon experiments in which massed practice was defined as permitting rest intervals of 8 seconds to 3 minutes. Much of the older literature, which did find greater differences between massed and distributed practice, used much longer intertest intervals—often 24 hours.

3. In verbal learning, meaningfulness and the degree of similarity between the items to be learned appear to be critical factors. It has been suggested that the process of verbal learning has two stages: (*a*) the responses are "acquired as responses"; e.g., a response word is distinguished from all other words—one learns that it *belongs* to the material to be learned—and (*b*) the word is associated or attached to some other stimulus word in the material (Underwood & Schulz, 1960). These stages are similar to the processes of detection and recognition in psychophysics: one must first detect the stimulus and then learn its relevance. Underwood (1961) suggests that when

FIGURE 15–2: *Both graphs show performance under massed and distributed practice. The efficiency of the two types of practice clearly differs as a function of whether the data are examined in terms of number of trials or number of days.*

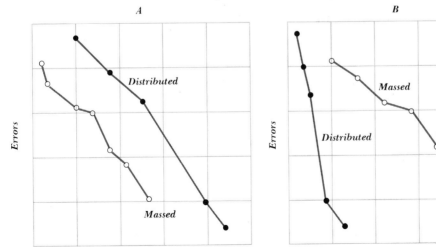

A

B

Time (days)

Trials

interference (e.g., interference from highly similar items in the material) occurs during the first stage, distributed practice may be expected to facilitate learning (see Underwood & Schulz, 1961a, 1961b; Underwood, 1957b). Interference may come from several sources: the investigators may build interference into the experiment by selecting stimulus items of a high degree of similarity; there may be individual differences among subjects; or a subject may associate words (as indicated by his confusing them in speech and writing) that are rarely associated by other persons.

4. The length of the rest period in verbal learning is a second critical determiner of the efficiency of learning. The rest period has two effects: (a) it may permit forgetting of correct responses, and (b) it may permit forgetting of incorrect responses. The former will hinder performance; the latter will improve it. There is evidence from studies which show more rapid learning under distributed practice that more errors are made in the first few trials by subjects learning under the distributed method than by those learning under the massed method (Underwood & Schulz, 1961a; 1961b). Thus, the two most critical factors affecting learning rate under massed and distributed practice are (a) length of the rest period and (b) amount of interference between the items to be learned.

5. Since the amount of interference is an important variable, it follows that the method used for acquisition is important. Paired-associate learning and serial learning may be expected to permit different kinds of interference during acquisition, so that distributed-practice effects are greater with serial than paired-associate learning.

6. The effect of *warming up* (many tasks are performed slowly during the first few moments and then spurt) favors massed practice. A writer often begins by staring into space, and perhaps writing a sentence. As he "warms up" to the task, words flow at a rapid, if not well-considered, rate. Distributed practice would appear to be detrimental to activities that require warming up. The student who is given 60 minutes to write a paper will perform differently from the student who is permitted to write 5 minutes on each of 12 successive days. The latter student will spend much of his time warming up.

7. Distributed practice offers the subject an opportunity to rehearse the material. During the rest period, the subject may repeat the material to himself. Thus, the so-called rest period is really used as an additional acquisition period. Some investigators require subjects to perform an irrelevant task during the rest period in order to limit the possibility of rehearsing the material. It is important, of course, that the interpolated activity not permit either positive or negative transfer in respect to the material being learned. Among the interpolated tasks that have been used are color naming and counting backward.

8. In general, retention is greater after learning by the distributed method (Hovland, 1940; Keppel, 1964). This is true even though subjects trained under massed practice have more trials (since they take longer to learn). Possibly, however, it is true that this finding occurs only under very special conditions.

9. It is possible that distributed practice affects performance, but not learning. This intriguing suggestion has been examined by using the paradigm of the Crespi effect (Chapter 14), in which the running speed of rats was measured when the amount of incentive was altered. Kientzle (1949) used the design of the Crespi experiment to investigate massed and distributed learning. The results are shown in Figure 15–3. The group receiving one-minute rest periods were shifted at trial 15 to no-rest, and the no-rest group were shifted to one-minute rest. The typical Crespi effect is observed, for the no-rest group show an immediate increase in performance rate, and the rest group show a decrease. By trial 20, both groups are performing at the same level. Note that a critical difference between this experiment and the design of the Crespi effect is that the effect of the rest interval was eliminated rather than reversed.

10. Learning tasks that require exploration or the selection of one of several alternatives, e.g., learning a maze, are apparently more easily learned under massed practice (T. W. Cook, 1944; S. C. Ericksen, 1942).

Reminiscence: It has been noted that under some conditions retention is greater on the first retention test after the first practice trial.

FIGURE 15-3: *Changes in performance when the intertrial interval is shifted. The experiment follows the paradigm of the Crespi effect. The groups were shifted at trial 15; one group received massed tests, and a second group received a one-minute rest between trials. The massed group apparently was learning more during the first 15 trials than is shown by its performance, for when it was shifted to distributed trials, the performance showed a rapid increase to the level of performance of the other group. (Data from Kientzle, 1949, as plotted by Woodworth & Schlosberg, 1954, p. 792.)*

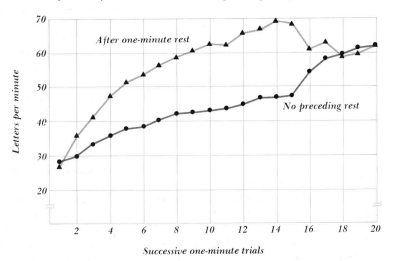

This finding may imply that some learning occurred between tests. The increase in retention score is called *reminiscence*. There is no question that reminiscence occurs with motor tasks. Reminiscence is thus a special case of the facilitation of retention after distributed practice. The fact that it is difficult to design and conduct experiments that adequately control for other possible sources of increase in retention scores, however, means that it is difficult to specify the exact conditions under which reminiscence occurs (see reviews by G. O. McGeoch, 1935; Buxton, 1943).

The phenomenon was first studied and named by Ballard (1913). He presented poetry to school children and conducted a recall test immediately after the learning session. Without forewarning, some of the students were tested for recall the following day, and others after 2 days, 3 days, and so on, up to 7 days. Figure 15-4 shows the results of three types of

material. All the materials indicate reminiscence, although the point of its occurrence varies. In addition, Ballard noted greater reminiscence among young children than among older children, a function we have found previously (Chapter 9) in regard to eidetic imagery. O. Williams (1926) repeated and extended these findings. Among the types of materials he used, he found evidence of reminiscence only when poetry was used. Moreover, he failed to find the effect among older children. Still, his findings did confirm the presence of reminiscence, and for this reason those who prefer to avoid the use of common terms to describe scientific phenomena refer to "reminiscence" as the *Ballard-Williams* phenomenon.

One difficulty with the studies of Ballard and O. Williams is that each subject received two recall tests: this permitted rehearsing during the interim and also permitted what-

FIGURE 15–4: *Reminiscence as a function of the type of material learned. The amount remembered immediately after learning is taken as the basis on which the percentage reproduced later is calculated. (A) "The Wreck of the Hesperus"; (B) "The Ancient Mariner"; (C) nonsense verses. (From Ballard, 1913, p. 5.)*

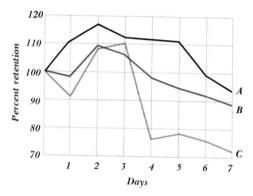

ever learning occurred during the first retention test to be transferred to the second retention test. Ward (1937) provided an improved design for tests of reminiscence by dividing the subjects into two groups. After the original learning, one group received a rest, and the other did not. Retention was measured by having the subjects relearn the material. In this design one group served as a control to measure the extent of learning immediately after practice. The design is limited by the kind of material that can be used; memorization of poetry, for example, is not very suitable to designs that require original learning to criterion, nor is it convenient to divide the subjects into two groups, equal on the basis of ability, when poetry is the material. The Ward design is similar in concept to designs used to measure the relationship between distributed- and massed-practice effects.

The problem of controlling rehearsal is a critical design problem and has received experimental attention. One common method for eliminating rehearsal is to require the subject to name colors during the intertest period. Irion (1949) and Thune (1950) have shown, however, that even the simple task of

naming colors facilitates later performance, presumably because it keeps the subject in the learning situation. In a direct attack on rehearsing, G. O. McGeoch (1935) merely asked subjects if they had rehearsed the material. She found that 84 percent of the young subjects and 70 percent of the older subjects reported rehearsing; however, those who rehearsed did no better on the retention tests than those who did not.

Hovland (1951) points out that it is necessary to show that reminiscence is a phenomenon of learning and not merely an artifact of the manner in which performance is measured. He suggests that the following controls are necessary for showing the presence of reminiscence: (1) no intervening trial must be permitted—even a recall trial permits additional learning; (2) rehearsal must be eliminated—a condition surely more easily mentioned than accomplished; (3) an activity should be used during the interval that permits neither positive nor negative transfer; (4) there should be equal motivation at each test; (5) the subject must have sufficient training on learning tasks to make the shift from tasks smooth and not totally disruptive; and (6) fatigue and similar phenomena must be eliminated. Clearly, the experimenter who decides to perform the conclusive experiment on reminiscence must solve many of the unsolved problems in other areas of human learning before he begins.

Qualities of Materials: By the qualities of materials, we refer to such factors as the meaning of the stimulus items, the frequency with which they occur—a point which determines the familiarity of the items—and the pronounceableness of items.

Ebbinghaus was so concerned with meaning that he invented nonsense syllables to eliminate the possibility that the meaning of the stimuli would affect performance. Later, Glaze (1928) showed that even the apparently harmless nonsense syllables possess meaning. In Chapter 7 we cited several techniques that have been used to measure meaning—word association tests, nonsense syllables and other "meaningless" stimuli, the semantic differential and some physiological procedures. The search for totally meaningless stimulus items is somewhat like the search for the fountain of youth. If, as some commentators suspect, there is no such thing as a totally meaningless item, it becomes necessary to measure the amount of meaningfulness that items possess. The technique of presenting the stimulus and asking the subjects if they form an association with the item has been most commonly used to measure meaningfulness. This procedure is designed to indicate the percentage of the specific population that associates to a given nonsense syllable: GOP has a high association value, and ZOK has a low association value, for example. The semantic differential provides a different measure of meaningfulness, for it attempts to measure the type of meaning ascribed to items. In addition, ranking and rating may be used to scale meaning.

Many studies show that speed of learning is related positively to the familiarity or meaningfulness of the items to be learned (see C. E. Noble, 1952a, 1952b, 1955; Goss & Nodine, 1965). Too much similarity between items, however, makes learning more difficult.

In one of the earliest studies of the qualities of the stimulus that affect ease of learning, Lyon (1914) found words of poetry easiest to learn, followed by words of prose, digits, and nonsense syllables. It is reasonable to assume that at least some poetry and prose are more meaningful than digits or nonsense syllables. If those items possessing the most meaning are learned most rapidly, then it is reasonable to assume that those items learned most rapidly have the most meaning. Consider a stimulus list, however, in which all letters are in lowercase except one word, which is entirely in capital letters, or consider a list of words in which all words are printed in black except for one word printed in red. The unusual or different items are commonly learned most rapidly; this is known as the *von Restorff effect*, after the gestalt psychologist who first studied it (von Restorff, 1933). G. A. Kimble and Dufort (1955) have studied the effect in paired-associate learning. The von Restorff effect would indicate that the items learned most rapidly are not necessarily the most meaningful, for they may have other characteristics that serve to make them significant in the experimental situation. Other variables, such as size, shape, and color of the items, have been investigated. In general, these characteristics appear to be unimportant unless they are used to isolate items from one another, as in the typical von Restorff pattern.

The affective states of pleasantness and unpleasantness appear to be another quality of the stimulus that affects learning. Some stimuli seem to be more pleasant than others and, following the psychoanalytic theory of forgetting, it has been suggested that unpleasant items will be forgotten more quickly than pleasant items. Several investigations have found that pleasant experiences are recalled more easily than unpleasant (cf. Jersild, 1931) and that either pleasant *or* unpleasant items are remembered more easily than supposedly neutral items (Koch, 1930). Although these findings do not necessarily prove the validity of the psychoanalytic theory of forgetting, they do indicate that recall is a function of the affective qualities attached to the stimuli.

Knowledge of Results: In discussing the concept of reinforcement (Chapter 12), we noted that informing a subject of the outcome of his behavior is sometimes regarded as reinforcing. The need to consider knowledge of results (KR) as a reinforcement occurs because subjects who are informed or corrected perform better in some tasks than subjects who are not. Thus, to theorists who consider reinforcement necessary for learning, KR must be called a reinforcer. It is probable, however, that treating knowledge of results as a reinforcing agent masks the importance of the phenomenon that subjects so informed learn more efficiently. It may be beneficial to consider KR as a form of *feedback,* for certainly in motor tasks and probably in verbal tasks kinesthetic feedback exists. If you are asked to draw a 3-inch line while blindfolded, the kinesthetic sensations accompanying the movement of the drawing "feed back" to the system information on where the hand is and how rapidly it is moving. This information is fed back to the hand and is used to determine the speed and direction that the hand should take. In this way, feedback provides KR. In experimental situations, an additional form of feedback is often provided by the experimenter: he may inform the subject that his performance was "half an inch off," "not the right word," or "You played D, not C." Only superficially do such instructions seem to be similar to reinforcement. Certainly there is a vast difference, at least in the precision with which the desired response is defined, between being given a pellet of food and being told to draw a longer line.

Research on KR has tended to imitate the techniques used in the study of reinforcement in subhuman animals. It is unlikely, however, that KR experienced by a human being is similar in effect to reinforcement in animal forms; there are two reasons for this: (1) KR does not satisfy a physiological need, and (2) rats do not respond to the same stimuli as human beings. Nevertheless, some general statements may be made regarding KR.

1. If practice is distributed and KR is given, the smaller the interval between trials, the better the performance (Ammons, 1956). Thus, KR appears to affect the efficiency of distributed practice.

2. In classical conditioning and instrumental training, the delay of reward is an important variable. Studies that have attempted to find whether delay of KR is also effective have generally failed to find that delay is of any importance (Saltzman, Kanfer, & Greenspoon, 1955; Bilodeau, 1966). It is strange that delay is of critical importance when reinforcement is used but of negligible importance when KR is used. This finding suggests either that KR is not reinforcing or that experimenters have not yet developed appropriate techniques for measuring the effects of KR.

3. The effect of KR depends upon the type of task the subject learns. Some tasks, such as handwriting or driving a car, require immediate feedback of KR. If KR is not immediate in driving, the subject may find himself off the road or in some other predicament without opportunity for further responses.

4. The most efficient KR is that which most precisely defines the correct response. For example, if a student is taking a multiple-choice examination and has selected an incorrect answer, the effect of KR is greater if he is informed of the right response than if he is informed only that his response was wrong. Similarly, "Push the third red button from the left" is more useful than "You pushed the wrong button." Other forms of KR, such as electric shock for wrong (or right) answers, candy, and verbal reinforcements (saying "Mm-hm") have unreliable effects on performance. Although many studies have shown these forms of KR to be effective, there is little parametric research which shows the degree of effectiveness of varying amounts of KR.

Overlearning: Generations of parents and teachers have regarded overlearning as valuable. The admonition to practice a composition to perfection and then some, has tortured numerous students who have been ready with the reply "I've already learned it." Does repeated practice of a successfully learned task improve performance? Certainly, repeated practice does improve performance; however, the amount of improvement is a negatively accelerated function. That is, one receives less and less in return when material is practiced after criterion has been reached.

Figure 15–5 shows the savings found as a function of the length of delay (number of days since learning) and as a function and the percentage of overlearning. The figure shows that overlearning provides less and less savings. If one has overlearned a task 50 percent (i.e., if one took 10 trials to reach criterion, 5 additional "overlearning" trials are given), a 20 percent savings is noted after two weeks, or approximately 19 percent increase over 0 percent overlearning. If one overlearns by 100 percent (after the original 10 trials, 10 additional trials were given), the percentage saved increases only by approximately 8 percent.

RETENTION AND FORGETTING

Immediate, Short-term, and Long-term Memory: Many investigators and theorists believe that differences in retention scores depend upon whether the recall measure is made shortly after acquisition of the material or at a later time. *Immediate memory* has been investigated for many years by measuring such features as memory span. Tests of memory span have been incorporated into intelligence tests on the assumption that the extent of the immediate memory span is also a measure of one's capacity to learn. Of course, the need to complete the administration of an intelligence test in a relatively short period largely determined the use of immediate memory span in such tests. *Short-term memory* is measured by retention or recall tests given a few seconds or, at most, a few minutes after acquisition. *Long-term memory* is measured some time after acquisition.

One purpose for investigating the different measures of memory is that certain explanations of the learning process, especially those based on projected chemical changes in the central nervous system, are sometimes pressed to explain how a chemical change can be sufficiently rapid to permit the rapid forgetting that occurs in short-term memory but sufficiently stable to permit retention in long-term memory. This problem is related to the *stimulus trace* concept of forgetting, in which it is suggested that each stimulus leaves its imprint upon the neural system but that the imprint decays in time. The process of decay results in forgetting. Stimulus trace theories usually emphasize the supposition that repeated associations somehow strengthen the trace and provide for greater memory and retention. Hebb (1949; 1961), for example, postulates both a transient trace (corresponding roughly with short-term memory) and a permanent trace (corresponding, again roughly, with long-term memory).

Two of the major variables in human learning studies are the rate of presentation of stimuli and the rate at which recall is required. In general, the faster the rate of pre-

FIGURE 15-5: *Retention curves obtained after different amounts of original learning. The figure is in terms of savings scores and the number of days since learning. Clearly, overlearning produces diminishing returns, both over time and as a function of the percentage of overlearning. (Data from Krueger, 1929, as plotted in G. A. Kimble, 1956, p. 279.)*

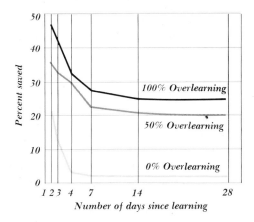

sentation, the slower the learning. Some experimenters, however, have found the reverse to be true with short-term memory; that is, the more rapid the rate of presentation, the better the recall (R. Conrad & Hille, 1958). Using slightly different experimental procedures, other investigators have found the expected results (Moray, 1960). The type of material used also affects short-term memory.

In a series of studies, Broadbent has investigated the relationship between short-term memory and the use of more than a single sensory system. This approach emphasizes the fact that in "real" life learning often occurs simultaneously through more than a single sensory system. For example, a train will stimulate our visual and auditory senses but not, we hope, our cutaneous sense. Broadbent suggests that when stimuli are presented through more than a single system, the subject's ability to shift his attention back and forth between the channels is restricted, in a manner similar to our inability to perceive both figure and ground at the same time. Further, it is suggested that stimuli entering a channel that is "unattuned" are stored in short-term memory until the subject can return his "attention" to them. The slower rate of presentation, the greater the number of shifts that are possible: hence, slow presentation should increase the storage of stimuli when more than a single channel is in use (Broadbent, 1956; 1957; 1958). Although this approach has provided additional information on short-term memory, it has also emphasized the importance of investigating learning as a function of more than a single sense.

Studies of short-term memory are particularly susceptible to the problem of controlling what occurs between the presentation of the material and the recall test. Two groups of investigators (K. E. Lloyd, L. S. Reid, & Feallock, 1960; Yntema & Meuser, 1960) have developed a technique which controls this interval and, at the same time, permits manipulation of other relevant variables. In this technique, the subjects are presented with a list of common nouns, such as "pine," "tin," and "polo." (Note that all these nouns are representatives of a larger class, e.g., "trees,"

"metals," and "sports.") At certain times, a signal consisting of the word for the major class name, such as "tree," notes a recall point. The major class name serves as a cue for the recall of the last word which was a member of the class. Figure 15–6 shows a sample sequence of this procedure. The term *storage load* refers to the number of items that the subject must retain at any given point in the sequence. The *average storage load,* as may be noted in the figure, is computed by summing the loads at each recall point and dividing by the number of recall points. The concept of storage load is useful in permitting measurement of the number of items that the subject is required to retain over the full sequence of stimuli. The Lloyd-Reid procedure, which was reported simultaneously by Yntema (Yntema & Mueser, 1960), permits the experimenter to control what occurs during the interval between presentation and recall and to vary the kind of material that is interpolated between these events by the choice of stimulus words used in the sequence. Investigations with this procedure have shown that the number of errors made in recall increases as the storage

FIGURE 15–6: *Sample sequences with different average storage loads. The lowercase letters represent items to be stored, and the capital letters indicate the recall points. The bottom line shows the words that replace the letters. In this sequence, the first recall point is at METAL. At this point the subject is storing three items ("pine," "tin," "polo"). The next recall point is TREE, and the subject is still storing three items ("pine," "polo," "copper"; "tin" has been dropped because it has already been recalled). At the third recall point, METAL, the storage load is two ("polo," "copper"). The final recall point is SPORT, and two items are stored ("polo," "hat"). (From K. E. Lloyd, L. S. Reid, & Feallock, 1960, p. 202.)*

							Serial position																
	a	*b*	*c*	*B*	*b*	*A*	*B*	*d*	*C*	*e*	*f*	*E*	*D*	*d*	*g*	*h*	*D*	*e*	*F*	*c*	*G*	*H E C*
Storage load				*3*		*3*	*2*		*2*			*3*	*2*				*4*		*4*		*4*	*3 2 1*

$\overline{X} = 2.8$

	pine	tin	polo	METAL	copper	TREE	METAL	hat	SPORT	dog ...
Storage load				*3*		*3*	*2*		*2*	

load is increased (K. E. Lloyd, L. S. Reid, & Feallock, 1960; L. S. Reid, K. E. Lloyd, Brackett, & W. F. Hawkins, 1961).

This approach also emphasizes the fact that in nonlaboratory learning situations learning is continuous. An organism is constantly bombarded with stimuli, some of which may never need to be recalled and others of which must be recalled almost immediately. For example, I may find a phone number, use it, and store it, but I have no way of knowing whether I shall ever need to recall the number or whether the operator will call back immediately to ask what number I called. Studies of the Lloyd-Reid kind—sometimes called *continuous-memory* experiments—emphasize the continuity in learning and the uncertainty in recall.

Other investigators have concentrated on testing short-term memory for a single item, rather than for a series of items given continuously. One advantage of this procedure is that the effects of transfer between items, which may be expected when items are presented serially as in the Lloyd-Reid paradigm, are minimized. L. R. Peterson and M. J. Peterson (1959) have developed a technique for evaluating short-term memory with a single stimulus, which has the advantage of controlling and manipulating the interval between stimulus presentation and recall. The investigators had their subjects follow this procedure: the experimenter spelled a group of letters to the subject (e.g., *CBG*) and then spoke a three-digit number (e.g., "306"). The subject had been instructed to count backward from the number as soon as it was presented. Meanwhile, the experimenter started a sensitive timer as soon as the syllable was spoken. When a predetermined interval was completed, the timer activated a light, which was the signal for the subject to repeat the consonant syllable.

Figure 15–7 shows the arrangement. Latency is regarded as the interval between the onset of the light and the completion of the subject's response. Using this procedure, the investigators varied the recall intervals from 3

to 18 seconds, in 3-second steps. Figure 15–8 shows the proportion of correct recalls (within 15 seconds of the light) plotted cumulatively as a function of latency. The functions are orderly and show that short-term memory is a function of the time permitted for forgetting. Note that retention is less than 10 percent after the 18-second delay. Compared with other procedures for measuring forgetting, this one provided extremely rapid forgetting.

The finding of such rapid forgetting in single-item memory has been clarified by further experimentation. To the suggestion that transfer effects were building up during the experiment, Keppel and Underwood (1962) studied the amount of transfer that occurs in successive retentions of single items. They found that inhibition increased as a function of the number of trials in which the subject participated. This finding suggests that transfer operates in a similar fashion on both short- and long-term memory. Indeed, it would appear that short-term memory and long-term

FIGURE 15–7: *The sequence of events under an experiment on short-term memory. The top line shows the passage of time in seconds. The second line shows the experimenter (E) presenting the stimulus (first the consonant, then the three-digit number). The third line shows the subject's behavior: he repeats the number and starts to count backward from it in threes. At the 3.5-second mark, or end of the recall interval, a light is turned on, and the subject must stop counting and recall the syllable. At 6 seconds the recall is complete, and the experimenter has stopped the timer. The recall interval (time from first hearing syllable until time to begin recall) is approximately 3 seconds. The latency (time from signal until recall is complete) is approximately 2.5 seconds. (From L. R. Peterson & M. J. Peterson, 1959, p. 194.)*

Sec	0	1	2	3	4	5	6...
E	*CHJ*	*506*					
S			*506*	*503*			*CHJ*

|←—Recall interval—→|←——Latency——→|

FIGURE 15-8: *Results from a study on short-term memory. The graph shows the number of correct recalls as cumulative functions of latency. Six different groups are used, ranging from 3 to 18 seconds. (From L. R. Peterson, & M. J. Peterson, 1959, p. 195.)*

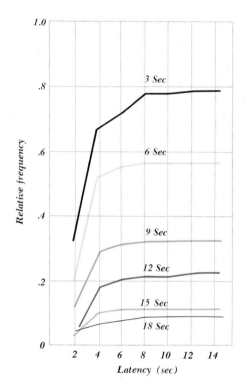

memory are affected by the same kinds of effects.

Theories of Forgetting: In general, very long-term retention and forgetting have not been so thoroughly investigated as acquisition. The reasons for this neglect are probably of a practical nature: it is difficult to find subjects willing to return for retention tests at the precise time when they are needed, and it is difficult to control the learning that occurs between acquisition and testing. Forgetting, however, as measured by retention, is of con-

siderable importance. We may distinguish two kinds of retention: *qualitative* and *quantitative*. Quantitative retention refers to the number of items recalled (e.g., six out of eight nonsense syllables) and qualitative retention refers to the kinds of items recalled (e.g., I can recall items concerned with food more readily than other items). Most laboratory studies have emphasized the quantitative, rather than the qualitative, attributes of memory.

The concepts of *disuse* and of *interference* are the two basic concepts of forgetting from which most theories are derived. Disuse assumes that stored memories are not used, and thus become weak and are forgotten. Interference theory, on the other hand, suggests that forgetting is a result of transfer: items are forgotten, not because they decay, but because some other item is remembered. The difficulty with the theory of disuse is that it is not a very helpful theory: it does not tell us where, neurologically, to look for the decay from disuse; it does not predict how memory will be changed as a function of the method used for acquisition and retention—in short, it is a barren approach. To the psychologist, interference theories have been more appealing, for they lead to testable hypotheses.

The degree of interference may be measured by varying the kinds of activities the subject performs between acquisition and retention testing. Since there should be little, if any, interference while one is sleeping, the study of the effect of sleep on forgetting has been examined. There is agreement that retention is better after sleep than after waking activities. Figure 15–9 shows the results of a study made by J. G. Jenkins and Dallenbach (1924; revised by Dallenbach, 1963), who had two subjects learn a list of 10 nonsense syllables. For the lists learned prior to the sleep interval, there was some forgetting during the first 2 hours, perhaps related to the subjects' passing from wakefulness to sleep. Sleep had a beneficial effect on recall, for after 2 hours the sleep group retained the same number of syllables through 8 hours, although the awake group showed a steady decline in memory. When stories, rather than nonsense syllables were used, there was no difference between sleep and awake groups in recall of the major themes of the story, but the subjects who slept during the interim recalled nonessential aspects of the material more clearly (Newman, 1939).

In an attempt to test the effect of inactivity, Hunter (1932) immobilized cockroaches by means of cold and tested them on a darkness avoidance test. He found that learning was retarded if the roaches were exposed to temperatures of 3 to 6°C for 2 to 4 hours. Minami and Dallenbach (1946) also tested the effect of activity. They used three groups of cockroaches: one was a forced-activity group, one a normal-resting activity group, and one an inactivity group. They found that retention was lowest for the forced-activity group.

Ebbinghaus (1913) first published the standard forgetting curve, the general shape of which has been consistently duplicated in a variety of experimental conditions. The function, like that shown in Figure 15–10, appears more similar to what one would expect if the decay theory of forgetting were appropriate than if the interference theory were correct. (For the opposite point of view see Bilodeau, 1961). If it is interference that causes forgetting, why should the function not be linear? Why should interference be most damaging shortly after learning but become less and less effective as time passes? These questions serve to show that in their present forms neither disuse nor interference theories are able to interpret all the facts of forgetting, although interference theory can account for many of them.

The gestalt position has attributes of both disuse and interference. On the whole, this position places greatest emphasis on the perceptual and organizational pattern of stimuli. In its simplest form, it suggests that forgetting is a function of the "wholeness" or "goodness" of the object. From these assumptions, gestalt

FIGURE 15–9: *The relationship between recall of nonsense syllables and the activity (sleeping or being awake) interpolated between acquisition and the retention test. The average number of syllables reproduced by the subjects after various time intervals of sleep and waking are shown. (From Dallenbach, 1963, p. 702.)*

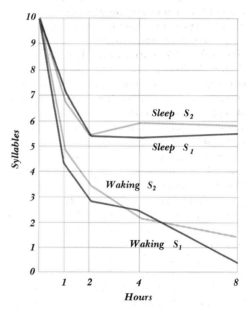

FIGURE 15–10: *Ebbinghaus's curve of retention. This is the classic shape of the forgetting curve. These data were derived by the savings method. (From J. A. McGeoch & Irion, 1952, p. 356; data from Ebbinghaus, 1913.)*

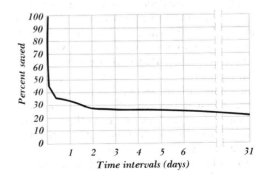

psychologists make predictions regarding the qualitative characteristics of memory. For example, if a figure is remembered, it will be remembered as a "better" figure than it actually was. Although the "goodness" of drawings is difficult to measure, studies that have required subjects to redraw items after different periods of time do appear to show that the recalled figures are smoother, less ragged, and, in general, represent a better "whole" (N. G. Hanawalt, 1937; Carmichael, H. P. Hogan, & Walter, 1932). One may argue that a figure is not forgotten; it merely becomes merged with other "good" figures, so that its original state of separateness is no longer noted. This postulation, of course, contains many of the elements of interference theory.

One of the more striking examples of the susceptibility of memory to procedural variables was reported by Zeigarnik (1927). She gave subjects 20 simple tasks. Half of the tasks were interrupted; i.e., the subjects were not permitted to finish. The other half were uninterrupted. When asked the nature of the tasks they had performed, the subjects were able to recall the interrupted tasks more often than the completed tasks. This phenomenon, known as the *Zeigarnik effect,* has received considerable attention from both gestalt psychologists and psychologists oriented more behavioristically. Although it appears that the effect occurs only under rather precise conditions (see Woodworth & Schlosberg, 1954, p. 692), the basic results have been duplicated in many laboratories.

The psychoanalytic approach to behavior has traditionally emphasized the role of *repression* in forgetting. In a postulate similar in structure to the law of effect, psychoanalytic theory states that unpleasant items (e.g., those producing anxiety, guilt, shame) are forgotten and become less easy to recall. Much of psychoanalytic therapy is based upon the presumably beneficial effect of recalling apparently forgotten events. Zeller (1950) obtained evidence for this general approach by using two tasks (nonsense-syllable learning and a

motor task) and by artificially varying the subjects' impressions of how well they did. In general, subjects recalled less of those tasks which they presumably failed than of those in which they supposedly succeeded. J. M. Levine and Murphy (1943) divided potential subjects into two groups, one which had reacted favorably to pro-Communist material and another which had reacted unfavorably. Both acquisition and retention were measured for material consisting of statements regarding the Soviet Union. The learning functions showed that the pro-Communist subjects learned the material more rapidly. The difference in original learning, however, masked possible differences in retention, thus showing a major difficulty in this type of experimental design.

One of the major concepts applied to verbal learning is *clustering*. Clustering refers to the fact that a word has an associative value with other words. Bousfield (1953) gave subjects a list of 60 words. He selected the words so that they would be of four categories—vegetables, professions, animals, and names—and arranged them randomly into lists. In recall tests, the subjects showed a greater-than-chance tendency to recall the words in clusters, according to category. Research on clustering and related research on linguistics have contributed the notion of human verbal learning as a *mediated process*. This term implies that recall is not necessarily direct but that some process mediates between learning and retention. For example, Bousfield and B. H. Cohen (1953) noted that "leopard" could result in the association "animal" (the more general class) but that the associations which followed were other members of the original class "animal," such as "tiger," or "dog."

G. A. Miller (1956) has suggested that memory is related to *chunks* of information: chunks are the composites of stimuli. For example, consider the word "horse": I do not normally recall the word by remembering the five discrete units—the letters—of which it is composed. Rather, I see the word as a chunk. Similarly, several words, digits, or other stimuli may make up a chunk. A sentence such as:

Are rivulets canoes of bookish mire

does not form a chunk, but

Oh, say can you see

does. The chunk may occur because of past learning and because of the meaningfulness of its parts. Miller suggests that the chunks are the basic units of memory and that although individuals may differ in the number of chunks they can learn and recall, they will learn a similar number of chunks regardless of the type of material. Whether one is learning a series of digits or poetry, it is the number of chunks into which the material is divisible which governs how much can be learned and recalled. According to this approach, we constantly recode material into chunks; that is, we carry around a finite number of pigeonholes into which material must be forced before it can be accumulated and reproduced. If the material is complicated, we put less in each pigeonhole. In other words, we code the material into recallable units. Clustering, then, represents one form of chunking behavior. Miller suggests that the average number of chunks that can be recalled is 7 ± 2, i.e., between 5 and 9.

Before considering some specific areas of retention in the following sections, we may note some general findings:

1. The amount retained is a negatively accelerated decay function. The greatest amount of forgetting occurs immediately after learning. As time passes, less and less is forgotten. Note, however, that as time passes, there is less to forget.

2. In general, overlearning results in greater retention than underlearning. By overlearning, we mean the continuation of learning trials after criterion (one correct reproduction, for example) has been reached. By underlearning, we mean stopping the learning process before criterion has been reached. In general, the more overlearning,

the better the retention. There is some evidence that this finding holds only for those experienced in memorizing (Cuff, 1927).

3. Jost (1897) suggested two laws of retention (*Jost's laws*). Although they are somewhat loosely stated by current standards, the laws are generally valid. The first states that "if two associations are now of equal strength but of different ages, the older one will lose strength more slowly with the further passage of time." The second law states that "if two associations are of equal strength and different ages, further study has greater value for the older one." The first law is predictable from the usual retention function, for the older the material, the less the loss through forgetting. The second law, originally conceived to explain massed and distributed practice, suggests that the older the material, the more effective is relearning.

4. Forgetting occurs less in the "real world" than in the laboratory. In the laboratory, conditions are established that lead to reasonably rapid learning and forgetting. This is necessary in order to establish the parameters of learning and forgetting. Outside the laboratory, human beings are able to remember material for long periods of time. Although the data are largely anecdotal, savings may amount to 44 percent after five years with prose (Worcester, 1923) and 7 percent after twenty-two years with stanzas from Don Juan (Ebbinghaus, 1911). These savings are probably strongly affected by learning to learn.

5. Motor tasks are easily relearned. Again, many of the data are fragmentary and anecdotal; however, a person who ceases to type for several years apparently loses only a third of the performance rate, and relearning is rapid (Swift, 1906). This appears to be true for playing musical instruments and for similar motor activities.

6. Retention is clearly influenced by the method used to measure it. Figure 15–11 shows the classic data of Luh (1922), who investigated retention as a function of recognition, relearning, reconstruction, written reproduction, and anticipation. Although all the decay functions are negatively accelerated, they differ in slope.

7. The relationship between speed of learning and amount of retention is not a simple one. For

FIGURE 15-11: *Retention curves obtained under five different methods of measuring retention. Although the functions are similar, the percentage of retention varies as a function of the method used. (From Luh, 1922, p. 22.)*

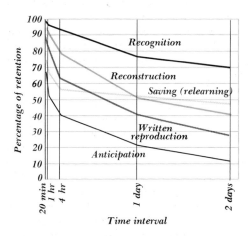

Indeed, a belief in some kind of transfer underlies all educational and training procedures. Moreover, transfer is involved in all experiments on learning: neither human nor rat subjects are "inexperienced" when placed in an experimental environment, for an organism has had some experiences which may be expected to transfer to the learning situations required in experiments. For this reason, among others, transfer is an influential concept in regard to the development of explanations of learning. When we speak of differentiation and stimulus or response generalization, we are concerned with transfer; when we discuss the learning or forgetting of stimulus items as a function of the interference of other stimuli, we are concerned with transfer. Although transfer has been studied in a number of animal forms, some of the most significant findings have come from work on human verbal learning.

Measuring Transfer: The experimental study of transfer presents problems similar to those found in studying reminiscence. Two general methods have been used to study transfer: the *pretest* method and the method of *successive practice.* The pretest is described by the following paradigm:

E	Pretest on A	Practice B	Posttest on A
C	Pretest on A	Nothing or neutral task	Posttest on A

The advantages of this design are (1) the subjects are "equated" on their ability to learn the eventual dependent variable (task A) at the onset of the experiment; (2) the direction of the transfer effect may be noted; i.e., it may be determined whether the effect is positive or negative by noting whether the experimental group's performance exceeds that of the control group on the posttest (positive transfer effect) or whether the performance is inferior to the control group (negative transfer effect).

There are, however, several disadvantages to this technique. The fact that the subjects

example, the method of measuring retention may affect the relationship. Underwood (1954) reports a zero correlation between time to learn and amount recalled but a high positive relationship between time to learn and time to relearn. It would appear that a person who learned rapidly might or might not show good recall, possibly because relearning is not a pure measure of retention, as we have noted.

TRANSFER

In an earlier day, some educators believed that the study of mathematics led to the development of an orderly mind and assumed that mastery of Greek and Latin generated elegant syntax and a substantial English vocabulary. This idea was based on the belief that *positive transfer* occurs in the process of education. A modern example of this idea is students who are taught to drive in mock-up cars in the expectation that whatever is learned in the mock-up will be transferred and yield appropriate driving behavior on the road.

are "matched" during the pretest does not ensure that *they will continue to learn at equally rapid rates.* It is possible that an apparent positive transfer effect could arise from the experimental group's having done better on the posttest because of reminiscence or some other factor which was unaccounted for by "matching" the groups during the pretest. To neutralize this difficulty, experimenters often use a short pretest (short, so as little learning will occur as is possible) and a task very similar to task B (similar, so that measuring performance on A can be an adequate measure of the effect on B). Both procedures present difficulties. By using a short pretest, the experimenter is unable to assess the course of learning task A; this is as if one assumed that all children of age two who are 32 inches tall would thereafter grow at the same rate. One must be certain to check for transfer at more than one point. If the pretest is short, task A is being tested at a relatively undeveloped state of learning. Reliance on the one-test procedure assumes that the course of learning can be accurately predicted from any point. As we have noted in our analogy with the eventual height of two-year-olds, this is an unlikely assumption. Moreover, transfer may affect learning in different ways, depending upon the degree of learning. For example, it is probable that a well-learned task, such as using the right foot on the accelerator, is more likely to be affected by negative transfer than a task that is not well learned. Certainly such factors as warming up may be overlooked by the pretest method. Often, however, these problems are relatively immaterial, and the pretest design succeeds in providing controls for the more serious problems.

The method of *successive practice* (Woodworth & Schlosberg, 1954) attempts to overcome the myopia of the pretest method by substituting a learning task in which the subject acquires the material presented in task A for the pretest. This procedure is often called the *single-group method* (Underwood, 1949). If it is assumed that A and B are equivalent tasks, then a control group is presumably unnecessary. The subjects merely learn A and then B. If the learning time for B is less than for A, it is assumed that there has been positive transfer; if A is learned more rapidly, then it is assumed that there has been negative transfer. The conclusion is reasonable, of course, so long as the experimenter can show that the tasks are *equal* in difficulty for the *subjects used.* This rather stiff requirement accounts for the observation that the method is rarely used; the assumption that the tasks are of equivalent difficulty greatly limits the type of subject matter that may be investigated under the single-group, successive-practice method. The use of a control group, however, permits selecting unequal tasks, as in the following paradigm:

E	Learn A	Learn B
C	—	Learn B

This design assumes that the subjects are somehow matched, so that neither group is superior in learning at the beginning of the experiment. The problem of matching subjects so that their rate of learning on a given task is equivalent, without using the material to be learned as a measure, is easily solved. To avoid both the problem of matching the groups and of using equivalent tasks, a pooled design may be used:

Group I	Learn A	Learn B
Group II	Learn B	Learn A

Note that if group II's learning of B is more efficient than group I's, we may assume that group I's learning of A hindered the learning of B. Similar comparisons may be made regarding group I's learning of task A. Experimenters are not limited, of course, to a single experimental group. Other groups may be added in order to investigate the role of subject matter, length of practice, or any of many variables that affect learning and transfer.

The statistical method chosen for showing the transfer effect is important. Two formulas are in common use. The first expresses transfer in percentages:

$$\frac{C-E}{C} \times 100$$

where

C = **control group's (or group II's) score on B**
E = **experimental group's (or group I's) score on B**

Assume that the measure is the number of trials to reach criterion (or any other measure in which the larger the number, the poorer the performance). A positive result indicates positive transfer, and a negative result indicates negative transfer. If the criterion is such that better performance is represented by a larger number (e.g., the number of items recalled correctly), the reverse will be true. The second formula is

$$\frac{E-C}{\text{Total possible score}} \times 100$$

where

E = **experimental group's score on B**
C = **control group's score on B**

Under this formula, the absence of transfer will yield a score of 0; 100 indicates complete transfer. A score of 100, for example, would mean that the same level of performance was reached as would have occurred had as much practice been devoted to the task used to measure transfer.

One difficulty with the second formula is that it assumes that the total possible score is known. Often it is, but on some experiments the total possible score may be infinite. Gagné, H. Foster, and Crowley (1948) suggest the following revision:

$$\frac{E - \text{initial } C \text{ score}}{\text{Final } C \text{ score} - \text{initial } C \text{ score}} \times 100$$

where

E = **experimental group's score on B**
C = **control group's score on B**

It may be recalled from our discussion of psychophysics that Weber had an uncanny ability to communicate important ideas to Fechner (such as Weber's law). In addition, he reported his observations on transfer to Fechner, and Fechner published them along with additional observations in 1858. Weber noted that children who had learned to write with the right hand were able to reproduce such writing with the left hand. Fechner commented on this at greater length. William James and Thorndike also studied transfer. Both were concerned with the assumption commonly made in education that the study of formal disciplines, such as Latin, aided the learning of other disciplines. William James (1890) had subjects learn verses of a poem. Then the subjects learned the verses of another poem and finally relearned the original material. Note that this design does not provide for a control group that does not participate in learning the verses of the second poem. James reported that little transfer occurred under these conditions, suggesting that the process of transfer was of limited value to education. Although James's implication was hasty, it is noteworthy that he suggested that the improvement he did notice came about because of an *increased facility to memorize.* That is, James suggested that *learning how to learn*—in this case, learning how to memorize —affected learning.

Some Kinds of Interference: There are a number of sources of interference and transfer in studies of human verbal learning. An example of several kinds is shown in Figure 15–12. Careful study of these sources will provide the student with the definitions of the basic kinds of interference. From the "prior state of the subject," the subject brings into the experimental design certain kinds of interference based on the instructions given

FIGURE 15–12: *Sources of interference in recall in studies of short-term memory. (Courtesy of Professor A. W. Melton.)*

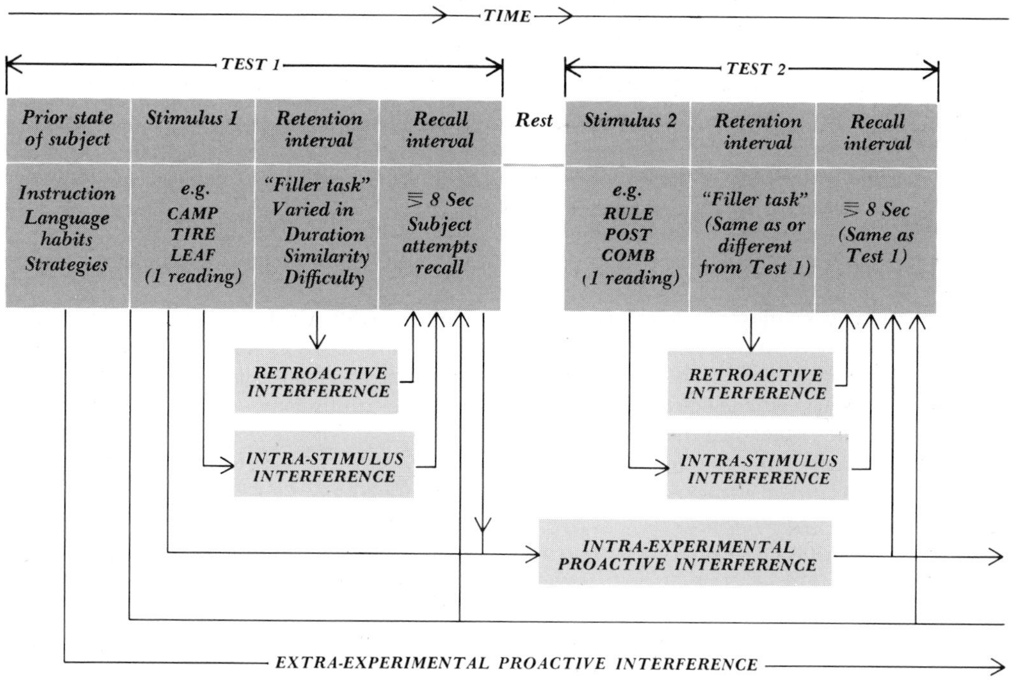

him in regard to the task, his previously learned language habits, and the strategies which he uses in the experiment. By strategies is meant the ways in which he goes about solving the problem posed by the experimenter's instructions. These variables lead to *extraexperimental-proactive interference.* Consider test 1. On the first reading, the subject learns stimuli, such as the words indicated in Figure 15–12. The retention interval contains a filler task, such as counting backward. These tasks may vary in the ways noted in Figure 15–12. Then recall is conducted. In short-term memory, the recall interval is less than eight seconds. Note that between these three events—presentation of the stimuli, the retention interval, and the recall interval—both *intrastimulus interference* and *retroactive interference* may occur. If a second test is given, as shown in Figure 15–12, we find the same

sources of interference within that test. However, the presentation of a second test introduces the possibility of *intraexperimental proactive interference.*

Experiment and Theory: The early literature on transfer was concerned primarily with *bilateral transfer,* i.e., transfer between hands or feet. Starting with William James, who probably represented the new interest in discovering principles of learning for the purpose of improving educational procedures, research on transfer was aimed toward pedagogical ends: the concern was whether the acquisition of specific subject matters influenced the learning of other subject matters. The rapid development of learning theories in the 1930s provided additional pressure to study transfer effects. The basic question that any theory of learning attempts to answer is

"How do new responses occur" and the principles of transfer are useful in answering this question. The problem of predicting the conditions under which transfer will occur and those which yield positive transfer has intrigued investigators for many years for both applied and theoretical reasons.

Edward L. Thorndike defended the position that ". . . a change in one function alters any other (function) only in so far as the two functions have as factors identical elements" (1913, vol. II, p. 358). This *identical elements* theory, although severely criticized by many commentators, has enjoyed a long history. In opposition to identical elements theory, some theorists have suggested that it is "general principles," rather than elements, which are transferred. The reader may recognize a similarity to the argument (Chapter 14) between absolute and relational theorists in discrimination learning.

Although the significance is not always appreciated, some form of transfer occurs whenever subjects are presented with verbal instructions. Battig (1956) has pointed out that in acquiring motor skills, the subject has two tasks: discovering what to do with the stimulus aspects of the task, such as the keys on a typewriter, and performing the task, including the kinesthetic movements necessary for completing the task. Verbal instructions can produce satisfactory learning for the *discovery* segment: one can explain the relationship between the keys on a typewriter and the production of typewritten material. This is a case of transfer, for performance on a task is altered by the interpolation of another task. It is also possible, of course, that verbal instructions can affect the *performance* aspect of motor learning. Battig's study (1956) showed that the more complex the motor skill, the less the transfer. That is, motor skills that require relatively little in the way of performance are greatly affected by the transfer created by verbal practice. Tasks that are relatively difficult to perform profit least from verbal transfer.

As may be expected from our discussion of meaningfulness in verbal learning, transfer is an important determiner of this form of learning. The effects of transfer may be investigated through paired-associate learning, where the degree of similarity between the stimulus and response may be controlled by the experimenter.

In a series of studies by D. Lewis and his associates (summarized by E. A. Bilodeau & I. McD. Bilodeau, 1961), the efficacy of negative transfer has been questioned. These studies suggest that when and if negative transfer does appear, it is likely to be ephemeral, disappearing after a few trials. Moreover, what appears to be an example of negative transfer sometimes becomes a positive transfer effect if trials are continued.

INCIDENTAL LEARNING

In most human learning experiments, the subjects are given instructions about the task they are to perform. They may be told, for example, to remember a list of words in order or to be prepared to recall as many items as possible from a selection of stimuli. These are experiments which involve *intentional learning*, for the experimenter is usually very careful to make certain that the subject understands the instructions. It is evident, however, that human beings, as well as animals, are capable of learning without being instructed to do so. Generally, in experiments involving intentional learning, data from subjects who clearly misunderstand the instructions and who attempt to learn the "wrong" thing are discarded. These discarded data provide information on a second type of learning—*incidental learning*. Studies of incidental learning are concerned with the learning that occurs even though subjects have not received instructions regarding the task to be learned.

Consider an experiment in which the experimenter asks the subject to memorize a list of nonsense syllables. Some of the syllables are in capital letters, and others are not, but this attribute of the stimuli is not mentioned in the instructions. After the subject succeeds in recalling the list, the experimenter asks him to name those syllables which were in capital letters and those which were not. Even though the subject was never instructed to learn this information, under most conditions he is able to show retention of such "irrelevant" characteristics of the stimuli. This is an illustration of incidental learning.

An example of a process similar to incidental learning has been found in the behavior of animals. If a rat is placed in a maze and permitted to explore (but without finding food or any reinforcer), his performance does not improve appreciably. That is, the number of "errors" he makes and the amount of time it takes him to reach the "goal" do not decrease. A second rat, serving as the control in this demonstration, finds food in the goal box. If he is hungry, we can expect his time to reach the goal and number of errors to decrease with repeated sessions in the maze. At this point, the first rat is made hungry and placed in the maze. Within a few trials his running speed and error rate are near those of the rat who has had more experience in finding the reinforcement. Apparently, the first rat was learning something during those trials in which he was permitted to explore the maze without reinforcement. This effect is called *latent learning,* for it suggests that the animal was *learning* during the exploratory trials but that this learning did not appear in his *performance* until the reinforcement was present—in this case, until the animal was hungry and food was in the goal box. Although there are basic differences between the concepts of latent learning and incidental learning, as well as between the designs of experiments concerned with them, both show that subjects may be learning something about characteristics of the stimuli or the experimental situation even when this learning does not appear immediately in performance.

Postman (1964) distinguishes two major types of studies of incidental learning: In the first type (type I), the subject is exposed to the stimuli and does not receive directions. Later he is tested unexpectedly on some attribute of the stimuli. In the second type of study (type II), the subject is directed to learn one task, but he is actually tested on some other task which was incidental to the first task. Our example of a subject who was instructed to learn a list of nonsense syllables but later asked to name the syllables that appeared in capital letters represents type II. The advantage of type I designs is that incidental learning may be measured without the presence of possible contamination due to directions having been given to the subject. Directions presumably permit the formation of a "set" to respond in a certain manner. By the same reasoning, type II designs are useful when the experimenter wishes to measure the effect of set or motivation.

J. G. Jenkins (1933) had students, who thought they were serving as experimenters in a laboratory experiment, read a list of nonsense syllables to student subjects. The subjects were directed to learn the words in order. The next day, without warning, both groups were asked to recall the words. The subjects (intentional group) recalled more words than the experimenters, although the experimenters were able to recall some of the words. The results uphold the belief in the ability of subjects to learn without specific directions and indicate that directions are instrumental in bringing about greater retention of the learning task.

The way in which the subject comes into contact with the stimuli is called the *orienting task,* and there is ample evidence that the nature of the orienting task is critical in determining the extent of incidental learning. For example, J. G. Jenkins (1933) reports that upon questioning the experimenters described in the above paragraph, he found that some had attempted to learn the list. Saltzman (1953; 1956) reports that the difference between the incidental and intentional learning scores may be due to the orienting task. He found that intentional learners generally perform better because they are not required to perform an orienting task. In a series of studies of incidental learning, Postman and his colleagues have further defined the relationship between intentional and incidental learning. There is less difference between intentional and incidental learning if the material is familiar and easy to learn than if it is difficult. Further, the kind and type of motivation provided to the subject through the instructions affects the efficiency of incidental learning (Postman & P. A. Adams, 1956; Postman, P. A. Adams, & Bohm, 1956; Postman, P. A. Adams, & L. W. Phillips, 1955; Postman & Tuma, 1954; Mechanic, 1962).

The presence and extent of incidental learning is determined primarily, therefore, by the attributes of the experimental situation: (1) the nature of the orienting task, (2) the type of material to be learned, and (3) the directions as to how it is to be learned.

VERBAL "CONDITIONING"

Traditionally in psychophysics, scaling, perception, and other areas of research, the verbal response of the subject has been used as a dependent variable. This assumes, more or less tacitly, that one's verbal behavior provides an accurate description of one's experiences.

Studies of operant training originally used a simple motor response, such as a bar press, as the dependent variable. Eventually, it became evident that verbal behavior, like motor behavior, was not immune to operant training. This evidence suggests that the trainability of verbal behavior is often used as a dependent variable.

Greenspoon (1951; 1955) instructed college students to say as many individual words as they could for 50 minutes. During the first half of the session the groups of subjects were reinforced under several conditions, including the experimenter's saying "Mm-hm" or "Uh-uh." In each of these groups, half of the subjects were reinforced for each plural noun (e.g., "trees") which they spoke. The remaining subjects were reinforced for all responses except plural nouns. A control group received

no reinforcements. During the second 25 minutes of the session, extinction was conducted; no reinforcements were given.

The group that received "Mm-hm" following their saying plural nouns increased the total number of plural nouns that they spoke. The group that heard "Uh-uh" after each plural noun showed a decrease in the number of that form of word, although the "Uh-uh" had different effects depending upon the class of responses that was being reinforced; "Mm-hm" served as a reinforcer in both classes. An important characteristic of the original Greenspoon study is that at the conclusion of testing, each subject was interviewed in order to determine whether he had noted the connection between his verbal behavior and the reinforcement. We shall note the importance of this procedure in our discussion of similar studies.

Since this study was reported, many aspects of verbal "conditioning," as the process has come to be called, have been investigated. The following are among the variables that have been studied:

1. *Magnitude of the class of responses that is reinforced* (Prutsman, 1961): Data suggest that some response classes may be too small to admit to ready "conditioning." For example, there are few pronouns in the English language compared with the number of nouns.

2. *Effect of different experimenters:* Matarazzo, Saslow, and Pareis (1960) found that some experimenters were able "conditioners" whereas others were not. Moreover, evidence shows that there is an interaction between the sex of the experimenter and the sex of the subject. Bachrach, Candland, and J. T. Gibson (1961) found that some subjects respond to reinforcers provided by male experimenters and others respond to those provided by female experimenters.

3. *The importance of the preconditioning situation:* In the conditioning of animals, it is a truism that the state of the animal prior to the onset of conditioning is an important determiner of the success of conditioning. Indeed, there is evidence that optimum conditioning occurs when the sub-

ject is aroused and excited to some degree. If verbal conditioning is similar to other forms of conditioning, one would expect the state of the subject prior to the onset of conditioning to affect conditioning. In one study, Kanfer and Karas (1959) provided different types of preconditioning experiences for four groups. All experimental subjects were asked to perform a task, for which they were either praised, criticized, or ignored. A control group received no preconditioning experience. All groups that interacted with the experimenters by working on the task emitted a greater number of conditioned responses than the subjects who had no interaction.

4. *The effect of instruction:* This variable has not received the attention it deserves. As an example of the potency of instructions in determining the ease of conditioning, however, Naumoff and Sidowski (1959) noted that subjects who were instructed to make the experimenter say "Good" as often as they could produced more conditioned verbal responses than subjects who did not have these instructions. This variable is, with little doubt, related to the problem of awareness. Most studies of verbal conditioning eliminate the data of subjects who report that they isolate the relationship between the experimenter's response and their behavior and who were aware of the reinforcer.

Medini (1957), for example, asked his subjects, after each group of 10 trials, if they had recognized any rule that determined when the experimenter said "Good." This procedure was continued until the subjects did recognize the relationship or until 200 trials had passed, whichever came first. A significant relationship between the speed at which a subject recognized the relationship and his degree of learning was found.

Other studies which have analyzed the role of awareness by interviews report that unaware subjects perform differently from subjects who are aware (e.g., Matarazzo, Saslow, & Pareis, 1960). We have noted that awareness plays an important role in classical conditioning; however, remarkably little is known about its role in operant training. Certainly, one curiosity is that so few of the subjects used in verbal conditioning studies are able to discover the relationship between the reinforcer and their speech. It is apparently not uncommon to find 90 percent of the subjects professing total unawareness, although in one detailed study (Krasner, Weiss, & Ullmann, 1959), 38 percent of the subjects reported some degree of awareness. It is likely that all through an experiment, the subjects attempt to figure out the relationship. Greenspoon (1951) reports a tendency for his subjects to continue naming the general class of responses if one response was reinforced. It may be recalled that Greenspoon reinforced plural nouns. He noted that if, for example, "potatoes" was reinforced, some subjects would continue naming vegetables until this behavior extingushed (or, presumably, until the plural name of a vegetable was given and reinforced).

There is ample evidence that subjects faced with a relatively unstructured situation of being asked to say all the words they can develop hypotheses which they test out along the way. If so, human verbal conditioning has some similarities to the behavior of rats which are trained to discriminate between shapes or colors. They too appear according to some investigators to form "hypotheses" concerning what the solution may be, and they appear to test them in an orderly fashion (cf. Krechevsky, 1932; 1938). Dulany (1961) has also suggested that the function of saying "Mm-hm" or of providing any other cue is to enable the subject to form hypotheses about the nature of the responses which are required of him. For example, Dulany questioned subjects who had received training in which "Mm-hm" followed each plural noun. Twenty-five percent of the subjects said that whenever they heard "Mm-hm," they assumed (hypothesized) that they were to continue to associate. Thus, if "Mm-hm" followed a plural noun, the subject hypothesized that further plural nouns were wanted. These subjects showed an acquisition of the response of saying plural nouns. The investigator suggests that rather than explain these experiments in terms of conditioning, we may assume that for the subjects the cue or reinforcer produces a set to associate. Thus, the subject forms hypotheses, based on the occurrence of the reinforcer, and tests out these hypotheses, often by continuing to say words in the same set as those reinforced.

5. *Distribution of reinforcement:* Although most investigators have found that omitting the reinforcer leads to a decrease in response rate, as in extinction, some reports suggest that omitting the reinforcer only redistributes the types of responses. Similarly, most investigators have found that acquisition conducted under continuous reinforcement is easier to extinguish than acquisition under the various partial reinforcement schedules.

6. *Punishment:* Although punishment is an important variable in operant training, it has not been used extensively in verbal conditioning studies. Generally, negative reinforcement has been investigated by saying "Wrong" or "Uh-uh." A. H. Buss and E. H. Buss (1956), for example, reported that using "Wrong" for incorrect responses but saying nothing for correct responses led to more efficient learning than saying "Right" for the correct response but nothing for the incorrect responses. This finding implies that negative reinforcement is comparatively more efficacious than positive reinforcement. (See Hovland, 1952, for an analysis of the effects of positive and negative reinforcement on concept learning.) We have noted this effect before in rats (cf. Muenzinger, 1934; see Chapter 12 of the present volume).

The implications of the discovery that language is "conditionable" are considerable. There is no question that much of human behavior is controlled by verbal behavior. We respond to the verbal behavior of others. Moreover, our own thought process is based on language. Finally, it would appear that attention should be given to the psychotherapeutic situation in which the therapist and the patient are, in effect, partaking in joint verbal conditioning (Greenspoon, 1962).

SAMPLES OF PERCEPTUAL-MOTOR LEARNING

Perceptual-motor learning describes those skills and activities which involve the integration and coordination of a perceptual system, such as vision or audition, with motor systems.

So many activities are of a perceptual-motor nature that we may distinguish some major differences between them. First, some activities require *fine* coordination (handwriting, tapping a telegraph key) whereas others require *gross* movement, or movements involving the coordination of many parts of the body (throwing a football, broadjumping). Second, some perceptual-motor responses require *single action* (a given, single response, such as depressing a brake following a particular stimulus such as a red light). Other responses involve *serial action* (either a chain of responses, such as those required for typing, or a *continuous* task, such as tracking a continually moving stimulus).

The distinction between fine and gross movements is not always obvious. Rather, the movements represent the ends of a continuum of perceptual-motor tasks. The distinction between single action and serial movements is useful when one considers the whole task or activity. The responses that constitute a serial-action task, however, may be reduced to the individual responses that make up the task. Moreover, although most activities are of a continuous nature, they are often reduced to their component tasks in the laboratory in order to permit the accumulation of data on how continuous tasks are learned.

Some Common Apparatuses and Techniques: Apparatuses and techniques used in studies of perceptual-motor learning are of two basic types: those which are selected because they simulate the activity under investigation and those which are expected to provide data that may be generalized to other perceptual-motor situations. Among the first type of apparatus are mock-up control panels for airplanes, mock-up cars for driving instruction, and typewriters with blank keys. The second type provides basic tasks which, although they have little direct relevance to everyday tasks, furnish information on such processes as transfer of training. The following are samples of the variety of tasks and apparatuses used in perceptual-motor experiments.

REACTION-TIME APPARATUS: One of the earliest questions asked by psychologists interested in differences among individuals was how rapidly a person could react to a stimulus. The reaction time most often measured is to visual or auditory stimuli, and sometimes to both simultaneously. Typically, the subject is instructed that when a light (or tone) appears (or sounds), he is to press a key or make some other response, which may be, perhaps, a verbal response. The time between the onset of the stimulus and the subject's reaction is called the *reaction time* (RT). Although RT experiments were originally made to assess the speed of transmission of the nervous system, later experiments were directed toward industrial and military concerns. For example, specialists in highway safety commonly separate the amount of time taken to stop a moving vehicle into two aspects, the RT of the subject and the amount of time needed for the vehicle to stop after the appropriate response has been made.

RT varies as a function of characteristics of both the stimulus and the subject. For example:

1. **RT to auditory or cutaneous stimuli is more rapid than to visual stimuli.**

2. **RT to light varies as a function of the area on the retina that is stimulated. The farther out on the periphery, the longer the RT.**

3. **In taste, salt has the most rapid RT, followed by sweet, sour, and bitter. Of course, the RT for taste will vary as a function of type and concentration of the stimulus, as well as the section of the tongue on which it is placed (Kiesow, 1903).**

4. **The more intense the stimulus, the more rapid the RT.**

5. **RT varies as a function of motivation. Compared with subjects given a normal RT examination, subjects given an incentive show more rapid RTs. Those punished by electric shock show even faster RTs (Johanson, 1922).**

6. *Disjunctive* **RT (e.g., the subject is instructed to respond to a red light by pressing a button with the left hand but to a green light by press-** ing a button with the right hand, *or* the subject is told to push a button when a red light appears but not when a green light appears) produces longer RTs than simple RT experiments. Moreover, the more similar the stimuli used in disjunctive RT, the longer the RT latency.

7. **RT (to tone) is a negative-decay function in respect to age, as shown in Figure 15–13.**

PURSUIT ROTOR: This apparatus is shown in Figure 15–14. The subject is instructed to keep the stylus in contact with the disk. The disk is usually rotated at a constant speed, but it may be rotated at different speeds. The pursuit rotor provides the opportunity to study the development of a continuous motor task; it is ordinarily employed in measuring the effects of massed and distributed practice on motor learning and fatigue.

MIRROR TRACING: Figure 15–15 shows a mirror-tracing apparatus. Although this apparatus is not often used in contemporary research, it was used in several classic experiments. Note that the image of the star which is perceived by the subject is reversed by the mirror. The subject is instructed to trace the path between the lines while watching the design through the mirror. The task is difficult and, not unusually, infuriating to subjects who have not attempted it before. Mirror tracing is particularly suitable for studying the effects of transfer and is most often used for this purpose. Bilateral transfer may be investigated by hav-

FIGURE 15–13: *Changes in reaction time as a function of age. (From Woodworth & Schlosberg, 1954, p. 36; data from Miles, 1942.)*

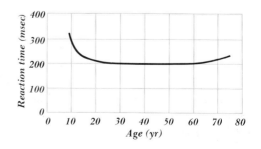

FIGURE 15-14: *A pursuit rotor. The subject is instructed to keep the stylus in contact with the disk while the disk is rotated at different speeds. (Courtesy of Lafayette Instrument Company.)*

FIGURE 15-15: *A mirror-tracing apparatus. The subject traces the star by following the course in the mirror. The apparatus is especially useful in experiments on transfer of training. (Courtesy of Lafayette Instrument Company.)*

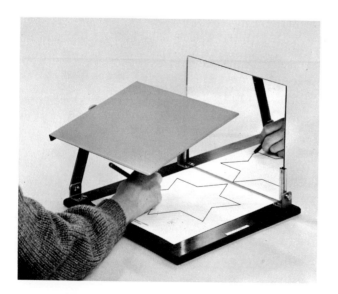

ing the subject use a different hand after he has performed with his preferred hand.

TRACKING: Like the pursuit rotor, tracking apparatuses employ a moving object. The subject must make movements with a wheel or some other device. A typical tracking task employs both a *target* and a *cursor*. In *pursuit tracking*, the target moves, and the subject manipulates the motion of the cursor in an attempt to match the movement of the target. This is similar to the motion one makes in sighting a gun at a moving object; the problem is to get the hairline of the gun sight (cursor) in line with the target. In *compensatory tracking*, the subject's task is to keep the target on some reference point. The subject attempts to keep the target in place by moving a device that controls its movements. Compensatory tracking is generally more difficult than pursuit tracking.

Because of the importance of tracking to many military and industrial skills, a considerable body of literature exists on the topic. Many studies have been concerned with finding the most efficient target size, rate of movement of the target, use of the hands (one hand versus two hands), and so on. Somewhat less is known about the effects of such standard psychological phenomena as massed versus distributed practice and transfer of training.

COMPLEX COORDINATION: Some perceptual-motor tasks require the simultaneous use of both feet and/or both hands in response to auditory and visual stimulation. Often these tasks employ mock-ups of actual perceptual-motor tasks, such as driving a car or flying an airplane. With the use of the mock-up, untrained persons can learn to operate machines without the complications that might result from the use of the real machine. In addition, investigators can measure the types of stimulus-response requirements that are most difficult, eliminate possible sources of negative transfer, and study the most efficient way for arranging controls.

SPECIFIC COORDINATION: Many tests purport to test perceptual-motor aptitude. An example is the *Purdue Pegboard* shown in Figure 15–16.

The test calls for assembling washers, pins, and other small parts in a designated way. Tests of perceptual-motor aptitude are more often valid for specific applications than for general applications.

Time-and-Motion Studies: The apparatuses we have mentioned, with the exception of tracking and the pursuit rotor, all provide information on discrete responses. That is, the apparatuses measure the number of errors or the amount of time taken to complete the task. In many perceptual-motor tasks, however, the behavior is serial, rather than single-action. Industrial psychology has long been concerned with analyzing continuous tasks. As early as 1881, investigators had begun to measure the components of continuous perceptual-motor tasks by time-and-motion studies (F. W. Taylor, 1911). The procedures involved filming the ongoing behavior and separating the components, such as the amount of time taken to grasp the tool, to carry it to the location where it was needed, to use it, and to return it to its place. The studies emphasized training workers to be efficient in their movements. A type of shorthand for the movements was devised by F. B. Gilbreth (1909, 1911; F. B. Gilbreth & L. M. Gilbreth, 1917), so that observers could record the motions while watching the workers. Similar techniques are used by contemporary investigators to study learning patterns. They have also been used for applied purposes, for example, to train finer discrimination in pitch perception (R. F. Wyatt, 1945).

Common Factors of Different Tests: The variety of perceptual-motor tasks suggests that there may be considerable overlap among them. Factor analysis (Chapter 5) is a useful mathematical tool for finding the common factors of different measures. Table 15–B shows one such analysis. From the table, it is clear that some tasks correlate very highly with others. It may therefore be presumed that these tasks are measuring the same ability or attribute. Accordingly, it is worthwhile, when attempting to measure general perceptual-

FIGURE 15-16: *The* Purdue Pegboard *used to measure coordination. The subject places the items (bolts, pins, and washers) in specified ways within the holes on the pegboard. (Courtesy of Lafayette Instrument Company.)*

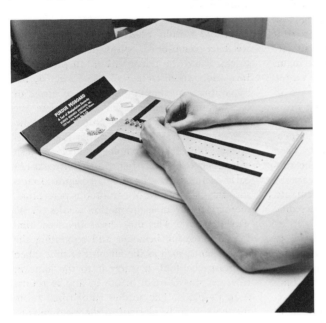

motor ability, to prepare a battery of tests, selected on the basis of their correlation. Fleishman has performed a number of analyses of the components of motor performance (1958; Fleishman & Hempel, 1956; Nicks & Fleishman, 1962).

Feedback: Emphasis on perceptual-motor behavior as continuous behavior has led to an appreciation of the importance of *feedback—* the process by which a given response acts as a stimulus for another response, so that information is transmitted between the two. The standard example of feedback is the relationship between a thermostat and a furnace: an increase in temperature affects the thermostat, the thermostat eventually affects the furnace by causing it to fire or shut down, and the activity of the furnace affects the thermostat. We may distinguish several kinds of feedback that are important in perceptual-motor tasks: In *delayed feedback* the normal temporal re-

lationship between perception and task is extended. For example, human beings continually receive auditory feedback when they speak, for they "hear their own voices." If this feedback is delayed, say, by using a tape recorder that feeds back what has been said with a one-minute delay, speech becomes halting and less precise. *Decreased feedback* occurs when the normal feedback is decreased in some fashion without necessarily altering the temporal relationship. Earplugs, which permit less sound to enter the ear, decrease feedback, for example.

One group of experimenters (R. A. Chase, Rapin, Gilden, Sutton, & Guilfoyle, 1961) studied the effects of different kinds and degrees of feedback on performance. In one study they asked subjects to tap a key continuously, at a specific rate, and with equal pressure. The tapping performance was evaluated under several conditions, including decreased auditory feedback in which a masking

TABLE 15-B: *A Factor Analysis.*
I is the speed of a single reaction, **II** is finger-hand speed in restricted oscillatory movements, **III** is forearm-and-hand speed in oscillatory movements of moderate extent, **IV** is steadiness, **V** is manipulation of spatial relations, and **VI** is unidentifiable or residual factors. The figures in boldface type are probably significant. (From R. H. Seashore, 1951, p. 1347.)

Test	I	II	III	IV	V	VI
Auditory simple reaction time	**.65**	.01	.03	—.03	—.06	—.10
Visual simple reaction time	**.64**	.15	.08	—.06	.15	.16
Auditory jump reaction time	**.48**	.20	.47	—.03	—.09	—.05
Vertical telegraph-key tapping	.03	**.89**	.04	.02	—.51	—.03
One-plate stylus tapping	.02	.22	**.40**	.12	.38	.18
Oscillometer, two-finger	.03	**.70**	—.03	.25	—.01	.05
Speed drill	**.54**	—.03	.26	.34	—.01	.20
Pursuit rotor	—.02	.09	.19	**.44**	**.44**	.23
Ataximeter, stand	—.04	.09	—.09	**.75**	.05	—.08
Spatial relations	.02	.03	.04	.01	**.58**	—.11

noise was presented through earphones, decreased visual feedback in which the subject's hand was hidden from view by a screen, vibration in which a stimulator was attached to the forearm in order to reduce kinesthetic feedback, the digital blocking of the finger, and under all four of these decreased feedback conditions together. The "audio" subjects, the "vibratory" subjects, and those who performed under all four conditions showed a decrement in performance. In another study, a more complex arrangement was used. The writers found that the conditions used to establish delayed sensory feedback did not greatly affect performance on the simple task. Identical conditions applied to a more complex task, however, had the effect of increasing the amount of pressure used by subjects and decreasing the rate of tapping.

Closed-circuit television provides another method for the study of feedback. Figure 15–17 shows a subject tracing a star pattern. The subject cannot observe her hand; rather, she observes her motions through the television screen. The image she perceives can be altered in a variety of ways. For example, it may be reversed, inverted, or both reversed and inverted.

Mirror-reversal drawing enables the investigation to observe the effect of reversal on

FIGURE 15–17: *The use of closed-circuit television in the study of motion and feedback. The camera is mounted overhead. The subject, who is tracing a star pattern, cannot see her hand directly. She watches her movements on the television monitor. The advantage of the use of television is that the image can be inverted, reversed, or both inverted and reversed (as shown here). (From K. U. Smith, 1962, p. 11.)*

motor behavior; however, closed-circuit television permits a variety of alterations. K. U. Smith (1962) arranged a camera over the shoulder of the subject. The camera recorded and reproduced the subject's handwriting from various angles. The subject was not permitted to observe his own writing behavior as he would be able to do in normal writing. A 0° angle was directly behind the subject, and a 180° angle was directly in front. The effects of different visual loci on handwriting are shown in Figure 15-18.

PROBLEM SOLVING

Problem solving, as noted in Chapter 12, involves activities not readily ascribable only to learning or conditioning. The fact that problem solving, or insightful behavior, cannot be placed neatly in categories does not imply that it is a separate entity but only that it contains certain experimental problems not commonly found in more familiar forms of learning. For example, problems may be solved without the presence of overt behavior: the subject may merely exclaim "Eureka!" Even without old and trustworthy overt behavior, investigators have shown cunning in formulating designs to measure problem solving. Many tasks have been used as the independent variables. The dependent variables have usually been (1) the amount of time needed to attain the solution to the problem or (2) the degree of correctness of the solution. Degree may be assessed by the actual time to solution, the number of times the problem is presented before the solution is attained, or the number and kinds of errors.

The task used is limited only by the inventiveness of the experimenters. The following are some commonly used problems:

FIGURE 15-18: *The effects on handwriting of displacing the locus of vision by 30°, 90°, and 180° in a horizontal plane. (From K. U. Smith, 1962, p. 12.)*

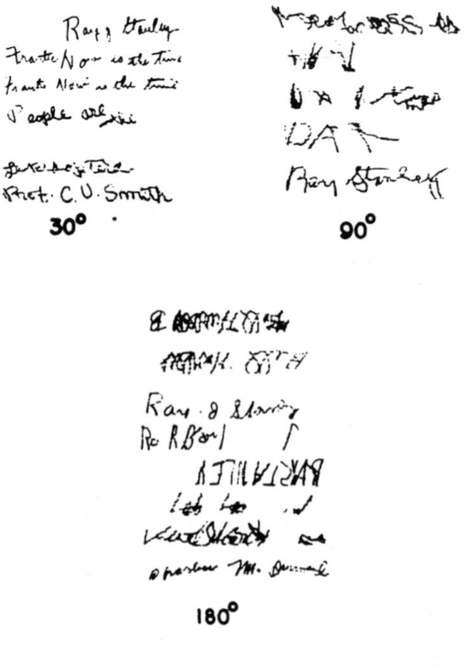

30°

90°

180°

1. *Umweg problem:* This is applicable to human beings and various kinds of animals. *Umweg* is German for *detour.* An animal or child is shown a desirable object, such as food or a toy. The subject must get around some kind of barrier before he can reach the object. In spite of the barrier, however, the object is in sight. Figure 15-19 shows the umweg problem used on a chicken and a monkey. The problem is, of course, to discover the principle of going away from an object in order eventually to get to it. The chicken is not notably successful in solving the umweg problem. Characteristically, he goes toward the object and retraces, but he will rarely make the required detour. Infants do not commonly solve the problem either, but older children have few difficulties. Since the umweg problem can be applied to many kinds of organisms, it has been used to compare the general intelligence of animals and to note how problem solving develops as one ages.

2. *Anagrams:* This familiar form of problem solving requires the subject to rearrange letters, such as *kobo*, into a meaningful word *(book).*

3. *Maier's string problem:* The subject is

FIGURE 15–19: *An example of the umweg problem. The chicken is unable to get to the food directly. In figure A, the chicken is trying to reach the food through the fence. In figure B, the apparently random pattern that the chicken has taken is shown. It is possible that the chicken could make the correct response of walking farther away from food and rounding the fence. Figure C and D show a monkey with the same problem. Immediately, he circles the fence and solves the umweg. (From Munn, 1957, p. 144. Reprinted with permission. Copyright 1957 by Scientific American, Inc. All rights reserved.)*

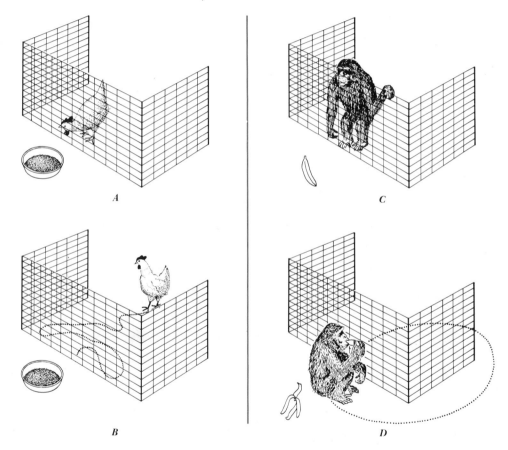

A

C

B

D

brought into a room which contains two strings dangling from the ceiling. He is instructed to tie them together, although they are spaced so far apart that he cannot hold both at once. A pair of pliers, a screwdriver, or some other heavy object, which appears to be irrelevant to the experiment, is placed elsewhere in the room. Some subjects solve the problem rapidly: they tie the pliers on one string and swing it. Then they wait by the other string until the first is thrust to them by its swing. Interestingly, some subjects do not solve the problem until the experimenter accidentally (supposedly) pushes against a string and sets it in motion. Some of these latter subjects, by the way, believe that they have solved the problem spontaneously: they fail to recall the experimenter's pushing the string.

4. *Problem boxes:* The principle of problem boxes is that the subject is required to escape from the box by performing appropriate acts. Thorndike's cats, for example, pushed against a pole. More complicated responses have also been required. Figure 15–20 shows a Healy puzzle box. Although this problem is extremely difficult, and probably unsolvable by animals, it provides an example of the way in which the solution to a problem may require a logical sequence of steps. Human beings solve this problem by the trial-and-error method. They either manipulate the parts until they find the correct solution, or they ponder the puzzle and then, as if through insight, solve the problem. When asked how they arrived at the solution, most subjects explain that they had thought of various solutions and discarded each solution as incorrect until the right one occurred. In effect, these subjects "internalize" their trial-and-error behavior.

5. *Concept formation:* In concept formation, the subject is asked to form abstractions based on some aspect of the stimuli, e.g., color or shape, in

FIGURE 15–20: *A Healy puzzle box. The closed box has a windowed lid. The subject observes the fastenings inside, which hold the box closed, and then attempts to remove them and open the box with the buttonhook. (Courtesy of C. H. Stoelting Company.)*

such a way that other stimuli may be identified. Figure 15–21 shows some of the stimuli used in a study by Heidbreder (1947). If you were given these stimuli mixed up, you would probably separate them into nine groups based on three concepts: concrete objects (faces, hats, and birds), number groupings (3, 4, and 6), and spatial forms ($\uparrow$, $\wedge$, $\bigcirc$). Generally, the experimenter rewards the correct response by saying "Right," or "Correct." The development of concept formation may be similar to the shaping technique used to enhance the speed with which operant learning occurs (Chapter 13).

There have been several explanations and descriptions of problem-solving behavior. We may group these explanations in three categories: (1) those which emphasize the *insight-ful* behavior that presumably occurs in some types of problem solving, (2) those which use the concept of *habit-family hierarchy* to account for some forms of problem-solving behavior, and (3) those which emphasize and attempt to study the supposed *mediating processes* that occur during problem solving.

Insight has been described as a sudden solution to a problem. Considerable disagreement exists regarding what insight, when applied to problem-solving behavior, really consists of. Some authorities claim it is an indivisible phenomenon, while others view it merely as a descriptive term that ignores the numerous simple behavioral components which combine to account for problem solving. The most commonly cited observation of insight is pro-

FIGURE 15–21: *Illustration of the materials used in one type of experiment on concept formation. The subject is asked to sort the pictures into groups; however, the criteria for group membership may vary. For example, one might separate the figures on the basis of numerosity. (From Heidbreder, 1947, p. 95.)*

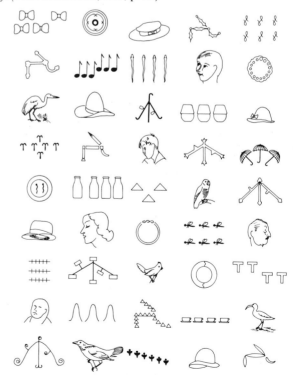

vided by W. Köhler (1917; 1927), who gave chimpanzees several problems, such as capturing a banana hanging from above by using poles or other implements (which could be fitted together) and boxes (which could be stacked upon one another). In observing the behavior of the animals, Köhler noted that they made few preparatory responses; that is, they did not appear to learn by trial and error, as had Thorndike's cats in a similar situation. Rather, they appeared to perceive a solution to the problem suddenly and then rush to complete the task by piling the boxes or putting together the poles in order to reach the fruit.

Some theorists use the presence or degree of insightful learning as one measure of intelligence. Many tests of human intelligence stress the ability of the subject to perform inventive acts and to rearrange stimuli in novel ways. For example, the commonly used *Wechsler Adult Intelligence Scale* includes a section in which testees are asked to arrange a set of pictures in appropriate order. Figure 15–22 shows a sample of this kind of test question and indicates the correct answer. Other theorists argue that solutions to such problems are not possible without prior experience and that the solutions represent stimulus or response generalization; that is, the solutions are really only extension of already learned responses. Clearly, this hypothesis is considerably

easier to subject to experimental test than the former suggestion that insightful learning is a type of learning disparate from other methods of acquiring responses and solving problems.

The idea that problem-solving behavior is based on the principles of stimulus or response generalization makes use of the concept of the habit-family hierarchy. This concept assumes that the organism possesses a series of habits which have been acquired throughout its lifetime and that these habits possess different probabilities of occurring, depending upon their previous history of reinforcement. Accordingly, these habits are arranged in a "family" of responses. Thus, the organism attempts to solve problems by moving down the habit-family hierarchy until an appropriate response is reached. The appropriate response is, of course, the one which succeeds in solving the problem. The advantage of the use of this concept is that the presence of habit-family hierarchies can be tested experimentally. The disadvantage is that the approach does not readily account for the observation that the organism does not try out all responses but that he appears to solve at least some part of the problem suddenly and insightfully. Nevertheless, following its introduction by Hull (1952), the concept of the habit-family hierarchy has received deserved experimental attention.

Those who find difficulties with both the insightful and the habit-family concepts have generally suggested the idea that mediating responses account for problem-solving behavior. Under some conditions, mediating responses can be measured. Several indirect examples of the possible presence of mediating responses are available. For example, the studies of Max (1934; 1935a; 1937), who measured minute muscle potential changes when subjects were asked to imagine themselves hitting a nail with a hammer or solving arithmetical problems, could serve as examples of measurable mediating responses. Counting represents a case of what is, possibly, mediating behavior, for it takes some ability to recognize that five people have something in common, namely, their numerical quality (Wesley, 1961). Koehler

FIGURE 15–22: *A sample picture arrangement test. The testee is given the three cards and asked to arrange them in a sensible order. In this example, B, C, A is correct. (Copyright, 1955, by The Psychological Corporation. Reproduced by permission.)*

A   *B*   *C*

(1943) trained a raven to discriminate between 76 piles of food with ratios between the piles such as 4:5 and 7:6. The training, however, took 12,000 trials and 800 hours! Fish appear to have considerable difficulty in learning the concept of number (Rossmon, 1959). There is some evidence that rats and other rodents are able to discriminate "twoness" from "threeness" (Wesley, 1961). Primates perform somewhat better.

Language may also represent an example of a mediating response. Happily, the human being is able to confer with himself without speaking out loud; he, at least, is capable of solving problems verbally without yielding overt indications of doing so. Colloquially, one refers to this as "thinking," but it is quite likely that much of what passes for thinking is silent verbal behavior, which still requires the use of words. Accordingly, before one can employ silent language, one must learn a language sufficiently well to abstract perceptions by applying names to them.

All these postulations have certain common elements, and as we consider the nature of these elements, we come nearer to an operational definition of both problem solving and insight. In all cases, insightful behavior is not specific learned behavior, but it does depend upon some previous learning. The "insight" appears in the form of the solution to a problem, but further training or practice can enhance performance of the task, thus indicating that problem solving is not devoid of learning. Moreover, the champanzee who used sticks and boxes to reach the banana must have previously learned something about the utility of these objects. Presumably, differences in previous learning are among the factors that account for individual differences in problem solving.

Birch (1945) used the Köhler stick problem on six chimpanzees. Four of the animals had no experience with getting food in the manner required by the problem; one had experience in getting food by pulling a string; and the sixth had experience in playing with sticks and using them for the general purpose of extending the reach of his arm. When presented with the Köhler problem, the monkey who had experience with sticks solved the problem in 12 seconds, and the one who had experience with pulling strings required 5 seconds. None of the inexperienced monkeys solved the problem during the first day of testing. Clearly, previous experience is important for insight in problem solving and may even account for the phenomenon. Indeed, when the four animals who did not learn were given sticks to play with for three days and then presented with the problem, all learned—or made the "insightful" response—within 20 seconds.

Problem solving and insightful behavior have been investigated by many experimenters. Unfortunately, the studies have not been organized in such a manner that information about the parameters and factors which affect problem-solving behavior is readily available. Most studies have been of the demonstrative sort; that is, they have shown that problem solving does or does not occur under specified conditions, as opposed to establishing the functional relationships that prevail. We shall review some illustrative experiments.

Several investigators have been concerned with controlling the type of learning that occurs before the problem-solving situation. In the older literature, controlling the pre-problem-solving experiences of the subjects was regarded as showing the effect of set. For example, Luchins (1942) gave subjects the problems shown in Table 15–C. All the problems (except number 1, which was used as a demonstration problem) may be solved by B-2C-A; i.e., "Fill the middle jar, and from it, fill the jar to the right twice and the jar to the left once, or B-2C-A" (Luchins, 1942, p. 2). Problem 7, however, is more simply solved by A-C. Of the 11 subjects, all used the tedious B-2C-A method on problem 7. On the other hand, if item 7 is given first, it is quickly solved by the more rapid solution. In short, the set, or *Einstellung* as it was called in the literature, is apparently responsible for the subjects' failure to see the more simple solution (Luchins and Luchins, 1959).

In a similar type of study, Rees and Israel (1935) used anagrams. The subjects were given

TABLE 15-C: *The Water-jar Problem.*
(From Luchins, 1942, p. 109.)

Problem	Given the following empty jars as measures			Obtain the required amount of water
	A	B	C	
1	3	29	3	20
2	21	127	3	100
3	14	163	25	99
4	18	43	10	5
5	9	42	6	21
6	20	59	4	31
7	23	49	3	20

practice anagrams: one group received anagrams that formed words associated with nature (e.g., "tree"), and the second group received anagrams that formed food words. Eventually both groups were given anagrams that could form words associated with either nature or food. There was a strong tendency for the set to determine the choice of the critical word: subjects trained on nature words tended to supply the answers associated with nature, and those trained on food words supplied the answers associated with food.

Contemporary theorists have sometimes replaced the concept of set with principles of reinforcement (e.g., A. W. Staats & C. K. Staats, 1963). Adamson (1959) set up experimental conditions similar to those employed in applying an intermittent reinforcement schedule. The subjects received anagrams, all of which had identical solution patterns. For example, *OOKB* and *USYB* are both solved by making the last letter the first. One group of subjects received six such anagrams (continuous reinforcement); a second group received the same six plus six others that were solvable by a different principle. The latter subjects received, then, six reinforcements for using the same sequence and six problems in which the solution was unreinforced. The principles of schedules of operant conditioning would suggest that the second group, the intermittent group, would take longer to acquire the response but that extinction should be more difficult (i.e., retention should be greater). When presented with a series of anagrams none of which followed the reinforced pattern, the intermittent group did take longer to extinguish the inappropriate "set" response during the extinction period. The measure used was the time to solve the anagrams.

One group of experimenters used the Maier string problem (Judson, Cofer, & Gelfand, 1956) but had subjects learn a list of words serially before introduction to the problem. Included in the list of words for some subjects was the sequence "rope-swing-pendulum." Another group learned the same list, although the critical words, "rope," "swing," and "pendulum" were not in that order. We might assume that those who had learned the words in sequence would perform better on the string problem than those who had learned the words out of sequence. The results tended to uphold this assumption.

Studies of this type strongly suggest that presolution experience is an important determiner of the rate of problem solving. Experimental rigor requires that the presolution tasks come immediately before the problem, but in everyday situations it is more likely that experiences of years ago are useful. Indeed, the ability to draw upon previous experiences and to use them in new ways is, no doubt, a major contributor to what is commonly called "intelligence."

The role of language in problem solving is difficult to assess, although with human beings language appears to be very important. Whether lower animals, particularly those who verbalize, such as dogs and cats, are able to "internalize" their verbalizations is a matter of pure conjecture. Gagné and E. C. Smith (1962) have provided data indicating that human subjects who are required to verbalize their thoughts while engaging in problem-solving behavior are superior in performance to those who are not required to do so. Certainly, language is of paramount importance in the thought process; however, the obvious difficulty of measuring the degree and kind of internalizations—the "private" experience of individuals—has not encouraged the research in this area that might be expected.

IMITATION

Imitation is a common learning technique, especially in higher animals. The young boy imitates his father's use of tools by repeating the actions he observes, and the girl attempts to duplicate her mother's domestic talents. Often, imitative learning appears to occur without any external reinforcing agent. Indeed, children often imitate responses that we should prefer to extinguish. Extinction is difficult, however, for the child seems to receive considerable satisfaction from imitating. The importance of the ability of the human being to learn by imitation is often overlooked. One reason for this neglect may be the fact that imitative behavior does not lend itself well to the theoretical framework supplied by operant-learning principles and by the principle that learning requires reinforcement. Nevertheless, imitation is an important part of most theories of personality, and the psychoanalytic approach to personality regards the process of identifying with the behavior of other persons through imitation as a major determiner of adult behavior.

Animals also learn by imitating. Welty (1934) reported that a fish can learn a maze more easily if he is permitted to observe another fish who has learned the maze previously. Rats are reported to learn a T maze more rapidly if they are permitted to observe another rat eating in the goal box (Baddeley, 1960). Finally, experimenters who have raised chimpanzees with the family in the home have reported descriptions of imitative behavior both between the chimpanzee and the child (W. N. Kellogg & L. A. Kellogg, 1933) and between the chimp and the "parent" (K. J. Hayes & C. Hayes, 1952).

Children have been the favorite subjects for investigators studying imitation, largely because imitative behavior is so common among children. N. E. Miller and Dollard (1941) used a situation in which one of two containers held a colored sticker with a picture of an animal which was used as a reward. The subject observed while a model took the first turn. The model performed several definite acts that were irrelevant to the task. For example, as she approached the boxes, she said "March, march, march"; then she struck at a doll left on the top of each box. The dependent variable was the number of such behaviors copied by the subject when his turn arrived. A control group was used in which the model took a detour to reach the boxes and removed the dolls from the boxes gently. Among preschool children, 28 percent copied the model's verbal statements, 44 percent copied the marching, and 88 percent imitated the aggression against the dolls. None of these actions appeared in the control group, although 75 percent did copy the detour.

Bandura has extended the study of imitative learning in a series of studies (Bandura, D. Ross, & S. A. Ross, 1963a; 1963b; 1963c). In a representative study (1963a), nursery school children either (1) saw a model act aggressively toward a doll, (2) watched a movie of the same scene, (3) watched a cartoon in which an animated cat aggressed against the doll, or (4) had none of these experiences (control group). As part of the experiment, the investigators sought to encourage aggression in the children. They took the children to a room containing interesting toys. After a child began playing with the toys, the experimenter told him that the toys were too good for him and that the experimenter was saving them for other children. Finally, each child was placed in a room with toys, including the doll, for twenty minutes. Imitation was measured by noting the number of times that the subject imitated the aggressive behavior. In total aggressiveness, the subjects who watched the real model and those who watched either the movie or the cartoon movie did not differ from one another; however, all three groups differed from the control group. Boys were more aggressive than girls on almost all measures. There was also a relationship between the sex of the model and the sex of the subject. Figure 15–23 shows the

FIGURE 15-23: *Imitation of aggressive behavior. Photograph sequence* A *shows the model performing the acts. Sequences* B *and* C *show two subjects imitating the aggressive behavior of the model. (From Bandura, D. Ross, & S. A. Ross, 1963a, p. 8.)*

model and some of the imitative behavior. Photograph sequence *A* shows the model acting out one aggressive scene, and sequences *B* and *C* show two subjects imitating the aggressive acts.

FATIGUE

Although fatigue is commonly regarded as a decrement in performance, it is important that the concept not be confused with extinction. A decrement in performance occurs during extinction; however, in extinction some condition has been introduced into, or removed from, the experimental procedure. Fatigue, on the other hand, occurs from sheer repetition of the performance. Although *mental fatigue*

is commonly regarded as having the same characteristics as *physical fatigue,* there are few data which support this assumption.

Most work on fatigue has been concerned with physical fatigue. If a muscle is stimulated repeatedly, it eventually loses its ability to respond to the stimulus. If the muscle is permitted to "rest," it regains its ability to respond. Thus, muscle fatigue occurs only when the requirements placed upon the muscle are greater that its ability. If the requirements are matched by the ability of the muscle to respond, it will continue to respond indefinitely without showing fatigue. The heart, for example, manages to respond at a steady rate for a long period of time. In older literature, physical fatigue was commonly measured with an *ergograph.* The ergograph is a device for measuring the output of energy of the finger or some other appendage. The subject is instructed to pull a weight with one finger as long and as rapidly as possible. Although individuals are highly variable in performing this task, eventually the finger tires, and the subject's ability to pull the weight is lessened. If the subject is permitted to rest for a few moments, he is usually able to start the task again with renewed vigor. Thus, the typical curve of physical fatigue follows the example of the muscle.

Other measures of physical fatigue are in more common use today. These include blood pressure, GSR, and other physiological determinations. The length of time taken for the heart rate to return to normal following exercise is a useful measure of the extent of the work and fatigue. A *respiration calorimeter,* which determines the amount of oxygen consumed in completing specified tasks has received considerable attention. The *electromyograph* (EMG) is used to measure the degree of tension in muscles. It is, therefore, a useful apparatus for measuring physical fatigue. Tension increases as a function of (1) amount of force required to complete the task, (2) amount of time in which the subject engages in the activity, and (3) motivation, usually provided by the experimenter through the instructions given to the subject (Eason, 1960; Gregg & Jarrard, 1958). Other experimenters have noted that skin conductance (GSR) is related to the warm-up effect. Using the pursuit rotor, Kling and Schlosberg (1961) found that the GSR decreased as the warm-up effect decreased.

Mental fatigue, such as that which may occur from repetitive verbal tasks (e.g., repeating a list of nonsense syllables until perfect recitation is possible), is often identified with boredom or monotony. Although fatigue and boredom have a detrimental effect upon performance, they also appear to be associated with highly variable performance (S. Wyatt, J. A. Fraser, & Stock, 1929). Under some conditions, work breaks, or rest periods, actually increase production, for the time lost in the pause is more than compensated for by an increase in production (Anastasi, 1964). Experimentally, it is difficult to separate the effects of fatigue from the effects of practice. As the subject is repeating a mental or verbal task, we may expect his performance to increase as a function of practice. At the same time, we expect the performance to decrease because of fatigue. Under most conditions the two effects are covariant, so that one cannot assess them as independent effects. The difficulty in designing experiments that effectively separate the two processes probably accounts for the lack of well-conducted studies on mental fatigue.

SOURCES

In the text, I have attempted to summarize the major studies—both those which contribute useful information and those which for one reason or another attract sufficient attention to provide impetus to research. Also, I have attempted to list major reviews of the literature within each topic. Among the following sources many were not noted in the text; however, they are useful to the student who wishes to consider the topics in greater detail.

Whole-Part and Massed-Distributed Learning: Among early experimental papers of value are Steffens (1900), Pechstein (1917), Lyon (1914), Leuba and Hyde (1905), Pyle (1913), Lorge (1930), Jost (1897), Ulrich (1915), B. A. Mayer and C. P. Stone (1931), Lashley (1918). On the influence of different kinds of material, see E. M. Hanawalt (1934), Barton (1921), T. W. Cook (1936; 1937), W. Meyer (1926), W. H. Winch (1924), Reed (1924a), G. O. McGeoch (1931b), C. E. Noble (1952a; 1952b; 1955), Bousfield (1961). On length of rest periods, see Lorge (1930), Travis (1937), G. A. Kimble (1949), S. T. H. Wright and D. W. Taylor (1949), Riley (1952). On the method used in acquisition, see Hovland (1949).

Reminiscence: On reminiscence as a function of the method of learning, see Hovland (1938a; 1938b; 1939), Ward (1937), Buxton and H. V.

Ross (1949), Melton and G. R. Stone (1942), Withey, Buxton, and Elkin (1949), English, Welborn, and Killian (1934), McClelland (1942), Archer (1953).

On reminiscence as a function of rest period, see H. M. Bell (1942), Ammons (1947), G. A. Kimble and Horenstein (1948), Melton (1941).

For theories, see Jost (1897 [although reminiscence had not yet been named, this paper anticipated the problem]), Gustafson and Irion (1951), Bills and C. Brown (1929), R. Dodge (1927), Telford (1931).

For motor learning, see Ammons (1947), Doré and Hilgard (1937; 1938), Leavitt and Schlosberg (1944), Snoddy (1935).

Meaningfulness: For the effect of different types of material, see J. A. McGeoch (1930), Reed (1924a; 1924b; 1938), M. G. Jones and English (1926), C. E. Noble (1952a; 1952b), Yavuz and Bousfield (1959).

On von Restorff's effect and "affective" characteristics, such as size, shape, and color, see T. Karwoski (1931), H. F. Adams and Dandison (1927), Newhall and Heim (1929), van Buskirk (1932), Brandt (1925) Pillsbury and Raush (1943), P. S. Siegel (1943), Stagner (1931), Koch (1930), Gordon (1925), Pintner and Forlano (1940). For reviews and criticisms, see G. M. Gilbert (1938), A. L. Edwards (1941), Sharp (1938).

For a cogent discussion of the usefulness of meaning as a concept in the study of human learning, see Bousfield (1961) and the accompanying comments by Osgood (1961) and Cofer (1961).

Knowledge of Results: For general reviews, E. A. Bilodeau and I. McD. Bilodeau (1961) is highly recommended. Other sources are Ammons (1956), J. S. Brown (1949), Fitts, M. E. Noble, Bahrick, and G. E. Briggs (1959a; 1959b). For information on delay of KR, see C. E. Noble and Alcock (1958), Denny, Allard, E. Hall, and Rokeach (1960), Greenspoon and Foreman (1956), E. A. Bilodeau and Ryan (1960), E. A. Bilodeau and I. McD. Bilodeau (1958), C. E. Noble and J. L. Noble (1958),

Holland and Henson (1956), Reynolds and J. A. Adams (1953). On the distinction between reinforcement and KR, see Goldbeck and L. J. Briggs (1962), Ugelow (1962), Carr (1959), Gagné and Bolles (1959), J. W. Moore and W. I. Smith (1964). For the relevance of KR to programmed instruction, see Lumsdaine and Glaser (1960).

On KR as a motivation or incentive condition, see Crafts and R. W. Gilbert (1934), Helmstadter and D. S. Ellis (1952).

Forgetting: On sleep as interference, see van Ormer (1932), Heine (1914). On animals, see Hoagland (1931), J. W. French (1942).

Papers of special interest which review and organize the data on interference theory are Underwood (1957b) and Postman (1961). For a thorough review of forgetting, covering research through 1950, see J. A. McGeoch and Irion (1952). Chapter 10 in J. A. McGeoch and Irion (1952) considers the role of affective tone, method of original learning, instruction and set, and pathological conditions in memory. On pathological conditions, also see Stratton (1919), and Penfield and Jasper (1954). For experimental work on interference, see G. E. Briggs (1954; 1957), G. E. Briggs, R. F. Thompson, and Brogden (1954), Gladis and Braun (1958), W. O. Jenkins and Postman (1949), Melton and J. M. Irwin (1940), Postman (1961), Underwood (1948), Waters and Peel (1935), K. E. Lloyd, L. S. Reid, and Feallock (1960), L. R. Peterson and M. J. Peterson (1959).

An important commentary is given by Underwood and Ekstrand (1966).

Immediate, Short-term, and Long-term Memory: Postman (1964) provides a thorough analysis of work in this area. For papers on the L. R. Peterson and M. J. Peterson procedure, see L. R. Peterson (1963), Murdock (1961a; 1961b), L. R. Peterson, Saltzman, Hillner, and V. Land (1962). On decay theory and short-term memory, see R. Conrad (1957), D. C. Fraser (1958), Moray (1960). On continuous-memory tasks, see Yntema and Mueser (1960), Shepard and M. Teghtsoonian (1961).

Transfer: On the history of transfer studies, see Woodworth and Schlosberg, 1954. Grose and Birney (1963) have reprinted a series of papers on transfer, some of historical interest. On measuring transfer, see Underwood (1949). Although not concerned directly with transfer, Underwood (1957a) presents two chapters on research designs which are required reading for those anticipating the construction of research designs to study transfer. Townsend (1953) presents an excellent and brief discussion of designs used in transfer studies. The presentation of these paradigms in diagramatic form is very useful. Also, see Melton (1964).

On theories of transfer, see Thorndike (1913), Sandiford (1928), Robinson (1927) J. A. McGeoch (1942), Osgood (1948; 1949; 1953), Deese (1958), E. A. Bilodeau and I. McD. Bilodeau (1961), Cofer (1961), and (although unindexed) Underwood and Schulz (1960).

The most thorough summary of the literature on transfer through 1954 is to be found in Woodworth and Schlosberg (1954). Hebb (1949) interprets transfer within the framework of his neurological theory.

Incidental Learning: This topic has received sporadic bursts of attention. In the period 1910 to 1920, the phenomenon of incidental learning was well established through the demonstrative studies of G. C. Myers (1913) and others. J. A. McGeoch and Irion (1952) cover the earlier literature. Postman (1964) provides an analysis of studies of incidental learning and discusses more recent experiments.

Verbal "Conditioning": For this area, the work of Dulany (1960; 1961; 1962) and Spielberger, Levin, and M. C. Shepard (1962) should be studied. Because of the diversity of research on verbal conditioning, very few general sources have been compiled. Greenspoon (1962) reviews the material justly, and two other sound reviewers, Krasner (1958) and Salzinger (1959), are available.

Perceptual-Motor Learning: A general review, which emphasizes the history of studies in this field, has been provided by R. H. Seashore (1951). Information on particular tests may be found in Anastasi (1961). Buros (1964), in *The Sixth Mental Measurements Yearbook*, presents reviews and information on the validity and reliability of tests. Some tests, which may be regarded as perceptual-motor, are included in the volume, although emphasis is on mental tests. Motor skills and perceptual-motor learning are reviewed regularly in the *Annual Review of Psychology*. Fitts (1964) presents a detailed and highly informative article on skill learning.

Problem Solving: Most introductory texts offer a discussion of problem solving. One of the more thorough presentations is provided by Munn (1961). D. J. Lewis (1963) offers an excellent chapter on problem solving and thinking. Gagné (1964) summarizes his research on problem solving and, in addition, offers an admirable discussion of the difficulties of this field of study. In the same volume, H. H. Kendler (1964) discusses work on concept formation.

Imitation: This has not been a favorite area for experimental psychology. The work by Bandura and R. H. Walters (1963) contains a chapter on their studies of imitative learning. The remainder of the book, although not concerned exclusively with imitation, is valuable. N. E. Miller and Dollard (1941) also discuss learning by imitation. Curiously, few introductory books mention imitative learning at all, and texts on conditioning and learning are of almost no help.

Fatigue: The most thorough account of studies of fatigue (particularly in the earlier literature) is found in Woodworth and Schlosberg (1954, pp. 798–809). Not surprisingly, much of the work in this area has been of an applied nature, relating particularly to such industrial problems as appropriate length of rest breaks. Anastasi (1964) reviews the studies and provides some general conclusions. Underwood (1949) comments upon some of the problems fatigue provides for experimental designs.

CHAPTER SIXTEEN

LEARNED AND NONLEARNED BEHAVIOR

INTRODUCTION

In an earlier day, a sharp distinction was drawn between supposedly innate behavior and acquired, or learned, behavior. As we have learned more about behavior, however, it has become clear that the sharp distinction served more to confuse our understanding of behavior than to aid it. When a behavioral pattern is observed, it may be analyzed in several ways, depending, primarily, on the procedures that elicit, eliminate, or modify the behavior. In some studies, genetic manipulation is used. In others, an interaction between the perceptual environment and physiological states is observed. The question is no longer whether a behavior is innate or learned but, rather, how we go about understanding it. When we discover that a behavior can be modified only by genetic manipulation, we have what may be described as a pure example of innately determined behavior. Nevertheless, for the purpose of analyzing behavior we ignore the dichotomy between innate and learned behavior and study the ways in which behavior may be modified.

Traditionally, unlearned, or instinctual behavior has been studied in animals by ethologists, ecologists, and comparative psychologists. Some investigators are concerned primarily with the behavior of animals; others use animals mainly to generalize their findings to human behavior, since animal behavior is relatively more easily controlled and manipulated than human behavior and instinctual patterns are more readily identified in animals. Tinbergen, among others, has argued that " . . . learning and many other higher processes are secondary modifications of innate mechanisms, and that therefore a study of learning processes has to be preceded by a study of the innate foundation of behavior" (1951, p. 6). Comparative psychologists, however, have tended to consider learned behavior more deserving of experimental attention.

In this chapter we shall consider the relationship between learned and nonlearned behavior and some representative work in such areas as imprinting and sexual activity. In addition, we shall discuss selected problem areas which have received a sufficient amount of experimental attention to provide examples of the complexity of the relationship between learned and nonlearned behavior.

THE CONCEPT OF NONLEARNED BEHAVIOR

The concept of instinctual, or nonlearned, behavior can be misleading, for it is tempting to describe many kinds of behavior as instinctual when they are not. For example, we read that "he inherited his temper from his father" or "he inherited his love of music from his aunt." It is unlikely that either anger or love of music is transmitted from one person to another in the same way that blue eyes and color blindness are transmitted. It is more likely that the aunt reinforced the love of music or that the child received gratification from imitating the father's temper. Accordingly, it is important that nonlearned behaviors, if they are to be separated at all from other kinds of behavior, be classified in such a way that they will not be confused with behaviors that are learnable, for when we divide behavior into this dichotomy, we make very important assumptions about the degrees and kinds of modification that are possible.

In trying to decide whether a behavior may be labeled nonlearned, we use the following criteria, none of which is definitive:

1. *Is the behavior characteristic of all members of the species?* If it is observed in only some organisms, we cannot immediately conclude that the behavior is nonlearned. It is still reasonable, however, to investigate whether the behavior is determined genetically. For example, mice of a certain strain walk in a distinctive fashion. They are called "waltzing mice." It has been shown that whether a particular mouse "waltzes" or not is purely a matter of his genetic inheritance. Thus, the behavior is nonlearned and is determined genetically, yet it is not a characteristic of all

members of the species. If the behavior *is* characteristic of all members of the species, this is evidence for the nonlearned classification, but the observation that some members do not display the behavior may indicate either learned or genetic determinants.

2. *Can the behavior be shown to be learned?* If the behavior is trainable, it is not nonlearned; on the other hand, if it is not shown to be trainable, we cannot be certain whether it is nonlearned or learned. For example, the development of some characteristics of speech in a child can be shown to be learnable; however, other aspects, such as the frequency with which particular phonemes are spoken in infancy, do not appear to be easily explainable by the rules of operant training. This is not conclusive evidence that the frequency of phonemes is entirely nonlearned, for the frequency may be learned in some other way, or an organism may be trainable at one age but not at another. Some theorists have urged that all behaviors be regarded as learned until investigation demonstrates that they cannot be learned. These theorists argue that their position is a necessary safeguard against the possibility that many learned behaviors will be erroneously classified as instinctual. Their fear is based on the fact that once a behavior has been described as instinctual, research on the learning process ends. Thus, a behavior can be incorrectly assigned to instinctual limbo. In general, it is sound experimental strategy to avoid classifying a behavior as unlearned unless exhaustive evidence indicates that it is truly not learned.

Two reservations deserve our attention: First, there is not always a clear distinction between learning and instinct. An instinctual response, for example, may remain dormant until some learning has occurred or until some point in maturation is attained. If one considers sexual behavior instinctual, it is clear that this behavior also depends upon maturation and learning. Second, it is probably a technical impossibility to show that a particular form of behavior *cannot* be learned, since final proof would require an infinite number of experiments. Nevertheless, when examined closely, many behaviors that appear to be totally instinctual, such as salmons' swimming upstream to spawn or the reproductive cycle of the dove, can be shown to be complex responses having both instinctual and learned qualities.

3. *Instinctual behavior is very complex.* "Complex" is, of course, a relative term. We use it, however, to distinguish instinctual behavior, which often involves a series of chained responses, from the simple, physiological reflexes (unconditioned responses), such as the patellar reflex. Although these reflexes are innate, they are the stuff of which instinctual behavior is made, rather than instinctual behaviors themselves. Stated in a different way, a third characteristic of instinctual behavior is that it is considerably more than reflexive behavior.

4. *Instinctual behavior is stereotyped.* The behavior pattern is essentially identical from time to time and from animal to animal. If one interrupts the pattern, the organism returns to finish the pattern. The gray goose, for example, appears to handle its eggs in an instinctual manner. If an egg is removed from the nest, the goose rolls the egg back in with its beak. If this behavior is interrupted, the animal may do other things, but she always returns to try to roll the egg.

5. *Instinctual behavior is often specific for a particular period of development.* For example, certain specifiable behaviors occur at various times during the reproductive cycle. These behaviors do not occur unless a certain period has been reached. Similarly, particular animals, such as the domestic chicken, demonstrates sensitive, or critical, periods of development. Certain responses either are learned during these periods or are incompletely or never learned.

Many other characteristics of instinctual behavior can be specified. No single characteristic, and probably no group of characteristics, is likely to account for all the instinctual phenomena that have been noted, for the concept of instinct subsumes a variety of behaviors.

Sensitive Periods: During certain periods in their lives, some animals appear to be more sensitive to certain kinds of stimulation than they are during other periods. An experienced electrician can often tolerate line voltage in his fingertips, but the same current could kill an infant. Clearly learning and experience as well as age and maturation are important in creating sensitive periods.

There are probably several kinds of sensitive periods. Some are primarily a function of maturation. Stimuli which may be sexually exciting to an eighteen-year-old may, one would hope, have little effect on a four-year-old. From the behavior of fowls, it is known that the *following response* may be altered by supplying the animal with appropriate visual stimulation at an appropriate age. If the same stimuli are presented at an inappropriate age, the following response is not altered. These sensitive periods are sometimes called *critical periods*. This name suggests an analogy to the concept of a critical period of embryology, where the term is used to refer to periods in the development of the fetus where stimuli or physiological events can alter the fetus. For example, if a mother develops German measles during a critical period in pregnancy, the fetus may be adversely affected. But if she contracts the disease after the critical period, no damage is done. Some investigators have reported that some responses learned during critical, or sensitive, periods are more difficult to extinguish than the same responses acquired at other times (Lorenz, 1935; 1937). The characteristics of sensitive periods may be clarified by a discussion of *imprinting*.

Imprinting: Possibly the first meaningful investigation of imprinting was reported by Heinroth (1910). He noted that for a few hours after birth geese would follow whatever large, moving object they first saw. Normally, this would be the mother goose. If a gosling was removed from the mother shortly after hatching and if it was presented with the sight of a human being in motion, it would follow the human being. Later, Lorenz (1937) investigated the phenomenon more thoroughly, leading a number of investigators to consider imprinting. For several reasons, imprinting is an interesting phenomenon to investigators. First, it has little resemblance to such traditional forms of learning as classical conditioning, operant training, or trial-and-error learning. The speed with which imprinting occurs argues against an explanation of the behavior within the traditional learning frameworks. Second, Heinroth and others have noted that imprinting will occur only within a sensitive period. Indeed, there is evidence (E. H. Hess, 1959c) that the imprinting period in one breed of fowl is between eight and twenty-two hours after hatching. If the response of following is not acquired during this sensitive period by the presentation of the proper stimulus, it is not likely that the response will ever be acquired. Third, imprinting may occur and be completed before acquisition of the ability to make the observable response. For example, a chick may become imprinted to a human being before the chick is able to follow the person; imprinting may then be retained until the chick reaches the appropriate maturation level at which he can make the following response.

Data on imprinting suggest that the phenomenon contains both instinctual and learned factors. Since these factors are difficult to separate, let us consider the information available on imprinting in order to note the methodological complications that attend experimental research on instinctual behaviors.

As is true of many other kinds of behavior, imprinting was noted and recorded long before its importance was understood. In 1873 Spalding (reprint, 1954) reported the phenomenon and stated that it was an instinctive, unlearned response. Lorenz (1937), who suggested the name *imprinting*, proposed the one fundamental distinction that separated imprinting from traditional learning, namely, that, once acquired, imprinting is irreversible. Learned responses are not irreversible; they may be extinguished. Since Lorenz's suggestion, the imprintability of a variety of animals has been examined. Some animals demonstrate the phenomenon, whereas others do not. Even within species, there are exceptions. Let us consider, however, three basic questions: First, is imprinting truly irreversible? That is, is it impossible to extinguish? Second, can the object to which the animal is imprinted serve as a reinforcer for other responses? That is, does the object have any reinforcing properties other than that of eliciting the following response? Third, what factors, if any, can be distinguished which enhance or inhibit imprinting?

The answer to the first question—whether imprinting is truly irreversible—appears to be negative. Moltz and Rosenblum (1958), for example, measured the amount of following generated by imprinted chickens for six days after the imprinting period. They showed that there was a statistically significant decrease in the amount of following.

The second question—whether the imprinted object possesses, or comes to possess, other qualities, especially the ability to serve as a reinforcer—has been considered most commonly by the use of operant training techniques. Both N. Peterson (1960) and Campbell and Pickleman (1961) have shown that an imprinted stimulus can serve as an operant reinforcer to both chicks and ducks. The basic question, however, is whether the imprinted stimulus maintains these reinforcing properties independently of the imprinting situation; i.e., are there some stimuli, notably those to which an organism imprints most readily, which have innately reinforcing properties. H. Hoffman, Toffey, Searle, and Kozma (1966) have shown that the imprinted stimulus may serve as a reinforcer in a variety of operant-training tasks, including scheduling and aversive training. Moreover, they have shown that although the imprinted stimulus could be an important factor in the emotional behavior of imprinted organisms, it did not have this function for older organisms. This finding, of course, supports the critical-period suggestion. A corollary study (W. R. Thompson & O'Kieffe, 1962) found that imprinted chicks showed less fear (measured by distress calls) to stressful auditory stimulation than nonimprinted chicks.

A procedural problem has hindered and sometimes confused work on imprinting, especially work on the question of the innate reinforcing properties of the stimulus. The usual dependent variable in imprinting studies is the following response. Thus, if an animal follows the stimulus, he is, by definition, imprinted. The question remains whether the animal can become imprinted without performing the following response; i.e., is the act of following necessary for imprinting? Baer and P. H. Gray (1960) confined newly hatched chicks, thus eliminating the possibility of their developing the following response. The investigators then forced either a black or a white guinea pig to pass by. The chicks showed significant preferences for the guinea pig they had seen. That is, chicks that had seen a white guinea pig preferred him in later preference tests. These writers argue that imprinting represents the learning of the attributes of the subject. Thus, following may make imprinting more stable or more efficient, but the following response itself is not necessary for imprinting to occur.

Third, we may inquire what factors inhibit or enhance imprinting. The critical period is, of course, one limiting factor. This period, in turn, appears to be limited by locomotor ability and the onset of fear responses. For example, E. H. Hess (1959a) reports a critical period for original imprinting. The period in the chicken, which occurs somewhere in the interval between four and thirty-six hours after hatching, is apparently related to the locomotive ability of the chick (for imprintability appears to peak with the peak in locomotive speed) and may be terminated by the onset of fear responses. Figure 16–1 shows this relationship. The critical period for imprintability may, however, also depend upon the stimulus. That is, although the foregoing may represent the critical period for objects of one type, P. H. Gray (1961) has shown that objects of particular colors may serve as imprinting objects for chicks as late as ten days of age. Guiton (1959) has shown that the imprinting period is related to the period of socialization of the chicken. It is also reported that if the object produces a loud sound whenever the subject is within 6 inches of it, imprinting is enhanced (Pitz & R. B. Ross, 1961).

From the studies of E. H. Hess and his colleagues (1957; 1959a; 1964), it would appear that imprinting is also a function of other factors: (1) the effort used in following the object, (2) the order in which imprinting stimuli are presented, and (3) the quality and quantity of other stimuli present during the imprinting period. For example, Hess has provided data to show that the more effort an animal expends in following the object, the greater the imprinting. Moreover, imprinting follows a law of *primacy,* which says, in effect, that whatever stimulus is presented first will be the one that is imprinted. Hess has also shown that punishment, in the form of electric current provided during the imprinting situation, can serve to enhance imprinting. These findings, coupled with the finding that locomotor ability and fear responses serve as the onset and termination of the critical period for imprinting, have led Hess to postulate a *law of effort* (1959b), in which all these factors are joined to produce an estimate of the degree of imprinting that a given experimental situation will produce. Sluckin and Salzen have noted, however, that they found no relationship between the distance a chick runs and his following behavior (1961). These writers point out that the law of effort fails to distinguish the chick who may not run but who has made an "effort" to do so.

Jaynes has collected data (1958a; 1958b) which show that chicks' ability to discriminate the imprinted object from other, but similar, objects increased with the number of exposures to the imprinted object. The implication of this finding is that the chick is still learning to discriminate the object after the supposed imprinting period has ended. It suggests that learning occurs after imprinting. The finding does not, of course, argue that the original imprinting is necessarily either learned or instinctual. As we have said, there are convincing data to suggest that original imprinting does not resemble the traditional acquisition of learned responses.

Maturation of the Ability to Learn: The data on imprinting suggest the possibility that

FIGURE 16-1: *Hypothetical and empirical curves of the critical period of chicks (White Rock stock) and mallard ducklings. The abscissa shows the age in hours, and the ordinate shows the percentage of animals exhibiting "fear" as measured by the animals' willingness to move. (From E. H. Hess, 1959b, p. 517.)*

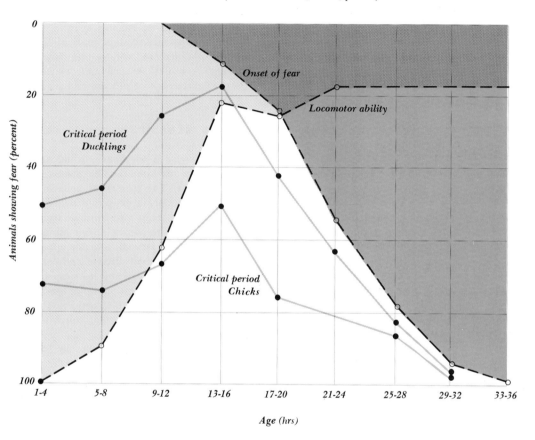

the ability to learn depends in part upon the existence of sensitive periods. Certainly, there is a widespread belief, at least in folklore, that old dogs do not learn new tricks and that the younger the organism, the more able it is to learn. There is no simple answer, however, to the question of whether young organisms learn more rapidly than older organisms. Experiments always experience the difficult problem of equating motivational levels and of training organisms of different ages. For example, a youngster might work hard to learn a task to gain a $5 reward, while an older

person might find the task infantile and the reward unattractive. Similarly, in animal research it is difficult to arrange experimental situations so that both old and young animals are equally motivated. In our discussions of conditioning and operant training (Chapters 13, 14) we have already noted some data on changes in learning ability as a function of age. It may be recalled that Mateer (1918) found the ease of classical conditioning of infants to increase from twelve to forty-eight months of age. Osipova (1926), however, using withdrawal rather than salivation, found that conditioning became more difficult with an increase in age. These studies may differ in their conclusions, but they show that learning may be expected to vary as a function of age.

It is, of course, one thing to point out changes in learning ability and quite another to be able to explain the causes of the changes. It has been shown, for example, that infant rhesus monkeys master discrimination and delayed-response problems by five months of age but do not show the acquisition of learning sets (learning to learn) until much later (W. A. Mason, Blazek, & Harlow, 1956). This finding raises the question of why some kinds of learning appear later than other kinds. No doubt increased age has at least one advantage: it provides time for the organism to acquire responses which can serve as "generalizers" when new tasks are to be learned.

One of the most enticing bits of evidence that something akin to critical or sensitive periods may exist for learning come from Hebb (1942). Hebb has suggested that some types of brain injury may cause specific speech defects at certain stages of language development. Loss or ablation of an area would produce no effect on one who had already learned to speak fluently but would result in a permanent defect if language behavior was not fully developed. In short, if this trauma occurs in a critical period—while speech is being developed—a permanent defect results. D. G. Freedman, King, and Elliot (1961) have found that puppies must react with human beings between 3½ and 13 weeks of age if the dogs are to become socialized as pets. Bowlby (1952) and others have argued that *maternal deprivation* at specific times in the child's life can cause permanent disability in the child, both physically and mentally. Some data suggest that children who are separated from their mothers for half a year during the first five years fail to develop certain social responses, such as the ability to use past experiences in new situations. These arguments, if reliable, would indicate the presence of critical periods in human development for the acquisition of certain responses.

Other workers have failed to find consistent age differences in learning. Munn (1954), for example, in reviewing the literature on reminiscence as a function of age, fails to find evidence that children and adults differ in this phenomenon. Another "negative" example comes from the work of J. G. Gilbert (1941) on immediate memory span in human beings from twenty to sixty years of age. He found no differences within this age range, although loss of short-term memory is a frequent characteristic of old age and senility.

SEXUAL BEHAVIOR

Sexual behavior is an area in which instinct and learning are combined to produce complex behavior. The pattern of behavior may be instinctual after appropriate stimuli have been provided, but it also contains many elements of learned responses. As one ascends the phylogenetic scale, sexual behavior appears to become more and more diverse and complex, although it seems reasonable to suppose that myopia from our position on top of the "scale" prohibits us from seeing the complexity of the supposedly totally instinctual responses of those lower on the scale.

In most, if not all, species some form of behavior prefaces copulation. In birds, a typical pattern is the locking of bills, accompanied by cooing—hence, the Homo sapiens phrase "billing and cooing." In some forms, this behavior may be led by a dominant male who struts or attacks the female. In a few forms, the female is dominant. Eventually, the female takes a submissive role by adopting the posture that is most efficient for copulation. The male also assumes an efficient posture. Many observers have commented on the stereotyped responses involved in sexual behavior of Aves, but it is reasonable to assume that individual differences could be found upon close examination.

Rodents (especially guinea pigs and rats) and domestic animals (cats and dogs) have been the mammals most commonly investigated. Little formal research has been performed on subhuman primates, although we may expect their sexual behavior to be phylogenetically most similar to that of man. The typical rodent mating behavior involves (from the point of view of the male) rendering the female relatively immobile by clasping the neck in the mouth and making a series of thrusts with the pelvic region. The female also provides a reasonably stereotyped pattern by engaging in lordosis, the posture which makes her receptive to the male, consisting primarily of an arching of the back and displaying of the genitals. Among domestic animals similar patterns are found. Many primates follow the pattern of rodents, for the male mounts *a tergum*. Some historical authorities cite evidence to show that the primary position for human sexual behavior varies as a function of the culture. This would imply that this rather basic aspect of behavior is at least partly learned.

The greatest amount of discussion regarding the relative influence of innate and learned behavior (as well as voluntary versus involuntary behavior) has centered around homosexual behavior, primarily because many cultures have strict laws which punish such behavior. Nevertheless, homosexual behavior is not uncommon among animals nor apparently among human beings (Kinsey, Pomeroy, & C. E. Martin, 1948). It is established that homosexual behavior may be altered through changing the hormonal structure of the individual. It is also clear, however, that the environmental factors, such as availability of members of the opposite sex, parental behavior toward children, and other factors make the possibility of homosexual behavior more likely in some individuals than in others.

Nest Building, Egg Laying, and Related Activities: Although one commonly associates the building of nests for the purpose of caring for the young with birds, some mammals also devote considerable behavior to nest construction. Among animals of both groups, the type and location of the nest varies. Since nest building is seasonal and since it correlates with the receptive period of the female, it is possible that both nest building and recep-

tivity are controlled by the same process. The most likely underlying process is the change which occurs in the hormonal structure of organisms as a function of climatic or cyclic changes. In most species, nest building can be enhanced by the injection of estrogen, one of the female sex hormones. Other species, however, appear to require something more than the hormone treatment. For example, it appears likely that the hormonal balance of some organisms depends upon external stimuli, such as the sight of the projected mate. Thus, some species exhibit what appears to be a reciprocal relationship, in which the hormonal balance of both male and female changes (with accompanying changes in behavior) as a function of the animals' stimulating each other through audition, vision, or the other sensory systems. This mutual stimulation may continue through the rearing of the young. To say that such behavior is instinctual is only to apply a useful adjective to a complicated relationship. Although the relationship may be instinctual, the mere use of the term as a descriptive label clearly leaves much unsaid.

In order to note more thoroughly the way in which complex mating and child-rearing behaviors may occur and in order to provide an example of the manner in which such complex behaviors are investigated, we shall consider a series of studies on the ringdove by Lehrman (1964). The ringdove exhibits well-ordered behavior patterns in the reproductive cycle. These behaviors are shown in Figure 16–2. Since the behaviors are observed throughout the species and do not appear to be learned, at least in the traditional meaning of the term, it is tempting to label the entire sequence as instinctual. No doubt, instinct plays a part, but nevertheless the careful observer will find that these complex behaviors are, if not learned, certainly dependent upon more factors than the term *instinct* would imply. Let us consider the questions that Lehrman and his colleagues asked and the way they investigated them:

1. When eggs are laid, both the female and the male sit on the eggs. Is this because the ringdove

will normally sit on any rounded object, or does he do so only under special conditions? In order to answer this, Lehrman kept male and female ringdoves in isolation for several weeks. Then he placed pairs in cages which contained both a nest bowl (see *A* and *B* of Figure 16–2) and two eggs. The result was that the doves ignored the eggs. Indeed, they proceeded to go through the normal courting and reproductive cycle—and sat only on their own newly laid eggs. In a control experiment in which pairs were placed in the cage seven days later, the doves hurriedly prepared the nests. Lehrman suggests (1964, p. 51) that two changes occur: First, the birds change "character"; they change from being interested in courtship to being interested in nest building. Second, they

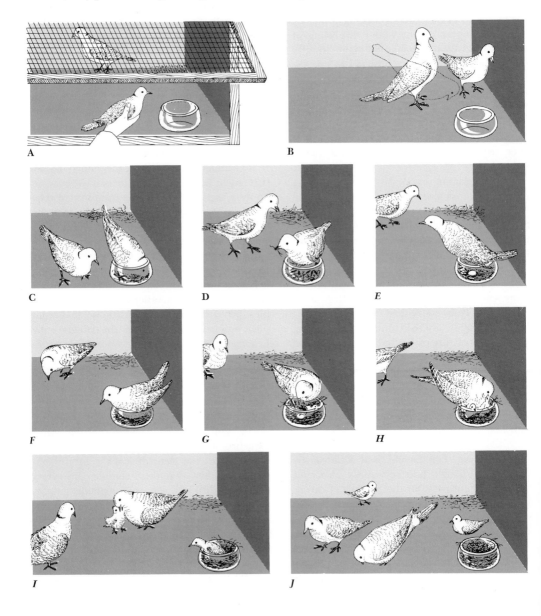

A

B

C

D

E

F

G

H

I

J

change from work in nest building to egg sitting. The first change occurs when a mate is introduced; the second occurs with nest-building activity.

2. What is the effect of the amount of time during which a mate and nest-building materials are available? Pairs of birds were placed in cages for different numbers of days. Some cages contained nesting material; others did not. The dependent variable was whether the birds sat or not. The percentage of sitting increased in both males and females, until almost 100 percent sat by the sixth day. The presence of nesting material had a salutary effect, for which both males and females the percentage was higher when nesting material was available.

These data suggest strongly that external stimuli, in addition to internal sexual stimuli, are important in determining the course of the reproductive cycle. Apparently, some stimuli associated with the mate are able to alter behavior. The probable location of this change is hormonal, for males and females were injected with the female hormone progesterone, over 90 percent of the eggs were sat upon within three hours after introduction to the cage. Normally, it will be recalled, the process of egg sitting would take five to seven days. This finding suggests that the hormonal secretions may be altered by external stimuli, such as sight of the male.

3. Is sight alone sufficient to generate egg-laying behaviors? It has been found that the female pigeon will lay eggs, even though she is separated from the male by a glass screen (H. L. Matthews, 1939). The African Mouth Breeder nests and lays infertile eggs when stimulated by the sight of another member of the species. Thus, it appears that the sight or sound of the mate is sufficient to induce egg-laying behavior. Data from the ringdove also show that the percentage of females ovulating increases as a function of the number of days during which association with a mate has been permitted. Moreover, ovulation and egg laying can be induced in the ringdove by permitting her to watch and/or hear a mate. Thus, it would appear that the stimuli from the male, along with the presence of nest-building materials, induces hormonal change which, in turn, provides the stimulus for incubation.

What stimuli from the male induce these changes? Lehrman (1965) used the ringdove-behind-glass technique but separated the males into two groups: those castrated and those intact. Most of the females provided with intact males ovulated, but few of the females associated with castrated males did so. This suggests that the stimuli are not simply auditory or visual but that they must be of a specific type.

It is clear that the reproductive behavior of these animals, although stereotyped, involves a complicated relationship between external

FIGURE 16–2: *Reproductive-behavior cycle begins soon after a male and a female ringdove are introduced into a cage containing nesting material (hay in this case) and an empty glass nest bowl (A). Courtship activity, on the first day, is characterized by the "bowing coo" of the male (B). The male and then the female utter a distinctive "nest call" to indicate their selection of a nesting site (C). There follows a week or more of cooperation in nest building (D), culminating in the laying of two eggs at precise times of day (E). The cycle continues as the adult birds take turns incubating the eggs (F), which hatch after about fourteen days (G). The newly hatched squabs are fed crop-milk, a liquid secreted in the gullets of the adults (H). The parents continue to feed them, albeit reluctantly, as the young birds learn to peck for grain themselves (I). When the squabs are between two and three weeks old, the adults ignore them, and once again a new cycle begins (J). (Lehrman, 1964, pp. 48–49. Reprinted with permission. Copyright 1964 by Scientific American, Inc. All rights reserved.)*

stimuli, such as the behavior of another animal, and internal behavior, such as hormonal secretions. It is also obvious that instinctual behavior is complex, that it involves more than internal stimuli, and that internal stimuli are, to some degree, regulated by external stimuli.

Mammals: The maternal behavior of mammals differs from that of birds in several aspects. One important difference is that the mammal usually has a relatively long period of pregnancy. At birth, some mammalian young are able to care for themselves fairly well, whereas others, including human beings, require parental care for long periods. Indeed, in human beings, the period of parental care (physical and social) runs to one-third of the lifetime of the individual.

Nest building is one of the more often investigated attributes of animal maternal behavior. Among the factors that affect nest building in mammals are time of year and climate (the higher the temperature for rodents, the less the nest building [Kinder, 1927; Koller, 1956]). That nest building in mammals also has a hormonal basis is shown by numerous experiments in which major glands have been removed. Thyroidectomy, for example, leads to an increase in nest building (Richter, 1941), and the injection of thyroid extracts decreases nest building, at least in the rat (Richter, 1942–1943). Since a portion of the pituitary controls the thyroid, removal of this portion *(hypophysectomy)* decreases the thyroid functioning and has the same effect as removing the thyroid; i.e., it increases nest-building behavior. Thus, it appears that nest building is a fairly discrete behavior under the control of a well-defined hormonal system. It is likely that the responsible hormone is progesterone. The production of progesterone occurs in the manufacturing of estrogen: most important, it is the only hormone that stimulates nest building in males. That it does not, however, have an effect on castrated males suggests that progesterone is, in some way, responsible for nest-building activities in the male and that its production in the female, along with estrogen, may account for the more impressive building behavior of the ladies.

As in birds, sensory stimuli can also alter the nest-building rate in mammals. Koller (1952; 1956), for example, has shown that if baby mice are placed in a cage with a nonpregnant mouse, the female mouse increases her nest-building activities. Moreover, there is some evidence that males can be induced to increase nest building with the presentation of babies.

The underlying processes that control sexual behavior grow more complex as one ascends the phylogenetic scale. The sexual behavior of lower organisms appears, perhaps deceptively, well ordered and stereotyped. It appears to be determined by the cyclic events of the reproductive cycle. In human beings, however, sexual behavior takes many forms and follows no seasonal pattern. Earlier literature suggested that sexual behavior came about because of the physiological state of the genitals. For example, it was suggested that in the male, as the seminal vesicles were filled, the sexual drive increased. This approach has a superficial resemblance to the homeostatic theory of the hunger and thirst drives: it assumes that the organism builds up and then satisfies a deficiency. The drive state, thus, increases and is satiated. Several observations suggest that this theory is not sufficient to explain all sexual behavior. Castrated animals do show sexual behavior. Further, the relationship between sexual deprivation and sexual behavior, which would be fairly direct if the homeostatic approach to sex were correct, is less than clear (see F. A. Beach, 1956). Experimental removal of various glands and appendages of animals also shows that sexually experienced animals do not lose their typical sexual behaviors when important vehicles for the behavior are removed. Less is known about the effect of such operations on animals who have never had sexual experience. It is possible that the experienced animal finds, through learning or conditioning, that the behavior is still rewarding, although the possibility of orgasm is removed.

Many personality theorists consider sexual behavior of considerable significance to personality. To Sigmund Freud (1856–1939) sexual energy occupied the position of a *Trieb,* a word which is usually translated into English as *drive.* Freud considered sexual energy an innate drive, although it was, obviously, capable of many transformations through experience and learning. Experimental psychology has long given tacit credence to this view by including sexual behavior as a basic drive along with hunger and thirst. Admittedly, however, sex differs from hunger and thirst in one important respect: although one most certainly dies from a lack of food or water, death from deprivation of the third primary drive, however imaginatively real, is unknown. Actually, the reasons for excluding sexual behavior from the restricted list of primary drives are more compelling than the reasons for including it. As F. A. Beach (1956) has argued, sex is not a homeostatic mechanism in the same sense that hunger and thirst are. There is no deprivation of the cellular structure such as occurs in hunger and thirst. The processes which produce hunger and thirst are reasonably well identified, although the exact relationships are sometimes unclear. Sexual behavior, however, appears to have no such simple antecedents as dryness in the mouth or absence of food in the stomach. Sexual behavior can be elicited by various external stimuli, and an exciter for one person may have no effect at all upon another.

Few experimental data exist concerning human sexual activity (Whalen, 1966). Available information is often of the statistical type, such as that provided by the two Kinsey reports (Kinsey, Pomeroy, & C. E. Martin, 1948; Kinsey, Pomeroy, C. E. Martin, & Gebhard, 1953). These reports provide statistical information on the frequency of various forms of sexual behavior in human beings as a function of such variables as age, education, and economic status. The writers provide occasional insights into the causes of certain forms of sexual behavior, although, understandably, experimental data are lacking.

Hormones: The gonads—the testes of the male and ovaries of the female—are inactive during the childhood of human beings. With puberty, however, the pituitary secretes *gonadotropins,* which influence the testicles and ovaries by encouraging the production of *androgen* (the primary male hormone) and *estrogen* (the primary female hormone). Androgen and estrogen are generic names. An important androgen is *testosterone.* An important estrogen is *progesterone,* which is active during pregnancy. These hormones encourage the development of secondary sexual characteristics, such as beard growth in the male and breast growth in the female, and eventually are responsible for the production of sperm in the male and eggs in the female. With pregnancy, the gonadotropin *prolactin* becomes influential. Although it is present without pregnancy, pregnancy releases its effect.

The relative effectiveness of hormones in mature organisms depends upon the species, for some species show seasonal cycles based on temperature and other physical factors of the environment and other species repond to the estrous cycle. Some animals are sexually active regardless of seasonal variations, whereas others reflect gonadal and hormonal changes which occur as a function of seasonal factors. In the human being, the male is apparently free from such influences, for he is able and willing to mate or to engage in sexual behavior at any convenient time. The human female is, to some extent, dependent upon menstrual cycles, for receptivity is related to the cyclic effect of menstruation. In other mammals, the estrous cycle has a similar, although often more pronounced, effect. Under nonpregnant conditions, estrous cycles are influenced by hormone secretion. If pregnancy occurs, other hormones appear. At the onset of pregnancy, the production of prolactin is increased. There is also an increase in secretion of both estrogen and progesterone.

The effects of the estrous cycle on sexual behavior have been observed often in rodents. The female rat, for example, has an estrous cycle lasting around five days. *Heat,* the period of maximal sexual receptivity, occurs only during a small portion of the cycle. In addition to changes in the vaginal structure, the animal becomes highly active. When the period has passed, the female is unreceptive. Indeed, she will commonly resist advances. Departure from this pattern occurs more frequently as one moves up the phylogenetic scale. Primates show a heightened receptivity during the heat period of the cycle, but the female is also occasionally receptive at other times. In human beings, the period of the cycle is even less important to female sexual receptivity, although it is clearly a factor.

Premature sexual behavior in the young of a species may occur if hormones are administered (P. T. Young, 1961). This has been noted in a variety of species as distinct as guppies and human beings. The hormone administration has two effects: first, the neuromuscular system becomes sufficiently matured for mating behavior to occur, and, second, the glands and organs necessary for such behavior mature. The effect of the level of maturity which the organism has reached when the hormones are administered has been studied by F. A. Beach and A. M. Holz (1946) among others. They castrated male rats at a variety of ages, ranging from one day to one year. Ninety days after the operation, each animal was given a dose of androgen and tested with a receptive female. The dependent variable was whether the animals copulated, ejaculated, or did nothing. In all the animals except the one-day-old group, copulation occurred, and most copulations led to ejaculation. The one-day-old animals failed to show normal penis growth, and this fact probably accounts for their disability. Castration, however, would exclude the action of the gonadal hormones. Thus, it would appear that, in the rat at least, the neuromuscular structure necessary for sexual behavior is present from birth and does not require gonadal secretions for maturation. It should be noted, however, that the rat requires little experience to perform satisfactorily. Since it is known that higher organisms, particularly human beings, require more ex-

perience, it is probably unjustified to generalize these findings to higher organisms.

Failure of the pituitary to secret appropriate hormones prevents the maturation of the gonads and the development of typical sexual patterns, just as castration before puberty in human males most often leads to disability. The effect of castration and hormonal deficiencies upon adult, experienced human beings varies, reflecting, no doubt, the dependence of the human being on experience as well as on internal secretions.

Among animals which have seasonal mating and sexual-behavior patterns, the administration of gonadal or pituitary hormones sets off the pattern regardless of the season. Among castrated, senile, or impotent animals, administration of the appropriate hormones (e.g., testosterone or progesterone) restores sexual behavior. In human beings, however, injection of these hormones is less effective. Impotent males do not necessarily respond to androgen. Both male and female homosexuals fail to shift from this pattern of sexual activity when the appropriate hormones are administered. Indeed, Ford and F. A. Beach (1951) report that administration of androgen to male homosexuals merely increases the sexual drive without altering the sexual pattern.

Homosexuality has been explained traditionally either genetically (implying that hormonal differences are responsible for the behavior) or experimentally (implying that experiences and learning are responsible). Attempts to alter homosexual behavior in the human being by altering the hormone balance have not been successful. Data from animals suggest that artificial alteration of the hormonal balance does affect the sexual behavior of lower organisms. Some male rats will demonstrate female mating and sexual patterns if injected with estrogen, and spayed females will show male behavior if injected with androgen. Even in the rat, however, the effects of hormone injections vary. These data, coupled with information from other species, including human beings, indicate that the patterns of both male and female behavior exist in all organisms and that the dominant pattern can be produced by changes in the hormonal balance (especially in lower mammals) and by experience (especially in higher animals).

Role of the Central Nervous System: Sexual behavior requires the cooperation of several physiological systems. Accordingly, we may expect the central nervous system to mediate some aspects of sexual behavior. In rodents and domestic animals, decortication does not alter sexual functioning in any essential way, although decorticated female rats do not take the initiative in sexual activity, as do normal female rats on some occasions (F. A. Beach, 1944). When more than 20 percent of the cortex is destroyed, some animals show disrupted copulatory behavior. The greater the loss, the more the animal is affected. The more sexually active the animal before the destruction of tissue, the greater the loss that is required for copulatory behavior to cease. When approximately 60 percent of the cortex is removed, the rat ceases to engage in sexual behavior. A sex difference appears when the role of the brain is considered. Large areas, such as the cortex or hippocampus, may be ablated in the female rodent without destroying the sexual responses; this is not true of the male of the species.

In some animals, destruction of portions of the sensory systems, leaving the cortex intact, serves to eliminate sexual behavior. This is true of the male rabbit, in which destruction of the olfactory lobes results in a loss of copulatory behavior. This is not true, interestingly, of the female rabbit, implying that this type of sensory stimulation is necessary for the eliciting of sexual behavior in one sex but not in the other. It is noteworthy that the olfactory bulbs may be destroyed in the male without altering copulatory behavior, provided little damage is done to the neocortex. This suggests that the need for sensory stimulation is not limited to olfaction but that sexual behavior may be aroused as long as the possibility of some sensory stimulation exists (F. A. Beach, 1940). The implication of these findings, provided they may be generalized to man, is that the male depends upon the higher, cortical centers for sexual behavior far more than the female—a finding that appears to contradict the common belief of Homo sapiens.

There is evidence that as one moves up the phylogenetic scale, the effects of decortication become more and more pronounced. Male cats, for example, lose their orientation and mount prematurely from the side. It is also reasonable to assume that the higher an organism is on the phylogenetic scale, the more capable he is of learning, and thus the more the learned responses will tend to override the purely physiological patterns of sexual behavior.

The spinal cord is an important component of sexual behavior, for, as we noted in Chapter 2, this connector between the brain and the periphery provides the location for reflex action such as ejaculation and tumescence in the male. In lower animals, sexual reflexes are common in both sexes. Male rodents, canines, and probably human beings show ejaculation and erection through stimulation of brain centers (Olds, 1962). Moreover, some semblances of the estrous cycle remain in cats and dogs whose spinal cord has been transected. These responses occur in castrated animals, and hormones do not appear to be essential for the female reflexes. Thus, the spinal cord may be said to control the more rudimentary reflexes involved in sexual behavior. In the brain, the hypothalamus, the amygdala, and other areas associated with the limbic system appear to be involved in the sexual process. These areas, as we shall discuss more fully in Chapter 17, are also associated with various behaviors generally classified as "emotional."

The study of sexual behavior in reptiles, amphibia, and lower mamals has not been extensive. This deficiency is unfortunate if one wishes to trace the instinctual aspect of sexual behavior through its phylogenetic development. Shaw (1962), studying the sexual behavior of the platyfish, has noted that mature sexual behavior is affected by social experiences early in the life of the organism. She isolated subjects taken by caesarean section and found that fish reared without seeing either the opposite sex of the species or the normal environment were greatly inhibited in performing the stereotyped sexual responses of this species. Fish that were not permitted to see mates but could see the general environment were not inhibited. Thus, it appears that the maturation of sexual behavior in this species of fish is a function of the general level of stimulation provided the organism but that observation of, or experience with, other members of the species is not necessary for sexual behavior.

ANALYSES OF SOME INSTINCTUAL BEHAVIORS

Every species, no doubt, possesses some behaviors which are instinctual. Only a few instinctual behaviors have been adequately described observationally, and considerably fewer have received the elucidation of experimental attention. To show the techniques used in the study of instincts and to show how data collected on one species may be useful in interpreting the behavior of another, we shall consider several topics that have encouraged more than casual experimental interest. These are (1) homing and migration among animals, (2) sucking behavior and licking at childbirth, (3) releasing mechanisms, as when an organism makes a stereotyped response to a specific external stimulus, (4) consummatory behavior, as shown by hoarding food, and (5) data on the possible physiological bases of instinctual behavior.

Homing and Migration: Homing refers to the capacity of a single animal to return to the place from which it was reared or released. *Migration* refers to the travel of groups of animals, coinciding with temperature and seasonal factors. Although training is of value, particularly in homing, it does not appear to be essential for successful homing. Migration

appears to require little, if any, learning. Homing is usually regarded as a characteristic of birds. Migration is found in birds as well as fish.

Many wild birds "home." Certain species of pigeon are reported to have unusual powers to relocate an area, and these birds have been used on many occasions as messengers. There are reliable reports that it is possible for a homing pigeon to travel across oceans in order to return home. Usually, the homing pigeon is "shaped" in the homing task by being repeatedly released farther and farther from home. Nevertheless, even without such training, the pigeon often appears to be able to find his way to the starting location.

The cues that birds use for migration have attracted the consideration of theorists. Unfortunately, experimental tests of the resulting postulations have not always served to resolve controversy. What appears to be simple to the bird is almost inexplicable to the human being who studies the bird. Two of the more favored hypotheses have been (1) that the birds make use of such physical factors as the wind patterns of the earth or the location of the magnetic field and (2) that temperature and its hormonal effects control the migratory pattern.

It is reasonable to suppose that migratory behavior is elicited and sustained by seasonal temperature changes. Several studies have suggested the importance of the sun to migration. At least in some species, the sun's rays are used to provide orientation to the bird, for orientation can be confused predictably by the use of artificial rays produced by mirrors (G. V. T. Matthews, 1955; Carthy, 1956; Griffin, 1964). Some birds appear to migrate only at night, thus making the sun theory appear to be inapplicable. Nocturnal migrating ability is usually attributed to the birds' memory or their use of the stars as navigating cues. Sauer (1958) has studied the night-migratory warbler and has found strong evidence that the warbler uses the stars for orientation. This species shows appropriate orientation when the stars are clear but has difficulty when the night is overcast and cloudy. Moreover, warblers who were raised in cages and not permitted to migrate demonstrated correct orientation when presented with a planetarium's reproduction of the night sky (Sauer, 1958).

The fact that birds go south when winter comes to the north suggests that temperature is a determining factor. Along with the change in climate, however, go other changes, such as increased difficulty in finding food on snowy, icy ground and decrease in the amount of daily illumination. These are, no doubt, important factors in migration, but they do not tell us the specific mechanisms that are used to guide the complicated behavior involved in migration.

An early indication of the importance of illumination came from Rowan (1931), who raised juncos in an aviary in which one group received a regular decrease in the amount of light daily (control group) and another received a regular increase in light (experimental group). The junco normally summers in Canada and winters in the central United States. The experimental procedure thus emulated fall and winter light durations for the control group and spring for the experimental group. Examination of the gonads showed that the control birds had testes or ovaries of normal size for winter and that the experimental birds had gonads most similar to those commonly noted in spring. Thus, it appears that the change in illumination alters the physiological structure of the organism. Again we note evidence that external stimuli can encourage or produce rather dramatic changes in basic structure. When the birds were freed in the winter, the controls remained nearby, but the experimental birds disappeared, ostensibly for a better climate.

This basic experiment was repeated with crows in order to determine where the released birds flew (Rowan, 1931). This type of bird normally migrates on an Alberta, Canada–Kansas, United States axis. The birds, treated like those in the junco study, were released in early November from Alberta. Examination of the gonads again showed changes commensurate with the changes in length of illumination. Information was obtained about

the released birds through the cooperation of local residents alerted to the experiment by radio and newspaper appeals. Approximately 50 percent of the released birds were eventually located. Of the control birds, none were found north of Alberta. Of the experimental birds, the majority were found in the far north. It appears that the lengthening or shortening of the illumination period is an appropriate stimulus for endocrinous changes in these birds and that these changes, in some way, lead the birds to change their habitat.

The migratory activities of fish have also received attention. The salmon has excited the greatest interest, and observation suggests that its spawning and reproductive behaviors resemble the migratory activities of birds. The stereotyped activities are related to the reproductive cycle, and there appears to be a relationship between external events and internal, physiological changes.

Roule (1933) has suggested that the movement of the salmon is, at first, a result of maturation. Toward the end of the second year of life, the young salmon migrate downstream. It may be recalled that the cutaneous layers of fish often contain photoreceptors. Since the amount of pigmentation decreases at this point in maturation, the photoreceptors become less protected by pigmentation. Thus, in order to escape the irritating effects of strong light, the salmon migrates to deeper water. Another possibility is that the irritating light renders the fish inert and they are swept downstream by the current. This suggestion is based on the observation that light produces inactivity in the salmon. Similar effects of light and dark on activity are well known in rodents, fowls, and perhaps man.

When the salmon have moved downstream, they usually remain within the mainstream of the river. Fresh-water rivers emptying into the ocean maintain a "stream," often for some miles, composed of the fresh water of the river. This oceanic river is less saline than the ocean as a whole. As the salmon grow larger, they require more and more oxygen. This oxygen requirement forces the salmon to migrate inward, toward the fresher water. The "upstream" migratory behavior may have basic similarities to the factors governing migration of birds. Hasler (1960) suggests that the salmon return to the stream from which they were hatched. Evidence for this comes from Donaldson and H. G. Allen (1957), who moved eggs from the stream in which they were laid to another stream. The salmon returned to the stream in which they were hatched, rather than to the stream inhabited by their parents. The salmon, however, continue their journey upstream, hurling themselves against the current for long periods. Various hypotheses have been suggested to account for this behavior; none is totally satisfactory. A good guess is that the salmon are able to identify chemical attributes of the water. Whatever the cues, salmon have remarkable retentive abilities, for some species have been tagged several thousands of miles from their home, yet when the gonads mature, these salmon are found to be making the trip home (Hasler, 1960).

The grunion has received less extensive study, although his spawning and migratory behavior is also predictable. When tides are at a particular point, the female grunion swims to shore, riding to the beach on a wave, digs a trough in the sand, deposits the eggs, and returns to sea on an outgoing wave. This behavior is so predictable that the exact time of a grunion "run" can be predicted by knowledge of the tides. The prediction is only valid for indicating the time of the run if there is a run, however; sometimes a predicted run does not occur.

Although many observations associated with migration are unexplained, perseverance has yielded explanations of some of the phenomena. The most reasonable and testable hypotheses relate internal physiological effects, such as maturation and reproductive cycle, and external stimuli, such as temperature and amount of oxygen.

The Sucking Reflex and Licking Behavior:
The sucking reflex is perhaps the clearest example of an innate behavior pattern in human beings and other mammals. Two rather distinct forces in psychology have shown interest in sucking behavior: the psychoanalytically inclined theorists, who consider the sucking response related to the general oral development of the human being, and psychologists and ethologists interested in instinctual behavior.

In the human being, the sucking response may be elicited shortly after birth by stimulating the mouth region of the infant. Nilsson (1965) has shown that this behavior begins during the prenatal period. The intensity and detail of the response vary, but the basic response is universal.

The fundamental experimental question is this: does sucking represent a need for food, or is it unrelated to the drive state of the organism? Information on this distinction comes primarily from work with dogs. D. M. Levy (1934) used six 2-day-old collies. Two remained with their mother, two were fed with "slow" nipples (which released the milk slowly, thus increasing the output of sucking responses), and two with "fast" nipples. If a separate sucking drive existed, one would expect the group fed with fast nipples to show more sucking behavior, since the drive would not be satisfied during feeding. The slow-nipple group, however, had reason to suck extensively during feeding. Thus, one would expect their sucking drive to be satisfied. The results, retrospectively, confirm this. The fast-nipple animals showed greater sucking behavior after eating, while sleeping, and at other times. W. T. James (1957) used a fistula technique and injected milk into the stomach of his subjects. He found no difference in sucking between injected subjects and noninjected controls. These data indicate that sucking is independent of food intake and that, conceptually, an organism needs to suck a certain amount: if the need is not satisfied while the animal is eating, the sucking behavior will occur in response to other stimuli.

The limited research conducted on sucking in the human being provides results opposite to those found in dogs. Whether this represents species difference or procedural difficulties is unclear. Data on human beings, however, have implications for the sometimes fashionable argument over breast versus bottle feeding. In one experiment, 60 neonates were studied in the hospital until ten days of age. Three groups were used: one received nutrition through cup feeding, another by bottle feeding, and a third by breast feeding. Among the many dependent variables measured, a finger-sucking test distinguished the groups. In this test, a finger was used to stimulate the mouth and cheeks of the neonate, and a record was kept of whether he attempted to suck the finger. The cup-fed babies showed little evidence of finger sucking; the breast group did suck the finger (H. V. Davis, Sears, H. C. Miller, and Brodbeck, 1948). Since the cup-fed babies would have little opportunity to suck during feeding, the Levy study would predict that they would show the greatest need to suck if the need were unrelated to feeding. The data suggest, on the contrary, that those who had an opportunity to suck (e.g., the breast-fed babies) showed the greatest need for sucking. This suggests, in turn, that sucking—or the need to continue to suck in nonnutritive situations—is learned. It may be argued that sucking comes to have secondary reinforcing values from its association with the pleasure of food intake or the reduction of the hunger drive. Certainly, this interpretation is reasonable in terms of the principles of classical conditioning and operant training, although validation would require extensive investigation of other variables, such as extinction, before it could be accepted.

Sucking behavior occurs in the kitten within an hour following birth and before the entire litter is delivered. Data collected by Rosenblatt, Turkewitz, and Schneirla (1962) show that the young kitten may spend eight hours per day sucking during the first month of life. During the second month, the frequency and duration of sucking decreases until weaning is completed. These observers note three periods: in the first, the female presents her teats to the kittens by arching over the young animals and stimulating the kittens tactually and thermally. During the second stage, generally from the third to the sixth week, sucking becomes a cooperative enterprise. The kittens approach the female, and the female cooperates by reclining in positions that encourage sucking. In the third stage, sucking is initiated more often by the kitten, until, at the end of the stage, the kittens must follow and coerce the mother into cooperation.

These investigators isolated some kittens in an incubator which contained a surrogate mother. The "mother" contained a nipple through which formula could be sucked. The sucking behavior of the isolated kittens was similar to that noted in the three stages associated with normal sucking; however, some differences in behavior were noted. When the kittens were returned to the real mother cat, some sucked immediately and others did not. The critical factor was the time at which the subject had been isolated. For example, all the kittens isolated between birth and 7 days of age sucked, as did those isolated from 6 to 23 and 18 to 33 days of age. Kittens isolated from 23 to 44 and from 2 to 44 days of age did not suck. These investigators favor an interpretation of their results which includes assessing both the maturational and experiential factors involved in behavior. Although the concept of the critical period is inviting, the writers point out that "every age-period is *critical* for the development of certain aspects of the *normal, progressive suckling pattern*" (Rosenblatt et al., 1962, p. 209).

In the domestic cat, Ewer (1959; 1961) found that during the first few weeks each kitten establishes ownership over a teat. Sometimes, but rarely, a kitten controls two teats. Each kitten gradually establishes ownership of one teat during the first days of life. Only rarely does the kitten use any other teat later. When a kitten is transferred with the first day of life to a foster mother, at first there is no response. Eventually it establishes ownership of a teat, but it is not necessarily the teat that has the same anatomical location as the original mother's teat. A similar relationship has been noted in pigs (Donald, 1937; McBride, 1963).

Another oral response, common in most mammals with the notable exception of human beings, is the licking behavior that occurs during parturition. Both cat and dog mothers lick the young as well as their own genital area. This behavior is commonly described as instinctual on the ground that it is difficult to show that it can have been learned. Some workers have ascribed the licking behavior to irritability of the female genitals following parturition and to chemical deficiencies during pregnancy.

Innate Releasing Mechanisms and Fixed Action Patterns: We have noted that instinctual behavior commonly appears at a predictable period in the development of the organism. The stereotyped behaviors associated with the reproductive cycle, such as mating and caring for the young, obviously require that the organism attain a particular period in development. It is possible, then, that an instinctual response might never occur, merely because the appropriate period has never arrived. This characteristic of instinctual behavior emphasizes the dependence of some instinctual behavior on external stimuli. Stimuli from outside the organism which serve to bring about an instinctual pattern of behavior are called *innate releasing mechanisms* (IRMs). Tinbergen points out (1951, p. 25) that although the study of the sensory limitations of animals tells us what the animal can or cannot perceive, it does not describe the stimuli to which the organism will respond. Certainly, an organism does not respond to all changes in sensory stimulation. Thus, according to Tinbergen, the investigation of the nature of the stimuli to which an animal responds provides the basis of the study of instinctual behavior.

As an example of a response worthy of study, Tinbergen nominates the reaction of the male stickleback fish to the red markings on the belly of other males. Tinbergen demonstrated the importance of this sensory stimulation to the fighting behavior of the fish by using the models shown in Figure 16–3. These models are very crude imitations of the species: the bottom four have little resemblance to the shape of the male stickleback, although all contain a red coloration in the belly region. The fish marked on top is an accurate

spatial representation of the fish, but it lacks the red area. When the models were placed in a tank, the fish reacted by fighting the four red-bellied models. Tinbergen concludes that this result shows that the male stickleback reacts to the red coloration and that the coloration is an IRM for the characteristic fighting behavior of the male of the species. Other IRMs have been described in a variety of species (Tinbergen, 1951; Thorpe, 1956, 1962).

Note that the fish has discriminated a certain characteristic of the stimulus and that this characteristic has served as an IRM. Note, too, that the fish has not responded to all the differentiable stimuli in his environment. The fact that he responds selectively, rather than in a general fashion, represents the "innateness" of the mechanism. Some innate mechanism presumably selects the stimuli to which he will react. Evidence for the innateness of the mechanism comes from the observation that animals reared in isolation or with other species show the behavior when the appropriate stimuli are presented.

The influence of classical conditioning or operant training on the IRM cannot be excluded. Lorenz (1957b) suggests that he was unable to continue observations on fear responses in ducks, because during the testing the animals became fearful at the sight of the observers putting the experimental apparatus in place. This suggests that the fear was becoming conditioned to visual and auditory cues. Adler and J. A. Hogan (1963) studied the aggressive behavior of the Siamese fighting fish and attempted to classically condition to a slight electric shock the extension of the gills which occurs in aggressive behavior. They were able to show suppression of the gill extension under these conditions.

The term *fixed action pattern* (FAP) has developed from the concept of IRMs. Like the IRM, the FAP is stereotyped and free from learning. Moltz (1965) suggests, however, two further characteristics of the FAP: that it is independent of "immediate external control" and that it is independent of "individual learning." The example of the graylag goose in retrieving eggs lost from the nest provides a neat example of the FAP. According to Moltz (1965, p. 29), when the goose is retrieving the egg, two separate motions are noted: "A sagittal movement that keeps the egg rolling in the bird's median plane, and a lateral or side-to-side movement that keeps it from deviating too far either to the right or left." Regardless of the shape of the eggs or of the terrain over which the goose is required to retrieve, the sagittal movement occurs. Thus, it is classified as an FAP. Moltz points out that if the egg rolls away accidentally, the goose continues to make the sagittal response, even though one egg (the stimulus) is no longer present. This observation implies that the sagittal movement does not require the presence of an external stimulus in order to maintain the response. The lateral movement is not considered an FAP, since it is under the constant influence of the egg. If the egg moves to the right or left, the goose compensates for the change and moves the egg on course. If the egg rolls away, the lateral action disappears. Thus, contact with the object is necessary for starting the response, and it is also necessary for sustaining the response once it has begun.

Evidence that FAPs should be considered unlearned responses comes from a variety of sources. First, they appear so quickly in the maturation of the young that it is unreasonable to postulate that the response could have been learned. Moreover, the FAP has been observed even when the appropriate structures are missing. For example, a drake that failed to develop the highly colored feather used in preening during courtship continued to make the preening FAP, even though the appropriate organ—the feather—was absent (Lorenz, 1955). The FAP is important to theory because of its fundamental nature. As a discrete, unlearned response, it may represent the equivalent of an atom of instinct, and study of individual FAPs may provide building blocks for theories of instinctual behavior.

Instinctual Consummatory Behavior: Rodents, among other mammals, are apt to store food, sometimes for later use and sometimes, apparently, merely for the pleasure of storing.

FIGURE 16-3: *Stickleback models. The models were used to determine the innate releasing mechanism for aggressive behavior in this fish. The model at the top is an accurate depiction of the stickleback, although it does not have the red belly. The four other models are less accurate representations, but they do have the red belly. The stickleback is aggressive toward the representations with the red belly, even though they have little else in common with the actual fish. (From Tinbergen, 1951, p. 28, after Tinbergen, 1948.)*

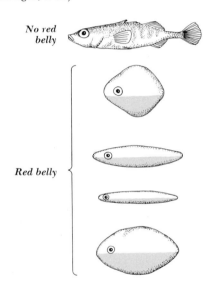

Squirrels hide food for the winter, rats accumulate food if convenient, and dogs bury bones for later recovery. Acquiring more food than is consumed is known as *hoarding,* and it has been investigated most extensively in rats. The most common experimental procedure is to place a food box in such a way that it is connected to the rats' home cage by an alley. The dependent variable is the number of pieces of food the rats transfer to the home cage for safekeeping. A number of factors affect the presence or rate of hoarding behavior. Experience with the food (Stellar & C. T. Morgan, 1943), temperature (McCleary & C. T. Morgan, 1946), and restriction of diet (C. T. Morgan, Stellar, & O. Johnson, 1943) are among the most often measured variables.

The physiological or behavioral reasons for hoarding are not well understood. Some authorities regard hoarding as an instinctual behavior (C. T. Morgan, 1947), although the chain of events which lead to the culmination of the instinct in eating are not described. Other writers consider hoarding a learned behavior (Marx, 1950), and still others regard it as a combination of instinctual and learned responses. We shall consider selections of the available reports:

Temperature: **Although temperature does affect the amount of hoarding, the exact relationship appears to depend upon the species. With satiated rats lowering the temperature may induce hoarding (McCleary & C. T. Morgan, 1946), but with mice an increase in temperature leads to hoarding (S. Ross & W. I. Smith, 1953).**

Hunger: **The fact that hungry animals exhibit hoarding behavior has sometimes confused interpretations of the literature. As it turns out, hunger is not a necessary condition for the onset of hoarding, but a food-deprived rat will eventually begin hoarding behavior.**

Food frustration: **If hungry rats are permitted to see and smell food but not permitted to eat it, the amount of hoarding increases (F. McCord, 1941). J. McV. Hunt (1941) provided feeding frustration in young rats at weaning and about one week later. Five months afterward, the subjects were tested in a hoarding apparatus along with nonfrustrated controls under conditions of both deprivation and satiation. The animals frustrated at weaning hoarded more when deprived, although the other age and satiation states did not produce differences in hoarding. This experiment suggests both the possibility of a critical period for hoarding behavior to be affected by food frustration and the possibility that the effects of food frustration may be long lasting.**

Although some of the factors that affect hoarding are known, the results of studies often appear to be contradictory. Certainly, it is impossible to make definitive statements regarding the nature of the behavior. It is possibly even more difficult to uncover the relative innateness or learnability of hoarding. Nevertheless, hoarding provides an excellent behavioral example of how investigation of an apparently innate activity can show how such behaviors are modifiable both by external and internal stimuli.

Physiological Basis of Instinct: Instinctual behavior represents a combination of many specific responses, but it is reasonable to assume that some center in the central nervous system maintains ultimate control over the behavior. Certainly, the ethological school looks to the central nervous system as the prime mover of instinctual behavior. Not surprisingly, the information available is minimal. Indeed, it is likely to remain so until some fortunate experiment locates such a center in the central nervous system or until new information about instinctual behavior suggests the location of such a center.

Evidence for the existence of central areas comes from the work of von Holst and his colleagues. Using the techniques of brain stimulation, they have reported an ability to elicit very specific chains of responses, such as searching for food or water, eating, drinking, sleeping, fighting, and "emotional behaviors," such as apparent disgust. Von Holst and von St. Paul (1962) report that the stimulation of two different areas of the brain at the same time results in a variety of interactions. Such stimulation may lead to (1) two behaviors occurring at the same time, (2) the behaviors alternating, (3) no response when two behaviors that cannot occur at the same time are stimulated, or (4) a combination of the behaviors that produces a totally new response. Figure 16–4 shows the stereotyped attack on a stuffed animal by an implanted chicken. Before stimulation, the chicken appears to have no interest in the stuffed animal. With stimulation, however, it attacks in a stereotyped manner. Figure 16–5 shows the chicken attacking the handler.

These findings most certainly do not contradict the ethological viewpoint. Neither do they necessarily validate it. The conceptualized viewpoint is that the neural centers increase in energy and that they are fired, or released, upon presentation of the appropriate stimulus. The centers form their own dominance hierarchy, and some can repress the reactions of others. Tinbergen (1951), for example, suggests a hierarchy of animal instincts running from the chasing and biting behavior noted in fighting to the rescuing of lost eggs. Clearly, these behaviors are influenced by external sen-

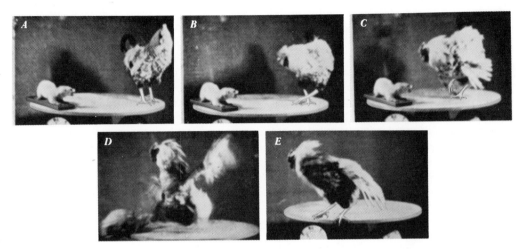

FIGURE 16–4: *The stereotyped attack by a chicken on a stuffed polecat produced by brain stimulation. (A) Before stimulation the cock stands to one side; (B) stimulation begins: the cock advances toward the polecat; (C) the cock in full enraged posture; (D) attack; (E) the enraged behavior continues. (From von Holst and von St. Paul, 1963, plate IVa.)*

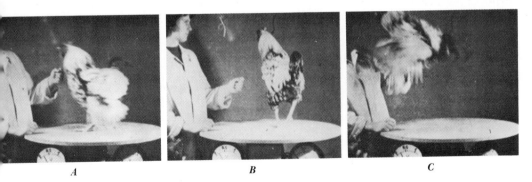

FIGURE 16–5: *The chicken attacks a normally well-liked handler. The aggressive behavior occurs during brain stimulation. (From von Holst and von St. Paul, 1963, plate IVb.)*

sory factors (e.g., the presence of a potential mate, as in the studies with the ringdove), hormonal influences (especially in animals displaying a seasonal reproductive cycle), and the energy built up by the centers of the central nervous system. When the center is released, through the removal of the inhibitory effect of some other·sensory stimulus or by external stimulation, the behavior occurs. Such behaviors occur at several levels. For example, when the stickleback performs his dance, we may note the actions of the muscles, the fins, or the rays of the fins. All these are interrelated, yet each is a step in the instinctual process which is activated by the central nervous system. This explanatory approach not only emphasizes the presence of neural centers which set off the responses but also shows that a perceptual motor hierarchy is involved.

The ethologists suggest that the study of animal behavior and animal sociology will reveal some traits of human beings which are kept from view because of the interference of learned behaviors. For example, they speculate that some instinctual responses, such as aggression, socialization, and reproductive behavior, may operate in many of the same ways that they operate among animals. Animal psychologists, to the contrary, consider instinctual behavior, if present, a relatively insignificant factor in the behavior of human beings. Thus, they concentrate on analysis of acquired responses. Both positions contribute to our understanding of instinctual processes. Indeed, the strong evidence that instinct and learning are related, as in the behavior of the ringdove, suggests that neither pure learning nor pure instinct exists as a separate entity.

SOURCES

The Concept of Instinct: F. A. Beach (1955) provides a general source of information on the development of the concept of instinct. Thorpe (1962) also provides a thoughtful commentary on the more recent developments in instinct theory. Birney and Teevan (1961)

have selected and edited original readings that trace the history of the concept.

The 1920-to-1930 period was the golden age of criticism of instinct theory. See, for example, Dunlap (1919), Kuo (1924), Eggan (1926), and Holt (1931). The 1950s provided something of a Renaissance for instinct criticism. See F. A. Beach (1955), Lehrman (1953), and Ginsburg (1952). Certainly, the concept of instinct has appealed to many theorists. W. James (1890) provides his customary thorough discussion of the usefulness and disadvantages of the concept. McDougall (1923; 1926; 1933) used the concept extensively in his analyses of behavior. It was he, more than any other person, who pushed the concept so far as to stimulate the detailed criticisms of instinct cited above.

Contemporary ethological work on instinct may be examined in a number of sources. A nontechnical introduction to the ethological viewpoint is found in Tinbergen (1951). The careful reader will note that the ethological views lead to a concept of research different from that of the experimental psychologist. Cofer and Appley (1964) have published an excellent chapter (chap. 3) on instinct and the ethological viewpoint. These writers' comments are an indication that neither the ethological nor the comparative viewpoints are totally reasonable. Tinbergen (1961) provides a more detailed ethological commentary than Lorenz (1952). Thorpe (1962) presents his usual reasoned discussion of instinct. Marler and Hamilton (1966) provide a thorough text on animal behavior.

Sensitive Periods, Imprinting, and the Maturation of Learnability: The concept of sensitive or critical periods is not new, although research on imprinting pushed the idea of critical periods to the foreground. Lorenz's (1935; 1937) original statements of imprinting should be consulted. Thorpe (1962) and Thorpe and Zangwill (1961) discuss sensitive periods.

Standard sources, such as Thorpe (1962), Bliss (1962) and Cofer and Appley (1964), include discussions of imprinting. The last-named source is particularly well detailed and reasoned. Reviews of imprinting and related phenomena are supplied by Moltz (1960) and E. H. Hess (1959b).

Sexual Behavior: One might expect this topic to account for a majority of the written words in any language, and perhaps it does. It would appear, however, to reverse the phrase, that people are so busy doing something about it that little is written about it, for there are few thoughtful treatises on the topic. Standard sources include, on a high level of difficulty, *Sex and Internal Secretions,* which has appeared in three editions (E. Allen, 1932; 1939; W. C. Young, 1961). These tomes present the most updated and detailed discussions of various aspects of sexual behavior. For experimental psychology, both Cofer and Appley (1964) and C. T. Morgan (1965) present useful discussions of the role of learning and instinct in sexual behavior.

F. A. Beach (1948) presents a lucid description and discussion of the role of hormones in the sexual behavior of a number of species. The excellent organization of this work makes it a reasonable place for the student to begin the study of sex and hormones; however, other readings would be necessary to cover the recent advances in this field. Ford and F. A. Beach (1951), in one of the most reasonable works on the subject, relate the physiology, psychology, and anthropology of sex. This book succeeds, particularly, in clarifying definitions, in untangling sources of confusion in the literature, and in bringing together diverse studies to form a comprehensive treatise on sexual behavior.

Since the purpose of the present chapter has been to show the relationship between innateness and learning, the reader should consult Riddle (1963), who provides an intensive criticism of Lehrman's work. The arguments presented are germane to more than the ringdove, for they attempt to drive to the heart of the distinction between learning and instinct. Also see Lehrman's reply (1963).

Nest Building, Egg Laying, and Related Activities: Information on invertebrates and fish may be found in F. A. Beach (1951), on birds in Gilliard (1958) and Lehrman (1961). Cofer and Appley (1964, p. 108) discuss nesting, retrieving, and other particular aspects of maternal behavior. Work on the relationship between physical contact and development in the monkey is provided by Harlow and Zimmermann (1959).

Analysis of Some Instinctual Behaviors

THE SUCKING REFLEX AND LICKING BEHAVIOR: The general theory of orality, as advanced by the psychoanalytic school, is best presented in Freud's second essay in *Three essays on the theory of sexuality* (1953). Further studies of sucking behavior in dogs are provided by S. Ross (1951a; 1951b), W. T. James (1959), and W. T. James and T. F. Gilbert (1957), and in human beings by Freeden (1948), Sears and Wise (1950), Yarrow (1954), and McKee and Honzik (1962).

HOMING AND MIGRATION: Griffin (1964) provides an unusual description of research on migration, including his work on bats. (See also Griffin, 1958.) G. V. T. Matthews's (1955) work in also very useful. He devotes considerable attention to the homing behavior of the pigeon.

CONSUMMATORY BEHAVIOR: Our discussion has been concerned directly with hoarding, because it has components of an instinctual response. Actually, consummatory behavior and appetitive behavior are cornerstones of the ethological framework, and the serious student would do well to approach consummatory behavior from this broader base. Thorpe (1962, chap. 2) presents an able analysis of the importance of appetitive behavior to instinct theory.

The age of consummate research on hoarding has passed; however, reviews may be found in Cofer and Appley (1964) and S. Ross, W. I. Smith, and Woessner (1955). The literature is detailed.

RELEASING MECHANISMS: The concepts of IRM and FAP are important in animal behavior, and work on them appears in many journals. Authorities differ in the significance they attach to these mechanisms. Moltz (1965) has presented a lucid review of the theoretical value of the FAP. Thorpe (1962) also comments extensively on these concepts and admirably relates the concepts to data. Tinbergen (1951; 1961) should be consulted for his description of the phenomena. The concept of the FAP derives from Lorenz, who called it *Erbkoordination*. See Thorpe (1962, p. 21) and Moltz (1965) for discussions of this topic.

PHYSIOLOGICAL BASIS OF INSTINCT: Although the relationship between instinct and innate or genetic determining factors has long been postulated, work on this relationship is difficult because of the technical problems associated with stimulation of the nervous system. The sources cited in the text provide the best introduction.

General Sources: In this chapter, I have emphasized the behavior of vertebrates. J. D. Carthy (1958) has published a thorough text on the behavior of invertebrates. Thorpe and Zangwill (1961) have edited a volume which covers both vertebrate and invertebrate behavior, presents a wide range of topics, and provides the reader with, at the least, an appreciation of the number of problems encountered in the study of animal behavior. Schiller (1957) has also edited a book on instinct which contains summaries and contributions basically from the ethological school. The chapters by Lorenz are particularly useful.

Tinbergen (1961) has written on the social behavior of animals, paying particular attention to the role of instinct in the development of social processes. Allee (1939; 1951) has written on social behaviors and cooperation among animals. Both books contain essentially the same text, although the 1951 edition is revised.

Probably the most detailed discussion of the behavior of domestic animals is provided by Hafez (1962). This edited work devotes separate chapters to animals, such as turkeys, rabbits, and swine (which are rarely reviewed), and to the more common domestic animals, such as dogs and cats. There are also chapters on pharmacology, genetics, and early experience. Bliss (1962) has edited a work which provides information on a variety of subjects, ranging from genetics through instinct and early experience to social behavior. Although the contributions are uneven in quality, they provide information on some novel problems.

The last three chapters of this book are concerned with complex forms of behavior and concepts. These are motivation and emotion, psychometrics, and the behavior of persons in groups. These areas have been selected from a number of conceptual areas of contemporary psychology because they receive appreciable experimental and theoretical attention.

Many psychologists have suggested that the study of psychology can proceed profitably without the inclusion of terms such as "motivation" and "emotion," for the terms are very loosely defined. Nevertheless, many investigators have examined behavior that contains emotional or motivational elements and found both valuable and interesting results.

Mental testing has been the most commonly applied use of psychological knowledge. Tests for the measurement of attitudes and abilities are often used in making such everyday decisions as who should go to college or who should be hired for a particular job. The techniques for the construction and interpretation of mental tests have become both complex and sophisticated in the past few years, and we devote a chapter to the topic of how mental tests are devised and used.

Recently, there has been increased experimental attention given to the fact the human beings are part of a society composed of other human beings. Little of our learned behavior occurs in isolation. Generally, the responses we acquire are learned in the company of other persons. Thus, other people become reinforcers and determinors of our behavior. The final chapter of this text is concerned with the special role that other people play in determining our behavior. Hopefully, it will be seen that our studies of the minute structures of the sensory systems and the minutiae of classical conditioning and operant training are relevant and, perhaps, logically prior to an understanding of the processes described in these chapters.

CHAPTER SEVENTEEN

EMOTION AND MOTIVATION

INTRODUCTION

Few persons would deny that *emotion* is an important attribute of many, if not all, psychological processes. Fewer persons, however, would offer a definition of emotion, and probably no one would suggest a definition that would find general, much less universal, acceptance. The fact that a concept is difficult to define, however—whether it be "emotion," "justice," or "freedom"—does not mean that we can ignore it.

The major difficulty with the concept of emotion is that psychology has never been able, if it has ever really tried, to divorce the common terms used to describe emotion (such as love, fear, and hate) from laboratory or theoretical usage, which requires precise terminology. Popular connotations render terms inoperable from an objective point of view. One does not deny that love exists, but the experimenter who designs an experiment to manipulate love is immediately criticized for whatever definition he may select. In learning theory, we have noted that popular terms are replaced with terms such as *pseudoconditioning* or *intermittent schedules.* The use of precisely defined terms, provided that pure jargon is avoided, provides the psychologist with a scientific vocabulary that avoids the traps of popular usage. Unfortunately, the use of precise terms often makes the language of a field needlessly esoteric. Given the difficulty of finding an appropriate meeting ground between popular and precise definitions, many psychologists have called a truce by defining emotional processes in operational terms. Thus, a change in the GSR of human beings or in the eliminative behavior of rodents represents emotional behavior. It is not surprising that experimental work on emotion has tended to use physiological measures, such as GSR, heart rate, and respiration, as dependent variables because of the comparative precision of measurement which is possible.

Most experimenters have ascribed to some form of homeostatic theory in their definition of emotion. Thus, emotion is considered a deviation from the normal state of the organism. *Motivation,* as a concept, has endured many of the problems that have plagued emotion, and this may be one of the reasons that emotion and motivation are sometimes treated as similar. Perhaps a more germane reason for equating the concepts is that many theorists regard emotional states as motivating. In explaining avoidance and escape learning, for example, theorists suggest that the reinforcement created by escape or avoidance is the diminution of fear reactions (a tacit emotion) resulting from the presence of unpleasant stimuli such as electric current. Note that this explanation draws upon both emotional and motivational concepts and incorporates the results into reinforcement theory. Note, too, that the explanation is dedicated to the concept of homeostasis, for escape or avoidance serves to return the organism to some supposedly normal state.

In this chapter, we shall discuss some methods of measuring emotion; some data on emotional processes, such as the use of facial and bodily expressions in human beings and animals to determine emotional states; induced emotion, in which drugs or the instructions provided by the experimenter are intended to provide an emotional state; the relationship between emotion and the central nervous system; and the major theoretical contributions that have attempted to unify the various characteristics of emotion into a single explanatory concept. Then we shall consider motivation by examining three current approaches to the question "What motivates organisms?"

SOME METHODS OF MEASURING EMOTION

There are four main methods of measuring emotion: The first involves some form of physiological recording; the dependent variable in this technique may include measurements of blood pressure, heart rate, muscle tension, or similar physiological responses. The second method involves less direct measurements, such as projective testing. The third is concerned with the effects on emotional re-

sponses produced by ablations or lesions of specific sections of the central nervous system. The fourth involves measurement of posture.

Physiological Measures: We may enumerate the physiological measures of emotion most easily by mentioning some of the apparatuses employed:

Ataximeter: **The ataximeter records body sway. If a subject is asked to stand motionless with his eyes closed, some movement will be recorded. It is well known that the amount of movement can be influenced by the experimenter. For example, the experimenter may tell the subject that he is "moving too much to the left." There are reports (Hull, 1933b) that the subject may be suggestible to the efforts of the experimenter. Although body sway is no longer a commonly used measure of emotion, reports of its use do appear occasionally in the literature.**

Automatograph: **The automatograph is used to record less gross motion than that measured by the ataximeter. Usually the subject places his arm or finger on a plate. Under the plate are microswitches, or strain gauges, which record the amount of movement exerted upon the plate. The observation that tremor occurs in the fingers following emotion-producing events is well known. The automatograph provides a method for measuring such movements.**

Electroencephalograph: **As noted in Chapter 2, the EEG is used for measuring the electric potentials emanating from the cortex and subcortical centers. Potentials picked up with scalp electrodes are amplified and recorded. Specific types of potentials have been identified that correlate with the behavior of the subject (e.g., whether he is asleep or awake). Although the EEG has not received widespread use in the study of emotion, possibly because of the difficulty of providing emotion-provoking situations while a subject is in the apparatus, there is reason to suspect that the EEG might be a useful technique for measuring change in emotion (Lindsley, 1951), although most often the emotional reaction interferes with the EEG readings.**

Phethysmograph and the GSR: **The phethysmograph measures volume changes in appendages,** such as the finger or hand, by measuring the constriction and dilation of blood vessels. Coupled with other devices, the phethysmograph is one of the most commonly used apparatuses for measuring emotion. As is true of many other such measures, however, there is often difficulty in establishing a response, for volume changes occur naturally over short periods of time. These "natural changes" often make assessment of the effect of the independent variable difficult. The galvanometer (PGR or GSR), which measures changes in the electrical resistance of the skin, presents similar difficulties (Woodworth & Schlosberg, 1954, chap. 6).

Pneumograph: The pneumograph measures changes in respiration. Usually, a rubber tube is placed around the chest. Changes in the elongation of the tubing, which reflect respiration, are recorded. The pneumograph provides a measure of the rate and depth of respiration. It is often used with other devices such the phethysmograph.

Sphygmomanometer: This instrument measures blood pressure. Blood pressure may be recorded in either of two ways: *absolute blood pressure,* which is measured at any specific moment, or *continuous blood pressure,* which is the more commonly measured and records the progressive differences between systolic and diastolic pressure. Data from various species are reported in Altman and Dittmer (1964).

Sphygmograph: The sphygmograph measures pulse. It is capable of recording both the rate and amplitude of the pulse beat. It is generally used with the sphygmomanometer.

The fact that members of a species show forms of emotion that are characteristic of the species has led to the development of a variety of emotion-measuring techniques. For example, the distress call that chickens emit when removed from other members of the species is sufficiently distinct from other vocalizations of the chicken to permit investigators to use this as a dependent variable in the study of animal emotionality. Similarly, rodents and some higher organisms commonly defecate and urinate when in the presence of apparently emotion-provoking situations. This behavior has led to the development of the *open field* as a measure of animal emotionality. In the simplest application of this measure, the animal is placed in a large and novel arena, and his activity, defecation, and urination are measured. Open-field defecation adapts with repeated experiences with the open field; it may be increased by the introduction of sudden strong stimuli, such as a bright light or electric current.

Projective Testing: The assessment of emotional states by projective-testing devices, such as the *Rorschach* and the *Thematic Apperception Test* (TAT), provides information on the emotional attitudes that a person has toward environmental events. The concern is not so much in measuring *how much* anger a person may experience but in understanding the *situations that produce* anger. In another sense, the use of projective tests theoretically bridges the gap between assessing an emotion and understanding the motivations that produce the emotional state. Projective tests are most commonly used to indicate the presence of socially unacceptable behavior. Thus, most basic research on projective techniques has been concerned with assessing their reliability and validity and with improving scoring and administration procedures, rather than with using them as dependent variables to measure emotion. One exception to this general statement is the widespread use of the *Taylor Manifest Anxiety Scale* (although it is not a projective test) to correlate "emotionality" with classical conditioning (Chapter 13) (see Duffy, 1962, for a summary of such research). With further refinement of projective techniques, both physiological and projective measures may be fruitfully used to assess the quality and quantity of emotional feelings.

Ablations and Lesions: Another method for the study of emotion emphasizes stimulation, ablation, or lesions of brain centers as the independent variable and uses a variety of tasks as the dependent variable. Escape and avoidance training are often used. It has been known for many years that certain areas of the central nervous system are correlated with emotional reactivity. The *limbic system,* which includes the septal area, amygdaloid complex, hypothalamus, portions of the thalamus, cingulate cortex, and hippocampus, was regarded as the seat of emotions by investigators earlier in this century. More recently investigators have discovered that the administration of a small amount of electric stimulation in the limbic system is rewarding; i.e., animals will learn a new response, such as the bar press, in order to receive the electric stimulation. A second area, identified more recently, is called the *reticular activating system* (RAS). As can be seen from Figure 17–1, the RAS includes parts of the medulla, hypothalamus, and nearby areas. Conceptually the RAS appears to have two primary systems: the formation located in the brainstem and the fibers that project from the thalamus to the cerebral cortex. The RAS contains synapses emanating from the sensory systems. Moreover, because of the relationship among the thalamus, the projected fibers, and the cerebral cortex, the cortex mediates between sensory impulses by returning such impulses through descending parts of the reticular formation. The RAS provides a feedback system which permits the cerebral cortex to become involved in sensory events. Moreover, the system permits the cortex to "anticipate" events. For example, it may be that the anticipation of pain, once such sensory impulses reach the cortex, is returned to the RAS, which serves the function of activating other responses. Since both systems are influenced by drugs and chemicals and show changes which appear to correlate with overt changes in emotionality, experimenters have altered the level of arousal of organisms by altering the physiological state of both the limbic system and the reticular activating system. For example, Bard and Mountcastle (1947) removed the limbic cortex of three cats. Afterward, all three cats displayed a lowered threshold for the rage reaction typical of cats, although the threshold returned to its normal level after a few weeks.

FIGURE 17–1: *Highly schematic diagram of the major connections to and from the reticular activating system (RAS). The RAS ascends in the core of the brainstem. It makes connections with cell bodies in the thalamus and the lateral hypothalamus and sends some fibers through the lateral hypothalamus directly into various structures in the rhinencephalon. As shown by the stippled arrows, some parts of the thalamus in turn diffuse the influence of the RAS over the neocortex, and some cells in the lateral hypothalamus send fibers into rhinencephalic structures for the same purpose. Shown schematically by the arrows are the three major sources of sensory input to the RAS: from all the sensory systems of the body, from the neocortex, and from the rhinencephalon. The fibers of the ventral portion of this system (interconnecting the RAS, the lateral hypothalamus, and the rhinencephalon) are carried in the important medial forebrain bundle. RAS = reticular activating system; Lat. Hy. = lateral hypothalamus; MFB = medial forebrain bundle. (From McCleary & R. Y. Moore, 1965, p. 27.)*

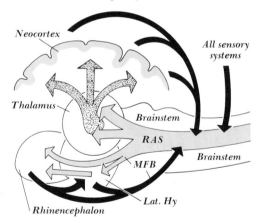

Posture: Since Charles Darwin's (1809–1882) work (1872) on bodily expression in animals and man, the observation has been amplified that certain emotions are reflected by facial expressions or by the stance an organism adopts. For example, the angry dog commonly assumes the position of "rage" in which the ears are alert and back, the whole body is tense, the lips are drawn back, and the teeth exposed. A similar reaction is observed among cats that are frightened. Techniques for the measurement of stature and body position are not well developed; however, such procedures as photographing the body position or facial expressions and comparing these responses with the emotion-provoking situation do suggest that the approach is reliable.

DEVELOPMENT OF ACTIVATION THEORY

A number of investigators are referred to by the general term *activation theorists*. The application of the word *theory* is misleading, for these investigators are united only in the belief that emotion represents extreme arousal rather than a separate psychological or physiological phenomenon. Arousal is thought of as a continuum extending from the amount of arousal evident in deep sleep to that evident in an angry human being. These theorists come closer than any other group to remaining faithful to the Latin origin of *emotion*, namely, *to move out*. In its development, *emotion* came to mean *physical agitation*. Activation theorists perceive emotion as a change in the psychological and physiological activation of the organism. Accordingly, these workers have concentrated on measuring basically physiological responses as dependent variables. Not surprisingly, activation theorists also have been greatly interested in the limbic system and the reticular activating system.

Activation theory, at least tacitly, assumes that emotion is an act of adjustment. That is, when an organism shows a rage reaction, one consequence is that the organism is presumably better able to cope physiologically with external events. The increase in amount of epinephrine secreted, among other endocrinous changes, serves to prepare the organism for more efficient behavior. By 1927 (Bills, 1927) it had been shown that performance on such tasks as verbal memorization or simple mathematics is improved when accompanied by the simultaneous performance of physical acts, such as squeezing a hand dynamometer. Additional research, however, shows that this finding is specific for certain situations. The results of the studies have led to the postulation of the inverted U-shaped relationship shown in Figure 17–2. This function suggests that learning or behavioral efficiency is correlated with an increase in arousal to an optimal level. After the optimal level, a continued increase in arousal or activation results in a decrement in efficiency: we are less efficient when sound asleep or when our emotions are aroused beyond a certain level. A person in a "blind rage" has surpassed the point at which the physiological changes responsible for the rage reaction serve to prepare him better for the stress experience. Rather, he becomes unable to cope effectively with environmental stress. It has been suggested that the inverted U-shaped function also holds for the relationship between simple learning and arousal. We noted in Chapter 13 that animals which are totally unaroused or which are exceptionally aroused do not learn so efficiently as those whose state of arousal is somewhere between these extremes (Hebb, 1955, 1958; Lindsley, 1957; Malmo, 1958; Schlosberg, 1954a, 1954b).

Curiously, although contemporary activation theory has tended to be nontheoretical, in the sense that its adherents rely more upon the generation of data than upon the development of theories, the origins of activation theory appear to lie in the purely theoretical contributions of William James and the successive experimental refinements of his postulation by Walter B. Cannon (1871–1945), Philip Bard, and J. W. Papez (1883–1958), among others.

In his classic textbook of psychology, William James made the following statement regarding emotion (1890, p. 449):

Our natural way of thinking about these coarser emotions is that the mental perception of some fact excites the mental affection called the

emotion, and that this latter state of mind gives rise to the bodily expression. My theory, on the contrary, is that the *bodily changes follow directly the perception of the exciting fact, and that our feeling of the same changes as they occur* IS the emotion. Common-sense says, we lose our fortune, are sorry and weep; we meet a bear, are frightened and run; we are insulted by a rival, are angry and strike. The hypothesis here to be defended says that this order of sequence is incorrect, that the one mental state is not immediately induced by the other, that the bodily manifestations must first be interposed between, and that the more rational statement is that we feel sorry because we cry, angry because we strike, or tremble, because we are sorry, angry, or fearful, as the case may be. Without the bodily states following on the perception, the latter would be purely cognitive in form, pale, colorless, destitute of emotional warmth. We might then see the bear, and judge it best to run, receive the insult and deem it right to strike, but we should not actually *feel* afraid or angry.

A few years before James's book was published the Danish physiologist, Carl Lange (1834–1900), had made a similar suggestion. Thus, the general statement that emotion *results from* physiological change rather than that emotion causes the physiological change is known as the *James-Lange theory*. Note that the theory specifically places emotion as a physiological event. It makes the suggestion, however, that we mistake the forest for the trees in our usual way of viewing emotion. Thus, to James and Lange, the perception produces a physiological change, and it is that physiological change that we interpret as emotion. The James-Lange postulation produced an appreciable amount of research; an unfortunate aspect of the theory, however, is that it is not directly testable.

In the next decade, Titchener, beginning in 1900, revitalized introspection, at least in American psychology. The *introspective* approach to the problems of emotion consisted of asking observers to report their conscious experience of the degree of pleasantness or

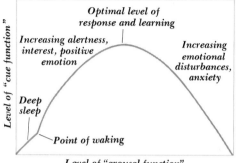

FIGURE 17-2: *Hypothetical inverted U-shaped relationship between behavioral efficiency or level of cue function and level of arousal. (From Hebb, 1955, p. 250.)*

unpleasantness felt in emotion-evoking situations. The introspective approach was not so outstandingly different from activation theory as might be supposed. If we consider that our conscious reports of our feelings reflect our sensations of changes in blood pressure, heart rate, and similar physiological responses, introspective techniques merely substitute a verbal report for physiological recordings. The attack on introspection by J. B. Watson, the pioneer behaviorist, placed particular emphasis on discrediting introspection as a psychological technique. Thus, the revealing findings of early introspective studies of emotion are still often submerged beneath the rubble of the Watsonian rebellion. Not surprisingly, the correlations between the physiological change and the conscious report of those changes by introspective techniques were never perfect. Worse, reports tended to vary not only from subject to subject but from laboratory to laboratory. On the other hand, it is evident that the relationship between physiological responses as measured by contemporary apparatuses and emotion is less than satisfactory for some of the same reasons.

Nafe (1924) attempted to overcome this problem by presenting subjects with a number of stimuli in a variety of sensory systems; he selected stimuli that would produce both pleasant and unpleasant experiences. He noted that observers came to describe feelings of pleasantness and unpleasantness in terms of pressure. Stimuli regarded as pleasant were also regarded as having the characteristic of bright pressure, and stimuli described as unpleasant were commonly described as having a dull pressure. Few contemporary psychologists are accustomed to discussing psychological phenomena in terms of affect, pleasantness, or feeling. Nevertheless, if properly defined, such processes are capable of investigation and may, indeed, provide useful starting points for further research.

The work of Walter B. Cannon, although it did not necessarily destroy the James-Lange theory, went far beyond James's speculation to show that the relationship between emotion and bodily state was appreciably more complex than James had suggested. For example, Cannon (1927; 1931) was able to show that removal of the sympathetic nervous system in cats did not destroy emotional behavior. The cats still displayed the common signs of anger and fear. Similarly, Sherrington (1906; reprinted 1961), some years earlier, had transected the visceral nerves of dogs and found that the dogs continued to show rage reactions. Supporters of the James-Lange approach commented, reasonably enough, that these experiments did not indicate whether or not these animals continued to *experience* emotion. This objection highlights one of the reasons why the James-Lange theory appears to be indestructible. There is no obvious method for determining whether or not animals, or human beings for that matter, are able to "feel." Nevertheless, Cannon and his coworkers clearly showed that emotional *behavior* could continue after the removal of the supposedly important physiological components of the emotion.

One of the most reasonable objections to the James-Lange approach is that it seems difficult for the sensory system to operate sufficiently rapidly to permit the immediate sensation of physiological change which would be required

by the theory. The rate of nervous conduction to the central nervous system, especially from the viscera and smooth muscles, is slow. Indeed, data suggest that emotional reactions appear far more promptly than would be feasible if the James-Lange position were accurate. A further difficulty with the James-Lange approach comes from data which show that subjects who were injected with epinephrine (and who should have shown heightened emotionality from increased autonomic activity) reported no arousal of emotion, although the usual physiological changes which accompany an increased discharge of epinephrine did occur (Marañon, 1924). Of course, the reliance upon the subjective report of subjects as to whether or not they felt emotion is open to criticism. More unfortunately, however, there appears to be no more adequate method of assessing emotionality following the injection of drugs and chemicals which excite the sympathetic nervous system. Although the criticisms by Cannon and others have failed to fell the James-Lange approach, it is noteworthy that, happily, these critics were compelled to produce most useful data to support their criticisms.

Cannon preferred the assumption that emotion is primarily thalamic. He suggested a relationship between the thalamus and the cortex in which, during an unemotional state, the cortex inhibits thalamic functioning. When an emotional situation occurs, the inhibition ceases; thus, the thalamus is the central structure in producing emotion. Cannon based his formulation on experimental findings. He had been able to show that decorticated animals showed rage reactions; however, with removal of the thalamus they did not. Moreover, if an animal received a lesion on only one side of the thalamus, a change in sensations occurred from the side of the body corresponding to the side of the thalamic destruction. Thus the role of the thalamus appeared to be rather specific. These data, of course, are open to the previously stated objection that the absence of a reaction does not prove the absence of feeling. That is, it is possible to imagine a decorticated animal whose thalamus has been removed who does not *respond* with the rage reaction but who in some way feels the emotion which he is unable to demonstrate behaviorally. In recent years, systems within the central nervous system have been found which appear to be important in emotional behavior and in activation theory.

We have noted that lesions and ablations of the limbic system and the RAS affect emotional states. Apparently, the limbic system has two distinct capacities: a lesion in the amygdala or cingulate cortex often renders an animal extremely tame, and a lesion on the septum often produces highly excitable animals. Klüver and Bucy (1939) first noted that monkeys became tame following lesions in the area of the temporal lobe. With refinements in technique, it appears that the exact area responsible for the docility is the amygdala. This finding has been reported for a number of primates and wilder animals. Thus, the amygdala appears to be responsible for, or at least a partner in, changes in emotional reactivity. In the rat, a lesion of the septum will often produce an animal who is hyperirritable. That is, following the brain lesion, the rat attacks other animals, the hands of his feeder, and the experimenters. Curiously, the lowered threshold for the rage response often dissipates after several weeks.

The hypothalamus appears to be concerned with both the rage and the placid reactions. For example, a cat which has been amygdalectomized may become irritable, rather than placid, if a lesion is applied to specific areas of the hypothalamus. Apparently, within the limbic system, the amygdala, the septum, and the hypothalamus are in some way behaviorally connected (they are clearly anatomically related) in such a manner that the placidity or excitability of an organism may be altered by the destruction of tissue in these areas.

A number of studies have dealt with the effects that lesions in various areas of the limbic system have on escape and avoidance learning. If we assume that both escape and avoidance learning are likely to generate fear reactions, then such studies are concerned with the effects of emotion and with the central nervous system. Moreover, such studies apply basic information on changes in learning patterns which occur as a result of the destruction of various anatomical pathways. A common experimental design involves the conditioned emotional response. Typically, in this design, the investigator presents a tone which is always followed by an unavoidable shock. The tone (CS) and the shock (US) are presented in some temporal arrangement so that the organism comes to respond to the tone as a signal, or cue, for the shock. Usually, the tone is then abruptly introduced into some other situation, such as the animal's eating situation. Under these conditions, the animal ordinarily ceases to eat. Thus, the tone comes to suppress the organism's behavior in some tasks quite distinct from the original conditioning situation. Consider an animal who has received the conditioning experience. He is now trained to bar-press for food. At a specified time while he is bar-pressing, the tone appears. The decline in bar-pressing rate attributable to the onset of tone is the measure of behavioral *suppression*. The technique is the one used by Mowrer and Aiken (1954) in the "hope and fear" discussed in Chapter 14.

Experimenters sometimes perform a brain lesion in a specified area before the suppression test. This design, then, investigates the retention of the conditioned emotional response. In other designs, the lesion may be applied before the conditioning session. In these, the effect of the specified area of the central nervous system on redevelopment of emotional response is being investigated.

In 1937, J. W. Papez published a paper which suggested that the thalamus, hypothalamus, and parts of the rhinencephalon were involved in emotional behavior. We now recognize this general area as the limbic system; however, in the late 1930s the importance of the "subcortical old brain" was only beginning to be recognized. Two years after Papez's paper, Klüver and Bucy (1939) removed the tips of the temporal lobes of monkeys and certain areas of the limbic system. These ablations produced a syndrome which included refusal to eat, apparent inability to recognize common objects visually, and hypersexuality. The finding that eating behavior was altered by these surgical procedures represented one of the earlier bits of information which indicated that the locus of appetitive behavior was in the limbic system. The more exact locus of this area now appears to be the hypothalamus.

As opposed to lesions and ablations, which destroy tissue, electrodes implanted in the limbic system may be used to provide small amounts of electric stimulation. A dramatic finding of experimenters using this technique is that electric stimulation of the limbic system may influence the overt bodily tension of an organism. For example, with appropriate stimulation, the organism produces the typical "attention" response in which the head is raised, the pupils are dilated, and the ears appear to be receptive to the slightest sound. In short, the animal reproduces all the behaviors we commonly associate with a dog or a cat at attention. When the electric stimulation is terminated, the organism's behavior immediately returns to a normal state. This finding provides further evidence that the limbic system, in addition to its concern with emotional processes, also controls the attentive ability of organisms. Needless to say, many other parts of the central nervous system, such as the cortex, play a role in both emotion and attention. Nevertheless, the fact that attention may be turned on and off like a light switch indicates the presence of some basic patterning in the limbic system for emotional and attentive responses. It is quite likely, however, that the appearance of these responses is dependent upon a complex network of anatomical pathways.

The RAS is divided into two components, the *descending* reticular system and the *ascending* reticular system (ARS). The former system appears to be primarily charged with the responsibility of inhibiting or suppressing output in the lower brainstem, e.g., in the medulla. The word *reticular* describes the ap-

pearance of the network of nerve fibers of which the system is composed. Under the microscope the stained fibers show considerable overlap, creating a system usually not unlike spider webs. The ARS makes contact with the neocortex. It receives nerve impulses from all sensory systems by means of afferent pathways. It also receives afferent pathways from the neocortex and the limbic system. Thus, the ARS is related to activation, for it is responsible for sending discharges to the higher brain centers. Two pathways are of interest: one pathway enters the thalamus, and the other enters the hypothalamus through the *medial forebrain bundle* (Chapter 2). In some manner, these pathways reach the neocortex. The great diffusion of fibers, as well as the complex network which permits anatomical pathways between many structures of the older brain (limbic system), the brainstem, and the cortex, enables the ARS to control, or at least to be concerned with, a number of behavioral patterns. Since the ARS is directly concerned with the level of activation or arousal of an organism, it is clear that the system is intimately concerned with behaviors commonly regarded as emotional.

The hypothalamus contains two distinct areas which affect behavior: the *medial* hypothalamic area and the *lateral* hypothalamic area. The medial area lies between fibers of the medial forebrain bundle, which originate in the rhinencephalon. The medial forebrain bundle has both the ascending and descending fibers. It is related to the connection between the hypothalamus and the reticular system. In addition, the medial area has anatomical connections with other parts of the limbic system. Therefore, the medial hypothalamic area serves as an important relay station in the reticular formation.

As we have noted, these areas are also involved in feeding behavior (Chapter 10). Collateral evidence that the reticular formation is important to the level of activation or arousal of the central nervous system comes from research that measured EEG output (Chapter 13) as a function of stimulation. EEG recordings show that sudden or intense stimulation produces characteristic changes in the EEG recording. Thus it is clear that some form of activation is occurring in the central nervous system in response to stimulation. When, for example, the sleeping cat is presented with a sudden noise, the typical high-voltage slow waves characteristic of sleep disappear, and small low-voltage waves of higher frequency appear. The latter pattern is most characteristic of an awake animal. Thus the EEG represents the change in level of arousal of an organism. Magoun (1963) showed that if one stimulates the reticular system of a sleeping cat, a characteristic EEG pattern indicating arousal appears. The same recordings are derived when the cat is actually stimulated by an external stimulus such as a loud noise. These data suggest a strong positive correlation between external events and the internal responses of the central nervous system.

Emotion and the Autonomic Nervous System: Some theorists have suggested that the degree of pleasantness and unpleasantness of emotional states is correlated with stimulation of the parasympathetic and sympathetic nervous systems. Activities which involve the parasympathetic system include salivation, secretion of gastric juices, thermoregulation, and certain muscular responses involved in sexual orgasm. Thus, it has been suggested that parasympathetic activity is correlated with the sensation of emotional pleasantness. Certain other parasympathetic activities, however, such as crying, are not generally regarded as pleasant. Accordingly, at the present time, only a rough correlation is known to exist between emotional state and either of the two nervous systems. Attempts to locate specified physiological changes that correlate with specific emotions (such as a syndrome of heightened blood pressure and increased heart rate for the emotion of fear but a decrease in blood pressure for love) have not been successful.

Some successful experimental attempts to distinguish the physiological basis of one emotion from another have been reported. For example, Ax (1953) used the two drugs epinephrine and norepinephrine. Both compositions are secreted by the adrenal gland, and both increase blood pressure, but epinephrine increases blood pressure by increasing the heart rate, and norepinephrine does so by constricting the blood vessels. The experimenter arranged situations calculated to bring about either fear or anger in college students. In one case, the students were led to believe that they had been strapped into an apparatus which was likely to cause physical pain. In other cases, another group of students was led to feel aggression toward an incompetent experimenter. The data suggest that the conditions created by the secretion of norepinephrine occurred in subjects from whom there had been an attempt to elicit anger, although the increased blood pressure in subjects in whom there had been an attempt to elicit fear were most like the symptoms produced by epinephrine.

Funkenstein (1955) has used the drug Mecholyl, which stimulates the parasympathetic system. The reaction of this drug to norepinephrine, however, is different from its reaction to epinephrine. When blood pressure has been increased by the secretion of norepinephrine, Mecholyl will create a *transient* decrease in blood pressure. When blood pressure has been increased by epinephrine, Mecholyl decreases the blood pressure and maintains the decreased rate for about twenty-five minutes. Funkenstein studied psychotic patients and noted that they could be differentiated into seven groups on the basis of their blood-pressure reactions to injections. That is, the groups were discovered to react differently to stressful situations, such as receiving an injection. Moreover, psychotic patients with high blood pressure reacted to an injection of Mecholyl in distinct ways. In one group, Mecholyl caused the transient drop; in the second group, the injection caused the depression of blood pressure for half an hour. Moreover, of the 42 patients who reacted to an injection of Mecholyl by a sharp decrease in blood pressure, 39 were responsive to electric-shock therapy; only

3 of the 21 subjects in the second group showed improvement with this form of therapy. Thus, Funkenstein suggested that the behavioral distinctions between the two groups of subjects might have been caused by specific emotional reactions.

Tests were also conducted on a group of medical students awaiting news of disposition of their application for internships. Mecholyl was administered to the students who showed elevated blood pressure during this highly emotion-provoking period. Those who tended to become angry at themselves over their emotion-provoking situation showed the characteristic transient reduction of blood pressure following Mecholyl response; those who were merely anxious showed a sharp decrease. Interestingly, the emotional characteristics of these groups disappeared when this period was over. After several weeks, when the internships had been announced and blood pressure had returned to a lower level, all students reacted identically to an injection of Mecholyl. Thus, the different responses in blood pressure could be traced directly to the emotional status of the subject at the time when the Mecholyl was applied. Specifically, from these kinds of studies it appears that the emotion of anger accompanies increased secretion of norepinephrine by the adrenals and fear accompanies an increased secretion of epinephrine. In a wider application of the findings it may be possible to identify emotions by characteristic physiological responses.

Emotion and Psychosomatic States: Whether emotion is the cause of physiological change or whether physiological change is the cause of emotion is, at least in our present state of knowledge, a chicken-or-egg problem. Nevertheless, it is clear that the relationship between emotion and physiological state is a two-way street. Certain physiological disturbances, such as the common ulcer, have been shown to be encouraged, if not directly caused, by the emotional state of the individual. Physiological disturbances that are created by the emotions are known as *psychosomatic* difficulties. The term *psychosomatic* is a combination of *psyche* (mind) and *soma* (body). As such, the term designates the intimate relationship between the mind and the body.

The term *ulcer* usually refers to irritation of the stomach and the intestinal lining. Most often, the source of the irritation is the acidity and the digestive enzyme working against the stomach lining. The psychoanalytic school (Alexander, 1950) has pointed out a suspected relationship between the type of gastrointestinal ulcer and the personality of the patient. There have been a number of attempts to produce ulcers in experimental animals by manipulating the environment. The fact that few of these attempts have been able to produce ulceration consistently indicates that the precise environmental conditions that lead to the creation of ulcers are probably highly specific to individual organisms.

Sawrey and Weisz (1956) maintained rats for thirty days in a specially designed apparatus which contained electric grillwork that the animal had to cross to obtain food or water. Experimental animals received shock; control animals did not. Both groups were deprived of food and water for forty-seven hours. It would be expected that the experimental group would experience "conflict" over their drive for food and water and their drive to avoid the painful electric stimulation. It is reported that up to 76 percent of the experimental animals developed gastrointestinal ulcers; none of the animals in the control group developed ulcers.

Porter, Brady, D. Conrad, J. W. Mason, Galambos, and Rioch (1958) have reported obtaining ulceration in monkeys required to bar-press at least once in every twenty-second period in order to avoid shock. The experimental conditions were carried out for six hours, followed by six hours of rest. Conditions for the control monkeys were the same, except that they could not manipulate the bar press. That is, if an experimental monkey failed to bar-press, both he and his control-group colleague received current. The control monkey did not have the choice of bar pressing to avoid the shock; he was, in short, a passive observer, although certainly not necessarily a passive recipient of the shock. Both experimental animals developed gastrointestinal lesions; the control animals did not. Brady, Porter, D. G. Conrad, and J. W. Mason (1958) extended the experimental situation for eighteen consecutive hours rather than the six-on and six-off procedure used in the earlier study. In this investigation, the experimental animals did not develop ulcers. The experimenters have suggested that the development of ulcers depends upon the schedule of stress. Unfortunately, the production of ulcers in monkeys is not well documented in the literature. Other experimenters have been unable to find ulceration following these or similar procedures. It is quite likely that ulcers are produced by emotional causes, but the precise conditions that lead to ulceration are not yet understood.

Stress and Emotion: The activationist approach to stress is represented by the work of Hans Selye and his collaborators. Animals subjected to environmental stress, such as intense temperature changes, show a characteristic bodily reaction. Although the reaction is complicated, it involves a greatly increased secretion of epinephrine as well as increased secretions of the several adrenal cortical hormones. These reactions are, of course, generally regarded as having a role in the production of emotion. Although Selye's work on stress has been devoted to biological stress, it is possible that some useful analogies may be found between reactions to stress and reactions to emotion-provoking situations. Certainly, most states that we would commonly call emotional also have the function of preparing the body to respond to the stress, if by stress we mean any stimulus that activates the autonomic nervous system beyonds its usual level of responsiveness.

Selye has suggested (1950) that we may distinguish three basic stages in the physiological reaction to stress. These stages constitute what Selye calls the *general-adaptation syndrome*

(GAS), or the overall reaction of the organism to stressful experiences. The first distinct stage of the syndrome is called the *alarm reaction* (AR). The AR consists of the basic, heightened responsiveness of the autonomic nervous system. Portions of this responsiveness are directed toward the biological change—change in size of capillaries and lowering of blood pressure, for example. Other portions are less specific. They may be compared to the general and nonspecific reactions that occur during "shock." If the stressful situation is minor, such as a cut on the finger or brief periods under cold temperatures, the reaction dissipates, and the organism does not go beyond the AR stage. Under more severe or continued stress, the reactions common to the AR stage are, to some extent, reversed. Blood pressure and temperature increase. Moreover, the adrenal cortex is enlarged. This stage is called *resistance to stress*. An important aspect of both stages is the release of the *adrenocorticotropic hormones* (ACTH) from the pituitary which, in turn, stimulate the production of hormones from the adrenal cortex. This series of physiological changes is basic to emotional behavior, for the results of these discharges, such as blood-pressure change, are commonly taken as measures of emotion. The final stage of the GAS is *exhaustion*. The organism's power to adapt to the stress is exhausted, with the result that permanent injury (as with an ulcer) or death is incurred.

The analogy between the body's reaction to physiological stress and its reaction to emotion-provoking situations may, of course, lead to unwarranted conclusions. For example, the fact that emotions are commonly thought to have different contents—as in the different feeling states of anger and love—remains, even though it is likely that stress reactions and emotional states have some physiological similarities.

Biochemical and Drug-produced Changes in Emotion: Many drugs and chemicals affect the emotional states of organisms by altering the level of activity. Tranquilizers serve to slow down the autonomic nervous system, whereas other drugs may serve to increase autonomic functioning. Thus we classify drugs as *stimulants* or *depressants,* depending upon their effect on the nervous system. Stimulants include caffeine, amphetamine, and LSD compounds. These drugs produce an increased level of arousal as measured by the EEG (Himwich, 1955).

For theoretical as well as for practical reasons, it is important to know how these drugs affect behavior, that is, what chemical reactions occur and where they occur within the central nervous system. Apparently, tranquilizers mainly affect the "old brain"—the hypothalamus and some components of the reticular system. It may be recalled that the hypothalamus is an important determiner of such reactions as temperature and blood pressure. Two commonly used drugs, reserpine and chlorpromazine, have been investigated intensively. The first is most commonly used to lower blood pressure and reduce hypertension. The second is widely reported to be useful in quieting psychotic behavior. Both are depressants (F. M. Berger, 1960), and both affect the EEG by producing a pattern similar to that found in the normal sleeping state. Although there are apparent differences in the effects produced by the two drugs, both are clearly capable of influencing emotional states.

Activity depends upon the relationship between the nervous systems and endocrinous changes, such as changes in adrenal secretion rate. Perhaps the two most important structures concerned with activity are the adrenals and the pituitary. The pituitary gland is commonly divided into the *anterior* and the *posterior* pituitary. The connections between the parts are subtle and complex. The anterior pituitary is apparently controlled by the hypothalamus; however, it affects the adrenal cortex and other structures (e.g., the gonads, Chapter 16) by the production of hormones—such as the adrenotropic and gonadotropic hormones—which influence emotional behavior. Epinephrine, which is secreted from the adrenal medulla, is extremely important in determining the stage of activation. Of significance is the fact that the amount of epinephrine found in the blood varies as a function of the emotional state of the individual. The adrenal cortex also secretes substances which affect homeostasis. It may be recalled from the work of Selye that the size of the adrenals may be altered by stressful situations.

There is a continuing search among investigators for biochemical measures of emotion. Hippuric acid, which is secreted by the kidneys, has been used as a measure (Basowitz, Persky, Korchin, & Grinker, 1955), as has the eosinophil level of the blood. If emotion is to be understood in terms of the complex biochemical and neurological relationships that correspond with our reports of internal, emotional feelings, it is clear that we are far from understanding even the simplest of relationships between emotional events and their effects upon the nervous system.

AN INTRODUCTION TO MOTIVATION

Research on motivation is hampered by the difficulty of finding a suitable definition of the concept and of acquiring appropriate techniques for measurement. Another important difficulty is that of determining whether emotion and motivation are really separate concepts. The literature of psychology abounds with treatises arguing the merits of separation and other treatises arguing that the concepts should be treated as similar, or even identical, phenomena. (See, for an overview, Duffy, 1934, 1948, 1957, 1962; Leeper, 1948; Leeper & Madison, 1959; Webb, 1948; P. T. Young, 1943, 1949, 1961; Cofer & Appley, 1964).

There is no question that one may experimentally alter performance by altering certain motivational aspects of a situation. A rat that is well trained to the bar-press response is not likely to perform for food if it is not hungry. The presence or absence of hunger is assuredly a motivational variable. On another level, there is ample evidence that two students, supposedly of equal ability, may differ widely in grade-getting behavior, ostensibly because of motivational variables. Like the concept of learning, motivation is a variable which we *infer* from behavior. The fact that it has less objective reality than blood pressure or temperature, however, should not deter us from investigating its properties.

In a very real sense, motivation may be said to be a part of all behavior. Conditioning, operant training, psychophysical measures, instinctual responses—all these categories of behavior may be influenced by motivational aspects of the situation. The difficulty is not that we do not know that the inferred variable "motivation" exists; the difficulty is that we do not know how to measure it. This deficiency is not created by a lack of attempts.

Motivation and Learning Theory: Learning theorists, such as Thorndike, tended to work with simple motivating drives, such as thirst, hunger, and avoidance of pain. Perhaps these drives are preferred by investigators because they are relatively easy to measure and to control, especially in work with animals. The preference has led, understandably, to the complaint that learning theory has been preoccupied with motivational variables that are rarely of concern to human beings. On the other hand, as learning theorists have commented, the complex human drives—the seeking of money or of women with blond hair—may perhaps best be understood, supremely, by thoroughly understanding the laws that govern more simple and hence more easily observed motivational states. There has been a persistent tendency for learning theories to accent homeostatic mechanisms as the basic motivational system of organisms. Thus, motivation is, at least implicitly, viewed as hedonistic: an organism performs appropriately if the outcome is satisfying, and he does not perform if the outcome is unpleasant. This statement, of course, is only a poor restatement of Thorndike's law of effect. It may be noted, however, that the law provides a clear interpretation of motivation as a hedonistic process. As we know from our discussion of learning

and conditioning, a hedonistic, law-of-effect interpretation of motivation is a useful working hypothesis, although it has obvious deficiencies in its inability to account for a number of behaviors which apparently fail to follow the hedonistic model.

We shall review, briefly, the general approach to motivation taken by three learning theorists. Among the influential learning theorists who attempted to measure motivational variables is Clark Hull (1884–1952). Hull's work (1943; 1951; 1952) furnishes us with an excellent example of an approach to, and some of the problems associated with, the quantifications of motivation. Hull attempted to show that performance could be predicted by identifying the relevant variables, such as drive level. These variables, which were given symbolic identifications, were then varied systematically in order to find the appropriate equations to predict performance. In its simplest form, drive (D) represents the hours of deprivation which an organism has undergone. D interacts with *habit strength* (sHr), which is a measure of the previous number of responses the organism has made, to produce the probability of the organism's making the response again. This probability is represented as the *excitatory potential* (sEr). Thus,

$$sEr = sHr \times D$$

Note that if either D or sHr is zero (i.e., if the animal is not hungry or has never performed the response), then sEr is zero, and the response will not occur. Thus the relationship between drive and habit strength is multiplicative: if either is zero, no response occurs. In this simplified version, the assumption is made that there is a perfect correlation between, say, hours of deprivation and hunger. This statement is not true empirically, however: the drive gradient is not linear. Thus D itself must be manipulated with other variables in order to determine its function. As these parameters were investigated, Hull later (1951, 1952) added other variables which affect drive, such as the incentive power of the reinforcer K (a hungry rat will respond differently to different types of reward) and the intensity of the stimulus (V) which evokes the response. Indeed, as it became necessary to add additional measures of motivation in order to predict accurately, other theorists questioned the usefulness of the multiplicative attribute of the formula and suggested that the parameters may be additive.

To show another approach, we shall consider the theoretical position of Edward C. Tolman (1886–1959; 1932, 1948, 1949, 1951, 1952, 1959), whose contributions to learning theory overlap those of Hull historically. Tolman's initial theory was published in 1932, but over the years it has undergone some revision. An essential difference between Hull's and Tolman's approaches to learning and motivation is that the Hullian system is patterned after classical mechanics—each environmental variable acts on the organism, and the organism responds in a predictable manner. Tolman's system, on the other hand, emphasized the biological purposiveness of behavior—organisms anticipate events and have cognitions regarding them. Thus, Tolman's work, although clearly behavioristically oriented in research and experimental design, had elements of the gestalt position. These two theorists attempted to explain and predict the same kinds of behavior, and both, in quite different ways, had to face the problem of motivation.

Perhaps the primary difference between Hull's and Tolman's outlooks was that Hull believed that drive developed from a lack of homeostasis and resulted in a more or less general level of arousal or motivation of the organism. That is, the hungry organism becomes restless, and his activity and exploratory behaviors increase. This relationship between activity and hunger is demonstrably true. Hull stopped short, however, of saying that the hungry rat *searched for food*. Tolman, on the other hand, emphasized the end result of the motivational state. To Tolman the hungry animal *expects* food. When food is found, the expectation is *confirmed*. This confirmation of expectations is the fundamental property of motivation. Tolman, then, pro-

vides the organism with cognitions; loosely put, organisms want, expect, confirm expectations, and "think ahead." For this reason, Tolman has been referred to as an *expectancy* theorist. The organism does not respond to a motivation or a drive randomly but expects confirmation and actively searches to confirm the expectations. Tolman (1932; 1951) listed primary needs (hunger, thirst, sex, exploration, curiosity, etc.), secondary needs (dominance, dependence), and tertiary needs, which are learned (such as the gain of money).

For comparison, consider the position taken by Edwin R. Guthrie (1885–1959; 1935, 1952). Guthrie built a theory of learning on the premise that all learning occurred on the first trial (that is, the first presentation of stimuli and the accompanying response) and that the function of repeated practice (which common experience tells us is necessary for correct performance) is to eliminate incorrect or inappropriate responses, rather than to strengthen the appropriate response. Since the role of reinforcement is to reduce the possibility of other responses being learned, motivation, in the traditional sense, is relatively unimportant to Guthrie's formulations. When a hungry rat runs down a maze containing food at the goal, one can assume that he is running *to* the food or that he is running *away* from painful hunger. Motivation, of whatever kind, serves to keep the organism active and aware of external stimuli. No doubt much of the popularity of Guthrie's position comes from the fact that the tricky problems of motivation are neatly avoided, or, as some might say, sidestepped. Indeed, the major contributors to our understanding of the learning process—B. F. Skinner and his colleagues, in their work on operant training (Chapter 13)—have given little attention to motivational variables. Certainly, Skinnerians *use* motivation: animals are deprived of food or water and rewarded with these substances for appropriate performance; but these forms of motivation are used to study the effects of reinforcement, schedules of reinforcement, and the like. They are not included because of an interest in motivation.

Neal E. Miller (1959), who has applied elements of Hullian theory to a range of experiments concerned with motivation and reinforcement, treats drive as "a strong stimulus which impels action" (N. E. Miller & Dollard, 1941, p. 18). Thus, intensity of motivation is directly correlated with intensity of the stimulus. The stimulus, of course, may be some external event, or it may be internal, physiological events, such as hunger pangs. It may be an innate motivational state, in the sense that hunger is an innate motivation of all organisms, or it may be acquired through learning. Drive reduction, in the form of a reduction in the intensity of the motivating stimulus, is probably necessary for learning; however, note that this concept of motivation is not necessarily homeostatic in outlook. How do we know whether a stimulus is sufficiently strong (i.e., sufficiently motivating) to "impel action"? If a new response can be learned which reduces or eliminates the stimulus, then the stimulus is motivating. For example, when the rat in the Miller-Mowrer box learns to press a bar or make some other new response in order to open the door between the shock and nonshock compartments, the stimulus has been sufficiently strong to be motivating.

The literature on learning in the 1930 to 1955 period is replete with studies investigating the merit of one approach over the other. If nothing more, all these approaches led to the collection of pages of data. In retrospect, some of the arguments which engaged many of the better theoretical and experimental minds seem relatively banal. The beginning student, however, is apt to see different approaches to the problem of motivation as black or white, when in reality the issues are so complex that an attempt at simplification (which we have offered above) does great disservice to the thoughtful work of many investigators. The argument is not whether animals possess cognitions or whether they have expectancies but whether any system can identify the crucial characteristic of learning and motivation which lead to the accurate prediction of behavior.

Motivation and Reinforcement: The assumptions of the learning theories we have sampled vary regarding the role of motivation, the role of reinforcement, and the way in which the two variables combine. As we noted in our discussion of the basic problems of learning (Chapter 12), we do not know whether reinforcement is necessary for learning or not. It now appears, however, that reinforcement—at least in the traditional sense of reinforcements which serve to restore the organism to its organic homeostasis—is not necessary for all kinds of learning. Examples of this appear in the literature from time to time, as, for example, when it was shown that rats would learn to run a T maze for saccharin, even though saccharin is nonnutritive (Sheffield & Roby, 1950; Sheffield, Roby & Campbell, 1954).

A more direct challenge to the homeostatic theory of motivation has come from work on *intracranial stimulation* (ICS). Olds and Milner (1954) and Olds (1955) were able to show that rats with electrodes (which could carry small amounts of electric current) chronically implanted in the septal area of the brain would learn the bar-press response when the response was followed by the brief application of electric current to the brain. Moreover, when the stimulation was eliminated, bar pressing ceased. Similar effects are found in other mammals, including cats, monkeys, and dolphins. Superficially, this phenomenon is similar to bar-pressing for food or other appetitive rewards. The fact that the rats were not deprived of any substance led to speculation that this was an instance of learning without apparent motivation in the homeostatic sense of the word. Several further findings from research on intracranial stimulation deserve attention:

1. The brain is differentially sensitive to placements: electrode placement in some areas produces greater response rates than in other areas.
2. Some areas appear to be negatively reinforcing; that is, the animal will learn a response in order to avoid stimulation.
3. Behavior under intracranial stimulation dif-

fers from behavior for positive reinforcement in several respects.

At least when the bar-press response is used, the response is learned quite rapidly. With electrodes properly implanted, an animal can be trained to bar-press far more quickly for the electric stimulation than for food. Similarly, extinction is very rapid; when the current is stopped, the animal ceases to respond after a few unreinforced responses. This is not true when food is used as the reinforcer.

On the other hand, bar pressing for food or water and bar pressing for electric stimulation have many factors in common. Although there is evidence that schedules of reinforcement, such as a VR schedule, produce similar cumulative records, particularly at lower ratios, it is apparent that such factors as duration and intensity of the electric stimulation are not directly comparable to amount of food or time permitted to eat. Thus, some of the apparent differences between the two forms of reinforcement may be cleared up when more is known about the scaled values of food and intracranial stimulation. For example, the rapid extinction observed under ICS training may be a cue to the fact that although all animals have had considerable experience with eating, this providing for the development of secondary reinforcing qualities, a normal animal has had no experience with ICS. This lack of experience thus prohibits the possibility of secondary reinforcement enhancing the length of the extinction process. Put another way, extinction under ICS may represent true extinction, unblemished by the previous behavioral history of the organism.

A further apparent difference is the high rates of responding which occur under ICS. Depending upon location of the placement, rats will make up to 5,000 responses in an hour (Olds, 1958). Note, however, that in bar pressing for ICS the animal does not take time out to eat a pellet, as he does under food-reinforcement conditions. Implants in certain areas, such as the hypothalamus, make the animal virtually insatiable; except when the animal is physically exhausted, he continues to bar-press. Other areas, such as the amygdala, do not produce insatiability. It is established that ICS bar-pressing rates can be influenced by food or water deprivation (Brady, Boren, D. Conrad, & Sidman, 1957). This has led to the reasonable speculation that the "pleasure center"—as Olds called the area which produces ICS responding—is somehow related to eating and drinking centers (Chapter 10).

Many experimenters have noted that animals bar-pressing for ICS stimulation show a tendency to nibble and chew at the bar. Hoebel and Teitelbaum (1962) implanted electrodes in the lateral hypothalamus of rats. The lateral hypothalamus is an area known to be concerned with eating behavior and also known to obtain high response rates from ICS. The rate of response was greatly decreased (1) by overfeeding the animal or (2) by providing stimulation in the ventromedial nucleus of the hypothalamus—called the *satiation center,* because ablation of the area creates hyperphagia.

Brain stimulation may be aversive as well as pleasurable (J. M. Delgado, Roberts, & N. E. Miller, 1954). If the implant is made in an aversive area, stimulation may be used in the same general manner that electric shock is used in escape and avoidance learning. For example, Roberts (1958a; 1958b) found that cats would learn a standard T maze if stimulation was turned off when the animal reached the goal box. Thus, the termination of the shock acted as a "positive reinforcer," much as if food had been in the goal box. Other areas appear to have both aversive and appetitive components. Bower and N. E. Miller (1958) found areas in the rat brain in which the electric stimulation was reinforcing at first but eventually became aversive.

Apparently, drive pathways exist in the central nervous system which can be artificially stimulated by the procedures of electrode placement. It is noteworthy that recent decades have seen the discovery of eating and satiation centers in the hypothalamus, areas (such as the reticular activating system) concerned with activity and sleep, and the general areas we have been discussing which appear to serve as either "pleasure centers" or "avoidance centers."

Learned Drives: The Example of Acquired Fear: It is clear that physiologically unlearned drives, such as hunger and thirst, exist. Few activities, however, particularly among man and higher animals, can be related directly to motivation for food or water. If motivation, drive, and reinforcement are necessary for learning to occur, as some theorists suppose, we may explain the development of more complex behavior in at least two ways: First, initial learning may indeed use basic, physiological drives, such as hunger, for motivation. The infant does indeed seek to be fed, and it is possible that through secondary reinforcement all other learning emanates from original motivation. Second, it is possible that many drives and motivations are learned. The learned drives are called *secondary drives*, in

analogy to the term *secondary reinforcement*. Perhaps the most commonly investigated secondary drive involves *anxiety*. The definition of what constitutes anxiety differs appreciably from theorist to theorist, and we shall discuss some of these concepts later in this chapter. For the moment let us consider anxiety an unpleasant emotional experience with heightened activation of the various central and peripheral systems associated with emotion.

In Figure 17–3, we can imagine an animal placed in the Miller-Mowrer box. He is on side *A*, and the current is activated. Assume that the door is open so that he may escape the shock by running to compartment *B*. Within the few trials, the animal learns to run to compartment *B* rapidly. Mowrer suggested (1939) that the stimuli accompanying placement in *A*—whether they be a tone or the grid floor and color of the compartment—come to evoke an emotional response. In compartment *A*, the animal's greatly increased defecation, freezing, and whining provide evidence of

FIGURE 17–3: *A Miller-Mowrer box. (From N. E. Miller, 1948, p. 90.)*

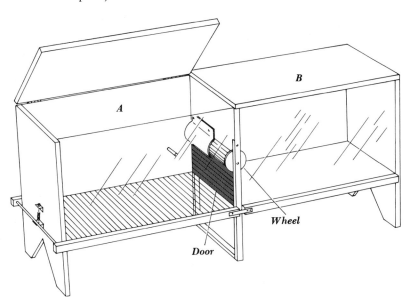

emotion. For convenience, the emotional response may be called anxiety. N. E. Miller (1948) used this situation to show the development of a secondary drive. Rats were placed in an apparatus such as that shown in Figure 17-3 and given a series of escape trials. Eventually, the shock was discontinued when the animals were placed in *A*, yet the rats continued to run to *B* without the negative reinforcement provided by the shock. Apparently, stimuli associated with compartment *A* acquired the power to evoke the escape response, even though the primary motivator—the current—was no longer used. Many phobias in human beings such as an apparently irrational fear of spiders or mirrors resemble the rat's behavior in the Miller-Mowrer box; escape behavior continues long after the original motivator has ceased to be present. In this experiment the stimuli once associated with shock came to have the power of a drive.

A drive-reduction theorist would point out that the reinforcement in this situation is the reduction in anxiety, for anxiety is assumed to be unpleasant and a decrease in anxiety is positively reinforcing. The ultimate test of whether a drive exists, however, is whether it may be used for the acquisition of a new response. Thus, the apparatus was altered, as shown in Figure 17-3, by placing a wheel between the two compartments. When the animal manipulates the wheel, the door opens, permitting access to compartment *B*. Like the bar in the Skinner box, the wheel provides opportunity for measuring a reasonably discrete response. Now the animal is returned to *A*. There is no shock. The animal shows the usual signs of emotion and eventually turns the wheel, opens the door, and escapes to *B*. On successive trials, the animal acquires the wheel-turning response, showing a learning curve very similar to that which we have noted for many other behaviors. Thus, the animal has learned a new response—wheel turning—without the presence of a primary drive. This experiment demonstrates two important principles: (1) escape or avoidance learning may be interpreted as an example of drive reduction

—the drive being anxiety—and (2) second-order drives may be learned. For example, the rats also learned to bar-press, thus showing the role of secondary drives.

Mowrer has pointed out a further interpretation of these data, namely, that both classical conditioning and operant training are involved in the development of the response. The original acquisition of the anxiety has the properties of a classically conditioned response, and learning to turn the wheel has the properties of operant training. Mowrer cautions us, however, against using a term such as anxiety to explain *itself:* we are still left with the question of how anxiety begins. That is, it is not sound science to say that an organism learned through anxiety, for anxiety itself is assumed to be a learned response (Mowrer, 1960a; 1960b).

The early psychoanalytic literature (see, for example, Freud, 1936; Ferenczi, 1950) contains examples of apparently comparable behaviors in human beings. Freud's analysis of a five-year-old boy's fear of horses follows similar explanatory principles, although Freud's interpretation includes the additional concept that anxiety in the boy developed from sexual "anxiety" associated with his relations with the father. Further, Freud's concept of anxiety at the time when he wrote this paper was neither so elaborate as it was to become nor so detailed as the contemporary physiologically based concept of anxiety.

Just as any "neutral" stimulus can come to serve as a secondary reinforcer, any neutral stimulus, it is reasonable to assume, can serve as a secondary-drive stimulus. Clearly, until much more is known about the distinction between primary drives (for example, shall we include sex?) and secondary, or acquired, drives, it is not always easy to separate one from the other except by examining the experimental operations employed in producing or studying the drives. How many acquired drives are there? Some theorists argue that anxiety alone is sufficient and that other drives may be shown to emanate from the drive reduction inherent in anxiety. Other theorists include the need for socializing or affiliation among the acquired drives. At any rate, one must guard against proliferating the number of acquired drives, just as one must guard against postulating many instincts.

SOME VIEWS ON HUMAN MOTIVATION

Human motivation is often thought to be totally different from animal motivation. One reason for this apparent cleavage is that few researchers ever work in both areas; i.e., experimenters are regarded as interested in animal motivation or human motivation, but rarely in just motivation. A study of the behavior of animals enables us to gather more precise data under better-controlled conditions than is possible with human beings. The question, of course, is whether by emphasizing precision we overlook our most important concern: what motivates men to make war, to work, or to love? In recent years, the work of the ethologists (Chapter 16) has penetrated the field of human motivation by suggesting that certain instinctual systems of animals may also exist in more elaborate form in human beings.

In this section we shall review, briefly, three representative approaches to human motivation: (1) The Freudian position has changed considerably over the years, and although those in sympathy with the psychoanalytic assumptions are not always in complete agreement, the psychoanalytic approach has had such a pervasive influence on psychological thought, especially among persons trained in disciplines other than psychology, that it deserves attention. (2) McClelland and his associates have attempted to develop a theory of motivation—indeed, a theory which attempts to predict the motivational level of different cultures and different centuries—basically through projective devices. These theorists have been concerned primarily with what they call the "achievement motive," but their work represents one of the better-developed contemporary theories of human-motivation measurement. (3) Finally, we shall consider some speculations made by ethologists concerning the relationship between human and animal motivation.

The Psychoanalytic Approach: When we speak of the "Freudian position" we refer to the general position that Freud developed through his own writings and those modifications and extensions made by others which have continued to receive attention in the psychoanalytic literature. Psychoanalysis, however, is heavily, if not entirely, devoted to the study of human motivation. It should be understood that in psychoanalysis, *all* behavior is assumed to be causal. The psychoanalytic outlook is not a purposive, or a teleological, view. Its framework is more similar to that of the Hullian system. All acts, even the blunders and malapropisms called "Freudian slips," have causes. Therefore, the psychoanalytic schools devote abundant attention to correlating specific behavior with its underlying causes. This accents the motivational relationships between causes and effects. In contrast to mechanistic theory, however, the psychoanalytic theory is not truly homeostatic. The psychoanalytic position is that there *is* a core of energy in the system (represented by the unknowable id) and that this energy must be dissipated by the other symbolic structures (e.g., ego, superego). The assumption, however, that the energy is homeostatic—that it results from deprivation and is satisfied by satiation—is not explicit in the system.

Perhaps the most unusual and distinctive feature of the Freudian concept of motivation is its *unconscious* content. In historical perspective, we may remember that the postulation of the basic Freudian system came at a time when psychology, in the tradition of Wundt, was a psychology of conscious experience, a psychology, to be a bit unjust, of psychophysics and of introspection of *conscious* processes. Parenthetically, the psychology of introspection led by Titchener and the psychology of psychoanalysis as practiced by

Freud were surprisingly identical in their emphasis on the individual's ability to describe strictly internal events, thoughts, and the like, and clearly different in respect to whether emphasis was on conscious material, such as colors, shapes, and the elements of perceptual events, or on unconscious material, such as dreams and fantasies.

The interpolation of an intervening variable, such as the unconscious, into behavior theory is a tricky task. We have already noted many of the difficulties with such intervening variables as mediation in verbal learning. The unconscious may well be regarded as the sovereign intervening variable. The experimental question is whether we can study the unconscious in such a way that we can predict its effect on behavior. If so, it is a useful intervening variable. One important source of data concerning the unconscious is that some events appear to alternate between the conscious and the unconscious. Perhaps, we cannot remember a name, but when we are reminded that the person embarrassed us in some fashion, the name returns.

The basis of motivation in the psychoanalytic position lies in the *id,* which contains "everything that is inherited . . . the instincts . . ." (Freud, trans. Strachey, 1949, p. 14). *Instinct* is not used here in precisely the same way that an ethologist would use the term, for the Freudians identify instincts by describing their operations, namely the *pleasure principle* and the *death wish.* The pleasure principle, in contemporary usage, refers to the concept that the id always seeks to gratify its instincts. Like an electric discharge, the instinctual energy of the id must be discharged *somewhere.* The death wish, again in contemporary usage, is similar to the *Nirvana principle,* which Freud postulated as the second of the two operations that characterize the id. This principle is that the organism seeks to keep the instinctual energy at a minimum. The principle is clearly related to the idea of a a death wish, which involves the regulation of the pleasure principle by an opposite process (i.e., a tendency to slow down) in order to keep the energy

emanating from the id (and thus the anxiety) at a minimum.

Freud added the concept of the death wish to the motivational system many years after the postulation of the pleasure principle. The acceptance of the death wish has not been universal among students of the psychoanalytic school; however, it does provide the motivational system with a balance much like the balance that exists between the sympathetic and parasympathetic nervous systems.

It is assumed that an organism attempts to reduce anxiety or excitation from the id as much as possible. Thus, so far, we are dealing with a tension-reduction system. Once instinctual energy from the id is discharged, one of several phenomena may occur. Sometimes, as in urinating, the energy is released in a relatively reflexive manner. The operation of the id's instincts directly, as in reflexive behavior, is referred to as the *primary process.* For a variety of reasons, such as our being taught to urinate only in certain places, eventually most id instincts cannot operate through the primary process. Thus, the other components, such as the *superego* and the *ego,* intervene to translate the instincts of the id into acceptable behaviors.

In the human being, the ego is the first symbolic structure to develop. The ego deals with reality directly. Thus, the *reality principle* comes to replace the pleasure principle with the development of the ego. The child learns that he is punished for urinating indiscriminately (i.e., pleasure principle) and that he must be "realistic." In facing reality, the child develops the superego. This form is part of the ego, yet remains separate from it. It contains what the ego has learned through its dealings with reality—the values of the parents and the society and other factors which reinforce what is "right" and what is "wrong."

Accordingly, the instinctual energy of the id is greatly transfigured by the time the correlative behavior occurs. Unless the energy has been reduced by the primary process—and very few behaviors can be—the original energy is reformed by the ego, which attempts to make the instinct acceptable to reality, and by the superego, which filters impulses. The ego develops many mechanisms to deal with instinctual energies. It may, as an example, attach the energy to something else *(displacement)*; e.g., instinctual energies aimed at one's mother become displaced toward one's wife. Or the energy may be *sublimated* into some artistic activity, such as painting. These *defense mechanisms* of the ego are a sampling of a number of such mechanisms that have been identified. All have in common the purpose of defending against anxiety caused by the instinctual urges of the id.

Our discussion of the Freudian system has omitted many of its characteristics, such as stages of development in childhood—anal, oral, and genital periods—for our intention has been to note the way in which motivation is conceived. The real motivators of behavior are unknown. Thus, the Freudian position furnishes us with a model of how motivators become translated into behaviors: it does not tell us precisely what the motivators are, although sexual behavior is most certainly an impressive candidate.

Need Achievement: The work of McClelland and his colleagues has not been directed toward understanding all motivations. The work of these experimenters, however, has furnished contemporary psychology with one of the few well-developed systems of measuring certain kinds of motivations. There are several essential characteristics and assumptions of this approach: First, motives are assumed to be learned; at least, it is assumed that the motives most important to human behavior are learned. Second, it is believed that learned motives can be examined by studying the fantasy life of the individual through projective testing. Third, if these assumptions are true, it should be possible to alter one's level of motivation (i.e., to produce a change in one's responses on the projective test) by furnishing conditions which would arouse motivation. Let us consider the development of this line of thinking in greater detail.

Motivation is defined as the learned expectation that a goal will produce either positive or negative reactions. In its simplest sense, the statement is similar to the law of effect, for it assumes that goals previously learned to be pleasant will motivate the organism toward such goals and the reverse will be true for goals that have produced negative reactions. Now, the affects which are attached to the goal —pleasure and pain—may indeed be innate, but the important point is that the anticipation of these goals is learned and thus the goals are available for study in the same way as any other learned behavior.

Although we might discover something about the strength of the goals simply by asking a person, the rationale used is that fantasy, as measured in a projective test, is a good index of motivation. This adoption of projective testing as the dependent variable in studies of motivation presumably accepts the rationale that at least some motivations are not part of conscious experience and they are not discovered merely by asking a person to define them. Thus, this group of investigators has consistently used as stimuli a series of cards from the TAT (C. D. Morgan & H. Murray, 1935; Tomkins, 1948). Usually, the subject is presented with the cards which show a situation, such as a boy holding a musical instrument and standing before a table, and asked the following questions: "What is happening?" "Who is the person?" "What has led up to this situation?" "What is being thought?" "What is wanted?" "What will happen?" Notice that these questions force the subject's attention to the past, present, and future characteristics of the situation.

The motivation which has received most attention has been *need achievement* (nAch) (H. A. Murray, 1938). The stories developed from the answers to the questions are scored in categories ranging from *unrelated imagery* (−1) through *doubtful imagery* (0) to categories, all rated +1, such as *achievement imagery* or *personal obstacle*. A story would receive a plus for the personal-obstacle category, for example, if achievement of a goal is made difficult by the presence of some event. A story related to the boy-and-violin card might indicate that the boy (presumably the subject) would become a great violinst, save for an accident which injured his fingers. Another "obstacle" might be a story in which the subject is too nervous to appear before an audience and hence cannot become a great concert violinist (McClelland, J. W. Atkinson, R. A. Clark, & Lowell, 1953). Although other projective tests could presumably be scored in similar ways, workers in this area have concentrated on the use of TAT-like cards as stimuli.

Clearly, the success of the system depends to a large extent upon the reliability and validity of the measuring device. It is reported that reliability between relatively untrained scorers in assessing the presence or absence of story material fitting the categories yields correlations above .90 (McClelland et al., 1953). The scoring system is apparently sufficiently lucid that little training is required for persons to agree on scoring. A second kind of reliability relating to whether an individual receives the same score with repeated administrations of the test is also important, however. Different studies have found this kind of reliability to vary from .22 to .78 (cf. Krumboltz & Farquhar, 1957; Haber & Alpert, 1958), although the amount of time between the tests varied in these studies. These data suggest several characteristics of the scoring method. First, they may indicate that, at least under some conditions, the procedure is unreliable. It is also possible, and perhaps likely, that need achievement is not a constant and that its "intensity" may vary appreciably within an individual over relatively short periods of time. If so, test-retest reliability tells us little about the reliability of the measure, for we may be measuring a variable that is highly quixotic. The validity of the scoring procedure is measured by the experimental procedures that are assumed to arouse motivation. Let us consider two early experiments which used the scoring procedure as the dependent variable but which attempted to vary the amount of motivational arousal as the independent variable.

J. W. Atkinson and McClelland (1948) attempted to assess the validity of the technique by using hunger, a motive that is not usually considered learned. Six pictures, along with the standard questionnaire were given to Navy personnel 1, 4, or 16 hours after eating. The stories were used to provide data for the development of the scoring protocol. Since the degree of hunger was represented in the stories, it was assumed that motivational states are reflected in the fantasy that accompanies storytelling. In an investigation of nAch the actual level of motivational arousal was varied (J. W. Atkinson, 1958b, chap. 3). In this study, college students were given four TAT cards and asked to write stories in response to the questions and to take a test, supposedly of "creative imagination," which consisted of solving anagrams and similar problems. The subjects were examined under six experimental conditions: relaxed, failure, neutral, success-failure, achievement-oriented, and success. Whether the instructions and explanations actually made the subjects "relaxed" or "neutral" is, for the most part, immaterial to the study. The success of the attempt to create such atmospheres can be judged only insofar as the stories differ under the different conditions.

In the "relaxed" group, a graduate student explained that the students were "trying out" some tests. The inference was that the test, not the group, was under observation. In the failure condition, the experimenters passed out the test without comment. The students took the test and scored it themselves. Then they completed a questionnaire whose purpose was to "ego-involve" the student. One question, for example, asked the subject to estimate his own IQ. An instructor talked about the tests, saying that they were used to measure intelligence and leadership qualities and had been widely used in the military and in government. He pointed out that they were being given in a number of institutions and gave norms on the test. The norms were such that almost all subjects scored in the lowest quartile. Six more tests were given, and each time most of the students fell in the lowest quartile. Then the test of "creative imagination," that is, the TAT cards with the usual directions, was given.

In the success condition, the procedure was the same as in the failure condition except that the quoted norms for each test showed that the subjects had done very well. In the success-failure group, the norms were such that most subjects appeared to score high on the first few tests but low on the remainder. In the achievement-oriented group, the instructions were the same as for the failure group, but no norms were announced. In the neutral group, the students were asked to do as well as they could; no norms were announced.

The writers assumed that the amount of induced nAch could be regarded as a continuum, with the relaxed condition at the low end and the failure condition at the high end. The nAch scores for the groups ranged from a mean of -1.00 for the relaxed group, through 3.30 (neutral), 5.82 (failure), and 6.00 (success-failure). The last two scores are, of course, very close together. Thus, it would appear that the methods used to induce different amounts of nAch were successful, in that the resulting scores differed from one another in a manner predictable from the assumptions of the experiment.

The general technique of assessing TAT cards for imagery has also been used to develop measures of other motives. We shall consider some of the ramifications and findings that this technique has produced.

A number of motives have been scrutinized. Among these are affiliation (Shipley & Veroff, 1952), fear (E. L. Walker & J. W. Atkinson, 1958), sex (R. A. Clark, 1955), power (Veroff, 1957), aggression (Feshbach, 1955), and "fear of failure" (R. A. Clark, Teevan, & Ricciuti, 1956). In measuring the amount of sexual material in the stories of sexually aroused and unaroused subjects, R. A. Clark (1952; 1955) showed slides of nude females or of landscapes. The subjects were asked to rate the former for attractiveness and the latter for aesthetic beauty. There was less sexual mate-

rial in the stories of the aroused group—the group which rated the nudes—than in those of the control group. The same variables were used on students attending a fraternity beer party. Under alcohol, both groups included more sexual content in their stories than did the groups tested in the classroom. The curious finding that the classroom control group showed more sexual content while evaluating landscapes than the experimental group evaluating nudes was attributed to anxiety produced by watching the slides and the presence of defense mechanisms to defend against the anxiety. Clark reexamined these results by evaluating the stories on the basis of sexual symbolism rather than overt sexual material. Clark found greater sexual symbolism, admittedly a difficult response to measure, in the stories of the experimental group. Both alcohol groups showed only small amounts of sexual symbolism, for most of the sexual content was manifest. This finding corroborates the comment that alcohol is the only known solvent of the superego. Moreover, the findings suggest that other motivations beside nAch may be examined through the McClelland procedure.

In order to assess the general validity of the technique, investigators have examined the relationship between nAch scores from the McClelland scoring procedure and other measures of performance. Although nAch has been shown to be related to other behaviors, such as scores on a verbal aptitude test, the correlations are rarely high. Lowell (1952) had high- and low-nAch subjects to take a test of both anagrams and arithmetic problems. On the anagram test, the two groups started out performing at the same level. By the end of the test the high-nAch subjects were unscrambling 50 percent more words per minute than they had at the beginning of the test; the low-nAch subjects were performing at the same rate as when they started. Thus, a relationship between improvement in performance and nAch exists. On the arithmetic test, neither group showed a change in performance, probably because the mathematical operations which the test required were so well known by the subjects that there was little opportunity for improvement. The high-nAch group, however, worked about 20 percent more problems per unit of time than the low-nAch group. McClelland et al. (1953, p. 232) report that college grades sometimes, but not always, correlate with nAch scores.

Finally, Atkinson (see McClelland et al., 1953, p. 244) has also reported that "level of aspiration" correlates with nAch. Students taking a final examination in a psychology course were asked to report to the testing room one hour before the examination. Half the class came, since the request indicated that attendance was voluntary. Those who came were given the standard nAch test and asked to indicate the grade they thought they would get on the final examination. This grade was used to assess the level of aspiration of the student. The correlation between nAch score and level of aspiration for the final examination was low, positive, and statistically insignificant. When the students' scores on the midterm were examined, however, the following relationship appeared: those students whose midterm grade was about the same as their overall grade-point standing showed a slightly negative, statistically insignificant, correlation between nAch and level of aspiration. Those whose midterm was quite different from their overall standing (i.e., they were doing unusually well or unusually poorly considering their overall standing) showed a positive and statistically significant correlation between nAch and level of aspiration. Thus, it appears that nAch and level of aspiration are not correlated when the level of aspiration is "realistic." Under less realistic circumstances, however, there is a significant correlation.

The McClelland procedures provide a method for measuring some forms of motivation by examining the fantasy life of an individual. Thus, the dependent variable is basically that of a projective technique. Many studies using the technique have attempted to arouse different levels and types of motivation

as the independent variable. Although there are many objections to the procedure and many experimental problems unsolved in its use (see Cofer & Appley, 1964, pp. 740–741), it has produced imaginative data on the measurement of motivations in human beings.

The Ethological Approach: It would be a misrepresentation to say that ethologists offer a unified theory of human motivation; it would be a greater error to think that they believe their observations of animal society have no bearing on human society and human motivation. There is a general belief among ethologists that human behavior is more extensively controlled by instincts than human beings care to admit. Since ethologists do not study human behavior directly, many of their comments regarding human motivation come from analogies of human behavior with animal behavior. Man is an animal. As such, his behavior may be viewed as an extension of instincts, the presence and development of which are more easily observable in animals lower on the phylogenetic scale. Among the instincts important to human behavior, Tinbergen has named movement, sex, food getting, and sleep (1951). There is further agreement, at least among those ethologists who have chosen to comment on the issue, that it is vital to examine the presence of *fixed action patterns* in human beings and that knowledge of human motivation can be gained from studying innate releasers (Chapter 16).

Unfortunately, the necessity of reasoning by analogy has brought ethologists under widespread attack from workers who emphasize the difficulty of generalizing across species. For example, Tinbergen (1951, p. 208) points out:

As a very simple example of how conscious reasoning may entirely distort our insight into the real causes underlying our behavior, one of the commonest conflicts between drive and reasoning may be taken. Mating behavior in man, not in the form of the accomplishment of the consummatory act, but in the preparatory, appetitive

stage of "love-making," proves, when studied etho-
logically, to be basically dependent on sex hormones and on external stimuli and it is on these
agents that our rational powers exact a regulating influence. Now every individual among us
who has the habit of self-observation, and who
has not forgotten his youth, knows how often the
urge has driven him "blindly," "against his better
judgment" to obey it, when there was a conflict
between better judgment and drive. Falling in
love changes one's entire outlook upon one's surroundings. Criminologists teach us that the number of crimes, even of serious ones like murder,
committed in obedience of the instinctive urge to
show off before a female is astonishingly high.
Quite different, but from our standpoint equally
significant, are murders due to sexual rivalry.

In discussing food seeking, admittedly a behavior which is rarely so important in human
beings as in animals, Tinbergen points out
that we can observe instances in human beings
in which "instinctive food seeking . . . conflicts
with reason" (1951, p. 208). He points to the
instances of widespread starvation, most typical of Asian countries but not unknown in the
Western world, particularly during wartime,
and draws our attention to "how relatively
weak reason is when it is up against really
powerful instinctive motivation."

From these two brief examples, we can see
the general way in which at least one ethologist views some problems of human motivation. On the whole, ethologists give relatively
little attention to human motivation. Tinbergen is one of the few workers who have
attempted to do so, and even he devotes only
6 pages of a 210-page book on instinct to human beings. There are, however, other comments in the ethological literature which provide analogies between human and animal
motivation. Lorenz (1943), for example, points
out that the parental instinct, which is regarded as a subclass of the reproductive instinct, is producible by the use of appropriate
"sign stimuli." Consider Figure 17–4. According to Lorenz, the stimuli in column *A* are re-

FIGURE 17–4: *Human baby and three
substitutes (column* A) *representing sign stimuli
that release parental reactions in man, as
compared with adult man and three animals
(column* B) *that do not release parental conduct.
(From N. Tinbergen,* The Study of Instinct, *
Oxford University Press, Fair Lawn, N.J., 1951,
p. 209, after Lorenz, 1943.)*

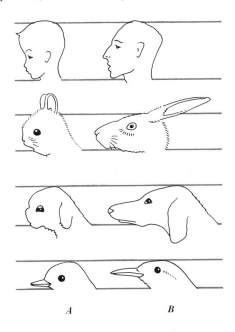

A   *B*

leasers for parental behavior in human beings,
whereas the four figures in column *B* are not.
Evidence that the two panels produce different
forms of behavior is supported only introspectively, but it is concluded from this example that a certain general shape—namely,
large forehead with short face—is responsible
for releasing the parental behavior. A short
forehead and elongated face do not have this
power. This example provides us with a relatively clear observation of the broad ethological approach—the search for forms, or signs,
which act as releasers for instinctual behavior,
as opposed to forms and signs which do not
release such behavior.

We may summarize the concern of ethologists for the study of human motivation, as well as this brief chapter, by citing Lorenz's comment (1950, pp. 266–267) that "...with atomic bombs in its hands and with the endogenous aggressive drives of an irascible ape in its central nervous system ... it is high time that the collective human intellect got some control on the necessary outlets for ... drives ... and some knowledge of human innate releasing mechanisms, especially those generating aggression."

SOURCES

There are several comprehensive works on emotion: Arnold (1960) has written a two-volume work on the topic (the first is on psychological aspects, the second on neurological and physiological aspects). Arnold's own approach to emotion is threaded throughout the volumes, and a reading of the full work, rather than selected chapters, is recommended. P. T. Young's work (1961), which covers both emotion and motivation, is an excellent source, as are his two earlier works (1936; 1943). In Woodworth and Schlosberg (1954) the three chapters on emotion provide a very useful introduction to the topic and serve as a very fine source of information on apparatuses and techniques used in the measurement of emotion. Candland (1962) has provided a source book of historical readings. Duffy's (1962) book, although concerned with activation and emotion, is a superior reference for most other aspects of emotion. See also chapter 11 of C. T. Morgan (1965) for a discussion of physiological aspects.

The field of motivation has not been deluged with truly general texts. Certainly, the most comprehensive and most useful is Cofer and Appley (1964). This book appears to discuss, sooner or later, everything that has been thought to be emotion or motivation. Criticisms of theory and research are both sharp and reasonable. Other sources tend to be concerned with more specific aspects of motivation. See Toman (1960) on the psychoanalytic approach. Stacey and DeMartino (1958) provide a book of current readings on human motivation; the book gives the flavor, and sometimes the aroma, of contemporary research. J. S. Brown's book (1961) is valuable for its Hullian orientation, as well as its interpretation of other aspects of human motivation. Rethlingshafer (1963) is oriented toward personality theory. J. F. Hall (1961) emphasizes the animal literature, as do Bindra (1959) and Fuller (1962). Both Bindra and Fuller are useful in showing how motivation has been investigated on a physiological and behavioral basis. For contemporary papers see the annual *Nebraska Symposium on Motivation* (M. R. Jones, 1954–1963; D. Levine, 1964–1966).

Methods of Measurement: For information on physiological recordings, see Lindsley (1951), P. T. Young (1948), R. Davis (1948), and Woodworth and Schlosberg (1954). For lesions and ablations see McCleary and R. Y. Moore (1965). For posture see Woodworth and Schlosberg (1954).

Activation: The use of the term *activation* received impetus from Lindsley's (1951) chapter on emotion. Duffy's (1962) work is a full-scale discussion of the activationist's approach to emotion, as well as of the measurement of other forms of behavior.

Limbic System and Reticular Activating System: McCleary and R. Y. Moore (1965) have published an excellent review of the subcortical mechanisms of behavior. The book, written at an appropriate level for students using this text, covers the physiological and neurological aspects of these areas in reasonable detail and discusses experiments and developments in this general area. Arnold (1960) also presents a short discussion of these topics (vol. 2, chap. 5).

Emotion, Psychosomatic States, and the Autonomic Nervous System: Literature in this area varies from the especially experimental, as found, for example, in the *Journal of Nervous and Mental Disease,* through speculations from neo-Freudians. For an analytic viewpoint, see Alexander (1950).

Biochemical and Drug-produced Changes in Emotion: Stress: See Selye (1956) for a popularized account of his concept of stress. For greater detail see the *Annual Reports on Stress* (Selye, 1951, and the subsequent dates for these reports).

An Introduction to Motivation: Works of value for an introduction to motivation are mentioned in the text; such works usually include discussions of emotion as well.

Motivation and Learning Theory: Bugelski (1956, chaps. 9, 10, 15) provides a review of the relationship between motivation and learning theory, as does Deese (1958, chaps. 5, 6) and Deese and Hulse (1967).

Learned Drives: The Example of Acquired Fear: The original works (Mowrer, 1939 and N. E. Miller, 1948) are suggested. In addition see Mowrer and Lamereaux (1946) as well as Mowrer's two excellent books (1960a; 1960b) and his review paper (1956).

Some Views on Human Motivation: The Psychoanalytic Approach: No single source adequately summarizes the psychoanalytic approach. The best understanding is gained from first reading Freud's works in chronological order and then the secondary reviews. If one must begin with a composite source, however, Munroe (1955) and C. S. Hall and Lindzey (1957) are recommended.

Need Achievement: The literature on need achievement is vast. Three books by McClelland and his associates (J. W. Atkinson, 1958a; McClelland, 1955; McClelland, J. W. Atkinson, R. A. Clark, & Lowell, 1953) contain many of the major studies. The scoring system appears in McClelland et al., 1953. McClelland's work on the achievement motive in various cultures appeared in 1962. For a summary of the work on various aspects of the McClelland system see Cofer and Appley, 1964. These writers present a fair evaluation of the work and provide information on some practical and conceptual problems.

The Ethologists: It is very difficult to summarize adequately the contributions ethologists have made to the study of human motivation. Certainly their occasional comments about extensions of animal motivation to human motivation fall far short of a systematic theory; nevertheless, the comments are often tantalizing. The interested reader is advised to read Tinbergen (1951, pp. 205–210), Lorenz (1950), part III of Thorpe and Zangwill (1961), Thorpe (1956; 1962), and Lorenz (1966). An excellent summary and criticism are provided by Cofer and Appley (1964, pp. 82–86).

CHAPTER EIGHTEEN

PSYCHOMETRICS: TESTS AND MEASUREMENT

INTRODUCTION

One of the dependent variables most commonly used on human beings is testing devices. Tests have two basic functions, both in their practical and their more theoretical applications. The first function is discrimination among individuals. When an IQ of 105 is assigned to one individual and an IQ of 115 to another individual, an attempt has been made to make a discrimination between them on the basis of "intelligence." Since the purpose of the test is to make such discriminations, it is necessary to ask whether the difference between 105 and 115 is a meaningful difference. This question, although psychometric in nature, is strikingly similar to the types of questions we ask in psychophysics or scaling when we inquire whether two stimuli differ from one another. The questions and the form of the answers posed by psychophysics are so similar to those posed by testing that the problems of testing become clearer if one recalls the basic psychophysical problems.

The second function of a test is the determination of whether an individual has changed in some measurable respect as a function of time or some other independent variable. If the person with an IQ of 115 is retested a year later and receives an IQ estimate of 50, it is probable that some variable has intervened between the two measures, such as brain damage. Similarly, we noted in Chapter 17 how McClelland and his associates have used the TAT as a dependent variable when need achievement is varied in subjects through the directions given by the experimenters.

The practical uses of tests are legion; we use them to assess students in course work; indeed, we use them in order to determine whether or not a student will have the opportunity of a college education. In clinical settings, tests are used to assess personality and to diagnose disorders. The use of tests has become so widespread that a variety of criticisms of them and of their use have been made (Hoffmann, 1962; Gross, 1962). In short, the use of tests has become something of a social issue. For this reason, as well as the fact that tests in one form or another are often used as dependent variables, it is worthwhile to understand how a sound test is constructed, how its reliability and validity are determined, and how it is used and evaluated.

Tests are of many kinds, and it is probably impossible to list definitive categories of them. However, we can discriminate certain gross differences between tests and between the ways in which they are constructed. For example, tests are often said to differ depending on whether they are *objective* or *subjective*. Actually, two different things are meant by this distinction. On the one hand we have the difference between a test which has definite answers (a history test which requires specific answers such as names and dates) and a test which requires more general answers (essay test). On the other hand, objective tests are those which can be scored by machine or by a person unfamiliar with the content (a multiple-choice examination), and subjective tests are those in which trained personnel are needed to score and interpret the results (the Rorschach and TAT). Tests in the subjective category are often *projective* tests in that the value of the test is that the subject projects attributes of his personality into the ambiguous stimuli incorporated in the test.

Another important distinction between tests is whether they attempt to evaluate how much a person knows (an *achievement* test) or whether they attempt to assess what is thought to be a relatively invariant capacity of the individual *(aptitude)*. Moreover, within the categories of either achievement or aptitude tests we may differentiate between those which attempt to measure a *specific* factor (such as musical ability) and those which attempt to assess *general* factors (such as intelligence).

In the manner of administration of the test, we may distinguish between tests which are *group*-administered and those which must be administered *individually*. Group tests are obviously less expensive and easier to give; generally, they are of an objective nature, as well. Some tests require individual administration.

For example, one test of intelligence requires the examiner to ask the subject the reasons for his selecting a particular answer, so that "partial credit" can be given.

We may also distinguish between *performance,* or nonlanguage, tests and those which require language. The usual IQ test, for example, requires that the subject be able to read and to write. However, in assessing the intelligence of young children or of illiterate subjects, a performance test is required in which the subject's responses are in the form of behavior—such as pointing to particular objects—rather than writing.

A BRIEF HISTORY OF TESTS AND MEASUREMENT

Testing and measurement arose as natural tools in the study of individual differences among persons, although the study of individual differences itself was a late development in the history of psychology. It may be recalled from our discussion of the development of psychophysics that the early psychophysicists tended to treat deviations as errors in their psychophysical methods, rather than as differences among individuals in perception. This approach characterized the psychology of the last century, and it was not until the last part of that century and the first part of this that the study of individual differences was undertaken. As the publication of textbooks and articles and the number of college courses offered on the topic testify, the study of individual differences probably reached its peak in the 1920s.

Sir Francis Galton is usually credited with establishing the study of individual differences and thus with being the pioneer of the science of testing and measurement. In 1882, he set up an "anthropomorphic booth" at a London museum where visitors could, for a small fee, be tested for acuteness of vision, hearing, reaction time, and other abilities. Thus Galton obtained the first appreciable amount of information on individual differences among human beings. As a pioneer, Galton developed most of the tests used in the anthropomorphic booth; some are still with us. The Galton whistle, for example, was used to test the TL for tone before the invention of audiooscillators. Nowadays, Galton whistles are used as dog whistles, and the two names are often used synonymously.

Galton believed that the acuteness of the sensory systems was related to general intellectual ability. His reasoning—not unlike that with which we have prefaced Chapter 3—was simply that as long as all information must come to the brain by way of the senses, it would follow that the more accurate the sensory apparatus, the more able the person (Galton, 1883). In addition to founding the study of individual differences and measurement, Galton made many other important contributions to psychology: (1) He was the first to apply descriptive statistics to psychological data. Individual differences, which tend to be normally distributed, are ideal data for the application of statistical devices, which were, in the last part of the century, just being developed by mathematicians. (2) Galton was among the first to use rating scales as a method of measuring psychological characteristics. (3) He introduced the use of free association as a psychological measure.

James McKeen Cattell (1860–1944) followed the traditional pattern of students of the late nineteenth century by taking his doctoral degree abroad. Working at Leipzig under Wilhelm Wundt, his dissertation was concerned with individual differences in reaction time—a topic which prompted Wundt to refer to the suggestion as *ganz amerikanisch* (Boring, 1950, p. 533). Returning to the United States, Cattell attempted to extend the use of tests to *mental tests*—a term which he coined (1890)—of reading, memory, learning ability, and similar factors. An exhibit was set up by Joseph Jastrow (1863–1945) at the Columbian Exposition in Chicago in 1893 in which people could take such tests, just as Galton had done eleven years earlier in London. Unfortunately, the future of the testing movement looked dim,

for few meaningful relations were found between test scores and actual success in school or work. Nevertheless, the idea of mental testing had taken hold, and even Hermann Ebbinghaus (1897)—whom we associate with the study of memory and the use of nonsense syllables (Chapter 15)—had joined the endeavor by developing tests of arithmetical ability, memory span, and sentence completion.

Impetus was given to the movement by the development of a successful test of mental ability by Alfred Binet (1857–1911), who with Simon (1873–1961) developed the Binet-Simon scale. This scale, developed at the request of the Paris school system, represented the first useful IQ test. Although Binet and his colleagues worked through many measures, including handwriting and palmistry, in an attempt to find meaningful measures, they finally concluded that the following device was most useful: Thirty problems, arranged in increasing order of difficulty, were developed. The level of difficulty was determined empirically by testing 50 normal and retarded children. This original scale was published in 1905. Three years later, the series was revised by eliminating unsuccessful items and increasing the total number of test items. Moreover, a different scoring system was used in which tests were divided into groups on the basis of the age at which the normal human being could answer them. Thus, norms were established for each age. A child's score on the test represented his *mental age*. For example, if a four-year-old child could answer all the tests successfully passed by five-year-olds but none of the tests passed by six-year-olds, he was said to have a mental age of five years.

In the United States, the concept of mental age was used by Terman (1916) in what was first known as the Terman-Binet and finally as the Stanford-Binet scale, reflecting the name of the university where Terman taught. Terman added an important contribution to the concept of mental age. He divided the mental age (MA) by the chronological age (CA). In our previous example, the MA of 5 would be divided by the CA of 4, yielding an intelligence quotient (IQ) of 1.25. In order to remove the decimal, the formula is multiplied by 100. Thus

$$IQ = \frac{MA}{CA} \times 100$$

Accordingly, when the IQ is above 100, the child is answering problems normally appropriate for older children; if the IQ is below 100, he is unable to answer questions normally answered by his own age. Theoretically, the mean IQ score of the population should be 100, and this mean should not change as a function of age. Thus, a sample of sixty-five-year-old persons should have a mean of 100, as should a sample of three-year-old children.

The tests of intelligence developed by Binet, Terman, and others were administered individually, but the mental-measurement movement received another boost with the advent of World War I and the development of group tests. In 1917, the American Psychological Association appointed a committee, with Robert M. Yerkes as chairman, to determine ways in which psychology could assist in the war. The committee set to work to develop means of rapidly classifying the recruits so that they could be assigned to an appropriate area of service. In the Army, intelligence tests were used. They were called Army Alpha and Army Beta tests. The former were for general testing, and the latter were used for illiterates or recruits who spoke only a foreign language. The large number of persons entering service made the individual administration of tests impossible; thus group tests were devised and administered for the first time. Moreover, the large number of persons taking the tests provided psychologists with sufficient data to evaluate the tests. After the war, the testing movement boomed. As early as 1908 G. Stanley Hall had warned of some of the problems associated with testing. During the years following 1920, the field of testing and measurement made many advances in the problem areas of evaluating reliability and validity. In addition, testing and measurement have turned to evaluating specific skills, rather than placing greatest emphasis on the search for instruments to measure such general factors as "intelligence."

After the development of mental testing, roughly in the 1920s, personality measurement began. The difficulty in assigning a precise date for the beginning of this form of testing comes from the fact that although questionnaires and free association tests were used in the 1890s, it is not certain that these would qualify as measures of personality by contemporary standards.

There are many kinds of tests which come under the heading of *personality tests*. Projective measures, such as the Rorschach, quite clearly are personality tests, for they attempt to measure emotional and motivational factors of the testees. However, even a measure of IQ tells us something about an individual. Personality tests do not necessarily require the use of paper and pencil. For example, some tests require the person to act out a problem, or their behavior is watched under certain conditions. These *situational tests* are also used to describe and predict personality even though the subject does not necessarily "take a test." Finally, questionnaires are often used as measures of personality. The subject may be asked to rate himself or others on certain measures. All these kinds of measures qualify as tests of personality. In the establishment of reliability and validity, personality tests do not appear to be so well founded or so accurate as tests of achievement and aptitude. Nevertheless, their wide use in diagnostic work means that their construction and accuracy deserves special attention.

DEVELOPING A TEST

Gulliksen (1950) reduces the problems of developing a test to five major categories, namely:

1. **"Writing and selecting the test items." The problems here, of course, are those concerned**

with knowing what kinds of items will be successful in discriminating among individuals on the desired basis. Although it is a simple matter to construct test items, it is a difficult matter to construct items which differentiate the people who answer the items. Thus, the selection of appropriate test items involves certain experimental techniques.

2. "Assigning a score to each person." In the best of all possible testing worlds, an answer is either right or wrong, and each individual gets a certain number right and a certain number wrong. However, this approach blatantly throws away whatever precision the measuring tool may have. Hence, the way in which the items are to be scored becomes an important item that influences reliability and validity.

3. "Determining the accuracy (reliability or *error of measurement*) of test scores." If we assume that a *true score* (T) exists for each person (i.e., a true or accurate number which represents his score) and that any deviation from this score, either because of a poor measuring instrument or because of a poor scoring system, is merely a deviation from the T score, then the assessment of reliability becomes a matter of assessing the *error of measurement*. We have noted on many occasions the importance of reliability in all phases of psychological measurement, from psychophysics to bar pressing.

4. "Determining the predictive value of the test scores (validity or *error of estimate*)." We have emphasized validity many times. The term *error of estimate* refers to the relationship between test scores and actual achievement, and the error contained in the prediction or estimate.

5. "Comparing the results with those obtained using other tests or other groups of subjects." How far can we generalize from the test? Does it measure the same thing as any other test? And as Gulliksen points out, "In making these comparisons, it is necessary to consider the effect of test length and group heterogeneity on the various measures of the accuracy and the predictive value of the test scores" (1950, p. 2).

The process of writing and selecting the items and of assigning a score to each person affect reliability and validity. Thus, it is useful first to note how it is that these two important measures, the error of measurement (reliability) and the error of estimate (or validity), are measured.

TYPES OF RELIABILITY

We have defined errors of measurement as a case of reliability; however, we should note that another type of error, a *sampling error*, often affects reliability. Sampling error, as the name implies, refers to inconsistent results when the same measure is applied to different samples of subjects. Thus a sampling error is different from an error of measurement, for in the latter there is inconsistency when the same measure is applied to the same subjects. Sampling errors involve problems in descriptive statistics and in determining and selecting random populations (Chapter 1). Our discussion of reliability, however, is critical for almost all kinds of psychological inquiry. Briefly, the problem of sampling is the same as the problem of how far one can generalize from experimental results. Is a sample of 20 rats from a laboratory colony sufficiently representative to permit the experimenter to generalize his findings to all other rats? Is a sample of 200 college sophomores of a certain college sufficient to permit the investigator to generalize to all people? To all college students? Or even to all college sophomores? Clearly the answer depends upon the appropriateness of the sampling procedures employed. If the college sample contains a random sample of all college students, then the sophomores are probably also representative. If not, the extent to which the findings can be generalized becomes questionable owing to sampling error. (For discussions of sampling and generalization, see Lyons, 1965; Underwood, 1957a, 1966.)

Test reliability refers to several different characteristics of a test. The first concerns whether the same test, given on different occasions, yields the same results. If person *A* is third among 50 students the first time the test is given, he should maintain the same relative position on the next administration of the test. If he does not occupy the same rank, the difference in rank on the two administrations of the test is a measure of the error. The error measured in this case is *temporal fluctuation*.

A second characteristic of test reliability is associated with the use of *parallel forms*. Parallel forms of a test have the same means and standard deviations, although the questions are different. Thus, we might compose a history test of 100 items. We could divide the test into two tests with 50 items each; however, simple division would not guarantee that the forms were parallel. If the forms of a test are truly parallel, it should not matter which form is given. If two tests are thought or known to be parallel, then reliability may be assessed by giving one form and then the other. As a check, half the subjects get one form first, and the remainder get the other form first.

Such assessments are grouped under the general heading of measures of *test-retest reliability*, since reliability is determined by a retest. There are at least two common methods, however, for assessing the reliability of a test without repeating its administration. These methods assess the test's internal consistency on the assumption that this is an important contributor to overall reliability.

The first measure based on a single administration of a test is the *split-half technique*. A simple form of this method involves correlating odd-numbered items of the test with even-numbered items. The higher the correlation, the higher the split-half reliability. In the second measure of internal consistency, a variety of formulas are available based on such factors as the number of persons responding correctly to an item and the number responding incorrectly. We shall discuss several of these formulas in greater detail shortly.

It is clear that the deceptively simple term *reliability* has many different operational meanings, depending upon the way in which reliability is assessed. It is also clear that each of the measures of reliability has difficulties which need to be considered in evaluating its

assessment of a test. For example, if the same test is given twice (retest with the same form), it is possible that some subjects will remember the items from the first test and other subjects will not. Thus the reliability may be artificially low or artificially high. In order to avoid this, one may use parallel forms, although their use always raises the question of how one ascertains whether they are truly parallel. The split-half, odd-even technique of assessing reliability assumes that all problems are of equal difficulty throughout the test—an assumption that frequently is not true. Each method has its drawbacks, each its advantages. Accordingly, the determination of reliability must be made in terms of what is most important for the experimenter or evaluator to know about the test.

CORRELATION, SPEARMAN-BROWN, AND KUDER-RICHARDSON TECHNIQUES

For the methods of assessing reliability, in which a test-retest reliability was found with or without parallel forms, a correlation coefficient between the ranks on the two tests is an expression of reliability. A correlation coefficient may vary from −1 through zero to +1. The first indicates a perfectly inverse relationship between the tests, and the last indicates a perfect relationship. The closer the correlation coefficient to 1 (whether it be positive or negative), the better the prediction. Thus, if the same test is administered twice and if the correlation coefficient between the first administration and second is +.96, we would know that the person who ranked third on the first administration ranked third, or nearby, on the readministration of the test. A high negative correlation would suggest that the subjects tend to reverse their score in relation to other subjects. (For information on the use of correlation, see Kendall, 1955).

When reliability is applied to internal consistency, a number of methods of assessment are available. In split-half reliability, it is usually unsafe to split the test in such a way that, for example, the first 50 questions are compared with the last 50. This procedure assumes that the testees do not become bored or fatigued as the test continues. The most precise technique for establishing split-half reliability is to determine the percentage of persons who answer each item correctly and the percentage who answer incorrectly. This percentage is regarded as the level of difficulty of each item. Items of equal difficulty may be placed in the two halves. If the items are arranged in accordance with level of difficulty, the odd-even approach (in which the odd items are correlated with the even-numbered items) is satisfactory.

Notice that the split-half approach reduces the number of items by half. Thus, a test with 100 items has 100 items to be compared if tested by the test-retest form of reliability. If the same test is evaluated by split-half reliability, however, only 50 items are compared. This fact becomes important when we consider the observation that the length of a test—in terms of the number of items—influences reliability directly. In general, the longer the test in terms of number of items, the more stable the evaluation. In order to determine the effect of making a test longer or shorter, the *Spearman-Brown* formula is often used. Thus

$$r = \frac{nr'}{1 + (n - 1)\, r'}$$

where

r = coefficient of correlation (reliability)

n = **number of times the test is lengthened or shortened (that is, with a 100-item test increased to 300 items, $n = 3$; if the test is shortened to 50 items, $n = 0.5$)**

r' = **obtained coefficient of correlation**

Consider a test of 50 items which has an obtained correlation (r') of +.5. If we increase the number of items to 100 (n, in the formula equals 2), we have

$$r = \frac{(2)\,(.5)}{1 + (2 - 1).5}$$

$$r = \frac{1}{1 + (1).5}$$

$$r = \frac{1}{1.5}$$

or

$$r = .67$$

Accordingly, in this case, doubling the length of the test served to increase the reliability from +.5 to +.67. Figure 18–1 shows the change in reliability as a function of increased test length for different initial reliabilities. It may be noted that as the number of items approaches infinity (as the length of the test is extended indefinitely), the reliability (r) approaches unity, or 1, for all the values of r'.

Now, assume that we have two tests. One test contains 10 items and has a reliability of .80. A second test contains 100 items and has a reliability of .85. Notice that the second and longer test is the more reliable of the two. We may wish to know whether lengthening the first test of 100 items will make it more reliable than the second test. Assuming that we are able to write an additional 90 items comparable to the first 10, the Spearman-Brown formula may be used to solve this problem. Thus

$$r = \frac{(10)(.80)}{1 + (10 - 1).80}$$

$$r = \frac{8}{1 + 7.20}$$

$$r = .975$$

Accordingly, if the test maker is able to increase the first test by 90 items and retain the original reliability of the first 10 items as he does so, the overall reliability is increased to .97. Needless to say, the test maker must consider whether it is worthwhile, practically, to give up a highly reliable 10-item test to construct a 100-item test whose reliability is .17 higher. Whether he chooses to do so or not depends upon such practical considerations as exactly how reliable the test must be to be useful and how much time he or the testees can devote to it.

A number of techniques for assessing reliability with a single administration of a test use data from performance on each test item. A series of formulas have been developed by Kuder and Richardson (1937); the most commonly used is as follows:

$$r = \left(\frac{n}{n-1}\right) \left[1 - \frac{\sum\limits_{g=1}^{n} S_g^2}{S_x^2}\right]$$

where

r = reliability coefficient of test
n = number of items on test
S_g^2 = variance of item g [equals $p_g (1-p_g)$ where p is the percentage getting the item correct]
S_x^2 = test variance

This formula follows the basic format of the Spearman-Brown formula; however, it contains an evaluation of the proportion of persons answering each item correctly and incorrectly. Since this determination is made in order to select items when a test is under construction, the formula requires only the knowledge which is already available. It may be noted that the formula also includes a measure of the variability (in terms of the standard deviation) of the total scores on the test.

The reliability of a test will vary depending upon a number of factors. Among these are the length of the test, level of difficulty of items, whether it is a *speed test* (in which the score is the number of items correct or number of items completed in a given length of time) or a *power test* (in which ample time is given for solution of the items and the score is the number of items that are correct, the num-

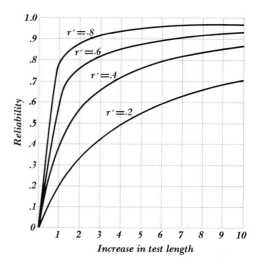

FIGURE 18-1: *A diagram showing the results derived from the equation regarding the effect on test reliability of changing the length of a test. The ordinate shows the augmented reliability, and the abscissa shows the change in test length. The curves show the obtained correlation. (From Gulliksen, 1950, p. 81.)*

ber incorrect, and the number left incomplete), and, of course, the particular measure of reliability that is used. Thus, to say that such-and-such a test has a reliability of .85 falls short of informing us of the usefulness of the test. It is necessary to indicate the kind of reliability that was measured. Moreover, a test may be highly reliable but be useless if it is not valid.

A second important factor which influences the reliability of a test is the homogeneity of the sample. The basic point is that the *range* (the difference between the highest and lowest scores of the sample) and the variability within the sample of scores affect the degree of correlation. In general, the more restricted the range, the lower the reliability. With appropriate formulas, however, it is possible to estimate the effect of a change in the variability of the sample on the reliability. The problem is crucial in situations where there is reason to suppose that the scores of some subjects were influenced by uncontrolled variables. Assume that an examiner arrives ten minutes late, so that the testees are permitted only fifty minutes to complete the test rather than the hour's time for which the test was constructed. This error in procedure is not likely to affect variance, for the error affected every subject. Assume, however, that a band practices outside the testing room and that the room is sufficiently large that only those students near the windows are able to hear the music, or noise, as the case may be. Here, the testees have been treated differently, and we would expect the variance to show this. If every testee hears the music, we would not expect a change in the variance. Since test administrations are rarely perfect, it is worthwhile to inquire about the effect of variability on reliability of the test.

Assuming that we have two groups taking the test under two different conditions and assuming that we know the reliability and variability (expressed as a standard deviation) we may, through appropriate formulas, find the change in reliability that can be expected from a change in variability (Gulliksen, 1950, chap. 10). Figure 18–2 shows the relationship between changes in reliability and changes in variability. The ordinate shows the reliability of one test (.64); the top horizontal scale shows that the reliability of the second is .91; we use the ordinate and read across at .64, as marked by the arrows, and we read down from the top horizontal line from .91. We note that the two lines intersect at the diagonal line marked 2.0. Thus, if the standard deviation were doubled (the meaning of the 2.0 diagonal line), we would expect a change in reliability from .64 to .91.

TYPES OF VALIDITY

Since validity, like reliability, may be measured in many ways, it is imprecise to speak of the validity of a test in absolute numbers.

The statement that the validity of a test is .64 tells us only that a correlation was performed between the test results and some other measure; however, the usefulness of the test will depend upon the measure selected for comparison. For example, assume that a test purports to assess mechanical aptitude. The test results are correlated with the ability of the subjects to repair an automobile, resulting in a correlation of .5. Now, the test is valid at the .5 level only if the repair of automobiles is considered the *criterion* of mechanical aptitude. Incidentally, it may be found that the test correlates .8 with IQ. The mechanical aptitude test, it would appear, is a more valid predictor of general intelligence than of ability to repair a car. Validity is always dependent upon the nature of the criterion. Just as reliability is specified in terms of the type of reliability of concern to us, so validity is expressed in terms of the *type* of measure of validity selected.

Five major types of validity measures will be discussed: (1) construct, (2) content, (3) face, (4) predictive, and (5) concurrent validity.

Construct Validity: The key word here is *construct,* for construct validity is concerned with validations of tests that measure a general construct, such˜as "intelligence" or "neurotic tendencies." The problem of assessing validity is complicated by the fact that the construct itself is rarely well defined. There is no simple technique for assessing construct validity; rather, information on such validity comes from many sources, including correlations with other tests which purport to measure similar or identical constructs, factor analyses (Chapter 5) of many tests, and whatever information can be gleaned from behavior, such as academic performance. Together, data from these sources may indicate that the construct is being measured adequately. Thus, there is no statistic to evaluate whether a test is high or low in construct validity. In general, construct validity may be expected to be only as accurate as the construct is well defined.

Consider, for example, a reliable IQ test. Its validity may be assessed in specific terms, such as whether persons with a high IQ do well in school. A high IQ, however, is certainly not the only predictor that a person will do well academically. Many other traits can be responsible. When we consider construct validity, we are assuming first that there is a general capacity (intelligence in this example) which is measurable. The Binet tests, which measure mental age against chronological age, clearly assume that as a child ages, he is able to perform more complicated tasks. Thus, changes in test performance as a function of increased age can serve as one method for assessing construct validity where the test assumes such improvement to occur.

Content Validity: In the evaluation of content validity, the questions or items on the test are examined to see if their content is suitable to the purpose of the test. Thus, content validity is useful in achievement tests. For example, the content validity of an examination in history would be assessed by determining whether the items dealt with historical subject matter. The validity of most examinations given in college or graduate school is determined in this fashion; i.e., the instructor composes questions which discriminate among students on the basis of specific areas which the instructor thinks are essential. Now if you were to take an examination in history and find on it a question regarding the role of the cortex in learning, you might reasonably claim that the test, or at least the question, is unfair. Essentially, you would be claiming that the question did not have content validity, for from the content of the question one could not predict how well you understood history.

There are many sources of error in preparing items for achievement tests, and since content validity is largely a matter of judgment on the part of the test maker, it is worthwhile to review some of the more common errors: First, unless one takes great care, it is natural to construct questions which have highly spe-

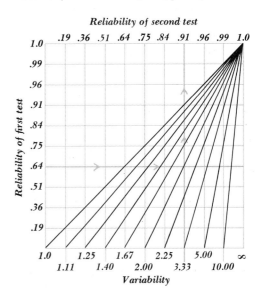

FIGURE 18–2: *Changes in reliability as a function of a change in standard deviation or variance. (From Gulliksen, 1950, p. 113.)*

cific answers, e.g., "In what year did Columbus discover America?" The danger, of course, is that the test will be formulated in a biased way, so that only questions with specific or easy-to-grade answers will be asked. Thus, the student who is prepared to discuss the reasons for Columbus's voyage has no chance to show his knowledge. Perhaps the best guard against this source of error is to stipulate in advance the areas to be covered.

A second common error is to make inappropriate generalizations from the results of an achievement test. For example, consider a multiple-choice test of spelling (Anastasi, 1961, p. 136). A sample item might be to select the correct spelling from the following: "restrant, restaurant, restaurent, resturant." The results will tell us whether an individual is able to recognize correctly spelled words from those which are spelled incorrectly, but it does not necessarily tell us much else. For example, it does not tell us whether a person can spell correctly from dictation. The test may be valid for the ability to discriminate correct spelling from incorrect spelling, but it does not guarantee that a person spells accurately in other situations.

It is preferable, when possible, to use empirical measures of validation. One empirical procedure is to use parallel forms of the test and to administer one form before a course (or some other independent variable) and the other after the course. The results suggest whether improvement has occurred and, if so, in which areas.

The evaluation of content validity is not useful on personality projective tests. Indeed, it may be highly dangerous. Simply, there is reasonable agreement on whether questions on history, chemistry, or psychology are valid questions—whether they relate to the particular field—and whether the questions denote achievement and mastery. It is a different matter, however, to design items which reveal the presence of neurosis or which are informative regarding personality traits. The danger, of course, is that what one person might consider a perfectly valid and revealing question would not be so considered by other persons. This fact has led to the rather common mistrust of projective, or personality, tests. To say that content validity is not an adequate measure of validity for tests of personality, however, is not to say that validation of them is not possible. The error in judgment involved is the confusion between content validity and *face validity*.

Face Validity: What a test *appears* to measure, as judged by the subjects, is face validity. Obviously this is not a real measure of validity, but it is extremely important, for if subjects do not *perceive* face validity, some are apt to become bored or angry, thus biasing the results. Most criticisms of tests come from those who mistake face validity for true validity and who "show" that such and such an item could not possibly be a valuable predictor.

First, let us note that, objectively, if the correct answer to the question, "How many ears do you have?" somehow manages to distinguish people who are good mechanics from those who are not, it is a useful and highly valid question. The issue of importance is whether or not it distinguishes among people in the way that the test constructor wishes. The question clearly lacks face validity, and it is understandable that persons who are not aware of the principles for establishing validity would be confused and often annoyed. As Anastasi (1961, p. 138) points out, there are ways in which face validity can be encouraged. For example, if a test of arithmetical reasoning is being given to astronauts, it is better that the questions be written with examples common to space exploration, rather than in terms of typical schoolbook problems such as "If three oranges cost 25 cents, how much money do I have to have in order to buy two dozen oranges?" Possibly, but not necessarily, improvement in face validity can affect objective validity by giving the subjects faith in the test.

Predictive Validity: As the name suggests, predictive validity is concerned with whether or not a test may be used to predict the future behavior of the subjects. Predictive validity is most conveniently used in personnel selection or similar situations in which future behavior must be evaluated. The results of the test are kept from persons who might have responsibility in assigning the subjects to positions in order to avoid *criterion contamination,* a term that refers to contaminating or biasing the criterion measure (e.g., success or failure in the position to which one is assigned). At a later date, the validity is assessed by comparing scores on the tests with performance. Often, an appropriate measure of validity requires that the investigation follow the behavior of persons who took the test but were not hired. In a college setting, for example, the admissions office might set a cutoff line for College Board scores: students scoring below the minimum, regardless of other attributes, would be excluded. This approach would require checking on students who were not admitted in order to see where they were admitted and how well they did. In *on-the-job* performance validation, the test scores would be compared with how well the subjects did at work.

The methods used by college admissions offices provide a clear example of the way predictive validity may be used. For a given school, a number of factors regarding applicants are considered, such as College Board scores, rank in secondary schools, and special skills. Often, these individual items are weighted so that a prediction of the likelihood of success of any given applicant can be obtained. For example, at a certain college, the equation resulting from these factors might be

Likelihood of eventual graduation = $.46C +$ $.21R + .10A + .23F$

where

C = **College Board scores**
R = **rank in secondary school class**
A = **number of extracurricular activities**
F = **finances, in terms of number of hours student will have to work to earn money during academic year**

Such equations differ from time to time within a school, and they most certainly differ widely among schools. The predictive validity of the factors included can be assessed by the obvious technique of comparing the prediction with actual facts, i.e., whether or not the student is graduated.

On the surface, predictive validity provides the most empirical, and hence the most trustworthy, technique we have discussed. Nevertheless, it is just as easy to misuse this method as the others. The need to follow those subjects who were tested but not enrolled or hired is an obvious, yet laborious, requirement. Moreover, the criterion selected must be adequate. The selection of a criterion is relatively simple in the example of admitting students to college: they either are graduated or they are not. Many criteria are appreciably less obvious.

What criteria do we use to distinguish good artists from bad artists?

Concurrent Validity: Often it is not practical to use predictive validity as an evaluation procedure; e.g., it is sometimes impossible to retest the subjects at a later date. Moreover, at times an experimenter only wishes to know how well a newly devised test correlates with already established information. For example, if an investigator has constructed a test with which he intends to predict college grade-point average, he may assess its validity by (1) giving the test to freshmen and correlating their grades at the end of four years with the test results—predictive validity—or (2) giving the test to seniors and comparing their grades with the test scores—concurrent validity. A complication from the use of concurrent validity is that one can be misled into making assumptions regarding nonexistent cause-and-effect relationships. In our previous example, one is tempted to assume, if the correlation between test scores and grades is high for seniors, that the test is a good predictor of grades. The test may be measuring other traits, however, such as motivation to succeed, and it may be that these other traits correlate highly with the attainment of high grades.

Concurrent validity is particularly useful in personality or diagnostic tests where the subjects are already clearly separated into groups, such as hospitalized psychotic patients or unhospitalized normal persons. If the test succeeds in showing that the scores of one group differ appreciably from the scores of the other group, the test has succeeded in diagnosing appropriately. Whether the test would continue to do so, i.e., whether the predictive validity would be as high, is another matter. Thus, concurrent validity is used to predict future situations.

Types of Questions Asked: We may summarize the five basic methods of assessing validity by showing the types of questions that each method attemps to answer. With an achievement test, usually evaluated by content validity, the question is "How much *has* X learned about Y?" With an aptitude test, which is most commonly evaluated by predictive validity, the question is "How much *will* X learn about Y?" For a diagnostic test, using concurrent validity, the question is "Has X had a course in American government, or has he not?" For a measure of some general factor, such as intelligence, and using construct validity, the question is "How intelligent is X?" And for an achievement test using face validity, "What does X think of Y?"

EXAMPLES OF TESTS

In this section, we shall review some sample tests in order to demonstrate the manner in which they are constructed and the ways in which reliability and validity have been measured. We shall discuss (1) a general-aptitude test, the Stanford-Binet test of intelligence, (2) a special-aptitude test, the Seashore test of musical talent, (3) an achievement test, and (4) a projective test, the *Tomkins-Horn Picture-Arrangement Test.*

A General-aptitude Test: Earlier in this chapter, we noted the contributions of Binet, Simon, and Terman to the concept of intelligence testing and ultimately to the theory of test construction. One crucial contribution was the use of a ratio between mental age and chronological age. The intelligence test developed from a 30-item test, with the items arranged in order of level of difficulty, to the use of the term IQ by Terman in the 1916 scale. More recently, the 1937 scale revised by Terman introduced the use of parallel forms of the test and standardization of the test on what was, up to that time, a remarkably large sample of the population. A revision of 1960 combined the two earlier forms of the test and eliminated items that had become obsolete in the intervening years. Obsoletion of items is a problem in most tests, for changes in clothing, modes of dress, and household furniture can

affect test results by decreasing face validity. When a subject takes a test which uses pictures of persons dressed in styles of thirty years ago, he may lose faith in the value of the test.

Since the 1937 Stanford-Binet test involved the basic labors of test construction, we shall consider the techniques that were used in constructing it. Approximately ten years of research were required to develop the items and to evaluate them on a sample of the population. The first step in the 1937 revision of the 1916 scale was to devise new items. Those items were tested on a small sample. The next step was to plot the percentage of subjects of each MA level who answered correctly or who answered incorrectly items on the 1916 test against the percentage who answered correctly or incorrectly the newly devised items. If a new item failed to correspond with the results of the earlier test, it was discarded at this point. When an appropriate number of items which corresponded with the results of the 1916 test items had been selected, the new test was administered to approximately three thousand children. Two forms of the test were used, L and M. Half the children took form L first, followed by form M; the other half took the tests in the reverse order. The time lapse between administration of the two tests was varied from one to seven days in order to provide a measure of the change in reliability between the two forms as a function of intertest interval.

In the analysis of the test items, plots were made of the percentage of subjects who answered each item correctly as a function of age, whether each item correlated positively with total score, and of the relationship between whether a subject answered a particular item correctly and his total score on the test. The first type of plot indicates whether the level of difficulty has been correctly identified, and the second evaluates the success in creating parallel forms. The third is concerned with the usefulness of individual items. One can imagine an item which is answered correctly by those whose total score on the test is low and answered incorrectly by those whose total score is high. Obviously, this item contributes little to the success of the test, for it discriminates against those who do well on the complete test. When this occurs in testing, it is a good guess that there is something wrong with the item. In achievement testing, such results imply that the question is ambiguous, so that the more able students perceive a variety of correct answers and the less able students perceive only a single answer—the answer the test constructor has chosen.

In selecting the items to be used in the two forms, the test makers considered other factors, such as sex of the subject, for it appears that some items are answered correctly more often by one sex than the other. This is not surprising if we consider that small boys and small girls are likely to have different play experiences. Items that showed a large discrepancy in the number answering correctly as a function of sex or other factors were discarded. Since not every item that showed a difference could be discarded, an attempt was made to account for this by including an equal number of items favoring each sex. One result of this procedure is that the test cannot evaluate sex differences—e.g., whether girls are more intelligent than boys—because this factor was eliminated from the test. The absence of any such differences only shows that the attempt to eliminate the effect of sex was successful.

For the 1937 revision, the tests were given in 11 states. An attempt was made to test different socioeconomic groups and to provide a wide sample of the total population. Today, when appropriately stratified samples of the population are widely used by polltakers and in the advertising field, the finding of a representative sample population appears to be an easy matter. These samples were not available in 1937, however, and it is remarkable that the sample population used for the revision was as varied as it was. Certain sampling inequalities did appear, including the testing of too few rural children in relation to the number of urban children. In any sample, it is easier to

acquire data from urban children, who are nicely bunched together in large cities. A second inequality was that the 1937 sample was limited to native-born white children. Nevertheless, the sample represented the greatest attempt to acquire data from a random sample of the population up to that time. It is important that those who interpret tests, such as this test of intelligence, know enough about its construction and the procedures for validation to know where scores on the test are likely to be in error. In this case, it may be difficult to generalize from the 1937 test to rural children, to immigrants, or to nonwhite subjects, since these were represented either inaccurately or not at all in the original sample.

The 1960 revision used a sample of approximately 4,500 subjects. There was no attempt to select a stratified sample, although every attempt was made to eliminate any major factor which would influence the result. Some items were excluded which tended to be obsolete or to be disproportionately answered correctly by subjects from certain income groups or certain regions of the country.

Figure 18–3 shows the items used in the standard Stanford-Binet test (1960 revision). The tasks include naming objects, putting blocks together into demonstrated shapes, noting which parts are absent from shapes (e.g., a finger missing from a hand), stringing beads, recognizing shapes, naming parts of the body, knowing the uses of objects, stating the relationship between objects, counting, recognizing verbal analogies, and interpreting proverbs.

Only a portion of the full test is given to any one subject. There is no need to administer all the items, for the purpose of the test is to discover the level at which the subject understands. Thus, the examiner commonly starts with items just below the level at which the subject is expected to operate. If the child answers these correctly, the examiner advances to more difficult items; if they are answered incorrectly, the examiner moves to a lower order of items. The level at which all tests are answered correctly is known as the *basal age;*

FIGURE 18–3: *The items used on the standard Stanford-Binet test to measure the general level of intelligence (1960 revision). (Courtesy of Houghton Mifflin Company, Boston.)*

the level at which all tests are answered incorrectly is the *ceiling age*. Thus, a seven-year-old child might have a basal age of 5 (denoting that he correctly answered all the items of the five-year-old level) and a ceiling age of 10 (denoting that he was able to answer at least one of the nine-year-old items but none of the ten-year-old items). There is not a sharp break between the basal and ceiling age. Most often, a child is able to answer some items in age levels more advanced than his chronological age, although he may be unable to answer some less advanced items. Mental age on the Stanford-Binet is computed by taking the basal age and adding to it "months" of credit for each additional test that is successfully completed.

One characteristic of this scoring procedure is that variability is a function of age. Thus, on the 1937 scale, an IQ of 100 at one age could correspond to an IQ of 105 at another age. Although this fact points out, once again, the necessity of understanding how scores are derived before interpreting them, it also makes clear the fact that in even such a well-developed test, the scores are relative, not absolute, indications of intelligence.

The reliability and validity of the Stanford-Binet have been assessed in numerous situations. It may be recalled that the 1937 test, in parallel forms, was administered in a counterbalanced design at intervals up to one week of intertest duration. One general statement that may be made from the test-retest reliabilities which this procedure provided is that the reliability, in terms of correlations, is higher (1) for older, as opposed to younger, subjects and (2) for subjects of lower IQ than for subjects of higher IQ. The correlations range upward from .8, and most are in the .9 to 1 range. The lower reliability for subjects of high IQs is not only a property of this test; it is a characteristic of most tests that use age as the major variable. The reasons for this are discussed by Anastasi (1961, p. 202) and Guilford (1954).

Academic achievement has been the criterion most often used for assessing measures of predictive and concurrent validity. Since the 1916 scale, these correlations have been reported to vary around .5 to .7. Bond (1940) reports the relationship between IQ score and the special type of academic achievement. For example, reading comprehension has a .73 correlation, although biology has a correlation of only .54. This is not surprising when we recall that the majority of items on the Stanford-Binet are of a verbal nature. Thus, it would be expected that the IQ score would correlate most highly with academic subjects which include verbal behavior. Correlations appear to be lower for college students—approximately .5 (Mitchell, 1943)—than for high school students. This finding probably reflects both the lower correlations which appear with high IQs discussed previously and the fact that the college population has less variation in IQ than the high school population. Moreover, it may reflect the importance of factors in addition to IQ, such as motivation, in college academic achievement.

Several long-term studies (Bradway, C. W. Thompson, & Cravens, 1958; Honzik, Macfarlane, & L. Allen, 1948) suggest strongly that although the reliability and validity of the Stanford-Binet, under the precise conditions described previously, are high, large increases or decreases in individual IQs over a period of time may be noted. IQ changes of as much as 50 points have been observed. In other cases, yearly increases or decreases have been observed. Moreover, there is ample evidence that the IQ score is related to training and experience. The sex differences in ability to answer certain items show that experience is an important factor. Larger than usual shifts in IQ are observed as a function of social and economic climate. There is no question that environmental factors influence IQ. Probably, the wisest conclusion is that IQ is a blend of innate factors and experience.

Special-aptitude Tests: The number of special-aptitude tests available is quite large. The tests vary from a test of color blindness to eliminate color-blind personnel from certain jobs where this deficiency would be troublesome to tests designed to measure artistic or musical ability. We have noted before the necessity of testing children for sensory disorders when there is evidence of unusual behavior or difficulties in speech and reading. Since these tests are most commonly used to spot deficiencies or to provide relatively quick information on job applicants, they tend to be designed for group testing and for quick administration and scoring.

In industry and in the military, special-aptitude tests are widely used for job placement. More appropriately, one should say that they are used for job exclusion; rarely does a test result indicate who should do which job. More often, the results indicate that certain persons would not do well at a particular job. In many positions, coordination is important, and a number of tests have been developed to measure various kinds of coordination. Similarly, tests may measure the ability to work with small parts, to sort objects according to size, or to place objects in particular places. Some special-aptitude tests are of the pencil and-paper variety; others are performance tests in the sense that the subject is required to perform the specific act, such as using tweezers to pick up small items.

One of the most widely used special aptitude tests is the *Seashore Measures of Musical Talents, Revised Edition* (C. E. Seashore, 1938; C. E. Seashore, D. Lewis, & Saetveit, 1960). This test has six parts; it measures pitch discrimination, loudness perception, rhythm, time, timbre, and tonal memory. The test is presented on phonograph records in order to assure standardization. It may be given as a group test. In many ways, the test is a psychophysical examination, for in the subtest the subject is presented with two tones and asked to indicate which is the higher (for pitch discrimination) or the louder (for loudness discrimination), whether one tone is played for a longer time than another (time test), whether the rhythms of two patterns are the same or different, whether two tones have different timbre qualities, and whether the subject can discriminate an altered tone in a sequence (tonal memory).

Each subtest is scored, and the subject's score is compared with norms and expressed in terms of percentiles. Reliability is approximately .55 to .85, using Kuder-Richardson. Content validity is assumed to be high, although it is important to note that the test is an examination of tonal sensitivity. It is reasonable to suppose that persons with good musical sensitivity would become better musicians than persons without such sensitivity, but the fact that one does have precise sensitivity hardly guarantees that one will, or can, become an accomplished musician. A few studies have used predictive validity and have found correlations which are generally low but positive (Lundin, 1953; Saetveit, D. Lewis, & C. E. Seashore, 1940).

Achievement Tests: Students are most familiar with achievement tests, and, not surprisingly, they tend to be extremely good critics of this kind of test construction. Achievement tests have a variety of uses besides that of assigning a grade to a student. They are often used to establish minimal performance levels in business and industry. The test that one takes to acquire a driver's license is an achievement test, for it is designed to determine whether one has enough information about driving to permit him to operate a car. If carefully designed and studied, the achievement tests used in the classroom may be used to indicate what a student has learned. In this way, although the test may be primarily a measure of the student's performance, the test results are a measure of the instructor's performance. One difficulty with achievement tests, especially as used in the classroom, is that there is often a long delay between the subject's selection of an answer and his being informed of whether he was right or wrong. This, of course, is the problem of knowledge of results or delay of reinforcement (Chapter 15). New techniques are being developed which permit immediate knowledge of results as a student takes a multiple-choice test.

One of the criticisms of achievement tests, especially the multiple-choice variety, is that the increasing use of such tests can lead to unwanted standardization of teaching procedures. That is, if a teacher's ability is evaluated by how well his students perform on a standardized achievement test, one would expect to find teachers teaching what they believe or know to be on the test, rather than what they think to be the essential matters of the course. Achievement tests, by their nature, tend to overemphasize certain attributes of course material. Moreover, not all kinds of subject matter are equally useful for conversion into achievement tests.

Achievement tests are usually evaluated by content validity. Thus in the construction of such a test it is vital that the items be given the most careful attention so that they do not evaluate irrelevant variables (such as reading speed).

Projective Tests: Projective tests may be arranged along a continuum of how projective they are. Unfortunately, the more projective tests, such as the Rorschach and the TAT, are difficult to explain in a textbook, for a proper understanding of their development and usefulness requires that the student have extensive practice with them. The *Tomkins-Horn Picture Arrangement Test* (PAT) which will serve as an example of a projective test, was developed as an attempt to make the TAT more amenable to objective interpretation. Its assumptions are identical to those of the more projective tests; however, it is also based on such useful experimental procedures as a sample of both normal and abnormal populations.

The PAT is designed for group testing and for machine scoring. It consists of 25 plates, each of which contains three pictures. Figure 18–4 shows a sample plate. The subject is asked to arrange the pictures in an order which he considers appropriate and to write a sentence regarding each picture. The pictures are identified by the triangle, circle, or

FIGURE 18-4: *One of the plates from the* Tomkins-Horn Picture Arrangement Test *(PAT). The subject is asked to arrange the three pictures in a meaningful order by placing the code number (triangle, circle, or rectangle) on the lines and writing a sentence regarding each picture (From Tomkins & J. B. Miner, 1957, p. 363.)*

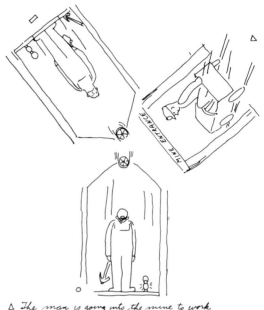

△ The man is going into the mine to work

○ He is going down the elevator of the mine shaft

□ He has finished his days work and going up the shaft

rectangle underneath each picture. Since each plate contains three pictures, six arrangements are possible. Since there are 25 plates, the number of possible combinations is 625. This number is sufficiently large that it would be rare for two individuals to arrange the pictures within all the plates the same way. If a test provided fewer alternatives, so that individuals did make identical arrangements, it would be likely that the test was not discriminating as well as possible. A test which, in effect, reports that two people are alike is obviously unable to assess all the characteristics of the individuals. The more different answers a test provides, however, the more diffi-

cult scoring becomes. The Rorschach, for example, permits an infinite number of answers. Thus, the scoring system has to be of a general nature in order to account for the various answers which may appear. The PAT provides for a large number of answers, but the number of arrangements is still sufficiently small that a scoring system may be developed.

The basic measure that the PAT provides is whether a particular arrangement on a specific plate is one usually or rarely made by persons of the same general level of intelligence, the same level of educational attainment, and the same age. Comparison may also be made on the basis of sex, marital status, religion, race, occupation of family head, occupation of the subject, class, rural or urban environment, and geographic location. The descriptive sentences required of the subjects were used originally by Tomkins and J. B. Miner (1957) to assess the adequacy of using the plates.

It often happens that two people will arrange the pictures within a given plate the same way. The important question, however, is whether these arrangements are indicative of personality traits. The arrangement a person selects contributes to *keys*. A key consists of several plates which have one or more characteristics in common. For example, the key for "high work" is composed of plates in which it is possible for the story to end with a scene depicting a working situation. The key for "restlessness" contains plates in which it is possible for the subject to arrange the pictures in such a way that one person is with a group, is alone, and is with a group again, or he is alone, with a group, and alone. For a plate to contribute to this key, there must be evidence that there have been distinct changes in socialization of an individual portrayed in the pictures. The keys are selected on the basis of common characteristics of the pictures. In all, there are 252 keys. Among the major keys are *sociophilia* (a preference for being with people, *sociophobia* (a preference for being alone), aggression, dependence, optimism, self-confidence, pessimism, hypochondriasis, high or low fantasy life, strong or weak affect, and high or low work endurance. Each key contains a set of subkeys, which may be understood most easily by the following example:

The major key entitled "general happy mood" is contributed to by seven arrangements. This key is defined as "a preference for, or expectation of, a happy mood or affect rather than unhappy mood or affect. This is indicated by a final situation in which the hero is shown laughing or smiling" (Tomkins & J. B. Miner, 1957, p. 125). The plates that make up this major key can be subdivided into three other keys, however: "a general happy mood in the non-work environ-

ment," "general happy mood in the work environment," and "general happy mood when alone." For interpretive reasons, it is as important to know for which keys a subject meets the requirements as it is to know for which he does not. For example, in the "general happy mood" keys, the behavior of the person who meets the requirements for "general happy mood when alone" and not for any of the other variants is clearly a different person from one who meets all the requirements of the "generally happy mood" keys.

The arrangement of the pictures within a particular plate is also considered in the analysis of this test. When a person arranges a plate in a way that is selected by less than 5 percent of his comparable population, that plate is considered a "plate rare." Table 18–A shows the percentage response frequencies for one of the PAT plates. The LOV (read rectangle, circle, triangle) combination is selected by 30.7 percent of the total sample; however, under the heading "class," we note that 19.7 percent of the lower class selected it compared with 30.4 percent of the middle class. The tables tell the scorer whether the responses to a particular plate may be considered rare.

In addition to data from the normal population, data were taken from approximately six hundred institutionalized persons with diagnoses ranging from organic conditions (such as brain damage) to schizophrenia. This sample provides information on the keys and "plate rares" which these individuals reach and permits a comparison of an individual's arrangements with arrangements provided by subjects for whom institutionalization is necessary.

Interpretation of the PAT, beyond computing "plate rares" and the keys which have been met, consists of working with the written comments of the subject and interpreting both sets of data clinically.

The problem of assessing the reliability of a test such as the PAT is that parallel forms are rarely available, and the typical split-half techniques are clearly inappropriate. Thus, the only procedure available for assessing relia-

TABLE 18-A: *Response Frequencies to One of the PAT Plates, Expressed as a Percentage of the Sample Population.* Background variables, such as age or religion, are placed along the first column at the left, and the percentage selecting each arrangement are shown in the right-hand columns. (From Tomkins and J. B. Miner, 1957, p. 180.)

Background variables	VOL	VLO	OLV	OVL	LVO	LOV
Education:						
0–6	7.8	24.9	15.6	8.7	13.3	29.8
7–8	8.2	23.4	16.0	8.7	16.9	26.7
9–11	11.8	27.4	13.5	4.7	12.2	30.4
12	7.5	24.6	15.3	3.9	13.8	34.8
13–15	10.3	23.4	18.7	3.7	13.1	30.9
16+	5.7	18.2	19.3	3.4	18.2	35.2
Sex:						
Male	9.2	25.5	16.4	5.5	16.0	27.2
Female	8.1	23.3	15.0	6.8	12.8	33.9
Marital status:						
Married	8.9	23.0	15.8	6.7	15.5	30.1
Single	8.0	27.8	13.4	5.1	11.0	34.6
Widowed	10.8	25.6	17.4	7.4	14.9	24.0
Religion:						
Protestant	9.1	23.3	15.1	6.4	15.4	30.7
Catholic	9.2	27.2	16.0	6.8	9.9	30.9
Jewish	2.0	28.6	22.4	0.0	16.3	30.6
Age:						
10–13	4.9	28.7	12.3	6.6	14.0	33.6
14–17	14.2	28.3	12.4	4.4	9.7	31.0
18–24	8.5	26.8	12.2	1.8	10.4	40.2
25–34	8.9	26.0	16.0	6.4	15.7	27.1
35–44	8.3	20.5	16.7	6.8	15.5	32.2
45–54	9.3	23.6	16.4	7.6	12.4	30.7
55–64	9.2	21.9	18.4	8.6	14.4	27.6
65+	6.6	24.3	17.8	5.9	19.7	25.7
Race:						
White	8.1	23.7	16.1	5.9	14.8	31.3
Negro	13.5	31.1	11.5	8.8	10.1	25.0
Occupation of family head:						
Professional	5.7	27.6	13.0	4.1	19.5	30.1
Farmers	10.0	22.2	15.0	6.1	13.3	33.3
Managers	8.6	26.7	15.5	6.0	12.1	31.0
Clerical	8.1	24.3	18.9	6.3	13.5	28.8
Sales	5.8	21.4	18.4	4.9	9.7	39.8
Skilled	7.8	26.9	16.3	6.5	12.6	29.8
Operatives	9.7	22.3	16.2	6.1	14.6	31.1
Service	9.2	24.4	13.7	7.6	18.3	26.7
Laborers	11.5	25.7	14.9	8.1	15.5	24.3

Background variables	VOL	VLO	OLV	OVL	LVO	LOV
Occupation of respondent:						
Professional, managers, farmers	9.7	24.9	17.3	4.3	18.4	25.4
Clerical, sales	6.7	25.2	17.8	7.4	11.9	31.1
Skilled	5.1	31.6	17.3	4.1	14.3	27.5
Operatives	12.8	17.9	16.7	7.1	15.4	30.1
Service, laborers	7.9	28.1	17.1	7.3	14.6	25.0
Housewives	8.3	21.5	15.2	7.2	13.2	34.7
Students	8.8	27.9	11.6	5.6	11.6	34.7
Retired	8.8	26.3	15.8	3.5	24.6	21.0
Class:						
Upper	15.2	19.6	19.6	10.9	10.9	23.9
Middle	8.5	25.9	18.1	3.2	13.8	30.4
Working	8.3	23.4	14.1	7.5	14.7	32.0
Lower	6.6	29.5	14.8	11.5	18.0	19.7
Rural-urban:						
Farm	12.2	23.2	15.3	7.0	13.5	28.8
Under 2,500	7.1	19.7	18.1	8.1	15.2	32.0
2,500–9,999	5.9	24.9	18.3	7.8	13.1	30.1
10,000–49,999	9.2	19.3	13.5	5.8	15.9	36.2
50,000–499,999	11.3	30.5	13.6	4.5	17.0	23.0
500,000+	6.4	30.3	14.8	3.8	10.6	34.1
Geographical:						
New England	6.5	29.0	21.5	7.5	15.1	20.4
Middle Atlantic	6.7	28.0	17.5	3.5	10.5	33.6
East Central	10.0	24.0	13.3	6.6	18.5	27.7
West Central	8.4	24.7	17.4	4.5	10.7	34.3
Border South	9.4	23.7	12.4	6.0	15.8	32.7
Deep South	5.7	26.4	15.1	7.5	15.1	30.2
Rocky Mountain	4.8	17.7	19.0	8.2	17.0	33.3
Pacific Coast	16.0	21.3	12.7	10.7	14.0	25.3
Intelligence:						
−79	8.4	24.4	18.3	9.2	15.3	24.4
80–90	12.6	25.1	8.8	9.6	14.2	29.7
91–110	8.2	25.3	15.6	5.9	14.4	30.6
111–119	6.8	24.5	21.5	3.4	11.8	32.1
120+	8.2	19.3	15.6	4.5	17.0	35.6
Total sample	8.7	24.5	15.7	6.2	14.3	30.7

bility is the test-retest method. We have noted previously that one characteristic of the test-retest method is that it assumes that the subject actually does not change during the interval and that the characteristic being measured does not vary. Therefore, any differences in scores of the two tests is attributed to errors in measurement of the test. It is possible, however, that some of the recorded error is due to changes in the behavior patterns of the individual taking the test. Tomkins and J. B. Miner (1957) retested a group of male college freshmen, some after three weeks and some after three years. In the three-week group, 33 percent of the responses were changed; in the three-year group 45 percent of the responses were changed. The distribution of choices remained almost the same, however. This finding suggests that although individuals changed their selections, for each subject who shifted away from a particular response, another subject shifted toward it, thus leaving the group means similar. Thus, for any given individual, the test-retest reliability is not high, but this may only mean that the characteristics being tested by the PAT are apt to change in time.

The assessment of validity of the test provides far more difficult problems than the measurement of reliability. As the authors of the test state, "The PAT was not designed to differentiate the variety of levels of psychological function with respect to all content areas. Therefore, one frequently can not tell whether a rare response indicates a wish, an expectation, or overt behavior" (Tomkins & J. B. Miner, 1957, p. 31). Said another way, it is difficult to construct a measure of the validity of a test unless we can specify what it is that the test purports to measure. Although one can assess validity by comparing overt behavior with test results, it is somewhat more difficult to measure fantasies and wishes. One individual might score high on the "high-work" key because he has just been warned that unless he produces, he will be fired, and another individual might score high on the same key because he is a very hard worker and

identifies himself with the person in the plate. Thus, little is known about the validity of the PAT.

The PAT represents, to an appreciable degree, an unusual test. It is projective in the sense that the subject is asked to arrange stimuli in whatever order he chooses, yet it is scorable through objective means. Its difficulties are clear: the reliability is not very high, and the validity is almost untestable. Nevertheless, it uses an adequate sample of the population for comparison and includes data on abnormal samples.

SOURCES

Although textbooks often separate the theory of tests from the practical aspects of giving tests, I have tried to emphasize that an understanding of tests requires knowledge of both the theory and application of the materials.

A number of texts on testing are available. The reader will find F. S. Freeman (1962) and Anastasi (1961) to be valuable. The former provides the greater amount of information on theory. Gulliksen (1950) presents a text devoted entirely to theory, and although the mathematics may at first seem difficult, a careful reading of the work shows this fear to be groundless. Gulliksen devotes appreciable attention to the problem of estimating reliability and validity, as does Guilford (1954) in his work on psychometric methods. I have made no attempt to discuss many of the subtle formulations available to the tester: rather, I have attempted to show the flavor and capacities of the theory of test construction by providing information on some of the most commonly used techniques.

History: F. S. Freeman (1962) and Anastasi (1961) have sections on the development of the testing movement. The most detailed discussion is provided by Boring (1950), who, in his thorough and charming fashion, shows how the movement developed and the influence it has had on psychology. This section is strongly recommended to the reader who wishes to understand tests in a historical context.

Types of Reliability and Validity: Gulliksen (1950) appears to be the most solid work in this field, although the years since its publication have produced different methods. Articles of professional quality appear in a number of journals, including *Psychometrika*.

Types of Tests: There are many tests, some of which are good and some bad. Buros's *The Sixth Mental Measurements Yearbook* (1964) is the best source for material on tests. The reader must be especially careful to ignore the title given a test and to pay strict attention to the ways in which validity has been assessed. Put another way, the question is not what the author of a test calls it but what the test actually tests. Unfortunately, many of the reviews which appear in Buros are short; however, they certainly provide the reader with general information about a given test. Both F. S. Freeman (1962) and Anastasi (1961) discuss a number of tests in detail. H. H. Anderson and G. L. Anderson (1951) have edited a book on projective tests. Each chapter is concerned with the theory, administration, and interpretation of a particular test.

We have noted, in the text, two criticisms of tests (Hoffmann, 1962; Gross, 1962). If read critically, Hoffmann's and Gross's books are valuable for two reasons: (1) to discover whether the objections are truly valid and (2) to note the types of confusion which may appear when the concepts of reliability, validity, and test construction are not fully appreciated.

CHAPTER NINETEEN

SOCIAL BEHAVIOR

BY RICHARD V. WAGNER

INTRODUCTION

The studies discussed in previous chapters are concerned with the relationship between the individual and his environment. Much of man's environment, however, is made up of other human beings, and much of his behavior is influenced by others. Indeed, it is difficult to find examples of human behavior that do not occur in *social context*, i.e., in the real or imagined presence of other persons.

The physician's slap on the baby's bottom is one of the first of a long and complex series of social stimuli to which the individual is subjected throughout life. Other people are involved in almost every nonreflexive response the individual makes. Often these people provide stimuli directly. The mother, for example, stimulates the child directly by offering her breast, to which the child responds by sucking, reflexively at first, purposefully later, or she may speak to him in a harsh voice, to which he responds by inhibiting a particular behavior. Sometimes the stimuli are contiguous to other stimuli and become associated with them. For example, the mother is usually present when the baby receives his bottle or when his diaper is changed; here, the important stimulus, from the child's point of view, is not the mother but the bottle and the removal of the unpleasant stimulus of a wet diaper. Through the principles of learning, the mother becomes associated with "bottle" and "removal of wet diaper" and ultimately comes to evoke many of the same responses that they do.

In industrialized countries today, few individuals work alone in the field or shop. We are constantly in contact with others. Even when no one is physically present, we sometimes behave in an environment of "imagined others," as if others were present.

Often the responses we make to other people then become stimuli for *them:* for example, A sees B and reacts to him; B notes this reaction and responds in turn; this causes a further response by A; and so on in a cyclic pattern of social behavior. Since social stimuli and the cyclic nature of interpersonal behavior are so pervading, it is appropriate that a discussion of the experimental approach of psychology should conclude with a discussion of social behavior.

For the purposes of this chapter, we shall define *social stimuli* as people or the acts of people, real or imagined, and *social behavior* as behavior in response to social stimuli. *Social interaction* will be used to refer to the cyclic pattern of social behavior described in the preceding paragraph.

The social psychologist is principally concerned with applying general scientific procedures and methodology, where possible, to the study of social stimuli, social behavior, and social interaction. This concern has led him to two different types of analysis, one in which he focuses on the *individual's* behavior in a social context and a second in which he concentrates on *group* behavior itself. As will be demonstrated in the next two sections, he generally applies one type of methodology to the study of the individual and another to the study of groups.

The Study of Individual Behavior in a Social Context: The investigation of individual behavior in a social context necessarily involves the consideration of social stimuli and social behavior. The analysis of social behavior is primarily a matter of categorizing and describing the types of behavior—aggression, affiliation, domination, etc.—that occur in social situations. The more critical analysis is of the social stimuli that evoke social behavior. Consequently, the social psychologist is interested in discovering what differences there are, if any, between objects and persons as "stimuli." When he discovers these, he applies general scientific procedures to the investigation of the effect of social stimuli on social behavior. Most social psychologists believe that, in a broad sense, the differences between social and object stimuli are differences of degree. One such difference is the degree of complexity of the relevant stimulus characteristics of object and social stimuli. There are, for example, few objects so complex as the human face.

The number of different facial expressions is almost unlimited, and each minute change in expression can produce a completely new stimulus configuration for a perceiver to respond to. Some of the cues in stimulus configurations are obvious and easily interpreted, such as a broad grin or a yawn. Others, such as a slightly raised eyebrow or a brief sardonic smile, are more subtle and may produce a stimulus configuration that is more difficult to detect and decipher. Of course, some objects are just as confounding as a face; an automobile may be comprehensible only to a garage mechanic. But the crucial factor is that the human face—a critical part of *every* social stimulus—presents a high degree of complexity, whereas the majority of objects have few or no complex stimulus characteristics.

A second difference between object and social stimuli is that the social stimulus is a human being and thus has many characteristics which the perceiver has but which an object obviously does not have. "Similarity" between stimulus and perceiver is an extremely complicated topic about which very little is known. Some phenomena relevant to the topic are empathy, sympathy, and the Freudian concept of identification: apparently, because of the social stimulus–perceiver similarity, the perceiver may respond to other people in a way that he seldom, if ever, responds to objects. We empathize and our leg "hurts" when we see someone kicked in the shins, but we feel no particular pain when a glass falls on the floor and breaks. We sympathize and feel "sorry" when we see a person whose face has been injured, but we do not feel sorry for the demolished car in which he was riding. And we often identify with, and unwittingly imitate, the behavior of persons we admire, but we do not usually attempt to emulate an admirable work of art.

A related issue is the fact that social stimuli have *eyes*—they can look back. Hence, the perceiver *knows*, consciously or unconsciously, that his response to a social stimulus can, in turn, be a stimulus to the perceived. Some persons, as stimuli, may present themselves in a particular way—for example, via a specific facial expression—in order to evoke a certain response by the perceiver or, if they are uncertain of what response may be forthcoming, in order to gain knowledge about the perceiver's reaction to particular stimuli. If the perceiver suspects that the person-stimulus is playing such a "game," his response to the stimulus may be altered to account for this possibility.

Parenthetically, it should be noted that this discussion of differences between object and social stimuli does not treat the question of differences between human beings and other animals as stimuli. One can argue that some nonhuman animals are as complex as human beings, that they are similar enough to human beings to evoke sympathetic and empathetic responses from human beings, and that they too have eyes and are capable of causing human beings to respond to them as if they were a part of the perceived-being-the-perceiver cycle. Where to place nonhuman animals as stimuli in relation to objects and persons is a question that we raise but leave unanswered.

Social Interaction and Small-group Behavior: Although the social psychologist acknowledges the importance of studying a particular social stimulus and a person's response to it, his attention has focused even more on social interaction, the cyclic pattern of stimulus-response sequences. Consequently, much of his interest has been on the analysis of *small-group behavior.*

What is a *small* group? Most social psychologists feel that a small group is one in which every member is aware of the individuality of every other member. This criterion excludes aggregates such as movie audiences or spectators at a sporting event, because they are too large for persons to become acquainted with one another's characteristics. It also rules out smaller aggregates of people who, for one reason or another, do not get to know one another in spite of the opportunity to do so. People in an elevator *could,* by this definition, become a small group, but generally they do not. Should the elevator break down, the individuals would almost inevitably begin to communicate and thus be transformed into a small group.

The distinction between the analysis of an *individual's* social stimulus–response behavior and social interaction in a small group is analogous to the distinction between the ultimate unit of analysis of the stucturalists and the gestaltists within the field of perception: a small group is "greater than the sum of its individual members" (Chapter 9). A description of the characteristics of each individual member is not sufficient to describe the group's characteristics or its behavior. This difference between "the group" and "the individual members of the group" can be discussed on both a conceptual and an empirical level.

Conceptually, a number of characteristics attributed to small groups are meaningless when applied to the individual. For example, groups can be described in terms of their power structure, that is, patterns of influence of the members upon one another. Consider a situation in which person A influences person B. Knowing that B responds to A in certain predictable ways may be meaningful, but it far from represents complete knowledge of their relationship, because the type of influence B receives from A may depend on A's perception of B's acceptance of the influence (e.g., does B accept it graciously or grudgingly?). The situation becomes even more complex when we add a third person C to the group. Perhaps A must receive permission from C before attempting to influence B. Or perhaps B and C can unite to withstand the pressure from A.

The application of the concept of power structure, along with many similar concepts which we shall describe later, is very useful in the analysis of small-group interaction but relatively meaningless in the analysis of a given individual's response to an isolated social stimulus.

Most research has indicated that group performance is superior to individual performance. M. Goldman (1965) compared group and individual performance on a task for which the subjects had varying abilities. He selected subjects of high (H), medium (M), and low (L) ability on the basis of their performance on one form of an intelligence test. Then he composed six types of two-person groups of various combinations of H, M, and L subjects (i.e., HH, MM, LL, HM, HL, and ML). He instructed each pair to complete a parallel form of the same intelligence test, to discuss, and to reach a mutual solution to each item. Comparisons of the scores of the pairs, both with their own previous scores on the first form of the test and with those of a random group of H, M, and L subjects who had taken both forms of the test individually, showed that subjects improved significantly more when working in pairs than when working as individuals. This was true even of the person who had performed very well on the first test and who had to work with a low performer on the second. This type of study suggests that, through a complex process of original ability, interstimulation, and convincing, groups are more likely to produce correct solutions to problems than are individuals. This is one empirical demonstration that the sum of individual characteristics does not describe a group. A further demonstration of this principle is Goldman's finding that two high performers working together *do not* improve their scores significantly more than a high and a low performer working together; if characteristics were additive, then one would find that a pair composed of two high performers would produce a single result significantly superior to that of a high and a low performer working together.

Although we have suggested the usefulness of studying social stimuli qua stimuli, we shall, in this chapter, concentrate on the study of social interaction in small groups. The chapter is limited in this way because individual social behavior is generally studied using the experimental procedures previously described in this book. Many of the concepts employed to describe different characteristics of social behavior have appeared previously (for example,

social motives such as the need for achievement, discussed in Chapters 17 and 18). Some of the instruments used to measure social variables have also appeared before (for example, the TAT, various checklists, and rating scales, discussed in Chapters 17 and 18). Investigations of variables related to small-group behavior, however, require methodology somewhat different from that described in previous chapters, primarily because individual social variables cannot be isolated from the context of the group and still maintain their original meaning. One cannot discuss a person's conformity, for example, without knowing his position in the group power structure, the sanctions the group can use against him, and the group's collective values.

General Techniques for Studying Small-group Behavior: In their extensive review of research conducted on small-group behavior in recent years, McGrath and Altman report that "in the last three decades at least 2,500 small group studies have been conducted and reported, and the rate of production appears to be accelerating.... Studies vary widely in rigor and methodological sophistication all the way from case studies, almost anecdotal in form, to highly complex programs of experimentation on extensive samples of groups" (1966, p. 67).

Four general types of experimental techniques are used in the study of small groups: *survey, field study, field experiment,* and *laboratory experiment.* These techniques may be evaluated in terms of a choice between minimizing artificiality and maximizing control. The more realistic the experimental setting, the less control the experimenter has over the variables, and thus the less certain he is that his results are a function of his experimental manipulations. Conversely, the greater the control, the less realistic is the setting, and hence the less generalizable are the results to similar situations in everyday life (see Chapter 1). In this section, we shall discuss the techniques and indicate the advantages and disadvantages of each.

SURVEY: Survey research involves the collection of descriptive information about people, typically by interviews or from documents and records compiled for other purposes. Usually surveys are designed to gather descriptions of a large number of people or variables. The data may range from facts and figures about the behavioral or demographic characteristics of persons (e.g., income, occupation, religion) to the attitudes, values, or beliefs they express to interviewers about a variety of people, objects, ideas, or events. The purpose of survey research may be simply to accumulate descriptive information about a representative sample of people at a given time.

D. R. Miller and Swanson (1958) used the survey to investigate the relationship between child-rearing practices and the type of employment of fathers. They interviewed 582 families in Detroit, Michigan, questioning the parents about how they raised their children (e.g., age at which children were weaned, specific type of punishment used in disciplining) and the nature of the father's occupation (e.g., what occupation, self-employed or not). They categorized occupations in two ways: (1) the position of the occupation in the social class hierarchy (professional and technical workers, managers, officials, and proprietors were considered upper middle class, clerical and sales workers were lower middle class, and so on); (2) the degree of "bureaucratization" of the occupation (a father was considered "entrepreneurial" if he was self-employed, gained half his income from profits, fees, or commissions, or was employed in an organization having two levels of supervision; he was classified "bureaucratic" if he worked for a salary in an organization having more than two levels of supervision).

The main predictions of Miller and Swanson were that children raised in entrepreneurial homes would be "encouraged to be highly rational, to exercise great self-control, to be self-reliant, and to assume an active, manipulative stance toward their environment" (1958, p. 57) and that those from bureaucratic homes would be encouraged "to be accommodative, to allow their impulses some spontaneous expression, and to seek direction from the organizational programs in which they participate" (1958, p. 58). These predictions were based on the assumption that parents involved in entrepreneurial occupations succeed if they are rational, self-reliant, and manipulate their environment, while those in bureaucratic employment progress if they are accommodative and do not actively attempt to manipulate others in the organization. Miller and Swanson expected that these occupational styles of life would generalize to the training of the children. They believed that feeding babies on schedule, early urinary and bowel training, and the use of symbolic rather than direct punishments (e.g., telling the child he had been bad, as opposed to spanking him) reflected attempts to help the child develop internal controls of behavior. Therefore, they predicted, correctly, that these practices would be more prevalent in entrepreneurial than in bureaucratic families.

Surveys may also be used to study the complex problem of the change in, or the development of, attitudes, values, perceptions, or behavior over long periods. Most of the analyses of consumer behavior fall in this category, as do many of the studies of voting behavior (cf., Katona, 1960; A. Campbell, Gurin, & W. E. Miller, 1954; A. Campbell, Converse, W. E. Miller, & Stokes, 1960).

As a methodology, the survey is not a very useful technique for studying small-group behavior, because descriptive data generally tell us very little about the actual processes of social interaction. But the survey may be valuably used to obtain suggestions about the nature of important variables involved in a topic the experimenter plans to investigate more intensively in the future. The 1958 study by D. R. Miller and Swanson is a case in point: two years later these investigators published an analysis of sociological and sociopsychological determinants of a person's use of particular mechanisms of defense against conflict (D. R. Miller & Swanson, 1960). Much of this latter research was derived from their 1958 survey study of social determinants of child-rearing practices.

Another example of the heuristic value of surveys is the series of studies of voting behavior conducted by Lazarsfeld and his associates (Lazarsfeld, Berelson, & Gaudet, 1944; Berelson, Lazarsfeld, & McPhee, 1954). These studies indicate a strong positive relationship between the voting preferences of an individual and those of his family. Although this does not seem to be surprising at first glance, it becomes significant when one looks at the data concerning persons who changed their voting intentions during the course of the political campaign. In the 1940 presidential elections, for example, only 3 percent of the subjects whose families were in unanimous agreement about their presidential choice changed their preferences between May and November of that year. However, 29 percent of those whose families were in disagreement with the respondent's preferred candidate in May switched their allegiances to the family's choice by November. In many cases, the persons who changed their choice did so in opposition to the preferences of other groups to which they belonged, such as friends and coworkers.

This is suggestive information about the influence one small (and crucial) group has on the individual member's behavior. The data imply that some small groups are more influential than others—in this case, the family is more influential than friends and coworkers. The need for an investigation of the differential characteristics of small groups became obvious because of these survey data.

The principal role of the survey in the analysis of small groups is an exploratory one. The survey method has certain liabilities, however. One is the lack of control over the variables examined. The researcher must be content with very general, suggestive data, and he learns either to tolerate the possibility that the relationships he finds between variables may be spurious or to reexamine the variables in another context in which he can control

them. The Lazarsfeld data, interesting as they were in their own right, were essentially a base from which other investigators examined the complex issues involving the family as a critical instance of small-group dynamics.

Similarly, there are questions about the quality of the information gathered in surveys. Misrepresentation of the truth by the subjects in any number of ways, from outright lying to subtle distortions, invalidates the data. In fact, a respondent's simple errors in memory can be a major nuisance to the survey researcher. Studies of child-rearing practices, such as those of D. R. Miller and Swanson, often rely upon parental recall of past treatment of their children. Most parents find it very difficult to report such treatment accurately, owing to the passage of time and, possibly, selective distortion of a potentially emotional topic.

Another limitation appears when the investigator attempts to make predictions about behavior on the basis of the subjects' stated attitudes. It is now generally accepted that people do not necessarily act in accord with their stated attitudes and hence prediction of consequent behavior is sometimes very unreliable. La Piere (1934) illuminated this problem. He and a Chinese couple traveled around the United States, stopping at numerous restaurants and hotels. Service was refused them only once. Later La Piere sent a questionnaire to the establishments asking whether they would accommodate Chinese guests. Slightly more than 50 percent of the questionnaires were returned. Over 90 percent of the respondents indicated that they would *refuse* service to Chinese persons. This simple study points out very clearly that it is a dangerous practice to make conclusions about behavior merely on the basis of the attitudes a person expresses. Despite these limitations, the survey technique for gathering information has been an asset to the sociopsychological study of groups.

FIELD STUDY: A field study is conducted in a natural setting. The researcher gathers his data in relative detail, according to general experimental procedures. He has no control over the variables, however, and therefore does not disrupt ongoing social processes. In essence, the experimenter takes advantage of a situation in which the variables are manipulated for him by natural circumstances (Chapter 1).

An illustration of a field study is Lieberman's analysis (1956) of the effects of role changes on a person's attitudes. He investigated changes in the attitudes toward management of industrial workers who were promoted to the position of foreman or elected as union stewards. He began by measuring the attitudes of all the workers at a particular plant. Within a year, 23 of the men were made foremen, and 35 were elected union stewards. With the

explanation of improving and updating his original questionnaire, Lieberman retested these 58 subjects and an equal number of persons whose positions had not changed. His results indicated that the new foremen had become significantly more promanagement and the stewards only slightly more prounion.

An economic recession ensued shortly after Lieberman's second survey. As a result of the recession and other factors, 8 of the foremen and 14 of the stewards were demoted to their original positions. Although the sample was small, Lieberman immediately prepared a survey to test the stability of the attitude change he had noted previously. His third test of those workers still employed by the company (Tables 19–A and 19–B) indicated that the workers-

TABLE 19–A: *Effects of Entering and Leaving the Foreman Role on Attitudes toward Management and Union.*
(Lieberman, 1956, p. 396.)

Attitude	Workers who became foremen and stayed foremen,* percent with attitude			Workers who became foremen and were later demoted,† percent with attitude		
	(W)‡ 1951	(F)‡ 1952	(F) 1954	(W) 1951	(F) 1952	(W) 1954
Rockwell is a good place to work	33	92	100	25	75	50
Management officers really care about the workers at Rockwell	8	33	67	0	25	0
Union should not have more say in setting labor standards	33	100	100	13	63	13
Satisfied with way incentive system works out at Rockwell	17	75	75	25	50	13
Worker's standard will not be changed just because he is a high producer	42	83	100	25	63	75
Ability should count more than seniority in promotions	33	58	75	25	50	38

* Total number of workers who became and remained foremen = 12.
† Total number of workers who became foremen and were later demoted = 8.
‡ W = Worker; F = Foreman

TABLE 19–B: *Effects of Entering and Leaving the Steward Role on Attitudes toward Management and Union.*
(Lieberman, 1956, p. 397.)

Attitude	Workers who were elected stewards and were later reelected,* percent with attitude			Workers who were elected stewards but were not later reelected,† percent with attitude		
	(W)‡ 1951	(S)‡ 1952	(S) 1954	(W) 1951	(S) 1952	(W) 1954
Rockwell is a good place to work	50	0	0	29	79	36
Management officers really care about the workers at Rockwell	0	0	0	14	14	0
Union should not have more say in setting labor standards	0	17	0	14	14	14
Satisfied with way incentive system works out at Rockwell	17	17	0	43	43	21
Worker's standard will not be changed just because he is a high producer	50	50	17	21	43	36
Ability should count more than seniority in promotions	67	17	17	36	36	21

* Total number of workers who were elected stewards and were later reelected = 6.
† Total number of workers who were elected stewards but later not reelected = 14.
‡ W = Worker; S = Steward

foremen-workers reverted to their original evaluations of management and union and that there was no consistent change in the attitudes of the workers-stewards-workers.

Lieberman suggests that the attitudes of the workers-foremen-workers changed much more than those of the workers-stewards-workers because of the greater discrepancy between the worker and foreman roles than between the worker and steward roles. The foremen worked full time in their new positions, while the stewards performed union duties only a few hours a week, spending the majority of their time operating in their previous worker positions. In addition, the foremen had to relinquish their union membership, while the stewards, of course, did not. Both these facts support Lieberman's contention that because of the dramatic difference between their old and new roles, the foremen had to change their attitudes to facilitate their adjustment to their new positions. The stewards, on the other hand, faced only minor changes in their roles and therefore had no need to reorient their evaluations of management or unions in order to perform their new duties adequately.

Lieberman has provided us with an excellent illustration of a field study. He can argue almost incontrovertibly that his presence as an experimenter had no important effect on the natural proceedings in the plant. He incorporated the administration of the attitude tests as a part of the normal procedures of industrial operations. He bided his time and let the "natural" changes in roles occur, and then gathered the critical data. He manipulated no variables but let the normal sequence of events manipulate them for him. This is probably as close as an experimenter can come to a study in which the experimental procedure has no effect on the group's usual behavior. Although it is conceivable that a survey might have provided a broad description of attitudes if conducted in a series of settings similar to Lieberman's, it seems very unlikely that it could have gathered this information in the detail provided by the field study.

The advantages of the field study are, then, the possibility of greater analytic depth than in a survey and the absence of a disruption of existing natural social processes. There is one important disadvantage, however. Because the experimenter has no control over the experimental situation, he is limited in the precision with which he can measure and manipulate variables; hence, he is less certain about the parameters of these variables and less certain of the lack of confounding or extraneous influences on his dependent variables. One could argue that a possible drawback to Lieberman's study was his lack of control over the process by which foremen and stewards return to workers' positions, which may have been a function of their deviant attitudes. Perhaps the foremen who were the least promanagement were the first to be demoted, and the stewards who were least clearly prounion were the ones not reelected. It is possible, then, that Lieberman's results had little to do with role change. Despite such limitations, field studies are very valuable as explorations of a topic and as confirmations in a natural setting of the generalizability of results of studies conducted under the controls available in a laboratory setting.

FIELD EXPERIMENT: In a field experiment, the investigation takes place in a natural setting, just as in the field study, but the experimenter has some control over the variables tested. An example is reported by M. Sherif (1958). He chose a summer camp for boys as the setting for his investigation of the formation and reduction of intergroup hostility. Intergroup tension or conflict was introduced by having the two groups into which the camp was divided compete in sports and games. Presumably as a result of this competition, the boys developed positive feelings toward members of their own group and negative feelings toward those in the other group.

Once the intergroup hostility had become stable, Sherif introduced two methods of reducing the tension: first, he allowed the groups to have a great deal of contact in favorable circumstances, such as at movies, at meals, and in noncompetitive recreational activities; second, he introduced several critical situations in which both groups would profit if they worked together and both would suffer if they did not. Sherif describes one of these "crises" in these words: "One day the two groups went on an outing at a lake some distance away. A large truck was to go to town for food. But when everyone was hungry and ready to eat, it developed that the truck would not start (we had taken care of that). The boys got a rope—the same rope they had used in their acrimonious tug-of-war—and all pulled together to start the truck" (1956, p. 58).

As Sherif predicted, the first means of reducing intergroup rivalry had little effect; the boys continued to push and shove members of the other group despite being engaged in pleasant, noncompetitive activities. On the other hand, the introduction of a series of *superordinate goals,* that is, situations in which neither group could succeed without a cooperative effort, had an enormous tension-reducing effect. In this second type of activity, group barriers dissolved, and the groups became unified.

Sherif's study has all the qualities of a field experiment: the setting was a natural one for the subjects; they were unaware that they were being manipulated by their counselors; and the experimenter had control over the variables introduced, such as amount of contact and nature of activities.

Generally, the field experiment combines the advantages of the field study (a natural setting) with general experimental procedures (control over variables). These positive qualities make it a very profitable experimental technique. One disadvantage of this type of experiment stems from the difficulties of finding a setting where one can establish the controls necessary for isolating the relevant experimental variables. Leaders of industries, school systems, or camps are understandably hesitant to permit the kinds of changes essential to a field experiment. The fact that some semblance of "naturalness" must be maintained in such a setting means that the experimenter can never be certain of the degree to which unexpected natural events may develop and disrupt his experiment. In the study of industrial groups, changes in labor legislation or major management-labor disputes might or might not produce tension in the group and obfuscate the effects of the experimental variables on the group's behavior.

LABORATORY EXPERIMENT: In a laboratory experiment, the investigator studies small-group behavior in an artificial setting—the laboratory. Generally, such studies are designed to isolate a few variables and examine them with as much precision and control as possible.

Many observers of industrial settings have noticed that the lines of communication affect the productivity of groups and the personal satisfaction of members of these groups. In order to study communication patterns, several investigators (e.g., Leavitt, 1951; Mulder, 1960) have used an apparatus in which the subjects' opportunities to communicate with one another are controlled by the experimenter.

In Leavitt's study five subjects were placed around a circular table with partitions between them, so that they could not see one another (see Figure 19–1). A large, thick pole, to which the partitions were attached, stood in the center of the table and was the site of message slots. Each compartment had eight slots in the center pole which allowed each subject to send and receive written notes from those in other compartments. By placing tape over particular slots, the experimenter could control who communicated with whom.

Leavitt compared the effects of four different communication patterns on group performance and on the satisfaction of members. Figure 19–2 shows these four patterns: (1) a circle, in which each subject can send messages to the two subjects sitting on either side of him; (2) a Y, in which one of the five subjects (C) can send and receive from three others, another (D) with two others, and the remaining three (A, B, and E) with only one other person; (3) a wheel, in which one subject (C) can exchange notes with all others, although all other subjects can exchange only with him; and (4) a chain, in which three subjects (B, C, and D) can communicate with two others, and the remaining two with only one other. Other variations are possible, of course, such as the "all-channels-open" situation (all subjects can communicate with one another), or directional patterns (not all the links are reciprocal—e.g., A can send to B, but B cannot send to A).

To study the effects of these patterns on group performance, Leavitt gave the groups a series of tasks. In a typical task each subject is given a list of words, and the group must discover which words all members have in common. The task is completed when every member of the group has the correct answer. Generally, Leavitt found that in the wheel and Y patterns work was more quickly completed and there were fewer changes in the organization of tasks than in the circle pattern. He attributes these results to there being greater centralization in the wheel and the Y than in the circle. By centralization Leavitt meant that fewer messages are needed to collect and distribute information to all members of the group. In the wheel, for example, C collects from A, B, D, and E simultaneously, decides on the correct answer, and immediately sends this information back to each of them. In the circle, however, information from A and E must go through another person before it gets

FIGURE 19–1: *Apparatus used for study of communication patterns.*

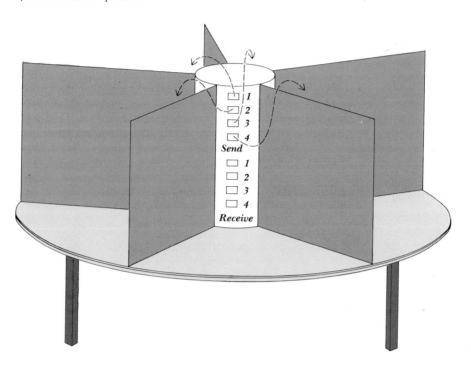

to *C* (assuming he has been chosen leader) and must go through an intermediary again before *A* and *E* receive the correct answer. The wheel requires fewer steps for collection and dissemination of information than does the circle. Hence, the wheel is more centralized than the circle.

In addition, Leavitt noted that member participation was directly related to centrality: person *C* in the wheel, the Y, and the chain sent and received the most communications and tended to emerge as the leader. Finally, Leavitt noted that member satisfaction is related to degree of centrality: in the wheel, person *C* enjoys the work very much, the other four much less so; in the Y, person *C* is the most satisfied, *D* the next, then *A* and *B*, and finally, *E*. Apparently, feeling that one is participating in completing the task is a determinant of satisfaction with one's work.

This study yields a variety of results, and the experimenter can be reasonably certain that they reflect differences in communication patterns more than other factors, such as inherent ability of members or the nature of the task. What he *cannot* say is that one can generalize from the laboratory directly to an industrial or military setting. Some clues about the relationship between communication and performance are available, but someone will have to apply these clues in the field in order to increase certainty of their value.

SMALL-GROUP BEHAVIOR

The study of small-group behavior is very complex, primarily because the majority of the relevant factors may be considered both independent and dependent variables. To facilitate

FIGURE 19-2: *Communication networks used in Leavitt's research. (Leavitt, 1951, p. 42.)*

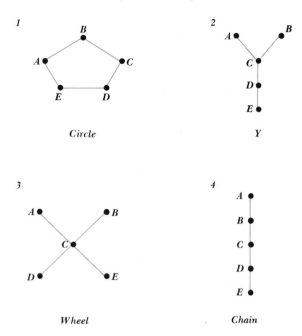

the exposition in the following pages, let us consider a hypothetical small group of seven college students and professors, serving as a committee to analyze the experiences students have during their first year in college, with a view to recommending changes in college procedures to improve the experiences.

Group cohesiveness and *performance* are two important factors which we can use to illustrate the complexity and interdependence of the variables one might study in the analysis of small-group behavior. In our hypothetical committee, group cohesiveness refers to the strength of the members' desire to remain together as a committee. If all the members enjoy being on the committee and would be loath to resign from it under any circumstances, we can say that the group is extremely cohesive. The group's performance refers to the product of its meetings. This product can be either tangible, such as a report, or intangible, such as the exchange of ideas about freshman experiences.

Cohesiveness and performance are interrelated. When one considers the degree to which the group's cohesiveness affects its performance, cohesiveness is the independent variable and performance the dependent variable. A hypothesis might be that the more positive feelings the members have toward the committee, the more time they will spend discussing freshman experiences, in relation to the time they spend conversing socially.

Or one can look at performance as the independent variable and cohesiveness as the dependent variable. A hypothesis might be that positive feelings toward the committee are dependent upon the extent to which the members feel they are progressing toward their ultimate goal—recommending changes to improve the student's first-year experiences.

Both hypotheses are true to some extent, as we shall show later. Therefore, we can say that the interrelationship of group cohesiveness and performance is very complex.

Figure 19–3 is a diagrammatic summary of the general variables considered in small-group research. This diagram suggests that one can characterize a group in terms of *group composition, group structure,* and the nature of the group *task* and the *environment* in which it is to be completed. In addition, one must consider the *group process* or patterns of interaction among these people.

FIGURE 19–3: *An illustration of the interdependence of variables affecting small-group behavior. (From Social Psychology: A Brief Introduction, by Joseph E. McGrath, preliminary edition, copyright, 1963, copyright 1964, by Holt, Rinehart and Winston, Inc., p. 70.)*

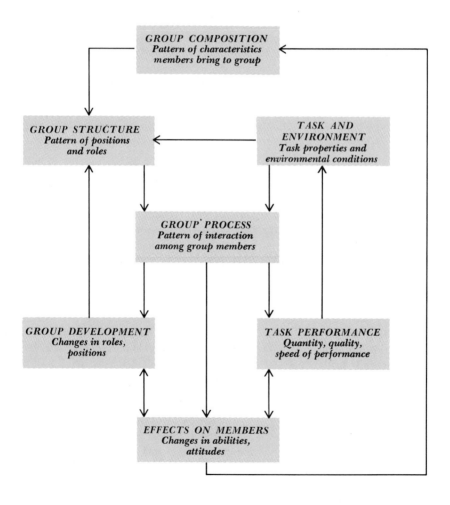

Group composition refers to the characteristics of members of the group. These characteristics may be relatively permanent, such as sex, race, physical and mental capacities, and basic values, or they may be relatively temporary, such as attitudes, interests, and opinions. Changes in group composition, that is, changes in members' attitudes, values, and so on, are referred to as *effects on members.*

Group structure indicates the interrelationships of the social positions occupied by members at the onset of the group process. A *social position* is "a set of expectations or acquired anticipatory reactions. That is to say, the person learns (*a*) to expect or anticipate certain actions from other persons and (*b*) that others have expectations of him" (Sarbin, 1954, p. 225). Suppose that in our committee concerned with freshman experiences one person has been designated as the leader. "Leader" is a social position because the person in this position expects certain behavior from the "followers" in the group and knows that they expect certain behavior from him. The actions of the leader are his *role.* If he is expected to make decisions about how the group should proceed to analyze its problem, then when he does so, he is performing his role.

Group structure, then, refers to the expected patterns of behavior within the group, or, put another way, the combined expectancies of how each member should act toward all other members and, in turn, how all others should act toward him. Some social positions are *explicit;* that is, they are openly and officially designated as having certain rights and obligations. Our student-faculty committee may have an official leader appointed by the president of the college. All members know that he is the person who informs the president about the committee's progress, who schedules committee meetings, and who delegates authority to individual members of the group. Other positions are *implicit;* that is, they are *not* officially defined according to certain rights and obligations but, instead, are unstated positions of which every member is aware. Our committee may have an unofficial

"jester," a person who keeps everyone laughing and happy to be a member of the group, who is looked to for diversion when the committee meetings become tense, and who is allowed to be witty and insulting in order to ease the hostility one member may be directing at another. Such an implicit tension-reducing position is common and very functional in many groups.

Several attempts have been made to delineate the many positions found in small groups. Benne and Sheats (1948) listed a number of functional positions which they believed to exist within most discussion groups. They noted such people as the "energizer," who attempts to instigate action, the "opinion giver," who states his opinion in response to someone else's suggestion, and the "evaluator-critic," who attempts to evaluate the positive and negative aspects of suggestions.

It is likely that the initial structure of a group will be ambiguous and tentative if the members of the group have not had prior contact. Most positions and roles evolve and become more or less established during the interaction process itself. A few positions may be defined prior to initial interaction (e.g., leadership or subcommittee membership), but this can only be done by fiat from an outside person or by someone who initially organized the group.

Some positions in a group structure may be more or less fixed and difficult to change. Our committee would probably have a permanent position of leader within its structure, primarily because the college president appointed a leader in the first place. Other positions may be flexible and easily changed. If the committee's first leader happens to be very dogmatic and authoritarian, the position of "jester" may be crucial in preventing resignations from the group. If leadership shifts to a less authoritarian person, the jester may no longer be functional and may change his behavior accordingly.

Groups can also differ in the degree to which their structure is determined prior to their initial meeting. At one extreme, the college president might appoint someone to organize a student-faculty committee, the appointee then outlining the functions each person is to fulfill throughout the group's existence. At the opposite extreme, the president might name the seven-person committee and ask the members to meet and decide on their own procedures.

Group development refers to changes in the group structure—changes in the role relationships and the positions of the various members of the group.

Task and environment refers to the nature of the task confronting the group and to the social situation in which the task must be performed. Obviously, tasks can vary greatly: they can be general and ambiguous, such as discussing and resolving a disagreement between management and workers in an industry, or they can be very specific, such as solving a series of mental puzzles or mathematical problems. They can require mental output, as in writing a new set of bylaws, or physical output, as in a construction task or a game of skill. The task can even be one in which the members are only to enjoy themselves in some way with no specific problems before them. Finally, tasks can vary in the degree to which members must cooperate to perform well. Solving simple arithmetic problems requires minimum cooperation, whereas winning at a game of tug-of-war demands maximum cooperation.

Environments can vary along several different dimensions. One such dimension is threat. A very amiable, relaxed experimenter may help to foster a nonthreatening environment, while a harsh, cold experimenter may create a threatening one. A group attempting to perform a task requiring maximum cooperation may find cooperating difficult when a threatening experimenter is present. Another dimension is the *size of the audience* observing the group. A group which functions smoothly when only an experimenter is present may not be able to concentrate on its task when a crowd is watching. A third factor is the *type of audience* observing the group. Before an

audience of students, members of our committee of seven may behave as they do when meeting alone; before a group of faculty members, they may act very subdued because of the status of their audience. Finally, the *naturalness* of the experimental setting must be considered: performing in a familiar environment, such as one's normal workroom in a factory, is very different from performing in a small laboratory room with one-way mirrors and a microphone in view. Because of the great variety of environments in which small-group research has taken place, an analysis of the potential effects of environmental differences is necessary for a complete understanding of the meaning of the research.

Task performance refers to the product of group interaction. Performance is usually measured in terms of the quantity and/or quality of the product. To illustrate, the performance of a group working on a series of mathematical problems might be measured by the *number* of problems completed correctly; the performance of a group trying to resolve a hypothetical labor-management dispute might be assessed by the *quality* of the solutions proposed.

Group process refers to the behavior of the persons within the group—their activities, their actions toward one another, what they say, what they do. Group process may be measured in terms of the acts of the members of the group toward one another, other persons, or objects; it may also be measured by the content of what the members say to one another or to others.

In the remainder of this chapter we shall discuss small-group behavior in terms of three major categories: group composition, group structure, and group process, or interaction. We have deliberately omitted a fourth category—task and environment—which appears in our diagram (Figure 19–3), primarily because the topic will be covered in the course of our discussion of the other three categories. For example, when we discuss the power structure of the group, we shall describe a study in which a threatening environment confronts the group. Or when we consider the effects of the size of the group on performance, we shall present studies showing that the effect of size is contingent upon whether the task the group is performing is "abstract" or "concrete."

Group Composition: We begin our detailed analysis of small-group research by considering the characteristics of the group members, both as they affect group behavior and as they are affected by group process.

The personal characteristics of the members play a major part in determining the nature of group interaction and the product of the interaction. The types of characteristics most often examined in this respect are (1) abilities, skills, and previous experiences relevant to the task or group situation, (2) attitudes, values, and interests, (3) personal demographic attributes, such as age, sex, and level of education, (4) personality as measured by standard personality tests, and (5) specific motives and social needs. We shall review some of the research that has examined the role of these characteristics in determining group behavior. Throughout the discussion, we must remember that the effect of these characteristics is almost always mediated by other group variables, including group structure and the nature of the task.

ABILITIES, SKILLS, AND EXPERIENCE: In small-group research, a member's abilities have been related to three types of variables: group performance, type of individual interaction within the group, and the member's position in the group structure. In a review of the literature, Heslin (1964) found that the general ability of members is positively related to the effectiveness of their group. "General ability," however, is rather ambiguous and a potentially misleading concept. It is logical to think not of such a global measure of ability but of those skills which are specifically relevant to the group's task. If one were to study ability as a determinant of a group's behavior in a tug-of-war, one would measure the members' physical strength, not their intelligence, which is fairly irrelevant to such a task.

Studies of specific abilities confirm the general hypothesis that greater ability leads to better task performance. An example of such studies is Rohde's investigation (1958) of the relationship between members' individual pretested ability on a serial maze task and subsequent performance of their groups. Rohde's equipment was designed so that all members of the group had to participate in order for them to complete the task. He found that the group's performance was significantly correlated with the individual scores of all the members of the group, thus demonstrating that each member's ability contributed to the total group performance.

In one sense, Rohde's study is a special case, because only one type of skill was required to perform the task. Other investigators (e.g., Thelen, 1949) have suggested that where more than one type of performance is demanded, the group's effectiveness is increased when the group is heterogeneous with regard to specific abilities—that is, the greater the distribution of skills throughout the group, the greater the performance. Although there are almost no studies directly supporting this latter contention, several investigations of leadership provide indirect evidence suggesting that heterogeneity of abilities does, in fact, contribute positively to group performance. Torrance (1954) notes that even though a group has all the requisite skills for a given task, this does not ensure that the people with these skills will be allowed to use them. Several factors may prevent their use. For example, Triandis, E. R. Hall, and Ewen (1965) suggest that heterogeneous attitudes may lead to "social stress" which disrupts the members' communication, thereby hampering their ability to capitalize on their respective skills. Comparing the performance of groups with varying combinations of heterogeneous and homogeneous abilities and attitudes, Triandis et al. found that groups whose members have heterogeneous attitudes perform more poorly than those whose members have homogeneous attitudes. This result is supported by their additional finding that when stress created by such heterogeneity was reduced or difficulties of communication were diminished, group performance improved markedly, presumably because of a more efficient use of their skills.

The power relations among members may also prevent a given member from communicating a critical bit of knowledge to the group. Torrance (1954) points this out in his investigation of the experiences of bomber crews confronted with the problem of surviving in a difficult environment after their bombers had been shot down. In some crews a very rigid command structure prevented persons low in the hierarchy from utilizing their skills to the fullest. In others, a flexible structure allowed for good communication among the crew members and the efficient use of everyone's skills.

Maier and Solem (1952) reached the same conclusion. They had groups attempt to solve a task requiring creative thinking. Some group leaders encouraged all members to participate in the resolution of the problem; other leaders merely acted as observers and did not encourage full participation. The former groups were superior to the latter in resolving the problem correctly, particularly when a minority of the members had the correct answer. Maier and Solem conclude that one of the crucial functions of a leader may be to allow minority opinions to be expressed, presumably because the skills or ideas of all are taken into consideration. Under such conditions, heterogeneity of ability is an asset to group performance.

This conclusion is strongly supported by the study by Maier and L. R. Hoffman (1965) of simulated industrial groups in which a foreman attempted to induce three workers to accept a reorganization of their work methods. The investigators noted the frequency with which the foremen referred to the workers as "problem employees" or as "idea men." Their results show that innovative solutions to the problem of work reorganization occurred more often in those groups led by foremen who perceived their subordinates as idea men than in those led by foremen who perceived the workers as problem employees. Again, it is concluded that the leaders who believe that the subordinates have potentially good ideas allow them to express these ideas, thereby increasing the quality of group performance.

Although Maier and Solem and Maier and Hoffman emphasize the importance of the leader's ability to permit the expression of minority opinions, a complementary study by L. R. Hoffman, Harburg, and Maier (1962) demonstrates the effect on performance of the followers' capacity to demand that they be heard. Hoffman et al. compared the quality of solutions to a hypothetical management-worker conflict of groups composed of varying combinations of dominant and "considerate" foremen and strongly committed and weakly committed workers. They found that, irrespective of the dominance or considerateness of the foreman, groups whose members were strongly committed to resist the foreman's proposals produced higher-quality solutions to the conflict than groups whose members were committed weakly to such resistance.

Individual performance can also be affected by certain attributes of ability. M. Goldman (1965) notes a very interesting effect that ability can have on the differences between working on a problem individually and working in pairs. The study, which we have described previously, in regard to *differences* between individual and group performance showed that a person's individual performance is better if he works with others than if he works alone. The increment is greatest, however, for persons of low ability, that is, those who performed poorly on the problem in previous trials. Goldman also notes that performance does not improve any more if the subject works with someone of his own ability than if he works with someone of less ability, but it improves significantly more if the partner is of greater ability than the subject himself.

In sum, there is ample evidence to support the contention that members' abilities are a determinant of group performance. One must, however, look at ability not solely in terms of a total of the group's skills but rather in terms of the distribution of these skills among the members, the structural possibilities of effectively using them, and their relevance to the group's task.

The nature of the individual members' interaction or behavior within the group is another variable related to ability. R. D. Mann (1959), in a review of the literature, reports a number of studies which indicate that intelligence is positively related to (1) total activity rate, that is, all the acts the person makes during the group's session; (2) task activity rate, which is limited to those acts which contribute to the group's attempts to cope with its task; and (3) positive socioemotional activity rate, consisting of those acts related to the maintenance of positive emotional feelings among the members of the group, such as agreeing, joking, and demonstrating solidarity. Intelligence is negatively related to negative socioemotional activity rate, consisting of those acts which adversely affect the feelings of the members of the group, such as disagreeing and showing antagonism. Although the studies Mann reports almost unanimously support these relationships, the correlations reported tend to be low. It seems, therefore, that intellectual ability is a definite but weak determinant of the type of behavior a member will display in a group.

To some extent, ability can also be examined as "learned ability," and one can consider previous experience a potential determinant of an individual's performance in a group. Harrison and McClintock (1965) examined this variable. They set up conditions for studying the extent to which being rewarded or punished monetarily for performance with a partner in a game affects a subject's cooperation or competition in subsequent games. For the initial condition, each subject was placed in a cubicle with a series of switches and told that when a light came on, he and a partner in another cubicle were to press a particular switch as quickly as possible. If both partners reacted fast enough, they would both receive a cent; if either failed to respond fast enough, both would lose a cent. This game was played 100 times. Persons in the rewarded group were informed that they

TABLE 19-C: *Payoff Matrix for the Prisoner's Dilemma Game.*

Player 2 choices	Player 1 choices	
	A	B
X	3,3	5,−1
Y	−1,5	0,0

had won on 85 of the 100 trials; those in the punished group lost on 85 of the 100 trials.

In an experiment designed to test the effects of these two conditions on subsequent, two-person cooperation, subjects then played the prisoners' dilemma game, half of each group doing so immediately and the other half one week later. In prisoners' dilemma (see Table 19–C), the partners may either cooperate on a series of trials and receive equal moderate rewards, or each may attempt to maximize his individual gains on each trial at the expense of the other; if both choose the latter alternative, ultimately neither wins. For example, if on the first trial player 1 chooses column A, and player 2 row X, both will win 3 points. If player 1 chooses A and player 2 chooses Y, player 1 will lose 1 point, and player 2 will gain 5 points. The first instance, where they both gain 3 points, is considered cooperation. The second, where one gains more and the other loses, is considered competition, and the following behavior is likely to occur: if on subsequent trials player 1 continues to select A while player 2 selects Y, player 1 will attempt to halt his losses by switching to column B, in which case neither player either wins or loses. The same sequence would occur were player 1 to try to gain 5 points by choosing B in the hope that player 2 would choose X: eventually player 2 would get tired of losing a point each time and switch to row Y, where both would receive zero points, that is, where they neither win nor lose.

Harrison and McClintock noted that persons who were rewarded for cooperating in the initial reaction-time game maintained higher levels of cooperative behavior than did control groups, both immediately after the initial game session and in a session one week later. On the other hand, players who lost in the reaction-time game showed little change in their cooperative behavior when they played the prisoners' dilemma game immediately afterward but showed much more competitive playing in sessions held one week later. Hence, these results suggest that prior experience in group situations can alter one's orientation toward group interaction in later groups.

Members of a group often occupy particular social positions within the group on the basis of their ability. Almost all the research relevant to this topic concerns the position of leader. Since we shall deal with leadership in detail in a later section, it is sufficient to say that Mann's review indicates that intelligence is positively related to leadership; that is, persons in positions of power have greater intelligence than other members of the group.

Whether or not persons with specific abilities assume leadership, or at least participate more in tasks for which they have special aptitude, varies greatly from group to group. Although there are no studies that treat this problem specifically, one can make some reasonable inferences from related studies. For example, one would surmise that the groups discussed by Maier and Solem (1952), in which leaders allowed minority opinions to be expressed, would be the type in which members with abilities relevant to particular tasks would be allowed to exercise leadership with respect to those tasks. Under such conditions, specific abilities can determine a member's position in the group structure.

ATTITUDES, VALUES, AND INTERESTS: The importance of this category for group behavior is restricted primarily to its effect on the attraction of group members to one another. The positive and negative feelings among members is one factor that affects the group's *cohesiveness*, which is defined as "the resultant of all the forces acting on all the members to remain in the group" (Cartwright & Zander, 1960, p. 74). Group cohesiveness is an important determinant of how effectively the group mem-

bers work together and will be discussed in greater detail in the section on Group Structure.

Some specific statements about the effects of attitudes, values, and interests on group behavior can be made. Numerous investigations have demonstrated the importance of homogeneity of these variables for the attraction between people. Newcomb (1961) measured the attitudes, values, and interests of 17 transfer students who were initially strangers but who subsequently lived together in a rooming house. He measured these variables before the students arrived at the house and several times during the following fifteen weeks. He also collected ratings of how much each person liked every other person in the house. The results of this study indicate that persons who have similar attitudes, values, and interests become friends. Newcomb noted further that friends' attitudes become more positively correlated as time goes on. One explanation of these results is that persons who have similar attitudes find an immediate mutual basis for talking with one another and, because of the ease of communication, manage to resolve their differences. Through small-group interaction, then, they arrive at mutual agreement on a number of issues on which they initially differed.

Specifically applying this idea of homogeneity of attitudes to group behavior, Fiedler, Meuwese, and Oonk (1961) found that groups homogeneous in religion show less interpersonal friction and perform better than groups heterogeneous in this variable. In a sense, one might look at homogeneity of attitudes, values, and interests as removing potential obstacles to effective group behavior. Most investigations suggest that homogeneity leads to more informal interaction, greater ease of communication, and increased satisfaction of the members within the group. The presence of these conditions would logically lead to better group performance. Free and open communication allows appropriate assignment of members to specific parts of the task plus sufficient feedback, so that correction of errors and general coordination of work can be easily accomplished. And, almost inevitably, satisfied members will work more diligently for the group than will unsatisfied ones. Hence, homogeneity of attitudes, values, and interests should lead to better group performance.

There is one possible exception to this generalization. Several studies indicate that homogeneity (or, at least, the members' perception of their homogeneity) leads to effective pressure on deviant members of the group to conform to the group's standards or norms (Festinger & Thibaut, 1951; Spitzer, 1964). This pressure to conform can detract from group performance when, for example, the deviant person has a very creative solution to problems confronting the group and the group rejects his solution because he is different or forces him to change from his deviant position. In this special case, homogeneity and its subsequent effects upon conformity can be harmful, because it suppresses the very creativity the group may need to perform its tasks successfully.

DEMOGRAPHIC VARIABLES: Demographic variables refer to attributes that describe a person physically and socially. Examples of physical demographic attributes are age, sex, race, height, and weight. Examples of social demographic attributes are religion, socioeconomic status, employment, residence, and level of education.

Demographic characteristics of members of groups can have diverse effects on the group's behavior. Great differences in age may result in stilted communication, with younger members hesitant to initiate ideas. Sex differences can have similar effects: women may feel that men should be the initiators in the group, and thus the ideas of the feminine members may be lost.

Willis's study (1966) of speakers' relationships and the distances from which they speak to each other dramatically illustrates the effects of demographic variables. He recorded the physical distance between people when they first began conversing and related these distances to their sex, race, age, and social rela-

tionship. His results indicate that, in general, people stand closer to their good friends than to general friends and acquaintances; this finding was much more common among women than among men. He further notes that (1) parents stand as far from their children as they do from strangers, (2) Negroes evoke a greater speaking distance than do Caucasians, both from other Negroes and from Caucasians, and (3) people stand closer to others of the same age than they do to persons younger than they. To the extent that speaking distance reflects the ease with which people communicate with one another, Willis's study indicates that age, sex, and race definitely affect group behavior.

Social status also determines the nature of interpersonal behavior. Strodtbeck, R. J. Simon, and C. Hawkins (1965), studying mock juries, found that persons of higher-status occupations have higher rates of participation, influence, personal satisfaction, and perceived competence in jury deliberations than do those of lower-status occupations. A related study (Strodtbeck & R. D. Mann, 1956) confirms the difference sex can make: men participate, give opinions, and orient the group more than do women, although women show more positive reactions, such as agreeing, joking, and showing solidarity. One of the end products of these differences is that men, as opposed to women, and higher-status persons, as opposed to lower-status ones, have a much greater chance of being elected foreman of the jury and, hence, of affecting the procedures in the deliberations—not an inauspicious effect.

B. M. Bass and Wurster (1953) noted similar effects: ". . . status tends to breed status," according to their research on oil-refinery supervisors. The supervisors' relative positions in the company hierarchy tended to be maintained when they met in informal groups away from their specific jobs. Persons treated with respect on the job were afforded equal respect when encountered informally. The data of Bass and Wurster suggest further that status is maintained most when the task of the informal group concerns issues relevant to the employment situation where the members have differential status; that is, if the group is informally discussing decisions related to management or business, their status differences persist more than if they are considering an irrelevant topic, such as means of improving high school teaching.

A somewhat different type of demographic characteristic has to do with the various roles that the individual performs. If there is conflict between the outside role of a person and the one he must play in the group, this conflict may affect his behavior. Burchard (1954) has noted the difficulties of chaplains working in battle. Presumably they are to teach peace, fellowship, and "Do unto others as you would have them do unto you," yet on the battlefield, chaplains must often act otherwise.

Cousins (1951) has noted a conflict particular to student monitors. On the one hand they are members of the student body and have loyalties to their student friends, and on the other they are expected to report to the administration any student deviations from the college rules. Is it any wonder that deans have difficulty recruiting the necessary number of student monitors and thus must resort to assistant deans to achieve the desired purpose? The studies we have discussed are quite disparate—social status and jury deliberations; age, sex, and race and speaking distance; and so on. Taken together, however, they support the contention that, in a variety of different ways, members' demographic characteristics can influence the manner in which they will interact as a group.

PERSONALITY CHARACTERISTICS: The personality characteristics of members are another set of variables which are presumed to have a great effect on group behavior. A number of studies have attempted to discover which characteristics have the most influence on the way members interact. Beginning with the most general statements that can be made, R. D. Mann (1959) reports that his review of about 150 studies of personality and performance in small groups shows that adjustment, extroversion, dominance, masculinity, conservatism, and interpersonal sensitivity are all related to

specific types of behavior. (He regarded these six characteristics as the basis of 350 of the over 500 different personality variables mentioned in the studies he reviewed.)

Broadly speaking, adjustment and extroversion were positively related to a member's perceived leadership, total activity rate, and popularity in the group, while conservatism was positively related to popularity but negatively related to leadership. Interpersonal sensitivity related positively to both leadership and popularity; dominance related positively to task contributions initiated and to leadership; and masculinity related slightly positively to leadership and popularity. In addition, his review finds that adjustment and dominance are negatively related to an individual's tendency to conform to the group's standards and opinions, while extroversion and conservatism are positively related to this tendency. Mann cautions, however, that many of the correlations between personality characteristics and performance are at a low level of significance. Although there is little doubt that such characteristics, in one way or another, affect the individual's and thus the group's behavior, the amount of variance they account for may be so low as to place their ultimate importance in question. Perhaps sensing the futility of correlational studies of endless numbers of personality characteristics such as those reviewed by Mann, several investigators have attempted a somewhat different analytic procedure by looking at the way the homogeneity or heterogeneity of these characteristics affects group behavior.

L. R. Hoffman (1959) and L. R. Hoffman and Maier (1961), for example, note that groups heterogeneous with regard to personality variables tend to produce more inventive solutions to problems presented them than do homogeneous groups. Tuckman (1964) shows that groups composed of homogeneously "abstract" individuals adopt a group structure which is much more flexible and open, where members are not rigidly hierarchized or unalterably set in positions, than do groups composed of homogeneously "concrete" members. The former groups also display more sensitivity to their environment, a greater orientation to information presented to them, and a more integrated strategy in approaching the problem. R. B. Cattell, Saunders, and Stice 1953) collected data from groups performing a variety of tasks and reported that groups heterogeneous in the characteristics of surgency, radicalism, character integration, and "adventuresomeness" make more accurate group judgments than groups homogeneous in these factors. On the other hand, groups heterogeneous in sensitivity, suspiciousness, and aggression have much greater difficulty in arriving at decisions than do groups homogeneous in these variables.

Other studies have noted the importance to group behavior of the relationship between leaders' and followers' personality characteristics (Haythorn, Couch, Haefner, Langham, & Carter, 1956; Sanford, 1952). The Haythorn et al. study compares the performance of groups with varying combination of high- and low-authoritarian leaders and followers. An authoritarian person (F) is one who is concerned primarily with power, desiring either to control or to be controlled. Observer ratings of the group sessions suggest that homogeneous groups (high F leader with high F followers and low F leader with low F followers) have higher morale, more effective communication, better cooperation, and less interpersonal conflict than heterogeneous groups. In addition, observers noted much less friction between leaders and followers in the homogeneous groups than in the heterogeneous ones.

These results are of particular importance, because they add a qualification to a well-known series of studies (Lewin & Lippitt, 1938; Lippitt, 1940; Lippitt & White, 1947) which have indicated that "democratic" leaders produce much higher morale, more satisfaction for members, and greater quality of performance than do autocratic or authoritarian leaders. Apparently these latter findings do not hold true when the members of the group themselves have an authoritarian orientation.

SOCIAL NEEDS: The "needs" with which the members enter the group have a direct bearing on the group's behavior. This fact is of great significance when the individual's needs are in conflict with the goals of the group. A study by Fouriezos, Hutt, and Guetzkow (1950) illustrates the problem. They noted that members of groups who measure high in "self-oriented need"—that is, who are concerned with satisfying a need or reaching a goal that has nothing to do with the group's goals—are much more dissatisfied with the group's behavior than are those with group orientations. In addition, the study indicated a tendency for groups composed of persons with self-oriented needs to be somewhat less productive than other groups. This result is supported by Stimpson and B. M. Bass (1964), who noted that "interaction-oriented" people have detrimental effects on the productivity of their groups. Presumably, such members are at cross purposes with the group goal, because they are more interested in socializing or in reaching another goal than in producing. However, the old story of the perfectly functioning group in which the three members have completely different motives for being in the group—three little boys making a lemonade stand, one because he just received a hammer and saw for his birthday which he wants to try out, the second because he wants to make money from the sale of lemonade, and the third because he enjoys being with the other two—makes good sense. The degree to which, as well as the way in which, an individual's needs affect the performance of his group is a function of the degree to which his needs can be satisfied *concomitantly* with the attainment of his group's goal.

Exploring this issue, E. J. Thomas (1957) notes the difference between *facilitative interdependence* and *"contriant" interdependence*. In the first, the better each member's performance, the greater is the reward for every member of the group. Each person's performance facilitates the movement of all toward their ultimate goals. In "contriant" interdependence the greater the performance (and hence reward) of one member, the less the reward received by the others. Thomas contends that needs are important to the extent that they determine whether member interdependence is to be facilitative or "contriant."

Research by Deutsch (1949) concerning competition and cooperation in small groups provides evidence indicating some of the results of the conditions Thomas describes. In this study, comparisons were made between groups told that the whole group would be rewarded on the basis of how well it performed in relation to other groups (cooperative condition) and those told that each member of the group would be ranked and rewarded in terms of how well he performed in relation to the other members of his group (competitive condition). Deutsch indicates that the cooperative groups showed greater quantity and quality of performance, greater division of labor, greater member satisfaction, greater friendliness, and fewer difficulties in communicating than did the competitive groups. This study is an example of a case in which members were sharing or competing for satisfaction of the same need or goal.

Diverse needs are similarly important in terms of the degree to which they are mutually exclusive. For example, in the Stimpson and Bass study mentioned earlier, one would speculate that the interaction-oriented members disrupted the group's performance because they were hampering the efforts of the members who wanted to complete the task as quickly and efficiently as possible. In effect, the interaction-oriented members were competing with the task-oriented ones for the time and energy of all the members of the group.

The personal characteristics that members bring into groups can affect their performance in the group. To a great extent, however, these characteristics have their effect through an interaction with other attributes of the group—for example, its structure, its communication patterns, and its goal.

Group Structure: Studies of group structure, defined as the pattern of role relationships among members of the group, have been extensive. Four different types of group structure are considered in such studies. One is the *task*

structure, which is the way the roles are set up in relation to the group's activity, or, operationally, who works with whom. The *power structure* is the pattern of power, authority, or influence within the group, that is, who influences whom. The *communication structure* refers to the pattern in which information is sent and received, that is, who sends messages to whom. The *affect structure* is the pattern of friendship relationships within the group, that is, who likes or dislikes whom. Before we consider these types of group structure, we shall discuss a related variable, *group size,* which can have significant effects on the group.

GROUP SIZE: Many investigators have noted that the distribution of activity within the groups is affected by the size of the group. Bales, Strodtbeck, Mills, and Roseborough (1951) studied the "basic initiation rate" of participation of members of groups of three to eight members. The basic initiation rate refers to the number of times during a given period that a person communicates with at least one other member of the group and whether his communication is relevant or irrelevant to the group's activity. Their results indicate that as the size of the group increases, the difference between participation of the most active member and second most active member and the rest of the members steadily increases. That is, the larger the group, the more the initiation of behavior rests in the hands of one or two active persons. Stephan and Mishler (1952), working with classroom groups of four to twelve members, found that as group size increased, the difference in the participation of the most active person (the class instructor) and the next most active member increased consistently. For example, the difference in the percentage of contributions made by the leader and the next most active participator is 14.7 in groups with four members, 19.4 in groups with five, 19.0 in groups with six, 24.8 in groups with seven, and so on, to 34.3 in groups with twelve members. In addition to this increasing difference between the participation of the leader and the next most active person, as group size increased, the differences among the participation rates of the remaining members became consistently smaller. For example, as the groups became larger, the participation rate of the second and third most active members gradually approached the rate of the least active members.

Evidence concerning the relationship between group size and the quality of the performance of the group is contradictory. Several studies suggest that some features of performance are negatively related to group size. Gibb (1951) used groups ranging from 1 to 96 members and found that the number of potential solutions to a group problem increased as group size increased. The number of solutions offered per member decreased, however. He reports further that many of the subjects in the larger groups felt constraints against participating. S. E. Seashore's study (1954) of 228 factory groups of different sizes supports this finding of a "feeling of inhibition" in large groups. He concludes that small groups (in his study, groups with 4 to 22 members) are more cohesive than large ones and that this greater cohesiveness leads to less restraint on communication. On the other hand, some investigations have concluded that performance is positively related to group size. South (1927) found that groups of six are better on abstract problems than are groups of three. The data of D. W. Taylor and Faust (1952) revealed essentially the same relationship for groups of four and two.

Slater (1958) suggests a resolution of this seemingly contradictory evidence. His research indicates that groups of approximately five are ideal in size. Groups smaller than five limit the range of talents, while groups larger than five waste manpower, lead to redundancy, tend to be disorganized, and place a greater feeling of constraint on participating and contributing to the solution of the problem. The results of South's study and that of Taylor and Faust do not contradict Slater's contention when it is recognized that the "larger" groups they were referring to were groups of only six and four members, respectively. Moreover, the studies cited which indicate a negative relationship

between size and performance used groups with as many as 96 members as the upper limit, which also fits clearly into Slater's designation of "large" small groups.

A further indication of the relationship between group size and performance is provided by Indik (1961; 1963). Utilizing organizations with from 15 to 2,983 members, he studied the relationship between size and member participation in an organization's activities, as measured by absenteeism and attendance at meetings. His data showed a significant negative correlation between size and participation; the larger the organization, the greater the absenteeism, and the lower the attendance at meetings. Indik suggested further that a series of intervening variables were producing this correlation, including the amount of communication, work specialization, members' attraction to the organization, members' satisfaction with their particular role in the organization, and their perception of the flexibility of the bureaucracy. He then computed partial correlations, effectively holding constant the intervening variables that he believed were contributing to the relationship he had previously found. When the effects of six such variables were eliminated in this manner, Indik found that the negative correlation between group size and participation had been reduced from $-.53$ to $-.08$. His work demonstrates very graphically that group size per se does not affect the members' participation but, rather, the artifacts of size—difficulties in communicating, rigidity or flexibility of the group, and so on.

It seems probable that increasing group size up to five or six members will result in an increase in quality of performance, especially on abstract problems where there is not just one simple, correct solution. With further increases in group size quality begins to decrease. These conclusions stem from the concomitant increase in the range of skills available for problem solving, organizational difficulties, constraints on participation, and redundancy with increases in group size. These conclusions do not necessarily apply to performance on "concrete" tasks. South notes that on simple tasks his three-man groups performed significantly faster and as accurately as the six-man groups. In concrete tasks, a range of skills is not as relevant as quick and efficient organization of the labor within the group.

TASK STRUCTURE: Task structure refers to the patterning of role relationships with regard to who does what and with whom toward completing the group's task, or, in other words, the division of labor in the group.

Task structures vary greatly. A six-person group confronting the problem of unloading boxes from a truck might set up a structure in which each member performed independently, each carrying a box at a time; or the members might divide up in pairs, two people carrying several boxes at once; or they might work as a total group and set up a "bucket-brigade" structure, standing in a line from the truck to their depository and passing the cartons from person to person. These are three examples of a number of ways in which the work on such a task can be divided.

The most frequent question asked by investigators of task structure is "What are the effects of the various means of dividing the labor upon group performance?" Before considering this problem, we should note that one of the crucial determinants of a group's efficiency is the degree to which the members possess the requisite skills for successfully performing the task they are assigned. The amount of talent available to the group sets limits on its potential capacity to handle its task. The task structure essentially determines the degree to which the potential is realized. This point will be demonstrated in the subsequent discussion of different structural factors.

Is it more efficient for one member of a group to do a number of different tasks, or for each man to do one task, or a very few tasks, many times? That is, is it better for work to be arranged so that one person does a number of different operations, as a tailor does when he makes a suit for a customer, or for several people to do one operation each,

as happens in clothing factories where one person cuts out all the sleeves, another sews the sleeves to the body of the jacket, and a third puts on the buttons? In one of the few studies undertaken to answer this question, Lanzetta and T. B. Roby (1956) required three-man groups to work on a task involving instrument readings. One of the independent variables was "degree of autonomy," or the degree to which each worker was dependent on the others for information necessary for the completion of the task. The task required of each group of three was to read simulated airplane instrument panels and to act on this information by adjusting switches controlling such factors as the steering mechanism, landing gear, and power setting. The subjects sat in separate booths and communicated via an "intercom" system. On each trial, four items of information were necessary for operating the control switches correctly.

Four different structures were established: (1) each member had all the information he needed directly available to him (high autonomy); (2) each was dependent upon *one* other person for three of the four items of information; (3) each was dependent upon himself for half the information and upon one other for the other half; and (4) each was dependent upon both other members for three of the four items of information (low autonomy). In addition, Lanzetta and Roby varied the difficulty of the task by increasing the amount of information given the subjects in a specific period and varying the randomness of its presentation. Performance was measured by the number of errors made in adjusting the control switches.

The results of this investigation indicate that the greater the autonomy of the task structure, the more accurate the performance of the group. In addition, the difficulty of the task does not modify the effect that the degree of autonomy has on performance. Thus, the rate of errors increases approximately equally for high- and low-autonomy groups as the task becomes more difficult. Lanzetta and Roby explain these data in terms of the number of "linkages" necessary in the completion of the task, that is, the number of times information must be relayed from one person to another before the task can be completed. For example, there are fewer linkages required to complete the task when information is directly available to the subject than when information comes from another source and must be relayed to the subject.

Lanzetta and Roby believe that to a great extent the relative inefficiency of low-autonomy groups is a function of the greater amount of communication necessary for this structure than for the high-autonomy structure. They speculate that if the former groups could set up an organized communication system, they would perform much better.

Three points about the relationship between division of labor and group productivity are noteworthy: First, division of labor into small parts can lead to greater productivity, because each worker can concentrate on his particular task, learn it well, and establish a set which will allow him to work efficiently. In a highly complex task, division of labor can have a very beneficial effect on productivity if each worker is assigned that part of the task which most precisely matches his particular skills.

Second, division of labor can result in a decrease in productivity to the extent that a loss of information (and thus of efficiency) can occur when various workers try to combine their parts of the task. Because a loss of information occurred when messages were relayed in their experiment, Lanzetta and Roby found that a division of labor was less efficient than having each person do the entire job himself.

Third, division of labor can affect productivity to the extent that it increases or decreases group morale. In E. J. Thomas's study (1957), which we discussed earlier, the division of labor and the members' perception of interdependence led to a feeling of "working together" to achieve a goal for the entire group, which resulted in an increase in morale and in productivity.

POWER STRUCTURE: Power structure refers to the patterns of influence and authority within the group, that is, who influences whom. Although power is generally defined in terms of influence, one must ask, "What kind of influence?" Is it influence based on force, on the ability to coerce another person to do or say what you want him to? Is it influence based on merely having a good idea that is accepted by others and therefore guides their behavior?

Bases of Social Power: J. R. P. French and Raven (1959) have helped to clarify this issue. They suggest that a person can attain social power, the ability to alter the behavior of others in a desired direction, in any one of five different ways. For illustrative purposes, we shall describe these different bases of social power in terms of the relationship between two persons, A and B.

First, A can have *reward* power if B perceives A as having the ability to control rewards for him. Parents often use this means of asserting power effectively: "You may use the car tonight if you'll take out the garbage, clean your room, and mow the lawn first." In this example, the parents are attempting to influence their son to do a number of chores, and they will be successful if he sees the parents as able to withhold the reward (use of the car) until he completes the chores (see Chapter 14).

Second, A can have *coercive* power if B perceives him as able to control punishments for him. Parents often use this power play as well: "Do *not* take the car this evening or you won't get your allowance." The power derives from the son's perception that the parents can and will withhold his allowance if he uses the car.

Third, A can have *legitimate* power if B perceives A as having the legitimate *right* to demand a given form of behavior. Students take examinations and write papers for a teacher because they perceive him as having the right to demand this work of them. These are examples of omission and punishment training described in Chapter 12.

Fourth, A can have *referent* power if B identifies with him. By "identify," French and

Raven mean that B is greatly attracted to A, likes him very much, or wants to be like him and thus takes on the characteristics of A. Hence, in order to maintain his relationship with A or in order to become more like him, B decides that his best course is to act like A and to express the same opinions as A. The "high school hero" is an excellent example of a person with referent power: the "high school senior, star football player, all-American boy," who has boys running around imitating him, agreeing with everything he says, and wishing they were just like him, influences their behavior considerably, and they his.

Fifth, A can have *expert* power if B perceives him as having special ability or knowledge. The native guide has expert power over the hunter to the extent that the hunter depends upon the guide to lead him through the jungle.

Considering these bases of social power within the context of a small group, we note three qualifications: First, a person's power in the group may be dependent upon one or a combination of these five bases. The leader of a country not only has legitimate power over his advisers by virtue of his election to office, but he can reward them (e.g., praise them to the press) and punish them (fire them). In addition, he may have a very attractive personality and thus have referent power, or he may be an expert in political machinations and be perceived by them as an aid in dealing with troublesome legislators.

Second, in most groups, *all* members have power to one extent or another. Benne and Sheats (1948) have supported this contention in their description of a variety of roles which may be performed by different members of a group. Each role implies that the member performing it alters the behavior of other members. For example, Benne and Sheats mention the role of "information giver." The person occupying this role presents information about the task confronting the group and changes the direction of the problem-solving process. Another is the "harmonizer," the person who changes behavior by resolving conflicts between group members. Another role is "energizer," which implies that this member provokes the group to action. Each of the people occupying these roles is exhibiting social power to some extent. Therefore, when we talk about social power, or about leadership, as we shall later in this section, we must realize that a person's power is relative to that of all other members of the group. We must speak of A's power relative to B's with regard to activity X, rather than A's power alone.

Third, we should note that most investigators believe that two basic types of behavior occur in all groups: *task-oriented* behavior and *socioemotional* behavior. Defined very simply, task-oriented behavior refers to acts related to working on the task confronting the group, while socioemotional behavior refers to acts concerned with the personal relationships among the members of the group. In our student-faculty committee studying the experiences of freshmen, when the group discusses means of handling problems faced by freshmen or plans programs to orient them to the college, the members are engaging in task-oriented behavior. When a member tells a joke or when the members take a coffee break, they are engaging in socioemotional behavior. Although we shall consider these two concepts in more detail in the section on group interaction, they do have relevance to power.

Several theorists (e.g., Bales, 1955; Thibaut & Kelley, 1959) have suggested that the predominant social power in the task and socioemotional areas of action is often divided between two people. We shall refer to the most powerful person in these areas as the *task leader* and the *socioemotional leader*. Rarely does one person fulfill both functions in a group. Studies have indicated that, in general, the socioemotional leader is the most liked person in the group; the task leader is not necessarily well liked but is more apt to be seen as a good organizer and an expert in dealing with the task the group must perform (e.g., Bales, 1955). In talking about leadership and trying to find the predominant person or persons in a group, one must look for leadership in these two areas, rather than search for one all-powerful leader.

The task leader is often dependent upon the socioemotional leader to execute his ideas and make his demands on the group. Leadership is often a thankless job, especially when there are annoying tasks which must be delegated. If there is friction between leader and followers, the group may reject the task leader's demands, despite their obvious importance to the success of the group, unless there is a socioemotional leader available to assuage the followers.

Determinants of the Distribution of Power: The distribution of power within groups can range from a situation in which virtually all the leadership functions are invested in one person to a situation in which the functions are distributed more or less equally throughout the membership. Several factors determine where any given group will fall along this continuum. One obvious factor is the amount of legitimate power delegated to a member by an outside authority. In the student-faculty committee, the president of the college may empower the chairman to make any decisions he wants to in his meetings with the committee, or he may ask him to work with the other members to come up with proposals acceptable to them all.

A second determinant of the centrality of leadership, or power, is the relationship between relevant personality characteristics of leaders and followers. Haythorn, Couch, Haefner, Langham, and Carter (1956) illustrated this factor in their study of groups composed of varying combinations of high- and low-authoritarian leaders and followers. Their findings that high-authoritarian leaders are less equalitarian, less concerned with gaining group approval, and more autocratic than low-authoritarian leaders and that high-authoritarian followers engage in less equalitarian behavior, in less "democratic" behavior than low-authoritarian followers suggest the effect that the leader's and the followers' personalities can have on the degree to which leadership is invested in one person. In a group composed of a leader and followers with opposing orientations toward authority, there must be a great deal of adjusting before the leadership style is ultimately established.

The ability of the leader to control the group's goals is a third determinant of the centrality of leadership. If the task is a very difficult one, for example, the "expert" may be accorded great power to execute his plans to complete the task.

Threats to the group constitute a fourth variable affecting the degree of centrality of power. Threats may come from other groups, as in a competitive situation, or from other external sources. Hamblin's study (1958) of leadership provides an example of such an outside threat. Hamblin set up groups of three people to play a modified shuffleboard game. The group had to learn, by trial and error, the special rules that had been introduced as a test of their ability. The group played, slowly but surely learning the various rules. Suddenly, Hamblin stymied them by changing the rules—procedures which had previously earned points now resulted in penalties. Faced by this crisis, the group immediately invested more authority in the person who had been their leader throughout the earlier part of the game. More specifically, the leader showed a sharp increase in "influence ratio" (each time a person made a suggestion to the group he was given a score for attempted influence). Concurrently, his "acceptance rate" increased precipitously (each time a person's suggestion was adopted, he was given a score for accepted influence). Parenthetically, we should note that when the leader's suggestions did not improve the group's performance—Hamblin's procedure ensured that they would not improve—leadership often shifted, just as absolutely, to another member of the group. Thus, the maintenance of centralized leadership by a given person during a crisis is contingent upon his ability to handle the crisis successfully.

The distribution of leadership, or power, in a group can be a function of (1) the power distribution imposed by an overriding authority, (2) the relationship between personality characteristics of the leaders and followers, (3) the ability of the leader to achieve group goals, and (4) the presence of external threats to the group.

Leadership: We have emphasized that power is seldom invested in a single person but is usually distributed in varying degrees among the members of the group. Nevertheless, we can discuss leadership as long as we do so only in reference to the most powerful person in the group and do not forget that his power is almost never absolute.

Perhaps the most famous study of leadership is the investigation of leadership styles and group performance reported by Lippitt and R. K. White (1947). They had adults serve as leaders in four clubs of eleven-year-old boys set up to engage in various craft and recreational activities. Each club was subjected to one of three different leadership styles by the adults: authoritarian, democratic, and laissez-faire. In the *authoritarian* pattern, the leader decided almost all the group's policies and the assignment of activities; he retained all information about the step-by-step procedures to be followed until each successive step was to be performed, and he kept apart from the group except to demonstrate particular parts of an activity. In the *democratic* pattern, the leader actively encouraged members to discuss group policies and activities and make decisions; when needed, he actively participated as an expert to assist the members in various phases of their activities, and he tried to act as an interested member of the group without actually going through all the group's activities himself. Finally, in the *laissez-faire* pattern, the leader passively allowed the members to make decisions about policies and activities, neither encouraging nor discouraging them to do so; he stated that he was available for help when asked but never offered assistance on his own; he maintained a friendly approach to the boys, although he never encouraged their personal contact with him. All the groups' meetings were watched and rated on several key factors by 11 trained observers. They rated such attributes of the members' behavior as the

quantity of social interactions of the boys and their leaders, the nature of this interaction (e.g., approach, response, refusal to respond), the nature of an individual's or a subgroup's activities and goals, and who initiated behavior.

Lippitt and White found a number of differences between the groups under the three leadership styles. The authoritarian groups tended to be either extremely aggressive or extremely apathetic. The aggressive authoritarian groups made many demands for attention from others, showed very little friendly, confiding behavior, made few suggestions concerning the group, and engaged in little "out-of-club" conversation and a medium amount of work-oriented conversation. The apathetic authoritarian groups, on the other hand, exhibited a great dependence upon the leader and made many demands for attention, very few group-oriented suggestions, little out-of-club conversation, and a great deal of work-oriented conversation.

The pattern of behavior shown by the democratic groups was quite different from that of the authoritarian groups. The members showed little dependence upon the leader, demanded little attention from him or from other members of the group, were generally friendly and confiding with one another, and engaged in more out-of-club and work-oriented conversation than any of the other groups.

The laissez-faire groups also exhibited a specific pattern of behavior. The members were similar to the democratic groups in being independent of the leader, demanding little attention, being generally friendly and confiding, and in making out-of-club conversation. They differed from the democratic groups, however, in continually asking for a great deal of information about the group's activities and in showing relatively little work-oriented conversation.

One particular statistic noted by Lippitt and White is relevant to productivity. They noted the differences in the time spent on work when the leader was *in* and when he was *out* of the workroom. For both the aggressive and apathetic authoritarian situations, the amount of work-related activity decreased more than 50 percent when the leader was not present. For the democratic groups, productivity remained about the same when he was in as when he was out of the room. And for the laissez-faire groups, strangely enough, work-related activity *increased* with the leader out of the room. This last result is explained by Lippitt and White as a function of strong leadership assertions by several powerful boys whenever the leader was absent.

In summary, it appears that the democratic style of leadership results in a fairly high work orientation and positive interpersonal relations among group members. The authoritarian style leads to either aggressive or apathetic reactions to the leader, along with somewhat stilted interpersonal relations, and a work orientation evident only when the leader is present. The laissez-faire situation leads to a disorganized approach to the work and fairly good interpersonal relations among members and the emergence of strong leaders within the group who direct the members in the formal leader's absence. Further evidence to support some of these conclusions appears in our discussion of the communication structure in a later section. Several externally imposed patterns of "who talks to whom" appear to be very similar to the leadership styles which have been discussed.

Limitations of Power: We have talked about the nature of influence from the point of view of the powerful person acting on the less powerful ones. There is another side, however: followers can, and often do, effectively limit the power of the leader. This is illustrated by Merei (1949). He examined twelve small groups of children from a day nursery. The children were judged to be nonleaders. They followed more than they led; they imitated more than they were imitated; and they demonstrated an average amount of participation and cooperation in group play. These children were allowed to play in groups for several days until they were judged by observers to have established group "traditions,"

that is, a series of norms concerning their mutual behavior. Then, Merei introduced a "leader" into each group. Leaders, who attended the same day nursery, were selected on the basis of being imitated and followed and of being generally more aggressive, dominant, and having more initiative than other children. Observers watched especially the degree to which a group accepted or rejected its leader's initiations and the responses of the leader to the group's reactions. For example, did the members of the group allow the leader to decide what games they would play? If not, did the leader try to fight or give up?

In all but one case, the leaders attempted but failed to change the groups' "traditional" procedures. The members either openly rejected the newcomer or ignored him. Typically, the leader then switched his strategy and imitated the group, accepting and acting according to the group's previously established norms. In some cases, he introduced several minor variations in the "traditional" rules and then, little by little, introduced changes in the group's behavior so that it coincided more with his desires. In other cases, the leader joined the others, learned all their rules, and then, at a later date, began ordering them again to do the very things which they *had* been doing, thus appropriating the leadership without changing any of the rules. Merei's study indicates that the ability of a leader to exert his influence is limited by the norms that the group has established. He can, however, begin to assert leadership within the group gradually as long as he does not actively challenge these norms.

Changes in Power: Few would disagree that a change in status is critically important to the individual member of a group. Several psychologists have investigated the effects of promotion and demotion, or the threat thereof, on group members' interpersonal behavior. Kelley's study (1951) of status and communication provides some valuable information on this issue. He established eight-person groups, which were further divided into four-person subgroups, to work on an assembly task. The two subgroups were put in separate rooms, and each was told that it was preparing items for the other to complete.

Kelley then created four different hierarchical positions: a permanent high-status position, a potentially temporary high-status position, a potentially temporary low-status position, and a permanent low-status position. Two people in each subgroup were told that they had the most important jobs of all, that of translating the words of the other group into patterns for the assembly of bricks (high status). One of these two was further told that he might have to change his job later for a low-status job in the other group (potentially temporary high status). The other two people were told that they had a relatively unimportant task, that the hard work was being done by the people in the other room while all they had to do was to follow directions (low status); one of these two people was further told that he might be able to change later to a high-status job in the other room (potentially temporary low status). Because he had no hope of moving higher, the permanently low-status person had the lowest position on the hierarchy. Because he had no fear of falling in status, the permanently high-status member occupied the highest position. Having established the power hierarchy, Kelley stimulated communication (notes) between the two rooms by introducing, at strategic points, counterfeit notes to each person, presumably from people in the other group. Some of the notes were relevant to the task, such as questions about the work; others were irrelevant, such as comments about the weather. His dependent variable was the nature of the replies made by each of the subjects.

Significant differences in the nature of the replies were found among the four different positions in the power hierarchy. First, the lower the subject's position in the hierarchy, the greater was the tendency to communicate things irrelevant to the task, perhaps as a means of escape from the disagreeable situation. The higher the person's position in the hierarchy, the greater the amount of communication relevant to the task. Second, Kelley's results indicated the presence of restraints against saying things that might diminish another person's judgment of the value of one's own position. Thus, the high-status people did not criticize their jobs to anyone else. Third, status differences produced restraints against criticizing people at a different level, unless one made the criticism directly to the person in question. Finally, the greatest rejection of other members of the group was shown by persons who were most unhappy in their positions, namely, those high-status subjects who could potentially become low-status, and those low-status people who were frustrated by having no possibility of change. These people, concludes Kelley, would be the ones most likely to disrupt the group process by hindering the effective establishment of group *morale*. This complex study provides an excellent transition to the third aspect of group structure: the communication structure of the group.

COMMUNICATION STRUCTURE: The communication structure of groups—the pattern of who talks to whom—has been the subject of a series of studies. Most studies have been conducted under artificial conditions, but nonetheless they have produced valuable insights into the nature of the communication structure. We shall consider first the communication structure affecting the group's performance and the satisfaction of the members within the group. Almost all the research concentrates on four categories of dependent variables: (1) the efficiency of the group, measured, for example, by the number of errors made by the group, the amount of time spent on the task, or the number of messages transmitted; (2) the organization of the group, including how it evolves and its consistency; (3) leadership in the group; and (4) satisfaction of members of the group, measured by their morale and their desire to remain members.

Bavelas (1948) introduced the topic of *communication networks* and their effect on group behavior. Since his initial statement, many studies have been conducted to test and extend his ideas (e.g., Leavitt, 1951; Guetzkow & H. A. Simon, 1955; Mulder, 1960). Leavitt's study, which illustrates the general approach taken in the majority of these investigations, was aimed directly at the four variables described in the preceding paragraph. The design of the research was presented in detail earlier in this chapter as an illustration of a laboratory experiment (see Figure 19–1). It will be recalled that Leavitt controlled the communication of the subjects in order to produce four communication networks (see Figure 19–2): the wheel, the Y, the chain, and the circle.

The task Leavitt assigned to the groups was simple. Each member of the group was given a card with five of six possible symbols on it. There was one symbol which appeared on all the cards; one of the other five was absent from at least one card. The task was to discover which symbol all cards had in common. To do this, the members *had* to communicate with one another.

Leavitt examined the group behavior of members in each network, and his results demonstrate clearly the effects of each pattern. The most *efficient* pattern was the wheel: the least time was needed, fewer errors were made than in any pattern other than the Y (which it matched), and fewer messages were needed to finish the task. The Y was second most efficient, the chain was third, and the circle least. The organization which evolved in the patterns was very consistent for all but the circle: the most central person, C, received messages from the peripheral members, compiled the information, and sent the answers back to the other members. In the circle, however, the typical procedure was for members to exchange information until anyone came up with an answer; this information was then circulated to the others. Except in the circle, then, *leadership* definitely rested in the hands of the most central person. Note that the wheel pattern is very similar to the authoritarian style described earlier in the study by Lippitt and R. K. White (1947). In terms of morale, or personal satisfaction with the group

experience, the central persons enjoyed the experience most. None of the peripheral members in the wheel, the Y, or the chain, however, enjoyed the task as much as did all the members in the circle.

Although Leavitt's study is a prototype of most of the investigations of communication patterns, one variation deserves mention: the comparison of the effects of one-way and two-way communication and of two different types of tasks on group efficiency. Heise and G. A. Miller (1951) set up five different groups of three men. Members communicated by using an intercommunication system, which was regulated according to one of the one-way and two-way communication networks illustrated in Figure 19–4. The groups were given two different tasks. The first was a sentence-construction task utilizing the same principles employed in Leavitt's experiment; for example, each member was given different parts of the sentence, and the group had to reconstruct the sentence from these parts. It was assumed that the members would have to communicate in order to complete the task. The second was an anagrams task, for which communication was helpful but not essential. Each person could do the anagrams on his own, but, owing to duplication, the final group product was not likely to be as great as it would be if the members worked together. Heise and Miller found that for the sentence-construction task there was an increase in efficiency (time required and number of statements made) from pattern 1 to pattern 5 as shown in Figure 19–4. For the anagrams task they found no significant differences among the five patterns. Since communication was necessary to complete the first task but not the second, communication structure, as a determinant of group efficiency, appears to be important *only* when communication is requisite to the successful completion of the task.

In addition to the extensions of these original studies, there have been several attempts to provide new approaches to the meaning of "communication patterns" within the context of a small working group, as Glanzer and R.

FIGURE 19-4: *Five nets used in the research of Heise and G. A. Miller. The arrows indicate the direction of communication from the talker to the listener. (Heise & G. A. Miller, 1951, p. 328.)*

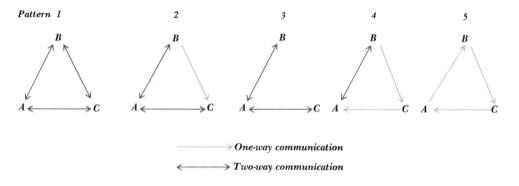

Glaser (1961) point out. We mentioned one such attempt in the section on Task Structure. Lanzetta and T. B. Roby (1956) looked at the various possibilities for communication in terms of autonomy and the direct or indirect accessibility of information pertinent to the task. Rosenberg and R. L. Hall (1958) viewed the problem in the context of feedback as reinforcement for one's original communication. For example, if the feedback is direct, subjects tend to work faster than if they are confronted by feedback about a partner's work. This approach to the communications structure has opened the topic to considerations involving learning theory (Chapters 12 to 15).

An interesting sidelight and example of the way in which "empirical accidents" can affect the psychologist's understanding of a particular phenomenon is pointed out in a study by Leavitt and Knight (1963). They note that we generally assume that the circle pattern is most efficient when it functions as a relay chain (Figure 19-5). *A* and *E* concurrently pass information to *B* and *D*, respectively, who subsequently pass it on to *C*. *C* integrates the information and passes it back along the same route. (In this case, *C* can be any member of the group—the issue is one of picking someone to be the focus of the group's operations.) One of the circle's inefficiencies is the amount of time wasted in setting up such an organi-

zation. The chain is established in such a way that this procedure is almost inevitably chosen. Leavitt and Knight note that the procedure involves five time periods for all members to receive the correct information: (1) *A* to *B* and *E* to *D;* (2) *B* and *D* to *C;* (3) *C* to *B;* (4) *C* to *D* and *B* to *A;* (5) *D* to *E* (Figure 19–5). They then present a different procedure by which the time periods can be cut to three (see Figure 19–6) when members swap, rather than relay, information. In addition they take into account the relative time necessary for each operation (e.g., writing one's information versus writing information for two people). By means of a series of such trades of information in which *C* is no longer the key person and persons *A* and *E* no longer sit by idly waiting for the ultimate result to be sent back to them, the time needed to complete the task can be greatly decreased.

Leavitt and Knight attribute the fact that this pattern or organization has never been used by experimental groups to (1) the difficulties of organizing such a pattern in a circle network and (2) the researchers' almost unanimous use of groups composed of an odd number of subjects. Had more research been conducted with groups of four subjects, for example, more efficient organizations, like that proposed by Leavitt and Knight, might have been developed. But with three- or five-man groups the shuttling of information to a central person appears more natural. Hence, an empirical accident (odd numbers of subjects) has been a partial cause of an unjustified assumption about what is the most efficient organization for one of these communication patterns.

The bulk of our discussion of communication structure has dealt with artificially imposed patterns of "who can communicate with whom." Most small groups, needless to say, have no such restrictions imposed on them; they are, in effect, networks in which all channels are potentially open. Several studies suggest, however, that there are a few factors which can partially, and perhaps completely, restrict communication among several members of a group. Norms in large businesses, for example, demand that you do not speak directly to the chairman of the board but rather to some special assistant to the chairman or to a secretary. Or in a student-faculty committee one member may have discovered that because of some personal conflict between himself and the committee chairman his suggestions are always rejected by the leader. To be effective, he may find it necessary to make his suggestions to another member of the committee, who, in turn, can present them to the chairman. Experimentally, Kelley's (1951) and Thibaut's (1950) studies indicate that communication can be restricted by status and the opportunity for mobility in the group: high-status persons are the focus of communication from other group members.

Seating position can also make a difference in the communication pattern. Hare and Bales (1963) note that in a group with the seating arrangements shown in Figure 19–7, the persons in seats 1, 3, and 5 tend to dominate the conversation when it is concerned with task-related information. Dominant people tend to choose a chair in one of these three positions. In addition, Hare and Bales note that distance between seats is a factor in communication. The greater the distance between two people, the more likely they are to direct task-related conversation to one another. Hence,

FIGURE 19–5: *Assumed solution for the circle network.*

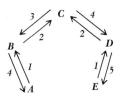

Step	Action	Information at the end of the step		
1	A→B E→D	A:a D:de	B:ab E:e	C:c
2	B→C D→C	A:a D:de	B:ab E:e	C:abcde
3	C→B	A:a D:de	B:abcde E:e	C:abcde
4	B→A C→D	A:abcde D:abcde	B:abcde E:e	C:abcde
5	D→E	A:abcde D:abcde	B:abcde E:abcde	C:abcde

the persons in positions 1 and 5 will converse more frequently than any other pair in the group. Persons sitting next to each other are more likely to engage in non-task-related conversation.

Although these studies do not cover all the information available concerning the facilitation and inhibition of communication between members of a group, they do indicate that differences in probability of communication between various members exist. Since communication is an inescapable attribute of any group's operation, the study of determinants of the patterns of communication, such as those we have described here, is vital to an ultimate understanding of small-group behavior.

AFFECT STRUCTURE: The affect structure of a group is the pattern of friendship within the group—who likes whom. To a great extent, this structure is interwoven with, and very de-

FIGURE 19-6: *Proposed solution for the circle network. (Leavitt & Knight, 1963, p. 262.)*

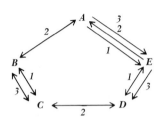

Step	Action	Information at the end of the step		
1	A→E; B→C; C→B; D→E; E→D	A:a; D:de	B:bc E:ade	C:bc
2	A→B; B→A; C→D; D→C; E→A	A:abcde; D:bcde;	B:abc E:ade	C:bcde
3	A→E; B→C; C→B; E→D	A:abcde C:abcde E:abcde		B:abcde D:abcde

FIGURE 19-7: *Seating positions in the research of Hare and Bales.*

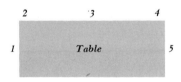

pendent upon, the task, communication, and power structures of the group. For example, it is more probable that a person will like someone with whom he can communicate freely and frequently than someone with whom communication is difficult. Hence, many of the points in our discussion of affect structure necessarily involve attributes of the task, communication, and power structures. We shall also consider the concept of *group cohesiveness,* which is the sum of the members' attraction to the group. This topic is included here

because a member's attraction to the group often reflects his attraction to specific members of the group, which essentially refers to features of the affect structure. Cohesiveness may also be based on other factors, however, such as the prestige gained from being a member of the group or the aid received in reaching a goal one cannot attain alone.

The number of investigations of the origins of interpersonal attraction has increased greatly since 1955, and many different variables have been examined. The variables can be grouped into four categories: (1) geographic and spatial proximity, (2) attractiveness, (3) similarity and complementarity of personal characteristics, and (4) instrumentality.

Geographic and Spatial Proximity: Variables that indicate the extent of interpersonal contiguity, such as those designating residence and membership in a given group, may be subsumed in this category. Proximity is assumed to affect patterns of friendship because it determines the amount of opportunity people have for contact with one another. Studies conducted on this topic attempt to discover the extent to which opportunity for contact is related to patterns of interpersonal attraction. Two examples should indicate the nature of most of these investigations.

Festinger, S. Schachter, and Back (1950) studied opportunity for contact and interpersonal attraction in two university housing projects. They discovered that the majority of close friendships which developed were between next-door neighbors. Moreover, they found that persons whose apartments were situated so that opportunity for contact with others in the project was maximized—such as those located next to a central stairway—developed closer friendships than residents living in less accessible apartments. M. Sherif and C. W. Sherif (1953) studied the formation of friendships between boys attending a summer camp. Initially the boys engaged in activities as a single large group, all of them living in the same bunkhouse. After several days, the experimenters divided the campers into two smaller contingents and observed the changes in friendships. They found that close friendships that had developed within the larger group soon dissolved and were replaced with new alliances within the subgroups.

In both these studies, geographic or spatial proximity was positively related to interpersonal attraction. That is, because of the spatial nature of the living conditions in the housing project and the camp, a person had more opportunity for contact with some people than with others. Both studies show that one is most likely to form a friendship with people with whom one has the most contact. One interpretation of this finding is that opportunity for contact operates as a necessary but not sufficient condition for developing a positive interpersonal relationship. Given two people who are equally desirable as friends, a person is more likely to develop a friendship with the one with whom he has the greater contact, because he will have a greater opportunity to discover the degree to which there is a basis for friendship. A slightly different, yet perhaps complementary, interpretation is that in a situation where one is forced into constant contact with others, life with them is much more enjoyable if one makes friends rather than remaining neutral or unfriendly. Two people who might never form a friendship under conditions where contact is optional might adopt a friendship to facilitate their interaction when they are forced together.

Attractiveness: This concept refers to qualities of a person which, in and of themselves, make him attractive to others. Although there have been a number of investigations of attractiveness, there is almost no consensus about which particular qualities compose this variable. A person's attractiveness might simply be a function of his "likeableness," that is, his apparent display of friendliness toward others. It might be a function of some characteristic that instills admiration on the part of others, such as his success in sports or in attracting members of the opposite sex. But these are all vague, almost meaningless phrases to the behavioral scientist.

Instead of referring to specific studies of personality characteristics and attractiveness,

we shall report the results of two extensive surveys of the literature on the topic. R. D. Mann reports that the general popularity of a person in a small group, which we shall assume is equivalent to attractiveness, is positively related to intelligence, adjustment, extroversion, masculinity, conservatism, and interpersonal sensitivity. He cautions, however, that in the large number of studies he reviewed, "in no case is the median correlation between an aspect of personality covered here . . . higher than .25, and most of the median correlations are closer to .15," indicating a very meager relationship between popularity and the referent variable (1959, p. 266).

A. J. Lott and B. E. Lott, reviewing the literature on group cohesiveness, conclude that ". . . attractiveness of an individual is enhanced by certain behavior which may be either temporary and situation bound or enduring and central to his personality. This behavior . . . can be described in terms of warmth, equalitarianism, good adjustment, sensitivity, helpfulness, and so on" (1965, p. 270). Note that Lott and Lott point out that these characteristics (which tend to project attractiveness) may not be the same for different people or for different situations. This suggests that it would be very difficult to designate specific qualities that are universally attractive within a culture. Consistent with this view is Mann's finding of low correlations between personality characteristics and popularity. It would seem that any meaningful study of personal characteristics and interpersonal attraction must include an analysis of the social context of the person's relationship, which would serve as a guide to predicting which attractive qualities are relevant to the relationship and which are not.

Similarity versus Complementarity: Another category of determinants of attraction between persons concerns the relationship between two persons' personal characteristics— their attitudes, values, interests, demographic characteristics (e.g., age and sex), social needs, etc. Three major hypotheses have been presented on this topic: First, some theorists (e.g., Newcomb, 1961) propose that *similarity* of two persons' characteristics leads to attraction between the persons. There is ample support for this position. An example is Newcomb's study (1961) of the formation of friendships among previously unacquainted college transfer students. He measured their attitudes and values before they arrived at the house he provided for them as well as the formation and maintenance of friendships during the subsequent fifteen weeks. Newcomb compared the similarity of the preacquaintance attitudes and values of pairs of persons who were friends and those who were not, during the first few weeks. Pairs who liked one another at the end of the fifteen-week period showed much more similarity in attitudes and values than did pairs who disliked each other after that long an acquaintance. Newcomb concluded that similarity of attitudes and values was a determinant of the affect structure in this group.

L. R. Hoffman and Maier (1966) present results which discredit the similarity hypothesis. They examined the development of attraction among members of four-person groups. The groups met two hours a week for eleven weeks to work together on tasks assigned them as part of a course in human relations. Groups were composed either of persons homogeneous or heterogeneous in personality characteristics. Attraction among members was assessed after the fifth, eighth, and eleventh weeks of meetings. Hoffman and Maier report no differences in the interpersonal attraction of members in either homogeneous or heterogeneous groups.

Most of the investigations of similarity consist of measuring the subjects' characteristics at a given point in time and correlating these with the characteristics of their best friends (e.g., Izard, 1960), or the persons to whom they are engaged (e.g., Banta & Hetherington, 1963), or their husbands or wives (e.g., Kelly, 1955). Besides Newcomb's study and that of Hoffman and Maier, there have been almost no longitudinal investigations of the development of interpersonal attraction.

A second hypothesis is that *complementarity* of two persons' characteristics leads to attraction between them. This conception was introduced by R. F. Winch (1958) in his study of married couples. He felt that in one type of variable—*social needs*—husbands and wives should have a certain degree of complementarity. Complementarity has two distinct attributes, according to Winch. First, for certain needs, if one partner is high in those needs, the other should be low in order for the marriage to constitute a viable relationship. For example, a very dominant husband would be attracted to a very nondominant wife. He could satisfy his need to dominate with no interference from her. Second, there are various *combinations* of social needs which should go together in a happy marriage. For example, if the husband is high in dominance, the wife should be high in deference (admiration and respect), low in aggressiveness, and low in exhibitionism (showing off, demanding attention from others, etc.). Using an interview he devised, Winch measured 15 social needs of a sample of married couples. Then he correlated the scores of each of the needs for each couple and found sufficient, though not overwhelming, support for his hypothesis.

A third hypothesis, essentially an extension of complementarity, suggests that combinations of two persons' social needs must be considered (1) in terms of the extent to which the needs imply gratification or frustration for the two people (e.g., one's high dominance with the other's low submissiveness leads to frustration) and (2) the extent to which the needs are relevant to the *social context* in which the two persons are interacting. For example, high aggressiveness in one person and high self-depreciation in the other should lead to some attraction, because the one's aggressiveness will be accepted by the other. Despite this theoretical "good match," such a partnership is not likely to last in an environment or institution where aggressiveness is an undesirable characteristic. In a monastery, an aggressive member would be rejected by a self-depreciating member, because the social norms in such a context are against aggressive behavior.

The concept of attraction as derived from

mutual gratification of social needs and modified by the social context of the relationship was proposed by D. R. Miller (1963) and tested by Wagner (1963) and Bermann (1964). In his study, Wagner used pairs of counselors working together in a summer camp. He compared the compatibility of combinations of relevant social needs of pairs who wanted to work together with those of pairs who did not. Dominance, for example, was considered a relevant social need, because counselors must make decisions when they work together. One counselor's need to dominate was therefore important to other counselors' desire to work with him. The results showed that counselors who wanted to work together were much better "matched" on the relevant social needs than those who did not want to be partners. Bermann's study compared pairs of student room-mates who wanted to continue living together with pairs who did not. He also found that the social needs of successfully paired room-mates were more compatible than those of unsuccessfully paired ones. A comparison of these studies provides an example of the importance of the "social context" to interpersonal attraction. In Wagner's study, compatibility on the need for achievement had no bearing on who wanted to work with whom; on the other hand, achievement was significantly better matched for happily paired room-mates than for unhappily paired room-mates according to the Bermann study. This difference between the two studies supports the contention that the social context is a highly important variable in the analysis of interpersonal relationships, since achievement was more relevant in a college setting than in a summer camp.

L. R. Hoffman and Maier (1966) concur. They suggest that the difference in the results of their study and Newcomb's of similarity and attraction can be explained in terms of the nature of the groups involved. Maier and Hoffman used working groups (members of a college course), and Newcomb used social groups (rooming-house residents). Perhaps similarity in personal characteristics is desirable when the main purpose of interacting is to enjoy oneself. Similarity loses its value when the purpose is to solve problems. This conclusion is supported indirectly by the L. R. Hoffman and Maier study (1961) which showed that heterogeneous groups perform better on problem-solving tasks than do homogeneous groups. Therefore, when task performance is important, homogeneity, or similarity, should not lead to higher interpersonal attraction among group members than heterogeneity.

Apparently some type of matching of personal characteristics helps to determine the extent to which members of a group will like one another. Some studies have found similarity of characteristics to be related to attraction. Others have found complementarity to be associated with attraction. One explanation of this discrepancy is that similarity is important when people are becoming acquainted; later, mutually gratifying combinations of needs are important for maintaining a relationship over a longer period of time. A person who likes art is likely to begin friendships among people who also like art. He develops his initial relationships with them on the basis of their similar interest. He does not, however, sustain intimate friendships with all the connoisseurs of art whom he knows. Instead, on the basis of his initial experiences with them, he selects those whom he finds the most enjoyable in this and in other activities. Continued mutual attraction is dependent upon something more substantial than a mutual interest in art, namely, mutually gratifying combinations of needs that would pervade an interpersonal relationship in a number of different contexts. This explanation is supported by Rosenfeld and Jackson (1965) who noted that similarity of friends' attitudes and values was higher for those who had been acquainted for less than one year than for those acquainted longer than one year.

Instrumentality: By instrumentality, we mean the degree to which one person can facilitate or interfere with another's attempt to attain a goal. The goal referred to is an external goal, one which is attained by task-oriented behavior. This differentiates instrumentality from the concept of mutual gratification of social needs discussed above, in which the reward was derived from the very process of interacting, irrespective of the activity in which the people engaged. The few studies relevant to this topic support the hypothesis that there is a positive relationship between a person's instrumentality and his attractiveness to other members of the group. Kleiner (1960), for example, studied groups of three people working on a task, one of whom was a stooge with prior knowledge of the task solutions. The stooge proved to be very instrumental in aiding the group to complete its work successfully. An analysis of the ratings of the other two members showed that they considered him significantly more attractive after they had worked together than before. Presumably his attractiveness increased because he had been instrumental in helping them reach their goal.

Jennings (1952) reports on popularity ratings of girls living in the New York State Training School for Girls. The data indicate that instrumentality in *interfering* with goal attainment is also central to the formation of affect structure. Jennings states that "to the underchosen (girls who were unattractive to others) ... are attributed twelve times as many incidences of actively or passively interfering with the group's activities, as to the over-chosen, while such incidences are practically missing for the average-chosen" (1952, p. 315). In other words, interference with goal attainment leads to rejection by group members, just as facilitation leads to acceptance. Both these investigations, then, support the contention that the ability to facilitate or to interfere with the group's attainment of a goal helps to determine attractiveness to the group and, consequently, the group's affect structure.

Effects of the Affect Structure: The affect structure of a group has a variety of effects on the group and its members. We shall discuss how this structure can affect (1) other types of group structure, (2) the members of the group, and (3) the productivity of the group.

General group structure: As indicated previously, the affect structure is intimately involved with the communication, power, and task structures of the group. A study by A. J. Lott and B. E. Lott (1961) illustrates the effect that mutual attraction among members of a group can have on communication. They required small groups of friends to discuss a topic for thirty minutes and recorded the frequency and direction of communication. The results demonstrate a direct relationship between the strength of mutual attraction and the frequency of communication among group members.

There is one important exception to this generalization. When a nonattractive member of the group expresses an opinion which deviates from the opinion held by the majority of the group, communication toward the deviant increases greatly. This has been demonstrated in a number of studies. Festinger and Thibaut (1951), for example, found that when a range of opinions exists in a group, there is more communication toward persons holding extreme opinions than toward those espousing less extreme positions. S. Schachter (1951), in a similar experiment, made a more extensive analysis and noted that at first the deviant is the focus of communication but as the other members perceive that he will not change his extreme opinion they eventually ignore him.

Two examples of research using group cohesiveness illustrate the effect "liking" can have on the power structure of a group. Back (1951) selected pairs of subjects and showed each partner separately a similar but not identical set of three pictures. Both partners were told they had seen the same pictures. The pairs were asked, first, to discuss the scenes they had been shown and then, independently, to write stories about them. Since the pictures each subject saw were slightly different from those seen by his partner, this procedure allowed the experimenter to measure influence or power by the extent each person wrote about scenes presented to the partner and never actually seen by the writer. Back found that subjects who were greatly attracted to their partner accepted more of his influence than did subjects not attracted to the partner.

Berkowitz (1957) conducted an investigation, also using pairs of subjects, which supports Back's results. He used a simulated army artillery-team procedure; one partner was the "observer," and the other the "battery commander." Using charts, the observer would "phone" the battery commander, informing him of the location of the "enemy." With this information and some "possibly unreliable" maps of the area, the battery commander was required to decide where the artillery should be aimed. The experimenter arranged the charts and maps so that there was an inevitable discrepancy between what the observer reported and what the commander saw on his "possibly unreliable" maps. As a result, the degree to which the commander relied on the observer's report for establishing the site of the target, in relation to what his maps showed, was used as a measure of the influence the observer had on the commander. Berkowitz's results, like those of Back, indicate that the more the commander was attracted to the observer, the more he was influenced by him. To generalize from these results, we conclude that the affect structure can produce an important effect on the power structure of a group.

There is very little direct evidence indicating the degree to which the affect structure determines the task structure of a group. It seems to be generally true that people who like one another also work well together (e.g., Berkowitz, 1956; Bjerstedt, 1961), but studies of this phenomenon indicate little about the initial selection of coworkers. In almost all the studies of selection of working partners, the subject's choice of partners is based on their previous experience in working together on other tasks; seldom is the selection made purely on the basis of whether they like one another apart from the context of work. Therefore, there is little support for the assumption that people who are friends will choose to work together. Indeed, the opposite view seems equally reasonable: people who are friends

spend much of their time socializing, which is not conducive to a high production rate; therefore, if the work is important, they may prefer *not* to work together. We conclude, then, that the effect that affect structure can have on task structure has not been clarified by research.

Members' characteristics: Most studies concerning affect, or attraction, have dealt with attraction of members to one another, or group cohesiveness, instead of attraction to specific members. The majority of the research on group cohesiveness (e.g., Berkowitz, 1957) has been focused on its effect on conformity. Most of the results of these studies demonstrate a positive relationship between high group cohesiveness and conformity: the more attracted a person is to the members of a group, the more he will conform to the norms the group has established.

Several investigations of affect between specific members of groups deserve mention. In his study of the development of friendships in a student boardinghouse, Newcomb (1961) measured changes in the students' attitudes over a period of fifteen weeks. He notes that the attitudes, values, and interests of people who were attracted to one another became more similar during that time. He believes that people become friends initially because they perceive a general agreement between their evaluations of a number of people, objects, and events. As the friendship continues, they communicate with each other and, in the process, resolve some of the inevitable differences that remain between their attitudes. Hence, their agreement increases as a result of their mutual attraction. The finding by Rosenfeld and Jackson (1965) that similarity of friends' attitudes was higher for those acquainted for less than one year than for those acquainted longer than one year suggests that the increase in agreement reaches an eventual plateau. L. R. Hoffman and Maier (1966) found such a plateau occurring after the eighth week of meetings of small groups engaged in problem-solving tasks.

Changes in self-perception and self-evaluation, which are a part of self-identity or the self-concept, have been the subject of several investigations of interpersonal attraction. Some theorists (e.g., D. R. Miller, 1963; C. R. Rogers, 1951) believe the self-concept to be a critical attribute of personality. Manis (1955) examined changes in students' perception of themselves during their first year in college and compared these changes with the perceptions held of them by a group of close friends and a group of nonfriends. His findings were that the subjects' self-perceptions change significantly more in the direction of their friends' perceptions of them than toward their nonfriends' perceptions of them. Sherwood (1965) studied the same phenomenon in a natural setting using a group of human-relations trainees. He measured each member's perception of himself and of every other member in the group. His results showed that during the two-week training session, members' self-perception shifted significantly toward the perception of them held by their two best friends in the group. There is, then, some slight evidence that a group member's friends can effect a change in some of his characteristics (e.g., attitudes and self-identity). Unfortunately, virtually no information is available about the relative degree to which other types of characteristics (e.g., abilities, intelligence, and social needs) can be altered by one's friends within the group.

Task performance: The effects of the affect structure on task performance of the group are complex. Almost all the relevant research considers affect structure in terms of the general attraction of the members to the group (cohesiveness), not in terms of specific patterns of friendship within the group. Some investigators have noted a consistent improvement in group performance as the cohesiveness of the group increased (e.g., Goodacre, 1951; 1953). Others have noted that cohesiveness can lead to lower productivity. The key to this confusion seems to be the concept of *group norms,* that is, the standards of behavior implicitly or explicitly established in the group. Highly cohesive groups will follow the group norms

more closely than will less cohesive ones. When the norms are to increase performance, performance will increase. When the norms are to decrease or maintain a given level of performance, the performance will be kept at the desired rate (S. Schachter, Ellertson, D. McBride, & Gregory, 1951). G. C. Homans (1950) emphasizes this latter point in his analysis of small teams of industrial workers. He notes that the high performance of the "rate-buster," the worker who produces more than anyone else and thus increases the chances that management will require other workers to increase their rate of production, is much more effectively suppressed in cohesive than in uncohesive groups. The cohesive team often develops a ritualized procedure of mentally and physically punishing the rate-buster, ultimately forcing him either to quit or to adhere to the production standards accepted by the other members of the team.

The generally greater productivity associated with high attractiveness among members of a group, in the absence of norms for either low or stable performance, can be attributed to two consequences of cohesiveness: First, in cohesive groups there is greater communication among members than in noncohesive groups. This apparently facilitates performance. Second, as noted earlier, there is greater conformity in cohesive groups than in noncohesive ones. As a result, there is less disruption of the group's efforts by persons who deviate from the group's norms and, consequently, greater concentration of effort on completing the task.

Three reasons, on the other hand, favor the interpretation that attraction between members can decrease group performance: First, it is possible that a leader—the one who must decide upon division of labor and other matters relevant to performance—may permit friendship to obscure his judgment in assigning members to the jobs for which they are best suited. Fiedler (1954) recognized the importance of a leader's ability to distinguish among the members' various abilities in his investigation of the relative success of several natural athletic and industrial work groups. He examined the perceptions the leaders (e.g., the captains of basketball teams) had of the characteristics of all the members of their groups. He then noted the discrepancy between each leader's perception of the members whom the leader most and least preferred in the group. Fiedler's findings were that the greater the discrepancy (that is, the greater the difference the leader perceived between these two people), the greater was the success of the group. Fiedler (1965) interprets this result in terms of the ability of the leader to divorce himself from the group and to use the various skills of the members in the most efficient manner possible, instead of being a friendly leader who tries to please everyone and make certain that no one's feelings are hurt by being assigned mediocre duties.

Second, the very activities in which friends engage socially may interfere with the group's performance. Socializing and working on a task may be mutually exclusive, depending, of course, on the difficulty of the task. This has not been demonstrated experimentally but is suggested in Wagner's data (1963) on the selection of working partners: in some instances, friends did not choose each other as partners, stating that they feared they would waste their time conversing instead of concentrating on their work.

Third, conformity, which tends to increase with general attraction among members of a group, can stifle certain types of creative skills. In tasks requiring inventive solutions, deviant opinions are often very valuable in helping the group to complete its task. Conformity inhibits deviation and thereby can lead to poor performance. Maier and Solem (1952) believe that this explains the difference in performance on a task requiring creativity between groups having a leader who merely observed the meetings and groups having a leader who led the discussions. The latter leaders allowed minority (that is, deviant, nonconforming) opinions to be stated and thus enhanced the probability that a creative, high-quality solution to the problem would emerge.

It appears that the affect structure as characterized by group cohesiveness plays an important part in the group's performance. It can help to improve performance by increasing the flow of communication, by determining who will be listened to and followed in the group, and by leading to conformity, which often increases performance in noncreative tasks. It can hinder group performance when the members conform to a group norm to limit their performance, when crucial persons allow their friendships to interfere with the assignment of duties according to ability, when the group spends an inordinate amount of time socializing instead of working, and when it inhibits deviant but potentially valuable creative ideas from being suggested as solutions to complex tasks.

Group Interaction: Group interaction is behavior engaged in by a group member which has consequences for other members. Interaction may consist of any type of behavior—talking, making facial expressions, writing messages, tapping a pencil on a table, silently working with another person on a common task, and so on. A facial expression such as a smile may encourage other members to continue talking. Tapping a pencil may irritate other members and disrupt the group. Working silently with a partner may encourage him to continue working, which he might not do without this companionship.

Group interaction is a neglected field in the study of small-group behavior. To some extent the neglect derives from the belief that interaction serves primarily as a vehicle by which an independent variable (e.g., particular communication patterns) has its effect on a dependent variable (e.g., group performance). Although most theorists admit that interaction can vary from group to group, they have shunned this variable in favor of other group characteristics which are somewhat more easily delineated. The position of interaction as an attribute of group behavior is somewhat analogous to that of the process of thinking as an attribute of individual behavior. Most people acknowledge that thinking is a behavioral process and are aware that there may be individual differences in the process. Because investigators are more interested in other variables (e.g., schedules of reinforcement) and the resulting behavior (e.g., extinction of a response), however, they tend to ignore the intervening process—thinking, in this case—and assume that individual differences will offset one another if they use a sufficiently large sample of subjects.

Despite this general neglect, a few investigators have examined the interaction process with great care, both because they believe that, as an attribute of behavior, interaction is intrinsically worthy of study and because they appreciate that as an intervening variable it can have an important bearing on the results of all investigations of group behavior. In addition, they feel that an analysis of interaction may allow an investigator to analyze and interpret his data more meaningfully. Newcomb, for example, became interested in interaction because he believed that his data showing that persons with similar attitudes become attracted to one another could be more clearly explained in terms of the *feedback* which occurs during interaction. That is, A begins to like B when he notes that B has reacted to him (feedback) by showing an interest in the same things that he, A, has expressed an interest in (Newcomb, R. H. Turner, & Converse, 1965).

Studies of the interaction process itself, irrespective of variables which may affect or be affected by it, have focused on two major factors: (1) two functionally different categories of interaction, one related to the emotional relationships among group members and the other to the task confronting the group, and (2) a sequence of functional phases through which most groups tend to pass during the course of their existence. We shall consider each of these topics in some detail.

TASK AND SOCIAL FUNCTIONS: The important distinction between acts related to the group's task and those concerned with the regulation of interpersonal relationships per se within the group was first outlined by Barnard (1938) and received further impetus and clarification from Jennings (1947) and Bales (1953). Jennings studied groups of girls living in a state training school and noticed that they made different choices of partners depending upon whether the partner was for leisure-time activities or for working together. The choice for leisure was based on the partner's ability to satisfy the chooser's personal emotional needs. The chooser enjoyed being with her partner regardless of the type of recreational activity in which they were involved. The choice for work was determined more by ability to work smoothly with the chooser and to contribute meaningfully to the group effort.

Bales also distinguishes two main types of interaction. He refers to groups whose primary purpose is to accomplish a task as *task-oriented groups,* and those concerned primarily with diversion, leisure, or recreational activities as *socioemotionally oriented groups.* Bales's main modification of Jennings's formulation was to suggest that these two types of groups seldom exist in pure form. Instead, Bales believes that the implied functions of each are complementary and must be performed in all groups, although the relative importance of each may differ from group to group. For example, when the student-faculty committee discusses plans for improving the orientation program for freshmen, they are performing task functions. It must be assumed, however, that in order to present a consensual design for improvements, they must cooperate with one another. Satisfaction in working with the members of the committee is central to cooperation. When they engage in acts that enhance this satisfaction, such as periodic social conversations, they are performing socioemotional functions. Bales maintains that both functions exist and are often interdependent in all groups. Therefore, he analyzed both task and socioemotional acts within groups, and he noted that some members tend to perform one type of activity more than another. He refers to the person engaged primarily in acts related to performing the task confronting the group as the *task specialist* and the one responsible for maintaining smooth, nonconflictual interpersonal relationships as the *socioemotional specialist*.

Bales finds that seldom is one person capable of performing both roles within the group. Instead, the functions are almost always divided among two or more people. Perhaps this occurs because the task specialist, if he is to lead well; must perform certain duties which almost inevitably lead to unhappiness for some of the group members. He must delegate responsibility to them according to their abilities, and those who are given the least desirable or least responsible tasks will feel slighted. Or he must evaluate the various suggestions made by the members, and those whose ideas are rejected may feel they have been unfairly treated. Therefore, the task specialist is not likely to be the most popular member of the group, which would make it difficult for him to serve as a socioemotional specialist as well. Instead, a secondary leader often emerges to fulfill the socioemotional role. He frequently acts as a liaison between the task specialist and the rest of the group. The task specialist, then, may become very dependent upon the socioemotional specialist if he is to lead effectively (Fiedler, 1954).

PHASES IN GROUP INTERACTION: A further and very important contribution of Bales and his associates was their initial analysis of the phases of interaction through which a group passes as it attempts to complete the task confronting it. Their analysis suggests that a problem-solving group goes through three distinguishable stages—orientation, evaluation, and control (Bales & Strodtbeck, 1951). The *orientation phase* consists of attempts of the members to acquaint themselves with the nature of their task and of suggesting possible approaches to it. The *evaluation phase* is composed of asking for and giving opinions, agreeing or disagreeing with them about the best way to resolve the problem. The *control phase* consists of acts aimed at bringing together the opinions and information from previous phases in an attempt to come to an ultimate

consensus about finishing the task. It is further characterized by an increase in positive and negative reactions toward others, with an emphasis on positive acts (e.g., agreement, tension release, and solidarity) if the group's efforts have been successful or on negative acts (e.g., disagreement, tension, and antagonism) if they have been unsuccessful.

An observation by Tuckman (1965) suggests that Bales's ideas warrant further examination in different social contexts. He reports that a fourth phase, coming between orientation and evaluation, frequently appears in groups whose primary purpose is to analyze the interpersonal relationships among members. An example is a therapeutic group in which the emphasis is upon why one acts toward others the way one does. Tuckman calls this phase *intragroup hostility* and says that it is characterized by uneasiness, unrest, and friction among members. He feels it is caused by the negative reaction of members to the emotional demands made upon them in such groups. The demands become difficult to endure when the novelty of the group experience, which occurs during the orientation stage, has extinguished. Task-oriented groups are generally much less exhausting emotionally and much more impersonal than groups of the kind Tuckman discusses. Hence they do not evoke such a negative response.

Bennis and H. A. Shepard (1956) present a different approach to the analysis of phases of group interaction. Their idea that group development passes through two major phases also derives from experiences in groups whose primary purpose is to consider the interpersonal relationships among members. Bennis and Shepard believe that in the first phase group members concentrate on resolving uncertainties about their relations to authority. This phase contains three subphases: (1) dependence-flight, characterized by the members' attempts to dispel anxiety arising from initial contact and uncertainty about the power structure of the group by appealing to a leader for direction; (2) counterdependence-flight, characterized by the members' disenchantment with a leader who cannot or will not reduce their anxiety by providing a strong power structure for the group and the eventual emergence of antagonism toward each other as a means of indirectly expressing their hostility toward the leader; and (3) resolution-catharsis, characterized by the members' assumption of responsibility for the group's progress.

Once the group has successfully negotiated these subphases, the members turn their attention to resolving uncertainties about their personal affective relationships to each other. This phase also contains three subphases: (1) enchantment-flight, characterized by an atmosphere of "sweetness and light" as the members attempt to dispel the memory of the anxiety and mutual antagonism evident in the previous phase; (2) disenchantment-flight, characterized by the members' fear of excessive intimacy and the realization that their positive feelings toward each other, which derive primarily from their relief at successfully negotiating the tense periods in previous subphases, are superficial; and (3) consensual validation, characterized by the members' rational acceptance of their responsibilities and affective feelings toward each other. Groups may stall at any one of these subphases and thereby fail to reach the point at which the members can communicate freely and contend rationally with the tasks or activities confronting them.

MEASURING GROUP INTERACTION: Group interaction must be measured by some type of observation of the group process. In one observational procedure, the observer may sit in the room during the group's meetings either as a participating member or as an outsider. This method has the advantage that the observer can see and hear almost everything that occurs during the meeting. It has the disadvantage that the observer's presence may disrupt the normal interaction that would occur were he not there. Many experienced observers believe that the effect of their presence virtually disappears after a short time. Deutsch (1949) supports their contention in his study of cooperation and competition in small groups observed over a period of three weeks.

Polansky, Lippitt, and Redl (1950) come to the opposite conclusion in their study of groups of boys in summer camps, although they admit that the ambiguity of the observers' role in the camp may have contributed to the unnatural behavior exhibited by the boys in the observers' presence (Heyns & Lippitt, 1954). There is an additional danger that, as a member of the group, the participant observer may become so involved in the ongoing events that his observations may be biased.

A second procedure is to observe the group from an adjoining room through a one-way mirror. Although this eliminates the potentially disrupting effect of the observer's presence in the room, it introduces a further problem of artificiality, because a microphone must be placed in front of the group. With such a cue the sophisticated subjects used in many experiments today are almost certain to be aware that they are being observed through the mirror on the wall of their meeting room.

Another common procedure is to film the group's meetings either for movies or for closed-circuit television. This procedure also eliminates the problem of the experimenter's presence and can be valuable if repeated observations of the same sessions are desirable. Unless cleverly concealed, however, cameras and microphones and the necessary lighting equipment produce an extremely artificial setting for group research. In addition, filming seldom captures all the behavior that occurs, since some group members may not be facing the cameras or may be partially hidden by other persons. Tape recordings are used occasionally to record group interaction, but they lack the visual factor which may reveal very informative facial expressions or a nervous tapping of someone's fingers. In addition, it is often difficult for the observer to know exactly who is talking to, or interacting with, whom.

It appears that all the observational procedures have both advantages and disadvantages. Personal observation in the room with the group or through a one-way mirror where the meeting room is not too obviously designed for such observation seem to be the least disruptive means of recording group interaction. Filming, while somewhat more artificial, allows for repeated observations of the same group sessions.

One can measure the nature of the interaction in two different ways: (1) classification of the members' interpersonal acts during the meetings and (2) general ratings of behavior of the members after the session has ended. Let us illustrate each of these procedures:

The *classification method* demands continual scoring of interpersonal acts, according to specified categories, as they occur. An example of one of the most frequently used classification systems is shown in Figure 19–8. The observer notes not only the type of behavior as it occurs (e.g., asks for or gives orientation) but who initiates and directs the act, to whom an act is directed, and who responds to it. In addition, it is possible to score acts according to the time period in which they occur, so that changes in interaction can be detected. Ulti-

mately the experimenter will have a record of the number and different types of acts made by each person, to whom they were directed, and the relative time of their occurrence.

When using the *rating method,* the experimenter observes a group's session and, when it is over, ranks or rates the interpersonal behavior of the individual members on a scale (perhaps a 7-point scale). He might rate each person on behavioral traits, such as aggressiveness, attempts to influence, or asking for help, or on more general factors, such as time spent talking, relevance of activity to the task, suggestions made, and information given. The problem with this method is that the observer must rely on his memory. Events occurring late in the session may overshadow earlier events, or highly emotional interaction may outweigh less emotional behavior.

Both the classification system and the post-session-rating system have advantages and disadvantages. The rating method has the value

FIGURE 19–8: *Observation categories used in Bales's interaction-process analysis. (R. F. Bales, 1952, p. 149.)*

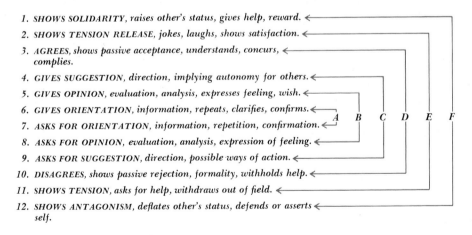

1. *SHOWS SOLIDARITY, raises other's status, gives help, reward.*
2. *SHOWS TENSION RELEASE, jokes, laughs, shows satisfaction.*
3. *AGREES, shows passive acceptance, understands, concurs, complies.*
4. *GIVES SUGGESTION, direction, implying autonomy for others.*
5. *GIVES OPINION, evaluation, analysis, expresses feeling, wish.*
6. *GIVES ORIENTATION, information, repeats, clarifies, confirms.*
7. *ASKS FOR ORIENTATION, information, repetition, confirmation.*
8. *ASKS FOR OPINION, evaluation, analysis, expression of feeling.*
9. *ASKS FOR SUGGESTION, direction, possible ways of action.*
10. *DISAGREES, shows passive rejection, formality, withholds help.*
11. *SHOWS TENSION, asks for help, withdraws out of field.*
12. *SHOWS ANTAGONISM, deflates other's status, defends or asserts self.*

A subclassification of system problems to which each pair of categories is most relevant:

A Problems of orientation   *D Problems of decision*

B Problems of evaluation   *E Problems of tension-management*

C Problems of control   *F Problems of integration*

of allowing certain acts to be given greater weight than others in the overall analysis of interaction. For example, in the classification system the same score would be recorded in "shows antagonism" for such diverse acts as hitting another member in the face or merely saying, "That's a lot of baloney!" to him. On the other hand, in a postsession rating, the observer is more likely to recall the former act than the latter and, therefore, to give it the greater weight than it probably deserves in his overall analysis.

Both systems demand that the observer make some inference about the meaning of group members' acts. The postsession rater can base his inferences on everything that occurred during the meeting, however, while the classifier must make his inferences immediately. The latter cannot correct his scoring on the basis of later acts which may clarify the meaning of earlier ones. In addition, the classifier is often so concerned about capturing and recording every individual act that he may miss the general progression of the group and, as a result, observe many acts out of context.

The classification system does have the advantage of being more objective than the rating system. It partially eliminates the problems of distorted memory. It has relatively clear-cut categories, and the observer takes most of the behavior at its face value. This reduces the distortion which may arise if the observer allows his own emotions to influence his interpretation of the meaning of an interpersonal act.

Carter, Haythorn, Meirowitz, and Lanzetta (1951) evaluated the relationship between these two methods of measuring group behavior, using both to score the same series of group meetings. Some observers scored behavior according to Bales's classification system (Figure 19–8) while the group was in session. Others rated the group members on a series of attributes after the session was over. Carter et al. correlated the scores for those attributes which both systems had in common (e.g., "shows antagonism" from Bales's system was considered the equivalent of "shows a personal feeling of aggressiveness or anger" from the

rating system). They then compared these correlations with the reliability scores they obtained for each of the methods separately. They noted that for those attributes showing *little* agreement between the two methods (correlations between +.30 and +.50), there was also little agreement between observers who used the *same* method for scoring the attribute. Similarly, for those attributes which showed great agreement between the two methods (correlations between +.50 and +.86), there was correspondingly great agreement between observers using the same method. Therefore, Carter et al. concluded that to some extent these two scoring systems were interchangeable. Both methods, however, are weak in the scoring of some attributes and strong in the scoring of others.

To a great extent, the variable of group interaction can be thought of as the "group structure in action": one can translate each of the four types of structure—task, power, communication, and affect—into activity that is interaction. For the task structure, for example, we would look at who is working with whom; for the power structure, who is attempting to influence whom; for the communication structure, who is talking to whom; and for the affect structure, who is showing positive or negative regard for whom. In each case, we can try to analyze the nature of the interpersonal acts that compose the interaction.

The variable of group interaction has been valuable in showing the importance of the different types of interpersonal orientation in the group—task or socioemotional—and in emphasizing the phases through which a group passes in its attempt to resolve problems confronting it. Group interaction can also serve as a means of analyzing the effects of other variables, such as attributes of group composition and structure, on group behavior.

For example, one could use a description of interaction as an explanation of the lower creativity shown by groups with autocratic leaders as compared with groups with democratic leaders. If one were to analyze the nature of the interaction using Bales's classification system, one would probably note that in the autocratic group the single leader makes most of the suggestions, gives most of the information, and makes most of the evaluations of ideas. In the democratic group there is a more even distribution among the members giving information, suggestions, and opinions. It would not be surprising, then, to find the autocratic group, which is essentially using the resources of just one person, less creative than the democratic, which is using the talents of many more.

As another example, S. Schachter's analysis (1951) of the reaction of group members to a person who deviates from the group norms shows that the deviate is rejected. The word *rejection* might be more specifically defined in terms of interaction to mean that no one talks to him any more, that they disagree with him continually, or that they physically leave him. Such a description in terms of interaction could be used very effectively to explain precisely what *rejection* means. Unfortunately, little systematic research has been conducted in this fashion. By so saying, we do not want to belittle the research which has focused on group interaction as an important group variable in and of itself. We are merely pointing out that its main use and analysis thus far have consisted of the delineation of task and social aspects of group behavior and the phases of group problem solving. Perhaps research on many of the variables discussed in previous sections could profit from analysis in terms of group interaction.

SOURCES

For the student interested in gaining a perspective on the position of social psychology in relation to general psychology and some of the other behavioral sciences, Lambert (1963) is recommended. An excellent historical account of the development of modern social psychology is presented by Allport (1954). The original and revised editions of the *Handbook of Social Psychology* (Lindzey, 1954; Lindzey & Aronson, 1967) give valuable and extensive reports of the major theoretical, methodological, and empirical work in social psychology.

For the student interested in specific theoretical approaches to the study of small-group behavior, several sources are available. Bales (1950) presents an approach which tends toward the sociological orientation within social psychology, concentrating primarily on group processes and less on the individuals within the group. His book also describes his methodological procedures for the analysis of the interaction process. The theoretical orientations of G. C. Homans 1950; 1961) and Thibaut and Kelley (1959) are focused on the nature of the interpersonal relationship, with interpersonal behavior viewed in terms of the "rewards and costs" of the interaction to the participants. Lewin (1951) has been an extremely influential force in the study of small-group behavior. His "field theoretical" approach, which encourages the inclusive analysis of the group and its members, incorporates principles of mathematical topology. Deutsch (1954) presents a readable analysis and synthesis of Lewin's basic formulations, and Cartwright (1958) discusses and extends Lewin's concepts in light of recent work in the field. Cartwright and Zander (1960) present research and theory relevant to many of the general principles of small-group behavior which have derived from Lewin's original formulations.

Berger, B. P. Cohen, Snell, and Zelditch (1962) present some of the formal mathematical models which are relevant to the analysis of small-group research. Specifically, they describe in some detail the models designed by (1) Cartwright and Harary (1956), extending F. Heider's (1946) homeostatic principles of cognitive balance to groups; (2) B. P. Cohen (1958), reinterpreting Asch's (1952) studies of conformity; and (3) Estes (1957) and R. C. Atkinson and Suppes (1958), applying Estes' and Burke's (1955) model of discrimination learning of individual subjects to group learning processes.

DeLamater, McClintock, and Becker (1965) provide an analysis of six different conceptual orientations to the study of small groups.

Their article demonstrates three of the basic dimensions on which theories can be compared and would assist the theoretically oriented student in gaining a perspective on the topic. McGrath and I. Altman (1966), noting that research on small groups has been characterized by the use of idiosyncratic terminology, have attempted to reduce the confusion by developing a system of classifying variables according to their basic commonalities. They have reviewed a sample of 250 studies in the field and, by cross classification, have summarized the research on the interrelationships among the major concepts applicable to small-group behavior. Although their systematic approach to the field is complex, it merits consideration by the serious student, because it exemplifies an increasing concern about the proliferation of studies and terms without a concomitant attempt to account for the commonalities present in many of the investigations.

A number of general collections of articles on research on small groups are available. Among these are Hare, Borgatta, and Bales (1955), Hare (1962) and Cartwright and Zander (1960).

The annual *Advances in Experimental Social Psychology* (Berkowitz, 1964–1966) includes both theoretical and review articles on small-group behavior. Among the articles in the 1965 edition, for example, are discussions of group problem solving (Hoffman, 1965), situational factors in conformity (V. L. Allen, 1965), social power (Schopler, 1965), and applications of Festinger's (1957) dissonance theory to interpersonal relations and group productivity (J. K. Adams, 1965).

Small-group research techniques are discussed in some detail in several volumes. Notable among these are Festinger and D. Katz (1953) and several chapters in the *Handbook of Social Psychology* (Lindzey, 1954; Lindzey & Aronson, 1967, vol. II).

Several reviews of the literature published in the *Psychological Bulletin* may be of interest to the student desiring to attain more detailed information about some of the attributes of small groups which have been discussed here. Lorge, Fox, Davitz, and Brenner (1958) review studies comparing group and individual performance. Group composition has been the subject of two articles. R. D. Mann (1959) reviews studies concerning the relationship between members' personality characteristics, their status in the group, and the group's performance. Heslin (1964) presents a summary of research predicting the task effectiveness of a group from the abilities and various key personality characteristics of the members. Three attributes of group structure have been reviewed. Thomas and Fink (1963) present evidence from 31 studies using group size as an independent variable, demonstrating the importance of this variable to such attributes of the group as performance, nature of interaction, and satisfaction of the members. Glanzer and R. Glaser (1961) review research on the effect of the communication and task structures upon group and individual behavior. A. J. Lott and B. E. Lott (1965) provide an extremely comprehensive summary of research on group cohesiveness, defined as interpersonal attraction. They have organized the literature in terms of cohesiveness as an independent and as a dependent variable interrelated with a variety of other attributes of small groups.

In addition, there have been several collections of articles concerning leadership and other characteristics of the group's power structure, among them Cartwright (1959) and Petrullo and B. M. Bass (1961). A review of the literature on one characteristic of group interaction is available. Tuckman (1965) has analyzed a number of investigations of the "developmental sequence in small groups," comparing the results with Bales's original formulations (1950) about different phases of group interaction in problem-solving groups. Finally, L. R. Hoffman (1965) and Collins and Guetzkow (1964) review a number of studies of factors determining group productivity measured by the members' performance on problem solving and "decision-making" tasks. H. B. Gerard (1967) reviews literature on the general topic of "group dynamics."

ACKNOWLEDGMENTS

In preparing a book of this scope an author receives aid of several kinds from many institutions and agencies. I am especially grateful to Mrs. Sidney Alpern Manning, who worked closely with me during the preparation of the final typescript. In addition to clarifying the text, Mrs. Manning undertook the difficult task of locating copyright holders of materials reproduced in this book and of preparing the index.

Professor Richard V. Wagner prepared Chapter 19. I am especially grateful for this contribution.

I am grateful to several colleagues who reviewed the type-script in various stages. They are Professors W. F. Battig, H. F. Harlow, D. W. Milne, W. Prokasy, W. I. Smith, Owen Anderson, L. R. Hoffman, J. J. Sherwood, and J. Harcle-rode. I am also grateful to those of my students who have contributed to this book in many ways. They are, in more or less chronological order, Z. Michael Nagy, Jack Culbert-son, Daniel Conklyn, Silas White, Douglas Bloomquist, Clemm Kessler, Charles Furst, Carl Stoltz, Ann Gallagher, Robert Lakatos, Robert Moyer, Ross Hartsough, Robert Pringle, James Koski, Donald MacNeil, T. James Matthews, Margaret Creaser Blackburn, Robert Orndoff, and Sanford Hyson.

I am indebted to the staff of the Ellen Clark Bertrand Library of Bucknell University, who tirelessly found articles and obscure facts for me. Miss Mildred Bolich, Miss Clara Stoner, and Mrs. Lois Wagner were especially helpful. Mrs. Ann Steinbach, Mrs. Jane Brumbach, and Mrs. Donna Coldren provided technical assistance. Professors P. L. Harriman and Wendell Smith have been generous in supporting this project in many ways.

Several investigators or their families provided me with useful information on their research or knowledge, which I requested. I would especially like to thank Karl M. Dallenbach, S. Howard Bartley, Mrs. Harold Schlosberg, E. Gombrich, Abraham Luchins, E. G. Boring, Israel Dvorine, Ralph Gerbrands, Masayasu Sato, S. S. Stevens, Mrs. Stephen Polyak, Bernard Beer, E. G. Wever, Philip Harriman, Powell Murchison, Gregory Razran, Milton Rosenberg, and N. Tinbergen.

I am grateful to the many investigators and their publishers who granted me permission to reproduce their words or data. Their names appear at the appropriate citation within the text.

REFERENCES AND AUTHOR INDEX

ABBREVIATIONS USED IN REFERENCES

Abh. — Abhandlungen (Proceedings)
abnorm.[1] — Abnormal
Abstr. — Abstract
Acad. — Academy, Academia, Academie
acoust. — acoustical
Agric. — Agriculture
Akad. — Akademie (Academy)
Akust. — Akusticheski (Acoustics)
Amer. — American
Amst. — Amsterdam
Anal. — Analysis
Anat. — Anatomy
anat. — anatomical
anim. — animal
Ann. — Annals
Annu. — Annual (noun)
annu. — annual (adj.)
Anthrop. — Anthropology
Anz. — Anzeige (Report)
appl. — applied
Arch. — Archives
Ass. — Association
Aviat. — Aviation

Bd. — Board
Behav. — Behavior
Ber. — Berichten (Reports)
biochem. — biochemical
Biol. — Biologie (Biology)
biophys. — biophysical
Brit. — Britain, British
Bull. — Bulletin
Bur. — Bureau
Byull. — Byulleten (Bulletin)

Canad. — Canadian
cell. — cellular
Cen. — Center
Chem. — Chemistry
chem. — chemical
Cl. — Classe (Class)
clin. — clinical

Co. — Company
Coll. — College
comp. — comparative
C.R. — Comptes-rendus (Reports)
Conf. — Confinia (Conference)
consult. — consulting
cont. — continued
Contr. — Contributions
Cytol. — Cytology

Def. — Deficiency
Develpm. — Development
Dis. — Disease
Disord. — Disorder
Dokl. — Doklady (Reports)
Dtsch. — Deutsche (German)

EEG — Electroencephalogram
Ed. — Editor
ed. — edition
Eds. — Editors
Educ. — Education
educ. — educational
Electroencephalog. — Electroencephalography
elem. — elementary
Embriol. — Embriology
Emp. — Empire
Endocrinol. — Endocrinology
Eng. — English
Engng. — Engineering
Engr — Engineer
essent. — essential
exp. — experimental

Fak. — Fakultat (Faculty)
Fat. — Fatigue
Fed. — Federation
fiziol. — fiziologicheskii (physiological)
Forsch. — Forschung (Researches)

gen. — general
genet. — genetic
Geol. — Geology
Gerontol. — Gerontology
ges. — gesamte
Ges. — Gesellschaft (Association)

[1] Abbreviations for adjectives are listed here with a small letter but are capitalized in the Bibliography when they occur at the beginning of a periodical title or when they are part of a proper name, such as the name of an organization.

Gosud. — Gosudarstvenngi (State University)

Harv. — Harvard
Hist. — History
hum. — human

Industr. — Industry
industr. — industrial
Inst. — Institute
int. — international
Invest. — Investigation, Investment
Ital. — Italian

J. — Journal
Jap. — Japanese
Jb. — Jahrbuch (Yearbook)
jurist. — juristisch (juridical)

Kbh. — Köbenhavn (Copenhagen)
Kinderheilk. — Kinderheilkunde (Child Medicine)
klin. — klinisch (clinical)
Kongr. — Kongress (Congress)

Lab. — Laboratory
Laryngol. — Laryngology
Leningr. — Leningrad
Lit. — Literarische (Letters)

Math. — Mathematics
Measmt — Measurement
Med. — Medicine
med. — medical
Mém. — Mémoirs
ment. — mental
Min. — Mining
Mitt. — Mittilungen (Reports)
mod. — modern
Mon. — Monthly (noun)
mon. — monthly (adj.)
Monogr. — Monograph
mot. — motor
Mschr. — Monatsschrift (Monthly) (noun)
Mus. — Museum

N. E. — New England
nat. — national, natural
nauch. — nauchnye (scientific)
Neërl. — Neërlandaises (Netherlands)

Nerv. — Nerve
nerv. — nervous
Neurol. — Neurology
neurol. — neurological
Neurophysiol. — Neurophysiology
Nervenkr. — Nervenkrankheit (Neurosis)
no. — Number (No. where following a period.)
n.s. — Original source not consulted (reference given is secondary source)

occup. — occupational
Ohrenheilk. — Ohrenheilkunde (Otology)
Ophthalmol. — Ophthalmology
Opin. — Opinion
opt. — optical
Ornithol. — Ornithology
Orthopsychiat. — Orthopsychiatry
Otol. — Otology
Otolaryngol. — Otolaryngology

Pap. — Paper
Pathol. — Pathology
Pediatr. — Pediatrics
Pedag. — Pedagogicheskik (Education)
percept. — perceptual
Perf. — Perfumery
Pers. — Personality
Phil. — Philosophy
phil. — philosophical
Phys. — Physics, Physik
phys. — physical, physisch
Physiol. — Physiologie, Physiology
physiol. — physiologica, physiological
Polon. — Polonica (Polish)
Proc. — Proceedings
Progr. — Progress
Psychiat. — Psychiatrie, Psychiatry
psychiat. — psychiatric
Psychol. — Psychologische, Psychology
psychol. — psychologic, psychological
Psychobiol. — Psychobiology
psychosom. — psychosomatic
Publ. — Publication, Public

Quart. — Quarterly (noun)
quart. — quarterly (adj.)

R. S. F. S. R. — Russian Socialist Federated Soviet Republic

Rec. — Record
Rep. — Report
Res. — Research
Resour. — Resource
Rev. — Review
rev. — revised
Rhinol. — Rhinology
Roy. — Royal

S. S. S. R. — Society Soviet Socialist Republic
Sachs. — Sachsischen (Business)
Scand. — Scandinavia
Sch. — School
Sci. — Science
scient. — scientific
Sem. — Seminar
Ser. — Series
Sinnesphysiol. — Sinnesphysiology
SitzBr. — Sitzungsberichte (Proceedings)
Soc. — Society
soc. — social
Sociol. — Sociology
sociol. — sociological
Stand. — Standards
Stud. — Studies, Student

Suppl. — Supplement
Syst. — System

Teach. — Teacher
tech. — technical
Th. — Theodule
Tierpsychol. — Tierpsychologie (Animal Psychology)
Trans. — Transactions, Translator
trans. — translation

u. — und (and)
Univer. — University

Verhl. — Verhandlungen (Proceedings)
Verslag. — Verslagen (Reports)
Vôl. — Volume (as in "Vol. 1")
vols. — volumes (as in "4 vols.")

WADC — Wright Air Development Center
Wiss. — Wissenschaften (Sciences)
Wschr. — Wochenschrift (Magazine)

Z. — Zeitschrift, Zhurnal (Journal)
Zool. — Zoologischen, Zoology

Abbott, P. S. The effect of temperature on taste in the white rat. Thesis, Brown Univer., 1953. (353)[1]

Ables, M. F. See Emers, R., Benjamin, R. M., & Ables, M. F., 1960.

Abrahams, H., Krakauer, D., & Dallenbach, K. M. Gustatory adaptation to salt. *Amer. J. Psychol.,* 1937, **49**, 462–469. (360)

Adams, H. F., & Dandison, B. Further experiments on the attention value of size and repetition in advertisements. *J. appl. Psychol.,* 1927, **11**, 483–489. (476)

Adams, J. A. See Reynolds, B., & Adams, J. A., 1953.

Adams, J. K. Laboratory studies of behavior without awareness. *Psychol. Bull.,* 1957, **54**, 383–405. (292–293)

Adams, J. R. See Dethier, V. G., Larsen, J. R., & Adams, J. R., 1963.

Adams, J. S. Inequity in social exchange. In L. Berkowitz (Ed.), *Advances in experimental social psychology.* New York: Academic, 1965. Pp. 267–299. (602)

Adams, P. A. See Postman, L., & Adams, P. A., 1956

Adams, P. A. See Postman, L., Adams, P. A., & Boehm, A. M., 1956.

Adams, P. A. See Postman, L., Adams, P. A., & Phillips, L. W., 1955.

Adamson, R. Inhibitory set in problem solving as related to reinforcement learning. *J. exp. Psychol.,* 1959, **58**, 280–282. (472)

Ades, H. W. Central auditory mechanisms. In J. Field, H. W. Magoun, & V. E. Hall (Eds.), *Handbook of physiology,* Vol. I. Washington, D.C.: American Physiological Society, 1959. Pp. 585–613. (152, 180, 183)

Adey, W. R. The sense of smell. In J. Field, H. W. Magoun, & V. E. Hall (Eds.), *Neurophysiology,* Vol. I. Washington, D.C.: American Physiological Society, 1959. Pp. 535–548. (348, 362)

Adler, N., & Hogan, J. A. Classical conditioning of an instinctive response in *Betta Splendens. Anim. Behav.,* 1963, **11**, 351–354. (497)

Adrian, E. D. Electrical responses of the human eye. *J. Physiol.,* 1945, **104**, 84–104. (227)

Adrian, E. D. Rod and cone components in the electric response of the eye. *J. Physiol.,* 1946, **105**, 24–37. (226)

Adrian, E. D. Olfactory discrimination. *Année psychol.,* 1951, **50**, 107–113. (344)

Adrian, E. D. The action of the mammalian olfactory organ. *J. Laryngol. Otol.,* 1956a, **70**, 1–14. (345)

Adrian, E. D. Problems of the modern physiology of the nervous and muscle systems. *Acad. Sci. Georgian S. S. R.,* 1956b, 13–19. (345)

Adrian, E. D. *The basis of sensation.* New York: Hafner, 1964 (327)

Adrian, E. D., & Ludwig, C. Nervous discharges from the olfactory organs of the fish. *J. Physiol.,* 1938, **94**, 441–460. (346)

Aiken, E. G. See Mowrer, O. H., & Aiken, E. G., 1954.

Akishige, Y. Experimentelle untersuchungen über die struktur des wahrenehomtungsraumes. Part II. *Mitt. Jurist-Lit. Fak.,* Kyushu, Japan: Kyushu University, 1937, No. 4, 23–118. (290)

Alcocer-Cuarón, C. See Lavín, A., Alcocer-Cuarón, C., & Hernandez-Peón, R., 1959.

Alcock, W. T. See Noble, C. E., & Alcock, W. T., 1958.

Alexander, F. *Psychosomatic medicine.* New York: Norton, 1950. (514, 531)

Allara, *Arch. ital. Anat. Embriol.,* 1939, **42**, 506–564. n.s. See Moncrieff, 1951, p. 157. (350)

Allard, M. See Denny, M. R., Allard, M., Hall, E., & Rokeach, M., 1960.

Allee, W. C. *The social life of animals.* London: Heinemann, 1939. (502)

Allee, W. C. *Cooperation among animals, with human implications.* New York: Abelard-Schuman, 1951. (502)

Allen, E. (Ed.) *Sex and internal secretions.* Baltimore: William & Wilkins, 1932. (501)

Allen, E. (Ed.) *Sex and internal secretions* (2nd Ed.) Baltimore: William & Wilkins, 1939. (501)

Allen, G. H. See Donaldson, L. R., & Allen, G. H., 1958.

---

[1] Numbers in parentheses at the end of an entry indicate the text pages on which references to the work appear.

Allen, L. See Honzik, M. P., Macfarlane, J. W., & Allen, L. 1948.

Allen, V. L. Situational factors in conformity. In L. Berkowitz (Ed.), *Advances in experimental social psychology*. New York: Academic, 1965. Pp. 133–175. (602)

Allison, E. G. See Kare, M. R., Black, R., & Allison, E. G., 1957.

Allison, V. C., & Katz, S. H. An investigation of stenches and odors for industrial purposes. *J. industr. Engng Chem.*, 1919, **11**, 336–338. (343)

Allport, G. W. The historical background of modern social psychology. In G. Lindzey (Ed.), *Handbook of social psychology*. Vol. I. Reading, Mass.: Addison-Wesley, 1954. Pp. 3–56. (601)

Alpert, R. See Haber, R. N., & Alpert, R., 1958.

Altman, I. See McGrath, J. E., & Altman, I., 1966.

Altman, P. L., & Dittmer, D. S. (Eds.) *Biology Data Book*. Washington, D.C.: Federation of American Societies for Experimental Biology, 1964. Pp. 239–241. (506)

Ames, A. *An interpretative manual for the demonstrations in the psychology research center, Princeton University: The nature of our perceptions, prehensions and behavior.* Princeton, N.J.: Princeton, 1955. (272)

Amitin, S. A. See Brush, F. R., & Amitin, S. A., 1960.

Ammons, R. B. Acquisition of motor skill: II. Rotary pursuit performance with continuous practice before and after a single rest. *J. exp. Psychol.*, 1947, **37**, 393–411. (476)

Ammons, R. B. Effects of knowledge of performance: A survey and tentative theoretical formulation. *J. gen. Psychol.*, 1956, **54**, 279–299. (444, 476)

Amoore, J. E., Johnston, J. W., & Rubin, M. The stereochemical theory of odor, *Scient. Amer.*, 1964, **210**, 42–49. (349)

Anand, B. K. Nervous regulation of food intake. *Physiol. Rev.*, 1961, **41**, 677–708. (336)

Anastasi, A. *Psychological testing*. New York: Macmillan, 1961. (477, 541–542, 546, 552–553)

Anastasi, A. *Fields of applied psychology*. New York: McGraw-Hill, 1964. (475, 477)

Anderson, G. L. See Anderson, H. H., & Anderson, G. L., 1951.

Anderson, H. H., and Anderson, G. L. (Eds.) *An introduction to projective techniques*. N.J., Prentice-Hall, 1951. (553)

Andreas, B. G. *Experimental psychology*. New York: Wiley, 1960. (34–35)

Andrews, G. C. *Diseases of the skin*. (5th ed.) Philadelphia: Saunders, 1963. (297)

Andrieux, C. Recherches expérimentales sur les mécanismes de défense. *Anneé psychol.*, 1954, **54**, 425–430. (292)

Anrep, G. V. Pitch discrimination in the dog. *J. Physiol.*, 1920, **53**, 367–385. (157)

Appel, J. B. Punishment and shock intensity. *Science*, 1963, **141**, 528–529. (421)

Appelberg, B. Species differences in the taste qualities mediated through the glossopharyngeal nerve. *Acta physiol. Scand.*, 1958, **44**, 129–137. (357)

Appley, M. H. See Cofer, C. N., & Appley, M. H., 1964.

Arab, V. M. See Dethier, V. G., & Arab, V. M., 1958.

Archer, E. J. Retention of serial nonsense syllables as a function of rest-interval responding rate and meaningfulness. *J. exp. Psychol.*, 1953, **45**, 245–252. (476)

Argentieri, D. *Leonardo's optics. Leonardo da Vinci*. New York: Reynal & Co., 1956 (281)

Armington, J. C. A component of the human electroretinogram associated with red color vision, *J. opt. Soc. Amer.*, 1952, **42**, 393–401. (227)

Arnold, M. B. *Emotion and personality*. New York: Columbia, 1960. 2 vols. (530)

Aronsohn, E., 1884. See Moncrieff, 1951, p. 94. (347)

Aronson, E. See Lindzey, G., & Aronson, E., 1967.

Asch, S. E. *Social psychology*. Englewood Cliffs, N.J.: Prentice-Hall, 1952. (601)

Aserinsky, E., & Kleitman, N. Regularly occurring periods of eye motility, and concomitant phenomena during sleep. *Science*, 1953, **118**, 273–274. (61)

Atkinson, J. W. (Ed.) *Motives in fantasy, ac-*

tion, and society. Princeton, N.J.: Van Nostrand, 1958a. (531)

Atkinson, J. W. Towards experimental analysis of human motivation in terms of motives, expectancies, and incentives. In Atkinson, J. W. (Ed.) *Motives in fantasy, action, and society.* Princeton, N.J.: Van Nostrand, 1958b. Pp. 288–305. (526)

Atkinson, J. W., & McClelland, D. C. The projective expression of needs: II. The effect of different intensities of the hunger drive on thematic apperception. *J. exp. Psychol.,* 1948, **38,** 643–658. (526)

Atkinson, J. W. See Walker, E. L., & Atkinson, J. W., 1958.

Atkinson, J. W. See McClelland, D. C., Atkinson, J. W., Clark, R. A., & Lowell, E. L., 1953.

Atkinson, R. C., & Suppes, P. An analysis of two-person game situations in terms of statistical learning theory. *J. exp. Psychol.,* 1958, **55,** 369–378. (601)

Atkinson, W. H. See Beebe-Center, J. G., Rogers, M. S., & Atkinson, W. H., 1955.

The atlas of normal anatomy. (med. stud. ed.) Pearle River, N.Y.: Lederle Laboratories. (182)

Attneave, F. *Applications of information theory to psychology: A summary of basic concepts, methods, and results.* New York: Holt, 1959. (212)

Ax, A. F. The physiological differentiation between fear and anger in humans. *Psychosom. Med.,* 1953, **15,** 433–442. (513)

Ayrapetyants, E. Sh. *Higher nervous function and the receptors of internal organs.* Moscow: Akad. Nauk S. S. S. R., 1952. (396)

Azrin, N. H. Punishment and recovery during fixed-ratio performance. *J. exp. Anal. Behav.,* 1959, **2,** 301–305. (421)

Azrin, N. H. Effects of punishment intensity during variable-interval reinforcement. *J. exp. Anal. Behav.,* 1960, **3,** 123–142. (421)

Azrin, N. H., & Holz, W. C. Punishment during fixed-interval reinforcement. *J. exp. Anal. Behav.,* 1961, **4,** 343–347. (421)

Azrin, N. H. See Holz, W. C., & Azrin, N. H., 1962.

Bachrach, A. J., Candland, D. K., & Gibson,

J. T. Experiments in verbal behavior. I. Group reinforcement of individual response. In I. Berg & B. Bass (Eds.), *Conformity and deviation.* New York: Harper & Row, 1961. Pp. 258–265. (458)

Back, K. Influence through social communication. *J. abnorm. soc. Psychol.,* 1951, **46,** 9–23. (592)

Back, K. See Festinger, L., Schachter, S., & Back, K., 1950.

Backlund, F. See Johansson, G., & Backlund, F., 1960.

Backman, E. L. Olfactology of the methylbenzene series. *Verslag. Akad. Wetenschappen Amst.,* 1917, **25,** 971–984. (348)

Baddeley, A. D. Enhanced learning of a position-habit with secondary reinforcement for the wrong response. *Amer. J. Psychol.,* 1960, **73,** 454–457. (473)

Baer, D. M., & Gray, P. H. Imprinting to a different species without overt following. *Percept. mot. Skills,* 1960, **10,** 171–174. (482)

Bahrick, H. P. See Fitts, P. M., Noble, M. E., Bahrick, H. P. & Briggs, G. E., 1959a.

Bahrick, H. P. See Fitts, P. M., Noble, M. E., Bahrick, H. P., & Briggs, G. E., 1959b.

Bailey, C. J. See Miller, N. E., Bailey, C. J., & Stevenson, J. A. F., 1950.

Bakan, D. The test of significance in psychological research. *Psy. Bull.,* 1966, **66,** 423–437. (35)

Baldus, C. *Untersuchung über Geruchsschwellen.* Wertheim: Bechstein, 1937. (343)

Bales, R. F. *Interaction process analysis: A method for the study of small groups.* Reading, Mass.: Addison-Wesley, 1950 (601–602)

Bales, R. F. Some uniformities of behavior in small social systems. In G. E. Swanson, T. M. Newcomb, & E. L. Hartley (Eds.), *Readings in social psychology,* New York: Holt, 1952. Pp. 146–159. (599)

Bales, R. F. The equilibrium problem in small groups. In T. Parsons, R. F. Bales, & E. A. Shils (Eds.), *Working papers in the theory of action.* Glencoe, Ill.: Free Press, 1953. Pp. 111–161. (596)

Bales, R. F. The equilibrium problem in small groups. In A. P. Hare, E. F. Borgatta, & R. F. Bales (Eds.), *Small groups: Studies in social interaction.* New York: Knopf, 1955. Pp. 424–456. (580)

Bales, R. F., & Strodtbeck, F. L. Phases in group problem solving. *J. abnorm. soc. Psychol.,* 1951, **46**, 485–495. (597)

Bales, R. F., Strodtbeck, F. L. Mills, T. M., & Roseborough, M. E. Channels of communication in small groups. *Amer. sociol. Rev.,* 1951, **16**, 461–468. (576)

Bales, R. F. See Hare, A. P., & Bales, R. F., 1963.

Bales, R. F. See Hare, A. P., Borgatta, E. F., & Bales, R. F., 1955.

Ballard, P. B. Obliviscence and reminiscence. *Brit. J. Psychol. (Monogr. Suppl.),* 1913, No. 2. (441–442)

Bandura, A. Psychotherapy as a learning process. *Psychol. Bull.,* 1961, **58**, 143–159. (387)

Bandura, A., & Walters, R. H. *Social learning and personality development.* New York: Holt, 1963. (477)

Bandura, A., Ross, D., & Ross, S. A. Imitation of film-mediated aggressive models. *J. abnorm. soc. Psychol.,* 1963a, **66**, 3–11. (473–474)

Bandura, A., Ross, D., & Ross, S. A. Vicarious reinforcement and imitative learning. *J. abnorm. soc. Psychol.,* 1963b, **67**, 601–607. (473)

Bandura, A., Ross, D., & Ross, S. A. A comparative test of the status envy, social power and the secondary-reinforcement theories of identificatory learning. *J. abnorm. soc. Psychol.,* 1963c, **67**, 527–534. (473)

Banta, T. J., & Hetherington, M. Relations between needs of friends and fiances. *J. abnorm. soc. Psychol.,* 1963, **66**, 401–404. (590)

Barber, S. B. Chemoreception and proprioception in Limmulus. *J. exp. Zool.,* 1956, **131**, 51–73. (353)

Bard, P., & Mountcastle, V. B. Some forebrain mechanisms involved in expression of rage with special reference to suppression of angry behavior. *Res. Publ. Ass. Res. nerv. ment. Dis.,* 1947, **27**, 362–404. (507)

Bare, J. K. See Pfaffman, C. Goff, W. R., & Bare, J. K., 1958.

Barnard, C. *The functions of the executive.* Cambridge, Mass.: Harvard, 1938. (596)

Barnes, W. T., Magoun, H. W., & Ranson, S. W. The ascending auditory pathway in the brain stem of the monkey. *J. comp. Neurol.,* 1943, **79**, 129–152. (180)

Bartleson, C. J. See Burnham, R. W., Hanes, R. M., & Bartleson, C. J., 1963.

Bartlett, C. J., Hermann, E., & Rettig, S. A comparison of six different scaling techniques. *J. soc. Psychol.,* 1960, **51**, 343–348. (141)

Bartlett, N. R. Thresholds as dependent on some energy relations and characteristics of the subject. In C. H. Graham (Ed.), *Vision and visual perception.* New York: Wiley, 1965. Pp. 154–184. (220, 246)

Bartley, S. H. Some factors in brightness discrimination. *Psychol. Rev.,* 1939, **46**, 337–358. (227, 238)

Bartley, S. H. *Vision.* Princeton, N.J.: Van Nostrand, 1941. (237)

Bartley, S. H. The psychophysiology of vision. In S. S. Stevens (Ed.), *Handbook of experimental psychology.* New York: Wiley, 1951, 921–984. (237, 246)

Bartley, S. H. *Principles of perception.* New York: Harper & Row, 1958. (237, 263)

Bartley, S. H., & Nelson, T. M. Some relations between sensory end results and neural activity in the optic pathway. *J. Psychol.,* 1963, **55**, 121–143. (228)

Barton, J. W. Smaller vs. larger units in learning the maze. *J. exp. Psychol.,* 1921, **4**, 418–429. (475)

Barylko-Pikielna, N. See Tilgner, D. J., & Barylko-Pikielna, N., 1959.

Bash, K. W. An investigation into a possible organic basis for the hunger drive. *J. comp. physiol. Psychol.,* 1939a, **28**, 109–135. (330)

Bash, K. W. Contribution to a theory of the hunger drive. *J. comp physiol. Psychol.,* 1939b, **28**, 137–160. (330)

Basowitz, H., Persky, H., Korchin, S. J., & Grinker, R. R. *Anxiety and stress: an interdisciplinary study of a life situation.* New York: McGraw-Hill, 1955. (516)

Bass, B. M., & Wurster, C. R. Effects of the nature of the problem on L G D performance. *J. appl. Psychol.,* 1953, **37**, 96–99. (573)

Bass, B. M. See Petrullo, L., & Bass, B. M., 1961.

Bass, B. M. See Stimpson, D. V., & Bass, B. M., 1964.

Bass, M. J., & Hull, C. L. The irradiation of a tactile conditioned reflex in man. *J. comp. Psychol.*, 1934, **17**, 47–65. (392)

Battersby, W. S. See Teuber, H. L. Battersby, W. S., & Bender, M. B., 1960.

Battig, W. F. Transfer from verbal pretraining to motor performance as a function of motor task complexity. *J. exp. Psychol.*, 1956, **51**, 371–378. (456)

Battig, W. F., and Spera, A. J. Rated association values of numbers from 0–100. *J. verb. Learng. verb. Behav.*, 1962, **1** (3), 200–202. (195)

Bavelas, A. A mathematical model for group structure. *Appl. Anthropol.*, 1948, **7**, 16–30. (584)

Bazett, H. C. Temperature sense in man. In *Temperature: Its measurement and control in science and industry.* New York: Reinhold, 1941. Pp. 489–501. (308)

Bazett, H. C., & McGlone, B. Studies in sensation: II. The mode of stimulation of cutaneous sensations of cold and warmth. *A. M. A. Arch. Neurol. Psychiat.*, 1932, **27**, 1031–1069. (305)

Bazett, H. C., McGlone, B., & Brocklehurst, R. J. The temperature in the tissues which accompany temperature sensations. *J. Physiol.*, 1930, **69**, 88–112. (305)

Bazett, H. C., McGlone, B., Williams, R. G., & Lufkin, H. M. Sensations: I. Depth, distribution and probable identification in the prepuce of sensory end-organs concerned in sensations of temperature and touch; thermometric conductivity. *A. M. A. Arch. Neurol. Psychiat.*, 1932, **27**, 489–517. (305, 310)

Beach, F. A. Effects of cortical lesions upon the copulatory behavior of male rats. *J. comp. physiol. Psychol.*, 1940, **29**, 193–239. (491)

Beach, F. A. Effects of injury to the cerebral cortex upon sexually-receptive behavior in the female rat. *Psychosom. Med.*, 1944, **6**, 40–55. (491)

Beach, F. A. *Hormones and behavior.* New York: Hoeber-Harper, 1948. (501)

Beach, F. A. Instinctive behavior: Reproductive activities. In S. S. Stevens (Ed.), *Handbook of experimental psychology.* New York: Wiley, 1951. Pp. 387–434. (501)

Beach, F. A. The descent of instinct. *Psychol. Rev.*, 1955, **62**, 401–410. (500)

Beach, F. A. Characteristics of masculine "sex drive." In M. R. Jones (Ed.), *Nebraska symposium on motivation.* Lincoln, Nebr.: University of Nebraska Press, 1956, 1–32. (488–489)

Beach, F. A., & Holz, A. M. Mating behavior in male rats castrated at various ages and injected with androgen. *J. exp. Zool.*, 1946, **101**, 91–142. (490)

Beach, F. A., Hebb, D. O., Morgan, C. T., & Nissen, H. W. (Eds.), *The neuropsychology of Lashley.* New York: McGraw-Hill, 1960. (428)

Beach, F. A. See Ford, C. S., & Beach, F. A., 1951.

Beach, L. See Cameron, D. E., Solyom, L., & Beach, L., 1961.

Beardslee, D. C., & Wertheimer, Michael (Eds.) *Readings in perception.* Princeton, N.J.: Van Nostrand, 1958. (276, 295)

Beasley, W. C. *National Health Survey,* United States Public Health Service, Hearing Study Series, Bulletin 5, 1938. (157)

Beatty, R. T. *Hearing in man and animals.* London: G. Bell, 1932. (148, 154)

Beck, C. J. See Sacia, C. F., & Beck, C. J., 1926.

Beck, L. H., & Miles, W. R. Some theoretical and experimental relations between infrared absorption and olfaction. *Science.* 1947, **106**, 511. (349)

Becker, G. See DeLamater, J. McClintock, C. G., & Becker, G., 1965.

Bednár, M., & Langfelder, O. Ueber das intravenöse (hämatogne) Reichen. *Mschr. Ohrenheilk.*, 1930, **64**, 1133–1139. (81, 350)

Beebe-Center, J. G., & Waddell, D. A general psychological scale of taste. *J. Psychol.*, 1948, **26**, 517–524. (360–361)

Beebe-Center, J. G. Rogers, M. S., & Atkinson, W. H. Intensive equivalences for sucrose and NaCl solutions. *J. Psychol.,* 1955, **39,** 371–372. (360)

Beebe-Center, J. G., Rogers, M. S., & O'Connell, D. N. Transmission of information about sucrose and saline solutions through the sense of taste. *J. Psychol.,* 1955, **39,** 157–160. (360)

Beer, B. See Hearst, E., Beer, B., Shaetz, G., & Galambos, R., 1960.

Beidler, L. M. A theory of taste stimulation. *J. gen. Physiol.,* 1954, **38,** 133–139. (353)

Beidler, L. M. Physiological basis of taste psychophysics. *Fed. Proc.,* 1957, **16,** 9. (361)

Beidler, L. M. The chemical senses. *Annu. Rev. Psychol.,* 1961. (351, 361–362)

Beidler, L. M. See Kimura, K., & Beidler, L. M., 1956.

Beischer, D. E. See Meek, J. C., Graybiel, A., Beischer, D. E., & Riopelle, A. J., 1961.

Békésy, G. von Über die Herstellung und Messung langsamer sinusförmiger Luftdruckschwankungen. *Ann. Physik,* 1936a, **25,** 413–432. (157)

Békésy, G. von Über die Hörschwelle und Fühlgrenze langsamer sinusförmiger Luftruchschwankungen. *Ann. Physik,* 1936b, **26,** 554–566. (157)

Békésy, G. von The variation of phase along the basilar membrane with sinusoidal vibrations. *J. Acoust. Soc. Amer.,* 1947, **19,** 452–460. (177)

Békésy, G. von, *Experiments in hearing.* (E. G. Wever, trans.) New York: McGraw-Hill, 1960. (183)

Békésy, G. von, Hearing theories and complex sounds. *J. acoust. Soc. Amer.,* 1963, **35,** 588–601. (180)

Békésy, G. von, & Rosenblith, W. A. The mechanical properties of the ear. In S. S. Stevens (Ed.), *Handbook of experimental psychology.* New York: Wiley, 1951, Pp. 1075–1115. (150, 183)

Bekhterev, V. M. *La Psychologie objective.* Paris: Alcan, 1913a. (384)

Bekhterev, V. M. *Objektive Psychologie oder Psychoreflexologie. Die Lehre von den Assoziationsreflexen.* Leipzig: B. G. Teubner Verlagsgesellschaft, 1913b. (384)

Bekhterev, V. M. *General principles of human reflexology.* (E. Murphy & W. Murphy Trans.) New York: International Publishers, 1928. (384, 392)

Bell, C. *Idea of a new anatomy of the brain: Submitted for the observation of his friends.* London: privately printed monograph, 1811. (n.s.) (62–63)

Bell, C. Idea of a new anatomy of the brain: Submitted for the observation of his friends. *J. Anat. Physiol.,* 1869, **3,** 153–166. (Reprint of Bell, 1811.) (n.s.) (62–63)

Bell, C. Idea of a new anatomy of the brain: Submitted for the observation of his friends. In W. Dennis, *Readings in the history of psychology.* New York: Appleton-Century-Crofts, 1948. Pp. 113–124. (Reprint of Bell, 1811.) (n.s.) (62–63)

Bell, H. M. Rest pauses in motor learning as related to Snoddy's hypothesis of mental growth. *Psychol. Monogr.,* 1942, **54,** No. 1. (476)

Bender, M. B. See Teuber, H. L., Battersby, W. S., & Bender, M. B., 1960.

Benjamin, R. M. See Emmers, R., Benjamin, R. M., & Ables, M. F., 1960.

Benne, K. D., & Sheats, P. Functional roles of group members. *J. soc. Issues,* 1948, **4,** 41–49. (567, 580)

Bennett, E. L. See Rosenzweig, M. R., Krech, D., & Bennett, E. L., 1960.

Bennis, W. G., & Shepard, H. A. A theory of group development. *Hum. Relat.,* 1956, **9,** 415–437. (597)

Berelson, B., Lazarsfeld, P. F., & McPhee, W. N., *Voting: A study of opinion formation in a presidential campaign.* Chicago: University of Chicago Press, 1954. (559)

Berelson, B. See Lazarsfeld, P. F., Berelson, B., & Gaudet, H., 1944.

Berger, E. See Graham, C. H., Hsia, Y., & Berger, E., 1955.

Berger, F. M. Classification of psychoactive drugs according to their chemical structures and sites of action. In L. Uhr & J. G. Miller (Eds.), *Drugs and behavior.* New York: Interscience Publishers, 1960. (516)

Berger, H. Über das Electrenkephalogram des Menschen. I. *Arch Psychiat. Nevenkr.,* 1929, **87,** 527–570 (58)

Berger, J., Cohen, B. P., Snell, J. L., & Zelditch, M. *Types of formalization in small-group research.* Boston: Houghton Mifflin, 1962. (601)

Berkeley, G. *An essay toward a new theory of vision.* 1709. In various editions. (271)

Berkowitz, L. Group norms among bomber crews: Patterns of perceived crew attitudes, "actual" attitudes, and crew liking related to aircrew effectiveness in Far Eastern combat. *Sociometry*, 1956, **19**, 141–153. (593)

Berkowitz, L. Liking for the group and the perceived merit of the group's behavior. *J. abnorm. soc. Psychol.*, 1957, **54**, 353–357. (593)

Berkowitz, L. (Ed.) *Advances in experimental social psychology*, Vols. 1–3. New York: Academic, 1964–1966. (602)

Bermann, E. A. Stability and compatibility in interpersonal relationships. Unpublished doctoral dissertation, Univ. of Michigan, 1964 (591)

Bernard, J. An experimental comparison of ranking and paired comparisons as methods of evaluating questionnaire items. *Publ. Amer. Sociol. Soc.*, 1934, **28**, 81–84. (141)

Bernhard, C. G., & Granit, R. Nerve as a model temperature end organ. *J. gen. Physiol.*, 1946, **29**, 257–265. (306–307)

Bexton, W. H. Some effects of perceptual isolation on human subjects. Doctoral thesis, 153, McGill Univ., Montreal, Canada. (289)

Bexton, W. H., Heron, W., & Scott, T. H. Effects of decreased variation in the sensory environment. *Canad. J. Psychol.*, 1954, **8**, 70–76. (289)

Bickford, R. G. Experiments relating to the itch sensation, its peripheral mechanism and central pathways. *Clin. Sci.*, 1938, **3**, 377–386. (313)

Biddulph, R. See Shower, E. G., & Biddulph, R., 1931.

Bidwell, S. Some curiosities of vision. *Proc. Roy. Inst. Great Britain*, 1898, **15**, (91), 354–365. (242)

Bills, A. G. The influence of muscular tension on the efficiency of mental work. *Amer. J. Psychol.*, 1927, **38**, 227–251. (508)

Bills, A. G., & Brown, C. The quantitative set. *J. exp. Psychol.*, 1929, **12**, 301–323. (476)

Bilodeau, E. (Ed.) *Acquisition of skills.* New York: Academic, 1966. (444)

Bilodeau, E. A., & Bilodeau, I. McD. Variation of temporal intervals among critical events in five studies of knowledge of results. *J. exp. Psychol.*, 1958, **55**, 603–612. (476)

Bilodeau, E. A., & Bilodeau, I. McD. Motor-skills learning. *Annu. Rev. Psychol.*, 1961, **12**, 243–280. (456, 476–477)

Bilodeau, E. A., & Ryan, F. J. A test for interaction of delay of knowledge of results and two types of interpolated activity. *J. exp. Psychol.*, 1960, **59**, 414–419. (476)

Bilodeau, I. McD. See Bilodeau, E. A., & Bilodeau, I. McD., 1958.

Bilodeau, I. McD. See Bilodeau, E. A., & Bilodeau, I. McD., 1961.

Bindra, O. *Motivation: A systematic reinterpretation.* New York: Ronald, 1959. (530)

Bindra, D. See Licklider, J. C. R., Bindra, D., & Pollack, I., 1948.

Bingham, W. E., Jr. A study of the relations which the galvanic skin response and sensory reference bear to judgments of the meaningfulness, significance, and importance of 72 words. *J. Psychol.*, 1943, **16**, 21–34. (195)

Birch, H. G. The relation of previous experience to insightful problem-solving. *J. comp. Psychol.*, 1945, **38**, 367–383. (471)

Birney, R. C., & Teevan, R. C. (Eds.), *Instinct*, Princeton, N.J.: Van Nostrand, 1961. (500)

Birney, R. C. See Grose, R. F., & Birney, R. C., 1963.

Birney, R. C. See Teevan, R. C., & Birney, R. C., 1961.

Biryukov, D. A. The nature of orienting reactions. In L. G. Voronin, A. N. Leont'yev, A. R. Luria, E. N. Sokolov, & O. S. Vinogradova (Eds.), *Orientivovochny refleks i orientirovochnoissledovatel'skaya deyatel'nost'.* (The orienting reflex and orienting-investigatory activity.) Moscow: Akad. Pedag. Nauk R. S. F. S. R., 1958. Pp. 20–25. (398)

Bishop, G. H. Responses to electrical stimulation of single sensory units of the skin. *J. Neurophysiol.*, 1943, **6**, 361–382. (320)

Bishop, G. H. The peripheral unit for pain. *J. Neurophysiol.*, 1944, **7**, 71–80. (322)

Bishop, G. H. Relation of pain sensory threshold to form of mechanical stimulator. *J. Neurophysiol.*, 1949, **12**, 51–57. (321)

Bitterman, M. E., & Kniffin, C. W. Manifest anxiety and "perceptual defense." *J. abnorm. soc. Psychol.*, 1953, **48**, 248–252. (292)

Bitterman, M. E., & Wodinsky, J. Simultaneous and successive discrimination. *Psychol. Rev.*, 1953, **60**, 371–376. (418)

Bjerstedt, A. Preparation, process, and product in small group interaction. *Hum. Relat.*, 1961, **14**, 183–189. (593)

Black, R. See Kare, M. R., Black, R., & Allison, E. G., 1957.

Blackwell, H. R. Psychophysical thresholds: Experimental studies of methods of measurement. *Univer. Mich. Engng Res. Inst. Bull.*, 1953, No. 36, 1–4, (100, 108)

Blake, R. R., & Ramsey, G. V. *Perception, an approach to personality.* New York: Ronald, 1951. (295)

Blank, A. A. The Luneberg Theory of binocular space perception. In S. Koch (Ed.), *Psychology: A study of a science.* Study I. *Conceptual and systematic.* Vol. I. *Sensory perceptual, and physiological formulations.* New York: McGraw-Hill, 1959. Pp. 395–426. (295)

Blazek, N. C. See Mason, W. A., Blazek, N. C., & Harlow, H. F., 1956.

Bliss, E. L. (Ed.) *Roots of behavior.* New York: Harper & Row, 1962. (500, 502)

Blondel, A., & Rey, J. Sur la perception des lumières brèves à la limite de leur portée. *C. R. séances Acad. Sci.*, 1911, **153**, 54–56. (231)

Bloom, G., Engstrom, H. The structure of the epithelial surface in the olfactory region. *Exp. Cell Res.*, 1952, **3**, 699–701. (340)

Blum, G. S. Perceptual defense revisited. *J. abnorm. soc. Psychol.*, 1955, **51**, 24–29. (292)

Blum, H. B. See Fabian, F. W., & Blum, H. B. 1943.

Bohm, A. M. See Postman, L., Adams, P. A., & Bohm, A. M., 1956.

Bolles, R. C. See Gagné, R. M., & Bolles, R. C., 1959.

Bond, E. A. Tenth grade abilities and achievements. *Teach. Coll. Contr. Educ.*, 1940, No. 813. (547)

Boren, J. J., Sidman, M., & Herrnstein, R. J. Avoidance, escape and extinction as functions of shock intensity. *J. comp. physiol. Psychol.*, 1959, **52**, 420–425. (411)

Boren, J. J. See Brady, J. V., Boren, J. J., Conrad, D., & Sidman, M., 1957.

Borgatta, E. F. See Hare, A. P., Borgatta, E. F., & Bales, R. F., 1955.

Boring, E. G. A new ambiguous figure. *Amer. J. Psychol.*, 1930, **42**, 444–445. (265)

Boring, E. G. *Sensation and perception in the history of experimental psychology.* New York: Appleton-Century-Crofts, 1942. (62, 107, 242, 245, 247, 249, 264, 284, 294, 313)

Boring, E. G. *A history of experimental psychology.* (2nd ed.) New York: Appleton-Century-Crofts, 1950. (35, 60–63, 86, 107, 247, 534, 552)

Boring, E. G., & Stevens, S. S. The nature of tonal brightness. *Proc. Nat. Acad. Sci.*, 1936, **22**, 514–521. (164)

Bouliere, F., Cendron, H., Rapaport, A. Modification avec l'age des seuils gustatifs de perception et de reconnaissance aux saveurs salés et sucrés, chez l'homme. *Gerontalogia*, 1958, **2**, 105–112. (355)

Bourne, G. See El-Baradi, A., & Bourne, G., 1951.

Bousfield, W. A. The occurrence of clustering in the recall of randomly arranged associates. *J. gen. Psychol.*, 1953, **49**, 229–240. (450)

Bousfield, W. A. The problem of meaning in verbal learning. In C. N. Cofer (Ed.), *Verbal learning and verbal behavior.* New York: McGraw-Hill, 1961, Pp. 81–90. (475–476)

Bousfield, W. A., & Cohen, B. H. The effects of reinforcement on the occurrence of clustering in the recall of randomly arranged associates. *J. Psychol.*, 1953, **36**, 67–81. (450)

Bousfield, W. A. See Yavuz, H. S., & Bousfield, W. A., 1959.

Bowden, J. W. See Lindsley, D. B., Bowden, J. W., & Magoun, H. W., 1949.

Bower, G. H., & Miller, N. E. Rewarding and

punishing effects from stimulating the same place in the rat's brain. *J. comp. physiol. Psychol.,* 1958, **51**, 669–674. (520)

Bower, G. H. See Hilgard, E. R., & Bower, G. H., 1966.

Bowlby, J. Maternal care and mental health. *World Hlth Organiz. Monogr.,* 1952, No. 2. (484)

Boynton, R. M., & Riggs, L. A. The effect of stimulus area and intensity upon the human retinal response. *J. exp. Psychol.,* 1951, **42**, 217–226. (227)

Brackett, H. R. See Reid, L. S., Lloyd, K. E., Brackett, H. R., & Hawkins, W. F., 1961.

Bradway, K. P. Thompson, C. W., & Cravens, R. B. Preschool IQ's after twenty-five years. *J. educ. Psychol.,* 1958, **49**, 278–281. (547)

Brady, J. V., Boren, J. J., Conrad, D., & Sidman, M. The effect of food and water deprivation upon intercranial self-stimulation. *J. comp. physiol. Psychol.,* 1957, **50**, 134–137. (520)

Brady, J. V., Porter, R. W., Conrad, D. G., & Mason, J. W. Avoidance behavior and the development of gastroduodenal ulcers. *J. exp. Anal. Behav.,* 1958, **1**, 69–73. (515)

Brady, J. V. See Hunt, H. F., & Brady, J. V., 1951.

Brady, J. V. See Porter, R. W., Brady, J. V., Conrad, D., Mason, J. W., Galambos, R., & Rioch, D. McD., 1958.

Brain, Lord. *Speech disorders.* London: Butterworth, 1961. (211–212)

Braly, K. See Katz, D., & Braly, K., 1933.

Brandt, E. R. The memory value of advertisements, with special reference to the use of color. *Arch. Psychol., N.Y.,* 1925, **13**, No. 79. (476)

Braun, H. W. See Gladis, M., & Braun, H. W., 1958.

Bray, C. W. See Wever, E. G., & Bray, C. W., 1930a.

Bray, C. W. See Wever, E. G., & Bray, C. W., 1930b.

Bray, C. W. See Wever, E. G., & Bray, C. W., 1937.

Bray, C. W. See Wever, E. G., Bray, C. W., & Willey, C. F., 1937.

Brazier, M. A. B. *The history of the electrical activity of the brain. The first half century.* New York: Macmillan, 1961. (58)

Breder, C., & Rasquin, P. Comparative studies in the light sensitivity of blind Characins from a series of Mexican caves. *Bull. Amer. Mus., Nat. Hist.,* 1947, **89**, 325–351. (279)

Brenner, J. See Lorge, I., Fox, D., Davitz, J., & Brenner, M., 1958.

Bretnall, E. P. See Tolman, E. C., Hall, C. S., & Bretnall, E. P., 1932.

Brewer, E. D. See Elsberg, C. A., Brewer, E. D., & Leyy, I., 1935.

Brickwedde, F. G. See Priest, I. G., & Brickwedde, F. G., 1926.

Bridgman, P. W. *The logic of modern physics.* New York: Macmillan, 1927. (20)

Briggs, G. E. Acquisition, extinction and recovery functions in retroactive inhibition. *J. exp. Psychol.,* 1954, **47**, 285–293. (476)

Briggs, G. E. Retroactive inhibition as a function of the degree of original and interpolated learning. *J. exp. Psychol.,* 1957, **53**, 60–67. (476)

Briggs, G. E., Thompson, R. F., & Brogden, W. J. Retention functions in reproductive inhibition. *J. exp. Psychol.,* 1954, **48**, 419–423. (476)

Briggs, G. E. See Fitts, P. M., Noble, M. E., Bahrick, H. P., & Briggs, G. E., 1959a.

Briggs, G. E. See Fitts, P. M., Noble, M. E., Bahrick, H. P., & Briggs, G. E., 1959b.

Briggs, L. J. See Goldbeck, R. A., & Briggs, L. J., 1962.

Briggs, M. H., & Kitto, G. B. The molecular basis of memory and learning. *Psychol. Rev.,* 1962, **69**, 537–541. (382)

Brindley, G. S. *Physiology of the retina and the visual pathway.* London: E. Arnold, 1960. (294)

Broadbent, D. E. *Perception and communication.* New York: Pergamon Press, 1958. (211)

Brobeck, J. R. Neural control of hunger, appetite and satiety. *Yale J. Biol. Med.,* 1957, **29**, 567–574. (336)

Brobeck, J. R. Food and temperature. *Recent Progr. Hormone Res.,* 1960, **16**, 439–459. (336)

Brobeck, J. R., Larsson, S., & Reyes, E. A study of the electrical activity of the hypothalamic feeding mechanism. *J. Physiol.*, 1956, **132**, 358–364. (331)

Broca, P. *Bull. Soc. anat.*, 2me sér., 1861, **6**, 330–357. (n.s.) (210)

Brocklehurst, R. J. See Bazett, H. C., McGlone, B., & Brocklehurst, R. J., 1930.

Brodbeck, A. J. See Davis, H. V., Sears, R. R., Miller, H. C., & Brodbeck, A. J., 1948.

Brödel, M. *Three unpublished drawings of the ear.* Philadelphia: Saunders, 1946. (n.s.) (182)

Brogden, W. J., Lipman, E. A., & Culler, E. The role of incentive in conditioning and extinction. *Amer. J. Psychol.*, 1938, **51**, 109–117. (426)

Brogden, W. J. See Briggs, G. E., Thompson, R. F., & Brogden, W. J., 1954.

Bromiley, R. B. Conditioned responses in a dog after removal of neocortex. *J. comp. physiol. Psychol.*, 1948, **41**, 102–110. (393–394)

Bronson, W. C. See Postman, L., Bronson, W. C., & Gropper, G. L., 1953.

Brown, C. See Bills, A. G., & Brown, C., 1929.

Brown, G. G. Perception of depth with disoriented vision. *Brit. J. Psychol.*, 1928, **19**, 117–146. (281)

Brown, J. L. The structure of the visual system. In C. H. Graham (Ed.), *Vision and visual perception.* New York: Wiley, 1965a. Pp. 39–59. (215, 218, 246)

Brown, J. L. Afterimages. In C. E. Graham (Ed.), *Vision and visual perception.* New York: Wiley, 1965b. Pp. 479–503. (246)

Brown, J. S. Gradients of approach and avoidance responses and their relation to level of motivation. *J. comp. physiol. Psychol.*, 1948, **41**, 450–465. (423–424)

Brown, J. S. A proposed program of research on psychological feedback (knowledge of results) in the performance of psycho-motor tasks. In Research planning conference on perceptual and motor skills. *USAF Hum. Resour. Res. Center conf. Rep.*, 1949, No. 49–2. (n.s.) (476)

Brown, J. S. *The motivation of behavior.* New York: McGraw-Hill, 1961. (530)

Brown, R. *Words and things.* New York: Free Press, 1958. (212)

Brown, R., Galanter, E., Hess, E. H., & Mandler, G. *New directions in psychology.* New York: Holt, 1962. (65, 108)

Brown, R. W. The relation between two methods of learning piano music. *J. exp. Psychol.*, 1933, **16**, 435–441. (437)

Brown, W. O. See Muenzinger, K. F., Brown, W. O., Crow, W. J., & Powlowski, R. F., 1952.

Bruner, J. S., & Goodman, C. C. Value and need as organizing factors in perception. *J. abnorm. soc. Psychol.*, 1947, **42**, 33–44. (291)

Brunswik, E. Zur entwicklung der Albedowahrnehmung. *Z. Psychol.*, 1928, **109**, 40–115. (290)

Brunswik, E. *Perception and the representative design of psychological experiments.* Berkeley, Calif.: University of California Press, 1956. (290)

Brush, F. R., & Amitin, S. A. Early experience and quinine hydrochloride preference. (abstract) Eastern Psychological Association, 1960. (354)

Bucy, P. C. See Klüver, H., & Bucy, P. C., 1939.

Buddenbrock, W. von. *Die Welt der Sinne.* (2nd ed.) Berlin: Springer, 1953. (246)

Buddenbrock, W. von. *The senses.* Ann Arbor, Mich.: Univer. of Michigan Press, 1958. (224, 246)

Bugelski, B. R. *A first course in experimental psychology.* New York: Holt, 1951. (34, 108)

Bugelski, B. R. *The psychology of learning.* New York: Holt, 1956. (383, 401, 531)

Bugelski, B. R. *An introduction to the principles of psychology.* New York: Holt, 1960. (265)

Buhler, C. *Kindheit und Jugend.* (3rd ed.) Leipzig: S. Hirzel Verlag, 1931. (206)

Buhler, R. A. Stress and flicker fusion. In W. H. Ittelson, & S. B. Kutash (Eds.), *Perceptual changes in psychopathology.* New Brunswick, N.J.: Rutgers University Press, 1961. (237)

Bujas, Z., & Chweitzer, A. Gout électrique par courants alternifs chez l'homme. *C. R. Soc. Biol.*, 1937, **126**, 1106–1109. (351)

Bunch. C. C. Age variations in auditory acuity. *Arch. Otolaryngol.*, 1929, **9**, 625–636. (156)

Burchard, W. Role conflicts of military chaplains. *Amer. sociol. Rev.*, 1954, **19**, 528–535. (574)

Burke, C. J. See Estes, W. K., & Burke, C. J., 1955.

Burnham, R. W., Hanes, R. M., & Bartleson, C. J. *Color: a guide to basic facts and concepts.* New York: Wiley, 1963. (294)

Buros, O. K. (Ed.) *Sixth ment. measmt yearb.* Highland Park, N.J.: Gryphon Press, 1964. (477, 553)

Burzlaff, W. Methodologische Beitrage zum Problem der garbenkonstanz. *Z. Psychol.*, 1931, **119**, 177–235. (290)

Bush, R. R. See Luce, R. D., Bush, R. R., & Galanter, E., 1963.

Buss, A. H., & Buss, E. H. The effect of verbal reinforcement combinations on conceptual learning. *J. exp. Psychol.*, 1956, **52**, 283–287. (460)

Buss, E. H. See Buss, A. H., & Buss, E. H., 1956.

Buswell, G. T. The relationship between eye perception and voice response in reading. *J. educ. Psychol.*, 1922, **12**, 217–227. (287)

Buxton, C. E. The status of research in reminiscence. *Psychol. Bull.*, 1943, **40**, 313–340. (441)

Buxton, C. E., & Ross, H. V. Relationship between reminiscence and type of learning technique in serial anticipation learning. *J. exp. Psychol.*, 1949, **39**, 41–46. (475)

Buxton, C. E. See Withey, S., Buxton, C. E., & Elkin, A., 1949.

Byrd, E., Gertman, S. Taste sensitivity in the aging persons. *Geriatrics*, 1959, **14**, 381–384. (355)

Caldwell, W. E. See Waters, R. H., Rethling-shafer, D. A., & Caldwell, W. E., 1960.

Cameron, D. E., & Solyom, L. Effects of ribonucleic acid on memory. *Geriatrics,* 1961, **16**, 74–81. (382)

Cameron, D. E., Solyom, L., & Beach, L. Further studies upon the effects of the administration of ribonucleic acid in aged patients suffering from memory (retention) failure. *Neuropsychopharmacology*, 1961, **2**, 351–355. (382)

Campbell, A., Converse, P. E., Miller, W. E., &

Stokes, D. E. *The American voter.* New York: Wiley, 1960. (558)

Campbell, A., Gurin, G., & Miller, W. E. *The voter decides.* New York: Harper & Row, 1954. (558)

Campbell, B. A., & Pickleman, J. R. The imprinting object as a reinforcing stimulus. *J. comp. physiol. Psychol.*, 1961, **54**, 592–596. (481)

Campbell, B. A., & Teghtsoonian, R. Electrical and behavioral effects of different types of shock stimuli on the rat. *J. comp. physiol. Pscyhol.*, 1958, **51**, 185–192. (421)

Campbell, B. A. See Sheffield, F. D., Roby, T. B., & Campbell, B. A., 1954.

Candland, D. K. *Emotion: Bodily change.* Princeton, N.J.: Van Nostrand, 1962. (530)

Candland, D. K. See Bachrach, A. J., Candland, D. K., & Gibson, J. T., 1961.

Candland, D. K. See Vernon, J. A., McGill, T. E., Gulick, W. L., & Candland, D. K., 1959.

Candland, D. K. See Vernon, J. A., McGill, T. E., Gulick, W. L., & Candland, D. K., 1961.

Cannon, W. B. The James-Lange theory of emotions: A critical examination and an alternative theory. *Amer. J. Psychol.*, 1927, **39**, 106–124. (510)

Cannon, W. B. Again the James-Lange and the thalamic theories of emotion. *Psychol. Rev.*, 1931, **38**, 281–295. (510)

Cannon, W. B. *The wisdom of the body.* New York: Norton, 1932. (55)

Cannon, W. B., & Washburn, A. L. An explanation of hunger. *Amer. J. Physiol.*, 1912, **29**, 441–454. (328)

Carlson, A. J. *The control of hunger in health and diseases.* Chicago: Univer. of Chicago Press, 1916. (330)

Carlson, A. J. See Luckhardt, A. B., & Carlson, A. J., 1915.

Carmichael, L. Sir Charles Bell: A contribution to the history of physiological psychology. *Psychol. Rev.*, 1926, **33**, 188–217. (63)

Carmichael, L., Hogan, H. P., & Walter, A. A. An experimental study of the effect of language on the reproduction of visually perceived form. *J. exp. Psychol.*, 1932, **15**, 73–86. (450)

Carr, W. J. *Self-instructional devices: A review of current concepts.* Wright-Patterson Air Force Base, Ohio: Aero-Space Medical Laboratory, Wright Air Development Center, August, 1959. WADC Technical Report, 59–503. (n.s.) (476)

Carroll, J. B. Diversity of vocabulary and the harmonic series law of word frequency distribution. *Psychol. Rec.*, 1938, **2**, 379–386. (198)

Carter, L., Haythorn, W., Meirowitz, B., & Lanzetta, J. The relation of categorizations and ratings in the observation of group behavior. *Hum. Relat.*, 1951, **4**, 239–254. (600)

Carter, L. See Haythorn, W. W., Couch, A., Haefner, D., Langham, P., & Carter, L., 1956.

Carthy, J. D. *Animal navigation: How animals find their way about.* London: G. Allen, 1956. (492)

Carthy, J. D. *An introduction to the behaviour of invertebrates.* London: G. Allen, 1958. (502)

Cartwright, D. See Lewin, K., 1951.

Cartwright, D. Lewinian theory as a contemporary systematic framework. In S. Koch (Ed.) *Psychology: A study of a science.* Study I. Conceptual and systematic. Vol. II. *General systematic formulations, learning, and special processes.* New York: McGraw-Hill, 1959. Pp. 7–91. (601)

Cartwright, D. (Ed.) *Studies in social power.* Ann Arbor, Mich.: Institute for Social Research, 1959. (602)

Cartwright, D., & Harary, F. Structural balance: A generalization of Heider's theory. *Psychol. Rev.*, 1956, **63**, 277–293. (601)

Cartwright, D., & Zander, A. (Eds.) *Group dynamics: Research and theory.* New York: Harper & Row, 1960. (572, 601–602)

Catania, A. C. See Lane, H. L., Catania, A. C., & Stevens, S. S., 1961.

Cattell, J. McK. Mental tests and measurements. *Mind*, 1890, **15**, 373–381. (534)

Cattell, J. McK. See Fullerton, G. S. & Cattell, J. McK., 1892.

Cattell, R. B., Saunders, D. R., & Stice, G. F.

The dimensions of syntality in small groups. *Hum. Relat.*, 1953, **6**, 331–356. (575)

Cendron, H. See Bouliere, F., Cendron, H., & Rapaport, A., 1958.

Chamberlain, T. J., Rothschild, G. H., & Gerard, R. W. Drugs affecting RNA and learning. *Proc. Nat. Acad. Sci. U. S.*, 1963, **49**, 918–924. (382)

Chapanis, A. How we see: A summary of basic principles. In *Human Factors in undersea warfare.* Washington, D.C.: National Research Council, 1949. Pp. 3–60. (220, 222, 231, 244)

Chapanis, A. The reconstruction of abbreviated printed messages. *J. exp. Psychol.*, 1954, **48**, 496–510. (203, 206–207)

Chapanis, A., Garner, W. R., & Morgan, C. T. *Applied experimental psychology: Human factors in engineering design.* New York: Wiley, 1949. (69, 73, 201, 212, 232, 246–247)

Charpy, A. See Poirier, P., & Charpy, A., 1907.

Chase, A. M. See Hecht, S., Haig, C., & Chase, A. M., 1937.

Chase, R. A., Rapin, I., Gilden, L., Sutton, S., & Guilfoyle, G. Studies on sensory feedback: II. Sensory feedback influences on keytapping motor tasks. *Quart. J. exp. Psychol.*, 1961, **13**, 153–167. (464)

Chen, H. P. See Irwin, O. C., & Chen, H. P., 1946.

Cherry, C. *On human communication.* New York: Wiley, 1957; New York: Science Editions, 1961a. (211)

Cherry, C. Two ears—but one world. In W. A. Rosenblith (Ed.), *Sensory Communication.* Cambridge, Mass.: M.I.T., 1961b. Pp. 99–118. (183, 211)

Chotlos, J. W. Studies in language behavior: IV. A statistical and comparative analysis of individual written language samples. *Psychol. Monogr.*, 1944, **56**, 75–111. (198)

Christensen, K. R. Isohedonic contours in the sucrose–sodium chloride area of gustatory stimulation. Ph.D. thesis, Univer. of Illinois, 1960. (360)

Church, J. *Language and the discovery of reality.* New York: Random House, 1961. (212)

Church, R. M. The varied effects of punishment on behavior. *Psychol. Rev.,* 1963, **70,** 369–402. (421, 428)

Churcher, B. G. A loudness scale for industrial noise measurement. *J. Acoust. Soc. Amer.,* 1935, **6,** 216–226. (161)

Chweitzer, A. See Bujas, Z., & Chweitzer, A., 1937.

Claridge, G. S. See O'Connor, N., & Claridge, G. S., 1958.

Clark, A. See Wald, G., & Clark, A., 1937.

Clark, B., & Graybiel, A. Human performance during adaptation to stress in the Pensacola Slow Rotation Room. *USN Sch. Aviat. Med. Res. Rep.,* 1960, No. 52. (335)

Clark, R. A. The projective measurement of experimentally induced levels of sexual motivation. *J. exp. Psychol.,* 1952, **44,** 391–399. (527)

Clark, R. A. The effects of sexual motivation on fantasy. In D. C. McClelland (Ed.), *Studies in motivation.* New York: Appleton-Century-Crofts, 1955. Pp. 44–57. (527)

Clark, R. A., Teevan, R., & Ricciuti, H. N. Hope of success and fear of failure as aspects of need for achievement. *J. abnorm. soc. Psychol.,* 1956, **53,** 182–186. (527)

Clark, R. A. See McClelland, D. C., Atkinson, J. W., Clark, R. A., & Lowell, E. L., 1953.

Clark, S. L. See Ranson, S. W., & Clark, S. L., 1959.

Clements, F. Racial differences in colour blindness. *Amer. J. phys. Anthrop.,* 1930, **14,** 417–432. (254)

Clisby, K. H. See Richter, C. P., & Clisby, K. H., 1941.

Cofer, C. N. (Ed.) *Verbal learning and verbal behavior.* New York: McGraw-Hill, 1961. (476–477)

Cofer, C. N., & Appley, M. H. *Motivation: Theory and research.* New York: Wiley, 1964. (500–501, 516, 528, 530–531)

Cofer, C. N. See Judson, A. J., Cofer, C. N., & Gelfand, S., 1956.

Cohen, B. H. See Bousfield, W. A., & Cohen, B. H., 1953.

Cohen, B. P. A probability model for conformity. *Sociometry,* 1958, **21,** 69–81. (601)

Cohen, B. P. See Berger, J., Cohen, B. P., Snell, J. L., & Zelditch, M., 1962.

Cohen, J., & Ogden, D. P. Taste blindness to

phenyl-thio-carbamide and related compounds. *Psychol. Bull.,* 1949, **46,** 490–498. (361)

Cohen, L. A. Analysis of position sense in human shoulder. *J. Neurophysiol.,* 1958, **21,** 550–562. (314)

Cohen, M. J., Landgren, S., Ström, L., & Zotterman, Y. Cortical reception of touch and taste in the cat. *Acta physiol. Scand.,* 1957, **40,** Suppl. 135, 1–50. (353, 358)

Cohen, T., & Gitman, L. Oral complaints and taste perception in the aged. *J. Gerontol.,* 1959, **14,** 294–298. (355)

Cohen, W. Color perception in the chromatic Ganzfeld. *Amer. J. Psychol.,* 1958a, **71,** 390–394. (282)

Cohen, W. Apparent movement of simple figures in the Ganzfeld. *Percept. mot. Skills,* 1958b, **8,** 32. (284)

Collins, B. E., & Guetzkow, H. *A social psychology of group processes for decision-making.* New York: Wiley, 1964. (602)

Comte, A. *Cours de philosophie positive.* Paris: Hachette, 1927. (34)

Conrad, D. See Brady, J. V., Boren, J. J., Conrad, D., & Sidman, M., 1957.

Conrad, D. G. See Brady, J. V. Porter, R. W., Conrad, D. G., & Mason, J. W., 1958.

Conrad, D. See Porter, R. W., Brady, J. V., Conrad, D. G., Mason, J. W., Galambos, R., & Rioch, D. McD., 1958.

Conrad, R. Decay theory of immediate memory. *Nature,* 1957, **179,** 831–832. (476)

Conrad, R., & Hille, B. A. The decay theory of immediate memory and paced recall. *Canad. J. Psychol.,* 1958, **12,** 1–6. (445)

Converse, P. E. See Campbell, A., Converse, P. E., Miller, W. E., & Stokes, D. E., 1960.

Cook, L., Davidson, A. B., Davis, D. J., Green, H., & Fellows, E. J. Ribonucleic acid: Effect on conditioned behavior in rats. *Science,* 1963, **141,** 268–269. (382)

Cook, S. W. The production of "experimental neurosis" in the white rat. *Psychosom. Med.,* 1939, **1,** 293–308. (401)

Cook, T. W. Factors in whole and part learning a visually perceived maze. *J. genet. Psychol.,* 1936, **49,** 3–32. (475)

Cook, T. W. Whole versus part learning the

spider maze. *J. exp. Psychol.,* 1937, **20,** 477–494. (475)

Cook, T. W. Factors in massed and distributed practice. *J. exp. Psychol.,* 1944, **34,** 325–334. (440)

Coover, J. E. Experiments in psychical research. *Psychical Res. Monogr.* No. 1. Stanford, Calif.: Stanford, 1917. (293)

Copenhaver, W. M. (Ed.), & Johnson, D. D. *Bailey's textbook of histology.* (Rev. ed.) Baltimore: Williams & Wilkins, 1958, (n.s.) (49)

Corning, W. C., & John, E. R. Effect of ribonuclease on retention of conditioned response in regenerated planarians. *Science,* 1961, **134,** 1363–1365. (382)

Costello, C. G. Constant errors in the measurement of kinesthetic figural after-effects. *Amer. J. Psychol.,* 1961, **74,** 473–474. (326)

Cotzin, M., & Dallenbach, K. M. Facial vision: The role of pitch and loudness in the perception of obstacles by the blind. *Amer. J. Psychol.,* 1950, **63,** 485–515. (169)

Cotzin, M. See Supa, M., Cotzin, M., & Dallenbach, K. M., 1944.

Couch, A. See Haythorn, W. W., Couch, A., Haefner, D., Langham, P., & Carter, L., 1956.

Coulson, A. H. See Graham, C. H., Sperling, H. G., Hsia, Y., & Coulson, A. H., 1961.

Cousins, A. N. Social equilibrium and the psychodynamic mechanisms. *Social Forces,* 1951, **30,** 202–209. (573)

Crafts, L. W. Whole and part methods with nonserial reactions. *Amer. J. Psychol.,* 1929, **41,** 543–563. (437)

Crafts, L. W. Whole and part methods with unrelated reactions. *Amer. J. Psychol.,* 1930, **42,** 591–601. (437)

Crafts, L. W. Whole and part methods with visual spatial material. *Amer. J. Psychol.,* 1932, **44,** 526–534. (437)

Crafts, L. W., & Gilbert, R. W. The effect of punishment during learning upon retention. *J. exp. Psychol.,* 1934, **17,** 73–84. (476)

Cramer, T. Über die Beziehung des Zwischenmediums zur den Transformations und Kontrasterscheinungen. *Z. Sinnesphysiol,* 1923, **54,** 215–242. (268)

Cravens, R. B. See Bradway, K. P., Thompson, C. W., & Cravens, R. B., 1958.

Crespi, L. P. Quantitative variation of incentive and performance in the white rat. *Amer. J. Psychol.,* 1942, **55,** 467–517. (411)

Crick, F. H. C. See Watson, J. D., & Crick, F. H. C., 1953.

Crow, W. J. See Muenzinger, K. F., Brown, W. O., Crow, W. J., & Powlowski, R. F., 1952.

Crowley, M. E. See Gagné, R. M., Foster, H., & Crowley, M. E., 1948.

Crozier, W. J., & Wolf, E. Theory and measurement of visual mechanisms. *J. gen. Physiol.,* 1941, **24,** 635–654. (237)

Crozier, W. J. See Holway, A. H., & Crozier, W. J., 1937a.

Crozier, W. J. See Holway, A. H., & Crozier, W. J., 1937b.

Cuff, N. B. The relation of overlearning to retention. *George Peabody cont. Educ.,* 1927, No. 43. (451)

Culler, E. See Shurrager, P. S., & Culler, E., 1940.

Culler, E. See Shurrager, P. S., & Culler, E., 1941.

Culler, E. See Brogden, W. J., Lipman, E. A., & Culler, E., 1938.

Culler, E. See Girden, E., Mettler, F. A., Finch, G., & Culler, E., 1936.

Culver, C. A. *Musical acoustics.* 4th ed. New York: McGraw-Hill, 1956. (71)

Cumming, W. W. See Schoenfeld, W. N., & Cumming, W. W., 1963.

Curry, R. *The mechanisms of the human voice.* New York: Longmans, 1940. (212)

Cuvier, G. L. C. F. D. *Memoires de la classe des sciences mathematiques et physiques de l'Institut de France,* 1808. Pp. 109–160. (n.s.) (63)

Dallenbach, K. M. The temperature spots and end-organs. *Amer. J. Psychol.,* 1927, **39,** 402–427. (302, 310)

Dallenbach, K. M. Pain: History and present status. *Amer. J. Psychol.,* 1939, **52,** 331–347. (321)

Dallenbach, K. M. Twitmyer and the conditioned reflex. *Amer. J. Psychol.,* 1959, **72,** 633–638. (386)

Dallenbach, K. M. Tables vs. graphs as a means of presenting experimental results. *Amer. J. Psychol.,* 1963, **76**, 700–702. (448–449)

Dallenbach, K. M. See Cotzin, M., & Dallenbach, K. M., 1950.

Dallenbach, K. M. See Jenkins, J. G., & Dallenbach, K. M., 1924.

Dallenbach, K. M. See Krakauer, D., & Dallenbach, 1937.

Dallenbach, K. M. See Minami, H., & Dallenbach, K. M., 1946.

Dallenbach, K. M. See Abrahams, H., Krakauer, D., & Dallenbach, K. M., 1937.

Dallenbach, K. M. See Supa, M., Cotzin, M., & Dallenbach, K. M., 1944.

Dandison, B. See Adams, H. F., & Dandison, B., 1927.

Dartnall, H. J. A. *The visual pigments.* London: Methuen, 1957. (246–247)

Darwin, C. *Expression of the emotions in man and animals.* London: J. Murray, 1872. (507)

David, M. See Hacaen, H., Talairach, J., David, M., & Dell, M. B., 1949.

David, M. See Talairach, J., Hecaen, H., David, M., Monnier, M., & de Ajuriaguerra, J., 1949.

Davidson, A. B. See Cook, L., Davidson, A. B., Davis, D. J., Green, H., & Fellows, E. J., 1963.

Davies, J. D. *Phrenology: Fad and science.* New Haven: Yale, 1955. (41)

Davies, J. T., & Taylor, F. H. Molecular shape, size and adsorption in olfaction. *2nd int. Conf. Surface Activity,* 195, Vol. IV. 329–340. (349)

Davies, J. T., & Taylor, F. H. The role of adsorption and molecular morphology in olfaction: The calculation of olfactory thresholds. *Biol. Bull.,* 1959, **117**, 222–238. (349)

Davis, D. J. See Cook, L., Davidson, A. B., Davis, D. J., Green, H., & Fellows, E. J., 1963.

Davis, H. Excitation of auditory receptors. In J. Field, H. W. Magoun, & V. E. Hall (Eds.), *Handbook of physiology.* Vol. I. Washington, D.C.: American Physiological Society, 1959. Pp. 565–584. (179–181, 183)

Davis, H. Peripheral coding of auditory information. In W. A. Rosenblith, (Ed.), *Sensory communication.* Cambridge, Mass.: M.I.T., 1961, Pp. 119–142. (183)

Davis, H., & Saul, L. J. Action currents in the auditory tracts of the midbrain of the cat. *Science,* 1931, **74**, 205–206. (151)

Davis, H., Morgan, C. T., Hawkins, J. E., Jr., Galambos, R., & Smith, F. W. Temporary deafness following exposure to loud tones and noise. *Acta Otolaryngol., Stockholm, Supple.* 88, 1950, 1–56. (173)

Davis, H. See Stevens, S. S., & Davis, H., 1938.

Davis, H. See Tasaki, I., Davis, H., & Legouix, J. P., 1952.

Davis, H. V., Sears, R. R., Miller, H. C., & Brodbeck, A. J. Effects of cup, bottle, and breast-feeding on oral activities of new born infants. *Pediatrics,* 1948, **3**, 549–558. (495)

Davis, R. Methods of measuring and recording action. In T. G. Andrews (Ed.), *Methods of psychology.* New York: Wiley, 1948. (530)

Davitz, J. See Lorge, I., Fox, D., Davitz, J., & Brenner, J., 1958.

Davson, H. (Ed.) *The eye.* New York: Academic, 1962. (245)

De Ajuriaguerra, J. See Talairach, J., Hecaen, H., David, M., Monnier, M., & de Ajuriaguerra, J., 1949.

Deese, J. *The psychology of learning* (2nd ed.) New York: McGraw-Hill, 1958. (371, 383, 401, 477, 531)

Deese, J., & Hulse, S. H. *The psychology of learning.* (3rd ed.) New York: McGraw-Hill, 1967. (383, 401, 531)

Deese, J., & Kellogg, W. N. Some new data on the nature of "spinal conditioning." *J. comp. physiol. Psychol.,* 1949, **42**, 157–160. (395)

Delafresnaye, J. F. (Ed.) *Brain mechanisms and consciousness.* Springfield, Ill.: Charles C Thomas, 1954. (428)

Delafresnaye, J. F. (Ed.) *Brain mechanisms and learning.* London: Blackwell, 1961. (428)

DeLamater, J., McClintock, C. G., & Becker, G. Conceptual orientations of contemporary small group theory. *Psychol. Bull.,* 1965, **64**, 402–412. (601)

Delgado, J. M., Roberts, W. W., & Miller, N.

E. Learning motivated by electrical stimulation of the brain. *Amer. J. Physiol.,* 1954, **179**, 587–593. (520)

Delgado, J. M. R. Cerebral structures involved in transmission and elaboration of noxious stimulation. *J. Neurophysiol.,* 1955, **18**, 261–275. (321)

Dell, M. B. See Hecaen, H., Talairach, J., David, M., & Dell, M. B., 1949.

De Lorenzo, A. J. Electron microscopic observations on the taste buds of the rabbit. *J. biophys. biochem. Cytol.,* 1958, **4**, 143–148. (351)

De Lorenzo, A. J. Studies on the ultrastructure and histophysiology of cell membranes, nerve fibers, and synaptic functions in chemoreceptors. In Y. Zotterman (Ed.), *Taste and olfaction.* New York: Macmillan, 1963. Pp. 5–18. (351–352)

DeMartino, M. F. See Stacey, C. L., & DeMartino, M. F., 1958.

Dember, W. N. *The psychology of perception.* New York: Holt, 1960. (246, 277, 295)

Dement, W., & Kleitman, N. Cyclic variations in EEG during sleep and their relation to eye movements, body motility, and dreaming. *EEG clin. Neurophysiol.,* 1957, **9**, 673–690. (61)

Dement, W., & Wolpert, E. A. The relation of eye movements, body motility, and external stimuli to dream content. *J. exp. Psychol.,* 55, 1958, 543–553. (61)

Dennis, W. Congenital cataract and unlearned behavior. *J. genet. Psychol.,* 1934, **44**, 340–351. (278)

Denny, M. R., Allard, M., Hall, E., & Rokeach, M. Supplementary report: Delay of knowledge of task and intertrial interval. *J. exp. Psychol.,* 1960, **60**, 327. (476)

DeRivera, J. See Lawrence, D. H., & DeRivera, J., 1954.

Dethier, V. G. Chemoreceptor mechanisms: Molecular structure and functional activity of nerve cells. In R. G. Greness, & L. Mullins (Eds.), *Amer. Inst. Biol. Sciences Publ.,* 1956, No. 1. Pp. 1–30. (361)

Dethier, V. G., & Arab, V. M. Effect of temperature on the contact chemo-receptors of the blowfly. *J. Insect Physiol.,* 1958, **2**, 153–161. (353)

Dethier, V. G., Larsen, J. R., & Adams, J. R. The fine structures of the olfactory receptors of the blowfly. In Y. Zotterman (Ed.), *Olfaction and taste.* Vol. I. New York: Macmillan, 1963, pp. 105–110. (246)

Deutsch, M. An experimental study of the effects of cooperation and competition upon group process. *Hum. Relat.,* 1949, **2**, 199–232. (576, 598)

Deutsch, M. Field theory in social psychology. In G. Lindzey (Ed.), *Handbook of social psychology.* Vol. 1. Reading, Mass.: Addison-Wesley, 1954. Pp. 181–222. (601)

Deutsch, J. A., & Deutsch, D. *Physiological psychology,* Homewood, Ill.: Dorsey, 1966. (63)

De Valois, R. L. Color vision mechanisms in the monkey. *J. gen. Physiol.,* 1960, **43**, 115–128. (228)

Diamant, H., Funakoshi, M., Ström, L., & Zotterman, Y. Electrophysiological studies on human taste nerves. In Y. Zotterman (Ed.), *Olfaction and taste.* New York: Macmillan, 1963. Pp. 193–203. (357)

Diamant, H. See Zotterman, Y., & Diamant, H., 1959.

Diamond, I. T., & Neff, W. D. Ablation of temporal cortex and discrimination of auditory patterns. *J. Neurophysiol.,* 1957, **20**, 300–315. (181)

Diamond, I. T. See Neff, W. D., Fisher, J. F., Diamond, I. T., & Yela, M., 1956.

Dietze, A. G. Kinesthetic discrimination: The difference limen for finger span. *J. Psychol.,* 1961, **51**, 165–168. (325)

Dingman, W., & Sporn, M. B. The incorporation of 8-azaguanine into rat brain RNA and its effect on maze-learning by the rat: An inquiry into the biochemical basis of memory. *J. psychiat. Res.,* 1961, **1**, 1–11. (382)

Dinnerstein, D. See Köhler, W., & Dinnerstein, D., 1947.

Dinsmoor, J. A. A discrimination based on punishment. *Quart. J. exp. Psychol.,* 1952, **4**, 27–45. (422)

Dittmer, D. S. See Altman, P. L., & Dittmer, D. S., 1964.

Doane, B. K. See Heron, W., Doane, B. K., & Scott, T. H., 1956.

Dodge, H. W., Jr. See Sem-Jacobsen, C. W., Petersen, M. C., Dodge, H. W., Jr., Jacks, Q. D., & Lazarte, J. A., 1956.

Dodge, R. Note on Professor Thorndike's experiment. *Psychol. Rev.*, 1927, **34**, 237–240. (476)

Dodge, R. See Gatti, A., & Dodge, R., 1929.

Dodt, E., & Zotterman, Y. The discharge of specific cold fibres at high temperatures (the paradoxical cold). *Acta physiol. Scand.*, 1952, **26**, 358–365. (306)

Dohlman, G. Some practical and theoretical points in labyrinthology. *Proc. Roy. Soc. Med.*, 1935, **28**, 1371–1380. (333–335)

Dohlman, G. Investigations in the function of the semicircular canals, *Acta Otolaryng., Stockh., Suppl.*, 1944, **51**, 211–219. (333)

Dohlman, G. Some aspects of the mechanism of vestibular hair cell stimulation. *Conf. Neurol.*, 1960, **20**, 169–180. (333)

Dolin, A. O., Zborovskaya, I. I., & Zamakhover, Sh. M. The role of the orienting-investigatory reflex in conditioned reflex activity. In L. G. Voronin, A. N. Leont'yev, A. R. Luria, E. N. Sokolov, & O. S. Vinogradova (Eds.), *Orientirovochny refleks i orientirovochno-issledovatel'skaya deyatel' nost'.* (The orienting reflex and orienting-investigatory activity.) Moscow: Akad. Pedag. Nauk R. S. F. S. R., 1958. Pp. 47–60. (398)

Dollard, J. See Miller, N. E., & Dollard, J., 1941.

Donald, H. P. The milk composition and growth of suckling pigs. *Emp. J. exp. Agric.*, 1937, **5**, 349–368. (n.s.) (495)

Donaldson, L. R., & Allen, G. H. Return of silver salmon, *Oncorhynchus bisutch* (Walbaum), to point of release. *Trans. Amer. Fisheries Soc.*, 1958, **87** (1957), 13–22. (494)

Doré, L. R., & Hilgard, E. R. Spaced practice and the maturation hypothesis. *J. Psychol.*, 1937, **4**, 245–259. (476)

Doré, L. R., & Hilgard, E. R. Spaced practice as a test of Snoddy's two processes in mental growth. *J. exp. Psychol.*, 1938, **23**, 359–374. (476)

du Bois-Reymond, E. *Untersuchungen über thierische Elektricität,* I, 1848, II (1), 1849, II (2), 1860–1884. Berlin: G. Reimer. (40)

Duffy, E. Emotion: An example of the need for reorientation in psychology. *Psychol. Rev.*, 1934, **41**, 184–198. (516)

Duffy, E. Leeper's "Motivational" theory of emotion. *Psychol. Rev.*, 1948, **55**, 324–328. (516)

Duffy, E. The psychological significance of the concept of "arousal" or "activation." *Psychol. Rev.*, 1957, **64**, 265–275. (516)

Duffy, E. *Activation and behavior.* New York: Wiley, 1962. (506, 516, 530)

Dufort, R. H. See Kimble, G. A., & Dufort, R. H., 1955.

Dufort, R. H. See Kimble, G. A., & Dufort, R. H., 1956.

Dufort, R. H. See Kimble, G. A., Mann, L. I., & Dufort, R. H., 1955.

Dulany, D. E., Jr. *Reinforcement of verbal behavior.* Final report of research supported by National Science Foundation, Grant G-4461, 1960 (477)

Dulany, D. E., Jr. Hypotheses and habits in verbal "operant conditioning." *J. abnorm. soc. Psychol.*, 1961, **63**, 251–263. (459, 477)

Dulany, D. E., Jr. The place of hypotheses and intentions: An analysis of verbal control in verbal conditioning. In C. W. Eriksen (Ed.), *Behavior and awareness: A symposium of research and interpretation.* Durham, N.C.: Duke, 1962. Pp. 102–129. (477)

Dunlap, K. Are there any instincts? *J. abnorm. soc. Psychol.*, 1919, **14**, 35–50. (500)

Dvorine, I. *Dvorine pseudo-isochromatic plates.* (2nd ed.) Baltimore: Scientific Publishing, 1953. (255)

Dyson, G. M. Raman effect and the concept of odor. *Perf. essent. Oil Rec.*, 1937, **28**, 13–19. (348)

Dyson, G. M. The scientific basis of odor. *Chem. & Industr.*, 1938, **57**, 647–651. (348)

Eason, R. G. Electromyographic study of local and generalized muscular impairment. *J. Appl. Physiol.*, 1960, **15**, 479–482. (475)

Ebbinghaus, H. *Über das Gedächtnis: Untersuchungen zur experimentellen Psychologie.*

Leipzig: Duncker & Humblot, 1885. (195, 430)

Ebbinghaus, H. Über eine neue Methode zur Prüfung geistiger Fähigkeiten und ihre Anwendung bei Schuokindern. *Z. Psychol.,* 1897, **13**, 401–459. (534)

Ebbinghaus, H. *Grundzüge der Psychologie.* Leipzig: Veit, 1911. (451)

Ebbinghaus, H. *Memory: A contribution to experimental psychology.* (H. A. Ruger, & C. E. Bussenius, Trans.) New York: Columbia, 1913. (430, 449)

Eckerson, A. B. See Odbert, H. S., Karwoski, T. F., & Eckerson, A. B., 1942.

Edridge-Green, F. W. *Colour blindness and colour perception.* London: 1891. (n.s.) See Pickford (1951).

Edridge-Green, F. W. *The physiology of vision.* London: 1920. (n.s.) See Pickford (1951).

Edwards, A. L. Political frames of reference as a factor influencing recognition. *J. abnorm. soc. Psychol.,* 1941, **36**, 34–50. (476)

Edwards, A. L. *Techniques of attitude scale construction.* New York: Appleton-Century-Crofts, 1957. (108, 143)

Edwards, A. L. *Experimental design in psychological research,* (Rev. ed.) New York: Holt, 1960. (34–35)

Edwards, W. Recent research on pain perception. *Psychol. Bull.,* 1950, **47**, 449–474. (323)

Egan, J. P., & Wiener, F. M. On the intelligibility of bands of speech in noise. *J. Acoust. Soc. Amer.* 1946, **18**, 435–441. (201)

Egan, J. P. See Postman, L., & Egan, J. P., 1949.

Egan, J. P. See Rosenblith, W. A., Miller, G. A., Egan, J. P., Hirsh, I. J., & Thomas, G. J., 1947.

Eggan, J. B. Is instinct an entity? *J. abnorm. soc. Psychol.,* 1926, **21**, 38–51. (500)

Egyhazi, E. See Hydén, H., & Egyhazi, E., 1962.

Egyhazi, E. See Hydén, H., & Egyhazi, E., 1963.

Ehrenfreund, D. An experimental test of the continuity theory of discrimination learning with pattern vision. *J. comp. physiol. Psychol.,* 1948, **41**, 408–422. (85)

Ehrenfreund, D. A study of the transposition

gradient. *J. exp. Psychol.,* 1952, **43**, 81–87. (418)

Eisenson, J. *The psychology of speech.* New York: Crofts, 1938. (212)

Ekstrand, B. R. See Underwood, B. J., & Ekstrand, B. R., 1966.

El-Baradi, A., & Bourne, G. Theory of tastes and odors. *Science,* 1951, **113**, 660–661. (361)

Elkin, A. See Withey, S., Buxton, C. E., & Elkin, A., 1949.

Ellertson, N. See Schachter, S., Ellertson, N., McBride, D., & Gregory, D., 1951.

Elliot, O. See Freedman, D. G., King, J. A., & Elliot, O., 1961.

Ellis, D. S. See Helmstader, G. C., & Ellis, D. S., 1952.

Ellis, K. See Howarth, C. I., & Ellis, K., 1961.

Ellis, W. D. *A sourcebook of Gestalt psychology.* New York: Harcourt, Brace & World, 1938. (295)

Elsberg, C. A., & Levy, I. The sense of smell: I. A new and simple method of quantitative olfactometry. *Bull. Neurol. Inst. N.Y.,* 1935, **4**, 5–19. (341 342)

Elsberg, C. A., Brewer, E. D., & Levy, I. Concerning conditions which may temporarily alter normal olfactory activity. *Bull. Neurol. Inst. N.Y.,* 1935, **4**, 31–34. (344)

Emery, D. A. See Köhler, W., & Emery, D. A., 1947.

Emmers, R., Benjamin, R. M., & Ables, M. F. Differential localization of taste and tongue tactile afferents in the rat thalamus. *Fed. Proc.,* 1960, **19**, 286 (abstract). (353)

Eng, E., & French, R. L. The determination of sociometric status. *Sociometry,* 1948, **11**, 368–371. (141)

Engen, T., & Pfaffman, C. Absolute judgments of odor quality. *J. exp. Psychol.,* 1960, **59**, 214–219. (343)

English, H. B. *A comprehensive dictionary of psychological and psychoanalytic terms.* New York: Longmans, 1958. (35)

English, H. B., Welborn, E. L., & Killian, C. D. Studies in substance memorization. *J. gen. Psychol.,* 1934, **11**, 233–260. (476)

English, H. B. See Jones, M. G., & English, H. B., 1926.

Engström, H., & Rytzner, C. The fine structure of taste buds and taste fibers. *Annu. Otol. Rhinol. Laryngol.*, 1956, **65**, 361–375. (351)

Engström, H. See Bloom, G., & Engström, H., 1952.

Epstein, A. N. See Teitelbaum, P., and Epstein, A. N., 1962.

Epstein, W. The influence of syntactical structure on learning. *Amer. J. Psychol.*, 1961, **74**, 80–85. (189)

Eriksen, C. W. The case for perceptual defense. *Psychol. Rev.*, 1954, **61**, 175–182. (292)

Eriksen, C. W., & Kuethe, K. L. Avoidance conditioning of verbal behavior without awareness: A paradigm of repression. *J. abnorm. soc. Psychol.*, 1956, **53**, 203–209. (293)

Ericksen, S. C. Variability of attack in massed and distributed practice. *J. exp. Psychol.*, 1942, **31**, 339–345. (440)

Erickson, R. D. See Pfaffmann, C., Erickson, R. D., Frommer, G. P., & Halpern, B. P., 1961.

Erulkar, S. D., & Fillenz, M. Single-unit activity in the lateral geniculate body of the cat. *J. Physiol.*, 1960, **154**, 206–218. (228)

Estes, W. K. An experimental study of punishment. *Psychol. Monogr.*, 1944, **57** (Whole No. 263). (421)

Estes, W. K. Toward a statistical theory of learning. *Psychol. Rev.*, 1950, **57**, 94–107. (372)

Estes, W. K. Of models and men. *Amer. Psychologist*, 1957, **12**, 609–617. (601)

Estes, W. K., & Burke, C. J. Application of a statistical model to simple discrimination learning in human subjects. *J. exp. Psych.*, 1955, **50**, 81–88. (601)

Evans, C. L. *Principles of human physiology.* (12th ed.) Philadelphia: Lea & Febiger, 1956. (311)

Evans, H. G. V. See Wright, R. H., Reid, C., & Evans, H. G. V., 1956.

Ewen, R. B. See Triandis, H. C., Hall, E. R., & Ewen, R. B., 1965.

Ewer, R. F. Suckling behaviour in kittens. *Behaviour*, 1959, **15**, 146–160. (495)

Ewer, R. F. Further observations on suckling behaviour in kittens, together with some general considerations of the interrelations of innate and acquired responses. *Behaviour*, 1961, **17**, 247–260. (495)

Ewert, P. H. A study of the effect of inverted retinal stimulation upon spatially coordinated behavior. *Genet. Psychol. Monogr.*, 1930, **7**, 177–363. (281)

Ewert, P. H. Factors in space localization during inverted vision: I. Interference. *Psychol. Rev.*, 1936, **43**, 522–546. (281)

Ewert, P. H. Factors in space localization during inverted vision: II. An explanation of interference and adaptation. *Psychol. Rev.*, 1937, **44**, 105 116. (281)

Fabian, F. W., & Blum, H. B. Relative taste potency of some basic food constitutents and their competitive and compensatory action. *Food Res.*, 1943, **8**, 179–183. (350)

Fairbanks, H. Studies in language behavior: II. The quantitative differentiation of samples of spoken language. *Psychol. Monogr.*, 1944, **56** (2), 19–38. (198)

Fantz, R. L. Form preferences in newly hatched chicks. *J. comp. physiol. Psychol.*, 1957, **50**, 422–430. (282, 289)

Fantz, R. L. Pattern vision in young infants. *Psychol. Rec.*, 1958, **8**, 43–48. (290)

Farquhar, W. W. See Krumboltz, J. D., & Farquhar, W. W., 1957.

Faust, W. L. See Taylor, D. W., & Faust, W. L., 1952.

Feallock, J. B. See Lloyd, K. E., Reid, L. S., & Feallock, J. B., 1960.

Fechner, G. T. Beobachtungen welche zu beweizen scheinen dass durch die Uebung der Glieder der einen Seite die der andern zugleich mit geübt werden. *Ber. Sachs ges. Wiss. Leipzig MathPhys. Cl.*, 1858, **10**, 70–76, (n.s.) (454)

Fechner, G. T. *Elemente der Psychophysik.* Leipzig: Breitkopf und Härtel, 1860. (86, 89, 430)

Fechner, G. T. *In Sachen der Psychophysik.* Leipzig: 1877. (101)

Fechner, G. T. *Revision der Hauptpunkte der Psychophysik.* Leipzig: Breitkopf und Härtel, 1882. (n.s.) (86)

Fechner, G. T. *Elements of psychophysics.* (H. S. Langfeld, Trans.) In B. Rand (Ed.),

The classical psychologists. Boston: Houghton Mifflin, 1912. Pp. 562–572. (89)

Feindel, W. H., Weddell, G., & Sinclair, D. C. Pain sensibility in a deep somatic structure. *J. Neurol. Neurosurg. Psychiat.,* 1948, **11,** 113–117. (323)

Feindel, W. H. See Weddell, G., Sinclair, D. C., & Feindel, W. H., 1948.

Feldman, M. P. Aversion therapy for sexual deviations: A critical review. *Psychol. Bull.,* 1966, **65,** 65–79. (387)

Fellows, E. J. See Cook, L., Davidson, A B., Davis, D. J., Green, H., & Fellows, E. J., 1963.

Ferenczi, S. *Sex in psychoanalysis: Contributions to psychoanalysis.* New York: Brunner, 1950. (522)

Fernberger, S. W. New phenomena of apparent visual movement. *Amer. J. Psychol.,* 1934, **46,** 309–314. (284)

Feshbach, S. The drive-reducing function of fantasy behavior. *J. abnorm. soc. Psychol.,* 1955, **50,** 3–11. (527)

Festinger, L. *A theory of cognitive dissonance.* New York: Harper & Row, 1957. (602)

Festinger, L., & Katz, D. (Eds.) *Research methods in the behavioral sciences.* New York: Holt, 1953. (602)

Festinger, L., & Thibaut, J. Interpersonal communication in small groups. *J. abnorm. soc. Psychol.,* 1951, **46,** 92–99. (573, 592)

Festinger, L., Schachter, S., & Back, K. *Social pressures in informal groups: A study of human factors in housing.* New York: Harper & Row, 1950. (588)

Fick, A. Die Lehre von der Lichtempfindung. In L. Hermann (Ed.), *Handbuch der physiologie.* Vol. 3, Part 1. Leipzig: Vogel, 1879. (260)

Fiedler, F. E. Assumed similarity measures as predictors of team effectiveness. *J. abnorm. soc. Psychol.,* 1954, **49,** 381–388. (594, 597)

Fiedler, F. E. The contingency model: A theory of leadership effectiveness. In H. Proshansky and B. Seidenberg (Eds.), *Basic studies in social psychology.* New York: Holt, 1965. Pp. 538–551. (595)

Fiedler, F. E. Meuwese, W. A. T., & Oonk, S. An exploratory study of group creativity in laboratory tasks. *Acta psychol.,* 1961, **18,** 100 119. (572)

Field, J., Magoun, H. W., & Hall, V. E. (Eds.) *Handbook of physiology.* Baltimore: Waverly Press, Vol. I, II, III. Washington, D.C. American Physiological Society, 1959. (183, 336)

Fillenz, M. See Erulkar, S. D., & Fillenz, M., 1960.

Finch, G. See Girden, E., Mettler, F. A., Finch, G. & Culler, E., 1936.

Fink, C. F. See Thomas, E. J., & Fink, C. F., 1963.

Firestone, F. A. See Geiger, P. H., & Firestone, F. A., 1933.

Fisher, J. F. See Neff, W. D., Fisher, J. F., Diamond, I. T., & Yela, M., 1956.

Fishman, I. Y. Single fiber gustatory impulses in rat and hamster. *J. cell. comp. Physiol.,* 1957, **49,** 319–334. (353)

Fitts, P. M. Perceptual-motor skill learning. In A. W. Melton (Ed.), *Categories of human learning.* New York: Academic, 1964. Pp. 243–285. (477)

Fitts, P. M., Noble, M. E., Bahrick, H. P., & Briggs, G. E. Skilled performance. Part I. *AF WADC Final Report.* I. S. Air Force, Dayton, Ohio, 1959a. (n.s.) (476)

Fleishman, E. A. An analysis of positioning movements and static reactions. *J. exp. Psychol.,* 1958, **55,** 13–24. (464)

Fleishman, E. A., & Hempel, W. E., Jr. Factorial analysis of complex psychomotor performance and related skills. *J. appl. Psychol.,* 1956, **40,** 96–104. (464)

Fleishman, E. A. See Nicks, D. C., & Fleishman, E. A., 1962.

Fletcher, H. *Speech and hearing.* Princeton, N.J.: Van Nostrand, 1929. (70, 212)

Fletcher, H. Newer concepts of the pitch, the loudness and the timbre of musical tones. *J. Franklin Inst.,* 1935, **220,** 405–429. (165)

Fletcher, H. Auditory patterns. *Rev. mod. Phys.,* 1940, **12,** 47–65. (162)

Flexner, J. B., Flexner, L. B., & Stellar, E. Memory in mice as affected by intracerebral puromycin. *Science,* 1963, **141,** 57–59. (382)

Flexner, L. B. See Flexner, J. B., Flexner, L. B., & Stellar, E., 1963.

Flieandt, Kai von. *The world of perception.* Homewood, Illinois: The Dorsey Press, 1966. (245)

Flourens, P. Recherches expérimentales sur les propriétés et les fonctions du système nerveux, dans les animaux vertébrés. Paris, 1824. (No Eng. trans.) (40)

Flourens, M. J. P. Expériences sur les canaux semicirculaires de l'oreille dans les oiseaux. *Mém. Acad. Roy. Sci., Paris,* 1830a, **9,** 455–466. n.s. (333)

Flourens, M. J. P. Expériences sur les canaux semicirculaires de l'oreille dans les mammifères. *Mém. Acad. Roy, Sci., Paris,* 1830b, **9,** 466–477. n.s. (333)

Foerster, O. The dermatones in man. *Brain,* 1933, **56,** 1–39. (303)

Foley, J. P. Observation on the effect of prolonged inverted retinal stimulation upon spatially coordinated behavior in the rhesus monkey. *Psychol. Bull.,* 1938, **35,** 701–702. (282)

Forbes, A., & Gregg, A. Electrical studies in mammalian reflexes: The correlation between strength of stimuli and direct and reflex nerve response. *Amer. J. Physiol.,* 1915, **39,** 172–235. (176)

Ford, C. S., & Beach, F. A. *Patterns of sexual behavior.* New York: Harper, 1951. (490, 501)

Foreman, S. See Greenspoon, J., & Foreman, S., 1956.

Forgus, R. H. The effect of early perceptual learning on the behavioral organization of adult rats. *J. comp. physiol. Psychol.,* 1954, **47,** 331–336. (288)

Forgus, R. H. Early visual and motor experience as determiners of complex maze-learning ability under rich and reduced stimulation. *J. comp. physiol. Psychol.,* 1955, **48,** 215–220. (288)

Forgus, R. H. Advantage of early over late perceptual experience in improving form discrimination. *Canad. J. Psychol.,* 1956, **10,** 147–155. (288)

Forlano, G. See Pintner, R., & Forlano, R., 1940.

Fossler, H. R. Disturbances in breathing during stuttering. *Psychol. Monogr.,* 1930, **4,** 1–32. (185)

Foster, H. See Gagné, R. M., Foster, H., & Crowley, M. E., 1948.

Fouriezos, N. T., Hutt, M. L., & Guetzkow, H. Measurement of self-oriented needs in discussion groups. *J. abnorm. soc. Psychol.,* 1950, **45,** 682–690. (575)

Fox, D. See Lorge, I., Fox, D., Davitz, J., & Brenner, M., 1958.

Frank, P. G. (Ed.) *The validation of scientific theories.* New York: Collier Books, 1961. (35)

Fraser, D. C. Recent experimental work in the study of fatigue. *Occup. Psychol.,* 1958, **32,** 258–263. (476)

Fraser, J. A. See Wyatt, S., Fraser, J. A., & Stock, F. G. L., 1929.

Freeden, R. C. Cup feeding of new-born infants. *Pediatrics,* 1948, **3,** 544–548. (501)

Freedman, D. G., King, J. A., & Elliot, O. Critical period in the social development of dogs. *Science,* 1961. **133,** 1016–1017. (484)

Freedman, J. L. See Mednick, S. A., & Freedman, J. L., 1960.

Freedman, S. J., Grunebaum, H. U., & Greenblatt, M. Perceptual and cognitive changes in sensory deprivation. In P. Solomon, P. E. Kubzansky, P. H. Leiderman, J. H. Mendelson, R. Trumbull, & D. Wexler (Eds.), *Sensory deprivation.* Cambridge, Mass.: Harvard, 1961. Pp. 58–71. (289)

Freeman, F. S. *Theory and practice of psychological testing.* (3rd ed.) New York: Holt, 1962. (552–553)

Freeman, J. T. Set or perceptual defenses. *J. exp. Psychol.,* 1954, **48,** 283–288. (292)

French, J. W. The effect of temperature on the retention of a maze habit in fish. *J. exp. Psychol.,* 1942, **31,** 79–87. (476)

French, J. R. P., & Raven, B. H. The bases of social power. In D. Cartwright (ed.), *Studies in social power.* Ann Arbor, Mich.: Univer. of Michigan Press, 1959. Pp. 150–167. (579)

French, R. L. See Eng, E., & French, R. L., 1948.

Freud, S. *Inhibitions, symptoms, and anxiety.* (A. Strachey, Trans.) London: L. & V. Woolf, 1936. (522)

Freud, S. *An outline of psychoanalysis.* (J. Strachey, authorized trans.), New York: Norton, 1949. (524)

Freud, S. Three essays on the theory of sexuality. In J. Strachey (Ed.), *The complete works of Sigmund Freud.* Vol. VII. London: Hogarth and Institute of Psycho-analysis, 1953. Pp. 125–249. (501)

Frings, H., & Jumber, J. Preliminary studies on the use of specific sound to repel Starlings *(Sturnus vulgaris)* from objectionable roosts. *Science,* 1954, **119**, 318–319. (209)

Fritsch, G., & Hitzig, E. Über de elektrische Erregbarkeit des Grosshirns., *Arch. Anat. Physiol.,* 1870. (No Eng. trans.) (n.s.) (40, 59)

Frohlich, F. W. *Grundzüge einer Lehre vom Licht- und Farbensinn: Ein Beitrag zur allgemeinen Physiologie der Sinne.* Jena: S. Fischer, 1921. (n.s.) (225)

Frommer, G. P. Electrophysiological analysis of gustatory, tongue temperature, and tactile representation in thalamus of albino rat. Ph.D. thesis, Brown Univer., 1961. (n.s.) (357)

Frommer, G. P. See Pfaffmann, C., Erickson, R. D., Frommer, G. P., & Halpern, B. P., 1961.

Fuller, J. J. *Motivation: A biological perspective.* New York: Random House, 1962. (530)

Fullerton, G. S., & Cattell, J. McK. On the perception of small differences. *Publ. Univer. Pa. Phil. Ser.,* 1892, No. 2. (101)

Fulton, J. F. (Ed.) *Textbook of physiology* (17th ed.) Philadelphia; Saunders, 1955. (63)

Funakoshi, M. See Diamant, H. Funakoshi, M., Ström, L., & Zotterman, Y., 1963.

Funkenstein, D. H. The physiology of fear and anger. *Scient. Amer.,* 1955, **192**, 74–80. (513)

Gagné, R. M. Problem solving. In A. W. Melton (Ed.), *Categories of human learning.* New York: Academic, 1964. Pp. 293–317. (477)

Gagné, R. M., & Bolles, R. C. A review of factors in learning efficiency. In E. Galanter (Ed.), *Automatic teaching: the state of the art.* New York: Wiley, 1959, Pp. 13–53. (476)

Gagné, R. M., & Smith, E. C., Jr. A study of the effects of verbalization on problem solving. *J. exp. Psychol.,* 1962, **63**, 12–18. (472)

Gagné, R. M., Foster, H., & Crowley, M. E. The measurement of transfer of training. *Psychol. Bull.,* 1948, **45**, 97–130. (454)

Gaito, J. A biochemical approach to learning and memory. *Psychol. Rev.,* 1961, **68**, 288–292. (382)

Galambos, R. Suppression of auditory nerve activity by stimulation of efferent fibers to the cochlea. *J. Neurophysiol.,* 1956, **19**, 424–437. (181)

Galambos, R. Some neural correlates of conditioning and learning. In E. R. Ramey, & D. S. O'Doherty (Eds.), *Electrical studies on the unanesthetized brain.* New York: Hoeber-Harper, 1960. Pp. 120–132. (395)

Galambos, R. See Davis, H., Morgan, C. T., Hawkins, J. E., Jr., Galambos, R., & Smith, F. W., 1950.

Galambos, R. See Hearst, E., Beer, B., Sheatz, G., & Galambos, R., 1960.

Galambos, R. See Porter, R. W., Brady, J. V., Conrad, D., Mason, J. W., Galambos, R., & Rioch, D. McD., 1958.

Galanter, E. Contemporary psychophysics. In R. Brown, E. Galanter, E. Hess, & G. Mandler (Eds.), *New directions in psychology.* New York: Holt, 1962. Pp. 87–156. (108–109)

Galanter, E. See Luce, R. D., & Galanter, E., 1963.

Galanter, E. See Brown, R., Galanter, E., Hess, E. H., & Mandler, G., 1962.

Galanter, E. See Luce, R. D., Bush, R. R., & Galanter, E., 1963.

Gall, F. J. *Anatomie et physiologie du système nerveux en general, et du cerveau en particulier.* 4 vols. Paris: D'Hautel, 1810–1819. (63)

Galton, F. Psychometric experiments. *Brain,* 1879, **2**, 149–162. (193)

Galton, F. *Inquiries into human faculty and its development.* London: Macmillan, 1883. (534)

Galvani, L. *De viribus electricitatis in motu musculari.* Bononiensi Scientiarum et Artium Instituto atque Academiae Commentarii, 1791. Pp. 363–418. (n.s.) (40)

Gamburg, A. L. Orienting and defensive reactions in simple and paranoid forms of schizophrenia. In L. G. Voronin, A. N.

Leont'yev, A. R. Luria, E. N. Sokolov, & O. S. Vinogradova (Eds.), *Orientirovochny refleks i orientirovochnoissledovatel'skaya deyatel'nost'.* (The orienting reflex and orienting-investigatory activity.) Moscow: Akad. Pedag. Nauk, 1958. Pp. 270–281. (n.s.) (399)

Ganz, L. Is the figural aftereffect an *aftereffect?* A review of its intensity, onset, decay, and transfer characteristics. *Psychol. Bull.,* 1966, 66, 151–165. (295)

Gardener, M. B. See Steinberg, J. C., Montgomery, H. C., & Gardener, M. B., 1940.

Gardner, R. W. Individual differences in figural after-effects and response to reversible figures. *Brit. J. Psychol.,* 1961, 52, 269–272. (326)

Garner, W. R. See Chapanis, A., Garner, W. R., & Morgan, C. T., 1949.

Gatenbein, M. M. Recherche sur le développement de la perception du mouvement avec l'âge. (Mouvement apparent dit stroboscopique). *Arch. Psychol.,* Genève, 1952, 33, 198–294. (290)

Gatti, A., & Dodge, R. Über die Unterschiedsempfinclichkeit bei Reizung eines einzelnen, isolierten Tastorgans. *Arch. ges. Psychol.,* 1929, 69, 405–425. (314)

Gaudet, H. See Lazarsfeld, P. F., Berelson, B., & Gaudet, H., 1944.

Gault, R. H. On the identification of certain vowel and consonantal elements in words by their tactual qualities and by their visual qualities as seen by lip readers. *J. abnorm. soc. Psychol.,* 1927, 22, 33–39. (317)

Gebhard, P. H. See Kinsey, A. C., Pomeroy, W. B., Martin, C. E., & Gebhard, P. H., 1953.

Geiger, P. H., & Firestone, F. A. The estimation of fractional loudness. *J. Acoust. Soc. Amer.,* 1933, 5, 25–30. (141)

Geldard, F. A. The description of a case of total color blindness. *J. Opt. Soc. Amer.,* 1933, 23, 256–260. (256)

Geldard, F. A. The perception of mechanical vibration: I. History of a controversy. *J. gen. Psychol.,* 1940a, 22, 243–269. (316)

Geldard, F. A. The perception of mechanical vibration: II. The response of pressure receptors. *J. gen. Psychol.,* 1940b, 22, 271–280. (316)

Geldard, F. A. The perception of mechanical vibration: III. The frequency function. *J. gen. Psychol.,* 1940c, 22, 281–289. (316)

Geldard, F. A. The perception of mechanical vibration: IV. Is there a separate "vibratory sense?" *J. gen. Psychol.,* 1940d, 22, 291–308. (316)

Geldard, F. A. *The human senses.* New York: Wiley, 1953. (62, 77, 79, 150, 168, 183, 219, 246–247, 294, 312–313, 336, 343, 348)

Geldard, F. A. Adventures in tactile literacy. *Amer. Psychol.,* 1957, 12, 115–124. (316)

Geldard, F. A. Some neglected possibilities of communication. *Science,* 1960, 131, 1583–1588. (316, 317)

Geldard, F. A. Cutaneous channels of communication. In W. A. Rosenblith (Ed.), *Sensory communication.* New York: Wiley, 1961. (316–317)

Gelfand, S. See Judson, A. J., Cofer, C. N., & Gelfand, S., 1956.

Gerard, H. B. Group dynamics. In *Annual Review of Psychology.* Palo Alto, Calif.: Annual Reviews, 1967. (602)

Gerard, R. W. See Chamberlain, T. J., Rothschild, G. H., & Gerard, R. W., 1963.

Gerebtzoff, M. A., & Phillipot, E. Lipidis and pigment olfactifs. *Acta Oto-Rhino-Larynol., Belg.,* 1957, 11, 297–300. (342)

Gergen, J. A., & MacLean, P. D. *A stereotaxic atlas of the squirrel monkey's brain.* Bethesda, Md.: National Institutes of Health, 1962. (59)

Gernandt, B. E. Vestibular mechanisms. In J. Field, H. W. Magoun, & V. E. Hall (Eds.), *Neurophysiology.* Vol. I. Washington, D.C.: American Physiological Society, 1959. Pp. 549–564. (336)

Gertman, S. See Byrd, E., & Gertman, S., 1959.

Geschwind, N., & Segal, J. R. Colors of all hues from binocular mixing of two colors. *Science,* 1960, 131, 608. (263)

Gesteland, R. C. Action potentials recorded from olfactory receptor neurons. Ph. D. thesis, Massachusetts Institute of Technology, 1961. (348)

Gesteland, R. C., Lettvin, J. Y., Pitts, W. H., &

Rojas, A. Odor specificities of the frog's olfactory receptors. In Y. Zotterman (Ed.), *Olfaction and taste.* Vol. I. New York: Macmillan, 1963. Pp. 19–35. (345–347)

Gewirtz, J. L. See Rheingold, H., Gewirtz, J. L., & Ross, H. W., 1959.

Gibb, J. R. The effects of group size and of threat reduction upon creativity in a problem-solving situation. *Amer. Psychologist,* 1951, **6**, 324. (Abstract.) (577)

Gibson, E. J., & Olum, V. Experimental methods for studying perception in children. In P. Mussen (Ed.), *Handbook of research methods in child development.* New York: Wiley, 1960. (294)

Gibson, E. J., & Walk, R. D. The effect of prolonged exposure to visually presented patterns on learning to discriminate them. *J. comp. physiol. Psychol.,* 1956, **49**, 239–242. (288)

Gibson, E. J., & Walk, R. D. The "Visual Cliff." *Scient. Amer.,* 1960, **202**, 64–71. (279, 281)

Gibson, E. J., Walk, R. D., Pick, H. L., & Tighe, T. J. The effect of prolonged exposure to visual patterns on learning to discriminate similar and different patterns. *J. comp. physiol. Psychol.,* 1958, **51**, 584–587. (288)

Gibson, J. J. *The perception of the visual world.* Boston: Houghton Mifflin, 1950. (267–268, 270, 272)

Gibson, J. J. Perception as a function of stimulation. In S. Koch (Ed.), *Psychology: A study of a science.* Study I. *Conceptual and systematic.* Vol. I. *Sensory, perceptual, and physiological formulations.* New York: McGraw-Hill, 1959, Pp. 456–501. (295)

Gibson, J. T. See Bachrach, A. J., Candland, D. K., & Gibson, J. T., 1961.

Gibson, K. S., & Tyndall, E. P. T. The visibility of radiant energy. *Scient. Pap. U.S. Bur. Stand.,* 1923, **19**, No. 475. (222)

Gilbert, G. M. The new status of experimental studies on the relationship of feeling to memory. *Psychol. Bull.,* 1938, **35**, 26–35. (476)

Gilbert, J. G. Memory loss in senescence. *J. abnorm. soc. Psychol.,* 1941, **36**, 73–86. (484)

Gilbert, L. C. Genetic study of eye movements in reading. *Elem. Sch. J.,* 1959, **59**, 328–335. (287)

Gilbert, R. W. See Crafts, L. W., & Gilbert, R. W., 1934.

Gilbert, T. F. See James, W. T., & Gilbert, T. F., 1957.

Gilbreth, F. B. *Bricklaying system.* New York: Clark, 1909. (463)

Gilbreth, F. B. *Motion study.* Princeton, N.J.: Van Nostrand, 1911. (463)

Gilbreth, F. B., & Gilbreth, L. M. *Applied motion study.* New York: Sturgis & Walton, 1917. (463)

Gilbreth, L. M. See Gilbreth, F. B., & Gilbreth, L. M., 1917.

Gilden, L. See Chase, R. A., Rapin, I., Gilden, L., Sutton, S., & Guilfoyle, G., 1961.

Gilliard, E. T. *Living birds of the world.* Garden City, N.Y.: Doubleday, 1958. (501)

Gilmer, B. von H. The glomus body as a receptor of cutaneous pressure and vibration. *Psychol. Bull.,* 1942, **39**, 73–93. (316)

Ginsberg, A. A reconstructive analysis of the concept "instinct." *J. Psychol.,* 1952, **33**, 235–277. (500)

Girden, E., Mettler, F. A., Finch, G., & Culler, E. Conditioned responses in a decorticate dog to acoustic, thermal, and tactile stimulation. *J. comp. Psychol.,* 1936, **21**, 367–385. (394)

Gitman, L. See Cohen, T., & Gitman, L., 1959.

Gladis, M., & Braun, H. W. Age differences in transfer and retroaction as a function of inter-task response similarity. *J. exp. Psychol.,* 1958, **55**, 25–30. (476)

Glanzer, M., & Glaser, R. Techniques for the study of group structure and behavior: II. Empirical studies of the effects of structure in small groups. *Psychol. Bull.,* 1961, **58**, 1–27. (585–586, 602)

Glaser, R. See Glanzer, M., & Glaser, R., 1961.

Glaser, R. M. See Lumsdaine, A. A., & Glaser, R. M., 1960.

Glass, L. See Hansen, R., & Glass, L., 1936.

Glaze, J. A. The association value of nonsense syllables. *J. genet. Psychol.,* 1928, **35**, 255–267. (194, 442)

Goetzl, F. R., & Stone, F. Diurnal variations

in acuity of olfaction and food intake. *Gastroenterology*, 1947, **9**, 444–452. (344)

Goff, W. R. See Pfaffmann, C., Goff, W. R., & Bare, H. K., 1958.

Gogel, W. C. See Hess, E. H., & Gogel, W. C., 1954.

Goldbeck, R. A., & Briggs, L. J. An analysis of response mode and feedback factors in automated instruction. In W. I. Smith, & J. W. Moore (Eds.), *Programmed learning*. Princeton, N.J.: Van Nostrand, 1962. Pp. 166–191. (476)

Goldberg, J. M., & Neff, W. D. Frequency discrimination after bilateral section of the brachium of the inferior colliculus. *J. comp. Neurol.*, 1961, **113**, 265–282. (181)

Goldiamond, I. Indicators of perception: I. Subliminal perception, subception, unconscious perception: An analysis in terms of psychophysical indicator methodology. *Psychol. Bull.*, 1958, **55**, 373–411. (292, 293)

Goldman, A. See von Frey, M., & Goldman, A., 1914.

Goldman, M. A comparison of individual and group performance for varying combinations of initial ability. *J. Pers. soc. Psychol.*, 1965, **1**, 210–216. (556, 570)

Goldstein, K. *Language and language disturbances*. New York: Grune & Stratton, 1948. (211)

Gombrich, E. H. How to read a painting. *Sat. Eve. Post*, 1961, **234**, 30, 64–65. (265)

Goodacre, D. M. The use of a sociometric test as a predictor of combat unit effectiveness. *Sociometry*, 1951, **14**, 148–152. (594)

Goodacre, D. M. Group characteristics of good and poor performing combat units. *Sociometry*, 1953, **16**, 168–178. (594)

Goodell, H. See Hardy, J. D., Wolff, H. G., & Goodell, H., 1940.

Goodell, H. See Hardy, J. D., Wolff, H. G., & Goodell, H., 1947.

Goodman, C. C. See Bruner, J. S., & Goodman, C. C., 1947.

Gordon, K. Class results with spaced and unspaced memorizing. *J. exp. Psychol.*, 1925, **8**, 337–343. (476)

Goss, A. E., & Nodine, C. F. *Paired-associates learning: The role of meaningfulness, fa-miliarity, and familiarization*. New York: Academic, 1965. (443)

Gottschaldt, K. Ueber den Einfluss der Erfahrung auf die Wahrnehmung von Figuren. *Psychol. Forsch.*, 1926, **8**, 261–317. (279)

Graham, C. H. Color theory. In S. Koch (Ed.), *Psychology: A study of a science*. Study I. *Conceptual and systematic*. Vol. I. *Sensory perceptual, and physiological formulations*. New York: McGraw-Hill, 1959. Pp. 145–287. (259–261, 294)

Graham, C. H. (Ed.) *Vision and visual perception*. New York: Wiley, 1965a. (246)

Graham, C. H. Some basic terms and methods. In C. H. Graham (Ed.), *Vision and visual perception*. New York: Wiley, 1965b. Pp. 60–67. (246)

Graham, C. H. Color: Data and theories. In C. H. Graham (Ed.), *Vision and visual perception*. New York: Wiley, 1965c. Pp. 414–451. (294)

Graham, C. H., & Hsia, Y. Luminosity curves for normal and dichromatic subjects including a case of unilateral color blindness. *Science*, 1954, **120**, 780. (257, 260)

Graham, C. H., & Hsia, Y. Color defect and color theory. *Science*, 1958, **127**, 675–682. (260)

Graham, C. H., Hsia, Y., & Berger, E. Luminosity functions for normal and dichromatic subjects including a case of unilateral color blindness. *J. Opt. Soc. Amer.*, 1955, **45**, 407. (257)

Graham, C. H., Sperling, H. G., Hsia, Y., & Coulson, A. H. The determination of some visual functions of a unilaterally color-blind subject: Method and results. *J. Psychol.*, 1961, **51**, 3–32. (260)

Graham, C. H. See Hsia, Y., & Graham, C. H., 1965.

Granit, R. The components of the retinal action potential in mammals and their relation to the discharge in the optic nerve. *J. Physiol.*, 1933, **77**, 207–239. (226–227)

Granit, R. Spectral properties of the visual receptor elements of the guinea pig. *Acta physiol. Scand.*, 1942, **3**, 318–328. (227)

Granit, R. *Sensory mechanisms of the retina*. New York: Oxford, 1947. (226)

Granit, R. *Receptors and sensory perception.* New Haven, Conn.: Yale, 1955. (225–226, 246)

Granit, R. The visual pathway. In H. Davson (Ed.), *The eye.* New York: Academic, 1962. Vol. 2. Pp. 537–763. (226)

Granit, R., & Harper, P. Comparative studies on the peripheral and central retina: II. Synaptic reactions in the eye. *Amer. J. Physiol.,* 1930, **95**, 211–218. (238)

Granit, R., & Skoglund, C. R. The effect of temperature on the artificial synapse formed by the cut end of the mammalian nerve. *J. Neurophysiol.,* 1945, **8**, 211–217. (306)

Granit, R. See Bernhard, C. G., & Granit, R., 1946.

Grant, D. A. See Norris, E. B., & Grant, D. A., 1948.

Gray, J. A. B., & Malcolm, J. L. The initiation of nerve impulses by mesenteric Pacinian corpuscles. *Proc. Roy. Soc.,* 1950, **137**, 96–114. (313)

Gray, J. A. B., & Matthews, P. B. C. A comparison of the adaptation of the Pacinian corpuscle with the accommodation of its own axon. *J. Physiol.,* 1951, **114**, 454–464. (313)

Gray, J. A. B., & Sato, M. Properties of the receptor potential in Pacinian corpuscles. *J. Physiol.,* 1953, **122**, 610–636. (313)

Gray, J. S. *Psychology applied to human affairs.* (2nd ed.) New York: McGraw-Hill, 1954. (212)

Gray, P. H. The releasers of imprinting: Differential reactions to color as a function of maturation. *J. comp. physiol. Psychol.,* 1961, **54**, 597–601. (482)

Gray, P. H. See Baer, D. M., & Gray, P. H., 1960.

Gray, W. S., & Leary, B. E. *What makes a book readable.* Chicago: University of Chicago Press, 1935. (198)

Graybiel, A. See Clark, B., & Graybiel, A., 1960.

Graybiel, A. See Meek, J. C., Graybiel, A., Beischer, D. E., & Riopelle, A. J., 1961.

Green, A. See Lacey, J. I., Smith, R. L., & Green, A., 1955.

Green, H. See Cook, L., Davidson, A. B., Davis, D. J., Green, H., & Fellows, E. J., 1963.

Green, H. C. See Potter, R. K., Kopp, G. A., & Green, H. C., 1947.

Greenblatt, M. See Freedman, S. J., Grunebaum, H. U., & Greenblatt, M., 1961.

Greenspoon, J. The effect of verbal and nonverbal stimuli on the frequency of members of two verbal response classes. Doctoral dissertation, Indiana Univer., 1951. (n.s.) (458–459)

Greenspoon, J. The reinforcing effect of two spoken sounds on the frequency of two responses. *Amer. J. Psychol.,* 1955, **68**, 409–416. (458)

Greenspoon, J. Verbal conditioning and clinical psychology. In A. J. Bachrach (Ed.), *Experimental foundations of clinical psychology.* New York: Basic Books, 1962. Pp. 510–553. (460, 477)

Greenspoon, J., & Foreman, S. Effect of delay of knowledge of results on learning a motor task. *J. exp. Psychol.,* 1956, **51**, 226–228. (476)

Greenspoon, J. See Saltzman, I. J., Kanfer, F. H., & Greenspoon, J., 1955.

Gregg, L. W., & Jarrard, L. F. Changes in muscle action potentials during prolonged work. *J. comp. physiol. Psychol.,* 1958, **51**, 532–535. (475)

Gregory, D. See Schechter, S., Ellertson, N., McBride, D., & Gregory, D., 1951.

Grice, G. R. The relation of secondary reinforcement to delayed reward in visual discrimination learning. *J. exp. Psychol.,* 1948, **38**, 1–16. (412)

Griffin, D. R. *Listening in the dark: The acoustic orientation of bats and men.* New Haven, Conn.: Yale, 1958. (501)

Griffin, D. R. *Bird migration.* Garden City, N.Y.: Anchor Books, Doubleday, 1964. (492, 501)

Grinker, R. R. See Basowitz, H., Persky, H., Kerchin, S. J., & Grinker, R. R., 1955.

Gropper, G. L. See Postman, L., Bronson, W. C., & Gropper, G. L., 1953.

Grose, R. F., & Birney, R. C. (Eds.) *Transfer of learning.* Princeton, N.J.: Van Nostrand, 1963. (477)

Gross, M. L. *The brain watchers.* New York: Random House, 1962. (553)

Grosslight, J. H., & Lively, B. L. The mynah bird *(Gracula religiosa)* as a laboratory organism: some general observations. *Psychol. Rec.,* 1963, 13, 1–9. (209)

Grossman, S. P. *Physiological psychology.* New York: Wiley, 1967. (63)

Grunebaum, H. U. See Freedman, S. J., Grunebaum, H. U., & Greenblatt, M., 1961.

Guetzkow, H., & Simon, H. A. The impact of certain communication nets upon organization and performance in task-oriented groups. *Mgmt Sci.,* 1955, 1, 233–250. (585)

Guetzkow, H. See Collins, B. E., & Guetzkow, H., 1964.

Guetzkow, H. See Fouriezos, N. T., Hutt, M. L., & Guetzkow, H., 1950.

Guilford, J. P. A generalized psychophysical law. *Psychol. Rev.,* 1932, 39, 73–85. (102)

Guilford, J. P. The determination of item difficulty when chance success is a factor. *Psychometrika,* 1936, 1, 259–264. (435)

Guilford, J. P. The computation of psychological values from judgments in absolute categories. *J. exp. Psychol.,* 1938, 22, 32–42. (141)

Guilford, J. P. *Psychosometric methods.* (2nd ed.) New York: McGraw-Hill, 1954. (87, 89, 96, 102, 108, 115, 142–143, 546, 552)

Guilford, J. P., & Holley, J. W. A factorial approach to the analysis of variance in esthetic judgments. *J. exp. Psychol.,* 1949, 39, 208–218. (139)

Guilfoyle, G. See Chase, R. A., Rapin, I., Gilden, L., Sutton, S., & Guilfoyle, G., 1961.

Guiton, P. Socialization and imprinting in Brown Leghorn chicks. *Anim. Behav.,* 1959, 7, 26–54. (482)

Gulick, W. L. See Vernon, J. A., McGill, T. E., Gulick, W. L., & Candland, D. K., 1959.

Gulick, W. L. See Vernon, J. A., McGill, T. E., Gulick, W. L., & Candland, D. K., 1961.

Gulliksen, H. *Theory of mental tests.* New York: Wiley, 1950. (435, 535–536, 539, 541, 552–553)

Gurin, G. See Campbell, A., Gurin, G., & Miller, W. E., 1954.

Gustafson, L. M., & Irion, A. L. Reminiscence in bilateral transfer. Paper read at Midwest Psychol. Ass., Chicago, April, 1951. (n.s.) (476)

Guthrie, E. R. *The psychology of learning.* New York: Harper & Row, 1935. (518)

Guthie, E. R. *The psychology of learning* (Rev. ed.). New York: Harper & Row, 1952. (272, 518)

Guttman, N. Equal reinforcement values for sucrose and glucose solutions compared with equal-sweetness values. *J. comp. physiol. Psychol.,* 1954, 47, 358–361. (411)

Guttman, N. Laws of behavior and facts of perception. In S. Koch (Ed.), *Psychology: A study of a science.* Study II. *Empirical substructure and relations with other sciences.* Vol. V, *The process areas, the person, and some applied fields: Their place in psychology and in science.* New York: McGraw-Hill, 1963. Pp. 114–178. (295)

Haber, R. N. & Alpert, R. The role of situation and picture cues in projective measurement of the achievement motive. In J. W. Atkinson (Ed.), *Motives in fantasy, action, and society.* Princeton, N.J.: Van Nostrand, 1958. Pp. 644–663. (526)

Habgood, J. S. Sensitization of sensory receptors in the frog's skin. *J. Physiol.,* 1950, 111, 195–213. (319)

Haefner, A. See Haythorn, W. W., Couch, A., Haefner, D., Langham, P., & Carter, L., 1956.

Hafez, E. S. E. *The behaviour of domestic animals.* Baltimore: Williams & Wilkins, 1962. (502)

Hahn, H. Über die Urasche der geschmacksempfindung. *Klin. Wschr.,* 1936, 15, 933–935. (353–354)

Haig, C. See Hecht, S., Haig, C., & Chase, A. M., 1937.

Hall, C. S., & Lindzey, G. *Theories of personality.* New York: Wiley, 1957. (531)

Hall, C. S. See Tolman, E. C., Hall, C. S., & Bretnall, E. P., 1932.

Hall, E. See Denny, M. R., Allard, M., Hall, E., & Rokeach, M., 1960.

Hall, E. R. See Triandis, H. C., Hall, E. R., & Ewen, R. B., 1965.

Hall, J. F. *Psychology of motivation.* Philadelphia: Lippincott, 1961. (530)

Hall, J. F. See Prokasy, W. F., & Hall, J. F., 1963.

Hall, J. F. See Slivinske, A. J., & Hall, J. F., 1960.

Hall, R. L. See Rosenberg, S., & Hall, R. L., 1958.

Hall, V. E. See Field, J., Magoun, H. W., & Hall, V. E., 1959.

Halpern, B. P. Gustatory responses in the medulla oblongata of the rat. Ph.D. thesis, Brown Univer., 1959. (n.s.) (358, 359)

Halpern, B. P. See Kare, M. R., & Halpern, B. P., 1961.

Halpern, B. P. See Pfaffmann, C., Erikson, R. D., Frommer, G. P., & Halpern, B. P., 1961.

Halstead, W. C. See Katz, J. J., & Halstead, W. C., 1950.

Ham, L. B., & Parkinson, J. S. Loudness and intensity relations. *J. Acoust. Soc. Amer.*, 1932, 3, 511–534. (141)

Hamblin, R. L. Leadership and crisis. *Sociometry*, 1958, 21, 322–335. (581)

Hamilton, M. A. See Laidlaw, R. W., & Hamilton, M. A., 1937.

Hammond, K. R., & Householder, J. E. *Introduction to the statistical method.* New York: Knopf, 1962. (35)

Hanawalt, E. M. Whole and part methods in trial and error learning: Human maze learning. *J. exp. Psychol.*, 1934, 17, 691–708. (450, 475)

Hanes, R. M. A scale of subjective brightness, *J. exp. Psychol.*, 1949, 39, 438–452. (141, 233)

Hanes, R. M. See Burnham, R. W., Hanes, R. M. & Bartleson, C. J., 1963.

Hansen, R., & Glass, L. Über den Geruchssinn in der Schwangerschaft. *Klin. Wschr.*, 1936, 15, 891–894. (n.s.) (344)

Harary, F. See Cartwright, D., & Harary, F., 1956.

Harburg, E. M. See Hoffman, L. R., Harburg, E. M., & Maier, N. R. F., 1962.

Hardy, J. D. Physiological responses to heat and cold. *Ann. Rev. Physiol.*, 1950, 12, 119–144. (319)

Hardy, J. D., & Oppel, T. W. Studies in temperature sensation: III. The sensitivity of

the body to heat and the spatial summation of the end organ responses. *J. clin. Invest.*, 1937, 16, 533–540. (308–309)

Hardy, J. D., Wolff, H. G., & Goodell, H. Studies on pain, a new method for measuring pain threshold: Observations on spatial summation of pain. *J. clin. Invest.*, 1940, 19, 649–657. (308)

Hardy, J. D., Wolff, H. G., & Goodell, H. Studies on pain: Discrimination of differences in intensity of a pain stimulus as a basis of a scale of pain intensity. *J. clin. Invest.*, 1947, 26, 1152–1158. (320)

Hardy, M. Observations on the innervation of the macula sacculi in man. *Anatom. Rec.*, 1934, 59, 403–418. (333)

Hare, A. P. *Handbook of small group research.* New York: Free Press, 1962. (602)

Hare, A. P., & Bales, R. F. Seating position and small group interaction. *Sociometry*, 1963, 26, 480–486. (587)

Hare, A. P., Borgatta, E. F., & Bales, R. F. (Eds.), *Small groups: Studies in social interaction.* New York: Knopf, 1955. (602)

Harlow, H. F. The formation of learning sets. *Psychol. Rev.*, 1949, 56, 51–65. (418)

Harlow, H. F., & Zimmermann, R. R. Affectional responses in the infant monkey. *Science*, 1959, 130, 421–432. (501)

Harlow, H. F. See Mason, W. A., Blazek, N. C., & Harlow, H. F., 1956.

Harper, P. See Granit, R., & Harper, P., 1930.

Harriman, P. L. *The new dictionary of psychology.* New York: Philosophical Library, 1947. (365)

Harriman, P. L. *Dictionary of psychology.* New York: Philosophical Library, 1959a, 1965. (35, 239)

Harriman, P. L. *Handbook of psychological terms.* Littlefield, Adams & Co., 1959b. (35)

Harris, J. D. Discrimination of pitch: Suggestions toward method and procedure. *Amer. J. Psychol.*, 1948, 61, 343–351. (159)

Harris, J. D. Pitch discrimination. *J. acoust. Soc. Amer.*, 1952, 24, 750–755.

Harris, J. D. See Rawnsley, A. I., & Harris, J. D., 1952.

Harrison, A. A., & McClintock, C. G. Previous experience within the dyad and cooperative game behavior. *J. Pers. soc. Psychol.*, 1965, 1, 671–675. (571)

Harrison, C. E. See Silverman, S. R., Harrison, C. E., & Lane, H. S., 1946.

Hasler, A. D. Guideposts of migrating fishes: New findings have added to our knowledge of how fish use olfactory and visual cues to find their way home. *Science*, 1960, 132, 785–792. (494)

Hawkes, G. R. Cutaneous communication: Absolute identification of electrical intensity level. *J. Psychol.*, 1960, 49, 203–212. (317)

Hawkes, G. R. Cutaneous discrimination of electrical intensity. *Amer. J. Psychol.*, 1961a, 74, 45–53. (318)

Hawkes, G. R. Information transmitted via electrical cutaneous stimulus duration. *J. Psychol.*, 1961b, 51, 293–298. (318)

Hawkins, C. See Strodtbeck, F. L., Simon, R. J., Hawkins, C., 1965.

Hawkins, J. E., Jr. See Davis, H., Morgan, C. T., Hawkins, J. E., Jr., Galambos, R., & Smith, F. W., 1950.

Hawkins, W. F. See Reid, L. S., Lloyd, K. E., Brackett, H. R., & Hawkins, W. F., 1961.

Hayes, C. See Hayes, K. J., & Hayes, C., 1951.

Hayes, C. See Hayes, K. J., & Hayes, C., 1952.

Hayes, K. J., & Hayes, C. The intellectual development of a home-raised chimpanzee. *Proc. Amer. Phil. Soc.*, 1951, 95, 105–109. (210)

Hayes, K. J., & Hayes, C. Imitation in a home-raised chimpanzee. *J. comp. physiol. Psychol.*, 1952, 45, 450–459. (473)

Haythorn, W. See Carter, L., Haythorn, W., Meirowitz, B., & Lanzetta, J., 1951.

Haythorn, W. W., Couch, A., Haefner, D., Langham, P., & Carter, L. The effects of varying combinations of authoritarian and equalitarian leaders and followers. *J. abnorm. soc. Psychol.*, 1956, 53, 210–219. (575, 581)

Head, H. *Studies in neurology.* London: Oxford, 1920. (303, 322, 324)

Hearst, E., Beer, B., Sheatz, G., & Galambos, R. Some electrophysiological correlates of conditioning in the monkey. *EEG clin. Neurophysiol.*, 1960, 12, 137–152. (59)

Hebb, D. O. The innate organization of vis-ual activity: I. Perception of figures by rats reared in total darkness. *J. genet. Psychol.*, 1937a, 51, 101–126. (279)

Hebb, D. O. The innate organization of visual activity: II. Transfer of response in the discrimination of brightness and size by rats reared in total darkness. *J. comp. Psychol.*, 1937b, 24, 277–299. (279)

Hebb, D. O. The effect of early and later brain injury upon test scores and the nature of normal adult intelligence. *Proc. Amer. Philos. Soc.*, 1942, 85, 275–292. (484)

Hebb, D. O. *The organization of behavior.* New York: Wiley, 1949. (323, 380, 385, 445, 477)

Hebb, D. O. Drives and the C.N.S. (conceptual nervous system). *Psychol. Rev.*, 1955, 62, 243–254. (62, 508–509)

Hebb, D. O. *A textbook of psychology.* Philadelphia: Saunders, 1958. (508)

Hebb, D. O. *The organization of behavior: A neurophysiological theory.* New York: Basic Books, 1961. (paperback) (445)

Hebb, D. O. See Beach, F. A., Hebb, D. O., Morgan, C. T., & Nissen, H. W., 1960.

Heber, R. F. Motor task performance of high grade mentally retarded males as a function of the magnitude of incentive. *Amer. J. ment. Defic.*, 1959, 63, 667–671. (412)

Hecaen, H., Talairach, J., David, M., & Dell, M. B. Coagulations limitées du thalamus dans les algies du syndrome thalamique: Resultats therapeutiques et physiologiques. *Rev. neurol.*, 1949, 81, 917–931. (322)

Hecaen, H. See Talairach, J., Hecaen, H., David, M., Monnier, M., & de Ajuriaguerra, J., 1949.

Hecht, S. Vision: II. The nature of the photoreceptor process. In C. Murchison (Ed.), *A handbook of general experimental psychology.* Worcester, Mass.: Clark University Press, 1934. Pp. 704–828. (231, 234, 240)

Hecht, S. Energy and vision. *Amer. Sci.*, 1944, 32, 159–177. (232)

Hecht, S., & Hsia, Y. Dark adaptation following light adaptation to red and white lights. *J. Opt. Soc. Amer.*, 1945, 35, 261–267. (241)

Hecht, S., & Mintz, E. U. The visibility of single lines at various illuminations and the retinal basis of visual resolution. *J. gen. Physiol.*, 1939, **22**, 593–612. (245)

Hecht, S., & Williams, R. E. The visibility of monochromatic radiation and the absorption spectrum of visual purple. *J. gen. Physiol.*, 1922, **5**, 1–34. (222)

Hecht, S., Haig, C., & Chase, A. M. The influence of light adaptation on subsequent dark adaptation in the eye. *J. gen. Physiol.*, 1937, **20**, 831–850. (241)

Hecht, S., Peskin, J. C., & Patt, M. Intensity discrimination in the human eye: II. The relation between ΔI/I and intensity for various parts of the spectrum. *J. gen. Physiol.*, 1938, **22**, 7–19. (233, 238)

Heidbreder, E. The attainment of concepts: III. The process. *J. Psychol.*, 1947, **24**, 93–138. (469)

Heider, F. Attitudinal and cognitive organization. *J. Psychol.*, 1946, **21**, 107–112. (601)

Heider, F. K., & Heider, G. M. A comparison of sentence structure of deaf and hearing children. *Psychol. Monogr.*, 1940, **52** (1), 42–103. (208)

Heider, G. M. See Heider, F. K., & Heider, G. M., 1940.

Heim, M. H. See Newhall, S. M., & Heim, M. H., 1929.

Heine, R. Über wiedererkennen und rückwirkende hemmung. *Z. Psychol.*, 1914, **68**, 161–236. (476)

Heinroth, O. Beitrage zur Biologie, namentlich Ethologie und Physiologie der Anatiden. *Verhl. 5. Int. Ornithol. Kongr.*, 1910, 589–702. (n.s.) (480)

Heise, G. A., & Miller, G. A. Problem solving by small groups using various communication nets. *J. abnorm. soc. Psychol.*, 1951, **46**, 327–335. (585–586)

Heise, G. A. See Miller, G. A., Heise, G. A., & Lichten, W., 1951.

Helmohltz, H. von. *Die Lehre von den Tonempfindungen* (1st ed.). Brunswick, Germany: Friedr. Vieweg & Sohn, 1863. (175)

Helmholtz, H. von. *Handbuch der physiologischen Optik.* Leipzig: Voss, 1st ed., 1867; 2nd ed., 1896; 3rd. ed., 1911. (175)

Helmholtz, H. von. *Handbuch der physiolo-gischen Optik.* Hamburg and Leipzig: Verlag, 1910. (246)

Helmholtz, H. von. *On the sensations of tone.* (A. J. Ellis, Trans.) New York: Dover, 1930. (175, 183)

Helmholtz, H. von. *Helmholtz' treatise on physiological optics.* (J. P. C., Southall, Trans. & Ed.) Vols. I and II. New York: Dover, 1962. (167, 239, 246)

Helmstader, G. C., & Ellis, D. S. Rate of manipulative learning as a function of goal-setting techniques. *J. exp. Psychol.*, 1952, **43**, 125–129. (476)

Helson, H. The fundamental propositions of Gestalt Psychology. *Psychol. Rev.*, 1933, **40**, 13–32. (275)

Helson, H. Fundamental problems in color vision: I. The principle governing changes in hue, saturation and lightness of non-selective samples in chromatic illumination. *J. exp. Psychol.*, 1938, **23**, 439–476. (103)

Helson, H. Adaptation level theory. In S. Koch (Ed.), *Psychology: A study of a science. Study I. Conceptual and systematic.* Vol. I. *Sensory, perceptual, and physiological.* New York: McGraw-Hill, 1958. Pp. 565–621. (295)

Helson, H. *Adaptation-level theory.* New York: Harper & Row, 1964. (103–104, 109)

Helson, H. See Michels, W. C., & Helson, H., 1949.

Hempel, W. E., Jr. See Fleishman, E. A., & Hempel, W. E., Jr., 1956.

Henle, M. *Documents of Gestalt psychology.* Berkeley, Calif.: University of California Press, 1961. (295)

Henle, M., & Hubbell, M. B. "Egocentricity" in adult conversation. *J. soc. Psychol.*, 1938, **9**, 227–234. (208)

Henning, H. *Der Geruch.* Leipzig: Barth, 1916. (79, 348)

Hensel, H. Heat and cold. *Ann. Rev. Physiol.*, 1959, **21**, 91–116. (336)

Hensel, H., & Zotterman, Y. Action potentials of cold fibers and intracutaneous temperature gradient. *J. Neurophysiol.*, 1951a, **14**, 377–385. (311)

Hensel, H., & Zotterman, Y. The response of mechanoreceptors to thermal stimulation. *J. Physiol.*, 1951b, **115**, 16–24. (306)

Hensel, H., & Zotterman, Y. Quantitative Beziehungen zwischen der Entaladung einzelner Kaltfasern der Temperatur. *Acta physiol. Scand.,* 1951c, **23**, 291. (76)

Henson, J. B. See Holland, J. G., & Henson, J. B., 1956.

Hering, E. Zur Lehre vom Lichtsinn. *Wein Akad. Wiss. Sitzbr.,* 1874, **69**, 85–104. (n.s.) (249, 258)

Hering, E. *Zur Lehre von Lichtsinne.* Vienna: Gerold's Sohn, 1878. (258)

Hering, E. *Grundzüge der Lehre von Lichtsinne.* Berlin: Springer, 1920. (249, 258)

Hermann, E. See Bartlett, C. J., Hermann, E., & Rettig, S., 1960.

Hernández-Peón, R., & Ibarra, G. C. Sleep induced by electrical or chemical stimulation of the forebrain. In R. Hernández-Peón (Ed.), The physiological basis of mental activity. *Electroencephalog. Clin. Neurophysiol. Suppl.,* 1963, **24**, 188–198. (62)

Hernández-Peón, R. See Lavín, A., Alcocer-Cuarón, C., Hernández-Peón, R., 1959.

Heron, W. T. The behavior of active and inactive rats in experimental extinction and discrimination problems. *Psychol. Rec.,* 1940, **4**, 23–31. (410–411)

Heron, W., Doane, B. K., & Scott, T. H. Visual disturbance after prolonged perceptual isolation. *Canad. J. Psychol.,* 1956, **10**, 13–18. (289)

Heron, W. See Bexton, W. H., Heron, W., & Scott, T. H., 1954.

Herrnstein, R. J. See Boren, J. J., Sidman, M., & Herrnstein, R. J., 1959.

Hertzman, M. See Witkin, H. A., Lewis, H. B., Hertzman, M., Machover, K., Meissner, P. B., & Wapner, S., 1954.

Heslin, R. Predicting group task effectiveness from member characteristics. *Psychol. Bull.,* 1964, **62**, 248–256. (569, 602)

Hess, E. See Brown, R., Galanter, E., Hess, E. H., & Mandler, G., 1962.

Hess, E. H. Space perception in the chick. *Scient. Amer.,* 1956, **195**, 71–80. (282)

Hess, E. H. Effects of meprobamate on imprinting in water fowl. *Ann. N.Y. Acad. Sci.,* 1957, **67**, 724–732. (482)

Hess, E. H. The relationship between imprinting and motivation. In M. R. Jones (Ed.), *Nebraska symposium on motivation.* Lincoln, Nebr.: University of Nebraska Press, 1959a. Pp. 44–77. (482)

Hess, E. H. Two conditions limiting critical age for imprinting. *J. comp. physiol. Psychol.,* 1959b, **52**, 515–518. (482–483, 501)

Hess, E. H. Imprinting. *Science,* 1959c, **130**, 133–141. (481)

Hess, E. H. Imprinting in birds. *Science,* 1964, **146**, 1128–1139. (482)

Hess, E. H., & Gogel, W. C. Natural preferences of the chick for objects of different colors. *J. Psychol.,* 1954, **38**, 483–493. (282, 289)

Hess, E. H. See Rheingold, H. L., & Hess, E. H., 1957.

Hess, W. See Lewis, T., & Hess, W., 1933.

Hess, W. R. *Das Zwischenhirn: Syndrome, Lokalization, Functionen* (2nd ed.). Basel: Schwabe, 1954a. (40)

Hess, W. R. *Diencephalon: Autonomic and extrapyramidal functions.* New York: Grune & Stratton, 1954b. (40)

Hetherington, A. W., & Ranson, S. W. Hypothalamic lesions and adiposity in the rat. *Anat. Rec.,* 1940, **78**, 149–172. (330)

Hetherington, M. See Banta, T. J., & Hetherington, M., 1963.

Heuser, G. See Selye, H. *Annual report on stress,* 1954.

Heyer, A. W. See Osgood, C. E., & Heyer, A. W., 1951.

Heyninx, A. Vibratory theory of odour. Thesis, Utrecht, 1917. (n.s.) (348)

Heyns, R. W., & Lippitt, R. Systematic observational techniques. In G. Lindzey (Ed.), *Handbook of social psychology.* Cambridge, Mass.: Addison-Wesley, 1954. Pp. 370–404. (598)

Higashihira, K. See Shimizu, M., Yanase, T., & Higashihira, K., 1959.

Hilgard, E. R. The saving score as a measure of retention. *Amer. J. Psychol.,* 1934, **46**, 337–339. (432)

Hilgard, E. R. Methods and procedures in the study of learning. In S. S. Stevens (Ed.), *Handbook of experimental psychology.* New York: Wiley, 1951. Pp. 517–567. (194, 383)

Hilgard, E. R. *Theories of learning.* (2nd ed.) New York: Appleton-Century-Crofts, 1956. (371)

Hilgard, E. R., & Bower, G. H. *Theories of learning.* (3rd ed.) New York: Appleton-Century-Crofts, 1966. (371)

Hilgard, E. R., & Humphreys, L. G. The effect of supporting and antagonistic voluntary instructions on conditioned discrimination. *J. exp. Psychol.,* 1938, **22**, 291–304. (424)

Hilgard, E. R., & Marquis, D. G. *Conditioning and learning.* New York: Appleton-Century-Crofts, 1940. (383, 401)

Hilgard, E. R. See Doré, L. R., & Hilgard, E. R., 1937.

Hilgard, E. R. See Doré, L. R., & Hilgard, E. R., 1938.

Hill, W. F. *Learning: A survey of psychological interpretations.* San Francisco: Chandler Publishing Co., 1963. (383)

Hille, B. A. See Conrad, R., & Hille, B. A., 1958.

Hillner, K. See Peterson, L. R., Saltzman, D., Hillner, K., & Land, V., 1962.

Himwich, H. Prospects in psychopharmacology. *J. nerv. ment. Dis.,* 1955, **122**, 413–423. (516)

Hirsch, J. Individual differences in behavior and their genetic basis. In E. L. Bliss (Ed.), *Roots of behavior.* New York: Harper & Row, 1962. Pp. 2–23. (428)

Hirsh, I. J. Binaural summation and interaural inhibition as a function of the level of masking noise. *Amer. J. Psychol.,* 1948, **61**, 205–213. (161)

Hirsh, I. J. *The measurement of hearing.* New York: McGraw-Hill, 1952. (182–183, 212)

Hirsh, I. J. See Rosenblith, W. A., Miller, G. A., Egan, J. P., Hirsh, I. J., & Thomas, G. J., 1947.

Hitzig, E. See Fritsch, G., & Hitzig, E., 1870.

Hoagland, H. A. A study of the physiology of learning in ants. *J. gen. Psychol.,* 1931, **5**, 21–41. (476)

Hochberg, J. E. *Perception.* Englewood Cliffs, N.J.: Prentice Hall, 1964. (295)

Hochberg, J. E., Triebel, W., & Seaman, G. Color adaptation under conditions of homogeneous visual stimulation *(Ganzfeld). J. exp. Psychol.,* 1951, **41**, 153–159. (282)

Hoebel, B. G., & Teitelbaum, P. Hypothalamic control of feeding and self-stimulation. *Science,* 1962, **135**, 375–377. (520)

Hoffman, H., Toffey, S., Searle, J. L, & Kozma, F. Behavioral control by an imprinted stimulus. *J. exp. Anal. Behav.,* 1966, **9**, 177–190. (481)

Hoffman, L. R. Homogeneity of member personality and its effect on group problem-solving. *J. abnorm. soc. Psychol.,* 1950, **58**, 27–32. (574)

Hoffman, L. R. Group problem solving. In L. Berkowitz (Ed.), *Advances in experimental social psychology.* New York: Academic, 1965. Pp. 99–132. (602)

Hoffman, L. R., & Maier, N. R. F. Quality and acceptance of problem solutions by members of homogeneous and heterogeneous groups. *J. abnorm. soc. Psychol.,* 1961, **62**, 401–407. (574, 591)

Hoffman, L. R., & Maier, N. R. F. An experimental reexamination of the similarity-attraction hypothesis. *J. Pers. soc. Psychol.,* 1966, **3**, 145–152. (590–591, 593)

Hoffman, L. R., Harburg, E. M., & Maier, N. R. F. Differences and disagreement as factors in creative group problem solving. *J. abnorm. soc. Psychol.,* 1962, **64**, 206–214. (570)

Hoffman, L. R. See Maier, N. R. F., & Hoffman, L. R., 1965. (602)

Hoffmann, B. *The tyranny of testing.* New York: Crowell-Collier, 1962. (553)

Hogan, H. P. See Carmichael, L. Hogan, H. P., & Walter, A. A., 1932.

Hogan, J. A. See Adler, N., & Hogan, J. A., 1963.

Holland, J. G., & Henson, J. B. Transfer of training between quickened and unquickened tracking systems. *J. appl. Psychol.,* 1956, **40**, 362–366. (476)

Holland, J. G., & Skinner, B. F. *The analysis of behavior.* New York: McGraw-Hill, 1961. (419, 427)

Holley, J. W. See Guilford, J. P., & Holley, J. W., 1949.

Holt, E. B. *Animal drive and the learning*

process: An essay toward radical empiricism. Vol. 1. New York: Holt, 1931. (500)

Holway, A. H., & Crozier, W. J. Differential sensitivity for somesthetic pressure. *Psychol. Rec.,* 1937a, 1, 170–176. (313)

Holway, A. H., & Crozier, W. J. The significance of area for differential sensitivity for somesthetic pressure. *Psychol. Rec.,* 1937b, 1, 178–184. (313)

Holz, A. M. See Beach, F. A., & Holz, A. M., 1946.

Holz, W. C., & Azrin, N. H. Interactions between the discriminative and aversive properties of punishment. *J. exp. Anal. Behav.,* 1962, 5, 229–234. (422)

Holz, W. C. See Azrin, N. H., & Holz, W. C., 1961.

Homans, G. C. *The human group.* New York: Harcourt, Brace & World, 1950. (594, 601)

Homans, G. C. *Social behavior: Its elementary forms.* New York: Harcourt, Brace & World, 1961. (601)

Homans, J. *A text-book of surgery.* (5th ed.) Springfield, Ill.: Charles C Thomas, 1945. (217)

Honzik, M. P., Macfarlane, J. W., & Allen, L. The stability of mental test performance between two and eighteen years. *J. exp. Educ.,* 1948, 17, 309–324. (547)

Honzik, M. P. See McKee, J. P., & Honzik, M. P., 1962.

Horava, A. See Selye, H. *Annual report on stress.*

Horenstein, B. R. See Kimble, G. A., & Horenstein, B. R., 1948.

Horst, P. A method for determining the absolute affective value of a series of stimulus evaluations. *J. educ. Psychol.,* 1932, 23, 418–440. (137)

Hoskins, A. B. The effectiveness of the part and whole methods of study. *George Peabody cont. Educ.,* 1936, No. 189. (437)

Householder, J. E. See Hammond, K. R., & Householder, J. E., 1962.

Hovland, C. I. The generalization of conditioned responses: I. The sensory generalization of conditioned responses with varying frequencies of tone. *J. gen. Psychol.,* 1937a, 17, 125–148. (392–393)

Hovland, C. I. The generalization of conditioned responses: II. The sensory generalization of conditioned responses with varying intensities of tone. *J. genet. Psychol.,* 1937b, 51, 279–291. (392)

Hovland, C. I. Experimental studies in rote-learning theory: I. Reminiscence following learning by massed and by distributed practice. *J. exp. Psychol.,* 1938a, 22, 201–224. (475)

Hovland, C. I. Experimental studies in rote-learning theory: II. Reminiscence with varying speeds of syllable presentation. *J. exp. Psychol.,* 1938b, 22, 338–353. (475)

Hovland, C. I. Experimental studies in rote-learning theory: IV. Comparison of reminiscence in serial and paired-associate learning. *J. exp. Psychol.,* 1939, 24, 466–484. (475)

Hovland, C. I. Experimental studies in rote-learning theory: VI. Comparison of retention following learning to same criterion by massed and distributed practice. *J. exp. Psychol.,* 1940, 26, 568–587. (440)

Hovland, C. I. Experimental studies in rote-learning theory: VIII. Distributed practice of paired-associates with varying rates of presentation. *J. exp. Psychol.,* 1949, 39, 714–718. (475)

Hovland, C. I. Human learning and retention. In S. S. Stevens (Ed.), *Handbook of experimental psychology.* New York: Wiley, 1951. Pp. 613–689. (442)

Hovland, C. I. A "communication analysis" of concept learning. *Psych. Rev.,* 1952, 59, 461–472. (460)

Howarth, C. I., & Ellis, K. The relative intelligibility threshold for one's own name compared with other names. *Quart. J. exp. Psychol.,* 1961, 13, 236–239. (203)

Howe, H. A. The relation of the Organ of Corti to audioelectric phenomena in deaf albino cats. *Amer. J. Physiol.,* 1935, 3, 187–191. (152)

Howell, W. C. Training on a vibratory communication system. Master's thesis, Univer. of Virginia, 1956. (n.s.) (317)

Howes, D. H., & Solomon, R. L. A note on McGinnies' "Emotionality and perceptual defense." *Psychol. Rev.*, 1950, **57**, 229–234. (292–293)

Hsia, Y. Photochemistry of vision. In C. H. Graham (Ed.), *Vision and visual perception.* New York: Wiley, 1965. Pp. 132–153. (246)

Hsia, Y., & Graham, C. H. Color blindness. In C. H. Graham, *Vision and visual perception.* New York: Wiley, 1965. Pp. 395–413. (258, 294)

Hsia, Y. See Graham, C. H., & Hsia, Y., 1954.

Hsia, Y. See Graham, C. H., & Hsia, Y., 1958.

Hsia, Y. See Hecht, S., & Hsia, Y., 1945.

Hsia, Y. See Graham, C. H., Hsia, Y., & Berger, E., 1955.

Hsia, Y. See Graham, C. H., Sperling, H. G., Hsia, Y., & Coulson, A. H., 1961.

Hubbel, M. B. See Henle, M., & Hubbell, M. B., 1938.

Hubel, D. H. Integrative processes in central visual pathways of the cat. *J. Opt. Soc. Amer,.* 1963, **53**, 58–66. (228)

Hugony, A. On the perception of vibrations by means of the tactual sense. *Z. Biol.*, 1935, **96**, 548–553. (316)

Hull, C. L. The meaningfulness of 320 selected nonsense syllables. *Amer. J. Psychol.*, 1933a, **45**, 730–734. (194)

Hull, C. L. *Hypnosis and suggestibility: An experimental approach.* New York: Appleton-Century-Crofts, 1933b. (505)

Hull, C. L. *Principles of behavior.* New York: Appleton-Century-Crofts, 1943. (411, 517)

Hull, C. L. *Essentials of behavior.* New Haven, Conn.: Yale, 1951. (517)

Hull, C. L. *A behavior system: An introduction to behavior theory concerning the individual organism.* New Haven, Conn.: Yale, 1952. (470, 517)

Hull, C. L. See Bass, M. J., & Hull, C. L., 1934.

Humphreys, L. S. See Hilgard, E. R., & Humphreys, L. G., 1938.

Hunt, E. L. Establishment of conditioned responses in chick embryos. *J. comp. physiol. Psychol.*, 1949, **42**, 107–117. (387)

Hunt, H. F., & Brady, J. V. Some quantitative and qualitative differences between "anxiety" and "punishment" conditioning. *Amer. Psychol.*, 1951, **6**, 276–277. (423)

Hunt, J. McV. The effects of infant feeding-frustration upon adult hoarding in the albino rat. *J. abnorm. soc. Psychol.*, 1941, **36**, 338–360. (498)

Hunt, J. McV. See Winnick, W. A., & Hunt, J. McV., 1951.

Hunter, W. S. The delayed reaction in animals and children. *Behav. Monogr.*, 1913, No. 6. (370)

Hunter, W. S. The effect of inactivity produced by cold upon learning and retention in the cockroach, *Latella germanica. J. genet. Psychol.*, 1932, **41**, 253–266. (449)

Hurvich, L. M., & Jameson, D. Spectral sensitivity of the fovea: I. Neutral adaptation. *J. Opt. Soc. Amer.*, 1953, **43**, 485–494. (230)

Hurvich, L. M., & Jameson, D. Some quantitative aspects of an opponent-colors theory: II. Brightness, saturation and hue in normal and dichromatic vision. *J. Opt. Soc. Amer.*, 1955, **45**, 602–616. (261)

Hurvich, L. M., & Jameson, D. An opponent-process theory of color vision. *Psychol. Rev.*, 1957, **64**, 384–404. (260–261)

Hurvich, L. M. See Jameson, D., & Hurvich, L. M., 1955.

Hutt, M. L. See Fouriezos, N. T., Hutt, M. L., & Guetzkow, H., 1950.

Hyde, W. See Leuba, J. H., & Hyde, W., 1905.

Hydén, H. Biochemical changes in glial cells and nerve cells at varying activity. In *Biochemistry of the central nervous system: Proc. 4th Int. Cong. Biochem.* Vol. 3. London: Pergamon Press, 1959. Pp. 64–89. (382)

Hydén, H. The neuron. In J. Brachet, & A. E. Mirsky (Eds.), *The cell*, Vol. IV. New York: Academic, 1960. Pp. 215–323. (383)

Hydén, H. Satellite cells in the nervous system. *Scient. Amer.*, 1961, **205**, 62–70. (382)

Hydén, H., & Egyhazi, E. Nuclear RNA changes of nerve cells during a learning experiment in rats. *Proc. Nat. Acad. Sci. U.S.*, 1962, **48**, 1366–1373. (382)

Hydén, H., & Egyhazi, E. Glial RNA changes during a learning experiment in rats. *Proc. Nat. Acad. Sci. U.S.*, 1963, **49**, 618–624. (382)

Hyman, R. *The nature of psychological inquiry.* Englewood Cliffs, N.J.: Prentice Hall, 1964. (34)

Ibarra, G. C. See Hernández-Peón, R. & Ibarra, G. C., 1963.

Iggo, A. A single unit analysis of cutaneous receptors with C afferent fibers. In G. E. W. Wolstenholme, & M. O'Connor (Eds.), *Pain and itch: Nervous mechanisms.* Boston: Little, Brown, 1959. (336)

Indik, B. P. Organization size and member participation. Unpublished doctoral dissertation, Univer. of Michigan, 1961. (n.s.) (577)

Indik, B. P. Some effects of organization size on member attitudes and behavior. *Hum. Relat.,* 1963, **16**, 369–384. (577)

Irion, A. L. Retention and warming-up effects in paired-associate learning. *J. exp. Psychol.,* 1949, **39**, 669–675. (442)

Irion, A. L. See Gustafson, L. M., & Irion, A. L., 1951.

Irion, A. L. See McGeoch, J. A., & Irion, A. L., 1952.

Irwin, J. M. See Melton, A. W., & Irwin, J. M., 1940.

Irwin, O. C. Infant speech: Consonantal sounds according to place of articulation. *J. Speech Hearing, Disord.,* 1947, **12**, 402–404. (205)

Irwin, O. C. Infant speech: Development of vowel sounds. *J. Speech Hearing Disord.,* 1948, **13**, 31–34. (205, 208)

Irwin, O. C., & Chen, H. P. Infant speech: Vowel and consonant frequency. *J. Speech Hearing Disord.,* 1946, **11**, 123–125. (205, 209)

Ishihara, S. *Series of plates designed as tests for color blindness.* Tokyo; Chicago: C. S. Stoelting, 1920. (255)

Israel, H. C. See Rees, H. J., & Israel, H. C., 1935.

Ittelson, W. H. *The Ames demonstrations in perception.* Princeton, N.J.: Princeton, 1952. (273)

Ittelson, W. H., & Kutash, S. B. (Eds.), *Perceptual changes in psychopathology.* New Brunswick, N.J.: Rutger's University Press, 1961. (295)

Izard, C. E. Personality similarity in friendship. *J. abnor. soc. Psychol.,* 1960, **61**, 47–51. (590)

Jacks, Q. D. See Sem-Jacobsen, C. W., Petersen, M. C., Dodge, H. W., Jr., Jacks, Q. D., & Lazarte, J. A., 1956.

Jackson, J. See Rosenfeld, H. M., & Jackson, J., 1965.

Jacobson, A. L. See McConnell, J. V., Jacobson, A. L., & Kimble, D. P., 1959.

Jacobson, E. Electrophysiology of mental activities. *Amer. J. Psychol.,* 1932, 44, 677–694. (195)

Jacobson, R. See McConnell, J. V., Jacobson, R., & Maynard, D. M., 1959.

Jacobson, R. See Zelman, A., Kabat, L., Jacobson, R., & McConnell, J. V., 1963.

Jaensch, E. R. *Eidetic imagery, and typological methods of investigation.* (O. Oeser, Trans.) New York: Harcourt, Brace & World, 1930. (295)

James, W. *The principles of psychology.* New York: Holt, 1890. 2 vols. (386, 454, 500, 508–509)

James, W. T. The effect of satiation on the sucking response in puppies. *J. comp. physiol. Psychol.,* 1957, **50**, 375–378. (494)

James, W. T. A further analysis of the effect of satiation on the sucking response in puppies. *Psychol. Rec.,* 1959, 9, 1–6. (501)

James, W. T., & Gilbert, T. F. Elimination of eating behavior by food injection in weaned puppies. *Psychol. Rep.,* 1957, **54** (3), 167–168. (501)

Jameson, D., & Hurvich, L. M. Some quantitative aspects of an opponent-colors theory: I. Chromatic responses and spectral saturation. *J. opt. Soc. Amer.,* 1955, **45**, 546–552. (261)

Jameson, D. See Hurvich, L. M., & Jameson, D., 1953.

Jameson, D. See Hurvich, L. M., & Jameson, D., 1955.

Jameson, D. See Hurvich, L. M., & Jameson, D., 1957.

Jarrard, L. W. See Gregg, L. W., & Jarrard, L. F., 1958.

Jarrett, R. F. See Postman, L., & Jarrett, R. F., 1952.

Jasper, H. See Penfield, W., & Jasper, H., 1954.

Jaynes, J. Imprinting: The interaction of learned and innate behavior: III. Practice effects on performance, retention and fear. *J. comp. physiol. Psychol.*, 1958a, **51**, 234–237. (482)

Jaynes, J. Imprinting: The interaction of learned and innate behavior: IV. Generalization and emergent discrimination. *J. comp. physiol. Psychol.*, 1958b, **51**, 238–242. (482)

Jenkins, J. G. Instruction as a factor in "incidental" learning. *Amer. J. Psychol.*, 1933, **45**, 471–477. (457)

Jenkins, J. G., & Dallenbach, K. M. Oblivescence during sleep and waking. *Amer. J. Psychol.*, 1924, **35**, 605–612. (448)

Jenkins, J. J., & Palermo, D. S. *Word association norms: Grade school through college,* University of Minnesota Press, 1964. (194)

Jenkins, W. L. Studies in thermal sensitivity: 9. The reliability of seriatim cold-mapping with untrained subjects. *J. exp. Psychol.*, 1939a, **24**, 278–293. (310)

Jenkins, W. L. Studies in thermal sensitivity: 10. The reliability of seriatim warm-mapping with untrained subjects. *J. exp. Psychol.*, 1939b, **24**, 439–449. (310)

Jenkins, W. L. Studies in thermal sensitivity: 11. Effects of stimulator size in seriatim cold-mapping. *J. exp. Psychol.*, 1939c, **25**, 302–306. (310)

Jenkins, W. L. Studies in thermal sensitivity: 12. Part-whole relation in seriatim cold-mapping. *J. exp. Psychol.*, 1939d, **25**, 373–388. (310)

Jenkins, W. L. Studies in thermal sensitivity: 14. Part-whole relations in seriatim warm-mapping. *J. exp. Psychol.*, 1940, **27**, 76–80. (310)

Jenkins, W. L. Studies in thermal sensitivity: 17. The topographical and functional relations of warm and cold. *J. exp. Psychol.*, 1941, **29**, 511–516. (310)

Jenkins, W. L. Somesthesis. In S. S. Stevens (Ed.), *Handbook of experimental psychology.* New York: Wiley, 1951. (310)

Jenkins, W. O., & Postman, L. An experimental analysis of set in rote learning: Retroactive inhibition as a function of changing set. *J. exp. Psychol.*, 1949, **39**, 69–72. (476)

Jennings, H. H. Sociometric differentiation of the psychegroup and the sociogroup. *Sociometry*, 1947, **10**, 71–79. (596)

Jennings, H. H. Leadership and sociometric choice. In G. E. Swanson, T. M. Newcomb, & E. L. Hartley (Eds.), *Readings in social psychology.* (Rev. ed.) New York: Holt, 1952. Pp. 312–318. (592)

Jersild, A. Memory for the pleasant as compared with the unpleasant, *J. exp. Psychol.*, 1931, **14**, 284–288. (443)

Johanson, A. M. The influence of incentive and punishment upon reaction-time. *Arch. Psychol., N.Y.*, 1922, No. 54. (461)

Johanson, G., & Backlund, F. A versatile eye-movement recorder. *Scand. J. Psychol.*, 1960, **1**, 181–186. (286)

John, E. R. See Corning, W. C., & John, E. R., 1961.

Johnson, D. D. See Copenhaver, W. M. (Ed.), & Johnson, D. D., 1958.

Johnson, E. P., & Riggs, L. A. Electroretinal and psychophysical dark adaptation curves. *J. exp. Psychol.*, 1951, **41**, 139–147. (227)

Johnson, G. L. *Philos. Trans. Roy. Soc. London,* Ser. B, 1901, **194**, (n.s.) (219)

Johnson, O. See Morgan, C. T., Stellar, E., & Johnson, O., 1943.

Jonckheere, T. Le procédé fragmentaire, et la procédé global dans la technique de la mémorisation. *Centenaire Th. Ribot,* 1939, 403–413. (437)

Jones, F. N. Scales of subjective intensity for odors of diverse chemical nature. *Amer. J. Psychol.*, 1958, **71**, 305–310. (343)

Jones, F. N. See Wenger, M. A., Jones, F. N., & Jones, M. H., 1956.

Jones, L. A. The fundamental scale of pure hue and retinal sensibility to hue differences. *J. Opt. Soc. Amer.*, 1917, **1**, 63–77. (231)

Jones, L. A., & Lowery, E. M. Retinal sensibility to saturation differences. *J. Opt. Soc. Amer.*, 1926, **13**, 25–34. (234)

Jones, M. G., & English, H. B. Notional vs. rote memory. *Amer. J. Psychol.*, 1926, **37**, 602–603. (476)

Jones, M. H. See Wenger, M. A., Jones, F. N., & Jones, M. H., 1956.

Jones, M. R. (Ed.) *Nebraska symposium on*

motivation. Lincoln, Nebr.: University of Nebraska Press, 1954–1963. (530)

Jost, A. Die Associationsfestigkeit in ihrer Abhangigkeit von der Verteilung der Wiederholungen. *Z. Psychol.*, 1897, **14**, 436–472. (451, 475–476)

Jouvet, M. Telencephalic and rhombencephalic sleep in the cat. In G. E. W. Wolstenholme, & M. O'Connor (Eds.), *The nature of sleep.* Ciba Foundation Symposium. Boston: Little, Brown, 1960. Pp. 188–208. (61)

Judd, D. B. Facts of color-blindness. *J. Opt. Soc. Amer.*, 1943, **33**, 294–307. (256–257)

Judd, D. B. Basic correlates of the visual stimulus. In S. S. Stevens (Ed.), *Handbook of experimental psychology.* New York: Wiley, 1951. Pp. 811–867. (246, 253, 294)

Judson, A. J., Cofer, C. N., & Gelfand, S. Reasoning as an associative process: II. "Direction" in problem solving as a function of prior reinforcement of relevant responses. *Psychol. Rep.*, 1956, **2**, 501–507. (472)

Jumber, J. See Frings, H., & Jumber, J., 1954.

Jung, C. G. *Studies in word-association.* (M. D. Eder, Trans.) London: Heinemann, 1919. (193)

Jung, J. *Untersuchung über Geruchschwellen.* Wurzburg: Mayr, 1936. (343)

Kabat, L. See Zelman, A., Kabat, L., Jacobson, R., & McConnell, J. V., 1963.

Kamin, L. J. The gradient delay of secondary reward in avoidance learning. *J. comp. physiol. Psychol.*, 1957a, **50**, 445–449. (413)

Kamin, L. J. The gradient delay of secondary reward in avoidance learning tested on avoidance trials only. *J. comp. physiol. Psychol.*, 1957b, **50**, 450–456. (413)

Kanfer, F., & Karas, S. Prior experimenter-subject interaction and verbal conditioning. *Psychol. Rep.*, 1959, **5**, 345–353. (459)

Kanfer, F. H. See Saltzman, I. J., Kanfer, F. H., & Greenspoon, J., 1955.

Kaplan, E. See Werner, H., & Kaplan, E., 1950.

Kaplon, M. D. See Wolfe, J. B., & Kaplon, M. D., 1941.

Karas, S. See Kanfer, F., & Karas, S., 1959.

Karbe, M. See Strughold, H., & Karbe, M., 1925.

Kare, M. R., & Halpern, B. P. (Eds.) *Physiological and behavioral aspects of taste.* Chicago: University of Chicago Press, 1961. (359, 362)

Kare, M. R., Black, R., & Allison, E. G. The sense of taste in the fowl. *Poultry Sci.*, 1957, **36**, 129–138. (353)

Karpman, B. See Woodrow, H., & Karpman, B., 1917.

Karsh, E. Effects of number of rewarded trials and intensity of punishment on running speed. *J. comp. physiol. Psychol.*, 1962, **55**, 44–51. (422)

Karwoski, T. The memory value of size. *J. exp. Psychol.*, 1931, **14**, 539–554. (476)

Karwoski, T. F., & Odbert, H. S. Color-music. *Psychol. Monogr.*, 1938, **50**, No. 2 (Whole no. 222). (198)

Karwoski, T. F., & Schachter, J. Psychological studies in semantics: III. Reaction times for similarity and difference. *J. soc. Psychol.*, 1948, **28**, 103–120. (193)

Karwoski, T. F. See Odbert, H. S., Karwoski, T. F., & Eckerson, A. B., 1942.

Katona, G. *The powerful consumer: Psychological studies of the American economy.* New York: McGraw-Hill, 1960. (558)

Katz, D., & Braly, K. Racial stereotypes of one hundred college students. *J. abnorm. soc. Psychol.*, 1933, **28**, 280–290. (137)

Katz, D. See Festinger, L., & Katz, D., 1953.

Katz, J. J., & Halstead, W. C. Protein organization and mental function. In W. C. Halstead (Ed.), Brain and behavior: A symposium. *Comp. Physiol. Monogr.*, 1950, **20**, No. 1. Berkeley, Calif.: University of California Press. Pp. 1–38. (381)

Katz, S. H., & Talbert, E. J. Intensities of odors and irritating effects of warning agents for inflammable and poisonous gases. *U.S. Bur. Mines Tech. Pap.*, No. 480, 1930. (n.s.) (343)

Katz, S. H. See Allison, V. C., & Katz, S. H., 1919.

Keibs, L. See Waetzmann, E., & Keibs, L., 1936a.

Keibs, L. Waetzmann, E., & Keibs, L., 1936b.

Keith, A. See Wrightson, T., & Keith, 1918.

Keller, F. S. *Learning: reinforcement theory.* New York: Random House, 1954. (427)

Keller, F. S., & Schoenfeld, W. N. *Principles of psychology.* New York: Appleton-Century-Crofts, 1950. (415)

Kelley, H. H. Communication in experimentally created hierarchies. *Hum. Relat.,* 1951, **4,** 39–56. (583, 587)

Kelley, H. H. See Thibaut, J. W., and Kelley, H. H., 1959.

Kellogg, L. A. See Kellogg, W. N., & Kellogg, L. A., 1933.

Kellogg, W. N., & Kellogg, L. A. *The ape and the child.* New York: McGraw-Hill, 1933. (473)

Kellogg, W. N. See Deese, J., & Kellogg, W. N., 1949.

Kendall, M. G. *Rank correlation methods* (2nd ed.) London: Griffin, 1955. (537)

Kendler, H. H. The concept of the concept. In A. W. Melton (Ed.), *Categories of human learning.* New York: Academic, 1964. Pp. 211–236. (477)

Kendler, T. S. An experimental investigation of transposition as a function of the difference between training and test stimuli. *J. exp. Psychol.,* 1950, **40,** 552–562. (418)

Kennelly, T. W. The role of similarity in retroactive inhibition. *Arch. Psychol., N.Y.,* 1941, **37,** No. 260. (433)

Kenshalo, D. R., & Nafe, J. P. A quantitative theory of feeling: 1960. *Psychol. Rev.,* 1962, **69,** 17–33. (76, 306, 310–311, 336)

Kenshalo, D. R. See Nafe, J. P., & Kenshalo, D. R., 1962.

Kent, G. H., & Rosanoff, A. J. A study of association in insanity. *Amer. J. Insanity,* 1910, **67,** 37–96, 317–390. (194)

Keppel, G. Facilitation in short- and long-term retention of paired associates following distribution practice in learning. *J. verb. Learn. verb. Behav.,* 1964, **3** (2), 91–111. (440)

Keppel, G., & Underwood, B. J. Proactive inhibition in short-term retention of single items. *J. verb. Learn. verb. Behav.,* 1962, **1,** 153–161. (447)

Kessen, W., & Kuhlman, C. (Eds.) Thought in the young child: Report of a conference on intellective development with particular attention to the work of Jean Piaget. Lafayette, Ind.: Society for research in child development, Inc., 1962. (290)

Kessen, W. See Mandler, G., & Kessen, W., 1959.

Kientzle, M. J. Ability patterns under distributed practice. *J. exp. Psychol.,* 1949, **39,** 532–537. (440–441)

Kiesow, F. Ein Beitrag zur Frage nach den Reaktionszeiten der Geschmacksempfindungen. *Z. Psychol.,* 1903, **33,** 453–461. (461)

Kiesow, F. See von Frey, M., & Kiesow, F., 1899.

Killian, C. D. See English, H. B., Welborn, E. L., & Killian, C. D., 1934.

Kilpatrick, F. P. (Ed.) *Explorations in transactional psychology.* New York: New York University Press, 1961. (295)

Kimble, D. P. See McConnell, J. V., Jacobson, A. L., & Kimble, D. P., 1959.

Kimble, G. A. Performance and reminiscence in motor learning as a function of the degree of distribution of practice. *J. exp. Psychol.,* 1949, **39,** 500–510. (475)

Kimble, G. A. Shock intensity and avoidance learning. *J. comp. physiol. Psychol.,* 1955, **48,** 281–284. (443)

Kimble, G. A. *Principles of general psychology.* New York: Ronald, 1956. (445)

Kimble, G. A. *Hilgard and Marquis' conditioning and learning.* New York: Appleton-Century-Crofts, 1961. (329, 365, 373, 383, 385, 400–401, 425)

Kimble, G. A., & Dufort, R. H. Meaningfulness and isolation as factors in verbal learning. *J. exp. Psychol.,* 1955, **50,** 361–368. (411)

Kimble, G. A., & Dufort, R. H. The associative factor in eyelid conditioning. *J. exp. Psychol.,* 1956, **52,** 386–391. (391)

Kimble, G. A., & Horenstein, B. R. Reminiscence in motor learning as a function of length of interpolated rest. *J. exp. Psychol.,* 1948, **38,** 239–244. (476)

Kimble, G. A., Mann, L. I., & Dufort, R. H. Classical and instrumental eyelid conditioning. *J. exp. Psychol.,* 1955, **49,** 407–417. (426)

Kimura, K., & Beidler, L. M. Microelectrode

study of taste bud of the rat. *Amer. J. Physiol.,* 1956, **187**, 610–611 (abstract). (356)

Kinder, E. F. A study of the nest-building activity of the albino rat. *J. exp. Zool.,* 1927, 47, 117–162. (488)

King, J. A. See Freedman, D. G., King, J. A., & Elliot, O., 1961.

Kinsey, A. C., Pomeroy, W. B., & Martin, C. E. *Sexual behavior in the human male.* Philadelphia: Saunders, 1948. (485, 489)

Kinsey, A. C., Pomeroy, W. B., Martin, C. E., & Gebhard, P. H. *Sexual behavior in the human female.* Philadelphia: Saunders, 1953. (489)

Kistiakowsky, G. B. On the theory of odors. *Science,* 1950. **112**, 154–155. (349)

Kitchell, R. L., Ström, L., & Zotterman, Y. Electrophysiological studies of thermal and taste reception in chickens and pigeons. *Acta physiol. Scand.,* 1959, **46**, 144–151. (353, 357)

Kitto, G. B. See Briggs, M. H., & Kitto, G. B., 1962.

Kleiner, R. J. The effects of threat reduction upon interpersonal attraction. *J. Pers.,* 1960, **28**, 145–155. (592)

Kleitman, N. The nature of dreaming. In G. E. W. Wolstenholme & M. O'Connor (Eds.), *The nature of sleep.* Ciba Foundation Symposium. Boston: Little, Brown, 1960. Pp. 349–374. (61)

Kleitman, N. *Sleep and wakefulness.* (Rev. ed.) Chicago: University of Chicago Press, 1963. (61)

Kleitman, N. See Aserinsky, E., & Kleitman, N., 1953.

Kleitman, N. See Dement, W., & Kleitman, N., 1957.

Klimova, V. I. The characteristics of components of some orienting reactions. In L. G. Voronin, A. N. Leont'yev, A. R. Luria, E. N. Sokolov, & O. S. Vinogradova (Eds.), *Orientirovochny refleks i orientirovochno-issledovatel'skaya deyatel'nost'.* (The orienting reflex and orienting-investigatory activity.) Moscow: Akad. Pedag. Nauk R. S. F. S. R., 1958. Pp. 76–80. (n.s.) (398)

Klimpfinger, S. Die Entwicklung der Gestalt Konstanz vom kind zum erwachsenen. *Arch. ges. Psychol.,* 1933, **88**, 599–628. (290)

Klineberg, F. L. Studies in measurement of the relations among sovereign states. *Psychometrika,* 1941, **6**, 335–352. (138)

Kling, J. W., & Schlosberg, H. Relation of skin conductance and rotary pursuit during extended practice. *Percept. mot. Skills,* 1961, **12**, 270. (475)

Klüver, H., & Bucy, P. C. Preliminary analysis of functions of the temporal lobe in monkeys. *A. M. A. Arch. Neurol. Psychiat.,* 1939, **42**, 979–1000. (511)

Kniffin, C. W. See Bitterman, M. E., & Kniffin, C. W., 1953.

Knight, K. E. See Leavitt, H, J., & Knight, K. E., 1963.

Knudsen, V. O. Hearing with the sense of touch. *J. gen. Psychol.,* 1928, **1**, 320–352. (316)

Koch, H. L. Some factors affecting the relative efficiency of certain modes of presenting material for memorizing. *Amer. J. Psychol.,* 1930, **42**, 370–388. (443, 476)

Koehler, O. Zahl-versuche an einem Kohlkraben und Vergleichsversuche an Menchen. *Z. Tierpsychol.,* 1943, **5**, 575–712. (n.s.) (470)

Koenigsberger, L. *Hermann von Helmholtz.* Brunswick, Germany: Friedr. Vieweg & Sohn, 1902–1903. 3 vols. (175)

Koester, T. The time error and sensitivity in pitch and loudness discrimination as a function of time interval and stimulus lever. *Arch. Psychol., N.Y.,* 1945, **41** (279), 1–69. (159)

Kohler, I. *Über Aufau und Wandlungen der Wahrenehmungswelt, insbesondere über 'bedingte Empfindungen'.* Vienna: Rudolph M. Rohrer, 1951a. (281)

Kohler, I. Warum sehen wir aufrecht? *Die Pyramide,* 1951b, **2**, 30–33. (281)

Kohler, I. Experiments with prolonged optical distortion. *Acta Psychol.,* 1955, **11**, 176–178. (Abstract.) (281)

Köhler, W., *Intelligenzprüfungen an Menschenaffen.* Berlin: Springer, 1917. (470)

Köhler, W. *The mentality of apes.* (E. Winter, Trans.) London: Kegan Paul, Trench, Trubar & Co., 1927. (470)

Köhler, W. Gestalt psychology today. *Amer. Psychol.*, 1959, **14**, 727–734. (295)

Köhler, W., & Dinnerstein, D. Figural after-effects in kinesthesis. In *Miscellanea Psychol. Albert Michotte,* 1944. Pp. 196–200. (242)

Köhler, W., & Emery, D. A. Figural after-effects in the third dimension of visual space. *Amer. J. Psychol.*, 1947, **60**, 159–201. (242)

Köhler, W., & Wallach, H. Figural after-effects and investigation of visual processes. *Proc. Amer. Phil. Soc.*, 1944, **88**, 269–357. (242–243)

Koller, G. Der Nestbau der weissen Maus und seine hormonale Auslösung. *Verhl. dtsch. zool. Ges.,* Freiburg, 1952, 160–168. (488)

Koller, G. Hormonale und psychische Steuerung beim Nestbau weiser Mause. *Zool. Anz.* (Suppl.), 1956, **19** (*Verh. dtsch. zool. Ges.,* 1955), 123–132. (488)

König, A. Die Grundempfindungen und ihre Itensitäts-Vertheilung im Spectrum. *SitzBr. Akad. Wiss.,* Berlin, 1886, Pp. 805–829. (n.s.) (260)

Kopp, G. A. See Potter, R. K., Kopp, G. A., & Green, H. C., 1947.

Korchin, S. J. See Basowitz, H., Persky, H., Korchin, S. J., & Grinker, R. R., 1955.

Korte, A. Kinematoskopische Untersuchungen. *Z. Psychol.*, 1915, **72**, 193–296. (284)

Kozma, F. See Hoffman, H., Toffey, S., Searle, J. L., & Kozma, F., 1966.

Krakauer, D., & Dallenbach, K. M. Gustatory adaptation to sweet, sour, bitter. *Amer. J. Psychol.*, 1937, **49**, 469–475. (360)

Krakauer, D. See Abrahams, H., Krakauer, D., & Dallenbach, K. M., 1937.

Krasner, L. Studies of the conditioning of verbal behavior. *Psychol. Bull.*, 1958, **55**, 148–170. (477)

Krasner, L., Weiss, R. L., & Ullmann, L. P. Responsivity to verbal conditioning as a function of two different measures of "awareness." Paper read at Amer. Psychol. Ass., Cincinnati, Ohio, 1959. (n.s.) (459)

Krasnogorski, N. I. Über die Bedingungsreflexe in Kindesalter. *Jb. Kinderheilk,* 1909, 69, 1–24. (387)

Krasnogorski, N. I. Über die Grundmechanis-men der Arbeit der Grosshirnrinde bie Kindern. *Jb. Kinderheilk,* 1913, **78**, 373–398. (387)

Krech, D. See Rosenzweig, M. R., Krech, D., & Bennett, E. L., 1960.

Krechevsky, I. "Hypotheses" in rats. *Psychol. Rev.*, 1932, **39**, 516–532. (459)

Krechevsky, I. A study of the continuity of the problem-solving process. *Psychol. Rev.,* 1938, 45, 107–133. (459)

Krueger, W. C. F. The effect of overlearning on retention. *J. exp. Psychol.*, 1929, **12**, 71–78. (445)

Krumboltz, J. D., & Farquhar, W. W. Reliability and validity of the nAchievement test. *J. consult. Psychol.*, 1957, **21**, 226–231. (526)

Kuder, G. F., & Richardson, M. W. The theory of the estimation of test reliability. *Psychometrika,* 1937, **2**, 151–160. (539)

Kuethe, K. L. See Eriksen, C. W., & Kuthe, K. L., 1956.

Kuhlman, C. See Kessen, W., & Kuhlman, C., 1962.

Kulby, D. See Martin, B., & Kulby, D., 1955.

Kuo, Z. Y. A psychology without heredity. *Psychol. Rev.*, 1924, **31**, 427–448. (500)

Kutash, S. B. See Ittelson, W. H., & Kutash, S. B., 1961.

Lacey, J. I., Smith, R. L., & Green, A. Use of conditioned autonomic responses in the study of anxiety. *Psychosom. Med.*, 1955, **17**, 208–217. (396–398)

Ladd, G. T., & Woodworth, R. S. *Elements of physiological psychology.* New York: Scribner, 1911. (335)

Ladd-Franklin, C. On theories of light sensation. *Mind,* 1893, **2**, 473–489. (249, 260)

Laffal, J. *Pathological and normal language.* New York: Atherton Press, 1961. (211)

Laget, P. Reproduction expérimentale de la vibration des cordes vocales, en l'absence de tout courant d'air, par stimulation électrique d'un recurrent du chien, avec observation stroboscopique de la response laryngée. *Rev. laryngol.,* 1953, **74**, 132–142. (185)

Laidlaw, R. W., & Hamilton, M. A. A study of thresholds in apperception of passive movement among normal control subjects.

Bull. Neurol. Inst., N.Y., 1937, **6**, 268–273. (325)

Lakenan, M. E. The whole and part methods of memorizing poetry and prose. *J. educ. Psychol.*, 1913, 4, 189–198. (437)

Lambert, W. W. Social psychology in relation to general psychology and other behavioral sciences. In S. Koch (Ed.), *Psychology: A study of a science.* Study II. *Empirical substructure and relations with other sciences.* Vol. VI. *Investigations of man as a socius: Their place in psychology and the social sciences.* New York: McGraw-Hill, 1963. Pp. 173–243. (601)

Lamoreaux, R. R. See Mowrer, O. H., & Lamoreaux, R. R., 1942.

Lamoreaux, R. R. See Mowrer, O. H., & Lamoreaux, R. R., 1946.

Land, E. H. Experiments in color vision. *Scient. Amer.*, 1959, **200**, 84–99. (250, 262, 264)

Land, V. See Peterson, L. R., Saltzman, D., Hillner, K., & Land, V., 1962.

Landauer, T. K. Two hypotheses concerning the biochemical basis of memory. *Psychol. Rev.*, 1964, **71**, 167–179. (382)

Landgren, S. Convergence of tactile, thermal, and gustatory impulses on single cortical cells. *Acta physiol. Scand.*, 1957, **40**, 210. (353)

Landgren, S. The thalamic and cortical reception of afferent impulses from the tongue. In G. E. W. Wolstenholme, & M. O'Connor (Eds.), *Pain and itch.* Ciba Foundation Study No. 1. London: Churchill, 1959. Pp. 69–83. (358)

Landgren, S. The response of thalamic and cortical neurons to electrical and physiological stimulation of the cat's tongue. In W. A. Rosenblith (Ed.), *Sensory communication.* New York: Wiley; Cambridge, Mass.: M.I.T., 1961. Pp. 437 454. (358)

Landgren, S. See Cohen, M. J., Landgren, S., Ström, L., & Zotterman, Y., 1957.

Lane, C. E. See Wegel, R. L., & Lane, C. E., 1924.

Lane, H. Psychophysical parameters of vowel perception. *Psychol. Monogr.*, 1962, **76**, No. 44 (Whole No. 563). (192)

Lane, H. L., Catania, A. C., & Stevens, S. S. Voice level: Autophonic scale, perceived loudness, and effect of sidetone. *J. Acoust. Soc. Amer.*, 1961, **33**, 160–167. (192)

Lane, H. S. See Silverman, S. R., Harrison, C. E., & Lane, H. S., 1946.

Langfelder, O. See Bednár, M., & Langfelder, O., 1930.

Langham, P. See Haythorn, W. W., Couch, A., Haefner, D., Langham, P., & Carter, L., 1956.

Lanier, L. H. An experimental study of cutaneous innervation. *Proc. Ass. Res. Nerv. ment. Dis.*, 1934, **15**, 437–456. (322)

Lanzetta, J. See Carter, L., Haythorn, W., Meirowitz, B., & Lanzetta, J., 1951.

Lanzetta, J. T., & Roby, T. B. Effects of work-group structure and certain task variables on group performance. *J. abnorm. soc. Psychol.*, 1956, **53**, 307–314. (578–579, 586)

La Piere, R. T. Attitudes vs. actions. *Soc. Forces*, 1934, **13**, 230–237. (559)

Larsen, J. R. See Dethier, V. G., Larsen, J. R., & Adams, J. R., 1963.

Larsson, S. See Brobeck, J. R., Larsson, S., & Reyes, E., 1956.

Lashley, K. S. A simple maze: With data on the relation of the distribution of practice to the rate of learning. *Psychobiol.*, 1918, **1**, 353–367. (475)

Lashley, K. S. Cerebral function in learning. *Psychobiol.*, 1920, **2**, 55–136. (427)

Lashley, K. S. Studies of cerebral function in learning: IV. Vicarious function after destruction of the visual areas. *Amer. J. Physiol.*, 1922, **59**, 44–71. (427)

Lashley, K. S. *Brain mechanisms and intelligence.* Chicago: University of Chicago Press, 1929. (427)

Lashley, K. S. Integrative functions of the cerebral cortex. *Physiol. Rev.*, 1933, **13**, 1–42. (427)

Lashley, K. S. Studies of cerebral function in learning: XI. The behavior of the rat in latch box situations. *Comp. psychol. Monogr.*, 1935a, **11** (2), 1–42. (427)

Lashley, K. S. Studies of cerebral function in learning: XII. Nervous structures concerned in the acquisition and retention of habits based on reactions to light. *Comp. psychol. Monogr.*, 1935b, **11** (2), 43–79. (427)

Lashley, K. S. An examination of the continuity theories applied to discriminative learning. *J. gen. Psychol.*, 1942, **26**, 241–265. (85)

Lashley, K. S., & Russell, J. T. The mechanism of vision: XI. A preliminary test of innate organization. *J. genet. Psychol.*, 1934, **45**, 136 144. (279)

Lastrucci, C. L. *The scientific approach: Basic principles of the scientific method.* Cambridge, Mass.: Schenkman, 1963. (34)

Latta, R. Notes on a case of successful operation for congenital cataract in an adult. *Brit. J. Psychol.*, 1904, **1**, 135–150. (279)

Lauenstein, L. Ansatz zu einer physiologischen Theorie des Vergleichs und der Zeitfehler. *Ps. Forsch.*, 1932, **17**, 130–177. (100)

Lavín, A., Alcocer-Cuarón, C., & Hernandez-Peón, R. Centrifugal arousal in the olfactory bulb. *Science,* 1959, **129**, 332–333. (346)

Lawrence, D. H., & DeRivera, J. Evidence for relational transposition. *J. comp. physiol. Psychol.*, 1954, **47**, 465–471. (418)

Lawrence, M. See Wever, E. G., & Lawrence, M., 1954.

Lawson, R. See Rosenthal, R., & Lawson, R., 1964.

Lazarsfeld, P. F., Berelson, B., & Gaudet, H. *The people's choice.* New York: Duell, Sloan, & Pearce, 1944. (559)

Lazarsfeld, P. F. See Berelson, B., Lazarsfeld, P. F., & McPhee, W. N., 1954.

Lazarte, J. A. See Sem-Jacobsen, C. W., Petersen, M. C., Dodge, H. W., Jr., Jacks, Q. D., & Lazarte, J. A., 1956.

Lazarus, R. S. Is there a mechanism of perceptual defense? A reply to Postman, Bronson, & Gropper. *J. abnorm. soc. Psychol.*, 1954, **49**, 396–398. (292)

Lazarus, R. S. Subception: fact or artifact? A reply to Eriksen. *Psychol. Rev.*, 1956, **63**, 343–347. (293)

Lazarus, R. S., & McCleary, R. A. Autonomic discrimination without awareness: A study of subception. *Psychol. Rev.*, 1951, **58**, 113–122. (293)

Leary, B. E. See Gray, W. S., & Leary, B. E., 1935.

Leavitt, H. J. Some effects of certain communication patterns on group performance. *J. abnorm. soc. Psychol.*, 1951, **46**, 38–50. (563, 565, 585)

Leavitt, H. J., & Knight, K. E. Most "efficient" solutions to communication networks: Empirical versus analytical search. *Sociometry,* 1963, **26**, 260–267. (586, 588)

Leavitt, H. J., & Schlosberg, H. The retention of verbal and of motor skills. *J. exp. Psychol.*, 1944, **34**, 404–417. (476)

Leber, T. Ueber das Vorkommen von Anomalien des Farbensinnes bei Krankheiten des Auges, nebst Bemerkungen uber einigen Formen von Amblyopic. *Arch. Ophthalmol.*, 1869, **15**, 26–107 (n.s.) (260)

Ledoux, A. Bioelectric activity of the nerve of the semicircular canals at rest and upon stimulation. *Conf. Neurol.*, 1960, **20**, 196–207. (334)

Lee, J. C. See Snider, R. S., & Lee, J. C., 1961.

Leeper, R. A motivational theory of emotion to replace "emotion as disorganized response." *Psychol. Rev.*, 1948, **55**, 5–21.

Leeper, R. W., & Madison, P. *Toward understanding personality.* New York: Appleton-Century-Crofts, 1959. (516)

Legouix, J. P. See Tasaki, I., Davis, H., & Legouix, J. P., 1952.

Lehrman, D. S. A critique of Konrad Lorenz' theory of instinctive behavior. *Quart. Rev. Biol.*, 1953, **28**, 337–363. (500)

Lehrman, D. S. Hormonal regulation of parental behavior in birds and infrahuman mammals. In W. C. Young (Ed.), *Sex and internal secretions.* (3rd ed.) Baltimore: Williams & Wilkins, 1961. Pp. 1268–1382. (501)

Lehrman, D. S. On the initiation of incubation behavior in doves. *Anim. behav.*, 1963, **11**, 433–438. (501)

Lehrman, D. S. The reproductive behavior of ring doves. *Scient. Amer.*, 1964, **211**, 48–54. (485–487)

Lehrman, D. S. Interaction between internal and external environments in the regulation of the reproductive cycle of the ring dove.

In F. A. Beach (Ed.), *Sex and behavior*. New York: Wiley, 1965. Pp. 355–380. (487)

Lele, P. P., & Weddell, G. The relationship between neurohistology and corneal sensibility. *Brain*, 1956, **79**, 119–154. (319)

Le Magnen, J. Étude d'une méthode d'analyse qualitative de l'olfaction. *Ann. Psychol.*, 1942–1943, **43–44**, 249–264. (342)

Le Magnen, J. Étude des facteurs dynamiques de l'excitation olfactive. *Ann. Psychol.*, 1944–1945, **45–46**, 77–89. (342)

Lettvin, J. Y. See Gesteland, R. C., Lettvin, J. Y., Pitts, W. H., & Rojas, A., 1963.

Leuba, J. H., & Hyde, W. An experiment in learning to make hand movements. *Psychol. Rev.*, 1905, **12**, 351–369. (475)

Levin, S. M. See Spielberger, C. D., Levin, S. M., & Shepard, M. C., 1962.

Levine, D. (Ed.) *Nebraska symposium on motivation*. Lincoln, Nebr.: University of Nebraska Press, 1964–1966. (530)

Levine, J. M., & Murphy, G. The learning and forgetting of controversial material. *J. abnorm. soc. Psychol.*, 1943, **38**, 507–517. (450)

Levy, D. M. Experiments on the sucking reflex and social behavior of dogs. *Amer. J. Orthopsychiat.*, 1934, **4**, 203–224. (494)

Levy, E. Z. See Ruff, G. E., & Levy, E. Z., 1959.

Levy, I. See Elsberg, C. A., & Levy, I., 1935.

Levy, I. See Elsberg, C. A., Brewer, E. D., & Levy, I., 1935.

Lewin, K., (Cartwright, D., Ed.), *Field theory in social science*. New York: Harper & Row, 1951. (601)

Lewin, K., & Lippitt, R. An experimental approach to the study of autocracy and democracy: A preliminary note. *Sociometry*, 1938, **1**, 292–300. (575)

Lewis, D. See Saetveit, J. G., Lewis, D., & Seashore, C. E., 1940.

Lewis, D. See Seashore, C. E., Lewis, D., & Saetveit, J. G., 1960.

Lewis, D. J. Partial reinforcement: A selective review of the literature since 1950. *Psychol. Bull.*, 1960, **57**, 1–28. (405)

Lewis, D. J. *Scientific principles of psychology*. Englewood Cliffs, N. J.: Prentice-Hall, 1963. (477)

Lewis, D. R. Psychological scales of taste. *J. Psychol.*, 1948, **26**, 437–446. (360)

Lewis, H. B. See Witkin, H. A., Lewis, H. B., Hertzman, M., Machovar, K., Meissner, P. B., & Wapner, S., 1954.

Lewis, T. *The blood vessels of the human skin and their responses*. London: Shaw, 1927. (311)

Lewis, T. *Pain*. New York: Macmillan, 1942. (303, 319)

Lewis, T., & Hess, W. Pain derived from the skin and the mechanism of its production. *Clin. Sci.*, 1933, **1**, 39–61. (319)

Lichten, W. See Miller, G. A., Heise, G. A., & Lichten, W., 1951.

Lichtenstein, P. E. Studies of anxiety: I. The production of a feeding inhibition in dogs. *J. comp. physiol. Psychol.*, 1950, **43**, 16–29. (423)

Lickley, J. D. *The nervous system*. New York: Longmans, 1912. (n.s.) (301)

Licklider, J. C. R. Basic correlates of the auditory stimulus. In S. S. Stevens (Ed.), *Handbook of experimental psychology*. New York: Wiley, 1951. Pp. 985–1039. (157, 160, 165, 182)

Licklider, J. C. R., & Miller, G. A. The perception of speech. In S. S. Stevens (Ed.), *Handbook of experimental psychology*. New York: Wiley, 1951. Pp. 1040–1074. (186, 204, 212)

Licklider, J. C. R., Bindra, D., & Pollack, I. The intelligibility of rectangular speech-waves. *Amer. J. Psychol.*, 1948, **61**, 1–20 (205)

Liddell, H. S. The experimental neurosis and the problem of mental disorder. *Amer. J. Psychiat.*, 1938, **94**, 1035–1043. (401)

Lieberman, S. The effects of changes in roles on the attitudes of role occupants. *Hum. Relat.*, 1956, **9**, 385–402. (560–562)

Lilly, J. C. Mental effects of reduction of ordinary levels of physical stimuli on intact, healthy persons. *Psychiat. Res. Rep.*, 1956, **5**, 1–9. (289)

Lilly, J. C. *Man and dolphin*. Garden City, N.Y.: Doubleday, 1961. (210)

Lindley, R. H. Association value and familiarity in serial verbal learning. *J. exp. Psychol.* 1960, **59**, 366–370. (194)

Lindsley, D. B. Emotion. In S. S. Stevens (Ed.), *Handbook of experimental psychology.* New York: Wiley, 1951. Pp. 473–516. (505, 530)

Lindsley, D. B. Psychophysiology and motivation. In M. R. Jones (Ed.), *Nebraska symposium on motivation.* Lincoln, Nebr.: University of Nebraska Press, 1957. Pp. 44–105. (508)

Lindsley, D. B. Psychophysiology and perception. In *Current trends in description and analysis of behavior.* Pittsburgh, Pa.: University of Pittsburgh Press, 1958. (238)

Lindsley, D. B., Bowden, J. W., & Magoun, H. W. Effect upon the EEG of acute injury to the brain stem activating system. *Electroencephalog. Clin. Neurophysiol.,* 1949, **1,** 475–486. (61)

Lindzey, G. (Ed.) *Handbook of social psychology.* Cambridge, Mass.: Addison-Wesley, 1954. (601–602)

Lindzey, G., & Aronson, E. *Handbook of social psychology.* Cambridge, Mass.: Addison-Wesley, 1967. Vol. 1–5. (601–602)

Lindzey, G. See Hall, C. S., & Lindzey, G., 1957.

Linely, B. L. See Grosslight, J. H., & Linely, B. L., 1963.

Lipman, E. A. See Brogden, W. J., Lipman, E. A., & Culler, E., 1938.

Lippitt, R. An experimental study of the effect of democratic and authoritarian group atmospheres. *Univ. Iowa Stud. Child Welf.,* 1940, **16,** 43–195. (575)

Lippitt, R., & White, R. K. An experimental study of leadership and group life. In T. M. Newcomb & E. L. Hartley (Eds.), *Readings in social psychology.* New York: Holt, 1947. Pp. 315–330. (575, 582, 585)

Lippitt, R. See Heyns, R. W., & Lippitt, R., 1954.

Lippitt, R. See Lewin, K., & Lippitt, R., 1938.

Lippitt, R. See Polansky, N., Lippitt, R., & Redl, F., 1950.

Lippold, O. C. J., Nicholls, J. G., & Redfearn, J. W. T. Electrical and mechanical factors in the adaptation of a mammalian muscle spindle. *J. Physiol.,* 1960, **153,** 209–217. (326)

Lloyd, D. P. C. The nerve membrane, excitation, and impulse conduction. In J. F. Fulton (Ed.), *Textbook of physiology.* (17th ed.) Philadelphia, Saunders, 1955. Pp. 7–29. (44)

Lloyd, K. E., Reid, L. S., & Feallock, J. B. Short-term retention as a function of the average number of items presented. *J. exp. Psychol.,* 1960, **60,** 201–207. (446–447, 476)

Lloyd, K. E. See Reid, L. S., Lloyd, K. E., Brackett, H. R., & Hawkins, W. F., 1961.

Lloyd, V. V. See Mueller, C. G., & Lloyd, V. V., 1948.

Loed, P. M. Premières données sur l'électro olfactogramme du Lapin. *J. Physiol.,* Paris, 1959, **51,** 85–92. (345)

Lohr, T. F. The effect of shock on the rat's choice of a path to food. *J. exp. Psychol.,* 1959, **58,** 312–318. (419)

Lorenz, K. Z. Der Kumpan in der Umwelt des Vogels. *J. Ornithol.,* 1935, **83,** 137–214, 289–413. (480, 500)

Lorenz, K. Z. The companion in the bird's world. *Auk,* 1937, **54,** 245–273. (480–481, 500)

Lorenz, K. Die angeborener Formen möglicher Erfahrung. *Z. Tierpsychol.,* 1943, **5,** 235–409. (529)

Lorenz, K. The comparative method in studying innate behavior patterns. In Physiological mechanisms in animal behavior. *Soc. Exp. Biol. Sympos.* No. 40. New York: Academic, 1950. Pp. 221–268. (530–531)

Lorenz, K. *King Solomon's ring.* New York: Crowell, 1952. (500)

Lorenz, K. Morphology and behavior patterns in closely allied species. In B. Schaffner (Ed.), *Trans. 1st Conf. Group Processes, 1954.* New York: Josiah Macy, Jr., Foundation, 1955. Pp. 168–220. (497)

Lorenz, K. The conception of instinctive behavior. (1937.) In C. H. Schiller (Ed.), *Instinctive behavior.* New York: International Universities Press, 1957a. Pp. 129–175. (502)

Lorenz, K. Comparative study of behavior. (1939.) In C. H. Schiller (Ed.), *Instinctive behavior.* New York: International Universities Press, 1957b. Pp. 239–263. (497)

Lorenz, K. *On aggression.* Harcourt, Brace & World, 1966. (531)

Lorge, I. The influence of regularly interpolated time intervals upon subsequent learning. *Teach. Coll. Contr. Educ.*, 1930, No. 438. (475)

Lorge, I., Fox, D., Davitz, J., & Brenner, M. A survey of studies contrasting the quality of group performance and individual performance, 1920–1957. *Psychol. Bull.*, 1958, **55**, 337–372. (602)

Lott, A. J., & Lott, B. E. Group cohesiveness, communication level, and conformity. *J. abnorm. soc. Psychol.*, 1961, **62**, 408–412. (592)

Lott, A. J., & Lott, B. E. Group cohesiveness as interpersonal attraction: A review of relationships with antecedent and consequent variables. *Psychol. Bull.*, 1965, **64**, 259–309. (589, 602)

Lott, B. E. See Lott, A. J., & Lott, B. E., 1961.

Lott, B. E. See Lott, A. J., & Lott, B. E., 1965.

Lowell, E. L. The effect of need for achievement on learning and speed of performance. *J. Psychol.*, 1952, **33**, 31–40. (527)

Lowell, E. L. See McClelland, D. C., Atkinson, J. W., Clark, R. A., & Lowell, E. L., 1953.

Lowery, E. M. See Jones, L. A., & Lowery, E. M., 1926.

Luce, R. D. Detection and recognition. In R. D. Luce, R. R. Bush, & E. Galanter (Eds.), *Handbook of mathematical psychology.* Vol. 1. New York: Wiley, 1963. (246)

Luce, R. D., & Galanter, E. Discrimination. In R. D. Luce, R. R. Bush, & E. Galanter (Eds.), *Handbook of mathematical psychology.* Vol. 1. New York: Wiley, 1963. (246)

Luchins, A. S. Mechanization in problem solving: The effect of Einstellung. *Psychol. Monogr.*, 1942, **54**, No. 248. (471–472)

Luchins, A. S., & Luchins, E. H. *Rigidity of behavior.* Eugene, Ore.: University of Oregon Books, 1959. (471)

Luchins, E. H. See Luchins, A. S., & Luchins, E. H., 1959.

Luchsinger, R., & Arnold, G. E. *Voice, speech, language, clinical communicology: its physiology and pathology.* (G. E. Arnold, & E. R. Finkbeiner, Trans.) Belmont, Calif.: Wadsworth, 1965. (212)

Luckhardt, A. B., & Carlson, A. J. Contributions to the physiology of the stomach: XVII. On the chemical control of the gastric hunger mechanisms. *Amer. J. Physiol.*, 1915, **36**, 37–46. (330)

Ludwig, C. See Adrian, E. D., & Ludwig, C., 1938.

Lufkin, H. M. See Bazett, H. C., McGlone, B., Williams, R. G., & Lufkin, H. M., 1932.

Luft. E. Über die unterschiedsempfindlichkeit für Tonhohen. *Philos. Stud., Wundt,* 1888, **4**, 511–540. (n.s.) (158)

Luh, C. W. The conditions of retention. *Psychol. Monogr.*, 1922, **31**, No. 142. (451–452)

Lumsdaine, A. A., & Glaser, R. M. (Eds.) *Teaching machines and programmed learning.* Washington, D.C.: National Education Association, 1960. (476)

Lundin, R. W. *An objective psychology of music.* New York: Ronald, 1953. (548)

Luria, A. R. *The role of speech in the regulation of normal and abnormal behavior.* Tizard, J. (Ed.) New York: Liveright, 1961. (212)

Lyon, D. O. The relation of length of material to time taken for learning and the optimum distribution of time. *J. educ. Psychol.*, 1914, **5**, 1–9. (443, 475)

Lyons, J. *A primer of experimental psychology.* New York: Harper & Row, 1965. (35, 536)

McAllister, W. R. Adaptation of the original response to a conditioned stimulus. *Iowa Acad. Sci.*, 153, **60**, 534–539. (391)

McBride, D. See Schachter, S., Ellertson, N., McBride, D., & Gregory, D., 1951.

McBride, G. The "teat order" and communication in young pigs. *Anim. Behav.*, 1963, **11**, 53–56. (495)

McCarthy, D. The language development of the preschool child. *Inst. Child Welf. Monogr. Ser.*, No. 4, Minneapolis: University of Minnesota Press, 1930. (208)

McCarthy, D. Language disorders and parent-child relationships. *J. Speech Hearing Disord.*, 1954, **19**, 514–523. (205, 208, 211)

MacCaslin, E. F. Successive and simultaneous discrimination as a function of stimulus similarity. *Amer. J. Psychol.*, 1954, **67**, 308–314. (418)

McCleary, R. A., & Moore, R. Y. *Subcortical*

mechanisms of behavior. New York: Basic Books, 1965. (507, 530)

McCleary, R. A., & Morgan, C. T. Food hoarding in rats as a function of environmental temperature. *J. comp. physiol. Psychol.,* 1946, **39**, 371–378. (497–498)

McCleary, R. A. See Lazarus, R. S., & McCleary, R. A., 1951.

McClelland, D. C. Studies in serial verbal discrimination learning: I. Reminiscence with two speeds of pair presentation. *J. exp. Psychol.,* 1942, **31**, 44–56. (476)

McClelland, D. C. (Ed.) *Studies in motivation.* New York: Appleton-Century-Crofts, 1955. (531)

McClelland, D. C. The achievement motive in economic growth. In G. Nielson (Ed.), *Proc. 14th Int. Cong. Appl. Psychol.* Vol. 2. *Personality research.* Copenhagen, Denmark: Minksgaard, 1962. Pp. 60–80. (531)

McClelland, D. C., Atkinson, J. W., Clark, R. A., & Lowell, E. L. *The achievement motive.* New York: Appleton-Century-Crofts, 1953. (526, 528, 531)

McClelland, D. C. See Atkinson, J. W., & McClelland, D. C., 1948.

McClintock, C. G. See Harrison, A. A., & McClintock, C. G., 1965.

McClintock, C. G. See DeLamater, J., McClintock, C. G., & Becker, G., 1965.

McConnell, J. V., Jacobson, A. L., & Kimble, D. P. The effects of regeneration upon retention of a conditioned response in the planarian. *J. comp. physiol. Psychol.,* 1959, **52**, 1–5. (381)

McConnell, J. V., Jacobson, R., & Maynard, D. M. Apparent retention of a conditioned reflex following total regeneration in the planarian. *Amer. Psychol.,* 1959, **14**, 410. (Abstract.) (382)

McConnell, J. V. See Thompson, R., & McConnell, J. V., 1955.

McConnell, J. V. See Zelman, A., Kabat, L., Jacobson, R., & McConnell, J. V., 1963.

McCord, C. P., & Witheridge, W. N. *Odors: physiology and control.* New York: McGraw-Hill, 1949. (362)

McCord, F. The effect of frustration on hoarding in rats. *J. comp. physiol. Psychol.,* 1941, **32**, 531–541. (498)

McCulloch, W. Introductory discussion. In H. von Foerster (Ed.), *Cybernetics.* New York: Josiah Macy, Jr., Foundation, 1950. (381)

MacDonald, A. The effect of adaptation to the unconditioned stimulus upon the formation of conditioned avoidance responses. *J. exp. Psychol.,* 1946, **36**, 1–12. (391)

McDougall, W. *Outline of psychology.* New York: Scribner, 1923. (500)

McDougall, W. *An introduction to social psychology.* Boston: Luce & Co., 1926. (500)

McDougall, W. *The energies of men.* New York: Scribner, 1933. (500)

Macfarlane, J. W. See Honzik, M. P., Macfarlane, J. W., & Allen, L., 1948.

McGeoch, G. O. The intelligence quotient as a factor in the whole-part problem. *J. exp. Psychol.,* 1931a, **14**, 333–358. (437)

McGeoch, G. O. The whole-part problem. *Psychol. Bull.,* 1931b, **28**, 713–739. (475)

McGeoch, G. O. The conditions of reminiscence. *Amer. J. Psychol.,* 1935, **47**, 65–89. (441–442)

McGeoch, J. A. The influence of associative value upon the difficulty of nonsense-syllable lists. *J. genet. Psychol.,* 1930, **37**, 420–430. (194, 476)

McGeoch, J. A. *The psychology of human learning: An introduction.* New York: Longmans, 1942. (433, 477)

McGeoch, J. A., & Irion, A. L. *The psychology of human learning.* New York: Longmans, 1952. (383, 412, 449, 476–477)

McGill, T. E. See Vernon, J. A., McGill, T. E., & Schiffman, H., 1958.

McGill, T. E. See Vernon, J. A., McGill, T. E., Gulick, W. L., & Candland, D. K., 1959.

McGill, T. E. See Vernon, J. A., McGill, T. E., Gulick, W. L., & Candland, D. K., 1961.

McGinnies, E. Emotionality and perceptual defense. *Psychol. Rev.,* 1949, **56**, 244–251. (292)

McGinnies, E. Discussion of Howes' and Solomon's note on "Emotionality and perceptual defense." *Psychol. Rev.,* 1950, **57**, 229–234. (293)

McGlone, B. See Bazett, H. C., & McGlone, B., 1932.

McGlone, B. See Bazett, H. C., McGlone, B., & Brocklehurst, R. J., 1930.

McGlone, B. See Bazett, H. C., McGlone, B., Williams, R. G., & Lufkin, H. M., 1932.

McGrath, J. E. *Social psychology: A brief introduction.* New York: Holt, 1964. (566)

McGrath, J. E., & Altman, I. *Small group research: A synthesis and critique of the field.* New York: Holt, 1966. (602)

McGuigan, F. J. *Experimental psychology: A methodological approach.* Englewood Cliffs, N.J.: Prentice-Hall, 1960. (34)

McKee, J. P., & Honzik, M. P. The sucking behavior of mammals: An illustration of the nature-nurture question. In L. Postman (Ed.), *Psychology in the making.* New York: Knopf, 1962. Pp. 585–661. (501)

MacLean, P. D. The limbic system and its hippocampal formation: Studies in animals and their possible application to man. *J. Neurophysiol.,* 1954, **11**, 29–44. (61)

MacLean, P. D. See Gergen, J. A., & MacLean, P. D., 1962.

MacNichol, E. F., Jr. National Institutes of Health Symposium on the electrophysiology of the visual system. *Amer. J. Ophthalmol.,* 1958, **46**, 26–39. (261)

MacNichol, E. F., Jr., Three-pigment color vision. *Scient. Amer.,* 1964, **211**, December, P. 48. (261–262)

McPhee, W. N. See Bereleson, B., Lazarsfeld, P. F., & McPhee, W. N., 1954.

Mach, E. *Grundlinien der Lehre von den Bewegungsempfindungen.* Leipzig: Engelman, 1875. (n.s.) (333)

Machover, K. See Witkin, H. A., Lewis, H. B., Hertzman, M., Machover, K., Meissner, P. B., & Wapner, S., 1954.

Madison, P. See Leeper, R. W., & Madison, P., 1959.

Magendie, F. Expériences sur les fonctions des racines des nerfs rachidiens. *J. physiol. expér. Pathol.,* 1822a, **2**, 276–279. (n.s.) (63)

Magendie, F. Expériences sur les fonctions des racines qui naissent de la moëlle épinière. *J. physiol. expér. Pathol.,* 1822b, **2**, 366–371. (n.s.) (63)

Magendie, F. *Leçons sur les fonctions et les maladies du système nerveux.* Paris, 1839. 2 vols. (63)

Magoun, H. W. *The waking brain.* Springfield, Ill.: Charles C Thomas, 1963. (383, 513)

Magoun, H. W. See Moruzzi, G., & Magoun, H. W., 1949.

Magoun, H. W. See Barnes, W. T., Magoun, H. W., & Ranson, S. W., 1943.

Magoun, H. W. See Field, J., Magoun, H. W., & Hall, V. E., 1959.

Magoun, H. W. See Lindsley, D. B., Bowden, J. W., & Magoun, H. W., 1949.

Maier, N. R. F., & Hoffman, L. R. Acceptance and quality of solutions as related to leaders' attitudes toward disagreement in group problem solving. *J. appl. behav. Science,* 1965, **1**, 373–386. (570)

Maier, N. R. F., & Solem, A. R. The contribution of a discussion leader to the quality of group thinking: The effective use of minority opinions. *Hum. Relat.,* 1952, **5**, 277–288. (570, 572, 595)

Maier, N. R. F. See Hoffman, L. R., & Maier, N. R. F., 1961.

Maier, N. R. F. See Hoffman, L. R., & Maier, N. R. F., 1966.

Maier, N. R. F. See Hoffman, L. R., Harburg, E. M., & Maier, N. R. F., 1962.

Malcolm, J. L. See Gray, J. A. B., & Malcolm, J. L., 1950.

Malmo, R. B. Measurement of drive: An unsolved problem in psychology. In M. R. Jones (Ed.), *Nebraska Symposium on motivation.* Lincoln, Nebr.: University of Nebraska Press, 1958. Pp. 229–265. (508)

Mandelbaum, J., & Sloan, L. L. Peripheral visual acuity. *Amer. J. Ophthalmol.,* 1947, **30**, 581–588. (232)

Mandler, G., & Kessen, W. *Language of psychology.* New York: Wiley, 1959. (35)

Mandler, G. See Brown, R., Galanter, E., Hess, E. H., & Mandler, G., 1962.

Manis, M. Social interaction and the self concept. *J. abnorm. soc. Psychol.,* 1955, **51**, 362–370. (594)

Mann, L. I. See Kimble, G. A., Mann, L. I., & Dufort, R. H., 1955.

Mann, R. D. A review of the relationships between personality and performance in small groups. *Psychol. Bull.*, 1959, **56**, 241–270. (571, 574, 589, 602)

Mann, R. D. See Strodtbeck, F. L., & Mann, R. D., 1956.

Marañon, G. Contribution à l'étude de l'action émotive de l'adrenaline. *Rev. franc. Endocrinol.*, 1924, **2**, 301–325. (n.s.) (510)

Marbe, K. Z. See Thumb, A., & Marbe, K. Z., 1901.

Marler, P. R., & Hamilton, W. J., *Mechanisms of animal behavior*, New York: Wiley, 1966. (500)

Marquis, D. G. See Hilgard, E. R., & Marquis, D. G., 1940.

Marriott, F. H. C. See Pirenne, M. H., & Marriott, F. H. C., 1958.

Martin, B., & Kubly, D. Results of treatment of enuresis by a conditioned response method. *J. consult. Psychol.*, 1955, **19**, 71–73. (401)

Martin, C. E. See Kinsey, A. C., Pomeroy, W. B., & Martin, C. E., 1948.

Martin, C. E. See Kinsey, A. C., Pomeroy, W. B., Martin, C. E., & Gebhard, P. H., 1953.

Maruhashi, J., Mizuguchi, K., & Tasaki, I. Action currents in single afferent nerve fibers elicited by stimulation of the skin of the toad and the cat. *J. Physiol.*, 1952, **117**, 129–151. (320)

Marx, M. H. A stimulus-response analysis of the hoarding habit in the rat. *Psychol. Rev.*, 1950, **57**, 80–93. (498)

Mason, J. W. See Brady, J. V., Porter, R. W., Conrad, D. G., & Mason, J. W., 1958.

Mason, J. W. See Porter, R. W., Brady, J. V., Conrad, D., Mason, J. W., Galambos, R., & Rioch, D. McD., 1958.

Mason, M. Changes in the galvanic skin response accompanying reports of changes in meaning during oral repetition. *J. gen. Psychol.*, 1941, **25**, 353–401. (195)

Mason, W. A., Blazek, N. C., & Harlow, H. F. Learning capacities of the infant rhesus monkey. *J. comp. physiol. Psychol.*, 1956, **49**, 449–453. (484)

Masserman, J. H. *Behavior and neurosis.* Chicago: University of Chicago Press, 1943. (401, 423)

Matarazzo, J. D., Saslow, G., & Pareis, E. N. Verbal conditioning of two response classes: Some methodological considerations. *J. abnorm. soc. Psychol.*, 1960, **61**, 190–206. (458–459)

Mateer, F. Some differences between normals and defectives not indicated by intelligence tests. *Rep. Amer. Psychol. Ass.*, December, 1916. (386)

Mateer, F. *Child behavior: A critical and experimental study of young children by the method of conditioned reflexes.* Boston: Badger, 1918. (380, 483)

Matthews, G. V. T. *Bird navigation.* London: Cambridge, 1955. (492, 501)

Matthews, H. L. Visual stimulation and ovulation in pigeons. *Proc. Roy. Soc. Biol.*, 1939, **126**, 557–560.

Matthews, P. B. C. See Gray, J. A. B., & Matthews, P. B. C., 1951.

Max, L. W. An experimental study of the motor theory of consciousness: I. Critique of earlier studies. *J. gen. Psychol.*, 1934, **11**, 112–125. (195, 470)

Max, L. W. An experimental study of the motor theory of consciousness: III. Action-current responses in deaf-mutes during sleep, sensory stimulation and dreams. *J. comp. Psychol.*, 1935a, **19**, 469–486. (195, 470)

Max, L. W. Breaking up a homosexual fixation by the conditioned reaction techniques: A case study. *Psychol. Bull.*, 1935b, **32**, 734. (401)

Max, L. W. An experimental study of the motor theory of consciousness: IV. Action-current responses in the deaf during awakening, kinaesthetic imagery, and abstract thinking. *J. comp. Phychol.*, 1937, **24**, 301–344. (195, 470)

Maybee, G. R. Flavor in food-classification and comparison of tests. *Canad. chem. Process. Industr.*, 1939, **23**, 115–118. (347)

Mayer, B. A., & Stone, C. P. The relative efficiency of distributed and massed practice in maze learning by young and adult albino rats. *J. genet. Psychol.*, 1931, **39**, 28–48. (475)

Mayer, J. The glucosity theory of regulation

of food intake and the problem of obesity. *Bull. N. E. med. Cen.,* 1952, **14**, 43–49. (n.s.) (336)

Mayer, J. Regulation of food intake and multiple etiology of obesity. In E. S. Eppright, P. Swanson, & C. A. Iverson (Eds.), *Weight control: A collection of papers presented at the weight control colloquium.* Ames, Iowa: Iowa State College Press, 1955. Pp. 29–48. (336)

Maynard, D. M. See McConnell, J. V., Jacobson, R., & Maynard, D. M., 1959.

Meader, C. L. See Pillsbury, W. B., & Meader, C. L., 1928.

Mechanic, A. Effects of orienting task, practice, and incentive on simultaneous incidental and intentional learning. *J. exp. Psychol.,* 1962, **64** (4), 393–399. (458)

Medini, S. Learning without awareness and its relationship to insight and the hysteric-obsessive dimension. Doctoral dissertation, New York University, 1957. (n.s.) (459)

Mednick, S. A. *Learning.* Englewood Cliffs, N.J.: Prentice-Hall, 1964. (383)

Mednick, S. A., & Freedman, J. L. Stimulus generalization. *Psychol. Bull.,* 1960, **57**, 169–200. (414)

Meek, J. C., Graybiel, A., Beischer, D. E., & Riopelle, A. J. Observations of canal sickness and adaptation in chimpanzees and squirrel monkeys in a slow rotation room. *USN Sch. Aviat. Rep.,* 1961, No. 59. (335)

Meirowitz, B. See Carter, L., Haythorn, W., Meirowitz, B., & Lanzetta, J., 1951.

Meissner, P. B. See Witkin, H. A., Lewis, H. B., Hertzman, M., Machover, K., Meissner, P. B., & Wapner, S., 1954.

Melton, A. W. The effect of rest pauses on the acquisition of the pursuitmeter habit. *Psychol. Bull.,* 1941, **38**, 719. (476)

Melton, A. W. (Ed.) *Categories of human learning.* New York: Academic, 1964. (477)

Melton, A. W., & Irwin, J. M. The influence of degree of interpolated learning on retroactive inhibition and the overt transfer of specific responses. *Amer. J. Psychol.,* 1940, **53**, 173–203. (476)

Melton, A. W., & Stone, G. R. The retention of serial lists of adjectives over short time intervals with varying rates of presentation. *J. exp. Psychol.,* 1942, **30**, 295–310. (476)

Melzack, R., & Wall, P. D. Pain mechanisms: A new theory. *Science,* 1965, **150**, 971–979. (323, 385)

Merei, F. Group leadership and institutionalization. *Hum. Relat.,* 1949, **2**, 23–29. (583)

Mettler, F. A. See Girden, E., Mettler, F. A., Finch, G., & Culler, E., 1936.

Meuwese, W. A. T. See Fiedler, F. E. Meuwese, W. A. T., & Oonk, S., 1961.

Meyer, M. An introduction to the mechanics of the inner ear. *Univer. Missouri Stud., Sci. Ser.,* 1907, **2** (1), 1–140. (n.s.) (177)

Meyer, W. Über Ganz und Teillernverfahren bei vorgeschriebenem Rezitieren. *Z. Psychol.,* 1926, **98**, 304–341. (475)

Michaels, K. M., Phillips, D. S., Wright, R. H., & Pustek, J. Odor and olfaction: A bibliography, 1948–1960. *Percept. mot. Skills,* 1962, **15**, 475–529. (362)

Michels, W. C., & Helson, H. A reformulation of the Fechner law in terms of adaptation-level applied to rating-scale data. *Amer. J. Psychol.,* 1949, **62**, 355–368. (104)

Michotte, A. *La perception de la causalité.* Louvain: Institut Supérieur de Philosophie, 1946. (284)

Michotte, A. *The perception of causality.* New York: Basic Books, 1963. (284–285)

Miles, W. R. Psychological aspects of ageing. In E. V. Cowdry (Ed.), *Problems of ageing.* Baltimore: Williams & Wilkins, 1942. (461)

Miles, W. R. See Beck, L. H., & Miles, W. R., 1947.

Miller, D. R. The study of social relationships: Situation, identity, and social interaction. In S. Koch (Ed.), *Psychology: A study of a science,* Study II. *Empirical substructure and relations with other sciences.* Vol. V. *The process areas, the person, and some applied fields: Their place in psychology and in science.* New York: McGraw-Hill, 1963. Pp. 639–737. (591, 594)

Miller, D. R., & Swanson, G. E. *The changing American parent.* New York: Wiley, 1958. (558)

Miller, D. R., & Swanson, G. E. *Inner Con-*

flict and defense. New York: Holt, 1960. (558)

Miller, G. A. The masking of speech. *Psychol. Bull.,* 1947, **44**, 105–129. (203)

Miller, G. A. *Language and communication.* New York: McGraw-Hill, 1951a. (185–186, 188, 201, 206, 209, 211)

Miller, G. A. Speech and languauge. In S. S. Stevens (Ed.), *Handbook of experimental psychology.* New York: Wiley, 1951b. Pp. 789–810. (212)

Miller, G. A. The magical number seven plus or minus two: Some limits on our capacity for processing information. *Psychol. Rev.,* 1956, **63**, 81–97. (456)

Miller, G. A., Heise, G. A., & Lichten, W. The intelligibility of speech as a function of the context of the test materials. *J. exp. Psychol.,* 1951, **41**, 329–335. (202–203)

Miller, G. A. See Heise, G. A., & Miller, G. A., 1951.

Miller, G. A. See Licklider, J. C. R., & Miller, G. A., 1951.

Miller, G. A. See Rosenblith, W. A. Miller, G. A., Egan, J. P., Hirsh, I. J., & Thomas, G. J., 1947.

Miller, H. C. See Davis, H. V., Sears, R. R., Miller, H. C., & Brodbeck, A. J., 1948.

Miller, J. G. Discrimination without awareness. *Amer. J. Psychol.,* 1939, **52**, 562–578. (292)

Miller, J. G. *Unconsciousness.* New York: Wiley, 1942. (293)

Miller, N. E. Experimental studies of conflict. In J. McV. Hunt (Ed.), *Personality and the behavior disorders.* Vol. I. New York: Ronald, 1944. Pp. 431–465. (423)

Miller, N. E. Studies of fear as an acquirable drive: I. Fear as motivation and fear-reduction as reinforcement in the learning of new responses. *J. exp. Psychol.,* 1948, **38**, 89–101. (521–522, 531)

Miller, N. E. Liberalization of basic S-R concepts: Extensions to conflict behavior, motivation, and social learning. In S. Koch (Ed.), *Psychology: A study of a science.* Study I. *Conceptual and systematic.* Vol. II. *General systematic formulations, learning, and spe-*

cial processes. New York: McGraw-Hill, 1959. Pp. 196–292. (423, 519)

Miller, N. E., & Dollard, J. *Social learning and imitation.* New Haven, Conn.: Yale, 1941. (473, 477, 518)

Miller, N. E., Bailey, C. J., & Stevenson, J. A. F. Decreased "hunger" but increased food intake resulting from hypothalamic lesions. *Science,* 1950, **112**, 256–259. (331)

Miller, N. E. See Bower, G. H., & Miller, N. E., 1958.

Miller, N. E. See Delgado, J. M., Roberts, W. W., & Miller, N. E., 1954.

Miller, W. E. See Campbell, A., Gurin, G., & Miller, W. E., 1954.

Miller, W. E. See Campbell, A., Converse, P. E., Miller, W. E., & Stokes, D. E., 1960.

Mills, T. M. See Bales, R. F., Strodtbeck, F. L., Mills, T. M., & Roseborough, M. E., 1951.

Milne, L. J., & Milne, M. Photosensitivity in invertebrates. In J. Field, H. W. Magoun, & V. E. Hall (Eds.), *Handbooks of physiology.* Vol. 1. Washington, D.C.: American Physiological Society, 1959. Pp. 621–647. (294)

Milne, M. See Milne, L. J., & Milne, M., 1959.

Milner, R. See Olds, J., & Milner, R., 1954.

Minami, H., & Dallenbach, K. M. The effect of activity upon learning and retention in the cockroach *Periplaneta americana. Amer. J. Psychol.,* 1946, **59**, 1–58. (449)

Miner, J. B. A case of vision acquired in adult life. *Psychol. Rev., Monogr. Suppl.,* 1905, **6** (4), 102–118. (279)

Miner, J. B. See Tomkins, S. S., & Miner, J. B., 1957.

Miner, R. W. Basic odor research correlation. *Ann. N. Y. Acad. Sci.,* 1954, **58**, 13–260. (362)

Mintz, E. U. See Hecht, S., & Mintz, E. U., 1939.

Mishler, E. G. See Stephan, F. F., and Mishler, E. G., 1952.

Mitchell, M. B. The revised Stanford-Binet for university students. *J. educ. Res.,* 1943, **36**, 507–511. (547)

Mizuguchi, K. See Maruhashi, J., Mizuguchi, K., & Tasaki, I., 1952.

Moiseyeva, N. A. Interoceptive conditioned reflexes from the ileocecal region. In K. M.

Bykov (Ed.), *Voprosy fiziologii interotseptsii.* Moscow: Akad. Nauk. S. S. S. R., 1952. Pp. 405–410. (n.s.) (396)

Moltz, H. Imprinting: Empirical basis of theoretical significance. *Psychol. Bull.,* 1960, **57**, 291–314. (501)

Moltz, H. Contemporary instinct theory and the fixed action pattern. *Psychol. Rev.,* 1965, **72**, 27–47. (496–497, 502)

Moltz, H., & Rosenblum, L. A. Imprinting and associative learning: The stability of the following response in Peking ducks *(Anas platyrhynchous). J. comp. physiol. Psychol.,* 1958, **51**, 580–583. (481)

Moncrieff, R. W. *The chemical senses.* (1st ed.) New York: Wiley, 1946. (349)

Moncrieff, R. W. *The chemical senses.* (2nd ed.) London: Hill, 1951. (339, 343, 347–349, 352–353, 361)

Moncrieff, R. W. *Odour Preferences.* New York: Wiley, 1966. (362)

Monnier, M. See Talairach, J., Hecaen, H., David, M., Monnier, M., & de Ajuriaguerra, J., 1949.

Montgomery, H. C. Do our ears grow old? *Bell Lab. Rec.,* 1932, **10**, 311. (157)

Montgomery, H. C. See Steinberg, J. C., Montgomery, H. C., & Gardener, M. B., 1940.

Moore, R. Y. See McLeary, R. A., & Moore, R. Y., 1965.

Moore, J. W., & Smith, W. I. Role of knowledge of results in programmed instruction. *Psychol. Rep.,* 1964, **14**, 407–423. (476)

Moray, N. Selective listening. Doctoral dissertation, Oxford University, 1960. (n.s.) (445, 476)

Morgan, C. D., & Murray, H. Method for investigating fantasies: The thematic apperception test. *Acta Neurol. Psychiat.,* 1935, **34**, 289–306. (525)

Morgan, C. T. The hoarding instinct. *Psychol. Rev.,* 1947, **54**, 335–341. (498)

Morgan, C. T. *Introduction to psychology.* (2nd ed.) New York: McGraw-Hill, 1961. (218, 265)

Morgan, C. T. *Physiological psychology.* (3rd ed.) New York: McGraw-Hill, 1965. (46, 53, 63, 183, 307, 336, 348, 393, 401, 501, 530)

Morgan, C. T., & Stellar, E. *Physiological psychology.* New York: McGraw-Hill, 1950. (63, 308, 336)

Morgan, C. T., Stellar, E., & Johnson, O. Food deprivation and hoarding in rats. *J. comp. Psychol.,* 1943, **35**, 275–295. (497)

Morgan, C. T. See McCleary, R. A., & Morgan, C. T., 1946.

Morgan, C. T. See Stellar, E., & Morgan, C. T., 1943.

Morgan, C. T. See Chapanis, A., Garner, W. R., & Morgan, C. T., 1949.

Morgan, C. T. See Davis, H., Morgan, C. T., Hawkins, J. E., Jr., Galambos, R., & Smith, F. W., 1950.

Morgan, C. T. See Beach, F. A., Hebb, D. O., Morgan, C. T., & Nissen, H. W., 1960.

Morgane, P. J. Distinct feeding and hunger motivating systems in the lateral hypothalamus of the rat. *Science,* 1961, **133**, 887–888. (331)

Morgenstern, O. See Neumann, J. von, & Morgenstern, O., 1947.

Moruzzi, G., & Magoun, H. W. Brain stem reticular formation and activation of the EEG. *Electroencephalog. Clin. Neurophysiol.,* 1949, **1**, 455–473. (61)

Mosteller, F., & Wallace, D. L. *Inference and disputed authorship: The Federalist.* Cambridge, Mass.: Addison-Wesley, 1964. (198)

Moulton, D. G. Electrical activity in the olfactory system of rabbits with indwelling electrodes. In Y. Zotterman (Ed.), *Olfaction and taste.* New York: Macmillan, 1963. Pp. 71–84. (346)

Mountcastle, V. B. Some functional properties of the somatic afferent system. In W. A. Rosenblith (Ed.), *Sensory communication.* New York: Wiley; Cambridge, Mass.: M.I.T. Press, 1961. Pp. 403–436. (336)

Mountcastle, V. B. See Bard, P., & Mountcastle, V. B., 1947.

Mountcastle, V. B. See Rose, J. E., & Mountcastle, V. B., 1959.

Mowrer, O. H. "Maturation" vs. "learning" in the development of vestibular and optokinetic nystagmus. *J. genet. Psychol.,* 1936, **48**, 383–404. (279)

Mowrer, O. H. A stimulus-response analysis

of anxiety and its role as a reinforcing agent. *Psychol. Rev.*, 1939, **46**, 553–565. (521, 531)

Mowrer, O. H. On the utility of parrots and other birds in the study of language development: A preliminary report. *Amer. Psychol.*, 1947a, **2**, 279–280. (Abstract.) (209)

Mowrer, O. H. On the dual nature of learning: A re-interpretation of "conditioning" and "problem solving." *Harv. educ. Rev.*, 1947b, **17**, 102–148. (403)

Mowrer, O. H. Two-factor learning theory reconsidered, with special reference to secondary reinforcement and the concept of habit. *Psychol. Rev.*, 1956, **63**, 114–128. (531)

Mowrer, O. H. *Learning theory and behavior.* New York: Wiley, 1960a. (419, 428, 522, 531)

Mowrer, O. H. *Learning theory and the symbolic processes.* New York: Wiley, 1960b. (428, 522, 531)

Mowrer, O. H., & Aiken, E. G. Contiguity vs. drive-reduction in conditioned fear: Temporal variations in conditioned and unconditioned stimulus. *Amer. J. Psychol.*, 1954, **67**, 26–38. (413–414, 511)

Mowrer, O. H., & Lamoreaux, R. R. Avoidance conditioning and signal duration. *Psychol. Monogr.*, 1942, **54** (5), 1–34. (376)

Mowrer, O. H., & Lamoreaux, R. R. Fear as an intervening variable in avoidance conditioning. *J. comp. Psychol.*, 1946, **39**, 29–50. (531)

Mowrer, O. H., & Mowrer, W. M. Enuresis: A method for its study and treatment. *Amer. J. Orthopsychiat.*, 1938, **8**, 436–459. (401)

Mowrer, W. M. See Mowrer, O. H., & Mowrer, W. M., 1938.

Moyer, K. E. Effect of delay between training and extinction on the extinction of an avoidance response. *J. comp. physiol. Psychol.*, 1958, **51**, 116–118. (376)

Mueller, C. G. Visual sensitivity. In *Ann. Rev. Psychol.* Stanford, Calif.: Stanford University Press, 1961. (246)

Mueller, C. G. *Sensory psychology.* Englewood Cliffs, N.J.: Prentice-Hall, 1965. (247)

Mueller, C. G., & Lloyd, V. V. Stereoscopic acuity for various levels of illumination. *Proc. Nat. Acad. Sci.*, 1948, **34**, 223–227. (274)

Muenzinger, K. F. Motivation in learning: I.

Electric shock for correct response in the visual discrimination habit. *J. comp. Psychol.*, 1934, **17**, 267–277. (419, 422, 460)

Muenzinger, K. F., & Wood, A. Motivation in learning: IV. The function of punishment as determined by its temporal relation to the act of choice in the visual discrimination habit. *J. comp. Psychol.*, 1935, **20**, 95–106. (422)

Muenzinger, K. F., Brown, W. O., Crow, W. J., & Powloski, R. F. Motivation in learning: XI. An analysis of electric shock for correct responses into its avoidance and accelerating components. *J. exp. Psychol.*, 1952, **43**, 115–119. (422)

Mueser, G. E. See Yntema, D. B., & Mueser, G. E., 1960.

Mulder, M. Communication, structure, decision structure, and group performance. *Sociometry*, 1960, **23**, 1–14. (563, 585)

Müller, A. Dipole theory of odour. *Perf. essent. Oil Rec.*, 1936, **27**, 202. (348)

Müller, J. *Handbuch der Physiologie des Gesichtsinnes.* Leipzig, 1826. (63)

Müller, J. *Elements of physiology.* Vol. I. (W. Baly, Trans.) London: Taylor & Walton, 1838. (63)

Munn, N. L. *Handbook of psychological research on the rat; An introduction to animal psychology.* Boston: Houghton Mifflin, 1950. (342)

Munn, N. L. Learning in children. In L. Carmichael (Ed.), *Manual of child psychology.* (2nd ed.) New York: Wiley, 1954. Pp. 374–458. (484)

Munn, N. L. *The evolution and growth of behavior.* Boston: Houghton Mifflin, 1955. (294)

Munn, N. L. The evolution of mind. *Scient. Amer.*, 1957, **196**, 140–150. (467)

Munn, N. L. *Psychology: Fundamentals of human adjustment.* (4th ed.) Boston: Houghton Mifflin Co., 1961. (215, 477)

Munroe, R. *Schools of psychoanalytic thought.* New York: Dryden Press, 1955. (531)

Munsell, S. H. *Munsell book of color.* Baltimore: Munsell Color Co., 1929. (Plate 3)

Murdock, B. B., Jr. Perceptual defense and

threshold measurements. *J. Pers.,* 1954, **22,** 565–571. (292)

Murdock, B. B., Jr. Short-term retention of single paired associates. *Psychol. Rep.,* 1961a, **8,** 280. (476)

Murdock, B. B., Jr. The retention of individual items. *J. exp. Psychol.,* 1961b, **62,** 618–625. (476)

Murphy, G. See Levine, J. M., & Murphy, G., 1943.

Murray, E. Anomalies in color vision. *Sci. Mon.,* New York, 1943, **57,** 322–331. (255)

Murray, H. See Morgan, C. D., & Murray, H., 1935.

Murray, H. A. *Explorations in personality.* Fair Lawn, N.J.: Oxford University Press, 1938. (525)

Mussen, P. H. (Ed.) *Handbook of research methods in child development.* New York: Wiley, 1960. (295)

Myers, G. C. A study in incidental memory. *Arch. Psychol., N.Y.,* 1913, **4,** No. 26. (477)

Myers, J. L. Secondary reinforcement: A review of recent experimentation. *Psychol. Bull.,* 1958, **55,** 284–301. (414)

Nafe, J. P. An experimental study of the effective qualities. *Amer. J. Psychol.,* 1924, **35,** 507–544. (509)

Nafe, J. P. A quantitative theory of feeling. *J. gen. Psychol.,* 1929, **2,** 199–211. (311)

Nafe, J. P. The pressure, pain, and temperature senses. In C. Murchison (Ed.), *Handbook of general experimental psychology.* Worcester, Mass.: Clark University Press, 1934. (311)

Nafe, J. P. Dr. W. L. Jenkins on the vascular theory of warmth and cold. *Amer. J. Psychol.,* 1938, **51,** 763–769. (311)

Nafe, J. P., & Kenshalo, D. R. Somesthetic senses. *Annu. Rev. Psychol.,* 1962, **13,** 201–224. (336)

Nafe, J. P., & Wagoner, K. S. The effect of thermal stimulation upon dilation and constriction of the blood vessels of the skin of a contralateral hand. *J. Psychol.,* 1936, **2,** 461–477. (306, 311)

Nafe, J. P., & Wagoner, K. S. The insensitivity of the cornea to heat and pain derived from

high temperature. *Amer. J. Psychol.,* 1937, **49,** 631–635. (319)

Nafe, J. P., & Wagoner, K. S. The nature of pressure adaptation. *J. gen. Psychol.,* 1941, **25,** 323–351. (315)

Nafe, J. P. See Kenshalo, D. R., & Nafe, J. P., 1962.

Nagaki, J., Yamashita, S., & Sato, M. Neural response of cat to taste stimuli of varying temperatures. *Jap. J. Physiol.,* 1964, **14,** 67–89. (354)

Naumoff, H., & Sidowski, J. Variables influencing verbal conditioning. Paper read at Western Psychol. Ass., San Jose, Calif., 1959. n.s. (459)

Neff, W. D. Discriminatory capacity of different divisions of the auditory system. In M. A. B. Brazier (Ed.), *Brain and behavior.* Vol. 1. Washington, D.C.: American Institute of Biological Sciences, 1961a. Pp. 205–216. (181)

Neff, W. D. Neural mechanisms of auditory discrimination. In W. A. Rosenblith (Ed.), *Sensory communication.* Cambridge, Mass.: M.I.T. Press, 1961b. Pp. 259–278. (183)

Neff, W. D., Fisher, J. F., Diamond, I. T., & Yela, M. Role of auditory cortex in discrimination requiring localization of sound in space. *J. Neurophysiol.,* 1956, **19,** 500–512. (181)

Neff, W. D. See Diamond, I. T., & Neff, W. D., 1957.

Neff, W. D. See Goldberg, J. M., & Neff, W. D., 1961.

Neff, W. S. A critical investigation of the visual apprehension of movement. *Amer. J. Psychol.,* 1936, **48,** 1–42. (284)

Nelson, T. M. See Bartley, S. H., & Nelson, T. M., 1963.

Netter, F. H. *The Ciba collection of medical illustrations.* Vol. I. *The nervous system.* New York: Ciba Pharmaceutical Products, Inc., 1957. (50, 54, 63, 182, 339)

Neuhaus, W. Experimentelle Unterschung der Scheinbewegung. *Arch. ges. Psychol.,* 1930, **75,** 315–458. (284)

Neumann, J. von, & Morgenstern, O. *Theory of games and economic behavior.* (2nd ed.) Princeton, N. J.: Princeton University Press, 1947. (112)

Newcomb, T. M. *The acquaintance process.* New York: Holt, 1961. (572, 589–590, 593)

Newcomb, T. M., Turner, R. H., & Converse, P. E. *Social psychology: The study of human interaction.* New York: Holt, 1965. (596)

Newhall, S. M., & Heim, M. H. Memory value of absolute size in magazine advertising. *J. appl. Psychol.,* 1929, **13,** 62–75. (476)

Newhall, S. M. See Nickerson, D., & Newhall, S. M., 1943.

Newman, E. B. Forgetting of meaningful material during sleep and waking. *Amer. J. Psychol.,* 1939, **52,** 65–71. (449)

Newman, E. B., Volkmann, J., & Stevens, S. S. On the method of bisection and its relation to a loudness scale. *Amer. J. Psychol.,* 1937, **49,** 134–137. (117)

Newman, E. B. See Stevens, S. S., & Newman, E. B., 1934.

Newman, E. B. See Stevens, S. S., & Newman, E. B., 1936a.

Newman, E. B. See Stevens, S. S., & Newman, E. B., 1936b.

Newman, E. B. See Stevens, S. S., Volkmann, J., & Newman, E. B., 1937.

Nicholls, J. G. See Lippold, O. C. J., Nicholls, J. G., & Redfearn, J. W. T., 1960.

Nickerson, D., & Newhall, S. M. A psychological color solid. *J. Opt. Soc. Amer.,* 1943, **33,** 419–422. (249–251)

Nicks, D. C., & Fleishman, E. A. What do physical fitness tests measure? A review of factor analytic studies. *Educ. psychol. Measmt,* 1962, **22,** 77–95. (464)

Niemer, W. T. See Snider, R. S., & Niemer, W. T., 1961.

Nilsson, L. Drama of life before birth. *Life,* 1965, **58,** 54–72a.

Nissen, H. W. See Beach, F. A., Hebb, D. O., Morgan, C. T., & Nissen, H. W., 1960.

Noble, C. E. An analysis of meaning. *Psychol. Rev.,* 1952a, **59,** 421–430. (443, 475–476)

Noble, C. E. The role of stimulus meaning (m) in serial verbal learning. *J. exp. Psychol.,* 1952b, **43,** 437–446. (443, 475–476)

Noble, C. E. Compound trial and error learning as a function of response availability

(Nr). *J. exp. Psychol.,* 1955, **49,** 93–96. (443, 475)

Noble, C. E., & Alcock, W. T. Human delayed-reward learning with different lengths of task. *J. exp. Psychol.,* 1958, **56,** 407–412. (476)

Noble, C. E., & Noble, J. L. Human trial-and-error learning under joint variation of locus of reward and type of pacing. *J. exp. Psychol.,* 1958, **56,** 103–109. (476)

Noble, J. L. See Noble, C. E., & Noble, J. L., 1958.

Noble, M. E. See Fitts, P. M., Noble, M. E., Bahrick, H. P., & Briggs, G. E., 1959a.

Noble, M. E. See Fitts, P. M., Noble, M. E., Bahrick, H. P., & Briggs, G. E., 1959b.

Nodine, C. F. See Goss, A. E., & Nodine, C. F., 1965.

Norris, E. B., & Grant, D. A. Eyelid conditioning as affected by verbally induced inhibitory set and counter reinforcement. *Amer. J. Psychol.,* 1948, **61,** 37–49. (424–425)

Nutting, P. G. The luminous equivalent of radiation. *Bull. Bur. Stand.,* 1908, **5,** 261–308. (n.s.) (231)

Oberlin, K. W. Variation in intensive sensitivity to lifted weights. *J. exp. Psychol.,* 1936, **19,** 438–455. (326)

O'Brien, C. C. Part and whole methods in the memorization of music. *J. educ. Psychol.,* 1943, **34,** 552–560. (437)

Ochs, S. *Elements of neurophysiology.* New York: Wiley, 1965. (163)

O'Connell, D. N. See Beebe-Center, J. G., Rogers, M. S., & O'Connell, D. N., 1955.

O'Connor, N., Claridge, G. S. A "Crespi effect" in male imbeciles. *Brit. J. Psychol.,* 1958, **49,** 42–48. (412)

Odbert H. S., Karwoski, T. F., & Eckerson, A. B. Studies in synesthetic thinking: I. Musical and verbal association of color and mood. *J. gen Psychol.,* 1942, **26,** 153–173. (198)

Odbert, H. S. See Karwoski, T. F., & Odbert, H. S., 1938.

Ogden, D. P. See Cohen, J., & Ogden, D. P., 1949.

Ogle, K. N. Theory of stereoscopic vision. In S. Koch (Ed.) *Psychology: A study of a sci-*

ence. Study I. *Conceptual and systematic.* Vol. I. *Sensory, perceptual, and physiological formulations.* New York: Mc-Graw-Hill, 1959. Pp. 362–394. (295)

Ohma, S. La classification des odeurs aromatiques en sous-classes. *Arch. Neerl. Physiol.,* 1922, **6**, 567–590. (343)

O'Kieffe, M. W. See Thompson, W. R., & O'Kieffe, M. W., 1962.

Olds, J. Physiological mechanisms of reward. In M. R. Jones (Ed.), *Nebraska symposium on motivation, 1955.* Lincoln, Nebr.: University of Nebraska Press, 1955. Pp. 73–139. (519)

Olds, J. Satiation effects in self-stimulation of the brain. *J. comp. physiol. Psychol.,* 1958, **51**, 675–678. (520)

Olds, J. Hypothalamic substrates of reward. *Physiol. Rev.,* 1962, **42**, 554–604. (491)

Olds, J., & Milner, R. Positive reinforcement produced by electrical stimulation of septal area and other regions of the rat brain. *J. comp. physiol. Psychol.* 1954, **47**, 419–427. (40, 59, 519)

Oléron, P. Reconstitution de textes Français ayant subi diners taux de mutilation. *Psychol. Francaise,* 1960, **5**, 161–174. (203)

Olum, V. See Gibson, E. J., & Olum, V., 1960.

Oonk, S. See Fiedler, F. E., Meuwese, W. A. T., & Oonk, S., 1961.

Oppel, T. W. See Hardy, J. D., & Oppel, T. W., 1937.

Orbison, W. D. The relative efficiency of whole and part methods of learning paired-associates as a function of the length of list. Doctoral dissertation Yale Univer., 1944. (n.s.) (437)

Ormsby, O. S. *A practical treatise on diseases of the skin.* (3rd ed.) Philadelphia: Lea & Febiger, 1927. (299–300)

Orton, S. T. *Reading, writing, and speech problems in children.* New York: Norton, 1937. (211)

Osepian, V. A. Development of the function of the taste analyzer in the first year of life. *Pavlov J. Higher nerv. Activ.,* 1958, **8**, 766–772. (354)

Osepian, V. A. Development of the function

of the taste analyzer in puppies. *Fiziol-Z., U.S.S.R.,* 1959, **45½**, 121–216. (354)

Osgood, C. E. Meaningful similarity and interference in learning. *J. exp. Psychol.,* 1946, **36**, 277–301. (434)

Osgood, C. E. An investigation into the causes of retroactive interference. *J. exp. Psychol.,* 1948, **38**, 132–154. (477)

Osgood, C. E. The similarity paradox in human learning. *Psychol. Rev.,* 1949, **56**, 132–143. (434, 477)

Osgood, C. E. *Method and theory in experimental psychology.* Fair Lawn, N.J.: Oxford, 1953. (178, 183, 204–205, 212, 244, 246, 274, 279, 294, 336, 383, 394, 428, 477)

Osgood C. E. Comments on Professor Bousfield's paper. In C. N. Cofer (Ed.), *Verbal learning and verbal behavior.* New York: McGraw-Hill 1961. Pp. 91–106. (476)

Osgood, C. E., & Heyer, A. W. A new interpretation of figural after-effects. *Psychol. Rev,,* 1952, **59**, 98–118. (243)

Osgood, C. E., Suci, G. J., & Tannenbaum, P. H. *The measure of meaning.* Urbana, Ill.: University of Illinois Press, 1957. (196–197)

Osgood, C. E. See Stagner, R., & Osgood, C. E., 1946.

Osipova, 1926. (483) See Razran, G. H. S., 1933.

Ottoson, D. Analysis of the electrical activity of the olfactory epithelium. *Acta physiol. Scand., Suppl.* 122, 1956, **35**, 7–83. (345)

Ottoson, D. Studies on slow potential in the rabbit's olfactory bulb and nasal mucosa. *Acta physiol. Scand.,* 1959, **47**, 136–148. (345)

Palermo, D. S. See Jenkins, J. J., & Palermo, D. S., 1964.

Papez, J. W. A proposed mechanism of emotion. *Arch. Neurol. Psychiat.,* 1937 **38**, 725–743. (511)

Pareis, E. N. See Matarazzo, J. D., Saslow, G., & Pareis, E. N., 1960.

Parkinson, J. S. See Ham, L. B., & Parkinson, J. S., 1932.

Patt, M. See Hecht, S., Peskin, J. C., & Patt, M., 1938.

Patton, H. D. See Ruch, T. C., Patton, H. D., Woodbury, J. W., & Towe, A. L., 1961.

Pavlov, I. P. *Conditioned reflexes: An investigation of the physiological activity of the cerebral cortex.* London: Oxford, 1927. (40, 391, 400–401)

Pavlov, I. P. *Lectures on conditioned reflexes.* (W. H. Gantt, Trans.) New York: International, 1928a. (40, 401)

Pavlov, I. P. *Lectures on conditioned reflexes.* New York: Liveright, 1928b. (40, 401)

Pavlov, I. P. The reply of a physiologist to psychologists. *Psychol. Rev.,* 1932, **39,** 91–98. (62)

Pavlov, I. P. *Conditioned reflexes: An investigation of the physiological activity of the cerebral cortex.* (G. V. Anrep, Trans. & Ed.) New York: Dover, 1960. (401)

Pechstein, L. A. Whole vs. part methods in motor learning. *Psychol. Monogr.,* 1917, No. 99. (475)

Peel, Z. E. See Waters, R. H., & Peel, Z. E., 1935.

Penfield, W., & Jasper, H. *Epilepsy and the functional anatomy of the brain.* Boston: Little, Brown, 1954. (476)

Perin, C. T. A quantitative investigation of the delay-of-reinforcement gradient. *J. exp. Psychol.,* 1943, **32,** 37–51. (412)

Perkins, N. L. Human reactions in a maze of fixed orientation. *Comp. Psychol. Monogr.,* 1927, No. 21. (437)

Persky, H. See Basowitz, H., Persky, H., Korchin, S. J., & Grinker, R. R., 1955.

Peskin, J. C. See Hecht, S., Peskin, J. C., & Patt, M., 1938.

Petersen, M. C. See Sem-Jacobsen, C. W., Petersen, M. C., Dodge, H. W., Jr., Jacks, Q. D., & Lazarte, J. A., 1956.

Peterson, J., & Peterson, J. K. Does practice with inverted lenses make vision normal? *Psychol. Monogr.,* 1938, **50** (5), 12–37. (281)

Peterson, J. K. See Peterson, J., & Peterson, J. K., 1938.

Peterson, L. R. Immediate memory: Data and theory. In C. N. Cofer, & B. S. Musgrave (Eds.), *Verbal behavior and learning.* New York: McGraw-Hill, 1963. Pp. 336–353. (476)

Peterson, L. R., & Peterson, M. J. Short-term retention of individual verbal items. *J. exp. Psychol.,* 1959, **58,** 193–198. (447–448, 476)

Peterson, L. R., Saltzman, D., Hillner, K., & Land, V. Recency and frequency in paired-associate learning. *J. exp. Psychol.,* 1962, **63,** 396–403. (476)

Peterson, M. J. See Peterson, L. R., & Peterson, M. J., 1959.

Peterson, N. Control of behavior by presentation of an imprinted stimulus. *Science,* 1960, **132,** 1395–1396. (481)

Petrullo, L., & Bass, B. M. (Eds.) *Leadership and interpersonal behavior.* New York: Holt, 1961. (602)

Pfaffmann, C. Gustatory afferent impulses. *J. cell. comp. Physiol.,* 1941, **17,** 243–258. (355)

Pfaffmann, C. Studying the senses of taste and smell. In T. G. Andrews (Ed.), *Methods of psychology.* New York: Wiley, 1948. Pp. 268–288. (341)

Pfaffmann, C. Taste and smell. In S. S. Stevens (Ed.), *Handbook of experimental psychology.* New York: Wiley, 1951. Pp. 1143–1171. (345, 360, 362)

Pfaffmann, C. Gustatory impulses in rat, cat, and rabbit. *J. Neurophysiol.,* 1955, **18,** 429–440. (355–356)

Pfaffmann, C. Afferent code for sensory quality. *Amer. Psychol.,* 1959, **14,** 226–232. (355, 362)

Pfaffmann, C., Goff, W. R., & Bare, J. K. An olfactometer for the rat. *Science,* 1958, **128,** 1007–1008. (342)

Pfaffmann, C., Erickson, R. D., Frommer, G. P., & Halpern, B. P. Gustatory discharges in rat medulla and thalamus. In W. A. Rosenblith (Ed.), *Sensory communication,* New York: Wiley, 1961. Pp. 455–474. (358, 360)

Pfaffmann, C. See Engen, T., & Pfaffmann, C., 1960.

Pfaffmann, C. See Warren, R. P., & Pfaffmann, C., 1959.

Philbrick, E. B., & Postman, L. A further analysis of "learning without awareness." *Amer. J. Psychol.,* 1955, **68,** 417–424. (293)

Phillipot, E. See Gerebtzoff, M. A., & Phillipot, E., 1957.

Phillips, D. S. See Michaels, K. M., Phillips, D. S., Wright, R. H., & Pustek, J., 1962.

Phillips, L. W. See Postman, L., Adams, P. A., & Phillips, L. W., 1955.

Piaget, J. *Le Langage et la pensée chez l'enfant.* Neuchâtel and Paris: Belachaux et Niestle, 1924. (208)

Piaget, J. *The language and thought of the child.* New York: Harcourt, Brace & World, 1926. (290)

Piaget, J. *The child's conception of the world.* New York: Harcourt, Brace & World, 1929. (290)

Piaget, J. *The child's conception of physical causality.* New York: Harcourt, Brace & World, 1930. (290)

Piaget, J. *The construction of reality in the child.* New York: Basic Books, 1954. (290)

Piccard, A. See Piccard, J., & Piccard, A., 1908.

Piccard, J., & Piccard, A. Odoriferous phenomena produced by shock. *Arch. Sci. Phys. Math.,* 1908, **25**, 425–429. (n.s.) (347)

Pick, H. L. See Gibson, E. J., Walk, R. D., Pick, H. L., & Tighe, T. J., 1958.

Pickford, R. W. *Individual differences in colour vision.* New York: Macmillan, 1951. (254–255, 257, 294)

Pickleman, J. R. See Campbell, B. A., & Pickleman, J. R., 1961.

Pieron, H. *The sensations.* New Haven, Conn.: Yale, 1952. (294)

Pilgram, F. J. See Schutz, H. G., & Pilgram, F. J., 1957.

Pillsbury, W. B., & Meader, C. L. *The psychology of langauge.* New York: Appleton-Century-Crofts, 1928. (212)

Pillsbury, W. B., & Rausch, H. L. An extension of the Köhler-Restorff inhibition phenomenon. *Amer. J. Psychol.,* 1943, **56**, 293–298. (476)

Pintner, R., & Forlano, G. The influence of pleasantly and unpleasantly toned words on retention. *J. soc. Psychol.,* 1940, **11**, 147–149. (476)

Pirenne, M. H. *Vision and the eye.* London: Chapman & Hall, 1948. (232, 245)

Pirenne, M. H., & Marriott, F. H. C. The quantum theory of light and the psychophysiology of vision. In S. Koch (Ed.), *Psychology: A study of a science.* Study I. *Conceptual and systematic.* Vol. I. *Sensory perceptual, and physiological formulations.*

New York: McGraw-Hill, 1959. Pp. 288–361. (294)

Pitts, W. H. See Gesteland, R. C., Lettvin, J. Y., Pitts, W. H., & Rojas, A., 1963.

Pitz, G. F., & Ross, R. B. Imprinting as a function of arousal. *J. comp. physiol. Psychol.,* 1961, **54**, 602–604. (482)

Pliny. *Naturalis historia.* Venetiis Nicolaus Jenson, 1472. (3)

Pliny. *Natural History.* Vol. 8. Book 32. (W. Melmoth, Trans.) New York: Macmillan, 1915.

Poirier, P., & Charpy, A. *Traité d'anatomie humaine.* Vol. V. Paris: Mason et Cie, 1907. (n.s.) (148)

Polansky, N., Lippitt, R., & Redl, F. An investigation of behavioral contagion in groups. *Hum. Relat.,* 1950, **3**, 319–348. (598)

Pollack, I. See Licklider, J. C. R., Bindra, D., & Pollack, I., 1948.

Poltyrew, S. S., & Zeliony, G. P. Grosshirnrinde und Assoziationsfunktion. *Z. Biol.,* 1930, **90**, 157–160. (393)

Polyak, S. L. *The retina.* Chicago: University of Chicago Press, 1941. (215–216)

Polyak, S. L. *The vertebrate visual system.* Chicago: University of Chicago Press, 1957. (218, 245–246)

Pomeroy, W. B. See Kinsey, A. C., Pomeroy, W. B., & Martin, C. E., 1948.

Pomeroy, W. B. See Kinsey, A. C., Pomeroy, W. B., Martin, C. E., & Gebhard, P. H., 1953.

Porter, R. W., Brady, J. V., Conrad, D., Mason, J. W., Galambos, R., & Rioch, D. McD. Some experimental observations on gastro-intestinal lesions in behaviorally conditioned monkeys. *Psychosom. Med.,* 1958, **20**, 379–394. (514)

Porter, R. W. See Brady, J. V., Porter, R. W., Conrad, D. G., & Mason, J. W., 1958.

Porz, R. See Strughold, H., & Porz, R., 1931.

Postman, L. On the problem of perceptual defense. *Psychol. Rev.,* 1953, **60**, 298–306. (292)

Postman, L. Spread of effect as a function of time and intraserial similarity. *Amer. J. Psychol.,* 1961, **74**, 493–505. (476)

Postman, L. (Ed.) *Psychology in the making.* New York: Knopf, 1962. (62, 245)

Postman, L. Perception and learning. In S. Koch (Ed.), *Psychology: A study of a science.* Study II. *Empirical substructure and relations with other sciences.* Vol. V. *The process areas, the person, and some applied fields: Their place in psychology and in science.* New York: McGraw-Hill, 1963. Pp. 30–113. (295)

Postman, L. Short-term memory and incidental learning. In A. W. Melton (Ed.), *Categories of human learning.* New York: Academic, 1964. Pp. 145–201. (457, 476–477)

Postman, L., & Adams, P. A. Studies in incidental learning: IV. The interaction of orienting task and stimulus materials. *J. exp. Psychol.,* 1956, **51**, 329–333. (458)

Postman, L., & Egan, J. P. *Experimental psychology: An introduction.* New York: Harper & Row, 1949. (246)

Postman, L., & Jarrett, R. F. An experimental analysis of "learning without awareness." *Amer. J. Psychol.,* 1952, **65**, 244–255. (293)

Postman, L., & Tolman, E. C. Brunswick's probabilistic functionalism. In S. Koch (Ed.), *Psychology: A study of a science.* Study I. *Conceptual and systematic.* Vol. I. *Sensory, perceptual, and physiological.* New York: McGraw-Hill, 1959. Pp. 502–564. (295)

Postman, L., & Tuma, A. H. Latent learning in human subjects. *Amer. J. Psychol.,* 1954, **67**, 119–123. (458)

Postman, L., Adams, P. A., & Bohm, A. M. Studies in incidental learning: V. Recall for order and associative clustering. *J. exp. Psychol.,* 1956, **51**, 334–342. (458)

Postman, L., Adams, P. A., & Phillips, L. W. Studies in incidental learning: II. The effects of association value and of the method of testing. *J. exp. Psychol.,* 1955, **49**, 1–10. (458)

Postman, L., Bronson, W. C., & Gropper, G. L. Is there a mechanism of perceptual defense? *J. abnorm. soc. Psychol.,* 1953, **48**, 215–224. (292)

Potsman, L. See Jenkins, W. O., & Postman, L., 1949.

Postman, L. See Philbrick, E. B., & Postman, L., 1955.

Potter, R. K., Kopp, G. A., & Green, H. C. *Visible Speech.* Princeton, N.J.: Van Nostrand, 1947. (190)

Powloski, R. F. See Muenzinger, K. F., Brown, W. O., Crow, W. J., & Powloski, R. F., 1952.

Prentice, W. C. H. The systematic psychology of Wolfgang Köhler. In S. Koch (Ed.), *Psychology: A study of a science.* Study I. *Conceptual and systematic.* Vol. I. *Sensory, perceptual, and physiological formulations.* New York: McGraw-Hill, 1959. Pp. 427–555. (295)

Priest, I. G., & Brickwedde, F. G. The minimum perceptible colormetric purity as a function of dominant wave-length with sunlight as neutral standard. *J. Opt. Soc. Amer.,* 1926, **13**, 306–307. (234)

Prince, J. H. *Comparative anatomy of the eye.* Springfield, Ill.: Charles C. Thomas, 1956. (223)

Prokasy, W. F. (Ed.) *Classical conditioning: A symposium.* New York: Appleton-Century-Crofts, 1965 (401)

Prokasy, W. F., & Hall, J. F. Primary stimulus generalization. *Psychol. Rev.,* 1963, **70**, 310–322. (392, 428)

Pronko, N. H. See Snyder, F. W., & Pronko, N. H., 1952.

Prutsman, T. Magnitude of response class as a variable in verbal conditioning. Doctoral dissertation, Florida State Univer., 1961. (n.s.) (458)

Pustek, J. See Michaels, K. M., Phillips, D. S., Wright, R. H., & Pustek, J., 1962.

Pyle, W. H. Economical learning. *J. educ. Psychol.,* 1913, **4**, 148–158. (475)

Rabideau, G. F. Differences in visual acuity measurements obtained with different types of targets. *Psychol. Monogr.,* 1955, **69**, No. 10 (Whole No. 395). (243)

Ramsey, G. V. See Blake, R. R., & Ramsey, G. V., 1951.

Rand, B. (Ed.) *Classical psychologists.* Boston: Houghton Mifflin, 1912. Pp. 530–544. (63, 89)

Ranson, S. W., & Clark, S. L. *The anatomy of the nervous system, its development and function.* (10th ed.) Philadelphia: Saunders, 1959. (63)

Ranson, S. W. See Hetherington, A. W., & Ranson, S. W., 1940.

Ranson, S. W. See Barnes, W. T., Magoun, H. W., & Ranson, S. W., 1943.

Rapaport, A. See Bouliere, F., Cendron, H., & Rapaport, A., 1958.

Rapin, I. See Chase, R. A., Rapin, I., Gilden, L., Sutton, S., & Guilfoyle, G., 1961.

Rasmussen, A. T. *Outlines of neuro-anatomy.* Dubuque, Iowa: Brown, 1943. (149)

Rasquin, P. See Breder, C., & Rasquin, P., 1947.

Raush, H. L. See Pillsbury, W. B., & Raush, H. L., 1943.

Raven, B. H. See French, J. R. P., & Raven, B. H., 1959.

Rawnsley, A. I., & Harris, J. D. Studies in short duration fatigue: II. Recovery time. *J. exp. Psychol.,* 1952, 43, 138–142. (168)

Rayleigh, J. W. S. Experiments on colour. *Nature,* 1881, 25, 64–66. (254)

Razran, G. H. S. Conditioned responses: An experimental study and a theoretical analysis. *Arch. Psychol. N.Y.,* 1935, No. 191. (195)

Razran, G. H. S. Salivating and thinking in different languages. *J. Psychol.,* 1936, 1, 145–151. (195)

Razran, G. A quantitative study of meaning by a conditioned salivary technique (semantic conditioning). *Science,* 1939, 90, 89–90. (396)

Razran, G. The observable unconscious and the inferable conscious in current Soviet psychophysiology: Interoceptive conditioning, semantic conditioning, and the orienting reflex. *Psychol. Rev.,* 1961, 68, 81–147. (286, 396, 398–399)

Redfearn, J. W. T. See Lippold, O. C. J., Nicholls, J. G., & Redfearn, J. W. T., 1960.

Redl, F. See Polansky, N., Lippitt, R., & Redl, F., 1950.

Reed, H. B. Part and whole methods of learning. *J. educ. Psychol.,* 1924a, 15, 107–115. (475–476)

Reed, H. B. Repetition and association in learning. *Ped. Sem.,* 1924b, 31, 147–155. (476)

Reed, H. B. Meaning as a factor in learning. *J. educ. Psychol.,* 1938, 29, 419–430. (476)

Rees, H. J., & Israel, H. C. An investigation of the establishment and operation of mental sets. *Psychol. Monogr.,* 1935, 46, No. 210. (471)

Reid, C. See Wright, R. H., Reid, C., & Evans, H. G. V., 1956.

Reid, L. S., Lloyd, K. E., Brackett, H. R., & Hawkins, W. F. Short-term retention as a function of average storage load and average load reduction. *J. exp. Psychol.,* 1961, 62, 518–522. (447)

Reid, L. S. See Lloyd, K. E., Reid, L. S., & Feallock, J. B., 1960.

Reid, R. L. An illusion of movement complementary to the horizontal-vertical illusion. *Quart. J. exp. Psychol.,* 1954, 6, 107–111. (326)

Rein, H. Ueber die Topographie der Warmemphindung. *Z. Biol.,* 1925, 82, 513–535. (77)

Rethlingshafer, D. *Motivation as related to personality.* New York: McGraw-Hill, 1963. (530)

Rethlingshafer, D. A. See Waters, R. H., Rethlingshafer, D. A., & Caldwell, W. E., 1960.

Rettig, S. See Barlett, C. J., Hermann, E., & Rettig, S., 1960.

Reuck, A. V. S. de, & Knight J. (Eds.) *Colour vision: physiology and experimental psychology.* Boston: Little, Brown, 1965. (294)

Rey, J. See Blondel, A., & Rey, J. 1911.

Reyes, E. See Brobeck, J. R., Larsson, S., & Reyes, E., 1956.

Reynolds, B., & Adams, J. A. Motor performance as a function of click reinforcement. *J. exp. Psychol.,* 1953, 45, 315–320. (476)

Rheingold, H. L., & Hess, E. H. The chick's "preference" for some visual properties of water. *J. comp. physiol. Psychol.,* 1957, 50, 417–421. (282, 290)

Rheingold, H., Gewirtz, J. L., & Ross, H. W. Social conditioning of vocalizations in the infant. *J. comp. physiol. Psychol.,* 1959, 52, 68–73. (209)

Ricciuti, H. N. See Clark, R. A., Teevan, R., & Ricciuti, H. N., 1956.

Rich, G. J. A study of tonal attributes. *Amer. J. Psychol.,* 1919, **30**, 121–164. (164)

Richardson, M. W. Multidimensional psychophysics. *Psychol. Bull.,* 1938, **35**, 659–660. (138)

Richardson, M. W. See Kuder, G. F., & Richardson, M. W., 1937.

Richter, C. P. The internal environment and behavior: V. Internal secretions. *Amer. J. Psychiat.,* 1941, **97**, 878–893. (488)

Richter, C. P. Total self-regulatory functions in animals and human being. *Harvey Lect.,* 1942–1943, **38**, 63–103. (33, 488)

Richter, C. P., & Clisby, K. H. Graying of hair produced by ingestion of phenylthiocarbamide. *Proc. Soc. Exp. Biol. Med.,* 1941, **48**, 684–687. (361)

Riddle, O. Prolactin or progesterone as key to parental behavior: A review. *Anim. Behav.,* 1963, **11**, 419–432. (501)

Riesen, A. H. The development of visual perception in man and chimpanzee. *Science,* 1947, **106**, 107–108. (279)

Riesen, A. H. Arrested vision. *Scient. Amer.,* 1950, **183**, 16–19. (279)

Riesen, A. H. Excessive arousal effects of stimulation after early sensory deprivation. In P. Solomon, P. E. Kubzansky, P. H. Leiderman, J. H. Mendelson, R. Trumbull, & D. Wexler (Eds.), *Sensory deprivation.* Cambridge, Mass.: Harvard, 1961. Pp. 34–40. (294)

Riesz, R. R. Differential intensity sensitivity of the ear for pure tones. *Physical Rev.,* 1928, **31**, 867–875. (161)

Riggs, L. A. Continuous and reproducible records of the electrical activity of the human retina. *Proc. Sec. Exp. Biol. Med.,* 1941, **48**, 204–207. (227)

Riggs, L. A. Electroretinography in cases of night blindness. *Amer. J. Ophthalmol.,* 1954, **38**, 70–78. (227)

Riggs, L. A. Electrical phenomena in vision. In A. Hollaender (Ed.), *Radiation biology.* Vol. III. *Visible and near-visible light.* New York: McGraw-Hill, 1956. Pp. 581–619. (227)

Riggs, L. A. Light as a stimulus for vision. In C. H. Graham (Ed.), *Vision and visual perception.* New York: Wiley, 1965a. Pp. 1–38. (227, 246)

Riggs, L. A. Electrophysiology of vision. In C. H. Graham (Ed.), *Vision and visual perception.* New York: Wiley, 1965b. Pp. 81–131. (227, 246)

Riggs, L. A. Visual acuity. In C. H. Graham (Ed.), *Vision and visual perception.* New York: Wiley, 1965c. Pp. 321–349. (246–247)

Riggs, L. A. See Boynton, R. M., & Riggs, L. A., 1951.

Riggs, L. A. See Johnson, E. P., & Riggs, L. A., 1951.

Riley, D. A. Rote learning as a function of distribution of practice and the complexity of the situation. *J. exp. Psychol.,* 1952, **43**, 88–95. (475)

Rioch, D. McD. See Porter, R. W., Brady, J. V., Conrad, D., Mason, J. W., Galambos, R., & Rioch, D. McD., 1958.

Riopelle, A. J. See Meek, J. C., Graybiel, A., Beischer, D. E., & Riopelle, A. J., 1961.

Roberts, W. W. Rapid escape learning without avoidance learning motivated by hypothalamic stimulation in cats. *J. comp. physiol., Psychol.,* 1958a, **51**, 391–399. (520)

Roberts, W. W. Both rewarding and punishing effects from stimulation of posterior hypothalamus of cats with same electrode at same intensity. *J. comp. physiol. Psychol.,* 1958b, **51**, 400–407. (520)

Roberts, W. W. See Delgado, J. M., Roberts, W. W., & Miller, N. E., 1954.

Robinson, E. S. The "similarity" factor in retroaction. *Amer. J. Psychol.,* 1927, **39**, 297–312. (433, 477)

Roby, T. B. See Sheffield, F. D., & Roby, T. B., 1950.

Roby, T. B. See Sheffield, F. D., Roby, T. B., & Campbell, B. A., 1954.

Roby, T. B. See Lanzetta, J. T., and Roby, T. B., 1956.

Rock, I. See Zuckerman, C. B., & Rock, I., 1957.

Rogers, C. R. *Client-centered therapy: Its current practice, implications, and theory.* Boston: Houghton Mifflin, 1951. (594)

Rogers, J. V. See Walters, G. C., & Rogers, J. V., 1963.

Rogers, M. S. See Beebe-Center, J. G., Rogers, M. S., & Atkinson, W. H., 1955.

Rogers, M. S. See Beebe-Center, J. G., Rogers, M. S., & O'Connell, D. N., 1955.

Rohde, K. J. Theoretical and experimental analysis of leadership ability. *Psychol. Rep.,* 1958, 4, 243–278. (569)

Rojas, A. See Gesteland, R. C., Lettvin, J. Y., Pitts, W. H., & Rojas, A., 1963.

Rokeach, M. See Denny, M. R., Allard, M., Hall, E., & Rokeach, M., 1960.

Rolando, L. *Saggio sopra la vera struttura del cervello e sopra le funzioni del sistema nervoso.* Turin, 1809. (n.s.) (40)

Rosanoff, A. J. See Kent, G. H., & Rosanoff, A. J., 1910.

Rose, J. E., & Mountcastle, V. B. Touch and kinesthesis. In J. Field, H. W. Magoun, V. E. Hall (Eds.), *Neurophysiology.* Vol. I. Washington, D.C.: American Physiological Society, 1959. Pp. 387–430. (305, 336)

Roseborough, M. E. See Bales, R. F., Strodtbeck, F. L., Mills, T. M., & Roseborough, M. E., 1951.

Rosenberg, S., & Hall, R. L. The effects of different social feedback conditions upon performance in dyadic teams. *J. arbnorm. soc. Psychol.,* 1958, **57,** 271–277. (586)

Rosenblatt, J. S., Turkewitz, G., & Schneirla, T. C. Development of sucking and related behavior in neonate kittens. In E. L. Bliss (Ed.), *Roots of behavior.* New York: Harper & Row, 1962. Pp. 198–210. (495)

Rosenblith, W. A. (Ed.) *Sensory communication.* New York: Wiley; Cambridge, Mass.: M.I.T. Press, 1961. (114, 183, 246, 361)

Rosenblith, W. A., Miller, G. A., Egan, J. P., Hirsh, I. J., & Thomas, G. J. An auditory afterimage? *Science,* 1947, **106,** 333–335. (168)

Rosenblith, W. A. See Békésy, G. von, & Rosenblith, W. A., 1951.

Rosenblum, L. A. See Moltz, H., & Rosenblum, L. A., 1958.

Roseborough, M. E. See Bales, R. F., Strodtbeck, F. L., Mills, T. M., & Roseborough, M. E., 1951.

Rosenfeld, H. M., & Jackson, J. Temporal mediation of the similarity-attraction hypothesis. *J. Pers.,* 1965, **33,** 649–656. (591, 593)

Rosenthal, R. Experiment effects in behavioral research. New York: Appleton-Century-Crofts, 1966. (18)

Rosenthal, R., & Lawson, R. A longitudinal study of the effects of experimenter bias on the operant learning of laboratory rats. *J. Psychiat. Res.,* 1964, **2,** 71–72. (18)

Rosenthal, S. R. Histamine as possible chemical mediator for cutaneous pain: Dual pain response to histamine. *Proc. Soc. Exp. Biol. Med.,* 1950, **74,** 167–170. (319)

Rosenzweig, M. R. Development of research on the physiological mechanisms of auditory localization. *Psychol. Bull.,* 1961, **58,** 376–389. (170, 183)

Rosenzweig, M. R., Krech, D., & Bennett, E. L. A search for relations between brain chemistry and behavior. *Psychol. Bull.,* 1960, **57,** 476–492. (381)

Rosner, B. S. Neural factors limiting cutaneous spatiotemporal discriminations. In W. A. Rosenblith (Ed.), *Sensory communication.* New York: Wiley; Cambridge, Mass.: M.I.T. Press, 1961. Pp. 725–738. (336)

Ross, D. See Bandura, A., Ross, D., & Ross, S. A., 1963a.

Ross, D. See Bandura, A., Ross, D., & Ross, S. A., 1963b.

Ross, D. See Bandura, A., Ross, D., & Ross, S. A., 1963c.

Ross, H. V. See Buxton, C. E., & Ross, H. V., 1949.

Ross, H. W. See Rheingold, H., Gewirtz, J. L., & Ross, H. W., 1959.

Ross, R. B. See Pitz, G. F., & Ross, R. B., 1961.

Ross, R. T. A linear relationship between paired comparisons and rank order. *J. exp. Psychol.,* 1955, **50,** 352–354. (141)

Ross, S. Sucking behavior in neonate dogs. *J. abnorm. soc. Psychol.,* 1951a, **46,** 142–149. (501)

Ross, S. Effects of early weaning on sucking behavior in cocker spaniel puppies. *Anat. Rec.,* 1951b, **111,** 492. (501)

Ross, S., & Smith, W. I. The hoarding behavior of the mouse: II. The role of deprivation, satiation, and stress. *J. genet. Psychol.,* 1953, **82**, 299–307. (498)

Ross, S., Smith, W. I., & Woessner, B. L. Hoarding: An analysis of experiments and trends. *J. genet. Psychol.,* 1955, **52**, 307–326. (501)

Ross, S. A. See Bandura, A., Ross, D., & Ross, S. A., 1963a.

Ross, S. A. See Bandura, A., Ross, D., & Ross, S. A., 1963b.

Ross, S. A. See Bandura, A., Ross, D., & Ross, S. A., 1963c.

Rossman, A. Über das "Zähl"-Veringägen der Fische. *Z. Tierpsychol.,* 1959, **16**, 1–18. (471)

Rothe, C. F. Regulation of visceral function by the autonomic nervous system. In E. E. Selkurt (Ed.), *Physiology.* Boston: Little, Brown, 1963. (56–57)

Rothman, S. *Physiology and biochemistry of the skin.* Chicago: University of Chicago Press, 1954. (336)

Rothschild, G. H. See Chamberlain, T. J., Rothschild, G. H., & Gerard, R. W., 1963.

Roule, L. *Fishes: Their journeys and migrations.* New York: Norton, 1933. (493)

Rowan, W. *The riddle of migration.* Baltimore: Williams & Wilkins, 1931. (493)

Ruben, R. J., & Sekula, J. Inhibition of central auditory response. *Science,* 1960, **131**, 163. (181)

Rubin-Rabson, G. Studies in the psychology of memorizing piano music: III. A comparison of the whole and the part approach. *J. educ. Psychol.,* 1940, **31**, 460–476. (437)

Ruch, T. C., Patton, H. D., Woodbury, J. W., & Towe, A. L. *Neurophysiology.* Philadelphia: Saunders, 1961. (47, 63, 315)

Ruff, G. E., & Levy, E. Z. Psychiatric research in space medicine. *Amer. J. Psychiat.,* 1959, **115**, 793–797. (289)

Ruffini, A. *Arch. Ital. de Biol.* Vol. 21. Turin, 1894. (301)

Russell, G. V. Interrelationships within the limbic and centrencephalic systems. In D. E. Sheer (Ed.), *Electrical stimulation of the brain.* Austin, Tex.: University of Texas Press, 1961. Pp. 167–181. (61)

Russell, J. T. See Lashley, K. S., & Russell, J. T., 1934.

Rutherford, W. New theory of hearing. *J. Anat. Physiol.,* 1886, **21**, 166–168. (177)

Ryan, F. J. See Bilodeau, E. A., & Ryan, F. J., 1960.

Rytzner, C. See Engstrom, H., & Rytzner, C., 1956.

Sacia, C. F., & Beck, C. J. The power of fundamental speech sounds. *Bell Syst. tech. J.,* 1926, **5**, 393–403. (186)

Saetveit, J. G., Lewis, D., & Seashore, C. E. Revision of the Seashore Measures of Musical Talents. *Univer. Iowa Stud. Aims, Progr. Rep.,* 1940, No. 65. (n.s.) (548)

Saetveit, J. G. See Seashore, C. E., Lewis, D., & Saetveit, J. G., 1960.

Sagara, M., & Oyama, T. Experimental studies on figural aftereffects in Japan. *Psychol. Bull.,* 1957, **54**, 327–338. (295)

Saltzman, I. J. The orienting task in incidental and intentional learning. *Amer. J. Psychol.,* 1953, **66**, 593–597. (457)

Saltzman, I. J. Comparisons of incidental and intentional learning with different orienting tasks. *Amer. J. Psychol.,* 1956, **69**, 274–277. (457)

Saltzman, I. J., Kanfer, F. H., & Greenspoon, J. Delay of reward and human motor learning. *Psychol. Rep.,* 1955, **1**, 139–142. (444)

Saltzman, D. See Peterson, L. R., Saltzman, D., Hillner, K., & Land, V., 1962.

Salzen, E. A. See Sluckin, W., & Salzen, E. A., 1961.

Salzinger, K. Experimental manipulation of verbal behavior: A review. *J. gen. Psychol.,* 1959, **61**, 65–94. (477)

Sandiford, P. *Education psychology: An objective study.* New York: Longmans, 1928. (477)

Sanford, F. H. The follower's role in leadership phenomena. In G. E. Swanson, T. M. Newcomb, & E. L. Hartley (Eds.), *Readings in social psychology.* (Rev. ed.) New York: Holt, 1952. Pp. 328–340. (575)

Santayana, G. *The life of reason.* New York: Scribner, 1934. (145)

Sarbin, T. R. Role theory. In G. Lindzay (Ed.), *Handbook of social psychology.* Cambridge, Mass.: Addison-Wesley, 1954. Pp. 223–258. (567)

Saslow, G. See Matarazzo, J. D., Saslow, G., & Pareis, E. N., 1960.

Sato, M. The effect of temperature change on the response of taste receptors. In Y. Zotterman (Ed.), *Olfaction and taste.* New York: Macmillan, 1963. Pp. 151–164. (353–355)

Sato, M. See Gray, J. A. B., & Sato, M., 1953.

Sato, M. See Nagaki, J., Yamashita, S., & Sato, M., 1964.

Sauer, E. G. F. Celestial navigation by birds. *Scient. Amer.,* 1958, **199**, 42–47. (492–493)

Saul, L. J. See Davis, H., & Saul, L. J., 1931.

Saunders, D. R. See Cattell, R. B., Saunders, D. R., & Stice, G. F., 1953.

Savin, H. B. Word-frequency effect and errors in the perception of speech. *J. Acoust. Soc. Amer.,* 1963, **35**, 200–206. (202)

Sawrey, W., & Weisz, J. D. An experimental method of producing gastric ulcers. *J. comp. physiol. Psychol.,* 1956, **49**, 269–270. (514)

Schachter, J. See Karwoski, T. F., & Schachter, J., 1948.

Schachter, S. Deviation, rejection and communication. *J. abnorm. soc. Psychol.,* 1951, **46**, 190–207. (592, 601)

Schachter, S., Ellertson, N., McBride, D., & Gregory, D. An experimental study of cohesiveness and productivity. *Hum. Relat.,* 1951, 4, 229–238. (594)

Schachter, S. See Festinger, L., Schachter, S., & Back, K., 1950.

Schaeffer, J. P. *Morris' human anatomy.* (11th ed.) New York: McGraw-Hill, 1953. (147)

Schäfer, E. A. See Sherrington, C. S., 1900.

Schellenberg, P. E. A group free association test for college students. Unpublished Ph.D. thesis, Univer. of Minnesota, 1930. (194)

Schiffman, H. See Vernon, J. A., McGill, T. E., & Schiffman, H., 1958.

Schiller, C. H. (Ed.) *Instinctive behavior: The development of a modern concept.* New York: International Universities Press, 1957. (502)

Schley, O. H. *Untersuchung über Geruchsschwellen.* Berlin: Funk, 1934. (343)

Schlosberg, H. A scale for the judgment of facial expressions in terms of two dimensions. *J. exp. Psychol.,* 1941, **29**, 497–510. (126)

Schlosberg, H. The description of facial expressions in terms of two dimensions. *J. exp. Psychol.,* 1952, 44, 229–237. (126–127)

Schlosberg, H. Three dimensions of emotion. *Psychol. Rev.,* 1954a, **61**, 81–88. (508)

Schlosberg, H. *Fatigue, effort and work output.* Presidential address, Eastern Psychological Association, New York City, April 9, 1954b. (508)

Schlosberg, H. In R. S. Woodworth, & H. Schlosberg (Eds.), *Experimental psychology.* New York: Holt, 1954c. P. 505. (287)

Schlosberg, H. See Kling, J. W., & Schlosberg, H., 1961.

Schlosberg, H. See Leavitt, H. J., & Schlosberg, H., 1944.

Schlosberg, H. See Woodworth, R. S., & Schlosberg, H., 1954.

Schottelius, B. A. See Tuttle, W. W., & Schottelius, B. A., 1965.

Schmitt, F. O. (Ed.) *Macromolecular specificity and biological memory.* Cambridge, Mass.: M.I.T. Press, 1962. (383)

Schneider, D. Electrophysiological investigation of insect olfaction. In Y. Zotterman (Ed.), *Olfaction and taste.* New York: Macmillan, 1963, 85–104. (346)

Schneirla, T. C. See Rosenblatt, J. S., Turkewitz, G., & Schneirla, T. C., 1962.

Schoenfeld, W. N., & Cumming, W. W. Behavior and perception. In S. Koch (Ed.), *Psychology: A study of a science.* Study II. *Empirical substructure and relations with other sciences.* Vol. V. *The process areas, the person, and some applied fields: Their place in psychology and in science.* New York: McGraw-Hill, 1963. Pp. 213–252. (295)

Schoenfeld, W. N. See Keller, F. S., & Schoenfield, W. N., 1950.

Schopler, J. Social power. In L. Berkowitz (Ed.), *Advances in experimental social psychology.* Vol. 2. New York: Academic, 1965. Pp. 177–218. (602)

Schulz, R. W. See Underwood, B. J., & Schulz, R. W., 1960.

Schulz, R. W. See Underwood, B. J., & Schulz, R. W., 1961a.

Schulz, R. W. See Underwood, B. J., & Schulz, R. W., 1961b.

Schutz, H. G., & Pilgrim, F. J. Differential sensitivity in gustation. *J. exp. Psychol.,* 1957, **54**, 41–48. (360)

Schwarz, F. *Central Min. Geol.,* 1913, 660–665. See Moncrieff, 1951. P. 95. (347)

Scott, T. H. See Bexton, W. H., Heron, W., & Scott, T. H., 1954.

Scott, T. H. See Heron, W., Doane, B. K., & Scott, T. H., 1956.

Scott, W. A., & Wertheimer, M. *Introduction to psychological research.* New York: Wiley, 1962. Chap. 1, P. 4. (4, 25, 34)

Seagoe, M. V. Qualitative wholes: A re-evaluation of the whole-part problem. *J. educ. Psychol.,* 1936a, **27**, 537–545. (437)

Seagoe, M. V. The influence of degree of wholeness on whole-part learning. *J. exp. Psychol.,* 1936b, **19**, 763–768. (437)

Seaman, G. See Hochberg, J. E., Triebel, W., & Seaman, G., 1951.

Searle, J. L. See Hoffman, H., Toffey, S., Searle, J. L., & Kozma, F., 1966.

Sears, R. R., & Wise, G. W. Relation of cup feeding in infancy to thumb-sucking and the oral drive. *Amer. J. Orthopsychiat.,* 1950, **20**, 123–138. (501)

Sears, R. R. See Davis, H. V., Sears, R. R., Miller, H. C., & Brodbeck, A. J., 1948.

Seashore, C. E. *Psychology of music.* New York: McGraw-Hill, 1938. (547)

Seashore, C. E., Lewis, D., & Saetveit, J. G. *Seashore Measures of Musical Talents.* New York: Psychological Corporation, 1960. (n.s.) (547)

Seashore, C. E. See Saetveit, J. G., Lewis, D., & Seashore, C. E., 1940.

Seashore, R. H. Work and motor performances. In S. S. Stevens (Ed.), *Handbook of experimental psychology.* New York: Wiley, 1951. Pp. 1341–1362. (465, 477)

Seashore, S. E. *Group cohesiveness in the industrial work group.* Ann Arbor, Mich.: University of Michigan Institute for Social Research, Survey Research Center, 1954. (577)

Sechenov, I. *Selected works.* Moscow: State Publishing House, 1935. (385)

Segal, J. R. See Geschwind, N., & Segal, J. R., 1960.

Seidel, R. J. A review of sensory preconditioning. *Psychol. Bull.,* 1959, **56**, 58–73. (390)

Sekula, J. See Ruben, R. J., & Sekula, J., 1960.

Selye, H. *The physiology and pathology of exposure to stress.* Montreal: Acta, 1950. (515)

Selye, H. *Annual report on stress,* Montreal: Acta, 1951; Selye H., & Horava, A., 1952, 1953, and Selye, H., & Heuser, G., 1954, New York: 1955–1956, Medical Publishers. (531)

Selye, H. *The stress of life.* New York: McGraw-Hill, 1956. (531)

Sem-Jacobsen, C. W., & Torkildsen, A. Depth recording and electrical stimulation in the human brain. In E. R. Ramey, & D. S. O'Doherty (Eds.), *Electrical studies on the unanesthetized brain.* New York: Harper-Hoeber, 1960. Pp. 280–288. (59)

Sem-Jacobsen, C. W., Petersen, M. C., Dodge, H. W., Jr., Jacks, Q. D., & Lazarte, J. A. Electrical activity of the olfactory bulb in man. *Amer. J. med. Sci.,* 1956, **232**, 243–251. (345)

Setzfand, W. On the dependence on frequency of the vibratory sensation in man. *Z. Biol.,* 1935, **96**, 236–240. (316)

Shannon, C. E. A mathematical theory of communication. *Bell Syst. tech. J.,* 1948, **27**, 379–423, 623–656. (191, 200)

Sharp, A. A. An experimental test of Freud's doctrine of the relation of hedonic tone to memory revival. *J. exp. Psychol.,* 1938, **22**, 395–418. (476)

Shaw, E. Environmental conditions and the appearance of sexual behavior in the platyfish. In E. L. Bliss (Ed.), *Roots of behavior,* New York: Harper & Row, 1962. Pp. 123–141. (491)

Sheats, P. See Benne, K. D., & Sheats, P., 1948.

Sheatz, G. See Hearst, E., Beer, B., Sheatz, G., & Galambos, R., 1960.

Sheer, D. E. (Ed.) *Electrical stimulation of the brain.* Austin, Tex.: University of Texas Press, 1961. (40)

Sheffield, F. D. Avoidance training and the contiguity principle. *J. comp. physiol, Psychol.,* 1948, **41**, 165–177. (426)

Sheffield, F. D., & Roby, T. B. Reward value

of a non-nutritive sweet taste. *J. comp. physiol. Psychol.,* 1950, **43**, 471–481. (519)

Sheffield, F. D., Roby, T. B., & Campbell, B. A. Drive reduction versus consummatory behavior as determinants of reinforcement. *J. comp. physiol. Psychol.,* 1954, **47**, 349–354. (519)

Shepard, H. A. See Bennis, W. G., & Shepard, H. A., 1956.

Shepard, M. C. See Spielberger, C. D., Levin, S. M., & Shepard, M. C., 1962.

Sherif, C. W. See Sherif, M., & Sherif, C. W., 1953.

Sherif, M. Experiments in group conflict. *Scient. Amer.,* 1956, **195** (5), 54–58. (562)

Sherif, M. Superordinate goals in the reduction of intergroup conflict. *Amer. J. Sociol.,* 1958, **63**, 349–356. (562)

Sherif, M., & Sherif, C. W. *Groups in harmony and tension.* New York: Harper & Row, 1953. (588)

Sherrington, C. S. Cutaneous sensations. In E. A. Schäfer (Ed.), *Text-book of physiology.* Vol. II. Edinburgh: Pentland, 1900. Pp. 920–1001. (315)

Sherrington, C. S. *The integrative action of the nervous system.* London: Constable, 1906. Republished as a paperbound, New Haven, Conn.: Yale, 1961. (81, 510)

Sherwood, J. J. Self-identity and referent others. *Sociometry,* 1965, **28**, 66–81. (594)

Shibuya, T. See Tagaki, S. F., & Shibuya, T., 1959.

Shimizu, M., Yanase, T., & Higashihira, K. Relations between gustatory senses and temperature of drinks. *Kaseigaku Kenkyu,* 1959, **6**, 26–28. (n.s.) (355)

Shipley, T. E., & Veroff, J. A. A projective measure of need for affiliation. *J. exp. Psychol.,* 1952, **43**, 349–356. (527)

Shirley, M. M. *The first two years: A study of twenty-five babies.* Vol. II. *Intellectual development.* Minneapolis: University of Minnesota Press, 1933a. (207)

Shirley, M. M. *The first two years: A study of twenty-five babies.* Vol. III. *Personality manifestations.* Minneapolis: University of Minnesota Press, 1933b. (207)

Shlaer, S. The relation between visual acuity and illumination. *J. gen. Physiol.,* 1937, **21**, 165–188. (245)

Shower, E. G., & Biddulph, R. Differential pitch sensitivity of the ear. *J. Acoust. Soc. Amer.,* 1931, **3**, 275–287. (158–159)

Shurrager, P. S., & Culler, E. Conditioning in the spinal dog. *J. exp. Psychol.,* 1940, **26**, 133–159. (394)

Shurrager, P. S., & Culler, E. Conditioned extinction of a reflex in the spinal dog. *J. exp. Psychol.,* 1941, **28**, 287–303. (394)

Sidman, M. Avoidance conditioning with brief shock and no exteroceptive warning signal. *Science,* 1953a, **118**, 157–158. (375)

Sidman, M. Two temporal parameters of the maintenance of avoidance behavior by the white rat. *J. comp. physiol. Psychol.,* 1953b, **46**, 253–261. (375)

Sidman, M. *Tactics of scientific research.* New York: Basic Books, 1960. (34)

Sidman, M. See Boren, J. J., Sidman, M., & Herrnstein, R. J., 1959.

Sidman, M. See Brady, J. V., Boren, J. J., Conrad, D., & Sidman, M., 1957.

Sidowski, J. See Naumoff, H., & Sidowski, J., 1959.

Siegel, A. I. Deprivation of visual form definition in the ring dove: I. Discriminatory learning. *J. comp. physiol. Psychol.,* 1953a, **46**, 115–119. (279)

Siegel, A. I. Deprivation of visual form definition in the ring dove: II. Perceptual-motor transfer. *J. comp. physiol. Psychol.* 1953b, **46**, 249–252. (279)

Siegel, P. S. Structure effects within a memory series. *J. exp. Psychol.,* 1943, **33**, 311–316. (476)

Silverman, S. R., Harrison, C. E., & Lane, H. S. *Tolerance for pure tones and speech in normal and hard-of-hearing ears. OSRD Report 6303.* St. Louis: Central Institute for the Deaf, 1946. (n.s.) (157)

Simon, H. A. See Guetzkow, H., & Simon, H. A., 1955.

Simon, R. J. See Strodtbeck, F. L., Simon, R. J., & Hawkins, C., 1965.

Sinclair, D. C. See Feindel, W. H., Weddell, G., & Sinclair, D. C., 1948.

Sinclair, D. C. See Weddell, G. Sinclair, D. C., & Feindel, W. H., 1948.

Sivian, L. J., & White, S. D. On minimum audible sound fields. *J. Acoust. Soc. Amer.,* 1933, 4, 288–321. (157)

Sjöqvist, O. Studies on pain conduction in the trigeminal nerve. A contribution to the surgical treatment of facial pain. *Acta Psychiat. Suppl.,* 1938, **17**, 139. (319)

Skinner, B. F. *The behavior of organisms: An experimental analysis.* New York: Appleton-Century-Crofts, 1938. (386, 403, 420, 427)

Skinner, B. F. *Science and human behavior.* New York: Macmillan, 1953. (35, 37, 62, 427)

Skinner, B. F. See Holland, J. G., & Skinner, B. F., 1961.

Skolund, C. R. See Granit, R., & Skolund, C. R., 1945.

Slater, P. E. Contrasting correlates of group size. *Sociometry,* 1958, **21**, 129–139. (577)

Slivinske, A. J., & Hall, J. F. The discriminability of tones used to test stimulus-generalization. *Amer. J. Psychol.,* 1960, **73**, 581–586. (392)

Sloan, L. L., & Wollach, L. A case of unilateral deuteranopia. *J. Opt. Soc. Amer.,* 1948, **38**, 502–509. (257)

Sloan, L. L. See Mandelbaum, J., & Sloan, L. L., 1947.

Sluckin, W., & Salzen, E. A. Imprinting and perceptual learning. *Quart. J. exp. Psychol.,* 1961, **13**, 65–77. (482)

Smith, C. E. Is memory a matter of enzyme induction? *Science,* 1962, **138**, 889. (382)

Smith, E. C., Jr. See Gagné, R. M., & Smith, E. C., Jr., 1962.

Smith, F. W. See Davis, H., Morgan, C. T., Hawkins, J. E., Jr., Galambos, R., & Smith, F. W., 1950.

Smith, K. R. The problem of stimulation deafness: II. Histological changes in the cochlea as a function of tonal frequency. *J. exp. Psychol.,* 1947, **37**, 304–317. (172)

Smith, K. R., & Wever, E. G. The problem of stimulation deafness: III. The functional and histological effects of a high-frequency stimulus. *J. exp. Psychol.,* 1949, **39**, 238–241. (172)

Smith, K. U. Discriminative behavior in animals. In C. P. Stone (Ed.), *Comparative psychology* (3rd ed.) Englewood Cliffs, N.J.: Prentice-Hall, 1951. (294)

Smith, K. U. *Delayed sensory feedback and behavior.* Philadelphia: Saunders, 1962. (465–466)

Smith, K. U., & Smith, W. M. *Perception and motion: An analysis of space-structure behavior.* Philadelphia: Saunders, 1962. (281)

Smith, M. K. Measurement of the size of general English vocabulary through the elementary grades and high school. *Genet. Psychol. Monogr.,* 1941, **24**, 311–345. (207, 209)

Smith, R. L. See Lacey, J. I., Smith, R. L., & Green, A., 1955.

Smith, W. I. See Moore, J. W., & Smith, W. I., 1964.

Smith, W. I. See Ross, S., & Smith, W. I., 1953.

Smith, W. I. See Ross, S., Smith, W. I., & Woessner, B. L., 1955.

Smith, W. M., & Warter, P. J. Eye movement and stimulus movement: New photoelectric electromechanical system for recording and measuring tracking motions of the eye. *J. Opt. Soc. Amer.,* 1960, **50**, 245–250. (286)

Smith, W. M. See Smith, K. U., & Smith, W. M., 1962.

Snell, J. See Berger, J., Cohen, B. P., Snell, J. L., & Zelditch, M., 1962.

Snider, R. S., & Lee, J. C. *A stereotaxic atlas of the monkey brain.* Chicago: University of Chicago Press, 1961. (59)

Snider, R. S., & Niemer, W. T. *A stereotaxic atlas of the cat brain.* Chicago: University of Chicago Press, 1961. (59)

Snoddy, G. S. *Evidence for two opposed processes in mental growth.* Lancaster, Pa.: Science Press, 1935. (476)

Snyder, C. W. See Snyder, F. W., & Snyder, C. W., 1957.

Snyder, F. W., & Pronko, N. H. *Vision with spatial inversion.* Wichita, Kans.: University of Wichita Press, 1952. (281)

Snyder, F. W., & Snyder, C. W. Vision with spatial inversion: A follow-up study. *Psychol. Rec.,* 1957, **7**, 20–31. (281)

Solem, A. R. See Maier, N. R. F., & Solem, A. R., 1952.

Solomon, R. L. Punishment. *Amer. Psychol.,* 1964, **19**, 239–253. (428)

Solomon, R. L., & Turner, L. H. Discriminative classical conditioning in dogs paralyzed by curare can later control discriminative avoidance responses in the normal state. *Psychol. Rev.,* 1962, **69**, 202–219. (394, 428)

Solomon, R. L., & Wynne, L. C. Traumatic avoidance learning: The principles of anxiety conservation and partial irreversibility. *Psychol. Rev.,* 1954, **61**, 353–385. (423)

Solomon, R. L. See Howes, D. H., & Solomon, R. L., 1950.

Solyom, L. See Cameron, D. E., & Solyom, L., 1961.

Solyom, L. See Cameron, D. E., Solyom, L., & Beach, L., 1961.

Sontag, L. W., & Wallace, R. F. The movement responses of the human fetus to sound stimuli. *Child Develm.,* 1935, **6**, 253–258. (387)

South, E. B. Some psychological aspects of committee work. *J. appl. Psychol.,* 1927, **11**, 348–368, 437–464. (577)

Southall, J. P. C. *Introduction to physiological optics.* Fair Lawn, N.J.: Oxford, 1937. (167, 239, 246)

Spalding, D. A. Instinct, with original observations on young animals. *Macmillan's Magazine,* 1873. (481)

Spalding, D. A. Instinct, with original observations on young animals. *Brit. J. anim. Behav.,* 1954, **2**, 2–11. (Reprint of 1873.) (481)

Spence, K. W. The nature of discrimination learning in animals. *Psychol. Rev.,* 1936, **43**, 427–449. (418)

Spence, K. W. The differential response in animals to stimuli varying within a single dimension. *Psychol. Rev.,* 1937, **44**, 430–444. (418)

Spence, K. W. The nature of the response in discrimination learning. *Psychol. Rev.,* 1952, **59**, 89–93. (417)

Spence, K. W. *Behavior theory and conditioning.* New Haven, Conn.: Yale, 1956. (412, 428)

Spera, A. J. See Battig, W. F., & Spera, A. J., 1962.

Sperling, H. G. See Graham, C. H., Sperling, H. G., Hsia, Y., & Coulson, A. H., 1961.

Sperry, R. W. Effect of 180 degree rotation of the retinal field on visuomotor coordination. *J. exp. Zool.,* 1943, **92**, 263–279. (282)

Sperry, R. W. Optic nerve regeneration with return of vision in anurans. *J. Neurophysiol.,* 1944, **7**, 57–59. (282)

Sperry, R. W. Restoration of vision after crossing of optic nerves and after contralateral transplantation of eye. *J. Neurophysiol.,* 1945, **8**, 15–28. (282)

Sperry, R. W. The eye and the brain. *Scient. Amer.,* 1956, **194**, 48. (282)

Sperry, R. W. Cerebral organization and behavior. *Science,* 1961, **133**, 1749–1757. (282)

Spielberger, C. D., Levin, S. M., & Shepard, M. C. The effects of awareness and attitude toward the reinforcement on the operant conditioning of verbal behavior. *J. Person.,* 1962, **30**, 106–121. (477)

Spitzer, S. P. Consensual states and communicative behavior. *Sociometry,* 1964, **27**, 510–515. (573)

Sporn, M. B. See Dingman, W., & Sporn, M. B., 1961.

Spurzheim, G. *Phrenology or the doctrine of the human mind.* 1825. (n.s.) (63)

Spurzheim, G. *The anatomy of the human brain.* 1826. (n.s) (63)

Spurzheim, G. *Outlines of phrenology.* Boston: Marsh, Capen, & Lyon, 1832. (63)

Staats, A. W., & Staats, C. K. *Complex human behavior: A systematic extension of learning principles.* New York: Holt, 1963. (212, 428, 472)

Staats, C. K. See Staats, A. W., & Staats, C. K., 1963.

Stacey, C. L., & DeMartina, M. F. (Eds.) *Understanding human motivation.* Cleveland, Ohio: Howard Allen, 1958. (530)

Stagner, R. The redintegration of pleasant and unpleasant experiences. *Amer, J. Psychol.,* 1931, **43**, 463–468. (476)

Stagner, R., & Osgood, C. E. Impact of war on a nationalistic frame of reference: I. Changes in general approval and qualitative patterning of certain stereotypes. *J. soc. Psychol.*, 1946, 24, 187–215. (196)

Staples, R. The response of infants to colour. *J. exp. Psychol.*, 1932, 15, 119–141. (254)

Steffens, L. Experimentelle beiträge zur lehre vom ökonomischen lernen. *Z. Psychol.*, 1900, 22, 321–380. (475)

Steinberg, J. C. Application of sound measuring instruments to the study of phonetic problems. *J. Acoust. Soc. Amer.*, 1934, 6, 16–24. (191)

Steinberg, J. C., Montgomery, H. C., & Gardener, M. B. Results of the World's Fair hearing tests. *J. Acoust. Soc. Amer.*, 1940, 12, 291–301. (157)

Steinhausen, W. Ueber den experimentellen nachweis der Ablenking der Cupula terminalis in der intakten Bogengangsampulle des Labyrinths bei der thermischen und adaquaten rotatorischen Reizung. XX *Z. Hals-Nas, -u. Ohrenheilk.*, 1931, 29, 216. (n.s.) (333)

Stellar, E., & Morgan, C. T. The roles of experience and deprivation on the onset of hoarding behavior in the rat. *J. comp. physiol. Psychol.*, 1943, 36, 47–55. (497)

Stellar, E. See Morgan, C. T., & Stellar, E., 1950.

Stellar, E. See Teitelbaum, P., & Stellar, E., 1954.

Stellar, E. See Flexner, J. B., Flexner, L. B., & Stellar, E., 1963.

Stellar, E. See Morgan, C. T., Stellar, E., & Johnson, O., 1943.

Stephan, F. F., & Mishler, E. G. The distribution of participation in small groups: An exponential approximation. *Amer. sociol. Rev.*, 1952, 17, 598–608. (576)

Stephens, J. M. Further notes on punishment and reward. *J. genet. Psychol.*, 1934, 44, 464–472. (419)

Stevens, S. S. The attributes of tones. *Proc. Nat. Acad. Sci., U.S.*, 1934, 20, 457–459. (164–166)

Stevens, S. S. Mathematics, measurement and psychophysics. In S. S. Stevens (Ed.), *Handbook of experimental psychology*. New York: Wiley, 1951. (108, 111–112, 142, 246)

Stevens, S. S. On the psychophysical law. *Psychol. Rev.*, 1957, 64, 153–181. (101, 122)

Stevens, S. S. Cross-modality validation of subjective scales for loudness, vibration, and electric shock. *J. exp. Psychol.*, 1959, 57, 201–209. (105)

Stevens, S. S. In H. Gulliksen, & S. Messick (Eds.), *Psychological Scaling: Theory and applications. Reports of a conference.* New York: Wiley, 1960. (109)

Stevens, S. S. The psychophysics of sensory function. In W. A. Rosenblith (Ed.), *Sensory communication.* New York: Wiley; Cambridge, Mass.: M.I.T. Press, 1961, 1–33. (109, 114, 165)

Stevens, S. S. The surprising simplicity of sensory metrics. *Amer. Psychol.*, 1962, 17, 29–39. (106–107, 109)

Stevens, S. S. A metric for the social consensus. *Science*, 1966, 151, 530–541. (109)

Stevens, S. S., & Davis, H. *Hearing.* New York: Wiley, 1938. (152, 161, 163–164, 182)

Stevens, S. S., & Newman, E. B. The localization of pure tones. *Proc. Nat. Acad. Sci., U.S.*, 1934, 20, 593–596. (169)

Stevens, S. S., & Newman, E. B. The localization of actual sources of sound. *Amer. J. Psychol.*, 1936a, 48, 298–306. (169–171)

Stevens, S. S., & Newman, E. B. On the nature of aural harmonics. *Proc. Nat. Acad. Sci., U.S.*, 1936b, 22, 669–762. (169)

Stevens, S. S., & Stone, G. Finger span: Ratio scale, category scale, and JND scale. *J. exp. Psychol.*, 1959, 57, 91–95. (326)

Stevens, S. S., & Volkmann, J. The relation of pitch to frequency: A revised scale. *Amer. J. Psychol.*, 1940, 53, 329–353. (116, 118, 161)

Stevens, S. S., Volkmann, J., & Newman, E. B. A scale for the measurement of the psychological magnitude pitch. *J. Acoust. Soc. Amer.*, 1937, 8, 185–190. (160)

Stevens, S. S. See Boring, E. G., & Stevens, S. S., 1936.

Stevens, S. S. See Lane, H. L., Catania, A. C., & Stevens, S. S., 1961.

Stevens, S. S. See Newman, E. B., Volkmann, J., & Stevens, S. S., 1937.

Stevenson, J. A. F. See Miller, N. E., Bailey, C. J., & Stevenson, J. A. F., 1950.

Stice, G. F. See Cattell, R. B., Saunders, D. R., & Stice, G. F., 1953.

Stimpson, D. V., & Bass, B. M. Dyadic behavior of self-, interaction-, and task-oriented subjects in a test situation. *J. abnorm. soc. Psychol.*, 1964, **68**, 558–562. (575)

Stock, F. G. L. See Wyatt, S., Fraser, J. A., & Stock, F. G. L., 1929.

Stokes, D. E. See Campbell, A., Converse, P. E., Miller, W. E., & Stokes, D. E., 1960.

Stone, C. P. See Mayer, B. A., & Stone, C. P., 1931.

Stone, F. See Goetzl, F. R., & Stone, F., 1947.

Stone, G. See Stevens, S. S., & Stone, G., 1959.

Stone, G. R. See Melton, A. W., & Stone, G. R., 1942.

Stone, L. S. Functional polarization in retinal development and its reestablishment in regenerating retinae of rotated grafted eyes. *Proc. Soc. Exp. Biol. Med.*, 1944, **57**, 13–14. (282)

Straker, A. See Vernon, P. E., & Straker, A., 1943.

Stratton, G. M. Vision without inversion of the retinal image. *Psychol. Rev.*, 1897a, **4**, 341–360. (281)

Stratton, G. M. Vision without inversion of the retinal image. *Psychol. Rev.*, 1897b, **4**, 463–481. (281)

Stratton, G. M. The spatial harmony of touch and sight. *Mind.* 1899, **8**, 492–505. (281)

Stratton, G. M. Retroactive hypermnesia and other emotional effects on memory. *Psychol. Rev.*, 1919, **26**, 474–486. (476)

Strodtbeck, F. L., & Mann, R. D. Sex role differentiation in jury deliberations. *Sociometry*, 1956, **19**, 3–11. (573)

Strodtbeck, F. L., Simon, R. J., & Hawkins, C. Social status in jury deliberations. In I. D. Steiner, & M. Fishbein (Eds.), *Current studies in social psychology.* New York: Holt, 1965. Pp. 333–342. (573)

Strodtbeck, F. L. See Bales, R. F., & Strodtbeck, F. L., 1951.

Strodtbeck, F. L. See Bales, R. F., Strodtbeck, F. L., Mills, T. M., & Roseborough, M. E., 1951.

Ström, L. See Cohen, M. J., Landgren, S., Ström, L., & Zotterman, Y., 1957.

Ström, L. See Diamant, H., Funakoshi, M., Ström, L., & Zotterman, Y., 1963.

Ström, L. See Kitchell, R. L., Ström, L., & Zotterman, Y., 1959.

Strughold, H. Ueber die Dichte und Schwellen der Schmerzpunkte der Epidermis in den verschiedenen Korperregionen. *Z. Biol.*, 1924, **80**, 367–380. (320)

Strughold, H., & Karbe, M. Die Topographie des Kaltsinnes auf Cornea und Conjunctiva. *Z. Biol.*, 1925, **83**, 189–200. (310)

Strughold, H., & Porz, R. Die Dichte der Kaltpunkte auf der Haut des menschilichen Körpers. *Z. Biol.*, 1931, **91**, 563–571. (77)

Stuvier, M. Biophysics of the sense of smell. Ph.D. thesis, Rijks University, 1958. (n.s.) (344)

Suci, G. J. See Osgood, C. E., Suci, G. J., & Tannenbaum, P. H., 1957.

Supa, M., Cotzin, M., & Dallenbach, K. M. "Facial vision": The perception of obstacles by the blind. *Amer. J. Psychol.*, 1944, **57**, 133–183. (169)

Suppes, P. See Atkinson, R. C., & Suppes, P., 1958.

Sutton, S. See Chase, R. A., Rapin, I., Gilden, L., Sutton, S., & Guilfoyle, G., 1961.

Svaetichin, G. Spectral response curves from single cones. *Acta physiol. Scand.*, 1957, **39**, 17–46. (261–262)

Swanson, G. E. See Miller, D. R., & Swanson, G. E., 1958.

Swanson, G. E. See Miller, D. R., & Swanson, G. E., 1960.

Sweet, W. H. Pain. In J. Field, H. W. Magoun, & V. E. Hall (Eds.), *Neurophysiology.* Vol. I. Washington, D.C.: American Physiological Society, 1959. Pp. 459–506. (320, 336)

Sweet, W. See White, J. C., & Sweet, W., 1955.

Swets, J. A. Is there a sensory threshold? *Science*, 1961, **134**, 168–177. (108)

Swets, J. A. (Ed.) *Signal detection and recognition by human observers: Contemporary readings.* New York: Wiley, 1964. (109)

Swift, E. J. Memory of skillful movements. *Psychol. Bull.*, 1906, **3**, 185–187. (451)

Takagi, S. F., & Shibuya, T. "On"- and "off"-responses of the olfactory epithelium. *Nature,* 1959, **184**, 60. (345)

Talairach, J., Hecaen, H., David, M., Monnier, M., & de Ajuriaguerra, J. Recherches sur la coagulation thérapeutique des structures sous-corticales chez l'homme. *Rev. neurol.,* 1949, **81**, 4–24. (322)

Talairach, J. See Hecaen, H., Talairach, J., David, M., & Dell, M. B., 1949.

Talbert, E. J. See Katz, S. H., & Talbert, E. J., 1930.

Tannenbaum, P. H. See Osgood, C. E., Suci, G. J., & Tannenbaum, P. H., 1957.

Tasaki, I. Nerve impulses in individual auditory nerve fibers of the guinea pig. *J. Neurophysiol.,* 1954, **17**, 97–122. (180–181)

Tasaki, I., Davis, H., & Legouix, J. P. Space-time pattern of cochlear microphonics (guinea pig) as recorded by differential electrodes. *J. Acoust. Soc. Amer.,* 1952, **24**, 502–519. (153)

Tasaki, I. See Maruhashi, J., Mizuguchi, K., & Tasaki, I., 1952.

Taylor, D. W., & Faust, W. L. Twenty questions: Efficiency in problem solving as a function of size of group. *J. exp. Psychol.,* 1952, **44**, 360–368. (577)

Taylor, D. W. See Wright, S. T. H., & Taylor, D. W., 1949.

Taylor, F. H. See Davies, J. T., & Taylor, F. H., 1957.

Taylor, F. H. See Davies, J. T., & Taylor, F. H., 1959.

Taylor, F. W. *The principles of scientific management.* New York: Harper & Row, 1911. (463)

Taylor, J. A. The relationship of anxiety to the conditioned eyelid response. *J. exp. Psychol.,* 1951, **41**, 81–92. (399–400)

Taylor, J. A. A personality scale of manifest anxiety. *J. abnorm. soc. Psychol.,* 1953, **48**, 285–290. (399)

Teevan, R. C., & Birney, R. C. (Eds.) *Color vision.* Princeton, N.J.: Van Nostrand, 1961. (294)

Teevan, R. C. See Birney, R. C., & Teevan, R. C., 1961.

Teevan, R. See Clark, R. A., Teevan, R., & Ricciuti, H. N., 1956.

Teghtsoonian, R. See Campbell, B. A., & Teghtsoonian, R., 1958.

Teitelbaum, P. Disturbances in feeding and drinking behavior after hypothalamic lesions. In M. R. Jones (Ed.), *Nebraska symposium on motivation, 1961.* Lincoln, Nebr.: University of Nebraska Press, 1961. Pp. 39–69. (336)

Teitelbaum, P., and Epstein, A. N. The lateral hypothalamic syndrome. *Psychol. Rev.,* 1962, **69**, 74–90. (40, 330)

Teitelbaum, P., & Stellar, E. Recovery from the failure to eat produced by hypothalamic lesions. *Science,* 1954, **120**, 894–895. (330)

Teitelbaum, P. See Hoebel, B. G., & Teitelbaum, P., 1962.

Telford, C. W. The refractory phase of voluntary and associative responses. *J. exp. Psychol.,* 1931, **14**, 1–36. (476)

Ten Cate, J. Konnen die bedingten Reaktionen sich auch ausserhalb der Grosshirnrinde bilden? *Arch. Neerl. Physiol.,* 1934, **19**, 469–481. (393)

Terman, L. M. *The measurement of intelligence.* Boston: Houghton Mifflin, 1916. (534)

Terman, L. M. *Genetic studies of genius.* Vol. I. *Mental and physical traits of a thousand gifted children.* Stanford, Calif.: Stanford University Press, 1925. (206)

Teuber, H. L., Battersby, W. S., & Bender, M. B. *Visual defects after penetrating missile wounds of the brain.* Cambridge, Mass.: Harvard, 1960. (235)

Thelen, H. A. Group dynamics in instruction: principles of least group size. *Sch. Rev.,* 1949, **57**, 139–148. (569)

Thibaut, J. An experimental study of the cohesiveness of underprivileged groups. *Hum. Relat.,* 1950, **3**, 251–278. (587)

Thibaut, J. W., & Kelley, H. H. *The social psychology of groups.* New York: Wiley, 1959. (580, 601)

Thibaut, J. See Festinger, L., & Thibaut, J., 1951.

Thomas, E. J. Effects of facilitative role interdependence on group functioning. *Hum. Relat.,* 1957, **10**, 347–366. (575, 579)

Thomas, E. J., & Fink, C. F. Effects of group size. *Psychol. Bull.,* 1963, **60**, 371–384. (602)

Thomas, G. J. Equal-volume judgments of tones. *Amer. J. Psychol.,* 1949, **62**, 182–201. (163)

Thomas, G. J. Neurophysiology of learning. *Annu. Rev. Psychol.,* 1962, **13**, 71–106. (427)

Thomas, G. J. See Rosenblith, W. A., Miller, G. A., Egan, J. P., Hirsh, I. J., & Thomas, G. J., 1947.

Thompson, C. W. See Bradway, K. P., Thompson, C. W., & Cravens, R. B., 1958.

Thompson, R., & McConnell, J. V. Classical conditioning in the planarian, *Dugesia dorotocephala. J. comp. physiol. Psychol.,* 1955, **48**, 65–68. (381, 387)

Thompson, R. F. *Foundations of physiological psychology.* New York: Harper & Row, 1967. (63)

Thompson, R. F. See Briggs, G. E., Thompson, R. F., & Brogden, W. J., 1954.

Thompson, W. R., & O'Kieffe, M. W. Imprinting: Its effect on the response to stress in chicks. *Science,* 1962, **135**, 918–919. (48)

Thorndike, E. L. Animal intelligence: An experimental study of the associative processes in animals. *Psychol. Monogr.,* 1898, No. 8. (367, 427)

Thorndike, E. L. Handwriting. *Teach. Coll. Rec.,* 1910, **11**, No. 2. (141)

Thorndike, E. L. *Educational psychology.* Vol. I. *The psychology of learning.* New York: Teachers College, 1913. (456, 477)

Thorndike, E. L. *Educational psychology.* Vol. II. *The psychology of learning.* New York: Teachers College, 1925. (373)

Thorndike, E. L. Reward and punishment in animal learning. *Comp. Psychol. Monogr.,* 1932a, **8**, No. 4. (419)

Thorndike, E. L. *The fundamentals of learning.* New York: Teachers College, 1932b. (419)

Thorndike, E. L., & Lorge, I. *The teachers wordbook of 30,000 words.* New York: Columbia Univer. Press, 1944. (199)

Thorpe, W. H. *Learning and instinct in animals.* Cambridge, Mass.: Harvard, 1956. (209, 428, 496, 531)

Thorpe, W. H. *Learning and instinct in animals.* (Rev. ed.) Cambridge, Mass.: Harvard, 1962. (428, 496, 500–502, 531)

Thorpe, W. H., & Zangwill, O. L. (Eds.) *Current problems in animal behavior.* London: Cambridge, 1961. (500–502, 531)

Thumb, A., & Marbe, K. Z. *Experimentelle Untersuchungen über die psychologischen Grundlagen der sprachlichen Analogiebildung.* Leipzig: Englemann, 1901. (n.s.) (193)

Thune, L. E. The effect of different types of preliminary activities on subsequent learning of paired-associate material. *J. exp. Psychol.,* 1950, **40**, 423–438. (442)

Thurstone, L. L. Psychophysical analysis. *Amer. J. Psychol.,* 1927a, **38**, 368–389. (102)

Thurstone, L. L. A law of comparative judgment. *Psychol. Rev.,* 1927b, **34**, 273–286. (103)

Thurstone, L. L., & Chave, E. J. *The measurement of attitude: A psychophysical method and some experiments with a scale for measuring attitude toward the church.* Chicago: University of Chicago Press, 1929. (137)

Tighe, T. J. See Gibson, E. J., Walk, R. D., Pick, H. L., & Tighe, T. J., 1958.

Tilgner, D. J., & Barylko-Pikielna, N. Threshold and minimum sensitivity of the taste sense. *Acta physiol. Polon.,* 1959, **10**, 741–754. (360)

Tinbergen, N. Social releasers and the experimental method required for their study. *Wilson Bull.,* 1948, **60**, 6–51. (497)

Tinbergen, N. *The study of instinct.* Fair Lawn, N.J.: Oxford, 1951. (478, 496–497, 499, 500, 502, 528–529, 531)

Tinbergen, N. *The herring gull's world.* (Rev. ed.) New York: Basic Books, 1961. (500, 502)

Tinker, M. A. Eye movements in reading. *J. educ. Res.,* 1936, **30**, 241–277. (286–287)

Tinker, M. A. Recent studies of eye movements in reading. *Psychol. Bull.,* 1958, **55**, 215–231. (286)

Tinklepaugh, O. L. Multiple delayed reaction with chimpanzees and monkeys. *J. comp. Psychol.,* 1932, **13**, 207–243. (370)

Titchener, E. B. *Experimental psychology: A manual of laboratory practice.* I.1. Qualitative, student's manual. New York: Macmillan, 1901a. (247)

Titchener, E. B. *Experimental psychology: A manual of laboratory practice.* I.2. Qualitative, instructor's manual. New York: Macmillan, 1901b. (247)

Titchener, E. B. *Experimental psychology.* New York: Macmillan, 1902. (335)

Titchener, E. B. *Experimental psychology: A manual of laboratory practice.* II.1. Quantitative, student's manual. New York: Macmillan, 1905a. (247)

Titchener, E. B. *Experimental psychology: A manual of laboratory practice.* II.2. Quantitative, instructor's manual, New York: Macmillan, 1905b. (247)

Tizard, J. See Luria, A. R., 1961.

Toffey, S. See Hoffman, H., Toffey, S., Searle, J. L., & Kozma, F., 1966.

Tolman, E. C. *Purposive behavior in animals and men.* New York: Appleton-Century-Crofts, 1932. (518)

Tolman, E. C. Cognitive maps in rats and men. *Psychol. Rev.,* 1948, **55**, 189–208. (518)

Tolman, E. C. There is more than one kind of learning. *Psychol. Rev.,* 1949, **56**, 144–155. (518)

Tolman, E. C. A psychological model. In T. Parsons, & E. Shils (Eds.), *Toward a general theory of action.* Cambridge, Mass.: Harvard, 1951. Pp. 279–361. (518)

Tolman, E. C. A cognition motivation model. *Psychol. Rev.,* 1952, **59**, 389–400. (518)

Tolman, E. C. Principles of purposive behavior. In S. Koch (Ed.), *Psychology: A study of a science.* Study I. *Conceptual and systematic.* Vol. II. *General systematic formulations, learning, and special processes.* New York: McGraw-Hill, 1959. Pp. 92–157. (518)

Tolman, E. C., Hall, C. S., & Bretnall, E. P. A disproof of the law of effect and a substitution of the laws of emphasis, motivation, and disruption. *J. exp. Psychol.,* 1932, **15**, 601–614. (419)

Tolman, E. C. See Postman, L., & Tolman, E. C., 1958.

Toman, W. *An introduction to psychoanalytic theory of motivation.* New York: Pergamon Press, 1960. (530)

Tomkins, S. S. *The thematic apperception test: The theory and practice of interpretation.* New York: Grune & Stratton, 1948. (525)

Tomkins, S. S., & Miner, J. B. *The Tomkins-*

Horn Picture Arrangement Test. New York: Springer Publishing Co., 1957. (549–552)

Torgerson, W. S. *A theoretical and empirical investigation of multidimensional scaling.* Ph.D. Thesis, Princeton Univer., 1951. (138)

Torgerson, W. S. *Theory and methods of scaling.* New York: Wiley, 1958. (112, 142–143)

Torkildsen, A. See Sem-Jacobsen, C. W., & Torkildsen, A., 1960.

Torrance, E. P. The behavior of small groups under the stress of conditions of "survival." *Amer. sociol. Rev.,* 1954, **19**, 751–755. (569–570)

Towe, A. L. See Ruch, T. C., Patton, H. D., Woodbury, J. W., & Towe, A. L., 1961.

Townsend, J. C. *Introduction to experimental method: For psychology and the social sciences.* New York: McGraw-Hill, 1953. (34, 35, 477)

Trautscholdt, M. Experimentelle Untersuchungen über die Association der Vorstellungen. *Philos. Stud.,* 1883, **1**, 213–250. (n.s.) (193)

Travis, R. C. The effect of the length of the rest period on motor learning. *J. Psychol.,* 1937, **3**, 189–194. (475)

Triandis, H. C., Hall, E. R., and Ewen, R. B., Member heterogeneity and dyadic creativity. *Hum. Relat.,* 1965, **18**, 33–56. (569)

Triebel, W. See Hochberg, J. E., Triebel, W., & Seaman, G., 1951.

Trincker, D. E. W. The transformation of mechanical stimulus into nervous excitement by the labyrinthine receptors. In Biological receptor mechanisms. *Sympos. Soc. Exp. Biol.,* 1962, **16**. (334)

Troland, L. T. *The principles of psychophysiology.* Princeton, N.J.: Van Nostrand, 1929a. 3 Vols. (246)

Troland, L. T. The psychophysiology of auditory qualities and attributes. *J. gen. Psychol.,* 1929b, **2**, 28–58. (177)

Tuckman, B. W. Personality structure, group composition, and group functioning. *Sociometry,* 1964, **27**, 469–487. (574)

Tuckman, B. W. Developmental sequence in small groups. *Psychol. Bull.,* 1965, **63**, 384–399. (597, 602)

Tuma, A. H. See Postman, L., & Tuma, A. H., 1954.

Turkevitz, G. See Rosenblatt, J. S., Turkewitz, G., & Schneirla, T. C., 1962.

Turner, L. H. See Solomon, R. L., & Turner, L. H., 1962.

Turner, R. H. See Newcomb, T. M., Turner, R. H., & Converse, P. E., 1965.

Tuttle, W. W., & Schottelius, B. A. *Textbook of physiology.* (15th ed.) St. Louis: Mosby, 1965. (45)

Twitmyer, E. B. A study of the knee-jerk. Doctoral dissertation, Univer. of Pennsylvania, 1902. (n.s.) (386)

Twitmyer, E. B. Knee-jerks without stimulation of the patellar tendon. Report to Amer. Psychol. Ass., 1904. (See Twitmyer, E. B., 1905.) (386)

Twitmyer, E. B. Knee-jerks without stimulation of the patellar tendon. *Psychol. Bull.,* 1905, **2**, 43. (Abstract.) (386)

Tyndall, E. P. T. See Gibson, K. S., & Tyndall, E. P. T., 1923.

Ugelow, A. Motivation and the automation of training: A literature review. Aerospace Medical Research Laboratories. *Wright Air Develpm. Cen., Tech. Rep.* MRL-TDR-62-15, Dayton, Ohio, March, 1962. (476)

Ullmann, L. P. See Krasner, L., Weiss, R. L., & Ullmann, L. P., 1959.

Ulrich, J. L. The distribution of effort in learning in the white rat. *Behav. Monogr.,* 1915, **2**, No. 10. (475)

Underwood, B. J. Retroactive and proactive inhibition after 5 and 48 hours. *J. exp. Psychol.,* 1948, **38**, 29–38. (476)

Underwood, B. J. *Experimental psychology.* New York: Appleton-Century-Crofts, 1949. (96, 108, 365, 453, 477)

Underwood, B. J. Speed of learning and amount retained: A consideration of methodology. *Psychol. Bull.,* 1954, **51**, 276–282. (452)

Underwood, B. J. *Psychological research.* New York: Appleton-Century-Crofts, 1957a. (35, 383, 477, 536)

Underwood, B. J. Interference and forgetting. *Psychol. Rev.,* 1957b, **64**, 49–60. (440, 476)

Underwood, B. J. Ten years of massed prac-

tice on distributed practice. *Psychol. Rev.,* 1961, **68**, 229–247. (439)

Underwood, B. J. *Experimental psychology.* Appleton-Century-Crofts, 1966. (536)

Underwood, B. J., & Ekstrand, B. R. An analysis of some shortcomings in the interference theory of forgetting. *Psychol. Rev.,* 1966, **73**, 540–549. (96, 108, 476)

Underwood, B. J., & Schulz, R. W. *Meaningfulness and verbal learning.* Philadelphia: Lippincott, 1960. (439, 477)

Underwood, B. J., & Schulz, R. W. Studies of distributed practice: XX. Sources of interference associated with differences in learning and retention. *J. exp. Psychol.,* 1961a, **61**, 228–235. (440)

Underwood, B. J., & Schulz, R. W. Studies of distributed practice: XXI. The effect of interference from language habits. *J. exp. Psychol.,* 1961b, **62**, 571–575. (440)

Underwood, B. J. See Keppel, G., & Underwood, B. J., 1962.

Van Buskirk, W. L. An experimental study of vividness in learning and retention. *J. exp. Psychol.,* 1932, **15**, 563–573. (476)

Van Ormer, E. B. Retention after intervals of sleep and of waking. *Arch. Psychol., N.Y.,* 1932, No. 137. (476)

Vasilevskaya, N. E. Interoceptive conditioned reflexes of the second order. *Dokl. Akad. Nauk S. S. S. R.,* 1948, **61**, 161–164. (n.s.) (396)

Vasilevskaya, N. E. The formation of second-order interoceptive conditioned reflexes with exteroceptive reinforcement. *Nauch. Byull. Leningr. Gosud. Univer.,* 1950, **26**, 21–23. (n.s.) (396)

Vernon, J. A., McGill, T. E., & Schiffman, H. Visual hallucinations during perceptual isolation. *Canad. J. Psychol.,* 1958, **12**, 31–34. (289)

Vernon, J. A., McGill, T. E., Gulick, W. L., & Candland, D. K. Effect of sensory deprivation on some perceptual and motor skills. *Percept. mot. Skills,* 1959, **9**, 91–97. (289)

Vernon, J. A., McGill, T. E., Gulick, W. L., & Candland, D. K. The effect of human isolation upon some perceptual and motor skills. In P. Solomon, P. E. Kubzansky, P. H. Leiderman, J. H. Mendelson, R. Trumbull, & D. Wexler (Eds.), *Sensory deprivation.* Cambridge, Mass.: Harvard, 1961. Pp. 41–57. (289)

Vernon, P. E., & Straker, A. Distribution of colour-blind men in Great Britain. *Nature,* 1943, **152,** 690. (254)

Veroff, J. Development and validation of a projective measure of power motivation. *J. abnorm. soc. Psychol.,* 1957, **54,** 1–8. (527)

Veroff, J. A. See Shipley, T. E., & Veroff, J. A., 1952.

Verplanck, W. S. *A glossary of some terms used in the objective science of behavior.* Washington, D.C.: American Psychological Association, 1957. (35)

Volkmann, J. See Stevens, S. S., & Volkmann, J., 1940.

Volkmann, J. See Newman, E. B., Volkmann, J., & Stevens, S. S., 1937.

Volkmann, J. See Stevens, S. S., Volkmann, J., & Newman, E. B., 1937.

Volkova, V. D. On certain characteristics of the formation of conditioned reflexes to speech stimuli in children. *Fiziol. Z. S.S.S.R.,* 1953, **39,** 540–548. (396)

Volta, A. On the electricity excited by the mere contact of conducting surfaces of different kinds. *Phil. Trans.,* 1800, **90,** 403–431. (40)

Volta, A. *Collezione dell' opere del cavaliere Conte Allesandro Volta.* Florence: G. Piatti, 1816. 3 Vols. (n.s.) (40)

Von Frey, M. Beitrage zur Physiologie des Schmerzsinns. *Abh. Sachs. ges. Wiss. Leipzig Math-Phys. Cl.,* 1894, 185–196, 283–296. (313)

Von Frey, M. Untersuchungen über die Sinnesfunctionen der menschlichen Haut: Druckempfindungen und Schmerz. *Abh. Sachs. Ges. Wiss. Math-Phys. Cl.,* 1896, **23,** 175–266. (310, 319)

Von Frey, M. Über die zur eben merklichen Erregung des Drucksinns erforderlichen Energiemengen. *Z. Biol.,* 1919, **70,** 333–347. (312)

Von Frey, M., & Goldman, A. Der zeitliche Verlauf der Einstellung bei den Druckempfindungen. *Z. Biol.,* 1914, **65,** 183–202. (314)

Von Frey, M., & Kiesow, F. Ueber die Func-

tion der Tastkörperchen. *Z. Psychol.,* 1899, **20,** 126–163. (312)

Von Frisch, K. *Bees: Their vision, chemical senses, and language.* Ithaca, N.Y.: Cornell, 1950. (158, 209)

Von Holst, E., & von St. Paul, U. Electrically controlled behavior. *Scient. Amer.,* 1962, **206,** 50–59. (498)

Von Holst, E., & von St. Paul, U. On the functional organizations of drives. *Anim. Behav.,* 1963, **11,** 1–20. (499)

Von Restorff, H. Über die wirkung von Bereichsbildungen im Spurenfeld: Analyse von Vorängen im Spurenfeld. *Psychol. Forsch.,* 1933, **18,** 229–342. (443)

Von St. Paul, U. See von Holst, E., von St. Paul, U., 1962.

Von St. Paul, U. See von Holst, E., & von St. Paul, U., 1963.

Von Senden, M. *Raum- und Gestaltauffassung bei operierten Blindgeborenen vor und nach der Operation.* Leipzig: Barth, 1932. (n.s.) (278)

Waddell, D. See Beebe-Center, J. G., & Waddell, D., 1948.

Waetzmann, E., & Keibs, L. Hörschwellenbestimmungen mit dem Thermophon und Messungen am Trommelfell. *Ann. Physik.,* 1936a, **26,** 141–144. (n.s.) (157)

Waetzmann, E., & Keibs, L. Theoretischer und experimenteller Vergleich von Hörschwellenmessungen. *Akust. Z.,* 1936b, **1,** 3–12, (n.s.) (157)

Wagner, R. V. Stability of working relationships. Unpublished doctoral dissertation, Univer. of Michigan, 1963. (591, 595)

Wagoner, K. S. See Nafe, J. P., & Wagoner, K. S., 1936.

Wagoner, K. S. See Nafe, J. P., & Wagoner, K. S., 1937.

Wagoner, K. S. See Nafe, J. P., & Wagoner, K. S., 1941.

Wald, G. Carotenoids and the visual cycle. *J. gen. Physiol.,* 1936, **19,** 351–371. (219)

Wald, G. The photoreceptor process in vision. In J. Field, H. W. Magoun, & V. E. Hall (Eds.), *Handbook of neurophysiology,* Vol. I. Washington, D.C.: American Physiological Society, 1949. Pp. 671–692. (220)

Wald, G., & Clark, A. Visual adaptation and chemistry of the rods. *J. gen. Physiol.,* 1937, **21,** 93–105. (239)

Walk, R. D. See Gibson, E. J., & Walk, R. D., 1956.

Walk, R. D. See Gibson, E. J., & Walk, R. D., 1960.

Walk, R. D. See Gibson, E. J., Walk, R. D., Pick, H. L., & Tighe, T. J., 1958.

Walker, E. L., & Atkinson, J. W. The expression of fear-related motivation in thematic apperception as a function of proximity to an atomic explosion. In J. W. Atkinson (Ed.), *Motives in fantasy, action and society.* Princeton, N.J.: Van Nostrand, 1958. Pp. 143–159. (527)

Walker, W. Über die Adaptionsvorgange der Jugendliehen und ihre Beziehung zu den transformationserscheinungen. *Z. Psychol.,* 1927, **103,** 323–383. (290)

Wall, P. D. Two transmission systems for skin sensation. In W. A. Rosenblith (Ed.), *Sensory communication.* New York: Wiley; Cambridge, Mass.: M.I.T. Press, 1961, 475–496. (307, 309, 336)

Wall, P. D. See Melzack, R., & Wall, P. D., 1965.

Wallace, D. L. See Mosteller, F., & Wallace, D. L., 1964.

Wallace, R. F. See Sontag, L. W., & Wallace, R. F., 1935.

Wallach, H. See Köhler, W., & Wallach, H., 1944.

Walls, G. L. *The vertebrate eye.* Bloomfield Hills, Mich.: Cranbrook Press, 1942. (245)

Walls, G. L. "Land! Land!" *Psychol. Bull.,* 1960, **57,** 29–48. (263)

Walsh, E. G. Perception of linear motion following unilateral labyrinthectomy: Variations of threshold, according to orientation of the head. *J. Physiol.,* 1960, **153,** 350–357. (335)

Walter, A. A. See Carmichael, L., Hogan, H. P., & Walter, A. A., 1932.

Walters, G. C., & Rogers, J. V. Aversive stimulation of the rat: Long term effects on subsequent behavior. *Science,* 1963, **142,** 70–71. (422)

Walters, R. H. See Bandura, A., & Walters, R. H., 1963.

Wapner, S. See Witkin, H. A., Lewis, H. B., Hertzman, M., Machover, K., Meissner, P. B., & Wapner, S., 1954.

Ward, L. B. Reminiscence and rote learning. *Psychol. Monogr.,* 1937, No. 220. (442, 475)

Warren, R. P., & Pfaffmann, C. Early experience and taste aversion. *J. comp. physiol. Psychol.,* 1959, **52,** 263–266. (354)

Warter, P. J. See Smith, W. M., & Warter, P. J., 1960.

Washburn, A. L. See Cannon, W. B., & Washburn, A. L., 1912.

Waters, R. H., & Peel, Z. E. Similarity in the form of original and interpolated learning and retroactive inhibition. *Amer. J. Psychol.,* 1935, **47,** 477–481. (476)

Waters, R. H., Rethlingshafer, D. A., & Caldwell, W. E. (Eds.) *Principles of comparative psychology.* New York: McGraw-Hill, 1960. (294, 427)

Watson, J. B. The place of the conditioned-reflex in psychology. *Psychol. Rev.,* 1916, **23,** 89–116. (385)

Watson, J. B. *Behaviorism.* New York: Norton, 1925. (386)

Watson, J. D., & Crick, F. H. C. Genetical implications of the structure of deoxyribonucleic acid. *Nature,* 1953, **171,** 964–967. (381)

Weale, R. A. *The eye and its function.* London: Hatton Press, 1960. (294)

Webb, W. B. "A motivational theory of emotions . . ." *Psychol. Rev.,* 1948, **55,** 329–335. (516)

Weber, E. H. Tastsinn und Gemeingefühl. *Handwörterbuch Physiol. Wagner,* 1846, **3** (2), 481–588. (n.s.) (76, 86)

Weber, E. H. *Arch. Anat. Physiol.,* 1847. (n.s.) (353)

Weddell, G. The pattern of cutaneous innervation in relation to cutaneous sensibility. *J. Anat.,* 1941a, **75,** 346–367. (75)

Weddell, G. The multiple innervation of sensory spots in the skin. *J. Anat., London,* 1941b, **75,** 441–446. (322)

Weddell, G. The anatomy of cutaneous sensibility. *Brit. med. Bull.,* 1945, **3,** 167–172. (301)

Weddell, G. The anatomy of pain sensibility. *J. Anat., London*, 1947, **81**, 374. (75)

Weddell, G., Sinclair, D. C., & Feindel, W. H. An anatomical basis for alterations in quality of pain sensibility. *J. Neurophysiol.*, 1948, **11**, 99–109. (323)

Weddell, G. See Lele, P. P., & Weddell, G., 1956.

Weddell, G. See Feindel, W. H., Weddell, G., & Sinclair, D. C., 1948.

Wegel, R. L. Physical data and physiology of excitation of the auditory nerve. *Ann. Otol., Rhinol., Laryngol.*, 1932, **41**, 740–779. (157, 163)

Wegel, R. L., & Lane, C. E. The auditory masking of one pure tone by another and its probable relation to the dynamics of the inner ear. *Physiol. Rev.*, 1924, **23**, 266–285. (166–167)

Weiss, R. L. See Krasner, L., Weiss, R. L., & Ullmann, L. P., 1959.

Weisz, J. D. See Sawrey, W., & Weisz, J. D., 1956.

Weitz, J. Vibratory sensitivity as affected by local anesthesia. *J. exp. Psychol.*, 1939, **25**, 48–64. (316)

Welborn, E. L. See English, H. B., Welborn, E. L., & Killian, C. D., 1934.

Welty, J. C. Experiments in group behavior of fishes. *Physiol. Zool.*, 1934, **7**, 85–128. (473)

Wenger, M. A., Jones, F. N., & Jones, M. H. *Physiological psychology*. New York: Holt, 1956. (38, 43, 52, 63, 80, 247, 294, 325, 336, 343, 365)

Wenzel, B. M. Problems of odor research from the view point of a psychologist. *Ann. N.Y. Acad. Sci.*, 1954, **58**, 58–61. (342)

Werner, H., & Kaplan, E. Development of word meaning through verbal context: An experimental study. *J. Psychol.*, 1950, **29**, 251–257. (208)

Werner, H. See Zeitz, K., & Werner, H., 1927.

Wertheimer, Max. Experimentelle Studien über das Sehen von Bewegung. *Z. Psychol.*, 1912, **61**, 161–265. (275, 283–284)

Wertheimer, Max. Untersuchungen zur Lehre von der Gestalt: II. *Psychol. Forsch.*, 1923, 4, 301–350. (275–276)

Wertheimer, Max. Principles of perceptual organization (Michael Wertheimer, Trans.) In D. C. Beardslee, & Michael Wertheimer (Eds.), *Readings in perception*. Princeton, N.J.: Van Nostrand, 1958. (275–278)

Wertheimer, Michael. See Beardslee, D. C., & Wertheimer, Michael, 1958.

Wertheimer, Michael. See Scott, W. A., & Wertheimer, Michael, 1962.

Wesley, F. The number concept: A phylogenetic review. *Psychol. Bull.*, 1961, **58**, 420–428. (470–471)

Wever, E. G. The upper limit of hearing in the cat. *J. comp. Psychol.*, 1930, **10**, 221–234. (157)

Wever, E. G. *Theory of hearing*. New York: Wiley, 1949. (151, 172, 177, 182–183)

Wever, E. G., & Bray, C. W. Auditory nerve impulses. *Science*, 1930a, **71**, 215. (151, 157, 177)

Wever, E. G., & Bray, C. W. Present possibilities for auditory theory. *Psychol. Rev.*, 1930b, **37**, 365–380. (151, 177)

Wever, E. G., & Bray, C. W. The perception of low tones and the resonance-volley theory. *J. Psychol.*, 1937, **3**, 101–114. (156, 177)

Wever, E. G., & Lawrence, M. *Physiological acoustics*. Princeton, N.J.: Princeton University Press, 1954. (183)

Wever, E. G., Bray, C. W., & Willey, C. F. The response of the cochlea to tones of low frequency. *J. exp. Psychol.*, 1937, **20**, 336–349. (152)

Wever, E. G. See Smith, K. R., & Wever, E. G., 1949.

Whalen, R. E. Sexual motivation. *Psychol. Rev.*, 1966, **73**, 151–164. (489)

White, J. C., & Sweet, W. H. *Pain: Its mechanisms and neurosurgical control*. Springfield, Ill.: Charles C Thomas, 1955. (336)

White, R. K. See Lippitt, R., & White, R. K., 1947.

White, S. D. See Sivian, L. J., & White, S. D., 1933.

White, S. H. Generalization of an instrumental response with variation in two attributes of the CS. *J. exp. Psychol.*, 1958, **56**, 339–343. (414)

Wiener, F. M. See Egan, J. P., & Wiener, F. M., 1946.

Wiener, M. Word frequency or motivation in perceptual defense. *J. abnorm. soc. Psychol.,* 1955, **51**, 214–218. (292)

Wilkins, L. T. Incentives and the young male worker in England. With some notes on ranking methodology. *Int. J. Opin. Attitude Res.,* 1950, 4, 541–562. (141)

Willey, C. F. See Wever, E. G., Bray, C. W., & Willey, C. F., 1937.

Williams, O. A study of the phenomenon of reminiscence. *J. exp. Psychol.,* 1926, **9**, 368–387. (441)

Williams, R. E. See Hecht, S., & Williams, R. E., 1922.

Williams, R. G. See Bazett, H. C., McGlone, B., Williams, R. G., & Lufkin, H. M., 1932.

Willis, F. N. Initial speaking distance as a function of the speakers' relationship. *Psychonom. Sci.,* 1966, **5**, 221–222. (573)

Winch, R. F. *Mate-selection: A study of complementary needs.* New York: Harper & Row, 1958. (590)

Winch, W. H. Should poems be learned by school children as "wholes" or in "parts"? *Brit. J. Psychol.,* 1924, **15**, 64–80. (475)

Windle, W. F. *Regeneration in the central nervous system.* Springfield, Ill.: Charles C Thomas, 1955. (43)

Winnick, W. A., & Hunt, J. McV. The effect of an extra stimulus upon strength of response during acquisition and extinction. *J. exp. Psychol.,* 1951, **41**, 205–215. (391)

Wischner, G. J. The effect of punishment on discrimination learning in a non-correction situation. *J. exp. Psychol.,* 1947, **37**, 271–284. (422)

Wise, G. W. See Sears, R. R., & Wise, G. W., 1950.

Witheridge, W. N. See McCord, C. P., & Witheridge, W. N., 1949.

Withey, S., Buxton, C. E., & Elkin, A. Control of rest interval activities in experiments on reminiscence in serial verbal learning. *J. exp. Psychol.,* 1949, **39**, 173–176. (476)

Witkin, H. A., Lewis, H. B., Hertzman, M., Machover, K., Meissner, P. B., & Wapner, S. *Personality through perception: An experimental and clinical study.* New York: Harper & Row, 1954. (290)

Wodinsky, J. See Bitterman, M. E., & Wodinsky, J., 1953.

Woessner, B. L. See Ross, S., Smith, W. I., & Woessner, B. L., 1955.

Wohlwill, J. F. Developmental studies of perception. *Psychol. Bull.,* 1960, **57**, 249–288. (290, 294–295)

Wolf, E. See Crozier, W. J., & Wolf, E., 1941.

Wolf, S. See Wolff, H. G., & Wolf S., 1958.

Wolfe, J. B., & Kaplon, M. D. Effect of amount of reward and consummative activity on learning in chickens. *J. comp. physiol. Psychol.,* 1941, **31**, 353–361. (412)

Wolff, H. G., & Wolf, S. Pain. (2nd ed.) Springfield, Ill.: Charles C Thomas, 1958. (321)

Wolff, H. G. See Hardy, J. D., Wolff, H. G., & Goodell, H., 1940.

Wolff, H. G. See Hardy, J. D., Wolff, H. G., & Goodell, H., 1947.

Wolfle, H. M. Conditioning as a function of the interval between the conditioned and the original stimulus. *J. gen. Psychol.,* 1932, **7**, 80–103. (389–390)

Wollach, L. See Sloan, L. L., & Wollach, L., 1948.

Wolpert, E. A. See Dement, W., & Wolpert, E. A., 1958.

Wood, A. See Muenzinger, K. F., & Wood, A., 1935.

Wood, A. G. A quantitative account of the course of auditory fatigue. Unpublished master's thesis, Univer. of Virginia, 1930. (n.s.) (168)

Woodbury, J. W. See Ruch, T. C., Patten, H. D., Woodbury, J. W., & Towe, A. L., 1961.

Woodrow, H., & Karpman, B. A new olfactometric technique and some results. *J. exp. Psychol.,* 1917, **2**, 431–437. (344)

Woodworth, R. S. *Dynamic psychology.* New York: Columbia, 1918. (335)

Woodworth, R. S. *Experimental psychology.* New York: Holt, 1938. (335, 401, 427)

Woodworth, R. S. *Psychology.* (4th ed.) New York: Holt, 1940. (351)

Woodworth, R. S., & Schlosberg, H. *Experimental psychology.* (Rev. ed.) New York: Holt, 1954. (96, 108, 115, 142–143, 195, 243, 247, 274, 284, 294–295, 305, 313, 335, 379, 383, 431, 441, 450, 453, 461, 477, 506, 530)

Woodworth, R. S. See Ladd, G., & Woodworth, R. S., 1911.

Woolsey, C. N. Organization of cortical auditory system. In W. A. Rosenblith (Ed.), *Sensory communication.* New York: Wiley; Cambridge, Mass.: M.I.T. Press, 1961. Pp. 235–258. (183)

Wooster, M. Certain factors in the development of a new spatial co-ordination. *Psychol. Monogr.,* 1923, **32**, No. 4 (Whole No. 146). (281)

Worcester, D. A. Retention after long periods. *J. educ. Psychol.,* 1923, **14**, 113–114. (451)

Wright, R. H., Reid, C., & Evans, H. G. V. Odour and molecular vibration: III. A new theory of olfactory stimulation. *Chem. Industr. (London),* 1956, 973–977. (349)

Wright, R. H. See Michaels, K. M., Phillips, D. S., Wright, R. H., & Pustek, J., 1962.

Wright, S. T. H., & Taylor, D. W. Distributed practice in verbal learning and the maturation hypothesis. *J. exp. Psychol.,* 1949, **39**, 527–531. (475)

Wright, W. D. A re-determination of the trichromatic coefficients of the spectral colours. *Trans. Opt. Soc. London,* 1928–1929, **30**, 141–164. (252)

Wright, W. D. *Researches on normal and defective colour vision.* London: Kimpton, 1946. (250)

Wright, W. D. *The measurement of colour.* New York: Macmillan, 1958. (294)

Wrightson, T., & Keith, A. An enquiry into the analytical mechanism of the internal ear, 1918. (177)

Wurster, C. R. See Bass, B. M., & Wurster, C. R., 1953.

Wyatt, R. F. Improvability of pitch discrimination. *Psychol. Monogr.,* 1945, **58**, No. 2. (463)

Wyatt, S., Fraser, J. A., & Stock, F. G. L. The effects of monotony in work. *Industr. Fat. Res. Bd. Rep.,* 1929, No. 56. (n.s.) (475)

Wylie, G. E. Whole vs. part methods of learning as dependent upon practice. Doctoral dissertation, Univer. of Chicago, 1928. (n.s.) (437)

Wynne, L. C. See Solomon, R. L., & Wynne, L. C., 1954.

Yamashita, S. See Nagaki, J., Yamashita, S., & Sato, M., 1964.

Yanase, T. See Shimizu, M., Yanase, T., & Higashihira, K., 1959.

Yarrow, L. J. The relationship between nutritive sucking experiences in infancy and non-nutritive sucking in childhood. *J. genet. Psychol.,* 1954, **84**, 149–162. (501)

Yavuz, H. S., & Bousfield, W. A. Recall of connotative meaning. *Psychol. Rep.,* 1959, **5**, 319–320. (476)

Yela, M. See Neff, W. D., Fisher, J. F., Diamond, I. T., & Yela, M., 1956.

Yntema, D. B., & Mueser, G. E. Remembering the present states of a number of variables. *J. exp. Psychol.,* 1960, **60**, 18–22. (446, 476)

Young, P. T. *Motivation of behavior: The fundamental determinants of human and animal activity.* New York: Wiley, 1936. (530)

Young, P. T. *Emotion in man and animal.* New York: Wiley, 1943. (516, 530)

Young, P. T. Motivation, feeling and emotion. In T. G. Andrews (Ed.), *Methods of psychology.* New York: Wiley, 1948. Pp. 348–390. (530)

Young, P. T. Emotion as disorganized response: A reply to Professor Leeper. *Psychol. Rev.,* 1949, **56**, 184–191. (516)

Young, P. T. Isohedonic contour maps. *Psychol. Rep.,* 1960, **7**, 478. (360)

Young, P. T. *Motivation and emotion: A survey of the determinants of human and animal activity.* New York: Wiley, 1961. (490, 516, 530)

Young, T. On the theory of light and colours. In *Lectures in natural philosophy.* Vol. 2. London: Printed for Joseph Johnson, St. Paul's Church Yard, by William Savage, 1807. Pp. 613–632. (248, 260)

Young, W. C. (Ed.) *Sex and internal secretions.* (3rd ed.) Baltimore: Williams & Wilkins, 1961. (501)

Your eyes do deceive you. *Life,* Jan. 16, 1950. Pp. 57–62. (269)

Zamakhover, Sh. M. See Dolin, A. D., Zborovskaya, I. I., & Zamakhover, Sh. M., 1958.

Zander, A. See Cartwright, D., & Zander, A., 1960.

Zangwill, O. L. *Cerebral dominance and its relation to physiological functions.* Edinburgh: Published for the William Ramsay Henderson Trust by Oliver & Boyd, 1960. (212)

Zangwill, O. L. See Thorpe, W. H., & Zangwill, O. L., 1961.

Zborovskaya, I. I. See Dolin, A. O., Zborovskaya, I. I., & Zamakhover, Sh. M., 1958.

Zeaman, D. Response latency as a function of the amount of reinforcement. *J. exp. Psychol.,* 1949, **39,** 466–483. (411)

Zeigarnik, B. Über das Behalten von erledigten und unerledigten Handlungen. *Psychol. Forsch.,* 1927, **9,** 1–85. (450)

Zeitz, K., & Werner, H. Über die dynamische Struktur der Bewegung. *Z. Psychol.,* 1927, **105,** 226–248. (284)

Zelditch, M. See Berger, J., Cohen, B. P., Snell, J. L., & Zelditch, M., 1962.

Zeliony, G. P. Effets de l'ablation des hemispheres cerebraux. *Rev. Med., Paris,* 1929, **46,** 191–214. (n.s.) (393)

Zeliony, G. P. See Poltyrew, S. S., & Zeliony, G. P., 1930.

Zeller, A. F. An experimental analogue of repression: II. The effect of individual failure and success on memory measured by relearning. *J. exp. Psychol.,* 1950, **40,** 411–422. (450)

Zelman, A., Kabat, L., Jacobson, R., & McConnell, J. V. Transfer of training through injection of "conditioned" RNA into untrained planarians. *Worm Runners Dig.,* 1963, **5,** 14–21. (382)

Zigler, M. J. Pressure adaptation time: A function of intensity and extensity. *Amer. J. Psychol.,* 1932, 44, 709–720. (314)

Zimmermann, R. R. See Harlow, H. F., & Zimmermann, R. R., 1959.

Zimney, G. H. *Method in experimental psychology.* New York: Ronald, 1961. (34)

Zipf, G. K. *The psycho-biology of language.* Boston: Houghton Mifflin, 1935. (199)

Zipf, G. K. The meaning-frequency relationship of words. *J. gen. Psychol.,* 1945, **33,** 251–256. (199–200)

Zipf, G. K. *Human behavior and the principle of least effort.* Cambridge, Mass.: Addison-Wesley, 1949. (199–200)

Zotterman, Y. Touch, pain and tickling: An electrophysiological investigation on cutaneous sensory nerves. *J. Physiol.,* 1939, **95,** 1–28. (320)

Zotterman, Y. Special senses: Thermal receptors. *Annu. Rev. Physiol.,* 1953, **15,** 357–372. (306, 336)

Zotterman, Y. Thermal sensation. In J. Field, H. W. Magoun, & V. E. Hall (Eds.), *Handbook of Physiology.* Vol. I. Washington, D.C.: American Physiological Society, 1959. (306, 311, 336)

Zotterman, Y. Studies in the neural mechanism of taste. In W. A. Rosenblith (Ed.), *Sensory communication.* New York: Wiley; Cambridge, Mass.: M.I.T. Press, 1961. Pp. 205–216. (357–358)

Zotterman, Y. (Ed.) *Olfaction and taste.* New York: Macmillan, 1963. (361)

Zotterman, Y., & Diamant, H. Has water a specific taste? *Nature,* 1959, **183,** 191–192. (353, 357)

Zotterman, Y. See Dodt, E., & Zotterman, Y., 1952.

Zotterman, Y. See Hensel, H., & Zotterman, Y., 1951a.

Zotterman, Y. See Hensel, H., & Zotterman, Y., 1951b.

Zotterman, Y. See Hensel, H., & Zotterman, Y., 1951c.

Zotterman, Y. See Kitchell, R. L., Ström, L., & Zotterman, Y., 1959.

Zotterman, Y. See Cohen, M. J., Landgren, S., Ström, L., & Zotterman, Y., 1957.

Zotterman, Y. See Diamant, H., Funakoshi, M., Ström, L., & Zotterman, Y., 1963.

Zuckerman, C. B., & Rock, I. A reappraisal of the roles of past experience and innate organizing processes in visual perception. *Psychol. Bull.,* 1957, **54,** 269–296. (295)

Zwaardemaker, H. Prufung des Geruchssinnes und der Geruche. In R. Abderhalden (Ed.), *Handbuch der biologisches Arbeitsmethoden,* Abt. V. Teil 7, Heft 3, 1920. (341)

Zwaardemaker, H. Odeur et chimisme. *Arch. Neerl. Phys.,* 1922, **6,** 336–354. (348)

Zwaardemaker, H. *L'Odorat.* Paris: Doin, 1925. (344–345)

Zyve, C. I. Conversations among children. *Teach. Coll. Rec.,* 1927, **29,** 46–61. (207)

SUBJECT INDEX

Ability, individual performance, effect on, 570
  in small group research, 569
  and task performance, 569–572
Accommodation, 223
  of lens, 217, 218, 271
  and oculomotor nerve, 53
Acetylcholene, 48, 381
Acid taste (see Sour taste)
Acquisition, 371, 374, 376, 378, 380, 416
  under fixed interval schedule, 409, 410
  under fixed ratio schedule, 407, 408
  under intracranial stimulation, 520
  under variable interval schedule, 409, 411
  under variable ratio schedule, 408, 410
Action potential, 43, 45, 46
  in audition, 180
Activation theory, 508, 509, 511
Acuity, 243–245, 287
  illumination intensity, relation to, 244,
    245
  measures of, 243–245
  sensory deprivation, effect of, 284
"Adam's apple," 185
Adaptation, 82
  auditory, 166, 167
  in classical conditioning, 391
  dark, 239–241
  definition, 45
  gustatory, 360
  to hue, 241
  kinesthetic, 326, 327
  light, 239–241
  in method of fractionation, 121
  olfactory, 344–347
  to pain, 321
  to pressure, 314–316, 326, 327
  to temperature, 76
  in vestibular sense, 335
  visual, 239
Adaptation level theory, 101, 103, 104
Adipsia, 330
Affect structure, 576, 587, 600
  and attractiveness, 581
  communication, effect on, 588, 592
  complementarity, effect on, 589–591
  and geographic proximity, 588, 589
  and instrumentality, 591, 592
  power structure, effect on, 592
  and spatial proximity, 588, 589
  task performance, effect on, 594, 595
  task structure, effect on, 593
Aftereffects, auditory, 167, 168
Aftereffects, figural, 242, 243, 316

  kinesthetic, 168, 326
  spatial, 242
  visual, 167, 168, 241, 242
Afterimages, negative, 168
  positive, 168
  visual, 71, 283
Afterpotential, 44–46
Ageusia, 361
Alarm reaction (AR), 515
Albedo, 268
All-or-none law, 44, 45
  and auditory theory, 176
  and cochlear potential, 152
  and vibratory sensitivity, 316
Alpha rhythm, 58, 395
Ames room, 272–274
Amphetamine and food intake, 331
Amplitude, 68, 146, 155
  cochlea, reproduction by, 151, 152
  and frequency, 160, 164
  loudness, relation to, 69, 161, 162
  and sound localization, 169, 170
  in speech, 186, 188
Ampulla, 332–335
Amygdala, 51, 60
  and emotion, 507, 511
  intracranial stimulation of, 520
  olfaction, role in, 340
  and sexual behavior, 51, 60, 491
Anagrams, 466
Analgesia, 318
Analysis, statistical, of language, 199–201
Anchoring, 104
Androgen, 489, 490
Angstrom, 221
Annulospiral (A2) endings, 325
Anosmia, 347, 348
Antrum, 339
Anvil (incus), 147, 150
Anxiety, 399, 400
  classical conditioning, effect in, 400
  in Freudian theory, 522
  as secondary drive, 521, 522
Aphasia, 210, 211
Apparatus, aesthesiometer, 315
  anomaloscope, 254
  ataximeter, 505
  audiooscillator, 14
  automatograph, 505
  Bárány chair, 333
  camera inodorata, 341–342
  campimeter, 235
  chronoscope, 10

Apparatus, double olfactometer, 341
electroencephalograph, 58, 505
electromyograph, 475
electronic devices, 10
electronic switching, 12
ergograph, 474, 475
Galton whistle, 534
galvanometer, 40, 44, 45
Howard-Dohlman apparatus, 274, 291
illuminometer, 12
Michotte disk, 285
Miller-Mowrer box, 521
mirror tracing, 461, 462
olfactorium, 341
operant training chamber, 406
oscilloscope, 12
perimeter, 235
plethysmograph, 505, 506
pneumograph, 506
Purdue pegboard, 463, 464
pursuit rotor, 461, 462
puzzle box, 367, 368, 468
radar, 45
radio, 45
reaction time, 461
respiration calorimeter, 475
for response recording, 12, 16–18
as source of error, 31
spectograph, 190
sphygomograph, 506
sphygomomanometer, 506
stereotaxic instrument, 59
for stimulus presentation, 12, 14, 15
tachistoscope, 292
telescope, 45
thermocouple, 305, 306
tracking, 463
Zwaardemaker's olfactometer, 341
Apparent size, 272
Apparent visual kinetics, 285
(See also Causality, visual)
Appetite, 328–330
Approach-avoidance gradient, 423, 424
Approximation to language, 200
Aqueous humor, 215, 217, 218
Arachnoid layer, 48
Argyll-Robertson effect, 217
Arousal, and emotion, 508, 509
and learning, 508
level of, 58, 61, 62
and limbic system, 62, 512
Articulation, and clipping, 202, 204
positions of, 187

Articulation, score and speech to-noise ratio, 202, 203
test, 201, 202
types of, 187
Articulator, 187
Aspirant, 187
Assimilation, 100
Association, continuous, 194
controlled, 193, 196
discrete, 194
free, 193
measures of, 194
reflex, 384
value of, in nonsense syllables, 194
in words, 443
Associationism, 39
Attitude, role change, effect of, 560–562
scaling of, 137
task performance, effect on, 569, 572
Attractiveness, 589
and instrumentality, 592
Audiometry, 155
Audition, 81
aftereffects in, 167, 168
nature of stimulus, 67–70, 146
pathology, 170
(See also Deafness; Displacusis; Otosclerosis; Presbyacusia; Tinnitus)
theory, 148, 150, 151, 154, 170
(See also Frequency theory; "Piano string" theory; Place theory; Telephone theory; Volley theory)
Auditory nerve (VIII), 53, 146–148, 150, 152, 170, 180, 181, 216, 297, 332, 333
Auditory stimulus, reaction time to, 461
Autokinetic effect, 284
Autonomic nervous system, 55
and emotion, 513, 514
(See also Parasympathetic nervous system; Sympathetic nervous system)
Autonomy of task structure, 578
Avoidance centers, 521
Avoidance gradient, 423, 424
Avoidance training, 374–376, 395, 420, 423, 505, 511
Awareness, 292–294
in verbal conditioning, 397, 459
Axon, 42, 44

b wave, 226
Ballard-Williams phenomenon (see Reminiscence)
Basal age, 545, 546
Basilar membrane, 147–150
destruction of, 171, 172

Basilar membrane, in Helmholtz' theory, 175
  in telephone theory, 176, 177
  and tonal frequency, 152, 153
  in travelling wave theory, 178, 179
Basket endings, 198, 300
  as pressure receptors, 313
  as touch receptors, 312
Beats, 163, 165, 166
Behavior, animal, 8, 42
  awareness, without, 293, 294
  control of, 2
  eating, 60, 61
  drinking, 60, 61
  homosexual, 485, 490
  insightful (*see* Insight)
  instinctual, 479
    definitional criteria, 479, 480
    physiological basis, 498–500
    sexual, 485
  learned versus unlearned, 365, 366
  licking, 494–496
  prediction of, 1–4, 38
  sexual, 484
    and central nervous system, 491, 492
    hormonal effects, 485, 487–490
    in mammals, 488
    in ringdove, 485
  small group, 556, 557, 559
  social, 555
  socioemotional, 580
  suppression of, 511
  task-oriented, 580
  voting, 559
Behaviorism, 275, 278, 385, 386
Bel, 69
Bell, Sir Charles, 39, 45
Benham's top, 238, 239
Beta rhythm, 58
Bezold-Brücke effect, 237, 261
Bidwell's ghosts, 242
Binaural equation, 161
Binet-Simon scale, 534
Bitter taste, 80, 349–352
  and electrical stimulation, 81
  threshold, 360
Blast injection technique, 341, 342
Blindness, night, 213
  regaining vision after, 278, 279
  and sound localization, 169
Bone conduction, 154
Brain, 42, 56, 57
  directional definitions in, 48
  parts of, 48, 50–53
  visceral, 60

Brightness, of light, 229, 230, 249
  differential threshold, 232, 233
  enhancement, 237, 238
  simultaneous contrast, 242
  of tone, 164
Bril, 122, 233
Brilliance, 72, 220
  (*See also* Luminosity)
Broca's area, 210
Bunsen-Roscoe law, 230, 231

Candlepower, 221
Cannon, Walter B., 55
Cattell, James McKeen, 534
Causalgia, 320
Causality, visual, 284, 285
Cause and effect, 9, 19, 37
  and correlation, 29, 30
Ceiling age, 546
Cell, bipolar, in audition, 180
  epithelial, 297
  ganglion, in vision, 215, 216
  gland, 42
  hair, auditory, 148, 150, 152, 177
    gustatory, 351
    olfactory, 339
  mitral, 345, 346
  muscle, 42
  nerve (*see* Neuron)
  olfactory, 339, 340
  response to stimulation, 43
  rods and cones, relation to, 216, 219
  sustenacular, 339, 351
  T, 323
  ventral horn, 55
Cell body, of nerve, 42
  unmylenated, 46
Cellular theory, 42
Central nervous system, and audition, 152, 180
  and classical conditioning, 393–395
  and cutaneous sensitivity, 302–305
  directional definitions, 48
  and emotion, 58, 60, 61, 510, 511
  and gustation, 358
  and instinct, 498
  and learning, 379–381
  and motivation, 61
  neurons of, 42, 48
  and olfaction, 339, 340
  and pain, 321–323
  regeneration in, 43
  and sexual behavior, 491, 492
  and speech pathology, 210

Central nervous system, and vision, 228
Central sulcus, 52
Cerebellum, 50, 51
Cerebrospinal fluid, 52, 53
Cerebrum, 50, 51
Chemical sensitivity, 337
Child rearing, and occupation, 558
Cholinesterase, 48, 351, 381
Chorda tympani, 352–354, 357–359
Choriod coat, 215–217
  in pecten, 223
Chroma, 250
Chromaticity diagram, 250, 251
Chunk, 450, 451
Ciliary muscles, 215, 217, 327
Classical conditioning, 40, 327, 366, 402, 522
  and anxiety, 400
  backward, 388–390
  with children, 386, 387
  cortex, role of, 393, 394
  delayed, 388
  and innate releasing mechanisms, 496
  instructions, role of, 423–425
  versus instrumental training, 386, 424–427
  interoceptive, 395, 396, 400
  and knowledge of results, 444
  to measure meaning, 195–196
  to measure threshold, 81, 385
  second-order, 396
  simultaneous, 388
  and spinal cord, 394, 395
  temporal factors, 388, 389
  trace, 388
  of verbal behavior, 396–398
  (*See also* Verbal conditioning)
Clipping, 202–206
Closure, principle of, 276, 277
Clustering, 196, 450
Cochlea, 147–150, 179
  in amphibia, 154
  and conduction deafness, 170
  development of, 154
  electrical activity in, 151, 152
  in Helmholtz' theory, 175
  lower gallery, 147, 148
  in mammal, 154
  sound analysis by, 180
  and stimulation deafness, 171
  upper gallery, 147, 148
Cochlear microphonic, 151
  (*See also* Cochlear potential)
Cochlear nucleus, 152, 180, 181
Cochlear potential, 151–153, 157

Cold sensitivity, 74, 76
  adaptation, 308
  nerve impulses, 306, 307
  paradoxical, 305, 311
  receptors for, 307
  spots, 75, 77, 301, 302, 305, 306, 311
Collumella auris, 154, 158
Color, 72
  chroma of, 250
  illumination, effect of, 72
  mixing, 252
  as multidimensional attribute, 138
  preference, in butterfly, 224
    innate, 296
  saturation, effect of, 72
  standardization of, 250
  value, 250
Color deficiency, 254–258
  and age, 254
  frequency of, 257
  genetic determinants, 257, 258
  as racial characteristic, 254
  and theory, 258–260
  types, 255
Color solid, 249–251
Color spindle, 249, 250
Color vision, in animals, 223
  development of, 252–254
  in periphery, 235
  theory, 222, 248, 249, 258
Common fate, principle of, 276, 277
Communication, and affect structure, 588, 592
  among animals, 209
  networks, 584–586
  patterns, 563–565, 600
  structure, 576, 584–588
Complementarity hypothesis, 590
Concept formation, 468, 469
Conditioned emotional response (CER), 395, 423,
    511
Cones, 215, 216, 218
  absolute threshold for wavelength, 221, 222
  and acuity, 244, 245
  adaptation, 239
  and brightness, 232
  and color vision, 219, 259
  distribution of, 219
  and illumination, 222
  number of, 219, 220
  pigment in, absorption spectrum of, 261, 262
Consonant, 187, 188, 205, 209
Constancy, 266
  brightness, 267, 268, 271, 291

Constancy, color, 267
  hue, 268
  learning of, 271
  size, 266–269
Constant error (CE), in method of average error, 95
  in method of constant stimuli, 96–97
  in method of limits, 93, 94
Constant flow technique, 342
Content analysis, 198
Continuous memory experiment, 447
Contrast, 242
Convergence, 271
Corium, 298–300
Cornea, 214, 215, 217
  pain sensitivity in, 319, 320
Corpus callosum, 51, 52
Correlation, 29, 30, 537
  and factor analysis, 139
Cortex, 49, 51
  and audition, 180, 181
  and classical conditioning, 393, 394
  and emotion, 507, 510, 511
  and gustation, 358
  and instrumental training, 427
  movement, relation to, 40, 59
  oxygen lack, effect, 53
  precentral, 305
  and sexual behavior, 491
  somesthetic, 52, 60
  and sound localization, 170, 181
  striate, 228
  visual, 228
Counterbalancing, 24, 26
  in method of average error, 98, 99
  in method of fractionation, 121
  in paired comparison, 134
  in ranking, 130
Cranial nerve (*see* Auditory nerve; Facial nerve; Glossopharyngeal nerve; Trigeminal nerve; Vagus nerve)
Crespi effect, 411, 412, 440, 441
Cribiform plate, 339
Crista, 332, 333
Criterion, 379
  contamination, 542
  external, 101, 142
  and validity, 540, 543
Critical flicker fusion (CFF), 236, 237
  and brightness, 237, 238
  (*See also* Flicker fusion)
Critical periods, 480
  in imprinting, 482, 483

Critical periods, and sucking reflex, 495
  (*See also* Sensitive periods)
Crocker-Henderson odor classification system, 79
Cross-modality comparison, 105, 107
Cue, depth, 271, 272
Cumulative record, 378, 380
Cuneate nucleus, 304
Cupula, 333, 335
Curare, 394
Cutaneous sensitivity, 45, 73, 296
  anesthetic, effect of, 74
  and central nervous system, 302–305
  communication with, 317, 318
  in cornea, 217
  and gustation, 352, 353
  in hunger, 328
  receptors for, 74, 298–302
  stimulus, nature of, 73–77
    RT to, 461
  in thirst, 328
Cyanopsin, 220

D-matrix, 197
Deafness, conduction, 170, 171
  high-tone, 174
  nerve, 170, 171
  and speech pathology, 210
  stimulation, 171–173
Death wish, 524
Decibel, definition of, 69
Decision theory, 105–107
Defense mechanism, 525
Delayed-reaction experiment, 370
Delta rhythm, 58, 395
Dendrites, 42
  and graded response, 44
Density of sound, 155, 162, 164
Deoxyribonucleic acid (DNA), 381, 382
Depressants, 516
Depression effect, 411, 412
Depth perception, 271, 272
  age, effect of, 291
  and learning, 274, 279, 281
  (*See also* Space perception)
Dermatome, 303
Design, experimental (*see* Experimental design)
Detour problem, 466, 467
Deuteranomaly, 255, 257, 258, 260
Dichromatism, 255–257, 260
Diphthong, 188
"Dipole" theory, 348
Discrimination in instrumental training, 414–419
Dispersion, 102, 132

Displacement, 525
Displacusis, 172, 173
Distributed practice (*see* Learning, distributed)
Disuse theory (*see* Forgetting, theories of)
Dol, 321
Dominator-modulator color theory, 259
Dorsal spinal ganglion, 55
Double alternation problem, 370, 371
Double hearing, 173
   (*See also* Displacusis)
Dreams, correlation with rapid eye movements, 61
Drive, 55
   homeostasis, relation to, 55
   in Hullian theory, 517
   learned (secondary), 521–523
   in Miller's theory, 519
   reduction, 330, 519, 522
   sexual energy as, 489
du Bois-Reymond, Émil, 40
Duplicity (duplexity) theory, 221, 222
Dura mater, 48
Dvorine pseudoisochromatic plates, 255

Ear, electrical response of, 151
   evolution of, 152–154
   in fish, 153
   inner, 147
   middle, 147, 150
   outer, 147
   structures of, 147
Eardrum (*see* Tympanic membrane)
Ebbinghaus, Hermann, 195, 430, 432, 534
Edridge-Green bead test, 255
Egg laying, 485–487
Ego, 524, 525
Einstellung, 277
   (*See also* Set)
Elation effect, 411, 412
Electrical recording, in central nervous system, 58
   in cutaneous sensitivity, 305
   in gustation, 353–358
   in macula, 334
   monophasic, 43
   of nerve, 44–46
   in olfactory system, 344–347
   in pyriform area, 340
   of speech, 189
   in thermal sensitivity, 306
   in vision, 225, 261
Electrical stimulation, of brain, 40, 58–60
   (*See also* Intracranial stimulation)
   and instinctual behavior, 498–500

Electrical stimulation, in limbic system, 512
Electricity, nature of, 40
Electrode, chronic implant of, 59, 60
Electroencephalogram (EEG), 58
   and classical conditioning, 395
   emotion, to measure, 505
   and limbic system, 573
   response to stimulation, 59
   rhythms, 58, 395
   and sleep, 61
Electroencephalography, 58
Electromagnetic spectrum, 72, 73
Electrooculogram (EOG), 285, 287
Electroretinogram (ERG), 225–227, 229
Emotion, and activation theory, 508, 509
   and arousal level, 61, 508, 509
   and autonomic nervous system, 55
   defining, method of, 504
   drug effects, 513–516
   and facial expression, 126, 127
   introspective approach, 509
   James-Lange theory, 509, 510
   motivation, relation to, 516
   physiological measurement of, 505, 506
   and pituitary, 51
   and psychosomatic states, 514, 515
   and reticular activating system, 61, 507, 511, 512
   and stress, 515
Empiricism, 39
Endocrine system, 51
Endolymphatic fluid, 148, 332–334
Environment, of small groups, 566, 567
   visual perception, effect on, 288, 289
Eosinophil, used as measure of emotion, 516
Epicritic pain system, 322, 323
Epidermis, layers of, 297, 298
Epinephrine, 513–516
Epithelium, 339, 346, 349
Equal-density contour, 164, 166
Equal-loudness contour, 161, 163, 166
Equal-pitch contour, 166
Equal-volume contour, 163, 166
Equipment (*see* Apparatus)
Equipotentiality, 394
Error, of anticipation, 92
   of estimate, 536
   of habituation, 92, 277
   of inclusion, 434
   of measurement, 536
   of movement, 99
   of omission, 434
   sampling, 536
   sources of, 31

Error, space, 99, 134
time, 98, 134
Escape training, 374, 375, 420, 505, 511, 522
Estrogen, 489
effect on nest building, 485, 488
Estrous cycle, 489, 490
Ethologist, motivational approach of, 523, 528–530
Eustachian tube, 147, 150
Excitation, 391
Excitatory potential, 517
Exhaustion, 515
Expectancy theory, 518
Experience, principle of, 276–278
visual, 287–289
Experiment, advantages of, 7
experimenter-manipulated, 7
field, 557, 562, 563
laboratory, to study small groups, 557, 563, 564
Experimental design, 6, 10, 21
counterbalanced, 24, 26
factorial, 26, 27
naturalistic, 21
one variable, 21
two-group, 22, 23
Experimental technique, 9, 10
"Experimenter contamination," 138
External auditory meatus (*see* Meatus, external auditory)
Exteroceptive senses, 81
Extinction, 374–378, 380, 426
under fixed interval schedule, 409
under fixed ratio schedule, 408, 409
in instrumental training, 366, 403, 407, 416
with intracranial stimulation, 520
punishment, effect of, 420
under variable ratio schedule, 408
Eye, adaptability of, 215
anatomy of, 214–216
evolution of, 223–225
movement, 285–287

Facial nerve (VII), 53
and cutaneous sensitivity, 304
and gustation, 352
and vestibular sensitivity, 332, 333
Factor analysis, 136–140
in perceptual-motor tasks, 463–465
and semantic differential, 197
variance in, 139
Fasciculus cuneatus, 304
Fasciculus gracilis, 304
Fatigue, 474, 475

Fatigue, auditory, 166, 168
(*See also* Adaptation, auditory)
Fatigue effects, 99, 100
and method of fractionation, 121
Fear, acquired, 521, 522
Fechner, Gustav Theodor, 85, 86, 89, 90, 101, 105, 110, 136, 213, 430
Fechner's law, 89, 90, 102, 104, 110
Feedback, 58
decreased, 464
delayed, 464
knowledge of results as, 443, 444
perceptual-motor tasks, effect on, 464–466
and social communication, 586, 596
Field studies, 9, 557, 559–562
Figure-ground relationship, 264, 266, 274
Fissure of Sylvius, 52
Fixation, visual, 223, 285, 287
Fixed action pattern, 496, 497, 528
Flicker fusion, 236–238
Flourens, Pierre, 40
Flower-spray endings (A1), 325
Foot-candle, 221
Foot-lambert, 221
Forbes-Gregg hypothesis, 176, 177
Forgetting, 375
curve of, 449
and extinction, 375
and inactivity, 449
and repression, 450
stimulus trace concept, 445
theories of, disuse, 448, 449
Gestalt, 449, 450
interference, 448, 449
psychoanalytic, 450
(*See also* Memory; Retention)
Fornix, 51, 60
Four corner test, 255
Fourier analysis, 189
Fovea, 215, 219–221, 223
Free nerve endings, 298, 300, 302, 304, 310
as pain receptors, 319, 323
as pressure receptors, 313
Frequency of sound, 68, 69, 146, 155
and amplitude, 160
and central nervous system, 180, 181
cochlea, reproduction by, 151, 152
and density, 164
fundamental, 70
loudness, relation to, 161, 165
pitch, relation to, 68, 116–118, 160, 161, 165
and sound localization, 169–171
and volume, 163

Frequency theory, 177
Freud, Sigmund, 385, 522
Fricatives, 187
Fullerton-Cattell principle, 101, 102
Functional relations, 24, 25
"Fundamental formula," 89

Gall, Franz Joseph, 40
Galton, Francis, 175, 193, 533, 534
Galvani, Luigi, 40
Galvanic skin resistance, 475
  to measure emotion, 506
  to measure meaning, 195
Galvanic skin response (GSR), 195, 293
Ganzfeld, 282
General adaptation syndrome, 515
Generalization, 426
  absolute theory of, 417
  gradient, 393
  in instrumental training, 414, 417
  perceptual, 274
  relational theory of, 417
  response, 392
  stimulus, 392
  in verbal conditioning, 397, 398
Generator potential and thermal sensitivity, 306, 307
Geniculate body, and vision, 215, 228
Gestalt psychology, 274–276, 283
  theory of forgetting, 449, 450
  and Tolman's theory, 518
Glossopharyngeal nerve (IX), 53
  and cutaneous sensitivity, 304
  and gustation, 352, 357
Glottis, 185, 186
Goals, superordinate, 562
Golgi-Mazzoni corpuscles, 298, 300, 325
Gonadotropins, 489
Good continuation, principle of, 276, 277
Good whole, principle of, 276, 277
Gracile nucleus, 304, 307
Gradient of deformation, 75, 312
Graphic analysis, of speech, 189, 191
Grating, 244, 245
Ground, 264, 266, 274
Group, cohesiveness, 565, 566, 572, 577, 588, 589
  composition of, 566, 567, 569
  control of, 6, 22, 23, 31
  cooperative versus competitive, 576
  development of, 568
  experimental, 6, 22
  interaction of (*see* Interaction, group)

Group, norms of, 594
  performance of, 565, 566
  personality characteristics, effect of, 574
  small, behavior of, 556, 557, 559
  socioemotionally oriented, 596
  structure of, 566–569
  task oriented, 596, 597
Group process, 566, 568
Group size, 576, 577
  and basic initiation rate, 576, 592, 593
Guessing, correction for, 434, 435
Gust, 122, 360, 361
Gustation, 81, 337
  adaptation, 360
  and age, 80, 350
  chemical effects, 350
  cutaneous sensitivity, relation to, 352, 353
  electrical activity, 80, 351, 353, 355–360
  learning, role of, 354, 355
  olfaction, relation, 77
  pathology, 361
  receptors for, 337, 350–353
  stimulus, nature of, 79–81
  temperature, role of, 353–355
  theory, 361
  threshold, 343, 352, 353, 358, 360
Guthrie, E. R., learning theory of, 518
Gyrus cinguli, 51

Habit, principle of, 277, 278
  strength, 517
Habit-family hierarchy, 469, 470
Hammer (malleus), 147, 150
Hedonism, 517
Heliocotrema, 147, 148, 180
Helmholtz, Hermann von, 41, 174, 175
  auditory theory of, 175, 176, 182
    (*See also* Place theory)
  color vision theory, 248, 258–261
Henning, Hans K. F., olfactory classification system of, 79
Hering, E., color vision theory of, 249, 258–261
Hippocampus, 60
  and emotion, 507
  sexual behavior, relation to, 61, 491
Hoarding, 497, 498
Holmgren's wool test, 255
Homeostasis, 55, 56
  and emotion, 504
  as motivational system, 517–519
  and reinforcement, 372, 519
  in sexual behavior, 488, 489

Homing, 492
Homosexuality, 485, 490
"Hope and fear" study, 413, 414, 511
Hormones and sexual behavior, 489–491
Hostility, intergroup, 562, 563
Hue, 72, 220, 249
  absolute threshold, 229
  adaptation, 241
  differential threshold, 229, 231, 249
  in Ganzfeld, 283
  illumination, relation to, 72
  and phi phenomenon, 284
  purity of (*see* Saturation)
  threshold, 228
  wavelength, relation to, 72, 229, 231
Hull, Clark, learning theory of, 517, 518
Hunger, 297, 324, 327–332
  and body chemistry, 330
  and hoarding, 498
  hypothalamus, role of, 330, 331
  pituitary, role of, 332
  specific, 331
  and stomach contractions, 328
Hydrocephalus, 53
Hyperalgesia, 319, 322, 323
Hyperphagia, 330, 331
Hypoalgesia, 74
Hypoglossal nerve (XII), 53
Hypophagia, 330
Hypophysectomy, 488
Hypothalamus, 51, 60
  and arousal, 62
  drugs, effect of, 516
  eating center in, 40, 51, 60–62, 520
  and emotion, 507, 511, 512
  food intake, role in, 330
  intracranial stimulation of, 520
  and sexual behavior, 491
  water intake, role in, 60, 61, 330
Hypothesis, experimental, 13, 18–21
  and law, 19
  null, 19

I fraction, 185
Id, 524, 525
Identical elements theory, 456
Illumination, 72, 229, 230
  and autokinetic effect, 284
  and color, 72
  differential threshold, 73
  hue, relation to, 72
  and migratory behavior, 493

Illumination, and phi phenomenon, 284
  and photoreceptors, 220–222
  threshold, 228
Illusion, 71
  kinesthetic, 326, 327
  Müller-Lyer, 94, 220
  visual, 213, 290
  waterfall, 283
Imitation, 473, 474
Imprinting, 480–483
Impulse, nerve, 43, 46–48
Incus (anvil), 147, 150
Individual differences, 533, 534
Inferior colliculi and audition, 152
Information theory, 191, 192
Inhibition, 391, 392, 426
Innate releasing mechanism (IRM), 496, 497
Insight, 368, 372, 418, 469–471
Instinct (*see* Behavior, instinctual)
Instrumental training, 366, 387
  and classical conditioning, 386, 424–427
  and innate releasing mechanism, 496
  instructions, role of, 423, 424
  and knowledge of results, 444
  neurological correlates, 427
  temporal effects, 412, 413
  (*See also* Operant training)
Instrumentality, 591, 592
Intelligence, and group performance, 571
  and leadership, 572
  operational definition of, 20, 21
  scaling of, 111
  [*See also* Test(s), intelligence]
Intelligence quotient (IQ), 535, 541, 544
Intelligibility, of speech, 201, 202
Intensity, of light, and acuity, 244, 245
  and adaptation, 240, 241
  and area, 231
  differential threshold, 232
  and duration, 230
  electrical recording of, 226, 227
  of speech, 186
  effect on intelligibility, 201
Interaction, group, 556, 557, 595, 596, 600, 601
  measures of, 598–600
  phases of, 597, 598
  social, 555
Interdependence, facilitative versus "contriant," 575, 576
Interests and task performance, 572, 573
Interference, forgetting theory, 448, 449
  types of, 455
  in verbal learning, 440

Interneuron, 46
Interoceptive senses, 81
Interposition, 271, 272
Interval of uncertainty, 92–94
Intracranial stimulation (ICS), 40, 59, 519, 520
Introspection, 385, 509
Iodopsin, 219
Ionic permeability, of membrane, 43
Ionization, 44
Iris, 53, 215, 217
Ishihara pseudoisochromatic plates, 255
Isohedonic contours, 360
Isosensitivity contour, 107, 108

James-Lange theory, 509, 510
Jost's laws, 451
Judgments, interval, 115
  multidimensional, 138, 139
  ratio, 115
  unidimensional, 138
Jung, Carl, 193

Kinesthesis, 81, 296, 324
  adaptation, 326, 327
  aftereffect, 168, 326
  receptors for, 296, 324, 325
  stimulus for, 82
  threshold, 325, 326
Knowledge of results, 373, 443, 444, 548
König, A., color vision theory of, 259, 260
Korte's laws, 284
Krause end bulbs, 298, 300
  as cold receptors, 301, 307, 310
Kuder-Richardson formula, 539

Ladd-Franklin, C., color vision theory of, 249, 259
Lamina quadrigemina, 51
Land effect, 250, 262–264
Landolt rings, 244, 245
Language, in animals, 209, 210
  approximations to, 200
  development of, 204–209
  learning of, 204
  as mediating response, 471
  problem solving, role in, 472, 473
  redundancy in, 189
  variability of, 198
Larynx, 185, 186
Latent addition, 44
Lateral, 187
Lateral bundle, 304

Lateral lemniscus and audition, 152
Law, 19, 20
  of comparative judgment, 101–103
  of effect, 373, 374, 419, 517
  of effort, 482
  of primacy, 482
  of roots, 55, 174
Leader, function of, 570
  personality characteristics of, 575
  socioemotional, 580, 581
  task, 580, 581
  and task performance, 570
Leadership, centrality of, 581
  and communication network, 585
  and intelligence, 572
  styles of, 582, 583
Learning, and affective state, 443
  and arousal, 508
  chemistry of, 379, 380
  correction method, 422
  definition, 365
  discrimination, 366, 367, 417, 427
  distributed, 26, 27, 369, 436–441, 444
  incidental, 456–458
  as increment, 371
  intentional, 456–458
  latent, 457
  to learn, 369, 418, 454
  massed, 20, 27, 369, 436–441
  and maturation, 365
  and meaningfulness, 442, 443
  motor, 369, 439
  neurophysiology of, 379, 380
  noncorrection method, 422
  paired associate, 431
  part, 26, 27, 369, 436, 437
  perceptual-motor, 460
  and performance, 365, 440
  probability, 8
  respondent, 403
    (*See also* Classical conditioning)
  reversal, 418
  serial, 431
  set, 418
  theories of, 372
  trial-and-error, 367–369
  Type I, 384
    (*See also* Classical conditioning)
  Type II, 384
    (*See also* Instrumental training)
  verbal, 369, 439, 440
  visual perception, role in, 278, 279, 281, 288
  whole, 26, 27, 369, 436, 437

Learning curve, 371
Leber-Fick-type fundamental, 260
Lemniscal pathway, and audition, 152, 180
Lens, 214, 215, 217
  accommodation of, 217, 218
Light, 71, 72
  as orientation cue, 224
Light-dark ratio (LDR), 237, 238
Limbic system, 60–62
  and attention, 512
  and eating behavior, 512
  and emotion, 61, 507, 511, 512
Limen, 65
  (*See also* Threshold)
Linear perspective, 272
Lingual nerve and gustation, 357
Linnaeus, Carl, classification system of, 78, 79
Lobes, frontal, 51
  occipital, 52, 215, 216, 219
  olfactory, 339, 491
  parietal, 52
  temporal, 52
    and audition, 149
Local action, 45, 46
Localization, in central nervous system, 394
  function of pinna in, 147
  sound, 169–171, 181
Loudness, 69, 146, 155
  amplitude, relation to, 69, 161, 162, 164
  and central nervous system, 181
  cross modal comparison with vibration, 107
  frequency, relation to, 69, 161, 165
  and generalization, 392, 393
  and nerve firing, 176
  perception of, in travelling wave theory, 179
    in volley theory, 177, 178
  pitch, relation to, 155
  scale of, 117
Lumen, 221
Luminosity, 220

Macula, 332–334
Macula lutea, 219, 221, 222
Magendie, François, 39
Malleus (hammer), 147, 150
Mammillary bodies, 51, 60
Marbe's law, 193
Masking, in audition, 163, 166, 167
  of olfactory stimulus, 344
  of speech, 202, 203
Mass action, 394
Massed practice (*see* Learning, massed)

Maternal deprivation, 484
Maturation and learning, 365, 483, 484
Meaning, development of, 208, 209
  in language, 192, 193
  measure of, 192–199
  of nonsense syllables, 194
  of stimulus items, 442, 443
  verbal learning, effect on, 443
  and visual perception, 195, 196
  of words, scaling, 124, 125
Meatus, 146
  external auditory, 147, 150
Medial bundle, in spinal cord, 304, 512
Medial geniculate body, and audition, 149
Mediating process, 469–471
Medulla, 50, 51
  and arousal, 61
  and audition, 152, 180, 181
  and cutaneous sensitivity, 302, 304
  and emotion, 507
  functions of, 51
  and gustation, 352, 358
  oxygen lack, effect of, 53
Medullary substance, 298
Meissner corpuscles, 298, 300
  as pressure receptors, 313
  and touch, 301
Mel, 118, 122, 160, 161
Memory, chemical basis, 381, 382
  immediate, 445
  long-term, 445
  short-term, 445–448
  span of, 445, 489
  (*See also* Forgetting; Retention)
Ménière's disease, 172
Meninges, 48, 49, 52
Mental age, 534, 546
Merkel disks, 298, 300
  as pressure receptors, 313
  and touch, 301
Meter-candle, 221
Method, adjustment, 94
  average error, 86, 90, 95, 98, 99
    and method of equal appearing intervals, 117
    and method of equal sense distances, 115, 116
  balanced values, 136, 137
  bisection, 115
  classification, 599, 600
  constant stimuli, 86, 90, 95–100, 133, 134
    to measure kinesthesis, 325
    and method of equal appearing intervals, 118
    and method of equal sense distances, 115, 116
  constant-stimulus differences, 95

Method, equal appearing intervals, 117–120, 138, 141
  equal sense distances, 115–117
  equation, 94
  experimental, 3
  field, 5, 9
  first choice, 136, 137
  fractionation, 116, 118, 120–123, 141
    to scale gustatory stimuli, 360
    to scale loudness, 161, 164
    to scale pitch, 160
  frequency, 95–98
  of immediate memory span, 431
  learning time, 432
  limits, 86, 90–94, 98
    and method of equal sense distances, 115, 116
  magnitude estimation, 122, 123
    to relate loudness and amplitude, 162, 165
  minimal change, 90
  multiple stimuli, 122–124, 141
  paired comparisons, 115, 124–126, 129, 130, 133–137, 141
  phylogenetic, 5, 8, 9
  pretest, 452, 453
  ranking, 115, 124, 125, 129–133, 141
  rating, 115, 124–130, 141
  ratio estimation, 122, 123
  ratio production, 122, 123
  retained numbers, 431
  right and wrong cases, 95
  savings, 432, 433
  scientific, 3, 9, 19
  similar attributes, 136–138
  simultaneous discrimination, 367
  single group, 453
  successive categories, 124, 138
  successive discrimination, 367
  successive practice, 452, 453
  systematic change, 5–9
  of triads, 134, 135
Migration, 492–494
Millilambert, 221
Millimicron, 221
Mind-body problem, 85
Minimal audible field (MAF), 160
Minimal audible pressure (MAP), 160
"Mini-max" problem, 27
Minimum separable tasks, 244
Minimum visible tasks, 244
Minnesota Multiphasic Personality Inventory (MMPI), 399, 400
Mitosis, 298
Monaural-binaural equation, 161

Monochromatism, 255–257
Motion perception, 283, 284
Motion sickness, 335
Motivation, 505
  emotion, relation to, 516
  ethological approach, 528–530
  latency measure of, 11
  and learning theory, Guthrie's approach, 518
    Hullian approach, 517, 518
    Tolman's approach, 518
  need achievement theory of, 523, 525–527
  psychoanalytic approach, 523, 524
  and reaction time, 461
  and reinforcement, 519–521
  secondary drive as, 521, 522
Movement, apparent, 283, 284
  eye, 316
  real, 283
  stroboscopic, 284
Mucosa, 339, 345, 346
Müller, Johannes, 39, 45, 174
Multiple choice problem, 370, 435
Munsell color system, 250
Myelin, 46
Myelination, 46, 48

n^{th} power law, 102
Nagel card test, 255
Nares, 338, 339
Nasal septum, 338
Nasalization, 187
Nasopharynx, 339
Nearness, principle of, 276
Need achievement theory, 523, 525–527
Needs, social, 575, 576, 590
Nerve, A-type, 46, 47
  afferent, 46
  B-type, 46, 47
  C-type, 46, 47
  coding by, 39
  cranial, 53, 54, 57
  efferent, 46
  electrical change in, 43
  fibers, characteristics of, 46, 47
  field of, 303
  myelinated, 46, 47
  peripheral, 46, 48
  sacral, 57
  spinal, 53, 55, 56
  unmyelinated, 46, 47
Nerve tracts, 49
Nerve transmission, and cerebrospinal fluid, 52, 53

Nerve transmission, chemical nature of, 40, 47
  electrical nature of, 40, 47
  and stimulus intensity, 45, 46
Nervous system (*see* Autonomic nervous system;
  Central nervous system; Parasympathetic nervous system; Peripheral nervous system; Sympathetic nervous system)
Nest building, 485, 487, 488
Neuron, 42–44, 46
  in central nervous system, 42, 48
  excitability cycle of, 44
  motor, 39
  sensory, 39
  structure of, 42, 43
Neuropsychiatric disorder, 38
Neurosis, experimental, 400, 401
Night blindness, 219, 222, 241
  in macula lutea, 221
Nirvana principle, 524
Noise, 70
  effect on speech perception, 202
  white, 70
Nonauditory labyrinth, 53, 81, 82, 146, 147, 152,
  296, 332, 333
Nonsense syllables, 194, 195
Norepinephrine, 513, 514
Nyctalopia, 219
Nystagmus, 334, 335

Occupation and child rearing practices, 558
Oculomotor nerve (III), 53
Odor, 78
  classification systems, 78, 79
  primary, 349
  vapor pressure, relation to, 78
Ohm, Georg Simon, 40
Olfactie, 341
Olfaction, 81, 337
  absolute threshold, 77
  adaptation, 344–347
  differential threshold, 77
  gustation, relation to, 77
  macrosomatic perception, 347
  masking, 344
  microsomatic perception, 348
  pathology, 347, 348
  stimulus for, 77–79, 338
  thresholds, 342–344
    measurement of, 340–342
Olfactory bulb, 345, 346
Olfactory cleft, 335, 339

Olfactory nerve, 53, 339, 340
Omission training, 374
On-off system, 226–228
Open field technique, 506
Operant training, 378
  to measure threshold, 84, 85
  (*See also* Instrumental training)
Operationism, 20, 21
Opponent color theory, 257
Optic chiasma, 51, 216, 218, 228
Optic disc, 215, 219
Optic nerve (II), 53, 215–218, 225, 226, 228
Organ of Corti, 148, 151
  and cochlear potential, 152
  in Helmholtz' theory, 175
  intense stimulation, effect of, 172
Organic sensibility, 324
Orienting reflex, 397–399
Orienting task, 457
Ossicles, 147, 148, 150, 158, 179
  and conduction deafness, 170
  and presbyacusia, 173
Otolith, 332
Otosclerosis, 172, 174
Oval window, 147, 148, 150
  in otosclerosis, 174
  and traveling wave theory, 179
Overlearning, 444, 445, 451
Overtone, 163, 166
Oxygen, need in brain, 43, 53

Pacinian corpuscles, 298–300, 302, 325
  as pressure receptors, 313
  and touch, 301
Pain sensitivity, 73, 74, 312, 318
  adaptation, 321
  and central nervous system, 321, 322
  cutaneous, 75
  epicritic system, 322
  internal, 75, 325
  protopathic system, 322
  referred, 320
  and somesthetic cortex, 52
  spots, 320
  stimulus for, 321
  theory of, 322–324
  threshold, 318–320
  and tissue damage, 75
  Weddell's two qualities, 75
Palate, nasal, 339
Papillae, 351, 352
Paradoxical sleep, 61

Parallax, 271
Paralog, 195
Parasympathetic nervous system, 55, 57
  and emotion, 513
  path of nerve fibers, 55
Part learning (*see* Learning, part)
Patterning, temporal, in vision, 238
Pavlov, Ivan P., 3, 40, 329, 384–386
Pavlovian conditioning (*see* Classical conditioning)
Pecten, 84, 223
Perception, definition, 263, 264
  learning, effect of, 84
  versus sensation, 264
  subliminal, 292–294
Perceptual defense, 291, 292
Perceptual organization, 274–276
  principles of, 276–278
Performance, group versus individual, 556, 557
Perilymph, 148, 332, 333
Perimetry, 234–236
Peripheral nerve field, 303
Peripheral nervous system, 47, 55
Persistence effect, 92
  (*See also* Error, of anticipation; Error, of habituation)
Personality, characteristics and task performance, 574
Pharynx, 339
Phase, and sound localization, 169, 170
Phenothiocarbamide, 361
Phi phenomenon, 284, 316
Phoneme, 188, 189, 192
Phonetic system, 187
Photon, 221, 232
Photoreceptor, 214, 215, 218, 219
  anabolic-catabolic reaction in, 259, 260
  in animals, 223
  duplicity of, 220–223, 234
Phrenology, 40, 41
Physiological zero, 308, 311
Physiology, definition of, 38
  relation to psychology, 36–39
Pia mater, 48
"Piano string" theory, 150, 175
Pinna, 147, 149, 150
Pitch, 68, 69, 146, 155
  absolute, 160
  equal contour, 166
  frequency, relation to, 68, 116–118, 155, 160, 161, 165
  perception of, in Helmholtz' theory, 175, 176
    in telephone theory, 177
    in traveling wave theory, 179

Pitch, perception of, in volley theory, 177, 178
  in speech, 186, 188
  threshold change and age, 173
  and tonal brightness, 164
Pituitary, 51
  and emotion, 516
  food intake, role in, 330
  and sexual behavior, 490
  water intake, role in, 332
Place theory, 177, 182
  (*See also* Helmholtz, auditory theory of)
"Pleasure center," 520, 521
Pleasure principle, 524
Plosives, 187
Point of subjective equality (PSE), 87, 88
  and method of average error, 95
  and method of constant stimuli, 97
  and method of equal sense distances, 115, 116
  and method of limits, 93, 94
Pons, 51
  and arousal, 61, 62
Porphyropsin, 220
Postcentral gyrus and cutaneous sensitivity, 302, 304
Posture, 327
  as reflection of emotion, 507, 508
Power, centrality of, 581
  changes in, 583, 584
  distribution of, 581
  limitations of, 583
  social, 579
  types of, 579, 580
Power function, 104–106
Power structure, 576, 579, 600
  affect structure, effect of, 592, 593
  of small group, 556
Practice effects, 99, 100
  in method of fractionation, 120, 121
Pragnanz, law of, 278, 279
Prediction of behavior, 1–4, 38
Preference, 64, 65
  gustatory, 353, 354, 360, 361
  innate, 289, 290
Presbyacusia, 173
Pressure sensitivity, 73, 74
  adaptation, 314–316, 326, 327
  patterning, 316
  receptors for, 312, 313
  response of dorsal horn cell to, 307, 309
  stimulus for, 74, 75, 312
  theory, gradient, 312, 313
Primary process, 524
Principle of least effort, 200

Problem solving, 369, 370, 372, 466
  and insight, 471
  presolution experience, effect of, 471, 472
Progesterone, 489, 490
  and egg sitting, 487
  and nest building, 488
Prolactin, 489
Proprioceptive sensitivity, 81, 82
Prosodic feature, 188
Protanomaly, 255, 257, 258, 260
Protopathic pain system, 322, 323
Proximity, and affect structure, 588, 589
  principle of, 276
Pseudoconditioning, 390, 391
Psychoanalytic theory, and forgetting, 450
  motivational approach of, 523–525
Psychological Abstracts, 3, 13
Psychophysics, and decision theory, 106, 107
  definition, 65, 83
  methods (*see* Method)
  and power function, 105
  as scaling technique, 110
  and speech perception, 192
Psychosomatic states, 514
Punishment, 373–375
  as discriminative stimulus, 422
  duration of, 421, 422
  of instrumental response, 420, 421
  intensity of, 421, 522
  partial schedule of, 421
  versus positive reinforcement, 419, 422, 423
  as suppressor, 421
  Thorndike's view of, 419
  in verbal conditioning, 460
Punishment training, 374, 375
Pupil, 217
Purity of light (*see* Saturation)
Purkinje phenomenon (shift), 222
Pyriform area, 346

Quantum theory, 71

Radiant energy, measure of, 220, 221
Radiant heat, 308, 309, 320, 321
Raman shift, 348, 349
Rapid eye movements (REM), 61
Rayleigh equation, 254
Reaction time, 11, 461
  apparatus, 461
  disjunctive, 461
  in word association, 193, 194

Reading, eye movements during, 287
Reality principle, 524
Recall, 431, 433
Recognition, 434–436, 451, 452
Reconstruction, 436, 451, 452
Recruitment, 174
Redundancy in language, 189
Reflex arc, 49, 385
Refractory period, 152
  absolute, 44
  and Forbes-Gregg hypothesis, 176
  relative, 44, 45
  and volley theory, 177
Reinforcement, 372, 373
  amount, 410, 411
  and classical conditioning, 386, 402, 403
  continuous, 405
  delay of, 412, 413, 548
  and imprinting, 481
  and instrumental training, 386, 402
  and motivation, 519–521
  negative, 372, 374, 375, 420
    (*See also* Punishment)
  number of, 411
  partial, 405
  primary, 377
  quality of, 410, 411
  role of, 372
  secondary, 376, 377, 413, 414
  and verbal conditioning, 460
  withdrawal of, 374
  (*See also* Punishment; Reward)
Reinforcement schedules, 375
  alternate, 406
  chained, 407
  conjunctive, 406, 407
  fixed interval, 405, 408–410, 415
  fixed ratio, 405, 407–409
  and genetic differences, 409–411
  interlocking, 407
  mixed, 407
  multiple, 407
  tandem, 407
  variable interval, 406, 409, 411
  variable ratio, 405, 408, 410
Reissner's membrane, 148, 149
Relearning, 433, 450, 451
Reliability, 29, 536, 537
  intermethod, 140
  intersession, 100
  intertest, 100
  intramethod, 140
  intratest, 100

Reliability, Kuder-Richardson formula for, 539
  of method of fractionation, 120
  sample, effect of homogeneity, 539, 540
  of scaling procedures, 140–142
  of *Seashore Measures of Musical Talents,* 547–
    548
  Spearman-Brown correction, 538, 539
  split-half, 537, 538
  of Stanford-Binet test, 546, 547
  test length, effect of increasing, 538, 539
  test-retest, 536, 537
  of *Tomkins-Horn Picture Arrangement Test,*
    548–552
  validity, relation to, 100, 101
  variability, effect of, 540, 541
Remaining sensibility, technique of, 303
Reminiscence, 440–442, 484
Repression, role in forgetting, 450
Research, types of, 4, 5
Resonance in speech, 186
Response, amplitude of, 11
  conditioned, 49, 384, 387–389
  definition, 83
  duration of, 11
  frequency of, 11
  generalization, 392
  latency of, 11
  rate of, 11
  recording of, 9, 12
  strengthening of, 371, 372
  unconditioned, 386–389
Response operating characteristic, 107
Retention, 430
  curve of, 449
  after distributed learning, 440
  after massed learning, 440
  measures of (*see* Method, savings; Recall; Recog-
    nition; Relearning)
  measuring method, effect of, 451, 452
  and overlearning, 451
  qualitative, 448
  quantitative, 448
Reticular activating system (RAS), 61
  and arousal, 61, 62, 512, 520
  and emotion, 507, 511, 512
Retina, 53, 215, 216, 218
  electrical recording from, 225–227
  and flicker fusion, 238
  nasal, 219
  in pecten, 223
  summation in, 232
  temporal, 219
Retinal disparity, 271

Retinal images, distorted, 281, 282
Reverberating circuit, 45, 46
  role in pain, 320
Reward, 373–375
Rhodopsin, 219
  role in adaptation, 239
Rhythms, 58, 395
Ribonucleic acid (RNA), 381, 382
Ricco's law, 230
Righting response, 81, 327
Rods, 215–220
  absolute threshold for wavelength in, 221, 222
  and acuity, 244, 245
  adaptation in, 239
  and brightness, 232
  and color vision, 219
  distribution of, 219
  and illumination, 222
  number of, 219, 220
Rolando, Luigi, 40
Role, 567
  changes, effect on attitude, 560–562
  conflict, effect of, 574
Rorschach test, 533, 535
  to measure emotion, 506, 548, 549
Round window, 147, 148
Ruffini cylinders, 298, 300, 301
  and warm sensitivity, 301, 310

S-potential, 261
Saccule, 332, 333
Salt taste, 80, 349, 350, 352–356, 358
  threshold, 360
Sampling, 31
  homogeneity, 539, 540
  random, 24, 31, 32, 126
  stratified, 32
  systematic, 31–33
Satiation center, 520
Saturation, 72, 220, 233, 249
  absolute threshold for, 234
  in chromaticity diagram, 251
  and color, 72
  differential threshold for, 72, 234
  relation to homogeneity of wavelength, 282
Scale, definition of, 110
  interval, 112–115, 118, 130
  nominal, 112–114, 124
  ordinal, 112–114, 124, 130
  ratio, 113–115, 123, 124, 130
Scaling, 105
  of frequency, 160

Scaling, methods of (*see* Method)
  multidimensional, 136–139
  of olfactory stimuli, 343
  of pain, 320, 321
  of pitch, 160
  unidimensional, 138
Schwann, Theodor, 42
Sclerotic coat, 215, 217
  in pecten, 223
Scotoma, 236
Seashore Measures of Musical Talents, 547, 548
Self-concept, 594
Semantic differential, to measure meaning, 196–198
  as scaling technique, 124, 125
Semicircular canals, 332, 333
  (*See also* Nonauditory labyrinth)
Sensation versus perception, 264
Sensitive periods, 480, 483, 484
  in imprinting, 481
  (*See also* Critical periods)
Sensitive spot, 301
  (*See also* Cold sensitivity, spots; Warm sensitivity, spots)
Sensitization, 390, 391
Sensory deprivation, 288, 289
Sensory preconditioning, 390, 391
Septal area, 60
  and emotion, 506, 510
  intracranial stimulation of, 520
Set, 276, 277, 471, 472
Shading as depth cue, 272
Shell shock, 38
Similarity, principle of, 276, 277
Similarity hypothesis, 489, 490
Sine wave, 68, 70
Sinus, 339
Skaggs-Robinson hypothesis, 433, 434
Skill and task performance, 569–571, 578
Skin, comunication through, 317, 318
  as cutaneous receptor, 73, 296
  deformation of, as pressure stimulus, 312
  differential sensitivity in, 301
  injury, effects of, 319, 320
  layers of, 297
    (*See also* Corium; Epidermis)
Sleep, 61, 62
  brain, role of, 40, 58
  and delta rhythms, 58
  and electroencephalogram, 58, 59, 61
  and limbic system, 62
  (*See also* Arousal)
Smell (*see* Olfaction)
Smell prism, 79

Snellen chart, 243, 244
Social context, 554
Social position, 567
Somatic areas, 305
Sone, 122, 161
Sound, generation of, 67, 68
  localization, 169–171, 181
  production of, in speech, 185
  transmission of, 67
    in ear, 148
Sound pressure level (SPL), 69
Sound wave, 68, 71
  analysis of, 70
  types of, 70
Sour taste, 80, 349, 350, 352, 353, 355
  electrically produced, 81, 351
  threshold for, 360
Space perception, 271
  age, effect of, 291
  learning, role of, 281
  (*See also* Depth perception)
Spearman-Brown formula, 538, 539
Specific nerve energies, doctrine of, 39, 45, 174, 175
Spectrogram, 189, 190
Speech, auditory perception of, 184
  development of, as discriminatory process, 415
  egocentricity of, 207, 208
  intelligibility of, 201, 202
  parts of, change with age, 207, 208
  pathology, 210, 211
  prosodic features of, 188
  psychophysical measure of, 192
  recording of, 189–191
  and respiration, 184, 185
  socialized, 208
  subvocal, 195, 385
Speech-to-noise ratio, 202, 203
Spike potential, 43, 44, 46
Spinal cord, 43, 56
  anatomy of, 48, 49
  and classical conditioning, 394, 395
  functions of, 49
  and gustatory sensitivity, 302, 304
  and sexual behavior, 491
Spinothalamic tract, lateral, role in pain, 302, 304
    role in thermal sensitivity, 302, 304
  ventral, role in touch, 302, 304
Spontaneous recovery, 375, 376, 426
Stage theory, 261, 262
Standard observer, 251
Stanford-Binet scale, 20, 21, 534, 544–547
Stapedius (stirrup muscle), 148
Stapes (stirrup), 147, 148, 150, 151, 172, 174, 179

Statistics, 19, 29–31
Stimulants, 516
Stimulus, comparison, 90
  conditioned, 376, 387, 389
  definition of, 83
  generalization, 392
  intensity, and nerve transmission of, 45, 46
  physical and mental, relation between, 86–88
  presentation of, 9, 12
  social, 555, 556
  S^D, 415
  S^Δ, 415
  subthreshold, 43
  suprathreshold, 43, 44
  unconditioned, 385, 387
Stirrup (*see* Stapes)
Storage load, 446
Strabismus, 287, 288
Strephosymbolia, 287
Stress, 515
  and critical flicker fusion, 237
String problem, 466–468, 472
Stuttering, 210, 211
Subarachnoid spaces, 52
Subcallosal gyrus, 340
Subception, 292
  (*See also* Perception, subliminal)
Subcutaneous tissue, 298
Sublimation, 525
Successive approximations, technique of, 416
Sucking reflex, 494, 495
Summation, areal, in vision, 232
  in classical conditioning, 390, 391
  in nerve, 44, 47
  spatial, in vision, 232
Superego, 524
Survey, 557–559
Sweet taste, 80, 349–353, 355, 356, 358
  threshold, 360
Sympathetic nervous system, 55, 56
  and emotion, 510, 513
  nerve fibers, path of, 55
  and s.C fibers, 47
Synapse, 42, 46, 47

Tabes dorsalis, 327
Tabula rasa, 214
Tactile sensitivity, receptor for, 312
  and somesthetic cortex, 52
  (*See also* Pressure sensitivity)
Talbot's law, 207
Task, leader, effect of, 570

Task, performance of, 568
  and ability, 569
    affect structure, effect of, 593
  and personality characteristics, 574
  and power structure, 569
  and small group, 566, 568
  structure of, 576, 578, 600
    affect structure, effect of, 595
    and autonomy, degree of, 578, 579
Taste, 349
  basic, 349, 351, 352
    (*See also* Bitter taste; Salt taste; Sour taste; Sweet taste)
  threshold, 360
Taste bud, 351–353, 356
Taste sensitivity (*see* Gustation)
Taylor Manifest Anxiety Scale (MAS), 399, 506
Teaching machines, 8
Tectorial membrane, 148, 149
Teleology, 33
Telephone theory, 176, 177
Temperature, and hoarding, 498
  and migratory behavior, 492
Temperature sensitivity (*see* Thermal sensitivity)
Tensor tympani (hammer muscle), 148
Terman-Binet scale, 534
Test(s), achievement, 533, 541, 544, 548
  aptitude, 533, 544, 547, 548
  Army Alpha, 535
  Army Beta, 535
  development of, 535, 536
  F, 29
  function of, 532
  group, 533
  individual, 533
  intelligence, 534, 535, 544–547
  mental, 534
  objective, 533
  performance, 533
  personality, 535, 542
  power, 539
  projective, 265, 291, 533, 535, 542, 548
    to measure emotion, 506
    need achievement theory, use in, 525
  situational, 535
  speed, 539
  subjective, 533
  t, 29
Testosterone, 489, 490
Tetartanopes, 255, 257
Texture, role in visual perception, 267, 270, 272
Thalamus, 51, 60
  and arousal, 61

Thalamus, and audition, 149, 180
  and cutaneous sensitivity, 302
  and emotion, 507, 510, 511
  and gustation, 352, 353, 357–359
  and pain, 322, 323
  and vision, 228
Thematic Apperception Test (TAT), 533, 548
  to measure emotion, 506
  to measure motivation, 525, 526
Theory, 4, 5, 20
Thermal fibers, 306, 307
Thermal gradients, 306
Thermal sensitivity, 74, 328
  blood supply, effect of, 306, 308
  nerve response, 306
  and somesthetic cortex, 52
  and spinal cord, 49
  theory, 76, 306, 310, 311
    concentration, 310, 311
    specific receptor, 310
  threshold, 308–310
  two systems, 305
  variability of, 305
  (*See also* Cold sensitivity; Warm sensitivity)
Thermal summation, 310
Thirst, 296, 324, 327, 328, 331, 332
  role of hypothalamus, 330–332
  role of pituitary, 332
Thorndike, Edward L., 367, 368, 402, 419, 456, 517
"Three bowl" experiment, 76
Threshold, absolute, amplitude, 160–162
    constant stimuli, determination by method of,
      96
    definition, 65
    frequency, 65, 156, 157
    hue, 229
    wavelength, 229
    (*See also* stimulus, *below;* terminal, *below*)
  brightness, 232, 233
  definition of, 65
  detection, 106, 107
    for wavelength, 229, 230
  determination of, 66
  differential, 65, 66, 86–88
    amplitude, 161
    constant stimuli, determination by method of,
      97–99
    frequency, 158–160
    hue, 229, 231, 249
    interval of uncertainty, relation to, 93
    limits, determination by method of, 92
    variation in, 66
    of wavelength, 229, 231

Threshold, feeling, 156, 157
  and flicker fusion, 236
    (*See also* Critical flicker fusion)
  gustatory, 343, 352, 353, 358, 360, 366
  history of concept, 84
  illumination, 73
  kinesthetic, 325, 326
  movement, 283
  of nerve, 43, 44
  olfactory, 77, 342–344
  pain, 303, 318–320
  pressure, 313, 314
  purity, 72
  recognition, 106
  of saturation, 72, 234
  series, 92, 93
  stimulus, amplitude, 161
    constant stimuli, determination by method of,
      95
    definition, 65, 66, 86, 107
    frequency, 70, 155, 156
    gustatory, 343, 358
    of hue, 229
    of light, 65
    olfactory, 65, 77, 342, 343
    of pain, 313, 321
    of pressure, 313
    of saturation, 234
    of taste, 65
    of touch, 65
    visual, 66
    of wavelength, 71, 73, 229
  terminal, auditory, 157, 158
    average error, determination by method of, 95
    constant stimuli, determination by method of,
      95–97
    definition, 65, 86
    of frequency, and age, 156
    gustatory, 360
    of hue, 229
    limits, determination by method of, 90–92
    pitch, decrease with age, 173
    of pressure, 313
    of wavelength, 71, 73, 229
  thermal, 308–310
  two-point, 314, 315
  vestibular, 335
  visual, 228–234, 292
Thyroid, effect on nest building, 488
Tickling, 74, 316
Timbre, 162, 163
Time-motion studies, 463
Tinnitus, 172, 335

Tolman, Edward C., learning theory of, 518
Tomkins-Horn Picture Arrangement Test (PAT), 548–552
Tonal gaps, 155
Tonal islands, 155
Tonal pleasantness, 168, 169
Tones, 165, 166
Tongue, nerves serving, 53
Tonotopic organization, 181
Touch sensitivity (*see* Tactile sensitivity)
Touch spots, 312
Tracking, compensatory, 463
    pursuit, 463
Tract, nerve, 42
Transfer, 369, 447, 452
    bilateral, 369, 455, 461
    measures of, 452–454
    negative, 369, 418, 419
    positive, 369, 452
    statistical computations in, 454
    theory of, 455, 456
        identical elements, 456
Transposition, 417
Traveling wave theory, 178, 179
Trichromatism, anomalous, 255–257
    normal, 255, 256
Trigeminal nerve, and cutaneous sensitivity, 304, 319, 352
    and gustation, 352
Trill, 187
Tristimulus color theory, 257–260
    (*See also* Helmholtz, color vision theory; Young's color theory)
Tritanomaly, 255, 257
Troland, 221, 232
Turbinates, 338, 339
Tympanic lamella, effect of intense stimulation on, 172
Tympanic membrane, 147, 150, 179, 352
    pain sensitivity in, 320
Type-token ratio (TTR), 198

Ulcer, 514, 515
Umweg problem, 466, 467
Uncus, 340
Undulatory theory (*see* Wave theory)
Utricle, 332–334

Vagus nerve (X), and cutaneous sensitivity, 301
    and gustation, 352
Validity, 100, 536, 540

Validity, concurrent, 540, 543, 544
    construct, 540, 541, 544
    content, 540–542, 544, 548
    face, 540, 542, 544
    intermethod, 140
    intramethod, 140
    of need achievement technique, 526–528
    predictive, 540, 542–544
    relation to reliability, 100, 101
    of scaling procedures, 142
    of *Seashore Measures of Musical Talents* test, 548
    of Stanford-Binet scale, 547
Value in Munsell color system, 250
Values and task performance, 572, 573
Variables, demographic, 573, 574
    dependent, 10, 11, 23, 27, 30
    independent, 10, 11, 21–25, 27, 30
Variance, types of, 139
Variation, in threshold measurement, 98–100
Vascular theory, 76
Veg, 122
Ventricular system, 52
Ventromedial nuclei, as satiation center, 330, 331
Verbal conditioning, 209, 396–398, 458–460
Vernier acuity, 244
Vestibular sensitivity, 81, 82, 296, 332–335
    adaptation, 335
    stimulus for, 82, 333
    threshold, 335
Vibratese, 317
Vibratory sensitivity, 74, **316**
    cross-modal comparison with loudness, 107
Vicarious functioning, 427
Vincent curve, 379
Visceral brain (*see* Limbic system)
Visibility curves, 221
Vision, and meaning, 195, 196
    nature of stimulus, 70–73
    photopic, 221, 222
    scotopic, 221, 222
Visual cliff, 279–281
Visual perception, 213, 214
    behaviorist's approach, 275
    development of, 290, 291
    Gestalt approach, 275
    learning, role of, 278, 279, 281
    and meaning, 195, 196
    and stimulation, effect of amount, 288, 289
    (*See also* Depth perception; Motion perception; Space perception)
Visual purple, 219
    (*See also* Rhodopsin)

Vitreous humor, 215, 217, 218
Vocabulary, development of, 206–208
 size of, in children, 207, 209
Vocal folds, 185–187
Volley theory, 177–180
Volta, Alessandro, 40, 59
Volume of sound, 155, 162–164
von Restorff effect, 443
Vowels, 187
 classification of, 188
 development of, 205, 208, 209

Wakefulness (*see* Arousal)
Warmth sensitivity, 74, 76
 adaptation, 308
 nerve impulses, 306, 307
 paradoxical, 305
 spots, 76, 77, 301, 302, 305, 306, 311
 threshold, 308
Watson, John B., 385
Wave theory, 71
Wavelength, 71, 72
 absolute threshold, 66, 229, 230
 adaptation to, 240, 241
 chromaticity diagram, 251
 differential threshold, 229, 231
 electrical response to, 226, 227
 in Ganzfeld, 283
 homogeneity of, 72, 220, 228, 233, 282
  (*See also* Saturation)
 measure of, 220, 221
 and photoreceptors, 220, 221
 relation to hue, 72, 229, 231
 terminal threshold, 66
 threshold, 71, 228
Weber, Ernst Heinrich, 86

Weber's ratio (fraction), 88–90, 102
 for audition, 158, 159
 for brightness, 232
 fingerspan, 326
 for gustation, 360
 for kinesthesis, 325, 326
 for olfaction, 343
 for pain, 321
 and power function, 105
 for pressure, 314
 for weight, 88
Wechsler Adult Intelligence Scale, 470
Wernicke's area, 210
Wever-Bray effect, 151
Whole learning (*see* Learning, whole)
Word, basic, 207, 209
 derived, 207
 first, 206
 root, 207
 taboo, 291
Word association, to measure meaning,
  193
 and reaction time, 193
 ´ types of, 193, 194
Word dumbness, 211
Wundt, Wilhelm, 39, 86, 534

Young's color theory, 248, 258–261
Young-Helmholtz color theory, 258, 261

z scores, conversion to, 132, 133
Zeigarnik effect, 450
Zipf's laws, 199, 200
Zwaardemaker, Hendrik, olfactory system of classi-
 fication, 79